Advanced Microeconomic Theory

PEARSON

Advanced Microeconomic Theory

THIRD EDITION

Geoffrey A. Jehle
Vassar College

Philip J. Reny
University of Chicago

Financial Times Prentice Hall is an imprint of

Harlow, England • London • New York • Boston • San Francisco • Toronto • Sydney • Singapore • Hong Kong
Tokyo • Seoul • Taipei • New Delhi • Cape Town • Madrid • Mexico City • Amsterdam • Munich • Paris • Milan

Pearson Education Limited
Edinburgh Gate
Harlow
Essex CM20 2JE
England

and Associated Companies throughout the world

Visit us on the World Wide Web at:
www.pearsoned.co.uk

First published 2011

ISBN: 978-0-273-73191-7

British Library Cataloguing-in-Publication Data
A catalogue record for this book is available from the British Library

Library of Congress Cataloging-in-Publication Data
A catalog record for this book is available from the Library of Congress

10 9 8 7 6 5
14 13 12

Typeset in 10/12 pt and Times-Roman by 75
Printed and bound in Great Britain by Ashford Colour Press Ltd, Gosport, Hampshire

To Rana and Kamran

G.A.J.

To Dianne, Lisa, and Elizabeth

P.J.R.

CONTENTS

PREFACE

In preparing this third edition of our text, we wanted to provide long-time readers with new and updated material in a familiar format, while offering first-time readers an accessible, self-contained treatment of the essential core of modern microeconomic theory.

To those ends, every chapter has been revised and updated. The more significant changes include a new introduction to general equilibrium with contingent commodities in Chapter 5, along with a simplified proof of Arrow's theorem and a new, careful development of the Gibbard-Satterthwaite theorem in Chapter 6. Chapter 7 includes many refinements and extensions, especially in our presentation on Bayesian games. The biggest change – one we hope readers find interesting and useful – is an extensive, integrated presentation in Chapter 9 of many of the central results of mechanism design in the quasi-linear utility, private-values environment.

We continue to believe that working through exercises is the surest way to master the material in this text. New exercises have been added to virtually every chapter, and others have been updated and revised. Many of the new exercises guide readers in developing for themselves extensions, refinements or alternative approaches to important material covered in the text. Hints and answers for selected exercises are provided at the end of the book, along with lists of theorems and definitions appearing in the text. We will continue to maintain a readers' forum on the web, where readers can exchange solutions to exercises in the text. It can be reached at *http://alfred.objects.net*.

The two full chapters of the Mathematical Appendix still provide students with a lengthy and largely self-contained development of the set theory, real analysis, topology, calculus, and modern optimisation theory which are indispensable in modern microeconomics. Readers of this edition will now find a fuller, self-contained development of Lagrangian and Kuhn-Tucker methods, along with new material on the Theorem of the Maximum and two separation theorems. The exposition is formal but presumes nothing more than a good grounding in single-variable calculus and simple linear algebra as a starting point. We suggest that even students who are very well-prepared in mathematics browse both chapters of the appendix early on. That way, if and when some review or reference is needed, the reader will have a sense of how that material is organised.

Before we begin to develop the theory itself, we ought to say a word to new readers about the role mathematics will play in this text. Often, you will notice we make certain assumptions purely for the sake of mathematical expediency. The justification for proceeding this way is simple, and it is the same in every other branch of science. These abstractions from 'reality' allow us to bring to bear powerful mathematical methods that, by the rigour of the logical discipline they impose, help extend our insights into areas beyond the reach of our intuition and experience. In the physical world, there is 'no such thing' as a frictionless plane or a perfect vacuum. In economics, as in physics, allowing ourselves to accept assumptions like these frees us to focus on more important aspects of the problem and thereby helps to establish benchmarks in theory against which to gauge experience and observation in the real world. This does not mean that you must wholeheartedly embrace every 'unrealistic' or purely formal aspect of the theory. Far from it. It is *always* worthwhile to cast a critical eye on these matters as they arise and to ask yourself what is gained, and what is sacrificed, by the abstraction at hand. Thought and insight on these points are the stuff of which advances in theory and knowledge are made. From here on, however, we will take the theory as it is and seek to understand it on its own terms, leaving much of its critical appraisal to your moments away from this book.

Finally, we wish to acknowledge the many readers and colleagues who have provided helpful comments and pointed out errors in previous editions. Your keen eyes and good judgements have helped us make this third edition better and more complete than it otherwise would be. While we cannot thank all of you personally, we must thank Eddie Dekel, Roger Myerson, Derek Neal, Motty Perry, Arthur Robson, Steve Williams, and Jörgen Weibull for their thoughtful comments.

Part I

Economic Agents

CHAPTER 1

CONSUMER THEORY

In the first two chapters of this volume, we will explore the essential features of modern consumer theory – a bedrock foundation on which so many theoretical structures in economics are built. Some time later in your study of economics, you will begin to notice just how central this theory is to the economist's way of thinking. Time and time again you will hear the echoes of consumer theory in virtually every branch of the discipline – how it is conceived, how it is constructed, and how it is applied.

1.1 PRIMITIVE NOTIONS

There are four building blocks in any model of consumer choice. They are the consumption set, the feasible set, the preference relation, and the behavioural assumption. Each is conceptually distinct from the others, though it is quite common sometimes to lose sight of that fact. This basic structure is extremely general, and so, very flexible. By specifying the form each of these takes in a given problem, many different situations involving choice can be formally described and analysed. Although we will tend to concentrate here on specific formalisations that have come to dominate economists' view of an individual consumer's behaviour, it is well to keep in mind that 'consumer theory' *per se* is in fact a very rich and flexible *theory of choice*.

The notion of a **consumption set** is straightforward. We let the consumption set, X, represent the set of all alternatives, or complete consumption plans, that the consumer can conceive – whether some of them will be achievable in practice or not. What we intend to capture here is the universe of alternative choices over which the consumer's mind is capable of wandering, unfettered by consideration of the realities of his present situation. The consumption set is sometimes also called the **choice set**.

Let each commodity be measured in some infinitely divisible units. Let $x_i \in \mathbb{R}$ represent the number of units of good i. We assume that only non-negative units of each good are meaningful and that it is always possible to conceive of having *no* units of any particular commodity. Further, we assume there is a finite, fixed, but arbitrary number n of different goods. We let $\mathbf{x} = (x_1, \ldots, x_n)$ be a vector containing different quantities of each of the n commodities and call $\mathbf{x}$ a **consumption bundle** or a **consumption plan**. A consumption bundle $\mathbf{x} \in X$ is thus represented by a point $\mathbf{x} \in \mathbb{R}^n_+$. Usually, we'll simplify things and just think of the consumption set as the *entire* non-negative orthant, $X = \mathbb{R}^n_+$. In this case, it is easy to see that each of the following basic requirements is satisfied.

ASSUMPTION 1.1 ***Properties of the Consumption Set,*** X

The minimal requirements on the consumption set are

1. $X \subseteq \mathbb{R}^n_+$.
2. X *is closed.*
3. X *is convex.*
4. $\mathbf{0} \in X$.

The notion of a **feasible set** is likewise very straightforward. We let B represent all those alternative consumption plans that are both conceivable and, more important, realistically obtainable given the consumer's circumstances. What we intend to capture here are precisely those alternatives that are *achievable* given the economic realities the consumer faces. The feasible set B then is that subset of the consumption set X that remains after we have accounted for any constraints on the consumer's access to commodities due to the practical, institutional, or economic realities of the world. How we specify those realities in a given situation will determine the precise configuration and additional properties that B must have. For now, we will simply say that $B \subset X$.

A **preference relation** typically specifies the limits, if any, on the consumer's ability to perceive in situations involving choice the form of consistency or inconsistency in the consumer's choices, and information about the consumer's tastes for the different objects of choice. The preference relation plays a crucial role in any theory of choice. Its special form in the theory of consumer behaviour is sufficiently subtle to warrant special examination in the next section.

Finally, the model is 'closed' by specifying some **behavioural assumption**. This expresses the guiding principle the consumer uses to make final choices and so identifies the ultimate objectives in choice. It is supposed that *the consumer seeks to identify and select an available alternative that is most preferred in the light of his personal tastes.*

1.2 Preferences and Utility

In this section, we examine the consumer's preference relation and explore its connection to modern usage of the term 'utility'. Before we begin, however, a brief word on the evolution of economists' thinking will help to place what follows in its proper context.

In earlier periods, the so-called 'Law of Demand' was built on some extremely strong assumptions. In the classical theory of Edgeworth, Mill, and other proponents of the utilitarian school of philosophy, 'utility' was thought to be something of substance. 'Pleasure' and 'pain' were held to be well-defined entities that could be measured and compared between individuals. In addition, the 'Principle of Diminishing Marginal Utility' was accepted as a psychological 'law', and early statements of the Law of Demand depended on it. These are awfully strong assumptions about the inner workings of human beings.

The more recent history of consumer theory has been marked by a drive to render its foundations as general as possible. Economists have sought to pare away as many of the traditional assumptions, explicit or implicit, as they could and still retain a coherent theory with predictive power. Pareto (1896) can be credited with suspecting that the idea of a measurable 'utility' was inessential to the theory of demand. Slutsky (1915) undertook the first systematic examination of demand theory without the concept of a measurable substance called utility. Hicks (1939) demonstrated that the Principle of Diminishing Marginal Utility was neither necessary, nor sufficient, for the Law of Demand to hold. Finally, Debreu (1959) completed the reduction of standard consumer theory to those bare essentials we will consider here. Today's theory bears close and important relations to its earlier ancestors, but it is leaner, more precise, and more general.

1.2.1 PREFERENCE RELATIONS

Consumer preferences are characterised *axiomatically*. In this method of modelling as few meaningful and distinct assumptions as possible are set forth to characterise the structure and properties of preferences. The rest of the theory then builds logically from these axioms, and predictions of behaviour are developed through the process of deduction.

These **axioms of consumer choice** are intended to give formal mathematical expression to fundamental aspects of consumer behaviour and attitudes towards the objects of choice. Together, they formalise the view that the consumer *can* choose and that choices are *consistent* in a particular way.

Formally, we represent the consumer's preferences by a *binary relation*, $\succsim$, defined on the consumption set, X. If $\mathbf{x}^1 \succsim \mathbf{x}^2$, we say that '$\mathbf{x}^1$ is at least as good as $\mathbf{x}^2$', for this consumer.

That we use a binary relation to characterise preferences is significant and worth a moment's reflection. It conveys the important point that, from the beginning, our theory requires relatively little of the consumer it describes. We require only that consumers make *binary* comparisons, that is, that they only examine two consumption plans at a time and make a decision regarding those two. The following axioms set forth basic criteria with which those binary comparisons must conform.

AXIOM 1: Completeness. *For all* $\mathbf{x}^1$ *and* $\mathbf{x}^2$ *in* X, *either* $\mathbf{x}^1 \succsim \mathbf{x}^2$ *or* $\mathbf{x}^2 \succsim \mathbf{x}^1$.

Axiom 1 formalises the notion that the consumer *can* make comparisons, that is, that he has the ability to discriminate and the necessary knowledge to evaluate alternatives. It says the consumer can examine *any* two distinct consumption plans $\mathbf{x}^1$ and $\mathbf{x}^2$ and decide whether $\mathbf{x}^1$ is at least as good as $\mathbf{x}^2$ or $\mathbf{x}^2$ is at least as good as $\mathbf{x}^1$.

AXIOM 2: Transitivity. *For any three elements* $\mathbf{x}^1$, $\mathbf{x}^2$, *and* $\mathbf{x}^3$ *in* X, *if* $\mathbf{x}^1 \succsim \mathbf{x}^2$ *and* $\mathbf{x}^2 \succsim \mathbf{x}^3$, *then* $\mathbf{x}^1 \succsim \mathbf{x}^3$.

Axiom 2 gives a very particular form to the requirement that the consumer's choices be *consistent*. Although we require only that the consumer be capable of comparing two alternatives at a time, the assumption of transitivity requires that those pairwise comparisons be linked together in a consistent way. At first brush, requiring that the evaluation of alternatives be transitive seems simple and only natural. Indeed, were they not transitive, our instincts would tell us that there was something peculiar about them. Nonetheless, this is a controversial axiom. Experiments have shown that in various situations, the choices of real human beings are not always transitive. Nonetheless, we will retain it in our description of the consumer, though not without some slight trepidation.

These two axioms together imply that the consumer can completely *rank* any finite number of elements in the consumption set, X, from best to worst, possibly with some ties. (Try to prove this.) We summarise the view that preferences enable the consumer to construct such a ranking by saying that those preferences can be represented by a *preference relation*.

DEFINITION 1.1 ***Preference Relation***

The binary relation $\succsim$ on the consumption set X is called a preference relation if it satisfies Axioms 1 and 2.

There are two additional relations that we will use in our discussion of consumer preferences. Each is determined by the preference relation, $\succsim$, and they formalise the notions of *strict preference* and *indifference*.

DEFINITION 1.2 ***Strict Preference Relation***

The binary relation $\succ$ on the consumption set X is defined as follows:

$$\mathbf{x}^1 \succ \mathbf{x}^2 \quad \textit{if and only if} \quad \mathbf{x}^1 \succsim \mathbf{x}^2 \quad \textit{and} \quad \mathbf{x}^2 \not\succsim \mathbf{x}^1.$$

The relation $\succ$ is called the strict preference relation induced by $\succsim$, or simply the strict preference relation when $\succsim$ is clear. The phrase $\mathbf{x}^1 \succ \mathbf{x}^2$ is read, '$\mathbf{x}^1$ is strictly preferred to $\mathbf{x}^2$'.

DEFINITION 1.3 ***Indifference Relation***

The binary relation $\sim$ on the consumption set X is defined as follows:

$$\mathbf{x}^1 \sim \mathbf{x}^2 \quad \textit{if and only if} \quad \mathbf{x}^1 \succsim \mathbf{x}^2 \quad \textit{and} \quad \mathbf{x}^2 \succsim \mathbf{x}^1.$$

The relation $\sim$ is called the indifference relation induced by $\succsim$, or simply the indifference relation when $\succsim$ is clear. The phrase $\mathbf{x}^1 \sim \mathbf{x}^2$ is read, '$\mathbf{x}^1$ is indifferent to $\mathbf{x}^2$'.

Building on the underlying definition of the preference relation, both the strict preference relation and the indifference relation capture the usual sense in which the terms 'strict preference' and 'indifference' are used in ordinary language. Because each is derived from the preference relation, each can be expected to share some of its properties. Some, yes, but not all. In general, both are transitive and neither is complete.

Using these two supplementary relations, we can establish something very concrete about the consumer's ranking of any two alternatives. For any pair $\mathbf{x}^1$ and $\mathbf{x}^2$, *exactly one* of three mutually exclusive possibilities holds: $\mathbf{x}^1 \succ \mathbf{x}^2$, or $\mathbf{x}^2 \succ \mathbf{x}^1$, or $\mathbf{x}^1 \sim \mathbf{x}^2$.

To this point, we have simply managed to formalise the requirement that preferences reflect an ability to make choices and display a certain kind of consistency. Let us consider how we might describe graphically a set of preferences satisfying just those first few axioms. To that end, and also because of their usefulness later on, we will use the preference relation to define some related sets. These sets focus on a single alternative in the consumption set and examine the ranking of all other alternatives relative to it.

DEFINITION 1.4 ***Sets in** X **Derived from the Preference Relation***

Let $\mathbf{x}^0$ be any point in the consumption set, X. Relative to any such point, we can define the following subsets of X:

1. $\succsim(\mathbf{x}^0) \equiv \{\mathbf{x} \mid \mathbf{x} \in X, \mathbf{x} \succsim \mathbf{x}^0\}$, *called the 'at least as good as' set.*
2. $\precsim(\mathbf{x}^0) \equiv \{\mathbf{x} \mid \mathbf{x} \in X, \mathbf{x}^0 \succsim \mathbf{x}\}$, *called the 'no better than' set.*
3. $\prec(\mathbf{x}^0) \equiv \{\mathbf{x} \mid \mathbf{x} \in X, \mathbf{x}^0 \succ \mathbf{x}\}$, *called the 'worse than' set.*
4. $\succ(\mathbf{x}^0) \equiv \{\mathbf{x} \mid \mathbf{x} \in X, \mathbf{x} \succ \mathbf{x}^0\}$, *called the 'preferred to' set.*
5. $\sim(\mathbf{x}^0) \equiv \{\mathbf{x} \mid \mathbf{x} \in X, \mathbf{x} \sim \mathbf{x}^0\}$, *called the 'indifference' set.*

A hypothetical set of preferences satisfying Axioms 1 and 2 has been sketched in Fig. 1.1 for $X = \mathbb{R}^2_+$. Any point in the consumption set, such as $\mathbf{x}^0 = (x^0_1, x^0_2)$, represents a consumption plan consisting of a certain amount x^0_1 of commodity 1, together with a certain amount x^0_2 of commodity 2. Under Axiom 1, the consumer is able to compare $\mathbf{x}^0$ with any and every other plan in X and decide whether the other is at least as good as $\mathbf{x}^0$ or whether $\mathbf{x}^0$ is at least as good as the other. Given our definitions of the various sets relative to $\mathbf{x}^0$, Axioms 1 and 2 tell us that the consumer must place *every* point in X into

Figure 1.1. Hypothetical preferences satisfying Axioms 1 and 2.

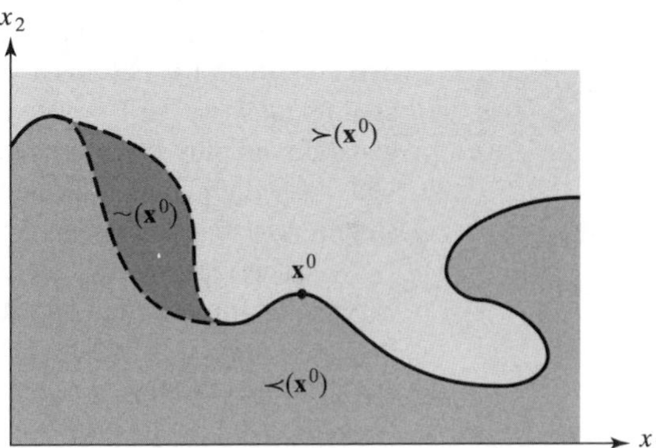

one of three mutually exclusive categories relative to $\mathbf{x}^0$; every other point is worse than $\mathbf{x}^0$, indifferent to $\mathbf{x}^0$, or preferred to $\mathbf{x}^0$. Thus, for any bundle $\mathbf{x}^0$ the three sets $\prec(\mathbf{x}^0)$, $\sim(\mathbf{x}^0)$, and $\succ(\mathbf{x}^0)$ *partition* the consumption set.

The preferences in Fig. 1.1 may seem rather odd. They possess only the most limited structure, yet they are entirely consistent with and allowed for by the first two axioms alone. Nothing assumed so far prohibits any of the 'irregularities' depicted there, such as the 'thick' indifference zones, or the 'gaps' and 'curves' within the indifference set $\sim(\mathbf{x}^0)$. Such things can be ruled out only by imposing additional requirements on preferences.

We shall consider several new assumptions on preferences. One has very little behavioural significance and speaks almost exclusively to the purely mathematical aspects of representing preferences; the others speak directly to the issue of consumer tastes over objects in the consumption set.

The first is an axiom whose only effect is to impose a kind of topological regularity on preferences, and whose primary contribution will become clear a bit later.

From now on we explicitly set $X = \mathbb{R}^n_+$.

AXIOM 3: Continuity. *For all $\mathbf{x} \in \mathbb{R}^n_+$, the 'at least as good as' set, $\succsim(\mathbf{x})$, and the 'no better than' set, $\precsim(\mathbf{x})$, are closed in $\mathbb{R}^n_+$.*

Recall that a set is closed in a particular domain if its complement is open in that domain. Thus, to say that $\succsim(\mathbf{x})$ is closed in $\mathbb{R}^n_+$ is to say that its complement, $\prec(\mathbf{x})$, is open in $\mathbb{R}^n_+$.

The continuity axiom guarantees that sudden preference reversals do not occur. Indeed, the continuity axiom can be equivalently expressed by saying that if each element $\mathbf{y}^n$ of a sequence of bundles is at least as good as (no better than) $\mathbf{x}$, and $\mathbf{y}^n$ converges to $\mathbf{y}$, then $\mathbf{y}$ is at least as good as (no better than) $\mathbf{x}$. Note that because $\succsim(\mathbf{x})$ and $\precsim(\mathbf{x})$ are closed, so, too, is $\sim(\mathbf{x})$ because the latter is the intersection of the former two. Consequently, Axiom 3 rules out the open area in the indifference set depicted in the north-west of Fig. 1.1.

Additional assumptions on tastes lend the greater structure and regularity to preferences that you are probably familiar with from earlier economics classes. Assumptions of this sort must be selected for their appropriateness to the particular choice problem being analysed. We will consider in turn a few key assumptions on tastes that are ordinarily imposed in 'standard' consumer theory, and seek to understand the individual and collective contributions they make to the structure of preferences. Within each class of these assumptions, we will proceed from the less restrictive to the more restrictive. We will generally employ the more restrictive versions considered. Consequently, we let axioms with primed numbers indicate alternatives to the norm, which are conceptually similar but slightly less restrictive than their unprimed partners.

When representing preferences over ordinary consumption goods, we will want to express the fundamental view that 'wants' are essentially unlimited. In a very weak sense, we can express this by saying that there will always exist some adjustment in the composition of the consumer's consumption plan that he can imagine making to give himself a consumption plan he prefers. This adjustment may involve acquiring more of some commodities and less of others, or more of all commodities, or even less of all commodities.

By this assumption, we preclude the possibility that the consumer can even *imagine* having all his wants and whims for commodities completely satisfied. Formally, we state this assumption as follows, where $B_\varepsilon(\mathbf{x}^0)$ denotes the open ball of radius ε centred at $\mathbf{x}^0$:[1]

AXIOM 4′: Local Non-satiation. *For all* $\mathbf{x}^0 \in \mathbb{R}^n_+$, *and for all* $\varepsilon > 0$, *there exists some* $\mathbf{x} \in B_\varepsilon(\mathbf{x}^0) \cap \mathbb{R}^n_+$ *such that* $\mathbf{x} \succ \mathbf{x}^0$.

Axiom 4′ says that within any vicinity of a given point $\mathbf{x}^0$, no matter how small that vicinity is, there will always be at least one other point $\mathbf{x}$ that the consumer prefers to $\mathbf{x}^0$. Its effect on the structure of indifference sets is significant. It rules out the possibility of having 'zones of indifference', such as that surrounding $\mathbf{x}^1$ in Fig. 1.2. To see this, note that we can always find some $\varepsilon > 0$, and some $B_\varepsilon(\mathbf{x}^1)$, containing nothing but points indifferent to $\mathbf{x}^1$. This of course violates Axiom 4′, because it requires there *always* be at least one point strictly preferred to $\mathbf{x}^1$, regardless of the $\varepsilon > 0$ we choose. The preferences depicted in Fig. 1.3 do satisfy Axiom 4′ as well as Axioms 1 to 3.

A different and more demanding view of needs and wants is very common. According to this view, more is always better than less. Whereas local non-satiation requires

Figure 1.2. Hypothetical preferences satisfying Axioms 1, 2, and 3.

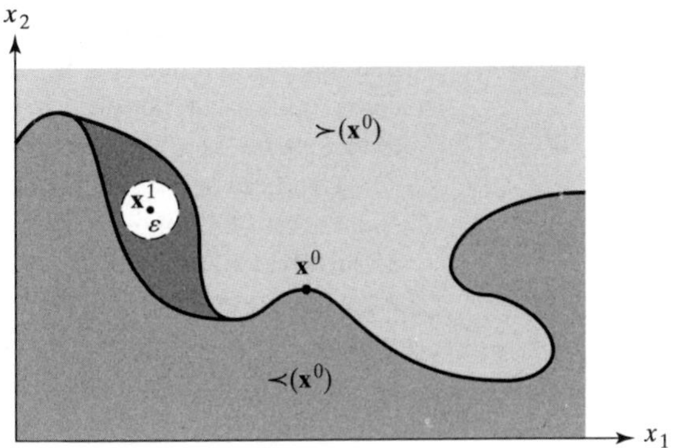

Figure 1.3. Hypothetical preferences satisfying Axioms 1, 2, 3, and 4′.

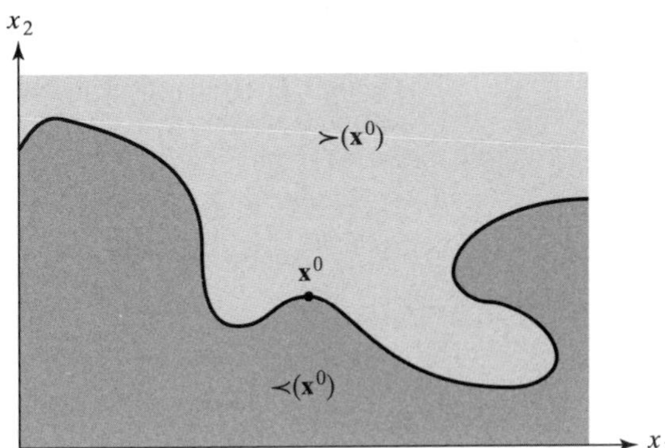

[1] See Definition A1.4 in the Mathematical Appendix.

that a preferred alternative nearby always exist, it does not rule out the possibility that the preferred alternative may involve less of some or even all commodities. Specifically, it does not *imply* that giving the consumer more of everything necessarily makes that consumer better off. The alternative view takes the position that the consumer will *always* prefer a consumption plan involving more to one involving less. This is captured by the axiom of *strict monotonicity*. As a matter of notation, if the bundle $\mathbf{x}^0$ contains at least as much of every good as does $\mathbf{x}^1$ we write $\mathbf{x}^0 \geq \mathbf{x}^1$, while if $\mathbf{x}^0$ contains *strictly* more of every good than $\mathbf{x}^1$ we write $\mathbf{x}^0 \gg \mathbf{x}^1$.

AXIOM 4: Strict Monotonicity. *For all* $\mathbf{x}^0, \mathbf{x}^1 \in \mathbb{R}^n_+$, *if* $\mathbf{x}^0 \geq \mathbf{x}^1$ *then* $\mathbf{x}^0 \succsim \mathbf{x}^1$, *while if* $\mathbf{x}^0 \gg \mathbf{x}^1$, *then* $\mathbf{x}^0 \succ \mathbf{x}^1$.

Axiom 4 says that if one bundle contains at least as much of every commodity as another bundle, then the one is at least as good as the other. Moreover, it is strictly better if it contains strictly more of every good. The impact on the structure of indifference and related sets is again significant. First, it should be clear that Axiom 4 implies Axiom 4′, so if preferences satisfy Axiom 4, they automatically satisfy Axiom 4′. Thus, to require Axiom 4 will have the same effects on the structure of indifference and related sets as Axiom 4′ does, plus some additional ones. In particular, Axiom 4 eliminates the possibility that the indifference sets in $\mathbb{R}^2_+$ 'bend upward', or contain positively sloped segments. It also requires that the 'preferred to' sets be 'above' the indifference sets and that the 'worse than' sets be 'below' them.

To help see this, consider Fig. 1.4. Under Axiom 4, no points north-east of $\mathbf{x}^0$ or south-west of $\mathbf{x}^0$ may lie in the same indifference set as $\mathbf{x}^0$. Any point north-east, such as $\mathbf{x}^1$, involves more of both goods than does $\mathbf{x}^0$. All such points in the north-east quadrant must therefore be strictly preferred to $\mathbf{x}^0$. Similarly, any point in the south-west quadrant, such as $\mathbf{x}^2$, involves less of both goods. Under Axiom 4, $\mathbf{x}^0$ must be strictly preferred to $\mathbf{x}^2$ and to all other points in the south-west quadrant, so none of these can lie in the same indifference set as $\mathbf{x}^0$. For any $\mathbf{x}^0$, points north-east of the indifference set will be contained in $\succ(\mathbf{x}^0)$, and all those south-west of the indifference set will be contained in the set $\prec(\mathbf{x}^0)$. A set of preferences satisfying Axioms 1, 2, 3, and 4 is given in Fig. 1.5.

Figure 1.4. Hypothetical preferences satisfying Axioms 1, 2, 3, and 4′.

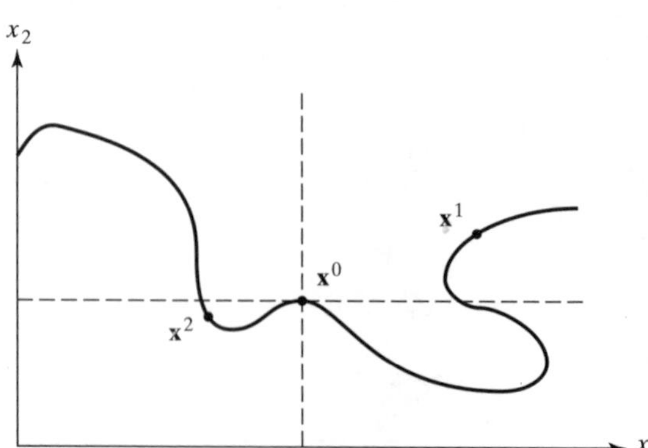

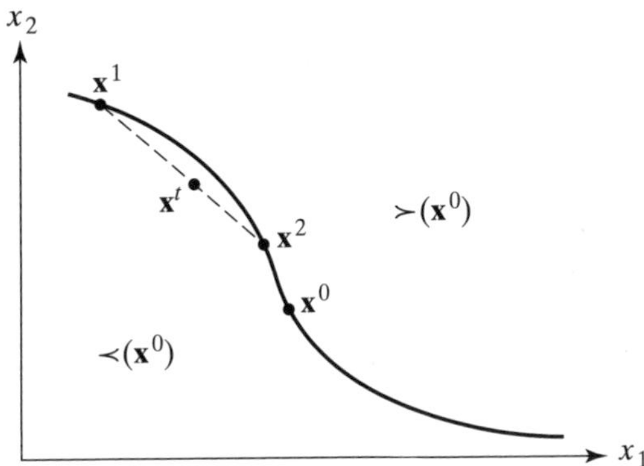

Figure 1.5. Hypothetical preferences satisfying Axioms 1, 2, 3, and 4.

The preferences in Fig. 1.5 are the closest we have seen to the kind undoubtedly familiar to you from your previous economics classes. They still differ, however, in one very important respect: typically, the kind of non-convex region in the north-west part of $\sim(\mathbf{x}^0)$ is explicitly ruled out. This is achieved by invoking one final assumption on tastes. We will state two different versions of the axiom and then consider their meaning and purpose.

AXIOM 5′: Convexity. *If* $\mathbf{x}^1 \succsim \mathbf{x}^0$, *then* $t\mathbf{x}^1 + (1-t)\mathbf{x}^0 \succsim \mathbf{x}^0$ *for all* $t \in [0, 1]$.

A slightly stronger version of this is the following:

AXIOM 5: Strict Convexity. *If* $\mathbf{x}^1 \neq \mathbf{x}^0$ *and* $\mathbf{x}^1 \succsim \mathbf{x}^0$, *then* $t\mathbf{x}^1 + (1-t)\mathbf{x}^0 \succ \mathbf{x}^0$ *for all* $t \in (0, 1)$.

Notice first that either Axiom 5′ or Axiom 5 – in conjunction with Axioms 1, 2, 3, and 4 – will rule out concave-to-the-origin segments in the indifference sets, such as those in the north-west part of Fig. 1.5. To see this, choose two distinct points in the indifference set depicted there. Because $\mathbf{x}^1$ and $\mathbf{x}^2$ are both indifferent to $\mathbf{x}^0$, we clearly have $\mathbf{x}^1 \succsim \mathbf{x}^2$. Convex combinations of those two points, such as $\mathbf{x}^t$, will lie within $\prec(\mathbf{x}^0)$, violating the requirements of both Axiom 5′ and Axiom 5.

For the purposes of the consumer theory we shall develop, it turns out that Axiom 5′ can be imposed without any loss of generality. The predictive content of the theory would be the same with or without it. Although the same statement does not quite hold for the slightly stronger Axiom 5, it does greatly simplify the analysis.

There are at least two ways we can intuitively understand the implications of convexity for consumer tastes. The preferences depicted in Fig. 1.6 are consistent with both Axiom 5′ and Axiom 5. Again, suppose we choose $\mathbf{x}^1 \sim \mathbf{x}^2$. Point $\mathbf{x}^1$ represents a bundle containing a proportion of the good x_2 which is relatively 'extreme', compared to the proportion of x_2 in the other bundle $\mathbf{x}^2$. The bundle $\mathbf{x}^2$, by contrast, contains a proportion of the other good, x_1, which is relatively extreme compared to that contained in $\mathbf{x}^1$. Although each contains a relatively high proportion of one good compared to the other, the consumer is indifferent between the two bundles. Now, any convex combination of $\mathbf{x}^1$ and $\mathbf{x}^2$, such as $\mathbf{x}^t$, will be a bundle containing a more 'balanced' combination of x_1

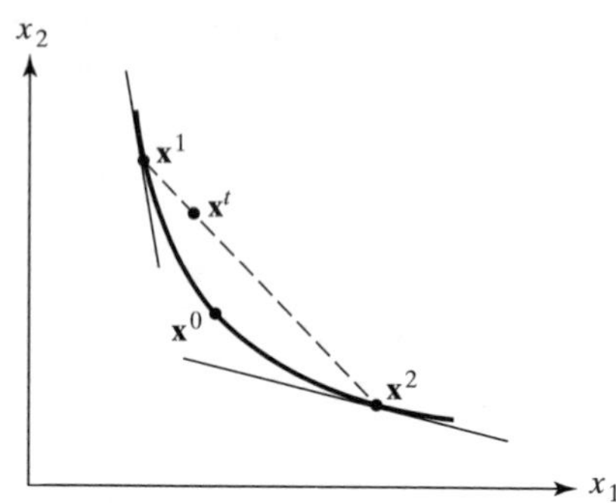

Figure 1.6. Hypothetical preferences satisfying Axioms 1, 2, 3, 4, and 5′ or 5.

and x_2 than does either 'extreme' bundle $\mathbf{x}^1$ or $\mathbf{x}^2$. The thrust of Axiom 5′ or Axiom 5 is to forbid the consumer from preferring such extremes in consumption. Axiom 5′ requires that any such relatively balanced bundle as $\mathbf{x}^t$ be no worse than either of the two extremes between which the consumer is indifferent. Axiom 5 goes a bit further and requires that the consumer strictly prefer any such relatively balanced consumption bundle to both of the extremes between which he is indifferent. In either case, some degree of 'bias' in favour of balance in consumption is required of the consumer's tastes.

Another way to describe the implications of convexity for consumers' tastes focuses attention on the 'curvature' of the indifference sets themselves. When $X = \mathbb{R}^2_+$, the (absolute value of the) slope of an indifference curve is called the **marginal rate of substitution of good two for good one**. This slope measures, at any point, the rate at which the consumer is just willing to give up good two per unit of good one received. Thus, the consumer is indifferent after the exchange.

If preferences are strictly monotonic, any form of convexity requires the indifference curves to be at least weakly convex-shaped relative to the origin. This is equivalent to requiring that the marginal rate of substitution not increase as we move from bundles such as $\mathbf{x}^1$ towards bundles such as $\mathbf{x}^2$. Loosely, this means that the consumer is no more willing to give up x_2 in exchange for x_1 when he has relatively little x_2 and much x_1 than he is when he has relatively much x_2 and little x_1. Axiom 5′ requires the rate at which the consumer would trade x_2 for x_1 and remain indifferent to be either constant or decreasing as we move from north-west to south-east along an indifference curve. Axiom 5 goes a bit further and requires that the rate be strictly diminishing. The preferences in Fig. 1.6 display this property, sometimes called the **principle of diminishing marginal rate of substitution** in consumption.

We have taken some care to consider a number of axioms describing consumer preferences. Our goal has been to gain some appreciation of their individual and collective implications for the structure and representation of consumer preferences. We can summarise this discussion rather briefly. The axioms on consumer preferences may be roughly classified in the following way. The axioms of *completeness* and *transitivity* describe a consumer who can make consistent comparisons among alternatives. The axiom of *continuity* is intended to guarantee the existence of topologically nice 'at least as good as' and 'no better than' sets, and its purpose is primarily a mathematical one. All other axioms serve to characterise consumers' *tastes* over the objects of choice. Typically, we require that tastes display some form of non-satiation, either weak or strong, and some bias in favour of balance in consumption, either weak or strong.

1.2.2 THE UTILITY FUNCTION

In modern theory, a utility function is simply a convenient device for summarising the information contained in the consumer's preference relation – no more and no less. Sometimes it is easier to work directly with the preference relation and its associated sets. Other times, especially when one would like to employ calculus methods, it is easier to work with a utility function. In modern theory, the preference relation is taken to be the primitive, most fundamental characterisation of preferences. The utility function merely 'represents', or summarises, the information conveyed by the preference relation. A utility function is defined formally as follows.

DEFINITION 1.5 ***A Utility Function Representing the Preference Relation*** $\succsim$

A real-valued function $u: \mathbb{R}^n_+ \rightarrow \mathbb{R}$ *is called a utility function representing the preference relation* $\succsim$*, if for all* $\mathbf{x}^0, \mathbf{x}^1 \in \mathbb{R}^n_+$, $u(\mathbf{x}^0) \geq u(\mathbf{x}^1) \Longleftrightarrow \mathbf{x}^0 \succsim \mathbf{x}^1$.

Thus a utility function represents a consumer's preference relation if it assigns higher numbers to preferred bundles.

A question that earlier attracted a great deal of attention from theorists concerned properties that a preference relation must possess to guarantee that it can be represented by a continuous real-valued function. The question is important because the analysis of many problems in consumer theory is enormously simplified if we can work with a utility function, rather than with the preference relation itself.

Mathematically, the question is one of *existence* of a continuous utility function representing a preference relation. It turns out that a subset of the axioms we have considered so far is precisely that required to guarantee existence. It can be shown that any binary relation that is *complete, transitive*, and *continuous* can be represented by a continuous real-valued utility function.[2] (In the exercises, you are asked to show that these three axioms are necessary for such a representation as well.) These are simply the axioms that, together, require that the consumer be able to make basically consistent binary choices and that the preference relation possess a certain amount of topological 'regularity'. In particular, representability does *not* depend on any assumptions about consumer tastes, such as convexity or even monotonicity. We can therefore summarise preferences by a continuous utility function in an extremely broad range of problems.

Here we will take a detailed look at a slightly less general result. In addition to the three most basic axioms mentioned before, we will impose the extra requirement that preferences be strictly monotonic. Although this is not essential for representability, to

[2]See, for example, Barten and Böhm (1982). The classic reference is Debreu (1954).

require it simultaneously simplifies the purely mathematical aspects of the problem and increases the intuitive content of the proof. Notice, however, that we will not require any form of convexity.

THEOREM 1.1 ***Existence of a Real-Valued Function Representing the Preference Relation*** $\succsim$

If the binary relation $\succsim$ *is complete, transitive, continuous, and strictly monotonic, there exists a continuous real-valued function,* $u\colon \mathbb{R}^n_+ \rightarrow \mathbb{R}$, *which represents* $\succsim$.

Notice carefully that this is only an *existence* theorem. It simply claims that under the conditions stated, at least one continuous real-valued function representing the preference relation is guaranteed to exist. There may be, and in fact there always will be, more than one such function. The theorem itself, however, makes no statement on how many more there are, nor does it indicate in any way what form any of them must take. Therefore, if we can dream up just *one* function that is continuous and that represents the given preferences, we will have proved the theorem. This is the strategy we will adopt in the following proof.

Proof: Let the relation $\succsim$ be complete, transitive, continuous, and strictly monotonic. Let $\mathbf{e} \equiv (1, \ldots, 1) \in \mathbb{R}^n_+$ be a vector of ones, and consider the mapping $u\colon \mathbb{R}^n_+ \rightarrow \mathbb{R}$ defined so that the following condition is satisfied:[3]

$$u(\mathbf{x})\mathbf{e} \sim \mathbf{x}. \tag{P.1}$$

Let us first make sure we understand what this says and how it works. In words, (P.1) says, 'take any $\mathbf{x}$ in the domain $\mathbb{R}^n_+$ and assign to it the number $u(\mathbf{x})$ such that the bundle, $u(\mathbf{x})\mathbf{e}$, with $u(\mathbf{x})$ units of every commodity is ranked indifferent to $\mathbf{x}$'.

Two questions immediately arise. First, does there always exist a number $u(\mathbf{x})$ satisfying (P.1)? Second, is it uniquely determined, so that $u(\mathbf{x})$ is a well-defined function?

To settle the first question, fix $\mathbf{x} \in \mathbb{R}^n_+$ and consider the following two subsets of real numbers:

$$A \equiv \{t \geq 0 \mid t\mathbf{e} \succsim \mathbf{x}\}$$
$$B \equiv \{t \geq 0 \mid t\mathbf{e} \precsim \mathbf{x}\}.$$

Note that if $t^* \in A \cap B$, then $t^*\mathbf{e} \sim \mathbf{x}$, so that setting $u(\mathbf{x}) = t^*$ would satisfy (P.1). Thus, the first question would be answered in the affirmative if we show that $A \cap B$ is guaranteed to be non-empty. This is precisely what we shall show.

---

[3]For $t \geq 0$, the vector $t\mathbf{e}$ will be some point in $\mathbb{R}^n_+$ each of whose coordinates is equal to the number t, because $t\mathbf{e} = t(1, \ldots, 1) = (t, \ldots, t)$. If $t = 0$, then $t\mathbf{e} = (0, \ldots, 0)$ coincides with the origin. If $t = 1$, then $t\mathbf{e} = (1, \ldots, 1)$ coincides with $\mathbf{e}$. If $t > 1$, the point $t\mathbf{e}$ lies farther out from the origin than $\mathbf{e}$. For $0<t<1$, the point $t\mathbf{e}$ lies between the origin and $\mathbf{e}$. It should be clear that for any choice of $t \geq 0$, $t\mathbf{e}$ will be a point in $\mathbb{R}^n_+$ somewhere on the ray from the origin through $\mathbf{e}$, i.e., some point on the 45° line in Fig. 1.7.

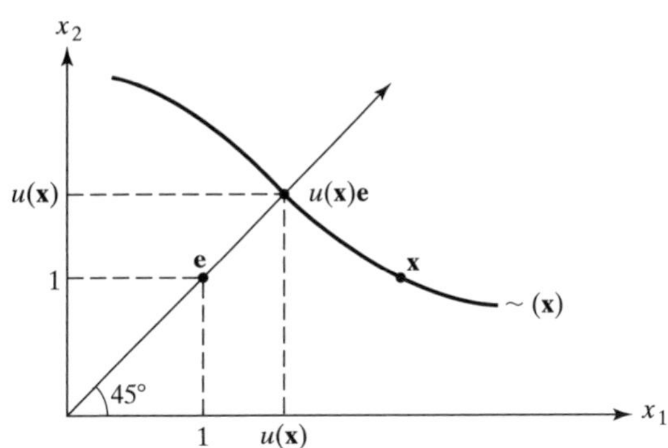

Figure 1.7. Constructing the mapping $u: \mathbb{R}^n_+ \to \mathbb{R}_+$.

According to Exercise 1.11, the continuity of $\succsim$ implies that both A and B are closed in $\mathbb{R}_+$. Also, by strict monotonicity, $t \in A$ implies $t' \in A$ for all $t' \geq t$. Consequently, A must be a closed interval of the form $[\underline{t}, \infty)$. Similarly, strict monotonicity and the closedness of B in $\mathbb{R}_+$ imply that B must be a closed interval of the form $[0, \bar{t}]$. Now for any $t \geq 0$, completeness of $\succsim$ implies that either $t\mathbf{e} \succsim \mathbf{x}$ or $t\mathbf{e} \precsim \mathbf{x}$, that is, $t \in A \cup B$. But this means that $\mathbb{R}_+ = A \cup B = [0, \bar{t}] \cup [\underline{t}, \infty]$. We conclude that $\underline{t} \leq \bar{t}$ so that $A \cap B \neq \emptyset$.

We now turn to the second question. We must show that there is *only one* number $t \geq 0$ such that $t\mathbf{e} \sim \mathbf{x}$. But this follows easily because if $t_1\mathbf{e} \sim \mathbf{x}$ and $t_2\mathbf{e} \sim \mathbf{x}$, then by the transitivity of $\sim$ (see Exercise 1.4), $t_1\mathbf{e} \sim t_2\mathbf{e}$. So, by strict monotonicity, it must be the case that $t_1 = t_2$.

We conclude that for every $\mathbf{x} \in \mathbb{R}^n_+$, there is exactly one number, $u(\mathbf{x})$, such that (P.1) is satisfied. Having constructed a utility function assigning each bundle in X a number, we show next that this utility function represents the preferences $\succsim$.

Consider two bundles $\mathbf{x}^1$ and $\mathbf{x}^2$, and their associated utility numbers $u(\mathbf{x}^1)$ and $u(\mathbf{x}^2)$, which by definition satisfy $u(\mathbf{x}^1)\mathbf{e} \sim \mathbf{x}^1$ and $u(\mathbf{x}^2)\mathbf{e} \sim \mathbf{x}^2$. Then we have the following:

$$\mathbf{x}^1 \succsim \mathbf{x}^2 \tag{P.2}$$

$$\Longleftrightarrow u(\mathbf{x}^1)\mathbf{e} \sim \mathbf{x}^1 \succsim \mathbf{x}^2 \sim u(\mathbf{x}^2)\mathbf{e} \tag{P.3}$$

$$\Longleftrightarrow u(\mathbf{x}^1)\mathbf{e} \succsim u(\mathbf{x}^2)\mathbf{e} \tag{P.4}$$

$$\Longleftrightarrow u(\mathbf{x}^1) \geq u(\mathbf{x}^2). \tag{P.5}$$

Here (P.2) $\Longleftrightarrow$ (P.3) follows by definition of u; (P.3) $\Longleftrightarrow$ (P.4) follows from the transitivity of $\succsim$, the transitivity of $\sim$, and the definition of u; and (P.4) $\Longleftrightarrow$ (P.5) follows from the strict monotonicity of $\succsim$. Together, (P.2) through (P.5) imply that (P.2) $\Longleftrightarrow$ (P.5), so that $\mathbf{x}^1 \succsim \mathbf{x}^2$ if and only if $u(\mathbf{x}^1) \geq u(\mathbf{x}^2)$, as we sought to show.

It remains only to show that the utility function $u: \mathbb{R}^n_+ \to \mathbb{R}$ representing $\succsim$ is continuous. By Theorem A1.6, it suffices to show that the inverse image under u of every open ball in $\mathbb{R}$ is open in $\mathbb{R}^n_+$. Because open balls in $\mathbb{R}$ are merely open intervals, this is equivalent to showing that $u^{-1}((a, b))$ is open in $\mathbb{R}^n_+$ for every $a<b$.

Now,

$$\begin{aligned} u^{-1}((a, b)) &= \{\mathbf{x} \in \mathbb{R}^n_+ \mid a < u(\mathbf{x}) < b\} \\ &= \{\mathbf{x} \in \mathbb{R}^n_+ \mid a\mathbf{e} \prec u(\mathbf{x})\mathbf{e} \prec b\mathbf{e}\} \\ &= \{\mathbf{x} \in \mathbb{R}^n_+ \mid a\mathbf{e} \prec \mathbf{x} \prec b\mathbf{e}\}. \end{aligned}$$

The first equality follows from the definition of the inverse image; the second from the monotonicity of $\succsim$; and the third from $u(\mathbf{x})\mathbf{e} \sim \mathbf{x}$ and Exercise 1.4. Rewriting the last set on the right-hand side gives

$$u^{-1}((a, b)) = \succ (a\mathbf{e}) \bigcap \prec (b\mathbf{e}). \tag{P.6}$$

By the continuity of $\succsim$, the sets $\precsim(a\mathbf{e})$ and $\succsim(b\mathbf{e})$ are closed in $X = \mathbb{R}^n_+$. Consequently, the two sets on the right-hand side of (P.6), being the complements of these closed sets, are open in $\mathbb{R}^n_+$. Therefore, $u^{-1}((a, b))$, being the intersection of two open sets in $\mathbb{R}^n_+$, is, by Exercise A1.28, itself open in $\mathbb{R}^n_+$. ∎

Theorem 1.1 is very important. It frees us to represent preferences either in terms of the primitive set-theoretic preference relation or in terms of a numerical representation, a continuous utility function. But this utility representation is never unique. If some function u represents a consumer's preferences, then so too will the function $v = u + 5$, or the function $v = u^3$, because each of these functions ranks bundles the same way u does. This is an important point about utility functions that must be grasped. If all we require of the preference relation is that it order the bundles in the consumption set, and if all we require of a utility function representing those preferences is that it reflect that ordering of bundles by the ordering of numbers it assigns to them, then any *other* function that assigns numbers to bundles in the same order as u does will *also* represent that preference relation and will itself be just as good a utility function as u.

This is known by several different names in the literature. People sometimes say the utility function is *invariant to positive monotonic transforms* or sometimes they say that the utility function is *unique up to a positive monotonic transform*. Either way, the meaning is this: if all we require of the preference relation is that rankings between bundles be meaningful, then all any utility function representing that relation is capable of conveying to us is *ordinal* information, no more and no less. If we know that one function properly conveys the ordering of bundles, then any transform of that function that preserves that ordering of bundles will perform all the duties of a utility function just as well.

Seeing the representation issue in proper perspective thus frees us and restrains us. If we have a function u that represents some consumers' preferences, it frees us to transform u into other, perhaps more convenient or easily manipulated forms, as long as the transformation we choose is order-preserving. At the same time, we are restrained by the explicit warning here that no significance whatsoever can be attached to the actual numbers assigned by a given utility function to particular bundles – only to the ordering of those numbers.[4] This conclusion, though simple to demonstrate, is nonetheless important enough to warrant being stated formally. The proof is left as an exercise.

THEOREM 1.2 ***Invariance of the Utility Function to Positive Monotonic Transforms***

Let $\succsim$ be a preference relation on $\mathbb{R}^n_+$ and suppose $u(\mathbf{x})$ is a utility function that represents it. Then $v(\mathbf{x})$ also represents $\succsim$ if and only if $v(\mathbf{x}) = f(u(\mathbf{x}))$ for every $\mathbf{x}$, where $f\colon \mathbb{R}\to\mathbb{R}$ is strictly increasing on the set of values taken on by u.

Typically, we will want to make some assumptions on tastes to complete the description of consumer preferences. Naturally enough, any additional structure we impose on preferences will be reflected as additional structure on the utility function representing them. By the same token, whenever we assume the utility function to have properties beyond continuity, we will in effect be invoking some set of additional assumptions on the underlying preference relation. There is, then, an equivalence between axioms on tastes and specific mathematical properties of the utility function. We will conclude this section by briefly noting some of them. The following theorem is exceedingly simple to prove because it follows easily from the definitions involved. It is worth being convinced, however, so its proof is left as an exercise. (See Chapter A1 in the Mathematical Appendix for definitions of strictly increasing, quasiconcave, and strictly quasiconcave functions.)

THEOREM 1.3 ***Properties of Preferences and Utility Functions***

Let $\succsim$ be represented by $u\colon \mathbb{R}^n_+\to\mathbb{R}$. Then:

1. *$u(\mathbf{x})$ is strictly increasing if and only if $\succsim$ is strictly monotonic.*
2. *$u(\mathbf{x})$ is quasiconcave if and only if $\succsim$ is convex.*
3. *$u(\mathbf{x})$ is strictly quasiconcave if and only if $\succsim$ is strictly convex.*

Later we will want to analyse problems using calculus tools. Until now, we have concentrated on the continuity of the utility function and properties of the preference relation that ensure it. Differentiability, of course, is a more demanding requirement than continuity. Intuitively, continuity requires there be no sudden preference reversals. It does not rule out 'kinks' or other kinds of continuous, but impolite behaviour. Differentiability specifically excludes such things and ensures indifference curves are 'smooth' as well as continuous. Differentiability of the utility function thus requires a stronger restriction on

[4]Some theorists are so sensitive to the potential confusion between the modern usage of the term 'utility function' and the classical utilitarian notion of 'utility' as a measurable quantity of pleasure or pain that they reject the anachronistic terminology altogether and simply speak of preference relations and their 'representation functions'.

preferences than continuity. Like the axiom of continuity, what is needed is just the right mathematical condition. We shall not develop this condition here, but refer the reader to Debreu (1972) for the details. For our purposes, we are content to simply assume that the utility representation is differentiable whenever necessary.

There is a certain vocabulary we use when utility is differentiable, so we should learn it. The first-order partial derivative of $u(\mathbf{x})$ with respect to x_i is called the **marginal utility of good** i. For the case of two goods, we defined the marginal rate of substitution of good 2 for good 1 as the absolute value of the slope of an indifference curve. We can derive an expression for this in terms of the two goods' marginal utilities. To see this, consider any bundle $\mathbf{x}^1 = (x_1^1, x_2^1)$. Because the indifference curve through $\mathbf{x}^1$ is just a function in the (x_1, x_2) plane, let $x_2 = f(x_1)$ be the function describing it. Therefore, as x_1 varies, the bundle $(x_1, x_2) = (x_1, f(x_1))$ traces out the indifference curve through $\mathbf{x}^1$. Consequently, for all x_1,

$$u(x_1, f(x_1)) = \text{constant}. \tag{1.1}$$

Now the marginal rate of substitution of good two for good one at the bundle $\mathbf{x}^1 = (x_1^1, x_2^1)$, denoted $MRS_{12}(x_1^1, x_2^1)$, is the absolute value of the slope of the indifference curve through (x_1^1, x_2^1). That is,

$$MRS_{12}(x_1^1, x_2^1) \equiv \left|f'(x_1^1)\right| = -f'(x_1^1), \tag{1.2}$$

because $f' < 0$. But by (1.1), $u(x_1, f(x_1))$ is a constant function of x_1. Hence, its derivative with respect to x_1 must be zero. That is,

$$\frac{\partial u(x_1, x_2)}{\partial x_1} + \frac{\partial u(x_1, x_2)}{\partial x_2} f'(x_1) = 0. \tag{1.3}$$

But (1.2) together with (1.3) imply that

$$MRS_{12}(\mathbf{x}^1) = \frac{\partial u(\mathbf{x}^1)/\partial x_1}{\partial u(\mathbf{x}^1)/\partial x_2}.$$

Similarly, when there are more than two goods we define the marginal rate of substitution of good j for good i as the ratio of their marginal utilities,

$$MRS_{ij}(\mathbf{x}) \equiv \frac{\partial u(\mathbf{x})/\partial x_i}{\partial u(\mathbf{x})/\partial x_j}.$$

When marginal utilities are strictly positive, the $MRS_{ij}(\mathbf{x})$ is again a positive number, and it tells us the rate at which good j can be exchanged per unit of good i with no change in the consumer's utility.

When $u(\mathbf{x})$ is continuously differentiable on $\mathbb{R}^n_{++}$ and preferences are strictly monotonic, the marginal utility of every good is virtually always strictly positive. That is,

$\partial u(\mathbf{x})/\partial x_i > 0$ for 'almost all' bundles $\mathbf{x}$, and all $i = 1, \ldots, n$.[5] When preferences are strictly convex, the marginal rate of substitution between two goods is always strictly diminishing along any level surface of the utility function. More generally, for any quasiconcave utility function, its Hessian matrix $\mathbf{H}(\mathbf{x})$ of second-order partials will satisfy

$$\mathbf{y}^{\mathrm{T}}\mathbf{H}(\mathbf{x})\mathbf{y} \leq 0 \qquad \text{for all vectors } \mathbf{y} \text{ such that} \qquad \nabla u(\mathbf{x}) \cdot \mathbf{y} = 0.$$

If the inequality is strict, this says that moving from $\mathbf{x}$ in a direction $\mathbf{y}$ that is tangent to the indifference surface through $\mathbf{x}$ [i.e., $\nabla u(\mathbf{x}) \cdot \mathbf{y} = 0$] reduces utility (i.e., $\mathbf{y}^{\mathrm{T}}\mathbf{H}(\mathbf{x})\mathbf{y} < 0$).

1.3 THE CONSUMER'S PROBLEM

We have dwelt upon how to structure and represent preferences, but these are only one of four major building blocks in our theory of consumer choice. In this section, we consider the rest of them and combine them all together to construct a formal description of the central actor in much of economic theory – the humble atomistic consumer.

On the most abstract level, we view the consumer as having a consumption set, $X = \mathbb{R}^n_+$, containing all conceivable alternatives in consumption. His inclinations and attitudes toward them are described by the preference relation $\succsim$ defined on $\mathbb{R}^n_+$. The consumer's circumstances limit the alternatives he is actually able to achieve, and we collect these all together into a feasible set, $B \subset \mathbb{R}^n_+$. Finally, we assume the consumer is motivated to choose the most preferred feasible alternative according to his preference relation. Formally, the consumer seeks

$$\mathbf{x}^* \in B \text{ such that } \mathbf{x}^* \succsim \mathbf{x} \text{ for all } \mathbf{x} \in B \tag{1.4}$$

To make further progress, we make the following assumptions that will be maintained unless stated otherwise.

ASSUMPTION 1.2 ***Consumer Preferences***

The consumer's preference relation $\succsim$ is complete, transitive, continuous, strictly monotonic, and strictly convex on $\mathbb{R}^n_+$. Therefore, by Theorems 1.1 and 1.3 it can be represented by a real-valued utility function, u, that is continuous, strictly increasing, and strictly quasiconcave on $\mathbb{R}^n_+$.

In the two-good case, preferences like these can be represented by an indifference map whose level sets are non-intersecting, strictly convex away from the origin, and increasing north-easterly, as depicted in Fig. 1.8.

[5] In case the reader is curious, the term 'almost all' means all bundles except a set having Lebesgue measure zero. However, there is no need to be familiar with Lebesgue measure to see that some such qualifier is necessary. Consider the case of a single good, x, and the utility function $u(x) = x + \sin(x)$. Because u is strictly increasing,

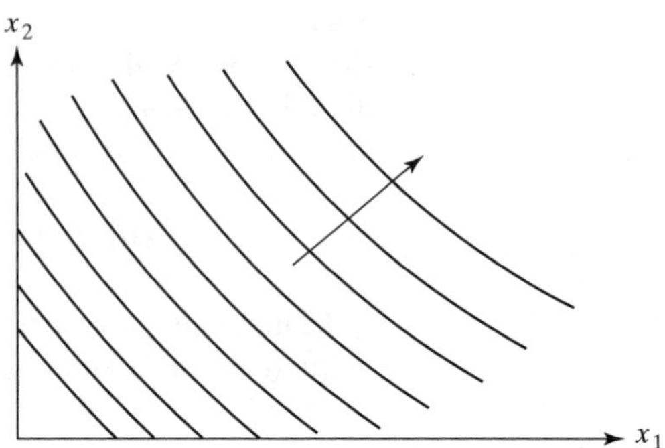

Figure 1.8. Indifference map for preferences satisfying Assumption 1.2.

Next, we consider the consumer's circumstances and structure the feasible set. Our concern is with an individual consumer operating within a **market economy**. By a market economy, we mean an economic system in which transactions between agents are mediated by markets. There is a market for each commodity, and in these markets, a price p_i prevails for each commodity i. We suppose that prices are strictly positive, so $p_i > 0, i = 1, \ldots, n$. Moreover, we assume the individual consumer is an *insignificant force* on every market. By this we mean, specifically, that the size of each market relative to the potential purchases of the individual consumer is so large that no matter how much or how little the consumer might purchase, there will be no perceptible effect on any market price. Formally, this means we take the vector of market prices, $\mathbf{p} \gg \mathbf{0}$, as *fixed* from the consumer's point of view.

The consumer is endowed with a fixed money income $y \geq 0$. Because the purchase of x_i units of commodity i at price p_i per unit requires an expenditure of $p_i x_i$ dollars, the requirement that expenditure not exceed income can be stated as $\sum_{i=1}^{n} p_i x_i \leq y$ or, more compactly, as $\mathbf{p} \cdot \mathbf{x} \leq y$. We summarise these assumptions on the economic environment of the consumer by specifying the following structure on the feasible set, B, called the **budget set:**

$$B = \{\mathbf{x} \mid \mathbf{x} \in \mathbb{R}^n_+, \mathbf{p} \cdot \mathbf{x} \leq y\}.$$

In the two-good case, B consists of all bundles lying inside or on the boundaries of the shaded region in Fig. 1.9.

If we want to, we can now recast the consumer's problem in very familiar terms. Under Assumption 1.2, preferences may be represented by a strictly increasing and strictly quasiconcave utility function $u(\mathbf{x})$ on the consumption set $\mathbb{R}^n_+$. Under our assumptions on the feasible set, total expenditure must not exceed income. The consumer's problem (1.4) can thus be cast *equivalently* as the problem of maximising the utility function subject to

---

it represents strictly monotonic preferences. However, although $u'(x)$ is strictly positive for most values of x, it is zero whenever $x = \pi + 2\pi k, k = 0, 1, 2, \ldots$

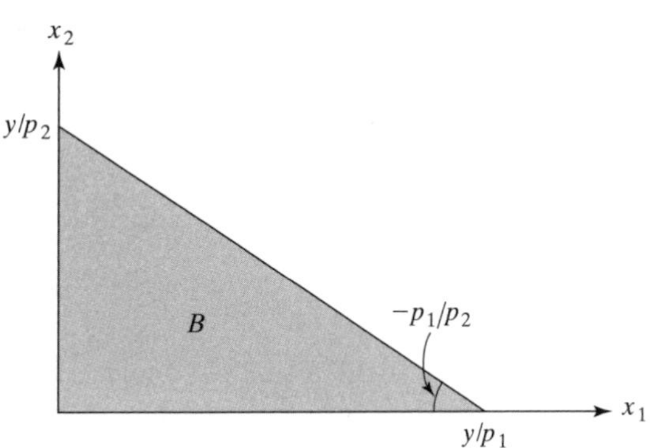

Figure 1.9. Budget set, $B = \{\mathbf{x} \mid \mathbf{x} \in \mathbb{R}^n_+,\ \mathbf{p} \cdot \mathbf{x} \le y\}$, in the case of two commodities.

the budget constraint. Formally, the consumer's **utility-maximisation problem** is written

$$\max_{\mathbf{x} \in \mathbb{R}^n_+} u(\mathbf{x}) \qquad \text{s.t.} \qquad \mathbf{p} \cdot \mathbf{x} \le \mathbf{y}. \tag{1.5}$$

Note that if $\mathbf{x}^*$ solves this problem, then $u(\mathbf{x}^*) \ge u(\mathbf{x})$ for all $\mathbf{x} \in B$, which means that $\mathbf{x}^* \succsim \mathbf{x}$ for all $\mathbf{x} \in B$. That is, solutions to (1.5) are indeed solutions to (1.4). The converse is also true.

We should take a moment to examine the mathematical structure of this problem. As we have noted, under the assumptions on preferences, the utility function $u(\mathbf{x})$ is real-valued and continuous. The budget set B is a non-empty (it contains $\mathbf{0} \in \mathbb{R}^n_+$), closed, bounded (because all prices are strictly positive), and thus compact subset of $\mathbb{R}^n$. By the Weierstrass theorem, Theorem A1.10, we are therefore assured that a maximum of $u(\mathbf{x})$ over B exists. Moreover, because B is convex and the objective function is strictly quasiconcave, the maximiser of $u(\mathbf{x})$ over B is *unique*. Because preferences are strictly monotonic, the solution $\mathbf{x}^*$ will satisfy the budget constraint with *equality*, lying *on*, rather than inside, the boundary of the budget set. Thus, when $y > 0$ and because $\mathbf{x}^* \ge 0$, but $\mathbf{x}^* \ne 0$, we know that $x_i^* > 0$ for at least one good i. A typical solution to this problem in the two-good case is illustrated in Fig. 1.10.

Clearly, the solution vector $\mathbf{x}^*$ depends on the parameters to the consumer's problem. Because it will be unique for given values of $\mathbf{p}$ and y, we can properly view the solution to (1.5) as a *function* from the set of prices and income to the set of quantities, $X = \mathbb{R}^n_+$. We therefore will often write $x_i^* = x_i(\mathbf{p}, y)$, $i = 1, \ldots, n$, or, in vector notation, $\mathbf{x}^* = \mathbf{x}(\mathbf{p}, y)$. When viewed as functions of $\mathbf{p}$ and y, the solutions to the utility-maximisation problem are known as ordinary, or **Marshallian demand functions**. When income and all prices other than the good's own price are held fixed, the graph of the relationship between quantity demanded of x_i and its own price p_i is the standard demand curve for good i.

The relationship between the consumer's problem and consumer demand behaviour is illustrated in Fig. 1.11. In Fig. 1.11(a), the consumer faces prices p_1^0 and p_2^0 and has income y^0. Quantities $x_1(p_1^0, p_2^0, y^0)$ and $x_2(p_1^0, p_2^0, y^0)$ solve the consumer's problem and

Figure 1.10. The solution to the consumer's utility-maximisation problem.

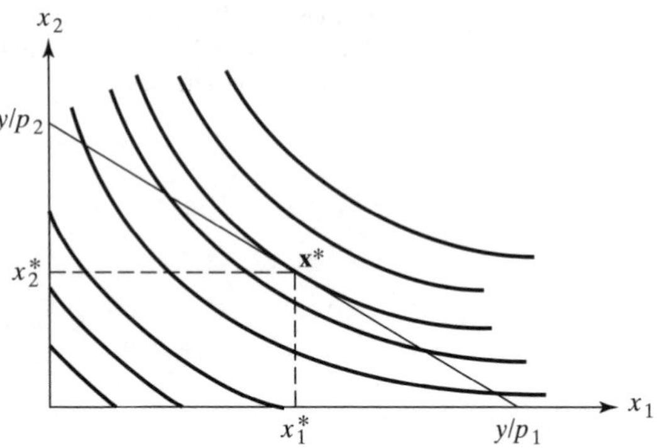

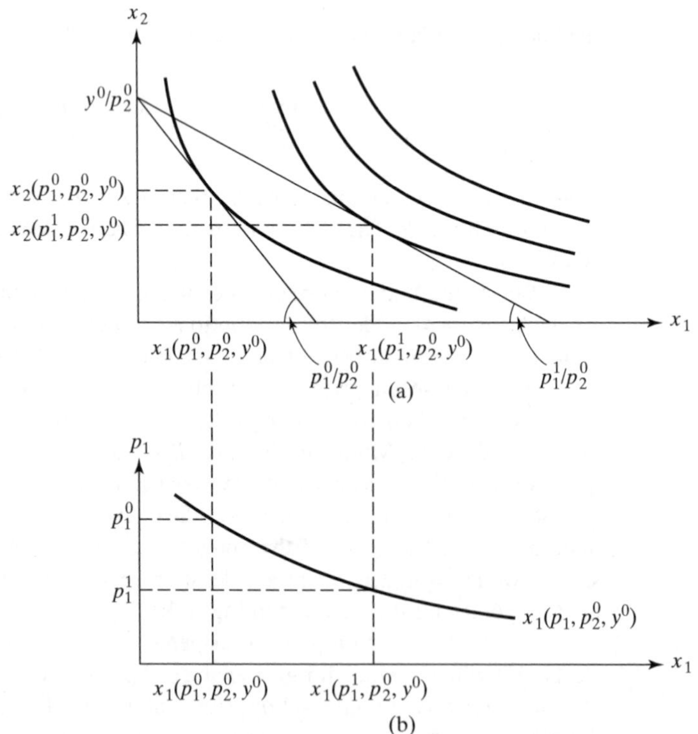

Figure 1.11. The consumer's problem and consumer demand behaviour.

maximise utility facing those prices and income. Directly below, in Fig. 1.11(b), we measure the price of good 1 on the vertical axis and the quantity demanded of good 1 on the horizontal axis. If we plot the price p_1^0 against the quantity of good 1 demanded at that price (given the price p_2^0 and income y^0), we obtain one point on the consumer's

Marshallian demand curve for good 1. At the same income and price of good 2, facing $p_1^1 < p_1^0$, the quantities $x_1(p_1^1, p_2^0, y^0)$ and $x_2(p_1^1, p_2^0, y^0)$ solve the consumer's problem and maximise utility. If we plot p_1^1 against the quantity of good 1 demanded at that price, we obtain another point on the Marshallian demand curve for good 1 in Fig. 1.11(b). By considering all possible values for p_1, we trace out the consumer's entire demand curve for good 1 in Fig. 1.11(b). As you can easily verify, different levels of income and different prices of good 2 will cause the position and shape of the demand curve for good 1 to change. That position and shape, however, will always be determined by the properties of the consumer's underlying preference relation.

If we strengthen the requirements on $u(\mathbf{x})$ to include differentiability, we can use calculus methods to further explore demand behaviour. Recall that the consumer's problem is

$$\max_{\mathbf{x} \in \mathbb{R}^n_+} u(\mathbf{x}) \qquad \text{s.t.} \qquad \mathbf{p} \cdot \mathbf{x} \leq y. \tag{1.6}$$

This is a non-linear programming problem with one inequality constraint. As we have noted, a solution $\mathbf{x}^*$ exists and is unique. If we rewrite the constraint as $\mathbf{p} \cdot \mathbf{x} - y \leq 0$ and then form the Lagrangian, we obtain

$$\mathcal{L}(\mathbf{x}, \lambda) = u(\mathbf{x}) - \lambda[\mathbf{p} \cdot \mathbf{x} - y].$$

Assuming that the solution $\mathbf{x}^*$ is strictly positive, we can apply Kuhn-Tucker methods to characterise it. If $\mathbf{x}^* \gg \mathbf{0}$ solves (1.6), then by Theorem A2.20, there exists a $\lambda^* \geq 0$ such that $(\mathbf{x}^*, \lambda^*)$ satisfy the following Kuhn-Tucker conditions:

$$\frac{\partial \mathcal{L}}{\partial x_i} = \frac{\partial u(\mathbf{x}^*)}{\partial x_i} - \lambda^* p_i = 0, \qquad i = 1, \ldots, n, \tag{1.7}$$

$$\mathbf{p} \cdot \mathbf{x}^* - y \leq 0, \tag{1.8}$$

$$\lambda^* \left[\mathbf{p} \cdot \mathbf{x}^* - y\right] = 0. \tag{1.9}$$

Now, by strict monotonicity, (1.8) must be satisfied with equality, so that (1.9) becomes redundant. Consequently, these conditions reduce to

$$\begin{aligned}
\frac{\partial \mathcal{L}}{\partial x_1} &= \frac{\partial u(\mathbf{x}^*)}{\partial x_1} - \lambda^* p_1 = 0, \\
&\vdots \\
\frac{\partial \mathcal{L}}{\partial x_n} &= \frac{\partial u(\mathbf{x}^*)}{\partial x_n} - \lambda^* p_n = 0, \\
&\mathbf{p} \cdot \mathbf{x}^* - y = 0.
\end{aligned} \tag{1.10}$$

What do these tell us about the solution to (1.6)? There are two possibilities. Either $\nabla u(\mathbf{x}^*) = \mathbf{0}$ or $\nabla u(\mathbf{x}^*) \neq \mathbf{0}$. Under strict monotonicity, the first case is possible, but quite unlikely. We shall simply assume therefore that $\nabla u(\mathbf{x}^*) \neq \mathbf{0}$. Thus, by strict monotonicity, $\partial u(\mathbf{x}^*)/\partial x_i > 0$, for some $i = 1, \ldots, n$. Because $p_i > 0$ for all i, it is clear from (1.7) that the Lagrangian multiplier will be strictly positive at the solution, because $\lambda^* = u_i(\mathbf{x}^*)/p_i > 0$. Consequently, for all j, $\partial u(\mathbf{x}^*)/\partial x_j = \lambda^* p_j > 0$, so marginal utility is proportional to price for all goods at the optimum. Alternatively, for any two goods j and k, we can combine the conditions to conclude that

$$\frac{\partial u(\mathbf{x}^*)/\partial x_j}{\partial u(\mathbf{x}^*)/\partial x_k} = \frac{p_j}{p_k}. \tag{1.11}$$

This says that at the optimum, the marginal rate of substitution between any two goods must be equal to the ratio of the goods' prices. In the two-good case, conditions (1.10) therefore require that the slope of the indifference curve through $\mathbf{x}^*$ be equal to the slope of the budget constraint, and that $\mathbf{x}^*$ lie on, rather than inside, the budget line, as in Fig. 1.10 and Fig. 1.11(a).

In general, conditions (1.10) are merely necessary conditions for a local optimum (see the end of Section A2.3). However, for the particular problem at hand, these necessary first-order conditions are in fact *sufficient* for a global optimum. This is worthwhile stating formally.

THEOREM 1.4 ***Sufficiency of Consumer's First-Order Conditions***

Suppose that $u(\mathbf{x})$ is continuous and quasiconcave on $\mathbb{R}^n_+$, and that $(\mathbf{p}, y) \gg \mathbf{0}$. If u is differentiable at $\mathbf{x}^*$, and $(\mathbf{x}^*, \lambda^*) \gg \mathbf{0}$ solves (1.10), then $\mathbf{x}^*$ solves the consumer's maximisation problem at prices $\mathbf{p}$ and income y.

Proof: We shall employ the following fact that you are asked to prove in Exercise 1.28: For all $\mathbf{x}, \mathbf{x}^1 \geq \mathbf{0}$, because u is quasiconcave, $\nabla u(\mathbf{x})(\mathbf{x}^1 - \mathbf{x}) \geq 0$ whenever $u(\mathbf{x}^1) \geq u(\mathbf{x})$ and u is differentiable at $\mathbf{x}$.

Now, suppose that $\nabla u(\mathbf{x}^*)$ exists and $(\mathbf{x}^*, \lambda^*) \gg \mathbf{0}$ solves (1.10). Then

$$\nabla u(\mathbf{x}^*) = \lambda^* \mathbf{p}, \tag{P.1}$$

$$\mathbf{p} \cdot \mathbf{x}^* = y. \tag{P.2}$$

If $\mathbf{x}^*$ is not utility-maximising, then there must be some $\mathbf{x}^0 \geq \mathbf{0}$ such that

$$u(\mathbf{x}^0) > u(\mathbf{x}^*),$$

$$\mathbf{p} \cdot \mathbf{x}^0 \leq y.$$

Because u is continuous and $y > 0$, the preceding inequalities imply that

$$u(t\mathbf{x}^0) > u(\mathbf{x}^*), \tag{P.3}$$
$$\mathbf{p} \cdot t\mathbf{x}^0 < y. \tag{P.4}$$

for some $t \in [0, 1]$ close enough to one. Letting $\mathbf{x}^1 = t\mathbf{x}^0$, we then have

$$\begin{aligned}\nabla u(\mathbf{x}^*)(\mathbf{x}^1 - \mathbf{x}^*) &= (\lambda^*\mathbf{p}) \cdot (\mathbf{x}^1 - \mathbf{x}^*)\\ &= \lambda^*(\mathbf{p} \cdot \mathbf{x}^1 - \mathbf{p} \cdot \mathbf{x}^*)\\ &< \lambda^*(y - y)\\ &= 0,\end{aligned}$$

where the first equality follows from (P.1), and the second inequality follows from (P.2) and (P.4). However, because by (P.3) $u(\mathbf{x}^1) > u(\mathbf{x}^*)$, (P.5) contradicts the fact set forth at the beginning of the proof. ∎

With this sufficiency result in hand, it is enough to find a solution $(\mathbf{x}^*, \lambda^*) \gg \mathbf{0}$ to (1.10). Note that (1.10) is a system of $n + 1$ equations in the $n + 1$ unknowns $x_1^*, \ldots, x_n^*, \lambda^*$. These equations can typically be used to solve for the demand functions $x_i(\mathbf{p}, y)$, $i = 1, \ldots, n$, as we show in the following example.

EXAMPLE 1.1 The function, $u(x_1, x_2) = (x_1^\rho + x_2^\rho)^{1/\rho}$, where $0 \neq \rho < 1$, is known as a **CES utility function**. You can easily verify that this utility function represents preferences that are strictly monotonic and strictly convex.

The consumer's problem is to find a non-negative consumption bundle solving

$$\max_{x_1, x_2} \left(x_1^\rho + x_2^\rho\right)^{1/\rho} \qquad \text{s.t.} \qquad p_1x_1 + p_2x_2 - y \leq 0. \tag{E.1}$$

To solve this problem, we first form the associated Lagrangian

$$\mathcal{L}(x_1, x_2, \lambda) \equiv \left(x_1^\rho + x_2^\rho\right)^{1/\rho} - \lambda(p_1x_1 + p_2x_2 - y).$$

Because preferences are monotonic, the budget constraint will hold with equality at the solution. Assuming an interior solution, the Kuhn-Tucker conditions coincide with the ordinary first-order Lagrangian conditions and the following equations must hold at the solution values x_1, x_2, and λ:

$$\frac{\partial \mathcal{L}}{\partial x_1} = \left(x_1^\rho + x_2^\rho\right)^{(1/\rho)-1} x_1^{\rho-1} - \lambda p_1 = 0, \tag{E.2}$$
$$\frac{\partial \mathcal{L}}{\partial x_2} = \left(x_1^\rho + x_2^\rho\right)^{(1/\rho)-1} x_2^{\rho-1} - \lambda p_2 = 0, \tag{E.3}$$
$$\frac{\partial \mathcal{L}}{\partial \lambda} = p_1x_1 + p_2x_2 - y = 0. \tag{E.4}$$

Rearranging (E.2) and (E.3), then dividing the first by the second and rearranging some more, we can reduce these three equations in three unknowns to only two equations in the two unknowns of particular interest, x_1 and x_2:

$$x_1 = x_2\left(\frac{p_1}{p_2}\right)^{1/(\rho-1)}, \tag{E.5}$$

$$y = p_1 x_1 + p_2 x_2. \tag{E.6}$$

First, substitute from (E.5) for x_1 in (E.6) to obtain the equation in x_2 alone:

$$\begin{aligned} y &= p_1 x_2\left(\frac{p_1}{p_2}\right)^{1/(\rho-1)} + p_2 x_2 \\ &= x_2\left(p_1^{\rho/(\rho-1)} + p_2^{\rho/(\rho-1)}\right)p_2^{-1/(\rho-1)}. \end{aligned} \tag{E.7}$$

Solving (E.7) for x_2 gives the solution value:

$$x_2 = \frac{p_2^{1/(\rho-1)}y}{p_1^{\rho/(\rho-1)} + p_2^{\rho/(\rho-1)}}. \tag{E.8}$$

To solve for x_1, substitute from (E.8) into (E.5) and obtain

$$x_1 = \frac{p_1^{1/(\rho-1)}y}{p_1^{\rho/(\rho-1)} + p_2^{\rho/(\rho-1)}}. \tag{E.9}$$

Equations (E.8) and (E.9), the solutions to the consumer's problem (E.1), are the consumer's Marshallian demand functions. If we define the parameter $r = \rho/(\rho - 1)$, we can simplify (E.8) and (E.9) and write the Marshallian demands as

$$x_1(\mathbf{p}, y) = \frac{p_1^{r-1}y}{p_1^r + p_2^r}, \tag{E.10}$$

$$x_2(\mathbf{p}, y) = \frac{p_2^{r-1}y}{p_1^r + p_2^r}. \tag{E.11}$$

Notice that the solutions to the consumer's problem depend only on its *parameters*, p_1, p_2, and y. Different prices and income, through (E.10) and (E.11), will give different quantities of each good demanded. To drive this point home, consider Fig. 1.12. There, at prices $p_1, \bar{p}_2$ and income $\bar{y}$, the solutions to the consumer's problem will be the quantities of x_1 and x_2 indicated. The pair $(p_1, x_1(p_1, \bar{p}_2, \bar{y}))$ will be a point on (one of) the consumer's demand curves for good x_1. □

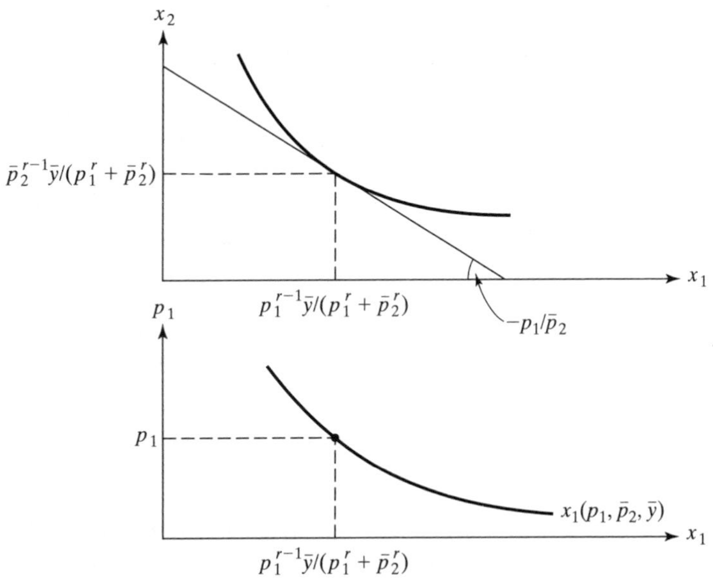

Figure 1.12. Consumer demand when preferences are represented by a CES utility function.

Finally, a word on the properties of the demand function $\mathbf{x}(\mathbf{p}, y)$ derived from the consumer's maximisation problem. We have made enough assumptions to ensure (by Theorem A2.21 (the theorem of the maximum)) that $\mathbf{x}(\mathbf{p}, y)$ will be continuous on $\mathbb{R}^n_{++}$. But we shall usually want more than this. We would like to be able to consider the slopes of demand curves and hence we would like $\mathbf{x}(\mathbf{p}, y)$ to be differentiable. From this point on, we shall simply assume that $\mathbf{x}(\mathbf{p}, y)$ is differentiable whenever we need it to be. But just to let you know what this involves, we state without proof the following result.

THEOREM 1.5 ***Differentiable Demand***

Let $\mathbf{x}^* \gg \mathbf{0}$ solve the consumer's maximisation problem at prices $\mathbf{p}^0 \gg \mathbf{0}$ and income $y^0 > 0$. If

- *u is twice continuously differentiable on $\mathbb{R}^n_{++}$,*
- *$\partial u(\mathbf{x}^*)/\partial x_i > 0$ for some $i = 1, \ldots, n$, and*
- *the bordered Hessian of u has a non-zero determinant at $\mathbf{x}^*$,*

then $\mathbf{x}(\mathbf{p}, y)$ is differentiable at $(\mathbf{p}^0, y^0)$.

1.4 INDIRECT UTILITY AND EXPENDITURE

1.4.1 THE INDIRECT UTILITY FUNCTION

The ordinary utility function, $u(\mathbf{x})$, is defined over the consumption set X and represents the consumer's preferences directly, as we have seen. It is therefore referred to as the **direct utility function**. Given prices $\mathbf{p}$ and income y, the consumer chooses a utility-maximising bundle $\mathbf{x}(\mathbf{p}, y)$. The level of utility achieved when $\mathbf{x}(\mathbf{p}, y)$ is chosen thus will be the highest level permitted by the consumer's budget constraint facing prices $\mathbf{p}$ and income y. Different prices or incomes, giving different budget constraints, will generally give rise to different choices by the consumer and so to different levels of maximised utility. The relationship among prices, income, and the maximised value of utility can be summarised by a real-valued function $v: \mathbb{R}^n_+ \times \mathbb{R}_+ \to \mathbb{R}$ defined as follows:

$$v(\mathbf{p}, y) = \max_{\mathbf{x} \in \mathbb{R}^n_+} u(\mathbf{x}) \quad \text{s.t.} \quad \mathbf{p} \cdot \mathbf{x} \leq y. \tag{1.12}$$

The function $v(\mathbf{p}, y)$ is called the **indirect utility function**. It is the maximum-value function corresponding to the consumer's utility maximisation problem. When $u(\mathbf{x})$ is continuous, $v(\mathbf{p}, y)$ is well-defined for all $\mathbf{p} \gg \mathbf{0}$ and $y \geq 0$ because a solution to the maximisation problem (1.12) is guaranteed to exist. If, in addition, $u(\mathbf{x})$ is strictly quasiconcave, then the solution is unique and we write it as $\mathbf{x}(\mathbf{p}, y)$, the consumer's demand function. The maximum level of utility that can be achieved when facing prices $\mathbf{p}$ and income y therefore will be that which is realised when $\mathbf{x}(\mathbf{p}, y)$ is chosen. Hence,

$$v(\mathbf{p}, y) = u(\mathbf{x}(\mathbf{p}, y)). \tag{1.13}$$

Geometrically, we can think of $v(\mathbf{p}, y)$ as giving the utility level of the highest indifference curve the consumer can reach, given prices $\mathbf{p}$ and income y, as illustrated in Fig. 1.13.

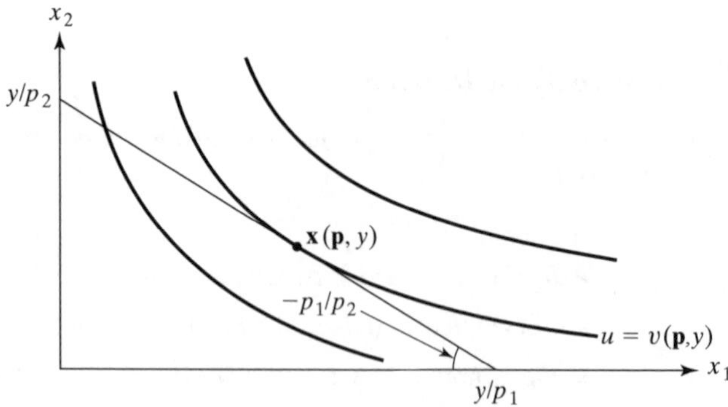

Figure 1.13. Indirect utility at prices $\mathbf{p}$ and income y.

There are several properties that the indirect utility function will possess. Continuity of the constraint function in $\mathbf{p}$ and y is sufficient to guarantee that $v(\mathbf{p}, y)$ will be continuous in $\mathbf{p}$ and y on $\mathbb{R}^n_{++} \times \mathbb{R}_+$. (See Section A2.4.) Effectively, the continuity of $v(\mathbf{p}, y)$ follows because at positive prices, 'small changes' in any of the parameters $(\mathbf{p}, y)$ fixing the location of the budget constraint will only lead to 'small changes' in the maximum level of utility the consumer can achieve. In the following theorem, we collect together a number of additional properties of $v(\mathbf{p}, y)$.

THEOREM 1.6 ***Properties of the Indirect Utility Function***

If $u(\mathbf{x})$ is continuous and strictly increasing on $\mathbb{R}^n_+$, then $v(\mathbf{p}, y)$ defined in (1.12) is

1. *Continuous on $\mathbb{R}^n_{++} \times \mathbb{R}_+$,*
2. *Homogeneous of degree zero in $(\mathbf{p}, y)$,*
3. *Strictly increasing in y,*
4. *Decreasing in $\mathbf{p}$,*
5. *Quasiconvex in $(\mathbf{p}, y)$.*

Moreover, it satisfies

6. *Roy's identity: If $v(\mathbf{p}, y)$ is differentiable at $(\mathbf{p}^0, y^0)$ and $\partial v(\mathbf{p}^0, y^0)/\partial y \neq 0$, then*

$$x_i(\mathbf{p}^0, y^0) = -\frac{\partial v(\mathbf{p}^0, y^0)/\partial p_i}{\partial v(\mathbf{p}^0, y^0)/\partial y}, \qquad i = 1, \ldots, n.$$

Proof: Property 1 follows from Theorem A2.21 (the theorem of the maximum). We shall not pursue the details.

The second property is easy to prove. We must show that $v(\mathbf{p}, y) = v(t\mathbf{p}, ty)$ for all $t > 0$. But $v(t\mathbf{p}, ty) = [\max u(\mathbf{x})$ s.t. $t\mathbf{p} \cdot \mathbf{x} \leq ty]$, which is clearly equivalent to $[\max u(\mathbf{x})$ s.t. $\mathbf{p} \cdot \mathbf{x} \leq y]$ because we may divide both sides of the constraint by $t > 0$ without affecting the set of bundles satisfying it. (See Fig. 1.14.) Consequently, $v(t\mathbf{p}, ty) = [\max u(\mathbf{x})$ s.t. $\mathbf{p} \cdot \mathbf{x} \leq y] = v(\mathbf{p}, y)$.

Intuitively, properties 3 and 4 simply say that any relaxation of the consumer's budget constraint can never cause the maximum level of achievable utility to decrease, whereas any tightening of the budget constraint can never cause that level to increase.

To prove 3 (and to practise Lagrangian methods), we shall make some additional assumptions although property 3 can be shown to hold without them. To keep things simple, we'll assume for the moment that the solution to (1.12) is strictly positive and differentiable, where $(\mathbf{p}, y) \gg \mathbf{0}$ and that $u(\cdot)$ is differentiable with $\partial u(\mathbf{x})/\partial x_i > 0$, for all $\mathbf{x} \gg \mathbf{0}$.

As we have remarked before, because $u(\cdot)$ is strictly increasing, the constraint in (1.12) must bind at the optimum. Consequently, (1.12) is equivalent to

$$v(\mathbf{p}, y) = \max_{\mathbf{x} \in \mathbb{R}^n_+} u(\mathbf{x}) \qquad \text{s.t.} \qquad \mathbf{p} \cdot \mathbf{x} = y. \tag{P.1}$$

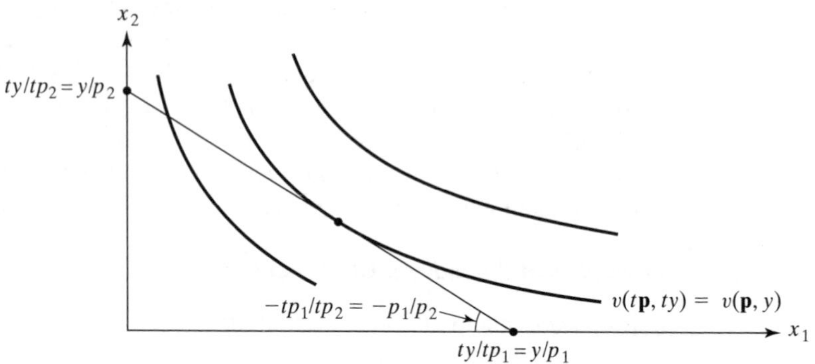

Figure 1.14. Homogeneity of the indirect utility function in prices and income.

The Lagrangian for (P.1) is

$$\mathcal{L}(\mathbf{x}, \lambda) = u(\mathbf{x}) - \lambda(\mathbf{p} \cdot \mathbf{x} - y). \tag{P.2}$$

Now, for $(\mathbf{p}, y) \gg \mathbf{0}$, let $\mathbf{x}^* = \mathbf{x}(\mathbf{p}, y)$ solve (P.1). By our additional assumption, $\mathbf{x}^* \gg \mathbf{0}$, so we may apply Lagrange's theorem to conclude that there is a $\lambda^* \in \mathbb{R}$ such that

$$\frac{\partial \mathcal{L}(\mathbf{x}^*, \lambda^*)}{\partial x_i} = \frac{\partial u(\mathbf{x}^*)}{\partial x_i} - \lambda^* p_i = 0, \qquad i = 1, \ldots, n. \tag{P.3}$$

Note that because both p_i and $\partial u(\mathbf{x}^*)/\partial x_i$ are positive, so, too, is λ^*.

Our additional differentiability assumptions allow us to now apply Theorem A2.22, the Envelope theorem, to establish that $v(\mathbf{p}, y)$ is strictly increasing in y. According to the Envelope theorem, the partial derivative of the maximum value function $v(\mathbf{p}, y)$ with respect to y is equal to the partial derivative of the Lagrangian with respect to y evaluated at $(\mathbf{x}^*, \lambda^*)$,

$$\frac{\partial v(\mathbf{p}, y)}{\partial y} = \frac{\partial \mathcal{L}(\mathbf{x}^*, \lambda^*)}{\partial y} = \lambda^* > 0. \tag{P.4}$$

Thus, $v(\mathbf{p}, y)$ is strictly increasing in $y > 0$. So, because v is continuous, it is then strictly increasing on $y \geq 0$.

For property 4, one can also employ the Envelope theorem. However, we shall give a more elementary proof that does not rely on any additional hypotheses. So consider $\mathbf{p}^0 \geq \mathbf{p}^1$ and let $\mathbf{x}^0$ solve (1.12) when $\mathbf{p} = \mathbf{p}^0$. Because $\mathbf{x}^0 \geq \mathbf{0}$, $(\mathbf{p}^0 - \mathbf{p}^1) \cdot \mathbf{x}^0 \geq 0$. Hence, $\mathbf{p}^1 {\cdot} \mathbf{x}^0 \leq \mathbf{p}^0 {\cdot} \mathbf{x}^0 \leq y$, so that $\mathbf{x}^0$ is feasible for (1.12) when $\mathbf{p} = \mathbf{p}^1$. We conclude that $v(\mathbf{p}^1, y) \geq u(\mathbf{x}^0) = v(\mathbf{p}^0, y)$, as desired.

Property 5 says that a consumer would prefer one of any two extreme budget sets to any average of the two. Our concern is to show that $v(\mathbf{p}, y)$ is quasiconvex in the vector of prices and income $(\mathbf{p}, y)$. The key to the proof is to concentrate on the budget sets.

Let B^1, B^2, and B^t be the budget sets available when prices and income are $(\mathbf{p}^1, y^1)$, $(\mathbf{p}^2, y^2)$, and $(\mathbf{p}^t, y^t)$, respectively, where $\mathbf{p}^t \equiv t\mathbf{p}^1 + (1-t)\mathbf{p}^2$ and $y^t \equiv y^1 + (1-t)y^2$. Then,

$$B^1 = \{\mathbf{x} \mid \mathbf{p}^1 \cdot \mathbf{x} \leq y^1\},$$
$$B^2 = \{\mathbf{x} \mid \mathbf{p}^2 \cdot \mathbf{x} \leq y^2\},$$
$$B^t = \{\mathbf{x} \mid \mathbf{p}^t \cdot \mathbf{x} \leq y^t\}.$$

Suppose we could show that every choice the consumer can possibly make when he faces budget B^t is a choice that could have been made when he faced either budget B^1 or budget B^2. It then would be the case that every level of utility he can achieve facing B^t is a level he could have achieved either when facing B^1 or when facing B^2. Then, of course, the *maximum* level of utility that he can achieve over B^t could be no larger than *at least one* of the following: the maximum level of utility he can achieve over B^1, or the maximum level of utility he can achieve over B^2. But if this is the case, then the maximum level of utility achieved over B^t can be no greater than the *largest* of these two. If our supposition is correct, therefore, we would know that

$$v(\mathbf{p}^t, y^t) \leq \max[v(\mathbf{p}^1, y^1), v(\mathbf{p}^2, y^2)] \qquad \forall\, t \in [0, 1].$$

This is equivalent to the statement that $v(\mathbf{p}, y)$ is quasiconvex in $(\mathbf{p}, y)$.

It will suffice, then, to show that our supposition on the budget sets is correct. We want to show that if $\mathbf{x} \in B^t$, then $\mathbf{x} \in B^1$ or $\mathbf{x} \in B^2$ for all $t \in [0, 1]$. If we choose either extreme value for t, B^t coincides with either B^1 or B^2, so the relations hold trivially. It remains to show that they hold for all $t \in (0, 1)$.

Suppose it were *not* true. Then we could find some $t \in (0, 1)$ and some $\mathbf{x} \in B^t$ such that $\mathbf{x} \notin B^1$ and $\mathbf{x} \notin B^2$. If $\mathbf{x} \notin B^1$ and $\mathbf{x} \notin B^2$, then

$$\mathbf{p}^1 \cdot \mathbf{x} > y^1$$

and

$$\mathbf{p}^2 \cdot \mathbf{x} > y^2,$$

respectively. Because $t \in (0, 1)$, we can multiply the first of these by t, the second by $(1-t)$, and preserve the inequalities to obtain

$$t\mathbf{p}^1 \cdot \mathbf{x} > ty^1$$

and

$$(1-t)\mathbf{p}^2 \cdot \mathbf{x} > (1-t)y^2.$$

Adding, we obtain

$$(t\mathbf{p}^1 + (1-t)\mathbf{p}^2) \cdot \mathbf{x} > ty^1 + (1-t)y^2$$

or

$$\mathbf{p}^t \cdot \mathbf{x} > y^t.$$

But this final line says that $\mathbf{x} \notin B^t$, contradicting our original assumption. We must conclude, therefore, that if $\mathbf{x} \in B^t$, then $\mathbf{x} \in B^1$ or $\mathbf{x} \in B^2$ for all $t \in [0, 1]$. By our previous argument, we can conclude that $v(\mathbf{p}, y)$ is quasiconvex in $(\mathbf{p}, y)$.

Finally, we turn to property 6, **Roy's identity**. This says that the consumer's Marshallian demand for good i is simply the ratio of the partial derivatives of indirect utility with respect to p_i and y *after a sign change*. (Note the minus sign in 6.)

We shall again invoke the additional assumptions introduced earlier in the proof because we shall again employ the Envelope theorem. (See Exercise 1.35 for a proof that does not require these additional assumptions.) Letting $\mathbf{x}^* = \mathbf{x}(\mathbf{p}, y)$ be the strictly positive solution to (1.12), as argued earlier, there must exist λ^* satisfying (P.3). Applying the Envelope theorem to evaluate $\partial v(\mathbf{p}, y)/\partial p_i$ gives

$$\frac{\partial v(\mathbf{p}, y)}{\partial p_i} = \frac{\partial \mathcal{L}(\mathbf{x}^*, \lambda^*)}{\partial p_i} = -\lambda^* x_i^*. \tag{P.5}$$

However, according to (P.4), $\lambda^* = \partial v(\mathbf{p}, y)/\partial y > 0$. Hence, (P.5) becomes

$$-\frac{\partial v(\mathbf{p}, y)/\partial p_i}{\partial v(\mathbf{p}, y)/\partial y} = x_i^* = x_i(\mathbf{p}, y),$$

as desired. ∎

EXAMPLE 1.2 In Example 1.1, the direct utility function is the CES form, $u(x_1, x_2) = (x_1^\rho + x_2^\rho)^{1/\rho}$, where $0 \neq \rho < 1$. There we found the Marshallian demands:

$$\begin{aligned} x_1(\mathbf{p}, y) &= \frac{p_1^{r-1} y}{p_1^r + p_2^r}, \\ x_2(\mathbf{p}, y) &= \frac{p_2^{r-1} y}{p_1^r + p_2^r}, \end{aligned} \tag{E.1}$$

for $r \equiv \rho/(\rho - 1)$. By (1.13), we can form the indirect utility function by substituting these back into the direct utility function. Doing that and rearranging, we obtain

$$\begin{aligned} v(\mathbf{p}, y) &= [(x_1(\mathbf{p}, y))^\rho + (x_2(\mathbf{p}, y))^\rho]^{1/\rho} \\ &= \left[\left(\frac{p_1^{r-1} y}{p_1^r + p_2^r}\right)^\rho + \left(\frac{p_2^{r-1} y}{p_1^r + p_2^r}\right)^\rho\right]^{1/\rho} \end{aligned} \tag{E.2}$$

$$= y\left[\frac{p_1^r + p_2^r}{(p_1^r + p_2^r)^{\rho}}\right]^{1/\rho}$$
$$= y\left(p_1^r + p_2^r\right)^{-1/r}.$$

We should verify that (E.2) satisfies all the properties of an indirect utility function detailed in Theorem 1.6. It is easy to see that $v(\mathbf{p}, y)$ is homogeneous of degree zero in prices and income, because for any $t > 0$,

$$\begin{aligned} v(t\mathbf{p}, ty) &= ty((tp_1)^r + (tp_2)^r)^{-1/r} \\ &= ty\left(t^r p_1^r + t^r p_2^r\right)^{-1/r} \\ &= tyt^{-1}\left(p_1^r + p_2^r\right)^{-1/r} \\ &= y\left(p_1^r + p_2^r\right)^{-1/r} \\ &= v(\mathbf{p}, y). \end{aligned}$$

To see that it is increasing in y and decreasing in $\mathbf{p}$, differentiate (E.2) with respect to income and any price to obtain

$$\frac{\partial v(\mathbf{p}, y)}{\partial y} = \left(p_1^r + p_2^r\right)^{-1/r} > 0, \tag{E.3}$$

$$\frac{\partial v(\mathbf{p}, y)}{\partial p_i} = -\left(p_1^r + p_2^r\right)^{(-1/r)-1} y p_i^{r-1} < 0, \qquad i = 1, 2. \tag{E.4}$$

To verify Roy's identity, form the required ratio of (E.4) to (E.3) and recall (E.1) to obtain

$$\begin{aligned} (-1)\left[\frac{\partial v(\mathbf{p}, y)/\partial p_i}{\partial v(\mathbf{p}, y)/\partial y}\right] &= (-1)\frac{-\left(p_1^r + p_2^r\right)^{(-1/r)-1} y p_i^{r-1}}{\left(p_1^r + p_2^r\right)^{-1/r}} \\ &= \frac{y p_i^{r-1}}{p_1^r + p_2^r} = x_i(\mathbf{p}, y), \qquad i = 1, 2. \end{aligned}$$

We leave as an exercise the task of verifying that (E.2) is a quasiconvex function of $(\mathbf{p}, y)$. □

1.4.2 THE EXPENDITURE FUNCTION

The indirect utility function is a neat and powerful way to summarise a great deal about the consumer's market behaviour. A companion measure, called the **expenditure function**, is equally useful. To construct the indirect utility function, we fixed market prices and

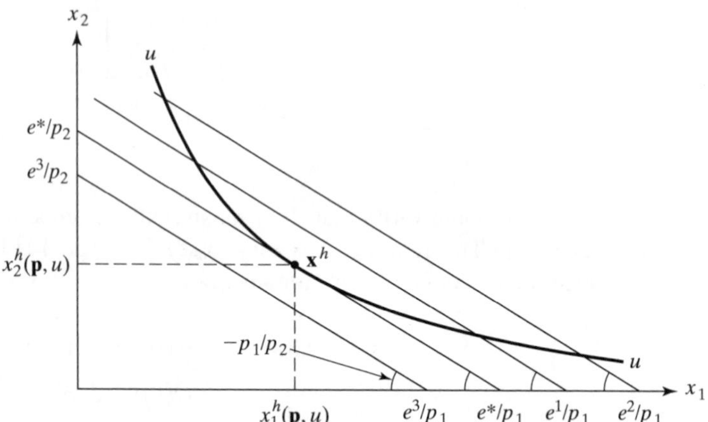

Figure 1.15. Finding the lowest level of expenditure to achieve utility level u.

income, and sought the maximum level of utility the consumer could achieve. To construct the expenditure function, we again fix prices, but we ask a different sort of question about the level of utility the consumer achieves. Specifically, we ask: what is the *minimum level of money expenditure* the consumer must make facing a given set of prices to achieve a given level of utility? In this construction, we ignore any limitations imposed by the consumer's income and simply ask what the consumer would have to spend to achieve some particular level of utility.

To better understand the type of problem we are studying, consider Fig. 1.15 and contrast it with Fig. 1.13. Each of the parallel straight lines in Fig. 1.15 depicts all bundles $\mathbf{x}$ that require the same level of total expenditure to acquire when facing prices $\mathbf{p} = (p_1, p_2)$. Each of these **isoexpenditure** curves is defined implicity by $e = p_1x_1 + p_2x_2$, for a different level of total expenditure $e > 0$. Each therefore will have the same slope, $-p_1/p_2$, but different horizontal and vertical intercepts, e/p_1 and e/p_2, respectively. Isoexpenditure curves farther out contain bundles costing more; those farther in give bundles costing less. If we fix the level of utility at u, then the indifference curve $u(\mathbf{x}) = u$ gives all bundles yielding the consumer that same level of utility.

There is no point in common with the isoexpenditure curve e^3 and the indifference curve u, indicating that e^3 dollars is insufficient at these prices to achieve utility u. However, each of the curves e^1, e^2, and e^* has at least one point in common with u, indicating that any of these levels of total expenditure is sufficient for the consumer to achieve utility u. In constructing the expenditure function, however, we seek the *minimum expenditure* the consumer requires to achieve utility u, or the lowest possible isoexpenditure curve that still has at least one point in common with indifference curve u. Clearly, that will be level e^*, and the least cost bundle that achieves utility u at prices $\mathbf{p}$ will be the bundle $\mathbf{x}^h = (x_1^h(\mathbf{p}, u), x_2^h(\mathbf{p}, u))$. If we denote the minimum expenditure necessary to achieve utility u at prices $\mathbf{p}$ by $e(\mathbf{p}, u)$, that level of expenditure will simply be equal to the cost of bundle $\mathbf{x}^h$, or $e(\mathbf{p}, u) = p_1x_1^h(\mathbf{p}, u) + p_2x_2^h(\mathbf{p}, u) = e^*$.

More generally, we define the **expenditure function** as the minimum-value function,

$$e(\mathbf{p}, u) \equiv \min_{\mathbf{x} \in \mathbb{R}^n_+} \mathbf{p} \cdot \mathbf{x} \qquad \text{s.t.} \qquad u(\mathbf{x}) \geq u \tag{1.14}$$

for all $\mathbf{p} \gg \mathbf{0}$ and all attainable utility levels u. For future reference, let $\mathcal{U} = \{u(\mathbf{x}) \mid \mathbf{x} \in \mathbb{R}^n_+\}$ denote the set of attainable utility levels. Thus, the domain of $e(\cdot)$ is $\mathbb{R}^n_{++} \times \mathcal{U}$.

Note that $e(\mathbf{p}, u)$ is well-defined because for $\mathbf{p} \in \mathbb{R}^n_{++}$, $\mathbf{x} \in \mathbb{R}^n_+$, $\mathbf{p} \cdot \mathbf{x} \geq 0$. Hence, the set of numbers $\{e | e = \mathbf{p} \cdot \mathbf{x}$ for some $\mathbf{x}$ with $u(\mathbf{x}) \geq u\}$ is bounded below by zero. Moreover because $\mathbf{p} \gg \mathbf{0}$, this set can be shown to be closed. Hence, it contains a smallest number. The value $e(\mathbf{p}, u)$ is precisely this smallest number. Note that any solution vector for this minimisation problem will be non-negative and will depend on the parameters $\mathbf{p}$ and u. Notice also that if $u(\mathbf{x})$ is continuous and strictly quasiconcave, the solution will be unique, so we can denote the solution as the function $\mathbf{x}^h(\mathbf{p}, u) \geq \mathbf{0}$. As we have seen, if $\mathbf{x}^h(\mathbf{p}, u)$ solves this problem, the lowest expenditure necessary to achieve utility u at prices $\mathbf{p}$ will be exactly equal to the cost of the bundle $\mathbf{x}^h(\mathbf{p}, u)$, or

$$e(\mathbf{p}, u) = \mathbf{p} \cdot \mathbf{x}^h(\mathbf{p}, u). \tag{1.15}$$

We have seen how the consumer's utility maximisation problem is intimately related to his observable market demand behaviour. Indeed, the very solutions to that problem – the Marshallian demand functions – tell us just how much of every good we should observe the consumer buying when he faces different prices and income. We shall now interpret the solution, $\mathbf{x}^h(\mathbf{p}, u)$, of the expenditure-minimisation problem as another kind of 'demand function' – but one that is not directly observable.

Consider the following mental experiment. If we fix the level of utility the consumer is permitted to achieve at some arbitrary level u, how will his purchases of each good behave as we change the prices he faces? The kind of 'demand functions' we are imagining here are thus *utility-constant* ones. We completely ignore the level of the consumer's money income and the utility levels he actually *can* achieve. In fact, we know that when a consumer has some level of income and we change the prices he faces, there will ordinarily be some change in his purchases and some corresponding change in the level of utility he achieves. To imagine how we might then construct our hypothetical demand functions, we must imagine a process by which whenever we lower some price, and so confer a utility gain on the consumer, we compensate by reducing the consumer's income, thus conferring a corresponding utility loss sufficient to bring the consumer back to the original level of utility. Similarly, whenever we increase some price, causing a utility loss, we must imagine compensating for this by increasing the consumer's income sufficiently to give a utility gain equal to the loss. Because they reflect the net effect of this process by which we match any utility change due to a change in prices by a compensating utility change from a hypothetical adjustment in income, the hypothetical demand functions we are describing are often called **compensated demand functions**. However, because John Hicks (1939) was the first to write about them in quite this way, these hypothetical demand functions are most commonly known as **Hicksian demand functions**. As we illustrate below, the

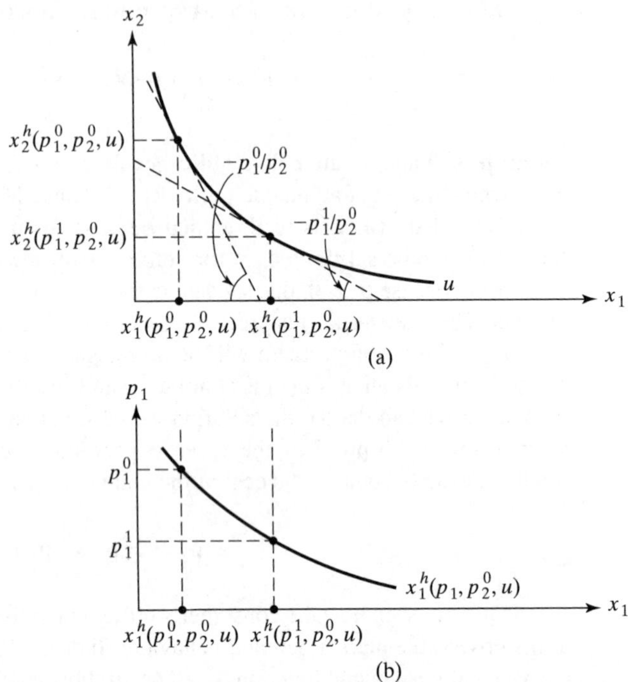

Figure 1.16. The Hicksian demand for good 1.

solution, $\mathbf{x}^h(\mathbf{p}, u)$, to the expenditure-minimisation problem is precisely the consumer's vector of Hicksian demands.

To get a clearer idea of what we have in mind, consider Fig. 1.16. If we wish to fix the level of utility the consumer can achieve at u in Fig. 1.16(a) and then confront him with prices p_1^0 and p_2^0, he must face the depicted budget constraint with slope $-p_1^0/p_2^0$. Note that his utility-maximising choices then coincide with the expenditure-minimising quantities $x_1^h(p_1^0, p_2^0, u)$ and $x_2^h(p_1^0, p_2^0, u)$. If we reduce the price of good 1 to $p_1^1 < p_1^0$, yet hold the consumer on the u-level indifference curve by an appropriate income reduction, his new budget line now has slope $-p_1^1/p_2^0$, and his utility-maximising choices change to $x_1^h(p_1^1, p_2^0, u)$ and $x_2^h(p_1^1, p_2^0, u)$. As before, if we fix price p_2^0 and we plot the own-price of good 1 in Fig. 1.16(b) against the corresponding hypothetical quantities of good 1 the consumer would 'buy' if constrained to utility level u, we would trace out a 'demand-curve-like' locus as depicted. This construction is the Hicksian demand curve for good 1, given utility level u. Clearly, there will be *different* Hicksian demand curves for different levels of utility – for different indifference curves. The shape and position of each of them, however, will always be determined by the underlying preferences.

In short, the solution, $\mathbf{x}^h(\mathbf{p}, u)$, to the expenditure-minimisation problem is precisely the vector of Hicksian demands because each of the hypothetical 'budget constraints' the consumer faces in Fig. 1.16 involves a level of expenditure exactly equal to the minimum level necessary at the given prices to achieve the utility level in question.

Thus, the expenditure function defined in (1.14) contains within it some important information on the consumer's Hicksian demands. Although the analytic importance of this construction will only become evident a bit later, we can take note here of the remarkable ease with which that information can be extracted from a knowledge of the expenditure function. The consumer's Hicksian demands can be extracted from the expenditure function by means of simple differentiation. We detail this and other important properties of the expenditure function in the following theorem.

THEOREM 1.7 ***Properties of the Expenditure Function***

If $u(\cdot)$ is continuous and strictly increasing, then $e(\mathbf{p}, u)$ defined in (1.14) is

1. *Zero when u takes on the lowest level of utility in $\mathcal{U}$,*
2. *Continuous on its domain $\mathbb{R}^n_{++} \times \mathcal{U}$,*
3. *For all $\mathbf{p} \gg \mathbf{0}$, strictly increasing and unbounded above in u,*
4. *Increasing in $\mathbf{p}$,*
5. *Homogeneous of degree 1 in $\mathbf{p}$,*
6. *Concave in $\mathbf{p}$.*

If, in addition, $u(\cdot)$ is strictly quasiconcave, we have

7. *Shephard's lemma: $e(\mathbf{p}, u)$ is differentiable in $\mathbf{p}$ at $(\mathbf{p}^0, u^0)$ with $\mathbf{p}^0 \gg \mathbf{0}$, and*

$$\frac{\partial e(\mathbf{p}^0, u^0)}{\partial p_i} = x_i^h(\mathbf{p}^0, u^0), \qquad i = 1, \ldots, n.$$

Proof: To prove property 1, note that the lowest value in $\mathcal{U}$ is $u(\mathbf{0})$ because $u(\cdot)$ is strictly increasing on $\mathbb{R}^n_+$. Consequently, $e(\mathbf{p}, u(\mathbf{0})) = 0$ because $\mathbf{x} = \mathbf{0}$ attains utility $u(\mathbf{0})$ and requires an expenditure of $\mathbf{p} \cdot \mathbf{0} = 0$.

Property 2, continuity, follows once again from Theorem A2.21 (the theorem of the maximum).

Although property 3 holds without any further assumptions, we shall be content to demonstrate it under the additional hypotheses that $\mathbf{x}^h(\mathbf{p}, u) \gg \mathbf{0}$ is differentiable $\forall\, \mathbf{p} \gg \mathbf{0}$, $u > u(\mathbf{0})$, and that $u(\cdot)$ is differentiable with $\partial u(\mathbf{x})/\partial x_i > 0$, $\forall\, i$ on $\mathbb{R}^n_{++}$.

Now, because $u(\cdot)$ is continuous and strictly increasing, and $\mathbf{p} \gg \mathbf{0}$, the constraint in (1.14) must be binding. For if $u(\mathbf{x}^1) > u$, there is a $t \in (0, 1)$ close enough to 1 such that $u(t\mathbf{x}^1) > u$. Moreover, $u \geq u(\mathbf{0})$ implies $u(\mathbf{x}^1) > u(\mathbf{0})$, so that $\mathbf{x}^1 \neq \mathbf{0}$. Therefore, $\mathbf{p} \cdot (t\mathbf{x}^1) < \mathbf{p} \cdot \mathbf{x}^1$, because $\mathbf{p} \cdot \mathbf{x}^1 > 0$. Consequently, when the constraint is not binding, there is a strictly cheaper bundle that also satisfies the constraint. Hence, at the optimum, the constraint must bind. Consequently, we may write (1.14) instead as

$$e(\mathbf{p}, u) \equiv \min_{\mathbf{x} \in \mathbb{R}^n_+} \mathbf{p} \cdot \mathbf{x} \qquad \text{s.t.} \qquad u(\mathbf{x}) = u. \tag{P.1}$$

The Lagrangian for this problem is

$$\mathcal{L}(\mathbf{x}, \lambda) = \mathbf{p} \cdot \mathbf{x} - \lambda[u(\mathbf{x}) - u]. \tag{P.2}$$

Now for $\mathbf{p} \gg \mathbf{0}$ and $u > u(\mathbf{0})$, we have that $\mathbf{x}^* = \mathbf{x}^h(\mathbf{p}, u) \gg \mathbf{0}$ solves (P.1). So, by Lagrange's theorem, there is a λ^* such that

$$\frac{\partial \mathcal{L}(\mathbf{x}^*, \lambda^*)}{\partial x_i} = p_i - \lambda^* \frac{\partial u(\mathbf{x}^*)}{\partial x_i} = 0, \qquad i = 1, \ldots, n. \tag{P.3}$$

Note then that because p_i and $\partial u(\mathbf{x}^*)/\partial x_i$ are positive, so, too, is λ^*. Under our additional hypotheses, we can now use the Envelope theorem to show that $e(\mathbf{p}, u)$ is strictly increasing in u.

By the Envelope theorem, the partial derivative of the minimum-value function $e(\mathbf{p}, u)$ with respect to u is equal to the partial derivative of the Lagrangian with respect to u, evaluated at $(\mathbf{x}^*, \lambda^*)$. Hence,

$$\frac{\partial e(\mathbf{p}, u)}{\partial u} = \frac{\partial \mathcal{L}(\mathbf{x}^*, \lambda^*)}{\partial u} = \lambda^* > 0.$$

Because this holds for all $u > u(\mathbf{0})$, and because $e(\cdot)$ is continuous, we may conclude that for all $\mathbf{p} \gg \mathbf{0}$, $e(\mathbf{p}, u)$ is strictly increasing in u on $\mathcal{U}$ (which includes $u(\mathbf{0})$).

That e is unbounded in u can be shown to follow from the fact that $u(\mathbf{x})$ is continuous and strictly increasing. You are asked to do so in Exercise 1.34.

Because property 4 follows from property 7, we shall defer it for the moment. Property 5 will be left as an exercise.

For property 6, we must prove that $e(\mathbf{p}, u)$ is a concave function of prices. We begin by recalling the definition of concavity. Let $\mathbf{p}^1$ and $\mathbf{p}^2$ be any two positive price vectors, let $t \in [0, 1]$, and let $\mathbf{p}^t = t\mathbf{p}^1 + (1 - t)\mathbf{p}^2$ be any convex combination of $\mathbf{p}^1$ and $\mathbf{p}^2$. Then the expenditure function will be concave in prices if

$$te(\mathbf{p}^1, u) + (1 - t)e(\mathbf{p}^2, u) \leq e(\mathbf{p}^t, u). \tag{P.4}$$

To see that this is indeed the case, simply focus on what it *means* for expenditure to be minimised at given prices. Suppose in particular that $\mathbf{x}^1$ minimises expenditure to achieve u when prices are $\mathbf{p}^1$, that $\mathbf{x}^2$ minimises expenditure to achieve u when prices are $\mathbf{p}^2$, and that $\mathbf{x}^*$ minimises expenditure to achieve u when prices are $\mathbf{p}^t$. Then the cost of $\mathbf{x}^1$ at prices $\mathbf{p}^1$ must be no more than the cost at prices $\mathbf{p}^1$ of *any other* bundle $\mathbf{x}$ that achieves utility u. Similarly, the cost of $\mathbf{x}^2$ at prices $\mathbf{p}^2$ must be no more than the cost at $\mathbf{p}^2$ of *any other* bundle $\mathbf{x}$ that achieves utility u. Now, if, as we have said,

$$\mathbf{p}^1 \cdot \mathbf{x}^1 \leq \mathbf{p}^1 \cdot \mathbf{x}$$

and

$$\mathbf{p}^2 \cdot \mathbf{x}^2 \leq \mathbf{p}^2 \cdot \mathbf{x}$$

for all $\mathbf{x}$ that achieve u, then these relations must *also* hold for $\mathbf{x}^*$, because $\mathbf{x}^*$ achieves u as well. Therefore, simply by virtue of what it means to minimise expenditure to achieve u at given prices, we know that

$$\mathbf{p}^1 \cdot \mathbf{x}^1 \leq \mathbf{p}^1 \cdot \mathbf{x}^*$$

and

$$\mathbf{p}^2 \cdot \mathbf{x}^2 \leq \mathbf{p}^2 \cdot \mathbf{x}^*.$$

But now we are home free. Because $t \geq 0$ and $(1-t) \geq 0$, we can multiply the first of these by t, the second by $(1-t)$, and add them. If we then substitute from the definition of $\mathbf{p}^t$, we obtain

$$t\mathbf{p}^1 \cdot \mathbf{x}^1 + (1-t)\mathbf{p}^2 \cdot \mathbf{x}^2 \leq \mathbf{p}^t \cdot \mathbf{x}^*.$$

The left-hand side is just the convex combination of the minimum levels of expenditure necessary at prices $\mathbf{p}^1$ and $\mathbf{p}^2$ to achieve utility u, and the right-hand side is the minimum expenditure needed to achieve utility u at the convex combination of those prices. In short, this is just the same as (P.5), and tells us that

$$te(\mathbf{p}^1, u) + (1-t)e(\mathbf{p}^2, u) \leq e(\mathbf{p}^t, u) \qquad \forall\, t \in [0, 1],$$

as we intended to show.

To prove property 7, we again appeal to the Envelope theorem but now differentiate with respect to p_i. This gives

$$\frac{\partial e(\mathbf{p}, u)}{\partial p_i} = \frac{\partial \mathcal{L}(\mathbf{x}^*, \lambda^*)}{\partial p_i} = x_i^* \equiv x_i^h(\mathbf{p}, u),$$

as required. Because $\mathbf{x}^h(\mathbf{p}, u) \geq \mathbf{0}$, this also proves property 4. (See Exercise 1.37 for a proof of 7 that does not require any additional assumptions. Try to prove property 4 without additional assumptions as well.) ∎

EXAMPLE 1.3 Suppose the direct utility function is again the CES form, $u(x_1, x_2) = (x_1^\rho + x_2^\rho)^{1/\rho}$, where $0 \neq \rho < 1$. We want to derive the corresponding expenditure function in this case. Because preferences are monotonic, we can formulate the expenditure minimisation problem (1.15)

$$\min_{x_1, x_2} p_1 x_1 + p_2 x_2 \qquad \text{s.t.} \qquad \left(x_1^\rho + x_2^\rho\right)^{1/\rho} - u = 0, \qquad x_1 \geq 0,\ x_2 \geq 0,$$

and its Lagrangian,

$$\mathcal{L}(x_1, x_2, \lambda) = p_1x_1 + p_2x_2 - \lambda\big[\big(x_1^\rho + x_2^\rho\big)^{1/\rho} - u\big]. \tag{E.1}$$

Assuming an interior solution in both goods, the first-order conditions for a minimum subject to the constraint ensure that the solution values x_1, x_2, and λ satisfy the equations

$$\frac{\partial \mathcal{L}}{\partial x_1} = p_1 - \lambda\big(x_1^\rho + x_2^\rho\big)^{(1/\rho)-1} x_1^{\rho-1} = 0, \tag{E.2}$$

$$\frac{\partial \mathcal{L}}{\partial x_2} = p_2 - \lambda\big(x_1^\rho + x_2^\rho\big)^{(1/\rho)-1} x_2^{\rho-1} = 0, \tag{E.3}$$

$$\frac{\partial \mathcal{L}}{\partial \lambda} = \big(x_1^\rho + x_2^\rho\big)^{1/\rho} - u = 0. \tag{E.4}$$

By eliminating λ, these can be reduced to the two equations in two unknowns,

$$x_1 = x_2\left(\frac{p_1}{p_2}\right)^{1/(\rho-1)}, \tag{E.5}$$

$$u = \big(x_1^\rho + x_2^\rho\big)^{1/\rho}. \tag{E.6}$$

Substituting from (E.5) into (E.6) gives

$$u = \left[x_2^\rho\left(\frac{p_1}{p_2}\right)^{\rho/(\rho-1)} + x_2^\rho\right]^{1/\rho} = x_2\left[\left(\frac{p_1}{p_2}\right)^{\rho/(\rho-1)} \times 1\right]^{1/\rho}.$$

Solving for x_2, and letting $r \equiv \rho/(\rho - 1)$, we obtain

$$\begin{aligned} x_2 &= u\left[\left(\frac{p_1}{p_2}\right)^{\rho/(\rho-1)} + 1\right]^{-1/\rho} = u\big[p_1^{\rho/(\rho-1)} + p_2^{\rho/(\rho-1)}\big]^{-1/\rho} p_2^{1/(\rho-1)} \\ &= u\big(p_1^r + p_2^r\big)^{(1/r)-1} p_2^{r-1}. \end{aligned} \tag{E.7}$$

Substituting from (E.7) into (E.5) gives us

$$\begin{aligned} x_1 &= up_1^{1/(\rho-1)} p_2^{-1/(\rho-1)} \big(p_1^r + p_2^r\big)^{(1/r)-1} p_2^{r-1} \\ &= u\big(p_1^r + p_2^r\big)^{(1/r)-1} p_1^{r-1}. \end{aligned} \tag{E.8}$$

The solutions (E.7) and (E.8) depend on the parameters of the minimisation problem, **p** and u. These are the Hicksian demands, so we can denote (E.7) and (E.8)

$$x_1^h(\mathbf{p}, u) = u\big(p_1^r + p_2^r\big)^{(1/r)-1} p_1^{r-1}, \tag{E.9}$$

$$x_2^h(\mathbf{p}, u) = u\big(p_1^r + p_2^r\big)^{(1/r)-1} p_2^{r-1}. \tag{E.10}$$

To form the expenditure function, we invoke equation (1.15) and substitute from (E.9) and (E.10) into the objective function in (E.1) to obtain

$$\begin{aligned} e(\mathbf{p}, u) &= p_1 x_1^h(\mathbf{p}, u) + p_2 x_2^h(\mathbf{p}, u) \\ &= u p_1 \big(p_1^r + p_2^r\big)^{(1/r)-1} p_1^{r-1} + u p_2 \big(p_1^r + p_2^r\big)^{(1/r)-1} p_2^{r-1} \\ &= u\big(p_1^r + p_2^r\big)\big(p_1^r + p_2^r\big)^{(1/r)-1} \\ &= u\big(p_1^r + p_2^r\big)^{1/r}. \end{aligned} \tag{E.11}$$

Equation (E.11) is the expenditure function we sought. We leave as an exercise the task of verifying that it possesses the usual properties. □

1.4.3 RELATIONS BETWEEN THE TWO

Though the indirect utility function and the expenditure function are conceptually distinct, there is obviously a close relationship between them. The same can be said for the Marshallian and Hicksian demand functions.

In particular, fix $(\mathbf{p}, y)$ and let $u = v(\mathbf{p}, y)$. By the definition of v, this says that at prices **p**, utility level u is the maximum that can be attained when the consumer's income is y. Consequently, at prices **p**, if the consumer wished to attain a level of utility at least u, then income y would be certainly large enough to achieve this. But recall now that $e(\mathbf{p}, u)$ is the *smallest* expenditure needed to attain a level of utility at least u. Hence, we must have $e(\mathbf{p}, u) \leq y$. Consequently, the definitions of v and e lead to the following inequality:

$$e(\mathbf{p}, v(\mathbf{p}, y)) \leq y, \qquad \forall\ (\mathbf{p}, y) \gg \mathbf{0}. \tag{1.16}$$

Next, fix $(\mathbf{p}, u)$ and let $y = e(\mathbf{p}, u)$. By the definition of e, this says that at prices **p**, income y is the smallest income that allows the consumer to attain at least the level of utility u. Consequently, at prices **p**, if the consumer's income were in fact y, then he could attain at least the level of utility u. Because $v(\mathbf{p}, y)$ is the *largest* utility level attainable at prices **p** and with income y, this implies that $v(\mathbf{p}, y) \geq u$. Consequently, the definitions of v and e also imply that

$$v(\mathbf{p}, e(\mathbf{p}, u)) \geq u \qquad \forall\ (\mathbf{p}, u) \in \mathbb{R}^n_{++} \times \mathcal{U}. \tag{1.17}$$

The next theorem demonstrates that under certain familiar conditions on preferences, both of these inequalities, in fact, must be equalities.

THEOREM 1.8 ***Relations Between Indirect Utility and Expenditure Functions***

Let $v(\mathbf{p}, y)$ and $e(\mathbf{p}, u)$ be the indirect utility function and expenditure function for some consumer whose utility function is continuous and strictly increasing. Then for all $\mathbf{p} \gg \mathbf{0}$, $y \geq 0$, and $u \in \mathcal{U}$:

1. $e(\mathbf{p}, v(\mathbf{p}, y)) = y$.
2. $v(\mathbf{p}, e(\mathbf{p}, u)) = u$.

Proof: Because $u(\cdot)$ is strictly increasing on $\mathbb{R}^n_+$, it attains a minimum at $\mathbf{x} = \mathbf{0}$, but does not attain a maximum. Moreover, because $u(\cdot)$ is continuous, the set $\mathcal{U}$ of attainable utility numbers must be an interval. Consequently, $\mathcal{U} = [u(\mathbf{0}), \bar{u})]$ for $\bar{u} > u(\mathbf{0})$, and where $\bar{u}$ may be either finite or $+\infty$.

To prove 1, fix $(\mathbf{p}, y) \in \mathbb{R}^n_{++} \times \mathbb{R}_+$. By (1.16), $e(\mathbf{p}, v(\mathbf{p}, y)) \leq y$. We would like to show in fact that equality must hold. So suppose not, that is, suppose $e(\mathbf{p}, u) < y$, where $u = v(\mathbf{p}, y)$. Note that by definition of $v(\cdot)$, $u \in \mathcal{U}$, so that $u < \bar{u}$. By the continuity of $e(\cdot)$ from Theorem 1.7, we may therefore choose $\varepsilon > 0$ small enough so that $u + \varepsilon < \bar{u}$, and $e(\mathbf{p}, u + \varepsilon) < y$. Letting $y_\varepsilon = e(\mathbf{p}, u + \varepsilon)$, (1.17) implies that $v(\mathbf{p}, y_\varepsilon) \geq u + \varepsilon$. Because $y_\varepsilon < y$ and v is strictly increasing in income by Theorem 1.6, $v(\mathbf{p}, y) > v(\mathbf{p}, y_\varepsilon) \geq u + \varepsilon$. But $u = v(\mathbf{p}, y)$ so this says $u \geq u + \varepsilon$, a contradiction. Hence, $e(\mathbf{p}, v(\mathbf{p}, y)) = y$.

To prove 2, fix $(\mathbf{p}, u) \in \mathbb{R}^n_{++} \times [u(\mathbf{0}), \bar{u}]$. By (1.17), $v(\mathbf{p}, e(\mathbf{p}, u)) \geq u$. Again, to show that this must be an equality, suppose to the contrary that $v(\mathbf{p}, e(\mathbf{p}, u)) > u$. There are two cases to consider: $u = u(\mathbf{0})$ and $u > u(\mathbf{0})$. We shall consider the second case only, leaving the first as an exercise. Letting $y = e(\mathbf{p}, u)$, we then have $v(\mathbf{p}, y) > u$. Now, because $e(\mathbf{p}, u(\mathbf{0})) = 0$ and because $e(\cdot)$ is strictly increasing in utility by Theorem 1.7, $y = e(\mathbf{p}, u) > 0$. Because $v(\cdot)$ is continuous by Theorem 1.6, we may choose $\varepsilon > 0$ small enough so that $y - \varepsilon > 0$ and $v(\mathbf{p}, y - \varepsilon) > u$. Thus, income $y - \varepsilon$ is sufficient, at prices $\mathbf{p}$, to achieve utility greater than u. Hence, we must have $e(\mathbf{p}, u) \leq y - \varepsilon$. But this contradicts the fact that $y = e(\mathbf{p}, u)$. ∎

Until now, if we wanted to derive a consumer's indirect utility and expenditure functions, we would have had to solve two separate constrained optimisation problems: one a maximisation problem and the other a minimisation problem. This theorem, however, points to an easy way to derive either one from knowledge of the other, thus requiring us to solve only one optimisation problem and giving us the choice of which one we care to solve.

To see how this would work, let us suppose first that we have solved the utility-maximisation problem and formed the indirect utility function. One thing we know about the indirect utility function is that it is *strictly increasing* in its income variable. But then, holding prices constant and viewing it only as a function of income, it must be possible to *invert* the indirect utility function in its income variable. From before,

$$v(\mathbf{p}, e(\mathbf{p}, u)) = u,$$

so we can apply that inverse function (call it $v^{-1}(\mathbf{p} : t)$) to both sides of this and obtain

$$e(\mathbf{p}, u) = v^{-1}(\mathbf{p} : u). \tag{1.18}$$

Whatever that expression on the right-hand side of (1.18) turns out to be, we know it will correspond exactly to the expression for the consumer's expenditure function – the expression we would eventually obtain if we solved the expenditure-minimisation problem, then substituted back into the objective function.

Suppose, instead, that we had chosen to solve the expenditure-minimisation problem and form the expenditure function, $e(\mathbf{p}, u)$. In this case, we know that $e(\mathbf{p}, u)$ is *strictly increasing* in u. Again supposing prices constant, there will be an inverse of the expenditure function in its utility variable, which we can denote $e^{-1}(\mathbf{p} : t)$. Applying this inverse to both sides of the first item in Theorem 1.8, we find that the indirect utility function can be solved for directly and will be that expression in $\mathbf{p}$ and y that results when we evaluate the utility inverse of the expenditure function at any level of income y,

$$v(\mathbf{p}, y) = e^{-1}(\mathbf{p} : y). \tag{1.19}$$

Equations (1.18) and (1.19) illustrate again the close relationship between utility maximisation and expenditure minimisation. The two are conceptually just opposite sides of the same coin. Mathematically, both the indirect utility function and the expenditure function are simply the appropriately chosen *inverses* of each other.

EXAMPLE 1.4 We can illustrate these procedures by drawing on findings from the previous examples. In Example 1.2, we found that the CES direct utility function gives the indirect utility function,

$$v(\mathbf{p}, y) = y\left(p_1^r + p_2^r\right)^{-1/r} \tag{E.1}$$

for any $\mathbf{p}$ and income level y. For an income level equal to $e(\mathbf{p}, u)$ dollars, therefore, we must have

$$v(\mathbf{p}, e(\mathbf{p}, u)) = e(\mathbf{p}, u)\left(p_1^r + p_2^r\right)^{-1/r}. \tag{E.2}$$

Next, from the second item in Theorem 1.8, we know that for any $\mathbf{p}$ and u,

$$v(\mathbf{p}, e(\mathbf{p}, u)) = u. \tag{E.3}$$

Combining (E.2) and (E.3) gives

$$e(\mathbf{p}, u)\left(p_1^r + p_2^r\right)^{-1/r} = u. \tag{E.4}$$

Solving (E.4) for $e(\mathbf{p}, u)$, we get the expression

$$e(\mathbf{p}, u) = u\left(p_1^r + p_2^r\right)^{1/r} \tag{E.5}$$

for the expenditure function. A quick look back at Example 1.3 confirms this is the same expression for the expenditure function obtained by directly solving the consumer's expenditure-minimisation problem.

Suppose, instead, we begin with knowledge of the expenditure function and want to derive the indirect utility function. For the CES direct utility function, we know from Example 1.3 that

$$e(\mathbf{p}, u) = u\left(p_1^r + p_2^r\right)^{1/r} \tag{E.6}$$

for any $\mathbf{p}$ and utility level u. Then for utility level $v(\mathbf{p}, y)$, we will have

$$e(\mathbf{p}, v(\mathbf{p}, y)) = v(\mathbf{p}, y)\left(p_1^r + p_2^r\right)^{1/r}. \tag{E.7}$$

From the first item in Theorem 1.8, for any $\mathbf{p}$ and y,

$$e(\mathbf{p}, v(\mathbf{p}, y)) = y. \tag{E.8}$$

Combining (E.7) and (E.8), we obtain

$$v(\mathbf{p}, y)\left(p_1^r + p_2^r\right)^{1/r} = y. \tag{E.9}$$

Solving (E.9) for $v(\mathbf{p}, y)$ gives the expression

$$v(\mathbf{p}, y) = y\left(p_1^r + p_2^r\right)^{-1/r} \tag{E.10}$$

for the indirect utility function. A glance at Example 1.2 confirms that (E.10) is what we obtained by directly solving the consumer's utility-maximisation problem. □

We can pursue this relationship between utility maximisation and expenditure minimisation a bit further by shifting our attention to the respective *solutions* to these two problems. The solutions to the utility-maximisation problem are the Marshallian demand functions. The solutions to the expenditure-minimisation problem are the Hicksian demand functions. In view of the close relationship between the two optimisation problems themselves, it is natural to suspect there is some equally close relationship between their respective solutions. The following theorem clarifies the links between Hicksian and Marshallian demands.

THEOREM 1.9 ***Duality Between Marshallian and Hicksian Demand Functions***

Under Assumption 1.2 we have the following relations between the Hicksian and Marshallian demand functions for $\mathbf{p} \gg \mathbf{0}$, $y \geq 0$, $u \in \mathcal{U}$, *and* $i = 1, \ldots, n$:

1. $x_i(\mathbf{p}, y) = x_i^h(\mathbf{p}, v(\mathbf{p}, y))$.
2. $x_i^h(\mathbf{p}, u) = x_i(\mathbf{p}, e(\mathbf{p}, u))$.

The first relation says that the Marshallian demand at prices **p** and income y is equal to the Hicksian demand at prices **p** and the utility level that is the maximum that can be achieved at prices **p** and income y. The second says that the Hicksian demand at any prices **p** and utility level u is the same as the Marshallian demand at those prices and an income level equal to the minimum expenditure necessary at those prices to achieve that utility level.

Roughly, Theorem 1.9 says that solutions to (1.12) are also solutions to (1.14), and vice versa. More precisely, if $\mathbf{x}^*$ solves (1.12) at $(\mathbf{p}, y)$, the theorem says that $\mathbf{x}^*$ solves (1.14) at $(\mathbf{p}, u)$, where $u = u(\mathbf{x}^*)$. Conversely, if $\mathbf{x}^*$ solves (1.14) at $(\mathbf{p}, u)$, then $\mathbf{x}^*$ solves (1.12) at $(\mathbf{p}, y)$, where $y = \mathbf{p} \cdot \mathbf{x}^*$. Fig. 1.17 illustrates the theorem. There, it is clear that $\mathbf{x}^*$ can be viewed either as the solution to (1.12) or the solution to (1.14). It is in this sense that $\mathbf{x}^*$ has a *dual* nature.

Proof: We will complete the proof of the first, leaving the second as an exercise.

Note that by Assumption 1.2, $u(\cdot)$ is continuous and strictly quasiconcave, so that the solutions to (1.12) and (1.14) exist and are unique. Consequently, the Marshallian and Hicksian demand fuctions are well-defined.

To prove the first relation, let $\mathbf{x}^0 = \mathbf{x}(\mathbf{p}^0, y^0)$, and let $u^0 = u(\mathbf{x}^0)$. Then $v(\mathbf{p}^0, y^0) = u^0$ by definition of $v(\cdot)$, and $\mathbf{p}^0 \cdot \mathbf{x}^0 = y^0$ because, by Assumption 1.2, $u(\cdot)$ is strictly increasing. By Theorem 1.8, $e(\mathbf{p}^0, v(\mathbf{p}^0, y^0)) = y^0$ or, equivalently, $e(\mathbf{p}^0, u^0) = y^0$. But

Figure 1.17. Expenditure minimisation and utility maximisation.

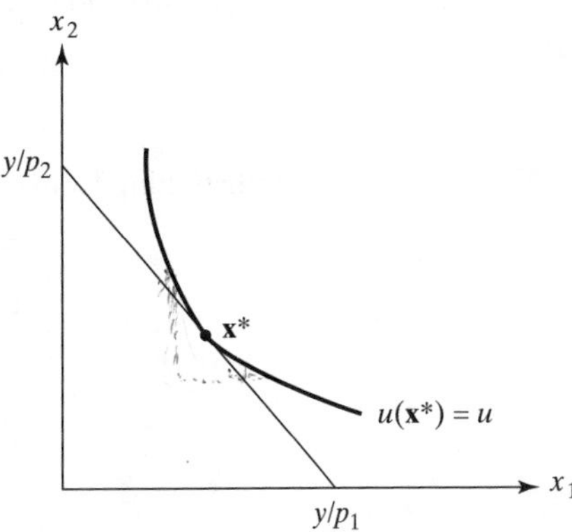

because $u(\mathbf{x}^0) = u^0$ and $\mathbf{p}^0 \cdot \mathbf{x}^0 = y^0$, this implies that $\mathbf{x}^0$ solves (1.14) when $(\mathbf{p}, u) = (\mathbf{p}^0, u^0)$. Hence, $\mathbf{x}^0 = \mathbf{x}^h(\mathbf{p}^0, u^0)$ and so $\mathbf{x}(\mathbf{p}^0, y^0) = \mathbf{x}^h(\mathbf{p}^0, v(\mathbf{p}^0, y^0))$. ∎

EXAMPLE 1.5 Let us confirm Theorem 1.9 for a CES consumer. From Example 1.3, the Hicksian demands are

$$x_i^h(\mathbf{p}, u) = u\left(p_1^r + p_2^r\right)^{(1/r)-1} p_i^{r-1}, \qquad i = 1, 2. \tag{E.1}$$

From Example 1.2, the indirect utility function is

$$v(\mathbf{p}, y) = y\left(p_1^r + p_2^r\right)^{-1/r}. \tag{E.2}$$

Substituting from (E.2) for u in (E.1) gives

$$\begin{aligned} x_i^h(\mathbf{p}, v(\mathbf{p}, y)) &= v(\mathbf{p}, y)\left(p_1^r + p_2^r\right)^{(1/r)-1} p_i^{r-1} \\ &= y\left(p_1^r + p_2^r\right)^{-1/r}\left(p_1^r + p_2^r\right)^{(1/r)-1} p_i^{r-1} \\ &= y p_i^{r-1}\left(p_1^r + p_2^r\right)^{-1} \\ &= \frac{y p_i^{r-1}}{p_1^r + p_2^r}, \qquad i = 1, 2. \end{aligned} \tag{E.3}$$

The final expression on the right-hand side of (E.3) gives the Marshallian demands we derived in Example 1.1 by solving the consumer's utility-maximisation problem. This confirms the first item in Theorem 1.9.

To confirm the second, suppose we know the Marshallian demands from Example 1.1,

$$x_i(\mathbf{p}, y) = \frac{y p_i^{r-1}}{p_1^r + p_2^r}, \qquad i = 1, 2, \tag{E.4}$$

and the expenditure function from Example 1.3,

$$e(\mathbf{p}, u) = u\left(p_1^r + p_2^r\right)^{1/r}. \tag{E.5}$$

Substituting from (E.5) into (E.4) for y yields

$$\begin{aligned} x_i(\mathbf{p}, e(\mathbf{p}, u)) &= \frac{e(\mathbf{p}, u) p_i^{r-1}}{p_1^r + p_2^r} \\ &= u\left(p_1^r + p_2^r\right)^{1/r} \frac{p_i^{r-1}}{p_1^r + p_2^r} \\ &= u p_i^{r-1}\left(p_1^r + p_2^r\right)^{(1/r)-1}, \qquad i = 1, 2. \end{aligned} \tag{E.6}$$

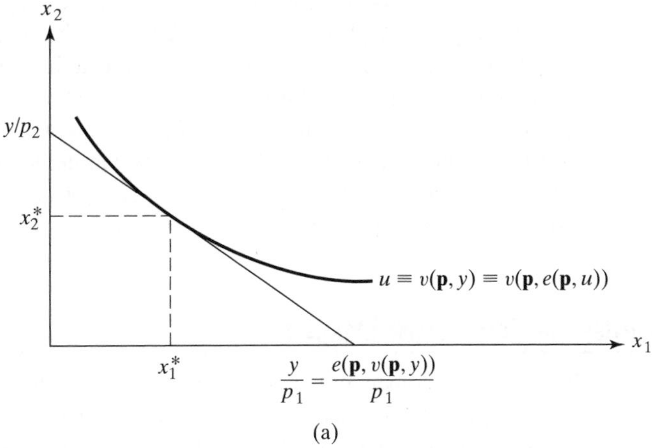

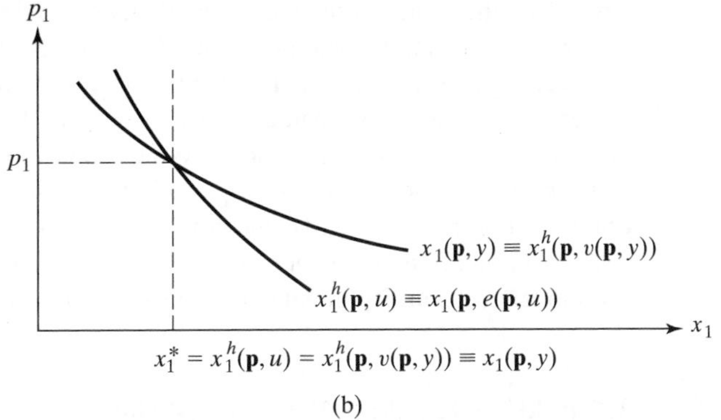

Figure 1.18. Illustration of Theorems 1.8 and 1.9.

The final expression on the right-hand side of (E.6) gives the Hicksian demands derived in Example 1.3 by directly solving the consumer's expenditure minimisation problem. □

To conclude this section, we can illustrate the four relations in Theorems 1.8 and 1.9. In Fig. 1.18(a), a consumer with income y facing prices $\mathbf{p}$ achieves maximum utility u by choosing x_1^* and x_2^*. That same u-level indifference curve therefore can be viewed as giving the level of utility $v(\mathbf{p}, y)$, and, in Fig. 1.18(b), point (p_1, x_1^*) will be a point on the Marshallian demand curve for good 1. Consider next the consumer's expenditure-minimisation problem, and suppose we seek to minimise expenditure to achieve utility u. Then, clearly, the lowest isoexpenditure curve that achieves u at prices $\mathbf{p}$ will *coincide* with the budget constraint in the previous utility-maximisation problem, and the expenditure minimising choices will again be x_1^* and x_2^*, giving the point (p_1, x_1^*) in Fig. 1.18(b) as a point on the consumer's Hicksian demand for good 1.

Considering the two problems together, we can easily see from the coincident intercepts of the budget constraint and isoexpenditure line that income y is an amount of money equal to the minimum expenditure necessary to achieve utility $v(\mathbf{p}, y)$ or that $y = e(\mathbf{p}, v(\mathbf{p}, y))$. Utility level u is both the maximum achievable at prices $\mathbf{p}$ and income y, so that $u = v(\mathbf{p}, y)$, and the maximum achievable at prices $\mathbf{p}$ and an income equal to the minimum expenditure necessary to achieve u, so that $u = v(\mathbf{p}, e(\mathbf{p}, u))$. Finally, notice that (p_1, x_1^*) must be a point on all three of the following: (1) the Hicksian demand for good 1 at prices $\mathbf{p}$ and utility level u, (2) the Hicksian demand for good 1 at prices $\mathbf{p}$ and utility level $v(\mathbf{p}, y)$, and (3) the Marshallian demand for good 1 at prices $\mathbf{p}$ and income y. Thus, $x_1(\mathbf{p}, y) = x_1^h(\mathbf{p}, v(\mathbf{p}, y))$ and $x_1^h(\mathbf{p}, u) = x_1(\mathbf{p}, e(\mathbf{p}, u))$, as we had hoped.

1.5 PROPERTIES OF CONSUMER DEMAND

The theory of consumer behaviour leads to a number of predictions about behaviour in the marketplace. We will see that *if* preferences, objectives, and circumstances are as we have modelled them to be, *then* demand behaviour must display certain observable characteristics. One then can test the theory by comparing these theoretical restrictions on demand behaviour to actual demand behaviour. Once a certain degree of confidence in the theory has been gained, it can be put to further use. For example, to statistically estimate consumer demand systems, characteristics of demand behaviour predicted by the theory can be used to provide *restrictions* on the values that estimated parameters are allowed to take. This application of the theory helps to improve the statistical precision of the estimates obtained. For both theoretical and empirical purposes, therefore, it is extremely important that we wring all the implications for observable demand behaviour we possibly can from our model of the utility-maximising consumer. This is the task of this section.

1.5.1 RELATIVE PRICES AND REAL INCOME

Economists generally prefer to measure important variables in *real*, rather than monetary, terms. This is because 'money is a veil', which only tends to obscure the analyst's view of what people truly do (or should) care about: namely, real commodities. Relative prices and real income are two such real measures.

By the **relative price** of some good, we mean the number of units of some other good that must be forgone to acquire 1 unit of the good in question. If p_i is the money price of good i, it will be measured in units of dollars per unit of good i. The money price of good j will have units of dollars per unit of good j. The relative price of good i in terms of good j measures the units of good j forgone per unit of good i acquired. This will be given by the price ratio p_i/p_j because

$$\frac{p_i}{p_j} = \frac{\$/\text{unit } i}{\$/\text{unit } j} = \frac{\$}{\text{unit } i} \cdot \frac{\text{unit } j}{\$} = \frac{\text{units of } j}{\text{unit of } i}.$$

By **real income**, we mean the maximum number of units of some commodity the consumer *could* acquire if he spent his entire money income. Real income is intended to reflect the consumer's total command over all resources by measuring his potential command over a single real commodity. If y is the consumer's money income, then the ratio y/p_j is called his real income in terms of good j and will be measured in units of good j, because

$$\frac{y}{p_j} = \frac{\$}{\$/\text{unit of } j} = \text{units of } j.$$

The simplest deduction we can make from our model of the utility-maximising consumer is that only *relative prices* and *real income* affect behaviour. This is sometimes expressed by saying that the consumer's demand behaviour displays an *absence of money illusion*. To see this, simply recall the discussion of Fig. 1.14. There, equiproportionate changes in money income and the level of all prices leave the slope (relative prices) and both intercepts of the consumer's budget constraint (real income measured in terms of any good) unchanged, and so call for no change in demand behaviour. Mathematically, this amounts to saying that the consumer's demand functions are homogeneous of degree zero in prices and income. Because the only role that money has played in constructing our model is as a unit of account, it would indeed be strange if this were not the case.

For future reference, we bundle this together with the observation that consumer spending will typically exhaust income, and we give names to both results.

THEOREM 1.10 ***Homogeneity and Budget Balancedness***

Under Assumption 1.2, the consumer demand function $x_i(\mathbf{p}, y)$, $i = 1, \ldots, n$, is homogeneous of degree zero in all prices and income, and it satisfies budget balancedness, $\mathbf{p} \cdot \mathbf{x}(\mathbf{p}, y) = y$ for all $(\mathbf{p}, y)$.

Proof: We already essentially proved homogeneity in Theorem 1.6, part 2, where we showed that the indirect utility function is homogeneous of degree zero, so that

$$v(\mathbf{p}, y) = v(t\mathbf{p}, ty) \quad \text{for all } t > 0.$$

This is equivalent to the statement

$$u(\mathbf{x}(\mathbf{p}, y)) = u(\mathbf{x}(t\mathbf{p}, ty)) \quad \text{for all } t > 0.$$

Now, because the budget sets at $(\mathbf{p}, y)$ and $(t\mathbf{p}, ty)$ are the same, each of $\mathbf{x}(\mathbf{p}, y)$ and $\mathbf{x}(t\mathbf{p}, ty)$ was feasible when the other was chosen. Hence, the previous equality and the strict quasiconcavity of u imply that

$$\mathbf{x}(\mathbf{p}, y) = \mathbf{x}(t\mathbf{p}, ty) \quad \text{for all } t > 0,$$

or that the demand for every good, $x_i(\mathbf{p}, y)$, $i = 1, \ldots, n$, is homogeneous of degree zero in prices and income.

We have already mentioned on numerous occasions that because $u(\cdot)$ is strictly increasing, $\mathbf{x}(\mathbf{p}, y)$ must exhaust the consumer's income. Otherwise, he could afford to purchase strictly more of every good and strictly increase his utility. We will refer to this relationship as **budget balancedness** from now on. ∎

Homogeneity allows us to completely eliminate the yardstick of money from any analysis of demand behaviour. This is generally done by arbitrarily designating one of the n goods to serve as *numéraire* in place of money. If its money price is p_n, we can set $t = 1/p_n$ and, invoking homogeneity, conclude that

$$\mathbf{x}(\mathbf{p}, y) = \mathbf{x}(t\mathbf{p}, ty) = \mathbf{x}\left(\frac{p_1}{p_n}, \ldots, \frac{p_{n-1}}{p_n}, 1, \frac{y}{p_n}\right).$$

In words, demand for each of the n goods depends only on $n-1$ *relative prices* and the consumer's *real income*.

1.5.2 INCOME AND SUBSTITUTION EFFECTS

An important question in our model of consumer behaviour concerns the response we should expect in quantity demanded when price changes. Ordinarily, we tend to think a consumer will buy more of a good when its price declines and less when its price increases, other things being equal. That this need not always be the case is illustrated in Fig. 1.19. In each panel, a utility-maximising consumer with strictly monotonic, convex preferences faces market-determined prices. In Fig. 1.19(a), a decrease in the price of good 1 causes the quantity of good 1 bought to increase, as we would usually expect. By contrast, in Fig. 1.19(b), a decrease in price causes no change in the amount of good 1 bought, whereas in Fig. 1.19(c), a decrease in price causes an absolute *decrease* in the amount of good 1

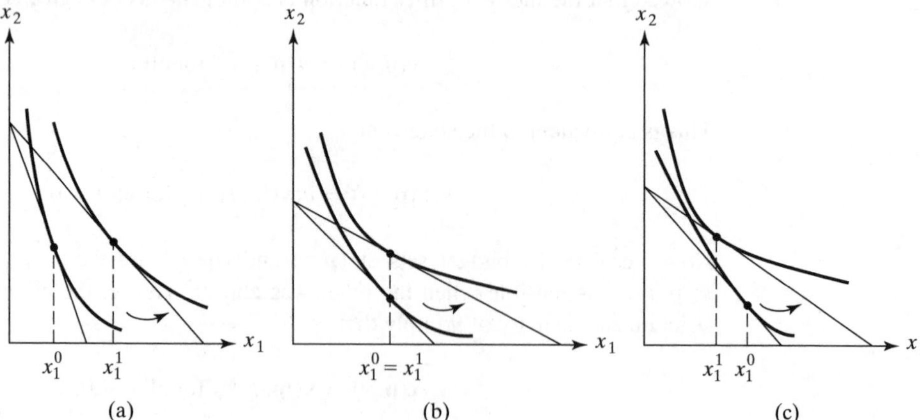

Figure 1.19. Response of quantity demanded to a change in price.

bought. Each of these cases is fully consistent with our model. What, then – if anything – does the theory predict about how someone's demand behaviour responds to changes in (relative) prices?

Let us approach it intuitively first. When the price of a good declines, there are at least two conceptually separate reasons why we expect some change in the quantity demanded. First, that good becomes relatively cheaper compared to other goods. Because all goods are desirable, even if the consumer's total command over goods were unchanged, we would expect him to substitute the relatively cheaper good for the now relatively more expensive ones. This is the **substitution effect** (*SE*). At the same time, however, whenever a price changes, the consumer's command over goods in general is *not* unchanged. When the price of any one good declines, the consumer's total command over all goods is effectively increased, allowing him to change his purchases of *all* goods in any way he sees fit. The effect on quantity demanded of this generalised increase in purchasing power is called the **income effect** (*IE*).

Although intuition tells us we can in some sense decompose the total effect (*TE*) of a price change into these two separate conceptual categories, we will have to be a great deal more precise if these ideas are to be of any analytical use. Different ways to formalise the intuition of the income and substitution effects have been proposed. We shall follow that proposed by Hicks (1939).

The Hicksian decomposition of the total effect of a price change starts with the observation that the consumer achieves some level of utility at the original prices before any change has occurred. The formalisation given to the intuitive notion of the substitution effect is the following: the substitution effect is that (hypothetical) change in consumption that *would* occur if relative prices were to change to their new levels but the maximum utility the consumer can achieve were kept the same as before the price change. The income effect is then defined as whatever is left of the total effect after the substitution effect. Notice that because the income effect is defined as a residual, the total effect is always completely explained by the sum of the substitution and the income effect. At first, this might seem a strange way to do things, but a glance at Fig. 1.20 should convince you of at least two things: its reasonable correspondence to the intuitive concepts of the income and substitution effects, and its analytical ingenuity.

Look first at Fig. 1.20(a), and suppose the consumer originally faces prices p_1^0 and p_2^0 and has income y. He originally buys quantities x_1^0 and x_2^0 and achieves utility level u^0. Suppose the price of good 1 falls to $p_1^1 < p_1^0$ and that the total effect of this price change on good 1 consumption is an increase to x_1^1, and the total effect on good 2 is a decrease to x_2^1. To apply the Hicksian decomposition, we first perform the hypothetical experiment of allowing the price of good 1 to fall to the new level p_1^1 *while holding the consumer to the original u^0 level indifference curve*. It is as if we allowed the consumer to face the new relative prices but reduced his income so that he faced the dashed hypothetical budget constraint and asked him to maximise against it. Under these circumstances, the consumer would *increase* his consumption of good 1 – the now relatively cheaper good – from x_1^0 to x_1^s, and would *decrease* his consumption of good 2 – the now relatively more expensive good – from x_2^0 to x_2^s. These hypothetical changes in consumption are the Hicksian

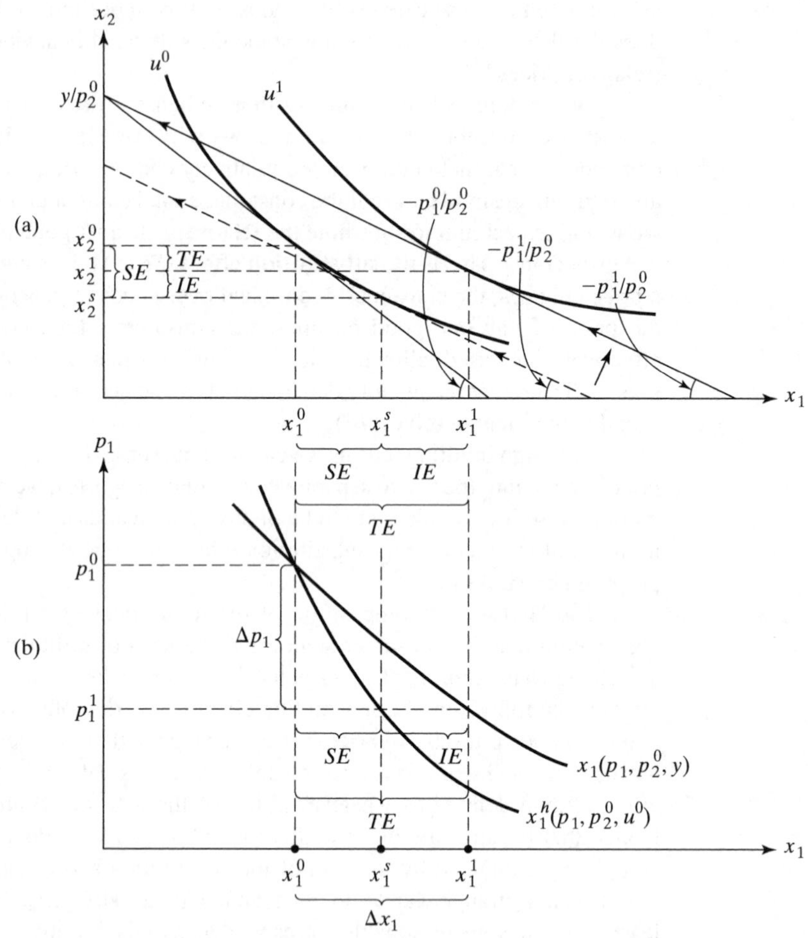

Figure 1.20. The Hicksian decomposition of a price change.

substitution effects on good 1 and good 2, and we regard them as due 'purely' to the change in relative prices with no change whatsoever in the well-being of the consumer. Look now at what is left of the total effect to explain. After hypothetical changes from x_1^0 and x_2^0 to x_1^s and x_2^s, the changes from x_1^s and x_2^s to x_1^1 and x_2^1 remain to be explained. Notice, however, that these are precisely the consumption changes that would occur if, at the new prices and the original level of utility u^0, the consumer were given an *increase in real income* shifting his budget constraint from the hypothetical dashed one out to the final, post price-change line tangent to u^1. It is in this sense that the Hicksian income effect captures the change in consumption due 'purely' to the income-like change that accompanies a price change.

Look now at Fig. 1.20(b), which ignores what is happening with good 2 and focuses exclusively on good 1. Clearly, (p_1^0, x_1^0) and (p_1^1, x_1^1) are points on the Marshallian demand curve for good 1. Similarly, (p_1^0, x_1^0) and (p_1^1, x_1^s) are points on the Hicksian demand curve for good 1, relative to the original utility level u^0. We can see that the Hicksian demand curve picks up *precisely* the pure *Hicksian* substitution effect of an own-price change. (Get it?) The Marshallian demand curve picks up the total effect of an own-price change. The two diverge from one another precisely because of, and in an amount equal to, the Hicksian income effect of an own-price change.

The Hicksian decomposition gives us a neat analytical way to isolate the two distinct forces working to change demand behaviour following a price change. We can take these same ideas and express them much more precisely, much more generally, and in a form that will prove more analytically useful. The relationships between total effect, substitution effect, and income effect are summarised in the *Slutsky equation*. The Slutsky equation is sometimes called the 'Fundamental Equation of Demand Theory', so what follows merits thinking about rather carefully.

Throughout the remainder of this chapter, Assumption 1.2 will be in effect, and, moreover, we will freely differentiate whenever necessary.

THEOREM 1.11 ***The Slutsky Equation***

Let $\mathbf{x}(\mathbf{p}, y)$ be the consumer's Marshallian demand system. Let u^* be the level of utility the consumer achieves at prices $\mathbf{p}$ and income y. Then,

$$\underbrace{\frac{\partial x_i(\mathbf{p}, y)}{\partial p_j}}_{TE} = \underbrace{\frac{\partial x_i^h(\mathbf{p}, u^*)}{\partial p_j}}_{SE} \underbrace{- x_j(\mathbf{p}, y)\frac{\partial x_i(\mathbf{p}, y)}{\partial y}}_{IE}, \qquad i, j = 1, \ldots, n.$$

Proof: The proof of this remarkable theorem is quite easy, though you must follow it quite carefully to avoid getting lost. We begin by recalling one of the links between Hicksian and Marshallian demand functions. From Theorem 1.9, we know that

$$x_i^h(\mathbf{p}, u^*) = x_i(\mathbf{p}, e(\mathbf{p}, u^*))$$

for any prices and level of utility u^*. Because this holds for all $\mathbf{p} \gg \mathbf{0}$, we can differentiate both sides with respect to p_j and the equality is preserved. The Hicksian demand on the left-hand side, because it depends only directly on prices, is straightforward to differentiate. The Marshallian demand on the right-hand side, however, depends directly on prices through its price argument, but it also depends indirectly on prices through the expenditure function in its income argument. We will have to apply the chain rule to differentiate the right-hand side. Keeping this in mind, we obtain

$$\frac{\partial x_i^h(\mathbf{p}, u^*)}{\partial p_j} = \frac{\partial x_i(\mathbf{p}, e(\mathbf{p}, u^*))}{\partial p_j} + \frac{\partial x_i(\mathbf{p}, e(\mathbf{p}, u^*))}{\partial y}\frac{\partial e(\mathbf{p}, u^*)}{\partial p_j}. \qquad \text{(P.1)}$$

Now if we look at (P.1) carefully, and remember the significance of the original level of utility u^*, we can make some critical substitutions. By assumption, u^* is the utility the consumer achieves facing $\mathbf{p}$ and y. Therefore, $u^* = v(\mathbf{p}, y)$. The minimum expenditure at prices $\mathbf{p}$ and utility u^* therefore will be the same as the minimum expenditure at prices $\mathbf{p}$ and utility $v(\mathbf{p}, y)$. From Theorem 1.8, however, we know that the minimum expenditure at prices $\mathbf{p}$ and maximum utility that can be achieved at prices $\mathbf{p}$ and income y is equal to income y. We have, therefore, that

$$e(\mathbf{p}, u^*) = e(\mathbf{p}, v(\mathbf{p}, y)) = y. \tag{P.2}$$

In addition, Theorem 1.7 tells us that the partial with respect to p_j of the expenditure function in (P.1) is just the Hicksian demand for good j at utility u^*. Because $u^* = v(\mathbf{p}, y)$, this must also be the Hicksian demand for good j at utility $v(\mathbf{p}, y)$, or

$$\frac{\partial e(\mathbf{p}, u^*)}{\partial p_j} = x_j^h(\mathbf{p}, u^*) = x_j^h(\mathbf{p}, v(\mathbf{p}, y)).$$

But look at the right-most term here. We know from Theorem 1.9 that the Hicksian demand at $\mathbf{p}$ and the maximum utility achieved at $\mathbf{p}$ and y is in turn equal to the Marshallian demand at $\mathbf{p}$ and y! Thus, we have that

$$\frac{\partial e(\mathbf{p}, u^*)}{\partial p_j} = x_j(\mathbf{p}, y). \tag{P.3}$$

[Beware here. Take note that we have shown the price partial of the expenditure function in (P.1) to be the Marshallian demand for good j, not good i.]

To complete the proof, substitute from (P.2) and (P.3) into (P.1) to obtain

$$\frac{\partial x_i^h(\mathbf{p}, u^*)}{\partial p_j} = \frac{\partial x_i(\mathbf{p}, y)}{\partial p_j} + \frac{\partial x_i(\mathbf{p}, y)}{\partial y} x_j(\mathbf{p}, y).$$

With a bit of rearranging, we have what we wanted to show:

$$\frac{\partial x_i(\mathbf{p}, y)}{\partial p_j} = \frac{\partial x_i^h(\mathbf{p}, u^*)}{\partial p_j} - x_j(\mathbf{p}, y)\frac{\partial x_i(\mathbf{p}, y)}{\partial y}, \qquad i, j = 1, \ldots, n. \qquad \blacksquare$$

Slutsky equations provide neat analytical expressions for substitution and income effects. They also give us an 'accounting framework', detailing how these must combine to explain any total effect of a given price change. Yet by themselves, the Slutsky relations do not answer any of the questions we set out to address. In fact, you might think that all this has only made it harder to deduce implications for *observable* behaviour from our theory. After all, the only thing we have done so far is decompose an observable total effect into (1) an observable income effect and (2) an *unobservable* substitution effect.

For example, consider what Slutsky tells us about the special case of an own-price change. From Theorem 1.11, we have that

$$\frac{\partial x_i(\mathbf{p}, y)}{\partial p_i} = \frac{\partial x_i^h(\mathbf{p}, u^*)}{\partial p_i} - x_i(\mathbf{p}, y)\frac{\partial x_i(\mathbf{p}, y)}{\partial y}. \tag{1.20}$$

The term on the left is the slope of the Marshallian demand curve for good i – the response of quantity demanded to a change in own price – and this is what we want to explain. To do that, however, we apparently need to know something about the first term on the right. This, however, is the slope of a *Hicksian* demand curve, and Hicksian demand curves are not directly observable. What can we know about Hicksian demand curves when we cannot even see them?

Surprisingly, our theory tells us quite a bit about Hicksian demands, and so quite a bit about substitution terms – whether we can see them or not. Whatever we learn about substitution terms then can be translated into knowledge about observable Marshallian demands via the Slutsky equations. This is how the Slutsky equations will help us, and this will be our strategy. We begin with a preliminary result on own-price effects that gives a hint of what is to come.

THEOREM 1.12 ***Negative Own-Substitution Terms***

Let $x_i^h(\mathbf{p}, u)$ be the Hicksian demand for good i. Then

$$\frac{\partial x_i^h(\mathbf{p}, u)}{\partial p_i} \leq 0, \qquad i = 1, \ldots, n.$$

Proof: This theorem tells us that Hicksian demand curves must always be as we have shown them in Fig. 1.16 and elsewhere: namely, negatively (non-positively) sloped with respect to their own price. The proof is easy.

The derivative property of the expenditure function, Theorem 1.7, part 7, tells us that for any $\mathbf{p}$ and u,

$$\frac{\partial e(\mathbf{p}, u)}{\partial p_i} = x_i^h(\mathbf{p}, u).$$

Differentiating again with respect to p_i shows that

$$\frac{\partial^2 e(\mathbf{p}, u)}{\partial p_i^2} = \frac{\partial x_i^h(\mathbf{p}, u)}{\partial p_i}, \qquad i = 1, \ldots, n.$$

By Theorem 1.7, part 6, the expenditure function is a concave function of $\mathbf{p}$. Therefore, by Theorem A2.5, all of its second-order own partial derivatives are non-positive, proving the theorem. ∎

We now have everything we need to spell out a modern version of the so-called Law of Demand. Classical economists like Edgeworth and Marshall assumed 'utility' was something measurable, and they believed in the Principle of Diminishing Marginal Utility. Classical statements of the Law of Demand were therefore rather emphatic: 'If price goes down, quantity demanded goes up.' This seemed generally to conform to observations of how people behave, but there were some troubling exceptions. The famous Giffen's paradox was the most outstanding of these. Although few in number, it seemed as though there were at least some goods for which a decrease in price was followed by a *decrease* in quantity demanded. This violated accepted doctrine, and classical theory could not explain it.

Modern theory makes fewer assumptions on preferences than classical theory did. In this sense, it is less restrictive and more widely applicable. Indeed, it is even capable of resolving Giffen's paradox. Look back at Fig. 1.19(c) and notice that the quantity of x_1 demanded does indeed decline as its own price declines. Nothing rules this out, so there is nothing paradoxical about Giffen's paradox in the context of modern theory. However, we do pay a price for greater generality: the modern Law of Demand must be more equivocal than its classical precursor.

In stating the law, we use some familiar terminology. A good is called **normal** if consumption of it increases as income increases, holding prices constant. A good is called **inferior** if consumption of it declines as income increases, holding prices constant.

THEOREM 1.13 ***The Law of Demand***

A decrease in the own price of a normal good will cause quantity demanded to increase. If an own price decrease causes a decrease in quantity demanded, the good must be inferior.

Proof: This follows easily from Theorem 1.12, if you use Theorem 1.11. You should do it yourself, so we leave it as an exercise. ∎

We actually know a great deal more about the Hicksian substitution terms than is contained in Theorem 1.12 and more about the Marshallian demands than is contained in Theorem 1.13. To move beyond the simple statements we have already made, we will have to probe the system of substitution terms a bit deeper. We first establish that 'cross-substitution terms' are *symmetric*.

THEOREM 1.14 ***Symmetric Substitution Terms***

Let $\mathbf{x}^h(\mathbf{p}, u)$ be the consumer's system of Hicksian demands and suppose that $e(\cdot)$ is twice continuously differentiable. Then,

$$\frac{\partial x_i^h(\mathbf{p}, u)}{\partial p_j} = \frac{\partial x_j^h(\mathbf{p}, u)}{\partial p_i}, \qquad i, j = 1, \ldots, n.$$

Proof: One is very hard pressed to directly comprehend the significance of this result. Remarkably, however, it can be shown that this symmetry condition is intimately related to the assumed transitivity of the consumer's preference relation! We shall not pursue this deep connection here, although we shall touch upon it somewhat later in this book.

In proving Theorem 1.12, we noted that the first-order price partial derivatives of the expenditure function give us the Hicksian demand functions, so the second-order price partials of the expenditure function will give us the *first-order* price partials of the Hicksian demands. Thus,

$$\frac{\partial}{\partial p_j}\left(\frac{\partial e(\mathbf{p},u)}{\partial p_i}\right)=\frac{\partial}{\partial p_j}\left(x_i^h(\mathbf{p},u)\right)$$

or

$$\frac{\partial^2 e(\mathbf{p},u)}{\partial p_j \partial p_i}=\frac{\partial x_i^h(\mathbf{p},u)}{\partial p_j} \tag{P.1}$$

for all i and j. By Young's theorem, the order of differentiation of the expenditure function makes no difference, so

$$\frac{\partial^2 e(\mathbf{p},u)}{\partial p_i \partial p_j}=\frac{\partial^2 e(\mathbf{p},u)}{\partial p_j \partial p_i}.$$

Together with (P.1), this gives us the conclusion,

$$\frac{\partial x_i^h(\mathbf{p},u)}{\partial p_j}=\frac{\partial x_j^h(\mathbf{p},u)}{\partial p_i}, \qquad i,j=1,\ldots,n.$$

∎

If we imagine arranging all n^2 substitution terms in the consumer's entire demand system into an $n \times n$ matrix, with the own-substitution terms on the diagonal and the cross-substitution terms off-diagonal, Theorems 1.12 and 1.14, together, tell us quite a bit about what that matrix will look like. Theorem 1.12 tells us that all elements along the principal diagonal will be non-positive, and Theorem 1.14 tells us the matrix will be symmetric. In fact, we can say even more than this about the matrix of substitution terms: it must be *negative semidefinite* as well.

THEOREM 1.15 ***Negative Semidefinite Substitution Matrix***

Let $\mathbf{x}^h(\mathbf{p},u)$ *be the consumer's system of Hicksian demands, and let*

$$\sigma(\mathbf{p},u)\equiv\begin{pmatrix}\dfrac{\partial x_1^h(\mathbf{p},u)}{\partial p_1} & \cdots & \dfrac{\partial x_1^h(\mathbf{p},u)}{\partial p_n}\\ \vdots & \ddots & \vdots \\ \dfrac{\partial x_n^h(\mathbf{p},u)}{\partial p_1} & \cdots & \dfrac{\partial x_n^h(\mathbf{p},u)}{\partial p_n}\end{pmatrix},$$

called the **substitution matrix**, *contain all the Hicksian substitution terms. Then the matrix* $\sigma(\mathbf{p}, u)$ *is negative semidefinite.*

Proof: The proof of this is immediate when we recall from the proof of the previous theorem that each term in this matrix is equal to one of the second-order price partial derivatives of the expenditure function. In particular, we have seen that $\partial x_i^h(\mathbf{p}, u)/\partial p_j = \partial^2 e(\mathbf{p}, u)/\partial p_j \partial p_i$ for all i and j, so in matrix form we must have

$$\begin{pmatrix} \dfrac{\partial x_1^h(\mathbf{p}, u)}{\partial p_1} & \cdots & \dfrac{\partial x_1^h(\mathbf{p}, u)}{\partial p_n} \\ \vdots & \ddots & \vdots \\ \dfrac{\partial x_n^h(\mathbf{p}, u)}{\partial p_1} & \cdots & \dfrac{\partial x_n^h(\mathbf{p}, u)}{\partial p_n} \end{pmatrix} = \begin{pmatrix} \dfrac{\partial^2 e(\mathbf{p}, u)}{\partial p_1^2} & \cdots & \dfrac{\partial^2 e(\mathbf{p}, u)}{\partial p_n \partial p_1} \\ \vdots & \ddots & \vdots \\ \dfrac{\partial^2 e(\mathbf{p}, u)}{\partial p_1 \partial p_n} & \cdots & \dfrac{\partial^2 e(\mathbf{p}, u)}{\partial p_n^2} \end{pmatrix}.$$

The matrix on the right is simply the Hessian matrix of second-order price partials of the expenditure function. From Theorem 1.7, the expenditure function is concave in prices. From Theorem A2.4, the Hessian matrix of a concave function is negative semidefinite. Because the two matrices are equal, the substitution matrix will therefore also be negative semidefinite. ∎

Having spent so much time exploring the properties of the unobservable Hicksian demand system, we are finally in a position to use that knowledge to say something rather concrete about the consumer's observable demand behaviour. We had a glimpse of how this might be done when we considered the 'Law of Demand'. There, we asked what the model of consumer behaviour implied for the unobservable, own-substitution effects, and then used the Slutsky relation to translate that into a statement on the relations that must hold between own-price and income responses in the consumer's observable Marshallian demand functions. In view of what we have now learned about the entire system of substitution terms, we need not limit ourselves to statements about own-price and income changes. We can, in fact, use our knowledge of the substitution *matrix* to make a comprehensive deduction about the effects of *all* price and income changes on the entire system of observable Marshallian demands.

THEOREM 1.16 ***Symmetric and Negative Semidefinite Slutsky Matrix***

Let $\mathbf{x}(\mathbf{p}, y)$ *be the consumer's Marshallian demand system. Define the* ijth *Slutsky term as*

$$\frac{\partial x_i(\mathbf{p}, y)}{\partial p_j} + x_j(\mathbf{p}, y)\frac{\partial x_i(\mathbf{p}, y)}{\partial y},$$

and form the entire $n \times n$ **Slutsky matrix** *of price and income responses as follows:*

$$\mathbf{s}(\mathbf{p}, y) =$$
$$\begin{pmatrix} \dfrac{\partial x_1(\mathbf{p}, y)}{\partial p_1} + x_1(\mathbf{p}, y)\dfrac{\partial x_1(\mathbf{p}, y)}{\partial y} & \cdots & \dfrac{\partial x_1(\mathbf{p}, y)}{\partial p_n} + x_n(\mathbf{p}, y)\dfrac{\partial x_1(\mathbf{p}, y)}{\partial y} \\ \vdots & \ddots & \vdots \\ \dfrac{\partial x_n(\mathbf{p}, y)}{\partial p_1} + x_1(\mathbf{p}, y)\dfrac{\partial x_n(\mathbf{p}, y)}{\partial y} & \cdots & \dfrac{\partial x_n(\mathbf{p}, y)}{\partial p_n} + x_n(\mathbf{p}, y)\dfrac{\partial x_n(\mathbf{p}, y)}{\partial y} \end{pmatrix}.$$

Then $\mathbf{s}(\mathbf{p}, y)$ *is symmetric and negative semidefinite.*

Proof: The proof of this is very simple. Let u^* be the maximum utility the consumer achieves at prices $\mathbf{p}$ and income y, so $u^* = v(\mathbf{p}, y)$. Solving for the ijth substitution term from the Slutsky equation in Theorem 1.11, we obtain

$$\frac{\partial x_i^h(\mathbf{p}, u^*)}{\partial p_j} = \frac{\partial x_i(\mathbf{p}, y)}{\partial p_j} + x_j(\mathbf{p}, y)\frac{\partial x_i(\mathbf{p}, y)}{\partial y}.$$

If now we form the matrix $\mathbf{s}(\mathbf{p}, y)$, it is clear from this that each element of that matrix is exactly equal to the corresponding element of the Hicksian substitution matrix $\sigma(\mathbf{p}, u^*)$. By Theorem 1.14, the substitution matrix is symmetric for all u, and by Theorem 1.15 it is negative semidefinite for all u, so it will be both symmetric and negative semidefinite at u^*, too. Because the two matrices are equal, the Slutsky matrix $\mathbf{s}(\mathbf{p}, y)$ must also be symmetric and negative semidefinite. ∎

Theorems 1.10 and 1.16 can be used as the starting point for testing the theory we have developed, or for applying it empirically. The requirements that consumer demand satisfy homogeneity and budget balancedness, and that the associated Slutsky matrix be symmetric and negative semidefinite, provide a set of *restrictions* on allowable values for the parameters in any empirically estimated Marshallian demand system – if that system is to be viewed as belonging to a price-taking, utility-maximising consumer. Are there *other* testable restrictions implied by the theory? This is a question we shall take up in the next chapter, but first we consider some important elasticity relations.

1.5.3 SOME ELASTICITY RELATIONS

To complete our discussion of consumer demand, we take a closer look at the implications of the budget-balancedness condition for the consumer's response to price and income changes. Here we need none of the heavy artillery we previously deployed. Instead, we only need to remind ourselves that the budget constraint imposes a kind of order and discipline on the consumer's response to any change in circumstances.

If $\mathbf{x}(\mathbf{p}, y)$ is the consumer's Marshallian demand function, budget balancedness says that the budget constraint must hold with *equality* at every set of prices and income, or that

$$y = \sum_{i=1}^{n} p_i x_i(\mathbf{p}, y).$$

Because this equality holds for *all* $\mathbf{p}$ and y, we know that if any single price or the consumer's income changes, it must hold both before and after the change. All consumer demand responses to price and income changes therefore must add up, or *aggregate*, in a way that preserves the equality of the budget constraint after the change. There are many such **comparative statics** experiments that we can perform on the budget constraint to determine how demand responses must aggregate together. Sometimes, these are expressed directly in terms of relations that must hold among various derivatives of the demand system. We will instead present them here in terms of relations that must hold among various price and income *elasticities* of demand. This will enable us to cast the results we obtain in an equivalent, but perhaps more intuitive and more readily useful way. We begin with some definitions for the record.

DEFINITION 1.6 ***Demand Elasticities and Income Shares***

Let $x_i(\mathbf{p}, y)$ be the consumer's Marshallian demand for good i. Then let

$$\eta_i \equiv \frac{\partial x_i(\mathbf{p}, y)}{\partial y} \frac{y}{x_i(\mathbf{p}, y)},$$
$$\epsilon_{ij} \equiv \frac{\partial x_i(\mathbf{p}, y)}{\partial p_j} \frac{p_j}{x_i(\mathbf{p}, y)}$$

and let

$$s_i \equiv \frac{p_i x_i(\mathbf{p}, y)}{y} \quad \textit{so that} \quad s_i \geq 0 \quad \textit{and} \quad \sum_{i=1}^{n} s_i = 1.$$

The symbol η_i denotes the **income elasticity** of demand for good i, and measures the percentage change in the quantity of i demanded per 1 per cent change in income. The symbol ϵ_{ij} denotes the **price elasticity** of demand for good i, and measures the percentage change in the quantity of i demanded per 1 per cent change in the price p_j. If $j = i$, ϵ_{ii} is called the **own-price elasticity** of demand for good i.[6] If $j \neq i$, ϵ_{ij} is called the **cross-price elasticity** of demand for good i with respect to p_j. The symbol s_i denotes the **income share**, or proportion of the consumer's income, spent on purchases of good i. These must of course be non-negative and sum to 1.

[6]Note that this has *not* been defined here, as is sometimes done, to guarantee that the own-price elasticity will be a positive number whenever demand is negatively sloped with respect to own price.

THEOREM 1.17 ***Aggregation in Consumer Demand***

Let $\mathbf{x}(\mathbf{p}, y)$ be the consumer's Marshallian demand system. Let η_i, ϵ_{ij}, and s_i, for $i, j = 1, \ldots, n$, be as defined before. Then the following relations must hold among income shares, price, and income elasticities of demand:

1. *Engel aggregation:* $\sum_{i=1}^{n} s_i \eta_i = 1$.
2. *Cournot aggregation:* $\sum_{i=1}^{n} s_i \epsilon_{ij} = -s_j, \quad j = 1, \ldots, n$.

Proof: We begin by recalling that the budget constraint requires

$$y = \mathbf{p} \cdot \mathbf{x}(\mathbf{p}, y) \tag{P.1}$$

for all $\mathbf{p}$ and y.

Engel aggregation says that the share-weighted income elasticities must always sum to one. To prove item 1, differentiate both sides of (P.1) with respect to income and get

$$1 = \sum_{i=1}^{n} p_i \frac{\partial x_i}{\partial y}.$$

Multiply and divide each element in the summation by $x_i y$, rearrange, and get

$$1 = \sum_{i=1}^{n} \frac{p_i x_i}{y} \frac{\partial x_i}{\partial y} \frac{y}{x_i}.$$

Substitute from the definitions to get

$$1 = \sum_{i=1}^{n} s_i \eta_i.$$

Cournot aggregation says that the share-weighted own- and cross-price elasticities must always sum in a particular way. To prove 2, we examine the effect of changing a single price, p_j. Differentiating both sides of (P.1) with respect to p_j, we obtain

$$0 = \left[\sum_{i \neq j}^{n} p_i \frac{\partial x_i}{\partial p_j} \right] + x_j + p_j \frac{\partial x_j}{\partial p_j},$$

where we have differentiated the jth term separately from the others to emphasise that the product rule must be used when differentiating the term $p_j x_j(\mathbf{p}, y)$. That noted, we can combine terms and rearrange to get

$$-x_j = \sum_{i=1}^{n} p_i \frac{\partial x_i}{\partial p_j}.$$

Multiply both sides of the equation by p_j/y and get

$$\frac{-p_j x_j}{y} = \sum_{i=1}^{n} \frac{p_i}{y} \frac{\partial x_i}{\partial p_j} p_j;$$

multiply and divide each element of the summation by x_i and get

$$\frac{-p_j x_j}{y} = \sum_{i=1}^{n} \frac{p_i x_i}{y} \frac{\partial x_i}{\partial p_j} \frac{p_j}{x_i}.$$

Marshallian Demands		
Homogeneity	$\mathbf{x}(\mathbf{p}, y) = \mathbf{x}(t\mathbf{p}, ty)$	for all $(\mathbf{p}, y)$, and $t > 0$
Symmetry	$\frac{\partial x_i(\mathbf{p}, y)}{\partial p_j} + x_j(\mathbf{p}, y)\frac{\partial x_i(p, y)}{\partial y}$	
	$= \frac{\partial x_j(\mathbf{p}, y)}{\partial p_i} + x_i(\mathbf{p}, y)\frac{\partial x_j(\mathbf{p}, y)}{\partial y}$	for all $(\mathbf{p}, y)$, and $i, j = 1, \ldots, n$
Negative semidefiniteness	$\mathbf{z}^T\mathbf{s}(\mathbf{p}, y)\mathbf{z} \leq 0$	for all $(\mathbf{p}, y)$, and $\mathbf{z}$
Budget balancedness	$\mathbf{p} \cdot \mathbf{x}(\mathbf{p}, y) = y$	for all $(\mathbf{p}, y)$,
Engel aggregation	$\sum_{i=1}^{n} s_i\eta_i = 1$	
Cournot aggregation	$\sum_{i=1}^{n} s_i\varepsilon_{ij} = -s_j$	for $j = 1, \ldots, n$
Hicksian Demands		
Homogeneity	$\mathbf{x}^h(t\mathbf{p}, u) = \mathbf{x}^h(\mathbf{p}, u)$	for all $(\mathbf{p}, u)$, and $t > 0$
Symmetry	$\frac{\partial x_i^h(\mathbf{p}, y)}{\partial p_j} = \frac{\partial x_j^h(\mathbf{p}, y)}{\partial p_i}$	for $i, j = 1, \ldots, n$
Negative semidefiniteness	$\mathbf{z}^T\sigma(\mathbf{p}, u)\mathbf{z} \leq 0$	for all $\mathbf{p}$, u, and $\mathbf{z}$
Relating the Two		
Slutsky equation	$\frac{\partial x_i(\mathbf{p}, y)}{\partial p_j}$	for all $(\mathbf{p}, y)$, $u = v(\mathbf{p}, y)$,
	$= \frac{\partial x_i^h(\mathbf{p}, u)}{\partial p_j} - x_j(\mathbf{p}, y)\frac{\partial x_i(\mathbf{p}, y)}{\partial y}$	and $i, j = 1, \ldots, n$

Figure 1.21. Properties of consumer demand.

Substituting from the definitions completes the proof:

$$-s_j = \sum_{i=1}^{n} s_i \epsilon_{ij}, \quad j = 1, \ldots, n. \qquad \blacksquare$$

Theorems 1.10 through 1.17, together, give us an accounting of some of the logical implications of utility-maximising behaviour. Homogeneity tells us how demand must respond to an overall, equiproportionate change in all prices and income simultaneously, and budget balancedness requires that demand always exhaust the consumer's income. The Slutsky equations give us qualitative information, or 'sign restrictions', on how the system of demand functions must respond to very general kinds of price changes, as well as giving us analytical insight into the unobservable components of the demand response to a price change: the income and substitution effects. Finally, the aggregation relations provide information on how the quantities demanded – first in response to an income change alone, then in response to a single price change – must all 'hang together' across the system of demand functions. In the next chapter, we will ask whether there are other implications of the theory we have developed. We end by pulling together all we have learned so far into Fig. 1.21.

1.6 EXERCISES

1.1 Let $X = \mathbb{R}^2_+$. Verify that X satisfies all five properties required of a consumption set in Assumption 1.1.

1.2 Let $\succsim$ be a preference relation. Prove the following:

(a) $\succ \subset \succsim$

(b) $\sim \subset \succsim$

(c) $\succ \cup \sim = \succsim$

(d) $\succ \cap \sim = \emptyset$

1.3 Give a proof or convincing argument for each of the following claims made in the text.

(a) Neither $\succ$ nor $\sim$ is complete.

(b) For any $\mathbf{x}^1$ and $\mathbf{x}^2$ in X, only *one* of the following holds: $\mathbf{x}^1 \succ \mathbf{x}^2$, or $\mathbf{x}^2 \succ \mathbf{x}^1$, or $\mathbf{x}^1 \sim \mathbf{x}^2$.

1.4 Prove that if $\succsim$ is a preference relation, then the relation $\succ$ is transitive and the relation $\sim$ is transitive. Also show that if $\mathbf{x}^1 \sim \mathbf{x}^2 \succsim \mathbf{x}^3$, then $\mathbf{x}^1 \succsim \mathbf{x}^3$.

1.5 If $\succsim$ is a preference relation, prove the following: For any $\mathbf{x}^0 \in X$,

(a) $\sim(\mathbf{x}^0) = \succsim(\mathbf{x}^0) \cap \precsim(\mathbf{x}^0)$

(b) $\succsim(\mathbf{x}^0) = \sim(\mathbf{x}^0) \cup \succ(\mathbf{x}^0)$

(c) $\sim(\mathbf{x}^0) \cap \succ(\mathbf{x}^0) = \emptyset$

(d) $\sim(\mathbf{x}^0) \cap \prec(\mathbf{x}^0) = \emptyset$

(e) $\prec(\mathbf{x}^0) \cap \succ(\mathbf{x}^0) = \emptyset$

(f) $\prec(\mathbf{x}^0) \cap \sim(\mathbf{x}^0) \cap \succ(\mathbf{x}^0) = \emptyset$

(g) $\prec(\mathbf{x}^0) \cup \sim(\mathbf{x}^0) \cup \succ(\mathbf{x}^0) = X$

1.6 Cite a credible example where the preferences of an 'ordinary consumer' would be unlikely to satisfy the axiom of convexity.

1.7 Prove that under Axiom 5′, the set $\succsim(\mathbf{x}^0)$ is a convex set for any $\mathbf{x}^0 \in X$.

1.8 Sketch a map of indifference sets that are all parallel, negatively sloped straight lines, with preference increasing north-easterly. We know that preferences such as these satisfy Axioms 1, 2, 3, and 4. Prove that they also satisfy Axiom 5′. Prove that they do not satisfy Axiom 5.

1.9 Sketch a map of indifference sets that are all parallel right angles that 'kink' on the line $x_1 = x_2$. If preference increases north-easterly, these preferences will satisfy Axioms 1, 2, 3, and 4′. Prove that they also satisfy Axiom 5′. Do they satisfy Axiom 4? Do they satisfy Axiom 5?

1.10 Sketch a set of preferences that satisfy Axioms 1, 2, 3, and 4, whose indifference sets are convex to the origin in some places and contain 'linear segments' in others. Prove that preferences such as these are consistent with Axiom 5′, but violate Axiom 5.

1.11 Show that if $\succsim$ is continuous, then the sets A and B defined in the proof of Theorem 1.1 are closed subsets of $\mathbb{R}$.

1.12 Suppose $u(x_1, x_2)$ and $v(x_1, x_2)$ are utility functions.

(a) Prove that if $u(x_1, x_2)$ and $v(x_1, x_2)$ are both homogeneous of degree r, then $s(x_1, x_2) \equiv u(x_1, x_2) + v(x_1, x_2)$ is homogeneous of degree r.

(b) Prove that if $u(x_1, x_2)$ and $v(x_1, x_2)$ are quasiconcave, then $m(x_1, x_2) \equiv \min\{u(x_1, x_2),\ v(x_1, x_2)\}$ is also quasiconcave.

1.13 A consumer has **lexicographic** preferences over $\mathbf{x} \in \mathbb{R}^2_+$ if the relation $\succsim$ satisfies $\mathbf{x}^1 \succsim \mathbf{x}^2$ whenever $x_1^1 > x_1^2$, or $x_1^1 = x_1^2$ and $x_2^1 \geq x_2^2$.

(a) Sketch an indifference map for these preferences.

(b) Can these preferences be represented by a continuous utility function? Why or why not?

1.14 Suppose that the preferences $\succsim$ can be represented by a continuous utility function. Show that $\succsim$ satisfies Axioms 1, 2, and 3.

1.15 Prove that the budget set, B, is a compact, convex set whenever $\mathbf{p} \gg \mathbf{0}$.

1.16 Prove the assertions made in the text that under Assumption 1.2:

(a) If $\mathbf{x}^*$ solves the consumer's problem, then $\mathbf{x}^*$ is unique.

(b) $\mathbf{x}^*$ will exhaust the consumer's income and satisfy $y = \mathbf{p} \cdot \mathbf{x}^*$.

1.17 Suppose that preferences are convex but not strictly convex. Give a clear and convincing argument that a solution to the consumer's problem still exists, but that it need not be unique. Illustrate your argument with a two-good example.

1.18 Consider a two-good case where $x_1^* > 0$ and $x_2^* = 0$ at the solution to the consumer's problem. State conditions, similar to those in (1.11), that characterise this solution and illustrate your answer with a diagram similar to Fig. 1.10.

1.19 Prove Theorem 1.2

1.20 Suppose preferences are represented by the **Cobb-Douglas** utility function, $u(x_1, x_2) = Ax_1^{\alpha}x_2^{1-\alpha}$, $0<\alpha<1$, and $A > 0$. Assuming an interior solution, solve for the Marshallian demand functions.

1.21 We have noted that $u(\mathbf{x})$ is invariant to positive monotonic transforms. One common transformation is the *logarithmic transform*, $\ln(u(\mathbf{x}))$. Take the logarithmic transform of the utility function in the preceding exercise; then, using that as the utility function, derive the Marshallian demand functions and verify that they are identical to those derived in the preceding exercise.

1.22 We can generalise further the result of the preceding exercise. Suppose that preferences are represented by the utility function $u(\mathbf{x})$. Assuming an interior solution, the consumer's demand functions, $\mathbf{x}(\mathbf{p}, y)$, are determined implicitly by the conditions in (1.10). Now consider the utility function $f(u(\mathbf{x}))$, where $f' > 0$, and show that the first-order conditions characterising the solution to the consumer's problem in both cases can be reduced to the same set of equations. Conclude from this that the consumer's demand behaviour is invariant to positive monotonic transforms of the utility function.

1.23 Prove Theorem 1.3.

1.24 Let $u(\mathbf{x})$ represent some consumer's monotonic preferences over $\mathbf{x} \in \mathbb{R}^n_+$. For each of the functions $f(\mathbf{x})$ that follow, state whether or not f *also* represents the preferences of this consumer. In each case, be sure to justify your answer with either an argument or a counterexample.

(a) $f(\mathbf{x}) = u(\mathbf{x}) + (u(\mathbf{x}))^3$

(b) $f(\mathbf{x}) = u(\mathbf{x}) - (u(\mathbf{x}))^2$

(c) $f(\mathbf{x}) = u(\mathbf{x}) + \sum_{i=1}^{n} x_i$

1.25 A consumer with convex, monotonic preferences consumes non-negative amounts of x_1 and x_2.

(a) If $u(x_1, x_2) = x_1^{\alpha}x_2^{(1/2)-\alpha}$ represents those preferences, what restrictions must there be on the value of parameter α? Explain.

(b) Given those restrictions, calculate the Marshallian demand functions.

1.26 A consumer of two goods faces positive prices and has a positive income. His utility function is

$$u(x_1, x_2) = x_1.$$

Derive the Marshallian demand functions.

1.27 A consumer of two goods faces positive prices and has a positive income. His utility function is

$$u(x_1, x_2) = \max[ax_1, ax_2] + \min[x_1, x_2], \qquad \text{where} \quad 0 < a < 1.$$

Derive the Marshallian demand functions.

1.28 In the proof of Theorem 1.4 we use the fact that if $u(\cdot)$ is quasiconcave and differentiable at $\mathbf{x}$ and $u(\mathbf{y}) \geq u(\mathbf{x})$, then $\nabla u(\mathbf{x}) \cdot (\mathbf{y} - \mathbf{x}) \geq 0$. Prove this fact in the following two steps.

(a) Prove that if $u(\mathbf{x}) \geq u(\mathbf{y})$ the quasiconcavity of $u(\cdot)$ and its differentiability at $\mathbf{x}$ imply that the derivative of $u((1-t)\mathbf{x} + t\mathbf{y})$ with respect to t must be non-negative at $t = 0$.

(b) Compute the derivative of $u((1-t)\mathbf{x} + t\mathbf{y})$ with respect to t evaluated at $t = 0$ and show that it is $\nabla u(\mathbf{x}) \cdot (\mathbf{y} - \mathbf{x})$.

1.29 An infinitely lived agent owns 1 unit of a commodity that he consumes over his lifetime. The commodity is perfectly storable and he will receive no more than he has now. Consumption of the commodity in period t is denoted x_t, and his lifetime utility function is given by

$$u(x_0, x_1, x_2, \ldots) = \sum_{t=0}^{\infty} \beta^t \ln(x_t), \qquad \text{where} \quad 0 < \beta < 1.$$

Calculate his optimal level of consumption in each period.

1.30 In the two-good case, the level sets of the indirect utility function in price space are sets of the form $\{(p_1, p_2) \mid v(p_1, p_2, y) = v^0\}$ for $v^0 \in \mathbb{R}$. These are sometimes called **price-indifference curves**. Sketch a possible map of price-indifference curves. Give separate arguments to support your claims as to their slope, curvature, and the direction of increasing utility.

1.31 Show that the indirect utility function in Example 1.2 is a quasiconvex function of prices and income.

1.32 In the statement of Theorem 1.6, we made the requirement that $u(\mathbf{x})$ be strictly increasing. How, if at all, must the statement of properties 1 through 6 be amended if we simply drop this requirement on preferences? Support your argument and illustrate any claims with a two-good case.

1.33 Let $v(\mathbf{p}, y)$ be some agent's indirect utility function. Show that demand behaviour is invariant to arbitrary, positive monotonic transforms of $v(\mathbf{p}, y)$. Conclude that any such transform of the indirect utility function can itself serve as the agent's indirect utility function.

1.34 Show that if $u(\mathbf{x})$ is continuous and strictly increasing, then for every $\mathbf{p} \gg \mathbf{0}$, $e(\mathbf{p}, u)$ is unbounded above in u.

1.35 Complete the proof of Theorem 1.7 by proving property 5.

1.36 Provide an alternative proof of Roy's identity by completing the following steps:

(a) Using the definition of v, show that if $\mathbf{p} \gg \mathbf{0}$ and $\mathbf{x}^0 = \mathbf{x}(\mathbf{p}^0, y^0)$, then $v(\mathbf{p}, \mathbf{p} \cdot \mathbf{x}^0) \geq v(\mathbf{p}^0, \mathbf{p}^0 \cdot \mathbf{x}^0)$ $\forall \mathbf{p} \gg \mathbf{0}$.

(b) Conclude that $f(\mathbf{p}) \equiv v(\mathbf{p}, \mathbf{p} \cdot \mathbf{x}^0)$ is minimised on $\mathbb{R}^n_{++}$ at $\mathbf{p} = \mathbf{p}^0$.

(c) Assume f is differentiable at $\mathbf{p}^0$. What value must its gradient have at $\mathbf{p}^0$?

(d) Prove Roy's identity using parts (a) to (c).

1.37 Provide an alternative proof of Shephard's lemma by completing the following steps:

(a) Using the definition of e, show that if $\mathbf{p}^0 \gg \mathbf{0}$ and $\mathbf{x}^0 = \mathbf{x}^h(\mathbf{p}^0, u^0)$, then $e(\mathbf{p}, u^0) \leq \mathbf{p} \cdot \mathbf{x}^0$ for all $\mathbf{p} \gg \mathbf{0}$ with equality when $\mathbf{p} = \mathbf{p}^0$.

(b) Conclude that $f(\mathbf{p}) \equiv e(\mathbf{p}, u) - \mathbf{p} \cdot \mathbf{x}^0$ is maximised on $\mathbb{R}^n_{++}$ at $\mathbf{p} = \mathbf{p}^0$.

(c) Assume that f is differentiable at $\mathbf{p}^0$. What value must its gradient have at $\mathbf{p}^0$?

(d) Assuming that $e(\mathbf{p}, u)$ is differentiable in $\mathbf{p}$, prove Shephard's lemma using parts (a) to (c).

1.38 Verify that the expenditure function obtained from the CES direct utility function in Example 1.3 satisfies all the properties given in Theorem 1.7.

1.39 Complete the proof of Theorem 1.9 by showing that $\mathbf{x}^h(\mathbf{p}, u) = \mathbf{x}(\mathbf{p}, e(\mathbf{p}, u))$.

1.40 Use Roy's identity and Theorem A2.6 to give an alternative proof that $x_i(\mathbf{p}, y)$ is homogeneous of degree zero in prices and income.

1.41 Prove that Hicksian demands are homogeneous of degree zero in prices.

1.42 Prove the modern Law of Demand given in Theorem 1.13. Prove that the *converse* of each statement in the Law of Demand is *not* true.

1.43 For expositional purposes, we derived Theorems 1.14 and 1.15 separately, but really the second one implies the first. Show that when the substitution matrix $\sigma(\mathbf{p}, u)$ is negative semidefinite, all own-substitution terms will be non-positive.

1.44 In a two-good case, show that if one good is inferior, the other good must be normal.

1.45 Fix $\mathbf{x}^0 \in \mathbb{R}^n_+$. Define the **Slutsky-compensated demand function** at $\mathbf{x}^0$, $\mathbf{x}^s(\mathbf{p}, \mathbf{x}^0)$, by $\mathbf{x}^s(\mathbf{p}, \mathbf{x}^0) = \mathbf{x}(\mathbf{p}, \mathbf{p} \cdot \mathbf{x}^0)$. Thus, Slutsky-compensated demand at $\mathbf{x}^0$ is that which would be made as prices change and the consumer's income is compensated so that he can always afford bundle $\mathbf{x}^0$. Let $\mathbf{x}^0 = \mathbf{x}(\mathbf{p}^0, y^0)$. Show that

$$\frac{\partial x_i^s(\mathbf{p}^0, \mathbf{x}^0)}{\partial p_j} = \frac{\partial x_i^h(\mathbf{p}^0, u^0)}{\partial p_j}, \qquad i, j = 1, \ldots, n,$$

where $u^0 = u(\mathbf{x}^0)$. Thus, the slopes of Hicksian and Slutsky-compensated demands are the same. Consequently, the Slutsky matrix is the matrix of slopes of Slutsky-compensated demands, and this is how it originally received its name.

1.46 We can derive yet another set of relations that must hold between price and income elasticities in the consumer's demand system. This one follows directly from homogeneity, and in fact can be considered simply a restatement of that principle. Prove that $\sum_{j=1}^n \epsilon_{ij} + \eta_i = 0$, $i = 1, \ldots, n$.

1.47 Suppose that $u(\mathbf{x})$ is a linear homogeneous utility function.

(a) Show that the expenditure function is multiplicatively separable in $\mathbf{p}$ and u and can be written in the form $e(\mathbf{p}, u) = e(\mathbf{p}, 1)u$.

(b) Show that the marginal utility of income depends on $\mathbf{p}$, but is independent of y.

1.48 Suppose that the expenditure function is multiplicatively separable in $\mathbf{p}$ and u so that $e(\mathbf{p}, u) = k(u)g(\mathbf{p})$, where $k(\cdot)$ is some positive monotonic function of a single variable, and $g\colon \mathbb{R}^n_+ \to \mathbb{R}_+$. Show that the income elasticity of (Marshallian) demand for every good is equal to unity.

1.49 You are given the following information about the demand functions and expenditure patterns of a consumer who spends all his income on two goods: (1) At current prices, the same amount is spent on both goods; (2) at current prices, the own-price elasticity of demand for good 1 is equal to -3.

(a) At current prices, what is the elasticity of demand for good 2 with respect to the price of good 1?

(b) Can statements (1) and (2) both hold at *all* prices? Why or why not?

1.50 Someone consumes a single good x, and his indirect utility function is

$$v(p, y) = G\left(A(p) + \frac{\bar{y}^{\eta} y^{1-\eta}}{1-\eta}\right), \qquad \text{where} \qquad A(p) = \int_{p}^{p^0} x(\xi, \bar{y}) d\xi,$$

and $G(\cdot)$ is some positive monotonic function of one variable.

(a) Derive the consumer's demand for x and show that it has constant income elasticity equal to η.

(b) Suppose the consumer has an income equal to $\bar{y}$, and the price of x rises from p to $p' > p$. Argue that the change in the consumer's utility caused by this price change can be measured by $-\int_{p}^{p'} x(\xi, \bar{y}) d\xi < 0$. Interpret this measure.

1.51 Consider the utility function, $u(x_1, x_2) = (x_1)^{1/2} + (x_2)^{1/2}$.

(a) Compute the demand functions, $x_i(p_1, p_2, y)$, $i = 1, 2$.

(b) Compute the substitution term in the Slutsky equation for the effects on x_1 of changes in p_2.

(c) Classify x_1 and x_2 as (gross) complements or substitutes.

1.52 Suppose $\underline{\eta}$ and $\bar{\eta}$ are lower and upper bounds, respectively, on the income elasticity of demand for good x_i over all prices and incomes. Then

$$\underline{\eta} \leq \frac{\partial x_i(\mathbf{p}, y)}{\partial y} \frac{y}{x_i(\mathbf{p}, y)} \leq \bar{\eta}$$

over all prices and incomes. Show that for any y and y^0,

$$\left(\frac{y}{y^0}\right)^{\underline{\eta}} \leq \frac{x_i(\mathbf{p}, y)}{x_i(\mathbf{p}, y^0)} \leq \left(\frac{y}{y^0}\right)^{\bar{\eta}}.$$

1.53 Agents A and B have the following expenditure functions. In each case, state whether or not the observable market behaviour of the two agents will be identical. Justify your answers.

(a) $e^A(\mathbf{p}, u)$ and $e^B(\mathbf{p}, u) = e^A(\mathbf{p}, 2u)$.

(b) $e^A(\mathbf{p}, u) = k(u)g(\mathbf{p})$, where $k'(u) > 0$, and $e^B(\mathbf{p}, u) = 2e^A(\mathbf{p}, u)$.

1.54 The n-good Cobb-Douglas utility function is

$$u(\mathbf{x}) = A \prod_{i=1}^{n} x_i^{\alpha_i},$$

where $A > 0$ and $\sum_{i=1}^{n} \alpha_i = 1$.

(a) Derive the Marshallian demand functions.

(b) Derive the indirect utility function.

(c) Compute the expenditure function.

(d) Compute the Hicksian demands.

1.55 Suppose

$$u(\mathbf{x}) = \sum_{i=1}^{n} f_i(x_i)$$

is strictly quasiconcave with $f_i'(x_i) > 0$ for all i. The consumer faces fixed prices $\mathbf{p} \gg \mathbf{0}$ and has income $y > 0$. Assume $\mathbf{x}(\mathbf{p}, y) \gg \mathbf{0}$.

(a) Show that if one good displays increasing marginal utility at $\mathbf{x}(\mathbf{p}, y)$, all other goods must display diminishing marginal utility there.

(b) Prove that if one good displays increasing marginal utility and all others diminishing marginal utility at $\mathbf{x}(\mathbf{p}, y)$, then one good is normal and all other goods are inferior.

(c) Show that if all goods display diminishing marginal utility at $\mathbf{x}(\mathbf{p}, y)$, then all goods are normal.

1.56 What restrictions must the $\alpha_i, f(y)$, $w(p_1, p_2)$, and $z(p_1, p_2)$ satisfy if each of the following is to be a legitimate indirect utility function?

(a) $v(p_1, p_2, p_3, y) = f(y)p_1^{\alpha_1} p_2^{\alpha_2} p_3^{\alpha_3}$

(b) $v(p_1, p_2, y) = w(p_1, p_2) + z(p_1, p_2)/y$

1.57 The **Stone-Geary utility function** has the form

$$u(\mathbf{x}) = \prod_{i=1}^{n} (x_i - a_i)^{b_i},$$

where $b_i \geq 0$ and $\sum_{i=1}^{n} b_i = 1$. The $a_i \geq 0$ are often interpreted as 'subsistence' levels of the respective commodities.

(a) Derive the associated expenditure and indirect utility functions. Note that the former is *linear* in utility, whereas the latter is proportional to the amount of 'discretionary income', $y - \sum_{i=1}^{n} p_i a_i$.

(b) Show that b_i measures the share of this 'discretionary income' that will be spent on 'discretionary' purchases of good x_i in excess of the subsistence level a_i.

1.58 The Stone-Geary expenditure function you derived in part (a) of the preceding exercise is a special case of the **Gorman polar form:**

$$e(\mathbf{p}, u) = a(\mathbf{p}) + ub(\mathbf{p}),$$

where $a(\mathbf{p})$ and $b(\mathbf{p})$ are both linear homogeneous and concave. Show that for a consumer with this expenditure function, the income elasticity of demand for every good approaches zero as $y \to 0$, and approaches unity as $y \to \infty$.

1.59 If $e(\mathbf{p}, u) = z(p_1, p_2)p_3^m u$, where $m > 0$, what restrictions must $z(p_1, p_2)$ satisfy for this to be a legitimate expenditure function?

1.60 Suppose $x_1(\mathbf{p}, y)$ and $x_2(\mathbf{p}, y)$ have equal income elasticity at $(\mathbf{p}^0, y^0)$. Show that $\partial x_1/\partial p_2 = \partial x_2/\partial p_1$ at $(\mathbf{p}^0, y^0)$.

1.61 Show that the Slutsky relation can be expressed in elasticity form as

$$\epsilon_{ij} = \epsilon_{ij}^h - s_j \eta_i,$$

where ϵ_{ij}^h is the elasticity of the Hicksian demand for x_i with respect to price p_j, and all other terms are as defined in Definition 1.6.

1.62 According to **Hicks' Third Law:**

$$\sum_{j=1}^{n} \frac{\partial x_i^h(\mathbf{p}, u)}{\partial p_j} p_j = 0, \quad i = 1, \ldots, n,$$

or equivalently, in elasticity form,

$$\sum_{j=1}^{n} \epsilon_{ij}^h = 0, \quad i = 1, \ldots, n.$$

Prove this and verify it for a consumer with the n-good Cobb-Douglas utility function in Exercise 1.54.

1.63 The substitution matrix of a utility-maximising consumer's demand system at prices $(8, p)$ is

$$\begin{pmatrix} a & b \\ 2 & -1/2 \end{pmatrix}.$$

Find a, b, and p.

1.64 *True or false?*

(a) When the ratio of goods consumed, x_i/x_j, is independent of the level of income for all i and j, then all income elasticities are equal to 1.

(b) When income elasticities are all *constant and equal*, they must all be equal to 1.

(c) If the utility function is homothetic, the marginal utility of income is independent of prices and depends only on income.

1.65 Show that the utility function is homothetic if and only if all demand functions are multiplicatively separable in prices and income and of the form $\mathbf{x}(\mathbf{p}, y) = \phi(y)\mathbf{x}(\mathbf{p}, 1)$.

1.66 A consumer with income y^0 faces prices $\mathbf{p}^0$ and enjoys utility $u^0 = v(\mathbf{p}^0, y^0)$. When prices change to $\mathbf{p}^1$, the cost of living is affected. To gauge the impact of these price changes, we may define a **cost of living index** as the ratio

$$I(\mathbf{p}^0, \mathbf{p}^1, u^0) \equiv \frac{e(\mathbf{p}^1, u^0)}{e(\mathbf{p}^0, u^0)}.$$

(a) Show that $I(\mathbf{p}^0, \mathbf{p}^1, u^0)$ is greater than (less than) unity as the outlay necessary to maintain base utility, u^0, rises (falls).

(b) Suppose consumer income also changes from y^0 to y^1. Show that the consumer will be better off (worse off) in the final period whenever y^1/y^0 is greater (less) than $I(\mathbf{p}^0, \mathbf{p}^1, u^0)$.

1.67 A cost of living index is introduced in the previous exercise. Suppose the consumer's direct utility function is $u(x_1, x_2) = \sqrt{x_1} + x_2$.

(a) Let base prices be $\mathbf{p}^0 = (1, 2)$, base income be $y^0 = 10$, and suppose $\mathbf{p}^1 = (2, 1)$. Compute the index I.

(b) Let base and final period prices be as in part (a), but now let base utility be u^0. Show that the value of the index I will vary with the base utility.

(c) It can be shown that when consumer preferences are homothetic, I will be *independent* of the base utility for any prices $\mathbf{p}^0$ and $\mathbf{p}^1$. Can you show it?

1.68 Show that the share of income spent on good x_i can always be measured by $\partial \ln[e(\mathbf{p}, u^*)]/\partial \ln(p_i)$, where $u^* \equiv v(\mathbf{p}, y)$.

CHAPTER 2

TOPICS IN CONSUMER THEORY

In this chapter, we explore some additional topics in consumer theory. We begin with duality theory and investigate more completely the links among utility, indirect utility, and expenditure functions. Then we consider the classic 'integrability problem' and ask what conditions a function of prices and income must satisfy in order that it qualify as a demand function for some utility-maximising consumer. The answer to this question will provide a complete characterisation of the restrictions our theory places on observable demand behaviour. We then examine 'revealed preference', an alternative approach to demand theory. Finally, we conclude our treatment of the individual consumer by looking at the problem of choice under uncertainty.

2.1 DUALITY: A CLOSER LOOK

As we have seen, the solutions to utility maximisation problems and expenditure minimisation problems are, in a sense, the same. This idea is formally expressed in Theorem 1.9. In this section, we shall explore further the connections among direct utility, indirect utility and expenditure functions. We will show that although our theory of the consumer was developed, quite naturally, beginning with axioms on preferences, an equivalent theory could have been developed beginning with axioms on expenditure behaviour. Indeed, we will show that every function of prices and utility that has all the properties of an expenditure function is in fact an expenditure function, i.e., there is a well-behaved utility function that generates it. Although this result is of some interest in itself, its real significance becomes clear when it is used to characterise completely the observable implications of our theory of the consumer's demand behaviour. This extraordinary characterisation will follow from the so-called 'integrability theorem' taken up in the next section. Given the importance of this result, this section can justifiably be viewed as preparation for the next.

2.1.1 EXPENDITURE AND CONSUMER PREFERENCES

Consider any function of prices and utility, $E(\mathbf{p}, u)$, that may or may not be an expenditure function. Now suppose that E satisfies the expenditure function properties 1 to 7 of

Theorem 1.7, so that it is continuous, strictly increasing, and unbounded above in u, as well as increasing, homogeneous of degree one, concave, and differentiable in $\mathbf{p}$. Thus, E 'looks like' an expenditure function. We shall show that E *must then be an expenditure function*. Specifically, we shall show that there must exist a utility function on $\mathbb{R}^n_+$ whose expenditure function is precisely E. Indeed, we shall give an explicit procedure for constructing this utility function.

To see how the construction works, choose $(\mathbf{p}^0, u^0) \in \mathbb{R}^n_{++} \times \mathbb{R}_+$, and evaluate E there to obtain the number $E(\mathbf{p}^0, u^0)$. Now use this number to construct the (closed) 'half-space' in the consumption set,

$$A(\mathbf{p}^0, u^0) \equiv \{\mathbf{x} \in \mathbb{R}^n_+ \mid \mathbf{p}^0 \cdot \mathbf{x} \geq E(\mathbf{p}^0, u^0)\},$$

illustrated in Fig. 2.1(a). Notice that $A(\mathbf{p}^0, u^0)$ is a closed convex set containing all points on and above the hyperplane, $\mathbf{p}^0 \cdot \mathbf{x} = E(\mathbf{p}^0, u^0)$. Now choose different prices $\mathbf{p}^1$, keep u^0 fixed, and construct the closed convex set,

$$A(\mathbf{p}^1, u^0) \equiv \{\mathbf{x} \in \mathbb{R}^n_+ \mid \mathbf{p}^1 \cdot \mathbf{x} \geq E(\mathbf{p}^1, u^0)\}.$$

Imagine proceeding like this for *all* prices $\mathbf{p} \gg \mathbf{0}$ and forming the infinite intersection,

$$A(u^0) \equiv \bigcap_{\mathbf{p} \gg \mathbf{0}} A(\mathbf{p}, u^0) = \{\mathbf{x} \in \mathbb{R}^n_+ \mid \mathbf{p} \cdot \mathbf{x} \geq E(\mathbf{p}, u^0) \text{ for all } \mathbf{p} \gg \mathbf{0}\}. \tag{2.1}$$

The shaded area in Fig. 2.1(b) illustrates the intersection of a finite number of the $A(\mathbf{p}, u^0)$, and gives some intuition about what $A(u^0)$ will look like. It is easy to imagine that as more and more prices are considered and more sets are added to the intersection, the shaded area will more closely resemble a *superior set* for some quasiconcave real-valued function. One might suspect, therefore, that these sets can be used to construct something

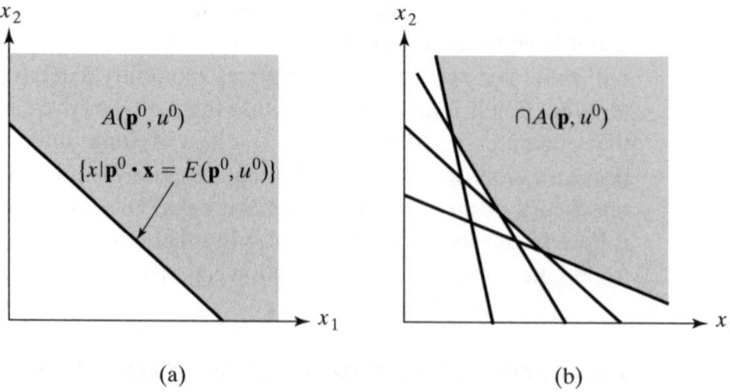

Figure 2.1. (a) The closed half-space $A(\mathbf{p}^0, u^0)$. (b) The intersection of a finite collection of the sets $A(\mathbf{p}, u^0)$.

very much like a direct utility function representing nice convex, monotonic preferences. This is indeed the case and is demonstrated by the following theorem.

THEOREM 2.1 ***Constructing a Utility Function from an Expenditure Function***

Let $E\colon \mathbb{R}^n_{++}\times\mathbb{R}_+\to\mathbb{R}_+$ *satisfy properties 1 through 7 of an expenditure function given in Theorem 1.7. Let* $A(u)$ *be as in (2.1). Then the function* $u\colon \mathbb{R}^n_+ \to \mathbb{R}_+$ *given by*

$$u(\mathbf{x}) \equiv \max\{u \geq 0 \mid \mathbf{x} \in A(u)\}$$

is increasing, unbounded above, and quasiconcave.

You might be wondering why we have chosen to define $u(\mathbf{x})$ the way we have. After all, there are many ways one can employ $E(\mathbf{p}, u)$ to assign numbers to each $\mathbf{x} \in \mathbb{R}^n_+$. To understand why, forget this definition of $u(\mathbf{x})$ and for the moment suppose that $E(\mathbf{p}, u)$ is in fact the expenditure function generated by some utility function $u(\mathbf{x})$. How might we recover $u(\mathbf{x})$ from knowledge of $E(\mathbf{p}, u)$? Note that by the definition of an expenditure function, $\mathbf{p} \cdot \mathbf{x} \geq E(\mathbf{p}, u(\mathbf{x}))$ for all prices $\mathbf{p} \gg \mathbf{0}$, and, typically, there will be equality for some price. Therefore, because E is strictly increasing in u, $u(\mathbf{x})$ is the largest value of u such that $\mathbf{p} \cdot \mathbf{x} \geq E(\mathbf{p}, u)$ for all $\mathbf{p} \gg \mathbf{0}$. That is, $u(\mathbf{x})$ is the largest value of u such that $\mathbf{x} \in A(u)$. Consequently, the construction we have given is just right for recovering the utility function that generated $E(\mathbf{p}, u)$ when in fact $E(\mathbf{p}, u)$ is an expenditure function. But the preceding considerations give us a strategy for showing that it is: first, show that $u(\mathbf{x})$ defined as in the statement of Theorem 2.1 is a utility function satisfying our axioms. (This is the content of Theorem 2.1.) Second, show that E is in fact the expenditure function generated by $u(\mathbf{x})$. (This is the content of Theorem 2.2.) We now give the proof of Theorem 2.1.

Proof: Note that by the definition of $A(u)$, we may write $u(\mathbf{x})$ as

$$u(\mathbf{x}) = \max\{u \geq 0 \mid \mathbf{p} \cdot \mathbf{x} \geq E(\mathbf{p}, u) \ \ \forall\, \mathbf{p} \gg \mathbf{0}\}.$$

The first thing that must be established is that $u(\mathbf{x})$ is well-defined. That is, it must be shown that the set $\{u \geq 0 \mid \mathbf{p} \cdot \mathbf{x} \geq E(\mathbf{p}, u) \ \ \forall\, \mathbf{p} \gg \mathbf{0}\}$ contains a largest element. We shall sketch the argument. First, this set, call it $B(\mathbf{x})$, must be bounded above because $E(\mathbf{p}, u)$ is unbounded above and increasing in u. Thus, $B(\mathbf{x})$ possesses an upper bound and hence also a least upper bound, $\hat{u}$. It must be shown that $\hat{u} \in B(\mathbf{x})$. But this follows because $B(\mathbf{x})$ is closed, which we will not show.

Having argued that $u(\mathbf{x})$ is well-defined, let us consider the claim that it is increasing. Consider $\mathbf{x}^1 \geq \mathbf{x}^2$. Then

$$\mathbf{p} \cdot \mathbf{x}^1 \geq \mathbf{p} \cdot \mathbf{x}^2 \qquad \forall\, \mathbf{p} \gg \mathbf{0}, \tag{P.1}$$

because all components of $\mathbf{x}^1$ are at least as large as the corresponding component of $\mathbf{x}^2$. By the definition of $u(\mathbf{x}^2)$,

$$\mathbf{p} \cdot \mathbf{x}^2 \geq E(\mathbf{p}, u(\mathbf{x}^2)) \qquad \forall\, \mathbf{p} \gg \mathbf{0}. \tag{P.2}$$

Together, (P.1) and (P.2) imply that

$$\mathbf{p} \cdot \mathbf{x}^1 \geq E(\mathbf{p}, u(\mathbf{x}^2)) \qquad \forall\, \mathbf{p} \gg \mathbf{0}. \tag{P.3}$$

Consequently, $u(\mathbf{x}^2)$ satisfies the condition: $\mathbf{x}^1 \in A(u(\mathbf{x}^2))$. But $u(\mathbf{x}^1)$ is the *largest* u satisfying $\mathbf{x}^1 \in A(u)$. Hence, $u(\mathbf{x}^1) \geq u(\mathbf{x}^2)$, which shows that $u(\mathbf{x})$ is increasing.

The unboundedness of $u(\cdot)$ on $\mathbb{R}^n_+$ can be shown by appealing to the increasing, concavity, homogeneity, and differentiability properties of $E(\cdot)$ in $\mathbf{p}$, and to the fact that its domain in u is all of $\mathbb{R}^n_+$. We shall not give the proof here (although it can be gleaned from the proof of Theorem 2.2 below).

To show that $u(\cdot)$ is quasiconcave, we must show that for all $\mathbf{x}^1, \mathbf{x}^2$, and convex combinations $\mathbf{x}^t$, $u(\mathbf{x}^t) \geq \min[u(\mathbf{x}^1), u(\mathbf{x}^2)]$. To see this, suppose that $u(\mathbf{x}^1) = \min[u(\mathbf{x}^1), u(\mathbf{x}^2)]$. Because E is strictly increasing in u, we know that $E(\mathbf{p}, u(\mathbf{x}^1)) \leq E(\mathbf{p}, u(x^2))$ and that therefore

$$tE(\mathbf{p}, u(\mathbf{x}^1)) + (1-t)E(\mathbf{p}, u(\mathbf{x}^2)) \geq E(\mathbf{p}, u(\mathbf{x}^1)) \quad \forall\, t \in [0, 1]. \tag{P.4}$$

From the definitions of $u(\mathbf{x}^1)$ and $u(\mathbf{x}^2)$, we know that

$$\begin{aligned} \mathbf{p} \cdot \mathbf{x}^1 &\geq E(\mathbf{p}, u(\mathbf{x}^1)) \qquad \forall\, \mathbf{p} \gg \mathbf{0}, \\ \mathbf{p} \cdot \mathbf{x}^2 &\geq E(\mathbf{p}, u(\mathbf{x}^2)) \qquad \forall\, \mathbf{p} \gg \mathbf{0}. \end{aligned}$$

Multiplying by $t \geq 0$ and $(1-t) \geq 0$, respectively, adding, and using (P.4) gives

$$\mathbf{p} \cdot \mathbf{x}^t \geq E(\mathbf{p}, u(\mathbf{x}^1)) \qquad \forall\, \mathbf{p} \gg \mathbf{0} \qquad \text{and} \qquad t \in [0, 1].$$

Consequently, by definition of $u(\mathbf{x}^t)$, $u(\mathbf{x}^t) \geq u(\mathbf{x}^1) = \min[u(\mathbf{x}^1), u(\mathbf{x}^2)]$ as we sought to show. ∎

Theorem 2.1 tells us we can begin with an expenditure function and use it to construct a direct utility function representing some convex, monotonic preferences. We actually know a bit more about those preferences. If we begin with them and derive the associated expenditure function, we end up with the function $E(\cdot)$ we started with!

THEOREM 2.2 ***The Expenditure Function of Derived Utility, u, is E***

Let $E(\mathbf{p}, u)$, defined on $\mathbb{R}^n_{++} \times \mathbb{R}^n_+$, satisfy properties 1 to 7 of an expenditure function given in Theorem 1.7 and let $u(\mathbf{x})$ be derived from E as in Theorem 2.1. Then for all non-negative *prices and utility,*

$$E(\mathbf{p}, u) = \min_{\mathbf{x}} \ \mathbf{p} \cdot \mathbf{x} \qquad \text{s.t.} \qquad u(\mathbf{x}) \geq u.$$

That is, $E(\mathbf{p}, u)$ is the expenditure function generated by derived utility $u(\mathbf{x})$.

Proof: Fix $\mathbf{p}^0 \gg \mathbf{0}$ and $u^0 \geq 0$ and suppose $\mathbf{x} \in \mathbb{R}^n_+$ satisfies $u(\mathbf{x}) \geq u^0$. Note that because $u(\cdot)$ is derived from E as in Theorem 2.1, we must then have

$$\mathbf{p} \cdot \mathbf{x} \geq E(\mathbf{p}, u(\mathbf{x})) \qquad \forall\, \mathbf{p} \gg \mathbf{0}.$$

Furthermore, because E is increasing in utility and $u(\mathbf{x}) \geq u^0$, we must have

$$\mathbf{p} \cdot \mathbf{x} \geq E(\mathbf{p}, u^0) \qquad \forall\, \mathbf{p} \gg \mathbf{0}. \tag{P.1}$$

Consequently, for any given prices $\mathbf{p}^0$, we have established that

$$E(\mathbf{p}^0, u^0) \leq \mathbf{p}^0 \cdot \mathbf{x} \qquad \forall\, \mathbf{x} \in \mathbb{R}^n_+ \qquad \text{s.t.} \qquad u(\mathbf{x}) \geq u^0. \tag{P.2}$$

But (P.2) then implies that

$$E(\mathbf{p}^0, u^0) \leq \min_{\mathbf{x} \in \mathbb{R}^n_+} \mathbf{p}^0 \cdot \mathbf{x} \qquad \text{s.t.} \qquad u(\mathbf{x}) \geq u^0. \tag{P.3}$$

We would like to show that the first inequality in (P.3) is an equality. To do so, it suffices to find a single $\mathbf{x}^0 \in \mathbb{R}^n_+$ such that

$$\mathbf{p}^0 \cdot \mathbf{x}^0 \leq E(\mathbf{p}^0, u^0) \quad \text{and} \quad u(\mathbf{x}^0) \geq u^0, \tag{P.4}$$

because this would clearly imply that the minimum on the right-hand side of (P.3) could not be greater than $E(\mathbf{p}^0, u^0)$.

To establish (P.4), note that by Euler's theorem (Theorem A2.7), because E is differentiable and homogeneous of degree 1 in $\mathbf{p}$,

$$E(\mathbf{p}, u) = \frac{\partial E(\mathbf{p}, u)}{\partial \mathbf{p}} \cdot \mathbf{p} \qquad \forall\, \mathbf{p} \gg \mathbf{0}, \tag{P.5}$$

where we use $\partial E(\mathbf{p}, u)/\partial \mathbf{p} \equiv (\partial E(\mathbf{p}, u)/\partial p_1, \ldots, \partial E(\mathbf{p}, u)/\partial p_n)$ to denote the vector of price-partial derivatives of E. Also, because $E(\mathbf{p}, u)$ is concave in $\mathbf{p}$, Theorem A2.4 implies that for all $\mathbf{p} \gg \mathbf{0}$,

$$E(\mathbf{p}, u^0) \leq E(\mathbf{p}^0, u^0) + \frac{\partial E(\mathbf{p}^0, u^0)}{\partial \mathbf{p}} \cdot (\mathbf{p} - \mathbf{p}^0). \tag{P.6}$$

But evaluating (P.5) at $(\mathbf{p}^0, u^0)$ and combining this with (P.6) implies that

$$E(\mathbf{p}, u^0) \leq \big(\partial E(\mathbf{p}^0, u^0)/\partial \mathbf{p}\big) \cdot \mathbf{p} \qquad \forall\, \mathbf{p} \gg \mathbf{0}. \tag{P.7}$$

Letting $\mathbf{x}^0 = \partial E(\mathbf{p}^0, u^0)/\partial \mathbf{p}$, note that $\mathbf{x}^0 \in \mathbb{R}^n_+$ because E is increasing in $\mathbf{p}$. We may rewrite (P.7) now as

$$\mathbf{p} \cdot \mathbf{x}^0 \geq E(\mathbf{p}, u^0) \qquad \forall\, \mathbf{p} \gg \mathbf{0}. \tag{P.8}$$

So, by the definition of $u(\cdot)$, we must have $u(\mathbf{x}^0) \geq u^0$. Furthermore, evaluating (P.5) at $(\mathbf{p}^0, u^0)$ yields $E(\mathbf{p}^0, u^0) = \mathbf{p}^0 \cdot \mathbf{x}^0$. Thus, we have established (P.4) for this choice of $\mathbf{x}^0$, and therefore we have shown that

$$E(\mathbf{p}^0, u^0) = \min_{\mathbf{x} \in \mathbb{R}^n_+} \mathbf{p}^0 \cdot \mathbf{x} \qquad \text{s.t.} \qquad u(\mathbf{x}) \geq u^0.$$

Because $\mathbf{p}^0 \gg \mathbf{0}$ and $u^0 \geq 0$ were arbitrary, we have shown that $E(\mathbf{p}, u)$ coincides with the expenditure function of $u(\mathbf{x})$ on $\mathbb{R}^n_{++} \times \mathbb{R}_+$. ∎

The last two theorems tell us that any time we can write down a function of prices and utility that satisfies properties 1 to 7 of Theorem 1.7, it will be a legitimate expenditure function for some preferences satisfying many of the usual axioms. We can of course then differentiate this function with respect to product prices to obtain the associated system of Hicksian demands. If the underlying preferences are continuous and strictly increasing, we can invert the function in u, obtain the associated indirect utility function, apply Roy's identity, and derive the system of Marshallian demands as well. Every time, we are assured that the resulting demand systems possess all properties required by utility maximisation. For theoretical purposes, therefore, a choice can be made. One can start with a direct utility function and proceed by solving the appropriate optimisation problems to derive the Hicksian and Marshallian demands. Or one can begin with an expenditure function and proceed to obtain consumer demand systems by the generally easier route of inversion and simple differentiation.

2.1.2 CONVEXITY AND MONOTONICITY

You may recall that after introducing the convexity axiom on preferences, it was stated that 'the predictive content of the theory would be the same with or without it'. This is an opportune time to support that claim and to investigate the import of the monotonicity assumption as well.

For the present discussion, let us suppose only that $u(\mathbf{x})$ is continuous. Thus, $u(\mathbf{x})$ need be neither increasing nor quasiconcave.

Let $e(\mathbf{p}, u)$ be the expenditure function generated by $u(\mathbf{x})$. As we know, the continuity of $u(\mathbf{x})$ is enough to guarantee that $e(\mathbf{p}, u)$ is well-defined. Moreover, $e(\mathbf{p}, u)$ is continuous.

Going one step further, consider the utility function, call it $w(\mathbf{x})$, generated by $e(\cdot)$ in the now familiar way, that is,

$$w(\mathbf{x}) \equiv \max\{u \geq 0 \mid \mathbf{p} \cdot \mathbf{x} \geq e(\mathbf{p}, u) \;\; \forall\, \mathbf{p} \gg \mathbf{0}\}.$$

A look at the proof of Theorem 2.1 will convince you that $w(\mathbf{x})$ is increasing and quasiconcave. Thus, regardless of whether or not $u(\mathbf{x})$ is quasiconcave or increasing, $w(\mathbf{x})$ will be both quasiconcave and increasing. Clearly, then, $u(\mathbf{x})$ and $w(\mathbf{x})$ need not coincide. How then are they related?

It is easy to see that $w(\mathbf{x}) \geq u(\mathbf{x})$ for all $\mathbf{x} \in \mathbb{R}^n_+$. This follows because by the definition of $e(\cdot)$, we have $e(\mathbf{p}, u(\mathbf{x})) \leq \mathbf{p} \cdot \mathbf{x} \;\; \forall\, \mathbf{p} \gg \mathbf{0}$. The desired inequality now follows from the definition of $w(\mathbf{x})$.

Thus, for any $u \geq 0$, the level-u superior set for $u(\mathbf{x})$, say $S(u)$, will be contained in the level-u superior set for $w(\mathbf{x})$, say, $T(u)$. Moreover, because $w(\mathbf{x})$ is quasiconcave, $T(u)$ is convex.

Now consider Fig. 2.2. If $u(\mathbf{x})$ happens to be increasing and quasiconcave, then the boundary of $S(u)$ yields the negatively sloped, convex indifference curve $u(\mathbf{x}) = u$ in Fig. 2.2(a). Note then that each point on that boundary is the expenditure-minimising bundle to achieve utility u at some price vector $\mathbf{p} \gg \mathbf{0}$. Consequently, if $u(\mathbf{x}^0) = u$, then for some $\mathbf{p}^0 \gg \mathbf{0}$, we have $e(\mathbf{p}^0, u) = \mathbf{p}^0 \cdot \mathbf{x}^0$. But because $e(\cdot)$ is strictly increasing in u, this means that $w(\mathbf{x}^0) \leq u = u(\mathbf{x}^0)$. But because $w(\mathbf{x}^0) \geq u(\mathbf{x}^0)$ always holds, we must then have $w(\mathbf{x}^0) = u(\mathbf{x}^0)$. Because u was arbitrary, this shows that in this case, $w(\mathbf{x}) = u(\mathbf{x})$ for all $\mathbf{x}$. But this is not much of a surprise in light of Theorems 2.1 and 2.2 and the assumed quasiconcavity and increasing properties of $u(\mathbf{x})$.

The case depicted in Fig. 2.2(b) is more interesting. There, $u(\mathbf{x})$ is neither increasing nor quasiconcave. Again, the boundary of $S(u)$ yields the indifference curve $u(\mathbf{x}) = u$.

Note that some bundles on the indifference curve *never* minimise the expenditure required to obtain utility level u regardless of the price vector. The thick lines in Fig. 2.2(c) show those bundles that *do* minimise expenditure at some positive price vector. For those bundles $\mathbf{x}$ on the thick line segments in Fig. 2.2(c), we therefore have as before that $w(\mathbf{x}) = u(\mathbf{x}) = u$. But because $w(\mathbf{x})$ is quasiconcave and increasing, the $w(\mathbf{x}) = u$ indifference curve must be as depicted in Fig. 2.2(d). Thus, $w(\mathbf{x})$ differs from $u(\mathbf{x})$ only as much as is required to become strictly increasing and quasiconcave.

Given the relationship between their indifference curves, it is clear that if some bundle maximises $u(\mathbf{x})$ subject to $\mathbf{p} \cdot \mathbf{x} \leq y$, then the same bundle maximises $w(\mathbf{x})$ subject to $\mathbf{p} \cdot \mathbf{x} \leq y$. (Careful, the converse is false.) Consequently, any observable demand behaviour that can be generated by a non-increasing, non-quasiconcave utility function, like $u(\mathbf{x})$, can *also* be generated by an increasing, quasiconcave utility function, like $w(\mathbf{x})$.

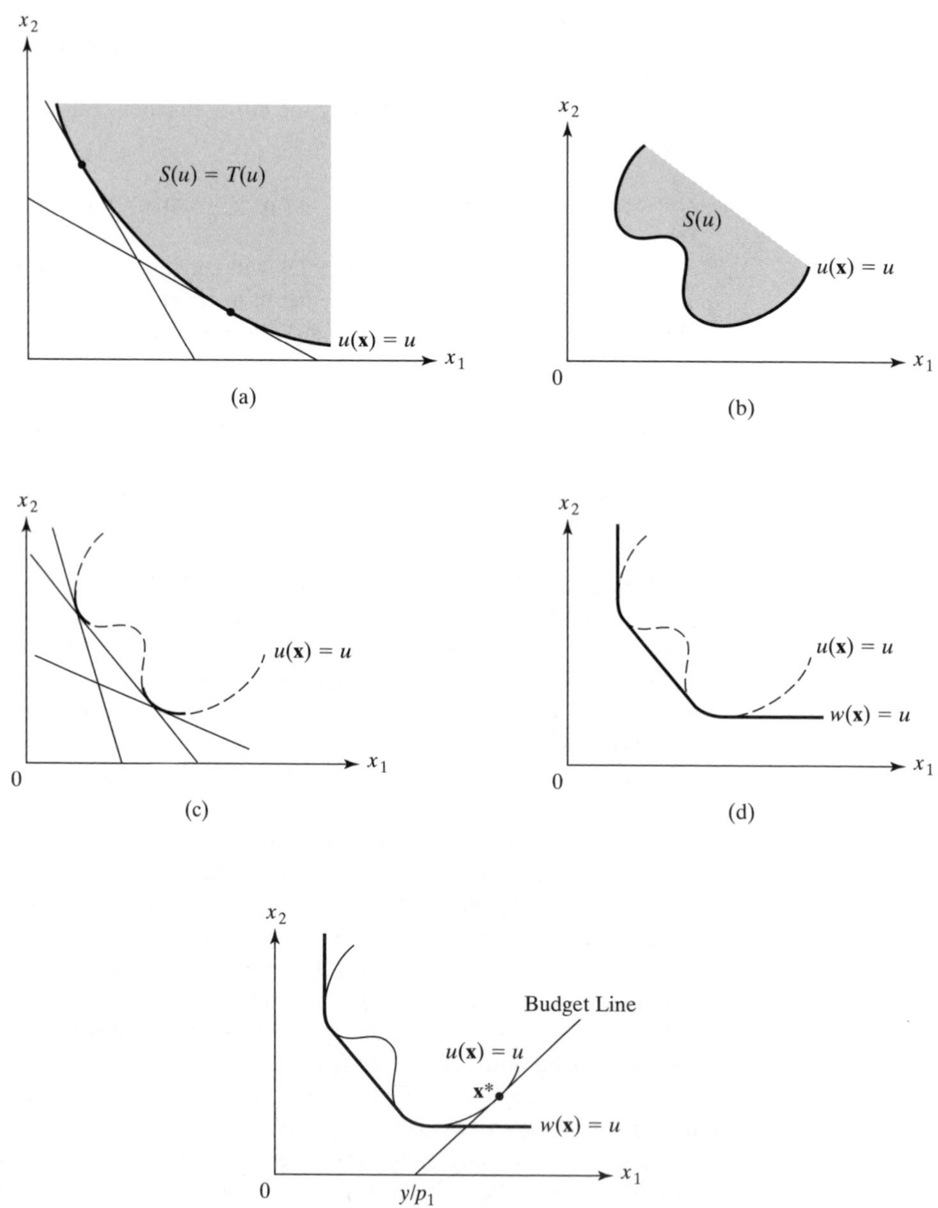

Figure 2.2. Duality between expenditure and utility.

It is in this sense that the assumptions of monotonicity and convexity of preferences have *no observable implications* for our theory of consumer demand.[1]

2.1.3 INDIRECT UTILITY AND CONSUMER PREFERENCES

We have seen how duality allows us to work from the expenditure function to the direct utility function. Because the expenditure and indirect utility functions are so closely related (i.e., are *inverses* of each other), it should come as no surprise that it is also possible to begin with an indirect utility function and work back to the underlying direct utility function. In this section, we outline the duality between direct and indirect utility functions.

Suppose that $u(\mathbf{x})$ generates the indirect utility function $v(\mathbf{p}, y)$. Then by definition, for every $\mathbf{x} \in \mathbb{R}^n_+$, $v(\mathbf{p}, \mathbf{p} \cdot \mathbf{x}) \geq u(\mathbf{x})$ holds for every $\mathbf{p} \gg \mathbf{0}$. In addition, there will typically be some price vector for which the inequality is an equality. Evidently, then we may write

$$u(\mathbf{x}) = \min_{\mathbf{p} \in \mathbb{R}^n_{++}} v(\mathbf{p}, \mathbf{p} \cdot \mathbf{x}). \tag{2.2}$$

Thus, (2.2) provides a means for recovering the utility function $u(\mathbf{x})$ from knowledge of only the indirect utility function it generates. The following theorem gives one version of this result, although the assumptions are not the weakest possible.

THEOREM 2.3 ***Duality Between Direct and Indirect Utility***

Suppose that $u(\mathbf{x})$ is quasiconcave and differentiable on $\mathbb{R}^n_{++}$ with strictly positive partial derivatives there. Then for all $\mathbf{x} \in \mathbb{R}^n_{++}$, $v(\mathbf{p}, \mathbf{p} \cdot \mathbf{x})$, the indirect utility function generated by $u(\mathbf{x})$, achieves a minimum in $\mathbf{p}$ on $\mathbb{R}^n_{++}$, and

$$u(\mathbf{x}) = \min_{\mathbf{p} \in \mathbb{R}^n_{++}} v(\mathbf{p}, \mathbf{p} \cdot \mathbf{x}). \tag{T.1}$$

Proof: According to the discussion preceding Theorem 2.3, the left-hand side of (T.1) never exceeds the right-hand side. Therefore, it suffices to show that for each $\mathbf{x} \gg \mathbf{0}$, there is some $\mathbf{p} \gg \mathbf{0}$ such that

$$u(\mathbf{x}) = v(\mathbf{p}, \mathbf{p} \cdot \mathbf{x}). \tag{P.1}$$

[1]Before ending this discussion, we give a cautionary note on the conclusion regarding monotonicity. The fact that the demand behaviour generated by $u(\mathbf{x})$ in the preceding second case could be captured by the increasing function $w(\mathbf{x})$ relies on the assumption that the consumer only faces non-negative prices. For example, if with two goods, one of the prices, say, p_2 were negative, then we may have a situation such as that in Fig. 2.2(e), where $\mathbf{x}^*$ is optimal for the utility function $u(\mathbf{x})$ but not for the increasing function $w(\mathbf{x})$. Thus, if prices can be negative, monotonicity is not without observable consequences.

So consider $\mathbf{x}^0 \gg \mathbf{0}$, and let $\mathbf{p}^0 = \nabla u(\mathbf{x}^0)$. Then by assumption, $\mathbf{p}^0 \gg \mathbf{0}$. Moreover, letting $\lambda^0 = 1$, and $y^0 = \mathbf{p}^0 \cdot \mathbf{x}^0$, we have

$$\frac{\partial u(\mathbf{x}^0)}{\partial x_i} - \lambda^0 p_i^0 = 0 \qquad i = 1, \ldots, n \tag{P.2}$$

and

$$\mathbf{p}^0 \cdot \mathbf{x}^0 = y^0. \tag{P.3}$$

Consequently, $(\mathbf{x}^0, \lambda^0)$ satisfy the first-order conditions for the consumer's maximisation problem $\max u(\mathbf{x})$ s.t. $\mathbf{p}^0 \cdot \mathbf{x} = y^0$. Moreover, by Theorem 1.4, because $u(\mathbf{x})$ is quasiconcave, these conditions are sufficient to guarantee that $\mathbf{x}^0$ solves the consumer's problem when $\mathbf{p} = \mathbf{p}^0$ and $y = y^0$. Therefore, $u(\mathbf{x}^0) = v(\mathbf{p}^0, y^0) = v(\mathbf{p}^0, \mathbf{p}^0 \cdot \mathbf{x}^0)$. Consequently, (P.1) holds for $(\mathbf{p}^0, \mathbf{x}^0)$, but because $\mathbf{x}^0$ was arbitrary, we may conclude that for every $\mathbf{x} \gg \mathbf{0}$, (P.1) holds for some $\mathbf{p} \gg \mathbf{0}$. ∎

As in the case of expenditure functions, one can show by using (T.1) that if some function $V(\mathbf{p}, y)$ has all the properties of an indirect utility function given in Theorem 1.6, then $V(\mathbf{p}, y)$ is in fact an indirect utility function. We will not pursue this result here, however. The interested reader may consult Diewert (1974).

Finally, we note that (T.1) can be written in another form, which is sometimes more convenient. Note that because $v(\mathbf{p}, y)$ is homogeneous of degree zero in $(\mathbf{p}, y)$, we have $v(\mathbf{p}, \mathbf{p} \cdot \mathbf{x}) = v(\mathbf{p}/(\mathbf{p} \cdot \mathbf{x}), 1)$ whenever $\mathbf{p} \cdot \mathbf{x} > 0$. Consequently, if $\mathbf{x} \gg \mathbf{0}$ and $\mathbf{p}^* \gg \mathbf{0}$ minimises $v(\mathbf{p}, \mathbf{p} \cdot \mathbf{x})$ for $\mathbf{p} \in \mathbb{R}^n_{++}$, then $\widehat{\mathbf{p}} \equiv \mathbf{p}^*/(\mathbf{p}^* \cdot \mathbf{x}) \gg \mathbf{0}$ minimises $v(\mathbf{p}, 1)$ for $\mathbf{p} \in \mathbb{R}^n_{++}$ such that $\mathbf{p} \cdot \mathbf{x} = 1$. Moreover, $v(\mathbf{p}^*, \mathbf{p}^* \cdot \mathbf{x}) = v(\widehat{\mathbf{p}}, 1)$. Thus, we may rewrite (T.1) as

$$u(\mathbf{x}) = \min_{\mathbf{p} \in \mathbb{R}^n_{++}} v(\mathbf{p}, 1) \qquad \text{s.t.} \qquad \mathbf{p} \cdot \mathbf{x} = 1. \tag{T.1$'$}$$

Whether we use (T.1) or (T.1′) to recover $u(\mathbf{x})$ from $v(\mathbf{p}, y)$ does not matter. Simply choose that which is more convenient. One disadvantage of (T.1) is that it always possesses *multiple* solutions because of the homogeneity of v (i.e., if $\mathbf{p}^*$ solves (T.1), then so does $t\mathbf{p}^*$ for all $t > 0$). Consequently, we could not, for example, apply Theorem A2.22 (the Envelope theorem) as we shall have occasion to do in what follows. For purposes such as these, (T.1′) is distinctly superior. ∎

EXAMPLE 2.1 Let us take a particular case and derive the direct utility function. Suppose that $v(\mathbf{p}, y) = y(p_1^r + p_2^r)^{-1/r}$. From the latter part of Example 1.2, we know this satisfies all necessary properties of an indirect utility function. We will use (T.1′) to recover $u(\mathbf{x})$. Setting $y = 1$ yields $v(\mathbf{p}, 1) = (p_1^r + p_2^r)^{-1/r}$. The direct utility function therefore will be the minimum-value function,

$$u(x_1, x_2) = \min_{p_1, p_2} \left(p_1^r + p_2^r\right)^{-1/r} \qquad \text{s.t.} \qquad p_1 x_1 + p_2 x_2 = 1.$$

First, solve the minimisation problem and then evaluate the objective function at the solution to form the minimum-value function. The first-order conditions for the Lagrangian require that the optimal p_1^* and p_2^* satisfy

$$-((p_1^*)^r + (p_2^*)^r)^{(-1/r)-1}(p_1^*)^{r-1} - \lambda^* x_1 = 0, \tag{E.1}$$

$$-((p_1^*)^r + (p_2^*)^r)^{(-1/r)-1}(p_2^*)^{r-1} - \lambda^* x_2 = 0, \tag{E.2}$$

$$1 - p_1^* x_1 - p_2^* x_2 = 0. \tag{E.3}$$

Eliminating λ^* from (E.1) and (E.2) gives

$$p_1^* = p_2^* \left(\frac{x_1}{x_2}\right)^{1/(r-1)}. \tag{E.4}$$

Substituting from (E.4) into (E.3) and using (E.4) again, after a bit of algebra, gives the solutions

$$p_1^* = \frac{x_1^{1/(r-1)}}{x_1^{r/(r-1)} + x_2^{r/(r-1)}}, \tag{E.5}$$

$$p_2^* = \frac{x_2^{1/(r-1)}}{x_1^{r/(r-1)} + x_2^{r/(r-1)}}. \tag{E.6}$$

Substituting these into the objective function and forming $u(x_1, x_2)$, we obtain

$$\begin{aligned} u(x_1, x_2) &= \left[\frac{x_1^{r/(r-1)} + x_2^{r/(r-1)}}{\left(x_1^{r/(r-1)} + x_2^{r/(r-1)}\right)^r}\right]^{-1/r} \\ &= \left[\left(x_1^{r/(r-1)} + x_2^{r/(r-1)}\right)^{1-r}\right]^{-1/r} \\ &= \left(x_1^{r/(r-1)} + x_2^{r/(r-1)}\right)^{(r-1)/r}. \end{aligned}$$

Defining $\rho \equiv r/(r-1)$ yields

$$u(x_1, x_2) = \left(x_1^\rho + x_2^\rho\right)^{1/\rho}. \tag{E.7}$$

This is the CES direct utility function we started with in Example 1.2, as it should be. □

The last duality result we take up concerns the consumer's *inverse demand functions*. Throughout the chapter, we have concentrated on the ordinary Marshallian demand functions, where quantity demanded is expressed as a function of prices and income.

Occasionally, it is convenient to work with demand functions in inverse form. Here we view the demand price for commodity i as a function of the *quantities* of good i and of all other goods and write $p_i = p_i(\mathbf{x})$. Duality theory offers a simple way to derive the system of consumer inverse demand functions, as the following theorem shows, where we shall simply assume differentiability as needed.

THEOREM 2.4 ***(Hotelling, Wold) Duality and the System of Inverse Demands***

Let $u(\mathbf{x})$ be the consumer's direct utility function. Then the inverse demand function for good i associated with income $y = 1$ is given by

$$p_i(\mathbf{x}) = \frac{\partial u(\mathbf{x})/\partial x_i}{\sum_{j=1}^{n} x_j(\partial u(\mathbf{x})/\partial x_j)}.$$

Proof: By the definition of $\mathbf{p}(\mathbf{x})$, we have $u(\mathbf{x}) = v(\mathbf{p}(\mathbf{x}), 1)$ and $[\mathbf{p}(\mathbf{x})] \cdot \mathbf{x} = 1$ for all $\mathbf{x}$. Consequently, by the discussion preceding Theorem 2.3 and the normalisation argument,

$$u(\mathbf{x}) = v(\mathbf{p}(\mathbf{x}), 1) = \min_{\mathbf{p} \in \mathbb{R}^n_{++}} v(\mathbf{p}, 1) \qquad \text{s.t.} \qquad \mathbf{p} \cdot \mathbf{x} = 1. \tag{P.1}$$

Consider now the Lagrangian associated with the minimisation problem in (P.1),

$$\mathcal{L}(\mathbf{p}, \lambda) = v(\mathbf{p}, 1) - \lambda(1 - \mathbf{p} \cdot \mathbf{x}).$$

Applying the Envelope theorem yields

$$\frac{\partial u(\mathbf{x})}{\partial x_i} = \frac{\partial \mathcal{L}(\mathbf{p}^*, \lambda^*)}{\partial x_i} = \lambda^* p_i^*, \qquad i = 1, \ldots, n, \tag{P.2}$$

where $\mathbf{p}^* = \mathbf{p}(\mathbf{x})$, and λ^* is the optimal value of the Lagrange multiplier. Assuming $\partial u(\mathbf{x})/\partial x_i > 0$, we have then that $\lambda^* > 0$.

Multiplying (P.2) by x_i and summing over i gives

$$\begin{aligned} \sum_{i=1}^{n} x_i \frac{\partial u(\mathbf{x})}{\partial x_i} &= \lambda^* \sum_{i=1}^{n} p_i^* x_i \\ &= \lambda^* \sum_{i=1}^{n} p_i(\mathbf{x}) x_i \\ &= \lambda^*, \end{aligned} \tag{P.3}$$

because $[\mathbf{p}(\mathbf{x})] \cdot \mathbf{x} = 1$. Combining (P.2) and (P.3) and recalling that $p_i^* = p_i(\mathbf{x})$ yields the desired result. ∎

EXAMPLE 2.2 Let us take the case of the CES utility function once again. If $u(x_1, x_2) = (x_1^\rho + x_2^\rho)^{1/\rho}$, then

$$\frac{\partial u(\mathbf{x})}{\partial x_j} = \left(x_1^\rho + x_2^\rho\right)^{(1/\rho)-1} x_j^{\rho-1}.$$

Multiplying by x_j, summing over $j = 1, 2$, forming the required ratios, and invoking Theorem 2.4 gives the following system of inverse demand functions when income $y = 1$:

$$p_1 = x_1^{\rho-1}\left(x_1^\rho + x_2^\rho\right)^{-1},$$
$$p_2 = x_2^{\rho-1}\left(x_1^\rho + x_2^\rho\right)^{-1}.$$

Notice carefully that these are precisely the solutions (E.5) and (E.6) to the first-order conditions in Example 2.1, after substituting for $r \equiv \rho/(\rho - 1)$. This is no coincidence. In general, the solutions to the consumer's utility-maximisation problem give Marshallian demand as a function of price, and the solutions to its dual, the (normalised) indirect utility-minimisation problem, give inverse demands as functions of quantity. □

2.2 INTEGRABILITY

In Chapter 1, we showed that a utility-maximising consumer's demand function must satisfy homogeneity of degree zero, budget balancedness, symmetry, and negative semidefiniteness, along with Cournot and Engel aggregation. But, really, there is some redundancy in these conditions. In particular, we know from Theorem 1.17 that both aggregation results follow directly from budget balancedness. There is another redundancy as well. Of the remaining four conditions, only budget balancedness, symmetry, and negative semidefiniteness are truly independent: homogeneity of degree zero is implied by the others. In fact, homogeneity is implied by budget balancedness and symmetry alone, as the following theorem demonstrates.

THEOREM 2.5 ***Budget Balancedness and Symmetry Imply Homogeneity***

If $\mathbf{x}(\mathbf{p}, y)$ satisfies budget balancedness and its Slutsky matrix is symmetric, then it is homogeneous of degree zero in $\mathbf{p}$ and y.

Proof: Recall from the proof of Theorem 1.17 that when budget balancedness holds, we may differentiate the budget equation with respect to prices and income to obtain for, $i = 1, \ldots, n$,

$$\sum_{j=1}^{n} p_j \frac{\partial x_j(\mathbf{p}, y)}{\partial p_i} = -x_i(\mathbf{p}, y), \tag{P.1}$$

and

$$\sum_{j=1}^{n} p_j \frac{\partial x_j(\mathbf{p}, y)}{\partial y} = 1. \tag{P.2}$$

Fix $\mathbf{p}$ and y, then let $f_i(t) = x_i(t\mathbf{p}, ty)$ for all $t > 0$. We must show that $f_i(t)$ is constant in t or that $f_i'(t) = 0$ for all $t > 0$.

Differentiating f_i with respect to t gives

$$f_i'(t) = \sum_{j=1}^{n} \frac{\partial x_i(t\mathbf{p}, ty)}{\partial p_j} p_j + \frac{\partial x_i(t\mathbf{p}, ty)}{\partial y} y. \tag{P.3}$$

Now by budget balancedness, $t\mathbf{p} \cdot \mathbf{x}(t\mathbf{p}, ty) = ty$, so that dividing by $t > 0$, we may write

$$y = \sum_{j=1}^{n} p_j x_j(t\mathbf{p}, ty). \tag{P.4}$$

Substituting from (P.4) for y in (P.3) and rearranging yields

$$f_i'(t) = \sum_{j=1}^{n} p_j \left[\frac{\partial x_i(t\mathbf{p}, ty)}{\partial p_j} + \frac{\partial x_i(t\mathbf{p}, ty)}{\partial y} x_j(t\mathbf{p}, ty) \right].$$

But the term in square brackets is the ijth entry of the Slutsky matrix, which, by assumption, is symmetric. Consequently we may interchange i and j within those brackets and maintain equality. Therefore,

$$\begin{aligned}
f_i'(t) &= \sum_{j=1}^{n} p_j \left[\frac{\partial x_j(t\mathbf{p}, ty)}{\partial p_i} + \frac{\partial x_j(t\mathbf{p}, ty)}{\partial y} x_i(t\mathbf{p}, ty) \right] \\
&= \left[\sum_{j=1}^{n} p_j \frac{\partial x_j(t\mathbf{p}, ty)}{\partial p_i} \right] + x_i(t\mathbf{p}, ty) \left[\sum_{j=1}^{n} p_j \frac{\partial x_j(t\mathbf{p}, ty)}{\partial y} \right] \\
&= \frac{1}{t} \left[\sum_{j=1}^{n} t p_j \frac{\partial x_j(t\mathbf{p}, ty)}{\partial p_i} \right] + x_i(t\mathbf{p}, ty) \frac{1}{t} \left[\sum_{j=1}^{n} t p_j \frac{\partial x_j(t\mathbf{p}, ty)}{\partial y} \right] \\
&= \frac{1}{t} [-x_i(t\mathbf{p}, ty)] + x_i(t\mathbf{p}, ty) \frac{1}{t} [1] \\
&= 0,
\end{aligned}$$

where the second-to-last equality follows from (P.1) and (P.2) evaluated at $(t\mathbf{p}, ty)$. ∎

Thus, if $\mathbf{x}(\mathbf{p}, y)$ is a utility-maximiser's system of demand functions, we may (compactly) summarise the implications for observable behaviour we have so far discovered in the following three items alone:

- *Budget Balancedness:* $\mathbf{p} \cdot \mathbf{x}(\mathbf{p}, y) = y$.
- *Negative Semidefiniteness: The associated Slutsky matrix* $\mathbf{s}(\mathbf{p}, y)$ *must be negative semidefinite.*
- *Symmetry:* $\mathbf{s}(\mathbf{p}, y)$ *must be symmetric.*

We would like to know whether or not this list is exhaustive. That is, are these the *only* implications for observable behaviour that flow from our utility-maximisation model of consumer behaviour? Are there perhaps other, additional implications that we have so far not discovered? Remarkably, it can be shown that this list is in fact complete – *there are no other independent restrictions imposed on demand behaviour by the theory of the utility-maximising consumer.*

But how does one even begin to prove such a result? The solution method is ingenious, and its origins date back to Antonelli (1886). The idea is this: suppose we are given a vector-valued function of prices and income, and that we are then somehow able to construct a utility function that generates precisely this same function as its demand function. Then, clearly, that original function must be consistent with our theory of the utility-maximising consumer because it is in fact the demand function of a consumer with the utility function we constructed. Antonelli's insight was to realise that if the vector-valued function of prices and income we start with satisfies just the three preceding conditions, then there must indeed exist a utility function that generates it as its demand function. The problem of recovering a consumer's utility function from his demand function is known as the **integrability problem**.

The implications of this are significant. According to Antonelli's insight, *if* a function of prices and income satisfies the three preceding conditions, it is the demand function for some utility-maximising consumer. We already know that *only if* a function of prices and income satisfies those same conditions will it be the demand function for a utility-maximising consumer. Putting these two together, we must conclude that those three conditions – and those three conditions alone – provide a complete and definitive test of our theory of consumer behaviour. That is, *demand behaviour is consistent with the theory of utility maximisation if and only if it satisfies budget balancedness, negative semidefiniteness, and symmetry*. This impressive result warrants a formal statement.

THEOREM 2.6 ***Integrability Theorem***

A continuously differentiable function $\mathbf{x}\colon \mathbb{R}^{n+1}_{++} \to \mathbb{R}^n_+$ *is the demand function generated by some increasing, quasiconcave utility function if (and only if, when utility is continuous, strictly increasing, and strictly quasiconcave) it satisfies budget balancedness, symmetry, and negative semidefiniteness.*

We now sketch a proof of Antonelli's result. However, we shall take the modern approach to this problem as developed by Hurwicz and Uzawa (1971). Their strategy of proof is a beautiful illustration of the power of duality theory.

Proof: (Sketch) Since we have already demonstrated the 'only if ' part, it suffices to prove the 'if' part of the statement. So suppose some function $\mathbf{x}(\mathbf{p}, y)$ satisfies budget balancedness, symmetry, and negative semidefiniteness. We must somehow show that there is a utility function that generates $\mathbf{x}(\cdot)$ as its demand function.

Consider an arbitrary expenditure function, $e(\mathbf{p}, u)$, generated by some increasing quasiconcave utility function $u(\mathbf{x})$, and suppose that $u(\mathbf{x})$ generates the Marshallian demand function $\mathbf{x}^m(\mathbf{p}, y)$. At this stage, there need be no relation between $\mathbf{x}(\cdot)$ and $e(\cdot)$, $\mathbf{x}(\cdot)$ and $u(\cdot)$, or $\mathbf{x}(\cdot)$ and $\mathbf{x}^m(\cdot)$.

But just for the sake of argument, suppose that $\mathbf{x}(\cdot)$ and $e(\cdot)$ happen to be related as follows:

$$\frac{\partial e(\mathbf{p}, u)}{\partial p_i} = x_i(\mathbf{p}, e(\mathbf{p}, u)), \qquad \forall\, (\mathbf{p}, u),\ i = 1, \ldots, n. \tag{P.1}$$

Can we then say anything about the relationship between $\mathbf{x}(\mathbf{p}, y)$ and the utility function $u(\mathbf{x})$ from which $e(\mathbf{p}, u)$ was derived? In fact, we can. If (P.1) holds, then $\mathbf{x}(\mathbf{p}, y)$ is the demand function generated by the utility function $u(\mathbf{x})$. That is, $\mathbf{x}(\mathbf{p}, y) = \mathbf{x}^m(\mathbf{p}, y)$.

We now sketch why this is so. Note that if Shephard's lemma were applicable, the left-hand side of (P.1) would be equal to $\mathbf{x}^h(\mathbf{p}, u)$, so that (P.1) would imply

$$\mathbf{x}^h(\mathbf{p}, u) = \mathbf{x}(\mathbf{p}, e(\mathbf{p}, u)) \qquad \forall\, (\mathbf{p}, u). \tag{P.2}$$

Moreover, if Theorem 1.9 were applicable, the Hicksian and Marshallian demand functions would be related as

$$\mathbf{x}^h(\mathbf{p}, u) = \mathbf{x}^m(\mathbf{p}, e(\mathbf{p}, u)) \qquad \forall\, (\mathbf{p}, u). \tag{P.3}$$

Putting (P.2) and (P.3) together yields

$$\mathbf{x}(\mathbf{p}, e(\mathbf{p}, u)) = \mathbf{x}^m(\mathbf{p}, e(\mathbf{p}, u)) \qquad \forall\, (\mathbf{p}, u). \tag{P.4}$$

But now recall that, as an expenditure function, for each fixed $\mathbf{p}$, $e(\mathbf{p}, u)$ assumes every non-negative number as u varies over its domain. Consequently, (P.4) is equivalent to

$$\mathbf{x}(\mathbf{p}, y) = \mathbf{x}^m(\mathbf{p}, y) \qquad \forall\, (\mathbf{p}, y)$$

as claimed. (Despite the fact that perhaps neither Shephard's lemma nor Theorem 1.9 can be applied, the preceding conclusion can be established.)

Thus, if the function $\mathbf{x}(\mathbf{p}, y)$ is related to an expenditure function according to (P.1), then $\mathbf{x}(\mathbf{p}, y)$ is the demand function generated by some increasing, quasiconcave utility function (i.e., that which, according to Theorem 2.1, generates the expenditure function).

We therefore have reduced our task to showing that there exists an expenditure function $e(\mathbf{p}, u)$ related to $\mathbf{x}(\mathbf{p}, y)$ according to (P.1).

Now, finding an expenditure function so that (P.1) holds is no easy task. Indeed, (P.1) is known in the mathematics literature as a system of **partial differential equations**. Although such systems are often notoriously difficult to actually solve, there is an important result that tells us precisely when a solution is guaranteed to exist. And, for our purposes, existence is enough.

However, before stating this result, note the following. If (P.1) has a solution $e(\mathbf{p}, u)$, then upon differentiating both sides by p_j, we would get

$$\frac{\partial^2 e(\mathbf{p}, u)}{\partial p_j \partial p_i} = \frac{\partial x_i(\mathbf{p}, e(\mathbf{p}, u))}{\partial p_j} + \frac{\partial e(\mathbf{p}, u)}{\partial p_j} \frac{\partial x_i(\mathbf{p}, e(\mathbf{p}, u))}{\partial y}.$$

By Shephard's lemma, using (P.2), and letting $y = e(\mathbf{p}, u)$, this can be written as

$$\frac{\partial^2 e(\mathbf{p}, u)}{\partial p_j \partial p_i} = \frac{\partial x_i(\mathbf{p}, y)}{\partial p_j} + x_j(\mathbf{p}, y) \frac{\partial x_i(\mathbf{p}, y)}{\partial y}. \tag{P.5}$$

Now note that the left-hand side of (P.5) is symmetric in i and j by Young's theorem. Consequently, (P.5) implies that the right-hand side must be symmetric in i and j as well. Therefore, symmetry of the right-hand side in i and j is a necessary condition for the existence of a solution to (P.1).

Remarkably, it turns out that this condition is also *sufficient* for the existence of a solution. According to **Frobenius' theorem**, a solution to (P.1) exists if and only if the right-hand side of (P.5) is symmetric in i and j. Take a close look at the right-hand side of (P.5). It is precisely the ijth term of the Slutsky matrix associated with $\mathbf{x}(\mathbf{p}, y)$. Consequently, because that Slutsky matrix satisfies symmetry, a function $e(\mathbf{p}, u)$ satisfying (P.1) is guaranteed to exist.

But will this function be a true expenditure function? Frobenius' theorem is silent on this issue. However, by Theorem 2.2, it *will* be an expenditure function if it has all the properties of an expenditure function listed in Theorem 1.7. We now attempt to verify each of those properties.

First, note that because $e(\mathbf{p}, u)$ satisfies (P.1), and because $\mathbf{x}(\mathbf{p}, y)$ is non-negative, $e(\mathbf{p}, u)$ is automatically increasing in $\mathbf{p}$, and Shephard's lemma is guaranteed by construction. Moreover, one can ensure it is continuous in $(\mathbf{p}, u)$, strictly increasing and unbounded in $u \in \mathbb{R}_+$, and that $e(\cdot, u) = 0$ when $u = 0$. As you are asked to show in Exercise 2.4, because (P.1) and budget balancedness are satisfied, $e(\cdot)$ must be homogeneous of degree 1 in $\mathbf{p}$. Thus, the only remaining property of an expenditure function that must be established is concavity in $\mathbf{p}$.

By Theorem A 2.4, $e(\cdot)$ will be concave in $\mathbf{p}$ if and only if its Hessian matrix with respect to $\mathbf{p}$ is negative semidefinite. But according to (P.5), this will be the case if and only if the Slutsky matrix associated with $\mathbf{x}(\mathbf{p}, y)$ is negative semidefinite, which, by assumption, it is.

Altogether we have established the following: *A solution $e(\cdot)$ to (P.1) exists and is an expenditure function if and only if* $\mathbf{x}(\mathbf{p}, y)$ *satisfies budget balancedness, symmetry, and negative semidefiniteness.* This is precisely what we set out to show. ∎

Although we have stressed the importance of this result for the theory itself, there are practical benefits as well. For example, if one wishes to estimate a consumer's demand function based on a limited amount of data, and one wishes to impose as a restriction that the demand function be utility-generated, one is now free to specify any functional form for demand as long as it satisfies budget balancedness, symmetry, and negative semidefiniteness. As we now know, any such demand function is guaranteed to be utility-generated.

To give you a feel for how one can actually recover an expenditure function from a demand function, we consider an example involving three goods.

EXAMPLE 2.3 Suppose there are three goods and that a consumer's demand behaviour is summarised by the functions

$$x_i(p_1, p_2, p_3, y) = \frac{\alpha_i y}{p_i}, \qquad i = 1, 2, 3,$$

where $\alpha_i > 0$, and $\alpha_1 + \alpha_2 + \alpha_3 = 1$.

It is straightforward to check that the vector of demands, $\mathbf{x}(\mathbf{p}, y)$, satisfies budget balancedness, symmetry, and negative semidefiniteness. Consequently, by Theorem 2.6, $\mathbf{x}(\mathbf{p}, y)$ must be utility-generated.

We shall be content to derive an expenditure function satisfying (P.1) in the previous proof. In Exercise 2.5, you are asked to go one step further and use the construction of Theorem 2.1 to recover a utility function generating the expenditure function obtained here. The utility function you recover then will generate the demand behaviour we began with here.

Our task then is to find $e(p_1, p_2, p_3, u)$ that solves the following system of partial differential equations

$$\frac{\partial e(p_1, p_2, p_3, u)}{\partial p_i} = \frac{\alpha_i e(p_1, p_2, p_3, u)}{p_i}, \qquad i = 1, 2, 3.$$

First, note that this can be rewritten as

$$\frac{\partial \ln(e(p_1, p_2, p_3, u))}{\partial p_i} = \frac{\alpha_i}{p_i}, \qquad i = 1, 2, 3. \tag{E.1}$$

Now, if you were asked to find $f(x)$ when told that $f'(x) = \alpha/x$, you would have no trouble deducing that $f(x) = \alpha \ln(x)$+constant. But (E.1) says just that, where $f = \ln(e)$. The only additional element to keep in mind is that when partially differentiating with respect to, say, p_1, all the other variables – p_2, p_3, and u – are treated as constants. With this in mind, it is easy to see that the three equations (E.1) imply the following three:

$$\begin{aligned}\ln(e(\mathbf{p},u)) &= \alpha_1\ln(p_1)+c_1(p_2,p_3,u),\\ \ln(e(\mathbf{p},u)) &= \alpha_2\ln(p_2)+c_2(p_1,p_3,u),\\ \ln(e(\mathbf{p},u)) &= \alpha_3\ln(p_3)+c_3(p_1,p_2,u),\end{aligned} \tag{E.2}$$

where the $c_i(\cdot)$ functions are like the constant added before to $f(x)$. But we must choose the $c_i(\cdot)$ functions so that all three of these equalities hold simultaneously. With a little thought, you will convince yourself that (E.2) then implies

$$\ln(e(\mathbf{p},u)) = \alpha_1\ln(p_1)+\alpha_2\ln(p_2)+\alpha_3\ln(p_3)+c(u),$$

where $c(u)$ is some function of u. But this means that

$$e(\mathbf{p},u) = c(u)p_1^{\alpha_1}p_2^{\alpha_2}p_3^{\alpha_3}.$$

Because we must ensure that $e(\cdot)$ is strictly increasing in u, we may choose $c(u)$ to be any strictly increasing function. It does not matter which, because the implied demand behaviour will be independent of such strictly increasing transformations. For example, we may choose $c(u) = u$, so that our final solution is

$$e(\mathbf{p},u) = up_1^{\alpha_1}p_2^{\alpha_2}p_3^{\alpha_3}.$$

We leave it to you to check that this function satisfies the original system of partial differential equations and that it has all the properties required of an expenditure function. □

2.3 REVEALED PREFERENCE

So far, we have approached demand theory by assuming the consumer has preferences satisfying certain properties (complete, transitive, and strictly monotonic); then we have tried to deduce all of the observable properties of market demand that follow as a consequence (budget balancedness, symmetry, and negative semidefiniteness of the Slutsky matrix). Thus, we have begun by assuming something about things we cannot observe – preferences – to ultimately make predictions about something we can observe – consumer demand behaviour.

In his remarkable *Foundations of Economic Analysis*, Paul Samuelson (1947) suggested an alternative approach. Why not *start and finish* with observable behaviour? Samuelson showed how virtually every prediction ordinary consumer theory makes for a consumer's observable market behaviour can also (and instead) be derived from a few simple and sensible assumptions about the consumer's observable *choices* themselves, rather than about his unobservable preferences.

The basic idea is simple: if the consumer buys one bundle instead of another affordable bundle, then the first bundle is considered to be **revealed preferred** to the second. The presumption is that by actually choosing one bundle over another, the consumer conveys important information about his tastes. Instead of laying down axioms on a person's preferences as we did before, we make assumptions about the consistency of the choices that are made. We make this all a bit more formal in the following.

DEFINITION 2.1 ***Weak Axiom of Revealed Preference (WARP)***

A consumer's choice behaviour satisfies WARP if for every distinct pair of bundles $\mathbf{x}^0$, $\mathbf{x}^1$ *with* $\mathbf{x}^0$ *chosen at prices* $\mathbf{p}^0$ *and* $\mathbf{x}^1$ *chosen at prices* $\mathbf{p}^1$,

$$\mathbf{p}^0 \cdot \mathbf{x}^1 \leq \mathbf{p}^0 \cdot \mathbf{x}^0 \Longrightarrow \mathbf{p}^1 \cdot \mathbf{x}^0 > \mathbf{p}^1 \cdot \mathbf{x}^1.$$

In other words, WARP holds if whenever $\mathbf{x}^0$ *is revealed preferred to* $\mathbf{x}^1$, $\mathbf{x}^1$ *is* never *revealed preferred to* $\mathbf{x}^0$.

To better understand the implications of this definition, look at Fig. 2.3. In both parts, the consumer facing $\mathbf{p}^0$ chooses $\mathbf{x}^0$, and facing $\mathbf{p}^1$ chooses $\mathbf{x}^1$. In Fig. 2.3(a), the consumer's choices satisfy WARP. There, $\mathbf{x}^0$ is chosen when $\mathbf{x}^1$ could have been, but was not, and when $\mathbf{x}^1$ is chosen, the consumer could not have afforded $\mathbf{x}^0$. By contrast, in Fig. 2.3(b), $\mathbf{x}^0$ is again chosen when $\mathbf{x}^1$ could have been, yet when $\mathbf{x}^1$ is chosen, the consumer could have chosen $\mathbf{x}^0$, but did not, violating WARP.

Now, suppose a consumer's choice behaviour satisfies WARP. Let $\mathbf{x}(\mathbf{p}, y)$ denote the choice made by this consumer when faced with prices $\mathbf{p}$ and income y. Note well that this is *not* a demand function because we have not mentioned utility or utility maximisation – it just denotes the quantities the consumer chooses facing $\mathbf{p}$ and y. To keep this point clear in our minds, we refer to $\mathbf{x}(\mathbf{p}, y)$ as a *choice function*. In addition to WARP, we make one

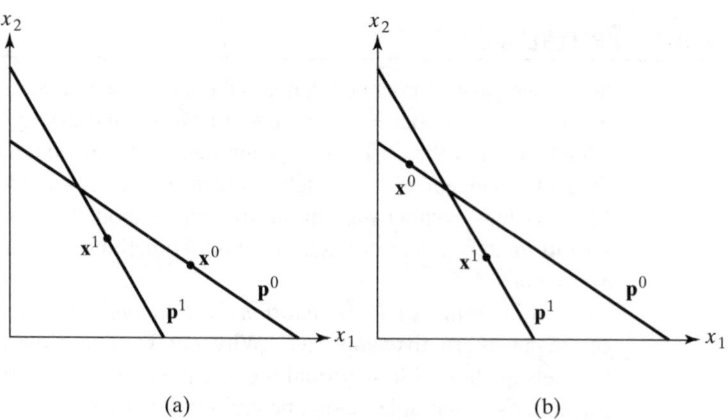

Figure 2.3. The Weak Axiom of Revealed Preference (WARP).

other assumption concerning the consumer's choice behaviour, namely, that for $\mathbf{p} \gg \mathbf{0}$, the choice $\mathbf{x}(\mathbf{p}, y)$ satisfies budget balancedness, i.e., $\mathbf{p} \cdot \mathbf{x}(\mathbf{p}, y) = y$. The implications of these two apparently mild requirements on the consumer's choice behaviour are rather remarkable.

The first consequence of WARP and budget balancedness is that the choice function $\mathbf{x}(\mathbf{p}, y)$ must be homogeneous of degree zero in $(\mathbf{p}, y)$. To see this, suppose $\mathbf{x}^0$ is chosen when prices are $\mathbf{p}^0$ and income is y^0, and suppose $\mathbf{x}^1$ is chosen when prices are $\mathbf{p}^1 = t\mathbf{p}^0$ and income is $y^1 = ty^0$ for $t > 0$. Because $y^1 = ty^0$, when all income is spent, we must have $\mathbf{p}^1 \cdot \mathbf{x}^1 = t\mathbf{p}^0 \cdot \mathbf{x}^0$. First, substitute $t\mathbf{p}^0$ for $\mathbf{p}^1$ in this, divide by t, and get

$$\mathbf{p}^0 \cdot \mathbf{x}^1 = \mathbf{p}^0 \cdot \mathbf{x}^0. \tag{2.3}$$

Then substitute $\mathbf{p}^1$ for $t\mathbf{p}^0$ in the same equation and get

$$\mathbf{p}^1 \cdot \mathbf{x}^1 = \mathbf{p}^1 \cdot \mathbf{x}^0. \tag{2.4}$$

If $\mathbf{x}^0$ and $\mathbf{x}^1$ are distinct bundles for which (2.3) holds, then WARP implies that the left-hand side in (2.4) must be strictly less than the right-hand side – a contradiction. Thus, these bundles cannot be distinct, and the consumer's choice function therefore must be homogeneous of degree zero in prices and income.

Thus, the choice function $\mathbf{x}(\mathbf{p}, y)$ must display one of the additional properties of a demand function. In fact, as we now show, $\mathbf{x}(\mathbf{p}, y)$ must display yet another of those properties as well.

In Exercise 1.45, the notion of Slutsky-compensated demand was introduced. Let us consider the effect here of Slutsky compensation for the consumer's choice behaviour. In case you missed the exercise, the Slutsky compensation is relative to some pre-specified bundle, say $\mathbf{x}^0$. The idea is to consider the choices the consumer makes as prices vary arbitrarily while his income is compensated so that he can just afford the bundle $\mathbf{x}^0$. (See Fig. 2.4.) Consequently, at prices $\mathbf{p}$, his income will be $\mathbf{p} \cdot \mathbf{x}^0$. Under these circumstances, his choice behaviour will be given by $\mathbf{x}(\mathbf{p}, \mathbf{p} \cdot \mathbf{x}^0)$.

Figure 2.4. A Slutsky compensation in income.

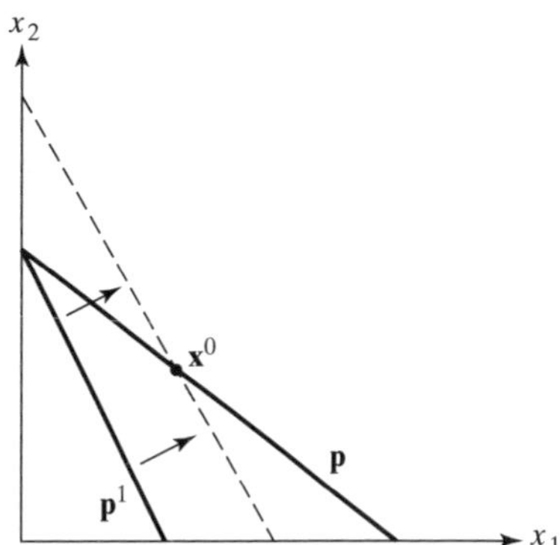

Now fix $\mathbf{p}^0 \gg \mathbf{0}$, $y^0 > 0$, and let $\mathbf{x}^0 = \mathbf{x}(\mathbf{p}^0, y^0)$. Then if $\mathbf{p}^1$ is *any other* price vector and $\mathbf{x}^1 = \mathbf{x}(\mathbf{p}^1, \mathbf{p}^1 \cdot \mathbf{x}^0)$, WARP implies that

$$\mathbf{p}^0 \cdot \mathbf{x}^0 \leq \mathbf{p}^0 \cdot \mathbf{x}^1. \tag{2.5}$$

Indeed, if $\mathbf{x}^1 = \mathbf{x}^0$, then (2.5) holds with equality. And if $\mathbf{x}^1 \neq \mathbf{x}^0$, then because $\mathbf{x}^1$ was chosen when $\mathbf{x}^0$ was affordable (i.e., at prices $\mathbf{p}^1$ and income $\mathbf{p}^1 \cdot \mathbf{x}^0$), WARP implies that $\mathbf{x}^1$ is not affordable whenever $\mathbf{x}^0$ is chosen. Consequently, the inequality in (2.5) would be strict.

Now, note that by budget balancedness:

$$\mathbf{p}^1 \cdot \mathbf{x}^0 = \mathbf{p}^1 \cdot \mathbf{x}(\mathbf{p}^1, \mathbf{p}^1 \cdot \mathbf{x}^0). \tag{2.6}$$

Subtracting (2.5) from (2.6) then implies that for all prices $\mathbf{p}^1$,

$$(\mathbf{p}^1 - \mathbf{p}^0) \cdot \mathbf{x}^0 \geq (\mathbf{p}^1 - \mathbf{p}^0) \cdot \mathbf{x}(\mathbf{p}^1, \mathbf{p}^1 \cdot \mathbf{x}^0). \tag{2.7}$$

Because (2.7) holds for all prices $\mathbf{p}^1$, let $\mathbf{p}^1 = \mathbf{p}^0 + t\mathbf{z}$, where $t > 0$, and $\mathbf{z} \in \mathbb{R}^n$ is arbitrary. Then (2.7) becomes

$$t[\mathbf{z} \cdot \mathbf{x}^0] \geq t[\mathbf{z} \cdot \mathbf{x}(\mathbf{p}^1, \mathbf{p}^1 \cdot \mathbf{x}^0)]. \tag{2.8}$$

Dividing by $t > 0$ gives

$$\mathbf{z} \cdot \mathbf{x}^0 \geq \mathbf{z} \cdot \mathbf{x}(\mathbf{p}^0 + t\mathbf{z}, (\mathbf{p}^0 + t\mathbf{z}) \cdot \mathbf{x}^0), \tag{2.9}$$

where we have used the fact that $\mathbf{p}^1 = \mathbf{p}^0 + t\mathbf{z}$.

Now for $\mathbf{z}$ fixed, we may choose $\bar{t} > 0$ small enough so that $\mathbf{p}^0 + t\mathbf{z} \gg \mathbf{0}$ for all $t \in [0, \bar{t}]$, because $\mathbf{p}^0 \gg \mathbf{0}$. Noting that (2.9) holds with equality when $t = 0$, (2.9) says that the function $f\colon [0, \bar{t}) \to \mathbb{R}$ defined by the right-hand side of (2.9), i.e.,

$$f(t) \equiv \mathbf{z} \cdot \mathbf{x}(\mathbf{p}^0 + t\mathbf{z}, (\mathbf{p}^0 + t\mathbf{z}) \cdot \mathbf{x}^0),$$

is maximised on $[0, \bar{t})$ at $t = 0$. Thus, we must have $f'(0) \leq 0$. But taking the derivative of $f(t)$ and evaluating at $t = 0$ gives (assuming that $\mathbf{x}(\cdot)$ is differentiable):

$$f'(0) = \sum_i \sum_j z_i \left[\frac{\partial x_i(\mathbf{p}^0, y^0)}{\partial p_j} + x_j(\mathbf{p}^0, y^0) \frac{\partial x_i(\mathbf{p}^0, y^0)}{\partial y} \right] z_j \leq 0. \tag{2.10}$$

Now, because $\mathbf{z} \in \mathbb{R}^n$ was arbitrary, (2.10) says that the matrix whose ijth entry is

$$\frac{\partial x_i(\mathbf{p}^0, y^0)}{\partial p_j} + x_j(\mathbf{p}^0, y^0) \frac{\partial x_i(\mathbf{p}^0, y^0)}{\partial y} \tag{2.11}$$

must be negative semidefinite. But this matrix is precisely the Slutsky matrix associated with the choice function $\mathbf{x}(\mathbf{p}, y)$!

Thus, we have demonstrated that if a choice function satisfies WARP and budget balancedness, then it must satisfy two other properties implied by utility maximisation, namely, homogeneity of degree zero and negative semidefiniteness of the Slutsky matrix.

If we could show, in addition, that the choice function's Slutsky matrix was symmetric, then by our integrability result, that choice function would actually be a demand function because we would then be able to construct a utility function generating it.

Before pursuing this last point further, it is worthwhile to point out that if $\mathbf{x}(\mathbf{p}, y)$ happens to be a utility-generated demand function then $\mathbf{x}(\mathbf{p}, y)$ must satisfy WARP. To see this, suppose a utility-maximising consumer has strictly monotonic and strictly convex preferences. Then we know there will be a unique bundle demanded at every set of prices, and that bundle will always exhaust the consumer's income. (See Exercise 1.16.) So let $\mathbf{x}^0$ maximise utility facing prices $\mathbf{p}^0$, let $\mathbf{x}^1$ maximise utility facing $\mathbf{p}^1$, and suppose $\mathbf{p}^0 \cdot \mathbf{x}^1 \leq \mathbf{p}^0 \cdot \mathbf{x}^0$. Because $\mathbf{x}^1$, though affordable, is not chosen, it must be because $u(\mathbf{x}^0) > u(x^1)$. Therefore, when $\mathbf{x}^1$ is chosen facing prices $\mathbf{p}^1$, it must be that $\mathbf{x}^0$ is not available or that $\mathbf{p}^1 \cdot \mathbf{x}^0 > \mathbf{p}^1 \cdot \mathbf{x}^1$. Thus, $\mathbf{p}^0 \cdot \mathbf{x}^1 \leq \mathbf{p}^0 \cdot \mathbf{x}^0$ implies $\mathbf{p}^1 \cdot \mathbf{x}^0 > \mathbf{p}^1 \cdot \mathbf{x}^1$, so WARP is satisfied.

But again what about the other way around? What if a consumer's choice function always satisfies WARP? Must that behaviour have been generated by utility maximisation? Put another way, must there exist a utility function that would yield the observed choices as the outcome of the utility-maximising process? If the answer is yes, we say the utility function **rationalises** the observed behaviour.

As it turns out, the answer is yes – and no. If there are only two goods, then WARP implies that there *will* exist some utility function that rationalises the choices; if, however, there are more than two goods, then even if WARP holds there need *not* be such a function.

The reason for the two-good exception is related to the symmetry of the Slutsky matrix and to transitivity.

It turns out that in the two-good case, budget balancedness together with homogeneity imply that the Slutsky matrix must be symmetric. (See Exercise 2.9.) Consequently, because WARP and budget balancedness imply homogeneity as well as negative semidefiniteness, then in the case of two goods, they also imply symmetry of the Slutsky matrix. Therefore, for two goods, our integrability theorem tells us that the choice function must be utility-generated.

An apparently distinct, yet ultimately equivalent, explanation for the two-good exception is that with two goods, the pairwise ranking of bundles implied through revealed preference turns out to have no intransitive cycles. (You are, in fact, asked to show this in Exercise 2.9.) And when this is so, there will be a utility representation generating the choice function. Thus, as we mentioned earlier in the text, there is a deep connection between the symmetry of the Slutsky matrix and the transitivity of consumer preferences.

For more than two goods, WARP and budget balancedness imply neither symmetry of the Slutsky matrix nor the absence of intransitive cycles in the revealed preferred to relation. Consequently, for more than two goods, WARP and budget balancedness are not equivalent to the utility-maximisation hypothesis.

This leads naturally to the question: how must we strengthen WARP to obtain a theory of revealed preference that *is* equivalent to the theory of utility maximisation? The answer lies in the 'Strong Axiom of Revealed Preference'.

The **Strong Axiom of Revealed Preference (SARP)** is satisfied if, for every sequence of distinct bundles $\mathbf{x}^0, \mathbf{x}^1, \ldots, \mathbf{x}^k$, where $\mathbf{x}^0$ is revealed preferred to $\mathbf{x}^1$, and $\mathbf{x}^1$ is revealed preferred to $\mathbf{x}^2, \ldots,$ and $\mathbf{x}^{k-1}$ is revealed preferred to $\mathbf{x}^k$, it is not the case that $\mathbf{x}^k$ is revealed preferred to $\mathbf{x}^0$. SARP rules out intransitive *revealed* preferences and therefore can be used to induce a complete and transitive preference relation, $\succsim$, for which there will then exist a utility function that rationalises the observed behaviour. We omit the proof of this and instead refer the reader to Houthakker (1950) for the original argument, and to Richter (1966) for an elegant proof.

It is not difficult to show that if a consumer chooses bundles to maximise a strictly quasiconcave and strictly increasing utility function, his demand behaviour must satisfy SARP (see Exercise 2.11). Thus, a theory of demand built only on SARP, a restriction on observable choice, is essentially *equivalent* to the theory of demand built on utility maximisation. Under both SARP and the utility-maximisation hypothesis, consumer demand will be homogeneous and the Slutsky matrix will be negative semidefinite *and* symmetric.

In our analysis so far, we have focused on revealed preference axioms and consumer choice *functions*. In effect, we have been acting as though we had an infinitely large collection of price and quantity data with which to work. To many, the original allure of revealed preference theory was the promise it held of being able to begin with actual data and work from the implied utility functions to predict consumer behaviour. Because real-world data sets will never contain more than a finite number of sample points, more recent work on revealed preference has attempted to grapple directly with some of the problems that arise when the number of observations is finite.

To that end, Afriat (1967) introduced the **Generalised Axiom of Revealed Preference (GARP)**, a slightly weaker requirement than SARP, and proved an analogue of the integrability theorem (Theorem 2.6). According to **Afriat's theorem**, a *finite* set of observed price and quantity data satisfy GARP if and only if there exists a continuous, increasing, and concave utility function that rationalises the data. (Exercise 2.12 explores a weaker version of Afriat's theorem.) However, with only a finite amount of data, the consumer's preferences are not completely pinned down at bundles 'out-of-sample'. Thus, there can be many different utility functions that rationalise the (finite) data.

But, in some cases, revealed preference does allow us to make certain 'out-of-sample' comparisons. For instance, consider Fig. 2.5. There we suppose we have observed the consumer to choose $\mathbf{x}^0$ at prices $\mathbf{p}^0$ and $\mathbf{x}^1$ at prices $\mathbf{p}^1$. It is easy to see that $\mathbf{x}^0$ is revealed preferred to $\mathbf{x}^1$. Thus, for any utility function that rationalises these data, we must have $u(\mathbf{x}^0) > u(\mathbf{x}^1)$, by definition. Now suppose we want to compare two bundles such as $\mathbf{x}$ and $\mathbf{y}$, which do not appear in our sample. Because $\mathbf{y}$ costs less than $\mathbf{x}^1$ when $\mathbf{x}^1$ was chosen, we may deduce that $u(\mathbf{x}^0) > u(\mathbf{x}^1) > u(\mathbf{y})$. Also, if more is preferred to less, the utility function must be increasing, so we have $u(\mathbf{x}) \geq u(\mathbf{x}^0)$. Thus, we have $u(\mathbf{x}) \geq u(\mathbf{x}^0) > u(\mathbf{x}^1) > u(\mathbf{y})$ for any increasing utility function that rationalises the observed data, and so we can compare our two out-of-sample bundles directly and

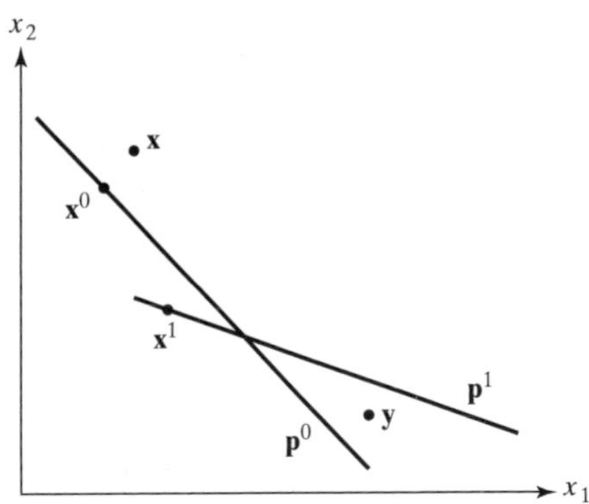

Figure 2.5. Recovering preferences that satisfy GARP.

conclude $u(\mathbf{x}) > u(\mathbf{y})$ for any increasing utility function that could possibly have generated the data we have observed.

But things do not always work out so nicely. To illustrate, say we observe the consumer to buy the single bundle $\mathbf{x}^1 = (1, 1)$ at prices $\mathbf{p}^1 = (2, 1)$. The utility function $u(\mathbf{x}) = x_1^2 x_2$ rationalises the choice we observe because the indifference curve through $\mathbf{x}^1$ is tangent there to the budget constraint $2x_1 + x_2 = 3$, as you can easily verify. At the same time, the utility function $v(\mathbf{x}) = x_1(x_2 + 1)$ will *also* rationalise the choice of $\mathbf{x}^1$ at $\mathbf{p}^1$ as this utility function's indifference curve through $\mathbf{x}^1$ will also be tangent at $\mathbf{x}^1$ to the same budget constraint. This would not be a problem if $u(\mathbf{x})$ and $v(\mathbf{x})$ were merely monotonic transforms of one another – but they are not. For when we compare the out-of-sample bundles $\mathbf{x} = (3, 1)$ and $y = (1, 7)$, in the one case, we get $u(3, 1) > u(1, 7)$, telling us the consumer prefers $\mathbf{x}$ to $\mathbf{y}$, and in the other, we get $v(3, 1) < v(1, 7)$, telling us he prefers $\mathbf{y}$ to $\mathbf{x}$.

So for a given bundle $\mathbf{y}$, can we find all bundles $\mathbf{x}$ such that $u(\mathbf{x}) > u(\mathbf{y})$ for every utility function rationalises the data set? A partial solution has been provided by Varian (1982). Varian described a set of bundles such that every $\mathbf{x}$ in the set satisfies $u(\mathbf{x}) > u(\mathbf{y})$ for every $u(\cdot)$ that rationalises the data. Knoblauch (1992) then showed that Varian's set is a *complete* solution – that is, it contains *all* such bundles.

Unfortunately, consumption data usually contain violations of GARP. Thus, the search is now on for criteria to help decide when those violations of GARP are unimportant enough to ignore and for practical algorithms that will construct appropriate utility functions on data sets with minor violations of GARP.

2.4 UNCERTAINTY

Until now, we have assumed that decision makers act in a world of absolute certainty. The consumer knows the prices of all commodities and knows that any feasible consumption bundle can be obtained with certainty. Clearly, economic agents in the real world cannot always operate under such pleasant conditions. Many economic decisions contain some element of *un*certainty. When buying a car, for example, the consumer must consider the future price of petrol, expenditure on repairs, and the resale value of the car several years later – none of which is known with certainty at the time of the decision. Decisions like this involve uncertainty about the outcome of the choice that is made. Whereas the decision maker may know the probabilities of different possible outcomes, the final result of the decision cannot be known until it occurs.

At first glance, uncertainty may seem an intractable problem, yet economic theory has much to contribute. The principal analytical approach to uncertainty is based on the pathbreaking work of von Neumann and Morgenstern (1944).

2.4.1 PREFERENCES

Earlier in the text, the consumer was assumed to have a preference relation over all consumption bundles $\mathbf{x}$ in a consumption set X. To allow for uncertainty we need only shift perspective slightly. We will maintain the notion of a preference relation but, instead of consumption bundles, the individual will be assumed to have a preference relation over **gambles**.

To formalise this, let $A = \{a_1, \ldots, a_n\}$ denote a finite set of **outcomes.** The a_i's might well be consumption bundles, amounts of money (positive or negative), or anything at all. The main point is that the a_i's themselves involve no uncertainty. On the other hand, we shall use the set A as the basis for creating gambles.

For example, let $A = \{1, -1\}$, where 1 is the outcome 'win one dollar', and -1 is the outcome 'lose one dollar'. Suppose that you have entered into the following bet with a friend. If the toss of a fair coin comes up heads, she pays you one dollar, and you pay her one dollar if it comes up tails. From your point of view, this gamble will result in one of the two outcomes in A: 1 (win a dollar) or -1 (lose a dollar), and each of these occurs with a probability of one-half because the coin is fair.

More generally, a **simple gamble** assigns a probability, p_i, to each of the outcomes a_i, in A. Of course, because the p_i's are probabilities, they must be non-negative, and because the gamble must result in some outcome in A, the p_i's must sum to one. We denote this simple gamble by $(p_1 \circ a_1, \ldots, p_n \circ a_n)$. We define the *set* of simple gambles $\mathcal{G}_S$ as follows.

DEFINITION 2.2 ***Simple Gambles***

Let $A = \{a_1, \ldots, a_n\}$ be the set of outcomes. Then $\mathcal{G}_S$, the set of simple gambles (on A), is given by

$$\mathcal{G}_S \equiv \left\{ (p_1 \circ a_1, \ldots, p_n \circ a_n) \mid p_i \geq 0, \sum_{i=1}^{n} p_i = 1 \right\}.$$

When one or more of the p_i's is zero, we shall drop those components from the expression when it is convenient to do so. For example, the simple gamble $(\alpha \circ a_1, 0 \circ a_2, \ldots, 0 \circ a_{n-1}, (1-\alpha) \circ a_n)$ would be written as $(\alpha \circ a_1, (1-\alpha) \circ a_n)$. Note that $\mathcal{G}_S$ contains A because for each i, $(1 \circ a_i)$, the gamble yielding a_i with probability one, is in $\mathcal{G}_S$. To simplify the notation further, we shall write a_i instead of $(1 \circ a_i)$ to denote this gamble yielding outcome a_i with certainty.

Returning to our coin-tossing example where $A = \{1, -1\}$, each individual, then, was faced with the simple gamble $(\frac{1}{2} \circ 1, \frac{1}{2} \circ -1)$. Of course, not all gambles are simple. For example, it is quite common for state lotteries to give as prizes tickets for the next lottery! Gambles whose prizes are themselves gambles are called **compound gambles**.

Note that there is no limit to the level of compounding that a compound gamble might involve. Indeed, the example of the state lottery is a particularly extreme case in point. Because each state lottery ticket might result in another lottery ticket as a prize, each ticket involves infinitely many levels of compounding. That is, by continuing to win lottery tickets as prizes, it can take any number of plays of the state lottery before the outcome of your original ticket is realised.

For simplicity only, we shall rule out infinitely layered compound gambles like the state lottery. The compound gambles we shall consider must result in an outcome in A after finitely many randomisations.

Let $\mathcal{G}$ then, denote the set of all gambles, both simple and compound. Although it is possible to give a more formal description of the set of compound gambles, and therefore of $\mathcal{G}$, for our purposes this is not necessary. Quite simply, a gamble can be viewed as a lottery ticket, which itself might result in one of a number of other (perhaps quite distinct) lottery tickets, and so on. But ultimately, after finitely many lotteries have been played, some outcome in A must result. So, if g is any gamble in $\mathcal{G}$, then $g = (p_1 \circ g^1, \ldots, p_k \circ g^k)$, for some $k \geq 1$ and some gambles $g^i \in \mathcal{G}$, where the g^i's might be compound gambles, simple gambles, or outcomes. Of course, the p_i's must be non-negative and they must sum to one.[2]

The objects of choice in decision making under uncertainty are gambles. Analogous to the case of consumer theory, we shall suppose that the decision maker has preferences, $\succsim$, over the set of gambles, $\mathcal{G}$. We shall proceed by positing a number of axioms, called **axioms of choice under uncertainty**, for the decision maker's preference relation, $\succsim$. As before, $\sim$ and $\succ$ denote the indifference and strict preference relations induced by $\succsim$. The first few axioms will look very familiar and so require no discussion.

AXIOM 1: Completeness. *For any two gambles, g and g' in $\mathcal{G}$, either $g \succsim g'$,* or *$g' \succsim g$.*

AXIOM 2: Transitivity. *For any three gambles g, g', g'' in $\mathcal{G}$, if $g \succsim g'$ and $g' \succsim g''$, then $g \succsim g''$.*

Because each a_i in A is represented in $\mathcal{G}$ as a degenerate gamble, Axioms G1 and G2 imply in particular that the finitely many elements of A are ordered by $\succsim$. (See

[2]For a formal definition of $\mathcal{G}$, proceed as follows. Let $\mathcal{G}_0 = A$, and for each $j = 1, 2, \ldots$, let $\mathcal{G}_j = \{(p_1 \circ g^1, \ldots, p_k \circ g^k) \mid k \geq 1; p_i \geq 0$ and $g^i \in \mathcal{G}_{j-1}\ \forall\, i = 1, \ldots, k$; and $\sum_{i=1}^{k} p_i = 1\}$. Then $\mathcal{G} = \cup_{j=0}^{\infty} \mathcal{G}_j$.

Exercise 2.16.) So let us assume without loss of generality that the elements of A have been indexed so that $a_1 \succsim a_2 \succsim \cdots \succsim a_n$.

It seems plausible then that no gamble is better than that giving a_1 with certainty, and no gamble is worse than that giving a_n with certainty (although we are not directly assuming this). That is, for any gamble g, it seems plausible that $(\alpha \circ a_1, (1-\alpha) \circ a_n) \succsim g$, when $\alpha = 1$, and $g \succsim (\alpha \circ a_1, (1-\alpha) \circ a_n)$ when $\alpha = 0$. The next axiom says that if indifference does not hold at either extreme, then it must hold for some intermediate value of α.

AXIOM 3: Continuity. *For any gamble g in $\mathcal{G}$, there is some probability, $\alpha \in [0, 1]$, such that $g \sim (\alpha \circ a_1, (1-\alpha) \circ a_n)$.*

Axiom G3 has implications that at first glance might appear unreasonable. For example, suppose that $A = \{\$1000, \$10, \text{'death'}\}$. For most of us, these outcomes are strictly ordered as follows: $1000 ≻ $10 ≻ 'death'. Now consider the simple gamble giving $10 with certainty. According to G3, there must be some probability α rendering the gamble ($\alpha \circ$ $1000, $(1-\alpha) \circ$ 'death') equally attractive as $10. Thus, if there is *no* probability α at which you would find $10 with certainty and the gamble ($\alpha \circ$ $1000, $(1-\alpha) \circ$ 'death') equally attractive, then your preferences over gambles do not satisfy G3.

Is, then, Axiom G3 an unduly strong restriction to impose on preferences? Do not be too hasty in reaching a conclusion. If you would drive across town to collect $1000 – an action involving *some* positive, if tiny, probability of death – rather than accept a $10 payment to stay at home, you would be declaring your preference for the gamble over the small sum with certainty. Presumably, we could increase the probability of a fatal traffic accident until you were just indifferent between the two choices. When that is the case, we will have found the indifference probability whose existence G3 assumes.

The next axiom expresses the idea that if two simple gambles each potentially yield only the best and worst outcomes, then that which yields the best outcome with the higher probability is preferred.

AXIOM 4: Monotonicity. *For all probabilities $\alpha, \beta \in [0, 1]$,*

$$(\alpha \circ a_1, (1-\alpha) \circ a_n) \succsim (\beta \circ a_1, (1-\beta) \circ a_n)$$

if and only if $\alpha \geq \beta$.

Note that monotonicity implies $a_1 \succ a_n$, and so the case in which the decision maker is indifferent among all the outcomes in A is ruled out.

Although most people will usually prefer gambles that give better outcomes higher probability, as monotonicity requires, it need not always be so. For example, to a safari hunter, death may be the worst outcome of an outing, yet the *possibility* of death adds to the excitement of the venture. An outing with a small probability of death would then be preferred to one with zero probability, a clear violation of monotonicity.

The next axiom states that the decision maker is indifferent between one gamble and another if he is indifferent between their realisations, and their realisations occur with the same probabilities.

AXIOM 5: Substitution. *If* $g = (p_1 \circ g^1, \ldots, p_k \circ g^k)$, *and* $h = (p_1 \circ h^1, \ldots, p_k \circ h^k)$ *are in* $\mathcal{G}$, *and if* $h^i \sim g^i$ *for every i, then* $h \sim g$.

Together with G1, Axiom G5 implies that when the agent is indifferent between two gambles he must be indifferent between all convex combinations of them. That is, if $g \sim h$, then because by G1 $g \sim g$, Axiom G5 implies $(\alpha \circ g, (1-\alpha) \circ h) \sim (\alpha \circ g, (1-\alpha) \circ g) = g$.

Our next, and final, axiom states that when considering a particular gamble, the decision maker cares only about the effective probabilities that gamble assigns to each outcome in A. This warrants a bit of discussion.

For example, suppose that $A = \{a_1, a_2\}$. Consider the compound gamble yielding outcome a_1 with probability α, and yielding a lottery ticket with probability $1 - \alpha$, where the lottery ticket itself is a simple gamble. It yields the outcome a_1 with probability β and the outcome a_2 with probability $1 - \beta$.

Now, taken all together, what is the effective probability that the outcome in fact will be a_1? Well, a_1 can result in two mutually exclusive ways, namely, as an immediate result of the compound gamble, or as a result of the lottery ticket. The probability of the first is clearly α. The probability of the second is $(1-\alpha)\beta$, because to obtain a_1 via the lottery ticket, a_1 must not have been the immediate result of the compound gamble *and* it must have been the result of the lottery ticket. So, all together, the probability that the outcome is a_1 is the sum, namely, $\alpha + (1-\alpha)\beta$, because the two different ways that a_1 can arise are mutually exclusive. Similarly, the effective probability that the outcome is a_2, is $(1-\alpha)(1-\beta)$.

To say that the decision maker cares only about the effective probabilities on the a_i's when considering the preceding compound gamble is to say that the decision maker is indifferent between the compound gamble and the simple gamble $(\alpha + (1-\alpha)\beta \circ a_1, (1-\alpha)(1-\beta) \circ a_2)$ that it induces.

Clearly, one can derive the (unique) effective probabilities on the a_i's induced by any compound gamble in a similar way. We shall not spell out the procedure explicitly here, as it is, at least conceptually, straightforward.

For any gamble $g \in \mathcal{G}$, if p_i denotes the effective probability assigned to a_i by g, then we say that g **induces the simple gamble** $(p_1 \circ a_1, \ldots, p_n \circ a_n) \in \mathcal{G}_S$. We emphasise that every $g \in \mathcal{G}$ induces a *unique* simple gamble. Our final axiom is then as follows.[3]

AXIOM 6: Reduction to Simple Gambles. *For any gamble* $g \in \mathcal{G}$, if $(p_1 \circ a_1, \ldots, p_n \circ a_n)$ *is the simple gamble induced by g, then* $(p_1 \circ a_1, \ldots, p_n \circ a_n) \sim g$.

Note that by G6 (and transitivity G2), an individual's preferences over all gambles – compound or otherwise – are completely determined by his preferences over simple gambles.

As plausible as G6 may seem, it does restrict the domain of our analysis. In particular, this would not be an appropriate assumption to maintain if one wished to model the behaviour of vacationers in Las Vegas. They would probably not be indifferent between

[3]In some treatments, Axioms G5 and G6 are combined into a single 'independence' axiom. (See Exercise 2.20.)

playing the slot machines many times during their stay and taking the single once and for all gamble defined by the effective probabilities over winnings and losses. On the other hand, many decisions under uncertainty are undertaken outside of Las Vegas, and for many of these, Axiom G6 is reasonable.

2.4.2 VON NEUMANN-MORGENSTERN UTILITY

Now that we have characterised the axioms preferences over gambles must obey, we once again ask whether we can represent such preferences with a continuous, real-valued function. The answer to that question is yes, which should come as no surprise. We know from our study of preferences under certainty that, here, Axioms G1, G2, and *some* kind of continuity assumption should be sufficient to ensure the existence of a continuous function representing $\succsim$. On the other hand, we have made assumptions in addition to G1, G2, and continuity. One might then expect to derive a utility representation that is more than just continuous. Indeed, we shall show that not only can we obtain a continuous utility function representing $\succsim$ on $\mathcal{G}$, we can obtain one that is linear in the effective probabilities on the outcomes.

To be more precise, suppose that $u\colon \mathcal{G} \to \mathbb{R}$ is a utility function representing $\succsim$ on $\mathcal{G}$.[4] So, for every $g \in \mathcal{G}$, $u(g)$ denotes the utility number assigned to the gamble g. In particular, for every i, u assigns the number $u(a_i)$ to the degenerate gamble $(1 \circ a_i)$, in which the outcome a_i occurs with certainty. We will often refer to $u(a_i)$ as simply the utility of the outcome a_i. We are now prepared to describe the linearity property mentioned above.

DEFINITION 2.3 ***Expected Utility Property***

The utility function $u\colon \mathcal{G} \to \mathbb{R}$ has the expected utility property if, for every $g \in \mathcal{G}$,

$$u(g) = \sum_{i=1}^{n} p_i u(a_i),$$

where $(p_1 \circ a_1, \ldots, p_n \circ a_n)$ is the simple gamble induced by g.

Thus, to say that u has the expected utility property is to say that it assigns to each gamble the expected value of the utilities that might result, where each utility that might result is assigned its effective probability.[5] Of course, the effective probability that g yields utility $u(a_i)$ is simply the effective probability that it yields outcome a_i, namely, p_i.

---

[4]The function $u(\cdot)$ represents $\succsim$ whenever $g \succsim g'$ if and only if $u(g) \ge u(g')$. See Definition 1.5.

[5]The expected value of a function x taking on the values $x_1, \ldots, x_n$ with probabilities $p_1, \ldots, p_n$, respectively, is defined to be equal to $\sum_{i=1}^{n} p_i x_i$. Here, the $u(a_i)$'s play the role of the x_i's, so that we are considering the expected value of utility.

Note that if u has the expected utility property, and if $g_s = (p_1 \circ a_1, \ldots, p_n \circ a_n)$ is a simple gamble, then because the simple gamble induced by g_s is g_s itself, we must have

$$u(p_1 \circ a_1, \ldots, p_n \circ a_n) = \sum_{i=1}^{n} p_i u(a_i), \qquad \forall \text{ probability vectors } (p_1, \ldots, p_n).$$

Consequently, the function u is completely determined on all of $\mathcal{G}$ by the values it assumes on the finite set of outcomes, A.

If an individual's preferences are represented by a utility function with the expected utility property, and if that person always chooses his most preferred alternative available, then that individual will choose one gamble over another if and only if the expected utility of the one exceeds that of the other. Consequently, such an individual is an **expected utility maximiser**.

Any such function as this will have some obvious analytical advantages because the utility of any gamble will be expressible as a linear sum involving only the utility of outcomes and their associated probabilities. Yet this is clearly a great deal to require of the function representing $\succsim$, and it is unlike anything we required of ordinary utility functions under certainty before. To help keep in mind the important distinctions between the two, we refer to utility functions possessing the expected utility property as **von Neumann-Morgenstern (VNM) utility functions**.

We now present a fundamental theorem in the theory of choice under uncertainty.

THEOREM 2.7 ***Existence of a VNM Utility Function on $\mathcal{G}$***

Let preferences $\succsim$ over gambles in $\mathcal{G}$ satisfy axioms G1 to G6. Then there exists a utility function $u\colon \mathcal{G} \to \mathbb{R}$ representing $\succsim$ on $\mathcal{G}$, such that u has the expected utility property.

Proof: As in our proof of the existence of a utility function representing the consumer's preferences in Chapter 1, the proof here will be constructive.

So, consider an arbitrary gamble, g, from $\mathcal{G}$. Define $u(g)$ to be the number satisfying

$$g \sim (u(g) \circ a_1, (1 - u(g)) \circ a_n).$$

By G3, such a number must exist, and you are asked to show in Exercise 2.19 that by G4 this number is unique. This then defines a real-valued function, u, on $\mathcal{G}$. (Incidentally, by definition, $u(g) \in [0, 1]$ for all g.)

It remains to show that u represents $\succsim$, and that it has the expected utility property. We shall begin with the first of these.

So let $g, g' \in \mathcal{G}$ be arbitrary gambles. We claim that the following equivalences hold

$$g \succsim g' \tag{P.1}$$

if and only if

$$(u(g) \circ a_1, (1 - u(g)) \circ a_n) \succsim (u(g') \circ a_1, (1 - u(g')) \circ a_n) \tag{P.2}$$

if and only if

$$u(g) \geq u(g'). \tag{P.3}$$

To see this, note that (P.1) iff (P.2) because $\succsim$ is transitive, and $g \sim (u(g) \circ a_1, (1 - u(g)) \circ a_n)$, and $g' \sim (u(g') \circ a_1, (1 - u(g')) \circ a_n)$, both by the definition of u. Also, (P.2) iff (P.3) follows directly from monotonicity (Axiom G4).

Consequently, $g \succsim g'$ if and only if $u(g) \geq u(g')$, so that u represents $\succsim$ on $\mathcal{G}$.

To complete the proof, we must show that u has the expected utility property. So let $g \in \mathcal{G}$ be an arbitrary gamble, and let $g_s \equiv (p_1 \circ a_1, \ldots, p_n \circ a_n) \in \mathcal{G}_S$ be the simple gamble it induces. We must show that

$$u(g) = \sum_{i=1}^{n} p_i u(a_i).$$

Because by G6 $g \sim g_s$, and because u represents $\succsim$, we must have $u(g) = u(g_s)$. It therefore suffices to show that

$$u(g_s) = \sum_{i=1}^{n} p_i u(a_i). \tag{P.4}$$

Now, for each $i = 1, \ldots, n$, by definition, $u(a_i)$ satisfies

$$a_i \sim (u(a_i) \circ a_1, (1 - u(a_i)) \circ a_n). \tag{P.5}$$

Let q^i denote the simple gamble on the right in (P.5). That is, $q^i \equiv (u(a_i) \circ a_1, (1 - u(a_i)) \circ a_n)$ for every $i = 1, \ldots, n$. Consequently, $q^i \sim a_i$ for every i, so that by the substitution axiom, G5,

$$g' \equiv (p_1 \circ q^1, \ldots, p_n \circ q^n) \sim (p_1 \circ a_1, \ldots, p_n \circ a_n) = g_s. \tag{P.6}$$

We now wish to derive the simple gamble induced by the compound gamble g'. Note that because each q^i can result only in one of the two outcomes a_1 or a_n, g' must result only in one of those two outcomes as well. What is the effective probability that g' assigns to a_1? Well, a_1 results if for any i, q^i occurs (probability p_i) and a_1 is the result of gamble q^i (probability $u(a_i)$). Thus, for each i, there is a probability of $p_i u(a_i)$ that a_1 will result. Because the occurrences of the q^i's are mutually exclusive, the effective probability that a_1 results is the sum $\sum_{i=1}^{n} p_i u(a_i)$. Similarly, the effective probability of

a_n is $\sum_{i=1}^n p_i(1 - u(a_i))$, which is equal to $1 - \sum_{i=1}^n p_i u(a_i)$, because the p_i's sum to one. Therefore, the simple gamble induced by g' is

$$g'_s \equiv \left(\left(\sum_{i=1}^n p_i u(a_i)\right) \circ a_1, \left(1 - \sum_{i=1}^n p_i u(a_i)\right) \circ a_n\right).$$

By the reduction axiom, G6, it must be the case that $g' \sim g'_s$. But the transitivity of $\sim$ together with (P.6) then imply that

$$g_s \sim \left(\left(\sum_{i=1}^n p_i u(a_i)\right) \circ a_1, \left(1 - \sum_{i=1}^n p_i u(a_i)\right) \circ a_n\right). \tag{P.7}$$

However, by definition (and Exercise 2.19), $u(g_s)$ is the unique number satisfying

$$g_s \sim (u(g_s) \circ a_1, (1 - u(g_s)) \circ a_n). \tag{P.8}$$

Therefore, comparing (P.7) with (P.8) we conclude that

$$u(g_s) = \sum_{i=1}^n p_i u(a_i),$$

as desired. ∎

The careful reader might have noticed that Axiom G1 was not invoked in the process of proving Theorem 2.7. Indeed, it is redundant given the other axioms. In Exercise 2.22, you are asked to show that G2, G3, and G4 together imply G1. Consequently, we could have proceeded without explicitly mentioning completeness at all. On the other hand, assuming transitivity and not completeness would surely have raised unnecessary questions in the reader's mind. To spare you that kind of stress, we opted for the approach presented here.

The upshot of Theorem 2.7 is this: if an individual's preferences over gambles satisfy Axioms G1 through G6, then there are utility numbers that can be assigned to the outcomes in A so that the individual prefers one gamble over another if and only if the one has a higher expected utility than the other.

The proof of Theorem 2.7 not only establishes the existence of a utility function with the expected utility property, but it also shows us the steps we might take in constructing such a function in practice. To determine the utility of any outcome a_i, we need only ask the individual for the probability of the best outcome that would make him indifferent between a best–worst gamble of the form $(\alpha \circ a_1, (1 - \alpha) \circ a_n)$ and the outcome a_i with certainty. By repeating this process for every $a_i \in A$, we then could calculate the utility associated with any gamble $g \in \mathcal{G}$ as simply the expected utility it generates. And if the individual's preferences satisfy G1 through G6, Theorem 2.7 guarantees that the utility function we obtain in this way represents her preferences.

EXAMPLE 2.4 Suppose $A = \{\$10, \$4, -\$2\}$, where each of these represent thousands of dollars. We can reasonably suppose that the best outcome is \$10 and the worst is −\$2.

To construct the VNM utility function used in the proof of Theorem 2.7, we first have to come up with indifference probabilities associated with each of the three outcomes. We accomplish this by composing best–worst gambles that offer \$10 and −\$2 with as yet unknown probabilities summing to 1. Finally, we ask the individual the following question for each of the three outcomes: 'What probability for the best outcome will make you indifferent between the best–worst gamble we have composed and the outcome a_i with certainty?' The answers we get will be the utility numbers we assign to each of the three ultimate outcomes. Suppose we find that

$$\$10 \sim (1 \circ \$10, 0 \circ -\$2), \qquad \text{so} \quad u(\$10) \equiv 1, \tag{E.1}$$

$$\$4 \sim (.6 \circ \$10, .4 \circ -\$2), \qquad \text{so} \quad u(\$4) \equiv .6, \tag{E.2}$$

$$-\$2 \sim (0 \circ \$10, 1 \circ -\$2), \qquad \text{so} \quad u(-\$2) \equiv 0. \tag{E.3}$$

Note carefully that under this mapping, the utility of the best outcome must always be 1 and that of the worst outcome must always be zero. However, the utility assigned to intermediate outcomes, such as \$4 in this example, will depend on the individual's attitude towards taking risks.

Having obtained the utility numbers for each of the three possible outcomes, we now have every bit of information we need to rank *all* gambles involving them. Consider, for instance,

$$g_1 \equiv (.2 \circ \$4, .8 \circ \$10), \tag{E.4}$$

$$g_2 \equiv (.07 \circ -\$2, .03 \circ \$4, .9 \circ \$10). \tag{E.5}$$

Which of these will the individual prefer? Assuming that his preferences over gambles satisfy G1 through G6, we may appeal to Theorem 2.7. It tells us that we need only calculate the expected utility of each gamble, using the utility numbers generated in (E.1) through (E.3), to find out. Doing that, we find

$$u(g_1) = .2u(\$4) + .8u(\$10) = .92,$$
$$u(g_2) = .07u(-\$2) + .03u(\$4) + .9u(\$10) = .918.$$

Because g_1 has the greater *expected utility*, it must be the preferred gamble! In similar fashion, using only the utility numbers generated in (E.1) through (E.3), we can rank *any* of the infinite number of gambles that could be constructed from the three outcomes in A.

Just think some more about the information we have uncovered in this example. Look again at the answer given when asked to compare \$4 with certainty to the best–worst gamble in (E.2). The best–worst gamble g offered there has an *expected value* of $E(g) = (.6)(\$10) + (.4)(-\$2) = \$5.2$. This exceeds the expected value \$4 he obtains under the simple gamble offering \$4 with certainty, yet the individual is indifferent between these two gambles. Because we assume that his preferences are monotonic, we can immediately conclude that he would *strictly* prefer the same \$4 with certainty to *every* best–worst gamble offering the best outcome with probability less than .6. This of course includes the one offering \$10 and −\$2 with equal probabilities of .5, even though that gamble and \$4 with certainty have the same expected value of \$4. Thus, in some sense, this individual prefers to *avoid* risk. This same tendency is reflected in his ranking of g_1 and g_2 in (E.4) and (E.5), as well. There he prefers g_1 to g_2, even though the former's expected value, $E(g_1) = \$8.80$, is *less* than the latter's, $E(g_2) = \$8.98$. Here, g_2 is avoided because, unlike g_1, it includes too much risk of the worst outcome. Later, we will get more precise about risk avoidance and its measurement, but this example should help you see that a VNM utility function summarises important aspects about an individual's willingness to take risks. □

Let us step back a moment to consider what this VNM utility function really does and how it relates to the ordinary utility function under certainty. In the standard case, if the individual is indifferent between two commodity bundles, both receive the same utility number, whereas if one bundle is strictly preferred to another, its utility number must be larger. This is true, too, of the VNM utility function $u(g)$, although we must substitute the word 'gamble' for 'commodity bundle'.

However, in the consumer theory case, the utility numbers themselves have *only* ordinal meaning. Any strictly monotonic transformation of one utility representation yields another one. On the other hand, the utility numbers associated with a VNM utility representation of preferences over gambles have content beyond ordinality.

To see this, suppose that $A = \{a, b, c\}$, where $a \succ b \succ c$, and that $\succsim$ satisfies G1 through G6. By G3 and G4, there is an $\alpha \in (0, 1)$ satisfying

$$b \sim (\alpha \circ a, (1 - \alpha) \circ c).$$

Note well that the probability number α is determined by, and is a reflection of, the decision maker's preferences. It is a meaningful number. One cannot double it, add a constant to it, or transform it in any way without also changing the preferences with which it is associated.

Now, let u be some VNM utility representation of $\succsim$. Then the preceding indifference relation implies that

$$\begin{aligned} u(b) &= u(\alpha \circ a, (1 - \alpha) \circ c) \\ &= \alpha u(a) + (1 - \alpha)u(c), \end{aligned}$$

where the second equality follows from the expected utility property of u. But this equality can be rearranged to yield

$$\frac{u(a) - u(b)}{u(b) - u(c)} = \frac{1 - \alpha}{\alpha}.$$

Consequently, the ratios of the differences between the preceding utility numbers are uniquely determined by α. But because the number α was itself uniquely determined by the decision maker's preferences, so, too, then is the preceding ratio of utility differences.

We conclude that the ratio of utility differences has inherent meaning regarding the individual's preferences and they must take on the same value for every VNM utility representation of $\succsim$. Therefore, VNM utility representations provide distinctly more than ordinal information about the decision maker's preferences, for otherwise, through suitable monotone transformations, such ratios could assume many different values.

Clearly, then, a strictly increasing transformation of a VNM utility representation might not yield another VNM utility representation. (Of course, it still yields a utility representation, but that representation need not have the expected utility property.) This then raises the following question: what is the class of VNM utility representations of a given preference ordering? From the earlier considerations, these must preserve the ratios of utility differences. As the next result shows, this property provides a complete characterisation.

THEOREM 2.8 ***VNM Utility Functions are Unique up to Positive Affine Transformations***

Suppose that the VNM utility function $u(\cdot)$ represents $\succsim$. Then the VNM utility function, $v(\cdot)$, represents those same preferences if and only if for some scalar α and some scalar $\beta > 0$,

$$v(g) = \alpha + \beta u(g),$$

for all gambles g.

Proof: Sufficiency is obvious (but do convince yourself), so we only prove necessity here. Moreover, we shall suppose that g is a simple gamble. You are asked to show that if u and v are linearly related for all simple gambles, then they are linearly related for all gambles. As before, we let

$$A = \{a_1, \ldots, a_n\} \qquad \text{and} \qquad g \equiv (p_1 \circ a_1, p_2 \circ a_2, \ldots, p_n \circ a_n),$$

where $a_1 \succsim \cdots \succsim a_n$, and $a_1 \succ a_n$.

Because $u(\cdot)$ represents $\succsim$, we have $u(a_1) \geq \cdots \geq u(a_i) \geq \cdots \geq u(a_n)$, and $u(a_1) > u(a_n)$. So, for every $i = 1, \ldots, n$, there is a unique $\alpha_i \in [0, 1]$ such that

$$u(a_i) = \alpha_i u(a_1) + (1 - \alpha_i) u(a_n). \tag{P.1}$$

Note that $\alpha_i > 0$ if and only if $a_i \succ a_n$.

Now, because $u(\cdot)$ has the expected utility property, (P.1) implies that

$$u(a_i) = u(\alpha_i \circ a_1, (1 - \alpha_i) \circ a_n),$$

which, because $u(\cdot)$ represents $\succsim$, means that

$$a_i \sim (\alpha_i \circ a_1, (1-\alpha_i) \circ a_n). \tag{P.2}$$

So, because $v(\cdot)$ also represents $\succsim$, we must have

$$v(a_i) = v(\alpha_i \circ a_1, (1-\alpha_i) \circ a_n).$$

And, because $v(\cdot)$ has the expected utility property, this implies that

$$v(a_i) = \alpha_i v(a_1) + (1-\alpha_i)v(a_n). \tag{P.3}$$

Together, (P.1) and (P.3) imply that

$$\frac{u(a_1)-u(a_i)}{u(a_i)-u(a_n)} = \frac{1-\alpha_i}{\alpha_i} = \frac{v(a_1)-v(a_i)}{v(a_i)-v(a_n)} \tag{P.4}$$

for every $i = 1, \ldots, n$ such that $a_i \succ a_n$ (i.e., such that $\alpha_i > 0$).

From (P.4) we may conclude that

$$(u(a_1)-u(a_i))(v(a_i)-v(a_n)) = (v(a_1)-v(a_i))(u(a_i)-u(a_n)) \tag{P.5}$$

whenever $a_i \succ a_n$. However, (P.5) holds even when $a_i \sim a_n$ because in this case $u(a_i) = u(a_n)$ and $v(a_i) = v(a_n)$. Hence, (P.5) holds for all $i = 1, \ldots, n$.

Rearranging, (P.5) can be expressed in the form

$$v(a_i) = \alpha + \beta u(a_i), \qquad \text{for all } i = 1, \ldots, n, \tag{P.6}$$

where

$$\alpha \equiv \frac{u(a_1)v(a_n) - v(a_1)u(a_n)}{u(a_1)-u(a_n)} \qquad \text{and} \qquad \beta \equiv \frac{v(a_1)-v(a_n)}{u(a_1)-u(a_n)}.$$

Notice that both α and β are constants (i.e., independent of i), and that β is strictly positive.

So, for any gamble g, if $(p_1 \circ a_1, \ldots, p_n \circ a_n)$ is the simple gamble induced by g, then

$$\begin{aligned} v(g) &= \sum_{i=1}^{n} p_i v(a_i) \\ &= \sum_{i=1}^{n} p_i(\alpha + \beta u(a_i)) \\ &= \alpha + \beta \sum_{i=1}^{n} p_i u(a_i) \\ &= \alpha + \beta u(g), \end{aligned}$$

where the first and last equalities follow because $v(\cdot)$ and $u(\cdot)$ have the expected utility property and the second equality follows from (P.6). ∎

Just before the statement of Theorem 2.8, we stated that the class of VNM utility representations of a single preference relation is characterised by the constancy of ratios of utility differences. This in fact follows from Theorem 2.8, as you are asked to show in an exercise.

Theorem 2.8 tells us that VNM utility functions are not completely unique, nor are they entirely ordinal. We can still find an infinite number of them that will rank gambles in precisely the same order and also possess the expected utility property. But unlike ordinary utility functions from which we demand only an order-preserving numerical scaling, here we must limit ourselves to transformations that multiply by a positive number and/or add a constant term if we are to preserve the expected utility property as well. Yet the less than complete ordinality of the VNM utility function must not tempt us into attaching undue significance to the absolute level of a gamble's utility, or to the difference in utility between one gamble and another. With what little we have required of the agent's binary comparisons between gambles in the underlying preference relation, we still cannot use VNM utility functions for interpersonal comparisons of well-being, nor can we measure the 'intensity' with which one gamble is preferred to another.

2.4.3 RISK AVERSION

In Example 2.4 we argued that the VNM utility function we created there reflected some desire to avoid risk. Now we are prepared to define and describe risk aversion more formally. For that, we shall confine our attention to gambles whose outcomes consist of different amounts of *wealth*. In addition, it will be helpful to take as the set of outcomes, A, all non-negative wealth levels. Thus, $A = \mathbb{R}_+$. Even though the set of outcomes now contains infinitely many elements, we continue to consider gambles giving only finitely many outcomes a strictly positive effective probability. In particular, a simple gamble takes the form $(p_1 \circ w_1, \ldots, p_n \circ w_n)$, where n is some positive integer, the w_i's are non-negative wealth levels, and the non-negative probabilities, $p_1, \ldots, p_n$, sum to 1.[6] Finally, we shall assume that the individual's VNM utility function, $u(\cdot)$, is differentiable with $u'(w) > 0$ for all wealth levels w.

We now investigate the relationship between a VNM utility function and the agent's attitude towards risk. The expected value of the simple gamble g offering w_i with probability p_i is given by $E(g) = \sum_{i=1}^{n} p_i w_i$. Now suppose the agent is given a choice between accepting the gamble g on the one hand or receiving with *certainty* the expected value of g on the other. If $u(\cdot)$ is the agent's VNM utility function, we can evaluate these two

[6]With this framework, it is possible to prove an expected utility theorem along the lines of Theorem 2.7 by suitably modifying the axioms to take care of the fact that A is no longer a finite set.

alternatives as follows:

$$u(g) = \sum_{i=1}^{n} p_i u(w_i),$$

$$u(E(g)) = u\left(\sum_{i=1}^{n} p_i w_i\right).$$

The first of these is the VNM utility of the gamble, and the second is the VNM utility of the gamble's expected value. If preferences satisfy Axioms G1 to G6, we know the agent prefers the alternative with the higher expected utility. When someone would rather receive the expected value of a gamble with certainty than face the risk inherent in the gamble itself, we say they are *risk averse*. Of course, people may exhibit a complete disregard of risk, or even an attraction to risk, and still be consistent with Axioms G1 through G6. We catalogue these various possibilities, and define terms precisely, in what follows.

As remarked after Definition 2.3, a VNM utility function on $\mathcal{G}$ is completely determined by the values it assumes on the set of outcomes, A. Consequently, the characteristics of an individual's VNM utility function over the set of simple gambles alone provides a complete description of the individual's preferences over all gambles. Because of this, it is enough to focus on the behaviour of u on $\mathcal{G}_S$ to capture an individual's attitudes towards risk. This, and the preceding discussion, motivate the following definition.

DEFINITION 2.4 ***Risk Aversion, Risk Neutrality, and Risk Loving***

Let $u(\cdot)$ be an individual's VNM utility function for gambles over non-negative levels of wealth. Then for the simple gamble $g = (p_1 \circ w_1, \ldots, p_n \circ w_n)$, the individual is said to be

1. *risk averse at g if $u(E(g)) > u(g)$,*
2. *risk neutral at g if $u(E(g)) = u(g)$,*
3. *risk loving at g if $u(E(g)) < u(g)$.*

If for every non-degenerate[7] simple gamble, g, the individual is, for example, risk averse at g, then the individual is said simply to be risk averse (or risk averse on $\mathcal{G}$ for emphasis). Similarly, an individual can be defined to be risk neutral and risk loving (on $\mathcal{G}$).

Each of these attitudes toward risk is *equivalent* to a particular property of the VNM utility function. In the exercises, you are asked to show that the agent is risk averse, risk neutral, or risk loving over some subset of gambles if and only if his VNM utility function is strictly concave, linear, or strictly convex, respectively, over the appropriate domain of wealth.

[7]A simple gamble is non-degenerate if it assigns strictly positive probability to at least two distinct wealth levels.

To help see the first of these claims, let us consider a simple gamble involving two outcomes:

$$g \equiv (p \circ w_1, (1-p) \circ w_2).$$

Now suppose the individual is offered a choice between receiving wealth equal to $E(g) = pw_1 + (1-p)w_2$ with certainty or receiving the gamble g itself. We can assess the alternatives as follows:

$$u(g) = pu(w_1) + (1-p)u(w_2),$$
$$u(E(g)) = u(pw_1 + (1-p)w_2).$$

Now look at Fig. 2.6. There we have drawn a chord between the two points $R = (w_1, u(w_1))$ and $S = (w_2, u(w_2))$, and located their convex combination, $T = pR + (1-p)S$. The abscissa of T must be $E(g)$ and its ordinate must be $u(g)$. (Convince yourself of this.) We can then locate $u(E(g))$ on the vertical axis using the graph of the function $u(w)$ as indicated. The VNM utility function in Fig. 2.6 has been drawn strictly concave in wealth over the relevant region. As you can see, $u(E(g)) > u(g)$, so the individual is *risk averse*.

In Fig. 2.6, the individual prefers $E(g)$ with certainty to the gamble g itself. But there will be *some* amount of wealth we could offer with certainty that would make him indifferent between accepting that wealth with certainty and facing the gamble g. We call this amount of wealth the **certainty equivalent** of the gamble g. When a person is risk averse and strictly prefers more money to less, it is easy to show that the certainty equivalent is *less* than the expected value of the gamble, and you are asked to do this in the exercises. In effect, a risk-averse person will 'pay' some positive amount of wealth to avoid the gamble's inherent risk. This willingness to pay to avoid risk is measured by the *risk premium*.

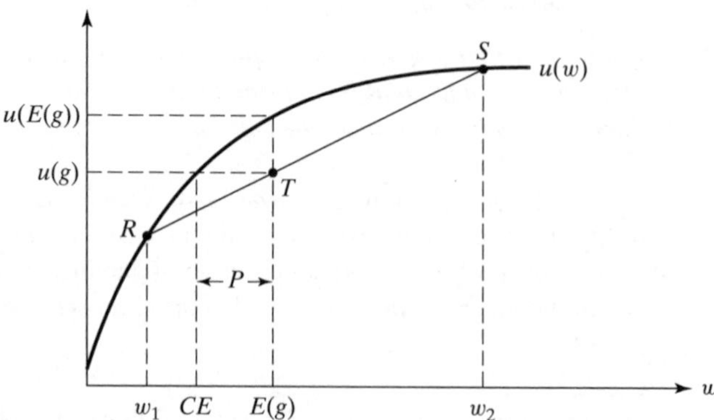

Figure 2.6. Risk aversion and strict concavity of the VNM utility function.

The certainty equivalent and the risk premium, both illustrated in Fig. 2.6, are defined in what follows.

DEFINITION 2.5 ***Certainty Equivalent and Risk Premium***

The certainty equivalent of any simple gamble g over wealth levels is an amount of wealth, CE, offered with certainty, such that $u(g) \equiv u(CE)$. The risk premium *is an amount of wealth, P, such that $u(g) \equiv u(E(g) - P)$. Clearly, $P \equiv E(g) - CE$.*

EXAMPLE 2.5 Suppose $u(w) \equiv \ln(w)$. Because this is strictly concave in wealth, the individual is risk averse. Let g offer 50–50 odds of winning or losing some amount of wealth, h, so that if the individual's initial wealth is w_0,

$$g \equiv ((1/2) \circ (w_0 + h), (1/2) \circ (w_0 - h)),$$

where we note that $E(g) = w_0$. The certainty equivalent for g must satisfy

$$\ln(CE) = (1/2)\ln(w_0 + h) + (1/2)\ln(w_0 - h) = \ln\left(w_0^2 - h^2\right)^{1/2}.$$

Thus, $CE = \left(w_0^2 - h^2\right)^{1/2} < E(g)$ and $P = w_0 - \left(w_0^2 - h^2\right)^{1/2} > 0$. □

Many times, we not only want to know whether someone is risk averse, but also *how* risk averse they are. Ideally, we would like a summary measure that allows us both to compare the degree of risk aversion across individuals and to gauge how the degree of risk aversion for a single individual might vary with the level of their wealth. Because risk aversion and concavity of the VNM utility function in wealth are equivalent, the seemingly most natural candidate for such a measure would be the second derivative, $u''(w)$, a basic measure of a function's 'curvature'. We might think that the greater the absolute value of this derivative, the greater the degree of risk aversion.

But this will not do. Although the *sign* of the second derivative does tell us whether the individual is risk averse, risk loving, or risk neutral, its *size* is entirely arbitrary. Theorem 2.8 showed that VNM utility functions are unique up to affine transformations. This means that for any given preferences, we can obtain virtually any size second derivative we wish through multiplication of $u(\cdot)$ by a properly chosen positive constant. With this and other considerations in mind, Arrow (1970) and Pratt (1964) have proposed the following measure of risk aversion.

DEFINITION 2.6 ***The Arrow-Pratt Measure of Absolute Risk Aversion***

The Arrow-Pratt measure of absolute risk aversion is given by

$$R_a(w) \equiv \frac{-u''(w)}{u'(w)}.$$

Note that the *sign* of this measure immediately tells us the basic attitude towards risk: $R_a(w)$ is positive, negative, or zero as the agent is risk averse, risk loving, or risk neutral, respectively. In addition, any positive affine transformation of utility will leave the measure unchanged: adding a constant affects neither the numerator nor the denominator; multiplication by a positive constant affects both numerator and denominator but leaves their ratio unchanged.

To demonstrate the effectiveness of the Arrow-Pratt measure of risk aversion, we now show that consumers with larger Arrow-Pratt measures are indeed more risk averse in a behaviourally significant respect: they have lower certainty equivalents and are willing to accept fewer gambles.

To see this, suppose there are two consumers, 1 and 2, and that consumer 1 has VNM utility function $u(w)$, and consumer 2's VNM utility function is $v(w)$. Wealth, w, can take on any non-negative number. Let us now suppose that *at every wealth level*, w, consumer 1's Arrow-Pratt measure of risk aversion is larger than consumer 2's. That is,

$$R_a^1(w) = -\frac{u''(w)}{u'(w)} > -\frac{v''(w)}{v'(w)} = R_a^2(w) \qquad \text{for all } w \geq 0, \tag{2.12}$$

where we are assuming that both u' and v' are always strictly positive.

For simplicity, assume that $v(w)$ takes on all values in $[0, \infty)$. Consequently, we may define $h\colon [0, \infty) \longrightarrow \mathbb{R}$ as follows:

$$h(x) = u(v^{-1}(x)) \qquad \text{for all } x \geq 0. \tag{2.13}$$

Therefore, h inherits twice differentiability from u and v with

$$h'(x) = \frac{u'(v^{-1}(x))}{v'(v^{-1}(x))} > 0, \qquad \text{and}$$

$$h''(x) = \frac{u'(v^{-1}(x))[u''(v^{-1}(x))/u'(v^{-1}(x)) - v''(v^{-1}(x))/v'(v^{-1}(x))]}{[v'(v^{-1}(x))]^2} < 0$$

for all $x > 0$, where the first inequality follows because $u', v' > 0$, and the second follows from (2.12). Therefore, h is a strictly increasing, strictly concave function.

Consider now a gamble $(p_1 \circ w_1, \ldots, p_n \circ w_n)$ over wealth levels. We can use (2.13) and the fact that h is strictly concave to show that consumer 1's certainty equivalent for this gamble is lower than consumer 2's.

To see this, let $\hat{w}_i$ denote consumer i's certainty equivalent for the gamble. That is,

$$\sum_{i=1}^{n} p_i u(w_i) = u(\hat{w}_1), \tag{2.14}$$

$$\sum_{i=1}^{n} p_i v(w_i) = v(\hat{w}_2). \tag{2.15}$$

We wish to show that $\hat{w}_1 < \hat{w}_2$.

Putting $x = v(w)$ in (2.13) and using (2.14) gives

$$\begin{aligned} u(\hat{w}_1) &= \sum_{i=1}^{n} p_i h(v(w_i)) \\ &< h\Big(\sum_{i=1}^{n} p_i v(w_i)\Big) \\ &= h(v(\hat{w}_2)) \\ &= u(\hat{w}_2), \end{aligned}$$

where the inequality, called **Jensen's inequality**, follows because h is strictly concave, and the final two equalities follow from (2.15) and (2.13), respectively. Consequently, $u(\hat{w}_1) < u(\hat{w}_2)$, so that because u is strictly increasing, $\hat{w}_1 < \hat{w}_2$ as desired.

We may conclude that consumer 1's certainty equivalent for any given gamble is lower than 2's. And from this it easily follows that if consumers 1 and 2 have the same initial wealth, then consumer 2 (the one with the globally lower Arrow-Pratt measure) will accept any gamble that consumer 1 will accept. (Convince yourself of this.) That is, consumer 1 is willing to accept fewer gambles than consumer 2.

Finally, note that in passing, we have also shown that (2.12) implies that consumer 1's VNM utility function is *more concave* than consumer 2's in the sense that (once again putting $x = v(w)$ in (2.13))

$$u(w) = h(v(w)) \qquad \text{for all } w \geq 0, \tag{2.16}$$

where, as you recall, h is a strictly concave function. Thus, according to (2.16), u is a 'concavification' of v. This is yet another (equivalent) expression of the idea that consumer 1 is more risk averse than consumer 2.

$R_a(w)$ is only a *local* measure of risk aversion, so it need not be the same at every level of wealth. Indeed, one expects that attitudes toward risk, and so the Arrow-Pratt measure, will ordinarily vary with wealth, and vary in 'sensible' ways. Arrow has proposed a simple classification of VNM utility functions (or utility function segments) according to how $R_a(w)$ varies with wealth. Quite straightforwardly, we say that a VNM utility function displays *constant, decreasing*, or *increasing* absolute risk aversion over some domain of wealth if, over that interval, $R_a(w)$ remains constant, decreases, or increases with an increase in wealth, respectively.

Decreasing absolute risk aversion (DARA) is generally a sensible restriction to impose. Under *constant* absolute risk aversion, there would be no greater willingness to accept a small gamble at higher levels of wealth, and under *increasing* absolute risk aversion, we have rather perverse behaviour: the greater the wealth, the more averse one becomes to accepting the same small gamble. DARA imposes the more plausible restriction that the individual be less averse to taking small risks at higher levels of wealth.

EXAMPLE 2.6 Consider an investor who must decide how much of his initial wealth w to put into a risky asset. The risky asset can have any of the positive or negative rates of return r_i with probabilities p_i, $i = 1, \ldots, n$. If β is the amount of wealth to be put into the risky asset, final wealth under outcome i will be $(w - \beta) + (1 + r_i)\beta = w + \beta r_i$. The investor's problem is to choose β to maximise the expected utility of wealth. We can write this formally as the single-variable optimisation problem

$$\max_{\beta} \sum_{i=1}^{n} p_i u(w + \beta r_i) \qquad \text{s. t.} \qquad 0 \le \beta \le w. \tag{E.1}$$

We first determine under what conditions a risk-averse investor will decide to put *no* wealth into the risky asset. In this case, we would have a corner solution where the objective function in (E.1) reaches a maximum at $\beta^* = 0$, so its first derivative must be non-increasing there. Differentiating expected utility in (E.1) with respect to β, then evaluating at $\beta^* = 0$, we therefore must have

$$\sum_{i=1}^{n} p_i u'(w + \beta^* r_i) r_i = u'(w) \sum_{i=1}^{n} p_i r_i \le 0.$$

The sum on the right-hand side is just the expected return on the risky asset. Because $u'(w)$ must be positive, the expected return must be non-positive. Because you can easily verify that the concavity of u in wealth is sufficient to ensure the concavity of (E.1) in β, we conclude that a risk-averse individual will abstain completely from the risky asset if and only if that asset has a *non-positive* expected return. Alternatively, we can say that a risk-averse investor will always prefer to place *some* wealth into a risky asset with a strictly positive expected return.

Now assume that the risky asset has a positive expected return. As we have seen, this means we can rule out $\beta^* = 0$. Let us also suppose that $\beta^* < w$. The first- and second-order conditions for an interior maximum of (E.1) tell us that

$$\sum_{i=1}^{n} p_i u'(w + \beta^* r_i) r_i = 0 \tag{E.2}$$

and

$$\sum_{i=1}^{n} p_i u''(w + \beta^* r_i) r_i^2 < 0, \tag{E.3}$$

respectively, where (E.3) is strict because of risk aversion.

Now we ask what happens to the amount of wealth devoted to the risky asset as wealth increases. Casual empiricism suggests that as wealth increases, a greater absolute amount of wealth is placed into risky assets, i.e., that risky assets are 'normal' rather than 'inferior' goods. We will show that this is so under DARA. Viewing β^* as a function of w, differentiating (E.2) with respect to w, we find that

$$\frac{d\beta^*}{dw} = \frac{-\sum_{i=1}^{n} p_i u''(w + \beta^* r_i) r_i}{\sum_{i=1}^{n} p_i u''(w + \beta^* r_i) r_i^2}. \tag{E.4}$$

Risk aversion ensures that the denominator in (E.4) will be negative, so risky assets will be 'normal' only when the numerator is also negative. DARA is sufficient to ensure this.

To see this, note that the definition of $R_a(w + \beta^* r_i)$ implies

$$-u''(w + \beta^* r_i) r_i \equiv R_a(w + \beta^* r_i) r_i u'(w + \beta^* r_i), \qquad i = 1, \ldots, n. \tag{E.5}$$

Under DARA, $R_a(w) > R_a(w + \beta^* r_i)$ whenever $r_i > 0$, and $R_a(w) < R_a(w + \beta^* r_i)$ whenever $r_i < 0$. Multiplying both sides of these inequalities by r_i, we obtain in both cases,

$$R_a(w) r_i > R_a(w + \beta^* r_i) r_i, \qquad i = 1, \ldots, n. \tag{E.6}$$

Substituting $R_a(w)$ for $R_a(w + \beta^* r_i)$ in (E.5) and using (E.6), we obtain

$$-u''(w + \beta^* r_i) r_i < R_a(w) r_i u'(w + \beta^* r_i), \qquad i = 1, \ldots, n.$$

Finally, taking expectations of both sides gives

$$-\sum_{i=1}^{n} p_i u''(w + \beta^* r_i) r_i < R_a(w) \sum_{i=1}^{n} p_i r_i u'(w + \beta^* r_i) = 0, \tag{E.7}$$

where the last equality follows from (E.2).

Thus, when behaviour displays DARA, (E.4) is positive and more wealth will be put into the risky asset as wealth increases. □

EXAMPLE 2.7 A risk-averse individual with initial wealth w_0 and VNM utility function $u(\cdot)$ must decide whether and for how much to insure his car. The probability that he will have an accident and incur a dollar loss of L in damages is $\alpha \in (0, 1)$. How much insurance, x, should he purchase?

Of course, the answer depends on the price at which insurance is available. Let us suppose that insurance is available at an actuarially fair price, i.e., one that yields insurance companies zero expected profits. Now, if ρ denotes the rate at which each dollar of insurance can be purchased, the insurance company's expected profits per dollar of insurance sold (assuming zero costs) will be $\alpha(\rho - 1) + (1 - \alpha)\rho$. Setting this equal to zero implies that $\rho = \alpha$.

So, with the price per dollar of insurance equal to α, how much insurance should our risk-averse individual purchase? Because he is an expected utility maximiser, he will choose that amount of insurance, x, to maximise his expected utility,

$$\alpha u(w_0 - \alpha x - L + x) + (1 - \alpha)u(w_0 - \alpha x). \tag{E.1}$$

Differentiating (E.1) with respect to x and setting the result to zero yields

$$(1 - \alpha)\alpha u'(w_0 - \alpha x - L + x) - \alpha(1 - \alpha)u'(w_0 - \alpha x) = 0,$$

which, on dividing by $(1 - \alpha)\alpha$, yields

$$u'(w_0 - \alpha x - L + x) = u'(w_0 - \alpha x).$$

But because the individual is risk averse, $u'' < 0$, so that the marginal utility of wealth is strictly decreasing in wealth. Consequently, equality of the preceding marginal utilities of wealth implies equality of the wealth levels themselves, i.e.,

$$w_0 - \alpha x - L + x = w_0 - \alpha x,$$

which implies that

$$x = L.$$

Consequently, with the availability of actuarially fair insurance, a risk-averse individual fully insures against all risk. Note that at the optimum, the individual's wealth is constant and equal to $w_0 - \alpha L$ whether or not he has an accident. □

2.5 EXERCISES

2.1 Show that budget balancedness and homogeneity of $\mathbf{x}(\mathbf{p}, y)$ are unrelated conditions in the sense that neither implies the other.

2.2 Suppose that $\mathbf{x}(\mathbf{p}, y) \in \mathbb{R}^n_+$ satisfies budget balancedness and homogeneity on $\mathbb{R}^{n+1}_{++}$. Show that for all $(\mathbf{p}, y) \in \mathbb{R}^{n+1}_{++}$, $\mathbf{s}(\mathbf{p}, y) \cdot \mathbf{p} = \mathbf{0}$, where $\mathbf{s}(\mathbf{p}, y)$ denotes the Slutsky matrix associated with $\mathbf{x}(\mathbf{p}, y)$.

2.3 Derive the consumer's direct utility function if his indirect utility function has the form $v(\mathbf{p}, y) = yp_1^{\alpha}p_2^{\beta}$ for negative α and β.

2.4 Suppose that the function $e(\mathbf{p}, u) \in \mathbb{R}_+$, not necessarily an expenditure function, and $\mathbf{x}(\mathbf{p}, y) \in \mathbb{R}^n_+$, not necessarily a demand function, satisfy the system of partial differential equations given in Section 2.2. Show the following:

(a) If $\mathbf{x}(\mathbf{p}, y)$ satisfies budget balancedness, then $e(\mathbf{p}, u)$ must be homogeneous of degree one in $\mathbf{p}$.

(b) If $e(\mathbf{p}, u)$ is homogeneous of degree one in $\mathbf{p}$ and for each $\mathbf{p}$, it assumes every non-negative value as u varies, then $\mathbf{x}(\mathbf{p}, y)$ must be homogeneous of degree zero in $(\mathbf{p}, y)$.

2.5 Consider the solution, $e(\mathbf{p}, u) = up_1^{\alpha_1} p_2^{\alpha_2} p_3^{\alpha_3}$ at the end of Example 2.3.

(a) Derive the indirect utility function through the relation $e(\mathbf{p}, v(\mathbf{p}, y)) = y$ and verify Roy's identity.

(b) Use the construction given in the proof of Theorem 2.1 to recover a utility function generating $e(\mathbf{p}, u)$. Show that the utility function you derive generates the demand functions given in Example 2.3.

2.6 A consumer has expenditure function $e(p_1, p_2, u) = up_1p_2/(p_1 + p_2)$. Find a *direct* utility function, $u(x_1, x_2)$, that rationalises this person's demand behaviour.

2.7 Derive the consumer's *inverse demand functions*, $p_1(x_1, x_2)$ and $p_2(x_1, x_2)$, when the utility function is of the Cobb-Douglas form, $u(x_1, x_2) = Ax_1^{\alpha} x_2^{1-\alpha}$ for $0 < \alpha < 1$.

2.8 The consumer buys bundle $\mathbf{x}^i$ at prices $\mathbf{p}^i$, $i = 0, 1$. Separately for parts (a) to (d), state whether these indicated choices satisfy WARP:

(a) $\mathbf{p}^0 = (1, 3)$, $\mathbf{x}^0 = (4, 2)$; $\mathbf{p}^1 = (3, 5)$, $\mathbf{x}^1 = (3, 1)$.

(b) $\mathbf{p}^0 = (1, 6)$, $\mathbf{x}^0 = (10, 5)$; $\mathbf{p}^1 = (3, 5)$, $\mathbf{x}^1 = (8, 4)$.

(c) $\mathbf{p}^0 = (1, 2)$, $\mathbf{x}^0 = (3, 1)$; $\mathbf{p}^1 = (2, 2)$, $\mathbf{x}^1 = (1, 2)$.

(d) $\mathbf{p}^0 = (2, 6)$, $\mathbf{x}^0 = (20, 10)$; $\mathbf{p}^1 = (3, 5)$, $\mathbf{x}^1 = (18, 4)$.

2.9 Suppose there are only two goods and that a consumer's choice function $\mathbf{x}(\mathbf{p}, y)$ satisfies budget balancedness, $\mathbf{p} \cdot \mathbf{x}(\mathbf{p}, y) = y \; \forall \; (\mathbf{p}, y)$. Show the following:

(a) If $\mathbf{x}(\mathbf{p}, y)$ is homogeneous of degree zero in $(\mathbf{p}, y)$, then the Slutsky matrix associated with $\mathbf{x}(\mathbf{p}, y)$ is symmetric.

(b) If $\mathbf{x}(\mathbf{p}, y)$ satisfies WARP, then the 'revealed preferred to' relation, R, has no intransitive cycles. (By definition, $\mathbf{x}^1 R \mathbf{x}^2$ if and only if $\mathbf{x}^1$ is revealed preferred to $\mathbf{x}^2$.)

2.10 Hicks (1956) offered the following example to demonstrate how WARP can fail to result in transitive revealed preferences when there are more than two goods. The consumer chooses bundle $\mathbf{x}^i$ at prices $\mathbf{p}^i$, $i = 0, 1, 2$, where

$$\mathbf{p}^0 = \begin{pmatrix} 1 \\ 1 \\ 2 \end{pmatrix} \quad \mathbf{x}^0 = \begin{pmatrix} 5 \\ 19 \\ 9 \end{pmatrix}$$

$$\mathbf{p}^1 = \begin{pmatrix} 1 \\ 1 \\ 1 \end{pmatrix} \quad \mathbf{x}^1 = \begin{pmatrix} 12 \\ 12 \\ 12 \end{pmatrix}$$

$$\mathbf{p}^2 = \begin{pmatrix} 1 \\ 2 \\ 1 \end{pmatrix} \quad \mathbf{x}^2 = \begin{pmatrix} 27 \\ 11 \\ 1 \end{pmatrix}.$$

(a) Show that these data satisfy WARP. Do it by considering all possible pairwise comparisons of the bundles and showing that in each case, one bundle in the pair is revealed preferred to the other.

(b) Find the intransitivity in the revealed preferences.

2.11 Show that if a consumer chooses bundles to maximise a strictly quasiconcave and strictly increasing utility function, his demand behaviour satisfies SARP.

2.12 This exercise guides you through a proof of a simplified version of Afriat's Theorem. Suppose that a consumer is observed to demand bundle $\mathbf{x}^1$ when the price vector is $\mathbf{p}^1$, and bundle $\mathbf{x}^2$ when the price vector is $\mathbf{p}^2$, ..., and bundle $\mathbf{x}^K$ when the price vector is $\mathbf{p}^K$. This produces the finite data set $D = \{(\mathbf{x}^1, \mathbf{p}^1), (\mathbf{x}^2, \mathbf{p}^2), \ldots, (\mathbf{x}^K, \mathbf{p}^K)\}$. We say that the consumer's choice behaviour satisfies GARP on the finite data set D if for every finite sequence, $(\mathbf{x}^{k_1}, \mathbf{p}^{k_1}), (\mathbf{x}^{k_2}, \mathbf{p}^{k_2}) \ldots, (\mathbf{x}^{k_m}, \mathbf{p}^{k_m})$, of points in D, if $\mathbf{p}^{k_1} \cdot \mathbf{x}^{k_1} \geq \mathbf{p}^{k_1} \cdot \mathbf{x}^{k_2}$, $\mathbf{p}^{k_2} \cdot \mathbf{x}^{k_2} \geq \mathbf{p}^{k_2} \cdot \mathbf{x}^{k_3}, \ldots,$ $\mathbf{p}^{k_{m-1}} \cdot \mathbf{x}^{k_{m-1}} \geq \mathbf{p}^{k_{m-1}} \cdot \mathbf{x}^{k_m}$, then $\mathbf{p}^{k_m} \cdot \mathbf{x}^{k_m} \leq \mathbf{p}^{k_m} \cdot \mathbf{x}^{k_1}$.

In other words, GARP holds if whenever $\mathbf{x}^{k_1}$ is revealed preferred to $\mathbf{x}^{k_2}$, and $\mathbf{x}^{k_2}$ is revealed preferred to $\mathbf{x}^{k_3}, \ldots,$ and $\mathbf{x}^{k_{m-1}}$ is revealed preferred to $\mathbf{x}^{k_m}$, then $\mathbf{x}^{k_1}$ is at least as expensive as $\mathbf{x}^{k_m}$ when $\mathbf{x}^{k_m}$ is chosen. (Note that SARP is stronger, requiring that $\mathbf{x}^{k_1}$ be strictly more expensive than $\mathbf{x}^{k_m}$.)

Assume throughout this question that the consumer's choice behaviour satisfies GARP on the data set $D = \{(\mathbf{x}^1, \mathbf{p}^1), (\mathbf{x}^2, \mathbf{p}^2), \ldots, (\mathbf{x}^K, \mathbf{p}^K)\}$ and that $\mathbf{p}^k \in \mathbb{R}^n_{++}$ for every $k = 1, \ldots, K$.

For each $k = 1, 2, \ldots, n$, define

$$\phi(\mathbf{x}^k) = \min_{k_1,\ldots,k_m} \mathbf{p}^{k_1} \cdot (\mathbf{x}^{k_2} - \mathbf{x}^{k_1}) + \mathbf{p}^{k_2} \cdot (\mathbf{x}^{k_3} - \mathbf{x}^{k_2}) + \ldots + \mathbf{p}^{k_m} \cdot (\mathbf{x}^k - \mathbf{x}^{k_m}),$$

where the minimum is taken over all sequences $k_1, \ldots, k_m$ of distinct elements of $\{1, 2, \ldots, K\}$ such that $\mathbf{p}^{k_j} \cdot (\mathbf{x}^{k_{j+1}} - \mathbf{x}^{k_j}) \leq 0$ for every $j = 1, 2, \ldots, m-1$, and such that $\mathbf{p}^{k_m} \cdot (\mathbf{x}^k - \mathbf{x}^{k_m}) \leq 0$. Note that at least one such sequence always exists, namely the 'sequence' consisting of one number, $k_1 = k$. Note also that there are only finitely many such sequences because their elements are distinct. Hence, the minimum above always exists.

(a) Prove that for all $k, j \in \{1, \ldots, K\}$, $\phi(\mathbf{x}^k) \leq \phi(\mathbf{x}^j) + \mathbf{p}^j \cdot (\mathbf{x}^k - \mathbf{x}^j)$ whenever $\mathbf{p}^j \cdot \mathbf{x}^k \leq \mathbf{p}^j \cdot \mathbf{x}^j$.

We next use the non-positive function $\phi(\cdot)$ to define a utility function $u\colon \mathbb{R}^n_+ \to \mathbb{R}$.

For every $\mathbf{x} \in \mathbb{R}^n_+$ such that $\mathbf{p}^k \cdot (\mathbf{x} - \mathbf{x}^k) \leq 0$ for at least one $k \in \{1, \ldots, K\}$, define $u(\mathbf{x}) \leq 0$ as follows:

$$u(\mathbf{x}) = \min_k(\phi(\mathbf{x}^k) + \mathbf{p}^k \cdot (\mathbf{x} - \mathbf{x}^k)),$$

where the minimum is over all $k \in \{1, \ldots, K\}$ such that $\mathbf{p}^k \cdot (\mathbf{x} - \mathbf{x}^k) \leq 0$.

For every $\mathbf{x} \in \mathbb{R}^n_+$ such that $\mathbf{p}^k \cdot (\mathbf{x} - \mathbf{x}^k) > 0$ for every $k \in \{1, \ldots, K\}$, define $u(\mathbf{x}) \geq 0$ as follows:

$$u(\mathbf{x}) = x_1 + \ldots + x_n.$$

(b) Prove that for every $k \in \{1, \ldots, K\}$, $u(\mathbf{x}^k) = \phi(\mathbf{x}^k)$.

(c) Prove that $u(\cdot)$ is strongly increasing i.e., $u(\mathbf{x}') > u(\mathbf{x})$ whenever every coordinate of $\mathbf{x}'$ is at least as large as the corresponding coordinate of $\mathbf{x}$ and at least one coordinate is strictly larger.

(d) Prove that for every $k \in \{1, \ldots, K\}$ and every $\mathbf{x} \in \mathbb{R}^n_+$, if $\mathbf{p}^k \cdot \mathbf{x} \leq \mathbf{p}^k \cdot \mathbf{x}^k$, then $u(\mathbf{x}) \leq u(\mathbf{x}^k)$ and therefore, by (c), the second inequality is strict if the first is strict.

(e) Prove that $u(\cdot)$ is quasiconcave.

Altogether, (a)–(e) prove the following: If a finite data set satisfies GARP, then there is a strongly increasing quasiconcave utility function that rationalises the data in the sense that each chosen bundle maximises the consumer's utility among all bundles that are no more expensive than the chosen bundle at the prices at which it was chosen. (Afriat's Theorem proves that utility function can, in addition, be chosen to be continuous and concave.)

(f) Prove a converse. That is, suppose that a strictly increasing utility function rationalises a finite data set. Prove that the consumer's behaviour satisfies GARP on that data set.

2.13 Answer the following.

(a) Suppose that a choice function $\mathbf{x}(\mathbf{p}, y) \in \mathbb{R}^n_+$ is homogeneous of degree zero in $(\mathbf{p}, y)$. Show that WARP is satisfied $\forall$ $(\mathbf{p}, y)$ iff it is satisfied on $\{(\mathbf{p}, 1) \mid \mathbf{p} \in \mathbb{R}^n_{++}\}$.

(b) Suppose that a choice function $\mathbf{x}(\mathbf{p}, y) \in \mathbb{R}^n_+$ satisfies homogeneity and budget balancedness. Suppose further that whenever $\mathbf{p}^1$ is not proportional to $\mathbf{p}^0$, we have $(\mathbf{p}^1)^T\mathbf{s}(\mathbf{p}^0, \mathbf{y})\mathbf{p}^1 < 0$. Show that $\mathbf{x}(\mathbf{p}, y)$ satisfies WARP.

2.14 Consider the problem of insuring an asset against theft. The value of the asset is \$$D$, the insurance cost is \$$I$ per year, and the probability of theft is p. List the four outcomes in the set A associated with this risky situation. Characterise the choice between insurance and no insurance as a choice between two gambles, each involving all four outcomes in A, where the gambles differ only in the probabilities assigned to each outcome.

2.15 We have assumed that an outcome set A has a finite number of elements, n. Show that as long as $n \geq 2$, the space $\mathcal{G}$ will always contain an infinite number of gambles.

2.16 Using Axioms G1 and G2, prove that at least one best and at least one worst outcome must exist in any finite set of outcomes, $A = \{a_1, \ldots, a_n\}$ whenever $n \geq 1$.

2.17 Let $A = \{a_1, a_2, a_3\}$, where $a_1 \succ a_2 \succ a_3$. The gamble g offers a_2 with certainty. Prove that if $g \sim (\alpha \circ a_1, (1 - \alpha) \circ a_3)$, the α must be *strictly* between zero and 1.

2.18 In the text, it was asserted that, to a safari hunter, death may be the worst outcome of an outing, yet an outing with the *possibility* of death is preferred to one where death is impossible. Characterise the outcome set associated with a hunter's choice of outings, and prove this behaviour violates the combined implications of Axioms G3 and G4.

2.19 Axiom G3 asserts the existence of an indifference probability for any gamble in $\mathcal{G}$. For a given gamble $g \in \mathcal{G}$, prove that the indifference probability is unique using G4.

2.20 Consider the following 'Independence Axiom' on a consumer's preferences, $\succsim$, over gambles: If

$$(p_1 \circ a_1, \ldots, p_n \circ a_n) \sim (q_1 \circ a_1, \ldots, q_n \circ a_n),$$

then for every $\alpha \in [0, 1]$, and every simple gamble $(r_1 \circ a_1, \ldots, r_n \circ a_n)$,

$$((\alpha p_1 + (1 - \alpha)r_1) \circ a_1, \ldots, (\alpha p_n + (1 - \alpha)r_n) \circ a_n)$$
$$\sim$$
$$((\alpha q_1 + (1 - \alpha)r_1) \circ a_1, \ldots, (\alpha q_n + (1 - \alpha)r_n) \circ a_n).$$

(Note this axiom says that when we combine each of two gambles with a third in the same way, the individual's ranking of the two new gambles is *independent* of which third gamble we used.) Show that this axiom follows from Axioms G5 and G6.

2.21 Using the definition of risk aversion given in the text, prove that an individual is risk averse over gambles involving non-negative wealth levels if and only if his VNM utility function is strictly concave on $\mathbb{R}_+$.

2.22 Suppose that $\succsim$ is a binary relation over gambles in $\mathcal{G}$ satisfying Axioms G2, G3, and G4. Show that $\succsim$ satisfies G1 as well.

2.23 Let u and v be utility functions (not necessarily VNM) representing $\succsim$ on $\mathcal{G}$. Show that v is a positive affine transformation of u if and only if for all gambles $g^1, g^2, g^3 \in \mathcal{G}$, with no two indifferent, we have

$$\frac{u(g^1) - u(g^2)}{u(g^2) - u(g^3)} = \frac{v(g^1) - v(g^2)}{v(g^2) - v(g^3)}.$$

2.24 Reconsider Example 2.7 and show that the individual will less than fully insure if the price per unit of insurance, ρ, exceeds the probability of incurring an accident, α.

2.25 Consider the quadratic VNM utility function $U(w) = a + bw + cw^2$.

(a) What restrictions if any must be placed on parameters a, b, and c for this function to display risk aversion?

(b) Over what domain of wealth can a quadratic VNM utility function be defined?

(c) Given the gamble

$$g = ((1/2) \circ (w + h), (1/2) \circ (w - h)),$$

show that $CE < E(g)$ and that $P > 0$.

(d) Show that this function, satisfying the restrictions in part (a), *cannot* represent preferences that display *decreasing* absolute risk aversion.

2.26 Let $u(w) = -(b - w)^c$. What restrictions on w, b, and c are required to ensure that $u(w)$ is strictly increasing and strictly concave? Show that under those restrictions, $u(w)$ displays *increasing* absolute risk aversion.

2.27 Show that for $\beta > 0$, the VNM utility function $u(w) = \alpha + \beta \ln(w)$ displays decreasing absolute risk aversion.

2.28 Let $u(x_1, x_2) = \ln(x_1) + 2\ln(x_2)$. If $p_1 = p_2 = 1$, will this person be risk loving, risk neutral, or risk averse when offered gambles over different amounts of income?

2.29 Using the definitions of risk aversion, certainty equivalent, and risk premium, prove that $CE < E(g)$ (or $P > 0$) for all $g \in \mathcal{G}$ is necessary and sufficient for risk aversion.

2.30 Prove that an individual is risk neutral if and only if each of the following is satisfied:

(a) The VNM utility function is linear in wealth.

(b) $C = E(g)$ for all $g \in \mathcal{G}$.

(c) $P = 0$ for all $g \in \mathcal{G}$.

What are the three equivalent necessary and sufficient conditions for risk *loving*?

2.31 Prove that for any VNM utility function, the condition $u'''(w) > 0$ is necessary but not sufficient for DARA.

2.32 If a VNM utility function displays constant absolute risk aversion, so that $R_a(w) = \alpha$ for all w, what functional form must it have?

2.33 Suppose a consumer's preferences over wealth gambles can be represented by a twice differentiable VNM utility function. Show that the consumer's preferences over gambles are independent of his initial wealth if and only if his utility function displays constant absolute risk aversion.

2.34 Another measure of risk aversion offered by Arrow and Pratt is their **relative risk aversion** measure, $R_r(w) \equiv R_a(w)w$. In what sense is $R_r(w)$ an 'elasticity'? If $u(w)$ displays constant *relative* risk aversion, what functional form must it have?

2.35 An investor must decide how much of initial wealth w to allocate to a risky asset with unknown rate of return r, where each outcome r_i occurs with probability p_i, $i = 1, \ldots, n$. Using the framework of Example 2.6, prove that if the investor's preferences display *increasing* absolute risk aversion, the risky asset must be an 'inferior' good.

2.36 Let S^i be the set of all probabilities of winning such that individual i will accept a gamble of winning or losing a small amount of wealth, h. Show that for any two individuals i and j, where $R_a^i(w) > R_a^j(w)$, it must be that $S^i \subset S^j$. Conclude that the more risk averse the individual, the smaller the set of gambles he will accept.

2.37 An infinitely lived agent must choose his lifetime consumption plan. Let x_t denote consumption spending in period t, y_t denote income expected in period t, and $r > 0$, the market rate of interest at which the agent can freely borrow or lend. The agent's intertemporal utility function takes the additively separable form

$$u^*(x_0, x_1, x_2, \ldots) = \sum_{t=0}^{\infty} \beta^t u(x_t),$$

where $u(x)$ is increasing and strictly concave, and $0 < \beta < 1$. The intertemporal budget constraint requires that the present value of expenditures not exceed the present value of income:

$$\sum_{t=0}^{\infty} \left(\frac{1}{1+r}\right)^t x_t \leq \sum_{t=0}^{\infty} \left(\frac{1}{1+r}\right)^t y_t.$$

(a) What interpretation can you give to parameter β?

(b) Write down the first-order conditions for optimal choice of consumption in period t.

(c) Assuming that consumption in all other periods remains constant, sketch an indifference curve showing the intertemporal trade-off between x_t and x_{t+1} alone. Carefully justify the slope and curvature you have depicted.

(d) How does consumption in period t vary with the market interest rate?

(e) Show that lifetime utility will always increase with an income increase in any period.

(f) If $\beta = 1/(1+r)$, what is the consumption plan of the agent?

(g) Describe the agent's consumption plan if $\beta > 1/(1+r)$ and if $\beta < 1/(1+r)$.

2.38 Consider a two-period version of the preceding exercise where

$$u(x_t) = -(1/2)(x_t - 2)^2 \qquad \text{and} \qquad t = 0, 1.$$

(a) If $y_0 = 1$, $y_1 = 1$, and $\beta = 1/(1+r)$, solve for optimal consumption in each period and calculate the level of lifetime utility the agent achieves.

Suppose, now, that the agent again knows that income in the initial period will be $y_0 = 1$. However, there is uncertainty about what next period's income will be. It could be high, $y_1^H = 3/2$; or it could be low, $y_1^L = 1/2$. He knows it will be high with probability 1/2. His problem now is to choose the initial period consumption, x_0; the future consumption if income is high, x_1^H; and the future consumption if income is low, x_1^L, to maximise (intertemporal) *expected utility*.

(b) Again, assuming that $\beta = 1/(1+r)$, formulate the agent's optimisation problem and solve for the optimal consumption plan and the level of lifetime utility.

(c) How do you account for any difference or similarity in your answers to parts (a) and (b)?

CHAPTER 3

THEORY OF THE FIRM

The second important actor on the microeconomic stage is the individual firm. We begin this chapter with aspects of production and cost that are common to all firms. Then we consider the behaviour of perfectly competitive firms – a very special but very important class. You will see we can now move rather quickly through much of this material because there are many formal similarities between producer theory and the consumer theory we just completed.

3.1 PRIMITIVE NOTIONS

Let us take a moment to remind ourselves just what a firm is. At its simplest, a firm is an entity created by individuals for some purpose. This entity will typically acquire inputs and combine them to produce output. Inputs are purchased on input markets and these expenditures are the firm's costs. Output is sold on product markets and the firm earns revenue from these sales.

Why would someone go to the considerable bother of creating a firm in the first place, and what guides such a person in the myriad decisions that must be made in the course of the firm's activities? Profit maximisation is the most common answer an economist will give, and it is an eminently reasonable one. Profit – the difference between revenue the firm earns from selling its output and expenditure it makes buying its inputs – is income to owners of the firm. These people are also consumers, and consumers get their satisfaction from the goods and services their income will buy. Clearly, the more profit the firm can make, the greater will be its owners' command over goods and services. In this view, firm owners will insist that all decisions on acquiring and combining inputs, and on marketing output, must serve the goal of maximising profit.

Of course, profit maximisation may not be the only motive behind firm behaviour, and economists have considered many others. Sales, market share, or even prestige maximisation are also possibilities. Each of these alternatives to profit maximisation – and others, too – have at least some superficial appeal. Yet the majority of economists continue to embrace the hypothesis of profit maximisation most of the time in most of their work.

There are good reasons for this tenacity. From an empirical point of view, assuming firms profit maximise leads to predictions of firm behaviour which are time and again borne out by the evidence. From a theoretical point of view, there is first the virtue of simplicity and consistency with the hypothesis of self-interested utility maximisation on the part of consumers. Also, many alternative hypotheses, such as sales or market-share maximisation, may be better viewed as short-run tactics in a long-run, profit-maximising strategy, rather than as ultimate objectives in themselves. Finally, there are identifiable market forces that *coerce* the firm towards profit maximisation even if its owners or managers are not themselves innately inclined in that direction. Suppose that some firm did not maximise profit. Then if the fault lies with the managers, and if at least a working majority of the firm's owners are non-satiated consumers, those owners have a clear common interest in ridding themselves of that management and replacing it with a profit-maximising one. If the fault lies with the owners, then there is an obvious incentive for any non-satiated entrepreneur outside the firm to acquire it and change its ways.

Like the hypothesis of utility maximisation for consumers, profit maximisation is the single most robust and compelling assumption we can make as we begin to examine and ultimately predict firm behaviour. In any choice the firm must make, we therefore will always suppose its decision is guided by the objective of profit maximisation. Which course of action best serves that goal will depend on the circumstances the firm faces – first, with respect to what is technologically possible; second, with respect to conditions on its input markets; and, finally, with respect to conditions on its product market. Clear thinking on firm behaviour will depend on carefully distinguishing between the firm's objective, which always remains the same, and its constraints, which are varied and depend on market realities beyond its control.

3.2 PRODUCTION

Production is the process of transforming inputs into outputs. The fundamental reality firms must contend with in this process is *technological feasibility*. The state of technology determines and restricts what is possible in combining inputs to produce output, and there are several ways we can represent this constraint. The most general way is to think of the firm as having a **production possibility set**, $Y \subset \mathbb{R}^m$, where each vector $\mathbf{y} = (y_1, \ldots, y_m) \in Y$ is a **production plan** whose components indicate the amounts of the various inputs and outputs. A common convention is to write elements of $\mathbf{y} \in Y$ so that $y_i < 0$ if resource i is used up in the production plan, and $y_i > 0$ if resource i is produced in the production plan.

The production possibility set is by far the most general way to characterise the firm's technology because it allows for multiple inputs and multiple outputs. Often, however, we will want to consider firms producing only a single product from many inputs. For that, it is more convenient to describe the firm's technology in terms of a **production function**.

When there is only one output produced by many inputs, we shall denote the amount of output by y, and the amount of input i by x_i, so that with n inputs, the entire vector of inputs is denoted by $\mathbf{x} = (x_1, \ldots, x_n)$. Of course, the input vector as well as the amount of output must be non-negative, so we require $\mathbf{x} \geq 0$, and $y \geq 0$.

A production function simply describes for each vector of inputs the amount of output that can be produced. The production function, f, is therefore a mapping from $\mathbb{R}^n_+$ into $\mathbb{R}_+$. When we write $y = f(\mathbf{x})$, we mean that y units of output (and no more) can be produced using the input vector $\mathbf{x}$. We shall maintain the following assumption on the production function f.[1]

ASSUMPTION 3.1 *Properties of the Production Function*

The production function, $f\colon \mathbb{R}^n_+ \to \mathbb{R}_+$, is continuous, strictly increasing, and strictly quasiconcave on $\mathbb{R}^n_+$, and $f(\mathbf{0}) = 0$.

Continuity of f ensures that small changes in the vector of inputs lead to small changes in the amount of output produced. We require f to be strictly increasing to ensure that employing strictly more of every input results in strictly more output. The strict quasiconcavity of f is assumed largely for reasons of simplicity. Similar to our assumption that consumer's preferences were strictly convex (so that u is strictly quasiconcave), we could do without it here without much change in the results we will present. Nonetheless, we can interpret the meaning of it. One interpretation is that strict quasiconcavity implies the presence of at least some complementarities in production. Intuitively, two inputs, labour and capital say, are to some degree complementary if very little production can take place if one of the inputs is low, even if the other input is high. In this sense, both inputs together are important for production. In such a situation, the average of two extreme production vectors, one with high labour and low capital and the other with low labour and high capital, will produce strictly more output than at least one of the two extreme input vectors, and perhaps even both. The assumption of strict quasiconcavity extends this idea to strict averages of all distinct pairs of input vectors. The last condition states that a positive amount of output requires positive amounts of some of the inputs.

When the production function is differentiable, its partial derivative, $\partial f(\mathbf{x})/\partial x_i$, is called the **marginal product** of input i and gives the rate at which output changes per additional unit of input i employed. If f is strictly increasing and everywhere continuously differentiable, then $\partial f(\mathbf{x})/\partial x_i > 0$ for 'almost all' input vectors. We will often assume for simplicity that the strict inequality always holds.

For any fixed level of output, y, the set of input vectors producing y units of output is called the y-level **isoquant**. An isoquant is then just a level set of f. We shall denote this set by $Q(y)$. That is,

$$Q(y) \equiv \{\mathbf{x} \geq 0 \mid f(\mathbf{x}) = y\}.$$

For an input vector $\mathbf{x}$, the **isoquant through x** is the set of input vectors producing the same output as $\mathbf{x}$, namely, $Q(f(\mathbf{x}))$.

[1] Compare this to Assumption 1.2 in Chapter 1.

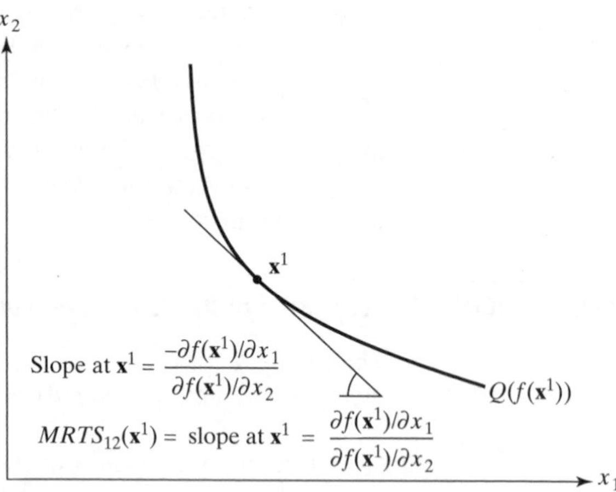

Figure 3.1. The marginal rate of technical substitution.

An analogue to the marginal rate of substitution in consumer theory is the **marginal rate of technical substitution (MRTS)** in producer theory. This measures the rate at which one input can be substituted for another without changing the amount of output produced. Formally, the marginal rate of technical substitution of input j for input i when the current input vector is $\mathbf{x}$, denoted $MRTS_{ij}(\mathbf{x})$, is defined as the ratio of marginal products,

$$MRTS_{ij}(\mathbf{x}) = \frac{\partial f(\mathbf{x})/\partial x_i}{\partial f(\mathbf{x})/\partial x_j}.$$

In the two-input case, as depicted in Fig. 3.1, $MRTS_{12}(\mathbf{x}^1)$ is the absolute value of the slope of the isoquant through $\mathbf{x}^1$ at the point $\mathbf{x}^1$.

In general, the MRTS between any two inputs depends on the amounts of *all* inputs employed. However, it is quite common, particularly in empirical work, to suppose that inputs can be classified into a relatively small number of types, with degrees of substitutability between those of a given type differing systematically from the degree of substitutability between those of different types. Production functions of this variety are called *separable*, and there are at least two major forms of separability. In the following definition, we use $f_i(\mathbf{x})$ as a shorthand for the marginal product of input i, i.e., for $\partial f(\mathbf{x})/\partial x_i$.

DEFINITION 3.1 ***Separable Production Functions***

Let $N = \{1, \ldots, n\}$ index the set of all inputs, and suppose that these inputs can be partitioned into $S > 1$ mutually exclusive and exhaustive subsets, $N_1, \ldots, N_S$. The production function is called weakly separable *if the MRTS between two inputs within the same group is independent of inputs used in other groups:*

$$\frac{\partial(f_i(\mathbf{x})/f_j(\mathbf{x}))}{\partial x_k} = 0 \qquad \text{for all} \quad i, j \in N_s \text{ and } k \notin N_s,$$

where f_i and f_j are the marginal products of inputs i and j. When $S > 2$, the production function is called strongly separable *if the MRTS between two inputs from any two groups, including from the same group, is independent of all inputs outside those two groups:*

$$\frac{\partial(f_i(\mathbf{x})/f_j(\mathbf{x}))}{\partial x_k} = 0 \qquad \text{for all} \quad i \in N_s,\ j \in N_t,\ \text{and } k \notin N_s \cup N_t.$$

The MRTS is one local measure of substitutability between inputs in producing a given level of output. Economists, however, have a penchant for measuring such things with unitless elasticities. Although there are several such measures, by far the most common is the *elasticity of substitution*, σ. Holding all other inputs and the level of output constant, the elasticity of substitution of input j for input i is defined as the percentage change in the input proportions, x_j/x_i, associated with a 1 per cent change in the MRTS between them.

DEFINITION 3.2 ***The Elasticity of Substitution***

For a production function $f(\mathbf{x})$, the elasticity of substitution of input j for input i at the point $\mathbf{x}^0 \in \mathbb{R}^n_{++}$ is defined as

$$\sigma_{ij}(\mathbf{x}^0) \equiv \left(\left. \frac{d \ln MRTS_{ij}(\mathbf{x}(r))}{d \ln r} \right|_{r = x_j^0/x_i^0} \right)^{-1},$$

where $\mathbf{x}(r)$ is the unique vector of inputs $\mathbf{x} = (x_1, \ldots, x_n)$ such that (i) $x_j/x_i = r$, (ii) $x_k = x_k^0$ for $k \neq i, j$, and (iii) $f(\mathbf{x}) = f(\mathbf{x}^0)$.[2]

The elasticity of substitution $\sigma_{ij}(\mathbf{x}^0)$ is a measure of the curvature of the *i*-*j* isoquant through $\mathbf{x}^0$ at $\mathbf{x}^0$. When the production function is quasiconcave, the elasticity of substitution can never be negative, so $\sigma_{ij} \geq 0$. In general, the closer it is to zero, the more 'difficult' is substitution between the inputs; the larger it is, the 'easier' is substitution between them.

When there are only two inputs we will write σ rather than σ_{12}. Let us consider a few two-input examples. In Fig. 3.2(a), the isoquant is linear and there is perfect substitutability between the inputs. There, σ is infinite. In Fig. 3.2(c), the two inputs are productive only in fixed proportions with one another – substitution between them is effectively impossible, and σ is zero. In Fig. 3.2(b), we have illustrated an intermediate case where σ is neither zero nor infinite, and the isoquants are neither straight lines nor right angles. In general, the closer σ is to zero, the more L-shaped the isoquants are and the more 'difficult' substitution between inputs; the larger σ is, the flatter the isoquants and the 'easier' substitution between them.

[2]That $\mathbf{x}(r)$ exists and is unique follows from Assumption 3.1.

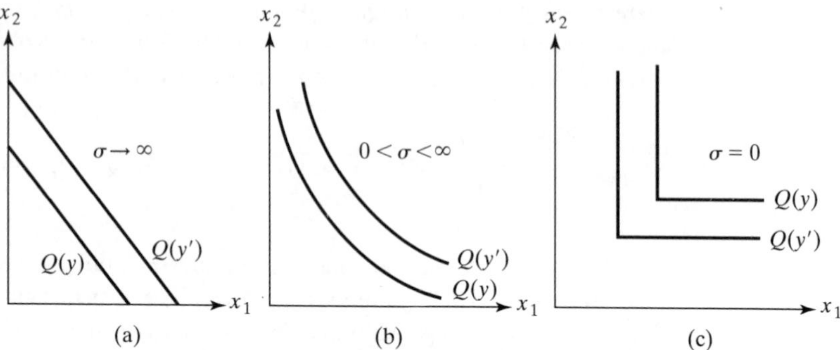

Figure 3.2. (a) σ is infinite and there is perfect substitutability between inputs. (b) σ is finite but larger than zero, indicating less than perfect substitutability. (c) σ is zero and there is no substitutability between inputs.

EXAMPLE 3.1 We are familiar with the CES utility function from demand theory. Perhaps it is time we see where this name comes from by considering the CES production function,

$$y = \left(x_1^\rho + x_2^\rho\right)^{1/\rho}$$

for $0 \neq \rho < 1$.

To calculate the elasticity of substitution, σ, note first that the marginal rate of technical substitution at an arbitrary point (x_1, x_2) is

$$MRTS_{12}(x_1, x_2) = \left(\frac{x_2}{x_1}\right)^{1-\rho}.$$

Hence, in this example the ratio of the two inputs alone determines MRTS, regardless of the quantity of output produced. Consequently, setting $r = x_2/x_1$,

$$\begin{aligned} \frac{d \ln MRTS_{12}(\mathbf{x}(r))}{d \ln r} &= \frac{d \ln r^{1-\rho}}{d \ln r} \\ &= (1-\rho)\frac{d \ln r}{d \ln r} \\ &= 1-\rho. \end{aligned}$$

Hence, according to Definition 3.2,

$$\sigma = \frac{1}{1-\rho},$$

which is a constant. This explains the initials CES, which stand for **constant elasticity of substitution**. □

With the CES form, the degree of substitutability between inputs is always the same, regardless of the level of output or input proportions. It is therefore a somewhat restrictive characterisation of the technology. On the other hand, different values of the parameter ρ, and so different values of the parameter σ, can be used to represent technologies with vastly different (though everywhere constant) substitutability between inputs. The closer ρ is to unity, the larger is σ; when ρ is equal to 1, σ is infinite and the production function is *linear*, with isoquants resembling those in Fig. 3.2(a).

Other popular production functions also can be seen as special cases of specific CES forms. In particular, it is easy to verify that

$$y = \left(\sum_{i=1}^{n} \alpha_i x_i^{\rho}\right)^{1/\rho}, \quad \text{where} \quad \sum_{i=1}^{n} \alpha_i = 1,$$

is a CES form with $\sigma_{ij} = 1/(1-\rho)$ for all $i \neq j$. It can be shown that as $\rho \to 0$, $\sigma_{ij} \to 1$, and this CES form reduces to the linear homogeneous Cobb-Douglas form,

$$y = \prod_{i=1}^{n} x_i^{\alpha_i}.$$

As $\rho \to -\infty$, $\sigma_{ij} \to 0$, giving the *Leontief* form as a limiting case, where

$$y = \min\{x_1, \ldots, x_n\}$$

with isoquants such as those in Fig. 3.2(c).

All CES production functions (including the limiting cases of Cobb-Douglas and Leontief) are members of the class of linear homogeneous production functions, and these are important in theoretical and applied work. Linear homogeneity imposes a great deal of additional structure on the production function. Among other things, linear homogeneous production functions will always be *concave* functions.

THEOREM 3.1 ***(Shephard) Homogeneous Production Functions are Concave***

Let $f(\mathbf{x})$ be a production function satisfying Assumption 3.1 and suppose it is homogeneous of degree $\alpha \in (0, 1]$. Then $f(\mathbf{x})$ is a concave function of $\mathbf{x}$.

Proof: Suppose first that $\alpha = 1$, i.e., that f is homogeneous of degree one. Take any $\mathbf{x}^1 \gg \mathbf{0}$ and $\mathbf{x}^2 \gg \mathbf{0}$ and let $y^1 = f(\mathbf{x}^1)$ and $y^2 = f(\mathbf{x}^2)$. Then $y^1, y^2 > 0$ because $f(\mathbf{0}) = 0$ and f is strictly increasing. Therefore, because f is homogeneous of degree one,

$$f\left(\frac{\mathbf{x}^1}{y^1}\right) = f\left(\frac{\mathbf{x}^2}{y^2}\right) = 1.$$

Because f is (strictly) quasiconcave,

$$f\left(\frac{t\mathbf{x}^1}{y^1} + \frac{(1-t)\mathbf{x}^2}{y^2}\right) \geq 1 \qquad \text{for all } t \in [0, 1]. \tag{P.1}$$

Now choose $t^* = y^1/(y^1 + y^2)$ and $(1 - t^*) = y^2/(y^1 + y^2)$. Then from (P.1),

$$f\left(\frac{\mathbf{x}^1}{y^1 + y^2} + \frac{\mathbf{x}^2}{y^1 + y^2}\right) \geq 1. \tag{P.2}$$

Again invoking the linear homogeneity of f and using (P.2) gives

$$f(\mathbf{x}^1 + \mathbf{x}^2) \geq y^1 + y^2 = f(\mathbf{x}^1) + f(\mathbf{x}^2). \tag{P.3}$$

Thus, (P.3) holds for all $\mathbf{x}^1, \mathbf{x}^2 \gg \mathbf{0}$. But the continuity of f then implies that (P.3) holds for *all* $\mathbf{x}^1, \mathbf{x}^2 \geq \mathbf{0}$.

To complete the proof for the $\alpha = 1$ case, consider any two vectors $\mathbf{x}^1 \geq \mathbf{0}$ and $\mathbf{x}^2 \geq \mathbf{0}$ and any $t \in [0, 1]$. Recall that linear homogeneity ensures that

$$f(t\mathbf{x}^1) = tf(\mathbf{x}^1), \tag{P.4}$$
$$f((1-t)\mathbf{x}^2) = (1-t)f(\mathbf{x}^2). \tag{P.5}$$

If we apply (P.3) and use (P.4) and (P.5), we conclude that

$$f(t\mathbf{x}^1 + (1-t)\mathbf{x}^2) \geq tf(\mathbf{x}^1) + (1-t)f(\mathbf{x}^2),$$

as desired.

Suppose now that f is homogeneous of degree $\alpha \in (0, 1]$. Then $f^{\frac{1}{\alpha}}$ is homogeneous of degree one and satisfies Assumption 3.1. Hence, by what we have just proven, $f^{\frac{1}{\alpha}}$ is concave. But then $f = \left[f^{\frac{1}{\alpha}}\right]^{\alpha}$ is concave since $\alpha \leq 1$. ∎

3.2.1 RETURNS TO SCALE AND VARYING PROPORTIONS

We frequently want to know how output responds as the amounts of different inputs are varied. For instance, in the **short run**, the period of time in which at least one input is fixed, output can be varied only by changing the amounts of some inputs but not others. As amounts of the variable inputs are changed, the proportions in which fixed and variable inputs are used are also changed. 'Returns to variable proportions' refer to how output responds in this situation. In the **long run**, the firm is free to vary all inputs, and classifying production functions by their 'returns to scale' is one way of describing how output responds in this situation. Specifically, returns to scale refer to how output responds when all inputs are varied in the *same* proportion, i.e., when the entire 'scale' of operation is

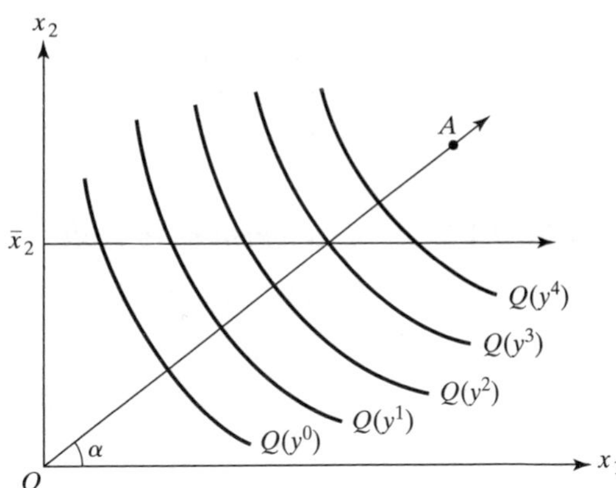

Figure 3.3. Returns to scale and varying proportions.

increased or decreased proportionally. In the two-input case, the distinction between these two attributes of the production function is best grasped by considering Fig. 3.3. Returns to varying proportions concern how output behaves as we move through the isoquant map along the horizontal at $\bar{x}_2$, keeping x_2 constant and varying the amount of x_1. Returns to scale have to do with how output behaves as we move through the isoquant map along a ray such as OA, where the levels of x_1 and x_2 are changed simultaneously, always staying in the proportion $x_2/x_1 = \alpha$.

Elementary measures of returns to varying proportions include the marginal product, $MP_i(\mathbf{x}) \equiv f_i(\mathbf{x})$, and the **average product**, $AP_i(\mathbf{x}) \equiv f(\mathbf{x})/x_i$, of each input. The **output elasticity of input** i, measuring the percentage response of output to a 1 per cent change in input i, is given by $\mu_i(\mathbf{x}) \equiv f_i(\mathbf{x})x_i/f(\mathbf{x}) = MP_i(\mathbf{x})/AP_i(\mathbf{x})$. Each of these is a local measure, defined at a point. The scale properties of the technology may be defined either locally or globally. A production function is said to have globally *constant, increasing*, or *decreasing* returns to scale according to the following definitions.

DEFINITION 3.3 ***(Global) Returns to Scale***

A production function $f(\mathbf{x})$ has the property of (globally):

1. *Constant returns to scale if $f(t\mathbf{x}) = tf(\mathbf{x})$ for all $t > 0$ and all $\mathbf{x}$;*
2. *Increasing returns to scale if $f(t\mathbf{x}) > tf(\mathbf{x})$ for all $t > 1$ and all $\mathbf{x}$;*
3. *Decreasing returns to scale if $f(t\mathbf{x}) < tf(\mathbf{x})$ for all $t > 1$ and all $\mathbf{x}$.*

Notice from these global definitions of returns to scale that a production function has constant returns if it is a (positive) linear homogeneous function. Notice carefully, however, that every homogeneous production function of degree *greater* (*less*) than one must have increasing (decreasing) returns, though the converse need not hold.

Note that many production functions satisfying Assumption 3.1 do not fall into any of the preceding three categories. Many technologies exhibit increasing, constant, and decreasing returns over only certain ranges of output. It is therefore useful to have a *local* measure of returns to scale. One such measure, defined at a point, tells us the instantaneous percentage change in output that occurs with a 1 per cent increase in all inputs. It is variously known as the *elasticity of scale* or the (overall) *elasticity of output*, and is defined as follows.

DEFINITION 3.4 ***(Local) Returns to Scale***

The elasticity of scale at the point $\mathbf{x}$ *is defined as*

$$\mu(\mathbf{x}) \equiv \lim_{t\to 1} \frac{d \ln[f(t\mathbf{x})]}{d \ln(t)} = \frac{\sum_{i=1}^{n} f_i(\mathbf{x})x_i}{f(\mathbf{x})}.$$

Returns to scale are locally constant, increasing, or decreasing as $\mu(\mathbf{x})$ *is equal to, greater than, or less than one. The elasticity of scale and the output elasticities of the inputs are related as follows:*

$$\mu(\mathbf{x}) = \sum_{i=1}^{n} \mu_i(\mathbf{x}).$$

EXAMPLE 3.2 Let us examine a production function with variable returns to scale:

$$y = k\left(1 + x_1^{-\alpha} x_2^{-\beta}\right)^{-1}, \tag{E.1}$$

where $\alpha > 0$, $\beta > 0$, and k is an upper bound on the level of output, so that $0 \le y < k$. Calculating the output elasticities for each input, we obtain

$$\mu_1(\mathbf{x}) = \alpha\left(1 + x_1^{-\alpha} x_2^{-\beta}\right)^{-1} x_1^{-\alpha} x_2^{-\beta},$$
$$\mu_2(\mathbf{x}) = \beta\left(1 + x_1^{-\alpha} x_2^{-\beta}\right)^{-1} x_1^{-\alpha} x_2^{-\beta},$$

each of which clearly varies with both scale and input proportions. Adding the two gives the following expression for the elasticity of scale:

$$\mu(\mathbf{x}) = (\alpha + \beta)\left(1 + x_1^{-\alpha} x_2^{-\beta}\right)^{-1} x_1^{-\alpha} x_2^{-\beta},$$

which also varies with $\mathbf{x}$.

Much neater expressions are obtained if we view these elasticities as functions of the level of output. From (E.1), we can write

$$x_1^{-\alpha} x_2^{-\beta} = \frac{k}{y} - 1. \tag{E.2}$$

Substituting from (E.1) and (E.2) gives

$$\mu_1^*(y) = \alpha\left(1 - \frac{y}{k}\right),$$

$$\mu_2^*(y) = \beta\left(1 - \frac{y}{k}\right).$$

Adding these again, we find that

$$\mu^*(y) = (\alpha + \beta)\left(1 - \frac{y}{k}\right).$$

Here it is clear that returns to each input, and overall returns to scale, decline monotonically as output increases. At $y = 0$, $\mu^*(y) = (\alpha + \beta) > 0$, and as $y \to k$, $\mu^*(y) \to 0$. If $\alpha + \beta > 1$, the production function exhibits increasing returns to scale for low levels of output, $0 \leq y < k[1 - 1/(\alpha + \beta)]$, locally constant returns at $y = k[1 - 1/(\alpha + \beta)]$, and decreasing returns for high levels of output, $k[1 - 1/(\alpha + \beta)] < y < k$. □

3.3 Cost

The firm's cost of output is precisely the expenditure it must make to acquire the inputs used to produce that output. In general, the technology will permit every level of output to be produced by a variety of input vectors, and all such possibilities can be summarised by the level sets of the production function. The firm must decide, therefore, which of the possible production plans it will use. If the object of the firm is to maximise profits, it will necessarily choose the least costly, or *cost-minimising*, production plan for every level of output. Note this will be true for all firms, whether monopolists, perfect competitors, or any thing between.

To determine the least costly method of production, the firm must consider the terms at which it can acquire inputs as well as the technological possibilities in production. These in turn depend on the circumstances it faces on its input markets. For example, the firm may face upward-sloping supply curves for some or all of its inputs, where the more it hires, the higher the per-unit price it must pay. Alternatively, the firm may be a small, insignificant force on its input markets, and so be able to hire as much or as little as it wants without affecting the prevailing market prices. In this case, we say that the firm is perfectly competitive on its input markets, because it has no power individually to affect prices on those markets. In either case, these circumstances must be taken into account in the firm's decisions.

We will assume throughout that firms are perfectly competitive on their input markets and that therefore they face fixed input prices. Let $\mathbf{w} = (w_1, \ldots, w_n) \geq \mathbf{0}$ be a vector of prevailing market prices at which the firm can buy inputs $\mathbf{x} = (x_1, \ldots, x_n)$. Because the firm is a profit maximiser, it will choose to produce some level of output while using that input vector requiring the smallest money outlay. One can speak therefore of 'the' cost of output y – it will be the cost at prices $\mathbf{w}$ of the least costly vector of inputs capable of producing y.

DEFINITION 3.5 ***The Cost Function***

The cost function, defined for all input prices $\mathbf{w} \gg \mathbf{0}$ *and all output levels* $y \in f(\mathbb{R}^n_+)$ *is the minimum-value function,*

$$c(\mathbf{w}, y) \equiv \min_{\mathbf{x} \in \mathbb{R}^n_+} \mathbf{w} \cdot \mathbf{x} \qquad s.t. \qquad f(\mathbf{x}) \geq y.$$

If $\mathbf{x}(\mathbf{w}, y)$ *solves the cost-minimisation problem, then*

$$c(\mathbf{w}, y) = \mathbf{w} \cdot \mathbf{x}(\mathbf{w}, y).$$

Let us consider the firm's cost-minimisation problem more closely. Because f is strictly increasing, the constraint will always be binding at a solution. Consequently, the cost-minimisation problem is equivalent to

$$\min_{\mathbf{x} \in \mathbb{R}^n_+} \mathbf{w} \cdot \mathbf{x} \qquad \text{s.t.} \qquad y = f(\mathbf{x}). \tag{3.1}$$

Let $\mathbf{x}^*$ denote a solution to (3.1). To keep things simple, we shall assume $\mathbf{x}^* \gg \mathbf{0}$, and that f is differentiable at $\mathbf{x}^*$ with $\nabla f(\mathbf{x}^*) \gg \mathbf{0}$. Thus, by Lagrange's theorem, there is a $\lambda^* \in \mathbb{R}$ such that

$$w_i = \lambda^* \frac{\partial f(\mathbf{x}^*)}{\partial x_i}, \qquad i = 1, \ldots, n.$$

Because $w_i > 0$, $i = 1, \ldots, n$, we may divide the preceding ith equation by the jth to obtain

$$\frac{\partial f(\mathbf{x}^*)/\partial x_i}{\partial f(\mathbf{x}^*)/\partial x_j} = \frac{w_i}{w_j}. \tag{3.2}$$

Thus, cost minimisation implies that the marginal rate of substitution between any two inputs is equal to the ratio of their prices.

From the first-order conditions, it is clear the solution depends on the parameters $\mathbf{w}$ and y. Moreover, because $\mathbf{w} \gg \mathbf{0}$ and f is strictly quasiconcave, the solution to (3.1) is unique. In Exercise 3.18, you are asked to show this, as well as that (3.1) always possesses a solution. So we can write $\mathbf{x}^* \equiv \mathbf{x}(\mathbf{w}, y)$ to denote the vector of inputs minimising the cost of producing y units of output at the input prices $\mathbf{w}$. The solution $\mathbf{x}(\mathbf{w}, y)$ is referred to as the firm's **conditional input demand**, because it is *conditional* on the level of output y, which at this point is arbitrary and so may or may not be profit maximising.

The solution to the cost-minimisation problem is illustrated in Fig. 3.4. With two inputs, an interior solution corresponds to a point of tangency between the y-level isoquant

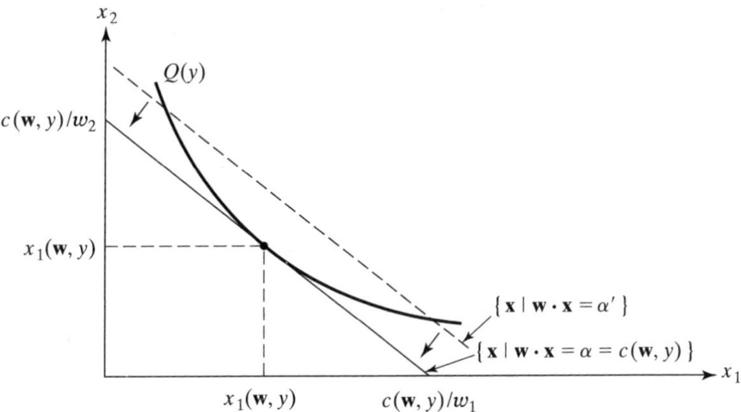

Figure 3.4. The solution to the firm's cost-minimisation problem. In the figure, $\alpha < \alpha'$.

and an **isocost** line of the form $\mathbf{w} \cdot \mathbf{x} = \alpha$ for some $\alpha > 0$. If $x_1(\mathbf{w}, y)$ and $x_2(\mathbf{w}, y)$ are solutions, then $c(\mathbf{w}, y) = w_1x_1(\mathbf{w}, y) + w_2x_2(\mathbf{w}, y)$.

EXAMPLE 3.3 Suppose the firm's technology is the two-input CES form. Its cost-minimisation problem (3.1) is then

$$\min_{x_1 \geq 0, x_2 \geq 0} \quad w_1x_1 + w_2x_2 \qquad \text{s.t.} \qquad \left(x_1^\rho + x_2^\rho\right)^{1/\rho} \geq y.$$

Assuming $y > 0$ and an interior solution, the first-order Lagrangian conditions reduce to the two conditions

$$\frac{w_1}{w_2} = \left(\frac{x_1}{x_2}\right)^{\rho-1}, \tag{E.1}$$

$$y = \left(x_1^\rho + x_2^\rho\right)^{1/\rho}. \tag{E.2}$$

Solving (E.1) for x_1, substituting in (E.2), and rearranging gives

$$y = x_2 w_2^{-1/(\rho-1)}\left(w_1^{\rho/(\rho-1)} + w_2^{\rho/(\rho-1)}\right)^{1/\rho}.$$

Solving this for x_2 and performing similar calculations to solve for x_1, we obtain the conditional input demands:

$$x_1 = y w_1^{1/(\rho-1)}\left(w_1^{\rho/(\rho-1)} + w_2^{\rho/(\rho-1)}\right)^{-1/\rho}, \tag{E.3}$$

$$x_2 = y w_2^{1/(\rho-1)}\left(w_1^{\rho/(\rho-1)} + w_2^{\rho/(\rho-1)}\right)^{-1/\rho}. \tag{E.4}$$

To obtain the cost function, we substitute the solutions (E.3) and (E.4) back into the objective function for the minimisation problem. Doing that yields

$$\begin{aligned} c(\mathbf{w}, y) &= w_1 x_1(\mathbf{w}, y) + w_2 x_2(\mathbf{w}, y) \\ &= y\left(w_1^{\rho/(\rho-1)} + w_2^{\rho/(\rho-1)}\right)^{(\rho-1)/\rho}. \end{aligned}$$

□

You may have noticed some similarities here with consumer theory. These similarities are in fact exact when one compares the cost function with the expenditure function. Indeed, consider their definitions.

$$\text{Expenditure Function}: \quad e(\mathbf{p}, u) \equiv \min_{\mathbf{x}\in\mathbb{R}^n_+} \mathbf{p}\cdot\mathbf{x} \quad \text{s.t.} \quad u(\mathbf{x}) \geq u.$$

$$\text{Cost Function}: \quad c(\mathbf{w}, y) \equiv \min_{\mathbf{x}\in\mathbb{R}^n_+} \mathbf{w}\cdot\mathbf{x} \quad \text{s.t.} \quad f(\mathbf{x}) \geq y.$$

Mathematically, the two functions are identical. Consequently, for every theorem we proved about expenditure functions, there is an equivalent theorem for cost functions. We shall state these theorems here, but we do not need to prove them. Their proofs are identical to those given for the expenditure function.

THEOREM 3.2 ***Properties of the Cost Function***

If f is continuous and strictly increasing, then $c(\mathbf{w}, y)$ is

1. *Zero when $y = 0$,*
2. *Continuous on its domain,*
3. *For all $\mathbf{w} \gg 0$, strictly increasing and unbounded above in y,*
4. *Increasing in $\mathbf{w}$,*
5. *Homogeneous of degree one in $\mathbf{w}$,*
6. *Concave in $\mathbf{w}$.*

Moreover, if f is strictly quasiconcave we have

7. *Shephard's lemma: $c(\mathbf{w}, y)$ is differentiable in $\mathbf{w}$ at $(\mathbf{w}^0, y^0)$ whenever $\mathbf{w}^0 \gg 0$, and*

$$\frac{\partial c(\mathbf{w}^0, y^0)}{\partial w_i} = x_i(\mathbf{w}^0, y^0), \qquad i = 1, \ldots, n.$$

EXAMPLE 3.4 Consider a cost function with the Cobb-Douglas form, $c(\mathbf{w}, y) = Aw_1^{\alpha} w_2^{\beta} y$. From property 7 of Theorem 3.2, the conditional input demands are obtained by differentiating with respect to input prices. Thus,

$$x_1(\mathbf{w}, y) = \frac{\partial c(\mathbf{w}, y)}{\partial w_1} = \alpha A w_1^{\alpha-1} w_2^{\beta} y = \frac{\alpha c(\mathbf{w}, y)}{w_1}, \tag{E.1}$$

$$x_2(\mathbf{w}, y) = \frac{\partial c(\mathbf{w}, y)}{\partial w_2} = \beta A w_1^{\alpha} w_2^{\beta-1} y = \frac{\beta c(\mathbf{w}, y)}{w_2}. \tag{E.2}$$

If we take the ratio of conditional input demands, we see that

$$\frac{x_1(\mathbf{w}, y)}{x_2(\mathbf{w}, y)} = \frac{\alpha}{\beta} \frac{w_2}{w_1}.$$

This tells us that the proportions in which a firm with this cost function will use its inputs depend only on relative input prices and are completely independent of the level or scale of output.

Now define the **input share**, $s_i \equiv w_i x_i(\mathbf{w}, y)/c(\mathbf{w}, y)$ as the proportion of total expenditure spent by the firm on input i. From (E.1) and (E.2), these are always constant and

$$s_1 = \alpha,$$
$$s_2 = \beta.$$

□

As solutions to the firm's cost-minimisation problem, the conditional input demand functions possess certain general properties. These are analogous to the properties of Hicksian compensated demands, so once again it is not necessary to repeat the proof.

THEOREM 3.3 ***Properties of Conditional Input Demands***

Suppose the production function satisfies Assumption 3.1 and that the associated cost function is twice continuously differentiable. Then

1. $\mathbf{x}(\mathbf{w}, y)$ *is homogeneous of degree zero in* $\mathbf{w}$,
2. *The substitution matrix, defined and denoted*

$$\sigma^*(\mathbf{w}, y) \equiv \begin{pmatrix} \frac{\partial x_1(\mathbf{w}, y)}{\partial w_1} & \cdots & \frac{\partial x_1(\mathbf{w}, y)}{\partial w_n} \\ \vdots & \ddots & \vdots \\ \frac{\partial x_n(\mathbf{w}, y)}{\partial w_1} & \cdots & \frac{\partial x_n(\mathbf{w}, y)}{\partial w_n} \end{pmatrix},$$

is symmetric and negative semidefinite. In particular, the negative semidefiniteness property implies that $\partial x_i(\mathbf{w}, y)/\partial w_i \leq 0$ *for all* i.

Homogeneous or, more generally, homothetic production technologies are quite common in theoretical and applied work. The cost and conditional input demands associated with these technologies have some special properties. Some of these are collected in what follows.

THEOREM 3.4 ***Cost and Conditional Input Demands when Production is Homothetic***

1. *When the production function satisfies Assumption 3.1 and is homothetic,*

   (a) *the cost function is multiplicatively separable in input prices and output and can be written* $c(\mathbf{w}, y) = h(y)c(\mathbf{w}, 1)$*, where* $h(y)$ *is strictly increasing and* $c(\mathbf{w}, 1)$ *is the unit cost function, or the cost of 1 unit of output;*

   (b) *the conditional input demands are multiplicatively separable in input prices and output and can be written* $\mathbf{x}(\mathbf{w}, y) = h(y)\mathbf{x}(\mathbf{w}, 1)$*, where* $h'(y) > 0$ *and* $\mathbf{x}(\mathbf{w}, 1)$ *is the conditional input demand for 1 unit of output.*

2. *When the production function is homogeneous of degree* $\alpha > 0$*,*

   (a) $c(\mathbf{w}, y) = y^{1/\alpha}c(\mathbf{w}, 1)$;

   (b) $\mathbf{x}(\mathbf{w}, y) = y^{1/\alpha}\mathbf{x}(\mathbf{w}, 1)$.

Proof: Part 2 can be proved by mimicking the proof of part 1, so this is left as an exercise. Part 1(b) follows from Shephard's lemma, so we need only prove part 1(a).

Let F denote the production function. Because it is homothetic, it can be written as $F(\mathbf{x}) = f(g(\mathbf{x}))$, where f is strictly increasing, and g is homogeneous of degree one.

For simplicity, we shall assume that the image of F is all of $\mathbb{R}_+$. Consequently, as you are asked to show in Exercise 3.5, $f^{-1}(y) > 0$ for all $y > 0$. So, for some $y > 0$, let $t = f^{-1}(1)/f^{-1}(y) > 0$. Note then that $f(g(\mathbf{x})) \geq y \Longleftrightarrow g(\mathbf{x}) \geq f^{-1}(y) \Longleftrightarrow g(t\mathbf{x}) \geq tf^{-1}(y) = f^{-1}(1) \Longleftrightarrow f(g(t\mathbf{x})) \geq 1$. Therefore, we may express the cost function associated with F as follows.

$$\begin{aligned} c(\mathbf{w}, y) &= \min_{\mathbf{x}\in\mathbb{R}^n_+} \mathbf{w}\cdot\mathbf{x} \quad \text{s.t.} \quad f(g(\mathbf{x})) \geq y \\ &= \min_{\mathbf{x}\in\mathbb{R}^n_+} \mathbf{w}\cdot\mathbf{x} \quad \text{s.t.} \quad f(g(t\mathbf{x})) \geq 1 \\ &= \frac{1}{t}\min_{\mathbf{x}\in\mathbb{R}^n_+} \mathbf{w}\cdot t\mathbf{x} \quad \text{s.t.} \quad f(g(t\mathbf{x})) \geq 1 \\ &= \frac{1}{t}\min_{\mathbf{z}\in\mathbb{R}^n_+} \mathbf{w}\cdot\mathbf{z} \quad \text{s.t.} \quad f(g(\mathbf{z})) \geq 1 \\ &= \frac{f^{-1}(y)}{f^{-1}(1)}c(\mathbf{w}, 1), \end{aligned}$$

where in the second to last line we let $\mathbf{z} \equiv t\mathbf{x}$.

Because f strictly increasing implies that f^{-1} is as well, the desired result holds for all $y > 0$. To see that it also holds for $y = 0$, recall that $c(\mathbf{w}, 0) = 0$, and note that $g(\mathbf{0}) = 0$, where the first equality follows from $F(\mathbf{0}) = 0$, and the second from the linear homogeneity of g. ∎

The general form of the cost function that we have been considering until now is most properly viewed as giving the firm's *long-run* costs. This is because we have supposed throughout that in choosing its production plan to minimise cost, the firm may freely choose the amount of *every* input it uses. In the short run, the firm does not have this luxury. It must usually contend with the fact that it has made fixed commitments, say, in leasing a plant of a particular size or machines of a particular type. When the firm is 'stuck' with fixed amounts of certain inputs in the short run, rather than being free to choose those inputs as optimally as it can in the long run, we should expect its costs in the short run to differ from its costs in the long run. To examine the relation between these two types of cost, let us begin by defining the firm's *short-run*, or *restricted*, cost function.

DEFINITION 3.6 ***The Short-Run, or Restricted, Cost Function***

Let the production function be $f(\mathbf{z})$, where $\mathbf{z} \equiv (\mathbf{x}, \bar{\mathbf{x}})$. Suppose that $\mathbf{x}$ is a subvector of variable inputs and $\bar{\mathbf{x}}$ is a subvector of fixed inputs. Let $\mathbf{w}$ and $\bar{\mathbf{w}}$ be the associated input prices for the variable and fixed inputs, respectively. The short-run, or restricted, total cost function is defined as

$$sc(\mathbf{w}, \bar{\mathbf{w}}, y; \bar{\mathbf{x}}) \equiv \min_{\mathbf{x}} \ \mathbf{w} \cdot \mathbf{x} + \bar{\mathbf{w}} \cdot \bar{\mathbf{x}} \qquad s.t. \qquad f(\mathbf{x}, \bar{\mathbf{x}}) \geq y.$$

If $\mathbf{x}(\mathbf{w}, \bar{\mathbf{w}}, y; \bar{\mathbf{x}})$ solves this minimisation problem, then

$$sc(\mathbf{w}, \bar{\mathbf{w}}, y; \bar{\mathbf{x}}) = \mathbf{w} \cdot \mathbf{x}(\mathbf{w}, \bar{\mathbf{w}}, y; \bar{\mathbf{x}}) + \bar{\mathbf{w}} \cdot \bar{\mathbf{x}}.$$

The optimised cost of the variable inputs, $\mathbf{w} \cdot \mathbf{x}(\mathbf{w}, \bar{\mathbf{w}}, y; \bar{\mathbf{x}})$, is called **total variable cost**. *The cost of the fixed inputs, $\bar{\mathbf{w}} \cdot \bar{\mathbf{x}}$, is called* **total fixed cost**.

Study the definition of short-run costs carefully. Notice it differs from the definition of generalised or long-run costs only in that the fixed inputs enter as parameters rather than as choice variables. It should be clear therefore that for a given level of output, long-run costs, where the firm is free to choose *all* inputs optimally, can never be greater than short-run costs, where the firm may choose some but not all inputs optimally.

This point is illustrated in Fig. 3.5 using isoquants and isocost curves. For simplicity we suppose that $w_1 = 1$, so that the horizontal intercepts measure the indicated costs, and the unnecessary parameters of the cost functions have been suppressed. If in the short run, the firm is stuck with $\bar{x}_2$ units of the fixed input, it must use input combinations A, C, and E, to produce output levels y^1, y^2, and y^3, and incur short-run costs of $sc(y^1)$, $sc(y^2)$, and $sc(y^3)$, respectively. In the long run, when the firm is free to choose

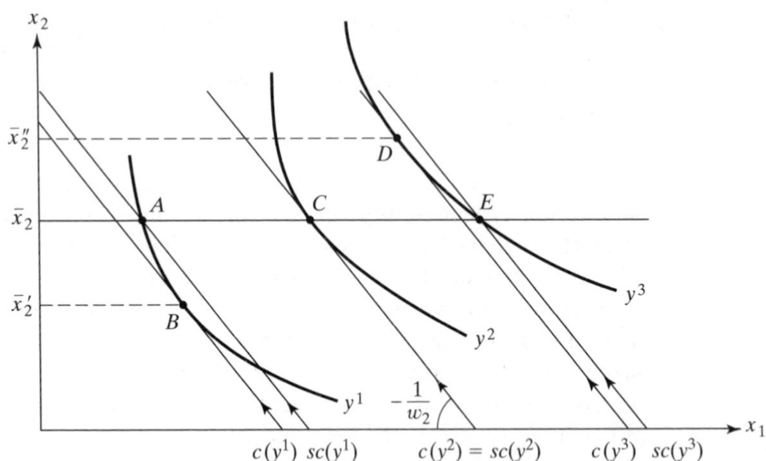

Figure 3.5. $sc(\mathbf{w}, \bar{\mathbf{w}}, y; \bar{\mathbf{x}}) \geq c(\mathbf{w}, \bar{\mathbf{w}}, y)$ for all output levels y.

both inputs optimally, it will use input combinations B, C, and D, and be able to achieve long-run costs of $c(y^1)$, $c(y^2)$, and $c(y^3)$, respectively. Notice that $sc(y^1)$ and $sc(y^3)$ are strictly greater than $c(y^1)$ and $c(y^3)$, respectively, and $sc(y^2) = c(y^2)$.

Look again at Fig. 3.5. Is the coincidence of long-run and short-run costs at output y^2 really a coincidence? No, not really. Why are the two costs equal there? A quick glance at the figure is enough to see it is because $\bar{x}_2$ units are exactly the amount of x_2 the firm would *choose* to use in the long run to produce y^1 at the prevailing input prices – that $\bar{x}_2$ units is, in effect, the cost-minimising amount of the fixed input to produce y^1. Thus, there can be no difference between long-run and short-run costs at that level of output. Notice further that there is nothing peculiar about this relationship of $\bar{x}_2$ and y^2. Long-run and short-run costs of y^1 would coincide if the firm were stuck with $\bar{x}_2'$ units of the fixed input, and long-run and short-run costs of y^3 would coincide if it were stuck with $\bar{x}_2''$ units of the fixed input. Each different level of the fixed input would give rise to a different short-run cost function, yet in each case, short-run and long-run costs would coincide for some particular level of output.

To explore this relationship a bit further, let $\bar{\mathbf{x}}(y)$ denote the optimal *choice* of the fixed inputs to minimise short-run cost of output y at the given input prices. Then we have argued that

$$c(\mathbf{w}, \bar{\mathbf{w}}, y) \equiv sc(\mathbf{w}, \bar{\mathbf{w}}, y; \bar{\mathbf{x}}(y)) \tag{3.3}$$

must hold for any y. Further, because we have chosen the fixed inputs to minimise short-run costs, the optimal amounts $\bar{\mathbf{x}}(y)$ must satisfy (identically) the first-order conditions for a minimum:

$$\frac{\partial sc(\mathbf{w}, \bar{\mathbf{w}}, y; \bar{\mathbf{x}}(y))}{\partial \bar{x}_i} \equiv 0 \tag{3.4}$$

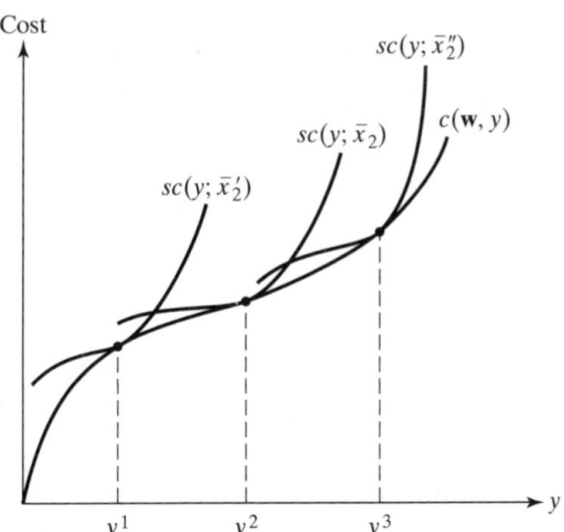

Figure 3.6. Long-run total cost is the envelope of short-run total cost.

for all fixed inputs i. Now differentiate the identity (3.3) and use (3.4) to see that

$$\frac{dc(\mathbf{w}, \bar{\mathbf{w}}, y)}{dy} = \frac{\partial sc(\mathbf{w}, \bar{\mathbf{w}}, y; \bar{\mathbf{x}}(y))}{\partial y} + \underbrace{\sum_i \frac{\partial sc(\mathbf{w}, \bar{\mathbf{w}}, y; \bar{\mathbf{x}}(y))}{\partial \bar{x}_i} \frac{\partial \bar{x}_i(y)}{\partial y}}_{=0}$$

$$= \frac{\partial sc(\mathbf{w}, \bar{\mathbf{w}}, y; \bar{\mathbf{x}}(y))}{\partial y}. \tag{3.5}$$

Let us tie the pieces together and see what we have managed to show. First, the short-run cost-minimisation problem involves more constraints on the firm than the long-run problem, so we know that $sc(\mathbf{w}, \bar{\mathbf{w}}, y; \bar{\mathbf{x}}) \geq c(\mathbf{w}, \bar{\mathbf{w}}, y)$ for all levels of output and levels of the fixed inputs. Second, for every level of output, (3.3) tells us that short-run and long-run costs will coincide for some short-run cost function associated with some level of the fixed inputs. Finally, (3.5) tells us that the *slope* of this short-run cost function will be equal to the slope of the long-run cost function in the cost–output plane. (Indeed, we could have derived this directly by appealing to Theorem A2.22, the Envelope theorem.) Now, if two functions take the same value at the same point in the plane, and if their slopes are equal, then they are tangent. This, then, establishes a familiar proposition from intermediate theory: the long-run total cost curve is the lower *envelope* of the entire family of short-run total cost curves! This is illustrated in Fig. 3.6.

3.4 Duality in Production

Given the obvious structural similarity between the firm's cost-minimisation problem and the individual's expenditure-minimisation problem, it should come as no surprise that there is a duality between production and cost just as there is between utility and expenditure.

The principles are identical. If we begin with a production function and derive its cost function, we can take that cost function and use it to generate a production function. If the original production function is quasiconcave, the derived production function will be identical to it. If the original production function is not quasiconcave, the derived production function is a 'concavication' of it. Moreover, any function with all the properties of a cost function generates some production function for which it is the cost function.

This last fact marks one of the most significant developments in modern theory and has had important implications for applied work. Applied researchers need no longer begin their study of the firm with detailed knowledge of the technology and with access to relatively obscure engineering data. Instead, they can estimate the firm's cost function by employing observable market input prices and levels of output. They can then 'recover' the underlying production function from the estimated cost function.

Again, we can make good use of the equivalence between cost functions and expenditure functions by stating the following theorem, which combines the analogues of Theorems 2.1 and 2.2, and whose proof follows from theirs.

THEOREM 3.5 ***Recovering a Production Function from a Cost Function***

Let $c\colon \mathbb{R}^n_{++} \times \mathbb{R}_+ \to \mathbb{R}_+$ *satisfy properties 1 to 7 of a cost function given in Theorem 3.2. Then the function* $f\colon \mathbb{R}^n_+ \to \mathbb{R}_+$ *defined by*

$$f(\mathbf{x}) \equiv \max\{y \geq 0 \mid \mathbf{w} \cdot \mathbf{x} \geq c(\mathbf{w}, y), \forall\, \mathbf{w} \gg \mathbf{0}\}$$

is increasing, unbounded above, and quasiconcave. Moreover, the cost function generated by f *is* c.

Finally, we can also state an integrability-type theorem for input demand. The basic question here is this: if $\mathbf{x}(\mathbf{w}, y)$ summarises the conditional input demand behaviour of some firm, under what conditions can we conclude that this behaviour is consistent with the hypothesis that each level of output produced by the firm was produced at minimum cost?

As in the case of demand, the answer will depend on being able to recover a cost function that generates the given input demands. That is, those demands will be consistent with cost minimisation at each output level if and only if there is a cost function c satisfying

$$\frac{\partial c(\mathbf{w}, y)}{\partial w_i} = x_i(\mathbf{w}, y), \quad i = 1, \ldots, n.$$

The following result should come as no surprise, and you are invited to convince yourself of it by mimicking the sketched proof of the integrability theorem in the case of consumer demand.

THEOREM 3.6 ***Integrability for Cost Functions***

A continuously differentiable function $\mathbf{x}(\mathbf{w}, y)$ *mapping* $\mathbb{R}^n_{++} \times \mathbb{R}_+$ *into* $\mathbb{R}^n_+$ *is the conditional input demand function generated by some strictly increasing, quasiconcave production function if and only if it is homogeneous of degree zero in* $\mathbf{w}$, *its substitution matrix, whose ijth entry is* $\partial x_i(\mathbf{w}, y)/\partial w_j$, *is symmetric and negative semidefinite, and* $\mathbf{w} \cdot \mathbf{x}(\mathbf{w}, y)$ *is strictly increasing in* y.

3.5 THE COMPETITIVE FIRM

In this section, we examine behaviour when the firm is both a perfect competitor on input markets *and* a perfect competitor on its output market. It is a perfect competitor on output markets if it believes the amount it produces and sells will have no effect on prevailing market prices. The competitive firm sees the market price for its product, assumes it will remain the same regardless of how much or how little it sells, and makes its plans accordingly. Such a firm is thus a **price taker** on both output and input markets.

One way to interpret the fact that the firm takes prices as given is to suppose that the firm has a choice regarding the price at which it sells its output and the prices at which it hires its inputs. If it attempts to sell its output at a price that is above the prevailing one, then it will make no sales, because in a competitive output market, consumers are perfectly informed about the lower price of the identical product elsewhere. On the other hand, the firm can sell all it desires at the prevailing price, so it has no incentive to charge any less. Consequently, it is always best for the firm to choose the price of its output equal to that price prevailing in the market. Thus, the firm *acts as if* it takes its output price as given. Similarly, the firm could not reduce the wages paid to the inputs below their prevailing rates, because in a competitive input market, the owners of those inputs then would sell their input services elsewhere, at the higher prevailing rate. And because once again the firm has no incentive to pay its inputs more than the prevailing rate, it will optimally choose to pay them exactly that rate.

While the assumption of price-taking behaviour and the conditions leading to it are extreme, they provide a tractable model of the firm that is capable of yielding important insights. The competitive firm therefore merits our careful study.

3.5.1 PROFIT MAXIMISATION

Profit is the difference between revenue from selling output and the cost of acquiring the factors necessary to produce it. The competitive firm can sell each unit of output at the market price, p. Its revenues are therefore a simple function of output, $R(y) = py$. Suppose the firm is considering output level y^0. If $\mathbf{x}^0$ is a feasible vector of inputs to produce y^0, and if $\mathbf{w}$ is the vector of factor prices, the cost of using $\mathbf{x}^0$ to produce y is simply $\mathbf{w} \cdot \mathbf{x}^0$. This plan would therefore yield the firm profits of $py^0 - \mathbf{w} \cdot \mathbf{x}^0$. There are two things worth noting here. First, output y^0 may not be the best level of output for the firm to produce. Second, even if it were the best level of output, input levels $\mathbf{x}^0$ may not be the best way to produce it. The firm therefore must make some decisions. It must decide both what level of output to produce and how much of which factors to use to produce it.

As usual, we suppose the overriding objective is to maximise profits. The firm therefore will choose that level of output and that combination of factors that solve the following problem:

$$\max_{(\mathbf{x},y)\geq\mathbf{0}} \; py - \mathbf{w}\cdot\mathbf{x} \qquad \text{s.t.} \qquad f(\mathbf{x}) \geq y, \tag{3.6}$$

where $f(\mathbf{x})$ is a production function satisfying Assumption 3.1. The solutions to this problem tell us how much output the firm will sell and how much of which inputs it will buy.

Once again, however, we may replace the inequality in the constraint by an equality, because the production function is strictly increasing. Consequently, because $y = f(\mathbf{x})$, we may rewrite the maximisation problem in terms of a choice over the input vector alone as

$$\max_{\mathbf{x}\in\mathbb{R}^n_+} \; pf(\mathbf{x}) - \mathbf{w}\cdot\mathbf{x}. \tag{3.7}$$

Let us assume that this profit-maximisation problem has an interior solution at the input vector $\mathbf{x}^* \gg 0$. [Hence, the profit-maximising amount of output produced is $y^* = f(\mathbf{x}^*)$.] Then the first-order conditions require that the gradient of the maximand be zero because there are no constraints. That is,

$$p\frac{\partial f(\mathbf{x}^*)}{\partial x_i} = w_i, \qquad \text{for every } i = 1, \ldots, n.$$

The term on the left-hand side, the product of the output price with the marginal product of input i, is often referred to as the **marginal revenue product** of input i. It gives the rate at which revenue increases per additional unit of input i employed. At the optimum, this must equal the cost per unit of input i, namely, w_i.

Assuming further that all the w_i are positive, we may use the previous first-order conditions to yield the following equality between ratios:

$$\frac{\partial f(\mathbf{x}^*)/\partial x_i}{\partial f(\mathbf{x}^*)/\partial x_j} = \frac{w_i}{w_j}, \qquad \text{for all } i, j,$$

or that the MRTS between any two inputs is equated to the ratio of their prices. This is precisely the same as the necessary condition for cost-minimising input choice we obtained in (3.2).

Indeed, it is possible to recast the firm's profit-maximisation problem in a manner that emphasises the necessity of cost minimisation. Instead of thinking about maximising profits in one step as was done above, consider the following two-step procedure. First, calculate for each possible level of output the (least) cost of producing it. Then choose that output that maximises the difference between the revenues it generates and its cost.

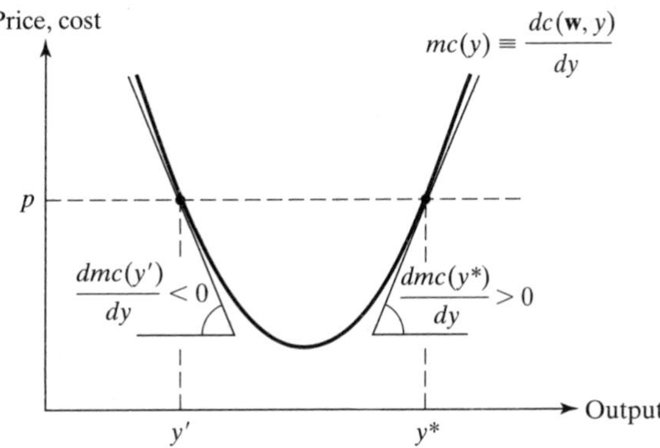

Figure 3.7. Output choice for the competitive firm. Profits are maximised at y^*, where price equals marginal cost, and marginal cost is non-decreasing.

The first step in this procedure is a familiar one. The least cost of producing y units of output is given by the cost function, $c(\mathbf{w}, y)$. The second step then amounts to solving the following maximisation problem:

$$\max_{y \geq 0} \; py - c(\mathbf{w}, y). \tag{3.8}$$

In Exercise 3.51, you are asked to verify that (3.7) and (3.8) are in fact equivalent.

If $y^* > 0$ is the optimal output, it therefore satisfies the first-order condition,

$$p - \frac{dc(\mathbf{w}, y^*)}{dy} = 0,$$

or output is chosen so that price equals marginal cost. Second-order conditions require that marginal cost be non-decreasing at the optimum, or that $d^2c(y^*)/dy^2 \geq 0$. Output choice is illustrated in Fig. 3.7.

3.5.2 THE PROFIT FUNCTION

When f satisfies Assumption 3.1 and is in addition strictly concave, solutions to the maximisation problem (3.6) – when they exist – will be unique for each price vector $(p, \mathbf{w})$. The optimal choice of output, $y^* \equiv y(p, \mathbf{w})$, is called the firm's **output supply function**, and the optimal choice of inputs, $\mathbf{x}^* \equiv \mathbf{x}(p, \mathbf{w})$, gives the vector of firm **input demand functions**. The latter are full-fledged demand functions because, unlike the conditional input demands that depend partly on output, these input demands achieve the ultimate objective of the firm; they maximise the firm's profit. The *profit function*, defined in what follows, is a useful tool for studying these supply and demand functions.

DEFINITION 3.7 ***The Profit Function***

The firm's profit function depends only on input and output prices and is defined as the maximum-value function,

$$\pi(p, \mathbf{w}) \equiv \max_{(\mathbf{x},y)\geq \mathbf{0}} py - \mathbf{w}\cdot\mathbf{x} \quad \text{s.t.} \quad f(\mathbf{x}) \geq y.$$

The usefulness of the profit function depends on certain preconditions being fulfilled. Not the least among these is that a maximum of profits actually exists. This is not as nitpicky as it may sound. To see this, let the technology exhibit increasing returns and suppose that $\mathbf{x}'$ and $y' = f(\mathbf{x}')$ maximise profits at p and $\mathbf{w}$. With increasing returns,

$$f(t\mathbf{x}') > tf(\mathbf{x}') \quad \text{for all} \quad t > 1.$$

Multiplying by $p > 0$, subtracting $\mathbf{w}\cdot t\mathbf{x}'$ from both sides, rearranging, and using $t > 1$ and the non-negativity of profits gives

$$pf(t\mathbf{x}') - \mathbf{w}\cdot t\mathbf{x}' > pf(\mathbf{x}') - \mathbf{w}\cdot\mathbf{x}' \quad \text{for all} \quad t > 1.$$

This says higher profit can always be had by increasing inputs in proportion $t > 1$ – contradicting our assumption that $\mathbf{x}'$ and $f(\mathbf{x}')$ maximised profit. Notice that in the special case of constant returns, no such problem arises if the maximal level of profit happens to be zero. In that case, though, the *scale* of the firm's operation is indeterminate because $(y', \mathbf{x}')$ and $(ty', t\mathbf{x}')$ give the same level of zero profits for all $t > 0$.

When the profit function is well-defined, it possesses several useful properties. Each will by now seem quite sensible and familiar.

THEOREM 3.7 ***Properties of the Profit Function***

If f satisfies Assumption 3.1, then for $p \geq 0$ and $\mathbf{w} \geq \mathbf{0}$, the profit function $\pi(p, \mathbf{w})$, where well-defined, is continuous and

1. *Increasing in p,*
2. *Decreasing in $\mathbf{w}$,*
3. *Homogeneous of degree one in $(p, \mathbf{w})$,*
4. *Convex in $(p, \mathbf{w})$,*
5. *Differentiable in $(p, \mathbf{w}) \gg \mathbf{0}$. Moreover, under the additional assumption that f is strictly concave (Hotelling's lemma),*

$$\frac{\partial\pi(p, \mathbf{w})}{\partial p} = y(p, \mathbf{w}), \quad \text{and} \quad \frac{-\partial\pi(p, \mathbf{w})}{\partial w_i} = x_i(p, \mathbf{w}), \quad i = 1, 2, \ldots, n.$$

Proof: Proofs of each property follow familiar patterns and so most are left as exercises. Here we just give a quick proof of convexity.

Let y and $\mathbf{x}$ maximise profits at p and $\mathbf{w}$, and let y' and $\mathbf{x}'$ maximise profits at p' and $\mathbf{w}'$. Define $p^t \equiv tp + (1-t)p'$ and $\mathbf{w}^t \equiv t\mathbf{w} + (1-t)\mathbf{w}'$ for $0 \leq t \leq 1$, and let y^* and $\mathbf{x}^*$ maximise profits at p^t and $\mathbf{w}^t$. Then

$$\pi(p, \mathbf{w}) = py - \mathbf{w} \cdot \mathbf{x} \geq py^* - \mathbf{w} \cdot \mathbf{x}^*,$$
$$\pi(p', \mathbf{w}') = p'y' - \mathbf{w}' \cdot \mathbf{x}' \geq p'y^* - \mathbf{w}' \cdot \mathbf{x}^*.$$

So, for $0 \leq t \leq 1$,

$$t\pi(p, \mathbf{w}) + (1-t)\pi(p', \mathbf{w}') \geq (tp + (1-t)p')y^* - (t\mathbf{w} + (1-t)\mathbf{w}') \cdot \mathbf{x}^*$$
$$= \pi(p^t, \mathbf{w}^t),$$

proving convexity. ∎

Note that by Hotelling's lemma, output supply and input demands can be obtained directly by simple differentiation. From this we can deduce restrictions on firm behaviour following from the hypothesis of profit maximisation. These are collected together in the following theorem.

THEOREM 3.8 ***Properties of Output Supply and Input Demand Functions***

Suppose that f is a strictly concave production function satisfying Assumption 3.1 and that its associated profit function, $\pi(\mathbf{p}, y)$, is twice continuously differentiable. Then, for all $p > 0$ and $\mathbf{w} \gg \mathbf{0}$ where it is well defined:

1. *Homogeneity of degree zero:*

$$y(tp, t\mathbf{w}) = y(p, \mathbf{w}) \quad \textit{for all} \quad t > 0,$$
$$x_i(tp, t\mathbf{w}) = x_i(p, \mathbf{w}) \quad \textit{for all} \quad t > 0 \quad \textit{and} \quad i = 1, \ldots, n.$$

2. *Own-price effects:*[3]

$$\frac{\partial y(p, \mathbf{w})}{\partial p} \geq 0,$$
$$\frac{\partial x_i(p, \mathbf{w})}{\partial w_i} \leq 0 \quad \textit{for all} \quad i = 1, \ldots, n.$$

[3] Although this follows from 3, we have stated it explicitly for emphasis.

3. The substitution matrix

$$\begin{pmatrix} \frac{\partial y(p,\mathbf{w})}{\partial p} & \frac{\partial y(p,\mathbf{w})}{\partial w_1} & \cdots & \frac{\partial y(p,\mathbf{w})}{\partial w_n} \\ \frac{-\partial x_1(p,\mathbf{w})}{\partial p} & \frac{-\partial x_1(p,\mathbf{w})}{\partial w_1} & \cdots & \frac{-\partial x_1(p,\mathbf{w})}{\partial w_n} \\ \vdots & \vdots & \ddots & \vdots \\ \frac{-\partial x_n(p,\mathbf{w})}{\partial p} & \frac{-\partial x_n(p,\mathbf{w})}{\partial w_1} & \cdots & \frac{-\partial x_n(p,\mathbf{w})}{\partial w_n} \end{pmatrix}$$

is symmetric and positive semidefinite.

Proof: Homogeneity of output supply and input demand follows from Hotelling's lemma and homogeneity of the profit function. Property 2 says output supply is increasing in product price and input demands are decreasing in their own input price. To see this, invoke Hotelling's lemma and express the supply and demand functions as

$$y(p,\mathbf{w}) = \frac{\partial \pi(p,\mathbf{w})}{\partial p},$$

$$x_i(p,\mathbf{w}) = (-1)\frac{\partial \pi(p,\mathbf{w})}{\partial \mathbf{w}_i}, \quad i = 1,\ldots,n.$$

Because these hold for all p and $\mathbf{w}$, differentiate both sides to obtain

$$\frac{\partial y(p,\mathbf{w})}{\partial p} = \frac{\partial^2 \pi(p,\mathbf{w})}{\partial p^2} \geq 0,$$

$$\frac{\partial x_i(p,\mathbf{w})}{\partial w_i} = (-1)\frac{\partial^2 \pi(p,\mathbf{w})}{\partial w_i^2} \leq 0, \quad i = 1,\ldots,n.$$

Each derivative on the right is a (signed) second-order own partial of $\pi(p,\mathbf{w})$. Because $\pi(p,\mathbf{w})$ is convex in p and $\mathbf{w}$, its second-order own partials are all non-negative, so the indicated signs obtain, proving 2.

It should be clear by now that the substitution matrix in item 3 is equal to the Hessian matrix of second-order partials of the profit function. This must be symmetric by Young's theorem and positive semidefinite by convexity of the profit function. (*Beware:* Note the *sign* of every term involving an input demand function.) ∎

Just as in the case of consumer demand, and conditional input demand, there is an integrability theorem for input demand and output supply. The reader is invited to explore this in an exercise.

EXAMPLE 3.5 Let the production function be the CES form,

$$y = \left(x_1^\rho + x_2^\rho\right)^{\beta/\rho}.$$

In Exercise 3.13, you will be asked to show that, when $\beta < 1$, this function exhibits decreasing returns to scale. Suppose, therefore, that $\beta < 1$ and that $0 \neq \rho < 1$.

Form the Lagrangian for the profit-maximisation problem in (3.6). By assuming an interior solution, the first-order conditions reduce to

$$-w_1 + p\beta\left(x_1^\rho + x_2^\rho\right)^{(\beta-\rho)/\rho} x_1^{\rho-1} = 0, \tag{E.1}$$

$$-w_2 + p\beta\left(x_1^\rho + x_2^\rho\right)^{(\beta-\rho)/\rho} x_2^{\rho-1} = 0, \tag{E.2}$$

$$\left(x_1^\rho + x_2^\rho\right)^{\beta/\rho} - y = 0. \tag{E.3}$$

Taking the ratio of (E.1) to (E.2) gives $x_1 = x_2(w_1/w_2)^{1/(\rho-1)}$. Substituting in (E.3) gives

$$x_i = y^{1/\beta}\left(w_1^{\rho/(\rho-1)} + w_2^{\rho/(\rho-1)}\right)^{-1/\rho} w_i^{1/(\rho-1)}, \qquad i = 1, 2. \tag{E.4}$$

Substituting these into (E.1) and solving for y gives the supply function,

$$y = (p\beta)^{-\beta/(\beta-1)}\left(w_1^{\rho/(\rho-1)} + w_2^{\rho/(\rho-1)}\right)^{\beta(\rho-1)/\rho(\beta-1)}. \tag{E.5}$$

From (E.4) and (E.5), we obtain the input demand functions,

$$x_i = w_i^{1/(\rho-1)}(p\beta)^{-1/(\beta-1)}\left(w_1^{\rho/(\rho-1)} + w_2^{\rho/(\rho-1)}\right)^{(\rho-\beta)/\rho(\beta-1)}, \qquad i = 1, 2. \tag{E.6}$$

To form the profit function, substitute from these last two equations into the objective function to obtain

$$\pi(p, \mathbf{w}) = p^{-1/(\beta-1)}\left(w_1^r + w_2^r\right)^{\beta/r(\beta-1)}\beta^{-\beta/(\beta-1)}(1-\beta), \tag{E.7}$$

where we let $r \equiv \rho/(\rho - 1)$.

Notice that if $\beta = 1$, the production function has constant returns and the profit function is undefined, as we concluded earlier. If $\beta > 1$, and the production function exhibits increasing returns, we could certainly form (E.7) as we have, but what would it give us? If you look closely, and check the second-order conditions, you will find that (E.5) and (E.6) give a local profit *minimum*, not maximum. Maximum profits with increasing returns is similarly undefined. □

The profit function we have defined so far is really best thought of as the *long-run* profit function, because we have supposed the firm is free to choose its output and all input levels as it sees fit. As we did for the cost function, we can construct a *short-run* or *restricted* profit function to describe firm behaviour when some of its inputs are variable and some are fixed.

The restricted profit function can be a powerful tool for several reasons. First, in many applications, it is most reasonable to suppose that at least *some* of the firm's inputs are in fixed supply. Under usual assumptions on technology, existence of these fixed inputs generally eliminates the indeterminacy and unboundedness of maximum firm profits. Finally, most properties of the general profit function with respect to output and input prices are preserved with respect to output price and prices of the *variable* inputs.

THEOREM 3.9 ***The Short-Run, or Restricted, Profit Function***

Suppose that $f\colon \mathbb{R}^n_+ \to \mathbb{R}_+$ is strictly concave and satisfies Assumption 3.1. For $k < n$, let $\bar{\mathbf{x}} \in \mathbb{R}^k_+$ be a subvector of fixed inputs and consider $f(\mathbf{x}, \bar{\mathbf{x}})$ as a function of the subvector of variable inputs $\mathbf{x} \in \mathbb{R}^{n-k}_+$. Let $\mathbf{w}$ and $\bar{\mathbf{w}}$ be the associated input prices for variable and fixed inputs, respectively. The short-run, *or* restricted, *profit function is defined as*

$$\pi(p, \mathbf{w}, \bar{\mathbf{w}}, \bar{\mathbf{x}}) \equiv \max_{y, \mathbf{x}} \; py - \mathbf{w} \cdot \mathbf{x} - \bar{\mathbf{w}} \cdot \bar{\mathbf{x}} \quad \text{s.t.} \quad f(\mathbf{x}, \bar{\mathbf{x}}) \geq y.$$

The solutions $y(p, \mathbf{w}, \bar{\mathbf{w}}, \bar{\mathbf{x}})$ and $\mathbf{x}(p, \mathbf{w}, \bar{\mathbf{w}}, \bar{\mathbf{x}})$ are called the short-run, or restricted, output supply and variable input demand functions, respectively.

For all $p > 0$ and $\mathbf{w} \gg \mathbf{0}$, $\pi(p, \mathbf{w}, \bar{\mathbf{w}}, \bar{\mathbf{x}})$ where well-defined is continuous in p and $\mathbf{w}$, increasing in p, decreasing in $\mathbf{w}$, and convex in $(p, \mathbf{w})$. If $\pi(p, \mathbf{w}, \bar{\mathbf{w}}, \bar{\mathbf{x}})$ is twice continuously differentiable, $y(p, \mathbf{w}, \bar{\mathbf{w}}, \bar{\mathbf{x}})$ and $\mathbf{x}(p, \mathbf{w}, \bar{\mathbf{w}}, \bar{\mathbf{x}})$ possess all three properties listed in Theorem 3.8 with respect to output and variable input prices.

Proof: The properties of $\pi(p, \mathbf{w}, \bar{\mathbf{w}}, \bar{\mathbf{x}})$ can be established simply by mimicking the proof of corresponding properties of $\pi(p, \mathbf{w})$ in Theorem 3.7. The only one there that does not carry over is homogeneity in variable input prices. The properties of short-run supply and demand functions can be established by mimicking the proof of Theorem 3.8, except in the case of homogeneity. To prove that requires a slight modification and is left as an exercise. ∎

EXAMPLE 3.6 Let us derive the short-run profit function for the constant-returns Cobb-Douglas technology. Supposing that x_2 is fixed at $\bar{x}_2$, our problem is to solve:

$$\max_{y, x_1} \; py - w_1 x_1 - \bar{w}_2 \bar{x}_2 \quad \text{s.t.} \quad x_1^{\alpha} \bar{x}_2^{1-\alpha} \geq y,$$

where $0 < \alpha < 1$. Assuming an interior solution, the constraint holds with equality, so we can substitute from the constraint for y in the objective function. The problem reduces to choosing the single variable x_1 to solve:

$$\max_{x_1} \; p x_1^{\alpha} \bar{x}_2^{1-\alpha} - w_1 x_1 - \bar{w}_2 \bar{x}_2. \tag{E.1}$$

The first-order condition on choice of x_1 requires that

$$\alpha p x_1^{\alpha-1} \bar{x}_2^{1-\alpha} - w_1 = 0.$$

Solving for x_1 gives

$$x_1 = p^{1/(1-\alpha)} w_1^{1/(\alpha-1)} \alpha^{1/(1-\alpha)} \bar{x}_2. \tag{E.2}$$

Substituting into (E.1) and simplifying gives the short-run profit function,

$$\pi(p, w_1, \bar{w}_2, \bar{x}_2) = p^{1/(1-\alpha)} w_1^{\alpha/(\alpha-1)} \alpha^{\alpha/(1-\alpha)} (1-\alpha)\bar{x}_2 - \bar{w}_2 \bar{x}_2. \tag{E.3}$$

Notice that because $\alpha < 1$, short-run profits are well-defined even though the production function exhibits (long-run) constant returns to scale.

By Hotelling's lemma, short-run supply can be found by differentiating (E.3) with respect to p:

$$\begin{aligned} y(p, w_1, \bar{w}_2, \bar{x}_2) &= \frac{\partial \pi(p, w_1, \bar{w}_2, \bar{x}_2)}{\partial p} \\ &= p^{\alpha/(1-\alpha)} w_1^{\alpha/(\alpha-1)} \alpha^{\alpha/(1-\alpha)} \bar{x}_2. \end{aligned}$$

We expect that this supply function is upward-sloping. Checking, we find that

$$\frac{\partial y(p, w_1, \bar{w}_2, \bar{x}_2)}{\partial p} = \frac{\alpha}{1-\alpha} p^{(2\alpha-1)/(1-\alpha)} w_1^{\alpha/(\alpha-1)} \alpha^{\alpha/(1-\alpha)} \bar{x}_2 > 0,$$

as expected. □

For one last perspective on the firm's short-run behaviour, let us abstract from input demand behaviour and focus on output supply. We can subsume the input choice problem into the short-run cost function and express short-run profits as

$$\pi(p, \mathbf{w}, \bar{\mathbf{w}}, \bar{\mathbf{x}}) = \max_y py - sc(y, \mathbf{w}, \bar{\mathbf{w}}, \bar{\mathbf{x}}).$$

The first-order condition tells us that for optimal output $y^* > 0$,

$$p = \frac{dsc(y^*)}{dy},$$

or that *price equals (short-run) marginal cost.*

Is 'price equals marginal cost' a foolproof rule for the competitive firm to follow in picking its short-run output? Let us suppose that price equals marginal cost at some $y^1 > 0$. Now the short-run total cost can be expressed as the sum of the total variable cost, $tvc(y)$, and the total fixed cost, tfc, where the former is the optimised cost of variable inputs and the latter the cost of fixed inputs. Ignoring unnecessary parameters, short-run profits can be expressed as

$$\pi^1 \equiv py^1 - tvc(y^1) - tfc.$$

What if π^1 is *negative*? Is it still best for the firm to produce y^1 even though it is making a loss? The preceding first-order condition tells us that *if* the firm is going to produce a positive level of output, then the profit-maximising (or loss-minimising) one would be y^1, where price equals marginal cost. However, the firm always has the option of shutting down and producing nothing. If it produces $y = 0$, it will have no revenues and need to buy no variable inputs, so variable costs are zero. However, the firm must still pay fixed costs, so profit (loss) if it shuts down would be

$$\pi^0 = p \cdot 0 - tvc(0) - tfc = -tfc < 0.$$

Clearly, a profit maximiser will choose between producing $y^1 > 0$ at a loss or 'producing' $y = 0$ at a loss according to which gives greater profit (smaller loss). The firm will produce $y^1 > 0$, therefore, only if $\pi^1 - \pi^0 \geq 0$ or only if

$$py^1 - tvc(y^1) \geq 0,$$

which in turn is equivalent to the requirement

$$p \geq \frac{tvc(y^1)}{y^1} \equiv avc(y^1).$$

We now have a complete description of output choice in the short run. If the firm produces a positive amount of output, then it will produce an amount of output where price equals marginal cost (and marginal cost is non-decreasing) and price is not below the average variable cost at that level of output. If price is less than the average variable cost where price equals marginal cost, the firm will shut down and produce no output.

One final comment on profit functions. Just as with cost functions, there is a full set of duality relations between profit functions and production functions. In both its long-run and short-run forms, every function with the required properties is the profit function for some production function with the usual properties. The analyst may choose therefore to begin with either a specification of the firm's technology or with a specification of the relevant profit function. See Diewert (1974) for details and Exercise 3.53 for an integrability result.

3.6 EXERCISES

3.1 The **elasticity of average product** is defined as $(\partial AP_i(\mathbf{x})/\partial x_i)(x_i/AP_i(\mathbf{x}))$. Show that this is equal to $\mu_i(\mathbf{x}) - 1$. Show that average product is increasing, constant, or decreasing as marginal product exceeds, is equal to, or is less than average product.

3.2 Let $y = f(x_1, x_2)$ be a constant returns-to-scale production function. Show that if the average product of x_1 is rising, the marginal product of x_2 is negative.

3.3 Prove that when the production function is homogeneous of degree one, it may be written as the sum $f(\mathbf{x}) = \sum_{i=1}^{n} MP_i(\mathbf{x})x_i$, where $MP_i(\mathbf{x})$ is the marginal product of input i.

3.4 Suppose the production function $F(\mathbf{x})$ is homothetic so that $F(\mathbf{x}) = f(g(\mathbf{x}))$ for some strictly increasing function f and some linear homogeneous function g. Take any point $\mathbf{x}^0$ on the unit isoquant so that $F(\mathbf{x}^0) = 1$. Let $\mathbf{x}^1$ be any point on the ray through $\mathbf{x}^0$ and suppose that $F(\mathbf{x}^1) = y$ so that $\mathbf{x}^1$ is on the y-level isoquant. Show that $\mathbf{x}^1 = t^*\mathbf{x}^0$, where $t^* = f^{-1}(y)/f^{-1}(1)$.

3.5 Suppose that F is a homothetic function so that it can be written as $F(\mathbf{x}) = f(g(\mathbf{x}))$, where f is strictly increasing, and g is homogeneous of degree one. Show that if the image of F is all of $\mathbb{R}_+, f^{-1}(y) > 0$ for all $y > 0$.

3.6 Let $f(x_1, x_2)$ be a production function satisfying Assumption 3.1, and suppose it is homogeneous of degree one. Show that the isoquants of f are *radially parallel*, with equal slope at all points along any given ray from the origin. Use this to demonstrate that the marginal rate of technical substitution depends only on input proportions. Further, show that MP_1 is non-decreasing and MP_2 is non-increasing in input proportions, $R \equiv x_2/x_1$. Show that the same is true when the production function is *homothetic*.

3.7 Goldman and Uzawa (1964) have shown that the production function is weakly separable with respect to the partition $\{N_1, \ldots, N_S\}$ if and only if it can be written in the form

$$f(\mathbf{x}) = g\left(f^1\left(\mathbf{x}^{(1)}\right), \ldots, f^S\left(\mathbf{x}^{(S)}\right)\right),$$

where g is some function of S variables, and, for each $i, f^i(\mathbf{x}^{(i)})$ is a function of the subvector $\mathbf{x}^{(i)}$ of inputs from group i alone. They have also shown that the production function will be strongly separable if and only if it is of the form

$$f(\mathbf{x}) = G\left(f^1\left(\mathbf{x}^{(1)}\right) + \cdots + f^S\left(\mathbf{x}^{(S)}\right)\right),$$

where G is a strictly increasing function of one variable, and the same conditions on the subfunctions and subvectors apply. Verify their results by showing that each is separable as they claim.

3.8 (a) Letting $f_i(\mathbf{x}) = \partial f(\mathbf{x})/\partial x_i$, show that,

$$\sigma_{ij}(\mathbf{x}) \equiv -\frac{x_i f_i(\mathbf{x}) + x_j f_j(\mathbf{x})}{f_j^2(\mathbf{x})f_{ii}(\mathbf{x}) + 2f_i(\mathbf{x})f_j(\mathbf{x})f_{ij}(\mathbf{x}) + f_i^2(\mathbf{x})f_{jj}(\mathbf{x})} \frac{f_i(\mathbf{x})f_j(\mathbf{x})}{x_i x_j}.$$

(b) Using the formula in (a), show that $\sigma_{ij}(\mathbf{x}) \geq 0$ whenever f is increasing and concave. (The elasticity of substitution is non-negative when f is merely quasiconcave but you need not show this.)

3.9 Suppose that the production function $f\colon \mathbb{R}^n_+ \to \mathbb{R}_+$ satisfies Assumption 3.1 and is twice continuously differentiable. Further, suppose that $\text{MRTS}_{ij}(\mathbf{x})$ depends only upon the ratio x_i/x_j and is independent of x_k for all k distinct from i and j. For every vector of input prices $\mathbf{w} \in \mathbb{R}^n_{++}$, suppose that the input vector $\zeta(\mathbf{w}) \in \mathbb{R}^n_{++}$ minimises the cost of producing $f(\zeta(\mathbf{w}))$ units of output. Prove that if $\mathbf{x}^0 = \zeta(\mathbf{w}^0)$, then

$$\sigma_{ij}(\mathbf{x}^0) = \left.\frac{d \ln \zeta_j(\mathbf{w})/\zeta_i(\mathbf{w})}{d \ln w_i/w_j}\right|_{\mathbf{w}=\mathbf{w}^0},$$

where you must show that the right-hand side is well-defined by showing that $\zeta_j(\mathbf{w})/\zeta_i(\mathbf{w})$ depends only on w_j/w_i and is independent of w_k for $k \neq i, j$. The above formula for the firm's elasticity of substitution is useful in empirical applications because the right-hand side can be computed from data on input prices and quantities, alone, without any direct information on the firm's production technology. Because only cost-minimisation is assumed, the firm need not be a perfect competitor in its output market since even a monopolist seeks to minimise the cost of producing output. (That is, when $\mathbf{w}$ is the observed vector of input prices and $\mathbf{x}$ is the observed vector of input demands, the above formula assumes that $\mathbf{x}$ minimises the cost of producing $y = f(\mathbf{x})$ units of output – a necessary condition for profit maximisation.)

3.10 A *Leontief* production function has the form

$$y = \min\{\alpha x_1, \beta x_2\}$$

for $\alpha > 0$ and $\beta > 0$. Carefully sketch the isoquant map for this technology and verify that the elasticity of substitution $\sigma = 0$, where defined.

3.11 Calculate σ for the Cobb-Douglas production function $y = Ax_1^{\alpha}x_2^{\beta}$, where $A > 0$, $\alpha > 0$, and $\beta > 0$.

3.12 The CMS (constant marginal shares) production function is the form $y = Ax_1^{\alpha}x_2^{1-\alpha} - mx_2$. Calculate σ for this function and show that, for $m \neq 0$ and $\alpha \neq 1$, AP_2 rises as $\sigma \to 1$. Under what conditions does this function reduce to a linear production function?

3.13 A generalisation of the CES production function is given by

$$y = A\left(\alpha_0 + \sum_{i=1}^{n} \alpha_i x_i^{\rho}\right)^{\beta/\rho}$$

for $A > 0$, $\alpha_0 \geq 0$, $\alpha_i \geq 0$, and $0 \neq \rho < 1$. Calculate σ_{ij} for this function. Show that when $\alpha_0 = 0$, the elasticity of scale is measured by the parameter β.

3.14 Calculate the elasticity of substitution for the production function in Example 3.2.

3.15 Show that the elasticity of substitution for any homothetic production function is equal to the elasticity of substitution for its linear homogeneous part alone.

3.16 Let

$$y = \left(\sum_{i=1}^{n} \alpha_i x_i^{\rho}\right)^{1/\rho}, \quad \text{where} \quad \sum_{i=1}^{n} \alpha_i = 1 \quad \text{and} \quad 0 \neq \rho < 1.$$

Verify that $\sigma_{ij} = 1/(1-\rho)$ for all $i \neq j$.

3.17 For the CES production function in the preceding exercise, prove the following claims made in the text.

(a) $\lim_{\rho \to 0} y = \prod_{i=1}^{n} x_i^{\alpha_i}$.

(b) $\lim_{\rho \to -\infty} y = \min\{x_1, \ldots, x_n\}$.

3.18 Suppose that f satisfies Assumption 3.1.

(a) Show that the minimisation problem (3.1) has a solution, $\mathbf{x}^*$, for all $(\mathbf{w}, y) \geq \mathbf{0}$ such that $y \in f(\mathbb{R}^n_+)$.

(b) Show that the solution to (3.1) is unique if, in addition, $\mathbf{w} \gg \mathbf{0}$.

3.19 Prove parts 1 through 4 in Theorem 3.2. Feel free to assume that $c(\mathbf{w}, y)$ is differentiable.

3.20 Prove parts 1 through 4 in Theorem 3.2. *Do not* feel free to assume that $c(\mathbf{w}, y)$ is differentiable.

3.21 What restrictions must there be on the parameters of the Cobb-Douglas form in Example 3.4 in order that it be a legitimate cost function?

3.22 Prove the rest of Theorem 3.3.

3.23 A real-valued function is called **superadditive** if $f(\mathbf{z}^1 + \mathbf{z}^2) \geq f(\mathbf{z}^1) + f(\mathbf{z}^2)$. Show that every cost function is superadditive in input prices. Use this to prove that the cost function is non-decreasing in input prices without requiring it to be differentiable.

3.24 *True or false?* 'If $\lambda(\mathbf{w}, y)$ is the Lagrangian multiplier associated with the firm's cost-minimisation problem, then $mc(\mathbf{w}, y) = \lambda(\mathbf{w}, y)$.'

3.25 Suppose the firm produces output $y > 0$. Show that $mc(y) = w_i/MP_i$ for every input i the firm uses, and $mc(y) \leq w_j/MP_j$ for every input j the firm does not use.

3.26 Calculate the cost function and conditional input demands for the Leontief production function in Exercise 3.8.

3.27 Prove Theorem 3.4, parts 1(b), 2(a), and 2(b).

3.28 A firm's technology possesses all the usual properties. It produces output using three inputs, with conditional input demands $x_i(w_1, w_2, w_3, y)$, $i = 1, 2, 3$. Some of the following observations are consistent with cost minimisation and some are not. If an observation is inconsistent, explain why. If it is consistent, give an example of a cost or production function that would produce such behaviour.

(a) $\partial x_2/\partial w_1 > 0$ and $\partial x_3/\partial w_1 > 0$.

(b) $\partial x_2/\partial w_1 > 0$ and $\partial x_3/\partial w_1 < 0$.

(c) $\partial x_1/\partial y < 0$ and $\partial x_2/\partial y < 0$ and $\partial x_3/\partial y < 0$.

(d) $\partial x_1/\partial y = 0$.

(e) $\partial(x_1/x_2)/\partial w_3 = 0$.

3.29 In Fig. 3.8, the cost functions of firms A and B are graphed against the input price w_1 for fixed values of w_2 and y.

(a) At wage rate w_1^0, which firm uses more of input 1? At w_1'? Explain.

(b) Which firm's production function has the higher elasticity of substitution? Explain.

3.30 Firm 1 has cost function $c^1(\mathbf{w}, y)$. Firm 2 has the following cost function. Will the input demand and output supply behaviour of the two firms be identical when

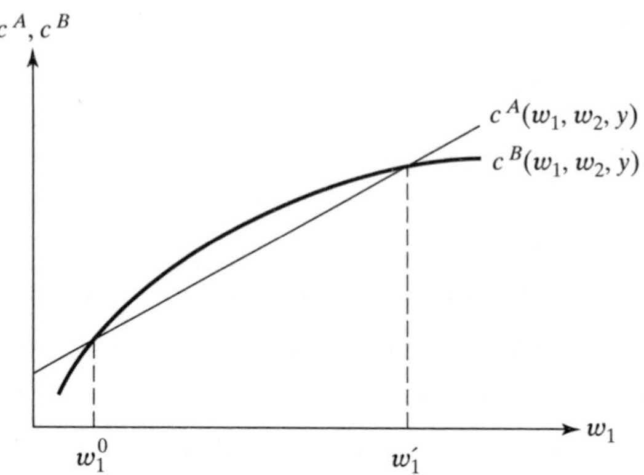

Figure 3.8. Cost functions.

(a) $c^2(\mathbf{w}, y) = (1/2)c^1(2\mathbf{w}, y)$?

(b) $c^2(\mathbf{w}, y) = c^1(\mathbf{w}, 2y)$?

3.31 The **output elasticity of demand for input** x_i is defined as

$$\epsilon_{iy}(w, y) \equiv (\partial x_i(\mathbf{w}, y)/\partial y)(y/x_i(\mathbf{w}, y)).$$

(a) Show that $\epsilon_{iy}(\mathbf{w}, y) = \phi(y)\epsilon_{iy}(\mathbf{w}, 1)$ when the production function is homothetic.

(b) Show that $\epsilon_{iy} = 1$, for $i = 1, \ldots, n$, when the production function has constant returns to scale.

3.32 Show that when average cost is declining, marginal cost must be less than average cost; when average cost is constant, marginal cost must equal average cost; and when average cost is increasing, marginal cost must be greater than average cost.

3.33 Let s_i be the input share for input i. Show that for any cost function, $s_i = \partial \ln[c(\mathbf{w}, y)]/\partial \ln(w_i)$. Verify by checking the Cobb-Douglas cost function.

3.34 It has been shown that the **translog cost function** is a (local) second-order approximation to an arbitrary cost function. It is given implicitly by the linear-in-logs form:

$$\ln(c) = \alpha_0 + \sum_{i=1}^{n} \alpha_i \ln(w_i) + \frac{1}{2}\sum_{i=1}^{n}\sum_{j=1}^{n} \gamma_{ij}\ln(w_i)\ln(w_j) + \ln(y).$$

If $\gamma_{ij} = \gamma_{ji}$ and $\sum_i \gamma_{ij} = 0$, for $i = 1, \ldots, n$, the substitution matrix is symmetric, as required.

(a) What restrictions on the parameters α_i are required to ensure homogeneity?

(b) For what values of the parameters does the translog reduce to the Cobb-Douglas form?

(c) Show that input shares in the translog cost function are linear in the logs of input prices and output.

3.35 Calculate the cost function and the conditional input demands for the *linear production function*, $y = \sum_{i=1}^{n} \alpha_i x_i$.

3.36 Derive the cost function for the two-input, constant-returns, Cobb-Douglas technology. Fix one input and derive the short-run cost function. Show that long-run average and long-run marginal cost are constant and equal. Show that for every level of the fixed input, short-run average cost and long-run average cost are equal at the minimum level of short-run average cost. Illustrate your results in the cost-output plane.

3.37 Prove each of the results you obtained in the preceding exercise for the general case of *any* constant returns-to-scale technology.

3.38 Show that when the production function is homothetic, the proportions in which the firm will combine any given pair of inputs is the same for every level of output.

3.39 Show that when the production function is homothetic, the conditional demand for every input must be non-increasing in its own price.

3.40 If the firm faces an upward-sloping supply curve for one input k, we can write the wage it must pay each unit of the input as $w_k = w_k(x_k)$, where $w_k' > 0$.

(a) Define the firm's cost function in this case and write down the first-order conditions for its optimal choice of each input.

(b) Define the elasticity of supply for input k as $\epsilon_k \equiv (dx_k(w_k)/dw_k)(w_k/x_k)$, and suppose that the firm uses a positive amount of input k in equilibrium. Show that Shephard's lemma applies only if $\epsilon_k \to \infty$.

3.41 Suppose the production function satisfies Assumption 3.1. Prove that the cost function is the linear-in-output form $c(\mathbf{w}, y) = y\phi(\mathbf{w})$ if and only if the production function has constant returns to scale.

3.42 We have seen that every Cobb-Douglas production function, $y = Ax_1^\alpha x_2^{1-\alpha}$, gives rise to a Cobb-Douglas cost function, $c(\mathbf{w}, y) = yAw_1^\alpha w_2^{1-\alpha}$, and every CES production function, $y = A(x_1^\rho + x_2^\rho)^{1/\rho}$, gives rise to a CES cost function, $c(\mathbf{w}, y) = yA(w_1^r + w_2^r)^{1/r}$. For each pair of functions, show that the converse is also true. That is, starting with the respective cost functions, 'work backward' to the underlying production function and show that it is of the indicated form. Justify your approach.

3.43 Show that **long-run average cost**, $lac(y) \equiv c(\mathbf{w}, \bar{\mathbf{w}}, y)/y$, is the lower envelope of **short-run average cost** $sac(y) \equiv sc(\mathbf{w}, \bar{\mathbf{w}}, y; \bar{\mathbf{x}})/y$, in the cost-output plane. Sketch your result in that plane, and be sure to include an accurate demonstration of the necessary relationship that must hold between **long-run marginal cost**, $lmc(y) \equiv dc(\mathbf{w}, \bar{\mathbf{w}}, y)/dy$, and **short-run marginal cost**, $smc(y; \bar{\mathbf{x}}) \equiv dsc(\mathbf{w}, \bar{\mathbf{w}}, y; \bar{\mathbf{x}})/dy$.

3.44 Derive the profit function for a firm with the Cobb-Douglas technology, $y = x_1^\alpha x_2^\beta$. What restrictions on α and β are required to ensure that the profit function is well-defined? Explain.

3.45 Suppose the production function is additively separable so that $f(x_1, x_2) = g(x_1) + h(x_2)$. Find conditions on the functions g and h so that input demands $x_1(p, \mathbf{w})$ and $x_2(p, \mathbf{w})$ are homogeneous of degree $1/2$ in $\mathbf{w}$.

3.46 Verify Theorem 3.7 for the profit function obtained in Example 3.5. Verify Theorem 3.8 for the associated output supply and input demand functions.

3.47 In deriving the firm's short-run supply function in Example 3.6, we ignored the shutdown condition by supposing an interior solution to the firm's profit-maximisation problem. Give a *complete* description of short-run supply behaviour in that Cobb-Douglas case.

3.48 The production function for some good is given by

$$y = x_2\left[\sin\left(\frac{x_1}{x_2} - \frac{\pi}{2}\right) + 1\right]$$

for $0 \leq x_1 \leq 2\pi$ and $0 < x_2 \leq 2\pi$ and $y = 0$ when $x_2 = 0$.

(a) What are the scale properties of this technology?

(b) On the same set of axes, sketch the marginal and average product of x_1 when $x_2 = 1$.

(c) If $w_1 = 1$, $w_2 = 2$, and $x_2 = 1$, derive the short-run cost and profit functions.

3.49 Derive the cost function for the production function in Example 3.5. Then solve $\max_y py - c(\mathbf{w}, y)$ and compare its solution, $y(p, \mathbf{w})$, to the solution in (E.5). Check that $\pi(p, \mathbf{w}) = py(p, \mathbf{w}) - c(\mathbf{w}, y(p, \mathbf{w}))$. Supposing that $\beta > 1$, confirm our conclusion that profits are *minimised* when the first-order conditions are satisfied by showing that marginal cost is decreasing at the solution. Sketch your results.

3.50 Prove that short-run supply and short-run variable input demands are homogeneous of degree zero in p and $\mathbf{w}$.

3.51 Let $c(\mathbf{w}, y)$ be the cost function generated by the production function f and suppose that (1) $\max_{y \geq 0} py - c(\mathbf{w}, y)$ and (2) $\max_{\mathbf{x} \in \mathbb{R}^n_+} pf(\mathbf{x}) - w \cdot \mathbf{x}$ have solutions $y^* \geq 0$ and $\mathbf{x}^* \geq \mathbf{0}$, respectively.

(a) Show that $\hat{y} = f(\mathbf{x}^*)$ solves (1).

(b) Show that if $c(\mathbf{w}, y^*) = \mathbf{w} \cdot \hat{\mathbf{x}}$ and $y^* = f(\hat{\mathbf{x}})$, then $\hat{\mathbf{x}}$ solves (2).

(c) Use parts (a) and (b) to show that $py^* - c(\mathbf{w}, y^*) = pf(\mathbf{x}^*) - \mathbf{w} \cdot \mathbf{x}^*$.

3.52 We can generalise the profit function for a firm producing *many* outputs rather than just one. If the firm produces the output vector $\mathbf{y} = (y_1, \ldots, y_m)$ from inputs $\mathbf{x} = (x_1, \ldots, x_n)$, the relationship between efficient input and output vectors can be written in terms of the *transformation function* as the implicit relation $T(\mathbf{y}, \mathbf{x}) = 0$. If $\mathbf{p}$ is a vector of product prices, the generalised profit function is $\pi(\mathbf{p}, \mathbf{w}) \equiv \max_{\mathbf{y},\mathbf{x}} \mathbf{p} \cdot \mathbf{y} - \mathbf{w} \cdot \mathbf{x}$ s.t. $T(\mathbf{y}, \mathbf{x}) = 0$. Show that this profit function has all the properties listed in Theorem 3.7, and that a generalised version of Hotelling's lemma applies.

3.53 Sketch an argument leading to the following integrability theorem for input demands and output supply of a competitive profit-maximising firm:

> *The continuously differentiable non-negative functions $x_i(p, \mathbf{w})$, $i = 1, \ldots, n$, and $y(p, \mathbf{w})$ defined on $\mathbb{R}^{n+1}_{++}$ are the input demand functions and the output supply function, respectively, generated by some increasing, quasiconcave production function if and only if they are homogeneous of degree zero in $(p, \mathbf{w})$, and their substitution matrix given in property 3 of Theorem 3.8 is symmetric and positive semidefinite.*

In particular, show that if the substitution matrix is symmetric and positive semidefinite, then there is a convex function $\Pi(p, \mathbf{w})$ whose derivatives are $-x_i(p, \mathbf{w})$ and $y(p, \mathbf{w})$. In addition, argue that $\Pi(p, \mathbf{w})$ is homogeneous of degree one in $(p, \mathbf{w})$.

3.54 Consider a firm with the cost function

$$c(w_1, w_2, y) = y^2(w_1 + w_2).$$

(a) On the same diagram, sketch the firm's marginal and average total cost curves and its output supply function.

(b) On a separate diagram, sketch the input demand for input x_1 against its own price w_1.

(c) On both diagrams, illustrate the effects of an increase in the price of input x_2.

3.55 A utility produces electricity to meet the demands of a city. The price it can charge for electricity is fixed and it must meet all demand at that price. It turns out that the amount of electricity demanded is always the same over every 24-hour period, but demand differs from day (6:00 A.M. to 6:00 P.M.) to night (6:00 P.M. to 6:00 A.M.). During the day, 4 units are demanded, whereas during the night only 3 units are demanded. Total output for each 24-hour period is thus always equal to 7 units. The utility produces electricity according to the production function

$$y_i = (KF_i)^{1/2}, \qquad i = \text{day, night},$$

where K is the size of the generating plant, and F_i is tons of fuel. The firm must build a single plant; it cannot change plant size from day to night. If a unit of plant size costs w_k per 24-hour period and a ton of fuel costs w_f, what size plant will the utility build? □

Part II

Markets and Welfare

CHAPTER 4

PARTIAL EQUILIBRIUM

In previous chapters we studied the behaviour of individual consumers and firms, describing optimal behaviour when market prices were fixed and beyond the agent's control. Here we begin to explore the consequences of that behaviour when consumers and firms come together in markets. First, we shall consider price and quantity determination in a single market or group of closely related markets. Then we shall assess those markets from a social point of view. Along the way, we pay special attention to the close relationship between a market's competitive structure and its social 'performance'.

4.1 PERFECT COMPETITION

In perfectly competitive markets, buyers and sellers are sufficiently large in number to ensure that no single one of them, alone, has the power to determine market price. Buyers and sellers are price takers, and each decides on a self-interested course of action in view of individual circumstances and objectives. A buyer's demand for any one good is, as we have seen, the outcome of a larger utility-maximising plan over all goods subject to the budget constraint. Similarly, a seller's supply of that good is the outcome of an overall profit-maximising plan subject to the selling price of that good, technological possibilities and input prices. Equilibrium in a competitive market thus requires the simultaneous compatibility of the disparate and often conflicting self-interested plans of a large number of different agents.

The demand side of a market is made up of all potential buyers of the good, each with their own preferences, consumption set, and income. We let $\mathcal{I} \equiv \{1, \ldots, I\}$ index the set of individual buyers and $q^i(p, \mathbf{p}, y^i)$ be i's non-negative demand for good q as a function of its own price, p, income, y^i, and prices, $\mathbf{p}$, for all other goods. Market demand for q is simply the sum of all buyers' individual demands

$$q^d(p) \equiv \sum_{i \in \mathcal{I}} q^i(p, \mathbf{p}, y^i). \tag{4.1}$$

There are several things worth noting in the definition of market demand. First, $q^d(p)$ gives the total amount of q demanded by all buyers in the market. Second, because each buyer's demand for q depends not only on the price of q, but on the prices of all other goods as well, so, too, does the market demand for q, though we will generally suppress explicit mention of this. Third, whereas a single buyer's demand depends on the level of his own income, market demand depends both on the *aggregate level* of income in the market and on its *distribution* among buyers. Finally, because individual demand is homogeneous of degree zero in all prices and the individual's income, market demand will be homogeneous of degree zero in all prices and the *vector* of buyers' incomes. Although several restrictions on an individual's demand system follow from utility maximisation, homogeneity is the *only* such restriction on the market demand for a single good.

The supply side of the market is made up of all potential sellers of q. However, we sometimes distinguish between firms that are potential sellers in the short run and those that are potential sellers in the long run. Earlier, we defined the short run as that period of time in which at least one input (for example, plant size) is fixed to the firm. Consistent with that definition, in the short-run market period, the number of potential sellers is fixed, finite, and limited to those firms that 'already exist' and are in some sense able to be up and running simply by acquiring the necessary variable inputs. If we let $\mathcal{J} \equiv \{1, \ldots, J\}$ index those firms, the **short-run market supply function** is the sum of individual firm short-run supply functions $q^j(p, \mathbf{w})$:

$$q^s(p) \equiv \sum_{j \in \mathcal{J}} q^j(p, \mathbf{w}). \tag{4.2}$$

Market demand and market supply together determine the price and total quantity traded. We say that a competitive market is in **short-run equilibrium** at price p^* when $q^d(p^*) = q^s(p^*)$. Geometrically, this corresponds to the familiar intersection of market supply and market demand curves drawn in the (p, q) plane. Note that by construction of market demand and market supply, market equilibrium is characterised by some interesting and important features: each price-taking buyer is buying his optimal amount of the good at the prevailing price, and each price-taking firm is selling its profit-maximising output at the same prevailing price. Thus, we have a true equilibrium in the sense that no agent in the market has any incentive to change his behaviour – each is doing the best he can under the circumstances he faces.

EXAMPLE 4.1 Consider a competitive industry composed of J identical firms. Firms produce output according to the Cobb-Douglas technology, $q = x^\alpha k^{1-\alpha}$, where x is some variable input such as labour, k is some input such as plant size, which is fixed in the short run, and $0 < \alpha < 1$. In Example 3.6, we derived the firm's short-run profit and supply functions with this technology. At prices p, w_x, and w_k, maximum profits are

$$\pi^j = p^{1/1-\alpha} w_x^{\alpha/\alpha-1} \alpha^{\alpha/1-\alpha}(1-\alpha)k - w_k k, \tag{E.1}$$

and output supply is

$$q^j = p^{\alpha/1-\alpha} w_x^{\alpha/\alpha-1} \alpha^{\alpha/1-\alpha} k. \tag{E.2}$$

If $\alpha = 1/2$, $w_x = 4$, and $w_k = 1$, then supposing each firm operates a plant of size $k = 1$, firm supply reduces to $q^j = p/8$. The market supply function with $J = 48$ firms will be

$$q^s = 48(p/8) = 6p. \tag{E.3}$$

Let market demand be given by

$$q^d = 294/p. \tag{E.4}$$

We can use (E.1) through (E.4) to solve for the short-run equilibrium price, market quantity, output per firm, and firm profits:

$$\begin{aligned} p^* &= 7, \\ q^* &= 42, \\ q^j &= 7/8, \\ \pi^j &= 2.0625 > 0. \end{aligned}$$

This equilibrium, at both market and individual firm levels, is illustrated in Fig. 4.1. (Note that short-run cost curves for firms with this technology can be derived from Exercise 3.36.) □

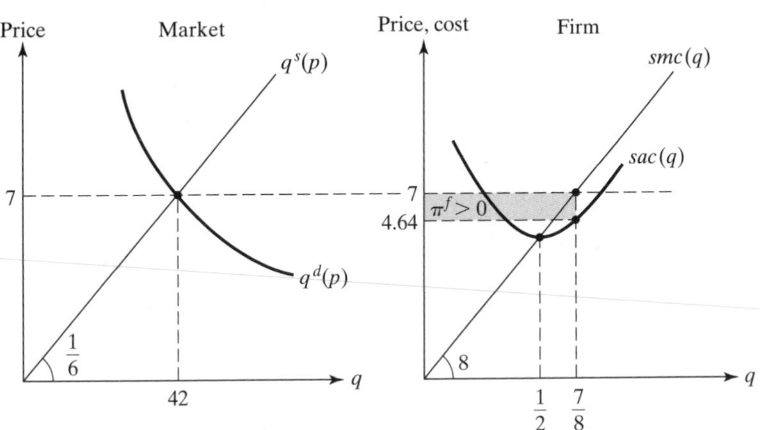

Figure 4.1. Short-run equilibrium in a single market.

In the long run, no inputs are fixed for the firm. Incumbent firms – those already producing – are free to choose optimal levels of all inputs, including, for example, the size of their plant. They are also free to leave the industry entirely. Moreover, in the long run, *new* firms may decide to begin producing the good in question. Thus, in the long run, there are possibilities of **entry** and **exit** of firms. Firms will enter the industry in response to positive long-run economic profits and will exit in response to negative long-run profits (losses).

In a long-run equilibrium, we shall require not only that the market clears but also that no firm has an incentive to enter or exit the industry. Clearly, then, long-run profits must be non-negative; otherwise, firms in the industry will wish to exit. On the other hand, because all firms have free access to one another's technology (in particular, firms currently not producing have access to the technology of every firm that is producing), no firm can be earning positive profits in the long run. Otherwise, firms outside the industry will adopt the technology of the firm earning positive profits and enter the industry themselves.

Thus, *two* conditions characterise long-run equilibrium in a competitive market:

$$
\begin{aligned}
q^d(\hat{p}) &= \sum_{j=1}^{\hat{J}} q^j(\hat{p}), \\
\pi^j(\hat{p}) &= 0, \qquad j = 1, \ldots, \hat{J}.
\end{aligned}
\tag{4.3}
$$

The first condition simply says the market must clear. The second says long-run profits for all firms in the industry must be zero so that no firm wishes to enter or exit the industry.

In contrast to the short run, where the number of firms is given and the market-clearing condition determines the short-run equilibrium price, the number of firms is not given in the long run. In the long run therefore, both the long-run equilibrium price $\hat{p}$ and the long-run equilibrium number of firms $\hat{J}$ must be determined jointly. Any such pair satisfying the market-clearing and zero-profit conditions in (4.3) constitute a long-run market equilibrium.

The next two examples demonstrate that the long-run number of firms is uniquely determined when long-run supply is upward-sloping but not when it is horizontal. On the other hand, because market demand is downward-sloping the long-run equilibrium price is uniquely determined in both cases.

EXAMPLE 4.2 Let inverse market demand be the linear form

$$p = 39 - 0.009q. \tag{E.1}$$

Technology for producing q is identical for all firms, and all firms face identical input prices. The long-run profit function for a representative firm is given by

$$\pi^j(p) = p^2 - 2p - 399, \tag{E.2}$$

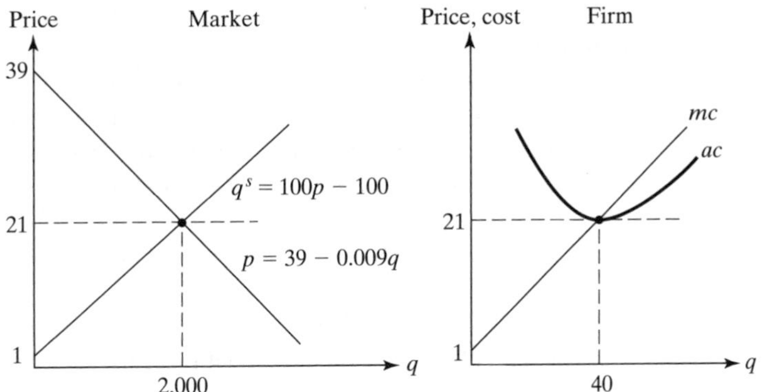

Figure 4.2. Long-run equilibrium in a competitive market.

so that its output supply function is

$$y^j = \frac{d\pi(p)}{dp} = 2p - 2. \tag{E.3}$$

Note that $y^j \geq 0$ requires $p \geq 1$.

In the long run, market-equilibrium price $\hat{p}$ and the equilibrium number of firms $\hat{J}$ must satisfy the two conditions (4.3). Thus, we must have

$$(1000/9)(39 - \hat{p}) = \hat{J}(2\hat{p} - 2),$$
$$\hat{p}^2 - 2\hat{p} - 399 = 0.$$

From the zero-profit condition, we obtain $\hat{p} = 21$. Substituting into the market-clearing condition gives $\hat{J} = 50$. From (E.3), each firm produces an output of 40 units in long-run equilibrium. This market equilibrium is illustrated in Fig. 4.2. □

EXAMPLE 4.3 Let us examine long-run equilibrium in the market of Example 4.1. There, technology was the constant-returns-to-scale form, $q = x^\alpha k^{1-\alpha}$ for x variable and k fixed in the short run. For $\alpha = 1/2$, $w_x = 4$, and $w_k = 1$, the short-run profit and short-run supply functions reduce to

$$\pi^j(p, k) = p^2k/16 - k, \tag{E.1}$$
$$q^j = pk/8. \tag{E.2}$$

With market demand of

$$q^d = 294/p \tag{E.3}$$

and 48 firms in the industry, we obtained a short-run equilibrium price of $p^* = 7$, giving firm profits of $\pi^j = 2.0625 > 0$.

In the long run, firms may enter in response to positive profits and incumbent firms are free to choose their plant size optimally. Market price will be driven to a level where maximum firm profits are zero. From (E.1), we can see that regardless of the firm's chosen plant size, this will occur only when $\hat{p} = 4$ because

$$\pi(\hat{p}, k) = k(\hat{p}^2/16 - 1) = 0 \tag{E.4}$$

for *all* $k > 0$ if and only if $\hat{p} = 4$.

The market-clearing condition with $\hat{J}$ firms, each operating a plant of size $\hat{k}$, requires that $q^d(\hat{p}) = q^s(\hat{p})$, or

$$\frac{294}{4} = \frac{4}{8}\hat{J}\hat{k}.$$

This is turn requires that

$$147 = \hat{J}\hat{k}. \tag{E.5}$$

Because at $\hat{p} = 4$ firm profits are zero regardless of plant size $\hat{k}$, long-run equilibrium is consistent with a wide range of market structures indeed. From (E.4) and (E.5), long-run equilibrium may involve a single firm operating a plant of size $\hat{k} = 147$, two firms each with plants $\hat{k} = 147/2$, three firms with plants $\hat{k} = 147/3$, all the way up to any number J of firms, each with a plant of size $147/J$. This indeterminacy in the long-run equilibrium number of firms is a phenomenon common to *all* constant-returns industries. You are asked to show this in the exercises. □

4.2 Imperfect Competition

Perfect competition occupies one polar extreme on a spectrum of possible market structures ranging from the 'more' to the 'less' competitive. **Pure monopoly**, the least competitive market structure imaginable, is at the opposite extreme. In pure monopoly, there is a single seller of a product for which there are no close substitutes in consumption, and entry into the market is completely blocked by technological, financial, or legal impediments.

The monopolist takes the market demand function as given and chooses price and quantity to maximise profit. Because the highest price the monopolist can charge for any given quantity, q, is inverse demand, $p(q)$, the firm's choice can be reduced to that of choosing q, alone. The firm would then set price equal to $p(q)$.

As a function of q, profit is the difference between revenue, $r(q) = p(q)q$, and cost, $c(q)$. That is, $\Pi(q) \equiv r(q) - c(q)$. If $q^* > 0$ maximises profit, it satisfies the first-order condition $\Pi'(q^*) \equiv r'(q^*) - c'(q^*) = 0$. This, in turn, is the same as the requirement that marginal revenue equal marginal cost:

$$mr(q^*) = mc(q^*). \tag{4.4}$$

Equilibrium price will be $p^* = p(q^*)$, where $p(q)$ is the inverse market demand function.

Let us explore the monopolist's output choice a bit further. Because $r(q) \equiv p(q)q$, differentiating to obtain marginal revenue gives

$$\begin{aligned} mr(q) &= p(q) + q\frac{dp(q)}{dq} \\ &= p(q)\left[1 + \frac{dp(q)}{dq}\frac{q}{p(q)}\right] \\ &= p(q)\left[1 + \frac{1}{\epsilon(q)}\right], \end{aligned} \tag{4.5}$$

where $\epsilon(q) = (dq/dp)(p/q)$ is the elasticity of market demand at output q. We assume that $\epsilon(q)$ is less than zero, i.e., that market demand is negatively sloped. By combining (4.4) and (4.5), q^* will satisfy

$$p(q^*)\left[1 + \frac{1}{\epsilon(q^*)}\right] = mc(q^*) \geq 0 \tag{4.6}$$

because marginal cost is always non-negative. Price is also non-negative, so we must have $|\epsilon(q^*)| \geq 1$. Thus, the monopolist never chooses an output in the *inelastic* range of market demand, and this is illustrated in Fig. 4.3.

Rearranging (4.6), we can obtain an expression for the percentage deviation of price from marginal cost in the monopoly equilibrium:

$$\frac{p(q^*) - mc(q^*)}{p(q^*)} = \frac{1}{|\epsilon(q^*)|}. \tag{4.7}$$

When market demand is less than infinitely elastic, $|\epsilon(q^*)|$ will be finite and the monopolist's price will exceed marginal cost in equilibrium. Moreover, price will exceed marginal cost by a greater amount the more market demand is *inelastic*, other things being equal.

As we have remarked, pure competition and pure monopoly are opposing extreme forms of market structure. Nonetheless, they share one important feature: Neither the pure competitor nor the pure monopolist needs to pay any attention to the actions of other firms in formulating its own profit-maximising plans. The perfect competitor individually cannot affect market price, nor therefore the actions of other competitors, and so only concerns itself with the effects of its own actions on its own profits. The pure monopolist completely

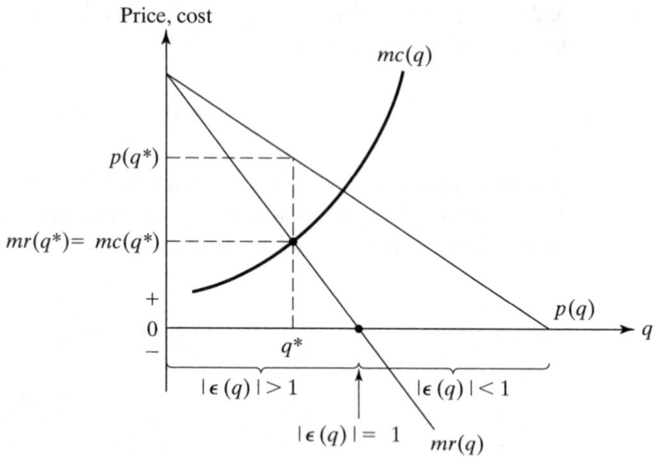

Figure 4.3. Equilibrium in a pure monopoly.

controls market price and output, and need not even be concerned about the possibility of entry because entry is effectively blocked.

Many markets display a blend of monopoly and competition simultaneously. Firms become more *interdependent* the smaller the number of firms in the industry, the easier entry, and the closer the substitute goods available to consumers. When firms perceive their interdependence, they have an incentive to take account of their rivals' actions and to formulate their own plans *strategically*. In Chapter 7, we shall have a great deal more to say about strategic behaviour and how to analyse it, but here we can take a first look at some of the most basic issues involved.

When firms are behaving strategically, one of the first things we need to do is ask ourselves how we should characterise *equilibrium* in situations like this. On the face of it, one might be tempted to reason as follows: because firms are aware of their interdependence, and because the actions of one firm may reduce the profits of others, will they not simply work together or *collude* to extract as much total profit as they can from the market and then divide it between themselves? After all, if they can work together to make the profit 'pie' as big as possible, will they not then be able to divide the pie so that each has at least as big a slice as they could otherwise obtain? Putting the legality of such collusion aside, there is something tempting in the idea of a **collusive equilibrium** such as this. However, there is also a problem.

Let us consider a simple market consisting of J firms, each producing output q^j. Suppose each firm's profit is adversely affected by an increase in the output of any other firm, so that

$$\Pi^j = \Pi^j(q^1, \ldots, q^j, \ldots, q^J) \quad \text{and} \quad \partial\Pi^j/\partial q^k < 0, \quad j \neq k. \tag{4.8}$$

Now suppose firms cooperate to maximise joint profits. If $\bar{\mathbf{q}}$ maximises $\sum_{j=1}^{J} \Pi^j$, it must satisfy the first-order conditions

$$\frac{\partial \Pi^k(\bar{\mathbf{q}})}{\partial q^k} + \sum_{j \neq k} \frac{\partial \Pi^j(\bar{\mathbf{q}})}{\partial q^k} = 0, \qquad k = 1, \ldots, J. \tag{4.9}$$

Note that (4.8) and (4.9) together imply

$$\frac{\partial \Pi^k(\bar{\mathbf{q}})}{\partial q^k} > 0, \qquad k = 1, \ldots, J.$$

Think what this means. Because *each* firm's profit is increasing in its own output at $\bar{\mathbf{q}}$, each can increase its *own* profit by increasing output away from its assignment under $\bar{\mathbf{q}}$ – provided, of course, that everyone else continues to produce their assignment under $\bar{\mathbf{q}}$! If even one firm succumbs to this temptation, $\bar{\mathbf{q}}$ will *not* be the output vector that prevails in the market.

Virtually all collusive solutions give rise to incentives such as these for the agents involved to cheat on the collusive agreement they fashion. Any appeal there may be in the idea of a collusive outcome as the likely 'equilibrium' in a market context is therefore considerably reduced. It is perhaps more appropriate to think of self-interested firms as essentially *non-cooperative*. To be compelling, any description of equilibrium in imperfectly competitive markets must take this into account.

The most common concept of non-cooperative equilibrium is due to John Nash (1951). In a **Nash equilibrium**, every agent must be doing the very best he or she can, given the actions of all other agents. It is easy to see that when all agents have reached such a point, none has any incentive to change unilaterally what he or she is doing, so the situation is sensibly viewed as an equilibrium.

In a market situation like the ones we have been discussing, the agents concerned are firms. There, we will not have a Nash equilibrium until every firm is maximising its own profit, given the profit-maximising actions of all other firms. Clearly, the joint profit-maximising output vector $\bar{\mathbf{q}}$ in (4.9) does not satisfy the requirements of a Nash equilibrium because, as we observed, *no* firm's individual profit is maximised at $\bar{\mathbf{q}}$ given the output choices of the other firms. Indeed, if $\mathbf{q}^*$ is to be a Nash equilibrium, each firm's output must maximise its own profit given the other firms' output choices. Thus, $\mathbf{q}^*$ must satisfy the first-order conditions:

$$\frac{\partial \Pi^k(\mathbf{q}^*)}{\partial q^k} = 0, \qquad k = 1, \ldots, J. \tag{4.10}$$

Clearly, there is a difference between (4.9) and (4.10). In general, they will determine quite different output vectors.

In what follows, we shall employ the Nash equilibrium concept in a number of different settings in which firms' decisions are interdependent.

4.2.1 COURNOT OLIGOPOLY

The following oligopoly model dates from 1838 and is due to the French economist Auguste Cournot (1838). Here we consider a simple example of **Cournot oligopoly** in the market for some homogeneous good. Suppose there are J identical firms, that entry by additional firms is effectively blocked, and that each firm has identical costs,

$$C(q^j) = cq^j, \qquad c \geq 0 \qquad \text{and} \qquad j = 1, \ldots, J. \tag{4.11}$$

Firms sell output on a common market, so market price depends on the total output sold by all firms in the market. Let inverse market demand be the linear form,

$$p = a - b\sum_{j=1}^{J} q^j, \tag{4.12}$$

where $a > 0$, $b > 0$, and we require $a > c$. From (4.11) and (4.12), profit for firm j is

$$\Pi^j(q^1, \ldots, q^j) = \left(a - b\sum_{k=1}^{J} q^k\right)q^j - cq^j. \tag{4.13}$$

We seek a vector of outputs $(\bar{q}^1, \ldots, \bar{q}^J)$ such that each firm's output choice is profit-maximising given the output choices of the other firms. Such a vector of outputs is called a **Cournot-Nash equilibrium**. This name gives due credit to Cournot, who introduced this solution to the oligopoly problem, and to Nash, who later developed the idea more generally.

So, if $(\bar{q}^1, \ldots, \bar{q}^J)$ is a Cournot-Nash equilibrium, $\bar{q}^j$ must maximise (4.13) when $q^k = \bar{q}^k$ for all $k \neq j$. Consequently, the derivative of (4.13) with respect to q^j must be zero when $q^k = \bar{q}^k$ for all $k = 1, \ldots, J$. Thus,

$$a - 2b\bar{q}^j - b\sum_{k \neq j} \bar{q}^k - c = 0,$$

which can be rewritten

$$b\bar{q}^j = a - c - b\sum_{k=1}^{J} \bar{q}^k. \tag{4.14}$$

Noting that the right-hand side of (4.14) is independent of which firm j we are considering, we conclude that all firms must produce the same amount of output in equilibrium. By letting $\bar{q}$ denote this common equilibrium output, (4.14) reduces to

$b\bar{q} = a - c - Jb\bar{q}$, which implies that

$$\bar{q} = \frac{a-c}{b(J+1)}. \tag{4.15}$$

By using (4.15), and doing a few calculations, the full set of market equilibrium values namely, firm output, total output, market price, and firm profits are as follows:

$$\begin{aligned}
\bar{q}^j &= (a-c)/b(J+1), \qquad j = 1, \ldots, J, \\
\sum_{j=1}^{J} \bar{q}^j &= J(a-c)/b(J+1), \\
\bar{p} &= a - J(a-c)/(J+1) < a, \\
\bar{\Pi}^j &= (a-c)^2/(J+1)^2 b.
\end{aligned}$$

Equilibrium in this Cournot oligopoly has some interesting features. We can calculate the deviation of price from marginal cost,

$$\bar{p} - c = \frac{a-c}{J+1} > 0, \tag{4.16}$$

and observe that equilibrium price will typically exceed the marginal cost of each identical firm. When $J = 1$, and that single firm is a pure monopolist, the deviation of price from marginal cost is greatest. At the other extreme, when the number of firms $J \to \infty$, (4.16) gives

$$\lim_{J\to\infty} (\bar{p} - c) = 0. \tag{4.17}$$

Equation (4.17) tells us that price will approach marginal cost as the number of competitors becomes large. Indeed, this limiting outcome corresponds precisely to what would obtain if any finite number of these firms behaved as perfect competitors. Thus, this simple model provides another interpretation of perfect competition. It suggests that perfect competition can be viewed as a limiting case of imperfect competition, as the number of firms becomes large.

4.2.2 BERTRAND OLIGOPOLY

Almost 50 years after Cournot, a French mathematician, Joseph Bertrand (1883), offered a different view of firm rivalry under imperfect competition. Bertrand argued it is much more natural to think of firms competing in their choice of price, rather than quantity. This small difference is enough to completely change the character of market equilibrium.

The issues involved stand out most clearly if we concentrate on rivalry between just two firms. In a simple **Bertrand duopoly**, two firms produce a homogeneous good, each has identical marginal costs $c > 0$, and no fixed cost. Though not at all crucial, for easy comparison with the Cournot case, we can again suppose that market demand is linear in total output, Q, and write

$$Q = \alpha - \beta p,$$

where p is market price.

Firms simultaneously declare the prices they will charge and they stand ready to supply all that is demanded of them at their price. Consumers buy from the cheapest source. Thus, the firm with the lowest price will serve the entire market demand at the price it has declared, whereas the firm with the highest price, if prices differ, gets no customers at all. If both firms declare the same price, then they share market demand equally, and each serves half.

Here each firm's profit clearly depends on its rival's price as well as its own. Taking firm 1 for example, for all non-negative prices below α/β (the price at which market demand is zero), profit will be

$$\Pi^1(p^1, p^2) = \begin{cases} (p^1 - c)(\alpha - \beta p^1), & c < p^1 < p^2, \\ \frac{1}{2}(p^1 - c)(\alpha - \beta p^1), & c < p^1 = p^2, \\ 0, & \text{otherwise.} \end{cases}$$

Note that firm 1's profit is positive as long as its price exceeds marginal cost. Other things being equal, it will be largest, of course, if firm 1 has the lowest price, and only half as large if the two firms charge the same price. Its profit need never be negative, however, because the firm can always charge a price equal to marginal cost and assure itself zero profits at worst. The situation for firm 2 is symmetrical. Thus, we shall suppose that each firm i restricts attention to prices $p^i \geq c$.

What is the Nash equilibrium in this market? It may be somewhat surprising, but in the unique Nash equilibrium, both firms charge a price equal to marginal cost, and both earn zero profit. Because profit functions here are discontinuous, we cannot argue the case by differentiating and solving first-order conditions. Instead, we just use some common sense.

Note that because the firm with the lowest price serves the entire market, each firm has an incentive to undercut its rival. It is this effect that ultimately drives the equilibrium price down to marginal cost. We now provide the formal argument.

First, note that if each firm chooses its price equal to c, then this is a Nash equilibrium. In this case, each firm serves half the market and earns zero profits because each unit is sold at cost. Moreover, by increasing its price, a firm ceases to obtain any demand at all because the other firm's price is then strictly lower. Consequently, it is not possible to earn more than zero profits. Therefore, each firm's price choice is profit-maximising given the other's.

Next we argue that there are no other Nash equilibria. Because each firm i chooses $p^i \geq c$, it suffices to show that here are no equilibria in which $p^i > c$ for some i. So let (p^1, p^2) be an equilibrium.

If $p^1 > c$, then because p^2 maximises firm 2's profits given firm 1's price choice, we must have $p^2 \in (c, p^1]$, because some such choice earns firm 2 strictly positive profits, whereas all other choices earn firm 2 zero profits. Moreover, $p^2 \neq p^1$ because if firm 2 can earn positive profits by choosing $p^2 = p^1$ and splitting the market, it can earn even higher profits by choosing p^2 just slightly below p^1 and supplying the entire market at virtually the same price. Therefore,

$$p^1 > c \Longrightarrow p^2 > c \qquad \text{and} \qquad p^2 < p^1.$$

But by switching the roles of firms 1 and 2, an analogous argument establishes that

$$p^2 > c \Longrightarrow p^1 > c \qquad \text{and} \qquad p^1 < p^2.$$

Consequently, if one firm's price is above marginal cost, both prices must be above marginal cost and each firm must be strictly undercutting the other, which is impossible.

In the Bertrand model, price is driven to marginal cost by competition among just *two* firms. This is striking, and it contrasts starkly with what occurs in the Cournot model, where the difference between price and marginal cost declines only as the number of firms in the market increases.

4.2.3 MONOPOLISTIC COMPETITION

Firms in both Cournot and Bertrand oligopolies sell a homogeneous product. In **monopolistic competition**, a 'relatively large' group of firms sell *differentiated* products that buyers view as close, though not perfect, substitutes for one another. Each firm therefore enjoys a limited degree of monopoly power in the market for its particular product variant, though the markets for different variants are closely related. Firms produce their products with a 'similar' technology. In a monopolistically competitive group, entry occurs when a new firm introduces a previously non-existent variant of the product.

Assume a potentially infinite number of possible product variants $j = 1, 2, \ldots$. The demand for product j depends on its own price and the prices of all other variants. We write demand for j as

$$q^j = q^j(\mathbf{p}), \text{ where } \partial q^j/\partial p^j < 0 \text{ and } \partial q^j/\partial p^k > 0 \text{ for k} \neq j, \tag{4.18}$$

and $\mathbf{p} = (p^1, \ldots, p^j, \ldots)$. In addition, we assume there is always some price $\tilde{p}^j > 0$ at which demand for j is zero, regardless of the prices of the other products.

Clearly, one firm's profit depends on the prices of *all* variants; being the difference between revenue and cost:

$$\Pi^j(\mathbf{p}) = q^j(\mathbf{p})p^j - c^j(q^j(\mathbf{p})). \tag{4.19}$$

Two classes of equilibria can be distinguished in monopolistic competition: short-run and long-run. In the short run, a fixed finite number of active firms choose price to maximise profit, given the prices chosen by the others. In a long-run equilibrium, entry and exit decisions can also be made. We consider each equilibrium in turn.

Let $j = 1, \ldots, \bar{J}$ be the active firms in the short run. For simplicity, set the price 'charged' by each inactive firm k to $\tilde{p}^k$ to ensure that each of them produces no output. (To ease notation, we shall drop explicit mention of inactive firms for the time being.)

Now suppose $\bar{\mathbf{p}} = (\bar{p}^1, \ldots, \bar{p}^{\bar{J}})$ is a Nash equilibrium in the short run. If $\bar{p}^j = \tilde{p}^j$, then $q^j(\bar{p}) = 0$ and firm j suffers losses equal to short-run fixed costs, $\Pi^j = -c^j(0)$. However, if $0 < \bar{p}^j < \tilde{p}^j$, then firm j produces a positive output and $\bar{\mathbf{p}}$ must satisfy the first-order conditions for an interior maximum of (4.19). These can be arranged in the form

$$\frac{\partial q^j(\bar{\mathbf{p}})}{\partial p^j}\left[mr^j(q^j(\bar{\mathbf{p}})) - mc^j(\mathbf{q}^j(\bar{\mathbf{p}}))\right] = 0, \tag{4.20}$$

where we have made use of (4.5). Because $\partial q^j/\partial p^j < 0$, this reduces to the familiar requirement that price and output be chosen to equate marginal revenue and marginal cost. As usual, the monopolistic competitor may have positive, negative, or zero short-run profit.

In the long run, firms will exit the industry if their profits are negative. To analyse the long run, we assume that each variant has arbitrarily close substitutes that can be produced at the same cost. Under this assumption, positive long-run profits for any single firm will induce the entry of arbitrarily many firms producing close substitutes. As usual, long-run

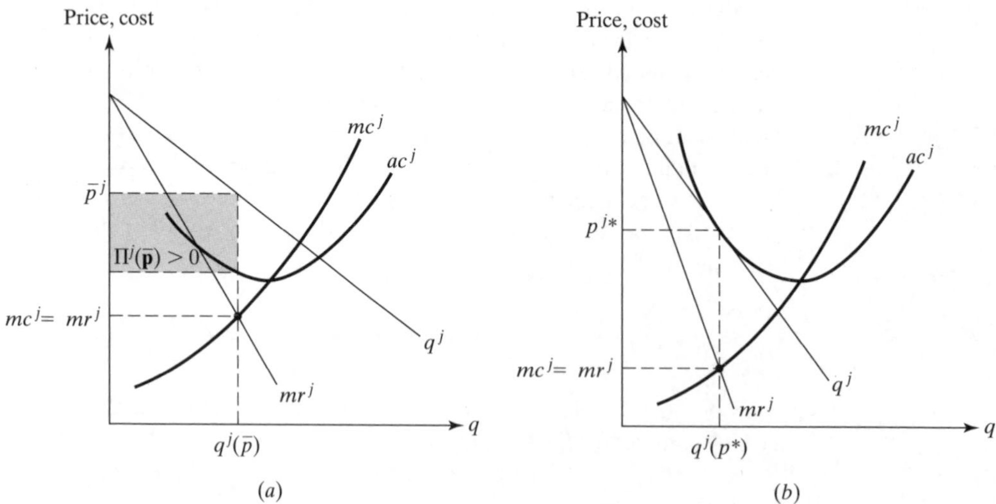

Figure 4.4. (a) Short-run and (b) long-run equilibrium in monopolistic competition.

equilibrium requires there to be no incentive for entry or exit. Consequently, because of our assumption, maximum achievable profits of all firms must be negative or zero, and those of every active firm must be exactly zero.

Suppose that $\mathbf{p}^*$ is a Nash equilibrium vector of long-run prices. Then the following *two* conditions must hold for all active firms j:

$$\frac{\partial q^j(\mathbf{p}^*)}{\partial p^j}\left[mr^j(q^j(\mathbf{p}^*)) - mc^j(\mathbf{q}^j(\mathbf{p}^*))\right] = 0, \tag{4.21}$$

$$\Pi^j(q^j(\mathbf{p}^*)) = 0. \tag{4.22}$$

Both short-run and long-run equilibrium for a representative active firm are illustrated in Fig. 4.4, which shows the tangency between demand and average cost in long-run equilibrium implied by (4.21) and (4.22).

4.3 EQUILIBRIUM AND WELFARE

To this point, we have been concerned with questions of price and quantity determination under different market structures. We have examined the agents' incentives and circumstances under competition, monopoly, and other forms of imperfect competition, and determined the corresponding equilibrium market outcome. In this section, we shift our focus from 'prediction' to 'assessment' and ask a different sort of question. Granted that different market structures give rise to different outcomes, are there means to assess these different market outcomes from a *social* point of view? Can we judge some to be 'better' or 'worse' than others in well-defined and meaningful ways? To answer questions like these, our focus must shift from the purely positive to the essentially normative.

Normative judgements invariably motivate and guide economic policy in matters ranging from taxation to the regulation of firms and industries. When government intervenes to change the laissez-faire market outcome, different agents will often be affected very differently. Typically, some will 'win' while others will 'lose'. When the welfare of the individual agent is an important consideration in formulating social policy, there are really two sorts of issues involved. First, we have to ask the positive question: how will the proposed policy affect the welfare of the individual? Second, we have to ask the much more difficult normative question: how should we weigh the different effects on different individuals together and arrive at a judgement of 'society's' interest? Here we concentrate on the first set of issues, and only dabble in the second, leaving their fuller treatment to a later chapter.

4.3.1 PRICE AND INDIVIDUAL WELFARE

It is often the case that the effect of a new policy essentially reduces to a change in prices that consumers face. Taxes and subsidies are obvious examples. To perform the kind of welfare analysis we have in mind, then, we need to know how the price of a good affects a person's welfare. To keep things simple, let us suppose the price of every other good except good q remains fixed throughout our discussion. This is the essence of the partial equilibrium approach.

So, if the price of good q is p, and the vector of all other prices is $\mathbf{p}$, then instead of writing the consumer's indirect utility as $v(p, \mathbf{p}, y)$, we shall simply write it as $v(p, y)$. Similarly, we shall suppress the vector $\mathbf{p}$ of other prices in the consumer's expenditure function, and in both his Hicksian and Marshallian demand functions. In fact, it will be convenient to introduce a **composite commodity**, m, as the amount of income spent on all goods other than q. If $\mathbf{x}(p, \mathbf{p}, y)$ denotes demand for the vector of all other goods, then the demand for the composite commodity is $m(p, \mathbf{p}, y) \equiv \mathbf{p} \cdot \mathbf{x}(p, \mathbf{p}, y)$, which we denote simply as $m(p, y)$. In Exercise 4.16, you are asked to show that if the consumer's utility function over all goods, $u(q, \mathbf{x})$, satisfies our standard assumptions, then the utility function over the two goods q and m, $\bar{u}(q, m) \equiv \max_{\mathbf{x}} u(q, \mathbf{x})$ subject to $\mathbf{p} \cdot \mathbf{x} \leq m$, also satisfies those assumptions. Moreover, we can use $\bar{u}$ to analyse the consumer's problem as if there were only two goods, q and m. That is, the consumer's demands for q and m, $q(p, y)$ and $m(p, y)$, respectively, solve

$$\max_{q,m} \bar{u}(q, m) \qquad \text{s.t.} \qquad pq + m \leq y,$$

and the maximised value of $\bar{u}$ is $v(p, y)$.

Consider now the following situation in which a typical practising economist might find himself. The local government is considering plans to modernise the community's water-treatment facility. The planned renovations will improve the facility's efficiency and will result in a decrease in the price of water. The cost of the improvements will be offset by a one-time 'water tax'. The question is: should the improvement be undertaken? If the preferences of the community are central, the issue reduces to this: would consumers be willing to pay the additional tax to obtain the reduction in the price of water?

To answer this question, let us suppose our economist has water demand data for each consumer. In particular, he knows each consumer's Marshallian demand curve corresponding to his current income level. It turns out that from this, he can determine quite accurately how much each consumer would be willing to pay for the price reduction. Let us see how this is done.

Consider a particular consumer whose income is y^0. Suppose that the initial price of water is p^0 and that it will fall to p^1 as a result of the improvement project. By letting v denote the consumer's indirect utility function, $v(p^0, y^0)$ denotes his utility before the price fall and $v(p^1, y^0)$ his utility after. Now the amount of income the consumer is willing to give up for the price decrease will be just enough so that at the lower price and income levels he would be just as well off as at the initial higher price and income levels. Letting CV denote this *change* in the consumer's income that would leave him as well off after the price fall as he was before, we have

$$v(p^1, y^0 + CV) = v(p^0, y^0). \tag{4.23}$$

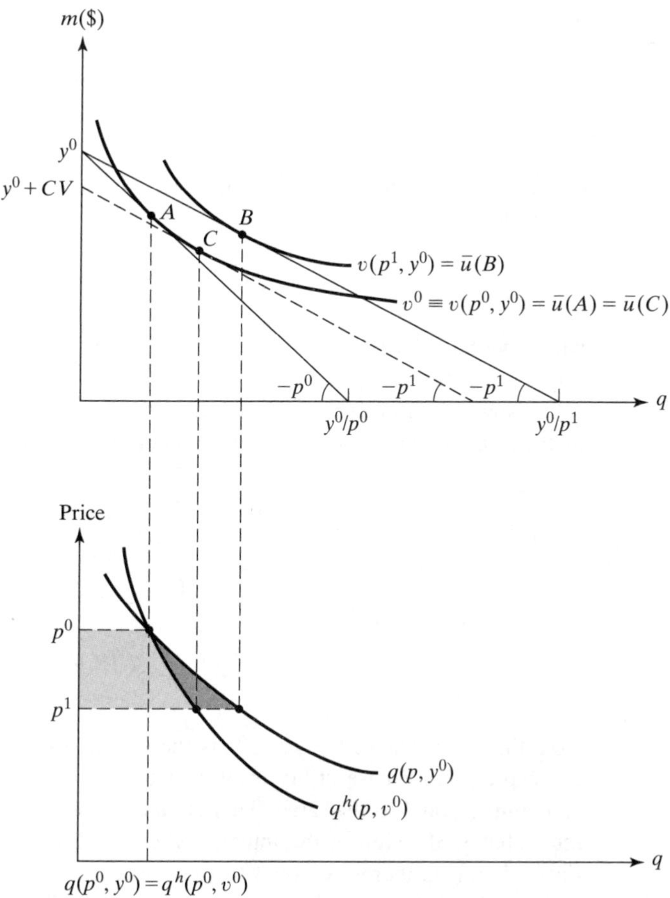

Figure 4.5. Prices, welfare, and consumer demand.

Note that in this example, CV is non-positive because v is non-increasing in p, increasing in y, and $p^1 < p^0$. CV would be non-negative for a price increase ($p^1 > p^0$). In either case, (4.23) remains valid. This change in income, CV, required to keep a consumer's utility constant as a result of a price change, is called the **compensating variation**, and it was originally suggested by Hicks.

The idea is easily illustrated in the upper portion of Fig. 4.5, where the indifference curves are those of $\bar{u}(q, m)$. The consumer is initially at A, enjoying utility $v(p^0, y^0)$. When price falls to p^1, the consumer's demand moves to point B and utility rises to $v(p^1, y^0)$. Facing the new price p^1, this consumer's income must be reduced to $y^0 + CV$ (recall $CV < 0$ here) to return to the original utility level $v(p^0, y^0)$ at point C.

Equation (4.23) and Fig. 4.5 suggest another way to look at CV. Using the familiar identity relating indirect utility and expenditure functions, and substituting from (4.23), we must have

$$e(p^1, v(p^0, y^0)) = e(p^1, v(p^1, y^0 + CV))$$
$$= y^0 + CV. \tag{4.24}$$

Because we also know that $y^0 = e(p^0, v(p^0, y^0))$, we can substitute into (4.24), rearrange, and write

$$CV = e(p^1, v^0) - e(p^0, v^0), \tag{4.25}$$

where we have let $v^0 \equiv v(p^0, y^0)$ stand for the consumer's base utility level facing base prices and income.

Now we know that the Hicksian demand for good q is (by Shephard's lemma) given by the price partial of the expenditure function. From that and (4.25), we can write

$$\begin{aligned} CV &= e(p^1, v^0) - e(p^0, v^0) \\ &= \int_{p^0}^{p^1} \frac{\partial e(p, v^0)}{\partial p} dp \\ &= \int_{p^0}^{p^1} q^h(p, v^0) dp. \end{aligned} \tag{4.26}$$

Note then that when $p^1 < p^0$, CV is the *negative* of the area to the left of the Hicksian demand curve for base utility level v^0 between p^1 and p^0, and if $p^1 > p^0$, CV is positive and simply equal to that area. This is taken care of automatically in (4.26) because one must change the sign of the integral when the limits of integration are interchanged. In Fig. 4.5, CV is therefore equal to the (negative of the) lightly shaded area between p^0 and p^1. Study (4.26) and Fig. 4.5 carefully. You will see, as common sense suggests, that if price rises ($p > p^0$), a positive income adjustment will be necessary to restore the original utility level ($CV > 0$), and if price declines ($p < p^0$), a negative income adjustment will restore the original utility level ($CV < 0$).

The compensating variation makes good sense as a dollar-denominated measure of the welfare impact a price change will have. Unfortunately, however, we have just learned that CV will always be the area to the left of some *Hicksian* demand curve, and Hicksian demand curves are not quite as readily observable as Marshallian ones. Of course, with enough data on the consumer's Marshallian demand system at different prices and income levels, one can recover via integrability methods the consumer's Hicksian demand and directly calculate CV. However, our economist only has access to the consumer's demand curve for this one good corresponding to one fixed level of income. And this is not generally enough information to recover Hicksian demand.

Despite this, we can still take advantage of the relation between Hicksian and Marshallian demands expressed by the Slutsky equation to obtain an estimate of CV. Recall that Marshallian demand picks up the total effect of a price change, and the Hicksian only picks up the substitution effect. The two will generally therefore diverge, and diverge precisely because of, the *income effect* of a price change. In the bottom portion of Fig. 4.5, this is illustrated for the case where q is a normal good by the horizontal deviation between the two curves everywhere but at p^0.

We would like to relate Hicks' idea of compensating variation to the notion of **consumer surplus**, because the latter is easily measured directly from Marshallian demand. Recall that at the price–income pair (p^0, y^0), consumer surplus, $CS(p^0, y^0)$, is simply the area under the demand curve (given y^0) and above the price, p^0. Consequently, the combined shaded areas in Fig. 4.5 equal the gain in consumer surplus due to the price fall from p^0 to p^1. That is,

$$\Delta CS \equiv CS(p^1, y^0) - CS(p^0, y^0) = \int_{p^1}^{p^0} q(p, y^0)dp. \tag{4.27}$$

As you can see, ΔCS will *always* be opposite in sign to CV, and it will diverge in absolute value from CV whenever demand depends in any way on the consumer's income, due to the income effect of a price change. Because we want to know CV but can only calculate ΔCS, a natural question immediately arises. How good an *approximation* of CV does ΔCS provide?

The answer is that as long as the price reduction from p^0 to p^1 is not too large, our economist can obtain a very good estimate indeed of each consumer's willingness to pay for the new water treatment facility. Based on this, an informed decision can be made as to who is taxed and by how much.

Before moving on, a word of warning: when only the market demand curve, as opposed to individual demand curves, is known, the change in consumer surplus (again for small price decreases, say) will provide a good approximation to the total amount of income that consumers are willing to give up for the price decrease. However, it may well be that some of them are willing to give up more income than others (heavy water users, for example). Consequently, market demand analysis might well indicate that total willingness to pay exceeds the total cost of the project, which would imply that there is *some* way to distribute the cost of the project among consumers so that everyone is better off after paying their part of the cost and enjoying the lower price. However, it would give no hint as to how that total cost should be distributed among consumers.

4.3.2 EFFICIENCY OF THE COMPETITIVE OUTCOME

In the example just considered, it seemed clear that the project should be implemented if after taking account of both the costs and benefits, everyone could be made better off. In general, when it is possible to make someone better off and no one worse off, we say that a **Pareto improvement** can be made. If there is no way at all to make a Pareto improvement, then we say that the situation is **Pareto efficient**. That is, a situation is Pareto efficient if there is no way to make someone better off without making someone else worse off.

The idea of Pareto efficiency is pervasive in economics and it is often used as one means to evaluate the performance of an economic system. The basic idea is that if an economic system is to be considered as functioning well, then given the distribution of resources it determines, it should not be possible to redistribute them in a way that results in a Pareto improvement. We shall pursue this idea more systematically in the next chapter. For now, we limit ourselves to the following question: which, if any, of the three types of market competition – perfect competition, monopoly, or Cournot oligopoly – function well in the sense that they yield a Pareto-efficient outcome?

Note that the difference between the three forms of competition is simply the prices and quantities they determine. For example, were a perfectly competitive industry taken over by a monopolist, the price would rise from the perfectly competitive equilibrium price to the monopolist's profit-maximising price and the quantity of the good produced and consumed would fall. Note, however, that in both cases, the price–quantity pair is a point on the market demand curve. The same is true of the Cournot-oligopoly solution. Consequently, we might just as well ask: which price–quantity pairs on the market demand curve yield Pareto-efficient outcomes? We now direct our attention toward providing an answer to this question.

To simplify the discussion, we shall suppose from now on that there is just one producer and one consumer. (The arguments generalise.) Refer now to Fig. 4.6, which depicts the consumer's (and therefore the market) Marshallian demand $q(p, y^0)$, his Hicksian-compensated demand $q^h(p, v^0)$, where $v^0 = v(p^0, y^0)$, and the firm's marginal cost curve, $mc(q)$. Note then that if this firm behaved as a perfect competitor, the equilibrium price–quantity pair would be determined by the intersection of the two curves, because a competitive firm's supply curve coincides with its marginal cost curve above the minimum of its average variable costs. (We have assumed that average variable costs are minimised at $q = 0$.)

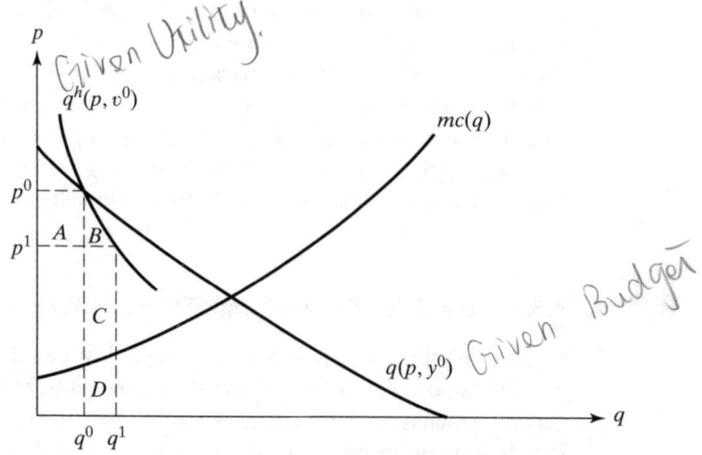

Figure 4.6. Inefficiency of monopoly equilibrium.

Consider now the price–quantity pair (p^0, q^0) on the consumer's demand curve above the competitive point in Fig. 4.6. We wish to argue that this market outcome is not Pareto efficient. To do so, we need only demonstrate that we can redistribute resources in a way that makes someone better off and no one worse off.

So, consider reducing the price of q from p^0 to p^1. What would the consumer be willing to pay for this reduction? As we now know, the answer is the absolute value of the compensating variation, which, in this case, is the sum of areas A and B in the figure. Let us then reduce the price to p^1 and take $A + B$ units of income away from the consumer. Consequently, he is just as well off as he was before, and he now demands q^1 units of the good according to his Hicksian-compensated demand.

To fulfil the additional demand for q, let us insist that the firm produce just enough additional output to meet it.

So, up to this point, we have lowered the price to p^1, increased production to q^1, and collected $A + B$ dollars from the consumer, and the consumer is just as well off as before these changes were made. Of course, the price–quantity change will have an effect on the profits earned by the firm. In particular, if $c(q)$ denotes the cost of producing q units of output, then the change in the firm's profits will be

$$\begin{aligned}[p^1q^1 - c(q^1)] - [p^0q^0 - c(q^0)] &= [p^1q^1 - p^0q^0] - [c(q^1) - c(q^0)] \\ &= [p^1q^1 - p^0q^0] - \int_{q^0}^{q^1} mc(q)dq \\ &= [C + D - A] - D \\ &= C - A.\end{aligned}$$

Consequently, if after making these changes, we give the firm A dollars out of the $A + B$ collected from the consumer, the firm will have come out strictly ahead by C dollars. We can then give the consumer the B dollars we have left over so that in the end, *both* the consumer and the firm are strictly better off as a result of the changes we have made.

Thus, beginning from the market outcome (p^0, q^0), we have been able to make both the consumer and the firm strictly better off simply by redistributing the available resources. Consequently, the original situation was not Pareto efficient.

A similar argument applies to price–quantity pairs on the consumer's Marshallian demand curve lying below the competitive point.[1] Hence, the only price–quantity pair that can possibly result in a Pareto-efficient outcome is the perfectly competitive one – and indeed it does. We shall not give the argument here because it will follow from our more general analysis in the next chapter. However, we encourage the reader to check that the particular scheme used before to obtain a Pareto improvement does not work when one begins at the competitive equilibrium. (No other scheme will produce a Pareto improvement either.)

---

[1] See Exercise 4.21.

Thus, our conclusion is that the only price–quantity pair yielding a Pareto-efficient outcome is the perfectly competitive one. In particular, neither the monopoly outcome nor the Cournot-oligopoly outcome is Pareto efficient.

Note well that we cannot conclude from this analysis that forcing a monopoly to behave differently than it would choose to must necessarily result in a Pareto improvement. It may well lower the price and increase the quantity supplied, but unless the consumers who are made better off by this change compensate the monopolist who is made worse off, the move will not be Pareto improving.

4.3.3 EFFICIENCY AND TOTAL SURPLUS MAXIMISATION

We have seen that consumer surplus is close to being a dollar measure of the gains going to the consumer as a result of purchasing the good in question. It is easier to find an exact way to measure the dollar value to the *producer* of selling the good to the consumer. This amount, called **producer surplus**, is simply the firm's revenue over and above its variable costs.

Now it would seem that to obtain an efficient outcome, the total surplus – the sum of consumer and producer surplus – must be maximised. Otherwise, both the producer and the consumer could be made better off by redistributing resources to increase the total surplus, and then dividing the larger surplus among them so that each obtains strictly more surplus than before.

But we must take care. Consumer surplus overstates the dollar benefits to the consumer whenever income effects are present and the good is normal. Despite this, however, under the assumption that demand is downward-sloping and the firm's marginal costs are rising, efficiency will not be achieved unless the sum of consumer and producer surplus is indeed maximised.

To see this, consider again the case of a single consumer and a single producer represented in Fig. 4.7 and consider an arbitrary price–quantity pair (p, q) on the demand curve (so that $p = p(q)$, where $p(\cdot)$ is inverse demand). Earlier we defined consumer surplus at (p, q) as the area under the demand curve and above the price p. It is easy to see that we can express that same area, and so consumer surplus, as the area under the inverse demand curve up to q minus the area of the rectangle $p(q)q$. Thus, we may express the sum of consumer and producer surplus as[2]

$$\begin{aligned} CS + PS &= \left[\int_0^q p(\xi)d\xi - p(q)q\right] + [p(q)q - tvc(q)] \\ &= \int_0^q p(\xi)d\xi - tvc(q) \\ &= \int_0^q [p(\xi) - mc(\xi)]d\xi. \end{aligned}$$

[2]The last line follows because $\int_0^q mc(\xi)d\xi = c(q) - c(0)$. Because $c(0)$ is fixed cost, and $c(q)$ is total cost, the difference $c(q) - c(0)$ is total variable cost, $tvc(q)$.

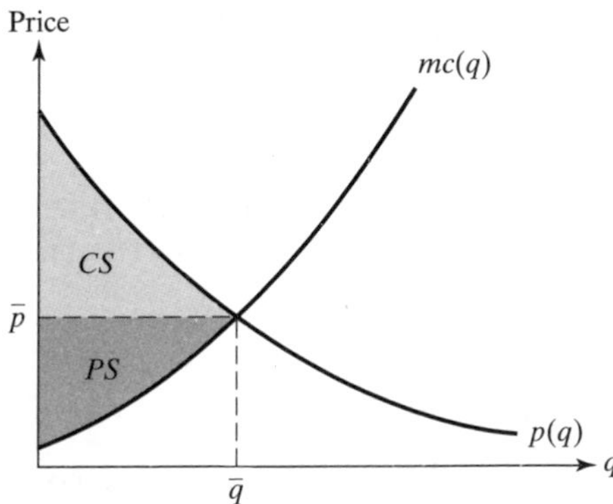

Figure 4.7. Consumer plus producer surplus is maximised at the competitive market equilibrium.

Choosing q to maximise this expression leads to the first-order condition

$$p(q) = mc(q),$$

which occurs precisely at the perfectly competitive equilibrium quantity when demand is downward-sloping and marginal costs rise, as we have depicted in Fig. 4.7.

In fact, it is this relation between price and marginal cost that is responsible for the connection between our analysis in the previous section and the present one. Whenever price and marginal cost differ, a Pareto improvement like the one employed in the previous section can be implemented. And, as we have just seen, whenever price and marginal cost differ, the total surplus can be increased.

Once again, a warning: although Pareto efficiency requires that the total surplus be maximised, a Pareto improvement need not result simply because the total surplus has increased. Unless those who gain compensate those who lose as a result of the change, the change is not Pareto improving.

We have seen that when markets are imperfectly competitive, the market equilibrium generally involves prices that exceed marginal cost. However, 'price equals marginal cost' is a necessary condition for a maximum of consumer and producer surplus. It should therefore come as no surprise that the equilibrium outcomes in most imperfectly competitive markets are *not* Pareto efficient.

EXAMPLE 4.4 Let us consider the performance of the Cournot oligopoly in Section 4.2.1. There, market demand is $p = a - bq$ for total market output q. Firms are identical, with marginal cost $c \geq 0$. When each firm produces the same output q/J, total surplus, $W \equiv cs + ps$, as a function of total output, will be

$$W(q) = \int_0^q (a - b\xi)d\xi - J\int_0^{q/J} cd\xi,$$

which reduces to

$$W(q) = aq - (b/2)q^2 - cq. \tag{E.1}$$

Because (E.1) is strictly concave, total surplus is maximised at $q^* = (a - c)/b$, where $W'(q^*) = 0$. Thus, the maximum potential surplus in this market will be

$$W(q^*) = \frac{(a-c)^2}{2b}. \tag{E.2}$$

In the Cournot-Nash equilibrium, we have seen that total market output will be $\bar{q} = J(a - c)/(J + 1)b$. Clearly, $\bar{q} < q^*$, so the Cournot oligopoly produces too little output from a social point of view. Total surplus in the Cournot equilibrium will be

$$W(\bar{q}) = \frac{(a-c)^2}{2b}\frac{J^2 + 2J}{(J+1)^2}, \tag{E.3}$$

with a **dead weight loss** of

$$W(q^*) - W(\bar{q}) = \frac{(a-c)^2}{(J+1)^2 2b} > 0. \tag{E.4}$$

By using (E.3), it is easy to show that total surplus increases as the number of firms in the market becomes larger. Before, we noted that market price converges to marginal cost as the number of firms in the oligopoly becomes large. Consequently, total surplus rises toward its maximal level in (E.2), and the dead weight loss in (E.4) declines to zero, as $J \to \infty$. □

4.4 EXERCISES

4.1 Suppose that preferences are identical and homothetic. Show that market demand for any good must be independent of the distribution of income. Also show that the elasticity of market demand with respect to the level of market income must be equal to unity.

4.2 Suppose that preferences are homothetic but not identical. Will market demand necessarily be independent of the distribution of income?

4.3 Show that if q is a normal good for every consumer, the market demand for q will be negatively sloped with respect to its own price.

4.4 Suppose that x and y are substitutes for all but one consumer. Does it follow that the market demand for x will be increasing in the price of y?

4.5 Show that the long-run equilibrium number of firms is indeterminate when all firms in the industry share the same constant returns-to-scale technology and face the same factor prices.

4.6 A firm j in a competitive industry has total cost function $c^j(q) = aq + b_jq^2$, where $a > 0$, q is firm output, and b_j is different for each firm.

(a) If $b_j > 0$ for all firms, what governs the amount produced by each of them? Will they produce equal amounts of output? Explain.

(b) What happens if $b_j < 0$ for all firms?

4.7 Technology for producing q gives rise to the cost function $c(q) = aq + bq^2$. The market demand for q is $p = \alpha - \beta q$.

(a) If $a > 0$, if $b < 0$, and if there are J firms in the industry, what is the short-run equilibrium market price and the output of a representative firm?

(b) If $a > 0$ and $b < 0$, what is the long-run equilibrium market price and number of firms? Explain.

(c) If $a > 0$ and $b > 0$, what is the long-run equilibrium market price and number of firms? Explain.

4.8 In the Cournot oligopoly of Section 4.2.1, suppose that $J = 2$. Let each duopolist have constant average and marginal costs, as before, but suppose that $0 \le c^1 < c^2$. Show that firm 1 will have greater profits and produce a greater share of market output than firm 2 in the Nash equilibrium.

4.9 In a **Stackelberg duopoly**, one firm is a 'leader' and one is a 'follower'. Both firms know each other's costs and market demand. The follower takes the leader's output as given and picks his own output accordingly (i.e., the follower acts like a Cournot competitor). The leader takes the follower's *reactions* as given and picks his own output accordingly. Suppose that firms 1 and 2 face market demand, $p = 100 - (q^1 + q^2)$. Firm costs are $c^1 = 10q^1$ and $c^2 = q^{22}$.

(a) Calculate market price and each firm's profit assuming that firm 1 is the leader and firm 2 the follower.

(b) Do the same assuming that firm 2 is the leader and firm 1 is the follower.

(c) Given your answers in parts (a) and (b), who would firm 1 want to be the leader in the market? Who would firm 2 want to be the leader?

(d) If each firm assumes what it wants to be the case in part (c), what are the equilibrium market price and firm profits? How does this compare with the Cournot-Nash equilibrium in this market?

4.10 (Stackelberg Warfare) In the market described in Section 4.2.1, let $J = 2$.

(a) Show that if, say, firm 1 is leader and firm 2 is follower, the leader earns higher and the follower earns lower profit than they do in the Cournot equilibrium. Conclude that each would want to be the leader.

(b) If both firms decide to act as leader and each assumes the other will be a follower, can the equilibrium be determined? What will happen in this market?

4.11 In the Cournot market of Section 4.2.1, suppose that each identical firm has cost function $c(q) = k + cq$, where $k > 0$ is fixed cost.

(a) What will be the equilibrium price, market output, and firm profits with J firms in the market?

(b) With free entry and exit, what will be the long-run equilibrium number of firms in the market?

4.12 In the Bertrand duopoly of Section 4.2.2, market demand is $Q = \alpha - \beta^p$, and firms have no fixed costs and identical marginal cost. Find a Bertrand equilibrium pair of prices, (p^1, p^2), and quantities, (q^1, q^2), when the following hold.

(a) Firm 1 has fixed costs $F > 0$.

(b) Both firms have fixed costs $F > 0$.

(c) Fixed costs are zero, but firm 1 has lower marginal cost than firm 2, so $c^2 > c^1 > 0$. (For this one, assume the low-cost firm captures the entire market demand whenever the firms charge equal prices.)

4.13 Duopolists producing substitute goods q_1 and q_2 face inverse demand schedules:

$$p_1 = 20 + \tfrac{1}{2}p_2 - q_1 \qquad \text{and} \qquad p_2 = 20 + \tfrac{1}{2}p_1 - q_2,$$

respectively. Each firm has constant marginal costs of 20 and no fixed costs. Each firm is a Cournot competitor in *price*, not quantity. Compute the Cournot equilibrium in this market, giving equilibrium price and output for each good.

4.14 An industry consists of many identical firms each with cost function $c(q) = q^2 + 1$. When there are J active firms, each firm faces an identical inverse market demand $p = 10 - 15q - (J - 1)\bar{q}$ whenever an identical output of $\bar{q}$ is produced by each of the other $(J - 1)$ active firms.

(a) With J active firms, and no possibility of entry or exit, what is the short-run equilibrium output q^* of a representative firm when firms act as Cournot competitors in choosing output?

(b) How many firms will be active in the long run?

4.15 When firms $j = 1, \ldots, J$ are active in a monopolistically competitive market, firm j faces the following demand function:

$$q^j = (p^j)^{-2}\left(\sum_{\substack{i=1\\ i\neq j}}^{J}(p^i)^{-1/2}\right)^{-2}, \qquad j = 1, \ldots, J.$$

Active or not, each of the many firms $j = 1, 2, \ldots$ has identical costs,

$$c(q) = cq + k,$$

where $c > 0$ and $k > 0$. Each firm chooses its price to maximise profits, given the prices chosen by the others.

(a) Show that each firm's demand is negatively sloped, with constant own-price elasticity, and that all goods are substitutes for each other.

(b) Show that if all firms raise their prices proportionately, the demand for any given good declines.

(c) Find the long-run Nash equilibrium number of firms.

4.16 Suppose that a consumer's utility function over all goods, $u(q, \mathbf{x})$, is continuous, strictly increasing, and strictly quasiconcave, and that the price $\mathbf{p}$ of the vector of goods, $\mathbf{x}$, is fixed. Let m denote the composite commodity $\mathbf{p} \cdot \mathbf{x}$, so that m is the amount of income spent on $\mathbf{x}$. Define the utility function $\bar{u}$ over the two goods q and m as follows.

$$\bar{u}(q, m) \equiv \max_{\mathbf{x}}\ u(q, \mathbf{x}) \quad \text{s.t.} \quad \mathbf{p} \cdot \mathbf{x} \leq m.$$

(a) Show that $\bar{u}(q, m)$ is strictly increasing and strictly quasiconcave. If you can, appeal to a theorem that allows you to conclude that it is also continuous.

(b) Show that if $q(p, \mathbf{p}, y)$ and $\mathbf{x}(p, \mathbf{p}, y)$ denote the consumer's Marshallian demands for q and $\mathbf{x}$, then, $q(p, \mathbf{p}, y)$ and $m(p, \mathbf{p}, y) \equiv \mathbf{p} \cdot \mathbf{x}(p, \mathbf{p}, y)$ solve

$$\max_{q,m} \ \bar{u}(q, m) \qquad \text{s.t.} \qquad pq + m \leq y.$$

and that the maximised value of $\bar{u}$ is $v(p, \mathbf{p}, y)$.

(c) Conclude that when the prices of all but one good are fixed, one can analyse the consumer's problem as if there were only two goods, the good whose price is not fixed, and the composite commodity, 'money spent on all other goods'.

4.17 Let $(q^0, \mathbf{x}^0) \gg \mathbf{0}$ maximise $u(q, \mathbf{x})$ subject to $p^0 q + \mathbf{p}^0 \cdot \mathbf{x} \leq y^0$. Show that if u is differentiable at $(q^0, \mathbf{x}^0)$ and $\nabla u(q^0, \mathbf{x}^0) \gg \mathbf{0}$, then the consumer would be willing to pay *strictly* more than $(p^0 - p^1)q^0$ for a reduction in the price of good q to p^1.

4.18 Willig (1976) has shown that when income elasticity of demand is independent of price, so that

$$\frac{\partial q(p, y)}{\partial y} \frac{y}{q(p, y)} \equiv \eta(y)$$

for all p and y in the relevant region, then for base price p^0 and income y^0, CS and CV are related, exactly, as follows:

$$-\Delta CS = \int_{y^0}^{CV+y^0} \exp\left(- \int_{y^0}^{\zeta} \frac{\eta(\xi)}{\xi} d\xi \right) d\zeta.$$

(a) Show that when income elasticity is constant but not equal to unity,

$$CV = y^0 \left[\frac{-\Delta CS}{y^0}(1 - \eta) + 1 \right]^{1/(1-\eta)} - y^0.$$

(b) Use this to show that when demand is independent of income, $-\Delta CS = CV$, so consumer surplus can then be used to obtain an exact measure of the welfare impact of a price change.

(c) Derive the relation between CV and ΔCS when income elasticity is unity.

(d) Finally, we can use the result in part (a) to establish a convenient rule of thumb that can be used to quickly gauge the approximate size of the deviation between the change in consumer surplus and the compensating variation when income elasticity is constant. Show that when income elasticity is constant and not equal to unity, we have $(CV - |\Delta CS|)/|\Delta CS| \approx (\eta |\Delta CS|)/2y^0$.

4.19 A consumer has preferences over the single good x and all other goods m represented by the utility function, $u(x, m) = \ln(x) + m$. Let the price of x be p, the price of m be unity, and let income be y.

(a) Derive the Marshallian demands for x and m.

(b) Derive the indirect utility function, $v(p, y)$.

(c) Use the Slutsky equation to decompose the effect of an own-price change on the demand for x into an income and substitution effect. Interpret your result briefly.

(d) Suppose that the price of x rises from p^0 to $p^1 > p^0$. Show that the consumer surplus area between p^0 and p^1 gives an *exact* measure of the effect of the price change on consumer welfare.

(e) Carefully illustrate your findings with a set of *two* diagrams: one giving the indifference curves and budget constraints on top, and the other giving the Marshallian and Hicksian demands below. Be certain that your diagrams reflect all qualitative information on preferences and demands that you have uncovered. Be sure to consider the two prices p^0 and p^1, and identify the Hicksian and Marshallian demands.

4.20 A consumer's demand for the single good x is given by $x(p, y) = y/p$, where p is the good's price, and y is the consumer's income. Let income be \$7. Find the compensating variation for an increase in the price of this good from \$1 to \$4.

4.21 Use a figure similar to Fig. 4.6 to argue that price–quantity pairs on the demand curve below the competitive price–quantity pair are not Pareto efficient.

4.22 A monopolist faces linear demand $p = \alpha - \beta q$ and has cost $C = cq + F$, where all parameters are positive, $\alpha > c$, and $(\alpha - c)^2 > 4\beta F$.

(a) Solve for the monopolist's output, price, and profits.

(b) Calculate the deadweight loss and show that it is positive.

(c) If the government requires this firm to set the price that maximises the sum of consumer and producer surplus, and to serve all buyers at that price, what is the price the firm must charge? Show that the firm's profits are negative under this regulation, so that this form of regulation is not sustainable in the long run.

4.23 (Ramsey Rule) Building from the preceding exercise, suppose a monopolist faces negatively sloped demand, $p = p(q)$, and has costs $C = cq + F$. Now suppose that the government requires this firm to set a price (p^*) that will maximise the sum of consumer and producer surplus, subject to the constraint that firm profit be non-negative, so that the regulation is sustainable in the long run. Show that under this form of regulation, the firm will charge a price greater than marginal cost, and that the percentage deviation of price from marginal cost ($(p^* - c)/p^*$) will be proportional to $1/\epsilon^*$, where ϵ^* is the elasticity of firm demand at the chosen price and output. Interpret your result.

4.24 Suppose that $(\bar{p}, \bar{q})$ are equilibrium market price and output in a perfectly competitive market with only two firms. Show that when demand is downward-sloping and marginal costs rise, $(\bar{p}, \bar{q})$ satisfy the second-order conditions for a maximum of consumer plus producer surplus.

4.25 (Welfare Bias in Product Selection) A monopolist must decide between two different designs for its product. Each design will have a different market demand and different costs of production. If design x^1 is introduced, it will have market demand and costs of

$$x^1 = \begin{cases} \dfrac{2}{p^1} + 6\tfrac{7}{8} - p^1, & \text{if} \quad 0 < p^1 \le 6\tfrac{7}{8}, \\ \dfrac{2}{p^1}, & \text{if} \quad p^1 > 6\tfrac{7}{8}, \end{cases}$$

$$c^1(x^1) = 5\tfrac{1}{8} + x^1.$$

If design x^2 is introduced, it will have the following market demand and costs:

$$x^2 = 7\tfrac{7}{8} - 1\tfrac{1}{8}p^2,$$
$$c^2(x^2) = 4\tfrac{1}{8} + x^2.$$

Note that the only difference in costs between these two designs is a difference in *fixed costs*.

(a) Calculate the price the firm would charge and the profits it would make if it introduced each design. Which design will it introduce?

(b) Carefully sketch the demand and marginal cost curves for both designs on the same set of axes. Does the firm's choice maximise consumer plus producer surplus? Is the outcome Pareto efficient?

4.26 A competitive industry is in long-run equilibrium. Market demand is linear, $p = a - bQ$, where $a > 0$, $b > 0$, and Q is market output. Each firm in the industry has the same technology with cost function, $c(q) = k^2 + q^2$.

(a) What is the long-run equilibrium price? (Assume what is necessary of the parameters to ensure that this is positive and less than a.)

(b) Suppose that the government imposes a per-unit tax, $t > 0$, on every producing firm in the industry. Describe what would happen in the long run to the number of firms in the industry. What is the post-tax market equilibrium price? (Again, assume whatever is necessary to ensure that this is positive and less than a.)

(c) Calculate the long-run effect of this tax on consumer surplus. Show that the loss in consumer surplus from this tax exceeds the amount of tax revenue collected by the government in the post-tax market equilibrium.

(d) Would a lump-sum tax, levied on producers and designed to raise the same amount of tax revenue, be preferred by consumers? Justify your answer.

(e) State the conditions under which a lump-sum tax, levied on *consumers* and designed to raise the same amount of revenue, would be preferred by consumers to either preceding form of tax.

4.27 A per-unit tax, $t > 0$, is levied on the output of a monopoly. The monopolist faces demand, $q = p^{-\epsilon}$, where $\epsilon > 1$, and has constant average costs. Show that the monopolist will increase price by more than the amount of the per-unit tax.

4.28 A firm under uncertainty faces gambles of the form $g = (p_1 \circ \pi_1, \ldots, p_n \circ \pi_n)$, where the π_i are profits and the p_i their probabilities of occurrence. The firm's owner has a VNM utility function over gambles in profit, and he is an expected utility maximiser. Prove that the firm's owner will always act to maximise *expected profit* if and only if he is *risk neutral*.

4.29 Consider a two-period monopoly facing the negatively sloped inverse demand function $p_t = p(q_t)$ in each period $t = 0, 1$. The firm maximises the present discounted value of profits, $PDV = \sum_{t=0}^{1}(1 + r)^{-t}\pi_t$, where $r > 0$ is the market interest rate, and π_t is period-t profit. In each of the following, assume that costs each period are increasing in that period's output and are strictly convex, and that PDV is strictly concave.

(a) If costs are $c_t = c(q_t)$ for $t = 0, 1$, show that the firm will 'short-run profit maximise' in each period by choosing output to equate marginal cost and marginal revenue in each period.

(b) Now suppose that the firm can 'learn by doing'. Its period-zero costs are simply $c_0 = c_0(q_0)$. Its period-one costs, however, depend on output in period zero; $c_1 = c_1(q_1, q_0)$, where $\partial c_1/\partial q_0 < 0$. Does the firm still 'short-run profit maximise' in each period? Why or why not? Interpret your results.

CHAPTER 5

GENERAL EQUILIBRIUM

Many scholars trace the birth of economics to the publication of Adam Smith's *The Wealth of Nations* (1776). Behind the superficial chaos of countless interdependent market actions by selfish agents, Smith saw a harmonising force serving society. This *Invisible Hand* guides the market system to an equilibrium that Smith believed possessed certain socially desirable characteristics.

One can ask many questions about competitive market systems. A fundamental one arises immediately: is Smith's vision of a smoothly functioning system composed of many self-interested individuals buying and selling on impersonal markets – with no regard for anything but their personal gain – a logically coherent vision at all? If so, is there one particular state towards which such a system will tend, or are there many such states? Are these fragile things that can be easily disrupted or are they robust?

These are questions of existence, uniqueness, and stability of general competitive equilibrium. All are deep and important, but we will only address the first.

In many ways, existence is the most fundamental question and so merits our closest attention. What is at issue is the logical coherence of the very *notion* of a competitive market system. The question is usually framed, however, as one of the existence of prices at which demand and supply are brought into balance in the market for every good and service simultaneously. The market prices of everything we buy and sell are principal determinants of what we can consume, and so, of the well-being we can achieve. Thus, market prices determine to a large extent 'who gets what' in a market economy.

In this chapter, we do not merely ask under what conditions a set of market-clearing prices exists. We also ask how well a market system solves the basic economic problem of distribution. We will begin by exploring the distribution problem in very general terms, then proceed to consider the existence of general competitive equilibrium itself. Along the way, we will focus particular scrutiny on Smith's claim that a competitive market system promotes society's welfare through no conscious collective intention of its members.

5.1 EQUILIBRIUM IN EXCHANGE

Here we explore the basic economic problem of distribution in a very simple society *without* organised markets. Our objective is to describe what outcomes might arise through a process of voluntary exchange. By examining the outcomes of this process, we can establish a benchmark against which the equilibria achieved under competitive market systems can be compared.

The society we consider is very stark. First, there is no production. Commodities exist, but for now we do not ask how they came to be. Instead, we merely assume each consumer is 'endowed' by nature with a certain amount of a finite number of consumable goods. Each consumer has preferences over the available commodity bundles, and each cares only about his or her individual well-being. Agents may consume their endowment of commodities or may engage in barter exchange with others. We admit the institution of private ownership into this society and assume that the principle of voluntary, non-coercive trade is respected. In the absence of coercion, and because consumers are self-interested, voluntary exchange is the only means by which commodities may be redistributed from the initial distribution. In such a setting, what outcomes might we expect to arise? Or, rephrasing the question, where might this system come to rest through the process of voluntary exchange? We shall refer to such rest points as barter equilibria.

To simplify matters, suppose there are only two consumers in this society, consumer 1 and consumer 2, and only two goods, x_1 and x_2. Let $\mathbf{e}^1 \equiv (e_1^1, e_2^1)$ denote the non-negative endowment of the two goods owned by consumer 1, and $\mathbf{e}^2 \equiv (e_1^2, e_2^2)$ the endowment of consumer 2. The total amount of each good available in this society then can be summarised by the vector $\mathbf{e}^1 + \mathbf{e}^2 = (e_1^1 + e_1^2, e_2^1 + e_2^2)$. (From now on, superscripts will be used to denote consumers and subscripts to denote goods.)

The essential aspects of this economy can be analysed with the ingenious **Edgeworth box**, familiar from intermediate theory courses. In Fig. 5.1, units of x_1 are measured along each horizontal side and units of x_2 along each vertical side. The south-west corner is consumer 1's origin and the north-east corner consumer 2's origin.

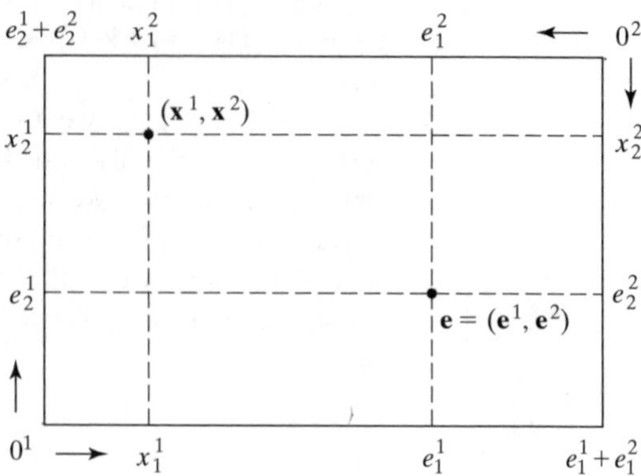

Figure 5.1. The Edgeworth box.

Increasing amounts of x_1 for consumer 1 are measured rightwards from 0^1 along the bottom side, and increasing amounts of x_1 for consumer 2 are measured leftwards from 0^2 along the top side. Similarly, x_2 for consumer 1 is measured vertically up from 0^1 on the left, and for consumer 2, vertically down on the right. The box is constructed so that its width measures the total endowment of x_1 and its height the total endowment of x_2.

Notice carefully that each point in the box has *four* coordinates – two indicating some amount of each good for consumer 1 and two indicating some amount of each good for consumer 2. Because the dimensions of the box are fixed by the total endowments, each set of four coordinates represents some division of the total amount of each good between the two consumers. For example, the point labelled **e** denotes the pair of initial endowments $\mathbf{e}^1$ and $\mathbf{e}^2$. Every other point in the box represents some other way the totals can be allocated between the consumers, and every possible allocation of the totals between the consumers is represented by some point in the box. The box therefore provides a complete picture of every feasible distribution of existing commodities between consumers.

To complete the description of the two-person exchange economy, suppose each consumer has preferences represented by a usual, convex indifference map. In Fig. 5.2, consumer 1's indifference map increases north-easterly, and consumer 2's increases south-westerly. One indifference curve for each consumer passes through *every* point in the box. The line labelled CC is the subset of allocations where the consumers' indifference curves through the point are tangent to each other, and it is called the **contract curve**. At any point off the contract curve, the consumers' indifference curves through that point must cut each other.

Given initial endowments at **e**, which allocations will be barter equilibria in this exchange economy? Obviously, the first requirement is that the allocations be somewhere,

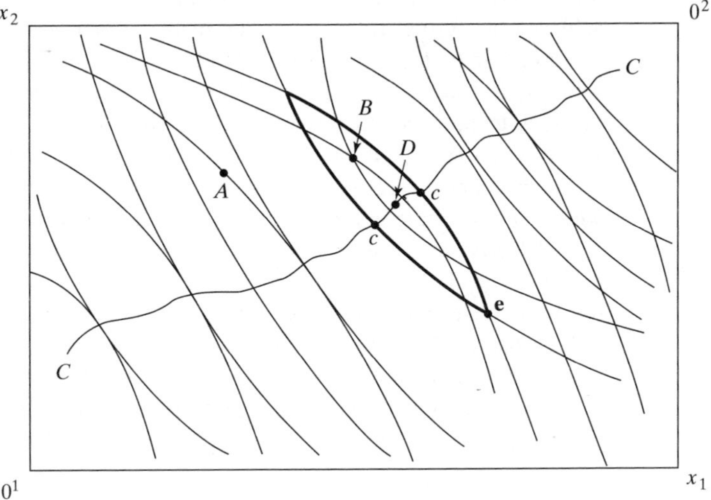

Figure 5.2. Equilibrium in two-person exchange.

'in the box', because only those are feasible. But not every feasible allocation can be a barter equilibrium. For example, suppose a redistribution from **e** to point A were proposed. Consumer 2 would be better off, but consumer 1 would clearly be worse off. Because this economy relies on voluntary exchange, and because consumers are self-interested, the redistribution to A would be refused, or 'blocked', by consumer 1, and so could not arise as an equilibrium given the initial endowment. By the same argument, all allocations to the left of consumer 1's indifference curve through **e** would be blocked by consumer 1, and all allocations to the right of consumer 2's indifference curve through **e** would be blocked by consumer 2.

This leaves only allocations inside and on the boundary of the lens-shaped area delineated by the two consumers' indifference curves through **e** as potential barter equilibria. At every point along the boundary, one consumer will be better off and the other no worse off than they are at **e**. At every allocation inside the lens, however, both consumers will be strictly better off than they are at **e**. To achieve these gains, the consumers must arrange a trade. Consumer 1 must give up some x_1 in exchange for some of consumer 2's x_2, and consumer 2 must give up some x_2 in exchange for some of consumer 1's x_1.

But are all allocations inside the lens barter equilibria? Suppose a redistribution to B within that region were to occur. Because B is off the contract curve, the two indifference curves passing through it must cut each other, forming another lens-shaped region contained entirely within the original one. Consequently, both consumers once again can be made strictly better off by arranging an appropriate trade away from B and inside the lens it determines. Thus, B and every such point inside the lens through **e** but off the contract curve can be ruled out as barter equilibria.

Now consider a point like D on segment cc of the contract curve. A move from **e** to any such point will definitely make both parties better off. Moreover, once the consumers trade to D, there are no feasible trades that result in further *mutual* gain. Thus, once D is achieved, no further trades will take place: D is a barter equilibrium. Indeed, any point along cc is a barter equilibrium. Should the consumers agree to trade and so find themselves at *any* allocation on cc, and should a redistribution to *any* other allocation in the box then be proposed, that redistribution would be blocked by one or both of them. (This includes, of course, any movement from one point on cc to another on cc.) Pick any point on cc, consider several possible reallocations, and convince yourself of this. Once on cc, we can be sure there will be no subsequent movement away.

Clearly, there are many barter equilibria toward which the system might evolve. We are content with having identified all of the possibilities. Note that these equilibria all share the property that once there, it is not possible to move elsewhere in the box without making at least one of the consumers worse off. Thus, each point of equilibrium in exchange is Pareto efficient in the sense described in Chapter 4.

Consider now the case of many consumers and many goods. Let

$$\mathcal{I} = \{1, \ldots, I\}$$

index the set of consumers, and suppose there are n goods. Each consumer $i \in \mathcal{I}$ has a preference relation, $\succsim^i$, and is endowed with a non-negative vector of the n goods, $\mathbf{e}^i = (e_1^i, \ldots, e_n^i)$. Altogether, the collection $\mathcal{E} = (\succsim^i, \mathbf{e}^i)_{i \in \mathcal{I}}$ defines an **exchange economy**.

What conditions characterise barter equilibria in this exchange economy? As before, the first requirement is that the assignment of goods to individuals not exceed the amounts available. Let

$$\mathbf{e} \equiv (\mathbf{e}^1, \ldots, \mathbf{e}^I)$$

denote the economy's endowment vector, and define an **allocation** as a vector

$$\mathbf{x} \equiv (\mathbf{x}^1, \ldots, \mathbf{x}^I),$$

where $\mathbf{x}^i \equiv (x_1^i, \ldots, x_n^i)$ denotes consumer i's bundle according to the allocation. The set of **feasible allocations** in this economy is given by

$$F(\mathbf{e}) \equiv \left\{ \mathbf{x} \,\middle|\, \sum_{i \in \mathcal{I}} \mathbf{x}^i = \sum_{i \in \mathcal{I}} \mathbf{e}^i \right\}, \tag{5.1}$$

and it contains all allocations of goods across individuals that, in total, exhaust the available amount of every good. The first requirement on $\mathbf{x}$ as a barter equilibrium is therefore that $\mathbf{x} \in F(\mathbf{e})$.

Now in the two-consumer case, we noted that if both consumers could be made better off by trading with one another, then we could not yet be at a barter equilibrium. Thus, at a barter equilibrium, no Pareto improvements were possible. This also carries over to the more general case. To formalise this, let us begin with the following.

DEFINITION 5.1 ***Pareto-Efficient Allocations***

A feasible allocation, $\mathbf{x} \in F(\mathbf{e})$, is Pareto efficient if there is no other feasible allocation, $\mathbf{y} \in F(\mathbf{e})$, such that $\mathbf{y}^i \succsim^i \mathbf{x}^i$ for all consumers, i, with at least one preference strict.

So, an allocation is Pareto efficient if it is not possible to make someone strictly better off without making someone else strictly worse off.

Now if $\mathbf{x} \in F(\mathbf{e})$ is not Pareto efficient, then there is another feasible allocation $\mathbf{y}$ making someone strictly better off and no one worse off. Consequently, the consumer who can be made strictly better off can arrange a trade with the others by announcing: 'I'll give each consumer i the bundle $\mathbf{y}^i$ in exchange for the bundle $\mathbf{x}^i$'. Because both allocations $\mathbf{x}$ and $\mathbf{y}$ are feasible, this trade is feasible. No consumer will object to it because it makes everyone at least as well off as they were before. Moreover it makes (at least) the one consumer strictly better off. Consequently, $\mathbf{x}$ would not be an equilibrium. Thus, to be a barter equilibrium, $\mathbf{x}$ must be feasible and Pareto efficient.

Suppose now that $\mathbf{x}$ is Pareto efficient. Can we move away from $\mathbf{x}$? No, we cannot. Because $\mathbf{x}$ is Pareto efficient, every other feasible allocation that makes someone better off must make at least one other consumer worse off. Hence, the latter consumer will not agree to the trade that is involved in the move.

So, we now know that *only* Pareto-efficient allocations are candidates for barter equilibrium, and whenever a Pareto-efficient allocation is reached, it will indeed be an equilibrium of our process of voluntary exchange. Thus, it remains to describe the set of Pareto-efficient allocations that can be reached through voluntary exchange.

Recall from the two-consumer case that not all Pareto-efficient allocations were equilibria there. That is, only those allocations on the contract curve and within the lens created by the indifference curves through the endowment point were equilibria. The reason for this was that the other Pareto-efficient allocations – those on the contract curve but outside the lens – made at least one of the consumers worse off than they would be by simply consuming their endowment. Thus, each such Pareto-efficient allocation was 'blocked' by one of the consumers.

Similarly, when there are more than two consumers, no equilibrium allocation can make any consumer worse off than he would be consuming his endowment. That consumer would simply refuse to make the necessary trade. But in fact there are now additional reasons you might refuse to trade to some Pareto-efficient allocation. Indeed, although you might prefer the bundle assigned to you in the proposed allocation over your own endowment, you might be able to find another consumer to strike a trade with such that you do even better as a result of that trade and he does no worse than he would have done had you both gone along with the proposed allocation. Consequently, although you *alone* are unable to block the proposal, you are able to block it *together with someone else*. Of course, the potential for blocking is not limited to coalitions of size 2. Three or more of you might be able to get together to block an allocation. With all of this in mind, consider the following.

DEFINITION 5.2 ***Blocking Coalitions***

Let $S \subset \mathcal{I}$ denote a coalition of consumers. We say that S blocks $\mathbf{x} \in F(\mathbf{e})$ if there is an allocation $\mathbf{y}$ such that:[1]

1. $\sum_{i \in S} \mathbf{y}^i = \sum_{i \in S} \mathbf{e}^i$.
2. $\mathbf{y}^i \succsim^i \mathbf{x}^i$ *for all $i \in S$, with at least one preference strict.*

Together, the first and second items in the definition say that the consumers in S must be able to take what they themselves have and divide it up differently among themselves so that none is worse off and at least one is better off than with their assignment under $\mathbf{x}$. Thus, an allocation $\mathbf{x}$ is blocked whenever some group, no matter how large or small, can do better than they do under $\mathbf{x}$ by simply 'going it alone'. By contrast, we say that an allocation is 'unblocked' if *no* coalition can block it. Our final requirement for equilibrium, then, is that the allocation be unblocked.

Note that this takes care of the two-consumer case because all allocations outside the lens are blocked by a coalition consisting of a single consumer (sometimes consumer 1, sometimes consumer 2). In addition, note that in general, if $\mathbf{x} \in F(\mathbf{e})$ is unblocked, then it must be Pareto efficient, because otherwise it would be blocked by the grand

[1] Note that there is no need to insist that $\mathbf{y} \in F(\mathbf{e})$, because one can always make it so by replacing the bundles in it going to consumers $j \notin S$ by $\mathbf{e}^j$.

coalition $S = \mathcal{I}$. This lets us summarise the requirements for equilibrium in exchange very compactly.

Specifically, *an allocation* $\mathbf{x} \in F(\mathbf{e})$ *is an equilibrium in the exchange economy with endowments* $\mathbf{e}$ *if* $\mathbf{x}$ *is not blocked by any coalition of consumers*. Take a moment to convince yourself that this definition reduces to the one we developed earlier when there were only two goods and two consumers.

The set of allocations we have identified as equilibria of the process of voluntary exchange is known as the 'core', and we define this term for future reference.

DEFINITION 5.3 ***The Core of an Exchange Economy***

The core of an exchange economy with endowment $\mathbf{e}$, *denoted* $C(\mathbf{e})$, *is the set of all unblocked feasible allocations.*

Can we be assured that every exchange economy possesses at least one allocation in the core? That is, must there exist at least one feasible and unblocked allocation? As we shall later show, the answer is yes under a number of familiar conditions.

We have argued that under ideal circumstances, including the costless nature of both the formation of coalitions and the acquisition of the information needed to arrange mutually beneficial trades, consumers are led, through the process of voluntary exchange, to pursue the attainment of allocations in the core. From this point of view, points in the core seem very far indeed from becoming a reality in a real-world economy. After all, most of us have little or no direct contact with the vast majority of other consumers. Consequently, one would be quite surprised were there not substantial gains from trade left unrealised, regardless of how the economy were organised – centrally planned, market-based, or otherwise. In the next section, we investigate economies organised by competitive markets. Prepare for a surprise.

5.2 EQUILIBRIUM IN COMPETITIVE MARKET SYSTEMS

In the preceding section, we examined a very primitive economic system based wholly on voluntary barter exchange. Here we take a first look at questions of equilibrium and distribution in a more sophisticated economic system. In a **perfectly competitive market system**, all transactions between individuals are mediated by impersonal markets. Consumers' market behaviour is guided solely by their personal self-interest, and each consumer, whether acting as buyer or seller, is individually insignificant on every market, with no power to affect prevailing prices. Equilibrium on each market separately is achieved when the totality of buyers' decisions are compatible with the totality of sellers' decisions at the prevailing market price. Equilibrium in the market *system* is achieved when the demands of buyers match the supplies of sellers at prevailing prices in every market simultaneously.

A noteworthy feature of the competitive model we shall develop here is its *decentralised* nature. Each consumer, fully aware of the prices of goods prevailing in all markets, demands a bundle that is best for him, *without the need to consider what other consumers might demand, being fully confident that sufficient production has taken place.* Similarly, producers, also fully aware of the prevailing prices of all goods (both inputs and outputs), choose amounts of production that maximise their profits, *without the need to consider how much other producers are producing, being fully confident that their output will be purchased.*

The naivete expressed in the decentralised aspect of the competitive model (i.e., that every agent acts in his own self-interest while ignoring the actions of others) should be viewed as a strength. Because in equilibrium consumers' demands *will* be satisfied, and because producers' outputs *will* be purchased, the actions of the other agents *can* be ignored and the *only* information required by consumers and producers is the *prevailing prices*. Consequently, the informational requirements of this model are minimal. This is in stark contrast to the barter model of trade developed in the previous section in which each consumer requires very detailed information about all other consumers' preferences and bundles.

Clearly, the optimality of ignoring others' actions requires that at prevailing prices consumer demands are met and producer supplies are sold. So, it is essential that prices are able to clear all markets simultaneously. But is it not rather bold to presume that a suitable vector of prices will ensure that the diverse tastes of consumers and the resulting totality of their demands will be exactly matched by the supplies coming from the production side of the market, with its many distinct firms, each being more or less adept at producing one good or another? The existence of such a vector of prices is not obvious at all, but the coherence of our competitive model requires such a price vector to exist.

To give you a feeling for the potential for trouble on this front, suppose that there are just three goods and that at current prices the demand for good 1 is equal to its supply, so this market is in equilibrium. However, suppose that there is excess demand for good 2 and excess supply of good 3, so that neither of these markets clears at current prices. It would be natural to suppose that one can achieve equilibrium in these markets by increasing the price of good 2 and decreasing the price of good 3. Now, while this might help to reduce the difference between demand and supply in these markets, these price changes may very well affect the demand for good 1! After all if goods 1 and 2 are substitutes, then increases in the price of good 2 can lead to increases in the demand for good 1. So, changing the prices of goods 2 and 3 in an attempt to equilibrate those markets can upset the equilibrium in the market for good 1.

The *interdependence* of markets renders the existence of an equilibrium price vector a subtle issue indeed. But again, the existence of a vector of prices that *simultaneously* clears all markets is *essential* for employing the model of the consumer and producer developed in Chapters 1 and 3, where we assumed that demands were always met and supplies always sold. Fortunately, even though it is not at all obvious, we can show (with a good deal of effort) that under some economically meaningful conditions, there *does* exist at least one vector of prices that simultaneously clears all markets. We now turn to this critical question.

5.2.1 EXISTENCE OF EQUILIBRIUM

For simplicity, let us first consider an economy without the complications of production in the model. Again let $\mathcal{I} = \{1, \ldots, I\}$ index the set of consumers and assume that each is endowed with a non-negative vector $\mathbf{e}^i$ of n goods. Further, suppose each consumer's preferences on the consumption set $\mathbb{R}^n_+$ can be represented by a utility function u^i satisfying the following.[2]

ASSUMPTION 5.1 ***Consumer Utility***

Utility u^i is continuous, strongly increasing, and strictly quasiconcave on $\mathbb{R}^n_+$.

On competitive markets, every consumer takes prices as given, whether acting as a buyer or a seller. If $\mathbf{p} \equiv (p_1, \ldots, p_n) \gg \mathbf{0}$ is the vector of market prices, then each consumer solves

$$\max_{\mathbf{x}^i \in \mathbb{R}^n_+} u^i(\mathbf{x}^i) \qquad \text{s.t.} \qquad \mathbf{p} \cdot \mathbf{x}^i \leq \mathbf{p} \cdot \mathbf{e}^i. \tag{5.2}$$

The constraint in (5.2) simply expresses the consumer's usual budget constraint but explicitly identifies the source of a consumer's income. Intuitively, one can imagine a consumer selling his entire endowment at prevailing market prices, receiving income, $\mathbf{p} \cdot \mathbf{e}^i$, and then facing the ordinary constraint that expenditures, $\mathbf{p} \cdot \mathbf{x}^i$, not exceed income. The solution $\mathbf{x}^i(\mathbf{p}, \mathbf{p} \cdot \mathbf{e}^i)$ to (5.2) is the consumer's demanded bundle, which depends on market prices and the consumer's endowment income. We record here a familiar result that we will need later.

THEOREM 5.1 ***Basic Properties of Demand***

If u^i satisfies Assumption 5.1 then for each $\mathbf{p} \gg \mathbf{0}$, the consumer's problem (5.2) has a unique solution, $\mathbf{x}^i(\mathbf{p}, \mathbf{p} \cdot \mathbf{e}^i)$. In addition, $\mathbf{x}^i(\mathbf{p}, \mathbf{p} \cdot \mathbf{e}^i)$ is continuous in $\mathbf{p}$ on $\mathbb{R}^n_{++}$.

Recall that existence of a solution follows because $\mathbf{p} \gg \mathbf{0}$ implies that the budget set is bounded, and uniqueness follows from the strict quasiconcavity of u^i. Continuity at $\mathbf{p}$ follows from Theorem A2.21 (the theorem of the maximum), and this requires $\mathbf{p} \gg \mathbf{0}$. We emphasise here that $\mathbf{x}^i(\mathbf{p}, \mathbf{p} \cdot \mathbf{e}^i)$ *is not continuous in* $\mathbf{p}$ *on all of* $\mathbb{R}^n_+$ because demand may well be infinite if one of the prices is zero. We will have to do a little work later to deal with this unpleasant, yet unavoidable, difficulty.

We can interpret the consumer's endowment $\mathbf{e}^i$ as giving the quantity of each of the n goods that he inelastically supplies on the various markets.

[2]Recall that a function is strongly increasing if strictly raising one component in the domain vector and lowering none strictly increases the value of the function. Note also that Cobb-Douglas utilities are neither strongly increasing nor strictly quasiconcave on all of $\mathbb{R}^n_+$ and so are ruled out by Assumption 5.1.

We now can begin to build a description of the system of markets we intend to analyse. The market demand for some good will simply be the sum of every individual consumer's demand for it. Market supply will be the sum of every consumer's supply. With n goods, the market system will consist of n markets, each with its market demand and market supply. Because consumers' demand for any one good depends on the prices of every good, the system of markets so constructed will be a completely *interdependent* system, with conditions in any one market affecting and being affected by conditions in every other market.

The earliest analysis of market systems, undertaken by Léon Walras (1874), proceeded along these lines, with each market described by separate demand and supply functions. Today, largely as a matter of convenience and notational simplicity, it is more common to describe each separate market by a single *excess demand function*. Then, the market system may be described compactly by a single n-dimensional *excess demand vector*, each of whose elements is the excess demand function for one of the n markets.

DEFINITION 5.4 Excess Demand

The aggregate excess demand function for good k is the real-valued function,

$$z_k(\mathbf{p}) \equiv \sum_{i\in\mathcal{I}} x_k^i(\mathbf{p}, \mathbf{p}\cdot\mathbf{e}^i) - \sum_{i\in\mathcal{I}} e_k^i.$$

The aggregate excess demand function is the vector-valued function,

$$\mathbf{z}(\mathbf{p}) \equiv (z_1(\mathbf{p}), \ldots, z_n(\mathbf{p})).$$

When $z_k(\mathbf{p}) > 0$, the aggregate demand for good k exceeds the aggregate endowment of good k and so there is excess demand for good k. When $z_k(\mathbf{p}) < 0$, there is excess supply of good k.

Aggregate excess demand functions possess certain properties. We detail these here.

THEOREM 5.2 Properties of Aggregate Excess Demand Functions

If for each consumer i, u^i satisfies Assumption 5.1, then for all $\mathbf{p} \gg \mathbf{0}$,

1. *Continuity:* $\mathbf{z}(\cdot)$ *is continuous at* $\mathbf{p}$.
2. *Homogeneity:* $\mathbf{z}(\lambda\mathbf{p}) = \mathbf{z}(\mathbf{p})$ *for all* $\lambda > 0$.
3. *Walras' law:* $\mathbf{p}\cdot\mathbf{z}(\mathbf{p}) = 0$.

Proof: Continuity follows from Theorem 5.1.

Homogeneity: A glance at the constraint in (5.2) should convince you that individual demands, and excess demands, are homogeneous of degree zero in prices. It follows immediately that aggregate excess demand is also homogeneous of degree zero in prices.

Walras' law: The third property, Walras' law, is important. It says that the *value* of aggregate excess demand will always be zero at *any* set of positive prices. Walras' law follows because when u^i is strongly increasing, each consumer's budget constraint holds with *equality*.

When the budget constraint in (5.2) holds with equality,

$$\sum_{k=1}^{n} p_k\big(x_k^i(\mathbf{p}, \mathbf{p}\cdot\mathbf{e}^i) - e_k^i\big) = 0.$$

Summing over individuals gives

$$\sum_{i\in\mathcal{I}}\sum_{k=1}^{n} p_k\big(x_k^i(\mathbf{p}, \mathbf{p}\cdot\mathbf{e}^i) - e_k^i\big) = 0.$$

Because the order of summation is immaterial, we can reverse it and write this as

$$\sum_{k=1}^{n}\sum_{i\in\mathcal{I}} p_k\big(x_k^i(\mathbf{p}, \mathbf{p}\cdot\mathbf{e}^i) - e_k^i\big) = 0.$$

This, in turn, is equivalent to the expression

$$\sum_{k=1}^{n} p_k\left(\sum_{i\in\mathcal{I}} x_k^i(\mathbf{p}, \mathbf{p}\cdot\mathbf{e}^i) - \sum_{i\in\mathcal{I}} e_k^i\right) = 0.$$

From Definition 5.4, the term in parentheses is the aggregate excess demand for good k, so we have

$$\sum_{k=1}^{n} p_k z_k(\mathbf{p}) = 0,$$

and the claim is proved. ∎

Walras' law has some interesting implications. For example, consider a two-good economy and suppose that prices are strictly positive. By Walras' law, we know that

$$p_1 z_1(\mathbf{p}) = -p_2 z_2(\mathbf{p}).$$

If there is excess demand in market 1, say, so that $z_1(\mathbf{p}) > 0$, we know immediately that we must have $z_2(\mathbf{p}) < 0$, or excess supply in market 2. Similarly, if market 1 is in equilibrium at $\mathbf{p}$, so that $z_1(\mathbf{p}) = 0$, Walras' law ensures that market 2 is also in equilibrium with $z_2(\mathbf{p}) = 0$. Both of these ideas generalise to the case of n markets. Any excess demand in the system of markets must be exactly matched by excess supply of equal value at the given prices somewhere else in the system. Moreover, if at some set of prices $n-1$ markets are in equilibrium, Walras' law ensures the nth market is also in equilibrium. This is often quite useful to remember.

Now consider a market system described by some excess demand function, $\mathbf{z}(\mathbf{p})$. We know that excess demand in any particular market, $z_k(\mathbf{p})$, may depend on the prices prevailing in *every* market, so that the system of markets is completely interdependent. There is a *partial equilibrium* in the single market k when the quantity of commodity k demanded is equal to the quantity of k supplied at prevailing prices, or when $z_k(\mathbf{p}) = 0$. If, at some prices $\mathbf{p}$, we had $\mathbf{z}(\mathbf{p}) = \mathbf{0}$, or demand equal to supply in *every* market, then we would say that the *system* of markets is in *general equilibrium*. Prices that equate demand and supply in every market are called **Walrasian**.[3]

DEFINITION 5.5 ***Walrasian Equilibrium***

A vector $\mathbf{p}^* \in \mathbb{R}^n_{++}$ *is called a Walrasian equilibrium if* $\mathbf{z}(\mathbf{p}^*) = \mathbf{0}$.

We now turn to the question of existence of Walrasian equilibrium. This is indeed an important question because it speaks directly to the logical coherence of Smith's vision of a market economy. One certainly cannot explore sensibly the social and economic properties of equilibria in market economies without full confidence that they exist, and without full knowledge of the circumstances under which they can be expected to exist. This central question in economic theory has attracted the attention of a great many theorists over time. We have mentioned that Walras was the first to attempt an answer to the question of existence by reducing it to a question of whether a system of market demand and market supply equations possessed a solution. However, Walras cannot be credited with providing a satisfactory answer to the question because his conclusion rested on the fallacious assumption that any system of equations with as many unknowns as equations always possesses a solution. Abraham Wald (1936) was the first to point to Walras' error by offering a simple counterexample: the two equations in two unknowns, $x^2 + y^2 = 0$ and $x^2 - y^2 = 1$, have no solution, as you can easily verify. Wald is credited with providing the first mathematically correct proof of existence, but his includes what many would regard as unnecessarily restrictive assumptions on consumers' preferences. In effect, he required that preferences be strongly separable and that every good exhibit 'diminishing marginal utility'. McKenzie (1954) and Arrow and Debreu (1954) were the first to offer significantly more general proofs of existence. Each framed their search for market-clearing prices as the search for a fixed point to a carefully chosen mapping and employed powerful fixed-point theorems to reach their conclusion. In what follows, we too shall employ the fixed-point method to demonstrate existence. However, we encourage the reader to consult both McKenzie (1954) and Arrow and Debreu (1954) for a more general treatment.

We begin by presenting a set of conditions on aggregate excess demand that guarantee a Walrasian equilibrium price vector exists.

[3]Note that we restrict attention to positive prices. Strictly speaking, there is no reason to do so. However, under our assumption that consumers' utility functions are strongly increasing, aggregate excess demand can be zero only if all prices are positive. See Exercise 5.3.

THEOREM 5.3 ***Aggregate Excess Demand and Walrasian Equilibrium***

Suppose $\mathbf{z}\colon \mathbb{R}^n_{++} \to \mathbb{R}^n$ *satisfies the following three conditions:*

1. $\mathbf{z}(\cdot)$ *is continuous on* $\mathbb{R}^n_{++}$*;*
2. $\mathbf{p} \cdot \mathbf{z}(\mathbf{p}) = 0$ *for all* $\mathbf{p} \gg \mathbf{0}$*;*
3. *If* $\{\mathbf{p}^m\}$ *is a sequence of price vectors in* $\mathbb{R}^n_{++}$ *converging to* $\bar{\mathbf{p}} \neq 0$, *and* $\bar{p}_k = 0$ *for some good k, then for some good k′ with* $\bar{p}_{k'} = 0$, *the associated sequence of excess demands in the market for good k′,* $\{z_{k'}(\mathbf{p}^m)\}$, *is unbounded above.*

Then there is a price vector $\mathbf{p}^* \gg \mathbf{0}$ *such that* $\mathbf{z}(\mathbf{p}^*) = \mathbf{0}$.

Before giving the proof, let us consider the three conditions in the theorem. The first two are familiar and are guaranteed to hold under the hypotheses of Theorem 5.2. Only the third, rather ominous-looking condition, is new. What it says is actually very easy to understand, however. It says roughly that if the prices of some but not all goods are arbitrarily close to zero, then the (excess) demand for at least one of those goods is arbitrarily high. Put this way, the condition sounds rather plausible. Later, we will show that under Assumption 5.1, condition 3 is satisfied.

Before getting into the proof of the theorem, we remark that it is here where the lack of continuity of consumer demand, and hence aggregate excess demand, on the boundary of the non-negative orthant of prices requires us to do some hard work. In particular, you will note that in a number of places, we take extra care to stay away from that boundary.

Proof: For each good, k, let $\bar{z}_k(\mathbf{p}) = \min(z_k(\mathbf{p}), 1)$ for all $\mathbf{p} \gg \mathbf{0}$, and let $\bar{\mathbf{z}}(\mathbf{p}) = (\bar{z}_1(\mathbf{p}), \ldots, \bar{z}_n(\mathbf{p}))$. Thus, we are assured that $\bar{z}_k(\mathbf{p})$ is bounded above by 1.

Now, fix $\varepsilon \in (0, 1)$, and let

$$S_\varepsilon = \left\{ \mathbf{p} \;\middle|\; \sum_{k=1}^{n} p_k = 1 \text{ and } p_k \geq \frac{\varepsilon}{1+2n} \quad \forall\, k \right\}.$$

In searching for $\mathbf{p}^*$ satisfying $\mathbf{z}(\mathbf{p}^*) = \mathbf{0}$, we shall begin by restricting our search to the set S_ε. It is depicted in Fig. 5.3 for the two-good case. Note how prices on and near the boundary of the non-negative orthant are excluded from S_ε. Note also that as ε is allowed to approach zero, S_ε includes more and more prices. Thus, we can expand the scope of our search by letting ε tend to zero. We shall do so a little later. For now, however, ε remains fixed.

Note the following properties of the set S_ε: it is compact, convex, and non-empty. Compactness follows because it is both closed and bounded (check this), and convexity can be easily checked. To see that it is non-empty, note that the price vector with each component equal to $(2 + 1/n)/(1 + 2n)$ is always a member because $\varepsilon < 1$.

For each good k and every $\mathbf{p} \in S_\varepsilon$, define $f_k(\mathbf{p})$ as follows:

$$f_k(\mathbf{p}) = \frac{\varepsilon + p_k + \max(0, \bar{z}_k(\mathbf{p}))}{n\varepsilon + 1 + \sum_{m=1}^{n} \max(0, \bar{z}_m(\mathbf{p}))},$$

Figure 5.3. The set S_ε in $\mathbb{R}^2_+$.

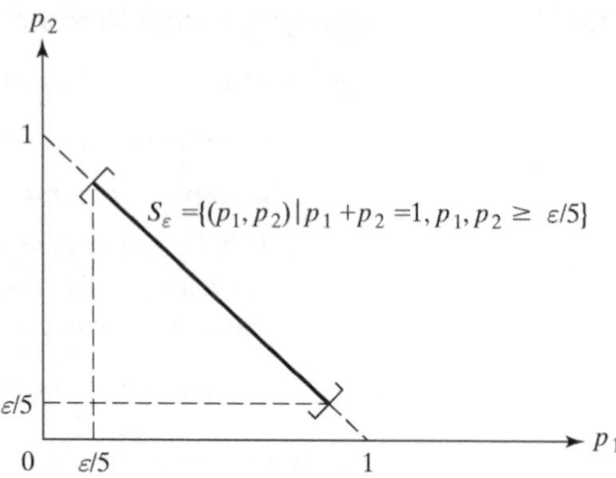

and let $f(\mathbf{p}) = (f_1(\mathbf{p}), \ldots, f_n(\mathbf{p}))$. Consequently, $\sum_{k=1}^n f_k(\mathbf{p}) = 1$ and $f_k(\mathbf{p}) \geq \varepsilon/(n\varepsilon + 1 + n \cdot 1)$, because $\bar{z}_m(\mathbf{p}) \leq 1$ for each m. Hence, $f_k(\mathbf{p}) \geq \varepsilon/(1 + 2n)$ because $\varepsilon < 1$. Therefore $f\colon S_\varepsilon \to S_\varepsilon$.

Note now that each f_k is continuous on S_ε because, by condition 1 of the statement of the theorem, $z_k(\cdot)$, and therefore $\bar{z}_k(\cdot)$, is continuous on S_ε, so that both the numerator and denominator defining f_k are continuous on S_ε. Moreover, the denominator is bounded away from zero because it always takes on a value of at least 1.

Therefore, f is a continuous function mapping the non-empty, compact, convex set S_ε into itself. We may then appeal to Brouwer's fixed-point theorem (Theorem A1.11) to conclude that there exists $\mathbf{p}^\varepsilon \in S_\varepsilon$ such that $f(\mathbf{p}^\varepsilon) = \mathbf{p}^\varepsilon$, or, equivalently, that $f_k(\mathbf{p}^\varepsilon) = p_k^\varepsilon$ for every $k = 1, 2, \ldots, n$. But this means, using the definition of $f_k(\mathbf{p}^\varepsilon)$ and rearranging, that for every k

$$p_k^\varepsilon \left[n\varepsilon + \sum_{m=1}^n \max(0, \bar{z}_m(\mathbf{p}^\varepsilon)) \right] = \varepsilon + \max(0, \bar{z}_k(\mathbf{p}^\varepsilon)). \tag{P.1}$$

So, up to this point, we have shown that for every $\varepsilon \in (0, 1)$ there is a price vector in S_ε satisfying (P.1).

Now allow ε to approach zero and consider the associated sequence of price vectors $\{\mathbf{p}^\varepsilon\}$ satisfying (P.1). Note that the price sequence is bounded, because $\mathbf{p}^\varepsilon \in S_\varepsilon$ implies that the price in every market always lies between zero and one. Consequently, by Theorem A1.8, some subsequence of $\{\mathbf{p}^\varepsilon\}$ must converge. To keep the notation simple, let us suppose that we were clever enough to choose this convergent subsequence right from the start so that $\{\mathbf{p}^\varepsilon\}$ itself converges to $\mathbf{p}^*$, say. Of course, $\mathbf{p}^* \geq \mathbf{0}$ and $\mathbf{p}^* \neq \mathbf{0}$ because its components sum to 1. We argue that in fact, $\mathbf{p}^* \gg \mathbf{0}$. This is where condition 3 enters the picture.

Let us argue by way of contradiction. So, suppose it is not the case that $\mathbf{p}^* \gg \mathbf{0}$. Then for some $\bar{k}$, we must have $p_{\bar{k}}^* = 0$. But condition 3 of the statement of the theorem then implies that there must be some good k' with $p_{k'}^* = 0$ such that $z_{k'}(\mathbf{p}^\varepsilon)$ is unbounded above as ε tends to zero.

But note that because $\mathbf{p}^\varepsilon \to \mathbf{p}^*$, $p^*_{k'} = 0$ implies that $p^\varepsilon_{k'} \to 0$. Consequently, the left-hand side of (P.1) for $k = k'$ must tend to zero, because the term in square brackets is bounded above by the definition of $\bar{\mathbf{z}}$. However, the right-hand side apparently does not tend to zero, because the unboundedness above of $z_{k'}(\mathbf{p}^\varepsilon)$ implies that $\bar{z}_{k'}(\mathbf{p}^\varepsilon)$ assumes its maximum value of 1 infinitely often. Of course, this is a contradiction because the two sides are equal for all values of ε. We conclude, therefore, that $\mathbf{p}^* \gg \mathbf{0}$.

Thus, $\mathbf{p}^\varepsilon \to \mathbf{p}^* \gg \mathbf{0}$ as $\varepsilon \to 0$. Because $\bar{\mathbf{z}}(\cdot)$ inherits continuity on $\mathbb{R}^n_{++}$ from $\mathbf{z}(\cdot)$, we may take the limit as $\varepsilon \to 0$ in (P.1) to obtain

$$p^*_k \sum_{m=1}^{n} \max(0, \bar{z}_m(\mathbf{p}^*)) = \max(0, \bar{z}_k(\mathbf{p}^*)) \tag{P.2}$$

for all $k = 1, 2, \ldots, n$. Multiplying both sides by $z_k(\mathbf{p}^*)$ and summing over k yields

$$\mathbf{p}^* \cdot \mathbf{z}(\mathbf{p}^*)\left(\sum_{m=1}^{n} \max(0, \bar{z}_m(\mathbf{p}^*))\right) = \sum_{k=1}^{n} z_k(\mathbf{p}^*) \max(0, \bar{z}_k(\mathbf{p}^*)).$$

Now, condition 2 in the statement of the theorem (Walras' law) says that $\mathbf{p}^*\mathbf{z}(\mathbf{p}^*) = 0$, so we may conclude that the left-hand side and therefore also the right-hand side of the preceding equation is zero. But because the sign of $\bar{z}_k(\mathbf{p}^*)$ is the same as that of $z_k(\mathbf{p}^*)$, the sum on the right-hand side can be zero only if $z_k(\mathbf{p}^*) \le 0$ for all k. This, together with $\mathbf{p}^* \gg \mathbf{0}$ and Walras' law implies that each $z_k(\mathbf{p}^*) = 0$, as desired. ∎

Thus, as long as on $\mathbb{R}^n_{++}$ aggregate excess demand is continuous, satisfies Walras' law, and is unbounded above as some, but not all, prices approach zero, a Walrasian equilibrium (with the price of every good strictly positive) is guaranteed to exist.

One might be tempted to try to obtain the same result without condition 3 on the unboundedness of excess demand. However, you are asked to show in Exercise 5.7 that the result simply does not hold without it.

We already know that when each consumer's utility function satisfies Assumption 5.1, conditions 1 and 2 of Theorem 5.3 will hold. (This is the content of Theorem 5.2.) It remains to show when condition 3 holds. We do so now.

THEOREM 5.4 ***Utility and Aggregate Excess Demand***

If each consumer's utility function satisfies Assumption 5.1, and if the aggregate endowment of each good is strictly positive (i.e., $\sum_{i=1}^{I} \mathbf{e}^i \gg \mathbf{0}$), then aggregate excess demand satisfies conditions 1 through 3 of Theorem 5.3.

Proof: Conditions 1 and 2 follow from Theorem 5.2. Thus, it remains only to verify condition 3. Consider a sequence of strictly positive price vectors, $\{\mathbf{p}^m\}$, converging to $\bar{\mathbf{p}} \neq \mathbf{0}$, such that $\bar{p}_k = 0$ for some good k. Because $\sum_{i=1}^{I} \mathbf{e}^i \gg \mathbf{0}$, we must have $\bar{\mathbf{p}} \cdot \sum_{i=1}^{I} \mathbf{e}^i > 0$. Consequently, $\bar{\mathbf{p}} \cdot \sum_{i=1}^{I} \mathbf{e}^i = \sum_{i=1}^{I} \bar{\mathbf{p}} \cdot \mathbf{e}^i > 0$, so that there must be at least one consumer i for whom $\bar{\mathbf{p}} \cdot \mathbf{e}^i > 0$.

Consider this consumer i's demand, $\mathbf{x}^i(\mathbf{p}^m, \mathbf{p}^m \cdot \mathbf{e}^i)$, along the sequence of prices. Now, let us suppose, by way of contradiction, that this sequence of demand vectors is bounded. Then, by Theorem A1.8, there must be a convergent subsequence. So we may assume without any loss (by reindexing the subsequence, for example) that the original sequence of demands converges to $\mathbf{x}^*$, say. That is, $\mathbf{x}^i(\mathbf{p}^m, \mathbf{p}^m \cdot \mathbf{e}^i) \to \mathbf{x}^*$.

To simplify the notation, let $\mathbf{x}^m \equiv \mathbf{x}^i(\mathbf{p}^m, \mathbf{p}^m \cdot \mathbf{e}^i)$ for every m. Now, because $\mathbf{x}^m$ maximises u^i subject to i's budget constraint given the prices $\mathbf{p}^m$, and because u^i is strongly (and, therefore, strictly) increasing, the budget constraint must be satisfied with equality. That is,

$$\mathbf{p}^m \cdot \mathbf{x}^m = \mathbf{p}^m \cdot \mathbf{e}^i$$

for every m.

Taking the limit as $m \to \infty$ yields

$$\bar{\mathbf{p}} \cdot \mathbf{x}^* = \bar{\mathbf{p}} \cdot \mathbf{e}^i > 0, \tag{P.1}$$

where the strict inequality follows from our choice of consumer i.

Now let $\hat{\mathbf{x}} = \mathbf{x}^* + (0, \ldots, 0, 1, 0, \ldots, 0)$, where the 1 occurs in the kth position. Then because u^i is strongly increasing on $\mathbb{R}^n_+$,

$$u^i(\hat{\mathbf{x}}) > u^i(\mathbf{x}^*). \tag{P.2}$$

In addition, because $\bar{p}_k = 0$, (P.1) implies that

$$\bar{\mathbf{p}} \cdot \hat{\mathbf{x}} = \bar{\mathbf{p}} \cdot \mathbf{e}^i > 0. \tag{P.3}$$

So, because u^i is continuous, (P.2) and (P.3) imply that there is a $t \in (0, 1)$ such that

$$u^i(t\hat{\mathbf{x}}) > u^i(\mathbf{x}^*),$$
$$\bar{\mathbf{p}} \cdot (t\hat{\mathbf{x}}) < \bar{\mathbf{p}} \cdot \mathbf{e}^i.$$

But because $\mathbf{p}^m \to \bar{\mathbf{p}}$, $\mathbf{x}^m \to \mathbf{x}^*$ and u^i is continuous, this implies that for m large enough,

$$u^i(t\hat{\mathbf{x}}) > u^i(\mathbf{x}^m)$$
$$\mathbf{p}^m \cdot (t\hat{\mathbf{x}}) < \mathbf{p}^m \cdot \mathbf{e}^i,$$

contradicting the fact that $\mathbf{x}^m$ solves the consumer's problem at prices $\mathbf{p}^m$. We conclude therefore that consumer i's sequence of demand vectors must be unbounded.

Now because i's sequence of demand vectors, $\{\mathbf{x}^m\}$, is unbounded yet non-negative, there must be some good k' such that $\{x^m_{k'}\}$ is unbounded above. But because i's income converges to $\bar{\mathbf{p}} \cdot \mathbf{e}^i$, the sequence of i's income $\{\mathbf{p}^m \cdot \mathbf{e}^i\}$ is bounded. (See Exercise 5.8.) Consequently, we must have $p^m_{k'} \to 0$, because this is the only way that the demand for good k' can be unbounded above and affordable. Consequently, $\bar{p}_{k'} = \lim_m p^m_{k'} = 0$.

Finally, note that because the aggregate supply of good k' is fixed and equal to the total endowment of it, and all consumers demand a non-negative amount of good k', the fact that i's demand for good k' is unbounded above implies that the aggregate excess demand for good k' is unbounded above. Consequently, beginning with the assumption that $\mathbf{p}^m \to \bar{\mathbf{p}} \neq \mathbf{0}$ and $\bar{p}_k = 0$ for some k, we have shown that there exists some good k', with $\bar{p}'_k = 0$, such that the aggregate excess demand for good k' is unbounded above along the sequence of prices $\{\mathbf{p}^m\}$, as desired. ∎

We now can state an existence result in terms of the more primitive elements of the model. The next theorem follows directly from Theorems 5.4 and 5.3.

THEOREM 5.5 ***Existence of Walrasian Equilibrium***

If each consumer's utility function satisfies Assumption 5.1, and $\sum_{i=1}^{I} \mathbf{e}^i \gg \mathbf{0}$, *then there exists at least one price vector,* $\mathbf{p}^* \gg \mathbf{0}$, *such that* $\mathbf{z}(\mathbf{p}^*) = \mathbf{0}$.

The assumption that utilities be strongly increasing is somewhat restrictive, although it has allowed us to keep the analysis relatively simple. As mentioned earlier, the otherwise very well-behaved Cobb-Douglas functional form of utility is not strongly increasing on $\mathbb{R}^n_+$. You are asked to show in Exercise 5.14 that existence of a Walrasian equilibrium with Cobb-Douglas preferences is nonetheless guaranteed.

When utilities satisfy Assumption 5.1, we know from Theorem 5.2 that the excess demand vector will be homogeneous of degree zero. The behavioural significance of homogeneity is that only relative prices matter in consumers' choices. Thus, if $\mathbf{p}^*$ is a Walrasian equilibrium in such an economy, we will have $\mathbf{z}(\mathbf{p}^*) = \mathbf{z}(\lambda\mathbf{p}^*) = \mathbf{0}$ for all $\lambda > 0$. So, should there exist some set of prices at which all markets clear, those markets will also clear at any other prices obtained by multiplying all prices by any positive constant. This fact often can be exploited to help simplify calculations when solving for Walrasian equilibria.

EXAMPLE 5.1 Let us take a simple two-person economy and solve for a Walrasian equilibrium. Let consumers 1 and 2 have identical CES utility functions,

$$u^i(x_1, x_2) = x_1^\rho + x_2^\rho, \qquad i = 1, 2,$$

where $0 < \rho < 1$. Let there be 1 unit of each good and suppose each consumer owns all of one good, so initial endowments are $\mathbf{e}^1 = (1, 0)$ and $\mathbf{e}^2 = (0, 1)$. Because the aggregate endowment of each good is strictly positive and the CES form of utility is strongly increasing and strictly quasiconcave on $\mathbb{R}^n_+$ when $0 < \rho < 1$, the requirements of Theorem 5.5 are satisfied, so we know a Walrasian equilibrium exists in this economy.

From (E.10) and (E.11) in Example 1.1, consumer i's demand for good j at prices $\mathbf{p}$ will be $x_j^i(\mathbf{p}, y^i) = p_j^{r-1} y^i / (p_1^r + p_2^r)$, where $r \equiv \rho/(\rho - 1)$, and y^i is the consumer's income. Here, income is equal to the market value of the endowment, so $y^1 = \mathbf{p} \cdot \mathbf{e}^1 = p_1$ and $y^2 = \mathbf{p} \cdot \mathbf{e}^2 = p_2$.

Because only *relative* prices matter, and because we know from Theorem 5.5 that there is an equilibrium in which all prices are strictly positive, we can choose a convenient normalisation to simplify calculations. Let $\bar{\mathbf{p}} \equiv (1/p_2)\mathbf{p}$. Here, $\bar{p}_1 \equiv p_1/p_2$ and $\bar{p}_2 \equiv 1$, so $\bar{p}_1$ is just the relative price of the good x_1. Because each consumer's demand at $\mathbf{p}$ is the same as the demand at $\bar{\mathbf{p}}$, we can frame our problem as one of finding an equilibrium set of relative prices, $\bar{\mathbf{p}}$.

Now consider the market for good 1. Assuming an interior solution, equilibrium requires $\bar{\mathbf{p}}^*$ where total quantity demanded equals total quantity supplied, or where

$$x_1^1(\bar{\mathbf{p}}^*, \bar{\mathbf{p}}^* \cdot \mathbf{e}^1) + x_1^2(\bar{\mathbf{p}}^*, \bar{\mathbf{p}}^* \cdot \mathbf{e}^2) = e_1^1 + e_1^2.$$

Substituting from before, this requires

$$\frac{\bar{p}_1^{*r-1}\bar{p}_1^*}{\bar{p}_1^{*r}+1} + \frac{\bar{p}_1^{*r-1}}{\bar{p}_1^{*r}+1} = 1.$$

Solving, we obtain $\bar{p}_1^* = 1$. We conclude that any vector $\mathbf{p}^*$ where $p_1^* = p_2^*$, equates demand and supply in market 1. By Walras' law, those same prices must equate demand and supply in market 2, so we are done. □

5.2.2 EFFICIENCY

We can adapt the Edgeworth box description of a two-person economy to gain useful perspective on the nature of Walrasian equilibrium. Fig. 5.4 represents an economy where preferences satisfy the requirements of Theorem 5.5. Initial endowments are (e_1^1, e_2^1) and (e_1^2, e_2^2), and the box is constructed so these two points coincide at $\mathbf{e}$, as before. At relative prices p_1^*/p_2^*, consumer 1's budget constraint is the straight line through $\mathbf{e}$ when viewed from 1's origin. Facing the same prices, consumer 2's budget constraint will coincide with that same straight line when viewed (upside down) from 2's origin. Consumer 1's most preferred bundle within her budget set is (x_1^1, x_2^1), giving the quantities of each good consumer 1 demands facing prices p_1^*/p_2^* and having income equal to the market value of her endowment, $p_1^*e_1^1 + p_2^*e_2^1$. Similarly, consumer 2's demanded bundle at these same prices with income equal to the value of his endowment is (x_1^2, x_2^2). Equilibrium in the market for good 1 requires $x_1^1 + x_1^2 = e_1^1 + e_1^2$, or that total quantity demanded equal total quantity supplied. This, of course, is equivalent to the requirement $x_1^2 - e_1^2 = e_1^1 - x_1^1$, or that consumer 2's *net* demand be equal to consumer 1's *net* supply of good 1. A similar description of equilibrium in the market for good 2 also can be given.

A little experimentation with different relative prices, and so different budget sets for the two consumers, should convince you that these conditions for market equilibrium will obtain only when the demanded bundles – viewed from the consumers' respective origins – coincide with the same point in the box, as in Fig. 5.4. Because by construction one indifference curve for each consumer passes through every point in the box, and because equilibrium requires the demanded bundles coincide, it is clear that equilibrium

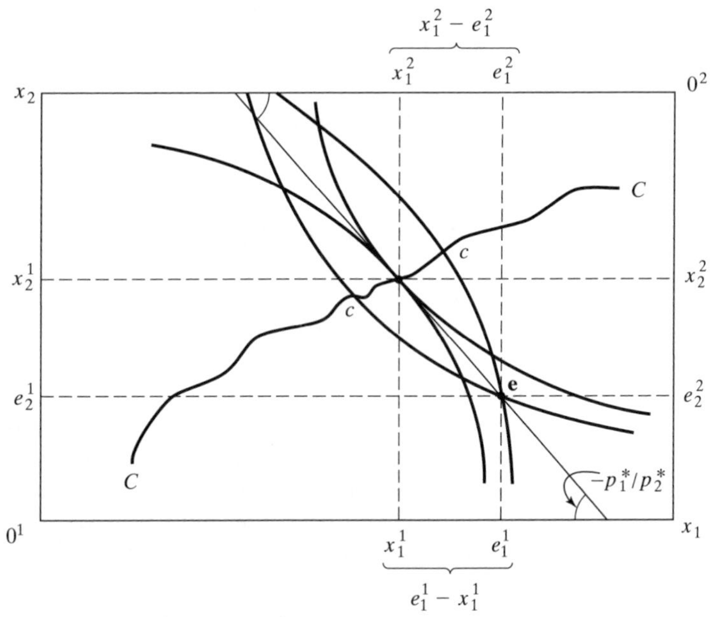

Figure 5.4. Walrasian equilibrium in the Edgeworth box.

will involve *tangency* between the two consumers' indifference curves through their demanded bundles, as illustrated in the figure.

There are several interesting features of Walrasian equilibrium that become immediately apparent with the perspective of the box. First, as we have noted, consumers' supplies and demands depend only on relative prices. Doubling or tripling all prices will not change the consumers' budget sets, so will not change their utility-maximising market behaviour. Second, Fig. 5.4 reinforces our understanding that market equilibrium amounts to the simultaneous compatibility of the actions of independent, decentralised, utility-maximising consumers.

Finally, Fig. 5.4 gives insight into the distributional implications of competitive market equilibrium. We have noted that equilibrium there is characterised by a tangency of the consumers' indifference curves through their respective demanded bundles. These bundles, in turn, give the final amount of each good owned and consumed by the consumer in the market system equilibrium. Thus, having begun with some initial distribution of the goods given by **e**, the maximising actions of self-interested consumers on impersonal markets has led to a redistribution of goods that is both 'inside the lens' formed by the indifference curves of each consumer through their respective endowments and 'on the contract curve'. In the preceding section, we identified allocations such as these as in the 'core' of the economy with endowments **e**. Thus, despite the fact that in the competitive market we have considered here, consumers do not require knowledge of other consumers' preferences or endowments, the allocation resulting from Walrasian equilibrium prices is in the core, at least for the Edgeworth box economy. As we now proceed to show, this remarkable property holds in general. We begin by defining some notation.

DEFINITION 5.6 ***Walrasian Equilibrium Allocations (WEAs)***

Let $\mathbf{p}^*$ be a Walrasian equilibrium for some economy with initial endowments $\mathbf{e}$, and let

$$\mathbf{x}(\mathbf{p}^*) \equiv (\mathbf{x}^1(\mathbf{p}^*, \mathbf{p}^* \cdot \mathbf{e}^1), \ldots, \mathbf{x}^I(\mathbf{p}^*, \mathbf{p}^* \cdot \mathbf{e}^I)),$$

where component i gives the n-vector of goods demanded and received by consumer i at prices $\mathbf{p}^*$. Then $\mathbf{x}(\mathbf{p}^*)$ is called a Walrasian equilibrium allocation, or WEA.

Now consider an economy with initial endowments $\mathbf{e}$ and feasible allocations $F(\mathbf{e})$ defined in (5.1). We should note some basic properties of the WEA in such economies. First, it should be obvious that any WEA will be feasible for this economy. Second, Fig. 5.4 makes clear that the bundle received by every consumer in a WEA is the most preferred bundle in that consumer's budget set at the Walrasian equilibrium prices. It therefore follows that any other allocation that is both feasible and preferred by some consumer to their bundle in the WEA must be too expensive for that consumer. Indeed, this would follow even if the price vector were not a Walrasian equilibrium. We record both of these facts as lemmas and leave the proof of the first and part of the proof of the second as exercises.

LEMMA 5.1 *Let $\mathbf{p}^*$ be a Walrasian equilibrium for some economy with initial endowments $\mathbf{e}$. Let $\mathbf{x}(\mathbf{p}^*)$ be the associated WEA. Then $\mathbf{x}(\mathbf{p}^*) \in F(\mathbf{e})$.*

LEMMA 5.2 *Suppose that u^i is strictly increasing on $\mathbb{R}^n_+$, that consumer i's demand is well-defined at $\mathbf{p} \geq \mathbf{0}$ and equal to $\hat{\mathbf{x}}^i$, and that $\mathbf{x}^i \in \mathbb{R}^n_+$.*

i. If $u^i(\mathbf{x}^i) > u^i(\hat{\mathbf{x}}^i)$, then $\mathbf{p} \cdot \mathbf{x}^i > \mathbf{p} \cdot \hat{\mathbf{x}}^i$.

ii. If $u^i(\mathbf{x}^i) \geq u^i(\hat{\mathbf{x}}^i)$, then $\mathbf{p} \cdot \mathbf{x}^i \geq \mathbf{p} \cdot \hat{\mathbf{x}}^i$.

Proof: We leave the first for you to prove as an exercise. So let us suppose that (i) holds. We therefore can employ it to prove (ii).

Suppose, by way of contradiction, that (ii) does not hold. Then $u^i(\mathbf{x}^i) \geq u^i(\hat{\mathbf{x}}^i)$ and $\mathbf{p} \cdot \mathbf{x}^i < \mathbf{p} \cdot \hat{\mathbf{x}}^i$. Consequently, beginning with $\mathbf{x}^i$, we may increase the amount of every good consumed by a small enough amount so that the resulting bundle, $\bar{\mathbf{x}}^i$, remains strictly less expensive than $\hat{\mathbf{x}}^i$. But because u^i is strictly increasing, we then have $u^i(\bar{\mathbf{x}}^i) > u^i(\mathbf{x}^i) \geq u^i(\hat{\mathbf{x}}^i)$, and $\mathbf{p} \cdot \bar{\mathbf{x}}^i < \mathbf{p} \cdot \hat{\mathbf{x}}^i$. But this contradicts (i) with $\mathbf{x}^i$ replaced by $\bar{\mathbf{x}}^i$. ∎

It bears noting, in general, that we have no reason to expect that when WEAs exist, they will be unique. Even in the two-person Edgeworth box economy, it is easy to construct examples where preferences satisfy very ordinary properties yet multiple Walrasian equilibrium allocations exist. Fig. 5.5 illustrates such a case. It seems prudent, therefore, to keep such possibilities in mind and avoid slipping into the belief that Walrasian equilibria

Figure 5.5. Multiple equilibria in a two-person market economy.

are 'usually' unique. As a matter of notation, then, let us give a name to the *set* of WEAs in an economy.

DEFINITION 5.7 ***The Set of WEAs***

For any economy with endowments $\mathbf{e}$, *let* $W(\mathbf{e})$ *denote the set of Walrasian equilibrium allocations.*

We now arrive at the crux of the matter. It is clear in both Figs. 5.4 and 5.5 that the WEAs involve allocations of goods to consumers that lie on the segment *cc* of the contract curve representing the *core* of those economies. It remains to show that WEAs have this property in arbitrary economies. Recall that $C(\mathbf{e})$ denotes the set of allocations in the core.

THEOREM 5.6 ***Core and Equilibria in Competitive Economies***

Consider an exchange economy $(u^i, \mathbf{e}^i)_{i\in\mathcal{I}}$. *If each consumer's utility function,* u^i, *is strictly increasing on* $\mathbb{R}^n_+$, *then every Walrasian equilibrium allocation is in the core. That is,*

$$W(\mathbf{e}) \subset C(\mathbf{e}).$$

Proof: The theorem claims that if $\mathbf{x}(\mathbf{p}^*)$ is a WEA for equilibrium prices $\mathbf{p}^*$, then $\mathbf{x}(\mathbf{p}^*) \in C(\mathbf{e})$. To prove it, suppose $\mathbf{x}(\mathbf{p}^*)$ is a WEA, and assume $\mathbf{x}(\mathbf{p}^*) \notin C(\mathbf{e})$.

Because $\mathbf{x}(\mathbf{p}^*)$ is a WEA, we know from Lemma 5.1 that $\mathbf{x}(\mathbf{p}^*) \in F(\mathbf{e})$, so $\mathbf{x}(\mathbf{p}^*)$ is feasible. However, because $\mathbf{x}(\mathbf{p}^*) \notin C(\mathbf{e})$, we can find a coalition S and another allocation $\mathbf{y}$ such that

$$\sum_{i\in S} \mathbf{y}^i = \sum_{i\in S} \mathbf{e}^i \tag{P.1}$$

and

$$u^i(\mathbf{y}^i) \geq u^i(\mathbf{x}^i(\mathbf{p}^*, \mathbf{p}^* \cdot \mathbf{e}^i)) \qquad \text{for all } i \in S, \tag{P.2}$$

with at least one inequality strict. (P.1) implies

$$\mathbf{p}^* \cdot \sum_{i \in S} \mathbf{y}^i = \mathbf{p}^* \cdot \sum_{i \in S} \mathbf{e}^i. \tag{P.3}$$

Now from (P.2) and Lemma 5.2, we know that for each $i \in S$, we must have

$$\mathbf{p}^* \cdot \mathbf{y}^i \geq \mathbf{p}^* \cdot \mathbf{x}^i(\mathbf{p}^*, \mathbf{p}^* \cdot \mathbf{e}^i) = \mathbf{p}^* \cdot \mathbf{e}^i, \tag{P.4}$$

with at least one inequality strict. Summing over all consumers in S, we obtain

$$\mathbf{p}^* \cdot \sum_{i \in S} \mathbf{y}^i > \mathbf{p}^* \cdot \sum_{i \in S} \mathbf{e}^i,$$

contradicting (P.3). Thus, $\mathbf{x}(\mathbf{p}^*) \in C(\mathbf{e})$ and the theorem is proved. ∎

Note that as a corollary to Theorem 5.5, we immediately have a result on the non-emptiness of the core. That is, under the conditions of Theorem 5.5, a Walrasian equilibrium allocation exists, and by Theorem 5.6, this allocation is in the core. Hence, the conditions of Theorem 5.5 guarantee that the core is non-empty.

Before moving on, we pause to consider what we have shown here. In a Walrasian equilibrium, each consumer acts completely independently of all other consumers in the sense that he simply chooses to demand a bundle that maximises his utility given the prevailing prices and given his income determined by the value of his endowment. In particular, he does not consider the amount demanded by others or the total amount supplied of any good. He knows only his own preferences and the prices at which he can carry out transactions.

Contrast this with the story of pure barter exchange with which we began the chapter. There, it was crucial that consumers actually could get together, take stock of the total resources available to them, and then exploit all potential gains from trade. In particular, each consumer would have to be keenly aware of when a mutually beneficial trade could be made with some other consumer – *any* other consumer! As we remarked earlier, it would be astonishing if such complete coordination could be even approximated, let alone achieved in practice. And even if it could be approximated, it would appear to require the aid of some central authority charged with coordinating the appropriate coalitions and trades.

But we have now shown in Theorem 5.6 that it is possible to achieve outcomes in the core *without* the aid of a central planner. Indeed, no one in our competitive economy requires direction or advice from anyone else. Each consumer simply observes the prices and places his utility-maximising demands and supplies on the market. In this sense, the competitive market mechanism is said to be **decentralised**.

Note, in particular, that because all core allocations are Pareto efficient, so, too, must be all Walrasian equilibrium allocations. Although we have proven more, this alone is quite remarkable. Imagine being charged with allocating all the economy's resources, so that in the end, the allocation is Pareto efficient. To keep you from giving all the resources to one person, let us also insist that in the end, every consumer must be at least as well off as they would have been just consuming their endowment. Think about how you might accomplish this. You might start by trying to gather information about the preferences of all consumers in the economy. (What a task that would be!) Only then could you attempt to redistribute goods in a manner that left no further gains from trade. As incredibly difficult as this task is, the competitive market mechanism achieves it, and more. To emphasise the fact that competitive outcomes are Pareto efficient, we state it as a theorem, called the *First Welfare Theorem*.

THEOREM 5.7 ***First Welfare Theorem***

Under the hypotheses of Theorem 5.6, every Walrasian equilibrium allocation is Pareto efficient.

Proof: The proof follows immediately from Theorem 5.6 and the observation that all core allocations are Pareto efficient. ∎

Theorem 5.7 provides some specific support for Adam Smith's contention that society's interests are served by an economic system where self-interested actions of individuals are mediated by impersonal markets. If conditions are sufficient to ensure that Walrasian equilibria exist, then regardless of the initial allocation of resources, the allocation realised in market equilibrium will be Pareto efficient.

It is extremely important to appreciate the scope of this aspect of competitive market systems. It is equally important to realise its limitations and to resist the temptation to read more into what we have shown than is justified. Nothing we have argued so far should lead us to believe that WEAs are necessarily 'socially optimal' if we include in our notion of social optimality any consideration for matters of 'equity' or 'justice' in distribution. Most would agree that an allocation that is not Pareto efficient is not even a candidate for the socially best, because it would always be possible to redistribute goods and make someone better off and no one worse off. At the same time, few could argue persuasively that every Pareto-efficient distribution has an equal claim to being considered the best or 'most just' from a social point of view.

In a later chapter, we give fuller consideration to normative issues such as these. For now, a simple example will serve to illustrate the distinction. Consider an economy with total endowments given by the dimensions of the Edgeworth box in Fig. 5.6. Suppose by some unknown means society has identified the distribution $\bar{\mathbf{x}}$ as the socially best. Suppose, in addition, that initial endowments are given by the allocation $\mathbf{e}$. Theorem 5.6 tells us that an equilibrium allocation under a competitive market system will be some allocation in $C(\mathbf{e})$, such as $\mathbf{x}'$, which in this case is quite distinct from $\bar{\mathbf{x}}$. Thus, while competitive market systems can improve on an initial distribution that is not itself Pareto efficient, there is no

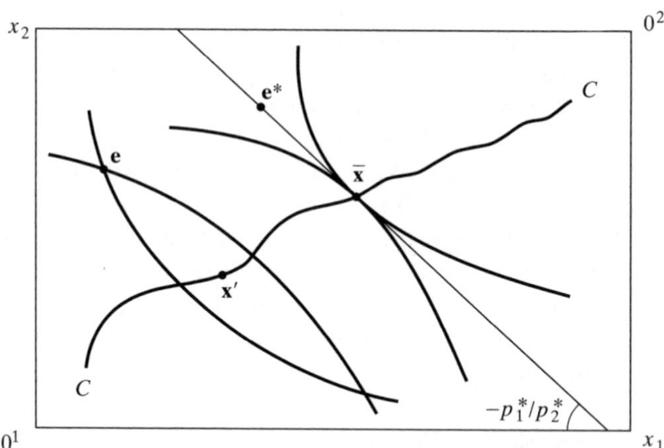

Figure 5.6. Efficiency and social optimality in a two-person economy.

assurance a competitive system, by itself, will lead to a final distribution that society as a whole views as best.

Before we become unduly pessimistic, let us consider a slightly different question. If by some means, we can determine the allocation we would like to see, can the power of a decentralised market system be used to achieve it? From Fig. 5.6, it seems this should be so. If initial endowments could be redistributed to $\mathbf{e}^*$, it is clear that $\bar{\mathbf{x}}$ is the allocation that would be achieved in competitive equilibrium with those endowments and prices $\mathbf{p}^*$.

In fact, this is an example of a rather general principle. It can be shown that under certain conditions, *any* Pareto-efficient allocation can be achieved by competitive markets and *some* initial endowments. This result is called the *Second Welfare Theorem.*

THEOREM 5.8 ***Second Welfare Theorem***

Consider an exchange economy $(u^i, \mathbf{e}^i)_{i\in\mathcal{I}}$ with aggregate endowment $\sum_{i=1}^{I} \mathbf{e}^i \gg \mathbf{0}$, and with each utility function u^i satisfying Assumption 5.1. Suppose that $\bar{\mathbf{x}}$ is a Pareto-efficient allocation for $(u^i, \mathbf{e}^i)_{i\in\mathcal{I}}$, and that endowments are redistributed so that the new endowment vector is $\bar{\mathbf{x}}$. Then $\bar{\mathbf{x}}$ is a Walrasian equilibrium allocation of the resulting exchange economy $(u^i, \bar{\mathbf{x}}^i)_{i\in\mathcal{I}}$.

Proof: Because $\bar{\mathbf{x}}$ is Pareto efficient, it is feasible. Hence, $\sum_{i=1}^{I} \bar{\mathbf{x}}^i = \sum_{i=1}^{I} \mathbf{e}^i \gg \mathbf{0}$. Consequently, we may apply Theorem 5.5 to conclude that the exchange economy $(u^i, \bar{\mathbf{x}}^i)_{i\in\mathcal{I}}$ possesses a Walrasian equilibrium allocation $\hat{\mathbf{x}}$. It only remains to show that $\hat{\mathbf{x}} = \bar{\mathbf{x}}$.

Now in the Walrasian equilibrium, each consumer's demand is utility maximising subject to her budget constraint. Consequently, because i demands $\hat{\mathbf{x}}^i$, and has endowment

$\bar{\mathbf{x}}^i$, we must have

$$u^i(\hat{\mathbf{x}}^i) \geq u^i(\bar{\mathbf{x}}^i) \qquad \text{for all } i \in \mathcal{I}. \tag{P.1}$$

But because $\hat{\mathbf{x}}$ is an equilibrium allocation, it must be feasible for the economy $(u^i, \bar{\mathbf{x}}^i)_{i\in\mathcal{I}}$. Consequently, $\sum_{i=1}^{I} \hat{\mathbf{x}}^i = \sum_{i=1}^{I} \bar{\mathbf{x}}^i = \sum_{i=1}^{I} \mathbf{e}^i$, so that $\hat{\mathbf{x}}$ is feasible for the original economy as well.

Thus, by (P.1), $\hat{\mathbf{x}}$ is feasible for the original economy and makes no consumer worse off than the Pareto-efficient (for the original economy) allocation $\bar{\mathbf{x}}$. Therefore, $\hat{\mathbf{x}}$ cannot make anyone strictly better off; otherwise, $\bar{\mathbf{x}}$ would not be Pareto efficient. Hence, every inequality in (P.1) must be an equality.

To see now that $\hat{\mathbf{x}}^i = \bar{\mathbf{x}}^i$ for every i, note that if for some consumer this were not the case, then in the Walrasian equilibrium of the new economy, that consumer could afford the average of the bundles $\hat{\mathbf{x}}^i$ and $\bar{\mathbf{x}}^i$ and strictly increase his utility (by strict quasiconcavity), contradicting the fact that $\hat{\mathbf{x}}^i$ is utility-maximising in the Walrasian equilibrium. ∎

One can view the Second Welfare Theorem as an affirmative answer to the following question: is a system that depends on decentralised, self-interested decision making by a large number of consumers capable of sustaining the socially 'best' allocation of resources, if we could just agree on what that was? Under the conditions stated before, the Second Welfare Theorem says yes, as long as socially 'best' requires, at least, Pareto efficiency.

Although we did not explicitly mention prices in the statement of the Second Welfare Theorem, or in its proof, they are there in the background. Specifically, the theorem says that there are Walrasian equilibrium prices, $\bar{\mathbf{p}}$, such that when the endowment allocation is $\bar{\mathbf{x}}$, each consumer i will maximise $u^i(\mathbf{x}^i)$ subject to $\bar{\mathbf{p}} \cdot \mathbf{x}^i \leq \bar{\mathbf{p}} \cdot \bar{\mathbf{x}}^i$ by choosing $\mathbf{x}^i = \bar{\mathbf{x}}^i$. Because of this, the prices $\bar{\mathbf{p}}$ are sometimes said to *support* the allocation $\bar{\mathbf{x}}$.

We began discussing the Second Welfare Theorem by asking whether redistribution to a point like $\mathbf{e}^*$ in Fig. 5.6 could yield the allocation $\bar{\mathbf{x}}$ as a WEA. In the theorem, we showed that the answer is yes if endowments were redistributed to $\bar{\mathbf{x}}$ itself. It should be clear from Fig. 5.6, however, that $\bar{\mathbf{x}}$ in fact will be a WEA for market prices $\bar{\mathbf{p}}$ under a redistribution of initial endowments to *any* point along the price line through $\bar{\mathbf{x}}$, including, of course, to $\mathbf{e}^*$. This same principle applies generally, so we have an immediate corollary to Theorem 5.8. The proof is left as an exercise.

COROLLARY 5.1 ***Another Look at the Second Welfare Theorem***

Under the assumptions of the preceding theorem, if $\bar{\mathbf{x}}$ is Pareto efficient, then $\bar{\mathbf{x}}$ is a WEA for some Walrasian equilibrium $\bar{\mathbf{p}}$ after redistribution of initial endowments to any allocation $\mathbf{e}^* \in F(\mathbf{e})$, such that $\bar{\mathbf{p}} \cdot \mathbf{e}^{*i} = \bar{\mathbf{p}} \cdot \bar{\mathbf{x}}^i$ for all $i \in \mathcal{I}$.

5.3 EQUILIBRIUM IN PRODUCTION

Now we expand our description of the economy to include production as well as consumption. We will find that most of the important properties of competitive market systems uncovered earlier continue to hold. However, production brings with it several new issues that must be addressed.

For example, the profits earned by firms must be distributed back to the consumers who own them. Also, in a single firm, the distinction between what constitutes an input and what constitutes an output is usually quite clear. This distinction becomes blurred when we look *across* firms and view the production side of the economy as a whole. An input for one firm may well be the output of another. To avoid hopelessly entangling ourselves in notation, it seems best to resist making any a priori distinctions between inputs and outputs and instead let the distinction depend on the context. Thus, we will view every type of good or service in a neutral way as just a different kind of *commodity*. We will suppose throughout that there is a fixed and finite number n of such commodities. In the case of producers, we will then adopt simple sign conventions to distinguish inputs from outputs in any particular context.

Again, we formalise the competitive structure of the economy by supposing consumers act to maximise utility subject to their budget constraints and that firms seek to maximise profit. Both consumers and firms are price takers.

5.3.1 PRODUCERS

To describe the production sector, we suppose there is a fixed number J of firms that we index by the set

$$\mathcal{J} = \{1, \ldots, J\}.$$

We now let $\mathbf{y}^j \in \mathbb{R}^n$ be a production plan for some firm, and observe the convention of writing $y_k^j < 0$ if commodity k is an input used in the production plan and $y_k^j > 0$ if it is an output produced from the production plan. If, for example, there are two commodities and $\mathbf{y}^j = (-7, 3)$, then the production plan requires 7 units of commodity one as an input, to produce 3 units of commodity two as an output.

To summarise the technological possibilities in production, we return to the most general description of the firm's technology, first encountered in Section 3.2, and suppose each firm possesses a production possibility set, $Y^j, j \in \mathcal{J}$. We make the following assumptions on production possibility sets.

ASSUMPTION 5.2 ***The Individual Firm***

1. *$\mathbf{0} \in Y^j \subseteq \mathbb{R}^n$.*
2. *Y^j is closed and bounded.*
3. *Y^j is strongly convex. That is, for all distinct $\mathbf{y}^1, \mathbf{y}^2 \in Y^j$ and all $t \in (0, 1)$, there exists $\bar{\mathbf{y}} \in Y^j$ such that $\bar{\mathbf{y}} \geq t\mathbf{y}^1 + (1-t)\mathbf{y}^2$ and equality does not hold.*

The first of these guarantees firm profits are bounded from below by zero, and the second that production of output always requires some inputs. The closedness part of the second condition imposes continuity. It says that the limits of possible production plans are themselves possible production plans. The boundedness part of this condition is very restrictive and is made only to keep the analysis simple to follow. Do not be tempted into thinking that it merely expresses the idea that resources are limited. For the time being, regard it as a simplifying yet dispensable assumption. We shall discuss the importance of removing this assumption a little later. The third assumption, strong convexity, is new. Unlike all the others, which are fairly weak restrictions on the technology, strong convexity is a more demanding requirement. In effect, strong convexity rules out constant and increasing returns to scale in production and ensures that the firm's profit-maximising production plan is unique. Although Assumption 5.2 does not impose it, all of our results to follow are consistent with the assumption of 'no free production' (i.e., $Y^j \cap \mathbb{R}^n_+ = \{\mathbf{0}\}$).

Each firm faces fixed commodity prices $\mathbf{p} \geq \mathbf{0}$ and chooses a production plan to maximise profit. Thus, each firm solves the problem

$$\max_{\mathbf{y}^j \in Y^j} \mathbf{p} \cdot \mathbf{y}^j \tag{5.3}$$

Note how our sign convention ensures that inputs are accounted for in profits as costs and outputs as revenues. Because the objective function is continuous and the constraint set closed and bounded, a maximum of firm profit will exist. So, for all $\mathbf{p} \geq \mathbf{0}$ let

$$\Pi^j(\mathbf{p}) \equiv \max_{\mathbf{y}^j \in Y^j} \mathbf{p} \cdot \mathbf{y}^j$$

denote firm j's profit function. By Theorem A2.21 (the theorem of the maximum), $\Pi^j(\mathbf{p})$ is continuous on $\mathbb{R}^n_+$. As you are asked to show in Exercise 5.23, strong convexity ensures that the profit-maximising production plan, $\mathbf{y}^j(\mathbf{p})$, will be unique whenever $\mathbf{p} \gg \mathbf{0}$. Finally, from Theorem A2.21 (the theorem of the maximum), $\mathbf{y}^j(\mathbf{p})$ will be continuous on $\mathbb{R}^n_{++}$. Note that for $\mathbf{p} \gg \mathbf{0}$, $\mathbf{y}^j(\mathbf{p})$ is a vector-valued function whose components are the firm's output supply and input demand functions. However, we often simply refer to $\mathbf{y}^j(\mathbf{p})$ as firm j's supply function. We record these properties for future reference.

THEOREM 5.9 ***Basic Properties of Supply and Profits***

If Y^j satisfies conditions 1 through 3 of Assumption 5.2, then for every price $\mathbf{p} \gg \mathbf{0}$, the solution to the firm's problem (5.3) is unique and denoted by $\mathbf{y}^j(\mathbf{p})$. Moreover, $\mathbf{y}^j(\mathbf{p})$ is continuous on $\mathbb{R}^n_{++}$. In addition, $\Pi^j(\mathbf{p})$ is well-defined and continuous on $\mathbb{R}^n_+$.

Finally, note that maximum firm profits are homogeneous of degree 1 in the vector of commodity prices. Each output supply and input demand function will be homogeneous of degree zero in prices. (See Theorems 3.7 and 3.8.)

Next we consider *aggregate* production possibilities economy-wide. We suppose there are no externalities in production between firms, and define the aggregate production possibilities set,

$$Y \equiv \left\{ \mathbf{y} \mid \mathbf{y} = \sum_{j \in \mathcal{J}} \mathbf{y}^j, \quad \text{where } \mathbf{y}^j \in Y^j \right\}.$$

The set Y will inherit all the properties of the individual production sets, and we take note of that formally.

THEOREM 5.10 ***Properties of*** Y

If each Y^j satisfies Assumption 5.2, then the aggregate production possibility set, Y, also satisfies Assumption 5.2.

We shall leave the proof of this as an exercise. Conditions 1, 3, and the boundedness of Y follow directly from those properties of the Y^j. The closedness of Y does not follow simply from the closedness of the individual Y^j's. However, under our additional assumption that the Y^j's are bounded, Y can be shown to be closed.

Now consider the problem of maximising *aggregate* profits. Under Theorem 5.10, a maximum of $\mathbf{p} \cdot \mathbf{y}$ over the aggregate production set Y will exist and be unique when $\mathbf{p} \gg \mathbf{0}$. In addition, the aggregate profit-maximising production plan $\mathbf{y}(\mathbf{p})$ will be a continuous function of $\mathbf{p}$. Moreover, we note the close connection between aggregate profit-maximising production plans and individual firm profit-maximising production plans.

THEOREM 5.11 ***Aggregate Profit Maximisation***

For any prices $\mathbf{p} \geq \mathbf{0}$, we have

$$\mathbf{p} \cdot \bar{\mathbf{y}} \geq \mathbf{p} \cdot \mathbf{y} \qquad \textit{for all} \quad \mathbf{y} \in Y$$

if and only if for some $\bar{\mathbf{y}}^j \in Y^j, j \in \mathcal{J}$, we may write $\bar{\mathbf{y}} = \sum_{j \in \mathcal{J}} \bar{\mathbf{y}}^j$, and

$$\mathbf{p} \cdot \bar{\mathbf{y}}^j \geq \mathbf{p} \cdot \mathbf{y}^j \qquad \textit{for all} \quad \mathbf{y}^j \in Y^j, \ j \in \mathcal{J}.$$

In words, the theorem says that $\bar{\mathbf{y}} \in Y$ maximises aggregate profit if and only if it can be decomposed into individual firm profit-maximising production plans. The proof is straightforward.

Proof: Let $\bar{\mathbf{y}} \in Y$ maximise aggregate profits at price $\mathbf{p}$. Suppose that $\bar{\mathbf{y}} \equiv \sum_{j \in \mathcal{J}} \bar{\mathbf{y}}^j$ for $\bar{\mathbf{y}}^j \in Y^j$. If $\bar{\mathbf{y}}^k$ does not maximise profits for firm k, then there exists some other $\tilde{\mathbf{y}}^k \in Y^k$ that gives firm k higher profits. But then the aggregate production vector $\tilde{\mathbf{y}} \in Y$ composed of $\tilde{\mathbf{y}}^k$ and the sum of the $\bar{\mathbf{y}}^j$ for $j \neq k$ must give higher aggregate profits than the aggregate vector $\bar{\mathbf{y}}$, contradicting the assumption that $\bar{\mathbf{y}}$ maximises aggregate profits at price $\mathbf{p}$.

Next, suppose feasible production plans $\bar{\mathbf{y}}^1, \ldots, \bar{\mathbf{y}}^j$ maximise profits at price $\mathbf{p}$ for the individual firms in $\mathcal{J}$. Then

$$\mathbf{p} \cdot \bar{\mathbf{y}}^j \geq \mathbf{p} \cdot \mathbf{y}^j \qquad \text{for } \mathbf{y}^j \in Y^j \text{ and } j \in \mathcal{J}.$$

Summing over all firms yields

$$\sum_{j \in \mathcal{J}} \mathbf{p} \cdot \bar{\mathbf{y}}^j \geq \sum_{j \in \mathcal{J}} \mathbf{p} \cdot \mathbf{y}^j \qquad \text{for } \mathbf{y}^j \in Y^j \text{ and } j \in \mathcal{J}.$$

Rearranging, we can write this as

$$\mathbf{p} \cdot \sum_{j \in \mathcal{J}} \bar{\mathbf{y}}^j \geq \mathbf{p} \cdot \sum_{j \in \mathcal{J}} \mathbf{y}^j \qquad \text{for } \mathbf{y}^j \in Y^j \text{ and } j \in \mathcal{J}.$$

But from the definitions of $\bar{\mathbf{y}}$ and Y, this just says

$$\mathbf{p} \cdot \bar{\mathbf{y}} \geq \mathbf{p} \cdot \mathbf{y} \qquad \text{for } \mathbf{y} \in Y,$$

so $\bar{\mathbf{y}}$ maximises aggregate profits at price $\mathbf{p}$, completing the proof. ∎

5.3.2 CONSUMERS

Formally, the description of consumers is just as it has always been. However, we need to modify some of the details to account for the distribution of firm *profits* because firms are owned by consumers. As before, we let

$$\mathcal{I} \equiv \{1, \ldots, I\}$$

index the set of consumers and let u^i denote i's utility function over the consumption set $\mathbb{R}^n_+$.

Before continuing, note that our assumption that consumer bundles are non-negative does not preclude the possibility that consumers supply goods and services to the market. Indeed, labour services are easily included by endowing the consumer with a fixed number of hours that are available for consumption. Those that are not consumed as 'leisure' are then supplied as labour services. If the consumer's only source of income is his endowment, then just as before, whether a consumer is a net demander or supplier of a good depends upon whether his (total) demand falls short of or exceeds his endowment of that good.

Of course, we must here also take account of the fact that consumers receive income from the profit earned by firms they own. In a *private ownership economy*, which we shall consider here, consumers own shares in firms and firm profits are distributed to shareholders. Consumer i's shares in firm j entitle him to some proportion $0 \leq \theta^{ij} \leq 1$ of the profits of firm j. Of course, these shares, summed over all consumers in the economy, must sum to 1. Thus,

$$0 \leq \theta^{ij} \leq 1 \qquad \text{for all } i \in \mathcal{I} \text{ and } j \in J,$$

where

$$\sum_{i \in \mathcal{I}} \theta^{ij} = 1 \qquad \text{for all } j \in J.$$

In our economy with production and private ownership of firms, a consumer's income can arise from two sources – from selling an endowment of commodities already owned, and from shares in the profits of any number of firms. If $\mathbf{p} \geq \mathbf{0}$ is the vector of market prices, one for each commodity, the consumer's budget constraint is

$$\mathbf{p} \cdot \mathbf{x}^i \leq \mathbf{p} \cdot \mathbf{e}^i + \sum_{j \in J} \theta^{ij} \Pi^j(\mathbf{p}). \tag{5.4}$$

By letting $m^i(\mathbf{p})$ denote the right-hand side of (5.4), the consumer's problem is

$$\max_{\mathbf{x}^i \in \mathbb{R}^n_+} u^i(\mathbf{x}^i) \qquad \text{s.t.} \qquad \mathbf{p} \cdot \mathbf{x}^i \leq m^i(\mathbf{p}). \tag{5.5}$$

Now, under Assumption 5.2, each firm will earn non-negative profits because each can always choose the zero production vector. Consequently, $m^i(\mathbf{p}) \geq 0$ because $\mathbf{p} \geq \mathbf{0}$ and $\mathbf{e}^i \geq \mathbf{0}$. Therefore, under Assumptions 5.1 and 5.2, a solution to (5.5) will exist and be unique whenever $\mathbf{p} \gg \mathbf{0}$. Again, we denote it by $\mathbf{x}^i(\mathbf{p}, m^i(\mathbf{p}))$, where $m^i(\mathbf{p})$ is just the consumer's income.

Recall from Chapter 1 that under the assumptions we made there (and also here), $\mathbf{x}^i(\mathbf{p}, y)$ is continuous in $(\mathbf{p}, y) \in \mathbb{R}^n_{++} \times \mathbb{R}^n_+$. Consequently, as long as $m^i(\mathbf{p})$ is continuous in $\mathbf{p}$, $\mathbf{x}^i(\mathbf{p}, m^i(\mathbf{p}))$ will be continuous in $\mathbf{p}$. By appealing to Theorem 5.9, we see that $m_i(\mathbf{p})$ is continuous on $\mathbb{R}^n_+$ under Assumption 5.2. Putting this all together we have the following theorem.

THEOREM 5.12 ***Basic Property of Demand with Profit Shares***

If each Y^j satisfies Assumption 5.2 and if u^i satisfies Assumption 5.1, then a solution to the consumer's problem (5.5) exists and is unique for all $\mathbf{p} \gg \mathbf{0}$. Denoting it by $\mathbf{x}^i(\mathbf{p}, m^i(\mathbf{p}))$, we have furthermore that $\mathbf{x}^i(\mathbf{p}, m^i(\mathbf{p}))$ is continuous in $\mathbf{p}$ on $\mathbb{R}^n_{++}$. In addition, $m_i(\mathbf{p})$ is continuous on $\mathbb{R}^n_+$.

This completes the description of the economy. Altogether, we can represent it as the collection $(u^i, \mathbf{e}^i, \theta^{ij}, Y^j)_{i \in \mathcal{I}, j \in \mathcal{J}}$.

5.3.3 EQUILIBRIUM

As in the case with no production, we can again define a real-valued aggregate excess demand function for each commodity market and a vector-valued aggregate excess demand function for the economy as a whole. Aggregate excess demand for commodity k is

$$z_k(\mathbf{p}) \equiv \sum_{i\in\mathcal{I}} x_k^i(\mathbf{p}, m^i(\mathbf{p})) - \sum_{j\in J} y_k^j(\mathbf{p}) - \sum_{i\in\mathcal{I}} e_k^i,$$

and the aggregate excess demand vector is

$$\mathbf{z}(\mathbf{p}) \equiv (z_1(\mathbf{p}), \ldots, z_n(\mathbf{p})).$$

As before (see Definition 5.5), a Walrasian equilibrium price vector $\mathbf{p}^* \gg \mathbf{0}$ clears all markets. That is, $\mathbf{z}(\mathbf{p}^*) = \mathbf{0}$.

THEOREM 5.13 ***Existence of Walrasian Equilibrium with Production***

Consider the economy $(u^i, \mathbf{e}^i, \theta^{ij}, Y^j)_{i\in\mathcal{I}, j\in\mathcal{J}}$. If each u^i satisfies Assumption 5.1, each Y^j satisfies Assumption 5.2, and $\mathbf{y} + \sum_{i\in\mathcal{I}} \mathbf{e}^i \gg \mathbf{0}$ for some aggregate production vector $\mathbf{y} \in \sum_{j\in\mathcal{J}} Y^j$, then there exists at least one price vector $\mathbf{p}^* \gg \mathbf{0}$, such that $\mathbf{z}(\mathbf{p}^*) = \mathbf{0}$.

Recall that when there was no production, we required the aggregate endowment vector to be strictly positive to guarantee existence. With production, that condition can be weakened to requiring that there is a feasible production vector for this economy whose net result is a strictly positive amount of every good (i.e., $\mathbf{y} + \sum_{i\in\mathcal{I}} \mathbf{e}^i \gg \mathbf{0}$ for some aggregate production vector $\mathbf{y}$).

Proof: We shall get the proof started, and leave the rest for you to complete as an exercise. The idea is to show that under the assumptions above, the aggregate excess demand function satisfies the conditions of Theorem 5.3. Because production sets are bounded and consumption is non-negative, this reduces to showing that some consumer's demand for some good is unbounded as some, but not all, prices approach zero. (However, you should check even this logic as you complete the proof for yourself.) Therefore, we really need only mimic the proof of Theorem 5.4.

So, consider a sequence of strictly positive price vectors, $\{\mathbf{p}^m\}$, converging to $\bar{\mathbf{p}} \neq \mathbf{0}$, such that $\bar{p}_k = 0$ for some good k. We would like to show that for some, possibly other, good k' with $\bar{p}_{k'} = 0$, the sequence $\{z_{k'}(\mathbf{p}^m)\}$, of excess demands for good k' is unbounded.

Recall that our first step in the proof of Theorem 5.4 was to identify a consumer whose income was strictly positive at the limit price vector $\bar{\mathbf{p}}$. This is where we shall use the new condition on net aggregate production.

Because $\mathbf{y} + \sum_{i=1}^{I} \mathbf{e}^i \gg \mathbf{0}$ for some aggregate production vector $\mathbf{y}$, and because the non-zero price vector $\bar{\mathbf{p}}$ has no negative components, we must have $\bar{\mathbf{p}} \cdot (\mathbf{y} + \sum_{i=1}^{I} \mathbf{e}^i) > 0$.

Consequently, recalling that both $m^i(\mathbf{p})$ and $\Pi^j(\mathbf{p})$ are well-defined for all $\mathbf{p} \geq \mathbf{0}$,

$$\begin{aligned}\sum_{i\in\mathcal{I}} m^i(\bar{\mathbf{p}}) &= \sum_{i\in\mathcal{I}}\left(\bar{\mathbf{p}}\cdot\mathbf{e}^i + \sum_{j\in\mathcal{J}}\theta^{ij}\Pi^j(\bar{\mathbf{p}})\right)\\ &= \sum_{i\in\mathcal{I}}\bar{\mathbf{p}}\cdot\mathbf{e}^i + \sum_{j\in\mathcal{J}}\Pi^j(\bar{\mathbf{p}})\\ &\geq \sum_{i\in\mathcal{I}}\bar{\mathbf{p}}\cdot\mathbf{e}^i + \bar{\mathbf{p}}\cdot\mathbf{y}\\ &= \bar{\mathbf{p}}\cdot\left(\mathbf{y}+\sum_{i=1}^{I}\mathbf{e}^i\right)\\ &> 0,\end{aligned}$$

where the first equality follows by the definition of $m^i(\bar{\mathbf{p}})$, the second follows because total non-endowment income is simply aggregate profits, and the weak inequality follows from Theorem 5.11, which ensures that the sum of individual firm maximised profits must be at least as large as maximised aggregate profits and hence aggregate profits from $\mathbf{y}$. Therefore, there must exist at least one consumer whose income at prices $\bar{\mathbf{p}}$, $m^i(\bar{\mathbf{p}})$, is strictly positive. The rest of the proof proceeds now as in the proof of Theorem 5.4, and we leave it for you to complete as an exercise. (You will need to use the result noted in Theorem 5.12 that $m^i(\mathbf{p})$ is continuous on $\mathbb{R}^n_+$.) ∎

As before, because excess demand is homogeneous of degree zero, when Walrasian equilibrium prices exist, they will not be unique. Also, note that once again the assumption that each u^i is strongly increasing (and strictly quasiconcave) on all of $\mathbb{R}^n_+$ rules out Cobb-Douglas utility functions. However, you are asked to show in Exercise 5.14 that, under Assumption 5.2 on the production sector, the aggregate excess demand function nonetheless satisfies all the conditions of Theorem 5.3 even when utilities are of the Cobb-Douglas form.

EXAMPLE 5.2 In the classic Robinson Crusoe economy, all production and all consumption is carried out by a single consumer. Robinson the consumer sells his labour time h (in hours) to Robinson the producer, who in turn uses the consumer's labour services for that amount of time to produce coconuts, y, which he then sells to Robinson the consumer. All profits from the production and sale of coconuts are distributed to Robinson the consumer.

With only one firm, the production possibility set for the firm and the economy coincide. Let that set be

$$Y = \{(-h, y) \mid 0 \leq h \leq b, \text{ and } 0 \leq y \leq h^{\alpha}\},$$

where $b > 0$, and $\alpha \in (0, 1)$.

So, for example, the production vector $(-2, 2^\alpha)$ is in the production set, which means that it is possible to produce 2^α coconuts by using 2 hours of Robinson's time.

The set Y is illustrated in Fig. 5.7(a), and it is easy to verify that it satisfies all the requirements of Assumption 5.2. Note that parameter b serves to bound the production set. Because this bound is present for purely technical purposes, do not give it much thought. In a moment, we will choose it to be large enough so that it is irrelevant.

As usual, the consumption set for Robinson the consumer is just the non-negative orthant, which in this two-good case is $\mathbb{R}^2_+$. Robinson's utility function is

$$u(h, y) = h^{1-\beta} y^\beta,$$

where $\beta \in (0, 1)$. Here, h denotes the number of hours consumed by Robinson (leisure, if you will), and y denotes the number of coconuts consumed. We will suppose that Robinson is endowed with $T > 0$ units of h (i.e., T hours), and no coconuts. That is, $\mathbf{e} = (T, 0)$.

We will now choose b large enough so that $b > T$. Consequently, in any Walrasian equilibrium, the constraint for the firm that $h \leq b$ will not be binding because in equilibrium the number of hours demanded by the firm cannot exceed the total available number of hours, T.

This economy satisfies all the hypotheses of Theorem 5.13 except that Robinson's utility function, being of the Cobb-Douglas form, is neither strongly increasing nor strictly quasiconcave on all of $\mathbb{R}^n_+$. However, as you are asked to show in Exercise 5.14, the resulting aggregate excess demand function nonetheless satisfies the conditions of Theorem 5.3. Consequently, a Walrasian equilibrium in strictly positive prices is guaranteed to exist. We now calculate one.

Let $p > 0$ denote the price of coconuts, y, and $w > 0$ denote the price per hour of Robinson's time, h. (Thus, it makes sense to think of w as a wage rate.) Consumer Robinson's budget set, before including income from profits, is depicted in Fig. 5.7(b), and Fig. 5.7(c) shows Robinson's budget set when he receives his (100 per cent) share of the firm's profits, equal to $\bar{\pi}$ in the figure.

To determine Walrasian equilibrium prices (w^*, p^*), we shall first determine the firm's supply function (which, in our terminology also includes the firm's demand for hours of labour), then determine the consumer's demand function, and finally put them together to find market-clearing prices. We begin with Robinson the firm. From this point, we use the terms firm and consumer and trust that you will keep in mind that both are in fact Robinson.

Because it never pays the firm to waste hours purchased, it will always choose $(-h, y) \in Y$, so that $y = h^\alpha$. Consequently, because we have chosen b large enough so that it will not be a binding constraint, the firm will choose $h \geq 0$ to maximise

$$ph^\alpha - wh.$$

When $\alpha < 1, h = 0$ will not be profit-maximising (as we shall see); hence, the first-order conditions require setting the derivative with respect to h equal to zero, i.e., $\alpha p h^{\alpha-1} - w = 0$. Rewriting this, and recalling that $y = h^\alpha$, gives the firm's demand for

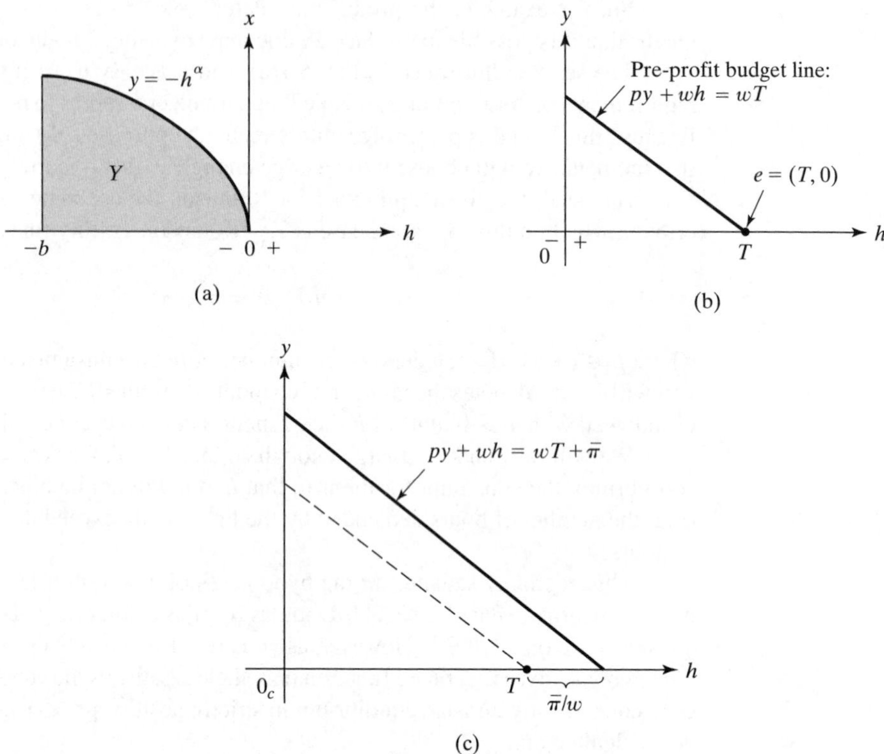

Figure 5.7. Production possibility set, Y, pre-profit budget line, and post-profit budget line in the Robinson Crusoe economy.

hours, denoted h^f, and its supply of output, denoted y^f, as functions of the prices w, p:[4]

$$h^f = \left(\frac{\alpha p}{w}\right)^{1/(1-\alpha)},$$

$$y^f = \left(\frac{\alpha p}{w}\right)^{\alpha/(1-\alpha)}.$$

Consequently, the firm's profits are

$$\pi(w, p) = \frac{1-\alpha}{\alpha} w \left(\frac{\alpha p}{w}\right)^{1/1-\alpha}.$$

Note that profits are positive as long as prices are. (This shows that choosing $h = 0$ is not profit-maximising just as we claimed earlier.)

[4]In case you are keeping track of sign conventions, this means that $(-h^f, y^f) \in Y$.

We now turn to the consumer's problem. Robinson's income is the sum of his endowment income, $(w, p) \cdot (T, 0) = wT$, and his income from his 100 per cent ownership in the firm, $\pi(w, p)$, the firm's profits. So the consumer's budget constraint, which will be satisfied with equality because his utility function is strictly increasing, is

$$py + wh = wT + \pi(w, p).$$

He chooses $(h, y) \geq (0, 0)$ to maximise utility subject to this constraint. By now, you are familiar with the demand functions of a consumer with Cobb-Douglas utility. He will spend the fraction $1 - \beta$ of his total income on h and fraction β of it on y. So, letting h^c and y^c denote the consumer's demands, we have

$$h^c = \frac{(1-\beta)(wT + \pi(w, p))}{w},$$

$$y^c = \frac{\beta(wT + \pi(w, p))}{p}.$$

We can now put all of this together to search for a price vector (w, p) that will clear both markets. There are two simplifications we can make, however. The first is that because aggregate excess demand is homogeneous of degree zero, and we are guaranteed a Walrasian equilibrium in strictly positive prices, we may set the Walrasian equilibrium price of y, p^*, equal to one without any loss. The second is that we need now only find a price w^* so that the market for h clears, because by Walras' law, the market for y will then clear as well.

It thus remains to find w^* such that $h^c + h^f = T$, or using the equations above and setting $p^* = 1$,

$$\frac{(1-\beta)(w^*T + \pi(w^*, 1))}{w^*} + \left(\frac{\alpha}{w^*}\right)^{1/(1-\alpha)} = T,$$

or

$$\frac{(1-\beta)(1-\alpha)}{\alpha}\left(\frac{\alpha}{w^*}\right)^{1/(1-\alpha)} + \left(\frac{\alpha}{w^*}\right)^{1/(1-\alpha)} = \beta T,$$

where we have substituted for the firm's profits to arrive at the second equality. It is straightforward now to solve for w^* to obtain the equilibrium wage

$$w^* = \alpha\left(\frac{1-\beta(1-\alpha)}{\alpha\beta T}\right)^{1-\alpha} > 0.$$

We invite you to check that for this value of w^*, and with $p^* = 1$, both markets do indeed clear.

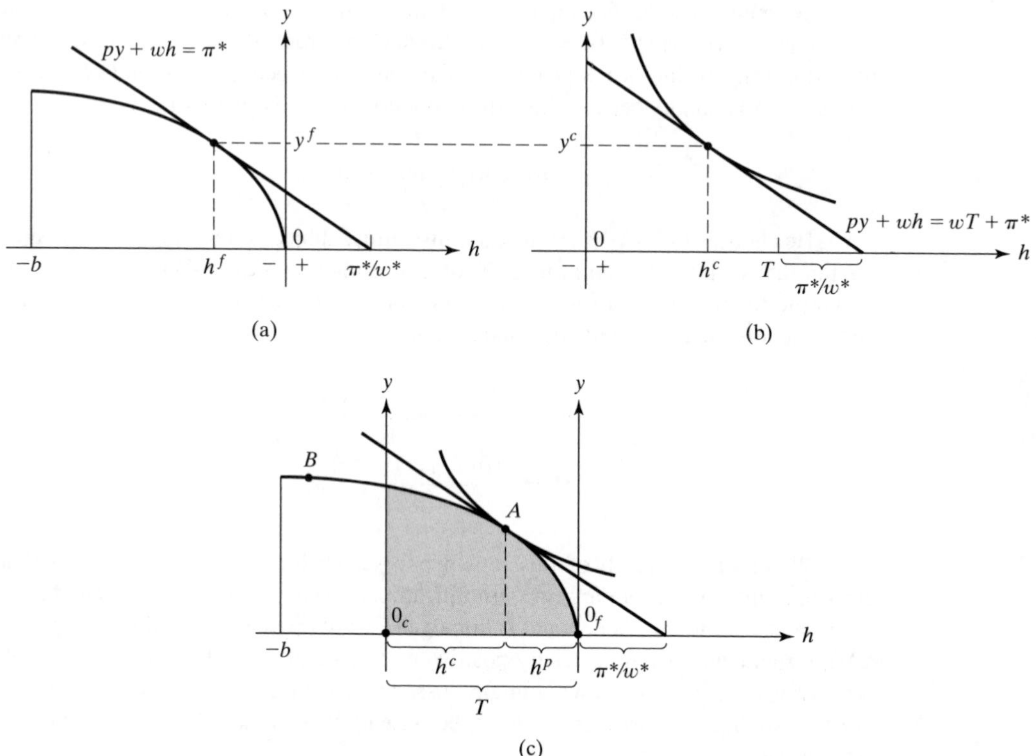

Figure 5.8. Equilibrium in a Robinson Crusoe economy.

We can illustrate the equilibrium diagrammatically. Fig. 5.8(a) shows the firm's profit-maximising solution. The line given by $\pi^* = py + wh$ is an **iso-profit line** for the firm, because profits are constant and equal to π^* for every (h, y) on it. Note that when $(h, y) \in Y, h \leq 0$, so that $py + wh$ is indeed the correct formula for profits in the figure. Also note that this iso-profit line (and all others) has slope $-w/p$. Moreover, the iso-profit line depicted yields the highest possible profits for the firm because higher profits would require a production plan above the π^* iso-profit line, and none of those is in the production set. Therefore, $\pi^* = \pi(w^*, 1)$.

Fig. 5.8(b) shows the consumer's utility-maximising solution given the budget constraint $py + wh = wT + \pi^*$. Note the slope of the consumer's budget constraint is $-w/p$, which is the same as the slope of the firm's iso-profit line.

Fig. 5.8(c) puts Figs. 5.8(a) and 5.8(b) together by superimposing the consumer's figure over the firm's, placing the point marked T in the consumer's figure onto the origin in the firm's figure. The origin for the consumer is marked as 0_c and the origin for the firm is 0_f. Point A shows the Walrasian equilibrium allocation.

Fig. 5.8(c) allows us to conclude that this competitive equilibrium with production is Pareto efficient. Consider the shaded region in the figure. With the origin at 0_f, the shaded region denotes the set of feasible production plans – those that can be actually implemented in this economy, taking into account the available resources. Any production plan in the shaded region can be carried out because it calls for no more than T hours, and this is the total number of hours with which the economy is endowed. On the other hand, a production plan like point B is technologically possible because it is in the production set, but it is infeasible because it requires more than T hours.

Switching our point of view, considering 0_c as the origin, the shaded region indicates the set of feasible consumption bundles for this economy. With this in mind, it is clear that the Walrasian allocation at A is Pareto efficient. It maximises Robinson's utility among all feasible consumption bundles.

Soon, we shall show that, just as in the case of a pure exchange economy, this is a rather general result even with production. □

We now return to the assumption of boundedness of the firms' production sets. As mentioned earlier, this assumption can be dispensed with. Moreover, there is very good reason to do so.

The production possibilities set is meant to describe the firm's technology, nothing more. It describes how much of various outputs can be produced with different amounts of various inputs. Thus, if the amount of inputs applied to the process increases without bound, so too might the amount of output produced. So, the first point is that there is simply no place in the description of the *technology* itself for bounds on the amounts of inputs that are available.

However, this might not impress a practical person. After all, who cares if it is *possible* to fill the universe with fountain pens if most of the universe were filled with ink! Is it not sufficient to describe the technology for only those production plans that are actually feasible? On the one hand, the answer is yes, because in equilibrium the production plans in fact be must feasible. But there is a more subtle and important difficulty. When we impose constraints on production possibilities based on aggregate supply, then we are implicitly assuming that *the firm takes these aggregate input constraints into account when making its profit-maximising decisions*. For example, if we bound the production set of a producer of pens because the supply of ink is finite, then at very low ink prices, the producer's demand for ink will be up against this constraint. But were it not for this constraint, the producer would demand even more ink at the current low price. Thus, by imposing this seemingly innocent feasibility constraint on production possibilities, we have severed the all-important connection between price and (excess) demand. And indeed, this is the essence of the competitive model. Producers (and consumers) make demand and supply decisions based on the prevailing prices, not on whether there is enough of the good to supply their demands (or vice versa). Thus, imposing boundedness on the production set runs entirely against the decentralised aspect of the competitive market that we are trying to capture. (A similar argument can be made against placing upper bounds on the consumption set.)

Fortunately, the boundedness assumption is not needed. However, do not despair that all of the hard work we have done has been wasted. It turns out that a standard method of proving existence without bounded production sets is to first prove it by placing artificial bounds on them (which is essentially what we have done) and then letting the artificial bounds become arbitrarily large (which we will not do). Under suitable conditions, this will yield a competitive equilibrium of the economy with unbounded production sets.

For the record, strict convexity of preferences and strong convexity of firm production possibility sets assumed in Theorem 5.13 are more stringent than needed to prove existence of equilibrium. If, instead, merely convexity of preferences and production possibility sets is assumed, existence can still be proved, though the mathematical techniques required are outside the scope of this book. If production possibility sets are convex, we allow the possibility of constant returns to scale for firms. Constant returns introduces the possibility that firm output supply and input demand functions will be set-valued relationships and that they will not be continuous in the usual way. Similarly, mere convexity of preferences raises the possibility of set-valued demand functions together with similar continuity problems. All of these can be handled by adopting generalised functions (called 'correspondences'), an appropriately generalised notion of continuity, and then applying a generalised version of Brouwer's fixed-point theorem due to Kakutani (1941). In fact, we can even do without convexity of individual *firm* production possibility sets altogether, as long as the *aggregate* production possibility set is convex. The reader interested in exploring all of these matters should consult Debreu (1959). But see also Exercise 5.22.

5.3.4 WELFARE

Here we show how Theorems 5.7 and 5.8 can be extended to an economy with production. As before, we focus on properties of the allocations consumers receive in a Walrasian equilibrium. In a production economy, we expand our earlier definition of Walrasian equilibrium allocations as follows.

DEFINITION 5.8 ***WEAs in a Production Economy***

Let $\mathbf{p}^* \gg \mathbf{0}$ be a Walrasian equilibrium for the economy $(u^i, \mathbf{e}^i, \theta^{ij}, Y^j)_{i\in\mathcal{I}, j\in\mathcal{J}}$. Then the pair $(\mathbf{x}(\mathbf{p}^*), \mathbf{y}(\mathbf{p}^*))$ is a Walrasian equilibrium allocation (WEA) where $\mathbf{x}(\mathbf{p}^*)$ denotes the vector, $(\mathbf{x}^1, \mathbf{x}^2, \dots, \mathbf{x}^I)$, whose ith *entry is the utility-maximising bundle demanded by consumer i facing prices $\mathbf{p}^*$ and income $m^i(\mathbf{p}^*)$; and where $\mathbf{y}(\mathbf{p}^*)$ denotes the vector, $(\mathbf{y}^1, \mathbf{y}^2, \dots, \mathbf{y}^J)$, of profit-maximising production vectors at prices $\mathbf{p}^*$. (Note then that because $\mathbf{p}^*$ is a Walrasian equilibrium, $\sum_{i\in\mathcal{I}} \mathbf{x}^i = \sum_{i\in\mathcal{I}} \mathbf{e}^i + \sum_{j\in\mathcal{J}} \mathbf{y}^j$).*

In other words, a consumption and production allocation is a WEA at prices $\mathbf{p}^*$ if (1) each consumer's commodity bundle is the most preferred in his budget set at prices $\mathbf{p}^*$, (2) each firm's production plan is profit-maximising in its production possibility set at prices $\mathbf{p}^*$, and (3) demand equals supply in every market.

We are now ready to extend the First Welfare Theorem to economies with production. Recall from our Robinson Crusoe example that the Walrasian equilibrium allocation there was such that no other feasible allocation could make Robinson better off. We now define Pareto efficiency when there are many consumers and firms based on the same idea.

Throughout the remainder of this section, we shall be concerned with the fixed economy $(u^i, \mathbf{e}^i, \theta^{ij}, Y^j)_{i\in\mathcal{I}, j\in\mathcal{J}}$. Thus, all definitions and theorems are stated with this economy in mind.

An allocation, $(\mathbf{x}, \mathbf{y}) = ((\mathbf{x}^1, \ldots, \mathbf{x}^I), (\mathbf{y}^1, \ldots, \mathbf{y}^J))$, of bundles to consumers and production plans to firms is **feasible** if $\mathbf{x}^i \in \mathbb{R}^n_+$ for all i, $\mathbf{y}^j \in Y^j$ for all j, and $\sum_{i\in\mathcal{I}} \mathbf{x}^i = \sum_{i\in\mathcal{I}} \mathbf{e}^i + \sum_{j\in\mathcal{J}} \mathbf{y}^j$.

DEFINITION 5.9 ***Pareto-Efficient Allocation with Production***

The feasible allocation $(\mathbf{x}, \mathbf{y})$ *is Pareto efficient if there is no other feasible allocation* $(\bar{\mathbf{x}}, \bar{\mathbf{y}})$ *such that* $u^i(\bar{\mathbf{x}}^i) \geq u^i(\mathbf{x}^i)$ *for all* $i \in \mathcal{I}$ *with at least one strict inequality.*

Thus, a feasible allocation of bundles to consumers and production plans to firms is Pareto efficient if there is no other feasible allocation that makes at least one consumer strictly better off and no consumer worse off.

It would be quite a task indeed to attempt to allocate resources in a manner that was Pareto efficient. Not only would you need information on consumer preferences, you would also require detailed knowledge of the technologies of all firms and the productivity of all inputs. In particular, you would have to assign individuals with particular skills to the firms that require those skills. It would be a massive undertaking. And yet, with apparently no central direction, the allocations obtained as Walrasian equilibria are Pareto efficient as we now demonstrate.

THEOREM 5.14 ***First Welfare Theorem with Production***

If each u^i *is strictly increasing on* $\mathbb{R}^n_+$, *then every Walrasian equilibrium allocation is Pareto efficient.*

Proof: We suppose $(\mathbf{x}, \mathbf{y})$ is a WEA at prices $\mathbf{p}^*$, but is not Pareto efficient, and derive a contradiction.

Because $(\mathbf{x}, \mathbf{y})$ is a WEA, it is feasible, so

$$\sum_{i\in\mathcal{I}} \mathbf{x}^i = \sum_{j\in\mathcal{J}} \mathbf{y}^j + \sum_{i\in\mathcal{I}} \mathbf{e}^i. \tag{P.1}$$

Because $(\mathbf{x}, \mathbf{y})$ is not Pareto efficient, there exists some feasible allocation $(\hat{\mathbf{x}}, \hat{\mathbf{y}})$ such that

$$u^i(\hat{\mathbf{x}}^i) \geq u^i(\mathbf{x}^i), \quad i \in \mathcal{I}, \tag{P.2}$$

with at least one strict inequality. By Lemma 5.2, this implies that

$$\mathbf{p}^* \cdot \hat{\mathbf{x}}^i \geq \mathbf{p}^* \cdot \mathbf{x}^i, \qquad i \in \mathcal{I}, \tag{P.3}$$

with at least one strict inequality. Summing over consumers in (P.3) and rearranging gives

$$\mathbf{p}^* \cdot \sum_{i \in \mathcal{I}} \hat{\mathbf{x}}^i > \mathbf{p}^* \cdot \sum_{i \in \mathcal{I}} \mathbf{x}^i. \tag{P.4}$$

Now (P.4) together with (P.1) and the feasibility of $(\hat{\mathbf{x}}, \hat{\mathbf{y}})$ tell us

$$\mathbf{p}^* \cdot \left(\sum_{j \in \mathcal{J}} \hat{\mathbf{y}}^j + \sum_{i \in \mathcal{I}} \mathbf{e}^i \right) > \mathbf{p}^* \cdot \left(\sum_{j \in \mathcal{J}} \mathbf{y}^j + \sum_{i \in \mathcal{I}} \mathbf{e}^i \right),$$

so

$$\mathbf{p}^* \cdot \sum_{j \in \mathcal{J}} \hat{\mathbf{y}}^j > \mathbf{p}^* \cdot \sum_{j \in \mathcal{J}} \mathbf{y}^j.$$

However, this means that $\mathbf{p}^* \cdot \hat{\mathbf{y}}^j > \mathbf{p}^* \cdot \mathbf{y}^j$ for some firm *j*, where $\hat{\mathbf{y}}^j \in Y^j$. This contradicts the fact that in the Walrasian equilibrium, $\mathbf{y}^j$ maximises firm *j*'s profit at prices $\mathbf{p}^*$. ∎

Next we show that competitive markets can support Pareto-efficient allocations after appropriate income transfers.

THEOREM 5.15 ***Second Welfare Theorem with Production***

Suppose that (i) each u^i satisfies Assumption 5.1, (ii) each Y^j satisfies Assumption 5.2, (iii) $\mathbf{y} + \sum_{i \in \mathcal{I}} \mathbf{e}^i \gg \mathbf{0}$ for some aggregate production vector $\mathbf{y}$, and (iv) the allocation $(\hat{\mathbf{x}}, \hat{\mathbf{y}})$ is Pareto efficient.

Then there are income transfers, $T_1, \ldots, T_I$, satisfying $\sum_{i \in \mathcal{I}} T_i = 0$, and a price vector, $\bar{\mathbf{p}}$, such that

1. *$\hat{\mathbf{x}}^i$ maximises $u^i(\mathbf{x}^i)$ s.t. $\bar{\mathbf{p}} \cdot \mathbf{x}^i \leq m^i(\bar{\mathbf{p}}) + T_i$, $i \in \mathcal{I}$.*
2. *$\hat{\mathbf{y}}^j$ maximises $\bar{\mathbf{p}} \cdot \mathbf{y}^j$ s.t. $\mathbf{y}^j \in Y^j$, $j \in \mathcal{J}$.*

Proof: For each $j \in \mathcal{J}$, let $\bar{Y}^j \equiv Y^j - \{\hat{\mathbf{y}}^j\}$, and note that so defined, each $\bar{Y}^j$ satisfies Assumption 5.2. Consider now the economy $\bar{\mathcal{E}} = (u^i, \hat{\mathbf{x}}^i, \theta^{ij}, \bar{Y}^j)_{i \in \mathcal{I}, j \in \mathcal{J}}$ obtained from the original economy by replacing consumer *i*'s endowment, $\mathbf{e}^i$, with the endowment $\hat{\mathbf{x}}^i$, and replacing each production set, Y^j, with the production set $\bar{Y}^j$. It is straightforward to show using hypotheses (i) to (iii) that $\bar{\mathcal{E}}$ satisfies all the assumptions of Theorem 5.13. Consequently, $\bar{\mathcal{E}}$ possesses a Walrasian equilibrium, $\bar{\mathbf{p}} \gg \mathbf{0}$, and an associated WEA, $(\bar{\mathbf{x}}, \bar{\mathbf{y}})$.

Now because $\mathbf{0} \in \bar{Y}^j$ for every firm *j*, profits of every firm are non-negative in equilibrium, so that each consumer can afford his endowment vector. Consequently,

$$u^i(\bar{\mathbf{x}}^i) \geq u^i(\hat{\mathbf{x}}^i), \quad i \in \mathcal{I}. \tag{P.1}$$

Next we shall argue that for some aggregate production vector $\tilde{\mathbf{y}}$, $(\bar{\mathbf{x}}, \tilde{\mathbf{y}})$ is feasible for the original economy. To see this, note that each $\bar{\mathbf{y}}^j \in \bar{Y}^j$ is of the form $\bar{\mathbf{y}}^j = \tilde{\mathbf{y}}^j - \hat{\mathbf{y}}^j$ for some $\tilde{\mathbf{y}}^j \in Y^j$, by the definition of $\bar{Y}^j$. Now, because $(\bar{\mathbf{x}}, \bar{\mathbf{y}})$ is a WEA for $\bar{\mathcal{E}}$, it must be feasible in that economy. Therefore,

$$\begin{aligned}\sum_{i\in\mathcal{I}} \bar{\mathbf{x}}^i &= \sum_{i\in\mathcal{I}} \hat{\mathbf{x}}^i + \sum_{j\in\mathcal{J}} \bar{\mathbf{y}}^j \\ &= \sum_{i\in\mathcal{I}} \hat{\mathbf{x}}^i + \sum_{j\in\mathcal{J}} (\tilde{\mathbf{y}}^j - \hat{\mathbf{y}}^j) \\ &= \sum_{i\in\mathcal{I}} \hat{\mathbf{x}}^i - \sum_{j\in\mathcal{J}} \hat{\mathbf{y}}^j + \sum_{j\in\mathcal{J}} \tilde{\mathbf{y}}^j \\ &= \sum_{i\in\mathcal{I}} \mathbf{e}^i + \sum_{j\in\mathcal{J}} \tilde{\mathbf{y}}^j,\end{aligned}$$

where the last equality follows from the feasibility of $(\hat{\mathbf{x}}, \hat{\mathbf{y}})$ in the original economy. Consequently, $(\bar{\mathbf{x}}, \tilde{\mathbf{y}})$ is feasible for the original economy, where $\tilde{\mathbf{y}} = \sum_{j\in\mathcal{J}} \tilde{\mathbf{y}}^j$.

We may conclude that every inequality in (P.1) must be an equality, otherwise $(\hat{\mathbf{x}}, \hat{\mathbf{y}})$ would not be Pareto efficient. But the strict quasiconcavity of u^i then implies that

$$\bar{\mathbf{x}}^i = \hat{\mathbf{x}}^i, \quad i \in \mathcal{I},$$

because otherwise some consumer would strictly prefer the average of the two bundles to $\bar{\mathbf{x}}^i$, and the average is affordable at prices $\bar{\mathbf{p}}$ because both bundles themselves are affordable. This would contradict the fact that $(\bar{\mathbf{x}}, \bar{\mathbf{y}})$ is a WEA for $\bar{\mathcal{E}}$ at prices $\bar{\mathbf{p}}$. Thus, we may conclude that

$$\hat{\mathbf{x}}^i \text{ maximises } u^i(\mathbf{x}^i) \quad \text{s.t.} \quad \bar{\mathbf{p}} \cdot \mathbf{x}^i \leq \bar{\mathbf{p}} \cdot \hat{\mathbf{x}}^i + \sum_{j\in\mathcal{J}} \theta^{ij} \bar{\mathbf{p}} \cdot \bar{\mathbf{y}}^j, \quad i \in \mathcal{I}.$$

But because utility is strongly increasing, the budget constraint holds with equality at $\mathbf{x}^i = \hat{\mathbf{x}}^i$, which implies that each consumer i's income from profits is zero. This means that every firm must be earning zero profits, which in turn means that $\bar{\mathbf{y}}^j = \mathbf{0}$ for every firm j.

We leave it as an exercise to show that because $\bar{\mathbf{y}}^j = \mathbf{0}$ maximises firm j's profits at prices $\bar{\mathbf{p}}$ when its production set is $\bar{Y}^j$, then (by the definition of $\bar{Y}^j$) $\hat{\mathbf{y}}^j$ maximises firm j's profits at prices $\bar{\mathbf{p}}$ when its production set is Y^j (i.e., in the original economy).

So altogether, we have shown the following:

$$\hat{\mathbf{x}}^i \text{ maximises } u^i(\mathbf{x}^i) \quad \text{s.t.} \quad \bar{\mathbf{p}} \cdot \mathbf{x}^i \leq \bar{\mathbf{p}} \cdot \hat{\mathbf{x}}^i, \quad i \in \mathcal{I}, \tag{P.2}$$

$$\hat{\mathbf{y}}^j \text{ maximises } \bar{\mathbf{p}} \cdot \mathbf{y}^j \quad \text{s.t.} \quad \mathbf{y}^j \in Y^j, \quad j \in \mathcal{J}. \tag{P.3}$$

Note then that setting $T_i \equiv \bar{\mathbf{p}} \cdot \hat{\mathbf{x}}^i - m^i(\bar{\mathbf{p}})$ provides the appropriate transfers, where $m^i(\bar{\mathbf{p}}) = \bar{\mathbf{p}} \cdot \mathbf{e}^i + \sum_{j \in \mathcal{J}} \theta^{ij} \bar{\mathbf{p}} \cdot \hat{\mathbf{y}}^j$ is consumer i's income in the original economy at prices $\bar{\mathbf{p}}$. These transfers sum to zero by the feasibility of $(\hat{\mathbf{x}}, \hat{\mathbf{y}})$, and when employed (in the original economy), they reduce each consumer's problem to that in (P.2). Consequently, both (1) and (2) are satisfied. ∎

5.4 CONTINGENT PLANS

Up to now we have considered the problem of how a market economy allocates resources through a competitive price system in what appears to be a static environment. There has been no mention of *time* in the model. So, for example, discussions of interest rates, inflation, borrowing, and lending seem to be out of reach. But in fact this is not so. The model we have developed is actually quite capable of including not only time, interest rates, borrowing, and lending, but also uncertainty about many things, including the future state of the economy, the value of stocks and bonds, and more. The key idea is to refine the notion of a good to include all of the characteristics of interest to us.

5.4.1 TIME

If we wish to include time in our model, then we simply index goods not only by what they are, e.g. apples, oranges, etc., but also by the date at which they are consumed (or produced). So instead of keeping track only of x_k, the amount of good k consumed by a consumer, we also keep track of the date t at which it is consumed. Thus, we let x_{kt} denote the amount of good k consumed at date t. If there are two goods, $k = 1, 2$, and two dates $t = 1, 2$, then a consumption bundle is a vector of four numbers $(x_{11}, x_{12}, x_{21}, x_{22})$, where, for example, x_{12} is the amount of good $k = 1$ consumed at date $t = 2$.

But if a consumption bundle is $(x_{11}, x_{12}, x_{21}, x_{22})$, then in keeping with our convention up to now, we should really think of each of the four coordinates of the consumption bundle as representing the quantities of *distinct goods*. That is, with two ‘ basic’ goods, apples and oranges, and two dates, today and tomorrow, we actually have four goods – apples today, apples tomorrow, oranges today, and oranges tomorrow.

5.4.2 UNCERTAINTY

Uncertainty, too, can be captured using the same technique. For example, suppose there is uncertainty about today's weather and that this is important because the weather might affect the desirability of certain products (e.g., umbrellas, sunscreen, vacations,. . .) and/or the production possibilities for certain products (e.g., agriculture). To keep things simple, let us suppose that there are just two possibilities for the state of the weather. In state $s = 1$ it rains, and in state $s = 2$ it is sunny. Then, analogous to what we did with time, we can index each good k with the state in which it is consumed (or produced) by letting x_{ks} denote the amount of good k consumed in state s, and letting y_{ks} denote the amount of good k produced in state s. This permits consumers to have quite distinct preferences over umbrellas when it is sunny and umbrellas when it rains, and it also permits production possibilities, for agricultural products for example, to be distinct in the two states. We can also model the demand for insurance by allowing a consumer's endowment vector to depend upon the state, with low endowments being associated with one state (fire or flood, for example) and high endowments with another.

5.4.3 WALRASIAN EQUILIBRIUM WITH CONTINGENT COMMODITIES

Let us put all of this together by incorporating both time and uncertainty. We will then step back and interpret the meaning of a Walrasian equilibrium of the resulting model.

There are N basic goods, $k = 1, 2, \ldots, N$, T dates, $t = 1, 2, \ldots, T$, and for each date t there are S_t mutually exclusive and exhaustive events $s_t = 1, 2, \ldots, S_t$ that can occur. Consequently, the *state of the world* at date t is described by the vector $(s_1, \ldots, s_t)$ of the t events that occurred at the start of dates 1 through t inclusive. A consumption bundle is a non-negative vector $\mathbf{x} = (x_{kts})$, where k runs from 1 to N, t runs from 1 to T, and given t, $s = (s_1, \ldots, s_t)$ is one of the $S_1S_2 \ldots S_t$ states of the world describing the events that have occurred up to date t. Thus, $\mathbf{x} \in \mathbb{R}^{NM}_{+}$, where $M = S_1 + S_1S_2 + \ldots + S_1S_2 \ldots S_T$ is the total number of date–state pairs (t, s).

There are J firms and each firm $j \in \mathcal{J}$ has a production possibilities set, Y^j, contained in $\mathbb{R}^{NM}$.

There are I consumers. Each consumer $i \in \mathcal{I}$ has preferences over the set of consumption bundles in $\mathbb{R}^{NM}_{+}$ and i's preferences are represented by a utility function $u^i(\cdot)$. Consumer i has an endowment vector $\mathbf{e}^i \in \mathbb{R}^{NM}_{+}$ and ownership share θ^{ij} of each firm $j \in \mathcal{J}$.[5] Note that the endowment vector $\mathbf{e}^i$ specifies that at date t and in state s, consumer i's endowment of the N goods is $(e^i_{1ts}, \ldots, e^i_{Nts})$.

In terms of our previous definitions, this is simply a private ownership economy with $n = NM$ goods. For example $x_{kts} = 2$ denotes two units of good kts or equivalently it denotes two units of the basic good k at date t in state s. Thus, we are treating the same basic good as distinct when consumed at distinct dates or in distinct states. After all, the amount one is willing to pay for an automobile delivered today might well be higher than the amount one is willing to pay for delivery of an otherwise identical automobile six months from today. From this perspective, treating the same basic good at distinct dates (or in distinct states) as distinct goods is entirely natural.

Under the hypotheses of Theorem 5.13, there is a price vector $\mathbf{p}^* \in \mathbb{R}^{NM}_{++}$ constituting a Walrasian equilibrium for this private ownership economy. In particular, demand must equal supply for each of the NM goods, that is for every basic good at every date and in every state of the world. Let us now understand what this means starting with firms.

For each firm $j \in \mathcal{J}$, let $\hat{\mathbf{y}}^j = (\hat{y}^j_{kts}) \in Y^j \subseteq \mathbb{R}^{NM}$ denote its (unique) profit-maximising production plan given the price vector $\mathbf{p}^*$. Consequently, at date t in state s, firm j will produce $\hat{y}^j_{kts}$ units of the basic good (output) k if $\hat{y}^j_{kts} \geq 0$ and will demand

[5] One could allow ownership shares to depend upon the date and the state, but we shall not do so.

$\left|\hat{y}^j_{kts}\right|$ units of the basic good (input) k if $\hat{y}^j_{kts} < 0$. Thus, $\hat{\mathbf{y}}^j$ is a profit-maximising *contingent production plan*, describing output supply and input demand for the N basic goods contingent upon each date and state. Let us now turn to consumers.

For each $i \in \mathcal{I}$, let $\hat{\mathbf{x}}^i = (\hat{x}^i_{kts}) \in \mathbb{R}^{NM}_+$ denote consumer i's (unique) utility-maximising affordable consumption bundle given prices $\mathbf{p}^*$ and income $m^i(\mathbf{p}^*)$. Consequently, at date t in state s consumer i will consume $\hat{x}^i_{kts}$ units of the basic good k. Thus $\hat{\mathbf{x}}^i$ is a utility-maximising affordable *contingent consumption plan* for consumer i, specifying his consumption of each of the basic goods contingent on each date and state.

Now, on the one hand, because demand equals supply for every good, we have

$$\sum_{i\in\mathcal{I}} \hat{x}^i_{kts} = \sum_{j\in\mathcal{J}} \hat{y}^j_{kts} + \sum_{i\in\mathcal{I}} e^i_{kts}, \quad \text{for every } k, t, s. \tag{5.6}$$

Consequently, at every date and in every state, demand equals supply for each of the basic goods. On the other hand, each consumer i has only a single budget constraint linking his expenditures on all goods as follows:

$$\sum_{k,t,s} p^*_{kts}\hat{x}^i_{kts} = \sum_{k,t,s} p^*_{kts}e^i_{kts} + \sum_{j\in\mathcal{J}} \theta^{ij} \sum_{k,t,s} p^*_{kts}\hat{y}^j_{kts}, \quad \text{for every } i \in \mathcal{I}. \tag{5.7}$$

In particular, when state s' occurs at date t', it may turn out that for some consumer(s) i,

$$\sum_{k} p^*_{kt's'}\hat{x}^i_{kt's'} > \sum_{k} p^*_{kt's'}e^i_{kt's'} + \sum_{j\in\mathcal{J}} \theta^{ij} \sum_{k} p^*_{kt's'}\hat{y}^j_{kt's'}.$$

That is, consumer i's expenditures on basic goods at date t' in state s' might exceed his income at that date and in that state. Does this make sense? The answer is 'yes, it absolutely makes sense'. Indeed, this budget shortfall is an expression of two important economic phenomena, namely borrowing and insurance. When one borrows at date t, one is effectively spending more than one's endowment and profit-share income at date t, and when one receives an insurance payment due to loss in state s (e.g., fire or flood) then again one is able to spend in state s more than one's endowment and profit-share income. On the other side of the coin, there can very well be some states and dates associated with budget surpluses (e.g., when one lends or when one provides insurance on states that did not occur).

But if each consumer's budget need balance only overall, as given in (5.7), then how is this Walrasian equilibrium allocation actually implemented? The answer is as follows. Think of a prior date zero at which firms and consumers participate in a market for binding contracts. A contract is a piece of paper on which is written a non-negative real number, a basic good k, a date t, and a state, s. For example, the contract $(107.6, k = 3, t = 2, s = 7)$ entitles the bearer to 107.6 units of basic good $k = 3$ at date $t = 2$ in state $s = 7$. Notice that each consumer's equilibrium net consumption bundle $\hat{\mathbf{x}}^i - \mathbf{e}^i = (\hat{x}^i_{kts} - e^i_{kts})$ can be reinterpreted as a vector of contracts. That is, for each k, t, and s, if $\hat{x}^i_{kts} - e^i_{kts} \geq 0$ then consumer i is entitled to receive from the market $\hat{x}^i_{kts} - e^i_{kts}$ units of basic good k at date t in state s. If $\hat{x}^i_{kts} - e^i_{kts} < 0$, consumer i is required to supply to the market $|\hat{x}^i_{kts} - e^i_{kts}|$ units of basic good k at date t in state s.

Similarly, each firm's production plan $\hat{\mathbf{y}}^j = (\hat{y}^j_{kts})$ can be reinterpreted as the vector of contracts requiring firm j to supply to the market $\hat{y}^j_{kts}$ units of basic good k at date t in state s if $\hat{y}^j_{kts} \geq 0$ and entitling firm j to receive from the market $\left|\hat{y}^j_{kts}\right|$ units of basic good k at date t in state s if $\hat{y}^j_{kts} < 0$.

Finally, note that if for each k, t, and s, the price of a contract per unit of basic good k at date t in state s is p^*_{kts}, then at date zero the market for contracts will clear with consumers maximising utility and firms maximising profits. When each date t arrives and any state s occurs, the contracts that are relevant for that date and state are executed. The market-clearing condition (5.6) ensures that this is feasible. After the initial trading of contracts in period zero, no further trade takes place. The only activity taking place as time passes and states occur is the execution of contracts that were purchased and sold at date zero.

Let us now provide several important remarks on this interpretation of our model. First, we have implicitly assumed that there is perfect monitoring in the sense that it is not possible for a firm or consumer to claim that he can supply more units of a basic good in state s at date t than he actually can supply. Thus, bankruptcy is assumed away. Second, it is assumed that there is perfect information in the sense that all firms and consumers are informed of the state when it occurs at each date. Otherwise, if only some agents were informed of the state, they might have an incentive to lie about which state actually did occur. Third, it is assumed that all contracts are perfectly enforced. Clearly, each of these assumptions is strong and rules out important economic settings. Nonetheless, it is quite remarkable how much additional mileage we are able to get from a model that appears entirely static and deterministic simply by reinterpreting its variables! The exercises explore this model further, examining how it provides theories of insurance, borrowing and lending, interest rates, and asset pricing.

5.5 CORE AND EQUILIBRIA

In this final section, we return to the world of pure exchange economies and pursue further the relation between the core of an economy and the set of Walrasian equilibrium allocations. As we have seen, every Walrasian equilibrium allocation is also a core allocation. On the other hand, simple Edgeworth box examples can be constructed that yield core allocations that are not Walrasian. Thus, it would seem that the connection between the two ideas is limited.

Edgeworth (1881), however, conjectured a more intimate relationship between Walrasian allocations and the core. He suggested that when the economy is 'large', and so when the Walrasian assumption of price-taking behaviour by consumers makes most sense, the distinction between core allocations and Walrasian equilibrium ones disappears. In considering that possibility anew, Debreu and Scarf (1963) extended Edgeworth's framework and proved him to be correct. Loosely speaking, they showed that as an economy becomes 'larger', its core 'shrinks' to include *only* those allocations that are Walrasian!

All in all, their result is heartening to those who believe in the special qualities of a market system, where the only information a consumer requires is the set of market prices he faces. It suggests a tantalising comparison between the polar paradigms of central planning and laissez-faire in very large economies. If the objective of the planning process is to identify and then implement some distribution of goods that is in the core, and if there are no other allocations in the core but those that would be picked out by a competitive market system, why go to the bother (and expense) of planning at all? To find the core, a central planner needs information on consumers' preferences, and consumers have selfish incentives to be less than completely honest in revealing that information to the planner. The *market* does not need to know anything about consumers' preferences at all, and in fact depends on consumers' selfishness. What is a vice in one case is a virtue of sorts in the other.

There is, of course, a great deal of loose language in this discussion. On a broad plane, the choice between planning and market systems would never hinge on efficiency alone. In addition, we know that core allocations from arbitrary initial endowments need not be equitable in any sense of the word. Planning may still be justified as a means of achieving a desired redistribution of endowments. On a narrower plane, there are technical issues unaddressed. What does it mean for an economy to be 'large', or to be 'larger', than another? Moreover, because an 'allocation' involves a vector of goods for each consumer, and because presumably a larger economy has a greater number of consumers, is not the 'dimensionality' of the core in large economies different from that in small economies? If so, how can we speak of the core 'shrinking'? We will answer each of these questions before we finish.

5.5.1 REPLICA ECONOMIES

To keep the analysis manageable, we follow Debreu and Scarf by formalising the notion of a large economy in a very particular way. We start with the idea of a basic exchange economy consisting of a finite but arbitrary finite number I of consumers, each with his or her own preferences and endowments. Now think of each consumer's preferences and/or endowments as making that consumer a different 'type' of consumer from all the rest. Two consumers with different preferences but the same endowments are considered different types. So, too, are two consumers with the same preferences but different endowments.[6] Thus, we now think of there being an arbitrary finite number of different *types* of consumers, and the basic exchange economy consists of one consumer of each type.

[6]In fact, we would also call two consumers with the same preferences and endowments different types even though the distinction would just be a formal one. For now, however, it is best to think of no two consumers as having both the same preferences and the same endowments.

Now imagine that each consumer suddenly acquires a twin. The twins are completely identical, having the same preferences and the same endowments. The new economy, consisting of all the original consumers and their twins, now has two consumers of each type rather than one. This new economy is clearly larger than the original one because it contains exactly twice as many consumers. We call this new economy the twofold *replica* of the original one. If each original consumer was tripled, or quadrupled, we could similarly construct threefold or fourfold replicas of the original economy, each in turn being larger than the preceding one in a well-defined way. Now you get the idea of a **replica economy**. It is one with a finite number of 'types' of consumers, an equal number of consumers of each type, and all individuals of the same type are *identical* in that they have identical preferences and identical endowments. Formally, we have the following definition and assumptions.

DEFINITION 5.10 ***An r-Fold Replica Economy***

Let there be I types of consumers in the basic exchange economy and index these types by the set $\mathcal{I} = \{1, \ldots, I\}$. By the r-fold replica economy, denoted $\mathcal{E}_r$, we mean the economy with r consumers of each type for a total of rI consumers. For any type $i \in \mathcal{I}$, all r consumers of that type share the common preferences $\succsim^i$ on $\mathbb{R}^n_+$ and have identical endowments $\mathbf{e}^i \gg \mathbf{0}$. We further assume for $i \in \mathcal{I}$ that preferences $\succsim^i$ can be represented by a utility function u^i satisfying Assumption 5.1.

Thus, when comparing two replica economies, we can unambiguously say which of them is larger. It will be the one having more of every type of consumer.

Let us now think about the core of the r-fold replica economy $\mathcal{E}_r$. Under the assumptions we have made, all of the hypotheses of Theorem 5.5 will be satisfied. Consequently, a WEA will exist, and by Theorem 5.5, it will be in the core. So we have made enough assumptions to ensure that the core of $\mathcal{E}_r$ is non-empty.

To keep track of all of the consumers in each replica economy, we shall index each of them by *two* superscripts, i and q, where $i = 1, \ldots, I$ runs through all the types, and $q = 1, \ldots, r$ runs through all consumers of a particular type. For example, the index $iq = 23$ refers to the type 2 consumer labelled by the number 3, or simply the third consumer of type 2. So, an allocation in $\mathcal{E}_r$ takes the form

$$\mathbf{x} = (\mathbf{x}^{11}, \mathbf{x}^{12}, \ldots, \mathbf{x}^{1r}, \ldots, \mathbf{x}^{I1}, \ldots, \mathbf{x}^{Ir}), \tag{5.8}$$

where $\mathbf{x}^{iq}$ denotes the bundle of the qth consumer of type i. The allocation is then feasible if

$$\sum_{i\in\mathcal{I}} \sum_{q=1}^{r} \mathbf{x}^{iq} = r \sum_{i\in\mathcal{I}} \mathbf{e}^i, \tag{5.9}$$

because each of the r consumers of type i has endowment vector $\mathbf{e}^i$.

The theorem below exploits this fact and the strict convexity of preferences.

THEOREM 5.16 ***Equal Treatment in the Core***

If $\mathbf{x}$ *is an allocation in the core of* $\mathcal{E}_r$*, then every consumer of type i must have the same bundle according to* $\mathbf{x}$*. That is, for every* $i = 1, \ldots, I$, $\mathbf{x}^{iq} = \mathbf{x}^{iq'}$ *for every* $q, q' = 1, \ldots, r$.

This theorem with the delightfully democratic name identifies a crucial property of core allocations in replica economies. It is therefore important that we not only believe equal treatment of like types occurs in the core but that we also have a good feel for why it is true. For that reason, we will give a leisurely 'proof' for the simplest, two-type, four-person economy. Once you understand this case, you should be able to derive the formal proof of the more general case for yourself, and that will be left as an exercise.

Proof: Let $I = 2$, and consider $\mathcal{E}_2$, the replica economy with two types of consumers and two consumers of each type, for a total of four consumers in the economy. Suppose that

$$\mathbf{x} \equiv (\mathbf{x}^{11}, \mathbf{x}^{12}, \mathbf{x}^{21}, \mathbf{x}^{22})$$

is an allocation in the core of $\mathcal{E}_2$. First, we note that because $\mathbf{x}$ is in the core, it must be feasible, so

$$\mathbf{x}^{11} + \mathbf{x}^{12} + \mathbf{x}^{21} + \mathbf{x}^{22} = 2\mathbf{e}^1 + 2\mathbf{e}^2 \tag{P.1}$$

because both consumers of each type have identical endowments.

Now suppose that $\mathbf{x}$ does not assign identical bundles to some pair of identical types. Let these be consumers 11 and 12, so $\mathbf{x}^{11}$ and $\mathbf{x}^{12}$ are distinct. Remember that they each have the same preferences, $\succsim^1$.

Because $\succsim^1$ is complete, it must rank one of the two bundles as being at least as good as the other. Let us assume that

$$\mathbf{x}^{11} \succsim^1 \mathbf{x}^{12}. \tag{P.2}$$

Of course, the preference may be strict, or the two bundles may be ranked equally. Figs. 5.9(a) and 5.9(b) illustrate both possibilities. Either way, we would like to show that because $\mathbf{x}^{11}$ and $\mathbf{x}^{12}$ are distinct, $\mathbf{x}$ cannot be in the core of $\mathcal{E}_2$. To do this, we will show that $\mathbf{x}$ can be blocked.

Now, consider the two consumers of type 2. Their bundles according to $\mathbf{x}$ are $\mathbf{x}^{21}$ and $\mathbf{x}^{22}$, and they each have preferences $\succsim^2$. Let us assume (again without loss of generality) that

$$\mathbf{x}^{21} \succsim^2 \mathbf{x}^{22}. \tag{P.3}$$

So, consumer 2 of type 1 is the worst off type 1 consumer, and consumer 2 of type 2 is the worst off type 2 consumer. Let us see if these *worst off* consumers of each type can get together and block the allocation $\mathbf{x}$.

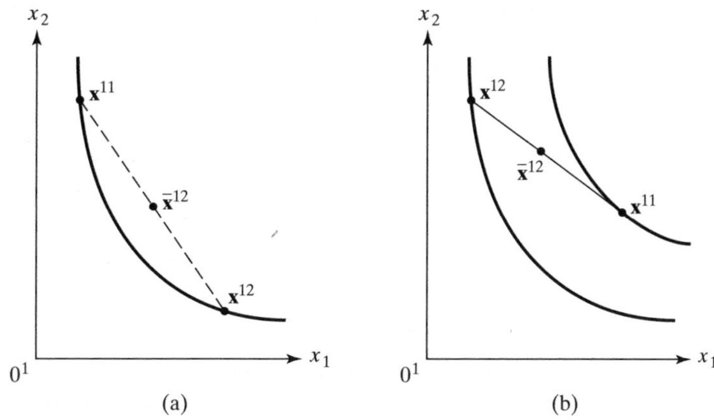

Figure 5.9. Demonstration of equal treatment in the core.

Let the bundles $\bar{\mathbf{x}}^{12}$ and $\bar{\mathbf{x}}^{22}$ be defined as follows:

$$\bar{\mathbf{x}}^{12} = \frac{\mathbf{x}^{11} + \mathbf{x}^{12}}{2},$$

$$\bar{\mathbf{x}}^{22} = \frac{\mathbf{x}^{21} + \mathbf{x}^{22}}{2}.$$

The first bundle is the average of the bundles going to the type 1 consumers and the second is the average of the bundles going to the type 2 consumers. See Fig. 5.9 for the placement of $\bar{\mathbf{x}}^{12}$.

Now, suppose it were possible to give consumer 12 the bundle $\bar{\mathbf{x}}^{12}$. How would this compare to giving him the bundle he's getting under $\bar{\mathbf{x}}$, namely, $\mathbf{x}^{12}$? Well, remember that according to (P.2), consumer 12 was the worst off consumer of type 1. Consequently, because bundles $\mathbf{x}^{11}$ and $\mathbf{x}^{12}$ are distinct, consumer 12 would strictly prefer $\bar{\mathbf{x}}^{12}$ to $\mathbf{x}^{12}$ because his preferences, $\succsim^1$, are strictly convex. That is,

$$\bar{\mathbf{x}}^{12} \succ^1 \mathbf{x}^{12}.$$

This is shown in Figs. 5.9(a) and 5.9(b).

Similarly, the strict convexity of consumer 22's preferences, $\succsim^2$, together with (P.3) imply

$$\bar{\mathbf{x}}^{22} \succsim^2 \mathbf{x}^{22},$$

where the preference need not be strict because we may have $\mathbf{x}^{21} = \mathbf{x}^{22}$.

The pair of bundles $(\bar{\mathbf{x}}^{12}, \bar{\mathbf{x}}^{22})$ therefore makes consumer 12 strictly better off and consumer 22 no worse off than the allocation $\mathbf{x}$. If this pair of bundles can be achieved by consumers 12 and 22 alone, then they can block the allocation $\mathbf{x}$, and the proof will be complete.

To see that together they can achieve $(\bar{\mathbf{x}}^{12}, \bar{\mathbf{x}}^{22})$, note the following:

$$\begin{aligned}\bar{\mathbf{x}}^{12} + \bar{\mathbf{x}}^{22} &= \frac{\mathbf{x}^{11} + \mathbf{x}^{12}}{2} + \frac{\mathbf{x}^{21} + \mathbf{x}^{22}}{2} \\ &= \tfrac{1}{2}(\mathbf{x}^{11} + \mathbf{x}^{12} + \mathbf{x}^{21} + \mathbf{x}^{22}) \\ &= \tfrac{1}{2}(2\mathbf{e}^1 + 2\mathbf{e}^2) \\ &= \mathbf{e}^1 + \mathbf{e}^2,\end{aligned}$$

where the third equality follows from (P.1). Consequently, the two worst off consumers of each type can together achieve a pair of bundles that makes one of them strictly better off and the other no worse off. The coalition $S = \{12, 22\}$ therefore can block $\mathbf{x}$. But this contradicts the fact that $\mathbf{x}$ is in the core.

We conclude then that $\mathbf{x}$ must give consumers of the same type the same bundle. ∎

Now that we have made clear what it means for one economy to be larger than another, and have demonstrated the equal treatment property in the core of a replica economy, we can clarify what we mean when we say the core 'shrinks' as the economy gets larger by replication. First, recognise that when we replicate some basic economy, we increase the number of consumers in the economy and so increase the number of bundles in an allocation. There should be no confusion about that. However, when we restrict our attention to *core* allocations in these economies, the equal-treatment property allows us to completely describe any allocation in the core of $\mathcal{E}_r$ by reference to a similar allocation in the basic economy, $\mathcal{E}_1$.

To see this, suppose that $\mathbf{x}$ is in the core of $\mathcal{E}_r$. Then by the equal treatment property, $\mathbf{x}$ must be of the form

$$\mathbf{x} = \Big(\underbrace{\mathbf{x}^1, \ldots, \mathbf{x}^1}_{r \text{ times}}, \underbrace{\mathbf{x}^2, \ldots, \mathbf{x}^2}_{r \text{ times}}, \ldots, \underbrace{\mathbf{x}^I, \ldots, \mathbf{x}^I}_{r \text{ times}}\Big),$$

because all consumers of the same type must receive the same bundle. Consequently, *core* allocations in $\mathcal{E}_r$ are just r-fold copies of allocations in $\mathcal{E}_1$ – i.e., the above core allocation is just the r-fold copy of the $\mathcal{E}_1$ allocation

$$(\mathbf{x}^1, \mathbf{x}^2, \ldots, \mathbf{x}^I). \tag{5.10}$$

In fact, this allocation is feasible in $\mathcal{E}_1$. To see this, note first that because $\mathbf{x}$ is a core allocation in $\mathcal{E}_r$, it must be feasible in $\mathcal{E}_r$. Therefore, we have

$$r\sum_{i\in\mathcal{I}} \mathbf{x}^i = r\sum_{i\in\mathcal{I}} \mathbf{e}^i,$$

which, dividing by r, shows that the allocation in (5.10) is feasible in the basic economy $\mathcal{E}_1$.

Altogether then, we have shown that every core allocation of the r-fold replica economy is simply an r-fold copy of some feasible allocation in the basic economy $\mathcal{E}_1$. Consequently, we can keep track of how the core changes as we replicate the economy simply by keeping track of those allocations in $\mathcal{E}_1$ corresponding to the core of each r-fold replica. With this in mind, define C_r as follows:

$$C_r \equiv \left\{ \mathbf{x} = (\mathbf{x}^1, \ldots, \mathbf{x}^I) \in F(\mathbf{e}) \mid \Big(\underbrace{\mathbf{x}^1, \ldots, \mathbf{x}^1}_{r \text{ times}}, \ldots, \underbrace{\mathbf{x}^I, \ldots, \mathbf{x}^I}_{r \text{ times}} \Big) \text{ is in the core of } \mathcal{E}_r \right\}.$$

We can now describe formally the idea that the core 'shrinks' as the economy is replicated.

LEMMA 5.3 *The sequence of sets $C_1, C_2, \ldots,$ is decreasing. That is $C_1 \supseteq C_2 \supseteq \ldots \supseteq C_r \supseteq \ldots$.*

Proof: It suffices to show that for $r > 1$, $C_r \subseteq C_{r-1}$. So, suppose that $\mathbf{x} = (\mathbf{x}^1, \ldots, \mathbf{x}^I) \in C_r$. This means that its r-fold copy cannot be blocked in the r-fold replica economy. We must show that its $(r-1)$-fold copy cannot be blocked in the $(r-1)$-fold replica economy. But a moment's thought will convince you of this once you realise that any coalition that blocks the $(r-1)$-fold copy in $\mathcal{E}_{r-1}$ could also block the r-fold copy in $\mathcal{E}_r$ – after all, all the members of that coalition are present in $\mathcal{E}_r$ as well, and their endowments have not changed. ∎

So, by keeping track of the allocations in the basic economy whose r-fold copies are in the core of the r-fold replica, Lemma 5.3 tells us that this set will get no larger as r increases. To see how the core actually shrinks as the economy is replicated, we shall look again at economies with just two types of consumers. Because we are only concerned with core allocations in these economies, we can exploit the equal-treatment property and illustrate our arguments in an Edgeworth box like Fig. 5.10. This time, we think of the preferences and endowments in the box as those of a *representative* consumer of each type.

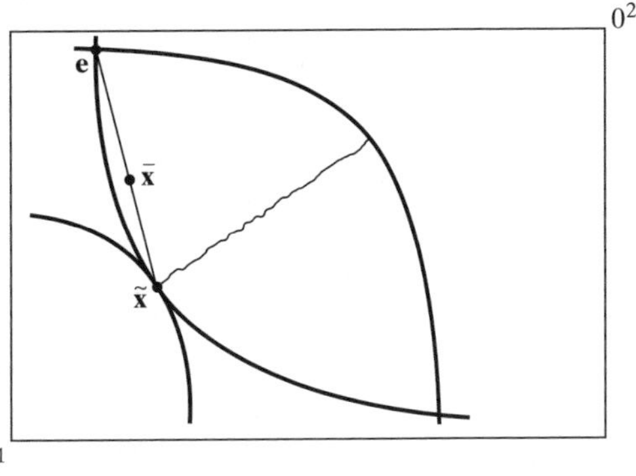

Figure 5.10. An Edgeworth box for a two-type replica economy.

In the basic economy with one consumer of each type, the core of $\mathcal{E}_1$ is the squiggly line between the two consumers' respective indifference curves through their endowments at $\mathbf{e}$. The core of $\mathcal{E}_1$ contains some allocations that are WEA and some that are not. The allocation marked $\tilde{\mathbf{x}}$ is *not* a WEA because the price line through $\tilde{\mathbf{x}}$ and $\mathbf{e}$ is not tangent to the consumers' indifference curves at $\tilde{\mathbf{x}}$. Note that $\tilde{\mathbf{x}}$ is on consumer 11's indifference curve through his endowment. If we now replicate this economy once, can the replication of this allocation be in the core of the larger four-consumer economy?

The answer is no; and to see it, first notice that any point along the line joining $\mathbf{e}$ and $\tilde{\mathbf{x}}$ is preferred to both $\mathbf{e}$ and $\tilde{\mathbf{x}}$ by both (there are now two) type 1's because their preferences are strictly convex. In particular, the midpoint $\bar{\mathbf{x}}$ has this property. Now consider the three-consumer coalition, $S = \{11, 12, 21\}$, consisting of both type 1's and one type 2 consumer (either one will do). Let each type 1 consumer have a bundle corresponding to the type 1 bundle at $\bar{\mathbf{x}}$ and let the lone type 2 consumer have a type 2 bundle like that at $\tilde{\mathbf{x}}$. We know that each type 1 strictly prefers this to the type 1 bundle at $\tilde{\mathbf{x}}$, and the type 2 consumer is just as well off. Specifically, we know

$$\begin{aligned} \bar{\mathbf{x}}^{11} &\equiv \tfrac{1}{2}(\mathbf{e}^1 + \tilde{\mathbf{x}}^{11}) \succ^1 \tilde{\mathbf{x}}^{11}, \\ \bar{\mathbf{x}}^{12} &\equiv \tfrac{1}{2}(\mathbf{e}^1 + \tilde{\mathbf{x}}^{12}) \succ^1 \tilde{\mathbf{x}}^{12}, \\ \tilde{\mathbf{x}}^{21} &\sim^2 \tilde{\mathbf{x}}^{21}. \end{aligned}$$

Are bundles $\{\bar{\mathbf{x}}^{11}, \bar{\mathbf{x}}^{12}, \tilde{\mathbf{x}}^{21}\}$ feasible for S? From the definitions, and noting that $\tilde{\mathbf{x}}^{11} = \tilde{\mathbf{x}}^{12}$, we have

$$\begin{aligned} \bar{\mathbf{x}}^{11} + \bar{\mathbf{x}}^{12} + \tilde{\mathbf{x}}^{21} &= 2\big(\tfrac{1}{2}\mathbf{e}^1 + \tfrac{1}{2}\tilde{\mathbf{x}}^{11}\big) + \tilde{\mathbf{x}}^{21} \\ &= \mathbf{e}^1 + \tilde{\mathbf{x}}^{11} + \tilde{\mathbf{x}}^{21}. \end{aligned} \tag{5.11}$$

Next recall that $\tilde{\mathbf{x}}$ is in the core of $\mathcal{E}_1$, so it must be feasible in the two-consumer economy. This implies

$$\tilde{\mathbf{x}}^{11} + \tilde{\mathbf{x}}^{21} = \mathbf{e}^1 + \mathbf{e}^2. \tag{5.12}$$

Combining (5.11) and (5.12) yields

$$\bar{\mathbf{x}}^{11} + \bar{\mathbf{x}}^{12} + \tilde{\mathbf{x}}^{21} = 2\mathbf{e}^1 + \mathbf{e}^2,$$

so the proposed allocation is indeed feasible for the coalition S of two type 1's and one type 2. Because we have found a coalition and an allocation they can achieve that makes two of them strictly better off and the other no worse off than their assignments under $\tilde{\mathbf{x}}$, that coalition blocks $\tilde{\mathbf{x}}$ in the four-consumer economy, ruling it out of the core of $\mathcal{E}_2$.

If we continue to replicate the economy, so that more consumers can form more coalitions, can we 'shrink' the core even further? If so, are there any allocations that are never ruled out and so belong to the core of every replica economy? The answer to both questions is yes, as we now proceed to show in the general case.

We would like to demonstrate that the set of core allocations for $\mathcal{E}_r$ converges to its set of Walrasian equilibrium allocations as r increases. Through the equal treatment property, we have been able to describe core allocations for $\mathcal{E}_r$ as r-fold copies of allocations in the basic economy. We now do the same for $\mathcal{E}_r$'s set of Walrasian equilibria.

LEMMA 5.4 *An allocation* $\mathbf{x}$ *is a WEA for* $\mathcal{E}_r$ *if and only if it is of the form*

$$\mathbf{x} = \Big(\underbrace{\mathbf{x}^1, \ldots, \mathbf{x}^1}_{r\ times}, \underbrace{\mathbf{x}^2, \ldots, \mathbf{x}^2}_{r\ times}, \ldots, \underbrace{\mathbf{x}^I, \ldots, \mathbf{x}^I}_{r\ times}\Big),$$

and the allocation $(\mathbf{x}^1, \mathbf{x}^2, \ldots, \mathbf{x}^I)$ *is a WEA for* $\mathcal{E}_1$.

Proof: If $\mathbf{x}$ is a WEA for $\mathcal{E}_r$, then by Theorem 5.5, it is in the core of $\mathcal{E}_r$, so that by Theorem 5.16 it must satisfy the equal treatment property. Hence, it must be an r-fold copy of some allocation in $\mathcal{E}_1$. We leave it as an exercise for you to show that this allocation in $\mathcal{E}_1$ is a WEA for $\mathcal{E}_1$. In addition, we leave the converse as an exercise. ∎

Lemma 5.4 says that as we replicate the economy, the set of Walrasian equilibria remains 'constant' in the sense that it consists purely of copies of Walrasian equilibria of the basic economy. Consequently, the set of Walrasian equilibria of the basic economy keeps track, exactly, of the set of Walrasian equilibria of the r-fold replicas.

We can now compare the set of core allocations for $\mathcal{E}_r$ with its set of Walrasian equilibrium allocations by comparing the set C_r – whose members are allocations for $\mathcal{E}_1$ – with the set of Walrasian equilibrium allocations for $\mathcal{E}_1$.

Because $C_1 \supset C_2 \supset \ldots$, the core is shrinking, as we have already seen. Moreover, $C_1 \supset C_2 \supset \ldots . \supset W_1(\mathbf{e})$, the set of WEAs for $\mathcal{E}_1$. To see this, note that by Lemma 5.4, the r-fold copy of a WEA for $\mathcal{E}_1$ is in the core of $\mathcal{E}_r$, which by the definition of C_r means that the original WEA for $\mathcal{E}_1$ is in C_r.

Now, as we replicate the economy and consider C_r, in the limit only those allocations satisfying $\mathbf{x} \in C_r$ for every $r = 1, 2, \ldots$ will remain. Thus, to say that the core shrinks to the set of competitive equilibria is to say that if $\mathbf{x} \in C_r$ for every r, then $\mathbf{x}$ is a competitive equilibrium allocation for $\mathcal{E}_1$. This is precisely what Debreu and Scarf have shown.

THEOREM 5.17 ***(Edgeworth-Debreu-Scarf) A Limit Theorem on the Core***

If $\mathbf{x} \in C_r$ *for every* $r = 1, 2, \ldots$, *then* $\mathbf{x}$ *is a Walrasian equilibrium allocation for* $\mathcal{E}_1$.

Before presenting the general argument, we will sharpen our intuition by considering the two-type Edgeworth box case. So, consider Fig. 5.11. Let us suppose, by way of contradiction, that some non-Walrasian equilibrium allocation, $\tilde{\mathbf{x}}$, is in C_r for every r. In particular, then, $\tilde{\mathbf{x}}$ is in the core of the basic two consumer economy consisting of one consumer of each type. In Fig. 5.11, this means that $\tilde{\mathbf{x}}$ must be within the lens and on the contract curve. That is, it must be on the squiggly line, and the consumers' indifference curves through $\tilde{\mathbf{x}}$ must be tangent.

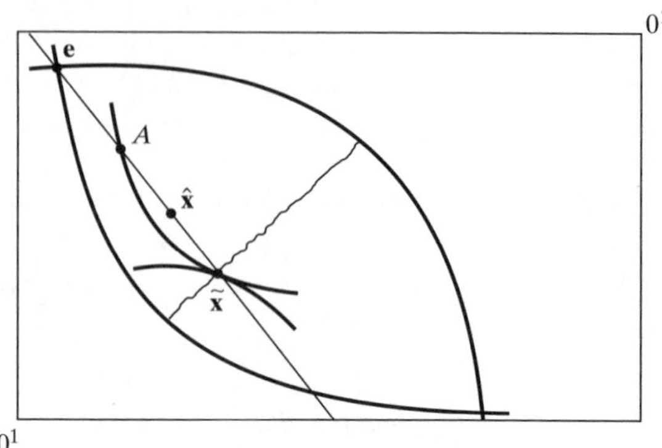

Figure 5.11. Illustration for the proof of Theorem 5.17.

Now consider the line joining the endowment point, **e**, and $\tilde{\mathbf{x}}$. This corresponds to a budget line for both consumers and an associated pair of prices p_1, p_2 for the two goods. Because $MRS^1_{12}(\tilde{\mathbf{x}}^1) = MRS^2_{12}(\tilde{\mathbf{x}})$, either $p_1/p_2 > MRS^1_{12}(\tilde{\mathbf{x}}^1)$, or $p_2/p_1 > MRS^2_{12}(\tilde{\mathbf{x}}^2)$. Note that equality cannot hold; otherwise, these prices would constitute a Walrasian equilibrium, and **x** would be a Walrasian equilibrium allocation. Fig. 5.11 depicts the first case. The second is handled analogously by reversing the roles of types 1 and 2.

As shown, the line from **e** to $\tilde{\mathbf{x}}$ therefore cuts the type 1's indifference curve at point A, and by strict convexity, lies entirely above it between A and $\tilde{\mathbf{x}}$. Thus, there exists some point like $\hat{\mathbf{x}}$ on the segment from A to $\tilde{\mathbf{x}}$, which a type 1 consumer strictly prefers to his bundle at $\tilde{\mathbf{x}}$. Because $\hat{\mathbf{x}}$ lies on the chord from **e** to $\tilde{\mathbf{x}}$, it can be expressed as a convex combination of **e** and $\tilde{\mathbf{x}}$. Thinking ahead a little, let us then write the type 1 bundle at $\hat{\mathbf{x}}$ as follows:

$$\hat{\mathbf{x}}^1 \equiv \frac{1}{r}\mathbf{e}^1 + \frac{r-1}{r}\tilde{\mathbf{x}}^1 \tag{5.13}$$

for some $r > 1$. Notice first that this is indeed a convex combination of the sort described because $1/r + (r-1)/r = 1$. For the record, let us recall that

$$\hat{\mathbf{x}}^1 \succ^1 \tilde{\mathbf{x}}^1. \tag{5.14}$$

Suppose, as can always be arranged, that r is an integer, and consider $\mathcal{E}_r$, the economy with r consumers of each type. Because we are assuming $\tilde{\mathbf{x}} \in C_r$, this means that the r-fold copy of $\tilde{\mathbf{x}}$ is in the core of $\mathcal{E}_r$. But can this be so? Not if we can find a coalition and an allocation that blocks it, and that is just what we will do.

This time, our coalition S consists of all r type 1 consumers and $r-1$ of the type 2 consumers. If we give each type 1 the bundle $\hat{\mathbf{x}}^1$, then from (5.14), each would prefer it to his assignment under $\tilde{\mathbf{x}}$. If we give each type 2 in the coalition a bundle $\tilde{\mathbf{x}}^2$ identical to her assignment under $\tilde{\mathbf{x}}$, each type 2 of course would be indifferent. Thus, we would have

$$\begin{aligned} \hat{\mathbf{x}}^1 &\succ^1 \tilde{\mathbf{x}}^1 && \text{for each of the } r \text{ type 1 consumers,} \\ \tilde{\mathbf{x}}^2 &\sim^2 \tilde{\mathbf{x}}^2 && \text{for each of the } (r-1) \text{ type 2 consumers.} \end{aligned} \tag{5.15}$$

Is such an allocation feasible for S? Summing over the consumers in S, their aggregate allocation is $r\hat{\mathbf{x}}^1 + (r-1)\tilde{\mathbf{x}}^2$. From the definition of $\hat{\mathbf{x}}^1$ in (5.13),

$$\begin{aligned} r\hat{\mathbf{x}}^1 + (r-1)\tilde{\mathbf{x}}^2 &= r\left[\frac{1}{r}\mathbf{e}^1 + \frac{r-1}{r}\tilde{\mathbf{x}}^1\right] + (r-1)\tilde{\mathbf{x}}^2 \\ &= \mathbf{e}^1 + (r-1)(\tilde{\mathbf{x}}^1 + \tilde{\mathbf{x}}^2). \end{aligned} \tag{5.16}$$

Now recall that $\tilde{\mathbf{x}}^1$ and $\tilde{\mathbf{x}}^2$ are, by assumption, in the core of the basic two-consumer economy. They therefore must be feasible for the two-consumer economy, so we know

$$\tilde{\mathbf{x}}^1 + \tilde{\mathbf{x}}^2 = \mathbf{e}^1 + \mathbf{e}^2. \tag{5.17}$$

Using (5.16) and (5.17), we find that

$$\begin{aligned} r\hat{\mathbf{x}}^1 + (r-1)\tilde{\mathbf{x}}^2 &= \mathbf{e}^1 + (r-1)(\tilde{\mathbf{x}}^1 + \tilde{\mathbf{x}}^2) \\ &= \mathbf{e}^1 + (r-1)(\mathbf{e}^1 + \mathbf{e}^2) \\ &= r\mathbf{e}^1 + (r-1)\mathbf{e}^2, \end{aligned}$$

confirming that the proposed allocation in (5.15) is indeed feasible for the coalition of r type 1's and $(r-1)$ type 2's. Because that allocation is feasible and strictly preferred by some members of S, and no worse for every member of S than the r-fold copy of $\tilde{\mathbf{x}}$, S blocks the r-fold copy of $\tilde{\mathbf{x}}$ and so it is not in the core of $\mathcal{E}_r$. We conclude that if $\mathbf{x} \in C_r$ for every r, then it must be a Walrasian equilibrium allocation in the basic economy.

We now give the general argument under two additional hypotheses. The first is that if $\mathbf{x} \in C_1$, then $\mathbf{x} \gg \mathbf{0}$. The second is that for each $i \in \mathcal{I}$, the utility function u^i representing $\succsim^i$ is differentiable on $\mathbb{R}^n_{++}$ with a strictly positive gradient vector there.

Proof: Suppose that $\tilde{\mathbf{x}} \in C_r$ for every r. We must show that $\tilde{\mathbf{x}}$ is a WEA for $\mathcal{E}_1$.

We shall first establish that

$$u^i((1-t)\tilde{\mathbf{x}}^i + t\mathbf{e}^i) \le u^i(\tilde{\mathbf{x}}^i), \qquad \forall\, t \in [0,1], \text{ and } \forall\, i \in \mathcal{I}. \tag{P.1}$$

To see that this inequality must hold, let us suppose that it does not and argue to a contradiction. So, suppose that for some $\bar{t} \in [0,1]$, and some $i \in \mathcal{I}$,

$$u^i((1-\bar{t})\tilde{\mathbf{x}}^i + \bar{t}\mathbf{e}^i) > u^i(\tilde{\mathbf{x}}^i).$$

By the strict quasiconcavity of u^i, this implies that

$$u^i((1-t)\tilde{\mathbf{x}}^i + t\mathbf{e}^i) > u^i(\tilde{\mathbf{x}}^i), \qquad \text{for all } t \in (0, \bar{t}].$$

Consequently, by the continuity of u^i, there is a positive integer, r, large enough such that

$$u^i\left(\left(1 - \frac{1}{r}\right)\tilde{\mathbf{x}}^i + \frac{1}{r}\mathbf{e}^i\right) > u^i(\tilde{\mathbf{x}}^i).$$

But we can now use precisely the same argument that we gave in the discussion preceding the proof to show that the r-fold copy of $\tilde{\mathbf{x}}$ is then not in the core of $\mathcal{E}_r$. But this contradicts the fact that $\tilde{\mathbf{x}} \in C_r$. We therefore conclude that (P.1) must hold.

Now, look closely at (P.1). Considering the left-hand side as a real-valued function of t on $[0, 1]$, it says that this function achieves a maximum at $t = 0$. Because this is on the lower boundary of $[0, 1]$ it implies that the derivative of the left-hand side is non-positive when evaluated at $t = 0$. Taking the derivative and evaluating it at $t = 0$ then gives

$$\nabla u^i(\tilde{\mathbf{x}}^i) \cdot (\mathbf{e}^i - \tilde{\mathbf{x}}^i) \leq 0, \qquad \text{for all } i \in I. \tag{P.2}$$

Now, because $\tilde{\mathbf{x}}$ is in the core of $\mathcal{E}_1$, it is Pareto efficient. Moreover, by our additional hypotheses, $\tilde{\mathbf{x}} \gg \mathbf{0}$, and each $\nabla u^i(\tilde{\mathbf{x}}^i) \gg \mathbf{0}$. Consequently, as you are asked to show in Exercise 5.27, the strictly positive gradient vectors, $\nabla u^1(\tilde{\mathbf{x}}^1), \ldots, \nabla u^I(\tilde{\mathbf{x}}^I)$, are proportional to one another and so to a common vector $\tilde{\mathbf{p}} \gg \mathbf{0}$. Consequently, there are strictly positive numbers, $\lambda_1, \ldots, \lambda_I$ such that

$$\nabla u^i(\tilde{\mathbf{x}}^i) = \lambda_i \tilde{\mathbf{p}}, \qquad \text{for all } i \in \mathcal{I}. \tag{P.3}$$

Together, (P.2), (P.3), and the positivity of each of the λ_i's give

$$\tilde{\mathbf{p}} \cdot \tilde{\mathbf{x}}^i \geq \tilde{\mathbf{p}} \cdot \mathbf{e}^i \qquad \text{for all } i \in \mathcal{I}. \tag{P.4}$$

Note that we would be finished if each inequality in (P.4) were an equality. For in this case, $\tilde{\mathbf{x}}^i$ would satisfy the first-order conditions for a maximum of the consumer's utility-maximisation problem subject to the budget constraint at prices $\tilde{\mathbf{p}}$. Moreover, under the hypotheses we have made, the first-order conditions are sufficient for a utility-maximising solution as well (see Theorem 1.4). That is, $\tilde{\mathbf{x}}^i$ would be a Walrasian equilibrium allocation for $\mathcal{E}_1$.

We now show that indeed each inequality in (P.4) must be an equality. Note that because $\tilde{\mathbf{x}} \in C_r$, it must be feasible in $\mathcal{E}_1$. Therefore,

$$\sum_{i \in \mathcal{I}} \tilde{\mathbf{x}}^i = \sum_{i \in \mathcal{I}} \mathbf{e}^i,$$

so that

$$\tilde{\mathbf{p}} \cdot \sum_{i \in \mathcal{I}} \tilde{\mathbf{x}}^i = \tilde{\mathbf{p}} \cdot \sum_{i \in \mathcal{I}} \mathbf{e}^i.$$

However, this equality would fail if for even one consumer i, the inequality in (P.4) were strict. ∎

We have shown that for large enough economies, only WEAs will be in the core. This astonishing result really does point towards some unique characteristics of large market economies and suggests itself as a sort of ultimate 'proof' of Adam Smith's intuitions about the efficacy of competitive market systems. The result does bear some scrutiny, however. First of all, it was obtained within the rather rigid context of replica economies with equal numbers of each type of consumer. Second, we cannot lose sight of the fact that the core itself is a very weak solution concept with arguable equity properties. To the extent that a 'good' solution to the distribution problem from society's point of view includes considerations of equity, even the broadest interpretation of this result does not provide support to arguments for pure laissez-faire. The 'equity' of *any* core allocation, and so of any WEA, depends on what the initial endowments are.

The first of these objections can be, and has been, addressed. Abandoning the rigid world of replica economies in favour of more flexible 'continuum economies', Aumann (1964), Hildenbrand (1974), and others have proved even stronger results without the assumption of equal numbers of each type. What then of the second objection cited? Well, if we want to use the market system to achieve the 'good society', the Second Welfare Theorem tells us that we can. All we need to do is decide where in the core we want to be and then redistribute 'endowments' or 'income' and use the market to 'support' that distribution. Ah, but there's the rub. How do we decide where we want to be? How does 'society' decide which distribution in the core it 'prefers'? This is the kind of question we take up in the next chapter.

5.6 EXERCISES

5.1 In an Edgeworth box economy, do the following:

(a) Sketch a situation where preferences are neither convex nor strictly monotonic and there is no Walrasian equilibrium.

(b) Sketch a situation where preferences are neither convex nor strictly monotonic yet a Walrasian equilibrium exists nonetheless.

(c) Repeat parts (a) and (b), but this time assume preferences are not continuous.

5.2 Let some consumer have endowments $\mathbf{e}$ and face prices $\mathbf{p}$. His indirect utility function is thus $v(\mathbf{p}, \mathbf{p} \cdot \mathbf{e})$. Show that whenever the price of a good rises by a sufficiently small amount, the consumer will be made worse off if initially he was a net demander of the good (i.e., his demand exceeded his endowment) and made better of if he was initially a net supplier of the good. What can you say if the price of the good rises by a sufficiently *large* amount?

5.3 Consider an exchange economy. Let $\mathbf{p}$ be a vector of prices in which the price of at least one good is non-positive. Show that if consumers' utility functions are strongly increasing, then aggregate excess demand cannot be zero in every market.

5.4 Derive the excess demand function $\mathbf{z}(\mathbf{p})$ for the economy in Example 5.1. Verify that it satisfies Walras' law.

5.5 In Example 5.1, calculate the consumers' Walrasian equilibrium allocations and illustrate in an Edgeworth box. Sketch in the contract curve and identify the core.

5.6 Prove Lemma 5.1 and complete the proof of Lemma 5.2.

5.7 Consider an exchange economy with two goods. Suppose that its aggregate excess demand function is $\mathbf{z}(p_1, p_2) = (-1, p_1/p_2)$ for all $(p_1, p_2) \gg (0, 0)$.

(a) Show that this function satisfies conditions 1 and 2 of Theorem 5.3, but not condition 3.

(b) Show that the conclusion of Theorem 5.3 fails here. That is, show that there is no $(p_1^*, p_2^*) \gg (0, 0)$ such that $\mathbf{z}(p_1^*, p_2^*) = (0, 0)$.

5.8 Let $\mathbf{p}^m$ be a sequence of strictly positive prices converging to $\bar{\mathbf{p}}$, and let a consumer's endowment vector be $\mathbf{e}$. Show that the sequence $\{\mathbf{p}^m \cdot \mathbf{e}\}$ of the consumer's income is bounded. Indeed, show more generally that if a sequence of real numbers converges, then it must be bounded.

5.9 Prove the corollary to Theorem 5.8. Extend the argument to show that, under the same assumptions, any Pareto-efficient allocation can be supported as a WEA for some Walrasian equilibrium $\bar{\mathbf{p}}$ and some distribution of *income*, $(R^1, \ldots, R^I)$, where R^i is the income distributed to consumer i.

5.10 In a two-person, two-good exchange economy with strictly increasing utility functions, it is easy to see that an allocation $\bar{\mathbf{x}} \in F(\mathbf{e})$ is Pareto efficient if and only if $\bar{\mathbf{x}}^i$ solves the problem

$$\max_{\mathbf{x}^i} u^i(\mathbf{x}^i) \quad \text{s.t.} \quad u^j(\mathbf{x}^j) \geq u^j(\bar{\mathbf{x}}^j),$$
$$x_1^1 + x_1^2 = e_1^1 + e_1^2,$$
$$x_2^1 + x_2^2 = e_2^1 + e_2^2$$

for $i = 1, 2$ and $i \neq j$.

(a) Prove the claim.

(b) Generalise this equivalent definition of a Pareto-efficient allocation to the case of n goods and I consumers. Then prove the general claim.

5.11 Consider a two-consumer, two-good exchange economy. Utility functions and endowments are

$$u^1(x_1, x_2) = (x_1 x_2)^2 \quad \text{and} \quad \mathbf{e}^1 = (18, 4),$$
$$u^2(x_1, x_2) = \ln(x_1) + 2\ln(x_2) \quad \text{and} \quad \mathbf{e}^2 = (3, 6).$$

(a) Characterise the set of Pareto-efficient allocations as completely as possible.

(b) Characterise the core of this economy.

(c) Find a Walrasian equilibrium and compute the WEA.

(d) Verify that the WEA you found in part (c) is in the core.

5.12 There are two goods and two consumers. Preferences and endowments are described by

$$u^1(x_1, x_2) = \min(x_1, x_2) \quad \text{and} \quad \mathbf{e}^1 = (30, 0),$$
$$v^2(\mathbf{p}, y) = y/2\sqrt{p_1 p_2} \quad \text{and} \quad \mathbf{e}^2 = (0, 20),$$

respectively.

(a) Find a Walrasian equilibrium for this economy and its associated WEA.

(b) Do the same when 1's endowment is $\mathbf{e}^1 = (5, 0)$ and 2's remains $\mathbf{e}^2 = (0, 20)$.

5.13 An exchange economy has two consumers with expenditure functions:

$$e^1(\mathbf{p}, u) = \left(3(1.5)^2 p_1^2 p_2 \exp(u)\right)^{1/3},$$
$$e^2(\mathbf{p}, u) = \left(3(1.5)^2 p_2^2 p_1 \exp(u)\right)^{1/3}.$$

If initial endowments are $\mathbf{e}^1 = (10, 0)$ and $\mathbf{e}^2 = (0, 10)$, find the Walrasian equilibrium.

5.14 Suppose that each consumer i has a strictly positive endowment vector, $\mathbf{e}^i$, and a Cobb-Douglas utility function on $\mathbb{R}^n_+$ of the form $u^i(\mathbf{x}) = x_1^{\alpha_1^i} x_2^{\alpha_2^i} \cdots x_n^{\alpha_n^i}$, where $\alpha_k^i > 0$ for all consumers i, and goods k, and $\sum_{k=1}^n \alpha_k^i = 1$ for all i.

(a) Show that no consumer's utility function is strongly increasing on $\mathbb{R}^n_+$, so that one cannot apply Theorem 5.5 to conclude that this economy possesses a Walrasian equilibrium.

(b) Show that conditions 1, 2, and 3 of Theorem 5.3 are satisfied so that one can nevertheless use Theorem 5.3 directly to conclude that a Walrasian equilibrium exists here.

(c) Prove that a Walrasian equilibrium would also exist with Cobb-Douglas utilities when production is present and each production set satisfies Assumption 5.2. Use the same strategy as before.

5.15 There are 100 units of x_1 and 100 units of x_2. Consumers 1 and 2 are each endowed with 50 units of each good. Consumer 1 says, 'I love x_1, but I can take or leave x_2'. Consumer 2 says, 'I love x_2, but I can take or leave x_1'.

(a) Draw an Edgeworth box for these traders and sketch their preferences.

(b) Identify the core of this economy.

(c) Find all Walrasian equilibria for this economy.

5.16 Consider a simple exchange economy in which consumer 1 has expenditure function

$$e^1(\mathbf{p}, u) = \begin{cases} \frac{1}{3}(p_1 + p_2)u & \text{for } p_2/2 < p_1 < 2p_2, \\ up_2 & \text{for } p_1 \geq 2p_2, \\ up_1 & \text{for } p_1 \leq p_2/2, \end{cases}$$

and consumer 2 has expenditure function

$$e^2(\mathbf{p}, u) = (p_1 + p_2)u \quad \text{for all } (p_1, p_2).$$

(a) Sketch the Edgeworth box for this economy when aggregate endowments are (1, 1). Identify the set of Pareto-efficient allocations.

(b) Sketch the Edgeworth box for this economy when aggregate endowments are (2, 1). Identify the set of Pareto-efficient allocations.

5.17 Consider an exchange economy with two identical consumers. Their common utility function is $u^i(x_1, x_2) = x_1^\alpha x_2^{1-\alpha}$ for $0 < \alpha < 1$. Society has 10 units of x_1 and 10 units of x_2 in all. Find endowments $\mathbf{e}^1$ and $\mathbf{e}^2$, where $\mathbf{e}^1 \neq \mathbf{e}^2$, and Walrasian equilibrium prices that will 'support' as a WEA the equal-division allocation giving both consumers the bundle (5, 5).

5.18 In a two-good, two-consumer economy, utility functions are

$$u^1(x_1, x_2) = x_1(x_2)^2,$$
$$u^2(x_1, x_2) = (x_1)^2 x_2.$$

Total endowments are $(10, 20)$.

(a) A social planner wants to allocate goods to maximise consumer 1's utility while holding consumer 2's utility at $u^2 = 8000/27$. Find the assignment of goods to consumers that solves the planner's problem and show that the solution is Pareto efficient.

(b) Suppose, instead, that the planner just divides the endowments so that $\mathbf{e}^1 = (10, 0)$ and $\mathbf{e}^2 = (0, 20)$ and then lets the consumers transact through perfectly competitive markets. Find the Walrasian equilibrium and show that the WEAs are the same as the solution in part (a).

5.19 (Scarf) An exchange economy has three consumers and three goods. Consumers' utility functions and initial endowments are as follows:

$$u^1(x_1, x_2, x_3) = \min(x_1, x_2) \qquad e^1 = (1, 0, 0),$$
$$u^2(x_1, x_2, x_3) = \min(x_2, x_3) \qquad e^2 = (0, 1, 0),$$
$$u^3(x_1, x_2, x_3) = \min(x_1, x_3) \qquad e^1 = (0, 0, 1).$$

Find a Walrasian equilibrium and the associated WEA for this economy.

5.20 In an exchange economy with two consumers, total endowments are $(e_1, e_2) \equiv (e_1^1 + e_1^2, e_2^1 + e_2^2)$. Consumer i requires s_j^i units of good j to survive, but consumers differ in that $(s_1^1, s_2^1) \neq (s_1^2, s_2^2)$. Consumers are otherwise identical, with utility functions $u^i = (x_1^i - s_1^i)^\alpha + (x_2^i - s_2^i)^\alpha$ for $0 < \alpha < 1$ and $i = 1, 2$.

(a) Suppose now that there is a single hypothetical consumer with initial endowments (e_1, e_2) and utility function $u = (x_1 - s_1)^\alpha + (x_2 - s_2)^\alpha$, where $s_j \equiv s_j^1 + s_j^2$ for $j = 1, 2$. Calculate $(\partial u/\partial x_1)/(\partial u/\partial x_2)$ for this consumer and evaluate it at $(x_1, x_2) = (e_1, e_2)$. Call what you've obtained p^*.

(b) Show that p^* obtained in part (a) must be an equilibrium relative price for good x_1 in the exchange economy previously described.

5.21 Consider an exchange economy with the two consumers. Consumer 1 has utility function $u^1(x_1, x_2) = x_2$ and endowment $e^1 = (1, 1)$ and consumer 2 has utility function $u^2(x^1, x^2) = x^1 + x^2$ and endowment $e^2 = (1, 0)$.

(a) Which of the hypotheses of Theorem 5.4 fail in this example?

(b) Show that there does not exist a Walrasian equilibrium in this exchange economy.

5.22 This exercise will guide you through a proof of a version of Theorem 5.4 when the consumer's utility function is quasiconcave instead of strictly quasiconcave and strictly increasing instead of strongly increasing.

(a) If the utility function $u\colon \mathbb{R}^n_+ \to \mathbb{R}$ is continuous, quasiconcave and strictly increasing, show that for every $\varepsilon \in (0, 1)$ the approximating utility function $v_\varepsilon : \mathbb{R}^n_+ \to \mathbb{R}$ defined by

$$v_\varepsilon(\mathbf{x}) = u\left(x_1^\varepsilon + (1-\varepsilon)\sum_{i=1}^n x_i^\varepsilon, \ldots, x_n^\varepsilon + (1-\varepsilon)\sum_{i=1}^n x_i^\varepsilon\right),$$

is continuous, strictly quasiconcave and strongly increasing. Note that the approximation to $u(\cdot)$ becomes better and better as $\varepsilon \to 1$ because $v_\varepsilon(\mathbf{x}) \to u(\mathbf{x})$ as $\varepsilon \to 1$.

(b) Show that if in an exchange economy with a positive endowment of each good, each consumer's utility function is continuous, quasiconcave and strictly increasing on $\mathbb{R}^n_+$, there are approximating utility functions as in part (a) that define an exchange economy with the same endowments and possessing a Walrasian equilibrium. If, in addition, each consumer's endowment gives him a positive amount of each good, show that any limit of such Walrasian equilibria, as the approximations become better and better (e.g., as $\varepsilon \to 1$ in the approximations in part (a)) is a Walrasian equilibrium of the original exchange economy.

(c) Show that such a limit of Walrasian equilibria as described in part (b) exists. You will then have proven the following result.
If each consumer in an exchange economy is endowed with a positive amount of each good and has a continuous, quasiconcave and strictly increasing utility function, a Walrasian equilibrium exists.

(d) Which hypotheses of the Walrasian equilibrium existence result proved in part (b) fail to hold in the exchange economy in Exercise 5.21?

5.23 Show that if a firm's production set is strongly convex and the price vector is strictly positive, then there is at most one profit-maximising production plan.

5.24 Provide a proof of Theorem 5.10.

5.25 Complete the proof of Theorem 5.13 by showing that $\mathbf{z}(\mathbf{p})$ in the economy with production satisfies all the properties of Theorem 5.3.

5.26 Suppose that in a single-consumer economy, the consumer is endowed with none of the consumption good, y, and 24 hours of time, h, so that $\mathbf{e} = (24, 0)$. Suppose as well that preferences are defined over $\mathbb{R}^2_+$ and represented by $u(h, y) = hy$, and production possibilities are $Y = \{(-h, y) \mid 0 \le h \le b$ and $0 \le y \le \sqrt{h}\}$, where b is some large positive number. Let p_y and p_h be prices of the consumption good and leisure, respectively.

(a) Find relative prices p_y/p_h that clear the consumption and leisure markets simultaneously.

(b) Calculate the equilibrium consumption and production plans and sketch your results in $\mathbb{R}^2_+$.

(c) How many hours a day does the consumer work?

5.27 Consider an exchange economy $(u^i, \mathbf{e}^i)_{i \in \mathcal{I}}$ in which each u^i is continuous and quasiconcave on $\mathbb{R}^n_+$. Suppose that $\bar{\mathbf{x}} = (\bar{\mathbf{x}}^1, \bar{\mathbf{x}}^2, \ldots, \bar{\mathbf{x}}^I) \gg \mathbf{0}$ is Pareto efficient, that each u^i is continuously differentiable in an open set containing $\bar{\mathbf{x}}^i$, and that $\nabla u^i(\bar{\mathbf{x}}^i) \gg \mathbf{0}$. Under these conditions, which differ somewhat from those of Theorem 5.8, follow the steps below to derive another version of the Second Welfare Theorem.

(a) Show that for any two consumers i and j, the gradient vectors $\nabla u^i(\bar{\mathbf{x}}^i)$ and $\nabla u^j(\bar{\mathbf{x}}^j)$ must be proportional. That is, there must exist some $\alpha > 0$ (which may depend on i and j) such that $\nabla u^i(\bar{\mathbf{x}}^i) = \alpha \nabla u^j(\bar{\mathbf{x}}^j)$. Interpret this condition in the case of the Edgeworth box economy.

(b) Define $\bar{\mathbf{p}} = \nabla u^1(\bar{\mathbf{x}}^1) \gg \mathbf{0}$. Show that for every consumer i, there exists $\lambda_i > 0$ such that $\nabla u^i(\bar{\mathbf{x}}^i) = \lambda_i \bar{\mathbf{p}}$.

(c) Use Theorem 1.4 to argue that for every consumer i, $\bar{\mathbf{x}}^i$ solves

$$\max_{\mathbf{x}^i} u^i(\mathbf{x}^i) \qquad \text{s.t.} \qquad \bar{\mathbf{p}} \cdot \mathbf{x}^i \leq \bar{\mathbf{p}} \cdot \bar{\mathbf{x}}^i.$$

5.28 Suppose that all of the conditions in Exercise 5.27 hold, except the strict positivity of $\bar{\mathbf{x}}$ and the consumers' gradient vectors. Using an Edgeworth box, provide an example showing that in such a case, it may not be possible to support $\bar{\mathbf{x}}$ as a Walrasian equilibrium allocation. Because Theorem 5.8 does not require $\bar{\mathbf{x}}$ to be strictly positive, which hypothesis of Theorem 5.8 does your example violate?

5.29 Consider an exchange economy $(u^i, \mathbf{e}^i)_{i \in I}$ in which each u^i is continuous and quasiconcave on $\mathbb{R}^n_+$. Suppose that $\bar{\mathbf{x}} = (\bar{\mathbf{x}}^1, \bar{\mathbf{x}}^2, \ldots, \bar{\mathbf{x}}^I) \gg \mathbf{0}$ is Pareto efficient. Under these conditions, which differ from those of both Theorem 5.8 and Exercise 5.27, follow the steps below to derive yet another version of the Second Welfare Theorem.

(a) Let $C = \{\mathbf{y} \in \mathbb{R}^n \mid \mathbf{y} = \sum_{i \in I} \mathbf{x}^i$, some $\mathbf{x}^i \in \mathbb{R}^n$ such that $u^i(\mathbf{x}^i) \geq u^i(\bar{\mathbf{x}}^i)$ for all $i \in I$, with at least one inequality strict$\}$, and let $Z = \{\mathbf{z} \in \mathbb{R}^n \mid \mathbf{z} \leq \sum_{i \in I} \mathbf{e}^i\}$. Show that C and Z are convex and that their intersection is empty.

(b) Appeal to Theorem A2.24 to show that there exists a non-zero vector $\mathbf{p} \in \mathbb{R}^n$ such that

$$\mathbf{p} \cdot \mathbf{z} \leq \mathbf{p} \cdot \mathbf{y}, \quad \text{for every } \mathbf{z} \in Z \text{ and every } \mathbf{y} \in C.$$

Conclude from this inequality that $\mathbf{p} \geq \mathbf{0}$.

(c) Consider the same exchange economy, except that the endowment vector is $\bar{\mathbf{x}} = (\bar{\mathbf{x}}^1, \bar{\mathbf{x}}^2, \ldots, \bar{\mathbf{x}}^I)$. Use the inequality in part (b) to show that in this new economy, $\mathbf{p}$ is a Walrasian equilibrium price supporting the allocation $\bar{\mathbf{x}}$.

5.30 Suppose that $\mathbf{y} = \mathbf{0}$ solves

$$\max_{\mathbf{y}} \mathbf{p} \cdot \mathbf{y} \qquad \text{s.t.} \qquad \mathbf{y} \in Y - \mathbf{y}^0.$$

Show that $\mathbf{y}^0$ solves

$$\max_{\mathbf{y}} \mathbf{p} \cdot \mathbf{y} \qquad \text{s.t.} \qquad \mathbf{y} \in Y.$$

5.31 Consider an economy with production in which there are many goods produced by the production sector, but each firm produces only one of them. Suppose also that each firm's output is given by a differentiable production function and that each consumer's utility function is differentiable as well.

Assume that this economy is in a Walrasian equilibrium with strictly positive prices and that all consumer's marginal utilities (of consumption goods) and all firm's marginal products (of inputs) are also strictly positive.

(a) Show that the *MRS* between any two consumption goods is the same for each consumer, and that it is equal to the ratio of their prices.

(b) Show that the *MRTS* between any two inputs is the same for every firm and equal to the ratio of their prices.

(c) What does this tell you about the information content of Walrasian equilibrium prices?

5.32 Consider a simple economy with two consumers, a single consumption good x, and two time periods. Consumption of the good in period t is denoted x_t for $t = 1, 2$. Intertemporal utility functions for the two consumers are,

$$u_i(x_1, x_2) = x_1 x_2, \; i = 1, 2,$$

and endowments are $e^1 = (19, 1)$ and $e^2 = (1, 9)$. To capture the idea that the good is perfectly storable, we introduce a firm producing storage services. The firm can transform one unit of the good in period one into one unit of the good in period 2. Hence, the production set Y is the set of all vectors $(y_1, y_2) \in \mathbb{R}^2$ such that $y_1 + y_2 \leq 0$ and $y_1 \leq 0$. Consumer 1 is endowed with a 100 per cent ownership share of the firm.

(a) Suppose the two consumers cannot trade with one another. That is, suppose that each consumer is in a Robinson Crusoe economy and where consumer 1 has access to his storage firm. How much does each consumer consume in each period? How well off is each consumer? How much storage takes place?

(b) Now suppose the two consumers together with consumer 1's storage firm constitute a competitive production economy. What are the Walrasian equilibrium prices, p_1 and p_2? How much storage takes place now?

(c) Interpret p_1 as a spot price and p_2 as a futures price.

(d) Repeat the exercise under the assumption that storage is costly, i.e., that Y is the set of vectors $(y_1, y_2) \in \mathbb{R}^2$ such that $\delta y_1 + y_2 \leq 0$ and $y_1 \leq 0$, where $\delta \in [0, 1)$. Show that the existence of spot and futures markets now makes both consumers strictly better off.

5.33 The contingent-commodity interpretation of our general equilibrium model permits us to consider time (as in the previous exercise) as well as uncertainty and more (e.g. location). While the trading of contracts nicely captures the idea of futures contracts and prices, one might wonder about the role that spot markets play in our theory. This exercise will guide you through thinking about this. The main result is that once the date zero contingent-commodity contracts market has cleared at Walrasian prices, there is no remaining role for spot markets. Even if spot markets were to open up for some or all goods in some or all periods and in some or all states of the world, no additional trade would take place. All agents would simply exercise the contracts they already have in hand.

(a) Consider an exchange economy with I consumers, N goods, and $T = 2$ dates. There is no uncertainty. We will focus on one consumer whose utility function is $u(\mathbf{x}_1, \mathbf{x}_2)$, where $\mathbf{x}_t \in \mathbb{R}^N_+$ is a vector of period-t consumption of the N goods.

Suppose that $\hat{\mathbf{p}} = (\hat{\mathbf{p}}_1, \hat{\mathbf{p}}_2)$ is a Walrasian equilibrium price vector in the contingent-commodity sense described in Section 5.4, where $\hat{\mathbf{p}}_t \in \mathbb{R}^N_{++}$ is the price vector for period-t

contracts on the N goods. Let $\hat{\mathbf{x}} = (\hat{\mathbf{x}}_1, \hat{\mathbf{x}}_2)$ be the vector of contracts that our consumer purchases prior to date 1 given the Walrasian equilibrium price-vector $\hat{\mathbf{p}} = (\hat{\mathbf{p}}_1, \hat{\mathbf{p}}_2)$.

Suppose now that at each date t, spot-markets open for trade.

(i) Because all existing contracts are enforced, argue that our consumer's available endowment in period t is $\hat{\mathbf{x}}_t$.

(ii) Show that if our consumer wishes to trade in some period t spot-market and if all goods have period t spot-markets and the period t spot-prices are $\hat{\mathbf{p}}_t$, then our consumer's period t budget constraint is,

$$\hat{\mathbf{p}}_t \cdot \mathbf{x}_t \leq \hat{\mathbf{p}}_t \cdot \hat{\mathbf{x}}_t.$$

(iii) Conclude that our consumer can ultimately choose any $(\mathbf{x}_1, \mathbf{x}_2)$ such that

$$\hat{\mathbf{p}}_1 \cdot \mathbf{x}_1 \leq \hat{\mathbf{p}}_1 \cdot \hat{\mathbf{x}}_1 \qquad \text{and} \qquad \hat{\mathbf{p}}_2 \cdot \mathbf{x}_2 \leq \hat{\mathbf{p}}_2 \cdot \hat{\mathbf{x}}_2.$$

(iv) Prove that the consumer can do no better than to choose $\mathbf{x}_1 = \hat{\mathbf{x}}_1$ in period $t = 1$ and $\mathbf{x}_2 = \hat{\mathbf{x}}_2$ in period $t = 2$ by showing that any bundle that is feasible through trading in spot-markets is feasible in the contingent-commodity contract market. You should assume that in period 1 the consumer is forward-looking, knows the spot-prices he will face in period 2, and that he wishes to behave so as to maximise his lifetime utility $u(\mathbf{x}_1, \mathbf{x}_2)$. Further, assume that if he consumes $\bar{\mathbf{x}}_1$ in period $t = 1$, his utility of consuming any bundle $\mathbf{x}_2$ in period $t = 2$ is $u(\bar{\mathbf{x}}_1, \mathbf{x}_2)$.

Because the consumer can do no better if there are fewer spot-markets open, parts (i)–(iv) show that if there is a period t spot-market for good k and the period t spot-price of good k is $\hat{p}_{kt}$, then our consumer has no incentive to trade. Since this is true for all consumers, this shows that spot-markets clear at prices at which there is no trade.

(b) Repeat the exercise with uncertainty instead of time. Assume N goods and two states of the world, $s = 1, 2$. What is the interpretation of the assumption (analogous to that made in part (iv) of (a)) that if the consumer would have consumed bundle $\bar{\mathbf{x}}_1$ had state $s = 1$ occurred, his utility of consuming any bundle $\mathbf{x}_2$ in state $s = 2$ is $u(\bar{\mathbf{x}}_1, \mathbf{x}_2)$?

The next question shows that spot-markets nevertheless have a role.

5.34 (Arrow Securities) Exercise 5.33 shows that when there are opportunities to trade a priori in any commodity contingent on any date, state, etc., there is no remaining role for spot-markets. Here we show that if not all commodities can be traded contingent on every date and state, then spot-markets do have a role. We will in fact suppose that there is only one 'commodity' that can be traded a priori, an *Arrow security* (named after the Nobel prize winning economist Kenneth Arrow). An Arrow security for date t and state s entitles the bearer to one dollar at date t and in state s and nothing otherwise.

We wish to guide you towards showing that if $\hat{\mathbf{p}} \gg \mathbf{0}$ is a Walrasian equilibrium price in the contingent-commodity sense of Section 5.4 when there are N goods as well as time and uncertainty, and $\hat{\mathbf{x}} \geq \mathbf{0}$ is the corresponding Walrasian allocation, then the same prices and allocation arise when only Arrow securities can be traded a priori and all other goods must be traded on spot-markets. This shows that as long as there is a contingent-commodity market for a unit of account (money), the full contingent-commodity Walrasian equilibrium can be implemented with the aid of spot-markets. We will specialise our attention to exchange economies. You are invited to conduct the same analysis for production economies.

Consider then the following market structure and timing. At date zero, there is a market for trade in Arrow securities contingent on any date and any state. The price of each Arrow security is one dollar, and each date t and state s security entitles the bearer to one dollar at date t and in state s, and nothing otherwise. Let a^i_{ts} denote consumer i's quantity of date t and state s Arrow securities. No consumer is endowed with any Arrow securities. Hence, consumer i's budget constraint for Arrow securities at date zero is,

$$\sum_{t,s} a^i_{ts} = 0.$$

At each date $t \geq 1$, the date-t event s_t is realised and all consumers are informed of the date-t state of the world $s = (s_1, \ldots, s_t)$. Each consumer i receives his endowment $\mathbf{e}^i_{st} \in \mathbb{R}^N_+$ of the N goods. Spot-markets open for each of the N goods. If the spot-price of good k is p_{kts}, then consumer i's date-t state-s budget constraint is,

$$\sum_k p_{kts} x^i_{kts} = \sum_k p_{kts} e^i_{kts} + a^i_{ts}.$$

Each consumer i is assumed to know all current and future spot prices for every good in every state (a strong assumption!). Consequently, at date zero consumer i can decide on the trades he will actually make in each spot-market for each good at every future date and in every state. At date zero consumer i therefore solves,

$$\max_{(a^i_{ts}),(x^i_{kts})} u^i((x^i_{kts}))$$

subject to the Arrow security budget constraint,

$$\sum_{t,s} a^i_{ts} = 0,$$

and subject to the spot-market budget constraint,

$$\sum_k p_{kts} x^i_{kts} = \sum_k p_{kts} e^i_{kts} + a^i_{ts} \geq 0,$$

for each date t and state s. (Note the inequality in the date-t state-s constraints. This ensures that there is no bankruptcy.)

(a) Argue that the above formulation implicitly assumes that at any date t, current and future utility in any state is given by $u^i(\cdot)$ where past consumption is fixed at actual levels and consumption in states that did not occur are fixed at the levels that would have been chosen had they occurred.

(b) The consumer's budget constraint in the contingent-commodity model of Section 5.4 specialised to exchange economies is,

$$\sum_{k,t,s} p_{kts} x^i_{kts} = \sum_{k,t,s} p_{kts} e^i_{kts}.$$

Show that (x^i_{kts}) satisfies this budget constraint if and only if there is a vector of Arrow securities (a^i_{st}) such that (x^i_{kts}) and (a^i_{st}) together satisfy the Arrow security budget constraint and each of the spot-market budget constraints.

(c) Conclude from (b) that any Walrasian equilibrium price and allocation of the contingent-commodity model of Section 5.4 can be implemented in the spot-market model described here and that there will typically be trade in the spot-markets. Show also the converse.

(d) Explain why the price of each Arrow security is one. For example, why should the price of a security entitling the bearer to a dollar today be equal to the price of a security entitling the bearer to a dollar tomorrow when it is quite possible that consumers prefer consumption today to the same consumption tomorrow? (Hint: Think about what a dollar will buy.)

(e) Repeat the exercise when, instead of paying the bearer in a unit of account, one date-t state-s Arrow security pays the bearer one unit of good 1 at date t in state s and nothing otherwise. What prices must be set for Arrow securities now in order to obtain the result in part (c)? How does this affect the consumer's Arrow security and spot-market budget constraints?

5.35 (Asset Pricing) We can use our general equilibrium Walrasian model to think about asset pricing. We do this in the simplest possible manner by considering a setting with $N = 1$ good, $T = 1$ period, and finitely many states, $s = 1, 2, \ldots, S$. Thus a consumption bundle $\mathbf{x} = (x_1, x_2, \ldots, x_S) \in \mathbb{R}^S_+$ describes the quantity of the good consumed in each state. Once again, we restrict attention to an exchange economy. There are I consumers and consumer i's utility function is $u^i(x_1, x_2, \ldots, x_S)$ and his endowment vector is $\mathbf{e}^i = (e^i_1, \ldots, e^i_S)$. Note that one unit of commodity s yields one unit of the good in state s. Hence, we can think of commodity s as an Arrow security for the good in state s. Because all Arrow securities are tradeable here, the market is said to be *complete*.

Before thinking about asset pricing, let us consider this simply as an exchange economy and suppose that $\hat{\mathbf{p}} \gg 0$ is a Walrasian equilibrium price vector and that $\hat{\mathbf{x}} = (\hat{\mathbf{x}}^1, \hat{\mathbf{x}}^2, \ldots, \hat{\mathbf{x}}^I)$ is the associated Walrasian equilibrium allocation. Therefore, for each consumer i, $\hat{\mathbf{x}}^i = (\hat{x}^i_1, \hat{x}^i_2, \ldots, \hat{x}^i_S)$ maximises $u^i(x_1, x_2, \ldots, x_S)$ subject to

$$\hat{p}_1 x_1 + \ldots + \hat{p}_S x_S = \hat{p}_1 e^i_1 + \ldots + \hat{p}_S e^i_S,$$

and markets clear. That is,

$$\sum_i \hat{x}^i_s = \sum_i e^i_s,$$

for every state $s = 1, 2, \ldots, S$.

It is convenient to normalise prices throughout this exercise so that they sum to one, i.e., so that $\hat{p}_1 + \ldots + \hat{p}_S = 1$. Then, because $(1, 1, \ldots, 1)$ is the bundle guaranteeing one unit of the good regardless of the state, $\hat{p}_k$ has the interpretation that it is the number of units of the good (i.e., the number of units of the bundle $(1, 1, \ldots, 1)$) that must be paid in order to receive one unit of the good in state k. Thus, each $\hat{p}_k$ is a real, as opposed to a nominal, price.

An *asset* yields in each state s some non-negative amount of the good. Thus an asset is a vector, $\alpha = (\alpha_1, \ldots, \alpha_S) \in \mathbb{R}^S_+$, where α_s denotes the amount of the good the asset yields in state s.

(a) Suppose that the Walrasian equilibrium prices $\hat{\mathbf{p}}$ are in effect and that in addition to markets for each Arrow security, a spot-market opens for trade in an asset $\alpha = (\alpha_1, \ldots, \alpha_S)$. There is zero aggregate supply of asset α but consumers are permitted to purchase both positive and negative quantities of it (negative demand is sometimes called taking a 'short position' in the asset) so long as bankruptcy can be avoided in every state. Argue that consumers would be indifferent to trading in this asset if its price were set equal to $\hat{\mathbf{p}} \cdot \alpha$ and hence that this price is consistent with zero excess demand for the asset. Show also that, given the price vector $\hat{\mathbf{p}}$ for the Arrow securities, $\hat{\mathbf{p}} \cdot \alpha$ is the only price consistent with market-clearing and the occurrence of trade in the asset α.

(b) Suppose that π_s is the probability that state s occurs and that all consumers agree on this. Further, suppose that each consumer's preferences are represented by a von Neumann-Morgenstern utility function, $v_i(x)$, assigning VNM utility to any quantity $x \geq 0$ of the good and that $v_i' > 0$. Further, assume that each consumer is strictly risk averse, i.e., that $v_i'' < 0$. Consequently, for each consumer i,

$$u^i(x_1, \ldots, x_S) = \sum_{s=1}^{S} \pi_s v_i(x_s).$$

(i) Suppose the total endowment of the good is constant across states, i.e., suppose that

$$\sum_i e_s^i = \sum_i e_{s'}^i, \text{ for all states, } s, s'.$$

Show that $\hat{\mathbf{p}} = (\pi_1, \ldots, \pi_S)$ is a Walrasian equilibrium in which each consumer's consumption is constant across all states and in which the equilibrium price of any traded asset $\alpha = (\alpha_1, \ldots, \alpha_S) \in \mathbb{R}_+^S$ is simply its expected value. Thus, when consumers are able to fully diversify their risk, no asset receives a premium over and above its expected value.

(ii) Suppose the total endowment of the good is not constant across states.

(1) Prove that $\hat{\mathbf{p}} \neq (\pi_1, \ldots, \pi_S)$ and, assuming $\hat{\mathbf{x}} \gg \mathbf{0}$, prove that no consumer's consumption is constant across all states.

(2) Argue that the price of any traded asset $\alpha = (\alpha_1, \ldots, \alpha_S) \in \mathbb{R}_+^S$ must be equal to,

$$\frac{E(v_1'(\tilde{x}^1)\tilde{\alpha})}{E(v_1'(\tilde{x}^1))} = \cdots = \frac{E(v_I'(\tilde{x}^I)\tilde{\alpha})}{E(v_I'(\tilde{x}^I))},$$

where E denotes mathematical expectation, $\tilde{x}^i$ is the random variable describing the amount of the good consumed by consumer i in equilibrium ($\tilde{x}^i = \hat{x}_s^i$ in state s), and $\tilde{\alpha}$ is the random variable describing the amount of the good the asset yields ($\tilde{\alpha} = \alpha_s$ in state s). Conclude, at least roughly, that the real price of an asset is higher the more negatively correlated are its returns with consumption – it is then more useful for diversifying risk. In particular, conclude that an asset whose returns are independent of any consumer's marginal utility of consumption has a price equal to its expected value. Thus, the price of an asset is not so much related to its variance but rather the extent to which it is correlated with consumption.

5.36 (Arbitrage Pricing) We shift gears slightly in this question by considering an arbitrage argument that delivers the same pricing of assets as derived in Exercise 5.35. Suppose once again that there is one good and S states. Suppose also that there are N assets, $\alpha^1, \alpha^2, \ldots, \alpha^N$, that can be traded, each being a vector in $\mathbb{R}_+^S$. Let the price of asset k be q_k. We shall normalise prices so that they are real prices. That is, q_k is the number of units of the good that must be given up to purchase one unit of asset k. Suppose an investor purchases x_k units of each asset k.

(a) Show that the (column) vector

$$A\mathbf{x} \in \mathbb{R}_+^S$$

is the induced asset held by the investor subsequent to his purchase, where A is the $S \times N$ matrix whose kth column is α^k, and $\mathbf{x} = (x_1, \ldots, x_N)$ is the vector of the investor's asset purchases.

(b) Argue that the vector

$$A\mathbf{x} - \mathbf{1}(\mathbf{q} \cdot \mathbf{x}) \in \mathbb{R}^S_+$$

describes the real net gain to the investor in every state, where $\mathbf{1}$ is the column vector of S 1's.

(c) Suppose that every coordinate of the real net gain vector

$$A\mathbf{x} - \mathbf{1}(\mathbf{q} \cdot \mathbf{x})$$

is strictly positive. Argue that the investor can earn arbitrarily large profits with an initial outlay of a single unit of the good by repurchasing $\mathbf{x}$ (or an affordable fraction of it) again and again using short sales to cover his expenses, and always guaranteeing against bankruptcy in any state.

(d) Conclude from (c) that for markets to clear, there can be no $\mathbf{x} \in \mathbb{R}^N$ such that every coordinate of the real net gain vector is strictly positive. (Parts (c) and (d) constitute an 'arbitrage-pricing' argument. We next turn to its consequences.)

(e) Let $C = \{\mathbf{y} \in \mathbb{R}^N : \mathbf{y} = A\mathbf{x} - \mathbf{1}(\mathbf{q} \cdot \mathbf{x}) \text{ for some } \mathbf{x} \in \mathbb{R}^N\}$. Conclude from part (d) that

$$C \cap \mathbb{R}^N_{++} = \emptyset,$$

and use the separating hyperplane theorem, Theorem A2.24, to conclude that there is a non-zero vector, $\hat{\mathbf{p}} \in \mathbb{R}^N$ such that

$$\hat{\mathbf{p}} \cdot \mathbf{y} \le \hat{\mathbf{p}} \cdot \mathbf{z},$$

for all $\mathbf{y} \in C$ and all $\mathbf{z} \in \mathbb{R}^N_{++}$. Show further that $\hat{\mathbf{p}} \ge \mathbf{0}$ because otherwise the right-hand side of the previous inequality could be made arbitrarily negative and therefore for any $\mathbf{y}$, the inequality would fail for some $\mathbf{z}$. Finally, normalise $\hat{\mathbf{p}} \ge \mathbf{0}$ so that its coordinates sum to one.

(f) Using the definition of C and the results from part (e), show that,

$$\left(\hat{\mathbf{p}}^T A - \mathbf{q}\right)\mathbf{x} \le 0, \text{ for all } \mathbf{x} \in \mathbb{R}^N.$$

Argue that the inequality cannot be strict for any $\mathbf{x} \in \mathbb{R}^N$ because the inequality would then fail for $-\mathbf{x}$. Conclude that,

$$\left(\hat{\mathbf{p}}^T A - \mathbf{q}\right)\mathbf{x} = 0, \text{ for all } \mathbf{x} \in \mathbb{R}^N,$$

and therefore that,

$$\mathbf{q} = \hat{\mathbf{p}}^T A,$$

i.e., that for each asset k,

$$q_k = \hat{\mathbf{p}} \cdot \alpha^k.$$

(g) Compare the result in part (f) with the pricing of the asset that arose from the general equilibrium model considered in part (a) of Exercise 5.35. In that exercise, we assumed that all Arrow securities were tradeable, i.e., we assumed that the market was *complete*. Conclude from the current exercise that if there are no opportunities for profitable arbitrage among the assets that are available for trade, then even if markets are incomplete there are implicit prices, given by $\hat{\mathbf{p}}$, for all Arrow securities. Moreover, the prices of all tradeable assets are derived from these underlying Arrow security prices.

5.37 Complete the proof of Lemma 5.4.

(a) Show that if an allocation $\mathbf{x}$ is an r-fold copy of the allocation $(\mathbf{x}^1, \mathbf{x}^2, \ldots, \mathbf{x}^I)$ in $\mathcal{E}_1$, and $\mathbf{x}$ is a WEA in $\mathcal{E}_r$, then $(\mathbf{x}^1, \mathbf{x}^2, \ldots, \mathbf{x}^I)$ is a WEA in $\mathcal{E}_1$.

(b) Show that if $(\mathbf{x}^1, \mathbf{x}^2, \ldots, \mathbf{x}^I)$ is a WEA in $\mathcal{E}_1$, then its r-fold copy is a WEA in $\mathcal{E}_r$.

5.38 Give a general proof of Theorem 5.16 that is valid for an arbitrary number I of consumer types and an arbitrary number r of consumers of each type.

5.39 (Cornwall) In an economy with two types of consumer, each type has the respective utility function and endowments:

$$u^{1q}(x_1, x_2) = x_1 x_2 \quad \text{and} \quad \mathbf{e}^1 = (8, 2),$$
$$u^{2q}(x_1, x_2) = x_1 x_2 \quad \text{and} \quad \mathbf{e}^2 = (2, 8).$$

(a) Draw an Edgeworth box for this economy when there is one consumer of each type.

(b) Characterise as precisely as possible the set of allocations that are in the core of this two-consumer economy.

(c) Show that the allocation giving $\mathbf{x}^{11} = (4, 4)$ and $\mathbf{x}^{21} = (6, 6)$ is in the core.

(d) Now replicate this economy once so there are two consumers of each type, for a total of four consumers in the economy. Show that the double copy of the previous allocation, giving $\mathbf{x}^{11} = \mathbf{x}^{12} = (4, 4)$ and $\mathbf{x}^{21} = \mathbf{x}^{22} = (6, 6)$, is *not* in the core of the replicated economy.

5.40 In a pure exchange economy, consumer i *envies* consumer j if $\mathbf{x}^j \succ^i \mathbf{x}^i$. (Thus, i envies j if i likes j's bundle better than his own.) An allocation $\mathbf{x}$ is therefore *envy free* if $\mathbf{x}^i \succsim^i \mathbf{x}^j$ for all i and j. We know that envy-free allocations will always exist, because the equal-division allocation, $\bar{\mathbf{x}} = (1/I)\mathbf{e}$, must be envy free. An allocation is called **fair** if it is both envy free *and* Pareto efficient.

(a) In an Edgeworth box, demonstrate that envy-free allocations need not be fair.

(b) Under Assumption 5.1 on utilities, prove that every exchange economy having a strictly positive aggregate endowment vector possesses at least one fair allocation.

5.41 There are two consumers with the following characteristics:

$$u^1(x_1, x_2) = e^{x_1} x_2 \quad \text{and} \quad \mathbf{e}^1 = (1, 1),$$
$$u^2(x_1, x_2) = e^{x_1} x_2^2 \quad \text{and} \quad \mathbf{e}^2 = (5, 5).$$

(a) Find the equation for the contract curve in this economy, and carefully sketch it in the Edgeworth box.

(b) Find a fair allocation of goods to consumers in this economy.

(c) Now suppose that the economy is replicated *three* times. Find a fair allocation of goods to consumers in this new economy.

5.42 There are two consumers with the following characteristics:

$$u^1(x_1, x_2) = 2x_1 + x_2 \quad \text{and} \quad \mathbf{e}^1 = (1, 6),$$
$$u^2(x_1, x_2) = x_1 + x_2 \quad \text{and} \quad \mathbf{e}^2 = (3, 4).$$

Find a fair allocation of goods to consumers.

5.43 Throughout, we have assumed that a consumer's utility depends only on his own consumption. Suppose, however, that consumers' utilities are *interdependent*, depending on their own consumption and that of everyone else as well. For example, in a two-good, two-person economy with total endowments $\mathbf{e}$, suppose that $u^1 = u^1(x_1^1, x_2^1, x_1^2, x_2^2)$ and $u^2 = u^2(x_1^2, x_2^2, x_1^1, x_2^1)$, where $\partial u^i/\partial x_1^j \neq 0$ and $\partial u^i/\partial x_2^j \neq 0$ for $i, j = 1, 2$ and $i \neq j$.

(a) What are the necessary conditions for a Pareto-efficient distribution of goods to consumers?

(b) Are the WEAs Pareto efficient in an economy like this? Why or why not?

5.44 In the text, we have called an allocation $\bar{\mathbf{x}}$ Pareto efficient if there exists no other feasible allocation $\mathbf{x}$ such that $\mathbf{x}^i \succsim^i \bar{\mathbf{x}}^i$ for all i and $\mathbf{x}^j \succ^j \bar{\mathbf{x}}^j$ for at least one j. Sometimes, an allocation $\bar{\mathbf{x}}$ is called Pareto efficient if there exists no other feasible allocation $\mathbf{x}$ such that $\mathbf{x}^i \succ^i \bar{\mathbf{x}}^i$ for all i.

(a) Show that when preferences are continuous and strictly monotonic, the two definitions are equivalent.

(b) Construct an example where the two definitions are *not* equivalent, and illustrate in an Edgeworth box.

5.45 (Eisenberg's Theorem) Ordinarily, a system of *market* demand functions need not satisfy the properties of an individual consumer's demand system, such as the Slutsky restrictions, negative semidefiniteness of the substitution matrix, and so forth. Sometimes, however, it is useful to know when the market demand system *does* behave as though it were generated from a single, hypothetical consumer's utility-maximisation problem. Eisenberg (1961) has shown that this will be the case when consumers' preferences can be represented by linear homogeneous utility functions (not necessarily identical), and when the distribution of income is fixed and independent of prices.

In particular, let $\mathbf{x}^i(\mathbf{p}, y^i)$ solve $\max_{\mathbf{x}^i \in \mathbb{R}^n_+} u^i(\mathbf{x}^i)$ subject to $\mathbf{p} \cdot \mathbf{x}^i = y^i$ for $i \in \mathcal{I}$. Let $\mathbf{x}(\mathbf{p}, y^*)$ solve $\max_{\mathbf{x} \in \mathbb{R}^n_+} U(\mathbf{x})$ subject to $\mathbf{p} \cdot \mathbf{x} = y^*$. If (1) $u^i(\mathbf{x}^i)$ is linear homogeneous for all $i \in \mathcal{I}$; (2) y^* is aggregate income and income shares are fixed so that $y^i = \delta^i y^*$ for $0 < \delta^i < 1$ and $\sum_{i \in \mathcal{I}} \delta^i = 1$; and (3)

$$U(\mathbf{x}) = \max \prod_{i \in \mathcal{I}} (u^i(\mathbf{x}^i))^{\delta^i} \quad \text{s.t.} \quad \mathbf{x} = \sum_{i \in \mathcal{I}} \mathbf{x}^i,$$

then $\mathbf{x}(\mathbf{p}, y^*) = \sum_{i \in \mathcal{I}} \mathbf{x}^i(\mathbf{p}, y^i)$, so the system of market demand functions behaves as though generated from a single utility-maximisation problem.

(a) Consider a two-good, two-person exchange economy with initial endowments $\mathbf{e}^1 = (\delta^1, \delta^1)$ and $\mathbf{e}^2 = (\delta^2, \delta^2)$, where $0 < \delta^1 < 1$ and $\delta^1 + \delta^2 = 1$. Verify that income shares are fixed and independent of prices $\mathbf{p} = (p_1, p_2)$.

(b) Solve for $U(\mathbf{x})$ in the economy of part (a) when

$$u^1(\mathbf{x}^1) = \left(x_1^1\right)^{\alpha}\left(x_2^1\right)^{1-\alpha},$$
$$u^2(\mathbf{x}^2) = \left(x_1^2\right)^{\beta}\left(x_2^2\right)^{1-\beta}$$

for $0 < \alpha < 1$ and $0 < \beta < 1$.

(c) Verify Eisenberg's theorem for this economy.

5.46 In an exchange economy with initial endowments $\mathbf{e}$, prove that the aggregate excess demand vector, $\mathbf{z}(\mathbf{p})$, is independent of the initial distribution of endowments if and only if preferences are identical and homothetic.

CHAPTER 6

SOCIAL CHOICE AND WELFARE

With only few exceptions, we have so far tended to concentrate on questions of 'positive economics'. We have primarily been content to make assumptions about agents' motivations and circumstances, and deduce from these the consequences of their individual and collective actions. In essence, we have characterised and predicted behaviour, rather than judged it or prescribed it in any way. In most of this chapter, we change our perspective from positive to normative, and take a look at some important issues in welfare economics. At the end of the chapter we return to positive economics and consider how individuals motivated by self-interest make the problem of social choice doubly difficult.

6.1 THE NATURE OF THE PROBLEM

When we judge some situation, such as a market equilibrium, as 'good' or 'bad', or 'better' or 'worse' than another, we necessarily make at least implicit appeal to some underlying ethical standard. People often differ in their systems of ethics and so differ in their judgements on the merits of a given situation. This obvious fact need not discourage us nor make us despair that normative economics is all 'just a matter of opinion'. On the contrary, there is such a thing as consistency in reasoning from premises to conclusions and so to prescriptions. Welfare economics helps to inform the debate on social issues by forcing us to confront the ethical premises underlying our arguments as well as helping us to see their logical implications.

Viewed broadly, our goal in much of this chapter is to study means of obtaining a consistent ranking of different social situations, or 'social states', starting from well-defined and explicit ethical premises. On the level of generality at which we shall work, a 'social state' can be just about anything: the election of a particular candidate to a political office, a particular way of dividing a pie among a group of people, adoption of a market-oriented form of organising society, or a particular way of distributing society's resources among its members. A social choice problem arises whenever any group of individuals must make a collective choice from among a set of alternatives before them.

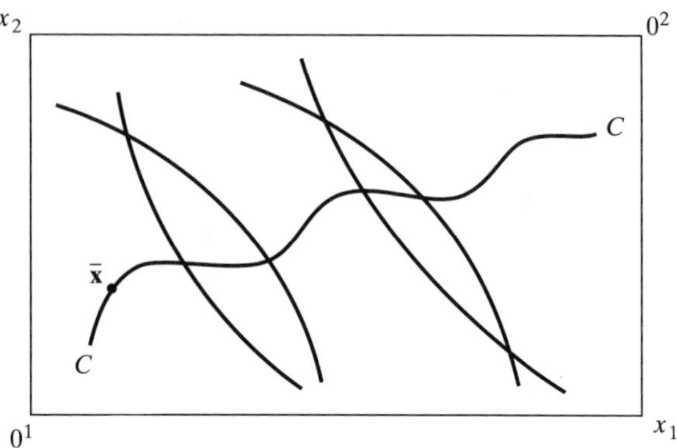

Figure 6.1. The distribution problem.

To make things a bit more concrete for just a moment, let us consider the distribution problem in a simple, two-good, two-person Edgeworth box economy, like the one depicted in Fig. 6.1. There, each point in the box represents some way of dividing society's fixed endowment of goods between its two members, so we can view each point in the box as one of the (mutually exclusive) alternate social states we could achieve. Each agent has his or her own preferences over these alternatives, and clearly these preferences are often at odds with one another. The social choice problem involved is easy to state. Which of the possible alternative distributions is best for society?

Although easy to state, the question is hard to answer. Perhaps without too much disagreement, points off the contract curve can be ruled out. Were one of these to be recommended as the best, it would be easy to find some other point on the contract curve that everyone prefers. Because it would be hard to argue with such unanimity of opinion, it is probably safe to say that our search for the best alternative ought to be restricted to the Pareto-efficient ones.

But which of these is best? Many will find it easy to say that wildly unequal alternatives such as $\bar{\mathbf{x}}$ must also be ruled out, even though they are Pareto efficient. Yet in doing so, appeal is being made to some additional ethical standard beyond the simple Pareto principle because that principle is silent on the essential question involved: namely, how may we trade off person 2's well-being for that of person 1 in the interests of society as a whole? In trying to make such trade-offs, does *intensity* of preference matter? If we think it does, other questions enter the picture. Can intensity of preference be known? Can people tell us how strongly they feel about different alternatives? Can different people's intense desires be compared so that a balancing of gains and losses can be achieved?

The questions are many and the problems are deep. To get very far at all, we will need to have a systematic framework for thinking about them. Arrow (1951) has offered such a framework, and we begin with a look at his path-breaking analysis of some of these problems.

6.2 SOCIAL CHOICE AND ARROW'S THEOREM

The formal structure we adopt is very simple and very general. There is some non-empty set X of mutually exclusive social states under consideration. While just about everything we do in this chapter can be accomplished whether the set X is finite or infinite, to keep things simple we will sometimes assume that X is finite and other times assume that it is infinite. We will be sure to let you know which of these we are assuming at all times. Society is composed of N individuals, where $N \geq 2$. Each individual i has his own preference relation, R^i, defined over the set of social states, X, with associated relations of strict preference, P^i, and indifference, I^i. Being a preference relation, each R^i is *complete* and *transitive*. Intuitively, we require nothing but that people be able to make binary comparisons between any two elements in X, and that those comparisons be consistent in the sense of being transitive. The set X has been defined very broadly, so keep in mind that its elements may range from the purely mundane to the purely spiritual. The relations R^i, therefore, also must be broadly construed. They need not merely reflect selfish attitudes towards material objects. They can also reflect the person's altruism, sense of kindness, or even their religious values.

Now recall that when preferences are complete and transitive, and X is finite the individual can completely order the elements of X from best to worst. The R^i, therefore, convey all the information we need to know to determine the individual's choice from among alternatives in X. To determine the *social* choice, however, we will need some ranking of the social states in X that reflects 'society's' preferences. Ideally, we would like to be able to compare any two alternatives in X from a social point of view, and we would like those binary comparisons to be consistent in the usual way. We have, then, the following definition.

DEFINITION 6.1 ***A Social Preference Relation***

A social preference relation, R, is a complete and transitive binary relation on the set X of social states. For x and y in X, we read xRy as the statement 'x is socially at least as good as y'. We let P and I be the associated relations of strict social preference and social indifference, respectively.

We take it for granted that the ranking of alternatives from a social point of view should depend on how individuals rank them. The problem considered by Arrow can be simply put. How can we go from the often divergent, but individually consistent, personal views of society's members to a single and consistent social view?

This is not an easy problem at all. When we insist on transitivity as a criterion for consistency in social choice, certain well-known difficulties can easily arise. For example, **Condorcet's paradox** illustrates that the familiar method of majority voting can fail to satisfy the transitivity requirement on R. To see this, suppose $N = 3, X = \{x, y, z\}$, and individual (strict) preferences over X are as follows

Person 1	Person 2	Person 3
x	y	z
y	z	x
z	x	y

In a choice between x and y, x would get two votes and y would get one, so the social preference under majority rule would be xPy. In a choice between y and z, majority voting gives yPz. Because xPy and yPz, transitivity of social preferences would require that xPz. However, with these individual preferences, z gets two votes to one for x, so majority voting here would give the social preference as zPx, thus violating transitivity. Note that in this example, the mechanism of majority rule is 'complete' in that it is capable of giving a best alternative in every possible pairwise comparison of alternatives in X. The failure of transitivity, however, means that within this set of three alternatives, no single best alternative can be determined by majority rule. Requiring completeness *and* transitivity of the social preference relation implies that it must be capable of placing every element in X within a hierarchy from best to worst. The kind of consistency required by transitivity has, therefore, considerable structural implications.

Yet consistency, alone, is not particularly interesting or compelling in matters of social choice. One can be perfectly consistent and still violate every moral precept the community might share. The more interesting question to ask might be put like this: how can we go from consistent individual views to a social view that is consistent and that *also* respects certain basic values on matters of social choice that are shared by members of the community? Because disagreement among individuals on matters of 'basic values' is in fact the very reason a problem of *social* choice arises in the first place, we will have to be very careful indeed in specifying these if we want to keep from trivialising the problem at the outset.

With such cautions in mind, however, we can imagine our problem as one of finding a 'rule', or function, capable of aggregating and reconciling the different individual views represented by the individual preference relations R^i into a single social preference relation R satisfying certain ethical principles. Formally, then, we seek a **social welfare function**, f, where

$$R = f(R^1, \ldots, R^N).$$

Thus, f takes an N-tuple of individual preference relations on X and turns (maps) them into a social preference relation on X.

For the remainder of this subsection we shall suppose that the set of social states, X, is finite.

Arrow has proposed a set of four conditions that might be considered minimal properties the social welfare function, f, should possess. They are as follows.

ASSUMPTION 6.1 *Arrow's Requirements on the Social Welfare Function*

U. Unrestricted Domain. *The domain of f must include all possible combinations of individual preference relations on X.*

WP. Weak Pareto Principle. *For any pair of alternatives x and y in X, if xP^iy for all i, then xPy.*

IIA. Independence of Irrelevant Alternatives. *Let $R = f(R^1, \ldots, R^N)$, $\tilde{R} = f(\tilde{R}^1, \ldots, \tilde{R}^N)$, and let x and y be any two alternatives in X. If each individual i ranks x versus y under R^i the same way that he does under $\tilde{R}^i$, then the social ranking of x versus y is the same under R and $\tilde{R}$.*

D. Non-dictatorship. *There is no individual i such that for all x and y in X, xP^iy implies xPy regardless of the preferences R^j of all other individuals $j \neq i$.*

Condition U says that f is able to generate a social preference ordering regardless of what the individuals' preference relations happen to be. It formalises the principle that the ability of a mechanism to make social choices should not depend on society's members holding any particular sorts of views. As we have seen before, this condition, together with the transitivity requirement on R, rules out majority voting as an appropriate mechanism because it sometimes fails to produce a transitive social ordering when there are more than three alternatives to consider.

Condition WP is very straightforward, and one that economists, at least, are quite comfortable with. It says society should prefer x to y if every single member of society prefers x to y. Notice that this is a *weak* Pareto requirement because it does not specifically require the social preference to be for x if, say, all but one strictly prefer x to y, yet one person is indifferent between x and y.

Condition IIA is perhaps the trickiest to interpret, so read it over carefully. In brief, the condition says that the social ranking of x and y should depend only on the individual rankings of x and y. Note that the individual preferences R^i and $\tilde{R}^i$ are allowed to differ in their rankings over pairs other than x, y. As you consider for yourself the reasonableness of IIA, think of what could happen if we failed to require it. For example, suppose that in the morning, all individuals rank z below both x and y, but some prefer x to y and others prefer y to x. Now suppose that given these individual preferences, the social welfare function leads to a social preference of x strictly preferred to y. So in the morning, if a choice were to be made between x and y, 'society' would choose x. As it happens, however, a choice between x and y is postponed until the afternoon. But by then, suppose that the individual preferences have changed so that now z is ranked *above* both x and y by all individuals. However, each individual's ranking of x versus y remains *unchanged*. Would it be reasonable for the social preference to now switch to y being ranked above x? IIA says it would not.

Condition D is a very mild restriction indeed. It simply says there should be no single individual who 'gets his way' on *every* single social choice, regardless of the views of everyone else in society. Thus, only the most extreme and absolute form of dictatorship is specifically excluded. Not even a 'virtual' dictator, one who always gets his way on all but *one* pair of social alternatives, would be ruled out by this condition alone.

Now take a moment to re-examine and reconsider each of these conditions in turn. Play with them, and try to imagine the kind of situations that could arise in a problem of social choice if one or more of them failed to hold. If, in the end, you agree that these are mild and *minimal* requirements for a reasonable social welfare function, you will find the following theorem astounding, and perhaps disturbing.

THEOREM 6.1 ***Arrow's Impossibility Theorem***

If there are at least three social states in X, then there is no social welfare function f that simultaneously satisfies conditions U, WP, IIA, and D.

Proof: The strategy of the proof is to show that conditions *U*, *WP*, and *IIA* imply the existence of a dictator. Consequently, if *U*, *WP*, and *IIA* hold, then *D* must fail to hold, and so no social welfare function can satisfy all four conditions.

The proof, following Geanakoplos (1996), proceeds in four steps. Note that axiom *U*, unrestricted domain, is used in each step whenever we choose or alter the preference profile under consideration. Unrestricted domain ensures that every such profile of preferences is admissible.

Step 1: Consider any social state, c. Suppose each individual places state c at the bottom of his ranking. By WP, the social ranking must place c at the bottom as well. See Fig. 6.2.

Step 2: Imagine now moving c to the top of individual 1's ranking, leaving the ranking of all other states unchanged. Next, do the same with individual 2: move c to the top of 2's ranking. Continue doing this one individual at a time, keeping in mind that each of these changes in individual preferences might have an effect on the social ranking. Eventually, c will be at the top of every individual's ranking, and so it must then also be at the top of the social ranking by WP. Consequently, there must be a *first* time during this process that the social ranking of c increases. Let individual n be the first such that raising c to the top of his ranking causes the social ranking of c to increase.

R^1	R^2	$\cdots$	R^N	R
x	x'	$\cdots$	x''	x'''
y	y'	$\cdots$	y''	y'''
.	.		.	.
.	.		.	.
.	.		.	.
c	c	$\cdots$	c	c

Figure 6.2. A consequence of *WP* and *U* in the proof of Arrow's theorem.

R^1	R^2	$\cdots$	R^n	$\cdots$	R^N	R
c	c	$\cdots$	c	$\cdots$	x''	c
x	x'	$\cdots$		$\cdots$	y''	
y	y'				$\cdot$	$\cdot$
$\cdot$	$\cdot$				$\cdot$	$\cdot$
$\cdot$	$\cdot$				$\cdot$	$\cdot$
$\cdot$	$\cdot$				$\cdot$	$\cdot$
w	w'	$\cdots$		$\cdots$	c	w'''

Figure 6.3. Axioms *WP*, *U*, and *IIA* yield a pivotal individual.

We claim that, as shown in Fig. 6.3, when c moves to the top of individual n's ranking, the social ranking of c not only increases but c also moves to the *top* of the social ranking.

To see this, assume by way of contradiction that the social ranking of c increases, but not to the top; i.e., αRc and $cR\beta$ for some states $\alpha, \beta \neq c$.

Now, because c is either at the bottom or at the top of every individual's ranking, we can change each individual i's preferences so that $\beta P^i\alpha$, while leaving the position of c unchanged for that individual. But this produces our desired contradiction because, on the one hand, $\beta P^i\alpha$ for every individual implies by WP that β must be strictly preferred to α according to the social ranking; i.e., $\beta P\alpha$. But, on the other hand, because the rankings of c relative to α and of c relative to β have not changed in any individual's ranking, *IIA* implies that the social rankings of c relative to α and of c relative to β must be unchanged; i.e., as initially assumed, we must have αRc and $cR\beta$. But transitivity then implies $\alpha R\beta$, contradicting $\beta P\alpha$. This establishes our claim that c must have moved to the top of the social ranking as in Fig. 6.3.

Step 3: Consider now any two distinct social states a and b, each distinct from c. In Fig. 6.3, change the profile of preferences as follows: change individual n's ranking so that aP^ncP^nb, and for every other individual rank a and b in any way so long as the position of c is unchanged for that individual. Note that in the new profile of preferences the ranking of a to c is the same for every individual as it was just *before* raising c to the top of individual n's ranking in Step 2. Therefore, by *IIA*, the social ranking of a and c must be the same as it was at that moment. But this means that aPc because at that moment c was still at the bottom of the social ranking.

Similarly, in the new profile of preferences, the ranking of c to b is the same for every individual as it was just *after* raising c to the top of individual n's ranking in Step 2. Therefore by *IIA*, the social ranking of c and b must be the same as it was at that moment. But this means that cPb because at that moment c had just risen to the top of the social ranking.

So, because aPc and cPb, we may conclude by transitivity that aPb. Note then that no matter how the others rank a and b, the social ranking agrees with individual n's ranking. By *IIA*, and because a and b were arbitrary, we may therefore conclude that for all social states a and b distinct from c

$$aP^n b \text{ implies } aPb.$$

That is, individual n is a dictator on all pairs of social states not involving c. The final step shows that individual n is in fact a dictator.

Step 4: Let a be distinct from c. We may repeat the above steps with a playing the role of c to conclude that some individual is a dictator on all pairs not involving a. However, recall that individual n's ranking of c (bottom or top) in Fig. 6.3 affects the social ranking of c (bottom or top). Hence, it must be individual n who is the dictator on all pairs not involving a. Because a was an arbitrary state distinct from c, and together with our previous conclusion about individual n, this implies that n is a dictator. ∎

Although here we have cast Arrow's theorem as an 'impossibility' result, the proof just sketched suggests it can also be stated as a 'possibility' result. That is, we have shown that any social welfare function satisfying the three conditions U, WP, and IIA must yield a social preference relation that exactly coincides with one person's preferences whenever that person's preferences are strict. As you are asked to explore in Exercise 6.3 this leaves several 'possibilities' for the social welfare function, although all of them are dictatorial according to condition D.

6.2.1 A DIAGRAMMATIC PROOF

The importance of Arrow's theorem warrants presenting another proof. Our second proof will be diagrammatic, dealing with the case of just two individuals. Together, we hope that the two proofs provide useful insight into the nature of this remarkable result.[1]

We shall depart from the setup of the previous section in several ways. First, we shall assume that X contains not just three or more social states, but infinitely many. Indeed, we assume that X is a non-singleton convex subset of $\mathbb{R}^K$ for some $K \geq 1$.[2]

Second, we assume that the individual preferences R^i on X can be represented by continuous utility functions, $u^i\colon X \to \mathbb{R}$. Thus, our domain of preferences is not completely unrestricted.[3]

Third, we assume that the social welfare function, f, maps profiles of continuous individual utility functions $\mathbf{u}(\cdot) = (u^1(\cdot), \ldots, u^N(\cdot))$ into a *continuous* utility function for society. Therefore, $f(u^1(\cdot), \ldots, u^N(\cdot))$ is a social utility function and $[f(u^1(\cdot), \ldots, u^N(\cdot))](x)$ is the utility assigned to the social state x. Note that the utility assigned to x, namely $[f(u^1(\cdot), \ldots, u^N(\cdot))](x)$, can in principle depend upon each individual's *entire utility function* $u^i(\cdot)$ and not just the utility $u^i(x)$ that each individual assigns to x.

[1] The diagrammatic idea of this proof is due to Blackorby, Donaldson, and Weymark (1984).

[2] This assumption can be weakened substantially. For example, the argument we shall provide is valid so long as $X \subseteq \mathbb{R}^K$ contains a point and a sequence of distinct points converging to it.

[3] If X were finite, every R^i would have a utility representation and every utility representation would be continuous. Hence, in the finite case, assuming continuity does not restrict the domain of preferences at all. This is why we assume an infinite X here, so that continuity has 'bite'.

For each continuous $\mathbf{u}(\cdot) = (u^1(\cdot), \ldots, u^N(\cdot))$ we henceforth let $f_{\mathbf{u}}$ denote the social utility function $f(u^1(\cdot), \ldots, u^N(\cdot))$ and we let $f_{\mathbf{u}}(x) = [f(u^1(\cdot), \ldots, u^N(\cdot))](x)$ denote the utility assigned to $x \in X$.

To maintain the idea that the social preference relation is determined only by the individual preference relations, R^i – an idea that is built into the previous section's treatment of Arrow's Theorem – it must be the case that the ordering of the social states according to $f_{\mathbf{u}} = f(u^1(\cdot), \ldots, u^N(\cdot))$ would be unchanged if any $u^i(\cdot)$ were replaced with a utility function representing the same preferences. Thus, because two utility functions represent the same preferences if and only if one is a strictly increasing transformation of the other, the social welfare function f must have the following property: if for each individual i, $u^i: X \to \mathbb{R}$ is continuous and $\psi^i: \mathbb{R} \to \mathbb{R}$ is strictly increasing and continuous, then

$$f_{\mathbf{u}}(x) \geq f_{\mathbf{u}}(y) \text{ if and only if } f_{\psi \circ \mathbf{u}}(x) \geq f_{\psi \circ \mathbf{u}}(y), \tag{6.1}$$

where $\psi \circ \mathbf{u}(\cdot) = (\psi^1(u^1(\cdot)), \ldots, \psi^N(u^N(\cdot)))$. That is, f must be order-invariant to strictly increasing continuous transformations of individual utility functions, where only continuous transformations ψ^i are considered to ensure that the transformed individual utility functions remain continuous.

Condition *U* in this setup means that the domain of f is the entire set of profiles of continuous individual utility functions. Condition *IIA* means precisely what it meant before, but note in particular it implies that whether $f_{\mathbf{u}}(x)$ is greater, less, or equal to $f_{\mathbf{u}}(y)$ can depend only on the vectors $\mathbf{u}(x) = (u^1(x), \ldots, u^N(x))$ and $\mathbf{u}(y) = (u^1(y), \ldots, u^N(y))$ and not on any other values taken on by the vector function $\mathbf{u}(\cdot) = (u^1(\cdot), \ldots, u^N(\cdot))$.[4] The meanings of conditions *WP* and *D* remain as before.

Consider now imposing the following additional condition on f.

PI. *Pareto Indifference Principle.* *If $u^i(x) = u^i(y)$ for all $i = 1, \ldots, N$, then $f_{\mathbf{u}}(x) = f_{\mathbf{u}}(y)$.*

The Pareto Indifference Principle requires society to be indifferent between two states if each individual is indifferent between them.

It can be shown (see Exercise 6.4 and also Sen (1970a)) that if f satisfies *U*, *IIA*, *WP*, and *PI*, then there is a strictly increasing continuous function, $W: \mathbb{R}^N \to \mathbb{R}$, such that for all social states x, y, and every profile of continuous individual utility functions $\mathbf{u}(\cdot) = (u^1(\cdot), \ldots, u^N(\cdot))$,

$$f_{\mathbf{u}}(x) \geq f_{\mathbf{u}}(y) \text{ if and only if } W(u^1(x), \ldots, u^N(x)) \geq W(u^1(y), \ldots, u^N(y)). \tag{6.2}$$

Condition (6.2) says that the social welfare function f can be summarised by a strictly increasing and continuous function W – that we will also call a social welfare function – that simply orders the vectors of individual utility numbers corresponding to

[4]As already noted, the social utility, $f_{\mathbf{u}}(x)$, assigned to the alternative x might depend on each individual's entire utility function. *IIA* goes a long way towards requiring that $f_{\mathbf{u}}(x)$ depend only on the vector of utilities $(u^1(x), \ldots, u^N(x))$.

the alternatives. Consequently, we may restrict our attention to this simpler yet equivalent form of a social welfare function. It is simpler because it states directly that the social utility of an alternative depends only on the vector of individual utilities of that alternative.

Our objective now is to deduce the existence of a dictator from the fact that W satisfies (6.2).

The property expressed in (6.1) that f is order-invariant to continuous strictly increasing transformations of individual utility functions has important implications for the welfare function W. For suppose $(u^1, \ldots, u^N)$ and $(\tilde{u}^1, \ldots, \tilde{u}^N)$ are utility vectors associated with two social states x and y. Combining (6.1) with (6.2) implies that W's ordering of $\mathbb{R}^N$ must be invariant to any continuous strictly increasing transformation of individual utility numbers. Therefore if W ranks x as socially better than y, i.e., if

$$W(u^1, \ldots, u^N) > W(\tilde{u}^1, \ldots, \tilde{u}^N),$$

then we must also have,

$$W(\psi^1(u^1), \ldots, \psi^N(u^N)) > W(\psi^1(\tilde{u}^1), \ldots, \psi^N(\tilde{u}^N))$$

for any N continuous strictly increasing functions, $\psi^i\colon \mathbb{R} \to \mathbb{R},\ i = 1, 2, \ldots, N$. Appreciating this is key to the argument that follows.

For the diagrammatic proof we assume that $N = 2$ so we can work in the plane.

To begin, consider an arbitrary point $\bar{\mathbf{u}}$ in Fig. 6.4, and try to imagine the social indifference curve on which it lies. For reference, the utility space has been divided into four regions relative to $\bar{\mathbf{u}}$, where the regions do not include the dashed lines. First, note that, by *WP*, all points in region I must be socially preferred to $\bar{\mathbf{u}}$. Similarly, $\bar{\mathbf{u}}$ must be socially preferred to all points in region III. Our problem, then, is to rank points in II, IV, and the excluded boundaries, relative to $\bar{\mathbf{u}}$.

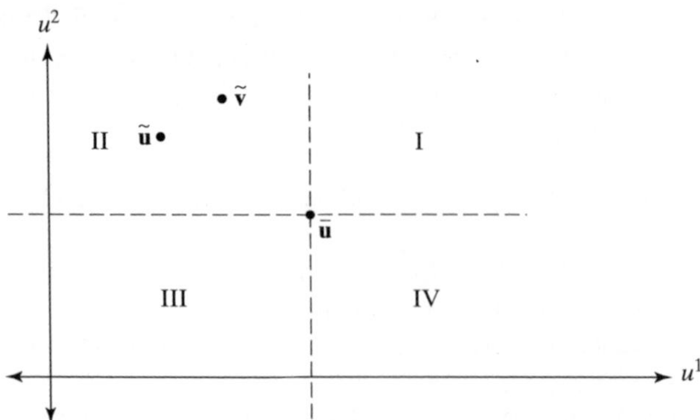

Figure 6.4. A diagrammatic proof of Arrow's theorem.

Now consider an arbitrary point $\tilde{\mathbf{u}}$ in II. One of the following must hold

$$W(\bar{\mathbf{u}}) > W(\tilde{\mathbf{u}}), \tag{6.3}$$

$$W(\bar{\mathbf{u}}) = W(\tilde{\mathbf{u}}), \tag{6.4}$$

$$W(\bar{\mathbf{u}}) < W(\tilde{\mathbf{u}}). \tag{6.5}$$

Suppose for the moment that $W(\bar{\mathbf{u}}) < W(\tilde{\mathbf{u}})$. Then because W's ordering of $\mathbb{R}^N$ is invariant to continuous strictly increasing transformations of utilities, that same ranking must be preserved when we apply *any* continuous strictly increasing transformations to the individuals' utilities. Suppose we choose two strictly increasing functions, ψ^1 and ψ^2, where

$$\psi^1(\bar{u}^1) = \bar{u}^1,$$
$$\psi^2(\bar{u}^2) = \bar{u}^2.$$

Now apply these functions to the coordinates of the point $\tilde{\mathbf{u}}$. Because $\tilde{\mathbf{u}}$ is in region II, we know that $\tilde{u}^1 < \bar{u}^1$ and $\tilde{u}^2 > \bar{u}^2$. Then because the ψ_i are strictly increasing, when applied to $\tilde{\mathbf{u}}$, we must have

$$\tilde{v}^1 \equiv \psi^1(\tilde{u}^1) < \psi^1(\bar{u}^1) = \bar{u}^1, \tag{6.6}$$

$$\tilde{v}^2 \equiv \psi^2(\tilde{u}^2) > \psi^2(\bar{u}^2) = \bar{u}^2. \tag{6.7}$$

Equations (6.6) and (6.7), together, inform us that the point $\tilde{\mathbf{v}} \equiv (\tilde{v}^1, \tilde{v}^2)$ must be somewhere in region II, as well. Because we have complete flexibility in our choice of the continuous strictly increasing ψ^i, we can, by an appropriate choice, map $\tilde{\mathbf{u}}$ into *any* point in region *II*.[5] But then because the social ranking of the underlying social states must be invariant to such transforms of individuals' utility, *every* point in region II must be ranked *the same way* relative to $\bar{\mathbf{u}}$! If, as we supposed, $W(\bar{\mathbf{u}}) < W(\tilde{\mathbf{u}})$, then every point in region II must be preferred to $\bar{\mathbf{u}}$. Yet nowhere in the argument did we use the fact that $W(\bar{\mathbf{u}}) < W(\tilde{\mathbf{u}})$. We could have begun by supposing any of (6.3), (6.4), or (6.5), and reached the same general conclusion by the same argument. Thus, under the invariance requirements on individual utility, *every* point in region II must be ranked in one of three ways relative to $\bar{\mathbf{u}}$: either $\bar{\mathbf{u}}$ is preferred, indifferent to, or worse than every point in region II. We will write this as the requirement that exactly one of the following must hold:

$$W(\bar{\mathbf{u}}) > W(\text{II}), \tag{6.8}$$

$$W(\bar{\mathbf{u}}) = W(\text{II}), \tag{6.9}$$

$$W(\bar{\mathbf{u}}) < W(\text{II}). \tag{6.10}$$

Note that (6.9) certainly cannot hold, for this would mean that all points in region II, being indifferent (under W) to $\bar{\mathbf{u}}$, are indifferent to one another. But this contradicts

[5]For example, to obtain $\psi^i(\tilde{u}^i) = \bar{u}^i$ and $\psi^i(\tilde{u}^i) = u^i$ we can choose the continuous function

$$\psi^i(t) \equiv \left[\frac{\bar{u}^i - u^i}{\bar{u}^i - \tilde{u}^i}\right] t + \left[\frac{u^i - \tilde{u}^i}{\bar{u}^i - \tilde{u}^i}\right] \bar{u}^i,$$

which is the form $\psi^i(t) = \alpha^i t + \beta^i$. Note that for any choice of (u^1, u^2) in region II, $\alpha^1, \alpha^2 > 0$.

W being strictly increasing because the point $\tilde{\mathbf{v}} \gg \tilde{\mathbf{u}}$ in region II (see Fig. 6.4) is strictly preferred to $\tilde{\mathbf{u}}$.

So, either $W(\bar{\mathbf{u}}) > W(\text{II})$ or $W(\bar{\mathbf{u}}) < W(\text{II})$. By a parallel argument to the one just given, we could consider points in region IV and show that either $W(\bar{\mathbf{u}}) > W(\text{IV})$ or $W(\bar{\mathbf{u}}) < W(\text{IV})$.

Now, suppose that $W(\bar{\mathbf{u}}) < W(\text{II})$. Then, in particular, $W(\bar{\mathbf{u}}) < W(\bar{u}^1 - 1, \bar{u}^2 + 1)$. Consider the pair of strictly increasing functions $\psi^1(u^1) = u^1 + 1$, $\psi^2(u^2) = u^2 - 1$. Applying these to $\bar{\mathbf{u}}$ and $(\bar{u}^1 - 1, \bar{u}^2 + 1)$ maps them into the points $(\bar{u}^1 + 1, \bar{u}^2 - 1)$ and $\bar{\mathbf{u}}$, respectively. But because W must be order-invariant to such transforms, these images must be ordered in the same way as their inverse images are ordered. Consequently, we must have $W(\bar{u}^1 + 1, \bar{u}^2 - 1) < W(\bar{\mathbf{u}})$. But this means that $\bar{\mathbf{u}}$ is strictly socially preferred to the point $(\bar{u}^1 + 1, \bar{u}^2 - 1)$ in region IV. Consequently, $\bar{\mathbf{u}}$ must be strictly socially preferred to every point in region IV.

So, we have shown that if $W(\bar{\mathbf{u}}) < W(\text{II})$, then $W(\bar{\mathbf{u}}) > W(\text{IV})$. A similar argument establishes that if $W(\bar{\mathbf{u}}) > W(\text{II})$, then $W(\bar{\mathbf{u}}) < W(\text{IV})$. Altogether, we have so far shown that

$$\text{either} \qquad W(\text{IV}) < W(\bar{\mathbf{u}}) < W(\text{II}), \tag{6.11}$$

$$\text{or} \qquad W(\text{II}) < W(\bar{\mathbf{u}}) < W(\text{IV}). \tag{6.12}$$

Now, note that if adjacent regions are ranked the same way relative to $\bar{\mathbf{u}}$, then the dashed line separating the two regions must be ranked that same way relative to $\bar{\mathbf{u}}$. For example, suppose regions I and II are ranked above $\bar{\mathbf{u}}$. Since by *WP* any point on the dashed line above $\bar{\mathbf{u}}$ is ranked above points in region II that lie strictly below it, transitivity implies this point on the dashed line must be ranked above $\bar{\mathbf{u}}$.

Consequently, if (6.11) holds, then because region I is ranked above $\bar{\mathbf{u}}$ and region III is ranked below, the social ranking must be as given in Fig. 6.5(a), where '+' ('−') denotes

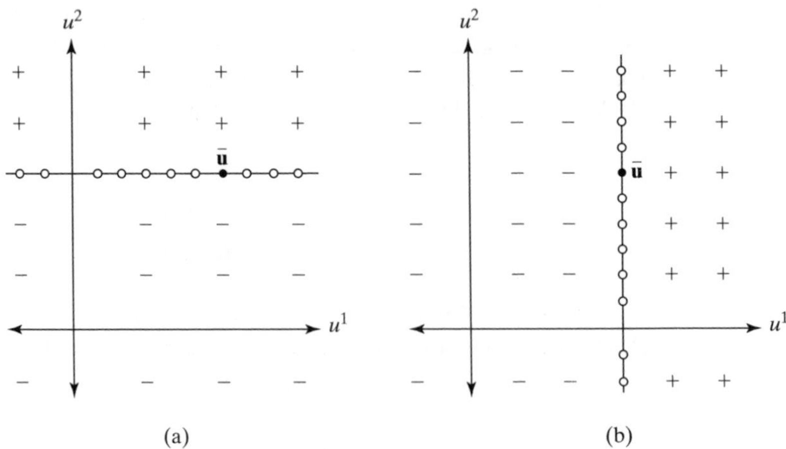

Figure 6.5. Social welfare possibilities under Arrow's conditions.

utility vectors $\mathbf{u} = (u^1, u^2)$ with $W(\mathbf{u})$ greater than (less than) $W(\bar{\mathbf{u}})$. But the continuity of W then implies that the indifference curve through $\bar{\mathbf{u}}$ is a horizontal straight line. On the other hand, if instead (6.12) holds so that Fig. 6.5(b) is relevant, then the indifference curve through $\bar{\mathbf{u}}$ would be a vertical straight line.

So, because $\bar{\mathbf{u}}$ was arbitrary, we may conclude that the indifference curve through every utility vector is either a horizontal or a vertical straight line. However, because indifference curves cannot cross one another, this means that either *all* indifference curves are horizontal straight lines, in which case individual 2 would be a dictator, or *all* indifference curves are vertical straight lines, in which case individual 1 is a dictator. In either case, we have established the existence of a dictator and the proof is complete.

6.3 Measurability, Comparability, and Some Possibilities

Arrow's theorem is truly disturbing. A very careful look at each of his requirements should impress you with their individual reasonableness and their collective economy. Only the very bold can be sanguine about dropping or relaxing any one of them. Yet the import of the theorem is that this is precisely what we must be prepared to do.

There have been various attempts to rescue social welfare analysis from the grip of Arrow's theorem. One has been to relax the requirements that must be satisfied by the social relation R. For example, replacing transitivity of R with a weaker restriction called 'acyclicity', and replacing the requirement that R order all alternatives from best to worse with the simpler restriction that we be merely capable of finding a best alternative among any subset, opens the way to several possible choice mechanisms, each respecting the rest of Arrow's conditions. Similarly, if transitivity is retained, but condition U is replaced with the assumption that individual preferences are 'single-peaked', Black (1948) has shown that majority voting satisfies the rest of Arrow's conditions, provided that the number of individuals is odd!

Another approach has proceeded along different lines and has yielded interesting results. Rather than argue with Arrow's conditions, attention is focused instead on the information assumed to be conveyed by individuals' preferences. In Arrow's framework, only the individuals' preference relations, R^i, are used as data in deriving the social preference relation $R = f(R^1, \ldots, R^N)$. Thus, if a society wants to implement f, it would obtain from each individual his ranking of the states from best to worst. From this data alone f would provide a ranking of the social states. Obviously, this process yields no information whatsoever about the strength of any particular individual's preferences for x in comparison to another individual's preference for y, nor does it yield any information about how much more one individual favours x over y in comparison to how much more another individual favours y over x. By design, Arrow's approach does not consider such information.

The alternative is to think about what would occur if such information were considered. Before merely pushing forward, a warning is in order. The idea that 'intensity of preference' can be compared in a coherent way across individuals is controversial at best. Nonetheless, the alternative approach to social choice that we are about to explore takes as a starting point – as an assumption – that such comparisons can be made in a meaningful way. We shall not attempt to justify this assumption. Let us just see what it can do for us.

The basic references for this line of work include Hammond (1976), d'Aspremont and Gevers (1977), Roberts (1980), and Sen (1984). Here, we will only consider a few of their findings to try and get the flavour.

To get us started, consider a situation with just two individuals. Suppose that individual 1 prefers state x to y and that individual 2 prefers y to x. In such a symmetric situation, more information might be useful in order to make a social choice. Indeed, suppose for example that society wishes to make its least well off individual as well off as as possible. It would then be useful to know whether individual 1's welfare from the state that he least prefers, namely y, is greater than 2's welfare from the state he least prefers, namely x. Suppose – and here is the important assumption – that the individual utility numbers provide this information. That is, suppose that i's utility function is $u^i(\cdot)$, that $u^1(y)$ is greater than $u^2(x)$, and that this is interpreted to mean that 1 *is better off at* y *than* 2 *is at* x. Armed with the additional information that the least well off individual is better off at y than at x, this society's social welfare function ranks y strictly above x.

Next, suppose that the two individual utility functions are $v^1(\cdot)$ and $v^2(\cdot)$ and that it is still the case that 1 prefers x to y and 2 prefers y to x, but now $v^1(y)$ is less than $v^2(x)$. That is, it is now the case that 1 is worse off at y than 2 is at x. Because the least well off individual is better off at x, this society now strictly prefers x to y *even though the individual rankings over x and y did not change.*

The point of this example is to demonstrate that if utilities carry more meaning than simply the ranking of states, then the social welfare function need not be invariant to strictly increasing utility transformations. The reason is that while strictly increasing transformations preserve utility comparisons between states for each individual separately, they need not preserve utility rankings between states across individuals. To guarantee that $\psi^i(u^i(x)) \geq \psi^j(u^j(y))$ whenever $u^i(x) \geq u^j(y)$, the utility transformations ψ^i and ψ^j must be strictly increasing and identical, i.e., $\psi^i = \psi^j$. Thus, the social welfare function f would need to be invariant only to strictly increasing utility transformations that are identical across individuals. This more limited set of restrictions allows more possibilities for f and a chance to avoid the impossibility result. When a social welfare function f is permitted to depend *only* on the ordering of utilities both for and across individuals, it must be invariant to *arbitrary*, but common, strictly increasing individual utility transformations. We will then say that f is **utility-level invariant**.

A second type of information that might be useful in making social choices is a measure of how much individual i gains when the social state is changed from x to y in comparison to how much individual j loses. In this case it is assumed that individual i's gain in the move from x to y is the difference in his utilities $u^i(y) - u^i(x)$ and that $u^i(y) - u^i(x) \geq u^j(x) - u^j(y)$ means that i's gain is at least as large as j's loss. Again, if a social welfare function is permitted to take such information into account then it need not be invariant to utility transformations that fail to preserve this information. It is not difficult to see that in order to preserve comparisons of utility differences across individuals, each individual i's utility transformation must be of the form $\psi^i(u^i) = a^i + bu^i$, where $b > 0$ is common to all individuals.

When a social welfare function f is permitted to depend *only* on the ordering of utility differences both for and across individuals, it must be invariant to arbitrary strictly increasing individual utility transformations of the form $\psi^i(u^i) = a^i + bu^i$, where $b > 0$. We'll then say that f is **utility-difference invariant**.

Other forms of measurability and interpersonal comparability can be imagined and combined in various ways, but we just stick with the two considered above. For later reference, we summarise the previous discussion as follows, where a social welfare function f maps profiles of utility functions into a social utility function.

DEFINITION 6.2 ***Measurability, Comparability, and Invariance***

1. *A social welfare function f is utility-level invariant if it is invariant to arbitrary, but common, strictly increasing transformations ψ applied to every individual's utility function. Hence, f is permitted to depend only on the ordering of utilities both for and across individuals.*
2. *A social welfare function f is utility-difference invariant if it is invariant to strictly increasing transformations of the form $\psi^i(u^i) = a^i + bu^i$, where $b > 0$ is common to each individual's utility transformation. Hence, f is permitted to depend only on the ordering of utility differences both for and across individuals.*

Throughout the remainder of this section we will assume that the set of social states X is a non-singleton convex subset of Euclidean space and that all social choice functions, f, under consideration satisfy **strict welfarism** (i.e., U, WP, IIA, and PI), where U means that f maps continuous individual utility functions into a continuous social utility function.[6] Consequently (see (6.2) and Exercise 6.4) we may summarise f with a strictly increasing continuous function $W: \mathbb{R}^N \to \mathbb{R}$ with the property that for every continuous $\mathbf{u}(\cdot) = (u^1(\cdot), \ldots, u^N(\cdot))$ and every pair of states x and y,

$$f_{\mathbf{u}}(x) \geq f_{\mathbf{u}}(y) \text{ if and only if } W(u^1(x), \ldots, u^N(x)) \geq W(u^1(y), \ldots, u^N(y)),$$

where we remind the reader that $f_{\mathbf{u}}(x)$ is the social utility assigned to x when the profile of individual utility functions is $\mathbf{u}(\cdot) = (u^1(\cdot), \ldots, u^N(\cdot))$.

The extent to which utility is assumed to be measurable and interpersonally comparable can best be viewed as a question of how much information society uses when making social decisions. This is quite distinct from the kind of ethical restrictions a society might wish those decisions to respect. There is, of course, some ethical content to the conditions U, WP, IIA and PI embodied in strict welfarism. However, a society may be willing to go further and build even more ethical values into its social welfare function. Each amounts to imposing an extra requirement on the strictly increasing and continuous social welfare function, W. Here, we consider only two.

[6] Sen (1970a) defines f to satisfy *welfarism* if f satisfies U, IIA, and PI.

DEFINITION 6.3 ***Two More Ethical Assumptions on the Social Welfare Function***

A. *Anonymity. Let* $\bar{\mathbf{u}}$ *be a utility N-vector, and let* $\tilde{\mathbf{u}}$ *be another vector obtained from* $\bar{\mathbf{u}}$ *after some permutation of its elements. Then* $W(\bar{\mathbf{u}}) = W(\tilde{\mathbf{u}})$.

HE. *Hammond Equity. Let* $\bar{\mathbf{u}}$ *and* $\tilde{\mathbf{u}}$ *be two distinct utility N-vectors and suppose that* $\bar{u}^k = \tilde{u}^k$ *for all k except i and j. If* $\bar{u}^i < \tilde{u}^i < \tilde{u}^j < \bar{u}^j$, *then* $W(\tilde{\mathbf{u}}) \geq W(\bar{\mathbf{u}})$.

Condition *A* simply says people should be treated symmetrically. Under *A*, the ranking of social states should not depend on the identity of the individuals involved, only the levels of welfare involved. Condition *HE* is slightly more controversial. It expresses the idea that society has a preference towards decreasing the dispersion of utilities across individuals. (Note that there is less dispersion of utilities under $\tilde{\mathbf{u}}$ than under $\bar{\mathbf{u}}$. Nevertheless, can you think of why one might object to ranking $\tilde{\mathbf{u}}$ above $\bar{\mathbf{u}}$?) In what follows, we use these conditions to illustrate how some well-known social welfare functions can be characterised axiomatically.

6.3.1 THE RAWLSIAN FORM

In the ethical system proposed by Rawls (1971), the welfare of society's worst-off member guides social decision making. In the following theorem, we give an axiomatic characterisation of this criterion of social welfare. The proof we provide is diagrammatic and so again we restrict ourselves to the case of $N = 2$.[7]

THEOREM 6.2 ***Rawlsian Social Welfare Functions***

A strictly increasing and continuous social welfare function W satisfies HE if and only if it can take the Rawlsian form, $W = \min[u^1, \ldots, u^N]$. *Moreover, W then satisfies A and is utility-level invariant.*

Proof: Suppose that W is continuous, strictly increasing and satisfies *HE*. We must show that it can take the form $W = \min[u^1, \ldots, u^N]$, i.e., that $W(\bar{\mathbf{u}}) \geq W(\tilde{\mathbf{u}})$ if and only if $\min[\bar{u}^1, \ldots, \bar{u}^N] \geq \min[\tilde{u}^1, \ldots, \tilde{u}^N]$.

We prove this diagrammatically only for $N = 2$ by once again characterising the map of social indifference curves. Consult Fig. 6.6 throughout the proof. To begin, choose an arbitrary point **a** on the 45° line and consider the infinite ray extending from **a** to the right. We shall first argue that every point on this ray is socially indifferent to **a** according to W.

Consider an arbitrary point $\bar{\mathbf{u}} = (\bar{u}^1, \bar{u}^2)$ on the ray. We wish to show that $W(\bar{\mathbf{u}}) = W(\mathbf{a})$. Let region *I* denote the region to the left of $\bar{\mathbf{u}}$ below the 45° and above the ray, and let region *II* denote the region to the left of $\bar{\mathbf{u}}$ below the 45° line and below the ray. Thus the ray is in neither region. Consider now an arbitrary point $\tilde{\mathbf{u}} = (\tilde{u}^1, \tilde{u}^2)$ in region *I*. One can easily see that to be in *I*, $\tilde{\mathbf{u}}$ must satisfy the inequalities $\bar{u}^2 < \tilde{u}^2 < \tilde{u}^1 < \bar{u}^1$. (Think

[7]For $N > 2$, see Exercise 6.8 and also Hammond (1976).

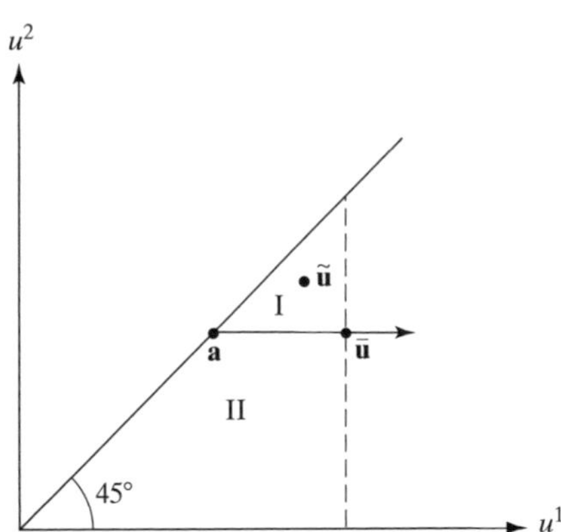

Figure 6.6. Proof of Theorem 6.2.

about this.) But then HE implies that $W(\tilde{\mathbf{u}}) \geq W(\bar{\mathbf{u}})$. Since $\tilde{\mathbf{u}}$ was an arbitrary point in I, the social utility of every point in I is at least $W(\bar{\mathbf{u}})$, which we write as $W(I) \geq W(\bar{\mathbf{u}})$.[8] As for region II, we must have $W(II) < W(\bar{\mathbf{u}})$ because every point in region II is south-west of $\bar{\mathbf{u}}$ and W is strictly increasing. Thus, we have shown that,

$$W(I) \geq W(\bar{\mathbf{u}}) > W(II). \tag{P.1}$$

Notice now that for every point on the line joining $\mathbf{a}$ and $\bar{\mathbf{u}}$ there are arbitrarily nearby points in region I each of which we have shown to receive social utility at least $W(\bar{\mathbf{u}})$ and there are arbitrarily nearby points in region II each of which we have shown to receive social utility less than $W(\bar{\mathbf{u}})$. Hence, by the continuity of W, every point on the line joining $\mathbf{a}$ and $\bar{\mathbf{u}}$ must receive social utility equal to $W(\bar{\mathbf{u}})$. In particular, $W(\mathbf{a}) = W(\bar{\mathbf{u}})$, as we wished to show. Because $\bar{\mathbf{u}}$ was an arbitrary point on the infinite ray starting at $\mathbf{a}$ and extending rightwards, we conclude that every point on this ray is socially indifferent to $\mathbf{a}$.

An analogous argument to that just given shows also that every point on the infinite ray starting at $\mathbf{a}$ and extending upwards is also socially indifferent to $\mathbf{a}$. Because W is strictly increasing, no other points can be indifferent to $\mathbf{a}$ and therefore the union of these two rays is the social indifference curve through $\mathbf{a}$. Because $\mathbf{a}$ was an arbitrary point on the 45° line, the social indifference map for W is therefore as shown in Fig. 6.7, with indifference curves further from the origin receiving higher social utility because W is strictly increasing. Thus W has the same indifference map as the function $\min[u^1, u^2]$, as desired.

Finally, we note that if $W = \min[u^1, \ldots, u^N]$ then A and HE are easily shown to be satisfied. Moreover, if $\psi : \mathbb{R} \to \mathbb{R}$ is strictly increasing, then $W(\psi(u^1), \ldots, \psi(u^N)) = \psi(W(u^1, \ldots, u^N))$ and therefore $W(\psi(u^1), \ldots, \psi(u^N)) \geq W(\psi(\tilde{u}^1), \ldots, \psi(\tilde{u}^N))$ if and only if $W(u^1, \ldots, u^N) \geq W(\tilde{u}^1, \ldots, \tilde{u}^N)$. Hence, W is utility-level invariant. ∎

[8]In fact, $W(I) > W(\bar{\mathbf{u}})$ because $N = 2$ and W is strictly increasing, but we will not need the strict inequality.

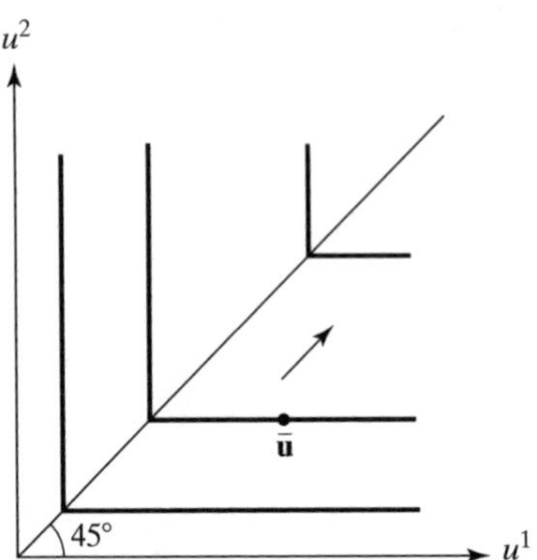

Figure 6.7. Social indifference curves for the (Rawlsian) social welfare function.

6.3.2 THE UTILITARIAN FORM

The utilitarian form is by far the most common and widely applied social welfare function in economics. Under a utilitarian rule, social states are ranked according to the linear sum of utilities. When ranking two social states, therefore, it is the linear sum of the individual utility differences between the states that is the determining factor. Consequently, statements of the form 'in the move from x to y, individual 1 gains more than individual 2' must be meaningful. Thus, utility differences must be comparable both for and across individuals and so we expect the utilitarian social choice function to be related to the property of utility-difference invariance. The theorem to follow shows that this is indeed the case. Once again, our proof covers the $N = 2$ case, the extension to $N > 2$ being straightforward.

THEOREM 6.3 ***Utilitarian Social Welfare Functions***

A strictly increasing and continuous social welfare function W satisfies A and utility-difference invariance if and only if it can take the utilitarian form, $W = \sum_{i=1}^{n} u^i$.

Proof: It is clear that if $W = \sum_{i=1}^{N} u^i$, then the conditions of the theorem are satisfied. It remains to show the converse. We will give a diagrammatic proof for the two-person case, but this can be extended to any number of individuals.

In Fig. 6.8, choose any point $\bar{\mathbf{u}} = (\bar{u}^1, \bar{u}^2)$ lying along the 45° line. Define the constant, $\gamma \equiv \bar{u}^1 + \bar{u}^2$ and consider the set of points $\Omega \equiv \{(u^1, u^2) \mid u^1 + u^2 = \gamma\}$. These are all the points lying on a straight line through $\bar{\mathbf{u}}$ with a slope of -1. Choose any point in Ω, distinct from $\bar{\mathbf{u}}$, such as $\tilde{\mathbf{u}}$. Point $\tilde{\mathbf{u}}^T$ is obtained by permuting the element of $\tilde{\mathbf{u}}$, and so $\tilde{\mathbf{u}}^T = (\tilde{u}^2, \tilde{u}^1)$ must also be in Ω. By condition A, $\tilde{\mathbf{u}}$ and $\tilde{\mathbf{u}}^T$ must be ranked the same way relative to $\bar{\mathbf{u}}$.

Now suppose that $W(\bar{\mathbf{u}}) > W(\tilde{\mathbf{u}})$. Under utility-difference dependence, this ranking must be invariant to transformations of the form $\alpha^i + bu^i$. Let $\psi^i(u^i) \equiv (\bar{u}^i - \tilde{u}^i) + u^i$, for $i = 1, 2$. Note carefully that both of these are in the allowable form. Taking note that $2\bar{u}^i = \tilde{u}^1 + \tilde{u}^2$ because $\bar{\mathbf{u}}$ is on the 45° line and both $\bar{\mathbf{u}}$ and $\tilde{\mathbf{u}}$ are in Ω, we apply

Figure 6.8. The utilitarian social welfare function.

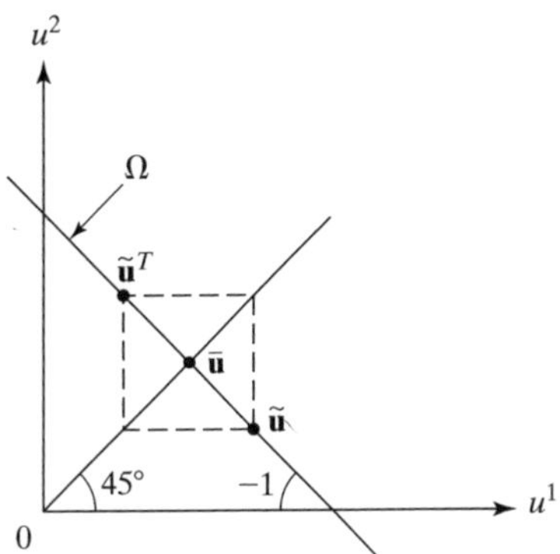

these transforms to $\tilde{\mathbf{u}}$ and obtain $(\psi^1(\tilde{u}^1), \psi^2(\tilde{u}^2)) = \bar{\mathbf{u}}$, and apply them to $\bar{\mathbf{u}}$ to obtain $(\psi^1(\bar{u}^1), \psi^2(\bar{u}^2)) = \tilde{\mathbf{u}}^T$. So, these transforms map $\tilde{\mathbf{u}}$ into $\bar{\mathbf{u}}$ and map $\bar{\mathbf{u}}$ into $\tilde{\mathbf{u}}^T$. Thus, if $W(\bar{\mathbf{u}}) > W(\tilde{\mathbf{u}})$, as we have assumed, then by the invariance requirement, we must likewise have $W(\tilde{\mathbf{u}}^T) > W(\bar{\mathbf{u}})$. But together these imply $W(\tilde{\mathbf{u}}^T) > W(\tilde{\mathbf{u}})$, violating A, so $W(\bar{\mathbf{u}}) > W(\tilde{\mathbf{u}})$ cannot hold. If, instead, we suppose $W(\tilde{\mathbf{u}}) > W(\bar{\mathbf{u}})$, then by using a similar argument, we get a similar contradiction. We therefore conclude that $W(\bar{\mathbf{u}}) = W(\tilde{\mathbf{u}})$. Condition A then tells us $W(\tilde{\mathbf{u}}^T) = W(\bar{\mathbf{u}}) = W(\tilde{\mathbf{u}})$. Now recall that $\tilde{\mathbf{u}}$ was chosen arbitrarily in Ω, so the same argument can be made for any point in that set, and so we have $W(\Omega) = W(\bar{\mathbf{u}})$.

Because W is strictly increasing, every point north-east of Ω must be strictly preferred to every point in Ω, and every point south-west must be strictly worse. Thus, Ω is indeed a social indifference curve, and the social indifference map is a set of parallel straight lines, each with a slope of -1, with social preference increasing north-easterly. This, of course, implies the social welfare function can be chosen to be of the form $W = u^1 + u^2$, completing the proof. ∎

If we drop the requirement of anonymity, the full range of *generalised utilitarian* orderings is allowed. These are represented by linear social welfare functions of the form $W = \sum_i a^i u^i$, where $a^i \geq 0$ for all i and $a^j > 0$ for some j. Under generalised utilitarian criteria, the welfare sum is again the important issue, but the welfare of different individuals can be given different 'weight' in the social assessment.

6.3.3 FLEXIBLE FORMS

To some extent, the greater the measurability and comparability of utility, the greater the range of social welfare functions allowed. For example, suppose that the social welfare function can depend upon the ordering of *percentage* changes in utility both for and across individuals, i.e., that information such as 'in going from x to y, the percentage increase in i's utility is greater than the percentage loss in j's utility', namely,

$$\frac{u^i(x) - u^i(y)}{u^i(x)} > \frac{u^j(x) - u^j(y)}{u^j(x)}$$

matters. Then the social welfare function need not be invariant to strictly increasing transformations unless they are identical and linear, (i.e., $\psi(u^i) = bu^i$, where $b > 0$ is common to all individuals) because only these are guaranteed to maintain the ordering of percentage changes in utility both for and across individuals. If the social welfare function f is permitted to depend *only* on the ordering of percentage changes in utility for and across individuals, then it must be invariant to *arbitrary*, but common, strictly increasing individual transformations of utility of the form $\psi(u^i) = bu^i$, where $b > 0$ is common to all individuals and we will then say that f is **utility-percentage invariant**.

Consequently, both the Rawlsian and utilitarian social welfare functions are permitted here. Indeed, a whole class of social welfare functions are now admitted as possibilities. When a continuous social welfare function satisfies strict welfarism, and is invariant to identical positive linear transformations of utilities, social indifference curves must be negatively sloped and radially parallel.

To see this, consider Fig. 6.9. First, choose an arbitrary point $\bar{\mathbf{u}}$. Clearly, as in the example sketched, the social indifference curve through $\bar{\mathbf{u}}$ must be negatively sloped because, by strict welfarism, W is strictly increasing. Now choose any other point on the ray OA through $\bar{\mathbf{u}}$. This point must be of the form $b\bar{\mathbf{u}}$ for some constant $b > 0$. Now choose any other point $\tilde{\mathbf{u}}$ such that $W(\bar{\mathbf{u}}) = W(\tilde{\mathbf{u}})$. By the invariance requirement, we must also have $W(b\bar{\mathbf{u}}) = W(b\tilde{\mathbf{u}})$, where $\tilde{\mathbf{u}}$ and $b\tilde{\mathbf{u}}$ are on the ray OB, as indicated.

We want to show that the slope of the tangent to the social indifference curve at $\bar{\mathbf{u}}$ is equal to the slope of the tangent at $b\bar{\mathbf{u}}$. First, note that the slope of the chord CC approximates the slope of the tangent at $\bar{\mathbf{u}}$, and the slope of the chord DD approximates the slope of the tangent at $b\bar{\mathbf{u}}$. Because the triangles OCC and ODD are similar, the slope of CC is equal to the slope of DD. Now imagine choosing our point $\tilde{\mathbf{u}}$ closer and closer to $\bar{\mathbf{u}}$ along the social indifference curve through $\bar{\mathbf{u}}$. As $\tilde{\mathbf{u}}$ approaches $\bar{\mathbf{u}}$, correspondingly $b\tilde{\mathbf{u}}$ approaches $b\bar{\mathbf{u}}$ along the social indifference curve through $b\bar{\mathbf{u}}$, and the chords CC and DD remain equal in slope. In the limit, the slope of CC converges to the slope of the tangent at $\bar{\mathbf{u}}$, and the slope of DD converges to the slope of the tangent at $b\bar{\mathbf{u}}$. Thus, the slope of the

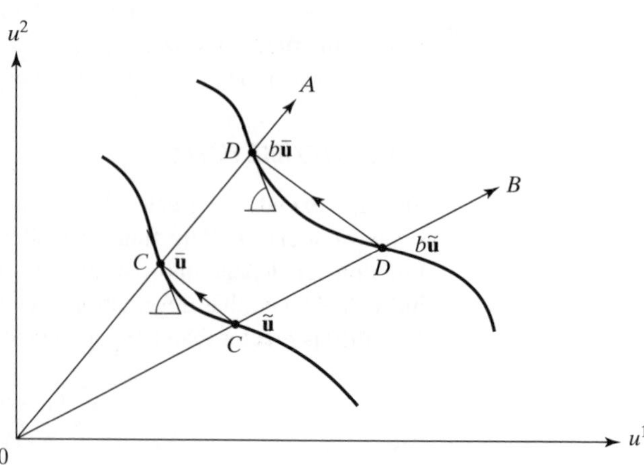

Figure 6.9. Radially parallel social indifference curves.

social indifference curve at $\bar{\mathbf{u}}$ must be equal to the slope of the curve at $b\bar{\mathbf{u}}$. Because $\bar{\mathbf{u}}$ and $b > 0$ were arbitrarily chosen, the slope of every social indifference curve must be the same at every point along a given ray, though, of course, slopes can differ across different rays.

A function's level curves will be radially parallel in this way if and only if the function is *homothetic*. Thus, strict welfarism and utility-percentage invariance allow any continuous, strictly increasing, homothetic social welfare function. If condition A is added, the function must be symmetric, and so its social indifference curves must be 'mirror images' around the 45° line. Sometimes a convexity assumption is also added. When the social welfare function is quasiconcave the 'socially at least as good as' sets are convex, and the ethical implication is that inequality in the distribution of welfare, *per se*, is not socially valued. Under strict quasiconcavity, there is a strict bias in favour of equality. (Do you see why?)

Because every homothetic function becomes a linear homogeneous function under some positive monotonic transform, for simplicity let us think in terms of linear homogeneous forms alone. Finally, suppose in addition to WP, A, and convexity, we add the *strong separability* requirement that the marginal rate of (social) substitution between any two individuals is independent of the welfare of all other individuals. Then the social welfare function must be a member of the CES family:

$$W = \left(\sum_{i=1}^{N}(u^i)^\rho\right)^{1/\rho}, \tag{6.13}$$

where $0 \neq \rho < 1$, and $\sigma = 1/(1-\rho)$ is the (constant and equal) elasticity of social substitution between any two individuals.

This is a very flexible social welfare function. Different values for ρ give different degrees of 'curvature' to the social indifference curves, and therefore build in different degrees to which equality is valued in the distribution of welfare. Indeed, the utilitarian form – which implies complete social indifference to how welfare is distributed – can be seen as a limiting case of (6.13) as $\rho \to 1$ ($\sigma \to \infty$). As $\rho \to -\infty$ ($\sigma \to 0$), (6.13) approaches the Rawlsian form, where the social bias in favour of equality is absolute. The range of possibilities is illustrated in Fig. 6.10.

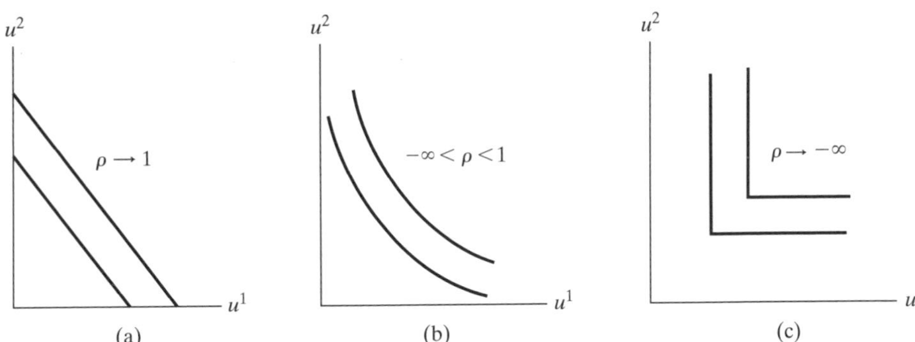

Figure 6.10. CES social welfare functions.

6.4 JUSTICE

Beyond the technical question of what must be assumed in the way of measurability and comparability of utility to sensibly apply a given social welfare function, there is the basic reality that the choice among such functions is effectively a choice between alternative sets of ethical values. On this score, then, matters of opinion really *are* involved. They rightfully belong in the very first stage of any analysis aimed at assessing the *social* significance of economic policies or institutions, when the choice of social welfare function is made.

The literature in economics and the literature in philosophy – one and the same in the days before Adam Smith – have combined again more recently to jointly consider the moral character of the choice that must be made. Guidance has been sought by appeal to axiomatic *theories of justice* that accept the social welfare approach to social decision making. Two broad historical traditions on these questions can be distinguished. One is the utilitarian tradition, associated with Hume, Smith, Bentham, and Mill. The other is the 'contractarian' tradition, associated with Locke, Rousseau, and Kant. More recently, these two traditions have been refined and articulated through the work of Harsanyi (1953, 1955, 1975) and Rawls (1971), respectively.

Both Harsanyi and Rawls accept the notion that a 'just' criterion of social welfare must be one that a rational person would choose if he were 'fair-minded'. To help ensure that the choice be fair-minded, each imagines an 'original position', behind what Rawls calls a 'veil of ignorance', in which the individual contemplates this choice without knowing what his personal situation and circumstances in society actually will be. Thus, each imagines the kind of choice to be made as a choice under uncertainty over who you will end up having to be in the society you prescribe. The two differ, however, in what they see as the appropriate decision rule to guide the choice in the original position.

Harsanyi's approach is remarkably straightforward. First, he accepts the von Neumann-Morgenstern axiomatic description of rationality under conditions of uncertainty. Thus, a person's preferences can be represented by a VNM utility function over social states, $u^i(x)$, which is unique up to positive affine transforms. By the **principle of insufficient reason**, he then suggests that a rational person in the original position must assign an equal probability to the prospect of being in any other person's shoes within the society. If there are N people in society, there is therefore a probability $1/N$ that i will end up in the circumstances of any other person j. Person i therefore must imagine those circumstances and imagine what his preferences, $u^j(x)$, would be. Because a person might end up with any of N possible 'identities', a 'rational' evaluation of social state x then would be made according to its *expected utility*:

$$\sum_{i=1}^{N}(1/N)u^i(x). \tag{6.14}$$

In a social choice between x and y, the one with the higher expected utility in (6.14) must be preferred. But this is equivalent to saying that x is socially preferred to y if and only if

$$\sum_{i=1}^{N}u^i(x) > \sum_{i=1}^{N}u^i(y),$$

a purely *utilitarian* criterion.

Rawls rejects Harsanyi's utilitarian rule for several reasons. Among them, he objects to the assignment of *any* probability to the prospect of being any particular individual because in the original position, there can be no empirical basis for assigning such probabilities, whether equal or not. Thus, the very notion of choice guided by expected utility is rejected by Rawls. Instead, he views the choice problem in the original position as one under *complete ignorance*. Assuming people are risk averse, he argues that in total ignorance, a rational person would order social states according to how he or she would view them were they to end up as society's worst-off member. Thus, x will be preferred to y as

$$\min[u^1(x), \dots, u^N(x)] > \min[u^1(y), \dots, u^N(y)], \tag{6.15}$$

a purely *maximin* criterion.

Ultimately, then, Rawls' own argument for the maximin over the utilitarian rests on the view that people are risk averse. But this cannot be a wholly persuasive argument, as Arrow (1973) has pointed out. For one thing, the VNM utility functions in Harsanyi's construction can be thought to embody any degree of risk aversion whatsoever. Thus, in Harsanyi's framework, nothing precludes individuals from being risk averse in the original position. Moreover, one need not reject the expected utility rule as a basis for choice to arrive at Rawls' criterion.

To see this, take any utility function $u^i(x)$ over social states with certainty. These same preferences, of course, can be represented equally well by the positive monotonic transform, $v^i(x) \equiv -u^i(x)^{-a}$, where $a > 0$. Now suppose $v^i(x)$ is i's VNM utility function over *uncertain* prospects. It is easy to convince yourself that the degree of risk aversion displayed by $v(x)$ is increasing in the parameter a. Now suppose, as Harsanyi does, (1) equal probabilities of having any identity, (2) an ordering of social states according to their expected utility, and so (3) a social welfare function

$$W = \sum_{i=1}^{N} v^i(x) \equiv -\sum_{i=1}^{N} u^i(x)^{-a}. \tag{6.16}$$

Because the ordering of states given by (6.16) has only ordinal significance, it will be exactly the same under the positive monotonic transform of W given by

$$W^* = (-W)^{-1/a} \equiv \left(\sum_{i=1}^{N} u^i(x)^{-a}\right)^{-1/a} \tag{6.17}$$

For $\rho \equiv -a < 0$, this is in the form of (6.11). We have already noted that as $\rho \to -\infty$ $(a \to \infty)$, this approaches the maximin criterion (6.13) as a limiting case. Thus, Rawls' maximin criterion – far from being incompatible with Harsanyi's utilitarianism – instead can be seen as a very special case of it, namely, the one that arises when individuals are *infinitely* risk averse.

On reflection, this makes a good deal of sense. Maximin decision rules are appealing in strategic situations where the interests of some rational and fully informed opponent are diametrically opposed to your own. In the kind of thought experiment required in the original position, there is little obvious justification for adopting such a decision rule, unless, of course, you are extremely (irrationally?) pessimistic.

Once again, your choice of social welfare function is a choice of distributional values and, therefore, a choice of ethical system. The choice is yours.

6.5 SOCIAL CHOICE AND THE GIBBARD-SATTERTHWAITE THEOREM

Up to this point in our analysis of the problem of social welfare, we have focused solely on the task of aggregating the preferences of many individuals into a single preference relation for society. This task, as we have seen, is a formidable one. Indeed, it cannot be carried out if we insist on all of Arrow's conditions.

Implicit in our analysis has been the assumption that the true preferences of each individual can be obtained and that society's preferences are then determined according to its social welfare function. But how, exactly, does society find out the preferences of its individual members? One possibility, of course, is to simply ask each individual to report his ranking of the social states. But this introduces a serious difficulty. Individuals would be better off lying about their preferences than reporting them truthfully if a false report leads to a better social state for them.[9] Thus, in addition to the problem of coherently aggregating individual rankings into a social ranking, there is the problem of finding out individual preferences in the first place. The purpose of this section is to address this latter issue head on.

Throughout this section the set of social states, X, is finite and each of the N individuals in society is permitted to have any preference relation at all on X. Thus, we are assuming unrestricted domain, U. Because the purpose of a social ranking of the states in X is presumably to allow society to make a choice from X, let us focus on that choice directly. Specifically, for each profile of individual rankings $\mathbf{R} = (R^1, \ldots, R^N)$, let $c(\mathbf{R}) \in X$ denote society's *choice* from X. We will assume that the range of $c(\cdot)$ is all of X. That is, for every social state $x \in X$ there is some profile of preferences $\mathbf{R}$ such that $c(\mathbf{R}) = x$. Otherwise, we could just as well eliminate the social state x from the set X. Any function $c(\cdot)$ mapping all profiles of individual preferences on X into a choice from X, and whose range is all of X is called a **social choice function**.[10]

Once again, we would like to avoid dictatorship and in the context of social choice functions a dictatorship is defined in the following natural way.

DEFINITION 6.4 ***Dictatorial Social Choice Function***

A social choice function $c(\cdot)$ is dictatorial if there is an individual i such that whenever $c(R^1, \ldots, R^N) = x$ it is the case that xR^iy for every $y \in X$.

---

[9]Another possibility is to attempt to infer an individual's preferences from his observed choice behaviour. But this too is problematic since an individual can alter his choice behaviour to profitably portray to society false preferences.

[10]Not all treatments of this topic include the full range condition in the definition of a social choice function, choosing instead to add the range condition separately. The present treatment is more convenient for our purposes.

Fix for the moment the preference profile, $\mathbf{R}^{-i}$, of all individuals but i and consider two possible preferences, R^i and $\tilde{R}^i$, for individual i. Let $c(R^i, \mathbf{R}^{-i}) = x$ and $c(\tilde{R}^i, \mathbf{R}^{-i}) = y$. Altogether then, we have a situation in which, when the others report the profile $\mathbf{R}^{-i}$, individual i, by choosing to report either R^i or $\tilde{R}^i$ can choose to make the social state either x or y. When would individual i have an incentive to lie about his preferences? Well, suppose his true preferences happen to be R^i and that given these preferences he strictly prefers y to x. If he reports honestly, the social state will be x. But if he lies and instead reports $\tilde{R}^i$, the social state will be y, a choice he strictly prefers. Hence, in this case, he has an incentive to misreport his preferences.

What property would a social choice function have to have so that under no circumstance would any individual have an incentive to misreport his preferences? It must have the following property called **strategy-proofness.**

DEFINITION 6.5 ***Strategy-Proof Social Choice Function***

A social choice function $c(\cdot)$ is strategy-proof when, for every individual, i, for every pair R^i and $\tilde{R}^i$ of his preferences, and for every profile $\mathbf{R}^{-i}$ of others' preferences, if $c(R^i, \mathbf{R}^{-i}) = x$ and $c(\tilde{R}^i, \mathbf{R}^{-i}) = y$, then xR^iy.

Definition 6.5 rules out exactly the situation described above and, with a little thought, you will convince yourself that if a social choice function is strategy-proof, no individual, no matter what his preferences might be, can ever strictly gain by misreporting his preferences no matter what the others report – even if the others lie about their preferences. Conversely, if a social choice function is not strategy-proof, then there is at least one circumstance (and perhaps many) under which some individual can strictly gain by misreporting his preferences.

Thus, requiring a social choice function to be strategy-proof ensures that it is optimal for individuals to report their preferences honestly and so society's choice will be based upon the true preferences of its individual members. Unfortunately, strategy-proofness has deep consequences. Indeed, reminiscent of Arrow's theorem we have another remarkable, though again negative, result due independently to Gibbard (1973) and Satterthwaite (1975).

THEOREM 6.4 ***The Gibbard-Satterthwaite Theorem***

If there are at least three social states, then every strategy-proof social choice function is dictatorial.

Our proof of Theorem 6.4 follows Reny (2001) and is broken into two parts.[11] Part I shows that a strategy-proof social choice function must exhibit two properties – Pareto-efficiency and monotonicity. Part II shows that any monotonic and Pareto-efficient social choice function is dictatorial. To prepare for the proof, we must first define **Pareto-efficient social choice functions** and **monotonic social choice functions**.

[11] In fact, because the full range condition in Reny (2001) is applied to the smaller domain of strict rankings, our Theorem 6.4 is a slightly stronger result. (At least on the face of it; see Exercise 6.22.)

DEFINITION 6.6 ***Pareto-Efficient Social Choice Function***

A social choice function $c(\cdot)$ is Pareto efficient if $c(R^1, \ldots, R^N) = x$ whenever xP^iy for every individual i and every $y \in X$ distinct from x.

Thus, a social choice function is Pareto efficient if whenever x is at the top of every individual's ranking, the social choice is x.

DEFINITION 6.7 ***Monotonic Social Choice Function***

A social choice function $c(\cdot)$ is monotonic if $c(R^1, \ldots, R^N) = x$ implies $c(\tilde{R}^1, \ldots, \tilde{R}^N) = x$ whenever for each individual i and every $y \in X$ distinct from x, $xR^iy \Longrightarrow x\tilde{P}^iy$.

Monotonicity says that the social choice does not change when individual preferences change so that every individual strictly prefers the social choice to any distinct social state that it was originally at least as good as. Loosely speaking, monotonicity says that the social choice does not change when the social choice rises in each individual's ranking. Notice that the individual rankings between pairs of social states other than the social choice are permitted to change arbitrarily.

We are now prepared to prove Theorem 6.4, but one more word before we do. We are *not* assuming either Pareto efficiency or monotonicity. Part 1 of our proof will *prove* that strategy-proofness implies Pareto efficiency and monotonicity. The *only* assumption Theorem 6.4 makes about the social choice function is that it is strategy-proof.

Proof: Suppose that X contains at least three social states and that $c(\cdot)$ is a strategy-proof social choice function. We must show that $c(\cdot)$ is dictatorial. To do so, we break the proof into two parts.

Part 1. *Strategy-proofness implies monotonicity and Pareto efficiency.*[12]

(a) *Monotonicity.* Let $(R^1, \ldots, R^N)$ be an arbitrary preference profile and suppose that $c(R^1, \ldots, R^N) = x$. Fix an individual, i say, and let $\tilde{R}^i$ be a preference for i such that for every $y \in X$ distinct from x, $xR^iy \Longrightarrow x\tilde{P}^iy$. We shall show that $c(\tilde{R}^i, \mathbf{R}^{-i}) = x$.

Suppose, by way of contradiction, that $c(\tilde{R}^i, \mathbf{R}^{-i}) = y \neq x$. Then, given that the others report $\mathbf{R}^{-i}$, individual i, when his preferences are R^i can report truthfully and obtain the social state x or he can lie by reporting $\tilde{R}^i$ and obtain the social state y. Strategy-proofness requires that lying cannot be strictly better than telling the truth. Hence we must have xR^iy. According to the definition of $\tilde{R}^i$, we then have $x\tilde{P}^iy$. Consequently, when individual i's preferences are $\tilde{R}^i$ he strictly prefers x to y and so, given that the others report $\mathbf{R}^{-i}$, individual i strictly prefers lying (reporting R^i and obtaining x) to telling the truth (reporting $\tilde{R}^i$ and obtaining y), contradicting strategy-proofness. We conclude that $c(\tilde{R}^i, \mathbf{R}^{-i}) = x$.

[12]Muller and Satterthwaite (1977) show that strategy-proofness is equivalent to what they call *strong-positive association*, which is equivalent to monotonicity when individual preferences do not display indifference.

Let $(R^1, \ldots, R^N)$ and $(\tilde{R}^1, \ldots, \tilde{R}^N)$ be preference profiles such that $c(R^1, \ldots, R^N) = x$, and such that for every individual i and every $y \in X$ distinct from x, $xR^iy \Longrightarrow x\tilde{P}^iy$. To prove that $c(\cdot)$ is monotonic, we must show that $c(\tilde{R}^1, \ldots, \tilde{R}^N) = x$. But this follows immediately from the result just proven – simply change the preference profile from $(R^1, \ldots, R^N)$ to $(\tilde{R}^1, \ldots, \tilde{R}^N)$ by switching, one at a time, the preferences of each individual i from R^i to $\tilde{R}^i$. We conclude that $c(\cdot)$ is monotonic.

(b) *Pareto Efficiency.* Let x be an arbitrary social state and let $\hat{\mathbf{R}}$ be a preference profile with x at the top of each individual's ranking. We must show that $c(\hat{\mathbf{R}}) = x$.

Because the range of $c(\cdot)$ is all of X, there is some preference profile $\mathbf{R}$ such that $c(\mathbf{R}) = x$. Obtain the preference profile $\tilde{\mathbf{R}}$ from $\mathbf{R}$ by moving x to the top of every individual's ranking. By monotonicity (proven above in (a)), $c(\tilde{\mathbf{R}}) = x$. Because $\hat{\mathbf{R}}$ places x at the top of every individual ranking and $c(\tilde{\mathbf{R}}) = x$, we can again apply monotonicity (do you see why?) and conclude that $c(\hat{\mathbf{R}}) = x$, as desired.

Part 2. $\#X \geq 3$ + *monotonicity* + *Pareto efficiency* $\Longrightarrow$ *dictatorship.*

The second part of the proof, like our first proof of Arrow's theorem, will use a series of well-chosen preference profiles to uncover a dictator. Given the results from Part 1, we can and will freely use the fact that $c(\cdot)$ is both monotonic and Pareto efficient. Also, in each of the particular figures employed in this proof, all individual rankings are strict. That is, no individual is indifferent between any two social states. We emphasise that this is not an additional assumption – we are *not* ruling out indifference. It just so happens that we are able to provide a proof of the desired result by considering a particular subset of preferences that do not exhibit indifference.

Step 1. Consider any two distinct social states $x, y \in X$ and a profile of strict rankings in which x is ranked highest and y lowest for every individual $i = 1, \ldots, N$. Pareto efficiency implies that the social choice at this profile is x. Consider now changing individual 1's ranking by strictly raising y in it one position at a time. By monotonicity, the social choice remains equal to x so long as y is below x in 1's ranking. But when y finally does rise above x, monotonicity implies that the social choice either changes to y or remains equal to x (see Exercise 6.18(a)). If the latter occurs, then begin the same process with individual 2, then 3, etc. until for some individual n, the social choice does change from x to y when y rises above x in n's ranking. (There must be such an individual n because y will eventually be at the top of every individual's ranking and by Pareto efficiency the social choice will then be y.) Figs. 6.11 and 6.12 depict the situations just before and just after individual n's ranking of y is raised above x.

Step 2. This is perhaps the trickiest step in the proof, so follow closely. Consider Figs. 6.13 and 6.14 below. Fig. 6.13 is derived from Fig. 6.11 (and Fig. 6.14 from Fig. 6.12) by moving x to the bottom of individual i's ranking for $i < n$ and moving it to the second last position in i's ranking for $i > n$. We wish to argue that these changes do not affect the social choices, i.e., that the social choices are as indicated in the figures.

R^1	$\cdots$	R^{n-1}	R^n	R^{n+1}	$\cdots$	R^N	Social Choice
y	$\cdots$	y	x	x	$\cdots$	x	
x	$\cdots$	x	y	$\cdot$		$\cdot$	
$\cdot$		$\cdot$	$\cdot$	$\cdot$		$\cdot$	x
$\cdot$		$\cdot$	$\cdot$	$\cdot$		$\cdot$	
$\cdot$		$\cdot$	$\cdot$	$\cdot$		$\cdot$	
$\cdot$		$\cdot$	$\cdot$	y	$\cdots$	y	

Figure 6.11.

R^1	$\cdots$	R^{n-1}	R^n	R^{n+1}	$\cdots$	R^N	Social Choice
y	$\cdots$	y	y	x	$\cdots$	x	
x	$\cdots$	x	x	$\cdot$		$\cdot$	y
$\cdot$		$\cdot$	$\cdot$	$\cdot$		$\cdot$	
$\cdot$		$\cdot$	$\cdot$	$\cdot$		$\cdot$	
$\cdot$		$\cdot$	$\cdot$	y	$\cdots$	y	

Figure 6.12.

R^1	$\cdots$	R^{n-1}	R^n	R^{n+1}	$\cdots$	R^N	Social Choice
y	$\cdots$	y	x	$\cdot$		$\cdot$	
$\cdot$		$\cdot$	y	$\cdot$		$\cdot$	x
$\cdot$		$\cdot$	$\cdot$	$\cdot$		$\cdot$	
$\cdot$		$\cdot$	$\cdot$	x	$\cdots$	x	
x	$\cdots$	x	$\cdot$	y	$\cdots$	y	

Figure 6.13.

R^1	$\cdots$	R^{n-1}	R^n	R^{n+1}	$\cdots$	R^N	Social Choice
y	$\cdots$	y	y	$\cdot$		$\cdot$	
$\cdot$		$\cdot$	x	$\cdot$		$\cdot$	
$\cdot$		$\cdot$	$\cdot$	$\cdot$		$\cdot$	y
$\cdot$		$\cdot$	$\cdot$	$\cdot$		$\cdot$	
$\cdot$		$\cdot$	$\cdot$	x	$\cdots$	x	
x	$\cdots$	x	$\cdot$	y	$\cdots$	y	

Figure 6.14.

First, note that the social choice in Fig. 6.14 must, by monotonicity, be y because the social choice in Fig. 6.12 is y and no individual's ranking of y versus any other social state changes in the move from Fig. 6.12 to Fig. 6.14 (see Exercise 6.18(b)). Next, note that the profiles in Figs. 6.13 and 6.14 differ only in individual n's ranking of x and y. So, because the social choice in Fig. 6.14 is y, the social choice in Fig. 6.13 must, by monotonicity, be either x or y (we used this same logic in Step 1 – see Exercise 6.18(a)). But

R^1	$\cdots$	R^{n-1}	R^n	R^{n+1}	$\cdots$	R^N	Social Choice
·		·	x	·		·	
·		·	z	·		·	
·		·	y	·		·	x
z	$\cdots$	z	·	z	$\cdots$	z	
y	$\cdots$	y	·	x	$\cdots$	x	
x	$\cdots$	x	·	y	$\cdots$	y	

Figure 6.15.

R^1	$\cdots$	R^{n-1}	R^n	R^{n+1}	$\cdots$	R^N	Social Choice
·		·	x	·		·	
·		·	z	·		·	
·		·	y	·		·	
·		·	·	·		·	x
·		·	·	·		·	
·		·	·	·		·	
z	$\cdots$	z	·	z	$\cdots$	z	
y	$\cdots$	y	·	y	$\cdots$	y	
x	$\cdots$	x	·	x	$\cdots$	x	

Figure 6.16.

if the social choice in Fig. 6.13 is y, then by monotonicity (see Exercise 6.18(b)), the social choice in Fig. 6.11 must be y, a contradiction. Hence, the social choice in Fig. 6.13 is x.

Step 3. Because there are at least three social states, we may consider a social state $z \in X$ distinct from x and y. Since the (otherwise arbitrary) profile of strict rankings in Fig. 6.15 can be obtained from the Fig. 6.13 profile without changing the ranking of x versus any other social state in any individual's ranking, the social choice in Fig. 6.15 must, by monotonicity, be x (see Exercise 6.18(b)).

Step 4. Consider the profile of rankings in Fig. 6.16 derived from the Fig. 6.15 profile by interchanging the ranking of x and y for individuals $i > n$. Because this is the only difference between the profiles in Figs. 6.15 and 6.16, and because the social choice in Fig. 6.15 is x, the social choice in Fig. 6.16 must, by monotonicity, be either x or y (see Exercise 6.18(a)). But the social choice in Fig. 6.16 cannot be y because z is ranked above y in every individual's Fig. 6.16 ranking, and monotonicity would then imply that the social choice would remain y even if z were raised to the top of every individual's ranking, contradicting Pareto efficiency. Hence the social choice in Fig. 6.16 is x.

Step 5. Note that an arbitrary profile of strict rankings with x at the top of individual n's ranking can be obtained from the profile in Fig. 6.16 without reducing the ranking of x versus any other social state in any individual's ranking. Hence, monotonicity (see Exercise 6.18(b)) implies that the social choice must be x whenever individual rankings are strict and x is at the top of individual n's ranking. You are asked to show in Exercise 6.19 that this implies that even when individual rankings are not strict and indifferences are present, the social choice must be at least as good as x for individual n whenever x is at least as good as every other social state for individual n. So, we may say that individual n is a dictator for the social state x. Because x was arbitrary, we have shown that for each social state $x \in X$, there is a dictator for x. But there cannot be distinct dictators for distinct social states (see Exercise 6.20). Hence there is a single dictator for all social states and therefore the social choice function is dictatorial. ∎

The message you should take away from the Gibbard-Satterthwaite theorem is that, in a rich enough setting, it is impossible to design a non-dictatorial system in which social choices are made based upon self-reported preferences without introducing the possibility that individuals can gain by lying. Fortunately, this does not mean that all is lost. In Chapter 9 we will impose an important and useful domain restriction, known as quasi-linearity, on individual preferences. This will allow us to escape the conclusion of the Gibbard-Satterthwaite theorem and to provide an introduction to aspects of the theory of mechanism design. Thus, the Gibbard-Satterthwaite theorem provides a critically important lesson about the limits of designing systems of social choice based on self-reported information and points us in the direction of what we will find to be rather fertile ground. But before we can develop this further, we must become familiar with the essential and powerful tools of **game theory**, the topic of our next chapter.

6.6 EXERCISES

6.1 Arrow (1951) shows that when the number of alternatives in X is restricted to just *two*, the method of majority voting does yield a social welfare relation that satisfies the conditions of Assumption 6.1. Verify, by example or more general argument, that this is indeed the case.

6.2 Show that the weak Pareto condition *WP* in Arrow's theorem can be replaced with the even weaker Pareto condition *VWP* (very weak Pareto) without affecting the conclusion of Arrow's theorem, where *VWP* is as follows.

VWP. 'If xP^iy for all i, then xPy'.

6.3 (a) Show that the social welfare function that coincides with individual i's preferences satisfies U, *WP*, and *IIA*. Call such a social welfare function an *individual i dictatorship*.

(b) Suppose that society ranks any two social states x and y according to individual 1's preferences unless he is indifferent in which case x and y are ranked according to 2's preferences unless he is indifferent, etc. Call the resulting social welfare function a *lexicographic dictatorship*. Show that a lexicographic dictatorship satisfies U, *WP* and *IIA* and that it is distinct from an individual i dictatorship.

(c) Describe a social welfare function distinct from an individual i dictatorship and a lexicographic dictatorship that satisfies U, *WP* and *IIA*.

6.4 Suppose that X is a non-singleton convex subset of $\mathbb{R}^K$ and that f is a social welfare function satisfying U in the sense that it maps every profile of continuous utility functions $\mathbf{u}(\cdot) = (u^1(\cdot), \ldots, u^N(\cdot))$ on X into a continuous social utility function $f_{\mathbf{u}}\colon X \to \mathbb{R}$. Suppose also that f satisfies *IIA*, *WP*, and *PI*.

Throughout this question you may assume that for any finite number of social states in X and any utility numbers you wish to assign to them, there is a continuous utility function defined on all of X assigning to those states the desired utility numbers. (You might wish to try and prove this. The hints section provides a solution.)

(a) Using U, IIA, and PI, show that if $\mathbf{u}(x) = \mathbf{v}(x')$ and $\mathbf{u}(y) = \mathbf{v}(y')$, then $f_{\mathbf{u}}(x) \geq f_{\mathbf{u}}(y)$ if and only if $f_{\mathbf{v}}(x') \geq f_{\mathbf{v}}(y')$.

Define the binary relation $\succsim$ on $\mathbb{R}^N$ as follows: $(a_1, \ldots, a_N) \succsim (b_1, \ldots, b_N)$ if $f_{\mathbf{u}}(x) \geq f_{\mathbf{u}}(y)$ for some vector of continuous utility functions $\mathbf{u}(\cdot) = (u^1(\cdot), \ldots, u^N(\cdot))$ and some pair of social states x and y satisfying $u^i(x) = a_i$ and $u^i(y) = b_i$ for all i.

(b) Show that $\succsim$ is complete.

(c) Use the fact that f satisfies WP to show that $\succsim$ is strictly monotonic.

(d) Use the result from part (a) to show that $\succsim$ is transitive. It is here where at least three social states are needed. (Of course, being non-singleton and convex, X is infinite so that there are many more states than necessary for this step.)

(e) It is possible to prove, using in particular the fact that X is non-singleton and convex, that $\succsim$ is continuous. But the proof is technically demanding. Instead, simply assume that $\succsim$ is continuous and use Theorems 1.1 and 1.3 to prove that there is a continuous and strictly increasing function $W\colon \mathbb{R}^N \to \mathbb{R}$ that represents $\succsim$. (You will need to provide a small argument to adjust for the fact that the domain of W is $\mathbb{R}^N$ while the domain of the utility functions in Chapter 1 is $\mathbb{R}^N_+$.)

(f) Show that for every profile of continuous utility functions $\mathbf{u}(\cdot) = (u^1(\cdot), \ldots, u^N(\cdot))$ on X and all pairs of social states x and y,

$$f_{\mathbf{u}}(x) \geq f_{\mathbf{u}}(y) \text{ if and only if } W(u^1(x), \ldots, u^N(x)) \geq W(u^1(y), \ldots, u^N(y)).$$

6.5 Recall the definition of a lexicographic dictatorship from Exercise 6.3.

(a) Suppose $N = 2$. As in Fig. 6.5, fix a utility vector $(\bar{u}_1, \bar{u}_2)$ in the plane and sketch the sets of utility vectors that are socially preferred, socially worse and socially indifferent to $(\bar{u}_1, \bar{u}_2)$ under a lexicographic dictatorship where individual 1's preferences come first and 2's second. Compare with Fig. 6.5. Pay special attention to the indifference sets.

(b) Conclude from Exercise 6.3 that our first proof of Arrow's theorem does not rule out the possibility of a lexicographic dictatorship and conclude from part (a) of this exercise that our second diagrammatic proof does rule out lexicographic dictatorship. What accounts for the stronger result in the diagrammatic proof?

6.6 In the diagrammatic proof of Arrow's theorem, the claim was made that in Fig. 6.4, we could show either $W(\bar{\mathbf{u}}) < W(\text{IV})$ or $W(\bar{\mathbf{u}}) > W(\text{IV})$. Provide the argument.

6.7 Provide the argument left out of the proof of Theorem 6.2 that the ray starting at $\mathbf{a}$ and extending upward is part of a social indifference curve.

6.8 This exercise considers Theorem 6.2 for the general case of $N \geq 2$. So, let $W\colon \mathbb{R}^N \to \mathbb{R}$ be continuous, strictly increasing and satisfy HE.

(a) Suppose that $\min[u^1, \ldots, u^N] = \alpha$. Show that $W(u^1 + \varepsilon, \ldots, u^N + \varepsilon) > W(\alpha, \alpha, \ldots, \alpha)$ for every $\varepsilon > 0$ because W is strictly increasing. Conclude by the continuity of W that $W(u^1, \ldots, u^N) \geq W(\alpha, \alpha, \ldots, \alpha)$.

(b) Suppose that $u^j = \min[u^1, \ldots, u^N] = \alpha$ and that $u^i > \alpha$. Using *HE*, show that $W(\alpha + \varepsilon, u^j, \mathbf{u}^{-ij}) \geq W(u^i, u^j - \varepsilon, \mathbf{u}^{-ij})$ for all $\varepsilon > 0$ sufficiently small, where $\mathbf{u}^{-ij} \in \mathbb{R}^{N-2}$ is the vector $(u^1, \ldots, u^N)$ without coordinates i and j.

(c) Using the continuity of W, conclude from (b) that if $\min[u^1, \ldots, u^N] = \alpha$, then for every individual i, $W(\alpha, \mathbf{u}^{-i}) \geq W(u^1, \ldots, u^N)$, where $\mathbf{u}^{-i} \in \mathbb{R}^{N-1}$ is the vector $(u^1, \ldots, u^N)$ without coordinate i.

(d) By successively applying the result from (c) one individual after another, show that if $\min[u^1, \ldots, u^N] = \alpha$, then $W(\alpha, \alpha, \ldots, \alpha) \geq W(u^1, \ldots, u^N)$.

(e) Using (a) and (d) and the fact that W is strictly increasing, show first that $W(u^1, \ldots, u^N) = W(\tilde{u}^1, \ldots, \tilde{u}^N)$ if and only if $\min(u^1, \ldots, u^N) = \min(\tilde{u}^1, \ldots, \tilde{u}^N)$ and then that $W(u^1, \ldots, u^N) \geq W(\tilde{u}^1, \ldots, \tilde{u}^N)$ if and only if $\min(u^1, \ldots, u^N) \geq \min(\tilde{u}^1, \ldots, \tilde{u}^N)$.

6.9 There are three individuals in society, $\{1, 2, 3\}$, three social states, $\{x, y, z\}$, and the domain of preferences is unrestricted. Suppose that the social preference relation, R, is given by pairwise majority voting (where voters break any indifferences by voting for x first then y then z) if this results in a transitive social order. If this does not result in a transitive social order the social order is $xPyPz$. Let f denote the social welfare function that this defines.

(a) Consider the following profiles, where P^i is individual i's strict preference relation:

Individual 1: xP^1yP^1z

Individual 2: yP^2zP^2x

Individual 3: zP^3xP^3y

What is the social order?

(b) What would be the social order if individual 1's preferences in (a) were instead yP^1zP^1x? or instead zP^1yP^1x?

(c) Prove that f satisfies the Pareto property, *WP*.

(d) Prove that f is non-dictatorial.

(e) Conclude that f does not satisfy *IIA*.

(f) Show directly that f does not satisfy *IIA* by providing two preference profiles and their associated social preferences that are in violation of *IIA*.

6.10 Aggregate income $\bar{y} > 0$ is to be distributed among a set $\mathcal{I}$ of individuals to maximise the utilitarian social welfare function, $W = \sum_{i \in \mathcal{I}} u^i$. Suppose that $u^i = \alpha^i (y^i)^\beta$, where $\alpha^i > 0$ for all $i \in \mathcal{I}$.

(a) Show that if $0 < \beta < 1$, income must be distributed equally if and only if $\alpha^i = \alpha^j$ for all i and j.

(b) Now suppose that $\alpha^i \neq \alpha^j$ for all i and j. What happens in the limit as $\beta \to 0$? How about as $\beta \to 1$? Interpret.

6.11 Suppose utility functions are strictly concave, strictly increasing, and differentiable for every agent in an n-good exchange economy with aggregate endowment $\mathbf{e} \gg \mathbf{0}$.

(a) Show that if $\mathbf{x}^* \gg \mathbf{0}$ is a WEA, then for some suitably chosen weights $\alpha^1, \ldots, \alpha^I > 0$, $\mathbf{x}^*$ maximises the (generalised) utilitarian social welfare function

$$W = \sum_{i \in \mathcal{I}} \alpha^i u^i(\mathbf{x}^i)$$

subject to the resource constraints

$$\sum_{i \in \mathcal{I}} x_j^i \le \sum_{i \in \mathcal{I}} e_j^i \qquad \text{for } j = i, \ldots, n.$$

(b) Use your findings in part (a) to give an alternative proof of the First Welfare Theorem 5.7.

6.12 The **Borda rule** is commonly used for making collective choices. Let there be N individuals and suppose X contains a finite number of alternatives. Individual i assigns a **Borda count**, $B^i(x)$, to every alternative x, where $B^i(x)$ is the number of alternatives in X to which x is preferred by agent i. Alternatives are then ranked according to their total Borda count as follows:

$$xRy \iff \sum_{i=1}^{N} B^i(x) \ge \sum_{i=1}^{N} B^i(y).$$

(a) Show that the Borda rule satisfies U, WP, and D in Assumption 6.1.

(b) Show that it does *not* satisfy *IIA*.

6.13 Individual i is said to be *decisive* in the social choice between x and y if xP^iy implies xPy, regardless of others' preferences. Sen (1970b) interprets 'liberal values' to imply that there are certain social choices over which each individual should be decisive. For example, in the social choice between individual i's reading or not reading a certain book, the preference of individual i should determine the social preference. Thus, we can view liberalism as a condition on the social welfare relation requiring that every individual be decisive over at least one pair of alternatives. Sen weakens this requirement further, defining a condition he calls **minimal liberalism** as follows:

L^*: there are at least two people k and j and two pairs of distinct alternatives (x, y) and (z, w) such that k and j are decisive over (x, y) and (z, w), respectively.

Prove that there exists *no* social welfare relation that satisfies (merely) the conditions U, WP, and L^*.

6.14 Atkinson (1970) proposes an index of equality in the distribution of income based on the notion of 'equally distributed equivalent income', denoted y_e. For any strictly increasing, symmetric, and quasiconcave social welfare function over income vectors, $W(y^1, \ldots, y^N)$, income y_e is defined as that amount of income which, if distributed to each individual, would produce the same level of social welfare as the given distribution. Thus, letting $\mathbf{e} \equiv (1, \ldots, 1)$ and $\mathbf{y} \equiv (y^1, \ldots, y^N)$, we have

$$W(y_e\mathbf{e}) \equiv W(\mathbf{y}).$$

Letting μ be the mean of the income distribution $\mathbf{y}$, an index of *equality* in the distribution of income then can be defined as follows:

$$I(\mathbf{y}) \equiv \frac{y_e}{\mu}.$$

(a) Show that $0 < I(\mathbf{y}) \le 1$ whenever $y_i > 0$ for all i.

(b) Show that the index $I(\mathbf{y})$ is always 'normatively significant' in the sense that for any two income distributions, $\mathbf{y}^1$, $\mathbf{y}^2$ with the same mean, $I(\mathbf{y}^1)$ is greater than, equal to, or less than $I(\mathbf{y}^2)$ if and only if $W(\mathbf{y}^1)$ is greater than, equal to, or less than $W(\mathbf{y}^2)$, respectively.

6.15 Blackorby and Donaldson (1978) built upon the work of Atkinson described in the preceding exercise. Let $W(\mathbf{y})$ be any strictly increasing, symmetric, and quasiconcave social welfare function defined over income distributions. The authors define a 'homogeneous implicit representation of W' as follows:

$$F(w, \mathbf{y}) \equiv \max_{\lambda}\{\lambda > 0 \mid W(\mathbf{y}/\lambda) \geq w\},$$

where $w \in \mathbb{R}$ is any 'reference level' of the underlying social welfare function. They then define their index of equality in the distribution of income as follows:

$$E(w, \mathbf{y}) \equiv \frac{F(w, \mathbf{y})}{F(w, \mu\mathbf{e})},$$

where, again, μ is the mean of the distribution $\mathbf{y}$ and $\mathbf{e}$ is a vector of 1's.

(a) Show that $F(w, \mathbf{y})$ is homogeneous of degree 1 in the income vector. Show that $F(w, \mathbf{y})$ is greater than, equal to, or less than unity as $W(y)$ is greater than, equal to, or less than w, respectively.

(b) Show that if $W(\mathbf{y})$ is homothetic, $E(w, \mathbf{y})$ is 'reference-level-free' so that $E(w, \mathbf{y}) = E^*(\mathbf{y})$ for all $\mathbf{y}$.

(c) Show that if $W(\mathbf{y})$ is homothetic, $E(w, \mathbf{y}) = I(\mathbf{y})$, where $I(\mathbf{y})$ is the Atkinson index defined in the preceding exercise. Conclude, therefore, that under these conditions, $E(w, \mathbf{y})$ is also normatively significant and lies between zero and 1.

(d) Suppose the social welfare function is the utilitarian form, $W = \sum_{i=1}^N y^i$. Show that $E(w, \mathbf{y}) = 1$, denoting 'perfect equality', regardless of the distribution of income. What do you conclude from this?

(e) Derive the index $E(w, \mathbf{y})$ when the social welfare function is the CES form

$$W(\mathbf{y}) = \left(\sum_{i=1}^{N} (y^i)^\rho\right)^{1/\rho}, \qquad 0 \neq \rho < 1.$$

6.16 Let $\mathbf{x} \equiv (\mathbf{x}^1, \ldots, \mathbf{x}^N)$ be an allocation of goods to agents, and let the economy's feasible set of allocations be T. Suppose $\mathbf{x}^*$ maximises the utilitarian social welfare function, $W = \sum_{i=1}^N u^i(\mathbf{x}^i)$, subject to $\mathbf{x} \in T$.

(a) Let ψ^i for $i = 1, \ldots, N$ be an arbitrary set of increasing functions of one variable. Does $\mathbf{x}^*$ maximise $\sum_{i=1}^N \psi^i(u^i(\mathbf{x}^i))$ over $\mathbf{x} \in T$? Why or why not?

(b) If in part (a), $\psi^i = \psi$ for all i, what would your answer be?

(c) If $\psi^i \equiv a^i + b^i u^i(\mathbf{x}^i)$ for arbitrary a^i and $b^i > 0$, what would your answer be?

(d) If $\psi^i \equiv a^i + b u^i(\mathbf{x}^i)$ for arbitrary a^i and $b > 0$, what would your answer be?

(e) How do you account for any similarities and differences in your answers to parts (a) through (d)?

6.17 From the preceding exercise, let $\mathbf{x}^*$ maximise the Rawlsian social welfare function, $W = \min[u^1(\mathbf{x}^1), \ldots, u^N(\mathbf{x}^N)]$ over $\mathbf{x} \in T$.

(a) If ψ^i for $i = 1, \ldots, N$ is an arbitrary set of increasing functions of one variable, must $\mathbf{x}^*$ maximise the function, $\min[\psi^1(u^1(\mathbf{x}^1)), \ldots, \psi^N(u^N(\mathbf{x}^N))]$, over $\mathbf{x} \in T$? Why or why not?

(b) If in part (a), $\psi^i = \psi$ for all i, what would your answer be?

(c) How do you account for your answers to parts (a) and (b)?

(d) How do you account for any differences or similarities in your answers to this exercise and the preceding one?

6.18 Suppose that $c(\cdot)$ is a monotonic social choice function and that $c(\mathbf{R}) = x$, where $R^1, \ldots, R^N$ are each strict rankings of the social states in X.

(a) Suppose that for some individual i, R^i ranks y just below x, and let $\tilde{R}^i$ be identical to R^i except that y is ranked just above x – i.e., the ranking of x and y is reversed. Prove that either $c(\tilde{R}^i, \mathbf{R}^{-i}) = x$ or $c(\tilde{R}^i, \mathbf{R}^{-i}) = y$.

(b) Suppose that $\tilde{R}^1, \ldots, \tilde{R}^N$ are strict rankings such that for every individual i, the ranking of x versus any other social state is the same under $\tilde{R}^i$ as it is under R^i. Prove that $c(\tilde{\mathbf{R}}) = x$.

6.19 Let $c(\cdot)$ be a monotonic social choice function and suppose that the social choice must be x whenever all individual rankings are strict and x is at the top of individual n's ranking. Show the social choice must be at least as good as x for individual n when the individual rankings are not necessarily strict and x is at least as good for individual n as any other social state.

6.20 Let x and y be distinct social states. Suppose that the social choice is at least as good as x for individual i whenever x is at least as good as every other social state for i. Suppose also that the social choice is at least as good as y for individual j whenever y is at least as good as every other social state for j. Prove that $i = j$.

6.21 Call a social choice function *strongly monotonic* if $c(\mathbf{R}) = x$ implies $c(\tilde{\mathbf{R}}) = x$ whenever for every individual i and every $y \in X$, $xR^iy \Longrightarrow x\tilde{R}^iy$.

Suppose there are two individuals, 1 and 2, and three social states, x, y, and z. Define the social choice function $c(\cdot)$ to choose individual 1's top-ranked social state unless it is not unique, in which case the social choice is individual 2's top-ranked social state among those that are top-ranked for individual 1, unless this too is not unique, in which case, among those that are top-ranked for both individuals, choose x if it is among them, otherwise choose y.

(a) Prove that $c(\cdot)$ is strategy-proof.

(b) Show by example that $c(\cdot)$ is not strongly monotonic. (Hence, strategy-proofness does not imply strong monotonicity, even though it implies monotonicity.)

6.22 Show that if $c(\cdot)$ is a monotonic social choice function and the finite set of social states is X, then for every $x \in X$ there is a profile, $\mathbf{R}$, of *strict* rankings such that $c(\mathbf{R}) = x$. (Recall that, by definition, every x in X is chosen by $c(\cdot)$ at some preference profile.)

6.23 Show that when there are just two alternatives and an odd number of individuals, the majority rule social choice function (i.e., that which chooses the outcome that is the top ranked choice for the majority of individuals) is Pareto efficient, strategy-proof and non-dictatorial.

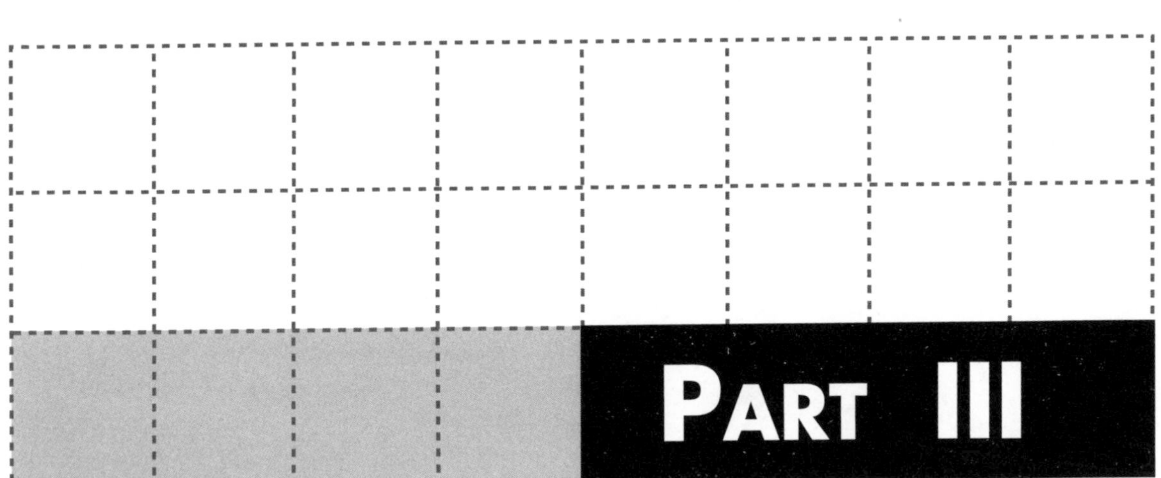

Part III

Strategic Behaviour

CHAPTER 7

GAME THEORY

When a consumer goes shopping for a new car, how will he bargain with the salesperson? If two countries negotiate a trade deal, what will be the outcome? What strategies will be followed by a number of oil companies each bidding on an offshore oil tract in a sealed-bid auction?

In situations such as these, the actions any one agent may take will have consequences for others. Because of this, agents have reason to act *strategically*. **Game theory** is the systematic study of how rational agents behave in strategic situations, or in *games*, where each agent must first know the decision of the other agents before knowing which decision is best for himself. This circularity is the hallmark of the theory of games, and deciding how rational agents behave in such settings will be the focus of this chapter.

The chapter begins with a close look at strategic form games and proceeds to consider extensive form games in some detail. The former are games in which the agents make a single, simultaneous choice, whereas the latter are games in which players may make choices in sequence.

Along the way, we will encounter a variety of methods for determining the outcome of a game. You will see that each method we encounter gives rise to a particular *solution concept*. The solution concepts we will study include those based on dominance arguments, Nash equilibrium, Bayesian-Nash equilibrium, backward induction, subgame perfection, and sequential equilibrium. Each of these solution concepts is more sophisticated than its predecessors, and knowing when to apply one solution rather than another is an important part of being a good applied economist.

7.1 STRATEGIC DECISION MAKING

The essential difference between strategic and non-strategic decisions is that the latter can be made in 'isolation', without taking into account the decisions that others might make. For example, the theory of the consumer developed in Chapter 1 is a model of non-strategic behaviour. Given prices and income, each consumer acts entirely on his own, without regard for the behaviour of others. On the other hand, the Cournot and Bertrand models of duopoly introduced in Chapter 4 capture strategic decision making on the part of the two firms. Each firm understands well that its optimal action depends on the action taken by the other firm.

To further illustrate the significance of strategic decision making consider the classic duel between a batter and a pitcher in baseball. To keep things simple, let us assume that the pitcher has only two possible pitches – a fastball and a curve. Also, suppose it is well known that this pitcher has the best fastball in the league, but his curve is only average. Based on this, it might seem best for the pitcher to always throw his fastball. However, such a non-strategic decision on the pitcher's part fails to take into account the batter's decision. For if the batter expects the pitcher to throw a fastball, then, being prepared for it, he will hit it. Consequently, it would be wise for the pitcher to take into account the batter's decision about the pitcher's pitch before deciding which pitch to throw.

To push the analysis a little further, let us assign some utility numbers to the various outcomes. For simplicity, we suppose that the situation is an all or nothing one for both players. Think of it as being the bottom of the ninth inning, with a full count, bases loaded, two outs, and the pitcher's team ahead by one run. Assume also that the batter either hits a home run (and wins the game) or strikes out (and loses the game). Consequently, there is exactly one pitch remaining in the game. Finally, suppose each player derives utility 1 from a win and utility -1 from a loss. We may then represent this situation by the matrix diagram in Fig. 7.1.

In this diagram, the pitcher (P) chooses the row, F (fastball) or C (curve), and the batter (B) chooses the column. The batter hits a home run when he prepares for the pitch that the pitcher has chosen, and strikes out otherwise. The entries in the matrix denote the players' payoffs as a result of their decisions, with the pitcher's payoff being the first number of each entry and the batter's the second. Thus, the entry $(1, -1)$ in the first row and second column indicates that if the pitcher throws a fastball and the batter prepares for a curve, the pitcher's payoff is 1 and the batter's is -1. The other entries are read in the same way.

Although we have so far concentrated on the pitcher's decision, the batter is obviously in a completely symmetric position. Just as the pitcher must decide on which pitch to throw, the batter must decide on which pitch to prepare for. What can be said about their behaviour in such a setting? Even though you might be able to provide the answer for yourself already, we will not analyse this game fully just yet.

However, we can immediately draw a rather important conclusion based solely on the ideas that each player seeks to maximise his payoff, and that each reasons strategically.

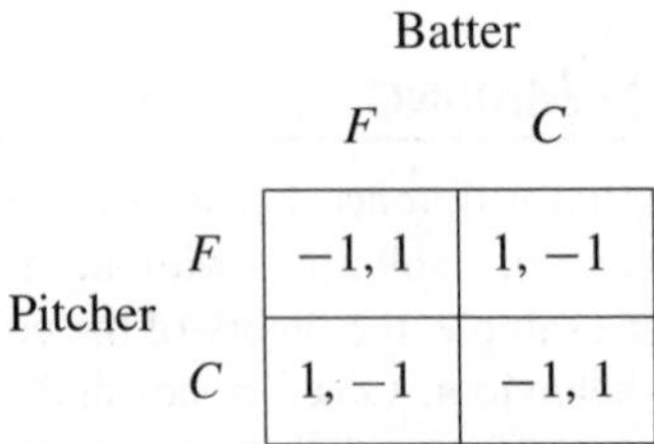

Pitcher \ Batter	F	C
F	$-1, 1$	$1, -1$
C	$1, -1$	$-1, 1$

Figure 7.1. The batter–pitcher game.

Here, each player must behave in a manner that is 'unpredictable'. Why? Because if the pitcher's behaviour were predictable in that, say, he always throws his fastball, then the batter, by choosing F, would be guaranteed to hit a home run and win the game. But this would mean that the batter's behaviour is predictable as well; he always prepares for a fastball. Consequently, because the pitcher behaves strategically, he will optimally choose to throw his curve, thereby striking the batter out and winning the game. But this contradicts our original supposition that the pitcher always throws his fastball! We conclude that the pitcher cannot be correctly predicted to always throw a fastball. Similarly, it must be incorrect to predict that the pitcher always throws a curve. Thus, whatever behaviour does eventually arise out of this scenario, it must involve a certain lack of predictability regarding the pitch to be thrown. And for precisely the same reasons, it must also involve a lack of predictability regarding the batter's choice of which pitch to prepare for.

Thus, when rational individuals make decisions strategically, each taking into account the decision the other makes, they sometimes behave in an 'unpredictable' manner. Any good poker player understands this well – it is an essential aspect of successful bluffing. Note, however, that there is no such advantage in non-strategic settings – when you are alone, there is no one to 'fool'. This is but one example of how outcomes among strategic decision makers may differ quite significantly from those among non-strategic decision makers. Now that we have a taste for strategic decision making, we are ready to develop a little theory.

7.2 Strategic Form Games

The batter–pitcher duel, as well as Cournot and Bertrand duopoly, are but three examples of the kinds of strategic situations economists wish to analyse. Other examples include bargaining between a labour union and a firm, trade wars between two countries, research-and-development races between companies, and so on. We seek a single framework capable of capturing the essential features of each of these settings and more. Thus, we must search for elements that are common among them. What features do these examples share? Well, each involves a number of participants – we shall call them 'players' – each of whom has a range of possible actions that can be taken – we shall call these actions 'strategies' – and each of whom derives one payoff or another depending on his own strategy choice as well as the strategies chosen by each of the other players. As has been the tradition, we shall refer to such a situation as a **game**, even though the stakes may be quite serious indeed. With this in mind, consider the following definition.

DEFINITION 7.1 ***Strategic Form Game***

A strategic form game is a tuple $G = (S_i, u_i)_{i=1}^N$, where for each player $i = 1, \ldots, N$, S_i is the set of strategies available to player i, and u_i: $\times_{j=1}^N S_j \to \mathbb{R}$ describes player i's payoff as a function of the strategies chosen by all players. A strategic form game is finite if each player's strategy set contains finitely many elements.

Note that this definition is general enough to cover our batter–pitcher duel. The strategic form game describing that situation, when the pitcher is designated player 1, is given by

$$\begin{aligned} S_1 &= S_2 = \{F, C\}, \\ u_1(F, F) &= u_1(C, C) = -1, \\ u_1(F, C) &= u_1(C, F) = 1, \quad \text{and} \\ u_2(s_1, s_2) &= -u_1(s_1, s_2) \qquad \text{for all} \quad (s_1, s_2) \in S_1 \times S_2. \end{aligned}$$

Note that two-player strategic form games with finite strategy sets can always be represented in matrix form, with the rows indexing the strategies of player 1, the columns indexing the strategies of player 2, and the entries denoting their payoffs.

7.2.1 DOMINANT STRATEGIES

Whenever we attempt to predict the outcome of a game, it is preferable to do so without requiring that the players know a great deal about how their opponents will behave. This is not always possible, but when it is, the solution arrived at is particularly convincing. In this section, we consider various forms of strategic dominance, and we look at ways we can sometimes use these ideas to solve, or narrow down, the solution to a game.

Let us begin with the two-player strategic form game in Fig. 7.2. There, player 2's payoff-maximising strategy choice depends on the choice made by player 1. If 1 chooses U (up), then it is best for 2 to choose L (left), and if 1 chooses D (down), then it is best for 2 to choose R (right). As a result, player 2 must make his decision strategically, and he must consider carefully the decision of player 1 before deciding what to do himself.

What will player 1 do? Look closely at the payoffs and you will see that player 1's best choice is actually *independent* of the choice made by player 2. Regardless of player 2's choice, U is best for player 1. Consequently, player 1 will surely choose U. Having deduced this, player 2 will then choose L. Thus, the only sensible outcome of this game is the strategy pair (U, L), with associated payoff vector $(3, 0)$.

The special feature of this game that allows us to 'solve' it – to deduce the outcome when it is played by rational players – is that player 1 possesses a strategy that is best for him *regardless of the strategy chosen by player 2*. Once player 1's decision is clear, then player 2's becomes clear as well. Thus, in two-player games, when one player possesses such a 'dominant' strategy, the outcome is rather straightforward to determine.

	L	R
U	3, 0	0, −4
D	2, 4	−1, 8

Figure 7.2. Strictly dominant strategies.

To make this a bit more formal, we introduce some notation. Let $S = S_1 \times \cdots \times S_N$ denote the set of joint pure strategies. The symbol, $-i$, denotes 'all players except player i'. So, for example, s_{-i} denotes an element of S_{-i}, which itself denotes the set $S_1 \times \cdots \times S_{i-1} \times S_{i+1} \times \cdots \times S_N$. Then we have the following definition.

DEFINITION 7.2 ***Strictly Dominant Strategies***

A strategy, $\hat{s}_i$, for player i is strictly dominant if $u_i(\hat{s}_i, s_{-i}) > u_i(s_i, s_{-i})$ for all $(s_i, s_{-i}) \in S$ with $s_i \neq \hat{s}_i$.

The presence of a strictly dominant strategy, one that is strictly superior to *all* other strategies, is rather rare. However, even when no strictly dominant strategy is available, it may still be possible to simplify the analysis of a game by ruling out strategies that are clearly *un*attractive to the player possessing them. Consider the example depicted in Fig. 7.3. Neither player possesses a strictly dominant strategy there. To see this, note that player 1's unique best choice is U when 2 plays L, but D when 2 plays M; and 2's unique best choice is L when 1 plays U, but R when 1 plays D. However, each player has a strategy that is particularly unattractive. Player 1's strategy C is always outperformed by D, in the sense that 1's payoff is strictly higher when D is chosen compared to when C is chosen *regardless* of the strategy chosen by player 2. Thus, we may remove C from consideration. Player 1 will never choose it. Similarly, player 2's strategy M is outperformed by R (check this) and it may be removed from consideration as well. Now that C and M have been removed, you will notice that the game has been reduced to that of Fig. 7.2. Thus, as before, the only sensible outcome is (3, 0). Again, we have used a dominance idea to help us solve the game. But this time we focused on the dominance of one strategy over *one* other, rather than over all others.

DEFINITION 7.3 ***Strictly Dominated Strategies***

Player i's strategy $\hat{s}_i$ strictly dominates another of his strategies $\bar{s}_i$, if $u_i(\hat{s}_i, s_{-i}) > u_i(\bar{s}_i, s_{-i})$ for all $s_{-i} \in S_{-i}$. In this case, we also say that $\bar{s}_i$ is strictly dominated in S.

As we have noticed, the presence of strictly dominant or strictly dominated strategies can simplify the analysis of a game enough to render it completely solvable. It is instructive to review our solution techniques for the games of Figs. 7.2 and 7.3.

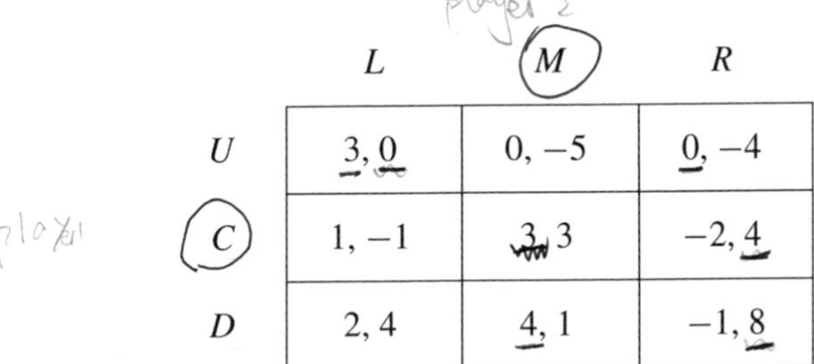

	L	M	R
U	3, 0	0, −5	0, −4
C	1, −1	3, 3	−2, 4
D	2, 4	4, 1	−1, 8

Figure 7.3. Strictly dominated strategies.

In the game of Fig. 7.2, we noted that U was strictly dominant for player 1. We were therefore able to *eliminate* D from consideration. Once done, we were then able to conclude that player 2 would choose L, or what amounts to the same thing, we were able to *eliminate* R. Note that although R is not strictly dominated in the original game, it is strictly dominated (by L) in the reduced game in which 1's strategy D is eliminated. This left the unique solution (U, L). In the game of Fig. 7.3, we first *eliminated* C for 1 and M for 2 (each being strictly dominated); then (following the Fig. 7.2 analysis) *eliminated* D for 1; then *eliminated* R for 2. This again left the unique strategy pair (U, L). Again, note that D is not strictly dominated in the original game, yet it is strictly dominated in the reduced game in which C has been eliminated. Similarly, R becomes strictly dominated only after both C and D have been eliminated. We now formalise this procedure of **iteratively eliminating** strictly dominated strategies.

Let $S_i^0 = S_i$ for each player i, and for $n \geq 1$, let S_i^n denote those strategies of player i surviving after the nth round of elimination. That is, $s_i \in S_i^n$ if $s_i \in S_i^{n-1}$ is not strictly dominated in S^{n-1}.

DEFINITION 7.4 ***Iteratively Strictly Undominated Strategies***

A strategy s_i for player i is iteratively strictly undominated in S (or survives iterative elimination of strictly dominated strategies) if $s_i \in S_i^n$, for all $n \geq 1$.

So far, we have considered only notions of *strict* dominance. Related notions of weak dominance are also available. In particular, consider the following analogues of Definitions 7.3 and 7.4.

DEFINITION 7.5 ***Weakly Dominated Strategies***

Player i's strategy $\hat{s}_i$ weakly dominates another of his strategies $\bar{s}_i$, if $u_i(\hat{s}_i, s_{-i}) \geq u_i(\bar{s}_i, s_{-i})$ for all $s_{-i} \in S_{-i}$, with at least one strict inequality. In this case, we also say that $\bar{s}_i$ is weakly dominated in S.

The difference between weak and strict dominance can be seen in the example of Fig. 7.4. In this game, neither player has a strictly dominated strategy. However, both D and R are weakly dominated by U and L, respectively. Thus, eliminating strictly dominated strategies has no effect here, whereas eliminating weakly dominated strategies isolates the unique strategy pair (U, L). As in the case of strict dominance, we may also wish to iteratively eliminate weakly dominated strategies.

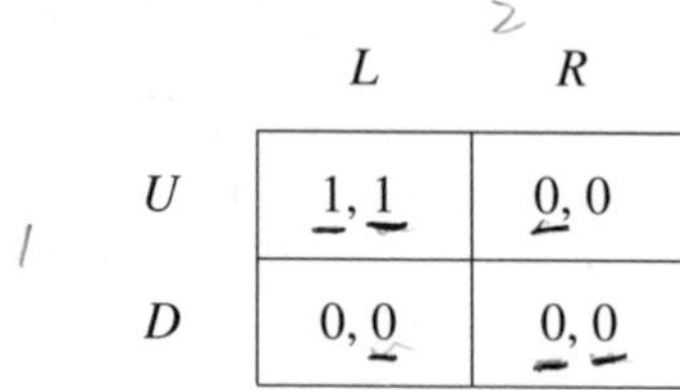

	L	R
U	1, 1	0, 0
D	0, 0	0, 0

Figure 7.4. Weakly dominated strategies.

With this in mind, let $W_i^0 = S_i$ for each player i, and for $n \geq 1$, let W_i^n denote those strategies of player i surviving after the nth round of elimination of weakly dominated strategies. That is, $s_i \in W_i^n$ if $s_i \in W_i^{n-1}$ is not weakly dominated in $W^{n-1} = W_1^{n-1} \times \cdots \times W_N^{n-1}$.

DEFINITION 7.6 ***Iteratively Weakly Undominated Strategies***

A strategy s_i for player i is iteratively weakly undominated in S (or survives iterative elimination of weakly dominated strategies) if $s_i \in W_i^n$ for all $n \geq 1$.

It should be clear that the set of strategies remaining after applying iterative weak dominance is contained in the set remaining after applying iterative strict dominance. You are asked to show this in one of the exercises.

To get a feel for the sometimes surprising power of iterative dominance arguments, consider the following game called 'Guess the Average' in which $N \geq 2$ players try to outguess one another. Each player must simultaneously choose an integer between 1 and 100. The person closest to one-third the average of the guesses wins \$100, whereas the others get nothing. The \$100 prize is split evenly if there are ties. Before reading on, think for a moment about how you would play this game when there are, say, 20 players.

Let us proceed by eliminating weakly dominated strategies. Note that choosing the number 33 weakly dominates all higher numbers. This is because one-third the average of the numbers must be less than or equal to $33\frac{1}{3}$. Consequently, regardless of the others' announced numbers, 33 is no worse a choice than any higher number, and if all other players happen to choose the number 34, then the choice of 33 is strictly better than all higher numbers. Thus, we may eliminate all numbers above 33 from consideration for all players. Therefore, $W_i^1 \subseteq \{1, 2, \ldots, 33\}$.[1] But a similar argument establishes that all numbers above 11 are weakly dominated in W^1. Thus, $W_i^2 \subseteq \{1, 2, \ldots, 11\}$. Continuing in this manner establishes that for each player, the only strategy surviving iterative weak dominance is choosing the number 1.

If you have been keeping the batter–pitcher duel in the back of your mind, you may have noticed that in that game, no strategy for either player is strictly or weakly dominated. Hence, none of the elimination procedures we have described will reduce the strategies under consideration there at all. Although these elimination procedures are clearly very helpful in some circumstances, we are no closer to solving the batter–pitcher duel than we were when we put it aside. It is now time to change that.

7.2.2 NASH EQUILIBRIUM

According to the theory of demand and supply, the notion of a market equilibrium in which demand equals supply is central. The theoretical attraction of the concept arises because in

[1]Depending on the number of players, other numbers may be weakly dominated as well. This is explored in the exercises.

such a situation, there is no tendency or necessity for anyone's behaviour to change. These regularities in behaviour form the basis for making predictions.

With a view towards making predictions, we wish to describe potential regularities in behaviour that might arise in a strategic setting. At the same time, we wish to incorporate the idea that the players are 'rational', both in the sense that they act in their own self-interest and that they are fully aware of the regularities in the behaviour of others. In the strategic setting, just as in the demand–supply setting, regularities in behaviour that can be 'rationally' sustained will be called **equilibria**. In Chapter 4, we have already encountered the notion of a Nash equilibrium in the strategic context of Cournot duopoly. This concept generalises to arbitrary strategic form games. Indeed, **Nash equilibrium**, introduced in Nash (1951), is the single most important equilibrium concept in all of game theory.

Informally, a joint strategy $\hat{s} \in S$ constitutes a Nash equilibrium as long as each individual, while fully aware of the others' behaviour, has no incentive to change his own. Thus, a Nash equilibrium describes behaviour that can be rationally sustained. Formally, the concept is defined as follows.

DEFINITION 7.7 ***Pure Strategy Nash Equilibrium***

Given a strategic form game $G = (S_i, u_i)_{i=1}^N$, the joint strategy $\hat{s} \in S$ is a pure strategy Nash equilibrium of G if for each player i, $u_i(\hat{s}) \geq u_i(s_i, \hat{s}_{-i})$ for all $s_i \in S_i$.

Note that in each of the games of Figs. 7.2 to 7.4, the strategy pair (U, L) constitutes a pure strategy Nash equilibrium. To see this in the game of Fig. 7.2, consider first whether player 1 can improve his payoff by changing his choice of strategy with player 2's strategy fixed. By switching to D, player 1's payoff falls from 3 to 2. Consequently, player 1 cannot improve his payoff. Likewise, player 2 cannot improve his payoff by changing his strategy when player 1's strategy is fixed at U. Therefore (U, L) is indeed a Nash equilibrium of the game in Fig. 7.2. The others can (and should) be similarly checked.

A game may possess more than one Nash equilibrium. For example, in the game of Fig. 7.4, (D, R) is also a pure strategy Nash equilibrium because neither player can strictly improve his payoff by switching strategies when the other player's strategy choice is fixed. Some games do not possess any pure strategy Nash equilibria. As you may have guessed, this is the case for our batter–pitcher duel game in Fig. 7.1, reproduced as Fig. 7.5.

Let us check that there is no pure strategy Nash equilibrium here. There are but four possibilities: (F, F), (F, C), (C, F), and (C, C). We will check one, and leave it to you to check the others. Can (F, F) be a pure strategy Nash equilibrium? Only if neither player can improve his payoff by unilaterally deviating from his part of (F, F). Let us begin with

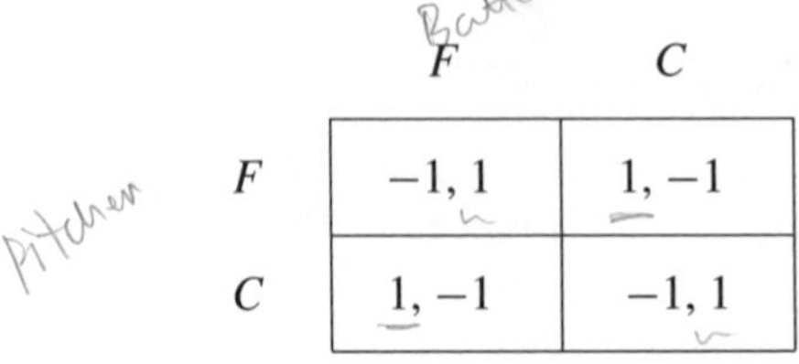

	F	C
F	$-1, 1$	$1, -1$
C	$1, -1$	$-1, 1$

Figure 7.5. The batter–pitcher game.

the batter. When (F, F) is played, the batter receives a payoff of 1. By switching to C, the joint strategy becomes (F, C) (remember, we must hold the pitcher's strategy fixed at F), and the batter receives -1. Consequently, the batter cannot improve his payoff by switching. What about the pitcher? At (F, F), the pitcher receives a payoff of -1. By switching to C, the joint strategy becomes (C, F) and the pitcher receives 1, an improvement. Thus, the pitcher *can* improve his payoff by unilaterally switching his strategy, and so (F, F) is not a pure strategy Nash equilibrium. A similar argument applies to the other three possibilities.

Of course, this was to be expected in the light of our heuristic analysis of the batter–pitcher duel at the beginning of this chapter. There we concluded that both the batter and the pitcher must behave in an unpredictable manner. But embodied in the definition of a pure strategy Nash equilibrium is that each player knows precisely which strategy each of the other players will choose. That is, in a pure strategy Nash equilibrium, everyone's choices are perfectly predictable. The batter–pitcher duel continues to escape analysis. But we are fast closing in on it.

Mixed Strategies and Nash Equilibrium

A sure-fire way to make a choice in a manner that others cannot predict is to make it in a manner that *you yourself* cannot predict. And the simplest way to do that is to *randomise* among your choices. For example, in the batter–pitcher duel, both the batter and the pitcher can avoid having their choice predicted by the other simply by tossing a coin to decide which choice to make.

Let us take a moment to see how this provides a solution to the batter–pitcher duel. Suppose that both the batter and the pitcher have with them a fair coin. Just before each is to perform his task, they each (separately) toss their coin. If a coin comes up heads, its owner chooses F; if tails, C. Furthermore, suppose that each of them is perfectly aware that the other makes his choice in this manner. Does this qualify as an equilibrium in the sense described before? In fact, it does. Given the method by which each player makes his choice, neither can improve his payoff by making his choice any differently. Let us see why.

Consider the pitcher. He knows that the batter is tossing a fair coin to decide whether to get ready for a fastball (F) or a curve (C). Thus, he knows that the batter will choose F and C each with probability one-half. Consequently, each of the pitcher's own choices will *induce a lottery* over the possible outcomes in the game. Let us therefore assume that the players' payoffs are in fact von Neumann-Morgenstern utilities, and that they will behave to maximise their expected utility.

What then is the expected utility that the pitcher derives from the choices available to him? If he were simply to choose F (ignoring his coin), his expected utility would be $\frac{1}{2}(-1) + \frac{1}{2}(1) = 0$, whereas if he were to choose C, it would be $\frac{1}{2}(1) + \frac{1}{2}(-1) = 0$. Thus, given the fact that the batter is choosing F and C with probability one-half each, the pitcher is indifferent between F and C himself. Thus, while choosing either F or C would give the pitcher his highest possible payoff of zero, so too would randomising between them with probability one-half on each. Similarly, given that the pitcher is randomising between F and C with probability one-half on each, the batter can also maximise his expected utility by randomising between F and C with equal probabilities. In short, the players' randomised choices form an equilibrium: each is aware of the (randomised) manner in which the other makes his choice, and neither can improve his expected payoff by unilaterally changing the manner in which his choice is made.

To apply these ideas to general strategic form games, we first formally introduce the notion of a mixed strategy.

DEFINITION 7.8 *Mixed Strategies*

Fix a finite strategic form game $G = (S_i, u_i)_{i=1}^N$. A mixed strategy, m_i, for player i is a probability distribution over S_i. That is, $m_i\colon S_i \to [0, 1]$ assigns to each $s_i \in S_i$ the probability, $m_i(s_i)$, that s_i will be played. We shall denote the set of mixed strategies for player i by M_i. Consequently, $M_i = \{m_i\colon S_i \to [0, 1] \mid \sum_{s_i \in S_i} m_i(s_i) = 1\}$. From now on, we shall call S_i player i's set of pure strategies.

Thus, a mixed strategy is the means by which players randomise their choices. One way to think of a mixed strategy is simply as a roulette wheel with the names of various pure strategies printed on sections of the wheel. Different roulette wheels might have larger sections assigned to one pure strategy or another, yielding different probabilities that those strategies will be chosen. The set of mixed strategies is then the set of all such roulette wheels.

Each player i is now allowed to choose from the set of mixed strategies M_i rather than S_i. Note that this gives each player i strictly more choices than before, because every pure strategy $\bar{s}_i \in S_i$ is represented in M_i by the (degenerate) probability distribution assigning probability one to $\bar{s}_i$.

Let $M = \times_{i=1}^N M_i$ denote the set of joint mixed strategies. From now on, we shall drop the word 'mixed' and simply call $m \in M$ a joint strategy and $m_i \in M_i$ a strategy for player i.

If u_i is a von Neumann-Morgenstern utility function on S, and the strategy $m \in M$ is played, then player i's expected utility is

$$u_i(m) \equiv \sum_{s \in S} m_1(s_1) \cdots m_N(s_N) u_i(s).$$

This formula follows from the fact that the players choose their strategies independently. Consequently, the probability that the pure strategy $s = (s_1, \ldots, s_N) \in S$ is chosen is the product of the probabilities that each separate component is chosen, namely $m_1(s_1) \cdots m_N(s_N)$. We now give the central equilibrium concept for strategic form games.

DEFINITION 7.9 *Nash Equilibrium*

Given a finite strategic form game $G = (S_i, u_i)_{i=1}^N$, a joint strategy $\hat{m} \in M$ is a Nash equilibrium of G if for each player i, $u_i(\hat{m}) \geq u_i(m_i, \hat{m}_{-i})$ for all $m_i \in M_i$.

Thus, in a Nash equilibrium, each player may be randomising his choices, and no player can improve his expected payoff by unilaterally randomising any differently.

It might appear that checking for a Nash equilibrium requires checking, for every player i, each strategy in the infinite set M_i against $\hat{m}_i$. The following result simplifies this task by taking advantage of the linearity of u_i in m_i.

THEOREM 7.1 ***Simplified Nash Equilibrium Tests***

The following statements are equivalent:

(a) $\hat{m} \in M$ is a Nash equilibrium.

(b) For every player i, $u_i(\hat{m}) = u_i(s_i, \hat{m}_{-i})$ for every $s_i \in S_i$ given positive weight by $\hat{m}_i$, and $u_i(\hat{m}) \geq u_i(s_i, \hat{m}_{-i})$ for every $s_i \in S_i$ given zero weight by $\hat{m}_i$.

(c) For every player i, $u_i(\hat{m}) \geq u_i(s_i, \hat{m}_{-i})$ for every $s_i \in S_i$.

According to the theorem, statements (b) and (c) offer alternative methods for checking for a Nash equilibrium. Statement (b) is most useful for computing Nash equilibria. It says that a player must be indifferent between all pure strategies given positive weight by his mixed strategy and that each of these must be no worse than any of his pure strategies given zero weight. Statement (c) says that it is enough to check for each player that no pure strategy yields a higher expected payoff than his mixed strategy in order that the vector of mixed strategies forms a Nash equilibrium.

Proof: We begin by showing that statement (a) implies (b). Suppose first that $\hat{m}$ is a Nash equilibrium. Consequently, $u_i(\hat{m}) \geq u_i(m_i, \hat{m}_{-i})$ for all $m_i \in M_i$. In particular, for every $s_i \in S_i$, we may choose m_i to be the strategy giving probability one to s_i, so that $u_i(\hat{m}) \geq u_i(s_i, \hat{m}_{-i})$ holds in fact for *every* $s_i \in S_i$. It remains to show that $u_i(\hat{m}) = u_i(s_i, \hat{m}_{-i})$ for every $s_i \in S_i$ given positive weight by $\hat{m}_i$. Now, if any of these numbers differed from $u_i(\hat{m})$, then at least one would be strictly larger because $u_i(\hat{m})$ is a strict convex combination of them. But this would contradict the inequality just established.

Because it is obvious that statement (b) implies (c), it remains only to establish that (c) implies (a). So, suppose that $u_i(\hat{m}) \geq u_i(s_i, \hat{m}_{-i})$ for every $s_i \in S_i$ and every player i. Fix a player i and $m_i \in M_i$. Because the number $u_i(m_i, \hat{m}_{-i})$ is a convex combination of the numbers $\{u_i(s_i, \hat{m}_{-i})\}_{s_i \in S_i}$, we have $u_i(\hat{m}) \geq u_i(m_i, \hat{m}_{-i})$. Because both the player and the chosen strategy were arbitrary, $\hat{m}$ is a Nash equilibrium of G. ∎

EXAMPLE 7.1 Let us consider an example to see these ideas at work. You and a colleague are asked to put together a report that must be ready in an hour. You agree to split the work into halves. To your mutual dismay, you each discover that the word processor you use is not compatible with the one the other uses. To put the report together in a presentable fashion, one of you must switch to the other's word processor. Of course, because it is costly to become familiar with a new word processor, each of you would rather that the other switched. On the other hand, each of you prefers to switch to the other's word processor rather than fail to coordinate at all. Finally, suppose there is no time for the two of you to

	WP	MW
WP	2, 1	0, 0
MW	0, 0	1, 2

Figure 7.6. A coordination game.

waste discussing the coordination issue. Each must decide which word processor to use in the privacy of his own office.

This situation is represented by the game of Fig. 7.6. Player 1's word processor is WP, and player 2's is MW. They each derive a payoff of zero by failing to coordinate, a payoff of 2 by coordinating on their own word processor, and a payoff of 1 by coordinating on the other's word processor. This game possesses two pure strategy Nash equilibria, namely, (WP, WP) and (MW, MW).

Are there any Nash equilibria in *mixed* strategies? If so, then it is easy to see from Fig. 7.6 that both players must choose each of their pure strategies with strictly positive probability. Let then $p > 0$ denote the probability that player 1 chooses his colleague's word processor, MW, and let $q > 0$ denote the probability that player 2 chooses *his* colleague's word processor WP. By part (b) of Theorem 7.1, each player must be indifferent between each of his pure strategies. For player 1, this means that

$$q(2) + (1 - q)(0) = q(0) + (1 - q)(1),$$

and for player 2, this means

$$(1 - p)(1) + p(0) = (1 - p)(0) + p(2).$$

Solving these yields $p = q = 1/3$. Thus, the (mixed) strategy in which each player chooses his colleague's word processor with probability $1/3$ and his own with probability $2/3$ is a third Nash equilibrium of this game. There are no others. □

The game of Example 7.1 is interesting in a number of respects. First, it possesses multiple Nash equilibria, some pure, others not. Second, one of these equilibria is inefficient. Notice that in the mixed-strategy equilibrium, each player's expected payoff is $2/3$, so that each would be strictly better off were either of the pure strategy equilibria played. Third, a mixed-strategy equilibrium is present even though this is *not* a game in which either player wishes to behave in an unpredictable manner.

Should we then ignore the mixed-strategy equilibrium we have found here, because in it, the mixed strategies are not serving the purpose they were introduced to serve? No. Although we first introduced mixed strategies to give players an opportunity to behave unpredictably if they so desired, there is *another* way to interpret the meaning of a mixed strategy. Rather than think of a mixed strategy for player 1, say, as deliberate randomisation on *his* part, think of it as an expression of *the other players' beliefs* regarding the pure strategy that player 1 will choose. So, for example, in our game of Fig. 7.6, player 1's equilibrium strategy placing probability 1/3 on MW and 2/3 on WP can be interpreted to reflect player 2's uncertainty regarding the pure strategy that player 1 will choose. Player 2 believes that player 1 will choose MW with probability 1/3 and WP with probability 2/3. Similarly, player 2's equilibrium mixed strategy here need not reflect the idea that player 2 deliberately randomises between WP and MW, rather it can be interpreted as player 1's beliefs about the probability that player 2 will choose one pure strategy or the other.

Thus, we now have *two* possible interpretations of mixed strategies at our disposal. On the one hand, they may constitute actual physical devices (roulette wheels) that players use to deliberately randomise their pure strategy choices. On the other hand, a player's mixed strategy may merely represent the beliefs that the others hold about the pure strategy that he might choose. In this latter interpretation, no player is explicitly randomising his choice of pure strategy. Whether we choose to employ one interpretation or the other depends largely on the context. Typically, the roulette wheel interpretation makes sense in games like the batter–pitcher duel in which the interests of the players are opposing, whereas the beliefs-based interpretation is better suited for games like the one of Fig. 7.6, in which the players' interests, to some extent, coincide.

Does every game possess at least one Nash equilibrium? Recall that in the case of pure strategy Nash equilibrium, the answer is no (the batter–pitcher duel). However, once mixed strategies are introduced, the answer is yes quite generally.

THEOREM 7.2 ***(Nash) Existence of Nash Equilibrium***

Every finite strategic form game possesses at least one Nash equilibrium.

Proof: Let $G = (S_i, u_i)_{i=1}^N$ be a finite strategic form game. To keep the notation simple, let us assume that each player has the same number of pure strategies, n. Thus, for each player i, we may index each of his pure strategies by one of the numbers 1 up to n and so we may write $S_i = \{1, 2, \ldots, n\}$. Consequently, $u_i(j_1, j_2, \ldots, j_N)$ denotes the payoff to player i when player 1 chooses pure strategy j_1, player 2 chooses pure strategy $j_2, \ldots,$ and player N chooses pure strategy j_N. Player i's set of mixed strategies is $M_i = \{(m_{i1}, \ldots, m_{in}) \in \mathbb{R}^n_+ \mid \sum_{j=1}^n m_{ij} = 1\}$, where m_{ij} denotes the probability assigned to player i's jth pure strategy. Note that M_i is non-empty, compact, and convex.

We shall show that a Nash equilibrium of G exists by demonstrating the existence of a fixed point of a function whose fixed points are necessarily equilibria of G. Thus, the remainder of the proof consists of three steps: (1) construct the function, (2) prove that it has a fixed point, and (3) demonstrate that the fixed point is a Nash equilibrium of G.

Step 1: Define $f\colon M \to M$ as follows. For each $m \in M$, each player i, and each of his pure strategies j, let

$$f_{ij}(m) = \frac{m_{ij} + \max(0, u_i(j, m_{-i}) - u_i(m))}{1 + \sum\limits_{j'=1}^{n} \max(0, u_i(j', m_{-i}) - u_i(m))}$$

Let $f_i(m) = (f_{i1}(m), \ldots, f_{in}(m))$, $i = 1, \ldots, N$, and let $f(m) = (f_1(m), \ldots, f_N(m))$. Note that for every player i, $\sum_{j=1}^{n} f_{ij}(m) = 1$ and that $f_{ij}(m) \geq 0$ for every j. Therefore, $f_i(m) \in M_i$ for every i, and so $f(m) \in M$.

Step 2: Because the numerator defining f_{ij} is continuous in m, and the denominator is both continuous in m and bounded away from zero (indeed, it is never less than one), f_{ij} is a continuous function of m for every i and j. Consequently, f is a continuous function mapping the non-empty, compact, and convex set M into itself. We therefore may apply Brouwer's fixed-point theorem (Theorem A1.11) to conclude that f has a fixed point, $\hat{m}$.

Step 3: Because $f(\hat{m}) = \hat{m}$, we have $f_{ij}(\hat{m}) = \hat{m}_{ij}$ for all players i and pure strategies j. Consequently, by the definition of f_{ij},

$$\hat{m}_{ij} = \frac{\hat{m}_{ij} + \max(0, u_i(j, \hat{m}_{-i}) - u_i(\hat{m}))}{1 + \sum_{j'=1}^{n} \max(0, u_i(j', \hat{m}_{-i}) - u_i(\hat{m}))}$$

or

$$\hat{m}_{ij} \sum_{j'=1}^{n} \max(0, u_i(j', \hat{m}_{-i}) - u_i(\hat{m})) = \max(0, u_i(j, \hat{m}_{-i}) - u_i(\hat{m})).$$

Multiplying both sides of this equation by $u_i(j, \hat{m}_{-i}) - u_i(\hat{m})$ and summing over j gives:

$$\begin{aligned} &\sum_{j=1}^{n} \hat{m}_{ij}[u_i(j, \hat{m}_{-i}) - u_i(\hat{m})] \sum_{j'=1}^{n} \max(0, u_i(j', \hat{m}_{-i}) - u_i(\hat{m})) \\ &\quad = \sum_{j=1}^{n} [u_i(j, \hat{m}_{-i}) - u_i(\hat{m})] \max(0, u_i(j, \hat{m}_{-i}) - u_i(\hat{m})). \end{aligned} \tag{P.1}$$

Now, a close look at the left-hand side reveals that it is zero, because

$$\begin{aligned} \sum_{j=1}^{n} \hat{m}_{ij}[u_i(j, \hat{m}_{-i}) - u_i(\hat{m})] &= \sum_{j=1}^{n} \hat{m}_{ij} u_i(j, \hat{m}_{-i}) - u_i(\hat{m}) \\ &= u_i(\hat{m}) - u_i(\hat{m}) \\ &= 0, \end{aligned}$$

where the first equality follows because the m_{ij}'s sum to one over j. Consequently, (P.1) may be rewritten

$$0 = \sum_{j=1}^{n} [u_i(j, \hat{m}_{-i}) - u_i(\hat{m})] \max(0, u_i(j, \hat{m}_{-i}) - u_i(\hat{m})).$$

But the sum on the right-hand side can be zero only if $u_i(j, \hat{m}_{-i}) - u_i(\hat{m}) \leq 0$ for every j. (If $u_i(j, \hat{m}_{-i}) - u_i(\hat{m}) > 0$ for some j, then the jth term in the sum is strictly positive. Because no term in the sum is negative, this would render the entire sum strictly positive.) Hence, by part (c) of Theorem 7.1, $\hat{m}$ is a Nash equilibrium. ∎

Theorem 7.2 is quite remarkable. It says that no matter how many players are involved, as long as each possesses finitely many pure strategies there will be at least one Nash equilibrium. From a practical point of view, this means that the search for a Nash equilibrium will not be futile. More importantly, however, the theorem establishes that the notion of a Nash equilibrium is coherent in a deep way. If Nash equilibria rarely existed, this would indicate a fundamental inconsistency within the definition. That Nash equilibria *always* exist in finite games is one measure of the soundness of the idea.

7.2.3 INCOMPLETE INFORMATION

Although a large variety of situations can be modelled as strategic form games, our analysis of these games so far seems to be subject to a rather important limitation. Until now, when we have considered iterative strict or weak dominance, or Nash equilibrium as our method of solving a game, we have always assumed that every player is perfectly informed of the payoffs of all other players. Otherwise, the players could not have carried out the calculations necessary for deriving their optimal strategies.

But many real-life situations involve substantial doses of incomplete information about the opponents' payoffs. Consider, for instance, two firms competing for profits in the same market. It is very likely that one or both of them is imperfectly informed about the other's costs of production. How are we to analyse such a situation? The idea is to add to it one more ingredient so that it becomes a strategic form game. We will then be able to apply any of the various solution methods that we have developed so far. These ideas were pioneered in Harsanyi (1967–1968).

The additional ingredient is a specification of each firm's beliefs about the other firm's cost. For example, we might specify that firm 1 believes that it is equally likely that firm 2 is a high- or low-cost firm. Moreover, we might wish to capture the idea that the costs of the two firms are correlated. For example, when firm 1's cost is low it may be more likely that firm 2's cost is also low. Hence, we might specify that when firm 1's cost is low he believes that 2's cost is twice as likely to be low as high and that when firm 1's cost is high he believes that 2's cost is twice as likely to be high as low. Before getting too far ahead, it is worthwhile to formalise some of our thoughts up to now.

Consider the following class of strategic situations in which information is incomplete. As usual, there are finitely many players $i = 1, \ldots, N$, and a pure strategy set, S_i, for each of them. In addition, however, there may be uncertainty regarding the payoffs of some of them. To capture this, we introduce for each player i a finite set, T_i, of possible 'types' that player might be. We allow a player's payoff to depend as usual on the chosen joint pure strategy, but also on his own type as well as on the types of the others. That is, player i's payoff function u_i maps $S \times T$ into $\mathbb{R}$, where $T = \times_{i=1}^{N} T_i$, and S is the set of joint pure strategies. Therefore, $u_i(s, t)$ is player i's von Neumann-Morgenstern utility when the joint pure strategy is s and the joint type-vector is t. Allowing player i's payoff to depend on another player's type allows us to analyse situations where information possessed by one player affects the payoff of another. For example, in the auctioning of offshore oil tracts, a bidder's payoff as well as his optimal bid will depend upon the likelihood that the tract contains oil, something about which other bidders may have information.

Finally, we introduce the extra ingredient that allows us to use the solutions we have developed in previous sections. The extra ingredient is a specification, for each player i and each of his types t_i, of the beliefs he holds about the types that the others might be. Formally, for each player i and each type $t_i \in T_i$, let $p_i(t_{-i}|t_i)$ denote the probability player i assigns to the event that the others' types are $t_{-i} \in T_{-i}$ when his type is t_i. Being a probability, we require each $p_i(t_{-i}|t_i)$ to be in $[0, 1]$, and we also require $\sum_{t_{-i}\in T_{-i}} p_i(t_{-i}|t_i) = 1$.

It is often useful to specify the players' beliefs so that they are in some sense consistent with one another. For example, one may wish to insist that two players would agree about which types of a third player have positive probability. A standard way to achieve this sort of consistency and more is to suppose that the players' beliefs are generated from a single probability distribution p over the joint type space T. Specifically, suppose that for each $t \in T$, $p(t) > 0$ and $\sum_{t\in T} p(t) = 1$. If we think of the players' joint type-vector $t \in T$ as being chosen by Nature according to p, then according to Bayes' rule (see also section 7.3.7.), player i's beliefs about the others' types when his type is t_i can be computed from p as follows:

$$p_i(t_{-i}|t_i) = p(t_i, t_{-i}) \Big/ \sum_{t'_{-i}\in T_{-i}} p(t_i, t'_{-i}).$$

If all the p_i can all be computed from p according to this formula, we say that p is a **common prior**.

The assumption that there is a common prior can be understood in at least two ways. The first is that p is simply an objective empirical distribution over the players' types, one that has been borne out through many past observations. The second is that the common prior assumption reflects the idea that differences in beliefs arise only from differences in information. Consequently, before the players are aware of their own types – and are therefore in an informationally symmetric position – each player's beliefs about the vector of player types must be identical, and equal to p.

Our ability to analyse a situation with incomplete information will not require the common prior assumption. We therefore shall not insist that the players' beliefs, the p_i, be generated from a common prior. Thus, we permit situations in which, for example, some type of player 1 assigns probability zero to a type of player 3 that is always assigned positive probability by player 2 regardless of his type. (Exercise 7.20 asks you to show that this situation is impossible with a common prior.)

Before we describe how to analyse a situation with incomplete information, we place all of these elements together.

DEFINITION 7.10 ***Game of Incomplete Information (Bayesian Game)***

A game of incomplete information is a tuple $G = (p_i, T_i, S_i, u_i)_{i=1}^N$*, where for each player* $i = 1, \ldots, N$*, the set* T_i *is finite,* $u_i\colon S \times T \to \mathbb{R}$*, and for each* $t_i \in T_i$*,* $p_i(\cdot|t_i)$ *is a probability distribution on* T_{-i}*. If in addition, for each player i, the strategy set* S_i *is finite, then G is called a finite game of incomplete information. A game of incomplete information is also called a Bayesian game.*

The question remains: how can we apply our previously developed solutions to incomplete information games? The answer is to associate with the incomplete information game G a strategic form game G^* in which each type of every player in the game of incomplete information is treated as a *separate player*. We can then apply all of our results for strategic form games to G^*. Of course, we must convince you that G^* captures all the relevant aspects of the incomplete information situation we started with. We will do all of this one step at a time. For now, let us start with an example.

EXAMPLE 7.2 Two firms are engaged in Bertrand price competition as in Chapter 4, except that one of them is uncertain about the other's constant marginal cost. Firm 1's marginal cost of production is known, and firm 2's is either high or low, with each possibility being equally likely. There are no fixed costs. Thus, firm 1 has but one type, and firm 2 has two types – high cost and low cost. The two firms each have the same strategy set, namely the set of non-negative prices. Firm 2's payoff depends on his type, but firm 1's payoff is independent of firm 2's type; it depends only on the chosen prices.

To derive from this game of incomplete information a strategic form game, imagine that there are actually *three* firms rather than two, namely, firm 1, firm 2 with high cost, and firm 2 with low cost. Imagine also that *each* of the three firms must simultaneously choose a price and that firm 1 believes that each of the firm 2's is equally likely to be his only competitor. Some thought will convince you that this way of looking at things beautifully captures all the relevant strategic features of the original situation. In particular, firm 1 must choose its price without knowing whether its competitor has high or low costs. Moreover, firm 1 understands that the competitor's price may differ according to its costs. □

In general then, we wish to associate with each game of incomplete information $G = (p_i, T_i, S_i, u_i)_{i=1}^N$, a strategic form game G^* in which each type of each player is itself a separate player. This is done as follows.

For each $i \in \{1, \ldots, N\}$ and each $t_i \in T_i$, let t_i be a player in G^* whose finite set of pure strategies is S_i.[2] Thus, $T_1 \cup \cdots \cup T_N$ is the finite set of players in G^*, and $S^* = S_1^{T_1} \times \cdots \times S_N^{T_N}$ is the set of joint pure strategies. It remains only to define the players' payoffs.

[2] We assume here that the type sets $T_1, \ldots, T_n$ are mutually disjoint. This is without loss of generality since the type sets, being finite, can always be defined to be subsets of integers and we can always choose these integers so that $t_i < t_j$ if $i < j$. Hence, there is no ambiguity in identifying a player in G^* by his type alone.

Let $s_i(t_i) \in S_i$ denote the pure strategy chosen by player $t_i \in T_i$. Given a joint pure strategy $s^* = (s_1(t_1), \ldots, s_N(t_N))_{t_1 \in T_1, \ldots, t_N \in T_N} \in S^*$, the payoff to player t_i is defined to be,

$$v_{t_i}(s^*) = \sum_{t_{-i} \in T_{-i}} p_i(t_{-i}|t_i) u_i(s_1(t_1), \ldots, s_N(t_N), t_1, \ldots, t_N).$$

Having defined finite sets of players, their finite pure strategy sets, and their payoffs for any joint pure strategy, this completes the definition of the strategic form game G^*.[3]

DEFINITION 7.11 ***The Associated Strategic Form Game***

Let $G = (p_i, T_i, S_i, u_i)_{i=1}^N$ be a game of incomplete information. The game G^* defined above is the strategic form game associated with the incomplete information game G.

Let us take a moment to understand why G^* captures the essence of the incomplete information situation we started with. The simplest way to see this is to understand player i's payoff formula. When pure strategies are chosen in G^* and player i's type is t_i, player i's payoff formula, namely,

$$\sum_{t_{-i} \in T_{-i}} p_i(t_{-i}|t_i) u_i(s_1(t_1), \ldots, s_N(t_N), t_1, \ldots, t_N)$$

captures the idea that player i is uncertain of the other players' types – i.e., he uses $p_i(t_{-i}|t_i)$ to assess their probability – and also captures the idea that the other players' behaviour may depend upon their types – i.e., for each j, the choice $s_j(t_j) \in S_j$ depends upon t_j.

By associating with each game of incomplete information G the well-chosen strategic form game, G^*, we have reduced the study of games of incomplete information to the study of games with complete information, that is, to the study of strategic form games. Consequently, we may apply any of the solutions that we have developed to G^*. It is particularly useful to consider the set of Nash equilibria of G^* and so we give this a separate definition.

DEFINITION 7.12 ***Bayesian-Nash Equilibrium***

A Bayesian-Nash equilibrium of a game of incomplete information is a Nash equilibrium of the associated strategic form game.

With the tools we have developed up to now, it is straightforward to deal with the question of existence of Bayesian-Nash equilibrium.

---

[3]If the type sets T_i are not disjoint subsets of positive integers, then this is 'technically' not a strategic form game in the sense of Definition 7.1, where players are indexed by positive integers. But this minor technical glitch can easily be remedied along the lines of the previous footnote.

THEOREM 7.3 ***Existence of Bayesian-Nash Equilibrium***

Every finite game of incomplete information possesses at least one Bayesian-Nash equilibrium.

Proof: By Definition 7.12, it suffices to show that the associated strategic form game possesses a Nash equilibrium. Because the strategic form game associated with a finite game of incomplete information is itself finite, we may apply Theorem 7.2 to conclude that the associated strategic form game possesses a Nash equilibrium. ∎

EXAMPLE 7.3 To see these ideas at work, let us consider in more detail the two firms discussed in Example 7.2. Suppose that firm 1's marginal cost of production is zero. Also, suppose firm 1 believes that firm 2's marginal cost is either 1 or 4, and that each of these 'types' of firm 2 occur with probability $1/2$. If the lowest price charged is p, then market demand is $8 - p$. To keep things simple, suppose that each firm can choose only one of three prices, 1, 4, or 6. The payoffs to the firms are described in Fig. 7.7. Firm 1's payoff is always the first number in any pair, and firm 2's payoff when his costs are low (high) are given by the second number in the entries of the matrix on the left (right).

In keeping with the Bertrand-competition nature of the problem, we have instituted the following convention in determining payoffs when the firms choose the same price. If both firms' costs are strictly less than the common price, then the market is split evenly between them. Otherwise, firm 1 captures the entire market at the common price. The latter uneven split reflects the idea that if the common price is above only firm 1's cost, firm 1 could capture the entire market by lowering his price slightly (which, if we let him, he could do and still more than cover his costs), whereas firm 2 would not lower his price (even if we let him) because this would result in losses.

We have now described the game of incomplete information. The associated strategic form game is one in which there are three players: firm 1, firm $2l$ (low cost), and firm $2h$ (high cost). Each has the same pure strategy set, namely, the set of prices $\{1, 4, 6\}$. Let p_1, p_l, p_h denote the price chosen by firms 1, $2l$, and $2h$, respectively.

Fig. 7.8 depicts this strategic form game. As there are three players, firm 1's choice of price determines the matrix, and firms $2l$ and $2h$'s prices determine the row and column, respectively, of the chosen matrix. For example, according to Fig. 7.8, if firm 1

	$p_l = 6$	$p_l = 4$	$p_l = 1$
$p_1 = 6$	6, 5	0, 12	0, 0
$p_1 = 4$	16, 0	8, 6	0, 0
$p_1 = 1$	7, 0	7, 0	7, 0

	$p_h = 6$	$p_h = 4$	$p_h = 1$
$p_1 = 6$	6, 2	0, 0	0, −21
$p_1 = 4$	16, 0	16, 0	0, −21
$p_1 = 1$	7, 0	7, 0	7, 0

Figure 7.7. A Bertrand-competition incomplete information game.

Firm 1 chooses $p_1 = 6$

	$p_h = 6$	$p_h = 4$	$p_h = 1$
$p_l = 6$	6, 5, 2	3, 5, 0	3, 5, −21
$p_l = 4$	3, 12, 2	0, 12, 0	0, 12, −21
$p_l = 1$	3, 0, 2	0, 0, 0	0, 0, −21

Firm 1 chooses $p_1 = 4$

	$p_h = 6$	$p_h = 4$	$p_h = 1$
$p_l = 6$	16, 0, 0	16, 0, 0	8, 0, −21
$p_l = 4$	12, 6, 0	12, 6, 0	4, 6, −21
$p_l = 1$	8, 0, 0	8, 0, 0	0, 0, −21

Firm 1 chooses $p_1 = 1$

	$p_h = 6$	$p_h = 4$	$p_h = 1$
$p_l = 6$	7, 0, 0	7, 0, 0	7, 0, 0
$p_l = 4$	7, 0, 0	7, 0, 0	7, 0, 0
$p_l = 1$	7, 0, 0	7, 0, 0	7, 0, 0

Figure 7.8. The associated strategic form game.

chooses $p_1 = 4$, firm $2l$ $p_l = 4$, and firm $2h$ $p_h = 4$, their payoffs would be 12, 6, and 0, respectively.

According to Definition 7.11, the payoffs in the strategic form game of Fig. 7.8 for firms $2l$ and $2h$ can be obtained by simply reading them off of the matrices from Fig. 7.7. This is because there is only one 'type' of firm 1. For example, according to Fig. 7.7, if the low-cost firm 2 chooses $p_l = 6$, then it receives a payoff of 5 if firm 1 chooses $p_1 = 6$. Note that this is reflected in the associated game of Fig. 7.8, where firm $2l$'s payoff is 5 when it and firm 1 choose a price of 6 regardless of the price chosen by firm $2h$.

The payoffs to firm 1 in the associated strategic form game of Fig. 7.8 are obtained by considering firm 1's beliefs about firm 2's costs. For example, consider the strategy in which firm $2l$ chooses $p_l = 1$, firm $2h$ chooses $p_h = 6$, and firm 1 chooses $p_1 = 4$. Now, if firm 2's costs are low (i.e., if firm 1 competes against firm $2l$), then according to Fig. 7.7, firm 1's payoff is zero. If firm 2's costs are high, then firm 1's payoff is 16. Because firm 1 believes that firm 2's costs are equally likely to be high or low, firm 1's expected payoff is 8. This is precisely firm 1's payoff corresponding to $p_1 = 4, p_l = 1$, and $p_h = 6$ in Fig. 7.8. One can similarly calculate firm 1's associated strategic form game (expected) payoff given in Fig. 7.8 for all other joint strategy combinations.

To discover a Bayesian-Nash equilibrium of the Bertrand-competition incomplete information game, we must look for a Nash equilibrium of the associated strategic form game of Fig. 7.8.

Finding one Nash equilibrium is particularly easy here. Note that firms $2l$ and $2h$ each have a weakly dominant strategy: choosing a price of 4 is weakly dominant for firm $2l$ and choosing a price of 6 is weakly dominant for firm $2h$. But once we eliminate the other strategies for them, firm 1 then has a strictly dominant strategy, namely, to choose a price of 4. To see this, suppose that $p_l = 4$ and $p_h = 6$. Then according to Fig. 7.8, firm 1's payoff is 3 if he chooses $p_1 = 6$, 12 if he chooses $p_1 = 4$, and 7 if he chooses $p_1 = 1$.

Consequently, there is a pure strategy Bayesian-Nash equilibrium in which two of the three firms choose a price of 4 while the third chooses a price of 6. You are invited to explore the existence of other Bayesian-Nash equilibria of this game in an exercise. Note that in contrast to the case of Bertrand competition with complete information, profits are not driven to zero here. Indeed, only the high-cost firm 2 earns zero profits in the equilibrium described here. □

7.3 EXTENSIVE FORM GAMES

So far, we have only considered strategic settings in which the players must choose their strategies simultaneously. We now bring dynamics explicitly into the picture, and consider strategic situations in which players may make choices in sequence.

In the game of 'take-away', there are 21 pennies on a table. You and your opponent alternately remove the pennies from it. The only stipulation is that on each turn, one, two, or three pennies must be removed. It is not possible to pass. The person who removes the last penny loses. What is the optimal way to play take-away, and if both players play optimally, who wins? We eventually will discover the answers to both questions.

Note that in take-away, players make their choices in sequence, with full knowledge of the choices made in the past. Consequently, our strategic form game model – in which players make their choices simultaneously, in ignorance of the others' choices – does not appear to provide an adequate framework for analysing this game.

In many parlour games such as this, players take turns in sequence and are perfectly informed of all previous choices when it is their turn to move. But in other games – parlour games and economic games – a player may not have perfect knowledge of every past move.

Consider, for example, a situation in which a buyer wishes to purchase a used car. The seller has the choice of repairing it or not. After deciding whether to make repairs, the seller chooses the price of the car. Subsequent to both of these decisions, he informs the buyer of the price. However, the buyer has no way of knowing whether the repairs were undertaken.[4]

There is a standard framework within which both sorts of dynamic situations – and many more – can be analysed. It is called an *extensive form game*. Informally, the elements of an extensive form game are (i) the players; (ii) Nature (or chance); (iii) the 'rules' of the game, including the order of play and the information each player has regarding the

[4]This assumes that it is impossible for the used-car salesperson to prove that the car has been repaired. In practice, this is not so far from the truth. Are higher prices a signal that the car was repaired? If so, how might an unscrupulous seller behave? For now, we wish only to observe that in this rather commonplace economic setting, the players move in sequence, yet the second mover (the buyer) is only partially informed of the choices made by the first mover.

previous moves of the others when it is his turn to play; and (iv) the payoffs to the players. Formally, these elements are contained in the following definition.[5]

DEFINITION 7.13 ***Extensive Form Game***

An extensive form game, denoted by Γ, is composed of the following elements:

1. *A finite set of players, N.*
2. *A set of actions, A, which includes all possible actions that might potentially be taken at some point in the game. A need not be finite.*
3. *A set of nodes, or histories, X, where*

   (i) X contains a distinguished element, x_0, called the initial node, or empty history,

   (ii) each $x \in X \backslash \{x_0\}$ takes the form $x = (a_1, a_2, \ldots, a_k)$ for some finitely many actions $a_i \in A$, and

   (iii) if $(a_1, a_2, \ldots, a_k) \in X \backslash \{x_0\}$ for some $k > 1$, then $(a_1, a_2, \ldots, a_{k-1}) \in X \backslash \{x_0\}$.

   A node, or history, is then simply a complete description of the actions that have been taken so far in the game.

   We shall use the terms history and node interchangeably. For future reference, let

   $$A(x) \equiv \{a \in A \mid (x, a) \in X\}$$

   denote the set of actions available to the player whose turn it is to move after the history $x \in X \backslash \{x_0\}$.
4. *A set of actions, $A(x_0) \subseteq A$, and a probability distribution, π, on $A(x_0)$ to describe the role of chance in the game. Chance always moves first, and just once, by randomly selecting an action from $A(x_0)$ using the probability distribution π. Thus, $(a_1, a_2, \ldots, a_k) \in X \backslash \{x_0\}$ implies that $a_i \in A(x_0)$ for $i = 1$ and only $i = 1$.*[6]
5. *A set of end nodes, $E \equiv \{x \in X \mid (x, a) \notin X$ for all $a \in A\}$. Each end node describes one particular complete play of the game from beginning to end.*

[5] The convention to employ sequences of actions to define histories is taken from Osborne and Rubinstein (1994). A classic treatment can be found in von Neumann and Morgenstern (1944).

[6] Allowing chance but one move at the start of the game might appear to be restrictive. It is not. Consider, for example, the board game Monopoly. Suppose that in a typical 2-hour game, the dice are rolled no more than once every 5 seconds. Thus, a conservative upper bound on the number of rolls of the dice is 2000. We could then equally well play Monopoly by having a referee roll dice and secretly choose 2000 numbers between 1 and 12 at the start of the game and then simply reveal these numbers one at a time as needed. In this way, it is without loss of generality that chance can be assumed to move exactly once at the beginning of the game.

6. *A function, $\iota\colon X\backslash(E \cup \{x_0\}) \to N$ that indicates whose turn it is at each decision node in X. For future reference, let*

$$X_i \equiv \{x \in X\backslash(E \cup \{x_0\}) \mid \iota(x) = i\}$$

denote the set of decision nodes belonging to player i.

7. *A partition, $\mathcal{I}$, of the set of decision nodes, $X\backslash(E \cup \{x_0\})$, such that if x and x′ are in the same element of the partition, then (i) $\iota(x) = \iota(x')$, and (ii) $A(x) = A(x')$.*[7] *$\mathcal{I}$ partitions the set of decision nodes into information sets. The information set containing x is denoted by $\mathcal{I}(x)$. When the decision node x is reached in the game, player $\iota(x)$ must take an action after being informed that the history of play is one of the elements of $\mathcal{I}(x)$. Thus, $\mathcal{I}(x)$ describes the information available to player $\iota(x)$ when after history x, it is his turn to move. Conditions (i) and (ii) ensure that player $\iota(x)$ cannot distinguish between histories in $\mathcal{I}(x)$ based on whether or not it is his turn to move or based on the set of available actions, respectively. For future reference, let*

$$\mathcal{I}_i \equiv \{\mathcal{I}(x) \mid \iota(x) = i, \ \textit{some}\ x \in X\backslash(E \cup \{x_0\})\}$$

denote the set of information sets belonging to player i.

8. *For each $i \in N$, a von Neumann-Morgenstern payoff function whose domain is the set of end nodes, $u_i\colon E \to \mathbb{R}$. This describes the payoff to each player for every possible complete play of the game.*

We write $\Gamma =< N, A, X, E, \iota, \pi, \mathcal{I}, (u_i)_{i\in N} >$. If the sets of actions, A, and nodes, X, are finite, then Γ is called a finite extensive form game.

Admittedly, this definition appears pretty complex, but read it over two or three times. You will soon begin to appreciate how remarkably compact it is, especially when you realise that virtually every parlour game ever played – not to mention a plethora of applications in the social sciences – is covered by it! Nevertheless, a few examples will help to crystallise these ideas.

EXAMPLE 7.4 Let us begin with the game of take-away described earlier. There are two players, so $N = \{1, 2\}$. A player can remove up to three coins on a turn, so let r_1, r_2, and r_3 denote the removal of one, two, or three coins, respectively. To formally model the fact that chance plays no role in this game, let $A(x_0) \equiv \{\bar{a}\}$ (i.e., chance has but one move). Thus, the set of actions is $A = \{\bar{a}, r_1, r_2, r_3\}$. A typical element of $X\backslash\{x_0\}$ then looks something like $\bar{x} = (\bar{a}, r_1, r_2, r_1, r_3, r_3)$. This would indicate that up to this point in the game, the numbers of coins removed alternately by the players were 1, 2, 1, 3, and 3, respectively. Consequently, there are 11 coins remaining and it is player 2's turn to move (because player

[7] A *partition* of a set is a collection of disjoint non-empty subsets whose union is the original set. Thus, an *element* of a partition is itself a set.

1 removes the first coin). Thus, $\iota(\bar{x}) = 2$. In addition, because each player is fully informed of all past moves, $\mathcal{I}(x) = \{x\}$ for every $x \in X$. Two examples of end nodes in take-away are $e_1 = (\bar{a}, r_1, r_2, r_1, r_3, r_3, r_3, r_3, r_3, r_2)$, and $e_2 = (\bar{a}, r_3, r_3, r_3, r_3, r_3, r_3, r_2, r_1)$, because each indicates that all 21 coins have been removed. The first indicates a win for player 2 (because player 1 removed the last two coins), and the second indicates a win for player 1. Thus, if a payoff of 1 is assigned to the winner, and -1 to the loser, we have $u_1(e_1) = u_2(e_2) = -1$, and $u_1(e_2) = u_2(e_1) = 1$. □

EXAMPLE 7.5 To take a second example, consider the buyer and seller of the used car. To keep things simple, assume that the seller, when choosing a price, has only two choices: high and low. Again there are two players, so $N = \{S, B\}$, where S denotes seller, and B, buyer. The set of actions that might arise is $A = \{$repair, don't repair, price high, price low, accept, reject$\}$. Because chance plays no role here, rather than give it a single action, we simply eliminate chance from the analysis. A node in this game is, for example, $x =$(repair, price high). At this node x, it is the buyer's turn to move, so that $\iota(x) = B$. Because at this node, the buyer is informed of the price chosen by the seller, but not of the seller's repair decision, $\mathcal{I}(x) = \{$(repair, price high), (don't repair, price high)$\}$. That is, when node x is reached, the buyer is informed only that one of the two histories in $\mathcal{I}(x)$ has occurred; he is not informed of which one, however. □

7.3.1 GAME TREES: A DIAGRAMMATIC REPRESENTATION

It is also possible to represent an extensive form game graphically by way of a 'game tree' diagram. To keep the diagram from getting out of hand, consider a four-coin version of take-away. Fig. 7.9 depicts this simplified game.

The small darkened circles represent the nodes and the lines joining them represent the actions taken. For example, the node labelled x takes the form $x = (\bar{a}, r_1, r_2)$ and denotes the history of play in which player 1 first removed one coin and then player 2 removed two. Consequently, at node x, there is one coin remaining and it is player 1's turn to move. Each decision node is given a player label to signify whose turn it is to move once that node is reached. The initial node is labelled with the letter C, indicating that the game begins with a chance move. Because chance actually plays no role in this game (which is formally indicated by the fact that chance can take but one action), we could have simplified the diagram by eliminating chance altogether. Henceforth we will follow this convention whenever chance plays no role.

Each end node is followed by a vector of payoffs. By convention, the ith entry corresponds to player i's payoff. So, for example, $u_1(e) = -1$ and $u_2(e) = 1$, where e is the end node depicted in Fig. 7.9.

The game tree corresponding to the buyer–seller game is shown in Fig. 7.10, but the payoffs have been left unspecified. The new feature is the presence of the ellipses composed of dashed lines that enclose various nodes. Each of these ellipses represents an **information set**. In the figure, there are two such information sets. By convention, singleton information sets – those containing exactly one node – are not depicted by enclosing the single node in a dashed circle. Rather, a node that is a member of a singleton

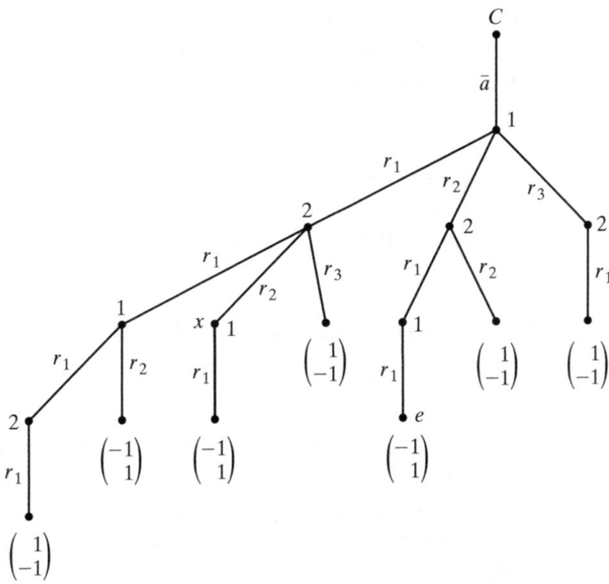

Figure 7.9. An extensive form game tree.

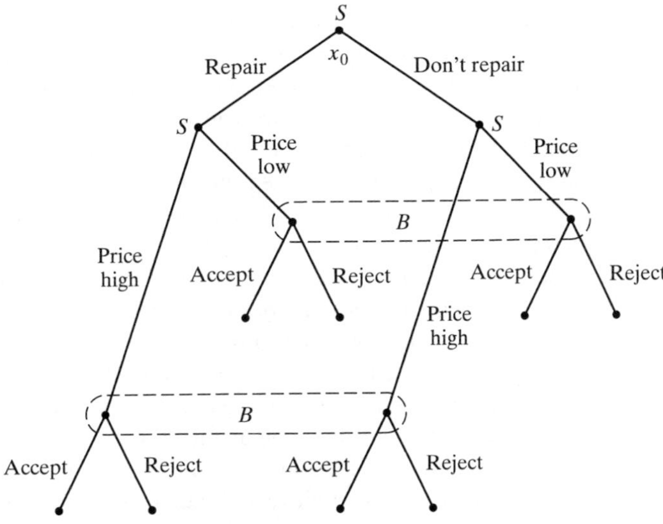

Figure 7.10. Buyer–seller game.

information set is simply left alone.[8] So, for example, the initial node, x_0, and the node (x_0, repair) are each the sole elements of two distinct information sets. Each information set is labelled with the single player whose turn it is to move whenever a node within that information set is reached. In this game, only the buyer has information sets that are not singletons.

Extensive form games in which every information set is a singleton, as in take-away, are called games of *perfect information*. All other games, like the buyer–seller game, are called games with *imperfect information*.

7.3.2 AN INFORMAL ANALYSIS OF TAKE-AWAY

We wish to develop informally two fundamental ideas in the course of analysing the game of take-away. The first is the notion of an extensive form game strategy, and the second is the notion of backward induction. A clear understanding of each of these ideas in this context will go a long way towards ensuring a clear understanding of more complex ideas in the sections that follow.

Our aim in this systematic analysis of take-away is to understand how two 'experts' would play the game. In particular, we seek to discover the 'best' course of action for every possible contingency that might arise. In the language of the extensive form, we wish to determine *an optimal action for each player at each decision node*.

A specification of an action at each decision node of a particular player constitutes what we shall call a (pure) **strategy** for that player. This notion is formally introduced in what follows. For the time being, it suffices to note that a strategy for player 1 in take-away must list a first move; a second move (for player 1) contingent on each potential first move of player 1 and each potential response by player 2, and so on. Consequently, armed with a strategy, a player can consult it whenever it is his turn, and it provides a suggested move given the history of play up to that point in the game. In particular, a player's strategy continues to provide advice even if he (mistakenly or deliberately) deviated from it in the past. For example, consider the following simple strategy for player 1: 'Remove one coin if the number remaining is odd, and two coins if the number remaining is even'. Even if player 1 deviates from this strategy by removing two coins on his first move, the strategy continues to provide advice for the remainder of the game. We now turn to the question of which strategies are sensible for the two players.

You may already have had some time to ponder over how to play well in the game of take-away. Nevertheless, at first blush, with 21 coins on the table, it is not at all clear how many coins the first player should remove. Of course, he must remove one, two, or three. Is one of these choices better than another? It is difficult to provide an immediate answer to this question because there are many moves remaining in the game. Thus, we cannot judge the soundness of the first move without knowing how the game will proceed thereafter.

To simplify matters, consider beginning with a much smaller number of coins. Indeed, if there were but one coin on the table, the player whose turn it is would lose,

[8]Note that the game trees of Fig. 7.9 were drawn with this convention in mind. There, all information sets are singletons.

because he would be forced to remove the last coin. Thus, one coin (remaining on the table) is a losing position. What about two coins? This is a winning position because the player whose turn it is can remove one coin, thereby leaving one coin remaining, which we already know to be a losing position for the other player. Similarly, both three and four coins are winning positions because removing two and three coins, respectively, leaves the opponent in the losing position of one coin. What about five coins? This must be a losing position because removing one, two, or three coins places one's opponent in the winning positions four, three, or two, respectively. Continuing in this manner, from positions nearest the end of the game to positions nearest the beginning, shows that positions 1, 5, 9, 13, 17, 21 are losing positions, and all others are winning positions.

Consequently, if two experts play take-away with 21 coins, the second player can always guarantee a win, *regardless* of how the first one plays. To see this, consider the following strategy for the second player that is suggested by our analysis of winning and losing positions: 'Whenever possible, always remove just enough coins so that the resulting position is one of the losing ones, namely, 1, 5, 9, 13, 17, 21; otherwise, remove one coin'. We leave it to the reader to verify that if the second player has done so on each of his previous turns, he can always render the position a losing one for his opponent. Because his opponent begins in a losing position, this completes the argument.

Note well the technique employed to analyse this game. Rather than start at the beginning of the game with all 21 coins on the table, we began the analysis at the end of the game – with one coin remaining, then two, and so on. This technique lies at the heart of numerous solution concepts for extensive form games. It is called **backward induction**. We shall return to it a little later. But before getting too far ahead of ourselves, we pause to formalise the idea of an extensive form game strategy.

7.3.3 EXTENSIVE FORM GAME STRATEGIES

As mentioned before, a (pure) strategy for a player in an extensive form game is a *complete description* of the choices that a player would make in any contingency that might arise during the course of play; it is a complete set of instructions that could be carried out by someone else on that player's behalf.

DEFINITION 7.14 ***Extensive Form Game Strategy***

Consider an extensive form game Γ as in Definition 7.13. Formally, a pure strategy for player i in Γ is a function $s_i\colon \mathcal{I}_i \to A$, satisfying $s_i(\mathcal{I}(x)) \in A(x)$ for all x with $\iota(x) = i$. Let S_i denote the set of pure strategies for player i in Γ.

Thus, a pure strategy for a player specifies for each of his information sets which action to take among those that are available. The fact that a player's choice of action can depend only on which information set he is currently faced with (as opposed to, say, the histories within the information set), ensures that the strategy properly reflects the informational constraints faced by the player in the game.

A player's pure strategies can be easily depicted in a game tree diagram by placing arrows on the actions that are to be taken when each information set is reached. For

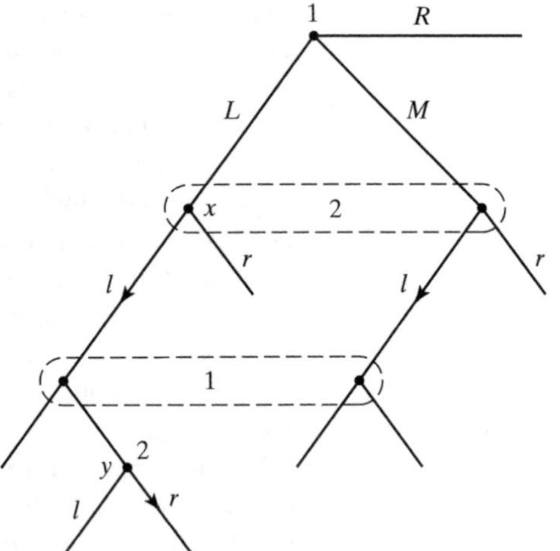

Figure 7.11. An extensive form game strategy.

example, Fig. 7.11 depicts the following pure strategy for player 2: choose l if $\mathcal{I}(x)$ is reached, and choose r if $\mathcal{I}(y)$ is reached.

It is important to note that a pure strategy for a player is indeed a complete description of how to play the game as that player. For example, suppose you are playing the black pieces in chess. A very small part of your pure strategy requires you to specify what move to make after white's first move. It is not enough to specify how you would react to a *single* opening move of white – say, P–K4 – even if you are virtually certain that this will be white's first move. Specifying a pure strategy requires you to say how you would react to *every* possible opening move of white. Indeed, you must specify how you would react to *every possible* (*legal*) *sequence* of moves ending with a move by white. Only then will you have specified a single pure strategy for black in the game of chess. The exercises ask you to formulate pure strategies for the games we have considered so far. You will see there that this alone can be a challenge.

7.3.4 STRATEGIES AND PAYOFFS

According to Definition 7.14, for each player i, S_i denotes that player's set of pure strategies in Γ. We shall assume that Γ is a finite game. Consequently, each of the sets S_i is also finite. Note that once a pure strategy has been chosen for each player, each player's actions during the course of play are completely determined save for the way they may be affected by chance moves. Thus, once chance's move is determined, the outcome of the game is completely determined by the players' pure strategies.

To see this, suppose that a_0 is chance's move. This determines the history $x_1 = a_0$, and the information set $\mathcal{I}(x_1)$ belonging to player $\iota(x_1) = 1$, say. Given player 1's strategy, s_1, player 1 takes the action $a_1 = s_1(\mathcal{I}(x_1))$, determining the history $x_2 = (x_1, a_1)$, and the information set $\mathcal{I}(x_2)$ belonging to player $\iota(x_2) = 2$, say. Given player 2's strategy, s_2, player 2 then takes the action $a_2 = s_2(\mathcal{I}(x_2))$, determining the history $x_3 = (x_2, a_2)$, and so on. We may continue this process until we inevitably (because the game is finite) reach an end node, e, say, yielding payoff $u_i(e)$ for each player $i \in N$. Consequently, given any joint pure strategy $s \in \times_{i \in N} S_i$, Nature's probability distribution π on $A(x_0)$ determines player i's expected utility, which we will denote by $u_i(s)$.

Note that the tuple $(S_i, u_i)_{i \in N}$ is then a strategic form game. It is called the **strategic form of Γ**, and we will refer back to it a little later.[9] For the moment, it suffices to note that therefore we can apply all of our strategic form game solution concepts to finite extensive form games. For example, a dominant strategy in the extensive form game Γ is simply a strategy that is dominant in the strategic form of Γ; a Nash equilibrium for the extensive form game Γ is simply a joint strategy that is a Nash equilibrium of the strategic form of Γ, and so on.

7.3.5 GAMES OF PERFECT INFORMATION AND BACKWARD INDUCTION STRATEGIES

An important subclass of extensive form games consists of those in which players are perfectly informed of all previous actions taken whenever it is their turn to move – i.e., those in which $\mathcal{I}(x) = \{x\}$ for all decision nodes x. These games are called **games of perfect information**.

Take-away is a game of perfect information as are chess, draughts, noughts and crosses, and many other parlour games. As an example of a simple perfect information game from economics, consider the following situation. There are two firms competing in a single industry. One is currently producing (the incumbent), and the other is not (the entrant). The entrant must decide whether to enter the industry or to stay out. If the entrant stays out, the status quo prevails and the game ends. If the entrant enters, the incumbent must decide whether to *fight* by flooding the market and driving the price down or to *acquiesce* by not doing so. In the status quo, the incumbent's payoff is 2, and the entrant's is 0. If the entrant enters the payoff to each firm is -1 if the incumbent fights, and it is 1 if the incumbent acquiesces. The game tree depicting this entry game is given in Fig. 7.12.

Clearly, the incumbent would like to keep the entrant out to continue enjoying his monopoly profits of 2. Will the entrant in fact stay out? This obviously depends on how the incumbent reacts to entry. If the incumbent reacts by fighting, then entering will lead to a payoff of -1 for the entrant and the entrant is better off staying out. On the other hand, if the incumbent acquiesces on entry, then the entrant should enter. Thus, it boils down to how the incumbent will react to entry.[10]

---

[9]Note that we have transformed an arbitrary finite extensive form game (which may well reflect a very complex, dynamic strategic situation) into a strategic form game. Thus, our earlier impression that strategic form games were only useful for modelling situations in which there are no explicit dynamics was rather naive. Indeed, based on our ability to construct the strategic form of any extensive form game, one might argue just the opposite; that from a theoretical point of view, it suffices to consider only strategic form games, because all extensive form games can be reduced to them! Whether or not the strategic form of an extensive form game is sufficient for carrying out an analysis of it is a current topic of research among game theorists. We will not develop this theme further here.

[10]Note the similarity here with our investigation of the solution to take-away. Here as there, one cannot assess the soundness of moves early in the game without first analysing how play will proceed later in the game.

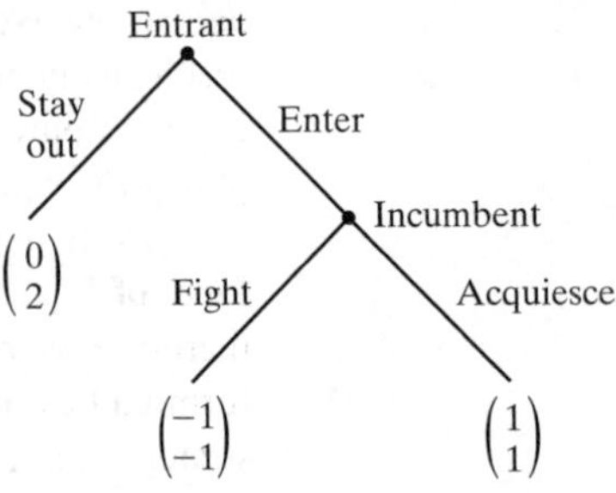

Figure 7.12. The entrant–incumbent game.

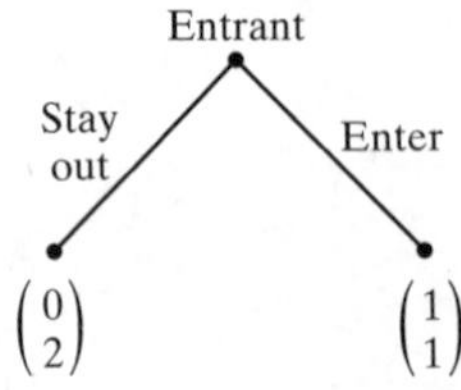

Figure 7.13. The reduced entrant–incumbent game.

So let us simply assume that the entrant has entered. What is best for the incumbent at this point in the game? Obviously, it is best for him to acquiesce because by doing so he receives a payoff of 1 rather than -1. Consequently, from the entrant's point of view, the game reduces to that given in Fig. 7.13, where we have simply replaced the incumbent's decision node and what follows with the payoff vector that will result once his decision node is reached. Clearly, the entrant will choose to enter because this yields a payoff of 1 rather than 0. Thus, once again we have arrived at a pair of strategies for the players by solving the game backwards. The strategies are the entrant enters and the incumbent acquiesces on entry.

Let us try this backward induction technique to solve the slightly more complex game of perfect information depicted in Fig. 7.14. We begin by analysing decision nodes preceding only end nodes. There are two such penultimate nodes and they are labelled x and y. Both belong to player 1. At x, player 1 does best to choose R', and at y he does best to choose L''. Consequently, the game of Fig. 7.14 can be reduced to that of Fig. 7.15, where the decision nodes x and y, and what follows, have been replaced by the payoffs that are now seen to be inevitable once x and y are reached. We now repeat this process on the reduced game. Here both w and z are penultimate decision nodes (this time belonging to player 2). If w is reached, player 2 does best by choosing r, and if z is reached, player 2 does best by choosing l'. Using these results to reduce the game yet again results in Fig. 7.16, where it is clear that player 1 will choose R. We conclude from this analysis that player 1 will choose the strategy (R, R', L'') and player 2 the strategy (r, l').[11] The outcome of employing these two strategies is that each player will receive a payoff of zero.

[11]The notation (R, R', L'') means that player 1 will choose R on his first move, R' if decision node x is reached, and L'' if decision node y is reached. Player 2's strategy (r, l') has a similar meaning.

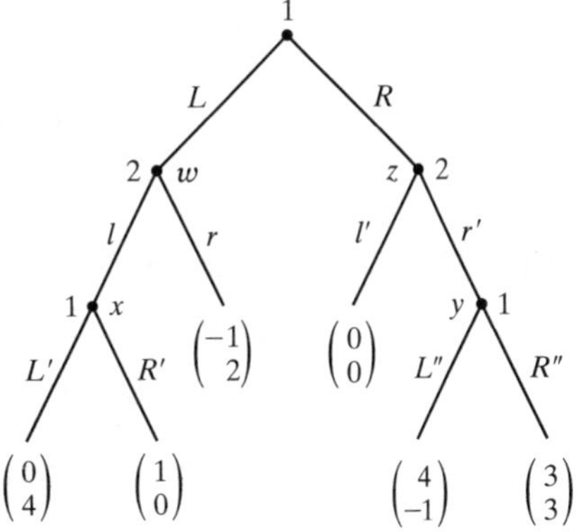

Figure 7.14. A backward induction exercise.

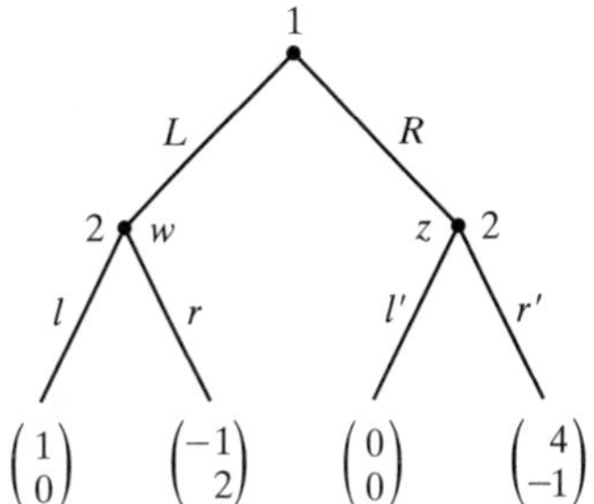

Figure 7.15. Applying backward induction reduces the game.

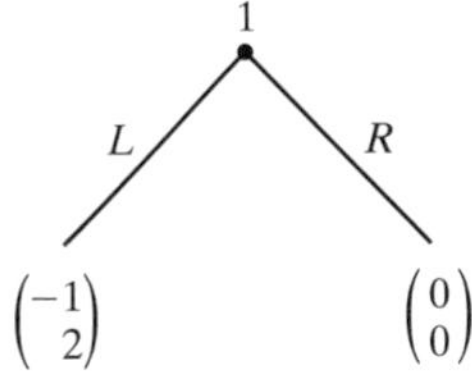

Figure 7.16. The final backward induction step.

It may seem a little odd that the solution to this game yields each player a payoff of zero when it is possible for each to derive a payoff of 3 by playing 'right' whenever possible. However, it would surely be a mistake for player 2 to play r' if node z is reached because player 1 will rationally choose L'' at y, not R'', because the former gives player 1 a higher payoff. Thus, player 2, correctly anticipating this, does best to choose l', for this yields player 2 a payoff zero, which surpasses the alternative of -1.[12]

[12]One might argue that the players ought to enter into a binding agreement to ensure the payoff vector (3, 3). However, by definition, the extensive form game includes all the possible actions that are available to the players. Consequently, if it is possible for the players to enter into binding agreements, this ought to be included in the extensive form game to begin with. Because in the game depicted these are not present, they are simply not available.

The preceding procedure can be used to obtain strategies in every game of perfect information. Such strategies are called **backward induction strategies**. To prepare for the definition, let us say that y **strictly follows** x if $y = (x, a_1, \ldots, a_k)$ for some $a_1, \ldots, a_k \in A$ and that y **immediately follows** x if $k = 1$. We say that y **weakly follows** x if $y = x$ or y strictly follows x.

DEFINITION 7.15 ***Backward Induction Strategies***

The joint (pure) strategy s is a backward induction strategy for the finite extensive form game Γ of perfect information if it is derived as follows. Call a node, x, penultimate in Γ if all nodes immediately following it are end nodes. For every penultimate node x, let $s_{\iota(x)}(x)$ be an action leading to an end node that maximises player $\iota(x)$'s payoff from among the actions available at x. Let u_x denote the resulting payoff vector. Remove the nodes and actions strictly following each penultimate node x in Γ and assign the payoff u_x to x, which then becomes an end node in Γ. Repeat this process until an action has been assigned to every decision node.[13] *This then yields a (backward induction) joint pure strategy s.*

The method for constructing a backward induction strategy given in Definition 7.15 is called the **backward induction algorithm**. Reflected in backward induction strategies is the idea that decisions made early in the game ought to take into account the *optimal* play of future players. We shall expand on this idea in the next section. Our discussion of backward induction is brought to a close by relating the backward induction strategies to the notion of a Nash equilibrium.

THEOREM 7.4 ***(Kuhn) Backward Induction and Nash Equilibrium***

If s is a backward induction strategy for the perfect information finite extensive form game Γ, then s is a Nash equilibrium of Γ.

Proof: Because a Nash equilibrium of Γ is simply a Nash equilibrium of its strategic form $(S_i, u_i)_{i\in N}$, it suffices to show that $u_i(s) \geq u_i(s'_i, s_{-i})$ for every player i and every $s'_i \in S_i$.

So, suppose that this is not the case. Then $u_i(s'_i, s_{-i}) > u_i(s)$ for some i and $s'_i \in S_i$. Consequently, there must be an action, a_1, taken by Nature, such that the end nodes e and e' induced respectively by s and $s' = (s'_i, s_{-i})$ given that action, satisfy $u_i(e') > u_i(e)$.

Therefore, the set of decision nodes x, where, were the game to begin there, player i could do better by using a strategy different from s_i, is non-empty because $x = a_1$ is a member of this set. Let $\bar{x}$ be a member of this set having no strict followers in the set.[14]

Thus, when the game begins at $\bar{x}$ and the other players employ s_{-i} thereafter, player i's payoff is strictly higher if he employs some strategy s''_i rather than s_i. Furthermore, because $\bar{x}$ has no strict followers among the set from which it was chosen, (1) $\bar{x}$ belongs to player i, and (2) all actions dictated by s_i at nodes belonging to i strictly following $\bar{x}$ cannot be improved upon.

---

[13]The finiteness of the game ensures that this process terminates.

[14]Such a node $\bar{x}$ exists (although it need not be unique) because the set of nodes from which it is chosen is finite and non-empty (see the exercises).

We may conclude, therefore, that when the game begins at $\bar{x}$ and the others employ s_{-i} thereafter, i's payoff if he takes the action at $\bar{x}$ specified by s_i'', but subsequently employs s_i, exceeds that when i employs s_i beginning at $\bar{x}$ as well as subsequently. But the latter payoff is i's backward induction payoff when the backward induction algorithm reaches node $\bar{x}$, and therefore must be the largest payoff that i can obtain from the actions available at $\bar{x}$ given that s (the backward induction strategies) will be employed thereafter. This contradiction completes the proof. ∎

Thus, every backward induction joint strategy tuple constitutes a Nash equilibrium. Because the backward induction algorithm always terminates in finite games with perfect information, we have actually established the following.

COROLLARY 7.1 ***Existence of Pure Strategy Nash Equilibrium***

Every finite extensive form game of perfect information possesses a pure strategy Nash equilibrium.

Although every backward induction strategy is a Nash equilibrium, not every Nash equilibrium is a backward induction strategy. To see this, note that although the unique backward induction strategy in the entrant–incumbent game of Fig. 7.12 involves the entrant entering and the incumbent acquiescing on entry, the following strategies also constitute a Nash equilibrium of the game: the entrant stays out, and the incumbent fights if the entrant enters. Note that *given* the strategy of the other player, neither player can increase his payoff by changing his strategy. Thus, the strategies do indeed form a Nash equilibrium.

However, this latter Nash equilibrium is nonsensical because it involves a threat to fight on the part of the incumbent that is not credible. The threat lacks credibility because it would not be in the incumbent's interest to actually carry it out if given the opportunity. The entrant ought to see through this and enter. It is precisely this sort of look-ahead capability of the entrant that is automatically embodied in backward induction strategies.

As we shall see, when there are multiple Nash equilibria, one can often eliminate one or more on the grounds that they involve incredible threats such as these.

7.3.6 GAMES OF IMPERFECT INFORMATION AND SUBGAME PERFECT EQUILIBRIUM

The backward induction technique is nicely tailored to apply to games with perfect information. It does not, however, immediately extend to other games. Consider, for example, the game in Fig. 7.17 in which player 1 has the option of playing a coordination game with player 2. Let us try to apply the backward induction technique to it.

As before, the first step is to locate all information sets such that whatever action is chosen at that information set, the game subsequently ends.[15] For the game in Fig. 7.17,

[15] Such information sets necessarily exist in finite games with perfect information. In general, however, this is not guaranteed when the (finite) game is one of imperfect information. You are asked to consider this in an exercise.

Figure 7.17. Coordination game with an option.

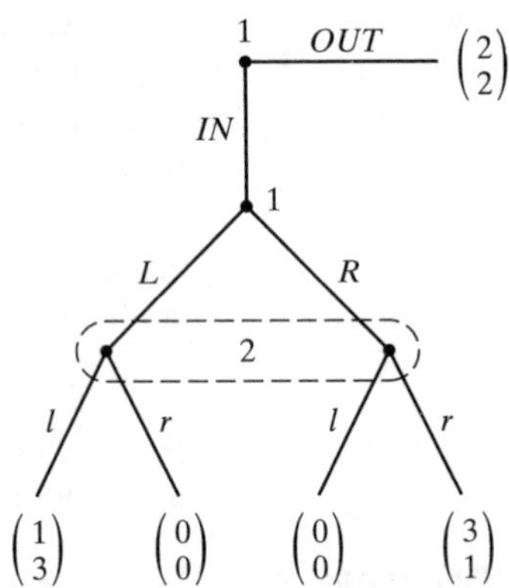

this isolates player 2's information set, i.e., the point in the game reached after player 1 has chosen *IN* and then *L* or *R*.

Note that when it is player 2's turn to play, taking either action *l* or *r* will result in the end of the game. Now, according to the backward induction algorithm, the next step is to choose an optimal action for player 2 there. But now we are in trouble because it is not at all clear which action is optimal for player 2. This is because player 2's best action depends on the action taken by player 1. If player 1 chose *L*, then 2's best action is *l*, whereas if player 1 chose *R*, then 2 should instead choose *r*. There is no immediate way out of this difficulty because, by definition of the information set, player 2 does not know which action player 1 has taken.

Recall the reason for solving the game backwards in the first place. We do so because to determine optimal play early in the game, we first have to understand how play will proceed later in the game. But in the example at hand, the reverse is also true. To determine optimal play later in the game (i.e., at player 2's information set), we must first understand how play proceeds earlier in the game (i.e., did player 1 choose *L* or *R*?). Thus, in this game (and in games of imperfect information quite generally), we must, at least to some extent, *simultaneously* determine optimal play at points both earlier and later in the game.

Let us continue with our analysis of the game of Fig. 7.17. Although we would like to first understand how play will proceed at the 'last' information set, let us give up on this for the preceding reasons, and do the next best thing. Consider moving one step backward in the tree to player 1's second decision node. Can we determine how play will proceed from that point of the game onwards? If so, then we can replace that 'portion' of the game, or subgame, with the resulting payoff vector, just as we did in the backward induction algorithm. But how are we to determine how play will proceed in the subgame beginning at player 1's second information set?

The idea, first developed in Selten (1965, 1975), is to consider the subgame as a game in its own right. (See Fig. 7.18.) Consider now applying the Nash equilibrium solution concept to the game of Fig. 7.18. There are two pure strategy Nash equilibria of this

Figure 7.18. A subgame.

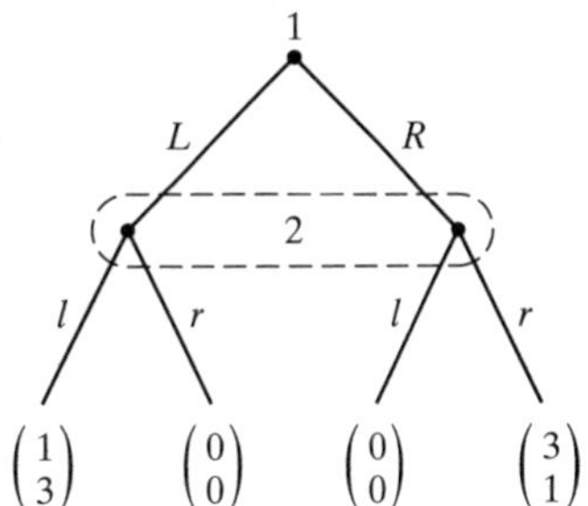

Figure 7.19. (a) Behaviour in the subgame; (b) the reduced game given behaviour in the subgame.

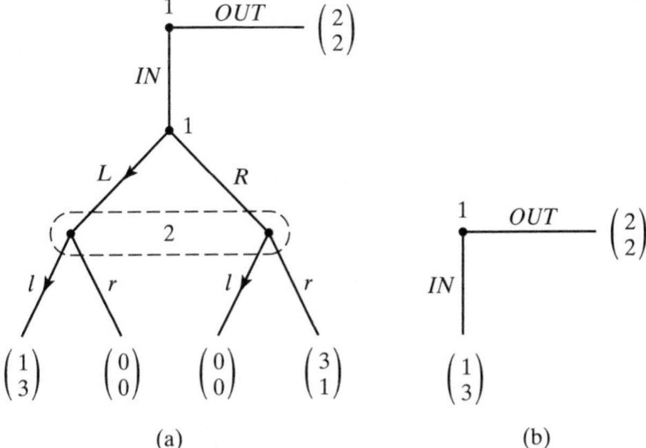

game: (L, l), and (R, r).[16] Let us suppose that when this subgame is reached in the course of playing the original game, one of these Nash equilibria will be played. For concreteness, suppose it is (L, l). Consequently, the resulting payoff vector will be $(1, 3)$ if the subgame is reached. We now can proceed analogously to the backward induction algorithm by replacing the entire subgame by the resulting payoff vector $(1, 3)$. (See Fig. 7.19.) Once done, it is clear that player 1 will choose *OUT* at his first decision node, because given the behaviour in the subgame, player 1 is better off choosing *OUT*, yielding a payoff of 2, than choosing *IN* and ultimately yielding a payoff of 1.

Altogether, the strategies previously derived are as follows. For player 1: *OUT* at his first decision node and L at his second; for player 2: l at his information set.

A couple of similarities with the perfect information case are worth noting. First, these strategies reflect the look-ahead capability of player 1 in the sense that his play at his first decision node is optimal based on the Nash equilibrium play later in the game. Thus, not only is player 1 looking ahead, but he understands that future play will be 'rational'

[16]There is also a mixed-strategy Nash equilibrium, but the discussion will be simplified if we ignore this for the time being.

in the sense that it constitutes a Nash equilibrium in the subgame. Second, these strategies form a Nash equilibrium of the original game.

The strategies we have just derived are called **subgame perfect equilibrium strategies**. As you may recall, there were two pure strategy Nash equilibria in the subgame, and we arbitrarily chose one of them. Had we chosen the other, the resulting strategies would have been quite different. Nonetheless, these resulting strategies, too, are subgame perfect according to the following definition. You are asked to explore this in an exercise.

To give a formal definition of subgame perfect equilibrium strategies, we must first introduce some terminology.

DEFINITION 7.16 ***Subgames***

A node, x, is said to define a subgame of an extensive form game if $\mathcal{I}(x) = \{x\}$ *and whenever y is a decision node following x, and z is in the information set containing y, then z also follows x.*

Thus, if a node x defines a subgame, then every player on every turn knows whether x has been reached. Fig. 7.20(a) shows a node x defining a subgame, and Fig. 7.20(b) shows a node x that does not. In the game depicted in Fig. 7.20(a), every node within player 1's non-singleton information set follows x. In contrast, nodes y and z are both members of player 3's information set in Fig. 7.20(b), yet only y follows x.

The subgame defined by a node such as x in Fig. 7.20(a) is denoted by Γ_x. Γ_x consists of all nodes following x, and it inherits its information structure and payoffs from the original game Γ. Fig. 7.21 depicts the subgame Γ_x derived from the game Γ in Fig. 7.20(a).

Given a joint pure strategy s for Γ, note that s naturally induces a joint pure strategy in every subgame Γ_x of Γ. That is, for every information set I in Γ_x, the induced pure strategy takes the same action at I that is specified by s at I.

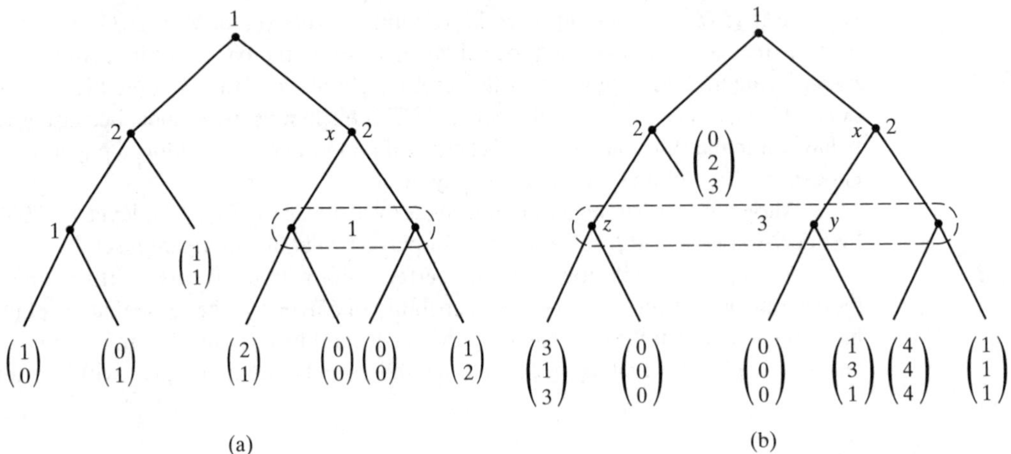

Figure 7.20. (a) Node x defines a subgame; (b) node x does not define a subgame.

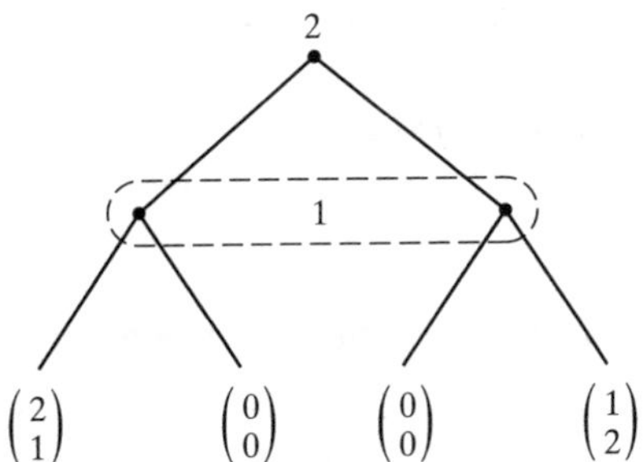

Figure 7.21. The subgame Γ_x from Γ in Fig. 7.20(a).

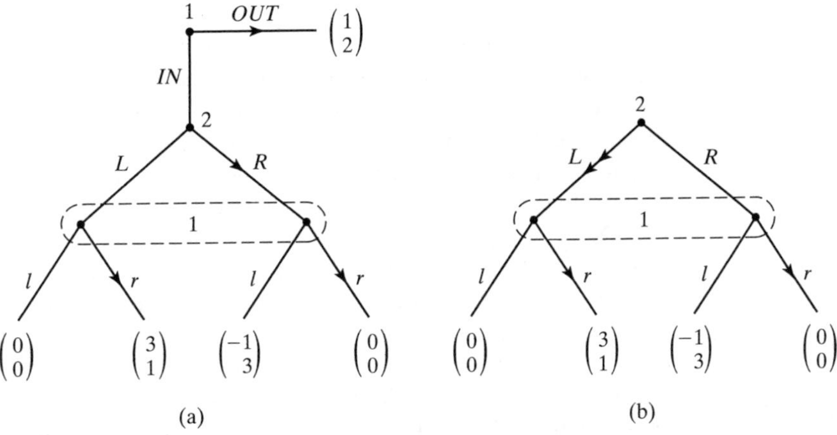

Figure 7.22. (a) A Nash, but not subgame perfect, equilibrium; (b) player 2's best response in the subgame.

DEFINITION 7.17 ***Pure Strategy Subgame Perfect Equilibrium***

A joint pure strategy s is a pure strategy subgame perfect equilibrium of the extensive form game Γ if s induces a Nash equilibrium in every subgame of Γ.

Note that because for any extensive form game Γ, the game itself is a subgame, a pure strategy subgame perfect equilibrium of Γ is also a pure strategy Nash equilibrium of Γ. Consequently, the subgame perfect equilibrium concept is a *refinement* of the Nash equilibrium concept. Indeed, this refinement is strict, as the example shown in Fig. 7.22 demonstrates.

The pure strategy depicted by the arrows in Fig. 7.22(a) is a Nash equilibrium because neither player can improve his payoff by switching strategies given the strategy of the other player. However, it is not subgame perfect. To see this, note that the strategies induced in the subgame beginning at player 2's node do not constitute a Nash equilibrium of the subgame. This is shown in Fig. 7.22(b) where the subgame has been isolated and the double arrow indicates a deviation that strictly improves player 2's payoff in the subgame.[17]

The next theorem shows that subgame perfection, which is applicable to all extensive form games, is a generalisation of backward induction, which applies only to perfect information games.

THEOREM 7.5 ***Subgame Perfect Equilibrium Generalises Backward Induction***

For every finite extensive form game of perfect information, the set of backward induction strategies coincides with the set of pure strategy subgame perfect equilibria.

Proof: We first argue that every backward induction strategy is subgame perfect. So let s denote a backward induction strategy. Because in a game with perfect information every node defines a subgame (see the exercises), we must argue that s induces a Nash equilibrium in the subgame defined by x for all x. But for each x, Γ_x, the subgame defined by x, is of course a perfect information game, and the strategy induced by s is clearly a backward induction strategy for the subgame. (To see this, think about how the backward induction strategy s is constructed, and then think about how backward induction strategies for the subgame would be constructed.) Consequently, we may apply Theorem 7.4 and conclude that the strategies induced by s form a Nash equilibrium of Γ_x.

Next we argue that every pure strategy subgame perfect equilibrium is a backward induction strategy. Let s be subgame perfect. It suffices to verify that s can be derived through the backward induction algorithm. Consider then any penultimate decision node. This node defines a one-player subgame, and because s is subgame perfect, it must assign a payoff-maximising choice for the player whose turn it is to move there (otherwise, it would not be a Nash equilibrium of the one-player subgame). Consequently, the action specified by s there is consistent with the backward induction algorithm. Consider now any decision node x having only penultimate decision nodes following it. This node defines a subgame in which at all nodes following it, the strategy s specifies a backward induction action. Because s induces a Nash equilibrium in this subgame, it must specify a payoff-maximising choice for player $\iota(x)$ at node x given that the choices to follow are backward induction choices (i.e., the choices induced by s). Consequently, the action specified at any such x is also consistent with the backward induction algorithm. Working our way back through the game tree in this manner establishes the result. ∎

Just as pure strategy Nash equilibria may fail to exist in some strategic form games, pure strategy subgame perfect equilibria need not always exist. Consider, for example, the game depicted in Fig. 7.23. Because the only subgame is the game itself, the set of pure strategy subgame perfect equilibria coincides with the set of pure strategy Nash equilibria

[17]Note that although player 2's payoff can be increased in the subgame, it cannot be increased in the original game. This is because the subgame in question is not reached by the original strategies. Indeed, Nash equilibrium strategies of the original game induce Nash equilibria in all subgames that are reached by the original strategies. Thus, it is precisely subgame perfection's treatment of unreached subgames that accounts for its distinction from Nash equilibrium. See the exercises.

Figure 7.23. A game with no pure strategy subgame perfect equilibrium.

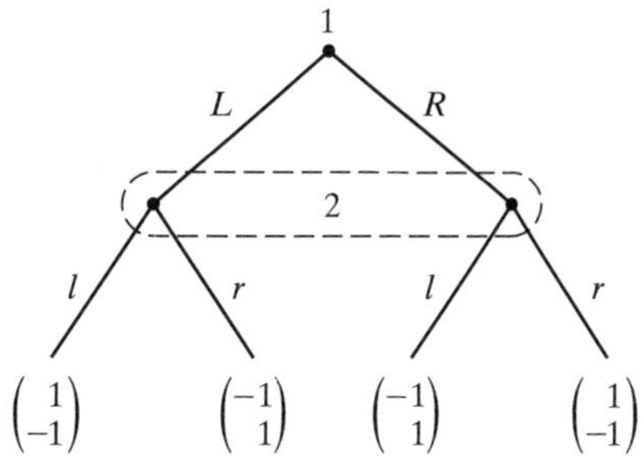

of this game. However, it is easy to verify that among the four possible joint pure strategies none constitutes a Nash equilibrium.

To guarantee the existence of at least one subgame perfect equilibrium, we must allow players the opportunity to randomise. The next section considers randomisation in extensive form games.

Mixed Strategies, Behavioural Strategies, and Perfect Recall

In strategic form games, there is a single natural way to randomise one's behaviour – assign probabilities to each pure strategy and then employ a randomisation device that chooses each strategy with its assigned probability.

In contrast, there are *two* ways one might go about randomising one's behaviour in an extensive form game. The first is a direct analogue of that used in strategic form games. Assign each pure strategy a probability, and before the game starts, employ the appropriate randomisation device to choose one of your pure strategies. With this method, you randomise once and for all at the beginning of the game. Once the pure strategy is chosen, your behaviour is determined by that pure strategy for the entire game; no further randomisation is undertaken.

The second method is to employ a randomisation device *whenever it is your turn to move*. Rather than randomising once and for all at the beginning of the game over your collection of pure strategies, you randomise, on each turn, over your current set of available actions. Thus, if during the course of play, it is your turn to move more than once, then you will employ a randomisation device more than once during the game. You may select a different randomisation device on each turn.

The first type of randomisation is called a *mixed strategy* in keeping with the terminology established for strategic form games. The second is called a *behavioural strategy*.

Formally, a **mixed strategy** m_i for player i is, as before, a probability distribution over player i's set of pure strategies S_i. That is, for each pure strategy $s_i \in S_i$, $m_i(s_i)$ denotes the probability that the pure strategy s_i is chosen. Consequently, we must have $m_i(s_i) \in [0, 1]$ and $\sum_{s_i \in S_i} m_i(s_i) = 1$.

On the other hand, a **behavioural strategy**, b_i, provides for each of player i's information sets a probability distribution over the actions available there. That is, $b_i(a, I) \in$

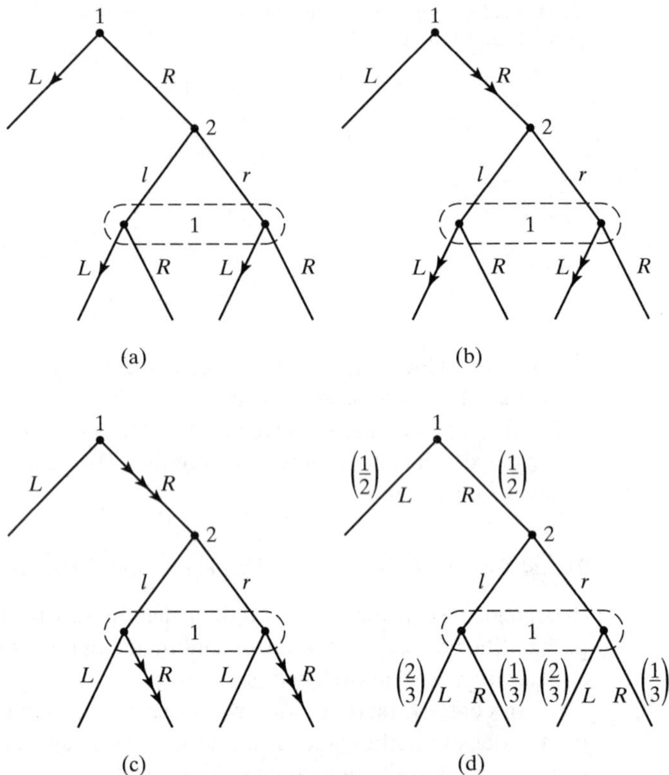

Figure 7.24. Equivalent behavioural strategies. The mixed strategy in which player 1 chooses pure strategy *LL* (part (a) indicated by single arrows) with probability 1/2, pure strategy *RL* (part (b) indicated by double arrows) with probability 1/3, and pure strategy *RR* (part (c) indicated by triple arrows) with probability 1/6 is equivalent to the behavioural strategy indicated in part (d), where the probabilities assigned to actions are given in parentheses.

[0, 1], and $\sum_{a\in A(I)} b_i(a, I) = 1$, for every information set I belonging to player i, where $A(I)$ denotes the set of actions available at the information set I.

In a game tree diagram, we denote a behavioural strategy by specifying beside each action the probability with which it is chosen (in parentheses). For example, Fig. 7.24(d) depicts the behavioural strategy for player 1 in which he chooses L and R with probability $1/2$ each at his first information set, and he chooses L and R with probability $2/3$ and $1/3$, respectively, at his second information set.

Although we will not provide a proof of this, it turns out that for all games that are of concern to us in this text, it makes no difference whatever whether players employ mixed or behavioural strategies. From a strategic point of view, they are entirely equivalent. That is, for each mixed strategy m_i belonging to player i, there is a behavioural strategy yielding player i precisely the same expected payoff as m_i, regardless of the strategies (mixed or behavioural) employed by the other players. Similarly, for each behavioural strategy, there is an equivalent mixed strategy.[18]

EXAMPLE 7.6 Figs. 7.24(a) to 7.24(c) depict three pure strategies for player 1 in the extensive form game there, namely, *LL*, *RL*, and *RR*. Consider the mixed strategy placing probability 1/2, 1/3, and 1/6, respectively, on these pure strategies. What then is this mixed strategy's equivalent behavioural strategy? To find out, we simply calculate the induced probability that each action is taken conditional on the information set at which it is available having been reached. For example, because player 1's first information set is necessarily reached, the induced probability that the action L is chosen there is $1/2$, as is the probability that R is chosen there [see Fig. 7.24(d)]. For player 1's second information set, note that it is reached only by the pure strategies *RL* and *RR*. Consequently, conditional on one of these pure strategies having been chosen, the probability that L is chosen at player 1's second information set is $2/3$, and the probability that R is chosen is $1/3$. Putting this together, Fig. 7.24(d) depicts the equivalent behavioural strategy. □

As mentioned, all games that will concern us in this text have the property that mixed and behavioural strategies are equivalent. This property is shared by all games with *perfect recall*.

DEFINITION 7.18 ***Perfect Recall***

An extensive form game has perfect recall if whenever two nodes x *and* $y = (x, a, a_1, \ldots, a_k)$ *belong to a single player, then every node in the same information set as* y *is of the form* $w = (z, a, a'_1, \ldots, a'_l)$ *for some node* z *in the same information set as* x.

Perfect recall says that each player always remembers what he knew in the past about the history of play. In particular, Definition 7.18 implies that any two histories (i.e., y and w) that a player's information set does not allow him to distinguish between can differ only in the actions taken by *other* players. So, in particular, no player ever forgets an action that he has taken in the past.

Fig. 7.25 depicts an extensive form game without perfect recall. Note that there is no behavioural strategy that is equivalent to the mixed strategy placing probability $1/2$ on

Figure 7.25. A game without perfect recall. Perfect recall fails because x and $y = (x, L)$ both belong to player 1, yet $w = (x, R)$ is in the same information set as y. Thus, player 1 cannot distinguish between the two histories (x, L) and (x, R) even though they differ in a past action of his.

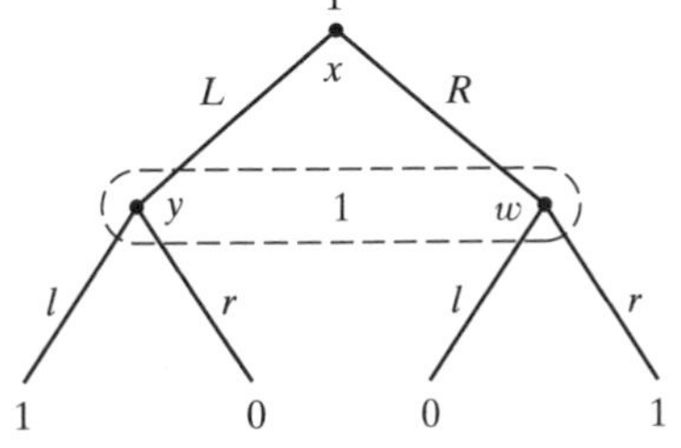

[18] Certain mixed (behavioural) strategies may admit multiple equivalent behavioural (mixed) strategies. See Kuhn (1953) for a complete analysis of the equivalence of mixed and behavioural strategies.

each of the pure strategies Ll and Rr, because any such behavioural strategy must place positive probability on both choices L and R at player 1's first information set, and it must also place positive probability on both choices l and r at 1's second information set. But it will then also place positive probability on the end nodes (L, r) and (R, l) that the original mixed strategy does not do.

Because of the equivalence of mixed and behavioural strategies in games with perfect recall, we have the luxury of using whichever is most convenient. Consequently, we shall restrict our attention to the sets of behavioural strategies for each player.

Subgame Perfect Equilibrium with Randomised Actions

Although subgame perfect equilibria in pure strategies are not guaranteed to exist (see the example in Fig. 7.23), subgame perfect equilibria in behavioural strategies do exist quite generally. Analogous to Definition 7.17, we have the following definition.

DEFINITION 7.19 ***Subgame Perfect Equilibrium***

A joint behavioural strategy b is a subgame perfect equilibrium of the finite extensive form game Γ if it induces a Nash equilibrium in every subgame of Γ.

Note that because behavioural and mixed strategies are equivalent in extensive form games with perfect recall, Theorem 7.1 ensures that a behavioural strategy constitutes a Nash equilibrium of a game (or a subgame) if no player has a pure strategy giving a higher payoff given the behavioural strategies of the others. This fact is helpful when both checking for and computing subgame perfect equilibria. The equivalence of mixed and behavioural strategies also guarantees that in games with perfect recall every subgame perfect equilibrium is a Nash equilibrium.

We now establish that subgame perfect equilibria exist quite generally.

THEOREM 7.6 ***(Selten) Existence of Subgame Perfect Equilibrium***

Every finite extensive form game with perfect recall possesses a subgame perfect equilibrium.

Proof: The proof employs a technique reminiscent of the backward induction algorithm. We shall construct the desired behavioural strategy in stages working from the end of the game back to the beginning.

Choose a subgame that contains no subgame but itself. This is always possible because the game is finite. By Theorem 7.2, this subgame has a Nash equilibrium in mixed strategies. Because the original game has perfect recall, the subgame does as well, and so the mixed strategy (in the subgame) has an equivalent behavioural strategy counterpart. Of course, being equivalent, this behavioural strategy also constitutes a Nash equilibrium in the subgame.

Now replace the subgame with the payoff vector determined by the equilibrium strategy in it. We have thus reduced the size of the game and have determined that part of the overall behavioural strategy within the subgame. We may now repeat the process for the reduced game, and so on, until we have completely determined a joint behavioural strategy for the original game. Observe that this algorithm must terminate because the game is finite.

That the behavioural strategy so determined constitutes a subgame perfect equilibrium follows in a manner that parallels the first half of the proof of Theorem 7.5. You are asked to fill in the details in an exercise. ∎

It is important to note that the assumption of perfect recall cannot be dispensed with. In a game without it, a subgame perfect equilibrium may not exist. This is considered in one of the exercises.

The process described in the proof is illustrated in Fig. 7.26(a) to 7.26(c). Note how subgame perfection echoes the theme of backward induction, namely, that optimal play early in the game is determined by that later in the game. In the next section, we develop a further refinement of Nash equilibrium in order to more fruitfully apply this central idea.

7.3.7 SEQUENTIAL EQUILIBRIUM

The game of Fig. 7.27 has a number of Nash equilibria. Because the game has only itself as a subgame, each of these is also subgame perfect. But are each of these subgame perfect equilibria sensible?

Consider the pure strategy subgame perfect equilibrium in which player 1 chooses L and player 2 chooses m. It is clearly a Nash equilibrium (and therefore subgame perfect) because neither player can improve their payoff by unilaterally changing their strategy. In particular, player 1 does not play M or R because according to this equilibrium, player 2 will respond by playing m and this would give player 1 a payoff of -1, rather than the 0 that he gets by playing L. Thus, the threat that player 2 will play m if given the opportunity is enough to convince player 1 to play L. But is player 2's threat a credible one? Does it make sense for player 1 to believe that 2 will choose m if reached? To answer this question, we must consider the decision problem faced by player 2 if player 1 does not choose L.

So, suppose that player 2 is reached. How can he decide which action to take? After all, his best action depends on the action chosen by player 1. If player 1 chooses M, then player 2's best action is r, whereas if player 1 chooses R, his best action is l.

Now because player 2 is not informed of player 1's action beyond knowing that player 1 chose either M or R, player 2 must form his own beliefs about which action player 1 chose. Let $p(x)$ and $p(y)$ denote the probabilities that player 2 places on nodes x and y having been reached given that it is his turn to move [hence, $p(x) + p(y) = 1$]. Given player 2's beliefs, we can assess the expected utility to him of choosing l, m, and r. These expected utilities are, respectively, $4p(y)$, 1, and $4p(x)$. Player 2 of course will make the choice that maximises his expected utility.

Because at this stage we do not know player 2's beliefs (i.e., $p(x)$ and $p(y)$), we cannot determine the choice he will make. However, we can say that he will never choose m. That is, regardless of the values of $p(x)$ and $p(y)$, m does not maximise 2's expected utility. To see this, simply note that the mixed strategy of choosing l and r with probability

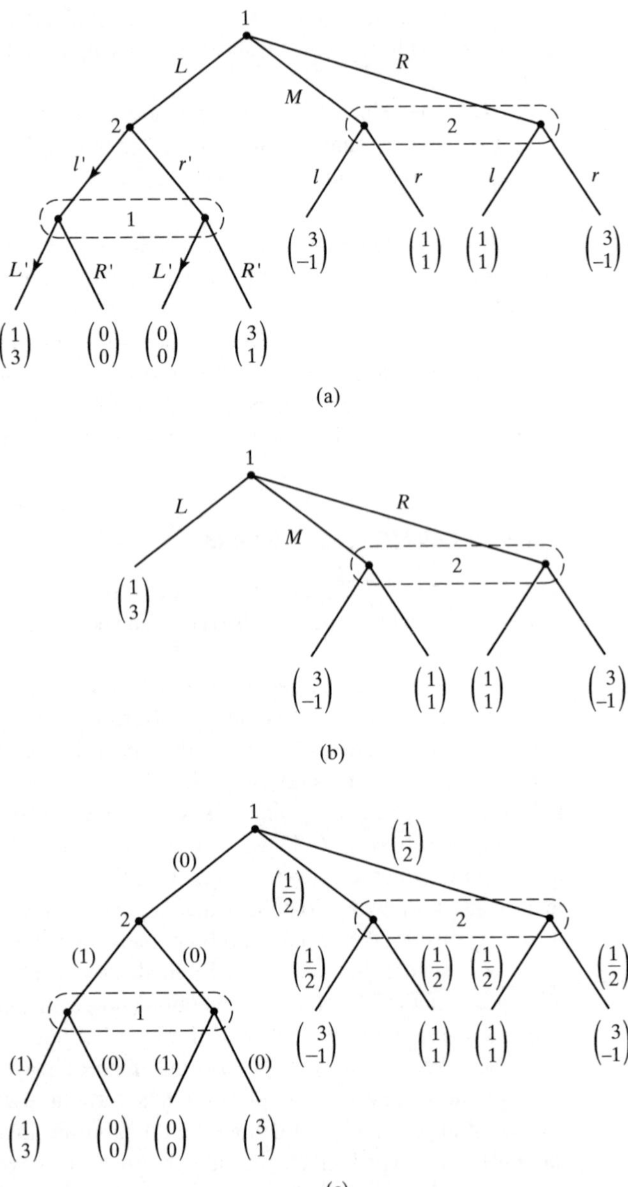

Figure 7.26. (a) Finding subgame perfect equilibria. The subgame defined by player 2's singleton information set contains no subgame but itself. The arrows depict a Nash equilibrium in this subgame. Replacing this subgame by the equilibrium payoff vector yields the reduced game in (b). (b) The reduced game. This game has only one subgame, namely, itself. It is not hard to verify that it possesses a unique Nash equilibrium: player 1 chooses M and R with probability $1/2$ each, and player 2 chooses l and r with probability $1/2$ each. (c) A subgame perfect equilibrium. (Can you find another?)

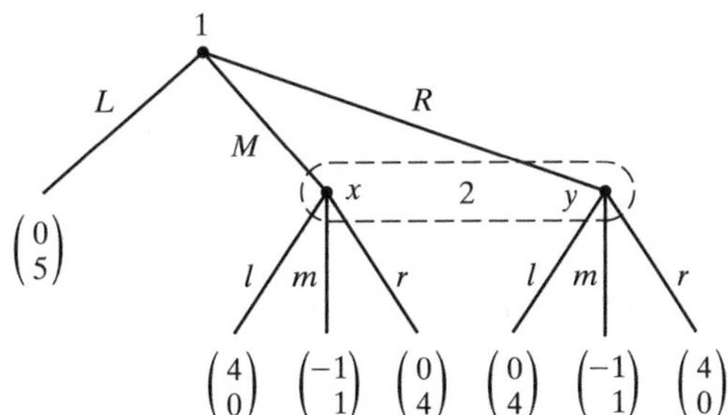

Figure 7.27. Not all subgame perfect equilibria are sensible.

1/2 each yields expected utility

$$p(x)\big(\tfrac{1}{2}(0) + \tfrac{1}{2}(4)\big) + p(y)\big(\tfrac{1}{2}(4) + \tfrac{1}{2}(0)\big) = 2(p(x) + p(y)) = 2,$$

which is strictly larger than the expected utility of 1 obtained by choosing m. Thus, regardless of the beliefs that player 2 might hold, at least one of l or r produces a strictly higher expected utility for player 2 than does m.

Consequently, contrary to the given subgame perfect equilibrium, player 2 will not play m if reached. Hence, this subgame perfect equilibrium is not a sensible one.

The reason that this subgame perfect equilibrium fails to be sensible is that subgame perfection does not discipline the behaviour of player 2 at his unreached information set. It fails to discipline 2's behaviour there because the unreached information set is not a singleton and therefore does not define a subgame.

However, as we have seen, by introducing beliefs for player 2 over the nodes within his information set once it has been reached, we *can* sensibly discipline his behaviour there. This can have a profound impact on the set of equilibrium outcomes. You are invited to show in an exercise that the only subgame perfect equilibrium in which m is given probability zero by player 2 (as we have argued it ought to be) has player 1 choosing L with probability zero.

We now formally introduce beliefs for the players over the nodes within their information sets for the purposes of refining the set of subgame perfect equilibria in the spirit of backward induction.

Beliefs and Their Connection to Strategies

As demonstrated in the example of Fig. 7.27, it makes good sense to consider the beliefs that players hold at their information sets regarding the history of play up to that point in the game.

Given an extensive form game Γ and a decision node x, let $p(x)$ denote the probability that player $\iota(x)$ assigns to the history x conditional on his information set $\mathcal{I}(x)$ having been reached. Thus, we must have $\sum_{x\in\mathcal{I}(y)} p(x) = 1$ for every decision node y. The function $p(\cdot)$ is called a **system of beliefs** because it embodies the beliefs of all players at each of their information sets regarding the history of play up to that point in the game.

In a game tree diagram, we will represent the system of beliefs, p, by placing the probability assigned to each node within each information set beside the respective node and in square brackets.

Because a player's beliefs about the history of play will typically have an important influence on his current behaviour, it is vital that these beliefs are formed in a sensible manner.

The question of interest to us is this: for a *given* behavioural strategy b, which systems of beliefs, p, are sensible? It is convenient to give the name **assessment** to a system of beliefs/behavioural strategy pair (p, b). Given such an ordered pair, (p, b), the beliefs p are interpreted as those that are held by the players given that the behavioural strategy b is being played. To rephrase our question then, *which assessments are sensible?*

For example, consider the game of Fig. 7.28. In it is depicted player 1's behavioural strategy as well as player 2's beliefs (left unspecified as α, β, and γ). Now, given player 1's strategy, player 2 can calculate the probability that each of his nodes has been reached given that one of them has by simply employing Bayes' rule. Thus, the only sensible beliefs for player 2, given 1's strategy, are $\alpha = 1/3$, $\beta = 1/9$, and $\gamma = 5/9$.

Thus, for an assessment (p, b) to be sensible, the system of beliefs p ought to be derived from the given joint behavioural strategy b using Bayes' rule whenever possible. That is, letting $P(x \mid b)$ denote the probability that node x is reached given the behavioural

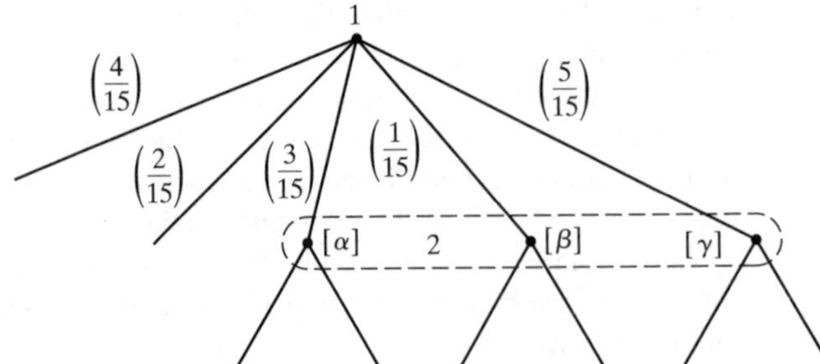

Figure 7.28. Using Bayes' rule. To see why Bayes' rule makes sense, imagine this game being played 1500 times with the strategy depicted for player 1. Out of the 1500 plays, on average, the two leftmost choices of player 1 would occur $400 + 200 = 600$ times, and the other choices would occur $300 + 100 + 500 = 900$ times. Therefore, 2's information set would be reached 900 times. Out of these 900, the leftmost node is reached 300 times, the middle node is reached 100 times, and the rightmost node is reached 500 times. Thus, from a frequency point of view, given that 2's information set has been reached, the probability of the leftmost node is $\alpha = 300/900 = 1/3$; the middle node is $\beta = 100/900 = 1/9$; and the rightmost node is $\gamma = 500/900 = 5/9$.

Figure 7.29. A restriction on beliefs beyond Bayes' rule.

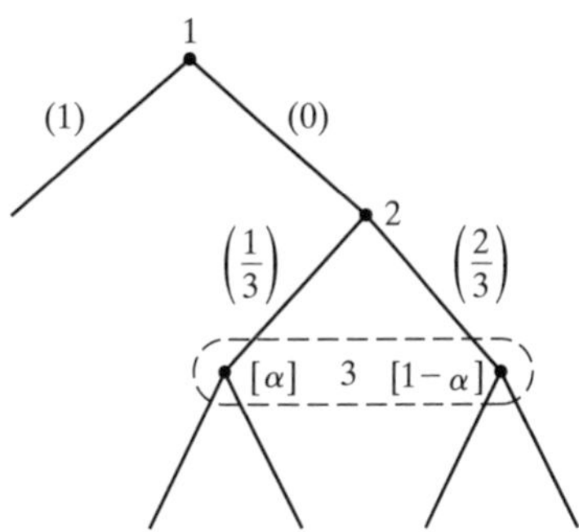

strategy b, Bayes' rule states that for every information set I, and every $x \in I$,

$$p(x) = \frac{P(x \mid b)}{\sum_{y \in I} P(y \mid b)}$$

whenever the denominator is positive – that is, whenever the information set is reached with positive probability according to b.[19]

We state this as our first principle.

Bayes' Rule: *Beliefs must be derived from strategies using Bayes' rule when possible.*

The phrase 'when possible' means at all information sets reached with positive probability according to the given joint strategy. Consequently, it is not always possible to employ Bayes' rule. For example, in the game of Fig. 7.29, given the behavioural strategies of players 1 and 2, player 3's information set is not reached (i.e., it is reached with probability zero). Thus, we cannot formally apply Bayes' rule in this circumstance to obtain 3's beliefs. Nonetheless, given player 2's strategy there does appear to be a unique sensible belief for player 3, namely $\alpha = 1/3$.

The reason that this is the only sensible belief is that player 2's behavioural strategy, strictly interpreted, means that he will play left with probability $1/3$ *if* player 1 plays right, even though player 1 is supposed to play left with probability one. Thus, player 2's mixed action already takes into account that player 1 must deviate from his strategy for 2's strategy to come into play. Consequently, when player 3 is reached, his only sensible belief is to place probability $1/3$ on player 2 having played left.

Are there still further restrictions we might consider imposing on the beliefs that accompany a given behavioural strategy? Well, in a word, yes. Consider Figs. 7.30 and 7.31, both of which specify a behavioural strategy for players 1 and 2. In each game, any choice of α and β between zero and one will suffice to render the resulting assessment compatible with Bayes' rule. Moreover, the type of argument used in the example of Fig. 7.29 is simply unavailable. Nonetheless, there is good reason to insist that in each case

[19] To keep the notation simple, we have not emphasised the fact that $P(x \mid b)$ also depends on chance's distribution π.

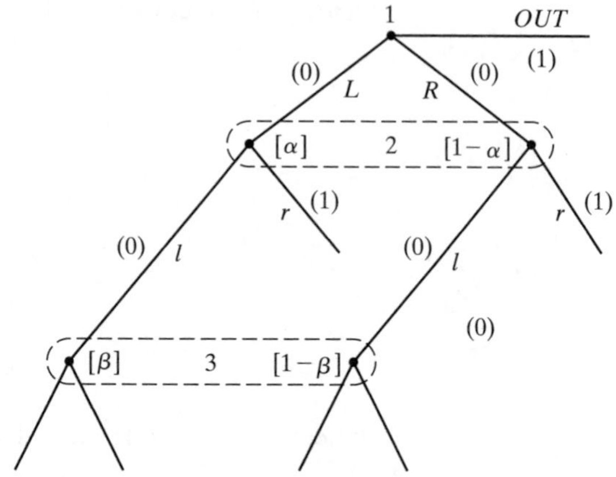

Figure 7.30. A restriction implied by common beliefs and independence.

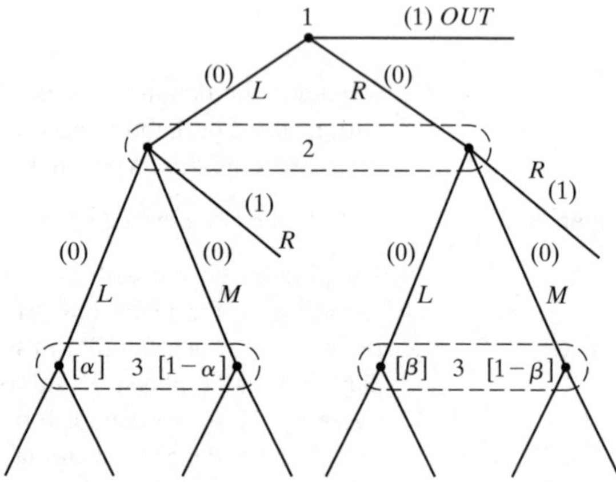

Figure 7.31. A restriction implied by independence.

$\alpha = \beta$. Indeed this equality follows from two additional principles that we intentionally describe only informally. They are as follows.

Independence: *Beliefs must reflect that players choose their strategies independently.*

Common Beliefs: *Players with identical information have identical beliefs.*

To see how these two principles lead to $\alpha = \beta$, consider Fig. 7.30. When player 2's information set is reached, α is the probability that player 2 places on player 1 having chosen L. Now, although this is not represented in the diagram, the principle of common beliefs implies that player 3 also places probability α on player 1 having chosen L at this point in the game (i.e., when given exactly the same information as player 2). But by independence of the players' strategies, finding out the strategy choice of player 2 provides player 3 with no information whatever regarding the strategy chosen by player

1.[20] Consequently, player 3's beliefs about player 1 must remain unchanged (i.e., equal to α on L by player 1) even after finding out that player 2 has chosen l. But this means that $\beta = \alpha$.

Similar reasoning can be applied to Fig. 7.31. Finding out whether or not player 1 played Left or Right should not (by independence) affect 3's beliefs about the probability that player 2 chose Left versus Middle, that is, $\alpha = \beta$. Note that the common beliefs principle is not needed in this case because the two information sets in question are owned by the same player.

Altogether, the three principles – Bayes' rule, independence, and common beliefs – suffice to yield all of the restrictions on beliefs we have considered so far in all previous examples. (You are asked in an exercise to show that independence yields the restriction $\alpha = 1/3$ in the game of Fig. 7.29.) Of course, this claim is only an informal one because the independence and common beliefs principles are stated only informally. What we really need is a formal definition of what it means for an assessment to be 'sensible', and this is what we now provide. After stating the definition, we will talk about how it relates to the three principles: Bayes' rule, independence, and common beliefs.

To prepare for the definition requires a little terminology. A behavioural strategy in a finite extensive form game is called **completely mixed** if it assigns strictly positive probability to every action at every information set. You are asked to show as an exercise that under a completely mixed strategy every information set is reached with strictly positive probability. Consequently, for such strategies, Bayes' rule alone uniquely determines the players' beliefs.

DEFINITION 7.20 ***Consistent Assessments***

An assessment (p, b) for a finite extensive form game Γ is consistent if there is a sequence of completely mixed behavioural strategies, b^n, converging to b, such that the associated sequence of Bayes' rule induced systems of beliefs, p^n, converges to p.

How does the definition of a consistent assessment relate to the principles of Bayes' rule, independence and common beliefs? As you are asked to show in Exercise 7.43, consistency implies Bayes' rule. Indeed, consistency is strictly more restrictive than Bayes' rule, and even more restrictive than Bayes' rule in every subgame. Because neither the independence principle nor the common beliefs principle are formally defined, we cannot formally relate them to consistency. However, we would like to suggest that consistency formalises both principles in a reasonable way. Consistency formalises the independence principle by insisting that beliefs are derived from limits of completely mixed strategies,

[20] Note that the independence principle applies even if player 2's single information set in Fig. 7.30 is split into two singleton information sets. In this case, player 2's decision of l or r may well depend on player 1's choice of L or R. Consequently, finding out whether player 2 chose l or r *does* provide player 3 with information regarding player 1's strategy choice. However, this does not violate the independence principle because in the new game, player 2's strategy set is $\{ll, lr, rl, rr\}$, not $\{l, r\}$, and according to the independence principle finding out which *strategy* player 2 has chosen must not provide player 3 with any information regarding the strategy choice of player 1.

which, by definition, incorporate independence. To see that consistency formalises the common beliefs principle, consider again the sequence of completely mixed strategies determining the players' beliefs. Each joint mixed strategy in the sequence can be thought of as a common belief that – prior to the play of the game when all players have the same information – all players share about how the joint pure strategy is chosen. The limit assessment is thus also a common belief. Let us now apply the definition of consistency to the examples we have considered so far. This will give us a feel for how it works.

In the example of Fig. 7.28, let b denote the behavioural strategy depicted there (2's behavioural strategy is irrelevant) and let $p = (\alpha, \beta, \gamma)$ denote the system of beliefs. For the assessment (p, b) to be consistent, there must be a sequence of assessments $(p^n, b^n) \to (p, b)$ with b^n completely mixed for every n, and p^n derived from b^n using Bayes' rule. But this means that along the sequence of behavioural strategies, the probabilities placed on the three rightmost choices of player 1 converge to $3/15$, $1/15$, and $5/15$, respectively. Therefore, because the sequence of beliefs is derived through Bayes' rule, $\alpha^n/\beta^n \to 3, \beta^n/\gamma^n \to 1/5$, and $\gamma^n/\alpha^n \to 5/3$, so that $\alpha^n \to 1/3, \beta^n \to 1/9$, and $\gamma^n \to 5/9$. Therefore, consistency of the assessment requires that $p = (\alpha, \beta, \gamma) = (1/3, 1/9, 5/9)$ precisely as we insisted upon before.

In Fig. 7.29, given the behavioural strategy depicted there, consistency requires $\alpha = 1/3$. This is because along any sequence of completely mixed strategies converging to the one in the figure, the probability that player 1 chooses right and 2 chooses right is, in the limit, twice as likely as that in which 1 chooses right and 2 chooses left. The conclusion follows from the requirement that the beliefs be derived from the limit of those derived along the sequence using Bayes' rule. We leave as an exercise verifying that consistency yields the restrictions previously discussed for the examples of Fig. 7.30 and 7.31 as well.

As mentioned, it can be proven that a consistent assessment satisfies our first principle, Bayes' rule, and we have suggested that it formalises our informal principles of independence and common beliefs. But one might worry that the rather mathematical definition of consistency goes beyond these principles in possibly unintended ways. However, it turns out that consistency can be shown to be *equivalent* to the following principles.[21]

(i) Players are able to assign relative probabilities, possibly infinite, to any pair of joint pure strategies.

(ii) The players' relative probabilities satisfy standard probability laws (e.g., Bayes' rule).

(iii) The players' relative probabilities coincide with the relative probabilities of an outside observer (common beliefs).

(iv) The outside observer's relative probabilities for the present strategic situation would not change after observing the outcome of any finite number of identical strategic situations (a form of independence related to 'infinite experience').

[21] See Kohlberg and Reny (1997).

In our opinion, the equivalence of consistency with these four principles indicates that consistency is an idealised restriction on beliefs. Of course, not all practical settings will conform to these ideals and one must therefore be careful not to apply consistency inappropriately. However, if one's goal is to understand strategic behaviour among idealised 'rational' players, then in light of the above equivalence, consistency is entirely reasonable.

Sequential Rationality

Now that we have explored the relationship between beliefs and strategies, we can return to the task of developing a sensible notion of backward induction for general extensive form games.

For games with perfect information, the backward induction solution amounts to insisting that all players make choices that are payoff-maximising whenever it is their turn to move. Subgame perfection attempts to extend this idea beyond perfect information games. However, as the example of Fig. 7.27 illustrates, subgame perfection is not quite strong enough to rule out behaviour that is suboptimal at every information set.

Now that we have endowed each player with beliefs about the history of play whenever it is that player's turn to move, it is straightforward to require that the choices made at each information set of every player be optimal there. Once this is done, we will have appropriately extended the backward induction idea to general extensive form games. We now formally pursue this line of thought.

Fix a finite extensive form game. Consider an assessment, (p, b), and an information set, I, belonging to player i. To check that player i's behavioural strategy, b_i, is optimal for i once his information set I is reached, we must be able to calculate the payoff to i of any other strategy he might employ once I is reached.

Let us first calculate i's payoff according to the assessment (p, b) given that his information set I has been reached. For each node x in I, we can use b to calculate player i's payoff beginning from x. To do this, simply treat x as if it defined a subgame. For each such x, let $u_i(b \mid x)$ denote this payoff number. Thus, $u_i(b \mid x)$ is the payoff to i if node x in I has been reached. Of course, player i does not know which node within I has been reached. But the system of beliefs, p, describes the probabilities that i assigns to each node in I. Consequently, player i's payoff according to (p, b), given that I has been reached, is simply the expected value of the numbers $u_i(b \mid x)$ according to the system of beliefs p, namely,

$$\sum_{x \in I} p(x) u_i(b \mid x).$$

We denote this payoff by $v_i(p, b \mid I)$. See Fig. 7.32 and 7.33 for an example in which $v_i(p, b \mid I)$ is calculated.

Now that we know how to calculate i's payoff from an arbitrary assessment conditional on one of his information sets having been reached, it is straightforward to compare this payoff to what he can obtain by changing his strategy at that point in the game, and this is the basis for the central definition of this section.

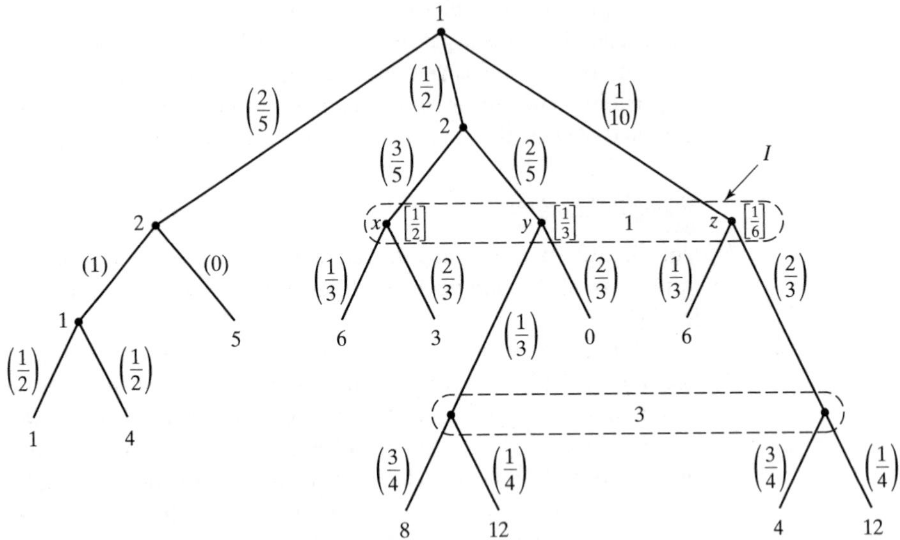

Figure 7.32. Payoffs conditional on an information set. See Fig. 7.33 for the calculation of 1's payoff conditional on I having been reached.

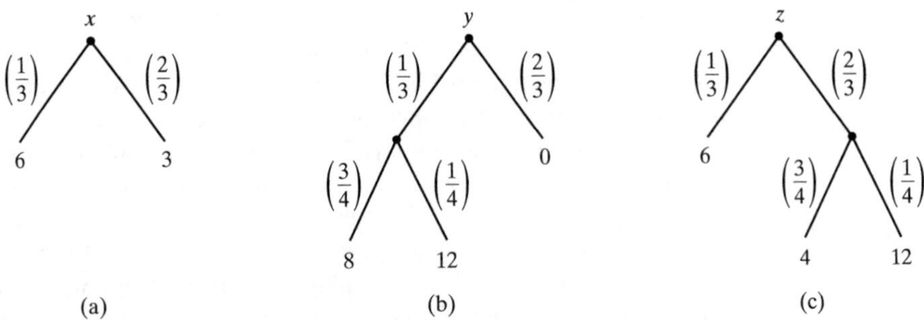

Figure 7.33. Calculating payoffs at an information set. Treating separately each node, x, y, and z within 1's information set labelled I in Fig. 7.32, we see from (a) that $u_1(b \mid x) = \frac{1}{3}(6) + \frac{2}{3}(3) = 4$, from (b) that $u_1(b \mid y) = \frac{1}{3}[\frac{3}{4}(8) + \frac{1}{4}(12)] + \frac{2}{3}[0] = 3$, and from (c) that $u_1(b \mid z) = \frac{1}{3}[6] + \frac{2}{3}[\frac{3}{4}(4) + \frac{1}{4}(12)] = 6$. Hence, $v_1(p, b \mid I) = p(x)u_1(b \mid x) + p(y)u_1(b \mid y) + p(z)u_1(b \mid z) = \frac{1}{2}(4) + \frac{1}{3}(3) + \frac{1}{6}(6) = 4$.

DEFINITION 7.21 ***Sequential Rationality***

An assessment (p, b) for a finite extensive form game is sequentially rational if for every player i, every information set I belonging to player i, and every behavioural strategy b_i' of player i,

$$v_i(p, b \mid I) \geq v_i(p, (b_i', b_{-i}) \mid I).$$

We also call a joint behavioural strategy, b, sequentially rational if for some system of beliefs, p, the assessment (p, b) is sequentially rational as above.

Thus, an assessment is sequentially rational if no player, *at any point in the game*, ever has an incentive to change his strategy. Note well that the italicised phrase '*at any point in the game*' refers not only to information sets reached with positive probability by the behavioural strategy b, but to *all* information sets.

The significance of the distinction is evident from the game of Fig. 7.27. As you may recall, the subgame perfect equilibrium in which player 1 plays L and 2 plays m was nonsensical precisely because player 2 would wish to switch from m if indeed his information set were reached. This nonsensical equilibrium would not be eliminated if we did not insist on checking for optimal behaviour at all information sets and instead only checked those that are reached with positive probability according to the given strategies. However, when we do insist that behaviour be optimal at all information sets, this subgame perfect equilibrium is eliminated. More formally, if b denotes the joint behavioural strategy depicted in Fig. 7.27, then there is no system of beliefs, p, such that the assessment (p, b) is sequentially rational. (See the exercises.)

Thus, not all subgame perfect equilibria (and, hence, not all Nash equilibria) are sequentially rational. Are there games possessing sequentially rational behavioural strategies that are not subgame perfect equilibria? The answer is yes, and the following example is a further reminder of the importance of establishing an appropriate connection between beliefs and strategies.

The game depicted in Fig. 7.34 is called 'matching pennies'. Each player has a penny and can choose to place it Heads up or Tails up in his palm. Player 1 wins 2's penny if the pennies match, and player 2 wins 1's penny if they fail to match. Player 1 chooses first, but keeps his palm closed until player 2 has made his choice. Thus, player 2 must choose Heads or Tails up without knowing the choice made by player 1.[22]

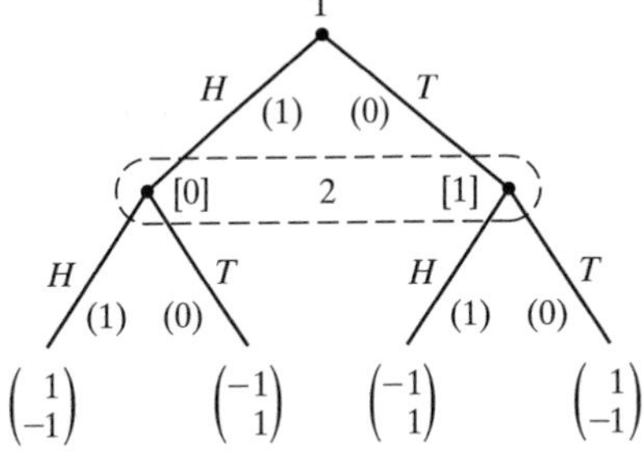

Figure 7.34. A sequentially rational assessment that is not a sequential equilibrium. Player 2's beliefs are not derived from the strategies using Bayes' rule.

[22]In effect, the players are making their choices simultaneously. Thus, this extensive form game is equivalent to the strategic form game in which the players' choices are in fact made simultaneously (i.e., the strategic form game of section 7.2, which we called the batter–pitcher duel; it is more commonly known in the game theory literature as matching pennies). In this sense, any strategic form game can be modelled as an extensive form game in which each of the players moves once in some fixed (but arbitrary) order and in which no player is informed of the choice made by any previous player.

The unique Nash equilibrium of this game, and hence the unique subgame perfect equilibrium, is for both players to randomise by choosing Heads and Tails with probability $1/2$ each. However, consider the assessment depicted in the figure in which both players choose *Heads* with probability 1, and player 2's beliefs place probability 1 on player 1 having chosen *Tails*. This assessment, although not a Nash equilibrium, is sequentially rational because player 1 is obtaining his highest possible payoff, and *according to 2's beliefs*, when his information set is reached, he, too, obtains his highest possible payoff. This is because according to 2's beliefs, player 1 has chosen *Tails* with probability one. Consequently, by choosing *Heads*, player 2's payoff is maximised – again, according to his beliefs.

Thus, sequentially rational assessments need not even be Nash equilibria. Clearly the difficulty with this example is that player 2's beliefs are not derived from the strategies via Bayes' rule.

Putting the notion of sequential rationality together with the three principles connecting beliefs with strategies discussed in the previous subsection – Bayes' rule, independence, and common beliefs – leads to the following important equilibrium concept introduced in Kreps and Wilson (1982).

DEFINITION 7.22 ***Sequential Equilibrium***

An assessment for a finite extensive form game is a sequential equilibrium if it is both consistent and sequentially rational.

Because (as you are asked to show in an exercise) consistent assessments do indeed satisfy Bayes' rule, the unique sequential equilibrium of the matching pennies game of Fig. 7.34 has each player choosing Heads with probability $1/2$.

It is instructive to apply the sequential equilibrium concept to a less transparent example.

EXAMPLE 7.7 Consider a variant of matching pennies, which we will call 'sophisticated matching pennies'. There are three players, each in possession of a penny. The objectives of the players are as follows: player 3 wishes to match the choice of player 1, and player 1 wishes for just the opposite. Player 2's role is to 'help' player 3 try to match player 1's choice. Thus, you can think of players 2 and 3 as being team members (although making independent choices) playing against player 1. There are four dollars at stake.

How exactly is player 2 allowed to help player 3 guess player 1's choice of Heads or Tails? The answer is of course embodied in the precise rules of the game, which we have not yet spelled out. They are as follows: player 1 begins by secretly placing his coin either Heads up or Tails up in his palm. Player 2 then does the same. Players 1 and 2 then reveal their coins to a referee (being careful not to reveal either coin to player 3). The referee then informs player 3 of whether or not the coins of players 1 and 2 match. Player 3 must then decide whether to choose Heads or Tails. If 3's choice matches 1's, then player 1 pays players 2 and 3 two dollars each. Otherwise, players 2 and 3 each pay player 1 two dollars. To make the game a little more interesting, we will also give players 1 and 2 the choice to

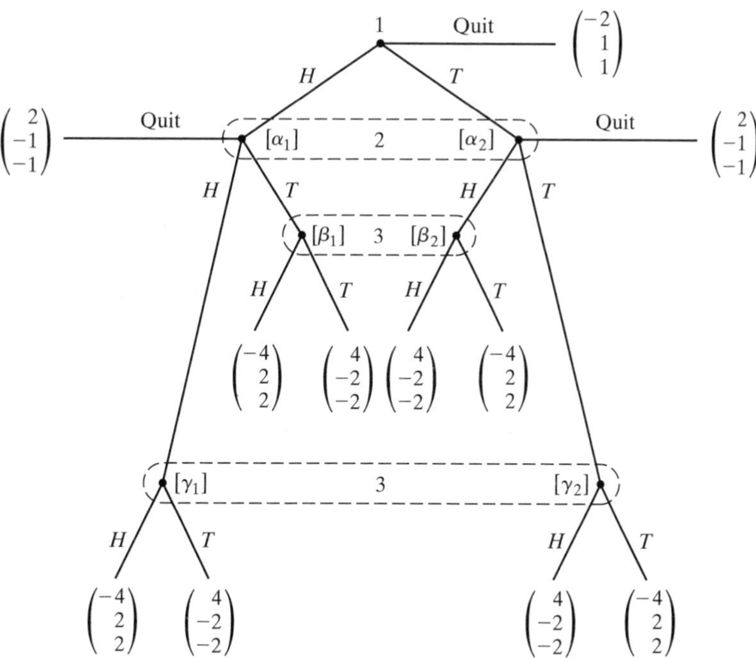

Figure 7.35. Sophisticated matching pennies.

quit on their turns. Quitting costs two dollars. So if player 1 quits, he must pay players 2 and 3 one dollar each, and if player 2 quits, players 2 and 3 each pay player 1 one dollar. The entire game is depicted in Fig. 7.35. You should check that the figure is compatible with the description just given.

This game possesses multiple sequential equilibria. It is instructive to demonstrate how one of these is calculated. You are asked to find the others in an exercise.

In the figure, we have indicated player 2's beliefs by α_i, and player 3's by β_i and γ_i. For expositional ease, we shall refer to player 3's information set with beliefs indicated by β_i as 3's 'beta' information set, and the other as 3's 'gamma' information set.

Let x and y denote the probabilities that players 1 and 2, respectively, place on Heads, and let $\bar{x}$ and $\bar{y}$ denote the probabilities they place on Tails. Let z_β and z_γ denote the probabilities that player 3 places on Heads at his information sets beta and gamma, respectively.

Thus, the vector $(\alpha_1, \beta_1, \gamma_1; x, \bar{x}, y, \bar{y}, z_\beta, z_\gamma)$ is an assessment for the game. We shall now search for a sequential equilibrium in which each of $x, \bar{x}, y, \bar{y}, z_\beta, z_\gamma$ is strictly between zero and one and in which players 1 and 2 never quit. Of course, there is no guarantee that such a sequential equilibrium exists. But if there is one, our search will discover it.

Let us then assume that each of x, $\bar{x}$, y, $\bar{y}$, z_β, z_γ is strictly between zero and one and that $x+\bar{x} = y+\bar{y} = 1$. Consequently, each information set is reached with positive probability, and so for the assessment to be consistent, it suffices that the beliefs be derived using Bayes' rule (see the exercises). Thus, for consistency, we must have

$$\alpha_1 = x, \qquad \beta_1 = \frac{x\bar{y}}{x\bar{y} + y\bar{x}}, \qquad \text{and} \qquad \gamma_1 = \frac{xy}{xy + \bar{x}\bar{y}}. \tag{E.1}$$

It remains to employ the conditions for sequential rationality.

Sequential rationality requires each player's strategy to be payoff-maximising at each of his information sets, given his beliefs and the strategies of the others. But recall the important fact that if a player is mixing between any number of choices and that player is maximising his payoff, then he must be indifferent between the choices. We shall use this fact to determine the players' strategies.

By using (E.1), direct calculation leads to the following:

$$\begin{aligned}
v_1(H \mid I_1) &= y(-4z_\gamma + 4(1 - z_\gamma)) + \bar{y}(-4z_\beta + 4(1 - z_\beta)), \\
v_1(T \mid I_1) &= y(4z_\beta - 4(1 - z_\beta)) + \bar{y}(4z_\gamma - 4(1 - z_\gamma)), \\
v_2(H \mid I_2) &= x(2z_\gamma - 2(1 - z_\gamma)) + \bar{x}(-2z_\beta + 2(1 - z_\beta)), \\
v_2(T \mid I_2) &= x(2z_\beta - 2(1 - z_\beta)) + \bar{x}(-2z_\gamma + 2(1 - z_\gamma))
\end{aligned} \tag{E.2}$$

$$\begin{aligned}
v_3(H \mid I_{3\beta}) &= \frac{x\bar{y}}{x\bar{y} + y\bar{x}}(2) + \frac{y\bar{x}}{x\bar{y} + y\bar{x}}(-2), \\
v_3(T \mid I_{3\beta}) &= \frac{x\bar{y}}{x\bar{y} + y\bar{x}}(-2) + \frac{y\bar{x}}{x\bar{y} + y\bar{x}}(2), \\
v_3(H \mid I_{3\gamma}) &= \frac{xy}{xy + \bar{x}\bar{y}}(2) + \frac{\bar{x}\bar{y}}{xy + \bar{x}\bar{y}}(-2), \\
v_3(T \mid I_{3\gamma}) &= \frac{xy}{xy + \bar{x}\bar{y}}(-2) + \frac{\bar{x}\bar{y}}{xy + \bar{x}\bar{y}}(2),
\end{aligned} \tag{E.3}$$

where, for example, (E.2) gives player 1's payoff of playing Heads at his information set denoted I_1, and (E.3) gives player 3's payoff of playing Tails at his beta information set denoted $I_{3\beta}$.

Now by the comment above, $x, \bar{x}, y, \bar{y}, z_\beta$, and z_γ must yield the following indifferences:

$$\begin{aligned}
v_1(H \mid I_1) &= v_1(T \mid I_1), \\
v_2(H \mid I_2) &= v_2(T \mid I_2), \\
v_3(H \mid I_{3\beta}) &= v_3(T \mid I_{3\beta}), \qquad \text{and} \\
v_3(H \mid I_{3\gamma}) &= v_3(T \mid I_{3\gamma}).
\end{aligned}$$

Because we are assuming that neither player quits in equilibrium, $\bar{x} = 1 - x$ and $\bar{y} = 1 - y$. With this in mind, we may use the last two indifferences above to solve for x and y, obtaining $x = \bar{x} = y = \bar{y} = 1/2$. Given this, the first two indifferences imply that $z_\beta = z_\gamma = 1/2$ as well.

Because player 3 has exactly two choices at each information set and he is indifferent between them, his behaviour is payoff-maximising at each of his information sets. It remains only to check that players 1 and 2 are maximising their payoffs. Thus, we must check that neither does better by quitting. That this is in fact the case follows because by quitting, players 1 and 2 obtain a negative payoff, whereas choosing Heads or Tails yields a payoff of 0.

Thus, the assessment $(\alpha_1, \beta_1, \gamma_1; x, \bar{x}, y, \bar{y}, z_\beta, z_\gamma)$ in which every entry is 1/2 is a sequential equilibrium.

Note that in the sequential equilibrium calculated here, each player receives a payoff of zero. Thus, player 3 is actually getting no significant help from player 2, because without player 2, the game would be a standard matching pennies game between players 1 and 3. In the exercises, you are asked to find all other sequential equilibria. You will discover that players 2 and 3 fare better in other equilibria. □

There is more we can learn from this example. Indeed, it is instructive to consider the assessment $(\alpha_1, \beta_1, \gamma_1; x, \bar{x}, y, \bar{y}, z_\beta, z_\gamma) = (1, 0, 0; 1, 0, 0, 0, 0, 0)$, in which player 1 chooses Heads with probability 1, player 2 quits with probability 1, and player 3 chooses Tails with probability 1.

This assessment seems rather silly because even though player 1 is sure to choose Heads, and player 3 would like to match it, player 3 chooses Tails, regardless of the choice of player 2. Despite this, the assessment is sequentially rational, and satisfies Bayes' rule! To see sequential rationality, note that player 1 is certainly maximising at his information set since player 2 quits. Also player 2 is maximising at his information set, because given his beliefs (which place probability 1 on player 1 having chosen Heads) and the strategy of player 3 (to choose Tails no matter what), player 3 is certain not to match player 1. Thus, it is best for 2 to quit. Finally, given that player 3 believes at each of his information sets that (if reached) player 1 has chosen Tails, it is indeed best for player 3 to also choose Tails. To verify Bayes' rule, simply note that the only non-singleton information set reached by the joint behavioural strategy is player 2's, and his beliefs are indeed those induced by Bayes' rule from the strategy.

Although this assessment satisfies Bayes' rule and is sequentially rational, it is not a sequential equilibrium. Indeed, it is not consistent. Intuitively, one senses that there is something wrong with player 3's beliefs. Before showing how the assessment formally violates the consistency condition embodied in Definition 7.20, it is helpful to first think about it intuitively. To do so, recall that consistency embodies three principles: Bayes' rule, independence, and common beliefs. Although the given assessment does satisfy Bayes' rule, it does not satisfy independence. Indeed, we shall argue that independence implies that one of β_2 or γ_2 must be zero. (Yet both are equal to 1 in the given assessment.)

Let $b_1(b_2)$ denote the left (right) node in player 3's beta information set, and let $g_1(g_2)$ denote the left (right) node in 3's gamma information set. Given the strategies, but before they are carried out, consider the following question pondered by player 3. 'What is the likelihood of node g_1 relative to node b_2?' We wish to argue that player 3's answer is: 'Node g_1 is infinitely more likely than node b_2'.[23]

The reason is as follows. From Fig. 7.35, note that the question can be rephrased as: 'Given that player 2 chooses Heads, what is the likelihood that player 1 chooses Heads relative to Tails?' But by independence, player 3 gains no information about 1's strategy choice by finding out the strategy choice of player 2. Consequently, the above question must have the same answer as the question: 'Given that player 2 chooses Quit, what is the likelihood that player 1 chooses Heads relative to Tails?' But the answer to the latter question must be that Heads by 1 is infinitely more likely than Tails given 2's choice to Quit, because this is precisely what the proposed strategies indicate. Hence, by independence, the answer to the original question must be the same – that g_1 is infinitely more likely than b_2.

An analogous argument shows that the answer to the question 'What is the likelihood of node b_1 relative to node g_2?' must be that the former is infinitely more likely than the latter. (Provide the argument.)

Finally, consider player 3's question: 'What is the likelihood of node g_1 relative to node b_1?' Although we cannot be certain of 3's answer, there are only two possibilities. Either g_1 is more likely (not necessarily infinitely more) than b_1 or it is not. If it is, then because b_1 is infinitely more likely than g_2, it must be the case that g_1 is infinitely more likely than g_2. But this is equivalent to saying that $\gamma_1 = 1$ and $\gamma_2 = 0$. Thus, in this case, $\gamma_2 = 0$.

On the other hand, if b_1 is at least as likely as g_1, then because g_1 is infinitely more likely than b_2, it must be the case that b_1 is infinitely more likely than b_2. But this is equivalent to saying that $\beta_1 = 1$ and $\beta_2 = 0$.

Consequently, independence implies that either $\gamma_2 = 0$, or $\beta_2 = 0$. We conclude that the given assessment does not satisfy independence.

This intuitive account does *not* constitute a formal demonstration that the assessment fails to be consistent. It is meant only to provide you with a little more insight into the nature of the difficulty with it. We will now formally show that the assessment fails to be consistent – and therefore that it is not a sequential equilibrium – by proving the following result.

CLAIM *If $(\alpha_1, \beta_1, \gamma_1, x, \bar{x}, y, \bar{y}, z_\beta, z_\gamma)$ is a consistent assessment for sophisticated matching pennies, then the beliefs must satisfy the following equality*

$$(\alpha_1)^2\beta_2\gamma_2 = (\alpha_2)^2\beta_1\gamma_1.$$

Before we give a proof of the claim, note that when $\alpha_1 = 1$ (as in the assessment we are analysing), the equation says that one of β_2 or γ_2 must be zero, precisely as we argued

[23] To say that one event is infinitely more likely than another simply means that conditional on one of the two having occurred, the one is assigned probability one, and the other is assigned probability zero. So, for example, given the players' strategies, and before the game begins, we would say that the choice of Heads by player 1 is infinitely more likely than the choice of Tails because the former has probability one and latter probability zero.

above using independence. Consequently, proving the claim does indeed demonstrate that the given sequentially rational assessment is not consistent and therefore not a sequential equilibrium.

Proof of the Claim: If the assessment $(\alpha_1, \beta_1, \gamma_1, x, \bar{x}, y, \bar{y}, z_\beta, z_\gamma)$ is consistent, then according to Definition 7.20, there is a completely mixed sequence of behavioural strategies $x^n, \bar{x}^n, y^n, \bar{y}^n, z^n_\beta, z^n_\gamma$ converging to $x, \bar{x}, y, \bar{y}, z_\beta, z_\gamma$, respectively, whose associated sequences of Bayes' rule induced beliefs $\alpha^n_1, \beta^n_1, \gamma^n_1$ converge to $\alpha_1, \beta_1, \gamma_1$, respectively.

Now, because all behavioural strategy probabilities are strictly positive along the sequence, we have the identity

$$\left(\frac{x^n}{\bar{x}^n}\right)^2 \frac{\bar{x}^n y^n}{x^n \bar{y}^n} \frac{\bar{x}^n \bar{y}^n}{x^n y^n} = 1, \qquad \text{for all } n.$$

But by Bayes' rule, we have

$$\begin{aligned} \frac{\alpha^n_1}{\alpha^n_2} &= \frac{x^n}{\bar{x}^n}, \\ \frac{\beta^n_2}{\beta^n_1} &= \frac{\bar{x}^n y^n}{x^n \bar{y}^n}, \qquad \text{and} \\ \frac{\gamma^n_2}{\gamma^n_1} &= \frac{\bar{x}^n \bar{y}^n}{x^n y^n} \end{aligned}$$

for all n. Consequently, we may substitute these expressions into the identity and rearrange to obtain

$$\left(\alpha^n_1\right)^2 \beta^n_2 \gamma^n_2 = \left(\alpha^n_2\right)^2 \beta^n_1 \gamma^n_1 \qquad \text{for every } n.$$

The desired result now follows by taking the limit of both sides as n tends to infinity. ∎

We end this section with the following theorem, which, on the one hand, indicates the overall coherence of the sequential equilibrium notion, and on the other shows that sequential equilibrium is indeed an extension of backward induction to general extensive form games.

THEOREM 7.7 ***(Kreps and Wilson) Existence of Sequential Equilibrium***

Every finite extensive form game with perfect recall possesses at least one sequential equilibrium. Moreover, if an assessment (p, b) is a sequential equilibrium, then the behavioural strategy b is a subgame perfect equilibrium.

We have explored many ideas in this chapter, from dominance, to Nash equilibrium, all the way through to sequential equilibrium. Along the way, we hope to have given the reader a sense of the richness of the theory of games as well as its tremendous power for shedding light on the outcomes of strategic situations involving rational players.

In the next chapter, we shall make good use of the game theoretic ideas we have developed here to understand the important economic consequences of informational asymmetries.

7.4 EXERCISES

7.1 Formulate the strategic form games associated with both Cournot and Bertrand duopoly.

7.2 For iterative elimination of strictly dominated strategies, show that the sets are nested and that the procedure terminates in finitely many rounds if the game is finite. Can you provide a tight upper bound on the number of iterations that might be required?

7.3 Our procedures for iteratively eliminating (weakly or strictly) dominated strategies eliminate all possible strategies each round. One might consider eliminating only some of those strategies that are dominated in each round. In this sense, one can alter the *order* in which dominated strategies are eliminated.

(a) Use the following game to show that the order in which weakly dominated strategies are eliminated can affect the outcomes that remain.

	L	M	R
U	2, 1	1, 1	0, 0
C	1, 2	3, 1	2, 1
D	2, −2	1, −1	−1, −1

(b) Prove that in a finite game, the order of elimination does not matter when one is eliminating strictly dominated strategies.

7.4 We have seen that one pure strategy can strictly dominate another pure strategy. Mixed strategies can also strictly dominate pure strategies, and they can strictly dominate other mixed strategies, too. To illustrate, consider the following two-player game.

	L	M	R
U	3, 0	0, −3	0, −4
D	2, 4	4, 5	−1, 8

(a) Convince yourself that neither of player 2's pure strategies L or R strictly dominates his pure strategy M.

(b) Show that the pure strategy M is strictly dominated by the mixed strategy in which player 2 chooses L and R each with probability $1/2$.

7.5 Consider the 'guess-the-average' game discussed at the end of section 7.2.1.

(a) Show that no pure strategy strictly dominates any other.

(b) Find a mixed strategy that strictly dominates 100.

(c) Show that 99 is not strictly dominated.

(d) Show that iterative elimination of *strictly* dominated strategies yields the unique choice of 1 for each of the N players, and that this requires 99 rounds of elimination.

(e) Show that when there are $N = 3$ players, and one applies the procedure of iterative weak dominance, then $W_i^1 = \{1, 2, \ldots, 14\}$, $W_i^2 = \{1, 2\}$, and $W_i^3 = \{1\}$ for every player i.

7.6 Show that any strategy surviving iterative weak dominance also survives iterative strict dominance.

7.7 A two-person game is called **zero-sum** if the players' payoffs always sum to zero. Let $u(x, y)$ denote player 1's payoff in a two-person, zero-sum game when player 1 chooses $x \in X$, and player 2 chooses $y \in Y$; consequently, player 2's payoff is $-u(x, y)$. Both X and Y are finite sets of pure strategies. The following questions all refer to this two-person, zero-sum game.

(a) Prove the **minimax theorem**. That is, prove that there exists a pair of mixed strategies m_1^*, m_2^* such that

$$\max_{m_1 \in M_1} \min_{m_2 \in M_2} u(m_1, m_2) = u(m_1^*, m_2^*) = \min_{m_2 \in M_2} \max_{m_1 \in M_1} u(m_1, m_2).$$

Interpret this result.

(b) Show that Nash equilibria are *interchangeable* in that if (m_1^*, m_2^*) and $(\bar{m}_1, \bar{m}_2)$ are two Nash equilibria, then $(m_1^*, \bar{m}_2)$ and $(\bar{m}_1, m_2^*)$ are also Nash equilibria. Conclude, therefore, that in two-person, zero-sum games, if there are multiple Nash equilibria, neither player need know which equilibrium strategy the other is using.

(c) Show that player 1's payoff (and therefore player 2's as well) is the same in every Nash equilibrium. This number is called the **value** of the game.

7.8 A game is **symmetric** if each player has the same set of pure strategies and $u_{\pi(i)}(s_{\pi(1)}, \ldots, s_{\pi(N)}) = u_i(s_1, \ldots, s_N)$ for each player i whenever the N-vector $(\pi(1), \ldots, \pi(N))$ is a permutation of $(1, \ldots, N)$. Prove that a finite symmetric game possesses a symmetric Nash equilibrium – a Nash equilibrium in which every player chooses the same strategy.

7.9 Prove that the value of a symmetric, two-person, zero-sum game is zero.

7.10 Calculate the set of Nash equilibria in the following games.

(a)

	L	R
U	1, 1	0, 0
D	0, 0	0, 0

Also show that there are two Nash equilibria, but only one in which neither player plays a weakly dominated strategy.

(b)

	L	R
U	$1, 1$	$0, 1$
D	$1, 0$	$-1, -1$

Also show that there are infinitely many Nash equilibria, only one of which has neither player playing a weakly dominated strategy.

(c)

	L	l	m	M
U	$1, 1$	$1, 2$	$0, 0$	$0, 0$
C	$1, 1$	$1, 1$	$10, 10$	$-10, -10$
D	$1, 1$	$-10, -10$	$10, -10$	$1, -10$

Also show that there is a unique strategy determined by iteratively eliminating weakly dominated strategies.

7.11 Two hunters are on a stag hunt. They split up in the forest and each have two strategies: hunt for a stag (S), or give up the stag hunt and instead hunt for rabbit (R). If they both hunt for a stag, they will succeed and each earn a payoff of 9. If one hunts for stag and the other gives up and hunts for rabbit, the stag hunter receives 0 and the rabbit hunter 8. If both hunt for rabbit then each receives 7. Compute all Nash equilibria for this game, called 'The Stag Hunt', depicted below. Which of these equilibria do you think is most likely to be played? Why?

	S	R
S	$9, 9$	$0, 8$
R	$8, 0$	$7, 7$

7.12 Call two games with the same strategy sets but different payoffs *strategically equivalent* if for each player i and any mixed strategies of the others, player i's ranking of his pure strategies in one game coincides with his ranking in the other. Consider again the Stag Hunt game, but suppose that player 1's payoff when the other player hunts stag is reduced by $\alpha \geq 0$ so that the game becomes,

	S	R
S	$9 - \alpha, 9$	$0, 8$
R	$8 - \alpha, 0$	$7, 7$

(a) Show that this game is strategically equivalent to the Stag Hunt game.

(b) Using only the operation of subtracting a constant from a player's payoff while holding fixed the other player's strategy, show that the Stag Hunt game is strategically equivalent to the pure coordination game,

	S	R
S	1, 1	0, 0
R	0, 0	7, 7

.

Which equilibrium do you think is most likely to be played in the pure coordination game? Why? Compare your answers to those you gave in Exercise 7.11. (If your answers are different ask yourself why, in light of the strategic equivalence of the two games.)

7.13 Consider the penalty kick in soccer. There are two players, the goalie and the striker. The striker has two strategies: kick to the goalie's right (R) or to the goalie's left (L). The goalie has two strategies: move left (L) or move right (R). Let α be the probability that the kick is stopped when both choose L and let β be the probability that the kick is stopped when both choose R. Assume that $0 < \alpha < \beta < 1$. Consequently, the striker is more skilled at kicking to the goalie's left. The payoff matrix is as follows.

		Kicker	
		L	R
Goalie	L	$\alpha, 1-\alpha$	0, 1
	R	0, 1	$\beta, 1-\beta$

(a) *Before analysing this game*, informally answer the following questions.

(i) Would you expect a striker who is more skilled at kicking to the goalie's left than to his right, to score more often when he kicks to the goalie's left?

(ii) If a striker's ability to score when kicking to the goalie's left rises (i.e. α decreases) how will this affect the percentage of times the striker scores when he chooses to kick to the goalie's left? Will it affect his scoring percentage when he kicks right?

(b) Find the unique Nash equilibrium.

(c) Answer again the questions in part (a). Based upon this, would it be wise to judge a striker's relative scoring ability in kicking left versus right by comparing the fraction of times he scores when he kicks right versus the fraction of times he scores when he kicks left?

(d) Show that knowing the fraction of times a goal was scored when both players chose L and the fraction of times a goal was scored when both players chose R would permit you to correctly deduce the player's scoring ability when kicking left and right.

(e) Could you correctly deduce the player's scoring ability when kicking left and right if you only had access to the striker's choice? If not, what can be deduced?

(f) Could you correctly deduce the player's scoring ability when kicking left versus right if you only had access to the goalie's choice? If not, what can be deduced?

7.14 Three firms use water from a lake for production purposes. Each firm has two pure strategies: purify sewage (P), or dump raw sewage (D). If zero or one firm chooses D, the water remains pure, but if two or three firms choose D, the water becomes polluted and each firm suffers a loss of 3. The cost of purification, P, is 1. Compute all Nash equilibria of this game.

7.15 Show that every finite game possesses a Nash equilibrium in which no player places positive probability on a weakly dominated pure strategy.

(a) Improve on this result by showing that every finite game possesses a Nash equilibrium m such that for each player i, m_i is not weakly dominated.

(b) Show that the result of part (a) requires finiteness by considering the Bertrand duopoly game introduced in Chapter 4.

7.16 Show that in a finite strategic form game, the set of strategies surviving iterative weak dominance is non-empty.

7.17 Consider the strategic form game depicted below. Each of two countries must simultaneously decide on a course of action. Country 1 must decide whether to keep its weapons or to destroy them. Country 2 must decide whether to spy on country 1 or not. It would be an international scandal for country 1 if country 2 could prove that country 1 was keeping its weapons. The payoff matrix is as follows.

	Spy	Don't Spy
Keep	$-1, 1$	$1, -1$
Destroy	$0, 2$	$0, 2$

(a) Does either player have a strictly dominant strategy?

(b) Does either player have a weakly dominant strategy?

(c) Find a Nash equilibrium in which neither player employs a weakly dominant strategy.

7.18 Reconsider the two countries from the previous exercise, but now suppose that country 1 can be one of two types, 'aggressive' or 'non-aggressive'. Country 1 knows its own type. Country 2 does not know country 1's type, but believes that country 1 is aggressive with probability $\varepsilon > 0$. The aggressive type places great importance on keeping its weapons. If it does so and country 2 spies on the aggressive type this leads to war, which the aggressive type wins and justifies because of the spying, but which is very costly for country 2. When country 1 is non-aggressive, the payoffs are as before (i.e., as in the previous exercise). The payoff matrices associated with each of the two possible types of country 1 are given below.

Country 1 is 'aggressive'
Probability ε

	Spy	Don't Spy
Keep	$10, -9$	$5, -1$
Destroy	$0, 2$	$0, 2$

Country 1 is 'non-aggressive'
Probability $1 - \varepsilon$

	Spy	Don't Spy
Keep	$-1, 1$	$1, -1$
Destroy	$0, 2$	$0, 2$

(a) What action must the aggressive type of country 1 take in any Bayesian-Nash equilibrium?

(b) Assuming that $\varepsilon < 1/5$, find the unique Bayes-Nash equilibrium. (Can you prove that it is unique?)

7.19 A community is composed of two types of individuals, good types and bad types. A fraction $\varepsilon > 0$ are bad, while the remaining fraction, $1 - \varepsilon > 0$ are good. Bad types are wanted by the police, while good types are not. Individuals can decide what colour car to drive, red or blue. Red cars are faster than blue cars. All individuals prefer fast cars to slow cars. Each day the police decide whether to stop only red cars or to stop only blue cars, or to stop no cars at all. They cannot stop all cars. Individuals must decide what colour car to drive. Individuals do not like being stopped, and police do not like stopping good individuals. A bad individual always tries to get away if stopped by the police and is more likely to get away if driving a red car. The payoff matrices associated with this daily situation are as follows.

Bad Individual
Probability ε

	Red Car	Blue Car
Stop Red	$5, -5$	$-10, 10$
Stop Blue	$-10, 15$	$10, -10$
Don't Stop	$-10, 15$	$-10, 10$

Good Individual
Probability $1 - \varepsilon$

	Red Car	Blue Car
Stop Red	$-1, -1$	$0, 0$
Stop Blue	$0, 5$	$-1, -6$
Don't Stop	$0, 5$	$0, 0$

Think of this as a Bayesian game and answer the following.

(a) Suppose that $\varepsilon < 1/21$. Find two pure strategy Bayes-Nash equilibria of this game.

(b) Suppose that $\varepsilon > 1/16$. Show that 'Don't Stop' is strictly dominated for the police by a mixed strategy.

(c) Suppose that $\varepsilon = 1/6$. Find the unique Bayes-Nash equilibrium. (Can you prove that it is unique?)

7.20 (a) Suppose that p is a common prior in a game of incomplete information assigning positive probability to every joint type vector. Show that if some type of some player assigns positive probability to some type, t_i, of another player i, then all players, regardless of their types, also assign positive probability to type t_i of player i.

(b) Provide a three-player game of incomplete information in which the players' beliefs cannot be generated by a common prior that assigns positive probability to every joint vector of types.

(c) Provide a two-player game of incomplete information in which the players' beliefs cannot be generated by a common prior that assigns positive probability to every joint vector of types and in which each player, regardless of his type, assigns positive probability to each type of the other player.

7.21 Our incomplete information games allow the players to have uncertainty about other players' payoffs. But what about uncertainty about other players' pure strategy sets? Show that uncertainty about a player's pure strategy set can be captured by uncertainty about his payoffs alone.

7.22 Show that there are other Bayesian-Nash equilibria of the two-firm Bertrand game in Example 7.3.

7.23 In this exercise we allow each player in a Bayesian game to have infinitely many types and we allow a player's beliefs about other players' types to be given by a probability density function. Payoff formulas and the definition of a Bayes-Nash equilibrium are precisely analogous to the finite type case with summations over types being replaced by integrals.

Consider a **first-price, sealed-bid auction** in which bidders simultaneously submit bids with the object going to the highest bidder at a price equal to their bid. Suppose that there are two bidders and that their values for the object are chosen independently from a uniform distribution over [0, 1]. Think of a player's type as being the value that player places on the object. A player's payoff is $v - b$ when he wins the object by bidding b and his value is v; his payoff is 0 if he does not win the object.

(a) Formulate this as a Bayesian game and find its associated strategic form game. Note that the associated strategic form game has infinitely many players.

(b) Let $b_i(v)$ denote the bid made by player i of type v. Show that there is a Bayesian-Nash equilibrium in which $b_i(v) = \alpha + \beta v$ for all i and v. Determine the values of α and β.

7.24 Modify the first-price, sealed-bid auction in the preceding exercise so that the loser also pays his bid (but does not win the object). This modified auction is called an **all-pay auction**.

(a) Show that there is a Bayesian-Nash equilibrium in which $b_i(v) = \gamma + \delta v + \phi v^2$ for all i and v.

(b) How do the players' bids compare to those in the first-price auction? What is the intuition behind this difference in bids?

(c) Show that, ex ante, the first-price auction and the all-pay auction generate the same expected revenue for the seller.

7.25 Fully describe two distinct pure strategies for each player in both the buyer–seller game and the simplified game of take-away. Calculate the payoffs associated with all four pairs of strategies.

7.26 List all pure strategies for both players in the extensive form games of Figs. 7.12 and 7.14. In addition, depict their associated strategic forms in a matrix diagram.

7.27 In Fig. 7.36, an insurance company (C), must consider whether to offer a cheap or costly automobile insurance policy to a driver (D). The company cannot observe whether the driver drives safely or recklessly, but can observe whether the driver has had an accident or not. The probability of an accident depends upon whether the driver drives safely or recklessly. If the driver drives safely he has an accident with probability 1/5. If he drives recklessly he has an accident with probability 4/5. If the driver drives safely he will not purchase the costly policy. This situation is modelled as an extensive form game in the figure below. The accident probabilities are modelled as randomisation by Nature and are given in square brackets in the figure. The driver's payoff is the top number in each payoff vector. For example, in the payoff vector $(2, -1)$ the driver's payoff is 2.

(a) Is there a Nash equilibrium in which the driver drives safely with probability one?

(b) Find the Nash equilibrium which maximises the probability that the driver drives safely.

7.28 Derive backward induction strategies for the games shown in Fig. 7.37 (p. 372).

(a) Which games admit multiple backward induction strategies?

(b) Prove that if a finite perfect information game has the property that no player is indifferent between any pair of end nodes, then the backward induction strategies are unique.

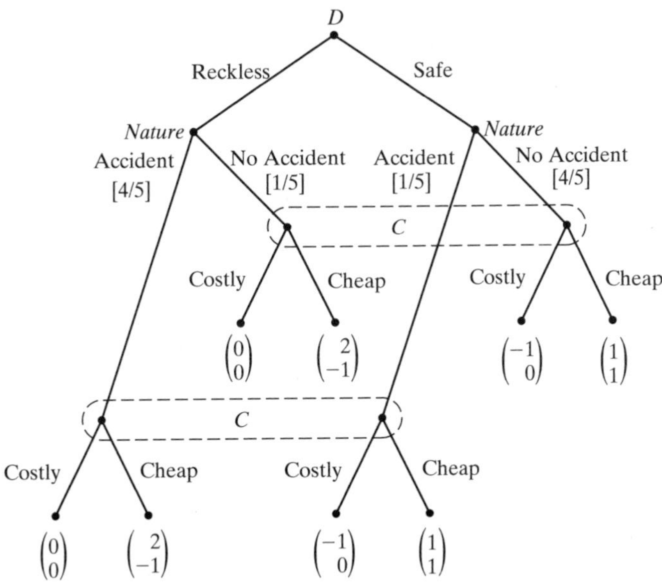

Figure 7.36. An insurance game.

(c) Give an example of a finite game of perfect information in which the backward induction strategies are not unique, but the payoff vector is.

7.29 The following game, taken from Reny (1992), is called 'Take-it-or-leave-it'. A referee is equipped with N dollars. He places one dollar on the table. Player 1 can either take the dollar or leave it. If he takes it, the game ends. If he leaves it, the referee places a second dollar on the table. Player two is now given the option of taking the two dollars or leaving them. If he takes them, the game ends. Otherwise the referee places a third dollar on the table and it is again player 1's turn to take or leave the three dollars. The game continues in this manner with the players alternately being given the choice to take all the money the referee has so far placed on the table and where the referee adds a dollar to the total whenever a player leaves the money. If the last player to move chooses to leave the N dollars the game ends with neither player receiving any money. Assume that N is public information.

(a) Without thinking too hard, how would you play this game if you were in the position of player 1? Would it make a difference if N were very large (like a million) or quite small (like 5)?

(b) Calculate the backward induction strategies. Do these make sense to you?

(c) Prove that the backward induction strategies form a Nash equilibrium.

(d) Prove that the outcome that results from the backward induction strategies is the unique outcome in any Nash equilibrium. Is there a unique Nash equilibrium?

7.30 Consider the extensive form without payoffs in Fig. 7.38. Suppose that the game either ends in a win for one player and a loss for the other, or a tie. That is, there are only three possible payoff

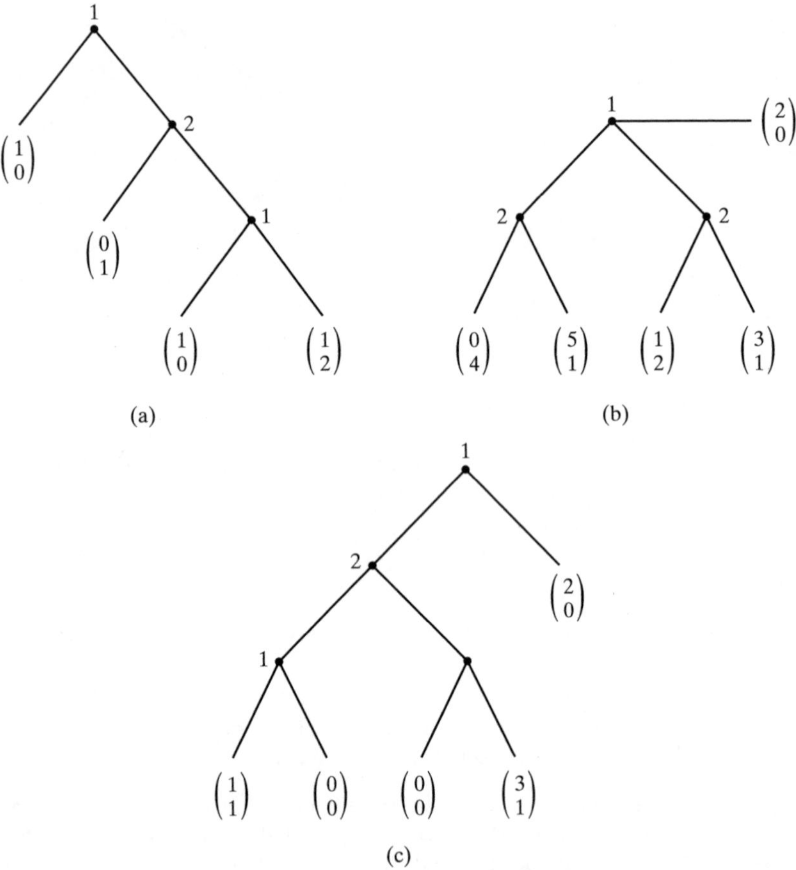

Figure 7.37.

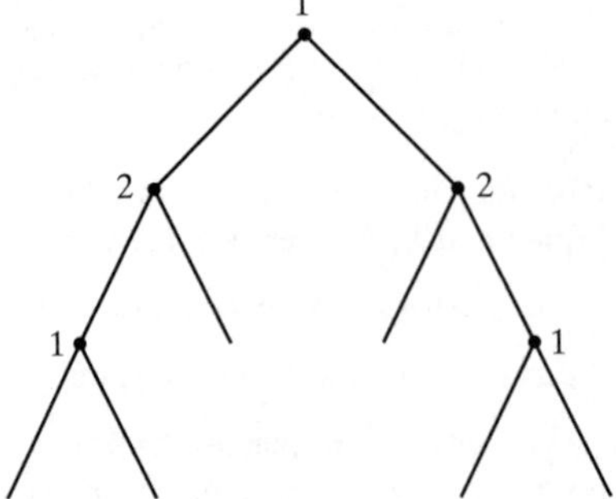

Figure 7.38.

vectors: $(0, 0)$, $(1, -1)$, and $(-1, 1)$. Construct four different games by assigning these payoffs in some fashion to the endpoints.

(a) Show that in each case, one of the players can ensure a win, or both can ensure a draw.

(b) Can you generalise this finding to some well-known parlour games (noughts and crosses, draughts, chess)?

7.31 Let Y denote a finite subset of nodes of some extensive form game. Prove that Y contains a node having no strict follower in Y.

7.32 Provide an example of a finite game of imperfect information and perfect recall in which there is no 'last' information set. That is, for every information set, there is a node, x, within it such that $(x, a) \in X$ is not an end node for some action a.

7.33 Find all subgame perfect equilibria in the game of Fig. 7.17.

7.34 Prove that for every extensive form game, the game itself is a subgame.

7.35 Show that if s is a pure strategy Nash equilibrium of an extensive form game, then s induces a Nash equilibrium in every subgame that is reached by s.

7.36 Argue that in every game of perfect information, every node defines a subgame.

7.37 Answer the following questions.

(a) Prove that every finite extensive form game with perfect information possesses at least one pure strategy subgame perfect equilibrium.

(b) Provide an example of a finite extensive form game having no pure strategy subgame perfect equilibrium.

7.38 Complete the proof of Theorem 7.6 on the existence of subgame perfect equilibrium.

7.39 Find all subgame perfect equilibria of the game in Fig. 7.26(a).

7.40 Answer the following questions for the game shown in Fig. 7.39.

(a) Calculate a Nash equilibrium for the game.

(b) Show that this game has no Nash equilibrium in behavioural strategies.

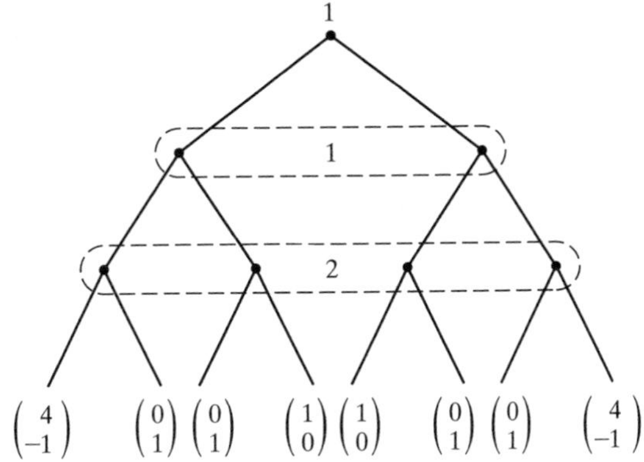

Figure 7.39.

(c) Conclude that this game does not possess a subgame perfect equilibrium.

(d) What is the source of the failure of existence?

7.41 Argue that for finite extensive form games, if a behavioural strategy, b, is completely mixed, then

(a) every information set is reached with positive probability.

(b) the assessment (p, b) is consistent if and only if p is derived from b using Bayes' rule.

7.42 Answer the following questions.

(a) Argue that the principle of independence implies that given the behavioural strategy depicted in the game of Fig. 7.29, the value of α must be $1/3$.

(b) Verify that given the behavioural strategies depicted in Figs. 7.30 and 7.31, consistency implies that in both cases the beliefs must satisfy $\alpha = \beta$.

7.43 Prove that if an assessment is consistent, then it satisfies Bayes' rule, and even Bayes' rule *in every subgame*. (The original assessment induces an assessment in each subgame. When each subgame is treated as a game in its own right, and the induced assessment on that subgame satisfies Bayes' rule, the original assessment is said to satisfy Bayes' rule in every subgame.)

7.44 Consider the game of Fig. 7.27. Let b denote the behavioural strategy in which player 1 plays L and player 2 plays m. Prove that for every system of beliefs, p, the assessment (p, b) is not sequentially rational. Find all sequentially rational assessments.

7.45 Find all sequential equilibria for the game of Fig. 7.35.

7.46 (a) Argue that the class of Bayesian games with a common prior is a subset of the class of extensive form games by showing that every Bayesian game with a common prior has strategy sets and payoff functions that are equivalent to those in the extensive form game in which Nature first chooses the players' types according to the prior, after which each player is simultaneously informed only of his own type, after which each player simultaneously takes an action.

(b) Consider a two-player Bayesian game with two types for each player and where all four vectors of types are equally likely. Draw the extensive form game (without specifying payoffs) as described in part (a).

(c) Prove that Bayes-Nash equilibrium of a Bayesian game induces a sequential equilibrium of the extensive form game described in part (a) and vice versa.

7.47 Consider the extensive form game in Fig. 7.40. An entrant must decide whether to enter a market in each of two periods. The market is already occupied by an incumbent, who may either be 'weak' or 'strong'. A weak incumbent is unable to cut its prices low enough to drive the entrant out if it attempts to enter. A strong incumbent can do so however. The probability that Nature chooses the strong incumbent is 1/4. The incumbent's payoff is the top number in each payoff vector. For example, in the payoff vector $(8, 0)$, the incumbent receives the payoff 8 and the entrant receives the payoff 0.

(a) Find a Nash equilibrium that is not subgame perfect.

(b) Find a sequentially rational assessment whose behavioural strategy part is not a subgame perfect equilibrium.

(c) Find an assessment, (p, b), that is sequentially rational and satisfies Bayes' rule.

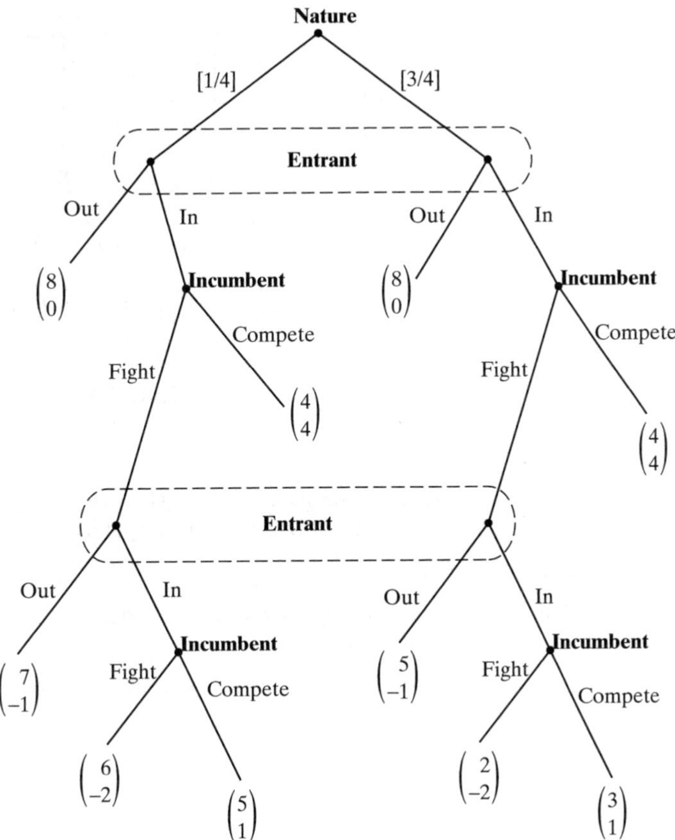
Nature
[1/4]
[3/4]
Entrant
Out
In
Out
In
(8, 0)
Incumbent
(8, 0)
Incumbent
Compete
Fight
(4, 4)
Compete
Fight
(4, 4)
Entrant
Out
In
Out
In
Incumbent
(7, –1)
Fight
Compete
(5, –1)
Incumbent
Fight
Compete
(6, –2)
(5, 1)
(2, –2)
(3, 1)

Figure 7.40.

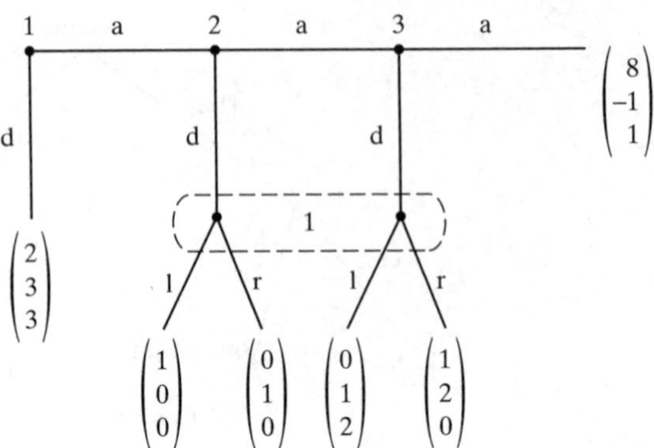

Figure 7.41.

7.48 Consider the extensive form game in Fig 7.41. Each of players 1, 2, and 3 can play down (d) or across (a), and player 1 can also play left (l) or right (r).

(a) Identify all subgames.

(b) Find a *pure strategy* subgame perfect equilibrium, b, such that (p, b) is not sequentially rational for any system of beliefs p.

(c) Find an assessment, (p, b), that is sequentially rational and satisfies Bayes' rule in every subgame.

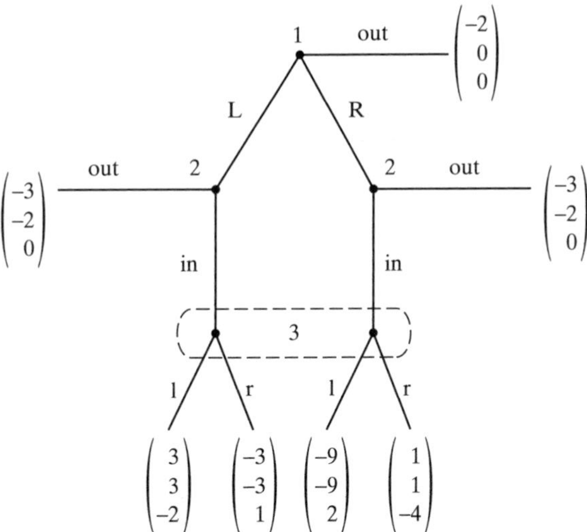

Figure 7.42.

7.49 Consider the extensive form game in Fig. 7.42.

(a) Find a subgame perfect equilibrium in which player 1 plays 'out' with probability one.

(b) Prove that there is no sequentially rational assessment in which player 2 plays out with probability one at each of his information sets.

(c) Find a sequentially rational assessment satisfying Bayes' rule.

CHAPTER 8

INFORMATION ECONOMICS

In the neoclassical theory of consumer and firm behaviour, consumers have perfect information about important features of the commodities they buy, such as their quality and durability. Firms have perfect information about the productivity of the inputs they demand. Because of this, it was possible to develop separately the theories of consumer demand and producer supply, and thereafter simply put them together by insisting on market-clearing prices.

One might hope that extending consumer and producer theory to include imperfect information would be as simple as incorporating decision making under uncertainty into those neoclassical models of consumer and producer behaviour. One might then derive theories of demand and supply under imperfect information, and simply put the two together once again to construct a theory of market equilibrium. Unfortunately, this approach would only make sense if the sources of the uncertainty on both sides of the market were exogenous and so not under the control of any agent involved.

Of course, the quality and durability of a commodity, for example, are not exogenous features. They are characteristics that are ultimately chosen by the producer. If consumers cannot directly observe product quality before making a purchase, then it may well be in the interest of the producer to produce only low-quality items. Of course, knowing this, consumers will be able to *infer* that product quality must be low and they will act accordingly. Thus, we cannot develop an adequate equilibrium theory of value under imperfect information without taking explicit account of the relevant *strategic* opportunities available to the agents involved. Notably, these strategic opportunities are significantly related to the *distribution of information* across economic agents.

A situation in which different agents possess different information is said to be one of **asymmetric information**. As we shall see, the strategic opportunities that arise in the presence of asymmetric information typically lead to *inefficient market outcomes*, a form of **market failure**. Under asymmetric information, the First Welfare Theorem no longer holds generally.

Thus, the main theme to be explored in this chapter is the important effect of asymmetric information on the efficiency properties of market outcomes. In the interest of simplicity and clarity, we will develop this theme within the context of one specific market: the market for insurance. By working through the details in our models of the insurance market, you will gain insight into how theorists would model other markets with similar informational asymmetries. By the end, we hope to have stimulated you to look for analogies and applications in your own field of special interest.

8.1 Adverse Selection

8.1.1 INFORMATION AND THE EFFICIENCY OF MARKET OUTCOMES

Consider a market for motor insurance in which many insurance companies sell insurance to many consumers.

Consumers are identical except for the exogenous probability that they are involved in an accident. Indeed, suppose that for $i = 1, 2, \ldots, m$, consumer i's accident probability is $\pi_i \in [0, 1]$, and that the occurrence of accidents is independent across consumers.[1] Otherwise, consumers are identical. Each has initial wealth w, suffers a loss of L dollars if an accident occurs, and has a continuous, strictly increasing, strictly concave von Neumann-Morgenstern utility of wealth function $u(\cdot)$. Consumers behave so as to maximise expected utility.

Insurance companies are identical. Each offers for sale full insurance only. That is, for a price, they promise to pay consumers L dollars if they incur an accident and zero dollars otherwise. For the moment, we will suppose that this full insurance policy is a lumpy good – that fractional amounts can be neither purchased nor sold. We also suppose that the cost of providing insurance is zero. Thus, if the full insurance policy sells for p dollars and is purchased by consumer i, then the insurance company's expected profits from this sale are $p - \pi_i L$. Insurance companies will be assumed to maximise expected profits.

Symmetric Information

Consider the case in which each consumer's accident probability can be identified by the insurance companies. Thus, there is no asymmetry of information here. What is the competitive (Walrasian) outcome in this benchmark setting in which all information is public?

To understand the competitive outcome here, it is important to recognise that the price of any particular commodity may well depend on the 'state of the world'. For example, an umbrella in the state 'rain' is a different commodity than an umbrella in the state 'sunny'. Consequently, these distinct commodities could command distinct prices.

The same holds true in this setting where a state specifies which subset of consumers have accidents. Because the state in which consumer i has an accident differs from that in which consumer j does, the commodity (policy) paying L dollars to consumer i when he has an accident differs from that paying L dollars to j when he does. Consequently, policies benefiting distinct consumers are in fact distinct commodities and may then command distinct prices.

[1] Thus, think of an accident as 'hitting a tree' as opposed to 'hitting another car'.

So, let p_i denote the price of the policy paying L dollars to consumer i should he have an accident. For simplicity, let us refer to this as the ith policy. We wish then to determine, for each $i = 1, 2, \ldots, m$, the competitive equilibrium price p_i^* of policy i.

Let us first consider the supply of policy i. If p_i is less than $\pi_i L$, then selling such a policy will result in expected losses. Hence, the supply of policy i will be zero in this case. On the other hand, if p_i is greater than $\pi_i L$, positive expected profits can be earned, so the supply of such policies will be infinite. Finally, if $p_i = \pi_i L$, then insurance companies break even on each policy i sold and hence are willing to supply any number of such policies.

On the demand side, if p_i is less than $\pi_i L$, then consumer i, being risk averse, will demand at least one policy i. This follows from our analysis in Chapter 2 where we showed that risk-averse consumers strictly prefer to fully insure than not to insure at all whenever actuarially fair insurance is available (i.e., whenever $p_i = \pi_i L$). The same analysis shows that if p_i exceeds $\pi_i L$, consumer i will purchase at most one policy i. (Recall that fractional policies cannot be purchased.)

By putting demand and supply together, the only possibility for equilibrium is when $p_i = \pi_i L$. In this case, each consumer i demands exactly one policy i and it is supplied by exactly one insurance company (any one will do). All other insurance companies are content to supply zero units of policy i because at price $p_i = \pi_i L$ all would earn zero expected profits.

We conclude that when information is freely available to all, there is a unique competitive equilibrium. In it, $p_i^* = \pi_i L$ for every policy $i = 1, 2, \ldots, m$. Note that in this competitive equilibrium, all insurance companies earn zero expected profits, and all consumers are fully insured.

We wish to argue that the competitive outcome is Pareto efficient – no consumer or insurance company can be made better off without making some other consumer or insurance company worse off. By constructing an appropriate pure exchange economy, one can come to this conclusion by appealing to the First Welfare Theorem. You are invited to do so in Exercise 8.1. We shall give a direct argument here.

In this setting, an *allocation* is an assignment of wealth to consumers and insurance companies *in each state*. An allocation is *feasible* if in every state, the total wealth assigned is equal to the total consumer wealth.

We now argue that no feasible allocation Pareto dominates the competitive allocation. Suppose, by way of contradiction, that some feasible allocation does Pareto dominate the competitive one. Without loss of generality, we may assume that the competitive allocation is dominated by a feasible allocation in which each consumer's wealth is the same whether or not he has an accident. (See Exercise 8.6.) Consequently, the dominating outcome guarantees each consumer i wealth $\bar{w}_i$. For this allocation to dominate the competitive one, it must be the case that $\bar{w}_i \geq w - \pi_i L$ for each i.

Now, because each consumer's wealth is certain, we may assume without loss that according to the dominating allocation, there is no transfer of wealth between any two consumers in any state. (Again, see Exercise 8.6.) Therefore, each consumer's wealth is directly transferred only to (or from) insurance companies in every state.

Consider then a particular consumer, i, and the insurance companies who are providing i with insurance in the dominating allocation. In aggregate, their expected profits from consumer i are

$$(1-\pi_i)(w-\bar{w}_i)+\pi_i(w-L-\bar{w}_i)=w-\pi_i L-\bar{w}_i, \tag{8.1}$$

because $\bar{w}_i - w$ (resp., $\bar{w}_i + L - w$) is the supplement to consumer i's wealth in states in which he does not have (resp., has) an accident, and the feasibility of the allocation implies that this additional wealth must be offset by a change in the aggregate wealth of insurance companies.

But we have already determined that the right-hand side of (8.1) is non-positive. So, letting EP_i^j denote company j's expected profits from consumer i, we have shown that in the dominating allocation,

$$w-\pi_i L-\bar{w}_i=\sum_j EP_i^j \leq 0 \qquad \text{for every consumer } i. \tag{8.2}$$

But each insurance company must be earning non-negative expected profits in the dominating allocation because each earns zero expected profits in the competitive allocation. Hence, we must also have

$$\sum_i EP_i^j \geq 0 \qquad \text{for every insurance company } j. \tag{8.3}$$

Summing (8.2) over i and (8.3) over j shows that each of the two inequalities must be equalities for every i and j. Consequently, each consumer's constant wealth and each firm's expected profits in the dominating allocation are identical to their competitive allocation counterparts. But this contradicts the definition of a dominating allocation and completes the argument that the competitive allocation is efficient.

Asymmetric Information and Adverse Selection

We now return to the more realistic setting in which insurance companies cannot identify consumers' accident probabilities. Although insurance companies can and do employ historical records of consumers to partially determine their accident probabilities, we will take a more extreme view for simplicity. Specifically, we shall suppose that insurance companies know only the distribution of accident probabilities among consumers and nothing else.

So let the non-degenerate interval $[\underline{\pi}, \bar{\pi}]$ contain the set of all consumer accident probabilities, and let F be a cumulative distribution function on $[\underline{\pi}, \bar{\pi}]$ representing the insurance companies' information. This specification allows either finitely many or a continuum of consumers. The possibility of allowing a continuum is convenient for examples. We will also suppose that both $\underline{\pi}$ and $\bar{\pi}$ are in the support of F.[2] Therefore, for each

[2]If there are finitely many consumers and therefore finitely many accident probabilities, this means simply that both $\underline{\pi}$ and $\bar{\pi}$ are given positive probability by F. More generally, it means that all non-degenerate intervals of the form $[\underline{\pi}, a)$ and $(b, \bar{\pi}]$ are given positive probability by F.

$\pi \in [\underline{\pi}, \bar{\pi}]$, $F(\pi)$ denotes the fraction of consumers having accident probability less than or equal to π. Equivalently, $F(\pi)$ denotes the probability that any particular consumer has accident probability π or lower. Insurance companies are otherwise exactly as before. In particular, they each sell only full insurance.

The impact of asymmetric information is quite dramatic. Indeed, even though policies sold to different consumers can potentially command distinct prices, in equilibrium they will not. The reason is quite straightforward. To see it, suppose to the contrary that the equilibrium price paid by consumer i exceeds that paid by consumer j. Because both consumers are actually purchasing a policy, the expected profits on each sale must be non-negative – otherwise the insurance company supplying the money-losing policy would not be profit-maximising. Consequently, because consumers i and j are identical to insurance companies from an accident probability point of view, the policy sold to consumer i must earn strictly positive expected profits. But then each insurance company would wish to supply an infinite amount of such a policy, which cannot be the case in equilibrium. This contradiction establishes the result: *There is a single equilibrium price of the full insurance policy for all consumers.*

Then let p denote this single price of the full insurance policy. We wish now to determine its equilibrium value, p^*.

Because positive expected profits result in infinite supply and negative expected profits result in zero supply, a natural guess would be to set $p^* = E(\pi)L$, where $E(\pi) = \int_{\underline{\pi}}^{\bar{\pi}} \pi dF(\pi)$ is the expected accident probability. Such a price is intended to render insurance companies' expected profits equal to zero. But does it?

To see that it might not, note that this price might be so high that only those consumers with relatively high accident probabilities will choose to purchase insurance. Consequently, companies would be *underestimating* the expected accident probability by using the unconditional expectation, $E(\pi)$, rather than the expectation of the accident probability *conditional on those consumers actually willing to purchase the policy*. By underestimating this way, profits would be strictly negative on average. Thus to find p^* we must take this into account.

For any accident probability π, the consumer buys a policy for price p only if the expected utility from doing so exceeds the expected utility from remaining uninsured: that is, only if[3]

$$u(w - p) \geq \pi u(w - L) + (1 - \pi)u(w).$$

Rearranging, and defining the function $h(p)$, we find that the policy will be purchased only if

$$\pi \geq \frac{u(w) - u(w - p)}{u(w) - u(w - L)} \equiv h(p).$$

[3]For simplicity, we assume that a consumer who is indifferent between buying the policy or not does in fact buy it.

Then we will call p^* a *competitive equilibrium price under asymmetric information* if it satisfies the following condition:

$$p^* = E(\pi \mid \pi \geq h(p^*))L, \tag{8.4}$$

where the expression $E(\pi \mid \pi \geq h(p^*)) = \left(\int_{h(p^*)}^{\bar{\pi}} \pi dF(\pi)\right) \Big/ \left(1 - F(h(p^*)\right)$ is the expected accident probability conditional on $\pi \geq h(p^*)$.

Note that a consumer with accident probability π will purchase the full insurance policy at price p as long as $\pi \geq h(p)$. Thus, condition (8.4) ensures that firms earn zero expected profits on each policy sold, conditional on the accident probabilities of consumers who actually purchase the policy. The supply of policies then can be set equal to the number demanded by consumers. Thus, the condition above does indeed describe an equilibrium.

An immediate concern is whether or not such an equilibrium exists. That is, does there necessarily exist a p^* satisfying (8.4)? The answer is yes, and here is why.

Let $g(p) = E(\pi \mid \pi \geq h(p))L$ for every $p \in [0, \bar{\pi}L]$, where $\bar{\pi}$ is the highest accident probability among all consumers. Note that the conditional expectation is well-defined because $h(p) \leq \bar{\pi}$ for every $p \in [0, \bar{\pi}L]$ (check this). In addition, because $E(\pi \mid \pi \geq h(p)) \in [0, \bar{\pi}]$, the function g maps the interval $[0, \bar{\pi}L]$ into itself. Finally, because h is strictly increasing in p, we know g is non-decreasing in p. Consequently, g is a non-decreasing function mapping a closed interval into itself. As you are invited to explore in the exercises, even though g need not be continuous, it must nonetheless have a fixed point $p^* \in [0, \bar{\pi}L]$.[4] By the definition of g, this fixed point is an equilibrium.

Having settled the existence question, we now turn to the properties of equilibria. First, there is no reason to expect a unique equilibrium here. Indeed, one can easily construct examples having multiple equilibria. But more importantly, equilibria need not be efficient.

For example, consider the case in which F is uniformly distributed over $[\underline{\pi}, \bar{\pi}] = [0,1]$. Then $g(p) = (1 + h(p))L/2$ is strictly increasing and strictly convex because $h(p)$ is. Consequently, as you are asked to show in an exercise, there can be at most two equilibrium prices. Any equilibrium price, p^*, satisfies $p^* = (1 + h(p^*))L/2$. But because $h(L) = 1$, $p^* = L$ is always an equilibrium, and it may be the only one. However, when $p^* = L$, (8.4) tells us the expected probability of an accident for those who buy insurance must be $E(\pi \mid \pi \geq h(L)) = 1$. Thus, in this equilibrium, all consumers will be uninsured except those who are certain to have an accident. But even these consumers have insurance only in a formal sense because they must pay the full amount of the loss, L, to obtain the policy. Thus, their wealth (and therefore their utility) remains the same as if they had not purchased the policy at all.

Clearly, this outcome is inefficient in the extreme. The competitive outcome with symmetric information gives every consumer (except those who are certain to have an accident) strictly higher utility, while also ensuring that every insurance company's expected

[4] Of course, if g is continuous, we can apply Theorem A1.11, Brouwer's fixed-point theorem. However, you will show in an exercise that if there are finitely many consumers, g cannot be continuous.

profits are zero. Here, the asymmetry in information causes a significant market failure in the insurance market. Effectively, no trades take place and therefore opportunities for Pareto improvements go unrealised.

To understand why prices are unable to produce an efficient equilibrium here, consider a price at which expected profits are negative for insurance companies. Then, other things being equal, you might think that raising the price will tend to increase expected profits. But in insurance markets, other things will *not* remain equal. In general, whenever the price of insurance is increased, the expected utility a consumer receives from buying insurance falls, whereas the expected utility from not insuring remains the same. For some consumers, it will no longer be worthwhile to buy insurance, so they will quit doing so. But who continues to buy as the price increases? Only those for whom the expected loss from *not* doing so is greatest, and these are precisely the consumers with the highest accident probabilities. As a result, whenever the price of insurance rises, the pool of customers who continue to buy insurance becomes riskier on average.

This is an example of **adverse selection**, and it tends here to have a negative influence on expected profits. If, as in our example, the negative impact of adverse selection on expected profits outweighs the positive impact of higher insurance prices, there can fail to be any efficient equilibrium at all, and mutually beneficial potential trades between insurance companies and relatively low-risk consumers can fail to take place.

The lesson is clear. In the presence of asymmetric information and adverse selection, the competitive outcome need not be efficient. Indeed, it can be dramatically inefficient.

One of the advantages of free markets is their ability to 'evolve'. Thus, one might well imagine that the insurance market would somehow adjust to cope with adverse selection. In fact, real insurance markets do perform a good deal better than the one we just analysed. The next section is devoted to explaining how this is accomplished.

8.1.2 SIGNALLING

Consider yourself a low-risk consumer stuck in the inefficient equilibrium we have just described. The equilibrium price of insurance is so high that you have chosen not to purchase any. If only there were some way you could convince one of the insurance companies that you are a low risk. They would then be willing to sell you a policy for a price you would be willing to pay.

In fact, there often *will* be ways consumers can credibly communicate how risky they are to insurance companies, and we call this kind of behaviour **signalling**. In real insurance markets, consumers can and do distinguish themselves from one another – and they do it by purchasing different types of policies. Although we ruled this out in our previous analysis by assuming only one type of policy, we can now adapt our analysis to allow it.

To keep things simple, we will suppose there are only two possible accident probabilities, $\underline{\pi}$ and $\bar{\pi}$, where $0 < \underline{\pi} < \bar{\pi} < 1$. We assume that the fraction of consumers having accident probability $\underline{\pi}$ is $\alpha \in (0, 1)$. Consumers with accident probability $\underline{\pi}$ are called *low-risk* consumers, and those with accident probability $\bar{\pi}$ are called *high-risk* consumers.

To model the idea that consumers can attempt to distinguish themselves from others by choosing different policies, we shall take a game theoretic approach.

Consider then the following extensive form game, which we will refer to as the **insurance signalling game**, involving two consumers (low-risk and high-risk) and a single insurance company:

- Nature moves first and determines which consumer will make a proposal to the insurance company. The low-risk consumer is chosen with probability α, and the high-risk consumer is chosen with probability $1 - \alpha$.
- The chosen consumer moves second. He chooses a *policy (B, p)*, consisting of a *benefit* $B \geq 0$ the insurance company pays him if he has an accident, and a *premium* $0 \leq p \leq w$ he pays to the insurance company whether or not he has an accident.[5]
- The insurance company moves last, not knowing which consumer was chosen by Nature, but knowing the chosen consumer's proposed policy. The insurance company either agrees to accept the terms of the consumer's policy or rejects them.

The extensive form of this game is shown in Fig. 8.1. When interpreting the game, think of the insurance company as being one of many competing companies, and think of the chosen consumer as a randomly selected member from the set of all consumers, of whom a fraction α are low-risk types and a fraction $1 - \alpha$ are high-risk types.

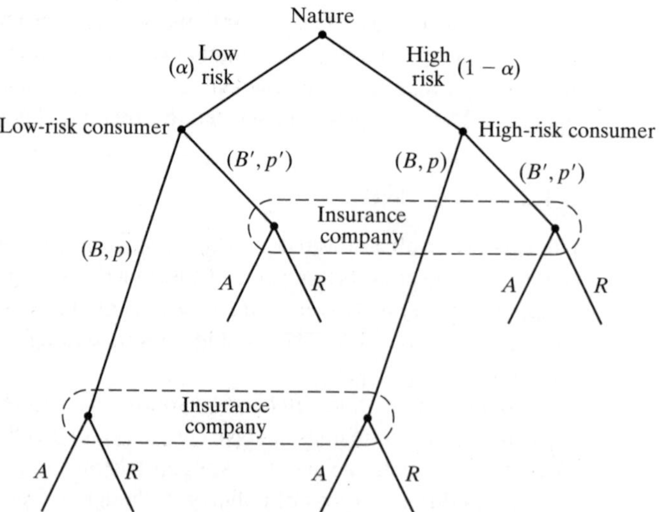

Figure 8.1. Insurance signalling game: a schematic diagram of the signalling extensive form game. The figure is complete except that it shows only two policy choices, (B, p) and (B', p'), available to the consumer when there are in fact infinitely many choices available.

[5]Note the slight change in our use of the term *policy*. It now refers to a benefit–premium *pair, (B, p)*, rather than simply the benefit. Restricting p to be no higher than w ensures that the consumer does not go bankrupt.

A pure strategy for the low-risk consumer is a specification of a policy $\psi_l = (B_l, p_l)$, and for the high-risk consumer, a policy $\psi_h = (B_h, p_h)$.

A pure strategy for the insurance company must specify one of two responses, either A (accept) or R (reject), for each potential policy proposed. Thus, a pure strategy for the insurance company is a response function, σ, where $\sigma(B, p) \in \{A, R\}$ for each policy (B, p). Note that σ depends only on the proposed policy and not on whether the consumer proposing it is low- or high-risk. This reflects the assumption that the insurance company does not know which risk type makes the proposal.

Once a policy is proposed, the insurance company formulates beliefs about the consumer's accident probability. Let probability $\beta(B, p)$ denote the insurance company's beliefs that the consumer who proposed policy (B, p) is the low-risk type.

We wish to determine the pure strategy sequential equilibria of this game.[6] There is, however, a purely technical difficulty with this. The definition of a sequential equilibrium requires the game to be finite, but the game under consideration is not – the consumer can choose any one of a continuum of policies.

Now, the definition of a sequential equilibrium requires the game to be finite only because the consistency condition is not easily defined for infinite games. However, as you will demonstrate in an exercise, when the consumer's choice set is restricted to any finite set of policies, so that the game becomes finite, *every* assessment satisfying Bayes' rule also satisfies the consistency condition. Consequently, in every finite version of the insurance signalling game, an assessment is a sequential equilibrium if and only if it is sequentially rational and satisfies Bayes' rule.

With this in mind, we define a sequential equilibrium for the (infinite) insurance signalling game in terms of sequential rationality and Bayes' rule, alone, as follows.

DEFINITION 8.1 ***Signalling Game Pure Strategy Sequential Equilibrium***

The assessment $(\psi_l, \psi_h, \sigma(\cdot), \beta(\cdot))$ is a pure strategy sequential equilibrium of the insurance signalling game if

1. *given the insurance company's strategy, $\sigma(\cdot)$, proposing the policy ψ_l maximises the low-risk consumer's expected utility, and proposing ψ_h maximises the high-risk consumer's expected utility;*
2. *the insurance company's beliefs satisfy Bayes' rule. That is,*
   (a) $\beta(\psi) \in [0, 1]$, for all policies $\psi = (B, p)$,
   (b) *if* $\psi_l \neq \psi_h$, *then* $\beta(\psi_l) = 1$ *and* $\beta(\psi_h) = 0$,
   (c) *if* $\psi_l = \psi_h$, *then* $\beta(\psi_l) = \beta(\psi_h) = \alpha$;
3. *for every policy $\psi = (B, p)$, the insurance company's reaction, $\sigma(\psi)$, maximises its expected profits given its beliefs $\beta(B, p)$.*

---

[6]See Chapter 7 for a discussion of sequential equilibrium. We have chosen to employ the sequential equilibrium concept here because we want to insist upon rational behaviour on the part of the insurance company at each of its information sets, and further that consumers take this into account.

Conditions (1) and (3) ensure that the assessment is sequentially rational, whereas condition (2) ensures that the insurance company's beliefs satisfy Bayes' rule. Because we are restricting attention to pure strategies, Bayes' rule reduces to something rather simple. If the different risk types choose different policies in equilibrium, then on observing the low- (high-) risk consumer's policy, the insurance company infers that it faces the low- (high-) risk consumer. This is condition 2.(b). If, however, the two risk types choose the same policy in equilibrium, then on observing this policy, the insurance company's beliefs remain unchanged and equal to its prior belief. This is condition 2.(c).

The basic question is this: can the low-risk consumer distinguish himself from the high-risk one here, and as a result achieve a more efficient outcome? It is not obvious that the answer is yes. For note that there is no direct connection between a consumer's risk type and the policy he proposes. That is, the act of purchasing less insurance does not decrease the probability that an accident will occur. In this sense, the signals used by consumers – the policies they propose – are *unproductive*.

However, despite this, the low-risk consumer can still attempt to signal that he is low-risk by demonstrating his willingness to accept a decrease in the benefit for a smaller compensating premium reduction than would the high-risk consumer. Of course, for this kind of (unproductive) signalling to be effective, the risk types must display different marginal rates of substitution between benefit levels, B, and premiums, p. As we shall shortly demonstrate, this crucial difference in marginal rates of substitution is indeed present.

Analysing the Game

To begin, it is convenient to define for each risk type the expected utility of a generic policy (B, p). So, let

$$u_l(B, p) = \underline{\pi} u(w - L + B - p) + (1 - \underline{\pi})u(w - p) \qquad \text{and}$$
$$u_h(B, p) = \bar{\pi} u(w - L + B - p) + (1 - \bar{\pi})u(w - p)$$

denote the expected utility of the policy (B, p) for the low- and high-risk consumer, respectively.

The following facts are easily established.

FACTS:

(a) $u_l(B, p)$ and $u_h(B, p)$ are continuous, differentiable, strictly concave in (B, p), strictly increasing in B, and strictly decreasing in p,

(b) $MRS_l(B, p)$ is greater than, equal to or less than $\underline{\pi}$ as B is less than, equal to, or greater than L. $MRS_h(B, p)$ is greater than, equal to, or less than $\bar{\pi}$ as B is less than, equal to, or greater than L.

(c) $MRS_l(B, p) < MRS_h(B, p)$ for all (B, p).

The last of these is often referred to as the **single-crossing property**. As its name suggests, it implies that indifference curves for the two consumer types intersect at most

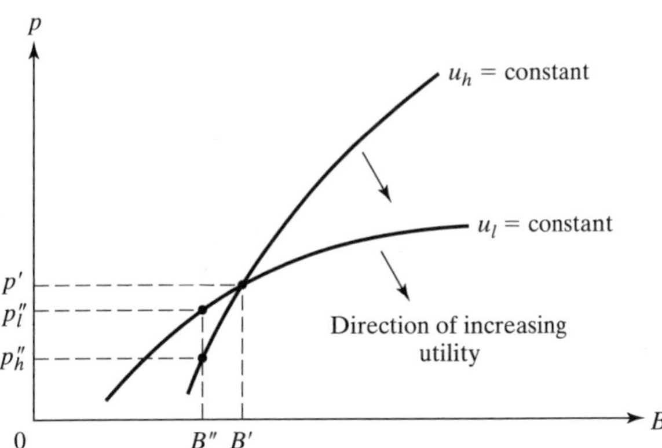

Figure 8.2. Single-crossing property. Beginning from policy (B', p'), the benefit is reduced to B''. To keep the low-risk type just as well off, the price must be reduced to p''_l. It must be further reduced to p''_h to keep the high-risk type just as well off.

once. Equally important, it shows that the different risk types display different marginal rates of substitution when faced with the same policy.

Fig. 8.2 illustrates facts (a) and (c). In accordance with fact (c), the steep indifference curves belong to the high-risk consumer and the flatter ones to the low-risk consumer. The difference in their marginal rates of substitution indicates that beginning from a given policy (B', p'), the low-risk consumer is willing to accept a decrease in the benefit to B'' for a smaller compensating premium reduction than would the high-risk consumer. Here, reducing the benefit is less costly to the low-risk consumer because he is less likely to have an accident.

The insurance company maximises expected profits. Now, in case it knows that the consumer is low-risk, it will accept any policy (B, p) satisfying $p > \underline{\pi} B$, because such a policy yields positive profits. Similarly, it will reject the policy if $p < \underline{\pi} B$. It is indifferent between accepting and rejecting the policy if $p = \underline{\pi} B$. If the insurance company knows the consumer is high-risk, then it accepts the policy (B, p) if $p > \bar{\pi} B$ and rejects it if $p < \bar{\pi} B$.

Fig. 8.3 illustrates the two zero-profit lines for the insurance company. The line $p = \underline{\pi} B$ contains those policies (B, p) yielding zero expected profits for the insurance company when the consumer is known to be low-risk. The line $p = \bar{\pi} B$ contains those policies yielding zero expected profits when the consumer is known to be high-risk. These two lines will play an important role in our analysis. Note that the low-risk zero profit line has slope $\underline{\pi}$, and the high-risk zero profit line has slope $\bar{\pi}$.

Now is a good time to think back to the competitive equilibrium for the case in which the insurance company can identify the risk types. There we showed that in the unique competitive equilibrium the price of full insurance, where $B = L$, is equal to $\underline{\pi} L$ for the low-risk consumer, and $\bar{\pi} L$ for the high-risk consumer. This outcome is depicted in Fig. 8.4. The insurance company earns zero profits on each consumer, each consumer purchases full insurance, and, by fact (b) above, each consumer's indifference curve is tangent to the insurance company's respective zero-profit line.

Returning to the game at hand, we begin characterising its sequential equilibria by providing lower bounds on each of the consumers' expected utilities, conditional on having been chosen by Nature. Note that the most pessimistic belief the insurance company might

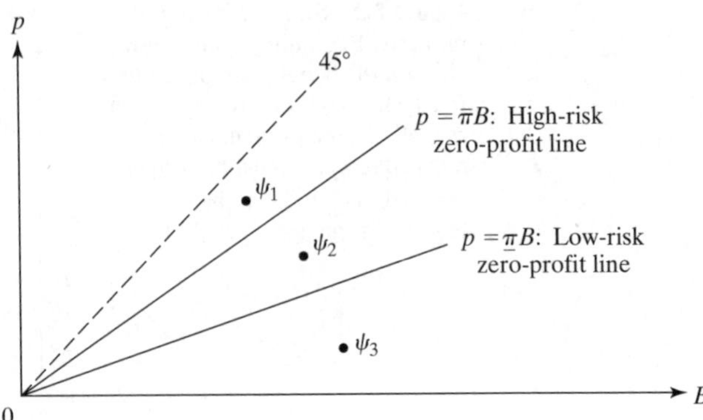

Figure 8.3. Zero-profit lines. Policy ψ_1 earns positive profits on both consumer types; ψ_2 earns positive profits on the low-risk consumer and negative profits on the high-risk consumer; ψ_3 earns negative profits on both consumer types.

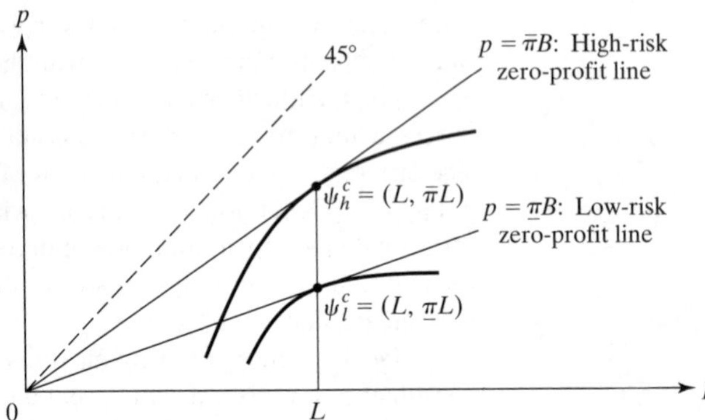

Figure 8.4. Competitive outcome, ψ_l^c and ψ_h^c denote the policies consumed by the low- and high-risk types in the competitive equilibrium when the insurance company can identify risk types. The competitive outcome is efficient.

have is that it faces the high-risk consumer. Consequently, both consumer-types' utilities ought to be bounded below by the maximum utility they could obtain when the insurance company believes them to be the high-risk consumer. This is the content of the next lemma.

LEMMA 8.1 *Let $(\psi_l, \psi_h, \sigma(\cdot), \beta(\cdot))$ be a sequential equilibrium, and let u_l^* and u_h^* denote the equilibrium utility of the low- and high-risk consumer, respectively, given that he has been chosen by Nature. Then*

1. $u_l^* \geq \tilde{u}_l$, *and*
2. $u_h^* \geq u_h^c$,

where $\tilde{u}_l \equiv \max_{(B,p)} u_l(B,p)$ s.t. $p = \bar{\pi}B \leq w$, and $u_h^c \equiv u_h(L, \bar{\pi}L)$ denotes the high-risk consumer's utility in the competitive equilibrium with full information.

Proof: Consider a policy (B, p) lying above the high-risk zero-profit line, so that $p > \bar{\pi}B$. We wish to argue that in equilibrium, the insurance company must accept this policy.

To see this, note that by accepting it, the company's expected profits given its beliefs $\beta(B,p)$ are

$$p - \{\beta(B,p)\underline{\pi} + (1-\beta(B,p))\bar{\pi}\}B \geq p - \bar{\pi}B > 0.$$

Consequently, accepting is strictly better than rejecting the policy because rejecting results in zero profits. We conclude that all policies (B,p) above the high-risk zero-profit line are accepted by the insurance company.

Thus, for any policy satisfying $\bar{\pi}B < p \leq w$, the low-risk consumer, by proposing it, can guarantee utility $u_l(B,p)$, and the high-risk consumer can guarantee utility $u_h(B,p)$. Therefore, because each risk type maximises expected utility in equilibrium, the following inequalities must hold for all policies satisfying $\bar{\pi}B < p \leq w$:

$$u_l^* \geq u_l(B,p) \quad \text{and} \tag{P.1}$$

$$u_h^* \geq u_h(B,p). \tag{P.2}$$

Continuity of u_l and u_h implies that (P.1) and (P.2) must in fact hold for all policies satisfying the weak inequality $\bar{\pi}B \leq p \leq w$. Thus, (P.1) and (P.2) may be rewritten as

$$u_l^* \geq u_l(B,p) \quad \text{for all} \quad \bar{\pi}B \leq p \leq w, \tag{P.3}$$

$$u_h^* \geq u_h(B,p) \quad \text{for all} \quad \bar{\pi}B \leq p \leq w. \tag{P.4}$$

But (P.3) is equivalent to (1) because utility is decreasing in p, and (P.4) is equivalent to (2) because, among all no better than fair insurance policies, the full insurance one uniquely maximises the high-risk consumer's utility. ∎

Fig. 8.5 illustrates Lemma 8.1. A consequence of the lemma that is evident from the figure is that the high-risk consumer must purchase insurance in equilibrium. This is because without insurance his utility would be $u_h(0,0)$ which, by strict risk aversion, is strictly less than u_h^c, a lower bound on his equilibrium utility.

The same cannot be said for the low-risk consumer even though it appears so from Fig. 8.5. We have drawn Fig. 8.5 for the case in which $MRS_l(0,0) > \bar{\pi}$, so that

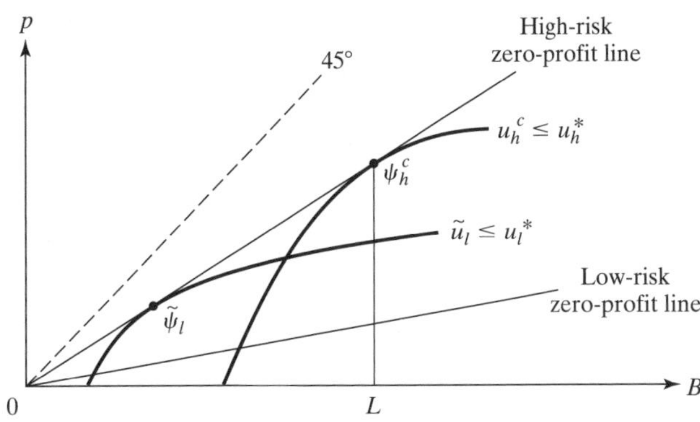

Figure 8.5. Lower bounds. Because all policies (B,p) above the high-risk zero-profit line are accepted by the insurance company in equilibrium, the low-risk consumer must obtain utility no smaller than $\tilde{u}_l = u_l(\tilde{\psi}_l)$ and the high-risk consumer utility no smaller than $u_h^c = u(\psi_h^c)$. Note that although in the figure $\tilde{\psi}_l \neq (0,0)$, it is possible that $\tilde{\psi}_l = (0,0)$.

$u_l(0, 0) < \tilde{u}_l$. However, in the equally plausible case in which $MRS_l(0, 0) < \bar{\pi}$ we have $u_l(0, 0) \geq \tilde{u}_l$. In this latter case, the low-risk consumer may choose not to purchase insurance in equilibrium (by making a proposal that is rejected) without violating the conclusion of Lemma 8.1.

The preceding lemma applies to every sequential equilibrium. We now separate the set of equilibria into two kinds: separating and pooling.

An equilibrium is a **separating equilibrium** if the different types of consumers propose different policies. In this way, the consumers separate themselves from one another and can be identified by the insurance company by virtue of the chosen policy. In contrast, an equilibrium is a **pooling equilibrium** if both consumer types propose the same policy. Consequently, the consumer types cannot be identified by observing the policy they propose. In summary, we have the following definition.

DEFINITION 8.2 ***Separating and Pooling Signalling Equilibria***

A pure strategy sequential equilibrium $(\psi_l, \psi_h, \sigma(\cdot), \beta(\cdot))$ is separating if $\psi_l \neq \psi_h$, while it is pooling otherwise.

With only two possible types of consumers, a pure strategy sequential equilibrium is either separating or pooling. Thus, it is enough for us to characterise the sets of separating and pooling equilibria. We begin with the former.

Separating Equilibria

In a separating equilibrium, the two risk types will propose different policies if chosen by Nature, and on the basis of this the insurance company will be able to identify them. Of course, each risk type therefore could feign the identity of the other simply by behaving as the other would according to the equilibrium.[7] The key conceptual point to grasp, then, is that in a separating equilibrium, *it must not be in the interest of either type to mimic the behaviour of the other*. Based on this idea, we can characterise the policies proposed and accepted in a separating pure strategy sequential equilibrium as follows.

THEOREM 8.1 ***Separating Equilibrium Characterisation***

The policies $\psi_l = (B_l, p_l)$ and $\psi_h = (B_h, p_h)$ are proposed by the low- and high-risk consumer, respectively, and accepted by the insurance company in some separating equilibrium if and only if

1. $\psi_l \neq \psi_h = (L, \bar{\pi} L)$.
2. $p_l \geq \underline{\pi} B_l$.

[7]There are other ways to feign the identity of the other type. For example, the low-risk type might choose a proposal that neither type is supposed to choose in equilibrium, but one that would nonetheless induce the insurance company to believe that it faced the high-risk consumer.

3. $u_l(\psi_l) \geq \tilde{u}_l \equiv \max_{(B,p)} u_l(B,p)$ *s.t.* $p = \bar{\pi}B \leq w$.

4. $u_h^c \equiv, u_h(\psi_h) \geq u_h(\psi_l)$.

Proof: Suppose first that $\psi_l = (B_l, p_l)$ and $\psi_h = (L, \bar{\pi}L)$ satisfy (1) to (4). We must construct a strategy $\sigma(\cdot)$ and beliefs $\beta(\cdot)$ for the insurance company so that the assessment $(\psi_l, \psi_h, \sigma(\cdot), \beta(\cdot))$ is a sequential equilibrium. It then will be clearly separating. The following specifications will suffice:

$$\beta(B,p) = \begin{cases} 1, & \text{if } (B,p) = \psi_l, \\ 0, & \text{if } (B,p) \neq \psi_l. \end{cases}$$

$$\sigma(B,p) = \begin{cases} A, & \text{if } (B,p) = \psi_l, \quad \text{or} \quad p \geq \bar{\pi}B, \\ R, & \text{otherwise.} \end{cases}$$

According to the beliefs $\beta(\cdot)$, any policy proposed other than ψ_l induces the insurance company to believe that it faces the high-risk consumer with probability one. On the other hand, when the policy ψ_l is proposed, the insurance company is sure that it faces the low-risk consumer. Consequently, the insurance company's beliefs satisfy Bayes' rule.

In addition, given these beliefs, the insurance company's strategy maximises its expected profits because, according to that strategy, the company accepts a policy if and only if it results in non-negative expected profits.

For example, the proposal $\psi_l = (B_l, p_l)$ is accepted because, once proposed, it induces the insurance company to believe with probability one that it faces the low-risk consumer. Consequently, the insurance company's expected profits from accepting the policy are $p_l - \underline{\pi}B_l$, which, according to (2), is non-negative. Similarly, the proposal $\psi_h = (L, \bar{\pi}L)$ is accepted because it induces the insurance company to believe with probability one that it faces the high-risk consumer. In that case, expected profits from accepting the policy are $\bar{\pi}L - \bar{\pi}L = 0$.

All other policy proposals (B, p) induce the insurance company to believe with probability one that it faces the high-risk consumer. Its expected profits from accepting such policies are then $p - \bar{\pi}B$. Thus, these policies are also accepted precisely when they yield non-negative expected profits given the insurance company's beliefs.

We have shown that given any policy (p, B), the insurance company's strategy maximises its expected profits given its beliefs. It remains to show that given the insurance company's strategy, both consumers are choosing policies that maximise their utility.

To complete this part of the proof, we show that no policy proposal yields the low-risk consumer more utility than ψ_l nor the high-risk consumer more than ψ_h. Note that because the insurance company accepts the policy (0, 0), and this policy is equivalent to a rejection by the insurance company (regardless of *which* policy was rejected), both consumers can maximise their utility by making a proposal that is accepted by the insurance company. We therefore may restrict our attention to the set of such policies that we denote by $\mathcal{A}$; i.e.,

$$\mathcal{A} = \{\psi_l\} \cup \{(B,p) \mid p \geq \bar{\pi}B\}.$$

Thus, it is enough to show that for all $(B, p) \in \mathcal{A}$ with $p \leq w$,

$$u_l(\psi_l) \geq u_l(B, p), \qquad \text{and} \tag{P.1}$$

$$u_h(\psi_h) \geq u_h(B, p). \tag{P.2}$$

But (P.1) follows from (3), and (P.2) follows from (1), (3), (4), and because $(L, \bar{\pi}L)$ is best for the high-risk consumer among all no better than fair policies.

We now consider the converse. So, suppose that $(\psi_l, \psi_h, \sigma(\cdot), \beta(\cdot))$ is a separating equilibrium in which the equilibrium policies are accepted by the insurance company. We must show that (1) to (4) hold. We take each in turn.

1. The definition of a separating equilibrium requires $\psi_l \neq \psi_h$. To see that $\psi_h \equiv (B_h, p_h) = (L, \bar{\pi}L)$, recall that Lemma 8.1 implies $u_h(\psi_h) = u_h(B_h, p_h) \geq u_h(L, \bar{\pi}L)$. Now because the insurance company accepts this proposal, it must earn non-negative profits. Hence, we must have $p_h \geq \bar{\pi}B_h$ because in a separating equilibrium, the insurance company's beliefs must place probability one on the high-risk consumer subsequent to the high-risk consumer's equilibrium proposal ψ_h. But as we have argued before, these two inequalities imply that $\psi_h = (L, \bar{\pi}L)$ (see, for example, Fig. 8.4).

2. Subsequent to the low-risk consumer's equilibrium proposal, (B_l, p_l), the insurance company places probability one on the low-risk consumer by Bayes' rule. Accepting the proposal then would yield the insurance company expected profits $p_l - \underline{\pi}B_l$. Because the insurance company accepts this proposal by hypothesis, this quantity must be non-negative.

3. This follows from (1) of Lemma 8.1.

4. According to the insurance company's strategy, it accepts policy ψ_l. Because the high-risk consumer's equilibrium utility is $u_h(\psi_h)$, we must have $u_h(\psi_h) \geq u_h(\psi_l)$. ∎

Fig. 8.6 illustrates the policies that can arise in a separating equilibrium according to Theorem 8.1. The high-risk consumer obtains policy $\psi_h^c \equiv, (L, \bar{\pi}L)$ and the low-risk consumer obtains the policy $\psi_l = (B_l, p_l)$, which must lie somewhere in the shaded region.

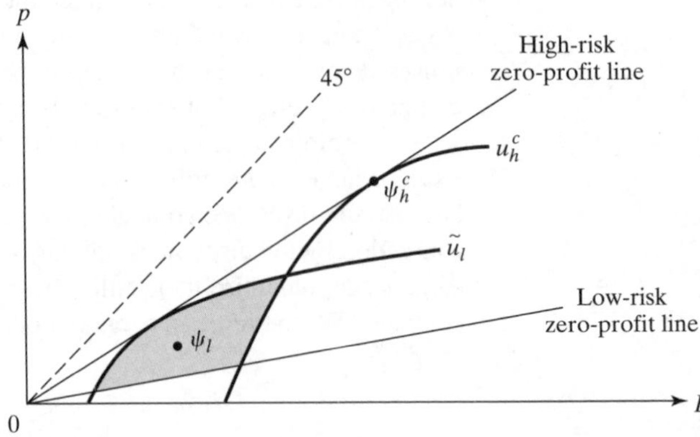

Figure 8.6. Potential separating equilibria. In a separating equilibrium in which both consumer types propose acceptable policies, the high-risk policy must be ψ_h^c and the low-risk policy, ψ_l, must be in the shaded region. Here, $MRS_l(0, 0) > \bar{\pi}$. A similar figure arises in the alternative case, noting that $MRS_l(0, 0) > \underline{\pi}$ always holds.

Note the essential features of the set of low-risk policies. Each is above the low-risk zero-profit line to induce acceptance by the insurance company, above the high-risk consumer's indifference curve through his equilibrium policy to ensure that he has no incentive to mimic the low-risk consumer, and below the indifference curve giving utility $\tilde{u}_l$ to the low-risk consumer to ensure that he has no incentive to deviate and be identified as a high-risk consumer.

Theorem 8.1 restricts attention to those equilibria in which both consumers propose acceptable policies. Owing to Lemma 8.1, this is a restriction only on the low-risk consumer's policy proposal. When $MRS_l(0, 0) \leq \bar{\pi}$, there are separating equilibria in which the low-risk consumer's proposal is rejected in equilibrium. However, you are asked to show in an exercise that each of these is payoff equivalent to some separating equilibrium in which the low-risk consumer's policy proposal is accepted. Finally, one can show that the shaded region depicted in Fig. 8.6 is always non-empty, even when $MRS_l(0, 0) \leq \bar{\pi}$. This requires using the fact that $MRS_l(0, 0) > \underline{\pi}$. Consequently, a pure strategy separating equilibrium always exists.

Now that we have characterised the policies that can arise in a separating equilibrium, we can assess the impact of allowing policy proposals to act as signals about risk. Note that because separating equilibria always exist, allowing policy proposals to act as signals about risk is always effective in the sense that it does indeed make it possible for the low-risk type to distinguish himself from the high-risk type.

On the other hand, there need not be much improvement in terms of efficiency. For example, when $MRS_l(0, 0) \leq \bar{\pi}$, there is a separating equilibrium in which the low-risk consumer receives the (null) policy (0, 0), and the high-risk consumer receives the policy $(L, \bar{\pi}L)$. That is, only the high-risk consumer is insured. Moreover, this remains an equilibrium outcome regardless of the probability that the consumer is high-risk![8] Thus, the presence of a bad apple – even with very low probability – can still spoil the outcome just as in the competitive equilibrium under asymmetric information wherein signalling was not possible.

Despite the existence of equilibria that are as inefficient as in the model without signalling, when signalling is present, there are always equilibria in which the low-risk consumer receives some insurance coverage. The one of these that is best for the low-risk consumer and worst for the insurance company provides the low-risk consumer with the policy labelled $\bar{\psi}_l$ in Fig. 8.7.

Because the high-risk consumer obtains the same policy ψ_h^c in every separating equilibrium, and so receives the same utility, the equilibrium outcome $(\bar{\psi}_l, \psi_h^c)$ is Pareto efficient among separating equilibria and it yields zero profits for the insurance company. This outcome is present in Fig. 8.7 regardless of the probability that the consumer is low-risk. Thus, even when the only competitive equilibrium under asymmetric information gives no insurance to the low-risk consumer (which occurs when α is sufficiently small), the low-risk consumer can obtain insurance, and market efficiency can be improved when signalling is possible.

We now turn our attention to the second category of equilibria.

[8]Or, according to our second interpretation, regardless of the proportion of high-risk consumers in the population.

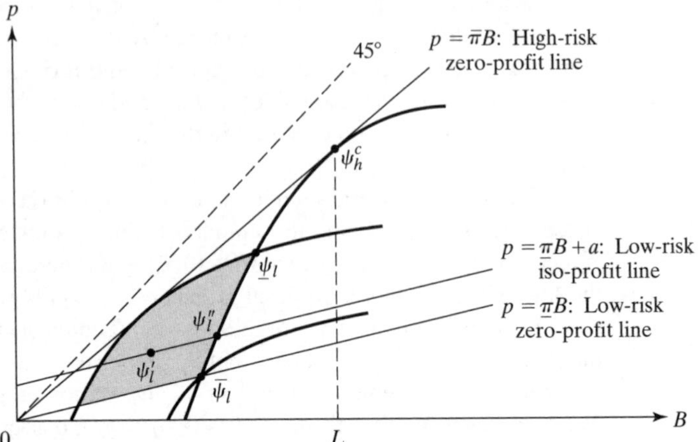

Figure 8.7. Separating equilibria. A pair of policies (ψ_l, ψ_h^c) is the outcome of a separating equilibrium if and only if $\psi_l \neq \psi_h$ and ψ_l is in the shaded region. Note that (ψ_l'', ψ_h^c) Pareto dominates (ψ_l', ψ_h^c). The high-risk consumer is indifferent between them as is the insurance company (ψ_l' and ψ_l'' are on the same low-risk iso-profit line, giving profits $a > 0$). But the low-risk consumer strictly prefers ψ_l'' to ψ_l' by fact (b). Consequently, among separating equilibria, only those with ψ_l between $\bar{\psi}_l$ and $\underline{\psi}_l$ are not Pareto dominated by some other separating equilibrium.

Pooling Equilibria

Recall that an equilibrium is a pooling one if the two types of consumers propose the same policy. By doing so, the insurance company cannot distinguish between them. Consequently, the low-risk consumer will be treated somewhat more like the high-risk consumer and vice versa. It is fair to say that in such equilibria, the high-risk consumer is mimicking the low-risk one.

To characterise the set of pooling equilibria, let us first consider the behaviour of the insurance company. If both consumers propose the same policy in equilibrium, then the insurance company learns nothing about the consumer's accident probability on hearing the proposal. Consequently, if the proposal is (B, p), then accepting it would yield the insurance company expected profits equal to

$$p - (\alpha\underline{\pi} + (1 - \alpha)\bar{\pi})B,$$

where, you recall, α is the probability that the consumer is low-risk.

Let

$$\hat{\pi} = \alpha\underline{\pi} + (1 - \alpha)\bar{\pi}.$$

Then the policy will be accepted if $p > \hat{\pi}B$, rejected if $p < \hat{\pi}B$, and the insurance company will be indifferent between accepting and rejecting if $p = \hat{\pi}B$.

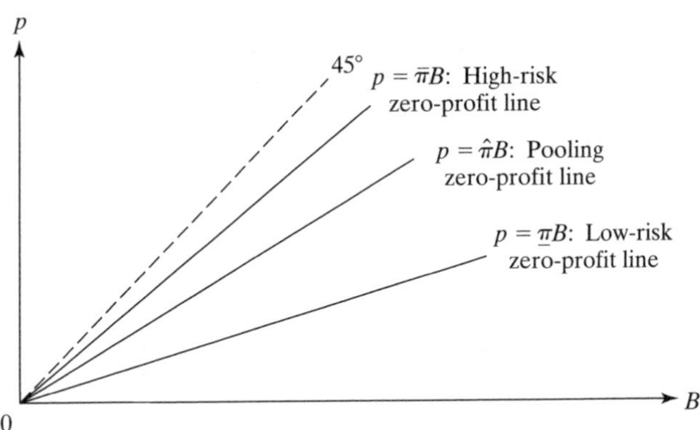

Figure 8.8. Pooling zero-profit line.

Owing to this, the set of policies (B, p) satisfying $p = \hat{\pi} B$ will play an important part in the analysis of pooling equilibria. Fig. 8.8 depicts the set of such policies. They lie on a ray through the origin called the *pooling zero-profit line*.

Now suppose that (B, p) is the pooling equilibrium proposal. According to Lemma 8.1, we must have

$$u_l(B, p) \geq \tilde{u}_l, \qquad \text{and} \qquad u_h(B, p) \geq u_h^c. \tag{8.5}$$

Moreover, as the discussion following the lemma points out, this policy must be accepted by the insurance company. Therefore, it must lie on or above the pooling zero-profit line, so we must have

$$p \geq \hat{\pi} B. \tag{8.6}$$

The policies satisfying the preceding three inequalities are depicted by the shaded region in Fig. 8.9. We now demonstrate that these are precisely the policies that can arise as pooling equilibrium outcomes.

THEOREM 8.2 ***Pooling Equilibrium Characterisation***

The policy $\psi' = (B', p')$ is the outcome in some pooling equilibrium if and only if it satisfies inequalities (8.5) and (8.6).

Proof: The discussion preceding the statement of the theorem shows that (B', p') must satisfy (8.5) and (8.6) in order that ψ' be the outcome of some pooling equilibrium. It suffices therefore to prove the converse.

Suppose that $\psi' = (B', p')$ satisfies (8.5) and (8.6). We must define beliefs $\beta(\cdot)$ and a strategy $\sigma(\cdot)$ for the insurance company so that $(\psi', \psi', \sigma(\cdot), \beta(\cdot))$ constitutes a sequential equilibrium.

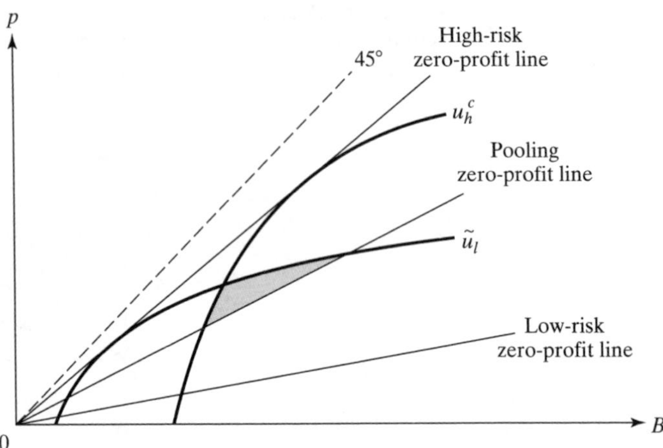

Figure 8.9. Pooling equilibria. The shaded region depicts the set of policies that can arise as pooling equilibria.

We follow the proof of Theorem 8.1 by choosing these functions as follows:

$$\beta(B, p) = \begin{cases} \alpha, & \text{if } (B, p) = \psi', \\ 0, & \text{if } (B, p) \neq \psi'. \end{cases}$$

$$\sigma(B, p) = \begin{cases} A, & \text{if } (B, p) = \psi', \quad \text{or} \quad p \geq \bar{\pi} B, \\ R, & \text{otherwise.} \end{cases}$$

Thus, just as in the proof of Theorem 8.1, the insurance company considers any deviation from the equilibrium proposal to have come from the high risk type. Consequently, it is profit-maximising to accept a proposal $(B, p) \neq \psi'$ only if $p \geq \bar{\pi} B$, as $\sigma(\cdot)$ specifies.

On the other hand, when the equilibrium policy, ψ', is proposed, Bayes' rule requires the insurance company's beliefs to be unchanged because this proposal is made by both risk types. Because $\beta(\psi') = \alpha$, the beliefs do indeed satisfy Bayes' rule. And given these beliefs, it is profit-maximising to accept the policy ψ', because by (8.6), it yields non-negative expected profits.

Thus, the insurance company's beliefs satisfy Bayes' rule, and given these beliefs, it is maximising expected profits subsequent to each policy proposal of the consumer. It remains to show that the two consumer types are maximising their utility given the insurance company's strategy.

By proposing ψ', the consumer (high- or low-risk) obtains the policy ψ'. By deviating to $(B, p) \neq \psi'$, the consumer obtains the policy $(0, 0)$ if the insurance company rejects the proposal (i.e., if $p < \bar{\pi} B$), and obtains the policy (B, p) if it is accepted (i.e., if $p \geq \bar{\pi} B$). Thus, proposing ψ' is optimal for risk type $i = l, h$ if

$$u_i(\psi') \geq u_i(0, 0), \qquad \text{and}$$
$$u_i(\psi') \geq u_i(B, p) \qquad \text{for all} \quad \bar{\pi} B \leq p \leq w.$$

But these inequalities follow from (8.5) (see Fig. 8.9). Therefore, $(\psi', \psi', \sigma(\cdot), \beta(\cdot))$ is a sequential equilibrium. ∎

As Fig. 8.9 shows, there are potentially many pooling equilibria. It is instructive to consider how the set of pooling equilibria is affected by changes in the probability, α, that the consumer is low-risk.

As α falls, the shaded area in Fig. 8.9 shrinks because the slope of the pooling zero-profit line increases, while everything else in the figure remains fixed. Eventually, the shaded area disappears altogether. Thus, if the probability that the consumer is high-risk is sufficiently high, there are no pooling equilibria.

As α increases, the shaded region in Fig. 8.9 expands because the slope of the pooling zero-profit line decreases. Fig. 8.10 shows that when α is large enough, there are pooling equilibria that make both consumer types better off than they would be in every separating equilibrium – even the low-risk consumer. This is not so surprising for the high-risk consumer. The reason this is possible for the low-risk consumer is that it is costly for him to separate himself from the high-risk consumer.

Effective separation requires the low-risk consumer to choose a policy that the high-risk consumer does not prefer to ψ_h^c. This restricts the low-risk consumer's choice and certainly reduces his utility below that which he could obtain in the absence of the high-risk consumer. When α is sufficiently high, and the equilibrium is a pooling one, it is very much like the high-risk consumer is not present. The cost to the low-risk consumer of pooling is then simply a slightly inflated marginal cost per unit of benefit (i.e., $\hat{\pi}$), over and above that which he would pay if his risk type were known (i.e., $\underline{\pi}$). This cost vanishes

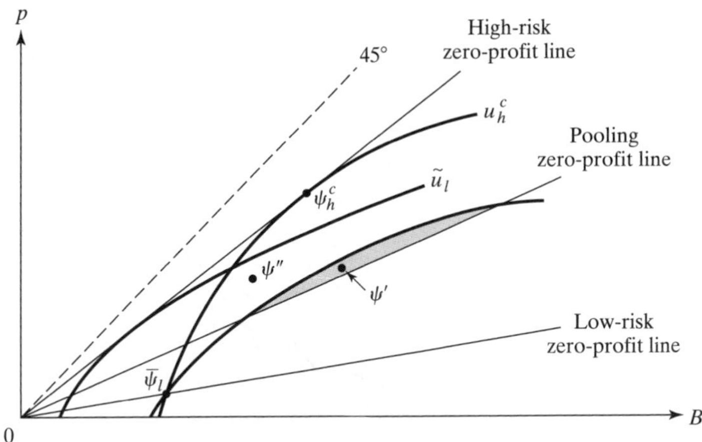

Figure 8.10. Pooling may dominate separation. The best separating equilibrium for consumers yields policies $\psi_l = \bar{\psi}_l$ and $\psi_h = \psi_h^c$. The pooling equilibrium outcome $\psi_l = \psi_h = \psi'$ in the shaded region is strictly preferred by both risk types. Other pooling equilibrium outcomes, such as $\psi_l = \psi_h = \psi''$, are not.

as α tends to one. On the other hand, the cost of separating himself from the high-risk consumer is bounded away from zero.

The reader may have noticed that in the proofs of Theorems 8.1 and 8.2, there was a common, and not so appealing, component. In each case, when constructing an equilibrium assessment, the beliefs assigned to the insurance company were rather extreme.

Recall that in both proofs, the insurance company's beliefs were constructed so that every deviation from equilibrium was interpreted as having been proposed by the *high-risk* consumer. Although there is nothing formally incorrect about this, it is perhaps worth considering whether or not such beliefs are reasonable.

Let us be clear before proceeding further. The beliefs constructed in proofs of Theorems 8.1 and 8.2 are perfectly in line with our definition of a sequential equilibrium for the insurance signalling game. What we are about to discuss is whether or not we wish to place *additional* restrictions on the insurance company's beliefs.

A Refinement

Are the beliefs assigned to the insurance company in the proofs of Theorems 8.1 and 8.2 reasonable? To see that they might not be, consider a typical pooling equilibrium policy, ψ', depicted in Fig. 8.11.

According to the equilibrium constructed in the proof of Theorem 8.2, were the consumer to propose instead the policy ψ'', the insurance company would believe that the consumer had a high accident probability and would reject the proposal. But do such beliefs make sense in light of the equilibrium ψ'? Note that by proposing the equilibrium policy ψ', the low-risk consumer obtains utility u_l^* and the high-risk consumer obtains

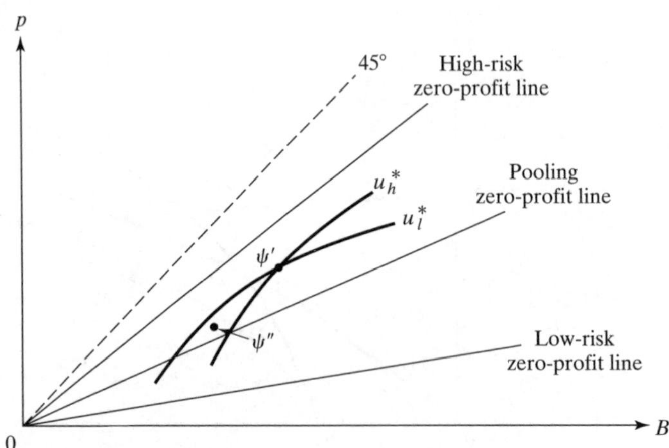

Figure 8.11. Are the firm's beliefs sensible? If ψ' is a pooling equilibrium outcome, then the proposal ψ'' is preferred only by the low-risk consumer. It also lies above the low-risk zero-profit line. Such a policy, ψ'', always exists because ψ' lies on or above the pooling zero-profit line, and $MRS_l(\psi') < MRS_h(\psi')$.

utility u_h^*. Moreover, $u_l^* < u_l(\psi'')$, and $u_h(\psi'') < u_h^*$. Therefore, whether the insurance company accepts or rejects the proposal ψ'', the high-risk consumer would be worse off making this proposal than making the equilibrium proposal ψ'. On the other hand, were the insurance company to accept the proposal ψ'', the low-risk consumer would be better off having made that proposal than having made the equilibrium proposal ψ'. Simply put, *only the low-risk consumer has any incentive at all in making the proposal ψ'', given that ψ' is the equilibrium proposal.*

With this in mind, it seems unreasonable for the insurance company to believe, after seeing the proposal ψ'', that it faces the high-risk consumer. Indeed, it is much more reasonable to insist that it instead believes it faces the low-risk consumer. Accordingly, we shall add the following restriction to the insurance company's beliefs. It applies to all sequential equilibria, not just pooling ones.

DEFINITION 8.3 ***(Cho and Kreps) An Intuitive Criterion***

A sequential equilibrium $(\psi_l, \psi_h, \sigma(\cdot), \beta(\cdot))$, yielding equilibrium utilities u_l^* and u_h^* to the low- and high-risk consumer, respectively, satisfies the intuitive criterion if the following condition is satisfied for every policy $\psi \neq \psi_l$ or ψ_h:

If $u_i(\psi) > u_i^*$ and $u_j(\psi) < u_j^*$, then $\beta(\psi)$ places probability one on risk type i, so that

$$\beta(\psi) = \begin{cases} 1 & \text{if} \quad i = l, \\ 0 & \text{if} \quad i = h. \end{cases}$$

Restricting attention to sequential equilibria satisfying the intuitive criterion dramatically reduces the set of equilibrium policies. Indeed, we have the following.

THEOREM 8.3 ***Intuitive Criterion Equilibrium***

There is a unique policy pair (ψ_l, ψ_h) that can be supported by a sequential equilibrium satisfying the intuitive criterion. Moreover, this equilibrium is the best separating equilibrium for the low-risk consumer (i.e., $\psi_l = \bar{\psi}_l$, and $\psi_h = \psi_h^c$; see Fig. 8.7).

Proof: We first argue that there are no pooling equilibria satisfying the intuitive criterion. Actually, we have almost already done this in our discussion of Fig. 8.11 preceding Definition 8.3. There we argued that if ψ' were a pooling equilibrium outcome, then there would be a policy ψ'' that is preferred only by the low-risk type, which, in addition, lies strictly above the low-risk zero-profit line (see Fig. 8.11). Consequently, if the low-risk type makes this proposal and the intuitive criterion is satisfied, the insurance company must believe that it faces the low-risk consumer. Because ψ'' lies strictly above the low-risk zero-profit line, the insurance company must accept it (by sequential rationality). But this means that the low-risk consumer can improve his payoff by deviating from ψ' to ψ''. This contradiction establishes the claim: there are no pooling equilibria satisfying the intuitive criterion.

Figure 8.12. The low-risk consumer can obtain $\bar{\psi}_l$.

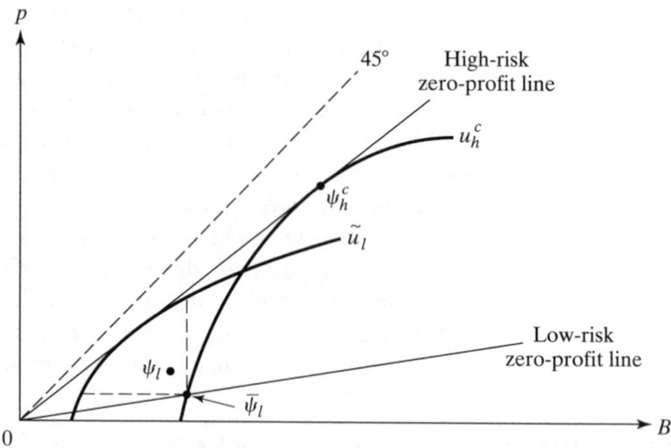

Suppose now that $(\psi_l, \psi_h, \sigma(\cdot), \beta(\cdot))$ is a separating equilibrium satisfying the intuitive criterion. Then, according to Lemma 8.1, the high-risk consumer's proposal must be accepted by the insurance company and his equilibrium utility, u_h^*, must be at least u_h^c (see Fig. 8.12).

Next, suppose by way of contradiction, that the low-risk consumer's equilibrium utility, u_l^*, satisfies $u_l^* < u_l(\bar{\psi}_l)$. Let $\bar{\psi}_l = (\bar{B}_l, \bar{p}_l)$ and consider the proposal $\psi_l^\varepsilon \equiv, (\bar{B}_l - \varepsilon, \bar{p}_l + \varepsilon)$ for ε positive and small. Then due to the continuity of $u_l(\cdot)$, the following inequalities hold for ε small enough. (See Fig. 8.12.)

$$\begin{aligned} u_h^* &\geq u_h^c > u_h(\psi_l^\varepsilon), \\ u_l(\psi_l^\varepsilon) &> u_l^*, \\ \bar{p}_l + \varepsilon &> \underline{\pi}(\bar{B}_l - \varepsilon). \end{aligned}$$

The first two together with the intuitive criterion imply that on seeing the proposal ψ_l^ε, the insurance company believes that it faces the low-risk consumer. The third inequality together with the sequential rationality property of the assessment imply that the insurance company must accept the proposal ψ_l^ε because it earns positive expected profits.

Hence, the low-risk consumer can achieve utility $u_l(\psi_l^\varepsilon) > u_l^*$ by proposing ψ_l^ε. But then u_l^* cannot be the low-risk consumer's equilibrium utility. This contradiction establishes that the low-risk consumer's equilibrium utility must be at least $u_l(\bar{\psi}_l)$. Thus, we have shown that the equilibrium utilities of the two consumer types must satisfy

$$\begin{aligned} u_l^* &\geq u_l(\bar{\psi}_l), \qquad \text{and} \\ u_h^* &\geq u_h(\psi_h^c). \end{aligned}$$

Now, these inequalities imply that the proposals made by both consumer types are accepted by the insurance company. Consequently, the hypotheses of Theorem 8.1 are satisfied. But according to Theorem 8.1, these two inequalities can hold in a sequential equilibrium only if (see Fig. 8.7)

$$\begin{aligned} \psi_l &= \bar{\psi}_l, \qquad \text{and} \\ \psi_h &= \psi_h^c. \end{aligned}$$

It remains to show that there is a separating equilibrium satisfying the intuitive criterion. We now construct one.

Let $\psi_l = \bar{\psi}_l$ and $\psi_h = \psi_h^c$. To define the insurance company's beliefs, $\beta(\cdot)$, in a manner that is compatible with the intuitive criterion, consider the following set of policies (see Fig. 8.13).

$$A = \{\psi \mid u_l(\psi) > u_l(\bar{\psi}_l) \text{ and } u_h(\psi) < u_h(\psi_h^c)\}.$$

This is the set of policies that only the low-risk type prefers to his equilibrium policy. We now define $\sigma(\cdot)$ and $\beta(\cdot)$ as follows.

$$\beta(B,p) = \begin{cases} 1, & \text{if } (B,p) \in A \cup \{\psi_l\} \\ 0, & \text{if } (B,p) \notin A \cup \{\psi_l\}. \end{cases}$$

$$\sigma(B,p) = \begin{cases} A, & \text{if } (B,p) = \psi_l, \text{ or } p \geq \bar{\pi} B, \\ R, & \text{otherwise.} \end{cases}$$

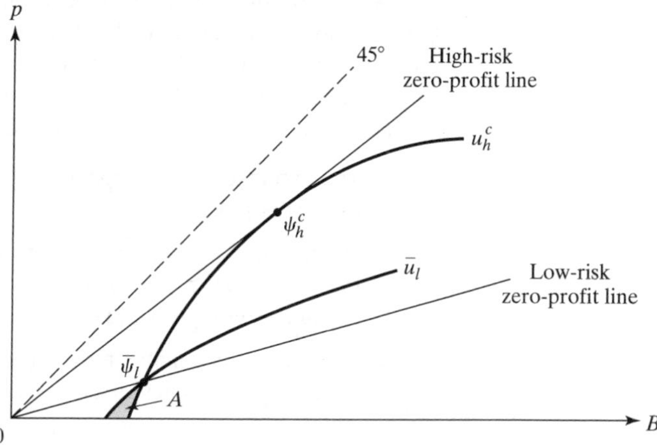

Figure 8.13. An equilibrium satisfying the intuitive criterion.

It is straightforward to check that by constriction, the beliefs satisfy the intuitive criterion. In addition, one can virtually mimic the relevant portion of the proof of Theorem 8.1 to conclude that the assessment $(\bar{\psi}_l, \psi_h^c, \sigma(\cdot), \beta(\cdot))$ constitutes a separating equilibrium. ∎

The inherent reasonableness of the additional restriction on the insurance company's beliefs embodied in the intuitive criterion suggests that the separating equilibrium that is best for the low-risk consumer is perhaps the most likely outcome in the signalling game. As we have discussed before, this particular outcome can outperform the competitive outcome under asymmetric information. Thus, signalling is indeed one way to improve the efficiency of this market.

There is another route towards improving the efficiency of competitive outcomes under asymmetric information. Indeed, in the insurance market of the real world, this alternative is the road more travelled.

8.1.3 SCREENING

When most consumers purchase motor insurance, they do not present the insurance company with a policy and await a reply, as in the model of the last section. Rather, the insurance company typically offers the consumer a menu of policies from which to choose, and the consumer simply makes a choice. By offering consumers a menu of policies, insurance companies are able to (implicitly) *screen* consumers by tailoring the offered policies so that high-risk types are induced to choose one particular policy, and low-risk types are induced to choose another. We now analyse such a model.

Again, we shall formulate the situation as an extensive form game. Although it was possible to illustrate the essential features of signalling using just a single insurance company, there are nuances of screening that require two insurance companies to reveal. Thus, we shall add an additional insurance company to the model.[9]

As before, there will be two consumers, low- and high-risk, occurring with probability α and $1 - \alpha$, respectively. And again, one can interpret this as there being many consumers, a fraction α of which is low-risk.

So consider the following 'insurance screening game' involving two insurance companies and two consumers. Fig. 8.14 depicts its extensive form.

- The two insurance companies move first by simultaneously choosing a finite list (menu) of policies.
- Nature moves second and determines which consumer the insurance companies face. The low-risk consumer is chosen with probability α, and the high-risk consumer with probability $1 - \alpha$.
- The chosen consumer moves last by choosing a single policy from one of the insurance companies' lists.

[9] We could also have included two insurance companies in the signalling model. This would not have changed the results there in any significant way.

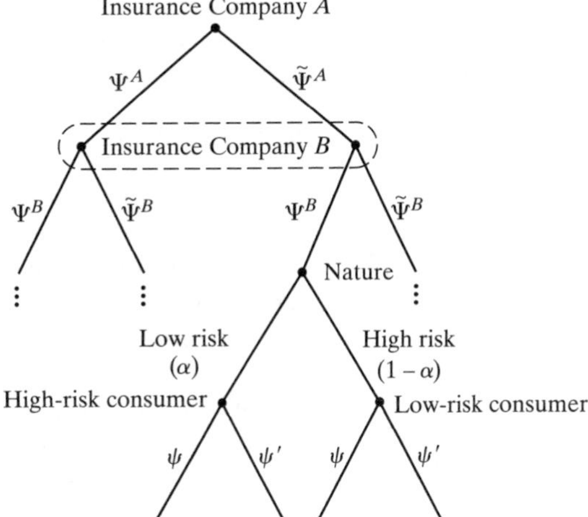

Figure 8.14. Insurance screening game. Note that, unlike the figure, the insurance companies actually have a continuum of actions. Thus, this game is not finite.

Now, because there are only two possible types of consumers, we may restrict the insurance companies to lists with at most two policies. Thus, a pure strategy for insurance company $j = A, B$ is a pair of policies $\Psi^j = (\psi_l^j, \psi_h^j)$. We interpret ψ_l^j (resp. ψ_h^j) as the policy that insurance company j includes in its list for the low- (resp., high-) risk consumer. However, keep in mind that the low- (resp., high-) risk consumer need not choose this policy because the insurance company cannot identify the consumer's risk type. The consumer will choose the policy yielding him the highest utility among those offered by the two insurance companies.

A pure strategy for consumer $i = l, h$ is a choice function $c_i(\cdot)$ specifying for each pair of policy pairs, (Ψ^A, Ψ^B), an insurance company and one of its policies or the null policy. Thus, we always give the consumers the option of choosing the null policy from either insurance company even if this policy is not formally on either company's list. This is simply a convenient way to allow consumers the ability not to purchase insurance. Thus, $c_i(\Psi^A, \Psi^B) = (j, \psi)$, where $j = A$ or B, and where $\psi = \psi_l^j, \psi_h^j$, or $(0, 0)$.

As is evident from Fig. 8.14, the only non-singleton information set belongs to insurance company B. However, note that no matter what strategies the players employ, this information set must be reached. Consequently, it is enough to consider the subgame perfect equilibria of this game. You are asked to show in an exercise that were the game finite (so that the sequential equilibrium definition can be applied), its set of sequential equilibrium outcomes would be identical to its set of subgame perfect equilibrium outcomes.

Again, we can split the set of pure strategy subgame perfect equilibria into two kinds: separating and pooling. In a separating equilibrium, the two consumer types make different policy choices, whereas in a pooling equilibrium, they do not.

DEFINITION 8.4 ***Separating and Pooling Screening Equilibria***

The pure strategy subgame perfect equilibrium $(\Psi^A, \Psi^B, c_l(\cdot), c_h(\cdot))$ is separating if $\psi_l \neq \psi_h$, where $(j_l, \psi_l) = c_l(\Psi^A, \Psi^B)$, and $(j_h, \psi_h) = c_h(\Psi^A, \Psi^B)$. Otherwise, it is pooling.

Note then that in a pooling equilibrium, although the two types of consumers must choose to purchase the same policy, they need not purchase it from the same insurance company.

Analysing the Game

We wish to characterise the set of subgame perfect equilibria of the insurance screening game. An important driving force of the analysis is a phenomenon called *cream skimming.*

Cream skimming occurs when one insurance company takes strategic advantage of the set of policies offered by the other by offering a policy that would attract away *only the low-risk consumers* from the competing company. The 'raiding' insurance company therefore gains only the very best consumers (the cream) while it leaves its competitor with the very worst consumers. In equilibrium, both companies must ensure that the other cannot skim its cream in this way. Note that at least two firms are required in order that cream skimming becomes a strategic concern. It is this that motivated us to introduce a second insurance company into the model.

We first provide a lemma that applies to all pure strategy subgame perfect equilibria.

LEMMA 8.2 *Both insurance companies earn zero expected profits in every pure strategy subgame perfect equilibrium.*

Proof: The proof of this result is analogous to that in the model of Bertrand competition from Chapter 4.

First, note that in equilibrium, each insurance company must earn non-negative profits because each can guarantee zero profits by offering a pair of null policies in which $B = p = 0$. Thus, it suffices to show that neither insurance company earns strictly positive expected profits.

Suppose by way of contradiction that company A earns strictly positive expected profits and that company B's profits are no higher than A's. Let $\psi_l^* = (B_l^*, p_l^*)$ and $\psi_h^* = (B_h^*, p_h^*)$ denote the policies chosen by the low- and high-risk consumers, respectively, in equilibrium. We then can write the total expected profits of the two firms as

$$\Pi \equiv \alpha(p_l^* - \underline{\pi} B_l^*) + (1-\alpha)(p_h^* - \bar{\pi} B_h^*) > 0.$$

Clearly, Π strictly exceeds company B's expected profits.

Now, we shall consider two cases.

Case 1: $\psi_l^* = \psi_h^* = (B^*, p^*)$. Consider the following deviation by company B. Company B offers the policy pair $\{(B^* + \varepsilon, p^*), (B^* + \varepsilon, p^*)\}$, where $\varepsilon > 0$. Clearly, each consumer type then will strictly prefer to choose the policy $(B^* + \varepsilon, p^*)$ from company B, and for ε small enough, company B's expected profits will be arbitrarily close to Π and so larger than they are in equilibrium. But this contradicts the equilibrium hypothesis.

Case 2: $\psi_l^* = (B_l^*, p_l^*) \neq \psi_h^* = (B_h^*, p_h^*)$. Equilibrium requires that neither consumer can improve his payoff by switching his policy choice to that of the other consumer. Together with this and the fact that the policy choices are distinct, the single-crossing property implies that at least one of the consumers strictly prefers his own choice to the other's; i.e., either

$$u_l(\psi_l^*) > u_l(\psi_h^*), \qquad \text{or} \tag{P.1}$$

$$u_h(\psi_h^*) > u_h(\psi_l^*). \tag{P.2}$$

Suppose then that (P.1) holds. Consider the deviation for company B in which it offers the pair of policies $\psi_l^\varepsilon = (B_l^* + \varepsilon, p_l^*)$ and $\psi_h^\varepsilon = (B_h^* + \beta, p_h^*)$, where $\varepsilon, \beta > 0$.

Clearly, each consumer $i = l, h$ strictly prefers policy ψ_i^ε to ψ_i^*. In addition, we claim that ε and $\beta > 0$ can be chosen arbitrarily small so that

$$u_l(\psi_l^\varepsilon) > u_l(\psi_h^\beta), \qquad \text{and} \tag{P.3}$$

$$u_h(\psi_h^\beta) > u_h(\psi_l^\varepsilon). \tag{P.4}$$

To see this, note that by (P.1), (P.3) will hold as long as ε and β are small enough. Inequality (P.4) then can be assured by fixing β and choosing ε small enough, because for $\beta > 0$ and fixed, we have

$$u_h(\psi_h^\beta) > u_h(\psi_h^*) \geq u_h(\psi_l^*) = \lim_{\varepsilon \to 0} u_h(\psi_l^\varepsilon),$$

where the weak inequality follows because, in equilibrium, the high-risk consumer cannot prefer any other policy choice to his own. See Fig. 8.15.

But (P.3) and (P.4) imply that subsequent to B's deviation, the low-risk consumer will choose the policy ψ_l^ε, and the high-risk consumer will choose the policy ψ_h^β. For ε and β small enough, this will yield company B expected profits arbitrarily close to Π and therefore strictly above B's equilibrium expected profits. But this is again a contradiction.

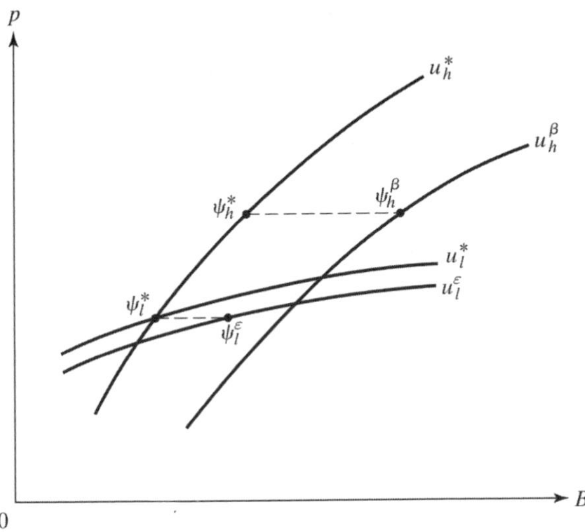

Figure 8.15. A difficult case: Depicted is the most troublesome case in which (P.1), $u_l^* \equiv, u_l(\psi_l^*) > u_l(\psi_h^*)$ holds, but $u_h^* \equiv, u_h(\psi_h^*) = u_h(\psi_l^*)$ so that (P.2) does not hold. For each $\beta > 0$, there is $\varepsilon > 0$ small enough so that $u_h^\beta \equiv, u_h(\psi_h^\beta) > u_l^\varepsilon \equiv, u_h(\psi_l^\varepsilon)$. When the policies ψ_l^ε and ψ_h^β are available, ψ_l^ε is strictly best for the low-risk consumer and ψ_h^β is strictly best for the high-risk consumer.

A similar argument leads to a contradiction if instead (P.2) holds, so we conclude that both insurance companies must earn zero expected profits in every subgame perfect equilibrium. ∎

Pooling Equilibria

One might suspect that the set of pooling equilibria would be whittled down by the cream-skimming phenomenon. Indeed, the setting seems just right for cream skimming when both consumer types are treated the same way. This intuition turns out to be correct with a vengeance. Indeed, cream skimming eliminates the possibility of any pooling equilibrium at all.

THEOREM 8.4 ***Non-existence of Pooling Equilibria***

There are no pure strategy pooling equilibria in the insurance screening game.

Proof: We shall proceed by way of contradiction.

Suppose the policy $\psi^* = (B^*, p^*)$ is chosen by both consumers in a subgame perfect equilibrium. By Lemma 8.2, the total expected profits of the two insurance companies must be zero, so

$$\alpha(p^* - \underline{\pi} B^*) + (1 - \alpha)(p^* - \bar{\pi} B^*) = 0. \tag{P.1}$$

Consider first the case in which $B^* > 0$. Then (P.1) implies that

$$p^* - \underline{\pi} B^* > 0. \tag{P.2}$$

Consequently, $p^* > 0$ as well, so that ψ^* does not lie on either axis as shown in Fig. 8.16. By the single-crossing property, there is a region, R (see Fig. 8.16), such that ψ^* is the limit of policies in R. Let ψ' be a policy in R very close to ψ^*.

Suppose now that insurance company A is offering policy ψ^* in equilibrium. If insurance company B offers policy ψ', and only ψ', then the high-risk consumer will choose

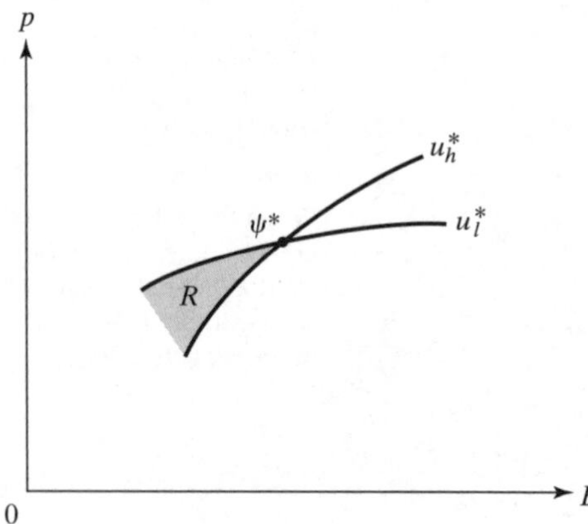

Figure 8.16. ψ^* lies on neither axis.

policy ψ^* (or one he is indifferent to) from the first insurance company, whereas the low-risk consumer will purchase ψ' from insurance company B. If ψ' is close enough to ψ^*, then by (P.2), insurance company B will earn strictly positive profits from this cream-skimming deviation, and so must be earning strictly positive profits in equilibrium. But this contradicts Lemma 8.2.

Consider now the case in which $B^* = 0$. By (P.1), this implies that $p^* = 0$ as well. Thus, ψ^* is the null policy, as in Fig. 8.17. But either company now can earn positive profits by offering the single policy $(L, \bar{\pi}L + \varepsilon)$ where $\varepsilon > 0$ is sufficiently small. It earns strictly positive profits because it earns strictly positive profits on both consumer types (it is above both the high- and low-risk zero-profit lines), and the high-risk consumer certainly will choose this policy over the null policy. This final contradiction completes the proof. ∎

Note the importance of cream skimming to the preceding result. This is a typical feature of competitive screening models wherein multiple agents on one side of a market compete to attract a common pool of agents on the other side of the market by simultaneously offering a menu of 'contracts' from which the pool of agents may choose.

Separating Equilibria

The competitive nature of our screening model also has an important impact on the set of separating equilibria, as we now demonstrate.

THEOREM 8.5 ***Separating Equilibrium Characterisation***

Suppose that ψ_l^* and ψ_h^* are the policies chosen by the low- and high-risk consumers, respectively, in a pure strategy separating equilibrium. Then $\psi_l^* = \bar{\psi}_l$ and $\psi_h^* = \psi_h^c$, as illustrated in Fig. 8.18.

Note then that the only possible separating equilibrium in the insurance screening model coincides with the *best* separating equilibrium for consumers in the insurance

Figure 8.17. ψ^* is the null policy.

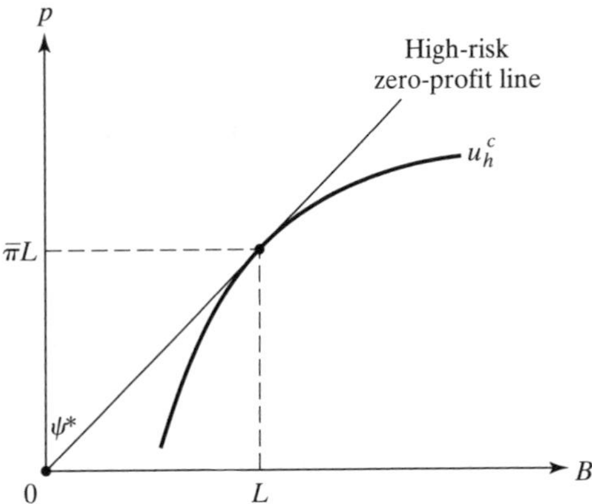

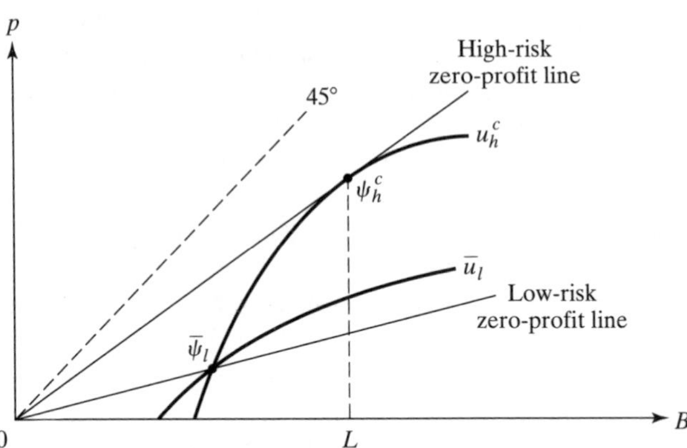

Figure 8.18. The only possible separating equilibrium. It coincides with the best separating equilibrium for consumers in the insurance signalling game from section 8.1.2.

signalling game from section 8.1.1. By Theorem 8.4, this will be the only possible equilibrium in the game.

Proof: The proof proceeds in series of claims.

Claim 1. *The high-risk consumer must obtain at least utility u_h^c. (See Fig. 8.18.)*

By Lemma 8.2, both insurance companies must earn zero profits. Consequently, it cannot be the case that the high-risk consumer strictly prefers the policy $(L, \bar{\pi}L + \varepsilon)$ to ψ_h^*. Otherwise, one of the insurance companies could offer just this policy and earn positive profits. (Note that this policy earns positive profits on both consumers.) But this means that

$$u_h(\psi_h^*) \geq u_h(L, \bar{\pi}L + \varepsilon) \quad \text{for all} \quad \varepsilon > 0.$$

The result follows by taking the limit of the right-hand side as $\varepsilon \to 0$, because $u_h(\cdot)$ is continuous and $\psi_h^c = (L, \bar{\pi}L)$.

Claim 2. *ψ_l^* must lie on the low-risk zero-profit line.*

Note that by Claim 1, ψ_h^* must lie on or below the high-risk zero-profit line. Thus, non-positive profits are earned on the high-risk consumer. Because by Lemma 8.2 the insurance companies' aggregate profits are zero, this implies that ψ_l^* lies on or above the low-risk zero-profit line.

So, suppose by way of contradiction that $\psi_l^* = (B_l^*, p_l^*)$ lies above the low-risk zero-profit line. Then $p_l^* > 0$. But this means that $B_l^* > 0$ as well because the low-risk consumer would otherwise choose the null policy (which is always available). Thus, ψ_l^* is strictly above the low-risk zero-profit line and not on the vertical axis as shown in Fig. 8.19.

Consequently, region R in Fig. 8.19 is present. Now if the insurance company which is *not* selling a policy to the high-risk consumer offers policies only strictly within region R, then only the low-risk consumer will purchase a policy from this insurance company. This is because such a policy is strictly preferred to ψ_l^* by the low-risk consumer and strictly worse than ψ_l^* (which itself is no better than ψ_h^*) for the high-risk consumer. This deviation

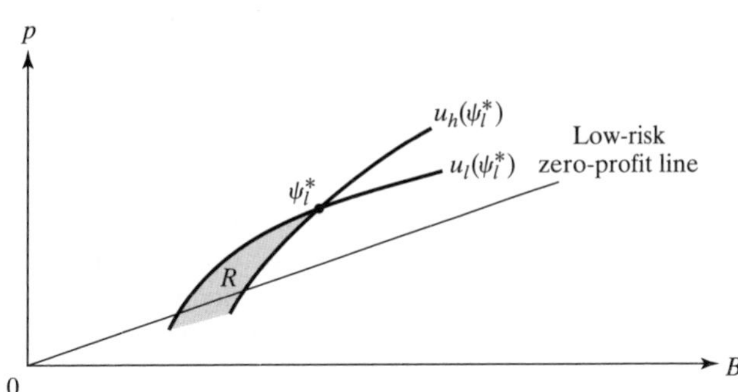

Figure 8.19. A cream-skimming region.

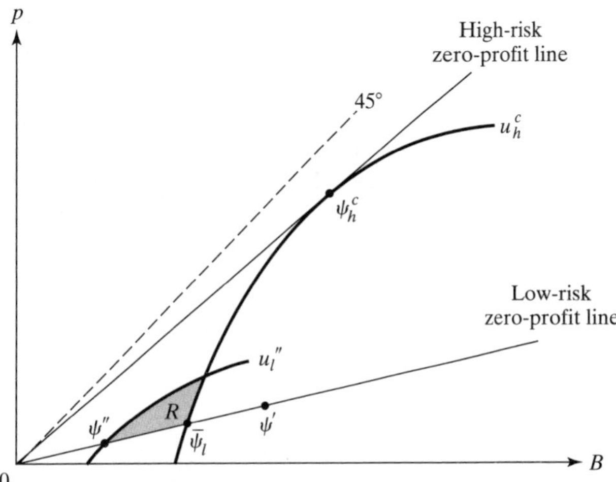

Figure 8.20. Another cream-skimming region.

would then result in strictly positive profits for this insurance company because all such policies are above the low-risk zero-profit line. The desired conclusion follows from this contradiction.

Claim 3. $\psi_h^* = \psi_h^c$.

By Claim 2, and Lemma 8.2, ψ_h^* must lie on the high-risk, zero-profit line. But by Claim 1, $u_h(\psi_h^*) \geq u_h(\psi_h^c)$. Together, these imply that $\psi_h^* = \psi_h^c$ (see Fig. 8.18).

Claim 4. $\psi_l^* = \bar{\psi}_l$.

Consult Fig. 8.20. By Claim 2, it suffices to show that ψ_l^* cannot lie on the low-risk zero-profit line strictly below $\bar{\psi}_l$ (such as ψ'') or strictly above $\bar{\psi}_l$ (such as ψ').

So, suppose first that $\psi_l^* = \psi'$. The high-risk consumer would then strictly prefer ψ' to ψ_h^c and thus would not choose ψ_h^c contrary to Claim 3.

Next, suppose that $\psi_l^* = \psi''$. Then the low-risk consumer obtains utility u_l'' in equilibrium (see Fig. 8.20). Moreover, region R is then present. Consider the insurance company that does *not* sell ψ_h^c to the high-risk consumer. Let this insurance company offer any policy strictly within region R. This policy will be purchased only by the low-risk consumer and will earn strictly positive profits. This contradiction proves Claim 4 and completes the proof. ∎

Note that Theorem 8.5 does not claim that a separating screening equilibrium exists. Together with Theorem 8.4, it says only that *if* a pure strategy subgame perfect equilibrium exists, it must be separating and the policies chosen by the consumers are unique.

Cream skimming is a powerful device in this screening model for eliminating equilibria. But it can be too powerful. Indeed, there are cases in which no pure strategy subgame perfect equilibrium exists at all.

Consider Fig. 8.21. Depicted there is a case in which no pure strategy equilibrium exists. To see this, it is enough to show that it is not an equilibrium for the low- and high-risk consumers to obtain the policies $\bar{\psi}_l$ and ψ_h^c as described in Theorem 8.5. But this is indeed the case, because either insurance company can deviate by offering only the policy ψ', which will be purchased by both consumer types (because it is strictly preferred by them to their equilibrium policies). Consequently, this company will earn strictly positive expected profits because ψ' is strictly above the pooling zero-profit line (which is the appropriate zero-profit line to consider because *both* consumer types will purchase ψ'). But this contradicts Lemma 8.2.

Thus, when α is close enough to one, so that the pooling zero-profit line intersects the $\bar{u}_l$ indifference curve (see Fig. 8.21), the screening model admits no pure strategy subgame

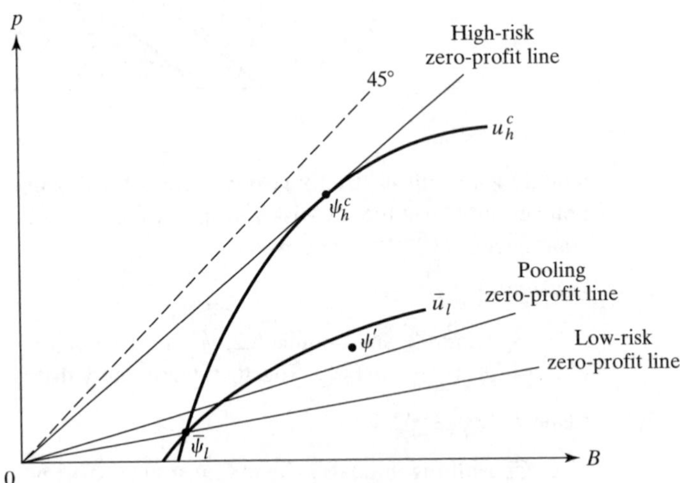

Figure 8.21. No equilibrium exists. If the best policies available for the low- and high-risk consumers are $\bar{\psi}_l$ and ψ_h^c, respectively, then offering the policy ψ' will attract both consumer types and earn positive profits because it lies above the pooling zero-profit line. No pure strategy subgame perfect equilibrium exists in this case.

perfect equilibrium.[10] One can show that there always exists a subgame perfect equilibrium in behavioural strategies, but we shall not pursue this. We are content to note that non-existence in this model arises only when the extent of the asymmetry of information is relatively minor, and in particular when the presence of high-risk consumers is small.

We next consider an issue that we have so far ignored. What is the effect of the availability of insurance on the driving behaviour of the consumer?

8.2 MORAL HAZARD AND THE PRINCIPAL–AGENT PROBLEM

Insurance companies are not naive. They understand well that once a consumer has purchased motor insurance, he may not drive with as much care as he did before he had insurance. Moreover, a consumer's incentive to drive carefully is likely to diminish with the amount of coverage. Unfortunately for insurance companies, they cannot observe the effort consumers direct toward safe driving. Thus, they must structure their policies so that the policies themselves induce the consumers to take an appropriate level of care.

When a *principal* (like the insurance company) has a stake in the action taken by an *agent* (the consumer), but the agent's action cannot be observed by the principal, the situation is said to involve **moral hazard**. The **principal–agent problem** is for the principal to design an incentive scheme so that the agent takes an appropriate action. We now explore these ideas in our insurance context.

To keep things simple, the model we shall consider involves a single insurance company and a single consumer. The consumer might incur an accident resulting in a varying amount of loss. There are L levels of losses, ranging from 1 dollar through L dollars, depending on the severity of the accident incurred. It is also possible that an accident is avoided altogether. It is convenient to refer to this latter possibility as an accident resulting in a loss of 0 dollars.

The probability of incurring an accident resulting in losses of $l \in \{0, 1, \ldots, L\}$ is given by $\pi_l(e) > 0$, where e is the amount of effort exerted towards safe driving. As discussed before, it is natural to think of these probabilities as being affected by such efforts. Note that $\sum_l \pi_l(e) = 1$ for each fixed effort level e.

To keep things simple, there are only two possible effort levels for the consumer. We let $e = 0$ denote low effort and $e = 1$ denote high effort. To capture the idea that higher effort results in a lower likelihood that the consumer will have a serious (i.e., expensive) accident, we make the following assumption.

ASSUMPTION 8.1 ***Monotone Likelihood Ratio***

$\pi_l(0)/\pi_l(1)$ *is strictly increasing in* $l \in \{0, 1, \ldots, L\}$.

[10] Even when the pooling zero-profit line does not intersect the $\bar{u}_l$ indifference curve, an equilibrium is not guaranteed to exist. There may still be a *pair* of policies such that one attracts the low-risk consumers making positive profits, and the other attracts the high-risk consumers (keeping them away from the first policy) making negative profits, so that overall expected profits are strictly positive.

The monotone likelihood ratio property says that conditional on observing the accident loss, l, the relative probability that low effort was expended versus high effort *increases* with l. Thus, one would be more willing to bet that the consumer exerted low effort when the observed accident loss is higher.

As in our previous models, the consumer has a strictly increasing, strictly concave, von Neumann-Morgenstern utility function, $u(\cdot)$, over wealth, and initial wealth equal to $w > L$. In addition, $d(e)$ denotes the consumer's disutility of effort, e. Thus, for a given effort level e, the consumer's von Neumann-Morgenstern utility over wealth is $u(\cdot) - d(e)$, where $d(1) > d(0)$.[11]

We assume that the insurance company can observe the amount of loss, l, due to an accident, but not the amount of accident avoidance effort, e. Consequently, the insurance company can only tie the benefit amount to the amount of loss. Let B_l denote the benefit paid by the insurance company to the consumer when the accident loss is l. Thus, a *policy* is a tuple $(p, B_0, B_1, \ldots, B_L)$, where p denotes the price paid to the insurance company in return for guaranteeing the consumer B_l dollars if an accident loss of l dollars occurs.

The question of interest is this: what kind of policy will the insurance company offer the consumer, and what are its efficiency properties?

8.2.1 SYMMETRIC INFORMATION

To understand the impact of the unobservability of the consumer's accident avoidance effort, we first shall consider the case in which the insurance company can observe the consumer's effort level.

Consequently, the insurance company can offer a policy that pays benefits *only if* a particular effort level was exerted. In effect, the insurance company can choose the consumer's effort level.

Thus, the insurance company wishes to solve the following problem:

$$\max_{e,p,B_0,\ldots,B_L} \quad p - \sum_{l=0}^{L} \pi_l(e)B_l, \quad \text{subject to} \tag{8.7}$$

$$\sum_{l=0}^{L} \pi_l(e)u(w - p - l + B_l) - d(e) \geq \bar{u},$$

where $\bar{u}$ denotes the consumer's reservation utility.[12]

---

[11] All of the analysis to follow generalises to the case in which utility takes the form $u(w, e)$, where $u(w, 0) > u(w, 1)$ for all wealth levels w.

[12] Because the consumer always can choose not to purchase insurance, $\bar{u}$ must be at least as large as $\max_{e\in\{0,1\}} \sum_{l=0}^{L} \pi_l(e)u(w - l) - d(e)$. However, $\bar{u}$ may be strictly larger than this if, for example, there are other insurance companies offering policies to the consumer as well.

According to the maximisation problem (8.7), the insurance company chooses a policy and an effort level to maximise its expected profits subject to the constraint that the policy yields the consumer at least his reservation utility – hence, the consumer will be willing to accept the terms of the policy and exert the required effort level.

The easiest way to solve (8.7) is to assume that $e \in \{0, 1\}$ is fixed and to then form the Lagrangian considered as a function of $p, B_0, \ldots, B_L$ only. This gives

$$\mathcal{L} = p - \sum_{l=0}^{L} \pi_l(e)B_l - \lambda\left[\bar{u} - \sum_{l=0}^{L} \pi_l(e)u(w - p - l + B_l) + d(e)\right].$$

The first-order conditions are

$$\frac{\partial \mathcal{L}}{\partial p} = 1 - \lambda\left[\sum_{l=0}^{L} \pi_l(e)u'(w - p - l + B_l)\right] = 0, \tag{8.8}$$

$$\frac{\partial \mathcal{L}}{\partial B_l} = -\pi_l(e) + \lambda\pi_l(e)u'(w - p - l + B_l) = 0, \qquad \forall\, l \geq 0, \tag{8.9}$$

$$\frac{\partial \mathcal{L}}{\partial \lambda} = \bar{u} - \sum_{l=0}^{L} \pi_l(e)u(w - p - l + B_l) + d(e) \leq 0, \tag{8.10}$$

where (8.10) holds with equality if $\lambda \neq 0$.

Note that the first condition, (8.8), is redundant because it is implied by the $(L + 1)$ equations in (8.9). Thus, the preceding is a system of at most $(L + 2)$ independent equations in $(L + 3)$ unknowns.

The equalities in (8.9) imply that $\lambda > 0$, and that

$$u'(w - p - l + B_l) = 1/\lambda, \quad \forall\, l \geq 0.$$

Hence, $B_l - l$ must be constant for all $l = 0, 1, \ldots, L$.

Because $\lambda > 0$, the first-order condition associated with the constraint must hold with equality, which implies that

$$u(w - p - l + B_l) = d(e) + \bar{u}, \quad \forall\, l \geq 0. \tag{8.11}$$

Because there are only $(L + 2)$ independent equations and $(L + 3)$ unknowns, we may set $B_0 = 0$ without any loss.[13] Thus, setting $l = 0$ in (8.11) gives us an equation in p alone and so determines p. Moreover, because $B_l - l$ is constant for all $l = 0, 1, \ldots, L$,

[13] Indeed, it was clear from the start that setting $B_0 = 0$ was harmless because changes in B_0 always can be offset by corresponding changes in the price p and in the benefit levels $B_1, \ldots, B_L$ without changing the consumer's utility or the insurance company's profits.

and because $B_0 - 0 = 0$, we therefore must have

$$B_l = l, \qquad \text{for all} \quad l = 0, 1, \ldots, L.$$

Therefore, for either fixed effort level $e \in \{0, 1\}$, the symmetric information solution provides full insurance to the consumer at every loss level. This is no surprise because the consumer is strictly risk averse and the insurance company is risk neutral. It is simply an example of efficient risk sharing. In addition, the price charged by the insurance company equates the consumer's utility from the policy at the required effort level with his reservation utility.

Now that we have determined for each effort level the optimal policy, it is straightforward to optimise over the effort level as well. Given $e \in \{0, 1\}$, the optimal benefit levels are $B_l = l$ for each l, so using (8.11) the optimal price $p(e)$ is given implicitly by

$$u(w - p(e)) = d(e) + \bar{u}. \tag{8.12}$$

Therefore, the insurance company chooses $e \in \{0, 1\}$ to maximise

$$p(e) - \sum_{l=0}^{L} \pi_l(e)l.$$

Note the trade-off between requiring high versus low effort. Because $d(0) < d(1)$, (8.12) implies that requiring *lower* effort allows the insurance company to charge a higher price, increasing profits. On the other hand, requiring *higher* effort reduces the expected loss due to an accident (by the monotone likelihood ratio property; see the exercises), and so also increases expected profits. One must simply check which effort level is best for the insurance company in any specific case.

What is important here is that regardless of which effort level is best for the firm, the profit-maximising policy always involves full insurance. This is significant and it implies that the outcome here is Pareto efficient. We have seen this sort of result before, so we shall not give another proof of it.

8.2.2 ASYMMETRIC INFORMATION

We now turn our attention to the more interesting case in which the consumer's choice of effort cannot be observed by the insurance company. The insurance company continues to seek the policy that will maximise expected profits. However, if it now cannot observe the effort level chosen by the consumer, how should it go about choosing the optimal policy?

Think of the problem this way. The insurance company must design a policy with a desired accident avoidance effort level in mind. However, because the consumer's effort level cannot be observed, the insurance company must ensure that *the nature of the policy renders it optimal for the consumer to voluntarily choose the desired effort level.*

This effectively adds an additional constraint to the insurance company's maximisation problem. The policy and effort level must be chosen not only to provide the consumer with at least his reservation utility; it must also induce the consumer to voluntarily choose the desired effort level. Thus, the insurance company's problem is

$$\max_{e,p,B_0,\ldots,B_L} p - \sum_{l=0}^{L} \pi_l(e)B_l \quad \text{subject to} \tag{8.13}$$

$$\sum_{l=0}^{L} \pi_l(e)u(w - p - l + B_l) - d(e) \geq \bar{u}, \quad \text{and} \tag{8.14}$$

$$\sum_{l=0}^{L} \pi_l(e)u(w - p - l + B_l) - d(e) \geq \sum_{l=0}^{L} \pi_l(e')u(w - p - l + B_l) - d(e'), \tag{8.15}$$

where $e, e' \in \{0, 1\}$ and $e \neq e'$.

The new constraint is (8.15). It ensures that e, the accident avoidance effort level that the insurance company has in mind when calculating its profits, is the same as that actually chosen by the consumer, for it guarantees that this effort level maximises the consumer's expected utility given the proposed policy.

We shall follow the same procedure as before in solving this problem. That is, we will first fix the effort level, e, and then determine for this particular effort level the form of the optimal policy. Once this is done for both effort levels, it is simply a matter of checking which effort level together with its associated optimal policy maximises the insurance company's profits.

The Optimal Policy for $e = 0$

Suppose we wish to induce the consumer to exert low effort. Among policies that have this effect, which is best for the insurance company? Although we could form the Lagrangian associated with this problem, it is simpler to take a different route.

Recall that if the incentive constraint (8.15) were absent, then the optimal policy when $e = 0$ is given by choosing $p, B_0, \ldots, B_L$ to satisfy

$$\begin{aligned} u(w - p) &= d(0) + \bar{u}, \\ B_l &= l, \qquad l = 0, 1, \ldots, L. \end{aligned} \tag{8.16}$$

Now, adding the incentive constraint to the problem cannot increase the insurance company's maximised profits. Therefore, if the solution to (8.16) satisfies the incentive constraint, then it must be the desired optimal policy. But, clearly, the solution does indeed satisfy (8.15). Given the policy in (8.16), the incentive constraint when $e = 0$ reduces to

$$d(0) \geq d(1),$$

which holds (strictly) by assumption.

Consequently, inducing the consumer to exert low effort in a manner that maximises profits requires the insurance company to offer the same policy as it would were effort observable.

The Optimal Policy for $e = 1$

Suppose now that we wish to induce the consumer to exert high effort. To find the optimal policy for the insurance company, we shall consider the effort level as fixed at $e = 1$ in the maximisation problem (8.13). Thus, the maximisation is over the choice variables $p, B_0, \ldots, B_L$. Also, because $e = 1$, we have $e' = 0$ in the incentive constraint (8.15).

The Lagrangian for this problem is then

$$\mathcal{L} = p - \sum_{l=0}^{L} \pi_l(1)B_l - \lambda\left[\bar{u} - \sum_{l=0}^{L} \pi_l(1)u(w - p - l + B_l) + d(1)\right] \tag{8.17}$$

$$- \beta\left[\sum_{l=0}^{L} \pi_l(0)u(w - p - l + B_l) - d(0) - \left(\sum_{l=0}^{L} \pi_l(1)u(w - p - l + B_l) - d(1)\right)\right],$$

where λ and β are the multipliers corresponding to constraints (8.14) and (8.15), respectively.

The first-order conditions are

$$\frac{\partial \mathcal{L}}{\partial p} = 1 - \lambda\left[\sum_{l=0}^{L}(\pi_l(1) + \beta(\pi_l(1) - \pi_l(0)))u'(w - p - l + B_l)\right] = 0, \tag{8.18}$$

$$\frac{\partial \mathcal{L}}{\partial B_l} = -\pi_l(1) + [\lambda\pi_l(1) + \beta(\pi_l(1) - \pi_l(0))]u'(w - p - l + B_l) = 0, \quad \forall\, l, \tag{8.19}$$

$$\frac{\partial \mathcal{L}}{\partial \lambda} = \bar{u} - \sum_{l=0}^{L} \pi_l(1)u(w - p - l + B_l) + d(1) \leq 0, \tag{8.20}$$

$$\frac{\partial \mathcal{L}}{\partial \beta} = \sum_{l=0}^{L}(\pi_l(0) - \pi_l(1))u(w - p - l + B_l) - d(0) + d(1) \leq 0, \tag{8.21}$$

where (8.20) and (8.21) hold with equality if $\lambda \neq 0$ and $\beta \neq 0$, respectively.

As in the previous problem, the first of these conditions (8.18) is implied by the next $L + 1$ given in (8.19). As before, this redundancy will allow us to set $B_0 = 0$ without loss of generality.

Now, (8.19) can be rewritten as

$$\frac{1}{u'(w - p + B_l - l)} = \lambda + \beta\left[1 - \frac{\pi_l(0)}{\pi_l(1)}\right]. \tag{8.22}$$

We now argue that both λ and β are non-zero.

Suppose that $\beta = 0$. Then (8.22) would imply that the left-hand side is constant in l, which implies that $w - p + B_l - l$ is constant in l. But this cannot hold because then condition (8.21) fails, as its left-hand side reduces to $d(0) - d(1)$, which is strictly negative. We conclude that $\beta \neq 0$.

To see that $\lambda \neq 0$, first note that the monotone likelihood ratio property implies that there is an l such that $\pi_l(0) \neq \pi_l(1)$. Because $\sum_l \pi_l(0) = \sum_l \pi_l(1) = 1$, there must exist l and l' such that $\pi_l(0) > \pi_l(1)$, and $\pi_{l'}(0) < \pi_{l'}(1)$. Consequently, the term in square brackets in (8.22) takes on both positive and negative values.

Now, if $\lambda = 0$, then because $\beta \neq 0$, the right-hand side of (8.22) takes on both positive and negative values. However, the left-hand side is always strictly positive. Therefore, $\lambda \neq 0$. Indeed, this argument shows that $\lambda > 0$.

The fact that both λ and β are non-zero implies that both constraints, (8.20) and (8.21), are binding in the optimal solution. Thus, the consumer is held down to his reservation utility, and he is just indifferent between choosing high and low effort.

To gain more insight into the optimal policy for $e = 1$, it is helpful to show that $\beta > 0$. So suppose that $\beta < 0$. The monotone likelihood ratio property then implies that the right-hand side of (8.22) is strictly increasing in l. Consequently $u'(w - p + B_l - l)$ is strictly decreasing in l, so that $B_l - l$, and therefore $u(w - p + B_l - l)$ are strictly increasing in l. But the latter together with the monotone likelihood ratio property imply that $\sum_l (\pi_l(1) - \pi_l(0))u(w - p + B_l - l) < 0$ (see Exercise 8.13). This contradicts (8.21), because $d(0) < d(1)$. We conclude that $\beta > 0$.

Now because $\beta > 0$, the monotone likelihood ratio property implies that the right-hand side of (8.22) is strictly decreasing, so that $u'(w - p + B_l - l)$ is strictly increasing. Consequently, the optimal policy must display the following feature:

$$l - B_l \text{ is strictly increasing in } l = 0, 1, \ldots, L. \tag{8.23}$$

Recall that we may set $B_0 = 0$ without any loss of generality. Consequently, condition (8.23) indicates that the optimal high-effort policy does not provide full insurance – rather, it specifies a deductible payment that increases with the size of the loss.

This is, of course, very intuitive. To give the consumer an incentive to choose high effort, there must be something in it for the consumer. When $l - B_l$ is strictly increasing, there is a positive utility benefit to exerting high effort, namely,

$$\sum_{l=0}^{L} (\pi_l(1) - \pi_l(0))u(w - p - l + B_l) > 0.$$

That this sum is strictly positive follows from (8.23) and the monotone likelihood ratio property (again, see Exercise 8.13). Of course, there is also a utility cost associated with high effort, namely, $d(1) - d(0) > 0$. The optimal policy is crafted so that the utility benefit of high effort just equals the utility cost.

The Optimal Policy and Efficiency

As we have seen, the policy that is best for the insurance company differs depending on whether it wishes to induce the consumer to choose high or low accident avoidance effort.

The overall optimal policy – the one that solves the maximisation problem (8.13) – is simply the one of these two that yields the larger expected profits.

Now, suppose that in the symmetric information case, the optimal effort level required of the consumer by the insurance company is *low*. Then precisely the same (full insurance) policy will be optimal in the asymmetric information case. This follows because this policy yields the same expected profits as in the symmetric information case, and the maximum expected profits when $e = 1$ is no higher in the asymmetric information case versus the symmetric information case because there is an additional constraint present under asymmetric information. Consequently, because the symmetric information outcome is Pareto efficient, so, too, will be the asymmetric information outcome in this case.

On the other hand, suppose that the optimal effort level required by the insurance company of the consumer is *high* in the symmetric information case. It may well be that the insurance company's maximised expected profits are substantially lower when it attempts to induce high effort in the asymmetric information case. Because expected profits conditional on low effort are identical in both the symmetric and asymmetric information cases, it may then be optimal for the insurance company in the asymmetric information setting to induce low effort by offering the full insurance policy. Although this would be optimal for the insurance company, it would not be Pareto efficient. For compared to the symmetric information solution, the consumer's utility is unchanged (and equal to $\bar{u}$), but the insurance company's profits are strictly lower.

Thus, once again, the effects of asymmetric information can reveal themselves in Pareto-inefficient outcomes.

8.3 INFORMATION AND MARKET PERFORMANCE

The distribution of information across market participants can have a profound and sometimes startling impact on market equilibrium. Indeed, as we have seen in this chapter, asymmetric equilibrium may cause markets to fail in that mutually beneficial trades go unexploited. This failure of market outcomes to be Pareto efficient is a most troubling aspect from a normative point of view.

We have devoted this chapter to a careful study of just one market – the market for insurance – and much of our analysis is drawn from Rothschild and Stiglitz (1976) and Wilson (1977). But the problems we have identified here are present in many other markets, too. Adverse selection arises in the market for used cars and in the market for labour – see, for example, Akerlof (1970) and Spence (1973). Moral hazard arises in the employer–employee relationship, in the doctor–patient relationship, and even in marriages – see, for example, Grossman and Hart (1983) and Holmstrom (1979a, 1982).

For the most part in this chapter we have concentrated on the disease and its symptoms, only occasionally hinting at a potential cure. We end this chapter by noting that very often these information problems can be mitigated if not surmounted. If adverse selection is the problem, signalling or screening can help. If moral hazard is the problem, contracts can be designed so that the agents' incentives lead them nearer to Pareto-efficient outcomes.

The analysis of markets with asymmetric information raises new questions and offers important challenges to economists. It is an area that offers few simple and broadly applicable answers, but it is one where all the analyst's creativity, insight, and logical rigour can pay handsome dividends.

8.4 EXERCISES

8.1 Consider the insurance model of section 8.1, but treat each insurance company as if it were a risk-neutral consumer with wealth endowment $\bar{w} \geq L$ in every state, where L is the size of the loss should one of the m risk-averse consumers have an accident. Also assume that the number of risk-neutral consumers exceeds the number of risk-averse ones. Show that the competitive equilibrium derived in section 8.1 is a competitive equilibrium in this exchange economy.

8.2 Suppose that in the insurance model with asymmetric information, a consumer's accident probability is a function of his wealth. That is, $\pi = f(w)$. Also suppose that different consumers have different wealth levels, and that $f' > 0$. Does adverse selection necessarily occur here?

8.3 In our insurance model of section 8.1, many consumers may have the same accident probability. We allowed policy prices to be person specific. Show that, with symmetric information, equilibrium policy prices depend only on probabilities, not on the particular individuals purchasing them.

8.4 Answer the following questions related to the insurance model with adverse selection.

(a) When there are finitely many consumers, F, the distribution of consumer accident probabilities is a step function. Show that $g : [0, \bar{\pi}L] \to [0, \bar{\pi}L]$ then is also a step function and that it is non-decreasing.

(b) Show that g must therefore possess a fixed point.

(c) More generally, show that a non-decreasing function mapping the unit interval into itself must have a fixed point. (Note that the function need not be continuous! This is a special case of a fixed-point theorem due to Tarski (1955)).

8.5 When analysing our insurance model with adverse selection, we claimed that when the distribution of accident probabilities is uniform on $[0, 1]$, there can be at most two competitive equilibrium prices. You will prove this in this exercise. Suppose that $f : [a, b] \to [a, b]$ is continuous and $f'' > 0$.

(a) Use the fundamental theorem of calculus to argue that if $f(x^*) = x^*$ and $f'(x^*) \geq 1$, then $f(x) > x$ for every $x > x^*$.

(b) Using an argument analogous to that in (a), show that if $f(x^*) = x^*$ and $f'(x^*) \leq 1$, then $f(x) > x$ for every $x < x^*$.

(c) Conclude from (a) and (b) that f has at most two fixed points.

(d) Conclude that there can be at most two competitive equilibrium prices in our insurance model with adverse selection when the distribution of accident probabilities is uniform on $[0, 1]$.

8.6 Suppose there are two states, 1 and 2. State 1 occurs with probability π, and w_i denotes a consumer's wealth in state i.

(a) If the consumer is strictly risk-averse and $w_1 \neq w_2$, show that an insurance company can provide him with insurance rendering his wealth constant across the two states so that he is better off and so that the insurance company earns positive expected profits.

(b) Suppose there are many consumers and many insurance companies and that a feasible allocation is such that each consumer's wealth is constant across states. Suppose also that in this allocation, some consumers are insuring others. Show that the same wealth levels for consumers and expected profits for insurance companies can be achieved by a feasible allocation in which no consumer insures any other.

8.7 (Akerlof) Consider the following market for used cars. There are many sellers of used cars. Each seller has exactly one used car to sell and is characterised by the quality of the used car he wishes to sell. Let $\theta \in [0, 1]$ index the quality of a used car and assume that θ is uniformly distributed on $[0, 1]$. If a seller of type θ sells his car (of quality θ) for a price of p, his utility is $u_s(p, \theta)$. If he does not sell his car, then his utility is 0. Buyers of used cars receive utility $\theta - p$ if they buy a car of quality θ at price p and receive utility 0 if they do not purchase a car. There is asymmetric information regarding the quality of used cars. Sellers know the quality of the car they are selling, but buyers do not know its quality. Assume that there are not enough cars to supply all potential buyers.

(a) Argue that in a competitive equilibrium under asymmetric information, we must have $E(\theta \mid p) = p$.

(b) Show that if $u_s(p, \theta) = p - \theta/2$, then every $p \in (0, 1/2]$ is an equilibrium price.

(c) Find the equilibrium price when $u_s(p, \theta) = p - \sqrt{\theta}$. Describe the equilibrium in words. In particular, which cars are traded in equilibrium?

(d) Find an equilibrium price when $u_s(p, \theta) = p - \theta^3$. How many equilibria are there in this case?

(e) Are any of the preceding outcomes Pareto efficient? Describe Pareto improvements whenever possible.

8.8 Show that in the insurance signalling game, if the consumers have finitely many policies from which to choose, then an assessment is consistent if and only if it satisfies Bayes' rule. Conclude that a sequential equilibrium is then simply an assessment that satisfies Bayes' rule and is sequentially rational.

8.9 Analyse the insurance signalling game when benefit B is restricted to being equal to L. Assume that the low-risk consumer strictly prefers full insurance at the high-risk competitive price to no insurance.

(a) Show that there is a unique sequential equilibrium when attention is restricted to those in which the insurance company earns zero profits.

(b) Show that among all sequential equilibria, there are no separating equilibria. Is this intuitive?

(c) Show that there are pooling equilibria in which the insurance company earns positive profits.

8.10 Consider the insurance signalling game.

(a) Show that there are separating equilibria in which the low-risk consumer's policy proposal is rejected in equilibrium if and only if $MRS_l(0, 0) \leq \bar{\pi}$.

(b) Given a separating equilibrium in which the low-risk consumer's policy proposal is rejected, construct a separating equilibrium in which it is accepted without changing any player's equilibrium payoff.

(c) Continue to consider this setting with one insurance company and two types of consumers. Also, assume low-risk consumers strictly prefer no insurance to full insurance at the high-risk competitive price. Show that when α (the probability that the consumer is low-risk) is low enough, the only competitive equilibrium under asymmetric information gives the low-risk consumer no insurance and the high-risk consumer full insurance.

(d) Returning to the general insurance signalling game, show that every separating equilibrium Pareto dominates the competitive equilibrium described in part (c).

8.11 Consider the insurance screening game. Suppose that the insurance companies had only finitely many policies from which to construct their lists of policies. Show that a joint strategy is a subgame perfect equilibrium if and only if there are beliefs that would render the resulting assessment a sequential equilibrium.

8.12 Consider the insurance screening game.

(a) Suppose there is only one insurance company, not two. Provide a diagram showing the unique pooling contract that is best for the low-risk consumer subject to non-negative expected profits for the insurance company.

(b) Prove that the pooling contract from part (a) does not maximise the low-risk consumer's expected utility among all menus of pairs of contracts subject to earning non-negative profits for the insurance company. Among those contracts, find the contract that maximises the low-risk consumer's expected utility.

(c) What contract maximises the insurance company's expected profits?

8.13 Consider the moral hazard insurance model where the consumer has the option of exerting either high or low accident avoidance effort (i.e., $e = 0$ or 1). Recall that $\pi_l(e) > 0$ denotes the probability that a loss of l dollars is incurred due to an accident. Show that if the monotone likelihood ratio property holds so that $\pi_l(0)/\pi_l(1)$ is strictly increasing in l, then $\sum_{l=0}^{L} \pi_l(0)x_l > \sum_{l=0}^{L} \pi_l(1)x_l$ for every increasing sequence of real numbers $x_1 < x_2 < \cdots < x_L$.

8.14 Consider the moral hazard insurance model.

(a) Show that when information is symmetric, the profit-maximising policy price is higher when low effort is induced compared to high effort.

(b) Let the consumer's reservation utility, $\bar{u}$, be the highest he can achieve by exerting the utility-maximising effort level when no insurance is available. Suppose that when information is asymmetric, it is impossible for the insurance company to earn non-negative profits by inducing the consumer to exert high effort. Show then that if there were no insurance available at all, the consumer would exert low effort.

8.15 Consider once again the moral hazard insurance model. Let the consumer's von Neumann-Morgenstern utility of wealth be $u(w) = \sqrt{w}$, let his initial wealth be $w_0 = \$100$, and suppose that there are but two loss levels, $l = 0$ and $l = \$51$. As usual, there are two effort levels, $e = 0$ and $e = 1$. The consumer's disutility of effort is given by the function $d(e)$, where $d(0) = 0$ and $d(1) = 1/3$. Finally, suppose that the loss probabilities are given by the following entries, where the rows correspond to effort and the columns to loss levels.

	$l = 0$	$l = 51$
$e = 0$	1/3	2/3
$e = 1$	2/3	1/3

So, for example, the probability that a loss of \$51 occurs when the consumer exerts high effort is 1/3.

(a) Verify that the probabilities given in the table satisfy the monotone likelihood ratio property.

(b) Find the consumer's reservation utility assuming that there is only one insurance company and that the consumer's only other option is to self-insure.

(c) What effort level will the consumer exert if no insurance is available?

(d) Show that if information is symmetric, then it is optimal for the insurance company to offer a policy that induces high effort.

(e) Show that the policy in part (d) will not induce high effort if information is asymmetric.

(f) Find the optimal policy when information is asymmetric.

(g) Compare the insurance company's profits in the symmetric and asymmetric information cases. Also, compare the consumer's utility in the two cases. Argue that the symmetric information solution Pareto dominates that with asymmetric information.

8.16 Consider the following principal–agent problem. The owner of a firm (the principal) employs a worker (the agent). The worker can exert low effort, $e = 0$, or high effort, $e = 1$. The resulting revenue, r, to the owner is random, but is more likely to be high when the worker exerts high effort. Specifically, if the worker exerts low effort, $e = 0$, then

$$r = \begin{cases} 0, & \text{with probability } 2/3 \\ 4, & \text{with probability } 1/3 \end{cases}.$$

If instead the worker exerts high effort, $e = 1$, then

$$r = \begin{cases} 0, & \text{with probability } 1/3 \\ 4, & \text{with probability } 2/3 \end{cases}.$$

The worker's von Neumann-Morgenstern utility from wage w and effort e is $u(w, e) = \sqrt{w} - e$. The firm's profits are $\pi = r - w$ when revenues are r and the worker's wage is w. A wage contract (w_0, w_4) specifies the wage, $w_r \geq 0$, that the worker will receive if revenues are $r \in \{0, 4\}$. When working, the worker chooses effort to maximise expected utility and always has the option (his only other option) of quitting his job and obtaining $(w, e) = (0, 0)$.

Find the wage contract $(w_0, w_4) \in [0, \infty)^2$ that maximises the firm's expected profits in each of the situations below.

(a) The owner can observe the worker's effort and so the contract can also be conditioned on the effort level of the worker. How much effort does the worker exert in the expected profit-maximising contract?

(b) The owner cannot observe the worker's effort and so the contract cannot be conditioned on effort. How much effort does the worker exert in the expected profit-maximising contract now?

8.17 A manager cannot observe the effort, e, of a worker, but can observe the output the worker produces. There are n effort levels available to the worker, $e_1 < \cdots < e_n$, and there are m output levels, $y_1 < \cdots < y_m$. Output depends stochastically on effort and $p(y \mid e)$ is the probability that the output level is y given that the worker exerts effort e. The worker's von Neumann-Morgenstern utility of receiving wage w when he exerts effort e is $u(w, e)$, strictly increasing in w and strictly decreasing in e. Note that the worker's 'wage' here is his *total* compensation.

Assume that $p(\cdot \mid \cdot)$ satisfies the strict monotone likelihood ratio property, i.e., that for every $i = 1, 2, \ldots, m$,

$$\frac{p(y_{i+1} \mid e)}{p(y_i \mid e)}$$

is strictly increasing in e.

(a) The manager wishes to offer the worker a wage contract so as to maximise his expected profits, where the worker's only other option is to stay at home and receive a wage of zero, and where the price per unit of output is fixed at one dollar (wages are also in dollars). Formulate the manager's optimisation problem. (What can the worker's wage depend upon?)

(b) Suppose that the optimal wage contract is such that the worker chooses effort level $e_i > e_1$. Prove that the wage contract must be *somewhere* strictly increasing in output (i.e., it must be the case that $w(y_i) < w(y_j)$ for some $y_i < y_j$). You may find the result from Exercise 8.13 useful here.

CHAPTER 9

AUCTIONS AND MECHANISM DESIGN

In most real-world markets, sellers do not have perfect knowledge of market demand. Instead, sellers typically have only statistical information about market demand. Only the buyers themselves know precisely how much of the good they are willing to buy at a particular price. In this chapter, we will revisit the monopoly problem under this more typical circumstance.

Perhaps the simplest situation in which the above elements are present occurs when a single object is put up for auction. There, the seller is typically unaware of the buyers' values but may nevertheless have some information about the distribution of values across buyers. In such a setting, there are a number of standard auction forms that the seller might use to sell the good – first-price, second-price, Dutch, English. Do each of these standard auctions raise the same revenue for the seller? If not, which is best? Is there a non-standard yet even better selling mechanism for the seller? To answer these and other questions, we will introduce and employ some of the tools from the theory of *mechanism design*.

Mechanism design is a general theory about how and when the design of appropriate institutions can achieve particular goals. This theory is especially germane when the designer requires information possessed only by others to achieve his goal. The subtlety in designing a successful mechanism lies in ensuring that the mechanism gives those who possess the needed information the incentive to reveal it to the designer. This chapter provides an introduction to the theory of mechanism design. We shall begin by considering the problem of designing a revenue-maximising selling mechanism. We then move on to the problem of efficient resource allocation. In both cases, the design problem will be subject to informational constraints – the agents possessing private information will have to be incentivised to report their information truthfully.

9.1 THE FOUR STANDARD AUCTIONS

Consider a seller with a single object for sale who wishes to sell the object to one of N buyers for the highest possible price. How should the seller go about achieving this goal? One possible answer is to hold an auction. Many distinct auctions have been put to use at one time or another, but we will focus on the following four standard auctions.[1]

[1] We shall assume throughout and unless otherwise noted that in all auctions ties in bids are broken at random: each tied bidder is equally likely to be deemed the winner.

- **First-Price, Sealed-Bid:** Each bidder submits a sealed bid to the seller. The highest bidder wins and pays his bid for the good.
- **Second-Price, Sealed-Bid:** Each bidder submits a sealed bid to the seller. The highest bidder wins and pays the second-highest bid for the good.
- **Dutch Auction:** The seller begins with a very high price and begins to reduce it. The first bidder to raise his hand wins the object at the current price.
- **English Auction:** The seller begins with very low price (perhaps zero) and begins to increase it. Each bidder signals when he wishes to drop out of the auction. Once a bidder has dropped out, he cannot resume bidding later. When only one bidder remains, he is the winner and pays the current price.

Can we decide even among these four which is best for the seller? To get a handle on this problem, we must begin with a model.

9.2 THE INDEPENDENT PRIVATE VALUES MODEL

A single risk-neutral seller wishes to sell an indivisible object to one of N risk-neutral buyers. The seller values the object at zero euros.[2] Buyer i's value for the object, v_i, is drawn from the interval $[0, 1]$ according to the distribution function $F_i(v_i)$ with density function $f_i(v_i)$.[3] We shall assume that the buyers' values are mutually independent. Each buyer knows his own value but not the values of the other buyers. However, the density functions, $f_1, \ldots, f_N$, are public information and so known by the seller and all buyers. In particular, while the seller is unaware of the buyers' exact values, he knows the distribution from which each value is drawn. If buyer i's value is v_i, then if he wins the object and pays p, his payoff (i.e., von Neumann-Morgenstern utility) is $v_i - p$, whereas his payoff is $-p$ if he must pay p but does not win the object.[4]

This is known as the 'independent, private values' model. **Independent** refers to the fact that each buyer's *private information* (in this case, each buyer's value) is independent of every other buyer's private information. **Private value** refers to the fact that once a buyer employs his own private information to assess the value of the object, this assessment would be unaffected were he subsequently to learn any other buyer's private information, i.e., each buyer's *private* information is sufficient for determining his *value*.[5]

Throughout this chapter, we will assume that the setting in which our monopolist finds himself is well-represented by the independent private values model. We can now

[2]This amounts to assuming that the object has already been produced and that the seller's use value for it is zero.

[3]Recall that $F_i(v_i)$ denotes the probability that i's value is less than or equal to v_i, and that $f_i(v_i) = F_i'(v_i)$. The latter relation can be equivalently expressed as $F_i(v_i) = \int_0^{v_i} f_i(x)dx$. Consequently, we will sometimes refer to f_i and sometimes refer to F_i since each one determines the other.

[4]Although such an outcome is not possible in any one of the four auctions above, there are other auctions (i.e., all-pay auctions) in which payments must be made whether or not one wins the object.

[5]There are more general models in which buyers with private information would potentially obtain yet *additional* information about the value of the object were they to learn *another buyer's* private information, but we shall not consider such models here.

begin to think about how the seller's profits vary with different auction formats. Note that with the production decision behind him and his own value equal to zero, profit-maximisation is equivalent to revenue-maximisation.

Before we can determine the seller's revenues in each of the four standard auctions, we must understand the bidding behaviour of the buyers across the different auction formats. Let us start with the first-price auction.

9.2.1 BIDDING BEHAVIOUR IN A FIRST-PRICE, SEALED-BID AUCTION

To understand bidding behaviour in a first-price auction, we shall, for simplicity, assume that the buyers are ex ante symmetric. That is, we shall suppose that for all buyers $i = 1, \ldots, N$, $f_i(v) = f(v)$ for all $v \in [0, 1]$.

Clearly, the main difficulty in determining the seller's revenue is in determining how the buyers, let us agree to call them *bidders* now, will bid. But note that if you are one of the bidders, then because you would prefer to win the good at a lower price rather than a higher one, you will want to bid low when the others are bidding low and you will want to bid higher when the others bid higher. Of course, you do not know the bids that the others submit because of the sealed-bid rule. Yet, *your optimal bid will depend on how the others bid.* Thus, the bidders are in a strategic setting in which the optimal action (bid) of each bidder depends on the actions of others. Consequently, to determine the behaviour of the bidders, we shall employ the game theoretic tools developed in Chapter 7.

Let us consider the problem of how to bid from the point of view of bidder i. Suppose that bidder i's value is v_i. Given this value, bidder i must submit a sealed bid, b_i. Because b_i will in general depend on i's value, let us write $b_i(v_i)$ to denote bidder i's bid when his value is v_i. Now, because bidder i must be prepared to submit a bid $b_i(v_i)$ for each of his potential values $v_i \in [0, 1]$, we may view bidder i's **strategy** as a *bidding function* $b_i \colon [0, 1] \to \mathbb{R}_+$, mapping each of his values into a (possibly different) non-negative bid.

Before we discuss payoffs, it will be helpful to focus our attention on a natural class of bidding strategies. It seems very natural to expect that bidders with higher values will place higher bids. So, let us restrict attention to *strictly increasing* bidding functions. Next, because the bidders are ex ante symmetric, it is also natural to suppose that bidders with the same value will submit the same bid. With this in mind, we shall focus on finding a strictly increasing bidding function, $\hat{b} \colon [0, 1] \to \mathbb{R}_+$, that is optimal for each bidder to employ, given that all other bidders employ this bidding function as well. That is, we wish to find a symmetric Nash equilibrium in strictly increasing bidding functions.

Now, let us suppose that we find a symmetric Nash equilibrium given by the strictly increasing bidding function $\hat{b}(\cdot)$. By definition it must be payoff-maximising for a bidder, say i, with value v to bid $\hat{b}(v)$ given that the other bidders employ the same bidding function $\hat{b}(\cdot)$. Because of this, we can usefully employ what may at first appear to be a rather mysterious exercise.

The mysterious but useful exercise is this: imagine that bidder i cannot attend the auction and that he sends a friend to bid for him. The friend knows the equilibrium bidding function $\hat{b}(\cdot)$, but he does not know bidder i's value. Now, if bidder i's value is v, bidder i would like his friend to submit the bid $\hat{b}(v)$ on his behalf. His friend can do this for him once bidder i calls him and tells him his value. Clearly, bidder i has no incentive to lie to his friend about his value. That is, among all the values $r \in [0, 1]$ that bidder i with value v can report to his friend, his payoff is maximised by reporting his true value, v, to his friend. This is because reporting the value r results in his friend submitting the bid $\hat{b}(r)$ on his behalf. But if bidder i were there himself he would submit the bid $\hat{b}(v)$.

Let us calculate bidder i's expected payoff from reporting an arbitrary value, r, to his friend when his value is v, given that all other bidders employ the bidding function $\hat{b}(\cdot)$. To calculate this expected payoff, it is necessary to notice just two things. First, bidder i will win only when the bid submitted for him is highest. That is, when $\hat{b}(r) > \hat{b}(v_j)$ for all bidders $j \neq i$. Because $\hat{b}(\cdot)$ is strictly increasing this occurs precisely when r exceeds the values of all $N-1$ other bidders. Letting F denote the distribution function associated with f, the probability that this occurs is $(F(r))^{N-1}$ which we will denote $F^{N-1}(r)$. Second, bidder i pays only when he wins and he then pays his bid, $\hat{b}(r)$. Consequently, bidder i's expected payoff from reporting the value r to his friend when his value is v, given that all other bidders employ the bidding function $\hat{b}(\cdot)$, can be written

$$u(r, v) = F^{N-1}(r)(v - \hat{b}(r)). \tag{9.1}$$

Now, as we have already remarked, because $\hat{b}(\cdot)$ is an equilibrium, bidder i's expected payoff-maximising bid when his value is v must be $\hat{b}(v)$. Consequently, (9.1) must be maximised when $r = v$, i.e., when bidder i reports his true value, v, to his friend. So, if we differentiate the right-hand side with respect to r, the resulting derivative must be zero when $r = v$. Differentiating yields

$$\frac{dF^{N-1}(r)(v - \hat{b}(r))}{dr} = (N-1)F^{N-2}(r)f(r)(v - \hat{b}(r)) - F^{N-1}(r)\hat{b}'(r). \tag{9.2}$$

Evaluating the right-hand side at $r = v$, where it is equal to zero, and rearranging yields,

$$(N-1)F^{N-2}(v)f(v)\hat{b}(v) + F^{N-1}(v)\hat{b}'(v) = (N-1)vf(v)F^{N-2}(v). \tag{9.3}$$

Looking closely at the left-hand side of (9.3), we see that it is just the derivative of the product $F^{N-1}(v)\hat{b}(v)$ with respect to v. With this observation, we can rewrite (9.3) as

$$\frac{dF^{N-1}(v)\hat{b}(v)}{dv} = (N-1)vf(v)F^{N-2}(v). \tag{9.4}$$

Now, because (9.4) must hold for every v, it must be the case that

$$F^{N-1}(v)\hat{b}(v) = (N-1)\int_0^v xf(x)F^{N-2}(x)dx + \text{constant}.$$

Noting that a bidder with value zero must bid zero, we conclude that the constant above must be zero. Hence, it must be the case that

$$\hat{b}(v) = \frac{N-1}{F^{N-1}(v)} \int_0^v xf(x)F^{N-2}(x)dx,$$

which can be written more succinctly as

$$\hat{b}(v) = \frac{1}{F^{N-1}(v)} \int_0^v xdF^{N-1}(x). \tag{9.5}$$

There are two things to notice about the bidding function in (9.5). First, as we had assumed, it is strictly increasing in v (see Exercise 9.1). Second, it has been uniquely determined. Hence, in conclusion, we have proven the following.

THEOREM 9.1 ***First-Price Auction Symmetric Equilibrium***

If N bidders have independent private values drawn from the common distribution, F, then bidding

$$\hat{b}(v) = \frac{1}{F^{N-1}(v)} \int_0^v xdF^{N-1}(x)$$

whenever one's value is v constitutes a symmetric Nash equilibrium of a first-price, sealed-bid auction. Moreover, this is the only symmetric Nash equilibrium.[6]

EXAMPLE 9.1 Suppose that each bidder's value is uniformly distributed on [0, 1]. Then $F(v) = v$ and $f(v) = 1$. Consequently, if there are N bidders, then each employs the bidding function

$$\begin{aligned}
\hat{b}(v) &= \frac{1}{v^{N-1}} \int_0^v xdx^{N-1} \\
&= \frac{1}{v^{N-1}} \int_0^v x(N-1)x^{N-2}dx \\
&= \frac{N-1}{v^{N-1}} \int_0^v x^{N-1}dx \\
&= \frac{N-1}{v^{N-1}} \frac{1}{N} v^N \\
&= v - \frac{v}{N}.
\end{aligned}$$

[6]Strictly speaking, we have not shown that this is an equilibrium. We have shown that *if* a symmetric equilibrium exists, then this must be it. You are asked to show that this is indeed an equilibrium in an exercise. You might also wonder about the existence of asymmetric equilibria. It can be shown that there are none, although we shall not do so here.

So, each bidder *shades* his bid, by bidding less than his value. Note that as the number of bidders increases, the bidders bid more aggressively. □

Because $F^{N-1}(\cdot)$ is the distribution function of the highest value among a bidder's $N-1$ competitors, the bidding strategy displayed in Theorem 9.1 says that each bidder bids the expectation of the second highest bidder's value conditional on his own value being highest. But, because the bidders use the *same strictly increasing* bidding function, having the highest value is equivalent to having the highest bid and so equivalent to winning the auction. So, we may say:

In the unique symmetric equilibrium of a first-price, sealed-bid auction, each bidder bids the expectation of the second-highest bidder's value conditional on winning the auction.

The idea that one ought to bid *conditional on winning* is very intuitive in a first-price auction because of the feature that one's bid matters only when one wins the auction. Because this feature is present in other auctions as well, this idea should be considered one of the basic insights of our strategic analysis.

Having analysed the first-price auction, it is an easy matter to describe behaviour in a Dutch auction.

9.2.2 BIDDING BEHAVIOUR IN A DUTCH AUCTION

In a Dutch auction, each bidder has a single decision to make, namely, 'At what price should I raise my hand to signal that I am willing to buy the good at that price?' Moreover, the bidder who chooses the highest price wins the auction and pays this price. Consequently, by replacing the word 'price' by 'bid' in the previous sentence we see that this auction is equivalent to a first-price auction! So, we can immediately conclude the following.

THEOREM 9.2 ***Dutch Auction Symmetric Equilibrium***

If N bidders have independent private values drawn from the common distribution, F, then raising one's hand when the price reaches

$$\frac{1}{F^{N-1}(v)} \int_0^v x dF^{N-1}(x)$$

whenever one's value is v constitutes a symmetric Nash equilibrium of a Dutch auction. Moreover, this is the only symmetric Nash equilibrium.

Clearly then, the first-price and Dutch auctions raise exactly the same revenue for the seller, ex post (i.e., for every realisation of bidder values $v_1, \ldots, v_N$).

We now turn to the second-price, sealed-bid auction.

9.2.3 BIDDING BEHAVIOUR IN A SECOND-PRICE, SEALED-BID AUCTION

One might wonder why we would bother considering a second-price auction at all. Is it not obvious that a first-price auction must yield higher revenue for the seller? After all, in a first-price auction the seller receives the *highest* bid, whereas in a second-price auction he receives only the *second-highest* bid.

While this might sound convincing, it neglects a crucial point: *The bidders will bid differently in the two auctions.* In a first-price auction, a bidder has an incentive to raise his bid to increase his chances of winning the auction, yet he has an incentive to reduce his bid to lower the price he pays when he does win. In a second-price auction, the second effect is absent because when a bidder wins, the amount he pays is independent of his bid. So, we should expect bidders to bid *more aggressively* in a second-price auction than they would in a first-price auction. Therefore, there is a chance that a second-price auction will generate higher expected revenues for the seller than will a first-price auction. When we recognise that bidding behaviour changes with the change in the auction format, the question of which auction raises more revenue is not quite so obvious, is it?

Happily, analysing bidding behaviour in a second-price, sealed-bid auction is remarkably straightforward. Unlike our analysis of the first-price auction, we need not restrict attention to the case involving symmetric bidders. That is, we shall allow the density functions $f_1, \ldots, f_N$, from which the bidders' values are independently drawn, to differ.[7]

Consider bidder i with value v_i, and let B denote the highest bid submitted by the other bidders. Of course, B is unknown to bidder i because the bids are sealed. Now, if bidder i were to win the auction, his bid would be highest and B would then be the second-highest bid. Consequently, bidder i would have to pay B for the object. In effect, then, the price that bidder i must pay for the object is the highest bid, B, submitted by the other bidders.

Now, because bidder i's value is v_i, he would strictly want to win the auction when his value exceeds the price he would have to pay, i.e., when $v_i > B$; and he would strictly want to lose when $v_i < B$. When $v_i = B$ he is indifferent between winning and losing. Can bidder i bid in a manner that guarantees that he will win when $v_i > B$ and that he will lose when $v_i < B$, even though he does not know B? The answer is yes. He can guarantee precisely this simply by bidding his value, v_i!

By bidding v_i, bidder i is the high bidder, and so wins, when $v_i > B$, and he is not the high bidder, and so loses, when $v_i < B$. Consequently, bidding his value is a payoff-maximising bid for bidder i *regardless of the bids submitted by the other bidders* (recall that B was the highest bid among any arbitrary bids submitted by the others). Moreover, because bidding below one's value runs the risk of losing the auction when one would have strictly preferred winning it, and bidding above one's value runs the risk of winning the auction for a price above one's value, bidding one's value is a weakly dominant bidding strategy. So, we can state the following.

[7] In fact, even the independence assumption can be dropped. (See Exercise 9.5.)

THEOREM 9.3 ***Second-Price Auction Equilibrium***

If N bidders have independent private values, then bidding one's value is the unique weakly dominant bidding strategy for each bidder in a second-price, sealed-bid auction.

This brings us to the English auction.

9.2.4 BIDDING BEHAVIOUR IN AN ENGLISH AUCTION

In contrast to the auctions we have considered so far, in an English auction there are potentially many decisions a bidder has to make. For example, when the price is very low, he must decide at which price he would drop out when no one has yet dropped out. But, if some other bidder drops out first, he must then decide at which price to drop out *given* the remaining active bidders, and so on. Despite this, there is a close connection between the English and second-price auctions.

In an English auction, as in a second-price auction, it turns out to be a dominant strategy for a bidder to drop out when the price reaches his value, regardless of which bidders remain active. The reason is rather straightforward. A bidder i with value v_i who, given the history of play and the current price $p < v_i$, considers dropping out can do no worse by planning to remain active a little longer and until the price reaches his value, v_i. By doing so, the worst that can happen is that he ends up dropping out when the price does indeed reach his value. His payoff would then be zero, just as it would be if he were to drop out now at price p. However, it might happen, were he to remain active, that all other bidders would drop out before the price reaches v_i. In this case, bidder i would be strictly better off by having remained active since he then wins the object at a price strictly less than his value v_i, obtaining a positive payoff. So, we have the following.

THEOREM 9.4 ***English Auction Equilibrium***

If N bidders have independent private values, then dropping out when the price reaches one's value is the unique weakly dominant bidding strategy for each bidder in an English auction.[8]

Given this result, it is easy to see that the bidder with the highest value will win in an English auction. But what price will he pay for the object? That, of course, depends on the price at which his *last remaining competitor* drops out of the auction. But his last remaining competitor will be the bidder with the *second-highest value*, and he will, like all bidders, drop out when the price reaches his value. Consequently, the bidder with highest value wins and pays a price equal to the second-highest value. Hence, we see that the outcome of the English auction is identical to that of the second-price auction. In particular, the English and second-price auctions earn exactly the same revenue for the seller, ex post.

---

[8]As in the second-price auction case, this weak dominance result does not rely on the independence of the bidder's values. It holds even if the values are correlated. However, it is important that the values are *private*.

9.2.5 REVENUE COMPARISONS

Because the first-price and Dutch auctions raise the same ex post revenue and the second-price and English auctions raise the same ex post revenue, it remains only to compare the revenues generated by the first- and second-price auctions. Clearly, these auctions need not raise the same revenue ex post. For example, when the highest value is quite high and the second-highest is quite low, running a first-price auction will yield more revenue than a second-price auction. On the other hand, when the first- and second-highest values are close together, a second-price auction will yield higher revenues than will a first-price auction.

Of course, when the seller must decide which of the two auction forms to employ, he does not know the bidders' values. However, knowing how the bidders bid as functions of their values, and knowing the distribution of bidder values, the seller can calculate the *expected revenue* associated with each auction. Thus, the question is, which auction yields the highest expected revenue, a first- or a second-price auction? Because our analysis of the first-price auction involved symmetric bidders, we must assume symmetry here to compare the expected revenue generated by a first-price versus a second-price auction. So, in what follows, $f(\cdot)$ will denote the common density of each bidder's value and $F(\cdot)$ will denote the associated distribution function.

Let us begin by considering the expected revenue, R_{FPA}, generated by a first-price auction (FPA). Because the highest bid wins a first-price auction and because the bidder with the highest value submits the highest bid, if v is the highest value among the N bidder values, then the seller's revenue is $\hat{b}(v)$. So, if the highest value is distributed according to the density $g(v)$, the seller's expected revenue can be written

$$R_{FPA} = \int_0^1 \hat{b}(v)g(v)dv.$$

Because the density, g, of the maximum of N independent random variables with common density f and distribution F is NfF^{N-1},[9] we have

$$R_{FPA} = N\int_0^1 \hat{b}(v)f(v)F^{N-1}(v)dv. \tag{9.6}$$

We have seen that in a second-price auction, because each bidder bids his value, the seller receives as price the second-highest value among the N bidder values. So, if $h(v)$ is the density of the second-highest value, the seller's expected revenue, R_{SPA}, in a second-price auction can be written

$$R_{SPA} = \int_0^1 vh(v)dv.$$

[9]To see this, note that the highest value is less than or equal to v if and only if all N values are, and that this occurs with probability $F^N(v)$. Hence, the distribution function of the highest value is F^N. Because the density function is the derivative of the distribution function the result follows.

Because the density, h, of the second-highest of N independent random variables with common density f and distribution function F is $N(N-1)F^{N-2}f(1-F)$,[10] we have

$$R_{SPA} = N(N-1)\int_0^1 vF^{N-2}(v)f(v)(1-F(v))dv. \tag{9.7}$$

We shall now compare the two. From (9.6) and (9.5) we have

$$\begin{aligned} R_{FPA} &= N\int_0^1 \left[\frac{1}{F^{N-1}(v)}\int_0^v x dF^{N-1}(x)\right] f(v)F^{N-1}(v)dv \\ &= N(N-1)\int_0^1 \left[\int_0^v xF^{N-2}(x)f(x)dx\right] f(v)dv \\ &= N(N-1)\int_0^1\int_0^v [xF^{N-2}(x)f(x)f(v)]dxdv \\ &= N(N-1)\int_0^1\int_x^1 [xF^{N-2}(x)f(x)f(v)]dvdx \\ &= N(N-1)\int_0^1 xF^{N-2}(x)f(x)(1-F(x))dx \\ &= R_{SPA}, \end{aligned}$$

where the fourth equality follows from interchanging the order of integration (i.e., from $dxdv$ to $dvdx$), and the final equality follows from (9.7).

EXAMPLE 9.2 Consider the case in which each bidder's value is uniform on [0, 1] so that $F(v) = v$ and $f(v) = 1$. The expected revenue generated in a first-price auction is

$$\begin{aligned} R_{FPA} &= N\int_0^1 \hat{b}(v)f(v)F^{N-1}(v)dv \\ &= N\int_0^1 \left[v - \frac{v}{N}\right] v^{N-1}dv \\ &= (N-1)\int_0^1 v^N dv \\ &= \frac{N-1}{N+1}. \end{aligned}$$

[10] One way to see this is to treat probability density like probability. Then the probability (density) that some particular bidder's value is v is $f(v)$ and the probability that exactly one of the remaining $N-1$ other bidders' values is above this is $(N-1)F^{N-2}(v)(1-F(v))$. Consequently, the probability that this particular bidder's value is v and it is second-highest is $(N-1)f(v)F^{N-2}(v)(1-F(v))$. Because there are N bidders, the probability (i.e., density) that the second-highest value is v is then $N(N-1)f(v)F^{N-2}(v)(1-F(v))$.

On the other hand, the expected revenue generated in a second-price auction is

$$\begin{aligned}R_{SPA} &= N(N-1)\int_0^1 vF^{N-2}(v)f(v)(1-F(v))dv \\ &= N(N-1)\int_0^1 v^{N-1}(1-v)dv \\ &= N(N-1)\left[\frac{1}{N}-\frac{1}{N+1}\right] \\ &= \frac{N-1}{N+1}.\end{aligned}$$

□

Remarkably, the first- and second-price auctions raise the *same* expected revenue, regardless of the common distribution of bidder values! So, we may state the following:

If N bidders have independent private values drawn from the common distribution, F, then all four standard auction forms (first-price, second-price, Dutch, and English) raise the same expected revenue for the seller.

This *revenue equivalence* result may go some way towards explaining why we see all four auction forms in practice. Were it the case that one of them raised more revenue than the others on average, then we would expect that one to be used rather than any of the others. But what is it that accounts for the coincidence of expected revenue in these auctions? Our next objective is to gain some insight into why this is so.

9.3 THE REVENUE EQUIVALENCE THEOREM

To explain the equivalence of revenue in the four standard auction forms, we must first find a way to fit all of these auctions into a single framework. With this in mind, we now define the notion of a *direct selling mechanism.*[11]

DEFINITION 9.1 ***Direct Selling Mechanism***

A direct selling mechanism is a collection of N probability assignment functions,

$$p_1(v_1,\ldots,v_N),\ldots,p_N(v_1,\ldots,v_N),$$

and N cost functions

$$c_1(v_1,\ldots,v_N),\ldots,c_N(v_1,\ldots,v_N).$$

For every vector of values $(v_1,\ldots,v_N)$ *reported by the N bidders,* $p_i(v_1,\ldots,v_N)\in[0,1]$ *denotes the probability that bidder i receives the object and* $c_i(v_1,\ldots,v_N)\in\mathbb{R}$

[11]Our presentation is based upon Myerson (1981).

denotes the payment that bidder i must make to the seller. The sum of the probabilities, $p_1(v_1, \ldots, v_N) + \cdots + p_N(v_1, \ldots, v_N)$ *is always no greater than unity.*

A direct selling mechanism works as follows. Because the seller does not know the bidders' values, he asks them to report them to him simultaneously. He then takes those reports, $v_1, \ldots, v_N$, which need not be truthful, and assigns the object to one of the bidders according to the probabilities $p_i(v_1, \ldots, v_N)$, $i = 1, \ldots, N$, keeping the object with the residual probability, and secures the payment $c_i(v_1, \ldots, v_N)$ from each bidder $i = 1, \ldots, N$. It is assumed that the entire direct selling mechanism – the probability assignment functions and the cost functions – are public information, and that the seller must carry out the terms of the mechanism given the vector of reported values.

Several points are worthy of note. First, although the sum of probabilities $p_1 + \cdots + p_N$ can never exceed unity, we allow this sum to fall short of unity because we want to allow the seller to keep the object.[12] Second, a bidder's cost may be negative. Third, a bidder's cost may be positive even when that bidder does not receive the object (i.e., when that bidder's probability of receiving the object is zero).

Clearly, the seller's revenue will depend on the reports submitted by the bidders. Will they be induced to report truthfully? If not, how will they behave? These are very good questions, but let us put them aside for the time being. Instead, we introduce what will turn out to be an extremely important special kind of direct selling mechanism, namely, those in which the bidders find it in their interest to report truthfully. These mechanisms are called *incentive-compatible*. Before introducing the formal definition, we introduce a little notation.

Consider a direct selling mechanism $(p_i(\cdot), c_i(\cdot))_{i=1}^N$. Suppose that bidder i's value is v_i and he considers reporting that his value is r_i. If all other bidders always report their values truthfully, then bidder i's expected payoff is

$$u_i(r_i, v_i) = \int_0^1 \cdots \int_0^1 (p_i(r_i, v_{-i})v_i - c_i(r_i, v_{-i}))f_{-i}(v_{-i})dv_{-i},$$

where $f_{-i}(v_{-i}) = f(v_1) \cdots f(v_{i-1})f(v_{i+1}) \cdots f(v_N)$ and $dv_{-i} = dv_1 \cdots dv_{i-1}dv_{i+1} \cdots dv_N$.

For every $r_i \in [0, 1]$, let

$$\bar{p}_i(r_i) = \int_0^1 \cdots \int_0^1 p_i(r_i, v_{-i})f_{-i}(v_{-i})dv_{-i}$$

and

$$\bar{c}_i(r_i) = \int_0^1 \cdots \int_0^1 c_i(r_i, v_{-i})f_{-i}(v_{-i})dv_{-i}.$$

[12]This is more generality than we need at the moment because the seller never keeps the object in any of the four standard auctions. However, this will be helpful a little later.

Therefore, $\bar{p}_i(r_i)$ is the probability that i receives the object when he reports r_i and $\bar{c}_i(r_i)$ is i's expected payment when he reports r_i, with both of these being conditional on all others always reporting truthfully. Consequently, bidder i's expected payoff when his value is v_i and he reports r_i can be written as

$$u_i(r_i, v_i) = \bar{p}_i(r_i)v_i - \bar{c}_i(r_i), \tag{9.8}$$

when all other bidders report their values truthfully.

We can now state the definition of an **incentive-compatible direct selling mechanism**.

DEFINITION 9.2 ***Incentive-Compatible Direct Selling Mechanisms***

A direct selling mechanism is incentive-compatible if when the other bidders always report their values truthfully, each bidder i's expected payoff is maximised by always reporting his value truthfully – i.e., the mechanism is incentive-compatible if for each bidder i, and for each of his values $v_i \in [0, 1]$, $u_i(r_i, v_i)$ as defined in (9.8) is maximised in $r_i \in [0, 1]$ when $r_i = v_i$. We shall then say that it is a Bayesian-Nash equilibrium for each bidder to always report his value truthfully.[13]

Note very carefully what the definition does *not* say. It does not say that reporting truthfully is best for a bidder regardless of the others' reports. It *only* says that a bidder can do no better than to report truthfully so long as all other bidders report truthfully. Thus, although truthful reporting is a Bayesian-Nash equilibrium in an incentive-compatible mechanism, it need not be a dominant strategy for any player.

You might wonder how all of this is related to the four standard auctions. We will now argue that each of the four standard auctions can be equivalently viewed as an incentive-compatible direct selling mechanism. In fact, understanding incentive-compatible direct selling mechanisms will not only be the key to understanding the connection between the four standard auctions, but it will be central to our understanding revenue-maximising auctions as well.

Consider a first-price auction with symmetric bidders. We would like to construct an 'equivalent' direct selling mechanism in which truth-telling is an equilibrium. To do this, we shall employ the first-price auction equilibrium bidding function $\hat{b}(\cdot)$. The idea behind our construction is simple. Instead of the bidders submitting bids computed by plugging their values into the equilibrium bidding function, the bidders will be asked to submit their values and the seller will then compute their equilibrium bids for them. Recall that because $\hat{b}(\cdot)$ is strictly increasing, a bidder wins the object in a first-price auction if and only if he has the highest value.

[13]This would in fact be a consequence of our Chapter 7 definition of Bayesian-Nash equilibrium but for the fact that we restricted attention to finite type spaces there.

Consider, then, the following direct selling mechanism, where $\hat{b}(\cdot)$ is the equilibrium bidding function for the first-price auction given in (9.5):

$$p_i(v_1, \ldots, v_N) = \begin{cases} 1, & \text{if } v_i > v_j \text{ for all } j \neq i \\ 0, & \text{otherwise,} \end{cases}$$

$$\text{and} \tag{9.9}$$

$$c_i(v_1, \ldots, v_N) = \begin{cases} \hat{b}(v_i), & \text{if } v_i > v_j \text{ for all } j \neq i \\ 0, & \text{otherwise.} \end{cases}$$

Look closely at this mechanism. Note that the bidder with the highest reported value, v, receives the object and he pays $\hat{b}(v)$ for it, just as he would have in a first-price auction equilibrium. So, if the bidders report their values truthfully, then the bidder with the highest value, v, wins the object and makes the payment $\hat{b}(v)$ to the seller. Consequently, if this mechanism is incentive-compatible, the seller will earn exactly the same ex post revenue as he would with a first-price auction.

To demonstrate that this mechanism is incentive-compatible we need to show that truth-telling is a Nash equilibrium. So, let us suppose that all other bidders report their values truthfully and that the remaining bidder has value v. We must show that this bidder can do no better than to report his value truthfully to the seller. So, suppose that this bidder considers reporting value r. He then wins the object and makes a payment of $\hat{b}(r)$ if and only if $r > v_j$ for all other bidders j. Because the other $N-1$ bidders' values are independently distributed according to F, this event occurs with probability $F^{N-1}(r)$. Consequently, this bidder's expected payoff from reporting value r when his true value is v is

$$F^{N-1}(r)(v - \hat{b}(r)).$$

But this is exactly the payoff in (9.1), which we already know is maximised when $r = v$. Hence, the direct selling mechanism (9.9) is indeed incentive-compatible.

Let us reconsider what we have accomplished here. Beginning with the equilibrium of a first-price auction, we have constructed an incentive-compatible direct selling mechanism whose truth-telling equilibrium results in the same ex post assignment of the object to bidders and the same ex post payments by them. In particular, it results in the same ex post revenue for the seller. Moreover, this method of constructing a direct mechanism is quite general. Indeed, beginning with the equilibrium of any of the four standard auctions, we can similarly construct an incentive-compatible direct selling mechanism that yields the same ex post assignment of the object to bidders and the same ex post payments by them. (You are asked to do this in an exercise.)

In effect, we have shown that each of the four standard auctions is equivalent to some incentive-compatible direct selling mechanism. Because of this, we can now gain insight into the former by studying the latter.

9.3.1 INCENTIVE-COMPATIBLE DIRECT SELLING MECHANISMS: A CHARACTERISATION

Because incentive-compatible mechanisms are so important, it is very helpful to know how to identify them. The following result provides a complete characterisation. It states that a direct mechanism is incentive-compatible if two conditions are met. First, it must be the case that reporting a higher value leads a bidder to expect that he will receive the object with higher probability. Second, the cost a bidder expects to pay must be related in a very particular way to the probability with which he expects to receive the object.

THEOREM 9.5 ***Incentive-Compatible Direct Selling Mechanisms***

A direct selling mechanism $(p_i(\cdot), c_i(\cdot))_{i=1}^N$ is incentive-compatible if and only if for every bidder i

(i) $\bar{p}_i(v_i)$ is non-decreasing in v_i and,

(ii) $\bar{c}_i(v_i) = \bar{c}_i(0) + \bar{p}_i(v_i)v_i - \int_0^{v_i} \bar{p}_i(x)dx$, for every $v_i \in [0, 1]$.

Proof: Suppose the mechanism is incentive-compatible. We must show that (i) and (ii) hold.

To see that (i) holds, note that by incentive compatibility, for all $r_i, v_i \in [0, 1]$,

$$\bar{p}_i(r_i)v_i - \bar{c}_i(r_i) = u_i(r_i, v_i) \leq u_i(v_i, v_i) = \bar{p}_i(v_i)v_i - \bar{c}_i(v_i).$$

Adding and subtracting $\bar{p}_i(v_i)r_i$ to the right-hand side, this implies

$$\bar{p}_i(r_i)v_i - \bar{c}_i(r_i) \leq [\bar{p}_i(v_i)r_i - \bar{c}_i(v_i)] + \bar{p}_i(v_i)(v_i - r_i).$$

But a careful look at the term in square brackets reveals that it is $u_i(v_i, r_i)$, bidder i's expected payoff from reporting v_i when his true value is r_i. By incentive compatibility, this must be no greater than $u_i(r_i, r_i)$, his payoff when he reports his true value, r_i. Consequently,

$$\begin{aligned}\bar{p}_i(r_i)v_i - \bar{c}_i(r_i) &\leq [\bar{p}_i(v_i)r_i - \bar{c}_i(v_i)] + \bar{p}_i(v_i)(v_i - r_i)\\ &\leq u_i(r_i, r_i) + \bar{p}_i(v_i)(v_i - r_i)\\ &= [\bar{p}_i(r_i)r_i - \bar{c}_i(r_i)] + \bar{p}_i(v_i)(v_i - r_i).\end{aligned}$$

That is,

$$\bar{p}_i(r_i)v_i - \bar{c}_i(r_i) \leq [\bar{p}_i(r_i)r_i - \bar{c}_i(r_i)] + \bar{p}_i(v_i)(v_i - r_i),$$

which, when rewritten, becomes

$$(\bar{p}_i(v_i) - \bar{p}_i(r_i))(v_i - r_i) \geq 0.$$

So, when $v_i > r_i$, it must be the case that $\bar{p}_i(v_i) \geq \bar{p}_i(r_i)$. We conclude that $\bar{p}_i(\cdot)$ is non-decreasing. Hence, (i) holds. (See also Exercise 9.7.)

To see that (ii) holds, note that because bidder i's expected payoff must be maximised when he reports truthfully, the derivative of $u_i(r_i, v_i)$ with respect to r_i must be zero when

$r_i = v_i$.[14] Computing this derivative yields

$$\frac{\partial u_i(r_i, v_i)}{\partial r_i} = \bar{p}_i'(r_i)v_i - \bar{c}_i'(r_i),$$

and setting this to zero when $r_i = v_i$ yields

$$\bar{c}_i'(v_i) = \bar{p}_i'(v_i)v_i. \tag{P.1}$$

Because v_i was arbitrary, (P.1) must hold for every $v_i \in [0, 1]$. Consequently,

$$\begin{aligned}\bar{c}_i(v_i) - \bar{c}_i(0) &= \int_0^{v_i} \bar{c}_i'(x)dx \\ &= \int_0^{v_i} \bar{p}_i'(x)xdx \\ &= \bar{p}_i(v_i)v_i - \int_0^{v_i} \bar{p}_i(x)dx,\end{aligned}$$

where the first equality follows from the fundamental theorem of calculus, the second from (P.1), and the third from integration by parts. Consequently, for every bidder i and every $v_i \in [0, 1]$,

$$\bar{c}_i(v_i) = \bar{c}_i(0) + \bar{p}_i(v_i)v_i - \int_0^{v_i} \bar{p}_i(x)dx, \tag{P.2}$$

proving (ii).

We must now show the converse. So, suppose that (i) and (ii) hold. We must show that $u_i(r_i, v_i)$ is maximised in r_i when $r_i = v_i$. To see this, note that substituting (ii) into (9.8) yields

$$u_i(r_i, v_i) = \bar{p}_i(r_i)v_i - \left[\bar{c}_i(0) + \bar{p}_i(r_i)r_i - \int_0^{r_i} \bar{p}_i(x)dx\right]. \tag{P.3}$$

This can be rewritten as

$$u_i(r_i, v_i) = -\bar{c}_i(0) + \int_0^{v_i} \bar{p}_i(x)dx - \left\{\int_{r_i}^{v_i} (\bar{p}_i(x) - \bar{p}_i(r_i))dx\right\},$$

where this expression is valid whether $r_i \le v_i$ or $r_i \ge v_i$.[15] Because by (i) $\bar{p}_i(\cdot)$ is non-decreasing, the integral in curly brackets is non-negative for all r_i and v_i. Consequently,

$$u_i(r_i, v_i) \le -\bar{c}_i(0) + \int_0^{v_i} \bar{p}_i(x)dx. \tag{P.4}$$

[14]We are ignoring two points here. The first is whether $u_i(r_i, v_i)$ is in fact differentiable in r_i. Although it need not be everywhere differentiable, incentive compatibility implies that it must be differentiable almost everywhere and that the analysis we shall conduct can be made perfectly rigorous. We will not pursue these details here. The second point we ignore is the first-order condition at the two non-interior values $v_i = 0$ or 1. Strictly speaking, the derivatives at these boundary points need not be zero. But there is no harm in this because these two values each occur with probability zero.

[15]Recall the convention in mathematics that when $a < b$, $\int_b^a f(x)dx = -\int_a^b f(x)dx$.

But, by (P.3), the right-hand side of (P.4) is equal to $u_i(v_i, v_i)$. Consequently,

$$u_i(r_i, v_i) \le u_i(v_i, v_i),$$

so that $u_i(r_i, v_i)$ is indeed maximised in r_i when $r_i = v_i$. ∎

Part (ii) of Theorem 9.5 says that if a direct mechanism is incentive-compatible there must be a connection between the probability assignment functions and the cost functions. In particular, it says that once the probability assignment function has been chosen and once a bidder's expected cost conditional on having value zero is chosen, the remainder of the expected cost function is chosen as well. To put it differently, under incentive compatibility a bidder's expected payment conditional on his value is completely determined by his expected payment when his value is zero and his probability assignment function. This observation is essential for understanding the following result.

THEOREM 9.6 ***Revenue Equivalence***

If two incentive-compatible direct selling mechanisms have the same probability assignment functions and every bidder with value zero is indifferent between the two mechanisms, then the two mechanisms generate the same expected revenue for the seller.

Proof: The seller's expected revenue is

$$\begin{aligned}
R &= \int_0^1 \cdots \int_0^1 \sum_{i=1}^N c_i(v_1, \ldots, v_N) f(v_1) \ldots f(v_N) dv_1 \ldots dv_N \\
&= \sum_{i=1}^N \int_0^1 \cdots \int_0^1 c_i(v_1, \ldots, v_N) f(v_1) \ldots f(v_N) dv_1 \ldots dv_N \\
&= \sum_{i=1}^N \int_0^1 \left[\int_0^1 \cdots \int_0^1 c_i(v_i, v_{-i}) f_{-i}(v_{-i}) dv_{-i} \right] f_i(v_i) dv_i \\
&= \sum_{i=1}^N \int_0^1 \bar{c}_i(v_i) f_i(v_i) dv_i \\
&= \sum_{i=1}^N \int_0^1 \left[\bar{c}_i(0) + \bar{p}_i(v_i) v_i - \int_0^{v_i} \bar{p}_i(x) dx \right] f_i(v_i) dv_i \\
&= \sum_{i=1}^N \int_0^1 \left[\bar{p}_i(v_i) v_i - \int_0^{v_i} \bar{p}_i(x) dx \right] f_i(v_i) dv_i + \sum_{i=1}^N \bar{c}_i(0),
\end{aligned}$$

where the fourth equality follows from the definition of $\bar{c}_i(v_i)$ and the fifth equality follows from (ii) of Theorem 9.5.

Consequently, the seller's expected revenue depends only on the probability assignment functions and the amount bidders expect to pay when their values are zero. Because a bidder's expected payoff when his value is zero is completely determined by his expected payment when his value is zero, the desired result follows. ∎

The revenue equivalence theorem provides an explanation for the apparently coincidental equality of expected revenue among the four standard auctions. We now see that this follows because, with symmetric bidders, each of the four standard auctions has the same probability assignment function (i.e., the object is assigned to the bidder with the highest value), and in each of the four standard auctions a bidder with value zero receives expected utility equal to zero.

The revenue equivalence theorem is very general and allows us to add additional auctions to the list of those yielding the same expected revenue as the four standard ones. For example, a first-price, all-pay auction, in which the highest among all sealed bids wins but *every* bidder pays an amount equal to his bid, also yields the same expected revenue under bidder symmetry as the four standard auctions. You are asked to explore this and other auctions in the exercises.

9.3.2 EFFICIENCY

Before closing this section, we briefly turn our attention to the allocative properties of the four standard auctions. As we have already noted several times, each of these auctions allocates the object to the bidder who values it most. That is, each of these auctions is efficient. In the case of the Dutch and the first-price auctions, this result relies on bidder symmetry. Without symmetry, different bidders in a first-price auction, say, will employ different strictly increasing bidding functions. Consequently, if one bidder employs a lower bidding function than another, then the one may have a higher value yet be outbid by the other.

9.4 DESIGNING A REVENUE MAXIMISING MECHANISM

By now we understand very well the four standard auctions, their equilibria, their expected revenue, and the relation among them. But do these auctions, each generating the same expected revenue (under bidder symmetry), maximise the seller's expected revenue? Or is there a better selling mechanism for the seller? If there is a better selling mechanism what form does it take? Do the bidders submit sealed bids? Do they bid sequentially? What about a combination of the two? Is an auction the best selling mechanism?

9.4.1 THE REVELATION PRINCIPLE

Apparently, finding a revenue-maximising selling mechanism is likely to be a difficult task. Given the freedom to choose any selling procedure, where do we start? The key observation is to recall how we were able to construct an incentive-compatible direct selling mechanism from the equilibrium of a first-price auction, and how the outcome of the first-price auction was exactly replicated in the direct mechanism's truth-telling equilibrium. As it turns out, the same type of construction can be applied to any selling procedure. That is, given an arbitrary selling procedure and a Nash equilibrium in which each bidder employs a strategy mapping his value into payoff-maximising behaviour under that selling procedure, we can construct an equivalent incentive-compatible direct selling mechanism. The requisite probability assignment and cost functions map each vector of values to the probabilities and costs that each bidder would experience according to the equilibrium strategies in the original selling procedure. So constructed, this direct selling mechanism is incentive-compatible and yields the same (probabilistic) assignment of the object and the same expected costs to each bidder as well as the same expected revenue to the seller.

Consequently, if some selling procedure yields the seller expected revenue equal to R, then so too does some incentive-compatible direct selling mechanism. But this means that *no selling mechanism among all conceivable selling mechanisms yields more revenue for the seller than the revenue-maximising, incentive-compatible direct selling mechanism.* We can, therefore, restrict our search for a revenue-maximising selling procedure to the (manageable) set of incentive-compatible direct selling mechanisms. In this way, we have simplified our problem considerably while losing nothing.

This simple but extremely important technique for reducing the set of mechanisms to the set of incentive-compatible direct mechanisms is an instance of what is called the **revelation principle**. This principle is used again and again in the theory of mechanism design and we will see it in action again in Section 9.5 when we consider the problem of achieving efficient outcomes in a private information setting.

9.4.2 INDIVIDUAL RATIONALITY

There is one additional restriction we must now consider. Because participation by the bidders is entirely voluntary, no bidder's expected payoff can be negative given his value. Otherwise, whenever he has that value, he will simply not participate in the selling mechanism. Thus, we must restrict attention to incentive-compatible direct selling mechanisms that are **individually rational**, i.e., that yield each bidder, regardless of his value, a non-negative expected payoff in the truth-telling equilibrium.

Now, in an incentive-compatible mechanism bidder i with value v_i will receive expected payoff $u_i(v_i, v_i)$ in the truth-telling equilibrium. So, an incentive-compatible direct selling mechanism is individually rational if this payoff is always non-negative, i.e., if

$$u_i(v_i, v_i) = \bar{p}_i(v_i)v_i - \bar{c}_i(v_i) \geq 0 \text{ for all } v_i \in [0, 1].$$

However, by incentive compatibility, (ii) of Theorem 9.5 tells us that

$$\bar{c}_i(v_i) = \bar{c}_i(0) + \bar{p}_i(v_i)v_i - \int_0^{v_i} \bar{p}_i(x)dx, \text{ for every } v_i \in [0, 1].$$

Consequently, an incentive-compatible direct selling mechanism is individually rational if and only if

$$u_i(v_i, v_i) = \bar{p}_i(v_i)v_i - \bar{c}_i(v_i) = -\bar{c}_i(0) + \int_0^{v_i} \bar{p}_i(x)dx \geq 0 \text{ for every } v_i \in [0, 1],$$

which clearly holds if and only if

$$\bar{c}_i(0) \leq 0. \tag{9.10}$$

Consequently, an incentive-compatible direct selling mechanism is individually rational if and only if each bidder's expected cost when his value is zero is non-positive.

9.4.3 AN OPTIMAL SELLING MECHANISM

We have now reduced the task of finding the optimal selling mechanism to maximising the seller's expected revenue among all individually rational, incentive-compatible direct selling mechanisms, $p_i(\cdot)$ and $c_i(\cdot)$, $i = 1, \ldots, N$. Because Theorem 9.5 characterises all incentive-compatible selling mechanisms, and because an incentive-compatible direct selling mechanism is individually rational if and only if $\bar{c}_i(0) \leq 0$, our task has been reduced to solving the following problem: choose a direct selling mechanism $p_i(\cdot)$, $c_i(\cdot)$, $i = 1, \ldots, N$, to maximise

$$R = \sum_{i=1}^{N} \int_0^1 \left[\bar{p}_i(v_i)v_i - \int_0^{v_i} \bar{p}_i(x)dx \right] f_i(v_i)dv_i + \sum_{i=1}^{N} \bar{c}_i(0)$$

subject to

(i) $\bar{p}_i(v_i)$ is non-decreasing in v_i,

(ii) $\bar{c}_i(v_i) = \bar{c}_i(0) + \bar{p}_i(v_i)v_i - \int_0^{v_i} \bar{p}_i(x)dx$, for every $v_i \in [0, 1]$,

(iii) $\bar{c}_i(0) \leq 0$,

where the expression for the seller's expected revenue follows from incentive compatibility precisely as in the proof of Theorem 9.6.

It will be helpful to rearrange the expression for the seller's expected revenue.

$$\begin{aligned} R &= \sum_{i=1}^{N} \int_0^1 \left[\bar{p}_i(v_i)v_i - \int_0^{v_i} \bar{p}_i(x)dx \right] f_i(v_i)dv_i + \sum_{i=1}^{N} \bar{c}_i(0) \\ &= \sum_{i=1}^{N} \left[\int_0^1 \bar{p}_i(v_i)v_i f_i(v_i)dv_i - \int_0^1 \int_0^{v_i} \bar{p}_i(x) f_i(v_i)dxdv_i \right] + \sum_{i=1}^{N} \bar{c}_i(0). \end{aligned}$$

By interchanging the order of integration in the iterated integral (i.e., from $dxdv_i$ to dv_idx), we obtain

$$R = \sum_{i=1}^{N}\left[\int_0^1 \bar{p}_i(v_i)v_if_i(v_i)dv_i - \int_0^1\int_x^1 \bar{p}_i(x)f_i(v_i)dv_idx\right] + \sum_{i=1}^{N}\bar{c}_i(0)$$

$$= \sum_{i=1}^{N}\left[\int_0^1 \bar{p}_i(v_i)v_if_i(v_i)dv_i - \int_0^1 \bar{p}_i(x)(1-F_i(x))dx\right] + \sum_{i=1}^{N}\bar{c}_i(0).$$

By replacing the dummy variable of integration, x, by v_i, this can be written equivalently as

$$R = \sum_{i=1}^{N}\left[\int_0^1 \bar{p}_i(v_i)v_if_i(v_i)dv_i - \int_0^1 \bar{p}_i(v_i)(1-F_i(v_i))dv_i\right] + \sum_{i=1}^{N}\bar{c}_i(0)$$

$$= \sum_{i=1}^{N}\int_0^1 \bar{p}_i(v_i)\left[v_i - \frac{1-F_i(v_i)}{f_i(v_i)}\right]f_i(v_i)dv_i + \sum_{i=1}^{N}\bar{c}_i(0).$$

Finally, recalling that

$$\bar{p}_i(r_i) = \int_0^1\cdots\int_0^1 p_i(r_i, v_{-i})f_{-i}(v_{-i})dv_{-i}$$

we may write

$$R = \sum_{i=1}^{N}\int_0^1\cdots\int_0^1 p_i(v_1,\ldots,v_N)\left[v_i - \frac{1-F_i(v_i)}{f_i(v_i)}\right]f_1(v_1)\ldots f_N(v_N)dv_1\ldots dv_N$$

$$+\sum_{i=1}^{N}\bar{c}_i(0),$$

or

$$R = \int_0^1\cdots\int_0^1\left\{\sum_{i=1}^{N}p_i(v_1,\ldots,v_N)\left[v_i - \frac{1-F_i(v_i)}{f_i(v_i)}\right]\right\}f_1(v_1)\ldots f_N(v_N)dv_1\ldots dv_N$$

$$+\sum_{i=1}^{N}\bar{c}_i(0). \tag{9.11}$$

So, our problem is to maximise (9.11) subject to the constraints (i)–(iii) above. For the moment, let us concentrate on the first term in (9.11), namely

$$\int_0^1 \cdots \int_0^1 \left\{ \sum_{i=1}^N p_i(v_1, \ldots, v_N) \left[v_i - \frac{1 - F_i(v_i)}{f_i(v_i)} \right] \right\} f_1(v_1) \ldots f_N(v_N) dv_1 \ldots dv_N. \quad (9.12)$$

Clearly, (9.12) would be maximised if the term in curly brackets were maximised for each vector of values $v_1, \ldots, v_N$. Now, because the $p_i(v_1, \ldots, v_N)$ are non-negative and sum to one or less, the $N + 1$ numbers $p_1(v_1, \ldots, v_N), \ldots, p_N(v_1, \ldots, v_N)$, $1 - \sum_{i=1}^N p_i(v_1, \ldots, v_N)$ are non-negative and sum to one. So, the sum above in curly brackets, which can be rewritten as

$$\sum_{i=1}^N p_i(v_1, \ldots, v_N) \left[v_i - \frac{1 - F_i(v_i)}{f_i(v_i)} \right] + \left(1 - \sum_{i=1}^N p_i(v_1, \ldots, v_N) \right) \cdot 0,$$

is just a weighted average of the $N + 1$ numbers

$$\left[v_1 - \frac{1 - F_1(v_1)}{f_1(v_1)} \right], \ldots, \left[v_N - \frac{1 - F_N(v_N)}{f_N(v_N)} \right], 0.$$

But then the sum in curly brackets can be no larger than the largest of these bracketed terms if one of them is positive, and no larger than zero if all of them are negative. Suppose now that no two of the bracketed terms are equal to one another. Then, if we define

$$p_i^*(v_1, \ldots, v_N) = \begin{cases} 1, \text{ if } v_i - \frac{1-F_i(v_i)}{f_i(v_i)} > \max\left(0, v_j - \frac{1-Fj(v_j)}{f_j(v_j)}\right) \text{ for all } j \neq i, \\ 0, \text{ otherwise,} \end{cases} \quad (9.13)$$

it must be the case that

$$\sum_{i=1}^N p_i(v_1, \ldots, v_N) \left[v_i - \frac{1 - F_i(v_i)}{f_i(v_i)} \right] \leq \sum_{i=1}^N p_i^*(v_1, \ldots, v_N) \left[v_i - \frac{1 - F_i(v_i)}{f_i(v_i)} \right].$$

Therefore, if the bracketed terms are distinct with probability one, we will have

$$R = \int_0^1 \cdots \int_0^1 \left\{ \sum_{i=1}^N p_i(v_1, \ldots, v_N) \left[v_i - \frac{1 - F_i(v_i)}{f_i(v_i)} \right] \right\} f_1(v_1) \ldots f_N(v_N) dv_1 \ldots dv_N$$

$$+ \sum_{i=1}^N \bar{c}_i(0)$$

$$\leq \int_0^1 \cdots \int_0^1 \left\{ \sum_{i=1}^{N} p_i^*(v_1, \ldots, v_N) \left[v_i - \frac{1 - F_i(v_i)}{f_i(v_i)} \right] \right\} f_1(v_1) \ldots f_N(v_N) dv_1 \ldots dv_N$$

$$+ \sum_{i=1}^{N} \bar{c}_i(0),$$

for all incentive-compatible direct selling mechanisms $p_i(\cdot), c_i(\cdot)$. For the moment, then, let us assume that the bracketed terms are distinct with probability one. We will introduce an assumption on the bidders' distributions that guarantees this shortly.[16]

Because constraint (iii) implies that each $\bar{c}_i(0) \leq 0$, we can also say that for all incentive-compatible direct selling mechanisms $p_i(\cdot), c_i(\cdot)$, the seller's revenue can be no larger than the following upper bound:

$$R \leq \int_0^1 \cdots \int_0^1 \left\{ \sum_{i=1}^{N} p_i^*(v_1, \ldots, v_N) \left[v_i - \frac{1 - F_i(v_i)}{f_i(v_i)} \right] \right\} f_1(v_1) \ldots f_N(v_N) dv_1 \ldots dv_N. \tag{9.14}$$

We will now construct an incentive-compatible direct selling mechanism that *achieves* this upper bound. Consequently, this mechanism will maximise the seller's revenue, and so will be optimal for the seller.

To construct this optimal mechanism, let the probability assignment functions be the $p_i^*(v_1, \ldots, v_N)$, $i = 1, \ldots, N$, in (9.13). To complete the mechanism, we must define cost functions $c_i^*(v_1, \ldots, v_N)$, $i = 1, \ldots, N$. But constraint (ii) requires that for each v_i, bidder i's expected cost and probability of receiving the object, $\bar{c}_i^*(v_i)$ and $\bar{p}_i^*(v_i)$, be related as follows

$$\bar{c}_i^*(v_i) = \bar{c}_i^*(0) + \bar{p}_i^*(v_i)v_i - \int_0^{v_i} \bar{p}_i^*(x)dx.$$

Now, because the $\bar{c}_i^*$ and $\bar{p}_i^*$ are averages of the c_i^* and p_i^*, this required relationship between *averages* will hold if it holds for *each and every* vector of values $v_1, \ldots, v_N$. That is, (ii) is guaranteed to hold if we define the c_i^* as follows: for every $v_1, \ldots, v_N$,

$$c_i^*(v_1, \ldots, v_N) = c_i^*(0, v_{-i}) + p_i^*(v_1, \ldots, v_N)v_i - \int_0^{v_i} p_i^*(x, v_{-i})dx. \tag{9.15}$$

To complete the definition of the cost functions and to satisfy constraint (iii), we shall set $c_i^*(0, v_2, \ldots, v_N) = 0$ for all i and all $v_2, \ldots, v_N$. So, our candidate for a revenue-maximising, incentive-compatible direct selling mechanism is as follows: for

[16]The assumption is given in (9.18).

every $i = 1, \ldots, N$ and every $v_1, \ldots, v_N$

$$p_i^*(v_1, \ldots, v_N) = \begin{cases} 1, \text{ if } v_i - \frac{1-F_i(v_i)}{f_i(v_i)} > \max\left(0, v_j - \frac{1-F_j(v_j)}{f_j(v_j)}\right) \text{ for all } j \neq i, \\ 0, \text{ otherwise;} \end{cases} \tag{9.16}$$

and

$$c_i^*(v_1, \ldots, v_N) = p_i^*(v_1, \ldots, v_N)v_i - \int_0^{v_i} p_i^*(x, v_{-i})dx. \tag{9.17}$$

By construction, this mechanism satisfies constraints (ii) and (iii), and it achieves the upper bound for revenues in (9.14). To see this, simply substitute the p_i^* into (9.11) and recall that by construction $\bar{c}_i^*(0) = 0$ for every i. The result is that the seller's revenues are

$$R = \int_0^1 \cdots \int_0^1 \left\{ \sum_{i=1}^N p_i^*(v_1, \ldots, v_N) \left[v_i - \frac{1 - F_i(v_i)}{f_i(v_i)} \right] \right\} f_1(v_1) \ldots f_N(v_N) dv_1 \ldots dv_N,$$

their maximum possible value.

So, if we can show that our mechanism's probability assignment functions defined in (9.16) satisfy constraint (i), then this mechanism will indeed be the solution we are seeking.

Unfortunately, the p_i^* as defined in (9.16) need not satisfy (i). To ensure that they do, we need to restrict the distributions of the bidders' values. Consider, then, the following assumption: For every $i = 1, \ldots, N$

$$v_i - \frac{1 - F_i(v_i)}{f_i(v_i)} \quad \text{is } \textit{strictly increasing} \text{ in } v_i. \tag{9.18}$$

This assumption is satisfied for a number of distributions, including the uniform distribution. Moreover, you are asked to show in an exercise that it holds whenever each F_i is any convex function, not merely that of the uniform distribution.[17] Note that in addition to ensuring that (i) holds, this assumption also guarantees that the numbers $v_1 - (1 - F_1(v_1))/f_1(v_1), \ldots, v_N - (1 - F_N(v_N))/f_N(v_N)$ are distinct with probability one, a requirement that we earlier employed but had left unjustified until now.

Let us now see why (9.18) implies that (i) is satisfied. Consider some bidder i and some fixed vector of values, v_{-i}, for the other bidders. Now, suppose that $\bar{v}_i > \underline{v}_i$ and that $p_i^*(\underline{v}_i, v_{-i}) = 1$. Then, by the definition of p_i^*, it must be the case that $\underline{v}_i - (1 - F_i(\underline{v}_i))/f_i(\underline{v}_i)$ is positive and strictly greater than $v_j - (1 - Fj(v_j))/f_j(v_j)$ for all $j \neq i$. Consequently, because $v_i - (1 - F_i(v_i))/f_i(v_i)$ is strictly increasing it must

[17]When this assumption fails, the mechanism we have constructed here is not optimal. One can nevertheless construct the optimal mechanism, but we shall not do so here. Thus, the additional assumption we are making here is only for simplicity's sake.

also be the case that $\bar{v}_i - (1 - F_i(\bar{v}_i))/f_i(\bar{v}_i)$ is both positive and strictly greater than $v_j - (1 - F_j(v_j))/f_j(v_j)$ for all $j \neq i$, which means that $p_i^*(\bar{v}_i, v_{-i}) = 1$. Thus, we have shown that if $p_i^*(v_i, v_{-i}) = 1$, then $p_i^*(v_i', v_{-i}) = 1$ for all $v_i' > v_i$. But because p_i^* takes on either the value 0 or 1, $p_i^*(v_i, v_{-i})$ is non-decreasing in v_i for every v_{-i}. This in turn implies that $\bar{p}_i^*(v_i)$ is non-decreasing in v_i, so that constraint (i) is indeed satisfied.

In the end then, our hard work has paid off handsomely. We can now state the following.

THEOREM 9.7 ***An Optimal Selling Mechanism***

If N bidders have independent private values with bidder i's value drawn from the continuous positive density f_i satisfying (9.18), then the direct selling mechanism defined in (9.16) and (9.17) yields the seller the largest possible expected revenue.

9.4.4 A CLOSER LOOK AT THE OPTIMAL SELLING MECHANISM

Let us see if we can simplify the description of the optimal selling mechanism by studying its details. There are two parts to the mechanism, the manner in which it allocates the object – the p_i^* – and the manner in which it determines payments – the c_i^*.

The allocation portion of the optimal mechanism is straightforward. Given the reported values $v_1, \ldots, v_N$, the object is given to the bidder i whose $v_i - (1 - F_i(v_i))/f_i(v_i)$ is strictly highest and positive. Otherwise, the seller keeps the object. But it is worth a little effort to try to interpret this allocation scheme.

What we shall argue is that $v_i - (1 - F_i(v_i))/f_i(v_i)$ represents the marginal revenue, $MR_i(v_i)$, that the seller obtains from increasing the probability that the object is assigned to bidder i when his value is v_i. To see this without too much notation we shall provide an intuitive argument. Consider the effect of increasing the probability that the object is awarded bidder i when his value is v_i. This enables the seller to increase the cost to v_i so as to leave his utility unchanged. Because the density of v_i is $f_i(v_i)$, the seller's revenue increases at the rate $v_i f_i(v_i)$ as a result of this change. On the other hand, incentive compatibility forces a connection between the probability that the good is assigned to bidder i with value v_i and the cost assessed to all higher values $v_i' > v_i$. Indeed, according to constraint (ii), increasing the probability that lower values receive the object reduces one-for-one the cost that all higher values can be assessed. Because there is a mass of $1 - F_i(v_i)$ values above v_i, this total reduction in revenue is $1 - F_i(v_i)$. So, altogether the seller's revenues increase by $v_i f_i(v_i) - (1 - F_i(v_i))$. But this is the total effect due to the density $f_i(v_i)$ of values equal to v_i. Consequently, the marginal revenue associated with each v_i is $MR_i(v_i) = v_i - (1 - F_i(v_i))/f_i(v_i)$.

The allocation rule now makes perfect sense. If $MR_i(v_i) > MR_j(v_j)$, the seller can increase revenue by reducing the probability that the object is assigned to bidder j and increasing the probability that it is assigned to bidder i. Clearly then, the seller maximises his revenue by assigning all probability (i.e., probability one) to the bidder with the highest $MR_i(v_i)$, so long as it is positive. If all the marginal revenues are negative, the seller does best by reducing all of the bidders' probabilities to zero, i.e., the seller keeps the object.

The payment portion of the mechanism is a little less transparent. To get a clearer picture of what is going on, suppose that when the (truthfully) reported values are $v_1, \ldots, v_N$, bidder i does not receive the object, i.e., that $p_i^*(v_i, v_{-i}) = 0$. What must bidder i pay according to the mechanism? The answer, according to (9.17), is

$$\begin{aligned} c_i^*(v_i, v_{-i}) &= p_i^*(v_i, v_{-i})v_i - \int_0^{v_i} p_i^*(x, v_{-i})dx \\ &= 0 \cdot v_i - \int_0^{v_i} p_i^*(x, v_{-i})dx. \end{aligned}$$

But recall that, by virtue of assumption (9.18), $p_i^*(\cdot, v_{-i})$ is non-decreasing. Consequently, because $p_i^*(v_i, v_{-i}) = 0$, it must be the case that $p_i^*(x, v_{-i}) = 0$ for every $x \leq v_i$. Hence the integral above must be zero so that

$$c_i^*(v_i, v_{-i}) = 0.$$

So, we have shown that according to the optimal mechanism, if bidder i does not receive the object, he pays nothing.

Suppose now that bidder i does receive the object, i.e., that $p_i^*(v_i, v_{-i}) = 1$. According to (9.17), he then pays

$$\begin{aligned} c_i^*(v_i, v_{-i}) &= p_i^*(v_i, v_{-i})v_i - \int_0^{v_i} p_i^*(x, v_{-i})dx \\ &= v_i - \int_0^{v_i} p_i^*(x, v_{-i})dx. \end{aligned}$$

Now, because p_i^* takes on the value 0 or 1, is non-decreasing and continuous from the left in i's value, and $p_i^*(v_i, v_{-i}) = 1$, there must be a largest value for bidder i, $r_i^* < v_i$, such that $p_i^*(r_i^*, v_{-i}) = 0$. Note that r_i^* will generally depend on v_{-i} so it would be more explicit to write $r_i^*(v_{-i})$. Note then that by the very definition of $r_i^*(v_{-i})$, $p_i^*(x, v_{-i})$ is equal to 1 for every $x > r_i^*(v_{-i})$, and is equal to 0 for every $x \leq r_i^*(v_{-i})$. But this means that

$$\begin{aligned} c_i^*(v_i, v_{-i}) &= v_i - \int_{r_i^*(v_{-i})}^{v_i} 1dx \\ &= v_i - (v_i - r_i^*(v_{-i})) \\ &= r_i^*(v_{-i}). \end{aligned}$$

So, when bidder i wins the object, *he pays a price, $r_i^*(v_{-i})$, that is independent of his own reported value.* Moreover, the price he pays is the maximum value he could have reported, given the others' reported values, without receiving the object.

Putting all of this together, we may rephrase the revenue-maximising selling mechanism defined by (9.16) and (9.17) in the following manner.

THEOREM 9.8 ***The Optimal Selling Mechanism Simplified***

If N bidders have independent private values with bidder i's value drawn from the continuous positive density f_i and each $v_i - (1 - F_i(v_i))/f_i(v_i)$ is strictly increasing, then the following direct selling mechanism yields the seller the largest possible expected revenue:

For each reported vector of values, $v_1, \ldots, v_N$, the seller assigns the object to the bidder i whose $v_i - (1 - F_i(v_i))/f_i(v_i)$ is strictly largest and positive. If there is no such bidder, the seller keeps the object and no payments are made. If there is such a bidder i, then only this bidder makes a payment to the seller in the amount r_i^*, where $r_i^* - (1 - F_i(r_i^*))/f_i(r_i^*) = 0$ or $\max_{j \neq i} v_j - (1 - F_j(v_j))/f_j(v_j)$, whichever is largest. Bidder i's payment, r_i^*, is, therefore, the largest value he could have reported, given the others' reported values, without receiving the object.

As we know, this mechanism is incentive-compatible. That is, truth-telling is a Nash equilibrium. But, in fact, the incentive to tell the truth in this mechanism is much stronger than this. In this mechanism it is, in fact, a *dominant strategy* for each bidder to report his value truthfully to the seller; even if the other bidders do not report their values truthfully, bidder i can do no better than to report his value truthfully to the seller. You are asked to show this in one of the exercises.

One drawback of this mechanism is that to implement it, the seller must know the distributions, F_i, from which the bidders' values are drawn. This is in contrast to the standard auctions that the seller can implement without any bidder information whatsoever. Yet there is a connection between this optimal mechanism and the four standard auctions that we now explore.

9.4.5 EFFICIENCY, SYMMETRY, AND COMPARISON TO THE FOUR STANDARD AUCTIONS

In the optimal selling mechanism, the object is not always allocated efficiently. Sometimes the bidder with the highest value does not receive the object. In fact, there are *two ways* that inefficiency can occur in the optimal selling mechanism. First, the outcome can be inefficient because the seller sometimes keeps the object, even though his value for it is zero and all bidders have positive values. This occurs when every bidder i's value v_i is such that $v_i - (1 - F_i(v_i))/f_i(v_i) \leq 0$. Second, even when the seller does assign the object to one of the bidders, it might not be assigned to the bidder with the highest value. To see this, consider the case of two bidders, 1 and 2. If the bidders are asymmetric, then for some $v \in [0, 1]$, $v - (1 - F_1(v))/f_1(v) \neq v - (1 - F_2(v))/f_2(v)$. Indeed, let us suppose that for this particular value, v, $v - (1 - F_1(v))/f_1(v) > v - (1 - F_2(v))/f_2(v) > 0$. Consequently, when both bidders' values are v, bidder 1 will receive the object. But, by continuity, even if bidder 1's value falls slightly to $v' < v$, so long as v' is close enough to v, the inequality $v' - (1 - F_1(v'))/f_1(v') > v - (1 - F_2(v))/f_2(v) > 0$ will continue to hold. Hence, bidder 1 will receive the object even though his value is strictly below that of bidder 2.

The presence of inefficiencies is not surprising. After all, the seller is a monopolist seeking maximal profits. In Chapter 4, we saw that a monopolist will restrict output below the efficient level so as to command a higher price. The same effect is present here. But, because there is only one unit of an indivisible object for sale, the seller here restricts supply by sometimes keeping the object, depending on the vector of reports. But this accounts for only the first kind of inefficiency. The second kind of inefficiency that arises here did not occur in our brief look at monopoly in Chapter 4. The reason is that there we assumed that the monopolist was unable to distinguish one consumer from another. Consequently, the monopolist had to charge all consumers the same price. Here, however, we are assuming that the seller *can* distinguish bidder i from bidder j and that the seller knows that i's distribution of values is F_i and that j's is F_j. This additional knowledge allows the monopolist to discriminate between the bidders, which leads to higher profits.

Let us now eliminate this second source of inefficiency by supposing that bidders are symmetric. Because the four standard auctions all yield the same expected revenue for the seller under symmetry, this will also allow us to compare the standard auctions with the optimal selling mechanism.

How does symmetry affect the optimal selling mechanism? If the bidders are symmetric, then $f_i = f$ and $F_i = F$ for every bidder i. Consequently, the optimal selling mechanism is as follows: if the vector of reported values is $(v_1, \ldots, v_N)$, the bidder i with the highest positive $v_i - (1 - F(v_i))/f(v_i)$ receives the object and pays the seller r_i^*, the largest value he could have reported, given the other bidder's reported values, without winning the object. If there is no such bidder i, the seller keeps the object and no payments are made.

But let us think about this for a moment. Because we are assuming that $v - (1 - F(v))/f(v)$ is strictly increasing in v, the object is actually awarded to the bidder i with the strictly highest value v_i, so long as $v_i - (1 - F_i(v_i))/f_i(v_i) > 0$ – that is, so long as $v_i > \rho^* \in [0, 1]$, where

$$\rho^* - \frac{1 - F(\rho^*)}{f(\rho^*)} = 0. \tag{9.19}$$

(You are asked to show in an exercise that a unique such ρ^* is guaranteed to exist.)

Now, how large can bidder i's reported value be before he is awarded the object? Well, he does not get the object unless his reported value is strictly highest and strictly above ρ^*. So, the largest his report can be without receiving the object is the largest of the other bidders' values or ρ^*, whichever is larger. Consequently, when bidder i does receive the object he pays either ρ^* or the largest value reported by the other bidders, whichever is larger.

Altogether then, the optimal selling mechanism is as follows: the bidder whose reported value is strictly highest and strictly above ρ^* receives the object and pays the larger of ρ^* and the largest reported value of the other bidders.

Remarkably, this optimal direct selling mechanism can be mimicked by running a second-price auction with reserve price ρ^*. That is, an auction in which the bidder with the highest bid strictly above the reserve price wins and pays the second-highest bid or the reserve price, whichever is larger. If no bids are above the reserve price, the seller keeps the object and no payments are made. This is optimal because, just as in a standard second-price auction, it is a dominant strategy to bid one's value in a second-price auction with a reserve price.

This is worth highlighting.

THEOREM 9.9 ***An Optimal Auction Under Symmetry***

If N bidders have independent private values, each drawn from the same continuous positive density f, where $v - (1 - F(v))/f(v)$ is strictly increasing, then a second price auction with reserve price ρ^* satisfying $\rho^* - (1 - F(\rho^*))/f(\rho^*) = 0$, maximises the seller's expected revenue.

You might wonder about the other three standard auctions. Will adding an appropriate reserve price render these auctions optimal for the seller too? The answer is yes, and this is left for you to explore in the exercises.

So, we have now come full circle. The four standard auctions – first-price, second-price, Dutch, and English – all yield the same revenue under symmetry. Moreover, by supplementing each by an appropriate reserve price, the seller maximises his expected revenue. Is it any wonder then that these auctions are in such widespread use?

9.5 DESIGNING ALLOCATIVELY EFFICIENT MECHANISMS

We now turn our attention away from profit maximisation and towards allocative efficiency. The basic question is how to achieve a Pareto-efficient outcome when critical pieces of information are held privately by individuals in society. Such information might include, for example, individual preferences, production costs, income, etc.

As in Chapter 6, we allow for a broad collection of circumstances by letting X denote the set of social states. To keep matters simple, we assume that X is finite. Once again, the members of X might be allocations in an exchange or production economy, candidates running for office, etc. We also introduce a distinguished good called 'money', whose role will be apparent shortly. Individuals will care about the social state $x \in X$ as well as about how much money they have. Thus, the social state does not completely describe all that is utility-relevant for individuals. For any fixed social state, an individual can use his money to purchase desirable commodities that are independent of, and have no effect upon, the social state.[18]

There are N individuals in society. To capture the idea that they might have critical pieces of private information, we introduce a set of possible 'types' for each individual. Let T_i denote the finite set of types of individual i. As in our Chapter 7 analysis of Bayesian games, we introduce probabilities over the players' types. In particular, we assume here that there is a common prior, q, where $q(t) > 0$ is the probability that the vector of

[18]It is also possible to interpret 'money' instead as a separate commodity that individuals directly desire. But we will stick with the monetary interpretation.

types of the N individuals is $t = (t_1, \ldots, t_N) \in T = \times_{i=1}^{N} T_i$. Moreover, we assume that the types are independent, so that $q(t) = q_1(t_1) \cdots q_N(t_N)$. Consequently, no individual's type provides any information about other individuals' types.[19]

9.5.1 QUASI-LINEAR UTILITY AND PRIVATE VALUES

For the remainder of this chapter, we shall restrict the domain of individual preferences to those that can be represented by *quasi-linear utility functions*. That is, if individual i has m dollars and $x \in X$ is the social state, his von Neumann-Morgenstern utility is

$$v_i(x, t_i) + m$$

when his type is $t_i \in T_i$.

Because we are interpreting m as money, $v_i(x, t_i)$ is correctly interpreted as the value, in dollars, that individual i places on the social state x when his type is t_i. Also, note that individual i's value for the social state $x \in X$ depends only on his type t_i and not on the types of the other individuals. Therefore, each individual has private values. Consequently, just as in Section 9.2, this is an *independent private values* model.[20] Let us consider an example.

EXAMPLE 9.3 Consider a small town with N individuals. The town has been selected by the state to receive either a new swimming pool (S) or a new bridge (B) and must decide which it wants. Thus, there are two social states, S and B, and therefore the set of social states is $X = \{S, B\}$. Each individual i in the town has quasi-linear preferences and has private information t_i regarding the value he places on the pool and on the bridge. Specifically, the values individual i places on the swimming pool (S) and on the bridge (B) are given by,

$$v_i(x, t_i) = \begin{cases} t_i + 5, & \text{if } x = S \\ 2t_i, & \text{if } x = B \end{cases},$$

where his type t_i is equally likely to take on any of the values $1, 2, \ldots, 9$ and where the types are independent across individuals.

Each individual is therefore as likely to strictly prefer the swimming pool over the bridge (i.e., $t_i \in \{1, 2, 3, 4\}$) as he is to strictly prefer the bridge over the swimming pool (i.e., $t_i \in \{6, 7, 8, 9\}$. Only the individual himself knows which of these is the case and by how much he prefers one social state over the other. And the more extreme an individual's type, the more he prefers one of the social states over the other. □

Quasi-linearity is a strong assumption. It implies that there is a common rate at which utility can be substituted across individuals regardless of the social state and regardless of

[19]None of our analysis here depends on finite type spaces. In particular, all of our formulae and conclusions are valid when, for example, each T_i is a Euclidean cube and each $q_i(t_i)$ is the probability density that i's type is t_i. In that case, summations over T, T_{-i} and T_i become integrals.

[20]In fact the single object model of Section 9.2 is itself a special case of a quasi-linear independent private values model.

individual types. Its advantage is that it yields a convenient characterisation of efficient social states. To see this most clearly, suppose that individuals have no private information, i.e., suppose there are no types. Individual i's utility function is then simply $v_i(x) + m$. Even though individuals care about both the social state and the amount of money they have, it turns out that the amount of money they end up with is more or less irrelevant to determining which social states are compatible with Pareto efficiency. Indeed, we claim the following:

With quasi-linear preferences, a social state $\hat{x} \in X$ is Pareto efficient if and only if it maximises the sum of the non-monetary parts of individual utilities, i.e., if and only if it solves,

$$\max_{x \in X} \sum_{i=1}^{N} v_i(x). \tag{9.20}$$

Let us see why this claim is true. Suppose, for example, that the social state happens to be $x \in X$ but that $y \in X$ satisfies,

$$\sum_{i=1}^{N} v_i(y) > \sum_{i=1}^{N} v_i(x). \tag{9.21}$$

We would like to show that a Pareto improvement is available. In fact, we shall show that a Pareto improvement can be obtained by switching the social state from x to y.

Now, even though (9.21) holds, merely switching the social state from x to y need not result in a Pareto improvement because some individual utilities may well fall in the move from x to y. The key idea is to compensate those individuals whose utilities fall by transferring to them income from individuals whose utilities rise. It is here where the common rate at which income translates into utility across individuals is absolutely central.

For each individual i, define the income transfer, τ_i, as follows:

$$\tau_i = v_i(x) - v_i(y) + \frac{1}{N}\sum_{i=1}^{N}(v_i(y) - v_i(x)).$$

If $\tau_i > 0$, then individual i receives τ_i dollars while if $\tau_i < 0$ individual i is taxed τ_i dollars. By construction, the τ_i sum to zero and so these are indeed income transfers among the N individuals.

After changing the state from x to y and carrying out the income transfers, the change in individual i's utility is,

$$v_i(y) + \tau_i - v_i(x),$$

which, by (9.21), is strictly positive. Hence, each individual is strictly better off after the change. This proves that the social state x is not Pareto efficient and establishes the 'only if' part of the claim in (9.20).[21] You are asked to establish the 'if' part of the claim in Exercise 9.26.

9.5.2 EX POST PARETO EFFICIENCY

There are several stages at which economists typically think about Pareto efficiency, the *ex ante stage* prior to individuals finding out their types, the *interim stage*, where each knows only his own type, and the *ex post stage* when all types are known by all individuals.

In general, the more uncertainty there is, the greater is the scope for mutually beneficial insurance. Hence, we expect ex ante Pareto efficiency to imply interim Pareto efficiency to imply ex post Pareto efficiency. We will focus here only on the latter, ex post Pareto efficiency.

Because individual preferences over social states are a function of individual types, $t_1, \ldots, t_N$, achieving ex post Pareto-efficient outcomes will typically require the social state to depend upon individual types. With this in mind, call a function $x: T \to X$ an *allocation function*. Thus, an allocation function specifies, for each vector of individual types, a social state in X.[22]

Analogous to the claim established in (9.20), ex post Pareto efficiency of an allocation function is characterised by maximisation of the sum of individual utilities. This leads us to the following definition.

DEFINITION 9.3 ***Ex Post Pareto Efficiency***

An allocation function $\hat{x}: T \to X$ is ex post Pareto-efficient if for each $t \in T$, $\hat{x}(t) \in X$ solves,

$$\max_{x \in X} \sum_{i=1}^{N} v_i(x, t_i),$$

where the maximisation is over all social states. We then also say that $\hat{x}(t)$ is an ex post efficient social state given $t \in T$.

Thus, $\hat{x}: T \to X$ is ex post Pareto efficient if for each type vector $t \in T$, the social state, $\hat{x}(t)$, maximises the sum of individual ex post utilities given t.

9.5.3 DIRECT MECHANISMS, INCENTIVE COMPATIBILITY AND THE REVELATION PRINCIPLE

Our question of interest is whether it is possible to always achieve an ex post efficient allocation, despite the fact that individual utilities are private information. How might we go about achieving this goal? The possibilities are in fact rather daunting. For example, we

[21] We implicitly assume that individuals whose transfers are negative, i.e., who are taxed, have sufficient income to pay the tax.

[22] We do not instead call this a social choice function, as in Section 6.5 of Chapter 6, because we do not require the range of $x(\cdot)$ to be all of X.

might ask individuals one at a time to publicly announce their type (of course they might lie). We might then ask whether anyone believes that someone lied about their type, suitably punishing (via taxes) those whose announcements are doubted by sufficiently many others – the hope being that this might encourage honest reports. On the other hand, we might not ask individuals to report their types at all. Rather, we might ask them to vote directly for the social state they would like implemented. But what voting system ought we employ? Plurality rule? Pairwise majority with ties broken randomly? Should the votes be by secret ballot? Or public and sequential? As you can sense, we could go on and on. There are endless possibilities for designing a system, or mechanism, in the pursuit of achieving our goal.

Fortunately, just as in the single-good revenue-maximisation setting, the **revelation principle** applies here and it allows us to limit our search to the set of incentive-compatible direct mechanisms. Before we discuss this second application of the revelation principle any further, it is useful to have on record two definitions. They are the extensions of Definitions 9.1 and 9.2 to the present more general setup.

DEFINITION 9.4 ***Direct Mechanisms***

A direct mechanism consists of a collection of probability assignment functions,

$$p^x(t_1, \ldots, t_N), \text{ one for each } x \in X,$$

and N cost functions,

$$c_1(t_1, \ldots, t_N), \ldots, c_N(t_1, \ldots, t_N).$$

For every vector of types $(t_1, \ldots, t_N) \in T$ reported by the N individuals, $p^x(t_1, \ldots, t_N) \in [0, 1]$ denotes the probability that the social state is $x \in X$ and $c_i(t_1, \ldots, t_N) \in \mathbb{R}$ denotes individual i's cost, i.e., the amount he must pay. Because some social state must be chosen, we require $\sum_{x\in X} p^x(t_1, \ldots, t_N) = 1$ for every $(t_1, \ldots, t_N) \in T$.

Because of the similarity between Definitions 9.1 and 9.4, there is little need for further discussion except to say that Definition 9.4 becomes equivalent to Definition 9.1 when (i) there is a single object available, (ii) there are $N + 1$ individuals consisting of N bidders and one seller, and (iii) the social states are the $N + 1$ allocations in which, either, one of the bidders ends up with the good or the seller ends up with the good. (See Exercise 9.28.)

Given a direct mechanism, $p, c_1, \ldots, c_N$, it is useful to define, as in Section 9.3, $u_i(r_i, t_i)$ to be individual i's expected utility from reporting that his type is $r_i \in T_i$ when his true type is $t_i \in T_i$ and given that all other individuals always report their types truthfully. That is,

$$u_i(r_i, t_i) = \sum_{t_{-i}\in T_{-i}} q_{-i}(t_{-i}) \left(\sum_{x\in X} p^x(r_i, t_{-i}) v_i(x, t_i) - c_i(r_i, t_{-i}) \right),$$

where $q_{-i}(t_{-i}) = \Pi_{j \neq i} q_j(t_j)$. As before, we can simplify this formula by defining

$$\bar{p}_i^x(r_i) = \sum_{t_{-i} \in T_{-i}} q_{-i}(t_{-i}) p^x(r_i, t_{-i}),$$

and

$$\bar{c}_i(r_i) = \sum_{t_{-i} \in T_{-i}} q_{-i}(t_{-i}) c_i(r_i, t_{-i}). \tag{9.22}$$

Then,

$$u_i(r_i, t_i) = \sum_{x \in X} \bar{p}_i^x(r_i) v_i(x, t_i) - \bar{c}_i(r_i) \tag{9.23}$$

DEFINITION 9.5 ***Incentive-Compatible Direct Mechanisms***

A direct mechanism is incentive-compatible if when the other individuals always report their types truthfully, each individual's expected utility is maximised by always reporting his type truthfully, i.e., the mechanism is incentive-compatible if for each individual i and for each of his types $t_i \in T_i$, $u_i(r_i, t_i)$ as defined in (9.23) is maximised in $r_i \in T_i$ when $r_i = t_i$. Or put yet another way, the mechanism is incentive-compatible if it is a Bayesian-Nash equilibrium for each individual to always report his type truthfully.[23]

With these definitions in hand, it is worthwhile to informally discuss how the revelation principle allows us to reduce our search to the set of incentive-compatible direct mechanisms. So, suppose that we manage to design some, possibly quite complex, extensive form game for individuals in society to play, where the payoffs to the individuals at the endpoints are defined by the utility they receive from some social state and income distribution at that endpoint. Because the strategies they choose to adopt may depend upon their types, any 'equilibrium' they play (i.e., Nash, subgame-perfect, sequential) will be a Bayesian-Nash equilibrium of the game's strategic form. Suppose that in some such Bayesian-Nash equilibrium, an ex post efficient social state is always certain to occur. We would then say that the given extensive form game (mechanism) successfully implements an ex post efficient outcome. According to the revelation principle, a direct incentive-compatible mechanism can do precisely the same thing. Here's how. Instead of having the individuals play their strategies themselves, design a new (direct) mechanism that simply plays their strategies for them after they report their types. Consequently, if the other individuals always report honestly, then, from your perspective, it is as if you are participating in the original extensive form game against them. But in that game, it was optimal for you to carry out the actions specified by your strategy conditional on your actual type. Consequently, it is optimal for you to report your type truthfully in the new direct mechanism so that those same actions are carried out on your behalf. Hence, the new direct

[23]Because the type spaces T_i are finite here, our Chapter 7 definition of a Bayesian-Nash equilibrium applies. If the type spaces are infinite we would simply define the truth-telling equilibrium to be a Bayesian-Nash equilibrium.

mechanism is incentive-compatible and always yields the same ex post efficient social state and income distribution as would the old. That's all there is to it!

As a matter of terminology, we call an incentive-compatible direct mechanism *ex post efficient* if it assigns probability one to a set of ex post efficient social states given any vector of reported types $t \in T$, i.e., if for every $t \in T$, $p^x(t) > 0$ implies $x \in X$ is ex post efficient when the vector of types is t.

9.5.4 THE VICKREY-CLARKE-GROVES MECHANISM

We now introduce one of the most important direct mechanisms in the theory of mechanism design, the Vickrey-Clarke-Groves (VCG) mechanism. As we shall see, it plays a central role in the theory we shall develop here. In particular, it will solve the ex post efficient allocation problem that we have so far set for ourselves.

An interesting feature of the VCG mechanism is that it can be thought of as a generalisation of a second-price auction. Recall that in a second-price auction for a single good, the highest bidder wins and pays the second-highest bid. As we know, it is therefore a dominant strategy for each bidder to bid his value, and so the bidder with highest value wins and pays the second highest value. This auction is sometimes described as one in which the winner 'pays his externality'. The reason is that if the winner were not present, the bidder with second highest value would have won. Thus, the winning bidder, by virtue of his presence, precludes the second-highest value from being realised – he imposes an externality. Of course, he pays for the good precisely the amount of the externality he imposes, and the end result is efficient.

The 'paying one's externality' idea generalises nicely to our current situation as follows. Let $\hat{x}\colon T \to X$ be an ex post efficient allocation function. That is, for each $t \in T$, let $\hat{x}(t)$ be a solution to,

$$\max_{x \in X} \sum_{i=1}^{N} v_i(x, t_i).$$

Such a solution always exists because X is finite. If there are multiple solutions choose any one of them. The ex post efficient allocation function $\hat{x}(\cdot)$ is therefore well-defined and it will remain fixed for the rest of this chapter.

Let us think about the externality imposed by each individual i on the remaining individuals under the assumption that ex post efficiency can be achieved. The trick to computing individual i's externality is to think about the difference his presence makes to the total utility of the others.

When individual i is present and the vector of types is $t \in T$, the social state is $\hat{x}(t)$ and the total utility of the others is,[24]

$$\sum_{j \neq i} v_j(\hat{x}(t), t_j).$$

[24]We can safely ignore the income individuals may have because we will ultimately be interested only in utility differences between different outcomes and therefore individual incomes will always cancel. In other words, it is harmless to compute utilities as if initial individual incomes are zero.

That was simple enough. But what is the total utility of the others when individual i is *not* present? This too is straightforward if we assume that in the absence of individual i – i.e., if society consists only of the $N-1$ individuals $j \neq i$ – the social state is chosen in an ex post efficient manner *relative to those who remain.*

For each $t_{-i} \in T_{-i}$, let $\tilde{x}^i(t_{-i}) \in X$ solve,

$$\max_{x \in X} \sum_{j \neq i} v_j(x, t_j).$$

That is, $\tilde{x}^i : T_{-i} \rightarrow X$ is an ex post efficient allocation function in the society without individual i.

It is now a simple matter to compute the difference that i's presence makes to the total utility of the others. Evidently, when the type vector is $t \in T$, the difference in the utility of the others when i is not present as compared to when he is present is,

$$\sum_{j \neq i} v_j(\tilde{x}^i(t_{-i}), t_j) - \sum_{j \neq i} v_j(\hat{x}(t), t_j).$$

Call this difference the *externality imposed by individual i.*

Note that one's externality is always non-negative and is typically positive because, by definition, $\tilde{x}^i(t_{-i}) \in X$ maximises the sum of utilities of individuals $j \neq i$ when their vector of types is t_{-i}. You should convince yourself that, in the case of a single good, each individual's externality is zero except for the individual with highest value, whose externality is the second highest value – just as it should be.

Consider now the following important mechanism, called the *VCG mechanism* after Vickrey, Clarke, and Groves, who independently provided important contributions leading to its development.[25]

DEFINITION 9.6 ***The Vickrey-Clarke-Groves Mechanism***

Each individual simultaneously reports his type to the designer. If the reported vector of types is $t \in T$, the social state $\hat{x}(t)$ is chosen. In addition, each individual i is assessed a monetary cost equal to,

$$c_i^{VCG}(t) = \sum_{j \neq i} v_j(\tilde{x}^i(t_{-i}), t_j) - \sum_{j \neq i} v_j(\hat{x}(t), t_j).$$

That is, each individual pays his externality based on the reported types. The c_i^{VCG} are called the VCG cost functions.

The key idea behind the VCG mechanism is to define individual costs so that each individual internalises the externality that, through his report, he imposes on the rest of society. Let us return to Example 9.3 to see what the VCG mechanism looks like there.

[25] See Vickrey (1961), Clarke (1971) and Groves (1973).

EXAMPLE 9.4 Consider the situation in Example 9.3. If the vector of reported types is $t \in T$, then it is efficient for the town to build the bridge if $\sum_i v_i(B, t_i) > \sum_i v_i(S, t_i)$.[26] Given the definition of the v_i, this leads to the following ex post efficient allocation function. For each $t \in T$,

$$\hat{x}(t) = \begin{cases} B, & \text{if } \sum_{i=1}^{N}(t_i - 5) > 0 \\ S, & \text{otherwise.} \end{cases}$$

According to the VCG mechanism, if the reported vector of types is $t \in T$, then the social state is $\hat{x}(t)$. It remains to describe the cost, $c_i^{VCG}(t)$, individual i must pay. Let us think about the externality that individual i imposes on the others. Suppose, for example, that the others report very high types, e.g., $t_j = 9$ for all $j \neq i$. Then, if there are at least two other individuals, the bridge will be built regardless of i's report. Indeed, the bridge will be built whether or not individual i is present. Hence, individual i's externality, and so also his cost, is zero in this case. Similarly, i's externality and cost will be zero whenever his presence does not change the outcome. With this in mind, let us say that individual i is pivotal for the social state $x \in \{S, B\}$ at the type vector $t \in T$ when, given reports t, his presence changes the social state from x' to x. For example, individual i is pivotal for B at $t \in T$ if $\sum_{j=1}^{N}(t_j - 5) > 0$ and $\sum_{j\neq i}(t_j - 5) \leq 0$, because the first (strict) inequality implies that the social state is B when he is present and the second (weak) inequality implies it is S when he is absent. In this circumstance, i's externality and cost is $c_i^{VCG}(t) = \sum_{j\neq i}(t_j + 5) - \sum_{j\neq i} 2t_j$, i.e., the difference between the others' total utility when he is absent and their total utility when he is present. Altogether then, $c_i^{VCG}(t)$ is as follows,

$$c_i^{VCG}(t) = \begin{cases} \sum_{j\neq i}(5 - t_j), & \text{if } i \text{ is pivotal for } B \text{ at } t \in T, \\ \sum_{j\neq i}(t_j - 5), & \text{if } i \text{ is pivotal for } S \text{ at } t \in T, \\ 0, & \text{otherwise.} \end{cases}$$

□

So far so good, but will the VCG mechanism actually succeed in implementing an ex post efficient outcome? By construction, the mechanism chooses an outcome that is ex post efficient based on the reported vector of types. However, individuals are free to lie about their types, and, if they do, the outcome will typically *not* be ex post efficient with respect to the *actual* vector of types. Hence, for this mechanism to work, it must induce individuals to report their types truthfully. Our next result establishes that the VCG mechanism does indeed do so.

THEOREM 9.10 ***Truth-Telling is Dominant in the VCG Mechanism***

In the VCG mechanism it is a weakly dominant strategy for each individual to report his type truthfully. Hence, the VCG mechanism is incentive-compatible and ex post efficient.

---

[26] We assume that the swimming pool is built if the two sums are equal.

Proof: We must show that truthful reporting is a weakly dominant strategy for an arbitrary individual i. Suppose then that the others report $t_{-i} \in T_{-i}$, which need not be truthful. Suppose also that individual i's type is $t_i \in T_i$ and that he reports $r_i \in T_i$. His utility would then be,[27]

$$v_i(\hat{x}(r_i, t_{-i}), t_i) - c_i^{VCG}(r_i, t_{-i}). \tag{P.1}$$

Note that $\hat{x}(\cdot)$ and $c^{VCG}(\cdot)$ are evaluated at i's reported type, r_i, while $v_i(x, \cdot)$ is evaluated at i's actual type, t_i. We must show that (P.1) is maximised when individual i reports truthfully, i.e., when $r_i = t_i$.

Substituting the definition of $c_i^{VCG}(r_i, t_{-i})$ into (P.1), i's utility can be written as,

$$\begin{aligned} v_i(\hat{x}(r_i, t_{-i}), t_i) - c_i^{VCG}(r_i, t_{-i}) &= v_i(\hat{x}(r_i, t_{-i}), t_i) - \left(\sum_{j\neq i} v_j(\tilde{x}^i(t_{-i}), t_j) \right. \\ &\qquad \left. - \sum_{j\neq i} v_j(\hat{x}(r_i, t_{-i}), t_j)\right) \\ &= \sum_{j=1}^{N} v_j(\hat{x}(r_i, t_{-i}), t_j) - \sum_{j\neq i} v_j(\tilde{x}^i(t_{-i}), t_j). \end{aligned} \tag{P.2}$$

Hence, we must show that setting $r_i = t_i$ maximises the right-hand side of the second equality (P.2). To see why this is so, note that r_i appears only in the first summation there and so it suffices to show that,

$$\sum_{j=1}^{N} v_j(\hat{x}(t_i, t_{-i}), t_j) \geq \sum_{j=1}^{N} v_j(\hat{x}(r_i, t_{-i}), t_j), \text{ for all } t_{-i} \in T_{-i}. \tag{P.3}$$

But by the definition of $\hat{x}(t_i, t_{-i})$,

$$\sum_{j=1}^{N} v_j(\hat{x}(t_i, t_{-i}), t_j) \geq \sum_{j=1}^{N} v_j(x, t_j), \text{ for all } x \in X.$$

Hence, in particular, (P.3) is satisfied because $\hat{x}(r_i, t_{-i}) \in X$ for all $r_i \in T_i$. ∎

To test your understanding of this proof and also of the VCG mechanism, you should try to show, with and without the aid of the proof, that it is a dominant strategy to tell the truth in the VCG mechanism that is explicitly defined in Example 9.4.

Several remarks are in order. First, because each individual's cost, $c_i^{VCG}(t)$, is always non-negative, the mechanism never runs a deficit and typically runs a surplus.

[27] We can safely ignore i's initial level of income since it simply adds a constant to all of our utility calculations.

Second, one might therefore wonder whether any individual would prefer to avoid paying his cost by not participating in the mechanism. To properly address this question we must specify what would happen if an individual were to choose not to participate. An obvious specification is to suppose that the VCG mechanism would be applied as usual, but only to those who do participate. With this in mind, we can show that it is an equilibrium for all N individuals to participate.

If all individuals participate and report truthfully (a dominant strategy), then individual i's payoff when the vector of types is t is,

$$v_i(\hat{x}(t), t_i) - c_i^{VCG}(t) = \sum_{j=1}^{N} v_j(\hat{x}(t), t_j) - \sum_{j \neq i} v_j(\tilde{x}^i(t_{-i}), t_j). \tag{9.24}$$

On the other hand, if individual i chooses not to participate, he avoids paying the cost $c_i^{VCG}(t)$, but the social state becomes instead $\tilde{x}^i(t_{-i})$, i.e., an ex post efficient social state for the $N-1$ participating individuals who report their types. Consequently, if individual i chooses not to participate his utility will be

$$v_i(\tilde{x}^i(t_{-i}), t_i). \tag{9.25}$$

By the definition of $\hat{x}(t)$,

$$\sum_{j=1}^{N} v_j(\hat{x}(t), t_j) \geq \sum_{j=1}^{N} v_j(\tilde{x}^i(t_{-i}), t_j),$$

because $\tilde{x}^i(t_{-i}) \in X$. Rearranging this, we obtain,

$$\sum_{j=1}^{N} v_j(\hat{x}(t), t_j) - \sum_{j \neq i} v_j(\tilde{x}^i(t_{-i}), t_j) \geq v_i(\tilde{x}^i(t_{-i}), t_i).$$

Hence, by (9.24), i's utility from participating, exceeds (9.25), his utility from not participating. Thus, it is an equilibrium for all individuals to voluntarily participate in the VCG mechanism.

Third, the dominance of truth-telling in the VCG mechanism might appear to contradict Theorem 6.4 (the Gibbard-Satterthwaite Theorem) of Chapter 6. Indeed, the function $\hat{x}(\cdot)$ maps vectors of types (which index individual utility functions) into social choices in such a way that no individual can ever gain by reporting untruthfully. That is, $\hat{x}(\cdot)$ is strategy-proof. Moreover, because we have assumed nothing about the range of $\hat{x}(\cdot)$, the range might very well be all of X (if not, simply remove those elements of X that are absent from the range). In that case, $\hat{x}(\cdot)$ is a strategy-proof social choice function. But it is certainly not dictatorial! (Consider the one-good case, for example.) But, rest assured, there is no contradiction because, in contrast to the situation in Chapter 6, we have restricted the domain of preferences here to those that are quasi-linear. This restriction permits us to avoid the negative conclusion of the Gibbard-Satterthwaite theorem.

9.5.5 ACHIEVING A BALANCED BUDGET: EXPECTED EXTERNALITY MECHANISMS

As already noted, the VCG mechanism runs a surplus because each individual's cost is non-negative, and sometimes positive, regardless of the reported vector of types. But what happens to the revenue that is generated? Does it matter? In fact, it does.

Suppose, for example, that there are no other individuals in society but the N individuals participating in the VCG mechanism. Then any revenue that is generated must either be redistributed or destroyed.

If any amount of the revenue is destroyed, the overall outcome, which consists of the social state plus the amount of money each individual possesses is clearly *not* ex post Pareto efficient. Therefore, destroying any portion of the revenue is simply not an option. Hence, the only option consistent with our goal is to redistribute the revenue among the N individuals. But this causes problems as well.

If the revenue is redistributed to the N individuals, then the costs, $c_i^{VCG}(t)$, are no longer the correct costs. They instead *overstate* actual costs because they do not take into account the redistributed revenue. Consequently, it is not at all clear that, once individuals take into account their share of the revenue that is generated, it remains a dominant strategy to report their types truthfully. And of course, if individuals lie about their types, the social state chosen will typically not be ex post efficient. This is a potentially serious problem. Fortunately, because individual utilities are quasi-linear and individual types are independent, this problem can be solved so long as revenue is redistributed in a sufficiently careful manner.

Before getting to the solution, let us note that if the revenue generated is redistributed among the N individuals, then the sum of the actual (net) payments made by all of them must be zero. For example, if there are just two individuals, and one of them ultimately ends up paying a dollar, then the other individual must receive that dollar because there is simply nowhere else for it to go. Thus, what we are really looking for are mechanisms in which the costs always add up to zero. Such mechanisms are called **budget-balanced**.

DEFINITION 9.7 ***Budget-Balanced Cost Functions***

The cost functions, $c_1, \ldots, c_N$, are budget-balanced if they sum to zero regardless of the reported vector of types, i.e., if

$$\sum_{i=1}^{N} c_i(t) = 0, \quad \textit{for every } t \in T.$$

If a direct mechanism's cost functions are budget-balanced then we say that the mechanism is budget-balanced as well.

Thus, a budget-balanced mechanism not only wastes no money, it is completely self-sufficient, requiring no money from the outside. We will now adjust the VCG costs so that they result in a budget-balanced mechanism.

When the vector of reported types is $t \in T$ individual i's VCG cost, $c_i^{VCG}(t)$, is his externality. Thus, according to the formula in (9.22), the quantity

$$\begin{aligned}\bar{c}_i^{VCG}(t_i) &= \sum_{t_{-i}\in T_{-i}} q_{-i}(t_{-i})c_i^{VCG}(t_i, t_{-i}) \\ &= \sum_{t_{-i}\in T_{-i}} q_{-i}(t_{-i})\left(\sum_{j\neq i} v_j(\tilde{x}^i(t_{-i}), t_j) - \sum_{j\neq i} v_j(\hat{x}(t), t_j)\right), \qquad (9.26)\end{aligned}$$

is i's *expected externality when his type is* t_i. It turns out that these expected externalities can be used to define costs in a way that delivers ex post efficiency and a balanced budget.

THEOREM 9.11 ***The Budget-Balanced Expected Externality Mechanism***

Consider the mechanism in which, when the vector of reported types is $t \in T$, the ex post efficient social state $\hat{x}(t)$ is chosen and individual i's cost is,

$$\bar{c}_i^{VCG}(t_i) - \bar{c}_{i+1}^{VCG}(t_{i+1}),$$

where the $\bar{c}_i^{VCG}(t_i)$ are defined by (9.26), and $i + 1 = 1$ when $i = N$. Then, this mechanism, which we call the budget-balanced expected externality mechanism, is incentive-compatible, ex post efficient, and budget-balanced. Furthermore, in the truth-telling equilibrium, every individual is voluntarily willing to participate regardless of his type.

The cost functions in the budget-balanced expected externality mechanism can be described as follows. Arrange the N individuals clockwise around a circular table. The mechanism requires each individual i to pay the person on his right his expected externality, $\bar{c}_i^{VCG}(t_i)$, given his reported type, t_i.[28] Mechanisms like this are sometimes called *expected externality mechanisms*.[29] Two points are worth emphasising. First, $\bar{c}_i^{VCG}(t_i) - \bar{c}_{i+1}^{VCG}(t_{i+1})$ is individual i's actual cost when the vector of reported types is $t \in T$. It is *not* his expected cost. Second, because individual i pays his expected externality to one person and receives another's expected externality, his actual cost is less than his expected externality. Hence his expected cost in the new mechanism is lower than in the original VCG mechanism.

Proof: The mechanism is clearly budget-balanced. (Do you see why?) Furthermore, if every individual always reports his type truthfully, then the ex post efficient social state $\hat{x}(t)$ will be chosen when the vector of types is $t \in T$. Hence it suffices to show that truthful reporting is a Bayesian-Nash equilibrium and that each individual is willing to participate.

---

[28]Paying one's externality to a single other individual keeps the formula for the new cost functions simple. But paying any number of the others one's expected externality would do just as well. See Exercise 9.29.

[29]See Arrow (1979) and d'Aspremont and Gérard-Varet (1979).

Let $u_i^{VCG}(r_i, t_i)$ denote individual i's expected utility in the VCG mechanism when his type is t_i and he reports that it is r_i, and when other individuals always report their types truthfully. Then,

$$u_i^{VCG}(r_i, t_i) = \sum_{t_{-i} \in T_{-i}} q(t_{-i}) v_i(\hat{x}(r_i, t_{-i}), t_i) - \bar{c}_i^{VCG}(r_i),$$

because the first term (the summation) is his expected utility from the social state, and the second, with the negative sign, is his expected cost given his report. We already know that truth-telling is a Bayesian-Nash equilibrium in the VCG mechanism (indeed it is a dominant strategy). Hence, $u_i^{VCG}(r_i, t_i)$ is maximised in r_i when $r_i = t_i$.

In the new mechanism, i's expected costs when he reports r_i and the others (in particular individual $i + 1$) report truthfully are,

$$\bar{c}_i^{VCG}(r_i) - \sum_{t_{i+1} \in T_{i+1}} q_{i+1}(t_{i+1}) \bar{c}_{i+1}^{VCG}(t_{i+1}).$$

Hence, his expected utility when he reports r_i in the new mechanism and when all others report truthfully is,

$$\sum_{t_{-i} \in T_{-i}} q(t_{-i}) v_i(\hat{x}(r_i, t_{-i}), t_i) - \bar{c}_i^{VCG}(r_i) + \bar{c}_{i+1},$$

where $\bar{c}_{i+1} = \sum_{t_{i+1} \in T_{i+1}} q_{i+1}(t_{i+1}) \bar{c}_{i+1}^{VCG}(t_{i+1})$ is a constant. But this last expression is equal to,

$$u_i^{VCG}(r_i, t_i) + \bar{c}_{i+1},$$

and so it too is maximised in r_i when $r_i = t_i$. Hence, truth-telling is a Bayesian-Nash equilibrium in the new mechanism.

Furthermore, because $\bar{c}_{i+1}$ is always non-negative (because it is equal to individual $i + 1$'s ex ante expected VCG cost), individual i is at least as well off in the new mechanism since he expects his costs to be weakly lower, regardless of his type. Hence, because individuals are willing to participate in the VCG mechanism regardless of their types, the same is true in the new mechanism. ∎

Note carefully that Theorem 9.11 does not say that truth-telling is a weakly dominant strategy in the new budget-balanced mechanism. It says only that truth-telling is a Bayesian-Nash equilibrium. Consequently, although we gain a balanced budget (and hence full efficiency) when we adjust the cost functions of the VCG mechanism, we lose the otherwise very nice property of dominant strategy equilibrium.[30]

[30] In fact, there are theorems stating that it is impossible to achieve both in a wide variety of circumstances. See Green and Laffont (1977) and Holmstrom (1979b).

EXAMPLE 9.5 Continuing with Examples 9.3 and 9.4, suppose that there are just two individuals, i.e., $N = 2$. As you are asked to show in Exercise 9.30, the cost formula given in Theorem 9.11 yields, for the two individuals here, budget-balanced cost functions that can be equivalently described by the following table.

If your reported type is:	1	2	3	4	5	6	7	8	9
You pay the other individual:	$\frac{10}{9}$	$\frac{2}{3}$	$\frac{1}{3}$	$\frac{1}{9}$	0	0	$\frac{1}{9}$	$\frac{1}{3}$	$\frac{2}{3}$

Let us understand why the entries in the table are as they are. The 'circular seating' description following Theorem 9.11 implies that the entries in the second row of the table are simply the expected VCG costs, i.e., the $\bar{c}_i^{VCG}(t_i)$. In particular, the fourth entry in the second row is $\bar{c}_1^{VCG}(4)$, individual 1's expected VCG cost when he reports that his type is $t_1 = 4$. By reporting $t_1 = 4 < 5$, he can be pivotal only for the swimming pool, and even then he is pivotal only when individual 2 reports $t_2 = 6$, in which case his VCG cost, i.e., his externality, is $c_1^{VCG}(4, 6) = 6 - 5$ (see Example 9.4). Because individual 2 reports truthfully and the probability that $t_2 = 6$ is $1/9$, individual 1's expected externality is therefore $\bar{c}_1^{VCG}(4) = \frac{1}{9}(6 - 5) = \frac{1}{9}$, as in the table.

Note that one's payment to the other individual is higher the more extreme is one's report. This is in keeping with the idea that, for correct incentives, individuals should pay their externality (but keep in mind that the amount paid according to the table is *not* one's cost, because each individual also receives a payment from the other individual). Indeed, the more extreme an individual's report, the more likely it is that he gets his way, or, equivalently, the less likely it is that the other individual gets their way. Requiring individuals to pay more when their reports are more extreme keeps them honest.

Thus, when $N = 2$, the budget-balanced expected externality mechanism for the town is as follows. The two individuals are asked to report their types and make payments to one another according to the table above. The bridge is built if the sum of the reports exceeds 10 and the swimming pool is built otherwise. This mechanism is incentive-compatible, ex post efficient, budget-balanced, and leads to voluntary participation. □

Theorem 9.11 provides an affirmative answer to the question of whether one can design a mechanism that ensures an ex post efficient outcome in a quasi-linear utility, independent private values setting. Thus, we have come quite a long way. But there are important situations that our analysis so far does not cover and it is now time to get to them.

9.5.6 PROPERTY RIGHTS, OUTSIDE OPTIONS, AND INDIVIDUAL RATIONALITY CONSTRAINTS

Up to now we have implicitly assumed that, on the one hand, individuals cannot be forced to give up their income and, on the other hand, they have no property rights over social states. These implicit assumptions show up in our analysis when we consider whether individuals are willing to participate in the mechanism.[31] Indeed, we presumed that when an individual chooses not to participate, two things are true. First, his income is unchanged, implying that he cannot be forced to give it up. Second, the set of social states available to the remaining individuals is also unchanged, implying that the individual himself has no control – i.e., no property rights – over them.

The 'no property rights over social states' assumption sometimes makes perfect sense. For example, when the mechanism is an auction and the N participating individuals are bidders, it is natural to suppose that no bidder has any effect on the availability of the good should he decide not to participate. But what if we include the seller as one of the individuals participating in the mechanism? It typically will not make sense to assume that the good will remain available to the bidders if the seller chooses not to participate.[32] Or, consider a situation in which a firm-owner has the technology to produce a good (at some cost) that a consumer might value. In this case too, the set of social states is not the same for the consumer alone as it is with the consumer and firm-owner together. Or, suppose one is interested in dissolving a partnership (e.g., a law firm, a marriage, etc.) efficiently, where each partner has rights to the property that is jointly owned. In order to cover these and other important situations we must generalise our model.

The key to accommodating property rights over social states is to be more flexible about individual participation decisions. To get us moving in the right direction, consider a situation involving a seller who owns an object and potential buyer. The seller's value for the object is some $v_s \in [0, 1]$ known only to the seller, and the buyer's value for the object is some $v_b \in [0, 1]$ known only to the buyer. If we wish to give the seller property rights over the object, then we cannot force him to trade it away. Consequently, the seller will participate in a mechanism only if he expects to receive utility at least v_s from doing so, because he can achieve this utility by not participating and keeping the object for himself. The notable feature of this example is that the value to the seller of not participating depends non-trivially on his private type, v_s. We will now incorporate this idea into our general model.

For each individual i, and for each $t_i \in T_i$, let $IR_i(t_i)$ denote i's expected utility when he does not participate in the mechanism and his type is t_i. Thus, in the example of the previous paragraph, letting individual 1 be the seller, we have $IR_1(v_s) = v_s$ for each $v_s \in [0, 1]$, and letting individual 2 be the buyer, we have $IR_2(v_b) = 0$ for each $v_b \in [0, 1]$.

DEFINITION 9.8 ***Individual Rationality***

An incentive-compatible direct mechanism is individually rational if for each individual i and for each $t_i \in T_i$, i's expected utility from participating in the mechanism and reporting truthfully when his type is t_i is at least $IR_i(t_i)$ when the others participate and always report their types truthfully.

[31] Participation in the mechanism, as always, implies a commitment to abide by its outcome.

[32] Note that in our treatment of auctions, the seller is always better off participating in the auction than not. Hence, this issue also arises there but is well taken care of.

Equivalently, an incentive-compatible direct mechanism, $p, c_1, \ldots, c_N$, is individually rational if the following individual rationality constraints are satisfied:

$$\sum_{x \in X} \bar{p}_i^x(t_i) v_i(x, t_i) - \bar{c}_i(t_i) \geq IR_i(t_i), \textit{ for every } i \textit{ and every } t_i \in T_i.$$

Thus, if an incentive-compatible direct mechanism is individually rational, it is optimal for each individual to voluntarily participate in the mechanism regardless of his type because his expected utility is at least as high when he participates as when he does not.

The individual rationality constraints appearing in Definition 9.8 are additional constraints, above and beyond the constraints imposed by incentive-compatibility and any other constraints of interest, such as ex post efficiency. The higher are the values $IR_i(t_i)$, the more difficult it will be to construct an incentive-compatible ex post efficient mechanism. Because property rights over social states often increase the $IR_i(t_i)$, their presence can create difficulties.

Note that we can always return to the model of no property rights over social states by defining $IR_i(t_i) = \min_{x \in X} v_i(x, t_i)$ since, given our harmless convention of zero initial income for each individual, this is the least utility one can expect when one's type is t_i.

Finally, note that introducing the functions, $IR_i(t_i)$, has an added benefit. They permit us to model the possibility that individuals have 'outside options', even if they have no property rights over the social states *per se*. For example, suppose that an individual has the opportunity to participate in one of several mechanisms and has no property rights over social states in any of them – e.g. think of a bidder considering which one of several auctions to attend. If you are designing one of the mechanisms, and $U_i^k(t_i)$ is individual i's expected utility from participating in any one of the other mechanisms $k = 1, \ldots, K$ when his type is t_i, then i will voluntarily participate in your mechanism only if his expected utility from doing so is at least $\max_k U_i^k(t_i)$. Consequently, to correctly assess i's participation decision in your mechanism we would define $IR_i(t_i) = \max_k U_i^k(t_i)$.

Let us take another look at Example 9.3 now that we can include property rights.

EXAMPLE 9.6 Reconsider Example 9.3 but suppose that the town itself must finance the building of either the bridge or the swimming pool and that building neither (i.e., 'Don't Build' (D)) is a third social state that is available. The types are as before as are the utilities for the bridge and pool. But we must specify utilities for building nothing. Suppose that individual 1 is the only engineer in town and that he would be the one to build the bridge or the pool. His utility for the social state D is

$$v_1(D, t_1) = 10,$$

while for every other individual $i > 1$,

$$v_i(D, t_i) = 0.$$

You may think of $v_1(D, t_1) = 10$ as the engineer's (opportunity) cost of building either the bridge or the pool. So, if the engineer cannot be forced to build (i.e., if he has property rights over the social state D), then the mechanism must give him at least an expected utility of 10 because he can ensure this utility simply by not building anything. Hence, for every $t \in T$, we have $IR_1(t_1) = 10$ and $IR_i(t_i) = 0$ for $i > 1$. As we now show, the expected externality mechanism that worked so beautifully without property rights no longer works.

Note that it is always efficient to build something, because total utility is equal to 10 if nothing is built, while it is strictly greater than 10 (assuming the engineer is not the only individual) if the swimming pool is built. Suppose there are just two individuals, the engineer and one other. The expected externality mechanism described in Example 9.5 fails to work because the engineer will sometimes refuse to build. For instance, if the engineer's type is $t_1 < 4$, then whatever are the reports, the mechanism will indicate that either the bridge or the pool be built and individual 2's payment to the engineer will be no more than 10/9. Consequently, even ignoring the payment the engineer must make to individual 2, the engineer's expected utility if he builds is strictly less than 10 because $\max(t_1 + 5, 2t_1) + 10/9 < 10$ when $t_1 < 4$. The engineer is therefore strictly better off exercising his right not to build. So, under the expected externality mechanism, the outcome is inefficient whenever $t_1 < 4$ because the engineer's individual rationality constraint is violated. □

Can the type of difficulty encountered in Example 9.6 be remedied? That is, is it always possible to design an incentive-compatible, ex post efficient, budget-balanced direct mechanism that is also individually rational? In general, the answer is 'No' (we will return to the specific case of Example 9.6 a little later). However, we can come to an essentially complete understanding of when it is possible and when it is not. Let us begin by providing conditions under which it is possible.[33]

9.5.7 THE IR-VCG MECHANISM: SUFFICIENCY OF EXPECTED SURPLUS

For each individual i, let $U_i^{VCG}(t_i)$ be his expected utility when his type is t_i in the truth-telling (dominant-strategy) equilibrium of the VCG mechanism. Hence,

$$U_i^{VCG}(t_i) = \sum_{t_{-i} \in T_{-i}} \sum_{x \in X} q_{-i}(t_{-i}) v_i(\hat{x}(t_i, t_{-i}), t_i) - \bar{c}_i^{VCG}(t_i).$$

As we now know, this mechanism need be neither budget-balanced nor individually rational.

Let us first try and achieve individual rationality in the simplest possible way, namely by giving a fixed amount of money to each individual so that they are willing to participate in the VCG mechanism no matter what their type. Let ψ_i denote the *participation subsidy* given to individual i. When will it be large enough so that he always chooses to participate in the VCG mechanism? The answer, of course, is that it must be such that,

$$U_i^{VCG}(t_i) + \psi_i \geq IR_i(t_i), \text{ for every } t_i \in T_i,$$

---

[33]The remainder of this chapter draws heavily from Krishna and Perry (1998). Another very nice treatment can be found in Williams (1999).

or equivalently, such that

$$\psi_i \geq IR_i(t_i) - U_i^{VCG}(t_i), \text{ for every } t_i \in T_i,$$

or finally, such that

$$\psi_i \geq \max_{t_i \in T_i}(IR_i(t_i) - U_i^{VCG}(t_i)).$$

Consequently, the *minimum* participation subsidy we must give to individual i (and it may be negative) so that he is willing to participate in the VCG mechanism regardless of his type, is

$$\psi_i^* = \max_{t_i \in T_i}(IR_i(t_i) - U_i^{VCG}(t_i)). \tag{9.27}$$

Using these minimum participation subsidies, we now define a new mechanism, called the *individually rational VCG mechanism*, or simply the IR-VCG mechanism. In the IR-VCG mechanism, each individual i reports his type and is given ψ_i^* dollars no matter what type he reports. If the vector of reports is t, the social state is $\hat{x}(t)$ and individual i must in addition pay his Vickrey cost, $c_i^{VCG}(t)$. Consequently, in total, individual i's cost is $c_i^{VCG}(t) - \psi_i^*$.

Because the participation subsidies, ψ_i^*, are handed out regardless of the reports, they have no effect on one's incentives to lie. Hence it remains a dominant strategy to report one's type truthfully. Moreover, by construction, the IR-VCG mechanism is individually rational and ex post efficient. Hence, the IR-VCG mechanism is incentive-compatible, ex post efficient, and individually rational. The only problem is that it might not be budget-balanced. To balance the budget, we might try the same trick used in Theorem 9.11, namely to seat the individuals around a circular table and have each one pay the person on their right their expected cost given their report. But there is a problem. Because the VCG costs have been reduced by the participation subsidies, it might be that an individual's expected cost is now negative. He would then not be *paying* the individual on his right. Instead, he would be *taking money away from* the individual on his right (who is also paying his expected cost to the individual on his right). This additional expense for him, the individual on his right, might lead to a violation of his individual rationality constraint. If so, our 'circular-table' trick balances the budget, but it results in a mechanism that is no longer individually rational. Thus, balancing the budget when expected costs are negative for some individuals requires a more sophisticated method than that described in Theorem 9.11, if indeed balancing the budget is possible at all.

Say that an incentive-compatible direct mechanism with cost functions $c_1, \ldots, c_N$, *runs an expected surplus* if, in the truth-telling equilibrium, ex ante expected revenue is non-negative, i.e., if

$$\sum_{t \in T} q(t) \left(\sum_{i=1}^{N} c_i(t) \right) \geq 0.$$

Note that the VCG mechanism runs an expected surplus because $c_i^{VCG}(t) \geq 0$ for every i and every t. On the other hand, the IR-VCG may or may not run an expected surplus because it reduces the expected surplus of the VCG mechanism by the amount of the participation subsidies. We can now state the following result, which holds for *any* incentive-compatible mechanism, not merely for the particular mechanisms we have considered so far.

THEOREM 9.12 ***Achieving a Balanced Budget***

Suppose that an incentive-compatible direct mechanism with cost functions $c_1, \ldots, c_N$ runs an expected surplus. For each individual i and every $t \in T$ replace the cost function c_i by the cost function,

$$c_i^B(t) = \bar{c}_i(t_i) - \bar{c}_{i+1}(t_{i+1}) + \bar{c}_{i+1} - \frac{1}{N}\sum_{j=1}^{N} \bar{c}_j,$$

where $\bar{c}_i(t_i)$ is defined by (9.22), $\bar{c}_i = \sum_{t \in T} q(t)c_i(t)$, and $i + 1 = 1$ when $i = N$. Then the resulting mechanism – with the same probability assignment function – is budget-balanced and remains incentive-compatible. Moreover, the resulting mechanism is weakly preferred by every type of every individual to the original mechanism. Therefore, if the original mechanism was individually rational, so is the new budget-balanced mechanism.

Analogous to the budget-balanced expected externality mechanism, the cost functions, c_i^B, defined in Theorem 9.12 can be described rather simply. Seat the N individuals in order, from 1 to N, clockwise around a circular table. If individual i reports t_i, he pays every other individual the fixed amount $\bar{c}_{i+1}/N$ and pays the individual on his right the additional amount $\bar{c}_i(t_i)$. That's it!

If you carefully trace through who pays whom how much when the vector of reports is t, you will find that, in the end, individual i's net cost is $c_i^B(t)$. Once again, the nice thing about this way of looking at the cost functions c_i^B is that it is 'obvious' that they balance the budget. Why? Because the N individuals are simply making payments among themselves. Hence, no money leaves the system (so no revenue is generated) and no money is pumped into the system (so no losses are generated). Therefore, the budget must balance. Let us now prove Theorem 9.12.

Proof: As we have already noted, the cost functions, $c_1^B, \ldots, c_N^B$, are budget-balanced. (For a more direct proof, add them up!)

Second, given the cost function c_i^B, individual i's expected cost when he reports r_i and the others report truthfully is,

$$\bar{c}_i^B(r_i) = \sum_{t_{-i} \in T_{-i}} q_{-i}(t_{-i})c_i^B(r_i, t_{-i}).$$

Substituting for the definition of $c_i^B(r_i, t_{-i})$ gives,

$$\begin{aligned}
\bar{c}_i^B(r_i) &= \sum_{t_{-i}\in T_{-i}} q_{-i}(t_{-i}) \left(\bar{c}_i(t_i) - \bar{c}_{i+1}(t_{i+1}) + \bar{c}_{i+1} - \frac{1}{N}\sum_{j=1}^{N} \bar{c}_j \right) \\
&= \bar{c}_i(r_i) - \left(\sum_{t_{i+1}\in T_{i+1}} q_{i+1}(t_{i+1})\bar{c}_{i+1}(t_{i+1}) \right) + \bar{c}_{i+1} - \frac{1}{N}\sum_{j=1}^{N} \bar{c}_j \\
&= \bar{c}_i(r_i) - \bar{c}_{i+1} + \bar{c}_{i+1} - \frac{1}{N}\sum_{j=1}^{N} \bar{c}_j \\
&= \bar{c}_i(r_i) - \frac{1}{N}\sum_{j=1}^{N} \bar{c}_j. \qquad \text{(P.1)}
\end{aligned}$$

Hence, individual i's expected cost when he reports r_i differs from the original by a fixed constant.

Given the original cost functions, c_i, let $u_i(r_i, t_i)$ denote individual i's expected utility from reporting r_i when his type is t_i and when all others report truthfully, and let $u_i^B(r_i, t_i)$ denote the analogous quantity with the new cost functions, c_i^B. Because the probability assignment function has not changed, the result from (P.1) and the formula in (9.23) imply,

$$u_i^B(r_i, t_i) = u_i(r_i, t_i) + \frac{1}{N}\sum_{j=1}^{N} \bar{c}_j. \qquad \text{(P.2)}$$

Therefore, because $u_i(r_i, t_i)$ is maximised in r_i when $r_i = t_i$, the same is true of $u_i^B(r_i, t_i)$ and we conclude that the new mechanism is incentive-compatible.

Finally, the assumption that the original mechanism runs an expected surplus means precisely that,

$$\sum_{j=1}^{N} \bar{c}_j \geq 0.$$

Consequently, evaluating (P.2) at $r_i = t_i$, the expected utility of every type of each individual is at least as high in the truth-telling equilibrium with the new cost functions as with the old. ∎

Let us note a few things about Theorem 9.12. First it provides explicit budget-balanced cost functions derived from the original cost functions that maintain incentive-compatibility. Second, not only do we achieve a balanced budget, we do so while ensuring that every individual, regardless of his type, is at least as well off in the truth-telling equilibrium of the new mechanism as he was in the old. Thus, if individuals were willing to participate in the old mechanism they are willing to participate in the new mechanism as well, regardless of their type.[34] Consequently, an immediate implication of Theorem 9.12 is the following.

THEOREM 9.13 ***IR-VCG Expected Surplus: Sufficiency***

Suppose that the IR-VCG mechanism runs an expected surplus, i.e., suppose that,

$$\sum_{t\in T}\sum_{i=1}^{N} q(t)(c_i^{VCG}(t) - \psi_i^*) \geq 0.$$

Then, the following direct mechanism is incentive-compatible, ex post efficient, budget-balanced, and individually rational: Each individual reports his type. If the reported vector of types is $t \in T$, then the social state is $\hat{x}(t)$, and individual i pays the cost,

$$\bar{c}_i^{VCG}(t_i) - \psi_i^* - \bar{c}_{i+1}^{VCG}(t_{i+1}) + \bar{c}_{i+1}^{VCG} - \frac{1}{N}\sum_{j=1}^{N}(\bar{c}_j^{VCG} - \psi_j^*),$$

where $\bar{c}_j^{VCG}(t_j)$ is defined by (9.26) and $\bar{c}_j^{VCG} = \sum_{t_j\in T_j} q_j(t_j)\bar{c}_j^{VCG}(t_j)$ is individual j's ex ante expected VCG cost.

The proof of Theorem 9.13 really is immediate because the IR-VCG mechanism is incentive-compatible, ex post efficient, and individually rational. So, if it runs an expected surplus, adjusting its cost functions, $c_i^{VCG}(t) - \psi_i^*$, according to Theorem 9.12, results in an incentive-compatible, ex post efficient, budget-balanced, and individually rational mechanism. You now need only convince yourself that the resulting mechanism is precisely that which is defined in Theorem 9.13. (Do convince yourself.)

Theorem 9.13 identifies expected surplus in the IR-VCG mechanism as a *sufficient* condition for the existence of a mechanism that satisfies all of our demands, i.e., incentive compatibility, ex post efficiency, budget-balancedness, and individual rationality. Moreover, Theorem 9.13 explicitly constructs such a mechanism.

EXAMPLE 9.7 In the light of Theorem 9.13, let us reconsider Example 9.6 when there are just two individuals, one of whom is the engineer. We know from Example 9.6 that the budget-balanced expected externality mechanism is not individually rational. In particular, when the engineer's type is low, he is better off not participating. Thus, the engineer's

[34]Theorem 9.12 remains true, and the proof is identical to that given here, even when the private value assumption fails – i.e., even when $v_i(x, t)$ depends on t_{-i} as well as on t_i. On the other hand, the proof given here depends crucially on the assumption that the types are independent across individuals.

participation subsidy ψ_1^* must be strictly positive. Let us check whether the IR-VCG mechanism runs an expected surplus here. According to (9.27),

$$\psi_1^* = \max_{t_1 \in T_1}(IR_1(t_1) - U_1^{VCG}(t_1)).$$

Because $IR_1(t_1) = 10$ for all $t_1 \in T_1$, we have,

$$\begin{aligned}\psi_1^* &= \max_{t_1 \in T_1}(10 - U_1^{VCG}(t_1)) \\ &= 10 - \min_{t_1 \in T_1} U_1^{VCG}(t_1).\end{aligned}$$

Thus, we must compute the minimum expected VCG utility over the engineer's types. It is not difficult to argue that the higher is the engineer's type, the better off he must be in the VCG mechanism (see Exercise 9.32). Hence, the minimum occurs when $t_1 = 1$, and his expected utility in the VCG mechanism is,

$$U_1^{VCG}(1) = (1 + 5) - \frac{10}{9},$$

because the pool will be built regardless of 2's report, and his expected *VCG* cost when his type is $t_1 = 1$ is, $\bar{c}_1^{VCG}(1) = 10/9$ (see Exercise 9.33). Hence,

$$\begin{aligned}\psi_1^* &= 10 - U_1^{VCG}(1) \\ &= 10 - 6 + \frac{10}{9} \\ &= \frac{46}{9}.\end{aligned}$$

Similarly, because $IR_2(t_2) = 0$ for all $t_2 \in T_2$ and because $\bar{c}_2^{VCG}(1) = 20/9$ (see Exercise 9.33),

$$\begin{aligned}\psi_2^* &= 0 - U_2^{VCG}(1) \\ &= 0 - ((1 + 5) - \frac{20}{9}) \\ &= -\frac{34}{9},\end{aligned}$$

so that,

$$\psi_1^* + \psi_2^* = \frac{4}{3}.$$

As you are asked to show in Exercise 9.33, the VCG's ex ante expected revenue here is $50/27 > 4/3$. Consequently, the IR-VCG mechanism runs an expected surplus and therefore it is possible to ensure that the outcome is ex post efficient even while respecting the engineer's individual rationality constraint. Exercise 9.33 asks you to explicitly provide a mechanism that does the job. □

9.5.8 THE NECESSITY OF IR-VCG EXPECTED SURPLUS

Up to this point in our analysis of the quasi-linear model we have assumed that the type set of each individual is finite. This was for simplicity only. Everything we have done up to now goes through with essentially no changes even when the type sets are infinite, e.g., intervals of real numbers ($T_i = [0, 1]$) or products of intervals of real numbers ($T_i = [0, 1]^K$).

But we now wish to show that an expected surplus in the IR-VCG mechanism is not only a sufficient condition but that it is also a *necessary condition* for the existence of an incentive-compatible, ex post efficient, budget-balanced, individually rational mechanism. And in order to do this, we must abandon finite type spaces. So, we will make the simplest possible assumption that suits our purposes. We will assume that each individuals' type space, T_i, is the unit interval $[0, 1]$.[35] We will continue to assume that the set of social states, X, is finite.

Our objective is modest. We wish to give the reader a good sense of why an expected surplus in the IR-VCG mechanism is also a necessary condition for ex post efficient mechanism design when type sets are intervals without always taking care of the finer technical details that arise with infinite type spaces.[36] Fortuitously, the notation largely remains as it has been except that sums over types are now integrals, and the probabilities, $q_i(t_i)$, are now probability density functions. So, for example, given a direct mechanism, $p, c_1, \ldots, c_N$, we now have for each individual i and type $t_i \in [0, 1]$,

$$\bar{p}_i^x(t_i) = \int_{T_{-i}} p_i^x(t_i, t_{-i}) q_{-i}(t_{-i}) dt_{-i}, \text{ for each } x \in X,$$

and

$$\bar{c}_i(t_i) = \int_{T_{-i}} c_i(t_i, t_{-i}) q_{-i}(t_{-i}) dt_{-i},$$

rather than their finite summation counterparts in (9.22). Consequently, individual i's expected utility from reporting r_i when his type is t_i and the others report truthfully is once again,

$$u_i(r_i, t_i) = \sum_{x \in X} \bar{p}_i^x(r_i) v_i(x, t_i) - \bar{c}_i(r_i),$$

exactly as in (9.23) where type sets are finite.

Now, suppose that the direct mechanism, $p, c_1, \ldots, c_N$, is incentive compatible. This implies that $u_i(r_i, t_i)$ is maximised in r_i at $r_i = t_i$. Assuming differentiability wherever we

[35] One can just as well allow type spaces to be Euclidean cubes. But we shall not do so here.

[36] E.g., measurability, continuity, or differentiability of probability assignment functions or cost functions.

need it, this yields the following first-order condition for every individual i and every $t_i \in (0, 1)$.

$$\left.\frac{\partial u_i(r_i, t_i)}{\partial r_i}\right|_{r_i=t_i} = \sum_{x\in X} \bar{p}_i^{x\prime}(t_i)v_i(x, t_i) - \bar{c}_i'(t_i) = 0,$$

so that

$$\bar{c}_i'(t_i) = \sum_{x\in X} \bar{p}_i^{x\prime}(t_i)v_i(x, t_i). \tag{9.28}$$

Consequently, if two mechanisms, $p, c_{A1}, \ldots, c_{AN}$, and $p, c_{B1}, \ldots, c_{BN}$ have the same probability assignment function, then the derivative of the expected costs in the A mechanism, $\bar{c}_{Ai}'(t_i)$, must satisfy (9.28) as must the derivative of the expected costs in the B mechanism, $\bar{c}_{iB}'(t_i)$. Hence, for all i and all $t_i \in (0, 1)$,

$$\bar{c}_{Ai}'(t_i) = \sum_{x\in X} \bar{p}_i^{x\prime}(t_i)v_i(x, t_i) = \bar{c}_{Bi}'(t_i).$$

That is, the derivatives of the expected cost functions must be identical. But then, so long as the fundamental theorem of calculus can be applied, the expected cost functions themselves must differ by a constant because,

$$\bar{c}_{Ai}(t_i) - \bar{c}_{Ai}(0) = \int_0^{t_i} \bar{c}_{Ai}'(s)ds = \int_0^{t_i} \bar{c}_{Bi}'(s)ds = \bar{c}_{Bi}(t_i) - \bar{c}_{Bi}(0).$$

In obtaining this conclusion we assumed differentiability of the mechanism and also that the derivative of expected cost is sufficiently well-behaved so that the fundamental theorem of calculus applies. These assumptions are in fact unnecessary for the result so long as, for example, $\partial v_i(x, t_i)/\partial t_i$ exists and is continuous in $t_i \in [0, 1]$ for each $x \in X$. Moreover, note that because (9.28) depends only on the *expected probabilities*, $\bar{p}_i^x$, it is enough that the two mechanisms have the same expected probability assignment functions. We state the following result without proof.

THEOREM 9.14 ***Costs Differ by a Constant***

Suppose that for each individual i, $\partial v_i(x, t_i)/\partial t_i$ exists and is continuous in $t_i \in [0, 1]$ for each $x \in X$. If two incentive-compatible mechanisms have the same expected probability assignment functions, $\bar{p}_i^x$, then for each i, individual i's expected cost functions in the two mechanisms differ by a constant (which may depend upon i).

From this we immediately obtain a general revenue equivalence result that is worthwhile stating in passing. It generalises Theorem 9.6.

THEOREM 9.15 ***A General Revenue Equivalence Theorem***

Suppose that for each individual i, $\partial v_i(x, t_i)/\partial t_i$ exists and is continuous in $t_i \in [0, 1]$ for each $x \in X$. If two incentive-compatible mechanisms have the same expected probability *assignment functions, $\bar{p}_i^x$, and every individual is indifferent between the two mechanisms when his type is zero, then the two mechanisms generate the same expected revenue.*

We leave the proof of Theorem 9.15 to you as an exercise (see Exercise 9.35). Another immediate consequence of Theorem 9.14 is the following. Suppose that for each $t \in T$ there is a unique ex post efficient social state. Then any two ex post efficient incentive-compatible mechanisms have the same probability assignment functions. Hence, by Theorem 9.14, because the VCG mechanism is incentive-compatible and ex post efficient, any other incentive compatible ex post efficient mechanism must have expected cost functions that differ from the VCG expected costs (i.e., the expected externalities) by a constant. Indeed, if you look back at all of the ex post efficient mechanisms we constructed, expected costs differ by a constant from the VCG expected costs. This fact is the basis of our next result.

The assumption that for each $t \in T$ there is a unique ex post efficient social state is very strong when there are finitely many social states.[37] Fortunately there are much weaker assumptions that have the same effect.

THEOREM 9.16 ***Maximal Revenue Subject to Efficiency and Individual Rationality***

Suppose that for each individual i, $\partial v_i(x, t_i)/\partial t_i$ exists and is continuous in $t_i \in [0, 1]$ for each $x \in X$. In addition, suppose that for each individual i and for each $t_{-i} \in T_{-i}$, there is, for all but perhaps finitely many $t_i \in T_i$, a unique ex post efficient social state given (t_i, t_{-i}). Then the IR-VCG mechanism generates the maximum ex ante expected revenue among all incentive-compatible, ex post efficient, individually rational direct mechanisms.

Proof: Because, for each $t_{-j} \in T_{-j}$ there is, for all but finitely many $t_j \in T_j$, a unique ex post efficient social state given (t_j, t_{-j}), the expected probability assignment functions, $\bar{p}_i^x(t_i)$, are uniquely determined by ex post efficiency. Consider then some incentive-compatible, ex post efficient, individually rational direct mechanism with cost functions $c_1, \ldots, c_N$. According to the fact just stated, its expected probability assignment functions must coincide with those of the IR-VCG mechanism. So, by Theorem 9.14, its expected cost functions differ by a constant from the expected cost functions, $\bar{c}_i^{VCG}(t_i) - \psi_i^*$, of the IR-VCG mechanism.[38] Hence, for some constants, $k_1, \ldots, k_N$,

$$\bar{c}_i(t_i) = \bar{c}_i^{VCG}(t_i) - \psi_i^* - k_i, \tag{P.1}$$

for every individual i and every $t_i \in T_i$.

Now, because the expected probability assignment functions in the two mechanisms are the same and because the mechanism with cost functions, c_i, is individually rational,

---

[37] Indeed, if each $v_i(x, t_i)$ is continuous in t_i, then uniqueness implies that $\hat{x}(t)$ must be constant. That is, there must be a single social state that is ex post efficient regardless of the vector of types. But in that case there is no problem to begin with since there is no uncertainty about which social state is ex post efficient.

[38] Keep in mind that all of our formulae, including those defing the ψ_i^*, must be adjusted from sums over types to integrals over types. But otherwise they are the same.

(P.1) says that starting with the VCG mechanism and adjusting it by giving to each individual i the participation subsidy $\psi_i^* + k_i$ renders it individually rational in addition to ex post efficient. But because the participation subsidies ψ_i^* are, by definition, the *smallest* such subsidies, it must be the case that $k_i \geq 0$ for all i. Hence, by (P.1),

$$\bar{c}_i(t_i) \leq \bar{c}_i^{VCG}(t_i) - \psi_i^*,$$

so that each individual, regardless of his type, expects to pay a lower cost in the mechanism with cost functions, c_i, than in the IR-VCG mechanism. Hence, the IR-VCG mechanism generates at least as much expected revenue. ∎

We can now prove the result we have been heading towards.

THEOREM 9.17 ***IR-VCG Expected Surplus: Necessity***

Suppose that for each individual i, $\partial v_i(x, t_i)/\partial t_i$ exists and is continuous in $t_i \in [0, 1]$ for each $x \in X$. In addition, suppose that for each individual i and for each $t_{-i} \in T_{-i}$, there is, for all but perhaps finitely many $t_i \in T_i$, a unique ex post efficient social state given (t_i, t_{-i}). If there exists an incentive-compatible, ex post efficient, budget-balanced, individually rational direct mechanism, then the IR-VCG mechanism runs an expected surplus.

Proof: If such a mechanism exists, then, because it is budget-balanced, its expected revenues are zero. On the other hand, by Theorem 9.16, the IR-VCG mechanism raises at least as much ex ante expected revenue. Therefore, the ex ante expected revenue raised by the IR-VCG mechanism must be non-negative. ∎

We can apply Theorem 9.17 to obtain a special case of an important impossibility result due to Myerson and Satterthwaite (1983).

EXAMPLE 9.8 Consider a buyer and a seller. The seller owns an indivisible object and both the buyer and seller have quasi-linear preferences and private values for the object. There are two social states, B (the buyer receives the object) and S (the seller receives the object). It is convenient to index the two individuals by $i = b$ for the buyer and $i = s$ for the seller. The buyer's type, t_b, and the seller's type, t_s, are each drawn uniformly and independently from $[0, 1]$. For each individual i, t_i is his value for the object. So, for example, $v_b(B, t_b) = t_b$ and $v_b(S, t_b) = 0$, and similarly for the seller. The seller has property rights over the object and so $IR_s(t_s) = t_s$ because the seller can always choose not to participate in the mechanism and keep his object. On the other hand, $IR_b(t_b) = 0$ because non-participation leaves the buyer with zero utility.

We wish to know whether there exists a direct mechanism that is incentive-compatible, ex post efficient, budget-balanced, and individually rational. According to Theorems 9.13 and 9.17 the answer is 'yes' if and only if the IR-VCG mechanism runs an expected surplus. So, let's check.

First, we compute the VCG cost functions. If the buyer's type is t_b, then it is efficient for the object to go to the buyer when $t_b > t_s$. In this case, the buyer's externality is $t_s - 0$

because, without the buyer, the seller receives the object and obtains utility t_s from the social state, but with the buyer, the buyer receives the object and the seller obtains utility zero from the social state. On the other hand, if $t_b < t_s$, the buyer's externality is zero because with or without him the seller receives the object. Hence,

$$c_b^{VCG}(t_b, t_s) = \begin{cases} t_s, & \text{if } t_b > t_s \\ 0 & \text{if } t_b < t_s. \end{cases}$$

There is no need to specify who receives the object when $t_b = t_s$ because this event occurs with probability zero and will have no effect on expected costs. Indeed, from what we already know, the buyer's expected cost given his type is:

$$\bar{c}_b^{VCG}(t_b) = \int_0^{t_b} t_s dt_s = \frac{1}{2}t_b^2.$$

Similarly, because within the VCG mechanism the buyer and seller are symmetric,[39]

$$\bar{c}_s^{VCG}(t_s) = \frac{1}{2}t_s^2.$$

Consequently, if $U_i^{VCG}(t_i)$ is individual i's expected utility in the VCG mechanism when his type is t_i, then

$$\begin{aligned} U_b^{VCG}(t_b) &= \int_0^{t_b} t_b dt_s - \bar{c}_b^{VCG}(t_b) \\ &= t_b^2 - \frac{1}{2}t_b^2 \\ &= \frac{1}{2}t_b^2, \end{aligned}$$

where the integral in the first line is the utility the buyer expects from receiving the object when that is the efficient social state. Similarly, by symmetry,

$$U_s^{VCG}(t_s) = \frac{1}{2}t_s^2.$$

The IR-VCG mechanism runs an expected surplus when the expected revenue from the VCG mechanism exceeds the sum of the participation subsidies, $\psi_b^* + \psi_s^*$. The

---

[39] The fact that the seller owns the object plays no role in the VCG mechanism, which always operates as if there are no property rights over social states.

expected revenue from the VCG mechanism is,

$$\begin{aligned}\int_0^1 \bar{c}_b^{VCG}(t_b)dt_b + \int_0^1 \bar{c}_s^{VCG}(t_s)dt_s &= \int_0^1 \frac{1}{2}t_b^2 dt_b + \int_0^1 \frac{1}{2}t_s^2 dt_s \\ &= \frac{1}{6} + \frac{1}{6} \\ &= \frac{1}{3}.\end{aligned}$$

On the other hand,

$$\begin{aligned}\psi_b^* &= \max_{t_b \in [0,1]} (IR_b(t_b) - U_b^{VCG}(t_b)) \\ &= \max_{t_b \in [0,1]} (0 - \frac{1}{2}t_b^2) \\ &= 0,\end{aligned}$$

and

$$\begin{aligned}\psi_s^* &= \max_{t_s \in [0,1]} (IR_s(t_b) - U_s^{VCG}(t_s)) \\ &= \max_{t_s \in [0,1]} (t_s - \frac{1}{2}t_s^2) \\ &= \frac{1}{2},\end{aligned}$$

so that

$$\psi_b^* + \psi_s^* = \frac{1}{2} > \frac{1}{3}.$$

Thus, we conclude that there *does not* exist an incentive-compatible, ex post efficient, budget-balanced, individually rational mechanism in this situation. □

There are several lessons to draw from Example 9.8. First, the example provides an explanation for the otherwise puzzling phenomenon of strikes and disagreements in bargaining situations. The puzzling thing about strikes is that one imagines that whatever agreement is eventually reached could have been reached without the strike, saving both sides time and resources. But the result in the example demonstrates that this 'intuition' is simply wrong. Sometimes there is no mechanism that can assure ex post efficiency – inefficiencies must occasionally appear. And one example of such an inefficiency is that associated with a strike.

Second, the example illustrates that property rights matter. A very famous result in law and economics is the 'Coase Theorem' which states, roughly, that if one's only interest is Pareto efficiency, property rights do not matter – e.g., whether a downstream fishery is given the legal right to clean water or an upstream steel mill is given the legal right to dump waste into the stream, the two parties will, through appropriate transfer payments to one another, reach a Pareto-efficient agreement. Our analysis reveals an important caveat, namely that the Coase Theorem can fail when the parties have private information about their preferences. If no individual has property rights over social states, we found that efficiency was always possible. However, when property rights are assigned (as in the buyer–seller example) an efficient agreement cannot always be guaranteed.

Third, the fact that property rights can get in the way of efficiency provides an important lesson for the privatisation of public assets (e.g. government sale of off-shore oil rights, or of radio spectrum for commercial communication (mobile phones, television, radio)). If the government's objective is efficiency, then it is important to design the privatisation mechanism so that it assigns the objects efficiently, if possible. This is because the assignment, by its nature, creates property rights. If the assignment is inefficient, and private information remains, the establishment of property rights may well lead to unavoidable, persistent, and potentially large efficiency losses.

Fourth, the example suggests that the lack of symmetry in ownership may play a role in the impossibility result. For example, a setting without property rights is one where property rights are symmetric and also one where it is possible to construct an ex post efficient budget-balanced mechanism with voluntary participation. In the exercises you are asked to explore this idea further (see also Cramton et al. (1987)).

An excellent question at this point is, 'What do we do when there does not exist an incentive-compatible, ex post efficient, budget-balanced, individually rational mechanism?' This is a terrific and important question, but one we will not pursue in this introduction to mechanism design. One answer, however, is that we do the next best thing. We instead search among all incentive-compatible mechanisms for those that cannot be Pareto improved upon either from the interim perspective (i.e., from the perspective of individuals once they know their type but no one else's), or from the ex ante perspective. An excellent example of this methodology can be found in Myerson and Satterthwaite (1983).

The theory of mechanism design is rich, powerful, and important, and, while we have only skimmed the surface here, we hope to have given you a sense of its usefulness in addressing the fundamental problem of resource allocation in the presence of private information.

9.6 EXERCISES

9.1 Show that the bidding strategy in (9.5) is strictly increasing.

9.2 Show in two ways that the symmetric equilibrium bidding strategy of a first-price auction with N symmetric bidders each with values distributed according to F, can be written as

$$\hat{b}(v) = v - \int_0^v \left(\frac{F(x)}{F(v)}\right)^{N-1} dx.$$

For the first way, use our solution from the text and apply integration by parts. For the second way, use the fact that $F^{N-1}(r)(v - \hat{b}(r))$ is maximised in r when $r = v$ and then apply the envelope theorem to conclude that $d(F^{N-1}(v)(v - \hat{b}(v))/dv = F^{N-1}(v)$; now integrate both sides from 0 to v.

9.3 This exercise will guide you through the proof that the bidding function in (9.5) is in fact a symmetric equilibrium of the first-price auction.

(a) Recall from (9.2) that

$$\frac{du(r,v)}{dr} = (N-1)F^{N-2}(r)f(r)(v - \hat{b}(r)) - F^{N-1}(r)\hat{b}'(r).$$

Using (9.3), show that

$$\begin{aligned}\frac{du(r,v)}{dr} &= (N-1)F^{N-2}(r)f(r)(v - \hat{b}(r)) - (N-1)F^{N-2}(r)f(r)(r - \hat{b}(r)) \\ &= (N-1)F^{N-2}(r)f(r)(v - r).\end{aligned}$$

(b) Use the result in part (a) to conclude that $du(r,v)/dr$ is positive when $r < v$ and negative when $r > v$, so that $u(r,v)$ is maximised when $r = v$.

9.4 Throughout this chapter we have assumed that both the seller and all bidders are risk neutral. In this question, we shall explore the consequences of risk aversion on the part of bidders.

There are N bidders participating in a first-price auction. Each bidder's value is independently drawn from [0,1] according to the distribution function F, having continuous and strictly positive density f. If a bidder's value is v and he wins the object with a bid of $b < v$, then his von Neumann-Morgenstern utility is $(v - b)^{\frac{1}{\alpha}}$, where $\alpha \geq 1$ is fixed and common to all bidders. Consequently, the bidders are risk averse when $\alpha > 1$ and risk neutral when $\alpha = 1$. (Do you see why?) Given the risk-aversion parameter α, let $\hat{b}_\alpha(v)$ denote the (symmetric) equilibrium bid of a bidder when his value is v. The following parts will guide you toward finding $\hat{b}_\alpha(v)$ and uncovering some of its implications.

(a) Let $u(r,v)$ denote a bidder's expected utility from bidding $\hat{b}_\alpha(r)$ when his value is v, given that all other bidders employ $\hat{b}_\alpha(\cdot)$. Show that

$$u(r,v) = F^{N-1}(r)(v - \hat{b}_\alpha(r))^{\frac{1}{\alpha}}.$$

Why must $u(r,v)$ be maximised in r when $r = v$?

(b) Use part (a) to argue that

$$[u(r,v)]^\alpha = [F^\alpha(r)]^{N-1}(v - \hat{b}_\alpha(r))$$

must be maximised in r when $r = v$.

(c) Use part (b) to argue that a first-price auction with the N risk-averse bidders above whose values are each independently distributed according to $F(v)$, is equivalent to a first-price auction with N *risk-neutral* bidders whose values are each independently distributed according to $F^\alpha(v)$. Use our solution for the risk-neutral case (see Exercise 9.2 above) to conclude that

$$\hat{b}_\alpha(v) = v - \int_0^v \left(\frac{F(x)}{F(v)}\right)^{\alpha(N-1)} dx.$$

(d) Prove that $\hat{b}_\alpha(v)$ is strictly increasing in $\alpha \geq 1$. Does this make sense? Conclude that as bidders become more risk averse, the seller's revenue from a first-price auction increases.

(e) Use part (d) and the revenue equivalence result for the standard auctions in the risk-neutral case to argue that when bidders are risk averse as above, a first-price auction raises *more* revenue for the seller than a second-price auction. Hence, these two standard auctions no longer generate the same revenue when bidders are risk averse.

(f) What happens to the seller's revenue as the bidders become infinitely risk averse (i.e., as $\alpha \to \infty$)?

9.5 In a private values model, argue that it is a weakly dominant strategy for a bidder to bid his value in a second-price auction even if the joint distribution of the bidders' values exhibits correlation.

9.6 Use the equilibria of the second-price, Dutch, and English auctions to construct incentive-compatible direct selling mechanisms for each of them in which the ex post assignment of the object to bidders as well as their ex post payments to the seller are unchanged.

9.7 Prove part (i) of Theorem 9.5 under the assumption that both $\bar{p}_i(v_i)$ and $\bar{c}_i(v_i)$ are differentiable at every $v_i \in [0, 1]$.

9.8 In a first-price, all-pay auction, the bidders simultaneously submit sealed bids. The highest bid wins the object and *every* bidder pays the seller the amount of his bid. Consider the independent private values model with symmetric bidders whose values are each distributed according to the distribution function F, with density f.

(a) Find the unique symmetric equilibrium bidding function. Interpret.

(b) Do bidders bid higher or lower than in a first-price auction?

(c) Find an expression for the seller's expected revenue.

(d) Both with and without using the revenue equivalence theorem, show that the seller's expected revenue is the same as in a first-price auction.

9.9 Suppose there are just two bidders. In a second-price, all-pay auction, the two bidders simultaneously submit sealed bids. The highest bid wins the object and both bidders pay the *second-highest* bid.

(a) Find the unique symmetric equilibrium bidding function. Interpret.

(b) Do bidders bid higher or lower than in a first-price, all-pay auction?

(c) Find an expression for the seller's expected revenue.

(d) Both with and without using the revenue equivalence theorem, show that the seller's expected revenue is the same as in a first-price auction.

9.10 Consider the following variant of a first-price auction. Sealed bids are collected. The highest bidder pays his bid but receives the object only if the outcome of the toss of a fair coin is heads. If the outcome is tails, the seller keeps the object and the high bidder's bid. Assume bidder symmetry.

(a) Find the unique symmetric equilibrium bidding function. Interpret.

(b) Do bidders bid higher or lower than in a first-price auction?

(c) Find an expression for the seller's expected revenue.

(d) Both with and without using the revenue equivalence theorem, show that the seller's expected revenue is exactly half that of a standard first-price auction.

9.11 Suppose all bidders' values are uniform on [0, 1]. Construct a revenue-maximising auction. What is the reserve price?

9.12 Consider again the case of uniformly distributed values on [0, 1]. Is a first-price auction with the same reserve price as in the preceding question optimal for the seller? Prove your claim using the revenue equivalence theorem.

9.13 Suppose the bidders' values are *i.i.d.*, each according to a uniform distribution on [1, 2]. Construct a revenue-maximising auction for the seller.

9.14 Suppose there are N bidders with independent private values where bidder i's value is uniform on $[a_i, b_i]$. Show that the following is a revenue-maximising, incentive-compatible direct selling mechanism. Each bidder reports his value. Given the reported values $v_1, \ldots, v_N$, bidder i wins the object if v_i is strictly larger than the $N - 1$ numbers of the form $\max[a_i, b_i/2 + \max(0, v_j - b_j/2)]$ for $j \neq i$. Bidder i then pays the seller an amount equal to the largest of these $N - 1$ numbers. All other bidders pay nothing.

9.15 A drawback of the direct mechanism approach is that the seller must know the distribution of the bidders' values to compute the optimal auction. The following exercise provides an optimal auction that is distribution-free for the case of two asymmetric bidders, 1 and 2, with independent private values. Bidder i's strictly positive and continuous density of values on [0, 1] is f_i with distribution F_i. Assume throughout that $v_i - (1 - F_i(v_i))/f_i(v_i)$ is strictly increasing for $i = 1, 2$.

The auction is as follows. In the first stage, the bidders each simultaneously submit a sealed bid. Before the second stage begins, the bids are publicly revealed. In the second stage, the bidders must simultaneously declare whether they are willing to purchase the object at the other bidder's revealed sealed bid. If one of them says 'yes' and the other 'no', then the 'yes' transaction is carried out. If they both say 'yes' or both say 'no', then the seller keeps the object and no payments are made. Note that the seller can run this auction without knowing the bidders' value distributions.

(a) Consider the following strategies for the bidders: In the first stage, when his value is v_i, bidder $i \neq j$ submits the sealed bid $b_i^*(v_i) = b_i$, where b_i solves

$$b_i - \frac{1 - F_j(b_i)}{f_j(b_i)} = \max\left(0, v_i - \frac{1 - F_i(v_i)}{f_i(v_i)}\right).$$

(Although such a b_i need not always exist, it will always exist if the functions $v_1 - (1 - F_1(v_1))/f_1(v_1)$ and $v_2 - (1 - F_2(v_2))/f_2(v_2)$ have the same range. So, assume this is the case.)

In the second stage each bidder says 'yes' if and only if his value is above the other bidder's first-stage bid.

Show that these strategies constitute an equilibrium of this auction. (Also, note that while the seller need not know the distribution of values, each bidder needs to know the distribution of the other bidder's values to carry out his strategy. Hence, this auction shifts the informational burden from the seller to the bidders.)

(b) (i) Show that in this equilibrium the seller's expected revenues are maximised.

(ii) Is the outcome always efficient?

(c) (i) Show that it is also an equilibrium for each bidder to bid his value and then to say 'yes' if and only if his value is above the other's bid.

(ii) Is the outcome always efficient in this equilibrium?

(d) Show that the seller's revenues are *not* maximal in this second equilibrium.

(e) Unfortunately, this auction possesses *many* equilibria. Choose any two strictly increasing functions g_i: $[0, 1] \to \mathbb{R}_2$ $i = 1, 2$, with a common range. Suppose in the first stage that bidder $i \neq j$ with value v_i bids $\tilde{b}_i(v_i) = b_i$, where b_i solves $g_j(b_i) = g_i(v_i)$ and says 'yes' in the second stage if and only if his value is strictly above the other bidder's bid. Show that this is an equilibrium of this auction. Also, show that the outcome is always efficient if and only if $g_i = g_j$.

9.16 Show that condition (9.18) is satisfied when each F_i is a convex function. Is convexity of F_i necessary?

9.17 Consider the independent private values model with N possibly asymmetric bidders. Suppose we restrict attention to *efficient* individually rational, incentive-compatible direct selling mechanisms; i.e., those that always assign the object to the bidder who values it most.

(a) What are the probability assignment functions?

(b) What then are the cost functions?

(c) What cost functions among these maximise the seller's revenue?

(d) Conclude that among *efficient* individually rational, incentive-compatible direct selling mechanisms, a second-price auction maximises the seller's expected revenue. (What about the other three standard auction forms?)

9.18 Call a direct selling mechanism $p_i(\cdot)$, $c_i(\cdot)$, $i = 1, \ldots, N$ *deterministic* if the p_i take on only the values 0 or 1.

(a) Assuming independent private values, show that for every incentive-compatible deterministic direct selling mechanism whose probability assignment functions, $p_i(v_i, v_{-i})$, are non-decreasing in v_i for every v_{-i}, there is another incentive-compatible direct selling mechanism with the *same* probability assignment functions (and, hence, deterministic as well) whose cost functions have the property that a bidder pays only when he receives the object and when he does win, the amount that he pays is independent of his reported value. Moreover, show that the new mechanism can be chosen so that the seller's expected revenue is the same as that in the old.

(b) How does this result apply to a first-price auction with symmetric bidders, wherein a bidder's payment depends on his bid?

(c) How does this result apply to an all-pay, first-price auction with symmetric bidders wherein bidders pay whether or not they win the auction?

9.19 Show that it is a weakly dominant strategy for each bidder to report his value truthfully in the optimal direct mechanism we derived in this chapter.

9.20 Under the assumption that each bidder's density, f_i, is continuous and strictly positive and that each $v_i - (1 - F_i(v_i))/f_i(v_i)$ is strictly increasing,

(a) Show that the optimal selling mechanism entails the seller keeping the object with strictly positive probability.

(b) Show that there is precisely one $\rho^* \in [0, 1]$ satisfying $\rho^* - (1 - F(\rho^*))/f(\rho^*) = 0$.

9.21 Show that when the bidders are symmetric, the first-price, Dutch, and English auctions all are optimal for the seller once an appropriate reserve price is chosen. Indeed, show that the optimal reserve price is the same for all four of the standard auctions.

9.22 You are hired to study a particular auction in which a single indivisible good is for sale. You find out that N bidders participate in the auction and each has a private value $v \in [0, 1]$ drawn independently from the common density $f(v) = 2v$, whose cumulative distribution function is $F(v) = v^2$. All you know about the auction rules is that the highest bidder wins. But you do not know what he must pay, or whether bidders who lose must pay as well. On the other hand, you do know that there is an equilibrium, and that in equilibrium each bidder employs the same strictly increasing bidding function (the exact function you do not know), and that no bidder ever pays more than his bid.

(a) Which bidder will win this auction?

(b) Prove that when a bidder's value is zero, he pays zero and wins the good with probability zero.

(c) Using parts (a) and (b), prove that the seller's expected revenue must be $1 - \frac{4N-1}{4N^2-1}$.

9.23 We have so far assumed that the seller has a single good for sale. Suppose instead that the seller has two identical goods for sale. Further, assume that even though there are two identical goods for sale, each bidder wishes to win just one of them (he doesn't care which one, since they are identical). There are N bidders and each bidder's single value, v, for either one of the goods is drawn independently from $[0, 1]$ according to the common density function $f(\cdot)$. So, if a bidder's value happens to be $v = 1/3$, he is willing to pay at most $1/3$ to receive one of the two goods.

Suppose that the seller employs the following auction to sell the two goods. Each bidder is asked to submit a sealed bid. The highest two bids win and the two winners each pay the third-highest bid. Losers pay nothing.

(a) Argue that a bidder can do no better in this auction than to bid his value.

(b) Find an expression for the seller's expected revenue. You may use the fact that the density, $g(v)$, of the third-highest value among the N bidder values is $g(v) = \frac{1}{6}N(N-1)(N-2)f(v)(1-F(v))^2F^{N-3}(v)$.

9.24 Consider again the situation described in Exercise 9.23, but now suppose that a different mechanism is employed by the seller to sell the two goods as follows. He randomly separates the N bidders into two separate rooms of $N/2$ bidders each (assume that N is even) and runs a standard first-price auction in each room.

(a) What bidding function does each bidder employ in each of the two rooms? (Pay attention to the number of bidders.)

(b) Assume that each bidder's value is uniformly distributed on $[0, 1]$ (therefore $f(v) = 1$ and $F(v) = v$ for all $v \in [0, 1]$

(i) Find the seller's expected revenue as a function of the total number of bidders, N.

(ii) By comparing your result in (i) with your answer to part (b) of Exercise 9.23, show that the seller's expected revenue is higher when he auctions the two goods simultaneously than when he separates the bidders and auctions the two goods separately.

(iii) Would the seller's expected revenue be any different if he instead uses a second-price auction in each of the two rooms?

(iv) Use your answer to (iii) to provide an intuitive – although perhaps incomplete – explanation for the result in (ii).

9.25 Suppose there are N bidders and bidder i's value is independently drawn uniformly from $[a_i, b_i]$.

(a) Prove that the seller can maximise his expected revenue by employing an auction of the following form. First, the seller chooses, for each bidder i, a possibly distinct reserve price ρ_i. (You must specify the optimal value of ρ_i for each bidder i.) Each bidder's reserve price is public information. The bidders are invited to submit sealed bids and the bidder submitting the highest positive bid wins. Only the winner pays and he pays his reserve price *plus* the second-highest bid, unless the second-highest bid is negative, in which case he pays his reserve price.

(b) Prove that each bidder has a weakly dominant bidding strategy in the auction described in (a).

9.26 Establish the 'if' part of the claim in (9.20). In particular, prove that if $\hat{x} \in X$ solves

$$\max_{x \in X} \sum_{i=1}^{N} v_i(x),$$

then, there is no $y \in X$ and no income transfers, τ_i, among the N individuals such that $v_i(y) + \tau_i \geq v_i(x)$ for every i with at least one inequality strict.

9.27 Justify the definition of ex post Pareto efficiency given in Definition 9.3 using arguments similar to those used to establish (9.20). The transfers may depend on the entire vector of types.

9.28 Show that Definition 9.4 is equivalent to Definition 9.1 when (i) there is a single object available, (ii) there are $N + 1$ individuals consisting of N bidders and one seller, and (iii) the social states are the $N + 1$ allocations in which, either, one of the bidders ends up with the good or the seller ends up with the good.

9.29 Consider the 'circle' mechanism described in Theorem 9.11. Instead of defining the new cost functions by paying the individual on one's right one's expected externality given one's type, suppose one pays each of the other individuals an equal share of one's expected externality. Prove that the conclusions of Theorem 9.11 remain valid.

9.30 Consider Examples 9.3–9.5.

(a) Show that the cost formula given in Theorem 9.11 for the budget-balanced expected externality mechanism yields cost functions that can be equivalently described by the following table.

If your reported type is:	1	2	3	4	5	6	7	8	9
You pay the other individual:	$\frac{10}{9}$	$\frac{2}{3}$	$\frac{1}{3}$	$\frac{1}{9}$	0	0	$\frac{1}{9}$	$\frac{1}{3}$	$\frac{2}{3}$

(b) We know that the mechanism described in Example 9.5 is incentive-compatible. Nonetheless, show by direct computation that, when individual 1's type is $t_1 = 3$ and individual 2 always reports truthfully, individual 1 can do no better than to report his type truthfully.

(c) Construct the table analogous to that in part (a) when the town consists of $N = 3$ individuals.

9.31 Consider Example 9.3. Add the social state 'Don't Build' (D) to the set of social states so that $X = \{D, S, B\}$. Suppose that for each individual i,

$$v_i(D, t_i) = k_i$$

is independent of t_i.

(a) Argue that one interpretation of k_i is the value of the leisure time individual i must give up towards the building of either the pool or the bridge. (For example, all the k_i might be zero except $k_1 > 0$, where individual 1 is the town's only engineer.)

(b) What are the interim individual rationality constraints if individuals have property rights over their leisure time?

(c) When is it efficient to build the pool? The bridge?

(d) Give sufficient conditions for the existence of an ex post efficient mechanism both when individuals have property rights over their leisure time and when they do not. Describe the mechanism in both cases and show that the presence of property rights makes it more difficult to achieve ex post efficiency.

9.32 Consider Examples 9.3–9.7 and suppose that the VCG mechanism is used there. Without making any explicit computations, show that each individual i's expected utility in the truth-telling equilibrium is non-decreasing in his type.

9.33 Consider Example 9.7.

(a) Compute the expected VCG costs for the engineer, $i = 1$, and for the other individual, $i = 2$, as a function of their types. Argue that the values in the second row of the table in Example 9.5 are valid for the engineer. Why are they not valid for the other individual, $i = 2$? Show that the expected VCG costs for $i = 2$ are given by the following table.

t_2 :	1	2	3	4	5	6	7	8	9
$\bar{c}_2^{VCG}(t_2)$:	$\frac{20}{9}$	$\frac{16}{9}$	$\frac{13}{9}$	$\frac{11}{9}$	$\frac{10}{9}$	$\frac{10}{9}$	$\frac{11}{9}$	$\frac{13}{9}$	$\frac{16}{9}$

(b) Compute the VCG mechanism's ex ante expected revenue.

(c) Use Theorem 9.13 to explicitly provide an incentive-compatible, ex post efficient, budget-balanced, individually rational mechanism.

(d) Because the engineer's opportunity cost of building is 10, it is always efficient to build something. Hence, it is not so surprising that a mechanism as in part (c) exists. Suppose instead that $K = 13$, so that it is efficient to build neither the bridge nor the pool if $t_1 = t_2 = 1$. By recomputing the participation subsidies, and the individuals' expected VCG costs, determine whether the IR-VCG mechanism runs an expected surplus now.

9.34 Show directly that the expected cost functions of any pair of mechanism among the VCG mechanism, the budget-balanced expected externality mechanism, the IR-VCG mechanism, and the mechanism defined in Theorem 9.13, differ by a constant.

9.35 Prove Theorem 9.15 by first showing that if an individual is indifferent between the two mechanisms when his type is zero, then his expected costs in the two mechanisms must be the same when his type is zero. Now apply Theorem 9.14 to conclude that the expected cost functions must be identical in the two mechanisms. Finally, conclude that expected revenues must be identical.

9.36 Reconsider Example 9.8. Suppose that the indivisible object is a business that is jointly owned by two partners whose preferences and private information are exactly as in Example 9.8. Let us call the partners individuals 1 and 2 here. Suppose that individual i's share of the business is $\alpha_i \in [0, 1]$ and that $\alpha_1 + \alpha_2 = 1$. The significance of the ownership shares is that they translate into individually rational utilities as follows. For $i = 1, 2$,

$$IR_i(t_i) = \alpha_i t_i, \quad \text{for all } t_i \in [0, 1].$$

Thus, each individual i has the right to a fraction α_i of the business. Suppose now that the partnership is to be dissolved.

(a) Under what conditions on the ownership shares, α_i, can the partnership be dissolved with an incentive-compatible, ex post efficient, budget-balanced, individually rational mechanism? Comment on the effect of asymmetric versus symmetric ownership shares.

(b) Can you generalise the result in (a) to N partners?

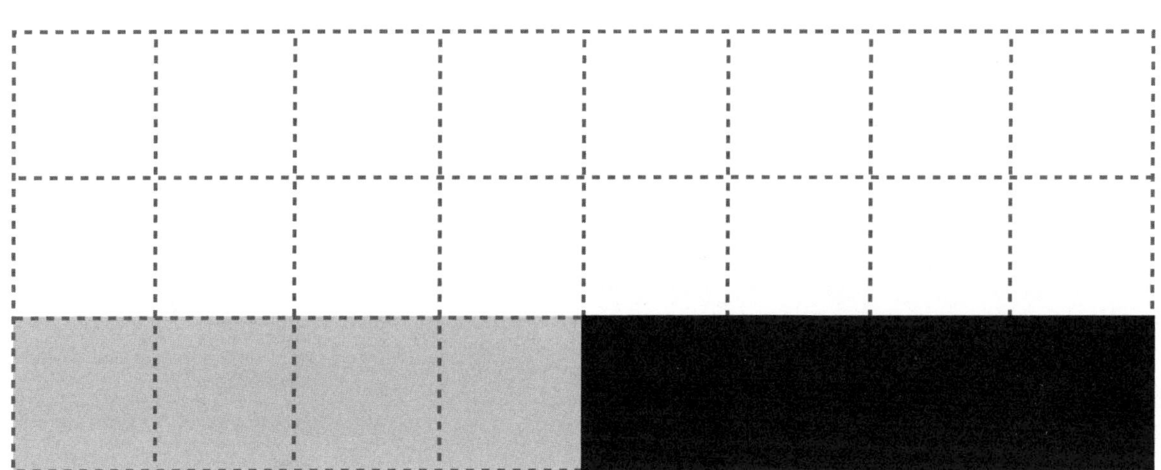

Mathematical Appendices

CHAPTER A1

SETS AND MAPPINGS

A1.1 ELEMENTS OF LOGIC

Important ideas in the economics literature are often stated in the form of **theorems**. A theorem is simply a statement deduced from other statements, and you should be familiar with them from your courses in mathematics. Theorems provide a compact and precise format for presenting the assumptions and important conclusions of sometimes lengthy arguments, and so help to identify immediately the scope and limitations of the result presented. Theorems must be proved, however, and a proof consists of establishing the validity of the statement in the theorem in a way that is consistent with the rules of logic. Here, we explain some of the language and simple rules of logic.

A1.1.1 NECESSITY AND SUFFICIENCY

Necessity and **sufficiency** are fundamental logical notions. In ordinary language, when you make the statement, 'A is necessary for B', what do you mean? When you make the statement, 'A is sufficient for B', what do you mean? It is worth a moment's reflection on the different meaning of these two statements.

Consider any two statements, A and B. When we say, 'A is necessary for B', we mean that A must hold or be true for B to hold or be true. For B to be true requires A to be true, so whenever B is true, we know that A must also be true. So we might have said, instead, that 'A is true *if* B is true', or simply that 'A *is implied by* B' (A $\Leftarrow$ B). There is, therefore, an equivalence in ordinary language and in logic among the phrases 'A is necessary for B', 'A if B', and 'A is implied by B'.

Suppose we know that 'A $\Leftarrow$ B' is a true statement. What if A is not true? Because A is necessary for B, when A is not true, then B cannot be true either. But does not this just say that 'B not true' is necessary for 'A not true'? Or that 'not B is implied by not A' ($\sim$B $\Leftarrow$ $\sim$A)? This latter form of the original statement is called the **contrapositive** form. Contraposition of the arguments in the statement *reverses* the direction of implication for a true statement.

Let us consider a simple illustration of these ideas. Let A be the phrase 'x is an integer less than 10'. Let B be the statement, 'x is an integer less than 8'. Clearly, A is necessary for B because 'x is an integer less than 10' is implied by the statement 'x is an integer less than 8'. If we form the contrapositive of these two statements, the statement $\sim$A becomes 'x is not an integer less than 10', and the statement $\sim$B becomes 'x is not an integer less than 8'. Beware that the statement '$\sim A \Leftarrow \sim B$' is *false*. The value of x could well be 9. We must *reverse* the direction of implication to obtain a contrapositive statement that is also true. The proper contrapositive statement, therefore, would be 'x is not an integer less than 8' implied by 'x is not an integer less than 10', or $\sim B \Leftarrow \sim A$.

The notion of necessity is distinct from that of *sufficiency*. When we say, 'A is sufficient for B', we mean that whenever A holds, B must hold. We can say, 'A is true *only if* B is true', or that 'A *implies* B' ($A \Rightarrow B$). Once again, whenever the statement $A \Rightarrow B$ is true, the contrapositive statement, $\sim B \Rightarrow \sim A$, is also true.

Two implications, '$A \Rightarrow B$' and '$A \Leftarrow B$', can both be true. When this is so, we say that 'A is necessary and sufficient for B', or that 'A is true if and only if B is true', or 'A iff B'. When A is necessary and sufficient for B, we say that the statements A and B are **equivalent** and write '$A \Longleftrightarrow B$'.

To illustrate briefly, suppose that A and B are the following statements: $A \equiv$ 'X is yellow', $B \equiv$ 'X is a lemon'. Certainly, if X is a lemon, then X is yellow. Here, A is necessary for B. At the same time, just because X is yellow does not mean that it must be a lemon. It could be a banana. So A is *not* sufficient for B. Suppose instead that the statements are $A \equiv$ 'X is a sour, yellow-skinned fruit' and $B \equiv$ 'X is a lemon'. Here, A is implied by B, or A is necessary for B. If X is a lemon, then it must be a yellow and sour fruit. At the same time, A implies B, or A is sufficient for B, because if X is a yellow and sour fruit, it must be a lemon. Because A is necessary and sufficient for B, there must be an *equivalence* between lemons and sour, yellow-skinned fruit.

A1.1.2 THEOREMS AND PROOFS

Mathematical theorems usually have the form of an implication or an equivalence, where one or more statements are alleged to be related in particular ways. Suppose we have the theorem '$A \Rightarrow B$'. Here, A is called the **premise** and B the **conclusion**. To prove a theorem is to establish the validity of its conclusion given the truth of its premise, and several methods can be used to do that.

In a **constructive proof**, we assume that A is true, deduce various consequences of that, and use them to show that B must also hold. This is also sometimes called a **direct proof**, for obvious reasons. There is also the **contrapositive proof**. In a contrapositive proof, we assume that B does *not* hold, then show that A cannot hold. This approach takes advantage of the logical equivalence between the claims '$A \Rightarrow B$' and '$\sim B \Rightarrow \sim A$' noted earlier, and essentially involves a constructive proof of the contrapositive to the original statement. Finally, there is a **proof by contradiction**, or **reductio ad absurdum**. Here, the strategy is to assume that A is true, assume that B is *not* true, and attempt to derive a logical contradiction. This approach relies on the fact that if $A \Rightarrow \sim B$ is false, then $A \Rightarrow B$ must be true. Sometimes, proofs by contradiction can get the job done very efficiently, yet because they involve no constructive chain of reasoning between A and B as the other two do, they seldom illuminate the relationship between the premise and the conclusion.

If we assert that A is *necessary and sufficient* for B, or that A $\Longleftrightarrow$ B, we must give a proof in 'both directions'. That is, both A $\Rightarrow$ B *and* B $\Rightarrow$ A must be established before a complete proof of the assertion has been achieved.

It never hurts to keep in mind the old saying that goes, 'Proof by example is no proof'. Suppose the statements A $\equiv$ 'x is a student' and B $\equiv$ 'x has red hair' are given, and we make the assertion A $\Rightarrow$ B. Then clearly finding one student with red hair and pointing him out to you is not going to convince you of anything. Examples are good for illustrating, but typically not for proving. In this book, we never pretend to have proven something by providing an example that merely illustrates the point. Occasionally, however, it is necessary to state some theorems without proof. It is hoped that being asked to accept things on faith just encourages you to explore beyond the scope of this book.

Finally, a sort of converse to the old saying about examples and proofs should be noted. Whereas citing 100 examples can never prove a certain property *always* holds, citing one solitary *counterexample* can *disprove* that the property always holds. For instance, to disprove the assertion about the colour of students' hair, you need simply point out one student with brown hair. A counterexample proves that the claim cannot *always* be true because you have found at least one case where it is not.

A1.2 ELEMENTS OF SET THEORY

A1.2.1 NOTATION AND BASIC CONCEPTS

The language and methods of set theory have thoroughly infiltrated microeconomic theory. No doubt the notion of a set and many basic rules of manipulating sets are familiar. Nonetheless, because we will encounter some of them repeatedly, it is best to review a few of the basics.

A **set** is any collection of elements. Sets can be defined by *enumeration* of their elements, e.g., $S = \{2, 4, 6, 8\}$, or by *description* of their elements, e.g., $S = \{x \mid x \text{ is a positive even integer greater than zero and less than } 10\}$. When we wish to denote membership or inclusion in a set, we use the symbol $\in$. For example, if $S = \{2, 5, 7\}$, we say that $5 \in S$.

A set S is a **subset** of another set T if every element of S is also an element of T. We write $S \subset T$ (S is contained in T) or $T \supset S$ (T contains S). If $S \subset T$, then $x \in S \Rightarrow x \in T$.

Two sets are **equal sets** if they each contain exactly the same elements. We write $S = T$ whenever $x \in S \Rightarrow x \in T$ and $x \in T \Rightarrow x \in S$. Thus, S and T are equal sets if and only if $S \subset T$ *and* $T \subset S$. For example, if $S = \{\text{integers}, x \mid x^2 = 1\}$ and $T = \{-1, 1\}$, then $S = T$.

A set S is **empty** or is an **empty set** if it contains no elements at all. For example, if $A = \{x \mid x^2 = 0 \text{ and } x > 1\}$, then A is empty. We denote the empty set by the symbol $\emptyset$ and write $A = \emptyset$.

The **complement** of a set S in a universal set U is the set of all elements in U that are not in S and is denoted S^c. If $U = \{2, 4, 6, 8\}$ and $S = \{4, 6\}$, then $S^c = \{2, 8\}$. More generally, for any two sets S and T in a universal set U, we define the **set difference** denoted $S \setminus T$, or $S - T$, as all elements in the set S that are not elements of T. Thus, we can think of the complement of the set S in U as the set difference $S^c = U \setminus S$.

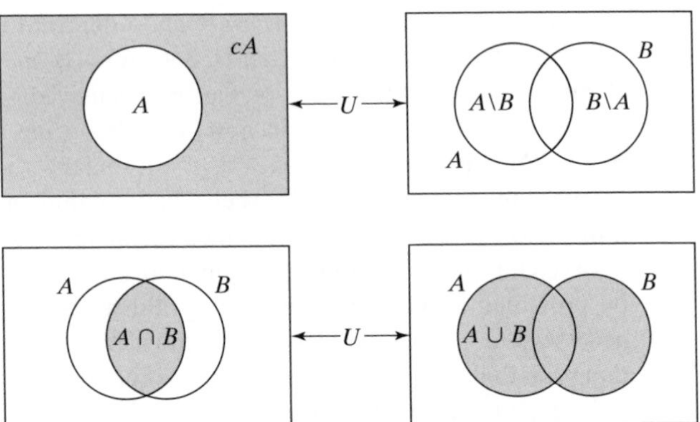

Figure A1. 1. Venn diagrams.

The basic operations on sets are **union** and **intersection**. They correspond to the logical notions of 'or' and 'and', respectively.[1] For two sets S and T, we define the *union* of S and T as the set $S \cup T \equiv \{x \mid x \in S \text{ or } x \in T\}$. We define the *intersection* of S and T as the set $S \cap T \equiv \{x \mid x \in S \text{ and } x \in T\}$. Some of these sets are illustrated in Fig. A1.1.

Sometimes we want to examine sets constructed from an arbitrary number of other sets. We could use some notation such as $\{S_1, S_2, S_3, \ldots\}$ to denote the set of all sets that concern us, but it is more common to collect the necessary (possibly infinite) number of integers starting with 1 into a set, $I \equiv \{1, 2, 3, \ldots\}$, called an **index set**, and denote the collection of sets more simply as $\{S_i\}_{i \in I}$. We would denote the union of all sets in the collection by $\cup_{i \in I} S_i$, and the intersection of all sets in the collection as $\cap_{i \in I} S_i$.

The product of two sets S and T is the set of 'ordered pairs' in the form (s, t), where the first element in the pair is a member of S and the second is a member of T. The product of S and T is denoted

$$S \times T \equiv \{(s, t) \mid s \in S, \ t \in T\}.$$

One familiar set product is the 'Cartesian plane'. This is the plane in which you commonly graph things. It is the visual representation of a set product constructed from the set of real numbers. The set of real numbers is denoted by the special symbol $\mathbb{R}$ and is defined as

$$\mathbb{R} \equiv \{x \mid -\infty < x < \infty\}.$$

If we form the set product

$$\mathbb{R} \times \mathbb{R} \equiv \{(x_1, x_2) \mid x_1 \in \mathbb{R}, \ x_2 \in \mathbb{R}\},$$

[1] In everyday language, the word 'or' can be used in two senses. One, called the *exclusive* 'or', carries the meaning 'either, but not both'. In mathematics, the word 'or' is used in the *inclusive* sense. The *inclusive* 'or' carries the meaning 'either or both'.

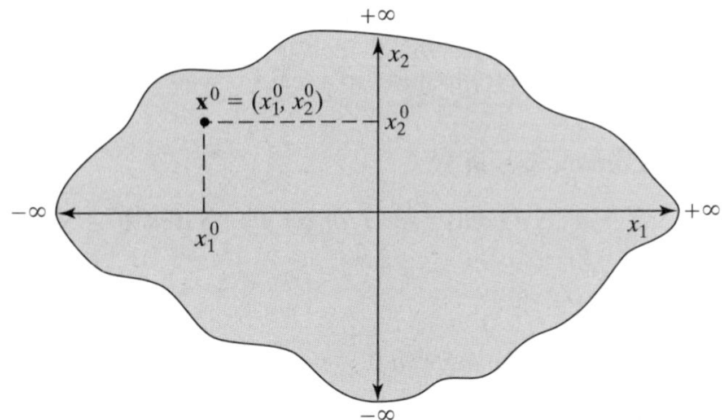

Figure A1. 2. The Cartesian plane, $\mathbb{R}^2$.

then any point in the set (any pair of numbers) can be identified with a point in the Cartesian plane depicted in Fig. A1.2. The set $\mathbb{R} \times \mathbb{R}$ is sometimes called 'two-dimensional Euclidean space' and is commonly denoted $\mathbb{R}^2$.

More generally, any n-tuple, or **vector**, is just an n-dimensional ordered tuple $(x_1, \ldots, x_n)$ and can be thought of as a 'point' in n-dimensional Euclidean space, or 'n-space'. As before, n-space is defined as the set product

$$\mathbb{R}^n \equiv \underbrace{\mathbb{R} \times \mathbb{R} \times \cdots \times \mathbb{R}}_{n \text{ times}} \equiv \{(x_1, \ldots, x_n) \mid x_i \in \mathbb{R},\ i = 1, \ldots, n\}.$$

We usually denote vectors or points in $\mathbb{R}^n$ with boldface type, so that $\mathbf{x} \equiv (x_1, \ldots, x_n)$.

Often, we want to restrict our attention to a subset of $\mathbb{R}^n$, called the 'non-negative orthant' and denoted $\mathbb{R}^n_+$, where

$$\mathbb{R}^n_+ \equiv \{(x_1, \ldots, x_n) \mid x_i \geq 0,\ i = 1, \ldots, n\} \subset \mathbb{R}^n.$$

We use the notation $\mathbf{x} \geq \mathbf{0}$ to indicate vectors in $\mathbb{R}^n_+$, where each component x_i is greater than or equal to zero. We use the notation $\mathbf{x} \gg \mathbf{0}$ to indicate vectors where *every* component of the vector is strictly positive. More generally, for any two vectors $\mathbf{x}$ and $\mathbf{y}$ in $\mathbb{R}^n$, we say that $\mathbf{x} \geq \mathbf{y}$ iff $x_i \geq y_i$, $i = 1, \ldots, n$. We say that $\mathbf{x} \gg \mathbf{y}$ if $x_i > y_i$, $i = 1, \ldots, n$.

A1.2.2 CONVEX SETS

Convex sets are basic building blocks in virtually every area of microeconomic theory. In theoretical work, convexity is most often assumed to guarantee that the analysis is mathematically tractable and that the results are clear-cut and 'well-behaved'. You will see that there is a very simple and intuitive way to think about convex sets. Once you have grasped the idea, you will see just how pervasive convexity is in the theory. Later, you will begin to appreciate the importance of convexity and its role in some fundamental optimisation problems in microeconomics. For now, we begin with a formal definition of a convex set and then try to develop a feel for what we have defined.

DEFINITION A1.1 ***Convex Sets in*** $\mathbb{R}^n$

$S \subset \mathbb{R}^n$ is a convex set if for all $\mathbf{x}^1 \in S$ and $\mathbf{x}^2 \in S$, we have

$$t\mathbf{x}^1 + (1-t)\mathbf{x}^2 \in S$$

for all t in the interval $0 \leq t \leq 1$.

This is not as bad as it seems at first, and you will quickly get used to what it says. Basically, it says that a set is convex if for *any* two points in the set, *all* weighted averages of those two points (where the weights sum to 1) are *also* points in the same set. Let us take the definition piece by piece, then put the pieces together to see what we get.

The kind of weighted average used in the definition is called a **convex combination**. We say that $\mathbf{z}$ is a convex combination of $\mathbf{x}^1$ and $\mathbf{x}^2$ if $\mathbf{z} = t\mathbf{x}^1 + (1-t)\mathbf{x}^2$ for some number t between zero and 1. Because t is between zero and 1, so is $(1-t)$, and the sum of the weights, $t + (1-t)$, will always equal 1. A convex combination $\mathbf{z}$ is thus a point that, in some sense, 'lies between' the two points $\mathbf{x}^1$ and $\mathbf{x}^2$.

To make this clearer, let us take a simple example. Consider the two points $x^1 \in \mathbb{R}$ and $x^2 \in \mathbb{R}$, where $x^1 = 8$ and $x^2 = 2$, represented in Fig. A1.3. The convex combination, $z = tx^1 + (1-t)x^2$, can be multiplied out and rewritten as

$$z = x^2 + t(x^1 - x^2).$$

If we think of the point x^2 as the 'starting point', and the difference $(x^1 - x^2)$ as the 'distance' from x^2 to x^1, then this expression says that z is a point located at the spot x^2 *plus* some proportion t, less than or equal to 1, of the distance between x^2 and x^1. If we suppose that t takes the value zero, then in our example, $z = x^2 = 2$. If t takes the value 1, then $z = x^1 = 8$. The extreme values of zero and 1 thus make the convex combination of any two points coincide with one of those two points. Values of t between zero and 1

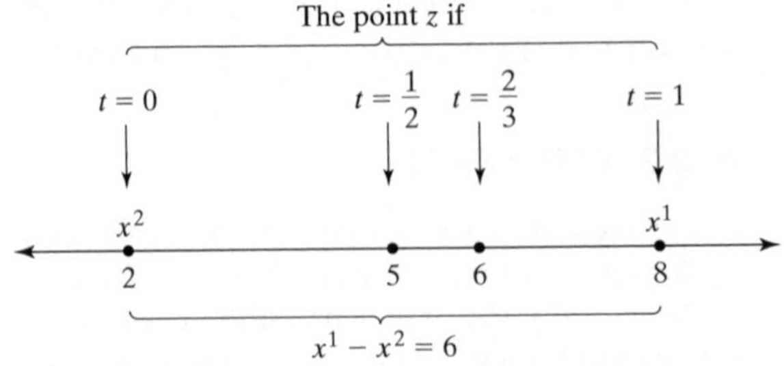

Figure A1.3. Convex combinations in $\mathbb{R}$.

will make the convex combination take some value in between the two points. If $t = 1/2$, then $z = x^2 + (1/2)(x^1 - x^2) = 2 + 3 = 5$, which is the midpoint of the interval between x^1 and x^2. If $t = 2/3$, then $z = x^2 + (2/3)(x^1 - x^2) = 2 + 4 = 6$, which is the point two-thirds of the distance between x^2 and x^1. You can see that as long as we choose a value of t in the interval $0 \leq t \leq 1$, the convex combination will always lie somewhere strictly in between the two points, or it will coincide with one of the points.

The second part of the definition of a convex set refers not just to some convex combinations of two points, but to *all* convex combinations of those points. In our example from the real line, notice that x^1, x^2, and every point in between x^1 and x^2 can be expressed as the convex combination of x^1 and x^2 for some value of t between zero and 1. The set of *all* convex combinations of x^1 and x^2 will therefore be the entire line segment between x^1 and x^2, including those two points.

These basic ideas carry over to sets of points in two dimensions as well. Consider the two vectors in $\mathbb{R}^2$, denoted $\mathbf{x}^1 = (x_1^1, x_2^1)$ and $\mathbf{x}^2 = (x_1^2, x_2^2)$. When we form the convex combination of vectors, we must be careful to observe the rules of scalar multiplication and vector addition. When a vector is multiplied by a scalar, the product is a vector, with *each component* of the vector multiplied by that scalar. When two vectors are added, the sum is a vector, with each component the sum of the corresponding components from the two vectors being added. So the convex combination of $\mathbf{x}^1$ and $\mathbf{x}^2$ will be

$$\begin{aligned}\mathbf{z} &= t\mathbf{x}^1 + (1-t)\mathbf{x}^2 \\ &= \left(tx_1^1, tx_2^1\right) + \left((1-t)x_1^2, (1-t)x_2^2\right) \\ &= \left(tx_1^1 + (1-t)x_1^2, tx_2^1 + (1-t)x_2^2\right).\end{aligned}$$

In Fig. A1.4, $\mathbf{x}^1$ and $\mathbf{x}^2$ are the points with coordinates (x_1^1, x_2^1) and (x_1^2, x_2^2), respectively. Their convex combination $\mathbf{z}$ has horizontal coordinate $tx_1^1 + (1-t)x_1^2 = x_1^2 + t(x_1^1 - x_1^2)$, or x_1^2 plus the proportion t of the distance between the horizontal coordinates of $\mathbf{x}^1$ and $\mathbf{x}^2$. Similarly, the vertical coordinate of $\mathbf{z}$ is $tx_2^1 + (1-t)x_2^2 = x_2^2 + t(x_2^1 - x_2^2)$, or x_2^2 plus the proportion t of the distance between the vertical coordinates of $\mathbf{x}^2$ and $\mathbf{x}^1$. Because each coordinate is the same proportion t of the distance between the respective horizontal and vertical coordinates, the point $\mathbf{z}$ will lie in that same proportion t of the distance between $\mathbf{x}^2$ and $\mathbf{x}^1$ along the chord connecting them. As we vary the proportion t, we will move the coordinates of $\mathbf{z}$ back and forth between x_1^1 and x_1^2 on the horizontal axis, and between x_2^1 and x_2^2 on the vertical axis, always keeping the horizontal and vertical coordinates of $\mathbf{z}$ at the same proportion of the distance between the respective coordinates of $\mathbf{x}^1$ and $\mathbf{x}^2$. As we vary t, then, we will continue to describe vectors that lie at different locations along the chord connecting $\mathbf{x}^1$ and $\mathbf{x}^2$. Just as before, any point along that chord can be described as a convex combination of $\mathbf{x}^1$ and $\mathbf{x}^2$ for some value of t between zero and 1. The set of *all* convex combinations of the vectors $\mathbf{x}^1$ and $\mathbf{x}^2$ is, therefore, precisely the set of all points on the chord connecting $\mathbf{x}^1$ and $\mathbf{x}^2$, including the endpoints.

Now look again at the definition of a convex set. Read it carefully and you will see that we could just as well have said that a set is convex if it contains all convex combinations of every pair of points in the set. We therefore have a very simple and intuitive

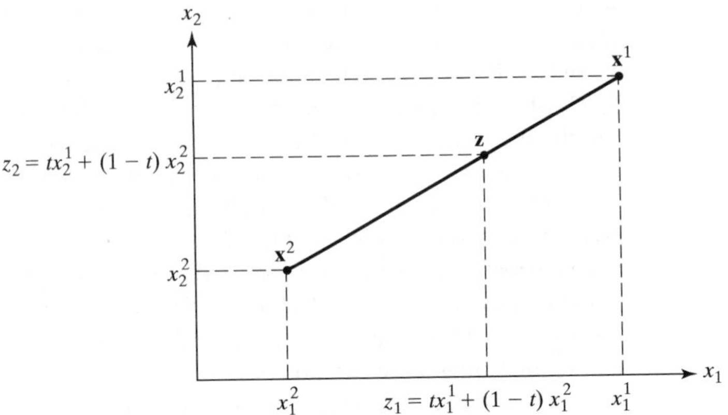

Figure A1.4. Some convex combinations in $\mathbb{R}^2$.

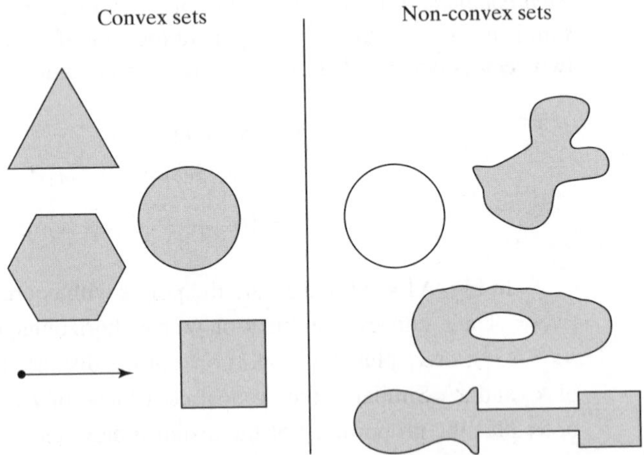

Figure A1.5. Convex and non-convex sets in $\mathbb{R}^2$.

rule defining convex sets: *A set is convex iff we can connect any two points in the set by a straight line that lies entirely within the set.* Examples of convex and non-convex sets are shown in Fig. A1.5. Notice that convex sets are all 'nicely behaved'. They have no holes, no breaks, and no awkward curvatures on their boundaries. They are nice sets.

We will end our discussion of convex sets for now by noting a simple but important property of sets constructed from convex sets.

THEOREM A1.1 ***The Intersection of Convex Sets is Convex***

Let S and T be convex sets in $\mathbb{R}^n$. Then $S \cap T$ is a convex set.

Proof: Let S and T be convex sets. Let $\mathbf{x}^1$ and $\mathbf{x}^2$ be any two points in $S \cap T$. Because $\mathbf{x}^1 \in S \cap T$, $\mathbf{x}^1 \in S$ and $\mathbf{x}^1 \in T$. Because $\mathbf{x}^2 \in S \cap T$, $\mathbf{x}^2 \in S$ and $\mathbf{x}^2 \in T$. Let $\mathbf{z} = t\mathbf{x}^1 + (1-t)\mathbf{x}^2$, for $t \in [0, 1]$, be any convex combination of $\mathbf{x}^1$ and $\mathbf{x}^2$. Because S is a convex set, $\mathbf{z} \in S$. Because T is a convex set, $\mathbf{z} \in T$. Because $\mathbf{z} \in S$ and $\mathbf{z} \in T$, $\mathbf{z} \in S \cap T$. Because every convex combination of any two points in $S \cap T$ is also in $S \cap T$, $S \cap T$ is a convex set. ∎

A1.2.3 RELATIONS AND FUNCTIONS

We have seen that any ordered pair (s, t) associates an element $s \in S$ to an element $t \in T$. The sets S and T need not contain numbers; they can contain anything. Any *collection* of ordered pairs is said to constitute a **binary relation** between the sets S and T.

A binary relation is defined by specifying some meaningful relationship that holds between the elements of the pair. For example, let S be the set of cities {Washington, London, Marseilles, Paris}, and T be the set of countries {United States, England, France, Germany}. The statement 'is the capital of' then defines a relation between these two sets that contains the elements {(Washington, United States), (London, England), (Paris, France)}. As this example shows, a binary relation $\mathcal{R}$ on $S \times T$ is always a subset of $S \times T$. When $s \in S$ bears the specified relationship to $t \in T$, we denote membership in the relation $\mathcal{R}$ in one of two ways: either we write $(s, t) \in \mathcal{R}$ or, more commonly, we simply write $s\mathcal{R}t$.

Many familiar binary relations are contained in the product of one set with itself. For example, let S be the closed unit interval, $S = [0, 1]$. Then the binary relation $\geq$, illustrated in Fig. A1.6, consists of all ordered pairs of numbers in S where the first one in the pair is greater than or equal to the second one. When, as here, a binary relation is a subset of the product of one set S with itself, we say that it is a relation *on* the set S.

We can build in more structure for a binary relation on some set by requiring that it possess certain properties.

DEFINITION A1.2 ***Completeness***

A relation $\mathcal{R}$ on S is complete if, for all elements x and y in S, $x\mathcal{R}y$ or $y\mathcal{R}x$.

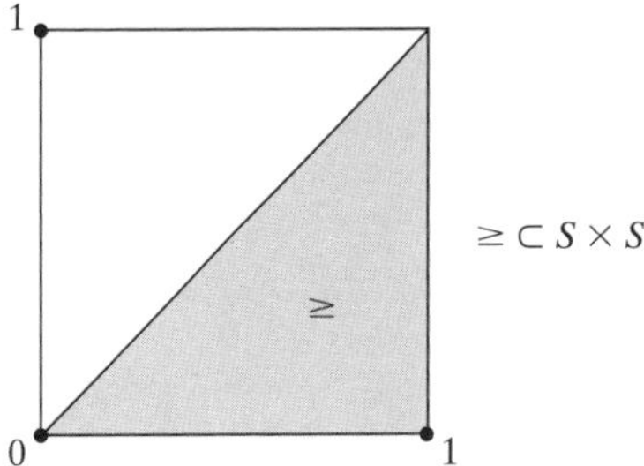

Figure A1.6. The relation $\geq$ on $S = [0, 1]$.

Suppose that $S = \{1, 2, \ldots, 10\}$, and consider the relation defined by the statement, 'is greater than'. This relation is *not* complete because one can easily find some $x \in S$ and some $y \in S$ where it is neither true that $x > y$ nor that $y > x$: for example, one could pick $x = y = 1$, or $x = y = 2$, and so on. The definition of completeness does not require the elements x and y to be distinct, so nothing prevents us from choosing them to be the same. Because no integer can be either less than or greater than itself, the relation 'is greater than' is not complete. However, the relation on S defined by the statement 'is at least as great as' *is* complete: for any two integers, whether distinct or not, one will always be at least as great as the other, as completeness requires.

DEFINITION A1.3 ***Transitivity***

A relation $\mathcal{R}$ on S is transitive if, for any three elements x, y, and z in S, $x\mathcal{R}y$ and $y\mathcal{R}z$ implies $x\mathcal{R}z$.

Both the relations just considered are transitive. If x is greater than y and y is greater than z, then x is certainly greater than z. The same is true for the relation defined by the statement 'is at least as great as'.

A **function** is a very common though very special kind of relation. Specifically, a function is a relation that associates each element of one set with a single, unique element of another set. We say that the function f is a **mapping** from one set D to another set R and write $f \colon D \to R$. We call the set D the **domain** and the set R the **range** of the mapping. If y is the point in the range mapped into by the point x in the domain, we write $y = f(x)$. To denote the entire set of points A in the range that is mapped into by a set of points B in the domain, we write $A = f(B)$. To illustrate, consider Fig. A1.7. Fig. A1.7(a) is *not* a function, because more than one point in the range is assigned to points in the

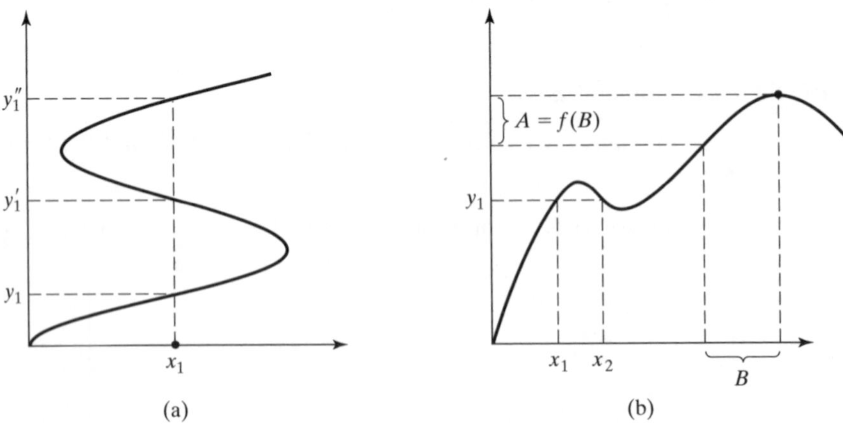

Figure A1.7. Functions and non-functions.

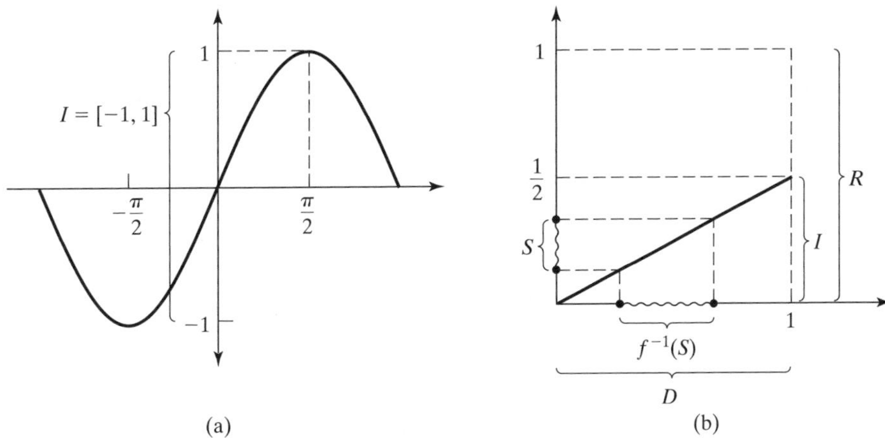

Figure A1.8. Domain, range, and image.

domain, such as x_1. Fig. A1.7(b) does depict a function because every point in the domain is assigned some unique point in the range.

The **image** of f is that set of points in the range into which some point in the domain is mapped, i.e., $I \equiv \{y \mid y = f(x), \text{ for some } x \in D\} \subset R$. The **inverse image** of a set of points $S \subset I$ is defined as $f^{-1}(S) \equiv \{x \mid x \in D, f(x) \in S\}$. The **graph** of the function f is familiar and is the set of ordered pairs $G \equiv \{(x, y) \mid x \in D, y = f(x)\}$. Some of these ideas are illustrated in Fig. A1.8. In Fig. A1.8(a), we have let $R = \mathbb{R}$, $D = \mathbb{R}$, and have graphed the function $y = \sin(x)$. The sine function, however, never takes values greater than 1 or less than -1. Its image is therefore the subset of the range consisting of the interval, $I = [-1, 1]$. In Fig. A1.8(b), we consider the function f: $[0, 1] \to [0, 1]$ given by $y = \frac{1}{2}x$. Here, we have chosen to restrict both the domain and the range to the unit interval. Once again, the image is a subset of the range $I = [0, \frac{1}{2}]$.

There is nothing in the definition of a function that prohibits more than one element in the domain from being mapped into the same element in the range. In Fig. A1.7(b), for example, both x_1 and x_2 are mapped into y_1, yet the mapping satisfies the requirements of a function. If, however, every point in the range is assigned to *at most* a single point in the domain, the function is called **one-to-one**. If the image is equal to the range – if every point in the range is mapped into by some point in the domain – the function is said to be **onto**. If a function is one-to-one and onto, then an **inverse function** f^{-1}: $R \to D$ exists that is also one-to-one and onto.

A1.3 A LITTLE TOPOLOGY

Topology is the study of fundamental properties of sets and mappings. In this section, we introduce a few basic topological ideas and use them to establish some important results about sets, and about continuous functions from one set to another. Although many of the

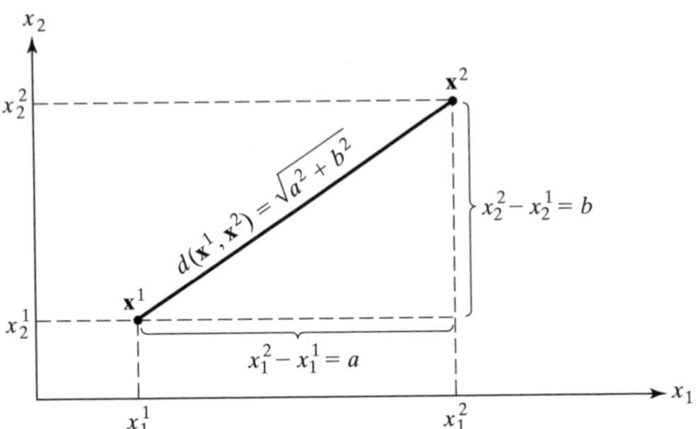

Figure A1.9. Distance in the plane.

ideas discussed here may be generalised to arbitrary types of sets, we confine ourselves to considering sets in $\mathbb{R}^n$, i.e., sets that contain real numbers or vectors of real numbers.

We begin by loosely describing the notion of a metric and a metric space. A **metric** is simply a measure of distance. A **metric space** is just a set with a notion of distance defined among the points within the set. The real line, $\mathbb{R}$, together with an appropriate function measuring distance, is a metric space. One such distance function, or metric, is just the absolute-value function. For any two points x^1 and x^2 in $\mathbb{R}$, the distance between them, denoted $d(x^1, x^2)$, is given by

$$d(x^1, x^2) = | x^1 - x^2 | .$$

The Cartesian plane, $\mathbb{R}^2$, is also a metric space. A natural notion of distance defined on the plane is inherited from Pythagoras. Choose any two points $\mathbf{x}^1 = (x_1^1, x_2^1)$ and $\mathbf{x}^2 = (x_1^2, x_2^2)$ in $\mathbb{R}^2$, as in Fig. A1.9. Construct the right triangle connecting the two points. If the horizontal leg is of length a and the vertical leg is length b, Pythagoras tells us the length of the hypotenuse – the distance between the points $\mathbf{x}^1$ and $\mathbf{x}^2$ – is equal to $\sqrt{a^2 + b^2}$. Now a^2 is just the square of the difference between the x_1 components of the two points, and b^2 is the square of the difference in their x_2 components. The length of the hypotenuse, or $d(\mathbf{x}^1, \mathbf{x}^2)$, is therefore

$$d(\mathbf{x}^1, \mathbf{x}^2) = \sqrt{a^2 + b^2} = \sqrt{\left(x_1^2 - x_1^1\right)^2 + \left(x_2^2 - x_2^1\right)^2}.$$

Whether it is obvious at first glance, both of these distance formulae can in fact be viewed as special cases of the same formula. For x^1 and x^2 in $\mathbb{R}$, the absolute value $| x^1 - x^2 |$ can be expressed as the square root of the product of $(x^1 - x^2)$ with itself. So we could write $d(x^1, x^2) = | x^1 - x^2 | = \sqrt{(x^1 - x^2)(x^1 - x^2)}$. For $\mathbf{x}^1$ and $\mathbf{x}^2$ in $\mathbb{R}^2$, if we can first apply the rules of *vector* subtraction to obtain the difference $(x^1 - x^2) =$

$(x_1^1 - x_1^2, x_2^1 - x_2^2)$, then apply the rules of *vector* (dot) multiplication to multiply this difference with itself, we obtain

$$\begin{aligned}(\mathbf{x}^1 - \mathbf{x}^2) \cdot (\mathbf{x}^1 - \mathbf{x}^2) &= \left(x_1^1 - x_1^2, x_2^1 - x_2^2\right) \cdot \left(x_1^1 - x_1^2, x_2^1 - x_2^2\right) \\ &= \left(x_1^1 - x_1^2\right)^2 + \left(x_2^1 - x_2^2\right)^2 \\ &= (-1)^2\left(x_1^2 - x_1^1\right)^2 + (-1)^2\left(x_2^2 - x_2^1\right)^2 \\ &= \left(x_1^2 - x_1^1\right)^2 + \left(x_2^2 - x_2^1\right)^2.\end{aligned}$$

Notice that this vector product produces a *scalar* that is precisely the same as the scalar beneath the radical in our earlier Pythagorean formula. Pythagoras tells us, therefore, that we can again measure the distance between two points as the square root of a product of the difference between the two points, this time the *vector* product of the *vector* difference of two points in the *plane*. Analogous to the case of points on the line, we can therefore write $d(\mathbf{x}^1, \mathbf{x}^2) = \sqrt{(\mathbf{x}^1 - \mathbf{x}^2) \cdot (\mathbf{x}^1 - \mathbf{x}^2)}$ for $\mathbf{x}^1$ and $\mathbf{x}^2$ in $\mathbb{R}^2$.

The distance between any two points in $\mathbb{R}^n$ is just a direct extension of these ideas. In general, for $\mathbf{x}^1$ and $\mathbf{x}^2$ in $\mathbb{R}^n$,

$$\begin{aligned}d(\mathbf{x}^1, \mathbf{x}^2) &\equiv \sqrt{(\mathbf{x}^1 - \mathbf{x}^2) \cdot (\mathbf{x}^1 - \mathbf{x}^2)} \\ &\equiv \sqrt{\left(x_1^1 - x_1^2\right)^2 + \left(x_2^1 - x_2^2\right)^2 + \cdots + \left(x_n^1 - x_n^2\right)^2},\end{aligned}$$

which we summarise with the notation $d(\mathbf{x}^1, \mathbf{x}^2) \equiv \parallel \mathbf{x}^1 - \mathbf{x}^2 \parallel$. We call this formula the **Euclidean metric** or **Euclidean norm**. Naturally enough, the metric spaces $\mathbb{R}^n$ that use this as the measure of distance are called **Euclidean spaces**.

Once we have a metric, we can make precise what it means for points to be 'near' each other. If we take any point $\mathbf{x}^0 \in \mathbb{R}^n$, we define the set of points that are less than a distance $\varepsilon > 0$ from $\mathbf{x}^0$ as the *open ε-ball with centre* $\mathbf{x}^0$. The set of points that are a distance of ε or less from $\mathbf{x}^0$ is called the *closed ε-ball with centre* $\mathbf{x}^0$. Notice carefully that any ε-ball is a *set* of points. Formally:

DEFINITION A1.4 *Open and Closed ε-Balls*

1. *The open ε-ball with centre $\mathbf{x}^0$ and radius $\varepsilon > 0$ (a real number) is the subset of points in $\mathbb{R}^n$:*

$$B_\varepsilon(\mathbf{x}^0) \equiv \{\mathbf{x} \in \mathbb{R}^n \mid \underbrace{d(\mathbf{x}^0, \mathbf{x}) < \varepsilon}_{\textit{strictly less than}} \}$$

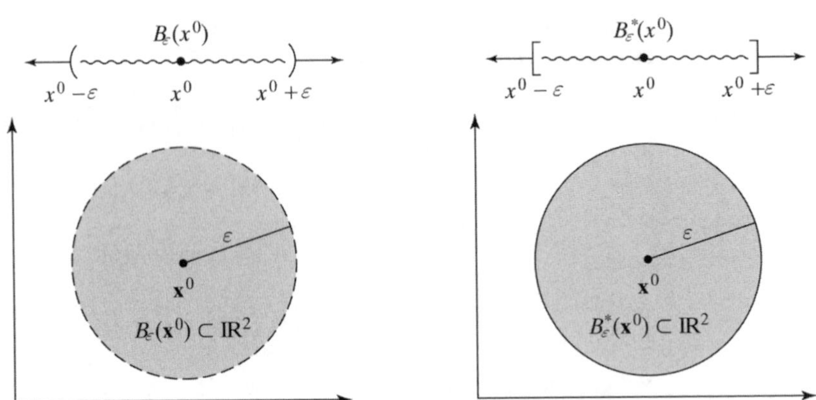

Figure A1.10. Balls in $\mathbb{R}$ and $\mathbb{R}^2$.

2. *The closed ε-ball with centre $\mathbf{x}^0$ and radius $\varepsilon > 0$ is the subset of points in $\mathbb{R}^n$:*

$$B^*_\varepsilon(\mathbf{x}^0) \equiv \{\mathbf{x} \in \mathbb{R}^n \mid \underbrace{d(\mathbf{x}^0, \mathbf{x}) \leq \varepsilon}_{\textit{less than or equal to}} \}$$

Some examples of open and closed balls are provided in Fig. A1.10. On the real line, the open ball with centre x^0 and radius ε is just the open interval $B_\varepsilon(x^0) = (x^0 - \varepsilon, x^0 + \varepsilon)$. The corresponding closed ball is the closed interval $B^*_\varepsilon(x^0) = [x^0 - \varepsilon, x^0 + \varepsilon]$. In $\mathbb{R}^2$, an open ball $B_\varepsilon(\mathbf{x}^0)$ is a disc consisting of the set of points inside, or on the interior of, the circle of radius ε around the point $\mathbf{x}^0$. The corresponding closed ball in the plane, $B^*_\varepsilon(\mathbf{x}^0)$, is the set of points inside and on the edge of the circle. In three-space, the open ball $B_\varepsilon(\mathbf{x}^0)$ is the set of points inside the sphere of radius ε. The closed ball $B^*_\varepsilon(\mathbf{x}^0)$ is the set of points inside and on the surface of the sphere. In $\mathbb{R}^4$ and higher dimensions, geometric intuition is rather difficult, but the idea remains the same.

We have a pretty good intuitive feel for what the difference is between open and closed intervals on the real line. The concept of the ε-ball allows us to formalise that difference and make the distinction applicable to sets in higher-dimensional spaces. We use the ε-ball to define open and closed *sets* and to establish some important results about them.

DEFINITION A1.5 ***Open Sets in*** $\mathbb{R}^n$

$S \subset \mathbb{R}^n$ is an open set if, for all $\mathbf{x} \in S$, there exists some $\varepsilon > 0$ such that $B_\varepsilon(\mathbf{x}) \subset S$.

The definition says that a set is open if around any point in it we can draw *some* open ball – no matter how small its radius may have to be – so that all the points in that ball will lie entirely in the set. This way of formalising things captures the essential aspects of the familiar open interval on the real line. Because an open interval (a, b) includes every point between a and b, but not a and b themselves, we can choose any point x in that interval, no matter how close to a or b, and find some small but positive ε such that the open ball (here the open interval) $B_\varepsilon(x) = (x - \varepsilon, x + \varepsilon)$ is contained entirely within the interval (a, b) itself. Thus, every open interval on the real line is an open set. Likewise, open discs and open spheres are open sets by this definition. More generally, any open ball is an open set.

To see this, let S be the open ball with centre $\mathbf{x}^0$ and radius ε in Fig. A1.11. If we take any other point $\mathbf{x}$ in S, it will always be possible to draw an open ball around $\mathbf{x}$ whose points all lie within S by choosing the radius of the ball around $\mathbf{x}$ carefully enough. Because $\mathbf{x}$ is in S, we know that $d(\mathbf{x}^0, \mathbf{x}) < \varepsilon$. Thus, $\varepsilon - d(\mathbf{x}^0, \mathbf{x}) > 0$. If we let $\varepsilon' = \varepsilon - d(\mathbf{x}^0, \mathbf{x}) > 0$, then it will always be the case that $B_{\varepsilon'}(\mathbf{x}) \subset S$ no matter how close we take $\mathbf{x}$ to the edge of the circle, as required. The following theorem is basic.

THEOREM A1.2 ***On Open Sets in*** $\mathbb{R}^n$

1. *The empty set, $\emptyset$, is an open set.*
2. *The entire space, $\mathbb{R}^n$, is an open set.*
3. *The union of open sets is an open set.*
4. *The intersection of any finite number of open sets is an open set.*

Proof: The second of these hardly requires any proof. Briefly, if we take any point in $\mathbb{R}^n$ and *any* $\varepsilon > 0$, then the set $B_\varepsilon(\mathbf{x})$ will of course consist entirely of points in $\mathbb{R}^n$ by the definition of the open ball. Thus, $B_\varepsilon(\mathbf{x}) \subset \mathbb{R}^n$, so $\mathbb{R}^n$ is open. Likewise, the first of these is

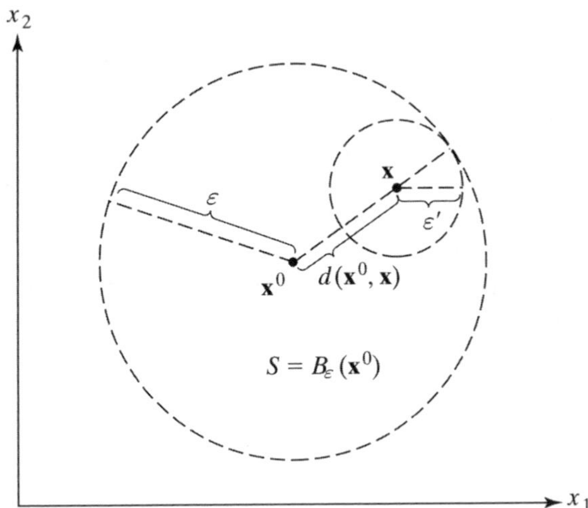

Figure A1.11. An open ball is an open set.

(vacuously) true. If there are *no* points in $\emptyset$, then it will of course be true that 'for every point in $\emptyset$, we can find an $\varepsilon, \ldots$' satisfying the definition of an open set.

The last two, however, are worth proving. We will prove (3) here, leaving the proof of (4) as an exercise.

Let S_i be an open set for all $i \in I$, where I is some index set. We must show that $\cup_{i \in I} S_i$ is an open set. So let $\mathbf{x} \in \cup_{i \in I} S_i$. Then $\mathbf{x} \in S_{i'}$ for some $i' \in I$. Because $S_{i'}$ is open, $B_\varepsilon(\mathbf{x}) \subset S_{i'}$ for some $\varepsilon > 0$. Consequently, $B_\varepsilon(\mathbf{x}) \subset \cup_{i \in I} S_i$, which shows that $\cup_{i \in I} S_i$ is open. ∎

Open sets have an interesting and useful property. They can always be described, exactly, as a collection of *different* open sets. A moment's reflection (perhaps more) should convince you of this. Suppose we start with some open set. Since our set is open, we can take each point in the set and 'surround' it with an open ball, all of whose points are contained within our set. Each of these open balls is itself an open set, as we illustrated in Fig. A1.11. Think now of the *union* of all these open balls. By Theorem A1.2, this union of open balls must be some open set. Can you think of a point in the set we started with that is not in this union of open balls? Can you think of a point that is in this union of open balls but that is not in our original set? If you answered 'no' to both of these questions, you have convinced yourself that the two sets are the same! This property of open sets is important enough to warrant the status of a theorem.

THEOREM A1.3 ***Every Open Set is a Collection of Open Balls***

Let S be an open set. For every $\mathbf{x} \in S$, choose some $\varepsilon_{\mathbf{x}} > 0$ such that $B_{\varepsilon_{\mathbf{x}}}(\mathbf{x}) \subset S$. Then,

$$S = \bigcup_{\mathbf{x} \in S} B_{\varepsilon_{\mathbf{x}}}(\mathbf{x}).$$

Proof: We have already looked at the ideas involved, so we can prove this rather quickly. Let $S \subset \mathbb{R}^n$ be open. Then, for each $\mathbf{x} \in S$, there exists some $\varepsilon_{\mathbf{x}} > 0$ such that $B_{\varepsilon_{\mathbf{x}}}(\mathbf{x}) \subset S$ because S is open. We have to show that $\mathbf{x} \in S$ implies that $\mathbf{x} \in \cup_{\mathbf{x} \in S} B_{\varepsilon_{\mathbf{x}}}(\mathbf{x})$, and we must show that $\mathbf{x} \in \cup_{\mathbf{x} \in S} B_{\varepsilon_{\mathbf{x}}}(\mathbf{x})$ implies that $\mathbf{x} \in S$.

If $\mathbf{x} \in S$, then $\mathbf{x} \in B_{\varepsilon_{\mathbf{x}}}(\mathbf{x})$ by the definition of the open ball around $\mathbf{x}$. But then $\mathbf{x}$ is in any union that includes this open ball, so in particular, we must have $\mathbf{x} \in \cup_{\mathbf{x} \in S} B_{\varepsilon_{\mathbf{x}}}(\mathbf{x})$, completing the first part of the proof.

Now, if $\mathbf{x} \in \cup_{\mathbf{x} \in S} B_{\varepsilon_{\mathbf{x}}}(\mathbf{x})$, then $\mathbf{x} \in B_{\varepsilon_{\mathbf{s}}}(\mathbf{s})$, for some $\mathbf{s} \in S$. But we chose every ε-ball so that it was entirely contained in S. Therefore, if $\mathbf{x} \in B_{\varepsilon_{\mathbf{s}}}(\mathbf{s}) \subset S$, we must have $\mathbf{x} \in S$, completing the second part of the proof.

∎

We use open sets to define closed sets.

DEFINITION A1.6 ***Closed Sets in $\mathbb{R}^n$***

S is a closed set if its complement, S^c, is an open set.

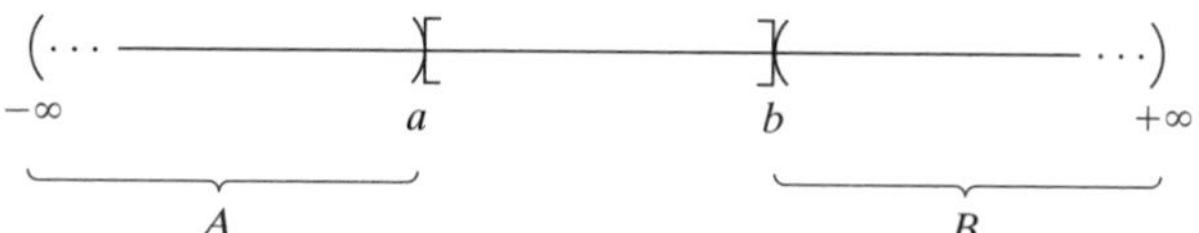

Figure A1. 12. A closed interval is a closed set.

It is worth taking a minute to see that this definition 'works', giving results that correspond to our intuition. To see that it does, consider the simplest case. We know that a closed interval in the real line is (or should be) a closed set. Does a closed interval satisfy the definition of a closed set? Consider the interval $[a, b] = \{x \mid x \in \mathbb{R}, a \leq x \leq b\}$ in Fig. A1.12. Now consider the two sets $A = \{x \mid x \in \mathbb{R},\ -\infty < x < a\}$ and $B = \{x \mid x \in \mathbb{R},\ b < x < +\infty\}$. A and B are the open intervals on either side of $[a, b]$. Because open intervals are open sets, A and B are open sets. By Theorem A1.2, the union of open sets is an open set, so $A \cup B = \{x \mid x \in \mathbb{R},\ -\infty < x < a \text{ or } b < x < +\infty\}$ is an open set. But $A \cup B$ is the *complement* of the set $[a, b]$ in $\mathbb{R}$. Because $[a, b]^c$ is an open set, $[a, b]$ is a closed set by the definition of closed sets, as we wanted to show. In higher-dimensional spaces, any closed ball is a closed set. In $\mathbb{R}^2$, a closed disk is a closed set, and in $\mathbb{R}^3$ a closed sphere is a closed set.

Loosely speaking, a set in $\mathbb{R}^n$ is open if it does not contain any of the points on its boundary, and is closed if it contains all of the points on its boundary. More precisely, a point $\mathbf{x}$ is called a **boundary point** of a set S in $\mathbb{R}^n$ if every ε-ball centred at $\mathbf{x}$ contains points in S as well as points not in S. The set of all boundary points of a set S is denoted ∂S. A set is open if it contains *none* of its boundary points; it is closed if it contains *all* of its boundary points. Pushing things a bit further, we can define what it means to be an interior point of a set. A point $\mathbf{x} \in S$ is called an **interior point** of S if there is *some* ε-ball centred at $\mathbf{x}$ that is entirely contained within S, or if there exist some $\varepsilon > 0$ such that $B_\varepsilon(\mathbf{x}) \subset S$. The set of all interior points of a set S is called its **interior** and is denoted *int* S. Looking at things this way, we can see that a set is open if it contains nothing but interior points, or if $S = int\ S$. By contrast, a set S is closed if it contains all its interior points *plus* all its boundary points, or if $S = int\ S \cup \partial S$. Fig. A1.13 illustrates some of these ideas for sets in $\mathbb{R}^2$. We will complete our discussion of open and closed sets by noting the corresponding properties of closed sets to those we noted for open sets in Theorem A1.2.

THEOREM A1.4 ***On Closed Sets in*** $\mathbb{R}^n$

1. *The empty set, ∅, is a closed set.*
2. *The entire space, $\mathbb{R}^n$, is a closed set.*
3. *The union of any finite collection of closed sets is a closed set.*
4. *The intersection of closed sets is a closed set.*

Proof: The empty set and the whole of $\mathbb{R}^n$ are the only two sets that are both open and closed in $\mathbb{R}^n$. We have seen that they are open in Theorem A1.2. To see that they are closed, notice that each is the complement of the other in $\mathbb{R}^n$. Because $\emptyset = \{\mathbb{R}^n\}^c$, and $\mathbb{R}^n$

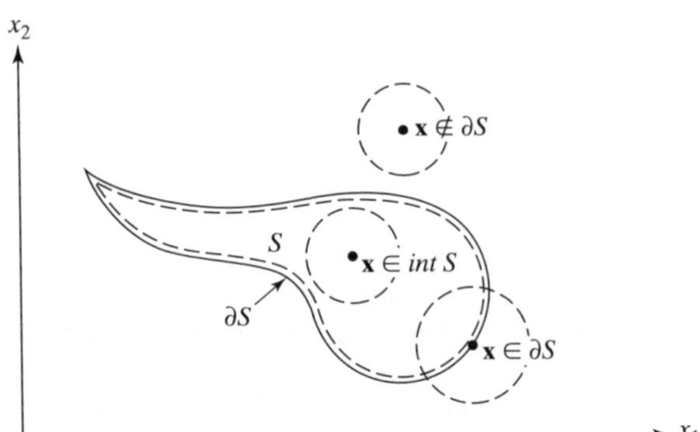

Figure A1.13. $S \cap \partial S = \emptyset$, and S is open. $S \cup \partial S$ is closed.

is open, $\emptyset$ must be closed by Definition A1.6. Similarly, because $\mathbb{R}^n = \emptyset^c$, and $\emptyset$ is open, $\mathbb{R}^n$ must be closed.

We again show how (3) may be proved, leaving the proof of (4) as an exercise. Let S_i be closed sets in $\mathbb{R}^n$, for all $i \in I$, where I is some finite index set. We want to show that $\cup_{i \in I} S_i$ is a closed set. Because S_i is closed, its complement S_i^c is an open set by Definition A1.6. By Theorem A1.2, the intersection $\cap_{i \in I} S_i^c$ is also open because the intersection of finitely many open sets is open. De Morgan's Law (Exercise A1.4) tells us that the complement of the intersection of a collection of sets is equal to the union of the complements of the sets in that collection, so that $(\cap_{i \in I} S_i^c)^c = \cup_{i \in I} S_i$. Because $\cap_{i \in I} S_i^c$ is open, its complement, $\cup_{i \in I} S_i$, is closed by the definition of closed sets. ∎

Another important concept is that of a *bounded set*. Very loosely, a set is bounded if it can be 'enclosed' in a ball. The following definition makes things more precise.

DEFINITION A1.7 ***Bounded Sets***

A set S in $\mathbb{R}^n$ is called bounded if it is entirely contained within some ε-ball (either open or closed). That is, S is bounded if there exists some $\varepsilon > 0$ such that $S \subset B_\varepsilon(\mathbf{x})$ for some $\mathbf{x} \in \mathbb{R}^n$.

By this definition, a set is bounded if we can always draw some ε-ball entirely around it. The definition becomes more intuitive if we confine ourselves to ε-balls centred at the *origin*, $\mathbf{0} \in \mathbb{R}^n$. From this perspective, S is bounded if there exists some finite distance ε such that every point in S is no farther from the origin than ε.

The open ball $B_{\varepsilon'}(\mathbf{x}^0)$ in Fig. A1.14 is a bounded set because it can be entirely contained within the ball centred at $\mathbf{x}^0$ but with radius $\varepsilon = \varepsilon' + 1$. Alternatively, we could say that $B_{\varepsilon'}(\mathbf{x}^0)$ is bounded because none of its points is farther than a distance ε' from the origin. Notice also that every open interval on the real line $(a, b) \subset \mathbb{R}$ is a bounded

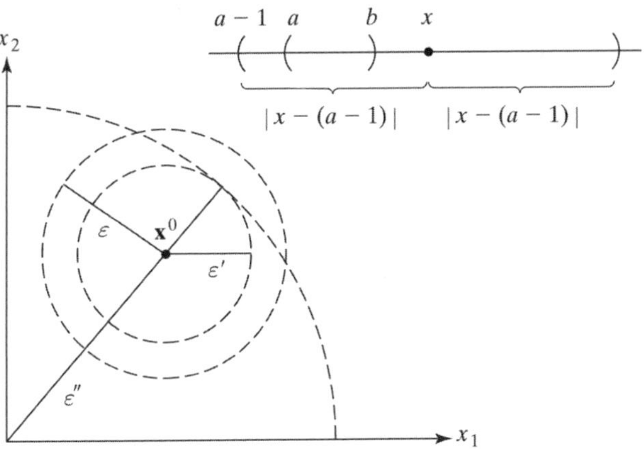

Figure A1. 14. Bounded sets in $\mathbb{R}$ and $\mathbb{R}^2$.

Figure A1. 15. Upper and lower bounds in subsets of real numbers.

set. Again, in Fig. A1.14, we can entirely contain the open interval (a, b) within the ball centred at $x \in \mathbb{R}$ with radius (for example) $\varepsilon = | x - (a-1) |$.

There is some particular terminology that applies to bounded sets from the real line. Let $S \subset \mathbb{R}$ be any non-empty set of real numbers. Any real number l (whether l is in S or not) for which $l \leq x$ for all $x \in S$ is called a **lower bound** for the set of numbers S. For example, if $S = \{4, 6, 8\}$, the number 1 is a lower bound for S, as is the number 4. Likewise, any real number u (whether u is in S or not) for which $x \leq u$ for all $x \in S$ is called an **upper bound** for S. In our previous example, $27 \notin S$ is an upper bound for S, as is the number $8 \in S$. A set of numbers $S \subset \mathbb{R}$ is **bounded from below** if it has a lower bound, and is **bounded from above** if it has an upper bound. The interval $(-\infty, 4)$ is bounded from above but is not bounded from below. Any set of numbers that is both bounded from above and bounded from below is of course bounded by Definition A1.7. (Make sure you see why.)

We have seen that any subset S of real numbers will generally have many lower bounds and many upper bounds. The largest number among those lower bounds is called the **greatest lower bound *(g.l.b.)*** of S. The smallest number among the upper bounds is called the **least upper bound *(l.u.b.)*** of S. The basic axioms of the real number system can be used to show that there will always exist a *g.l.b.* and a *l.u.b.* for any bounded subset of $\mathbb{R}$.

Consider the open and closed intervals (a, b) and $[a, b]$ depicted in Fig. A1.15. It is intuitively obvious from the figure, and easy to prove in general, that any closed subset in

$\mathbb{R}$ will contain its *g.l.b.* and its *l.u.b.* By contrast, any open subset in $\mathbb{R}$ will *not* contain its *g.l.b.* or its *l.u.b.* In Fig. A1.15(a), a is the *g.l.b.* and b is the *l.u.b.* of the open interval (a, b), and neither is contained within that interval. In Fig. A1.15(b), a is the *g.l.b.* and b is the *l.u.b.* of the closed interval $[a, b]$, and both are contained within that interval. This result is worth recording for future reference.

THEOREM A1.5 ***Upper and Lower Bounds in Subsets of Real Numbers***

1. *Let S be a bounded open set in $\mathbb{R}$ and let a be the g.l.b. of S and b be the l.u.b. of S. Then $a \notin S$ and $b \notin S$.*
2. *Let S be a bounded closed set in $\mathbb{R}$ and let a be the g.l.b. of S and b be the l.u.b. of S. Then $a \in S$ and $b \in S$.*

Proof: We will dwell here only long enough to indicate the way one might prove this theorem. We will prove it for the case of the *g.l.b.* in both instances, leaving the parts on the *l.u.b.* for exercises.

Let $S \subset \mathbb{R}$ be open, and let a be the *g.l.b.* of S. The theorem asserts that $a \notin S$. We will suppose that $a \in S$ and derive a contradiction.

Let $a \in S$. Because $a \in S$ and S is open, there exists some $\varepsilon > 0$ such that the open ball $B_\varepsilon(a) \subset S$, because this is true for all points in an open set. In particular, the single point $a - \frac{1}{2}\varepsilon \in S$. But because $a - \frac{1}{2}\varepsilon < a$ and $a - \frac{1}{2}\varepsilon \in S$, a cannot be a lower bound for S. Because it is not a lower bound, it cannot be a greatest lower bound because we have found at least one point in S that is less than a. By assuming the *g.l.b.* a is in S, we have derived a contradiction. Thus, we must conclude that $a \notin S$, as was to be shown.

To prove the theorem for the case of closed sets, let $S \subset \mathbb{R}$ be closed and bounded, and let a be the *g.l.b.* of S. Then, by definition of any lower bound, $a \leq x$ for all $x \in S$. If $a = x$ for some $x \in S$, then $a \in S$ and our job is done. Suppose, therefore, that a is *strictly less* than every point in S.

If $a < x$ for all $x \in S$, then $a \notin S$, so $a \in S^c$. Because S is a closed set, its complement is an open set. If $a \in S^c$ and S^c is open, there exists some $\varepsilon > 0$ such that all points in the open ball $B_\varepsilon(a) = (a - \varepsilon, a + \varepsilon)$ are contained in S^c by the definition of open sets. If $a < x$ for all $x \in S$ *and* $B_\varepsilon(a) \subset S^c$, then *every* point in the interval $(a - \varepsilon, a + \varepsilon)$ must be strictly less than every point in S, too. [If this were not the case, we would have $x \leq a - \varepsilon < a$ for some $x \in S$, contradicting the claim that a is a lower bound for S, or we would have $x \in B_\varepsilon(a) \subset S^c$, contradicting $x \in S$.] In particular, the point $a + \frac{1}{2}\varepsilon \in (a - \varepsilon, a + \varepsilon)$ and $a + \frac{1}{2}\varepsilon < x$ for all $x \in S$. But then $a + \frac{1}{2}\varepsilon$ is a lower bound for S and $a + \frac{1}{2}\varepsilon > a$, so a is not the *greatest* lower bound of S, contradicting our original assumption. We must conclude, therefore, that $a \in S$. ∎

We have discussed closed sets and bounded sets. Subsets of $\mathbb{R}^n$ that are both closed *and* bounded are called **compact sets**, and these are very common in economic applications. We will note the following for future reference.[2]

[2]Compactness is actually a topological property all its own. However, the Heine-Borel theorem shows that for sets in $\mathbb{R}^n$ that property is *equivalent* to being closed and bounded.

DEFINITION A1.8 ***(Heine-Borel) Compact Sets***

A set S in $\mathbb{R}^n$ is called compact if it is closed and bounded.

Any open interval in $\mathbb{R}$ is *not* a compact set. It may be bounded, as we have seen, but it is not closed. Similarly, an open ball in $\mathbb{R}^n$ is not compact. However, every closed and bounded interval in $\mathbb{R}$ is compact, as is every closed ball with finite radius in $\mathbb{R}^n$. All of $\mathbb{R}^n$ is not compact because, although it may be closed, it is not bounded.

A1.3.1 CONTINUITY

The last topological concept we will consider is continuity. In most economic applications, we will either want to *assume* that the functions we are dealing with are continuous functions or we will want to *discover* whether they are continuous when we are unwilling simply to assume it. In either instance, it is best to have a good understanding of what it means for a function to be continuous and what the properties of continuous functions are.

Intuitively, we know what a continuous function is. The function in Fig. A1.16(a) is continuous, whereas the function in Fig. A1.16(b) is not. Basically, a function is continuous if a 'small movement' in the domain does not cause a 'big jump' in the range. We can, however, get a bit more precise than that. For simple functions like those in Fig. A1.16, the following definition of continuity should be familiar from your single-variable calculus course.

A function $f: \mathbb{R} \to \mathbb{R}$ is *continuous at a point* x^0 if, for all $\varepsilon > 0$, there exists a $\delta > 0$ such that $d(x, x^0) < \delta$ implies that $d(f(x), f(x^0)) < \varepsilon$. A function is called a *continuous function* if it is continuous at every point in its domain.

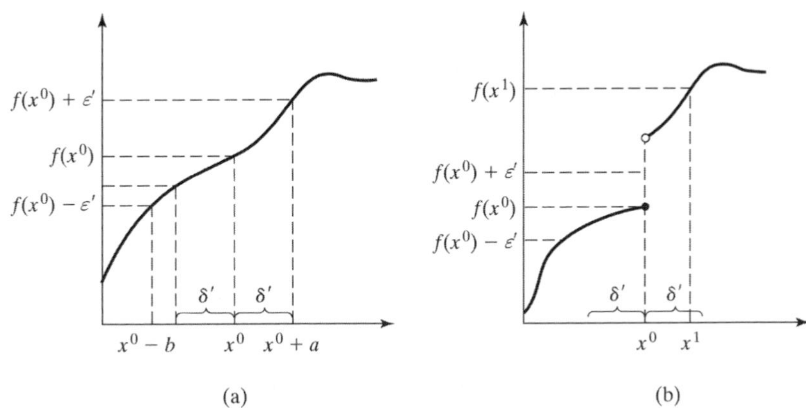

Figure A1.16. Continuity and discontinuity.

Let us take a moment to see that this definition gives results that correspond to our intuition about functions such as those in Fig. A1.16. Consider Fig. A1.16(b) first and we shall see why it fails to be continuous at x^0 according to the earlier definition. The definition requires that for *any* $\varepsilon > 0$, we be able to find *some* $\delta > 0$ such that whenever a point x lies within a distance δ of x^0, its image $f(x)$ will lie within a distance ε of $f(x^0)$. Suppose that we pick $\varepsilon' > 0$. A moment's reflection will convince you that there is *no* $\delta > 0$ satisfying this condition. To see this, notice that within any positive δ distance from x^0, such as δ', there will be points to the right of x^0, such as x^1. Every point like x^1 is mapped by f into points like $f(x^1)$ on the upper segment of the curve, well beyond a distance ε' from the image of $x^0, f(x^0)$. Because we have found at least one $x^0 \in \mathbb{R}$ and $\varepsilon > 0$ such that no $\delta > 0$ satisfying the condition exists, the function fails to be continuous under the definition given.

On the other hand, it is clear that the function in Fig. A1.16(a) *does* satisfy the definition. To convince yourself that it does, consider this: suppose we pick some $x^0 \in \mathbb{R}$ and some $\varepsilon > 0$, such as ε'. The points $f(x^0) + \varepsilon'$ and $f(x^0) - \varepsilon'$ are mapped into by points $x^0 + a$ and $x^0 - b$, respectively. Now, if for this $\varepsilon' > 0$, we choose δ as the smaller of $a > 0$ and $b > 0$, which in this case is a, we can be sure that the image of every point within a distance $\delta' = a$ on either side of x^0 is mapped into a point no farther than a distance ε' of $f(x^0)$! Thus, f satisfies the definition of continuity at the point x^0.

The definition of continuity we have been considering is fine for characterising the simple functions we have just been examining. It captures in a precise logical way how our intuition tells us a continuous function should behave. If we look at that definition closely, however, we will see that we can express exactly the same ideas more compactly and in a language that makes those ideas more easily applied to situations involving a much broader class of functions than just the very simple ones.

The simple definition of continuity tells us essentially that a function is continuous at a point x^0 in the domain if for all $\varepsilon > 0$, there exists a $\delta > 0$ such that any point less than a distance δ away from x^0 (therefore *every* point less than a distance δ away from x^0) is mapped by f into some point in the range that is less than a distance ε away from $f(x^0)$. Now, we know how to characterise the entire set of points a distance less than δ from x^0 in the domain. That is precisely the open ball centred at x^0 with radius δ, $B_\delta(x^0)$. In set notation, we denote the set of points in the range mapped into by the points in $B_\delta(x^0)$ as $f(B_\delta(x^0))$. Similarly, if $f(x^0)$ is the image of the point x^0, we can denote the set of points in the *range* that lie a distance less than ε away from $f(x^0)$ by the open ball centred at $f(x^0)$ with radius ε, $B_\varepsilon(f(x^0))$. To say that every point in $B_\delta(x^0)$ is mapped by f into some point no farther than ε from $f(x^0)$ is thus equivalent to saying that every point in $f(B_\delta(x^0))$ is in the set $B_\varepsilon(f(x^0))$, or that $f(B_\delta(x^0)) \subset B_\varepsilon(f(x^0))$. Fig. A1.17, reproducing Fig. A1.16(a), illustrates how these sets correspond to the more familiar terminology.

Fig. A1.17 is useful, but we need to build on the intuition behind it and to generalise these ideas about continuity in two directions. First, we want a definition of continuity that applies to functions from domains in $\mathbb{R}^m$, not merely in $\mathbb{R}$. Second, we need to account for functions over domains that are subsets of $\mathbb{R}^m$, rather than the whole of the space.[3]

[3]For example, $f(x) = \sqrt{x}$ has domain equal to $\mathbb{R}_+ \subset \mathbb{R}$.

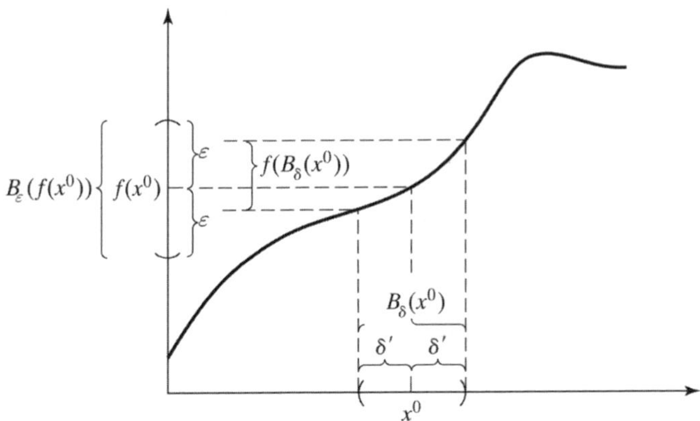

Figure A1. 17. Cauchy continuity.

Before, we implicitly assumed that the domain of f was *all* of $\mathbb{R}$. When that is the case, we are assured that for any $x^0 \in \mathbb{R}$ and any $\delta > 0$, the ball $B_\delta(\mathbf{x}^0)$ is contained entirely within the domain of f so that $f(B_\delta(\mathbf{x}^0))$ is well defined. However, when the domain D of some function f is only a subset of $\mathbb{R}^m$, we need not concern ourselves with all points in $\mathbb{R}^m$ within distance δ of $\mathbf{x}^0$, but only those in D within distance δ of $\mathbf{x}^0$, namely, $B_\delta(\mathbf{x}^0) \cap D$. The following definition generalises the notion of continuity in both these directions.

DEFINITION A1.9 ***(Cauchy) Continuity***

Let D be a subset of $\mathbb{R}^m$, and let $f\colon D \to \mathbb{R}^n$. The function f is continuous at the point $\mathbf{x}^0 \in D$ if for every $\varepsilon > 0$, there is a $\delta > 0$ such that

$$f(B_\delta(\mathbf{x}^0) \cap D) \subset B_\varepsilon(f(\mathbf{x}^0)).$$

If f is continuous at every point $\mathbf{x} \in D$, then it is called a continuous function.

This definition of continuity focuses entirely on the relation between one set in the image (the image of an open set in the domain) and another open set in the image. It would be nice to know what, if any, properties of sets are preserved under continuous mappings when we move back and forth between the image and the domain. Our intuition suggests to us that a continuous function is a sufficiently 'regular' and predictable animal that basic properties like openness and closedness are probably preserved in moving from the domain to the range. Unfortunately, this is an instance where intuition fails. Except in a very particular case to be mentioned later, we cannot take it for granted that every property of sets in the domain is preserved in the image when those sets are mapped by continuous functions. In particular, it is *not* true that a continuous function always maps an open set in the domain into an open set in the range, or that closed sets are mapped into closed sets. For example, the continuous function $f(x) = a$ maps *every* point in the domain, thus every open set of points in the domain, into the single point a in the range. In Exercise A1.25, you will convince yourself that a single point is a closed set, not an open set; so, our intuition fails us.

When, as in Definition A1.9, we allow the domain of a function to be some (possibly strict) subset D of $\mathbb{R}^m$, it no longer makes sense to define open sets in the domain in terms of open balls in $\mathbb{R}^m$ because these balls may lie partially, or entirely, outside of D. We need to develop and use an appropriate language that accounts for possibilities of this sort. We are thus led naturally to the following idea.

DEFINITION A1.10 ***Open Sets in*** D

Let D be a subset of $\mathbb{R}^m$. Then a subset S of D is open in D if for every $\mathbf{x} \in S$ there is an $\varepsilon > 0$ such that $B_\varepsilon(\mathbf{x}) \cap D \subset S$.

Thus, a set is open in D if for every point in the set, all nearby points are either in the set or outside of D. Note that if $D = \mathbb{R}^m$, this coincides with our definition of an open set in $\mathbb{R}^m$. Also note that D is always open in D.

As before, we define closedness in terms of openness.

DEFINITION A1.11 ***Closed Sets in*** D

Let D be a subset of $\mathbb{R}^m$. A subset S of D is closed in D if its complement in D, the set $\{\mathbf{x} \in D \mid \mathbf{x} \notin S\}$, is open in D.

Although we cannot, in general, be sure of what will happen as we move from the domain to the range under a continuous mapping, we *can* say quite a bit about what happens as we move the other way – from the range to the domain. In fact, there is an intimate relation between the continuity of a function and the properties of sets in the range and the properties of their *inverse images* in the domain. The next theorem establishes a series of equivalencies between the continuity of a function and the preservation of basic properties of sets under its *inverse mapping*.

THEOREM A1.6 ***Continuity and Inverse Images***

Let D be a subset of $\mathbb{R}^m$. The following conditions are equivalent:

1. *$f: D \rightarrow \mathbb{R}^n$ is continuous.*
2. *For every open ball B in $\mathbb{R}^n$, $f^{-1}(B)$ is open in D.*
3. *For every open set S in $\mathbb{R}^n$, $f^{-1}(S)$ is open in D.*

Proof: We shall show that *(1)* $\Rightarrow$ (2) $\Rightarrow$ (3) $\Rightarrow$ *(1)*.

(1) $\Rightarrow$ *(2)*. Suppose that *(1)* holds and let B be an open ball in $\mathbb{R}^n$. Choose any $\mathbf{x} \in f^{-1}(B)$. Clearly then, $f(\mathbf{x}) \in B$. Because B is open in $\mathbb{R}^n$, there is an $\varepsilon > 0$ such that $B_\varepsilon(f(\mathbf{x})) \subset B$. And by the continuity of f, there is a $\delta > 0$ such that $f(B_\delta(\mathbf{x}) \cap D) \subset$

$B_\varepsilon(f(\mathbf{x})) \subset B$. Consequently, $B_\delta(\mathbf{x}) \cap D \subset f^{-1}(B)$. Because $\mathbf{x} \in f^{-1}(B)$ was arbitrary, we conclude that $f^{-1}(B)$ is open in D, so that *(2)* holds.

(2) $\Rightarrow$ *(3)*. Suppose that *(2)* holds and that S is open in $\mathbb{R}^n$. By Theorem A1.3, S can be written as the union of open balls B_i, $i \in I$, so that $S = \cup_{i \in I} B_i$. Therefore, $f^{-1}(S) = f^{-1}(\cup_{i \in I} B_i) = \cup_{i \in I} f^{-1}(B_i)$. Because by *(2)* every set $f^{-1}(B_i)$ is open in D, $f^{-1}(S)$ is the union of open sets in D. Hence, by Exercise A1.28, $f^{-1}(S)$ is also open in D. Because S was an arbitrary open set in $\mathbb{R}^n$, this proves *(3)*.

(3) $\Rightarrow$ *(1)*. Suppose that *(3)* holds and choose $\mathbf{x} \in D$ and $\varepsilon > 0$. Then because $B_\varepsilon(f(\mathbf{x}))$ is open in $\mathbb{R}^n$, *(3)* implies that $f^{-1}(B_\varepsilon(f(\mathbf{x})))$ is open in D. Because $\mathbf{x} \in f^{-1}(B_\varepsilon(f(\mathbf{x})))$, this implies that there is a $\delta > 0$ such that $B_\delta(\mathbf{x}) \cap D \subset f^{-1}(B_\varepsilon(f(\mathbf{x})))$. But this implies that $f(B_\delta(\mathbf{x}) \cap D) \subset B_\varepsilon(f(\mathbf{x}))$. Therefore, f is continuous at $\mathbf{x}$. Because $\mathbf{x}$ was chosen arbitrarily from D, *(1)* holds and the proof is complete. ∎

This is a very general and very powerful theorem. If we know something about the inverse image of open sets or open balls in the range, we can use this theorem to conclude whether the function involved is continuous. By the same token, if we know that the function involved is continuous, we can use this theorem to tell us what properties the inverse images of open balls and open sets in the range must possess. Still, it would be nice to be able to say *something* about what happens to sets in the *domain* when they are mapped into sets in the range. As you were warned earlier, we cannot say as much as we think we would like to. Nonetheless, we can say something. In particular, it can be shown that if S is a *compact* subset in the domain, and if f is a continuous function, then the image set $f(S)$ in the range of f is also a compact set. This, at last, is at least one intuitively appealing result! Unfortunately, though, the proof takes us farther afield than we care to go. Because it is an important result, it is worth recording here for future reference. The interested (and equipped) reader can consult the reference for a proof.

THEOREM A1.7 ***The Continuous Image of a Compact Set is a Compact Set***

If D is a compact subset of $\mathbb{R}^m$ and $f: D \to \mathbb{R}^n$ is a continuous function, then the image of D under f, namely $f(D)$, is a compact subset of $\mathbb{R}^n$.

Proof: See Royden (1963) for a complete proof. ∎

Finally, we introduce the notion of a *sequence*.

DEFINITION A1.12 ***Sequences in*** $\mathbb{R}^n$

A sequence in $\mathbb{R}^n$ is a function mapping some infinite subset I of positive integers into $\mathbb{R}^n$. We shall denote a sequence by $\{\mathbf{x}^k\}_{k \in I}$, where $\mathbf{x}^k \in \mathbb{R}^n$ for every $k \in I$.

If the members of a sequence $\{\mathbf{x}^k\}$ become arbitrarily close to a particular point in $\mathbb{R}^n$ for all k large enough, then we say that the sequence **converges** to the point. Formally, we have the following.

DEFINITION A1.13 *Convergent Sequences*

The sequence $\{\mathbf{x}^k\}_{k \in I}$ converges to $\mathbf{x} \in \mathbb{R}^n$ if for every $\varepsilon > 0$, there is a $\bar{k}$ such that $\mathbf{x}^k \in B_\varepsilon(\mathbf{x})$ for all $k \in I$ exceeding $\bar{k}$.

In $\mathbb{R}^1$, for example, the sequence $1, 1/2, 1/3, \ldots$ converges to zero, even though zero is not a member of the sequence. On the other hand, the sequence $1, 2, 3, \ldots$ does not converge to any real number. Thus, not all sequences are convergent. Indeed, even sequences whose members are bounded need not converge. For example, the sequence $1, -1, 1, -1, \ldots$ is bounded, but it does not converge. On the other hand, if we consider only every other member of this sequence beginning with the first, we would get the (sub)sequence $1, 1, 1, \ldots$, which clearly converges to 1. This example can be generalised into an important result. To provide it, we need a few more definitions.

DEFINITION A1.14 *Bounded Sequences*

A sequence $\{\mathbf{x}^k\}_{k \in I}$ in $\mathbb{R}^n$ is bounded if for some $M \in \mathbb{R}$, $\| \mathbf{x}^k \| \leq M$ for all $k \in I$.

DEFINITION A1.15 *Subsequences*

$\{\mathbf{x}^k\}_{k \in J}$ is a subsequence of the sequence $\{\mathbf{x}^k\}_{k \in I}$ in $\mathbb{R}^n$, if J is an infinite subset of I.

We can now state the following important result.

THEOREM A1.8 *On Bounded Sequences*

Every bounded sequence in $\mathbb{R}^n$ has a convergent subsequence.

Proof: For a proof, see Royden (1963), or any good text in real analysis. ∎

It turns out that we could have defined open and closed sets in terms of sequences. Indeed, we end this section with a result that you are invited to prove for yourself.

THEOREM A1.9 *Sequences, Sets, and Continuous Functions*

Let D be a subset of $\mathbb{R}^n$, and let $f\colon D \to \mathbb{R}^m$. Then

1. *D is open if and only if for each $\mathbf{x} \in D$, if $\{\mathbf{x}^k\}_{k=1}^\infty$ converges to $\mathbf{x}$, then for some $\bar{k}$, $\mathbf{x}^k \in D$ for all $k \geq \bar{k}$.*
2. *D is closed if and only if for every sequence $\{\mathbf{x}^k\}_{k=1}^\infty$ of points in D converging to some $\mathbf{x} \in \mathbb{R}^n$, it is also the case that $\mathbf{x} \in D$.*
3. *f is continuous if and only if whenever $\{\mathbf{x}^k\}_{k=1}^\infty$ in D converges to $\mathbf{x} \in D$, $\{f(\mathbf{x}^k)\}_{k=1}^\infty$ converges to $f(\mathbf{x})$.*

A1.3.2 SOME EXISTENCE THEOREMS

To conclude this section, we consider some very powerful topological results, each with important applications in microeconomic theory. All are in a class of theorems known as 'existence theorems'. An existence theorem specifies conditions that, if met, guarantee that something exists. Two points are worth keeping in mind in our discussion of existence theorems. First, the conditions in these theorems are generally *sufficient*, not necessary conditions. This means that when the conditions of the theorem are present, the existence of the subject is guaranteed. At the same time, should the conditions *not* be met in some instance, the subject may still exist. We just cannot be sure in general and a priori. Second, although these theorems assure us that something exists, they generally give us no clue what it may look like, or where we may find it! They therefore provide potent and often indispensable links in the construction of rigorous 'abstract' arguments, but provide very feeble assistance in actually solving 'practical' problems.

The first theorem we consider is a fundamental result in *optimisation* theory. Many problems in economics involve maximising or minimising a function defined over some subset of $\mathbb{R}^n$. In later sections, we will examine how calculus techniques can be used to help identify and characterise the solutions to problems of this sort. We will pay particular attention to problems of maximising or minimising functions that map vectors in $\mathbb{R}^n$ into numbers of $\mathbb{R}$. Functions of this sort are called **real-valued functions**, and we turn to a detailed examination of this class of functions in the next section. Here, however, we can use a bit of the topology we have learned to establish one of the most widely invoked existence theorems known as the *Weierstrass theorem*. The Weierstrass theorem specifies sufficient conditions under which the existence of a maximum and a minimum of a function is assured.

THEOREM A1.10 ***(Weierstrass) Existence of Extreme Values***

Let $f\colon S \to \mathbb{R}$ be a continuous real-valued mapping where S is a non-empty compact subset of $\mathbb{R}^n$. Then there exists a vector $\mathbf{x}^* \in S$ and a vector $\tilde{\mathbf{x}} \in S$ such that

$$f(\tilde{\mathbf{x}}) \leq f(\mathbf{x}) \leq f(\mathbf{x}^*) \ \textit{for all} \ \mathbf{x} \in S.$$

Proof: Since f is continuous and S is compact, we know by Theorem A1.7 that $f(S)$ is a compact set. Because f is real-valued, $f(S) \subset \mathbb{R}$. Since $f(S)$ is compact, it is closed and bounded. By Theorem A1.5, any closed and bounded subset of real numbers contains its *g.l.b.*, call it a, and its *l.u.b.*, call it b. By definition of the image set, there exists some $\mathbf{x}^* \in S$ such that $f(\mathbf{x}^*) = b \in f(S)$ and some $\tilde{\mathbf{x}} \in S$ such that $f(\tilde{\mathbf{x}}) = a \in f(S)$. Together with the definitions of the *g.l.b.* and the *l.u.b.*, we have $f(\tilde{\mathbf{x}}) \leq f(\mathbf{x})$ and $f(\mathbf{x}) \leq f(\mathbf{x}^*)$ for all $\mathbf{x} \in S$. ∎

The sense of Theorem A1.10 is illustrated in Fig. A1.18. In both (a) and (b), $f\colon \mathbb{R} \to \mathbb{R}$ is a continuous real-valued function. In Fig. A1.18(a), the subset $S = [1, 2]$ is closed, bounded, and so compact. Because f is continuous, a minimum, $f(\tilde{x})$, and a maximum, $f(x^*)$, will, respectively, coincide with the *g.l.b.* and the *l.u.b.* in the image set $f(S)$. To see

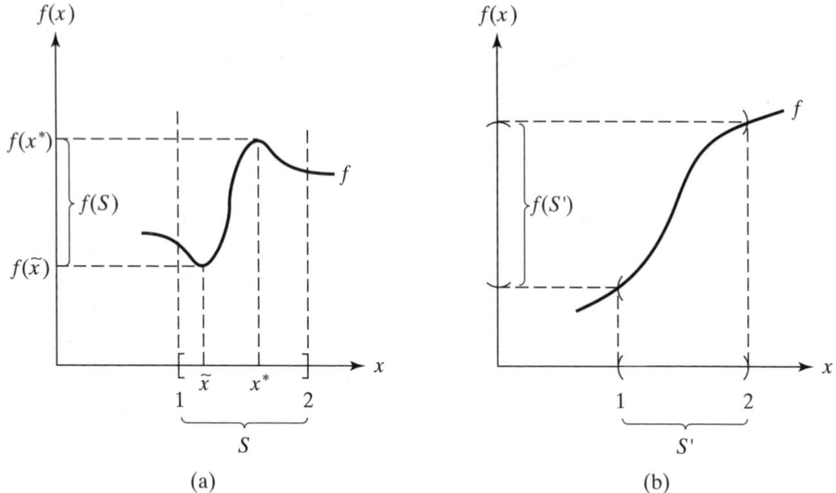

Figure A1. 18. The Weierstrass theorem: (a) A minimum and a maximum are guaranteed to exist, (b) Neither a minimum nor a maximum exists.

what can go wrong, however, consider Fig. A1.18(b). There we let the subset of the domain be $S' = (1, 2)$, which is not compact. It is bounded, but is not closed. Clearly, no minimum or maximum of f over S' exists in this case. Because S' is open, we can move closer and closer to either end of the open interval without ever reaching the endpoint itself. These movements are mapped into lower or higher values of f, respectively, never reaching either a minimum or a maximum value.

Next, let us turn our attention to a general method for determining whether systems of simultaneous equations with as many equations as variables admit at least one solution. Because the systems we encounter need not be linear, we wish to find a vector $\mathbf{x} = (x_1, \ldots, x_n)$ that simultaneously solves each of the n possibly non-linear equations,

$$\begin{aligned} g_1(x_1, \ldots, x_n) &= 0 \\ &\vdots \\ g_n(x_1, \ldots, x_n) &= 0. \end{aligned} \tag{A1.1}$$

If the domain of each of the functions g_i is a subset S of $\mathbb{R}^n$, then obviously we seek a solution $(x_1, \ldots, x_n) \in S$. An equivalent way to write the system of equations in (A1.1) is to define $f_i(x_1, \ldots, x_n) = g_i(x_1, \ldots, x_n) - x_i$. Then (A1.1) becomes,

$$\begin{aligned} f_1(x_1, \ldots, x_n) &= x_1 \\ &\vdots \\ f_n(x_1, \ldots, x_n) &= x_n. \end{aligned} \tag{A1.2}$$

Letting $f: S \to \mathbb{R}^n$ be defined by $f(\mathbf{x}) = (f_1(\mathbf{x}), \ldots, f_n(\mathbf{x}))$, we see that $\mathbf{x}^* \in S$ is a solution to (A1.1) and (A1.2) if and only if $f(\mathbf{x}^*) = \mathbf{x}^*$. Such a vector is called a **fixed point** of the function f. The term 'fixed point' is used because, should such a point exist, it will be one that is left undisturbed, or 'unmoved', by the function in going from the domain to the range. The function f merely takes $\mathbf{x}^*$ and maps it right back into itself.

Suppose we are confronted with a system of equations in the form of (A1.1). A basic question is whether the equations are mutually consistent, i.e., whether a solution to the system exists. As we have seen, this is equivalent to asking whether there is a fixed point for the vector-valued function f defined by the left-hand side of (A1.2). Many profound questions about the consistency of microeconomic systems have been answered by reformulating the question as one of the existence of a fixed point. The view of a competitive economy as a system of interrelated markets has been shown to be logically consistent by this means. The famous minimax theorem as well as Nash's equilibrium existence theorem in game theory have also been demonstrated this way. In these and other cases, some form of fixed-point theorem plays a central role. One especially fundamental theorem provides us with sufficient conditions under which a solution to systems of equations like (A1.2) is guaranteed to exist.

THEOREM A1.11 ***The Brouwer Fixed-Point Theorem***

Let $S \subset \mathbb{R}^n$ be a non-empty compact and convex set. Let $f: S \to S$ be a continuous function. Then there exists at least one fixed point of f in S. That is, there exists at least one $\mathbf{x}^* \in S$ such that $\mathbf{x}^* = f(\mathbf{x}^*)$.

Proof: We will restrict our proof of Brouwer's theorem to the special case in which S is the unit simplex in $\mathbb{R}^n_+$. That is, $S = \{(x_1, \ldots, x_n) \in \mathbb{R}^n_+ \mid \sum_{i=1}^n x_i = 1\}$. It is straightforward to check that this set is non-empty, compact and convex. (But do check this!) For $i = 1, \ldots, n$ and $\mathbf{x} = (x_1, \ldots, x_n) \in S$, let $f_i(\mathbf{x})$ denote the ith coordinate of the vector $f(\mathbf{x})$. Consequently, because $f(\mathbf{x}) \in S$, the n coordinates of $f(\mathbf{x})$ sum to one, i.e., $\sum_{i=1}^n f_i(\mathbf{x}) = 1$ for every $\mathbf{x} \in S$. Consider the following claim. For every $k = 1, 2, \ldots,$ there exist n points, $\mathbf{x}^{1,k}, \ldots, \mathbf{x}^{n,k} \in S$, all within a single $1/k$-ball, such that,

$$x_i^{i,k} \geq f_i(\mathbf{x}^{i,k}), \quad \text{for } i = 1, 2, \ldots, n. \tag{P.1}$$

Let us put aside the proof of this claim for the moment and focus instead on what it says and what it implies. The claim says that no matter how small a radius you have in mind, there are n points in S, all within a single ball of the radius you specified, with the property that the ith coordinate of the ith point is weakly greater than the ith coordinate of its image under f.

What does the claim imply? Clearly, the claim implies that there are n sequences of points in S, $\{\mathbf{x}^{1,k}\}_{k=1}^{\infty}, \ldots, \{\mathbf{x}^{n,k}\}_{k=1}^{\infty}$, such that (P.1) holds for every k. Because S is compact, it is bounded. Therefore, by Theorem A1.8, there is a common subsequence along which each sequence converges. (Why common? Think of $\{(\mathbf{x}^{1,k}, \ldots, \mathbf{x}^{n,k})\}_{k=1}^{\infty}$ as a single sequence in S^n.) Moreover, because the kth points in the sequences are within distance $1/k$ from one another, the subsequences must converge to the *same* point, $\mathbf{x}^* \in \mathbb{R}^n$ say. (Prove this!) And because the compactness of S implies that S is closed, we have that $\mathbf{x}^* \in S$. Summarising, there is an infinite subset K of the indices $k = 1, 2, \ldots$ such that each of the subsequences, $\{\mathbf{x}^{1,k}\}_{k \in K}, \ldots, \{\mathbf{x}^{n,k}\}_{k \in K}$, converges to $\mathbf{x}^* \in S$. Taking the limit of both sides of the inequality in (P.1) as $k \in K$ tends to infinity gives,

$$x_i^* = \lim_{k \to \infty, k \in K} x_i^{i,k} \geq \lim_{k \to \infty, k \in K} f_i(\mathbf{x}^{i,k}) = f_i(\mathbf{x}^*), \text{ for } i = 1, 2, \ldots, n,$$

where the second equality follows from the continuity of f. Hence, $\mathbf{x}^* = (x_1^*, \ldots, x_n^*) \in S$ satisfies,

$$x_i^* \geq f_i(\mathbf{x}^*), \text{ for } i = 1, 2, \ldots, n. \tag{P.2}$$

Because both $\mathbf{x}^*$ and $f(\mathbf{x}^*)$ are in S, their coordinates sum to one, i.e., both sides of (P.2) sum to one. But this is possible only if each inequality in (P.2) is in fact an equality. Hence, we have shown that $\mathbf{x}^* = f(\mathbf{x}^*)$, as desired!

Therefore (P.1) implies that f has a fixed point and so it suffices to prove (P.1). We will do so only for the special case of $n = 3$. The ideas used in our proof generalise to any number of dimensions. Consequently, the proof given here provides one way to see why Brouwer's theorem is true in general.

From this point in the proof onward we set $n = 3$. Therefore, $S = \{(x_1, x_2, x_3) \in \mathbb{R}_+^3 \mid x_1 + x_2 + x_3 = 1\}$ is the unit simplex in $\mathbb{R}^3$, the flat triangular surface shown in Figure A1.19. Rewriting (P.1) for the present special case in which $n = 3$, we wish to show that for every $k = 1, 2, \ldots$, there are three points, $\mathbf{a}$, $\mathbf{b}$, $\mathbf{c} \in S$, all within a single $1/k$-ball,

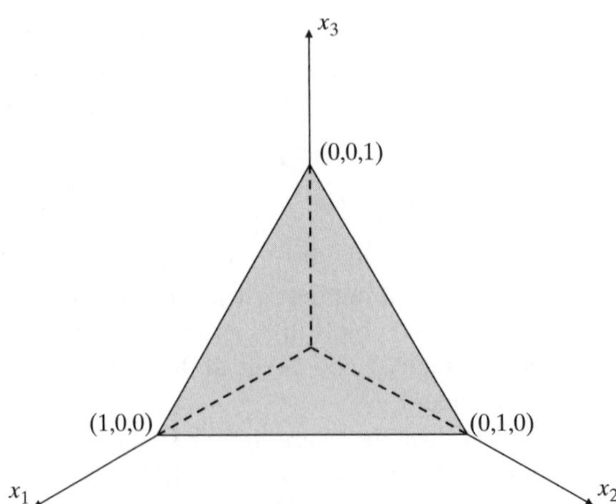

Figure A1.19. The two-dimensional unit simplex.

Figure A1. 20. A subdivision of the simplex.

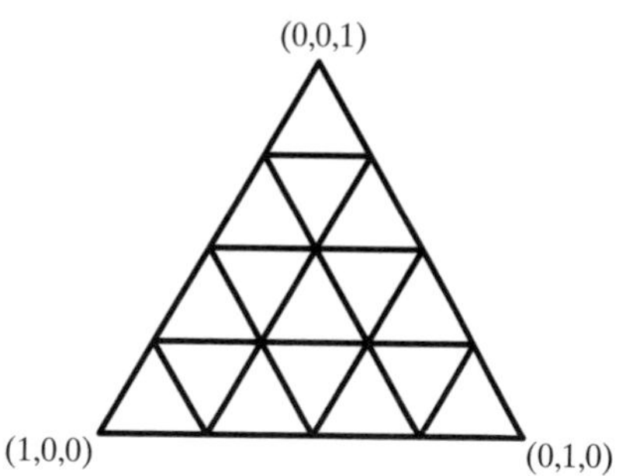

such that,

$$\begin{aligned} a_1 &\geq f_1(\mathbf{a}), \\ b_2 &\geq f_2(\mathbf{b}), \quad \text{and} \\ c_3 &\geq f_3(\mathbf{c}), \end{aligned} \tag{P.3}$$

where we have suppressed the dependence of **a**, **b**, and **c** on k.

So, fix k and divide the triangle S, which is equilateral, into smaller equilateral triangles as shown in Fig. A1.20. Choose the subdivision to be fine enough so that each of the smaller triangles fits into a $1/k$-ball.[4] If one of the vertices in the subdivision is a fixed point of f, then we may take $\mathbf{a} = \mathbf{b} = \mathbf{c}$ to be the fixed point and we are done. Thus, we may assume that no vertex in the subdivision is a fixed point of f. The proof will be complete if we can show that the vertices, **a**, **b**, and **c** of at least one of the small triangles in the subdivision must satisfy (P.3).

Working with Fig. A1.20 as an example, we begin by assigning to each vertex in the subdivision a number, or 'label', 1, 2, or 3. The following rule must be followed.

$$\text{The vertex } \mathbf{x} \text{ can be assigned the label } i \text{ only if } x_i > f_i(\mathbf{x}). \tag{P.4}$$

So, for example, if $\mathbf{x} = (1/4, 1/4, 1/2)$ is a vertex and $f(\mathbf{x}) = (0, 2/3, 1/3)$, then we can assign **x** the label 1 or 3, but not 2. If a labelling of each of the vertices in the subdivision satisfies (P.4), then the labelling is called *feasible*. As we have just seen, there can be more than one feasible labelling of a subdivision. But are we sure that there exists at least one feasible labelling? The answer is yes, because we have assumed that no vertex is a fixed point of f. Therefore for any vertex **x**, at least one $i \in \{1, 2, 3\}$ must satisfy $x_i > f_i(\mathbf{x})$ (Do you see why?), and so there is at least one feasible label for each vertex.

Fig. A1.21 is an example of a typical feasible labelling. Note that regardless of the function f, the vertices $(1, 0, 0)$, $(0, 1, 0)$, and $(0, 0, 1)$, of the original triangle S must be assigned the labels 1, 2, and 3, respectively. Furthermore, any vertex on the bottom edge

[4]This can always be done, for example, by dividing each of the three sides of the original triangle into $1/k$ equal intervals and then joining 'opposite' interval markers with lines that are parallel to the sides of the triangle.

Figure A1.21. A typical feasible labelling.

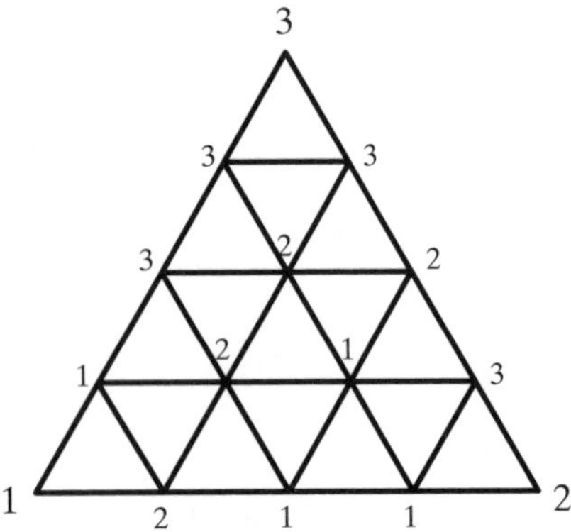

(i.e., any vertex that is a convex combination of the vertices $(1, 0, 0)$ and $(0, 1, 0)$) must be assigned the label 1 or 2, and cannot be assigned the label 3 because its third coordinate is zero. Similarly, the labels of left-edge vertices must be either 1 or 3 and the labels of right-edge vertices must be either 2 or 3. On the other hand, the labels assigned to vertices in the interior of triangle S can, in principle, be either 1, 2, or 3.

Our objective is to show that for any feasible labelling, at least one of the small triangles must be *completely labelled*, i.e., must have vertices labelled 1, 2, and 3. If this is the case, i.e., if the vertices **a**, **b**, and **c** of some small triangle have labels 1, 2, and 3, respectively, then according to (P.4),

$$
\begin{aligned}
a_1 &> f_1(\mathbf{a}), \\
b_2 &> f_2(\mathbf{b}), \quad \text{and} \\
c_3 &> f_3(\mathbf{c}),
\end{aligned}
$$

and so (P.3) is satisfied and we are done.

How can we show that at least one of the small triangles in any feasibly-labelled subdivision must be completely labelled? We will do so using a careful counting argument. In particular, fix a feasible labelling, e.g., as in Fig. A1.21. Consider now each of the small triangles in the subdivision as pieces in a puzzle. Separate the pieces while maintaining the labels on their vertices as shown in Fig. A1.22. Each of the pieces has three labels, one for each vertex. Take each piece and count the number of '1–2 edges', it contains, i.e., edges that have one endpoint labelled 1 and the other endpoint labelled 2. For example, a piece labelled 1,2,3 has one 1–2 edge, a piece labelled 1,1,2 has two 1–2 edges, and a piece labelled 1,1,3 has zero 1–2 edges.

We claim that the total number of 1–2 edges must always be odd. (Test this by counting the number of 1–2 edges in Fig. A1.22.) To see why, let us start by counting the number of 1–2 edges appearing along the bottom edge of the large triangle S. Go back to Fig. A1.21, and start from the $(1, 0, 0)$ vertex at the bottom left of the triangle and move to

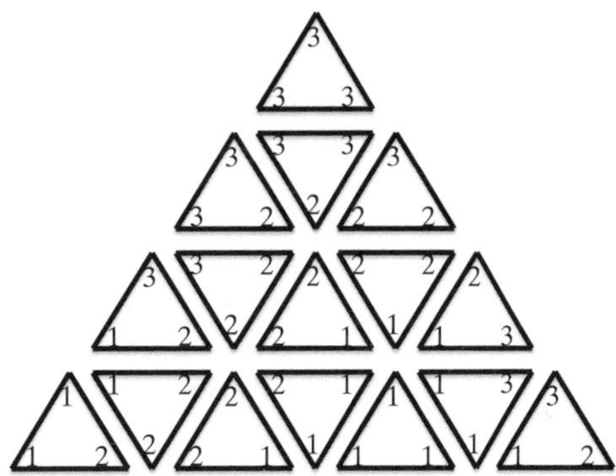

Figure A1.22. The exploded view.

the right keeping count of the number of 1–2 edges as we go.[5] Note that the first time we encounter a 2, the number of 1–2 edges goes from zero to one. We may then, in general, encounter a number of 2's in a row, in which case our total count of 1–2 edges does not change. Our count will increase to two only if we encounter a vertex labelled 1. But if we do, that cannot be the end of it. We must eventually encounter a vertex labelled 2 because the right-most vertex has label 2. So, *if* our 1–2 edge count gets to two *it cannot stop there.* It must get at least to three, at which point the current vertex is labelled 2. The same logic implies that our count can never end at an even number because our count of 1–2 edges becomes even precisely when the previous vertex has label 2 and the current vertex has label 1. Hence, there must be at least one more 1–2 edge because the last label is 2. Because the count cannot end with an even number, it must end with an odd number, i.e., there are an odd number of 1–2 edges along the bottom edge of the triangle.

Where else can 1–2 edges occur? As we have already observed, they cannot occur on either of the other two edges of the large triangle. Consequently, the only other place they can occur is within the interior of S, and we claim that the total number of 1–2 edges in the interior of S is even. To see why, look now at Fig. A1.22 and note that any interior edge has a twin adjacent to it with same labels. This is because the two endpoints of any interior edge and of its twin edge are in fact the same two points in S and hence are assigned the same pair of labels. Consequently, interior 1–2 edges come in pairs and hence there must be an even number of such edges.

Altogether then, when the subdivision is exploded into its separate pieces, the total number of 1–2 edges appearing along the bottom edge of S is odd (there are 3 such edges in Fig. A1.22) and the total number of 1–2 edges appearing in the interior of S is even (there are 12 such edges in Fig. A1.22). Since 1–2 edges can appear nowhere else, there must in total be an odd number of them.

The final step is to argue that if, looking at all the separate small triangles, there are an odd number of 1–2 edges, then there must be an odd number of completely labelled

[5]The order in which the 1–2 labels occur is not important. In particular, a small triangle edge along the bottom of the large triangle whose left endpoint is 2 and whose right endpoint is 1 is considered a 1–2 edge.

triangles (and hence there must be at least one!). Why? Let us count again the number of 1–2 edges in a different way. How many 1–2 edges are there if we focus only on the triangles that are *not* completely labelled? Some of these triangles have no 1–2 edges. But all others have exactly *two* 1–2 edges because their labels must be either 1,1,2; or 1,2,2 (draw such labelled triangles and count the 1–2 edges). Consequently, the total number of 1–2 edges among triangles that are not completely labelled is *even*. But since we know there are an odd number of 1–2 edges altogether, there must therefore be an odd number of completely labelled triangles since each of these has precisely one 1–2 edge.[6] ∎

When S is a non-empty closed interval $[a, b]$, Brouwer's theorem is illustrated in Fig. A1.23. Briefly stated, if f is a continuous mapping from $[a, b]$ into itself, Brouwer's theorem guarantees that the graph of f will cross the 45° line at least one time within the square $[a, b] \times [a, b]$. In the illustration offered, f performs that crossing three times. This is to alert you that no reference is made in Brouwer's theorem to the uniqueness of fixed points when the conditions of the theorem are met, only to their existence. In fact, Fig. A1.23 can be taken as a counterexample to any such 'theorem' you may be tempted to construct yourself!

We leave you with a homely thought experiment that you can perform for yourself and ponder in the morning. Consider a cup of coffee. Think of the molecules in that coffee as idealised points in $\mathbb{R}^3$, and the set of all molecules in your cup as a compact convex set in $\mathbb{R}^3$. Now lift up the cup and gently move it around so that the coffee is stirred in a 'continuous' way, i.e., no splashing! Let the molecules come back to rest. Brouwer's theorem guarantees that at least one molecule in your cup is exactly where it was to begin with!

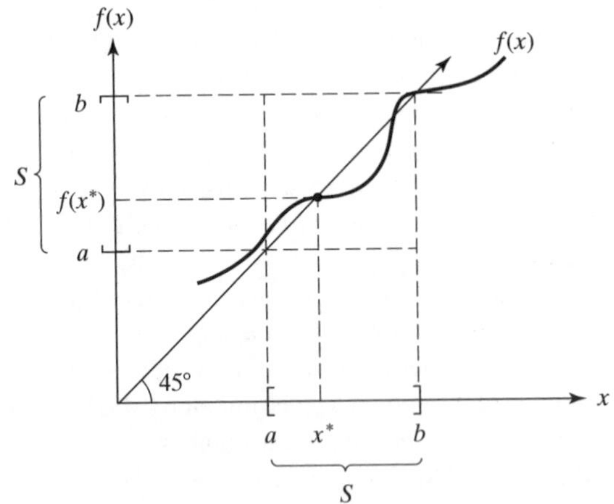

Figure A1.23. Brouwer's fixed-point theorem.

[6]The fact that a feasibly labelled subdivision of the simplex must have an odd number of completely labelled subtriangles is called Sperner's lemma, and it generalises to any number of dimensions.

A1.4 REAL-VALUED FUNCTIONS

Real-valued functions are commonly encountered in microeconomic theory. Consumer utility functions, firm production functions, and firm cost functions are just a few of the most familiar. Formally:

DEFINITION A1.16 ***Real-Valued Functions***

$f: D \to R$ is a real-valued function if D is any set and $R \subset \mathbb{R}$.

Simply stated, f is real-valued if it maps elements of its domain into the real line. If the domain is a subset of $\mathbb{R}^n$, a real-valued function maps vectors in $\mathbb{R}^n$ into points in $\mathbb{R}$. The functions $y = ax_1 + bx_2$, $y = \sqrt{z^2 + w^2}$, and $y = \sum_{i=1}^{n} a_i x_i^2$ are all examples of real-valued functions because in each case, the left-hand side is a real number. The class of real-valued functions is, of course, extremely broad. In this section, we will introduce some particular types of real-valued functions and explore their important properties.

The real-valued functions in typical economic applications tend to be ones that either rise or fall in a regular way over their domain. These are called *increasing* and *decreasing* functions and we should define these terms carefully for future reference. Here, we distinguish between three types of increasing function.

DEFINITION A1.17 ***Increasing, Strictly Increasing and Strongly Increasing Functions***

Let $f: D \to \mathbb{R}$, where D is a subset of $\mathbb{R}^n$. Then f is increasing *if $f(\mathbf{x}^0) \geq f(\mathbf{x}^1)$ whenever $\mathbf{x}^0 \geq \mathbf{x}^1$. If, in addition, the inequality is strict whenever $\mathbf{x}^0 \gg \mathbf{x}^1$, then we say that f is* strictly increasing. *If, instead, $f(\mathbf{x}^0) > f(\mathbf{x}^1)$ whenever $\mathbf{x}^0$ and $\mathbf{x}^1$ are distinct and $\mathbf{x}^0 \geq \mathbf{x}^1$, then we say that f is* strongly increasing.

Look carefully at these definitions and recall how we use the symbols $\geq$ and $\gg$ in the case of vector relations. We have defined a function as increasing whenever an increase in one or more of the components x_i of the vector $\mathbf{x} = (x_1, \ldots, x_n)$ never causes the value of the function to decrease. We have called the function strictly increasing whenever an increase in all components of $\mathbf{x}$ causes the value of the function to strictly increase. We have defined a function as strongly increasing whenever an increase in one or more of the x_i causes the value of the function to strictly increase. Before reading on, notice the hierarchy here: an increasing function need not be strictly increasing, and a strictly increasing function need not be strongly increasing, but every strongly increasing function is strictly increasing, and every strictly increasing function is increasing.

Decreasing functions are defined analogously, and we make similar distinctions.

DEFINITION A1.18 ***Decreasing, Strictly Decreasing and Strongly Decreasing Functions***

Let $f: D \to \mathbb{R}$, where D is a subset of $\mathbb{R}^n$. Then f is decreasing *if $f(\mathbf{x}^0) \leq f(\mathbf{x}^1)$ whenever $\mathbf{x}^0 \geq \mathbf{x}^1$. If, in addition, the inequality is strict whenever $\mathbf{x}^0 \gg \mathbf{x}^1$, then we say that f is* strictly decreasing. *If, instead,* $f(\mathbf{x}^0) < f(\mathbf{x}^1)$ *whenever* $\mathbf{x}^0$ *and* $\mathbf{x}^1$ *are distinct and* $\mathbf{x}^0 \geq \mathbf{x}^1$, *then we say that* f *is* strongly decreasing.

A1.4.1 RELATED SETS

We have seen that a function is a particular kind of relation between two sets. We have also remarked that the graph of a function is a related set that sometimes provides an easy and intuitive way of thinking about the function. There are some other sets related to a function that have become commonplace in the tool kit and lexicon of economic theory. Like the graph, some of these have particularly simple geometric representations and they often provide us with equivalent but simpler ways of thinking about and manipulating the functions themselves. This is especially true for real-valued functions, for which the range is some subset of the real line. After defining some related sets and establishing their relation to the function and to each other in general, we will consider some specific types of real-valued functions and the specific properties of their related sets.

The notion of a level set (or level curve) is undoubtedly quite familiar to you, albeit perhaps under a different name. Many familiar objects in microeconomics, such as indifference curves, isoquants, iso-profit lines, and so forth, are all level sets of real-valued functions. A level set is the set of all elements in the domain of a function that map into the same number, or 'level', in the range. Thus, any two elements in the same level set will, by definition, generate exactly the same number in the range when plugged into the function itself. Formally:

DEFINITION A1.19 ***Level Sets***

$L(y^0)$ is a level set of the real-valued function $f: D \rightarrow R$ iff $L(y^0) = \{x \mid x \in D, f(x) = y^0\}$, where $y^0 \in R \subset \mathbb{R}$.

Notice these are sets in the *domain* of the function. Because we can construct one level set for any value in its image, we can *completely* represent the function by these sets in its domain, thus reducing by one the number of dimensions needed to represent the function. It is this characteristic of level sets that you have seen so often exploited in the construction of indifference maps, isoquant maps, and so forth: level sets allow us to study functions of three variables, which normally require awkward three-dimensional graphs to depict, by focusing upon sets in the simple two-dimensional plane. Some level sets for the function of three variables, $y = f(x_1, x_2)$, are depicted in Fig. A1.24.

We should note another property of level sets. We saw before that the map $f: D \rightarrow R$ is a function if and only if it assigns a *single* number in the range to each element in the domain. Therefore, two different level sets of a function can never cross or intersect each other. If they did, that would mean two different numbers were being assigned to that one element in the domain where they cross. This, of course, would violate the definition of a function.

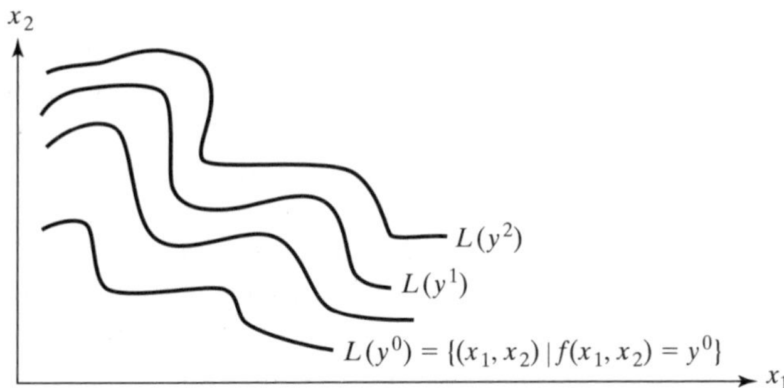

Figure A1. 24. Level sets in $\mathbb{R}^2$.

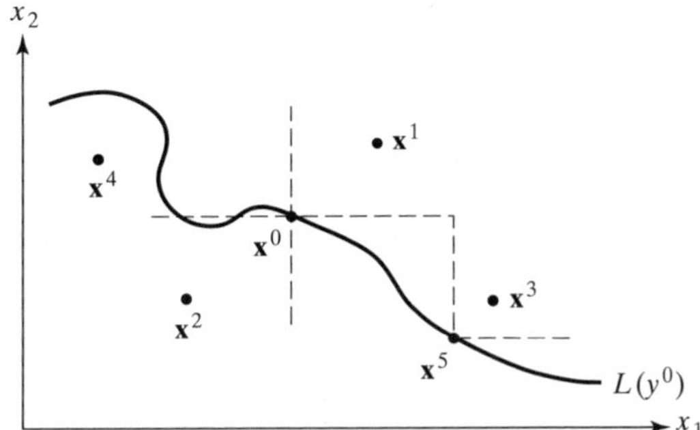

Figure A1. 25. A level set relative to a point $\mathbf{x}^0$.

Finally, we should make an observation on notation. For many purposes, it is convenient to think in terms of level sets relative to particular points in the domain, rather than relative to points in the range. Because a real-valued function maps any point $\mathbf{x}^0$ in its domain into *some* point or level $f(\mathbf{x}^0) = y^0$ in its range, it is simply a matter of notational convenience which way we define the level set. Thus, consistent with our earlier definition, we can define the level set *relative to the point* $\mathbf{x}^0$ as the set of all points in the domain that map into the same level in the range as $\mathbf{x}^0$ maps into. Formally:

DEFINITION A1.20 ***Level Sets Relative to a Point***

$\mathcal{L}(\mathbf{x}^0)$ *is a level set relative to* $\mathbf{x}^0$ *if* $\mathcal{L}(\mathbf{x}^0) = \{\mathbf{x} \mid \mathbf{x} \in D, f(\mathbf{x}) = f(\mathbf{x}^0)\}$.

Consider the level set for $f(\mathbf{x}) = y^0$ in Fig. A1.25. Because the point $\mathbf{x}^0$ is on the y^0 level set for $f(\mathbf{x})$, we know that $f(\mathbf{x}^0) = y^0$. What do we know about points elsewhere in the domain, such as $\mathbf{x}^1$ and $\mathbf{x}^2$? If $f(\mathbf{x})$ is a *strictly increasing* function, we know that $f(\mathbf{x}^1) > f(\mathbf{x}^0)$ and that $f(\mathbf{x}^2) < f(\mathbf{x}^0)$. This is clear because the coordinates of the vector $\mathbf{x}^1(\mathbf{x}^2)$ are both strictly greater (smaller) than those of $\mathbf{x}^0$, and a strictly increasing function assigns larger (smaller) numbers to vectors with larger (smaller) components. This is fairly straightforward. But what do we know about other points on the same side of $L(y^0)$ as $\mathbf{x}^1$ or $\mathbf{x}^2$, such as $\mathbf{x}^3$ or $\mathbf{x}^4$? Clearly, whether the function is increasing or decreasing, points like $\mathbf{x}^3$ and $\mathbf{x}^4$ must give rise to a value of the function that is in the same relation to y^0 as those given by the points $\mathbf{x}^1$ and $\mathbf{x}^2$, respectively. If $f(\mathbf{x})$ is strictly increasing, $f(\mathbf{x}^1)$ and $f(\mathbf{x}^3)$ must both be greater than y^0, while $f(\mathbf{x}^2)$ and $f(\mathbf{x}^4)$ must both be less than y^0. If $f(\mathbf{x})$ is strictly decreasing, $f(\mathbf{x}^1) < y^0, f(\mathbf{x}^3) < y^0$, and $f(\mathbf{x}^2) > y^0, f(\mathbf{x}^4) > y^0$. This is clear because, for example, $\mathbf{x}^3$ is in the same relation to some other point on $L(y^0)$, such as $\mathbf{x}^5$, as $\mathbf{x}^1$ is in to $\mathbf{x}^0$. Because $\mathbf{x}^0$ and $\mathbf{x}^5$ are both on $L(y^0)$, we know that $f(\mathbf{x}^0) = f(\mathbf{x}^5) = y^0$. We can then make the same kind of argument as before to determine whether $\mathbf{x}^3$ gives a value of the function greater or less than $\mathbf{x}^5$ does, depending on whether $f(\mathbf{x})$ is strictly increasing or decreasing. If $f(\mathbf{x})$ is strictly increasing, $f(\mathbf{x}^1) > f(\mathbf{x}^0) = y^0$ and $f(\mathbf{x}^3) > f(\mathbf{x}^5) = y^0$. If $f(\mathbf{x})$ is strictly decreasing, $f(\mathbf{x}^1) < f(\mathbf{x}^0) = y^0$ and $f(\mathbf{x}^3) < f(\mathbf{x}^5) = y^0$.

Thinking along these lines, we can define some additional sets to divide up the domain of a function in useful ways.

DEFINITION A1.21 ***Superior and Inferior Sets***

1. *$S(y^0) \equiv \{\mathbf{x} \mid \mathbf{x} \in D, f(\mathbf{x}) \geq y^0\}$ is called the superior set for level y^0.*
2. *$I(y^0) \equiv \{\mathbf{x} \mid \mathbf{x} \in D, f(\mathbf{x}) \leq y^0\}$ is called the inferior set for level y^0.*
3. *$S'(y^0) \equiv \{\mathbf{x} \mid \mathbf{x} \in D, f(\mathbf{x}) > y^0\}$ is called the strictly superior set for level y^0.*
4. *$I'(y^0) \equiv \{\mathbf{x} \mid \mathbf{x} \in D, f(\mathbf{x}) < y^0\}$ is called the strictly inferior set for level y^0.*

The superior set contains all points in D that give the function a value *equal to or greater than* the value y^0, and the strictly superior set contains all points giving a value *strictly greater than* y^0. The inferior set contains all points that give the function a value *less than or equal to* y^0, and the strictly inferior set contains all points giving a value *strictly less than* y^0. Because the level set itself contains all points that give the function the value y^0, these sets are clearly related. The following theorem makes these relationships clear. Its proof is left as an exercise.

THEOREM A1.12 ***Superior, Inferior, and Level Sets***

For any $f: D \to R$ and $y^0 \in R$:

1. *$L(y^0) \subset S(y^0)$.*
2. *$L(y^0) \subset I(y^0)$.*
3. *$L(y^0) = S(y^0) \cap I(y^0)$.*
4. *$S'(y^0) \subset S(y^0)$.*
5. *$I'(y^0) \subset I(y^0)$.*
6. *$S'(y^0) \cap L(y^0) = \emptyset$.*

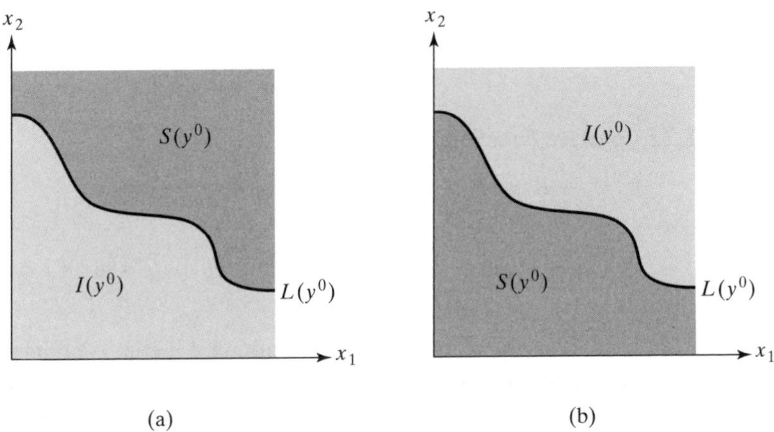

Figure A1.26. Level, inferior, and superior sets for (a) an increasing function and (b) a decreasing function.

7. $I'(y^0) \cap L(y^0) = \emptyset$.
8. $S'(y^0) \cap I'(y^0) = \emptyset$.

Fig. A1.26 illustrates the superior and inferior sets for two different functions, one increasing and the other decreasing. When $f(\mathbf{x})$ is *increasing*, $S(y^0)$ will always lie on and above the level set $L(y^0)$, and $I(y^0)$ will always lie on and below $L(y^0)$. $S'(y^0)$, if not empty, will always lie strictly above the level set $L(y^0)$, and $I'(y^0)$ will always lie strictly below it. When $f(\mathbf{x})$ is *decreasing*, $S(y^0)$ will lie on and below the level set $L(y^0)$, and $I(y^0)$ will lie on and above it. $S'(y^0)$, if not empty, will lie strictly below $L(y^0)$, and $I'(y^0)$ will lie strictly above $L(y^0)$.

A1.4.2 CONCAVE FUNCTIONS

For the remainder of this section, we will restrict our attention to real-valued functions whose domains are *convex sets*. This will virtually always be the case in subsequent work and will generally be understood to be the case even if not explicitly stated. For now, though, we should try to be careful and state our assumptions and notation clearly.

ASSUMPTION A1.1 ***Real-Valued Functions Over Convex Sets***

Throughout this section, whenever $f\colon D \rightarrow R$ is a real-valued function, we will assume $D \subset \mathbb{R}^n$ is a convex set. When we take $\mathbf{x}^1 \in D$ and $\mathbf{x}^2 \in D$, we will let $\mathbf{x}^t \equiv t\mathbf{x}^1 + (1-t)\mathbf{x}^2$, for $t \in [0, 1]$, denote the convex combination of $\mathbf{x}^1$ and $\mathbf{x}^2$. Because D is a convex set, we know that $\mathbf{x}^t \in D$.

In economics, we often encounter concave real-valued functions over convex domains. Concave functions are defined as follows.

DEFINITION A1.22 ***Concave Functions***

$f: D \to R$ is a concave function if for all $\mathbf{x}^1, \mathbf{x}^2 \in D$,

$$f(\mathbf{x}^t) \geq tf(\mathbf{x}^1) + (1-t)f(\mathbf{x}^2) \quad \forall\, t \in [0, 1].$$

Loosely, according to this definition, f is concave if its value at a convex combination of two points is no smaller than the convex combination of the two values. The definition corresponds nicely to a very simple geometric property of the graph of the function.

Let us consider the simple concave function of one variable graphed in Fig. A1.27. Now take two points on its graph, (x^1, y^1) and (x^2, y^2), and draw in the chord connecting them. We know from our previous discussion of convex sets that when we form any convex combination of the elements in the domain, x^1 and x^2, we get a point, x^t, some proportion of the distance between x^1 and x^2. If we form the same convex combination of the corresponding elements in the range $y^1 = f(x^1)$ and $y^2 = f(x^2)$, we will get a point $y^t = tf(x^1) + (1-t)f(x^2)$ the same proportion of the distance between $f(x^1)$ and $f(x^2)$ as x^t is of the distance between x^1 and x^2. If we plot the point (x^t, y^t), it must therefore lie on the straight-line chord connecting the points $(x^1, f(x^1))$ and $(x^2, f(x^2))$. The abscissa of (x^t, y^t) is the convex combination of x^1 and x^2, and the ordinate is the same convex combination of the numbers generated when f is evaluated at x^1 and x^2. For f to be concave, the vertical distance to the point $(x^t, f(x^t))$ must be at least as great as the vertical distance to the point to the chord (x^t, y^t); i.e., we must have $f(x^t) \geq y^t = tf(x^1) + (1-t)f(x^2)$. Here the vertical distance to the graph above x^t is strictly greater than the vertical distance to the chord above x^t, so the requirement is satisfied.

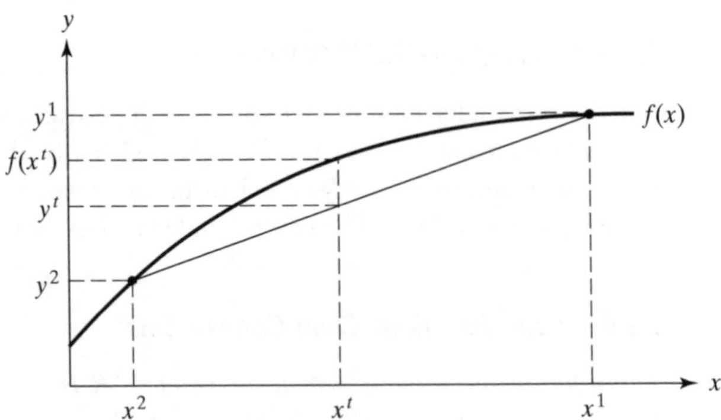

Figure A1.27. A concave function.

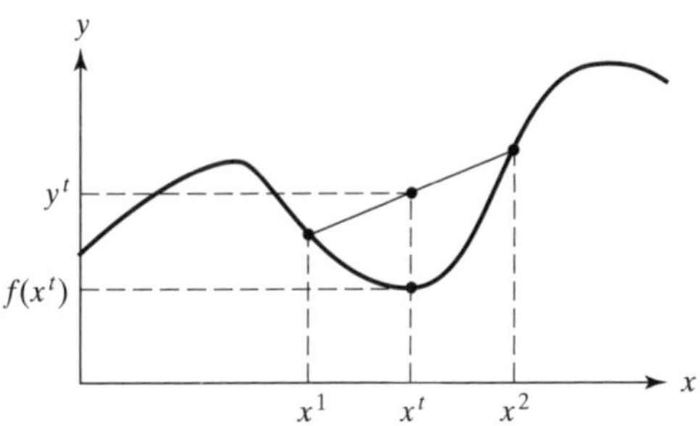

Figure A1. 28. Concave and non-concave regions.

If we now consider all values of $t \in [0, 1]$, we trace out every point on the abscissa between x^1 and x^2. For each value of t, the same argument would hold. The vertical distance to the graph exceeds (or equals) the vertical distance to the chord at every value of x^t. This suggests a very simple and intuitive rule: *A function is concave iff for every pair of points on its graph, the chord joining them lies on or below the graph.*

To see what happens when concavity fails to hold, consider the function in Fig. A1.28. This function is concave over the regions $[0, x^1]$ and $[x^2, \infty)$, as you can readily see by drawing chords between points on the graph within each of those regions. It is *not* concave, however, over the region $[x^1, x^2]$. Here we can construct the chord between $(x^1, f(x^1))$ and $(x^2, f(x^2))$ and find a t (say, $t = 1/2$) such that the convex combination of the points on the graph, (x^t, y^t), lies strictly *above* the point $(x^t, f(x^t))$. Because we have found two points in the domain and at least one $t \in [0, 1]$ such that $f(x^t) < tf(x^1) + (1 - t)f(x^2)$, the definition of concavity is violated.

Look again at Figs. A1.27 and A1.28. Can you sense what it is that distinguishes the concave function in Fig. A1.27 from the non-concave one in Fig. A1.28? Look at the area below the graph in Fig. A1.27 and below the concave regions of the graph in Fig. A1.28. Compare these to the areas below the non-concave region of Fig. A1.28. The points below the graph of all concave regions appear to be 'nicely behaved' in a way which we have seen before. In particular, the set of points *underneath* the graph of the concave regions of both functions are *convex sets*. The set of points beneath the non-concave region of Fig. A1.28 is *not* a convex set. This relationship between a concave function and the set of points beneath its graph is in fact a very general and intimate one. It holds for *all* concave functions, not just for the functions of a single variable. It is important enough to warrant stating as a theorem.

THEOREM A1.13 ***Points On and Below the Graph of a Concave Function Form a Convex Set***

Let $A \equiv \{(\mathbf{x}, y) \mid \mathbf{x} \in D, f(\mathbf{x}) \geq y\}$ *be the set of points 'on and below' the graph of* $f: D \rightarrow R$, *where* $D \subset \mathbb{R}^n$ *is a convex set and* $R \subset \mathbb{R}$. *Then,*

$$f \text{ is a concave function} \iff A \text{ is a convex set.}$$

We will shortly encounter several theorems like this one establishing the *equivalence* between a certain type of function and related convex sets. The proofs of some will be omitted and proofs of others will be left as exercises. Because it is important to develop your intuition for these relationships, we will give a proof for this theorem here. To make things as clear as possible, we will take an extended and leisurely approach.

Proof: (*Extended*) Because the theorem asserts an *equivalence* between concavity of the function and convexity of the set A, we will have to break up the theorem and give a proof in 'both directions'. We will have to show that f concave $\Rightarrow A$ convex *and* that A convex $\Rightarrow f$ concave.

First part: f concave $\Rightarrow A$ convex.

Assume f is a concave function. Then for $\mathbf{x}^t \equiv t\mathbf{x}^1 + (1-t)\mathbf{x}^2$ and by the definition of concave functions,

$$f(\mathbf{x}^t) \geq tf(\mathbf{x}^1) + (1-t)f(\mathbf{x}^2) \quad \text{for all } \mathbf{x}^1, \mathbf{x}^2 \in D, \text{ and } t \in [0, 1]. \tag{P.1}$$

Take any two points $(\mathbf{x}^1, y^1) \in A$ and $(\mathbf{x}^2, y^2) \in A$. By definition of A,

$$f(\mathbf{x}^1) \geq y^1 \quad \text{and} \quad f(\mathbf{x}^2) \geq y^2. \tag{P.2}$$

To prove that A is a convex set, we must show that the convex combination $(\mathbf{x}^t, y^t) \equiv (t\mathbf{x}^1 + (1-t)\mathbf{x}^2, ty^1 + (1-t)y^2)$ is also in A for all $t \in [0, 1]$. Because D is a convex set by assumption, we know $\mathbf{x}^t \in D$ for all $t \in [0, 1]$. Thus, we need only show that $f(\mathbf{x}^t) \geq y^t$ for all $t \in [0, 1]$ to establish $(\mathbf{x}^t, y^t) \in A$. But that is easy. From (P.2), we know that $f(\mathbf{x}^1) \geq y^1$ and $f(\mathbf{x}^2) \geq y^2$. Multiplying the first of these by $t \geq 0$ and the second by $(1-t) \geq 0$ gives us $tf(\mathbf{x}^1) \geq ty^1$ and $(1-t)f(\mathbf{x}^2) \geq (1-t)y^2$ $\forall\, t \in [0, 1]$. Adding these last two inequalities together gives us

$$tf(\mathbf{x}^1) + (1-t)f(\mathbf{x}^2) \geq ty^1 + (1-t)y^2.$$

Using (P.1), and remembering that $y^t \equiv ty^1 + (1-t)y^2$, gives us

$$f(\mathbf{x}^t) \geq y^t.$$

Thus, $(\mathbf{x}^t, y^t) \in A$, so A is a convex set.

That completes the first part of the proof and establishes that f concave $\Rightarrow A$ is a convex set. We need to prove the second part next.

Second part: A convex $\Rightarrow f$ concave.

Here we assume that A is a convex set and must show that f is therefore a concave function. The strategy for this part of the proof is to pick *any* two points in the domain D of f but two *particular* points in the set A, namely, the two points in A that are on, rather than beneath, the graph of f corresponding to those two points in its domain. If we can use the convexity of the set A to establish that f must satisfy the definition of a concave function at these two points in its domain, we will have established the assertion in general because those two points in the domain are chosen arbitrarily.

Choose $\mathbf{x}^1 \in D$ and $\mathbf{x}^2 \in D$, and let y^1 and y^2 satisfy

$$y^1 = f(\mathbf{x}^1) \text{ and } y^2 = f(\mathbf{x}^2). \tag{P.3}$$

The points $(\mathbf{x}^1, y^1)$ and $(\mathbf{x}^2, y^2)$ are thus in A because they satisfy $\mathbf{x}^i \in D$ and $f(\mathbf{x}^i) \geq y^i$ for each i. Now form the convex combination of these two points, $(\mathbf{x}^t, y^t)$. Because A is a convex set, $(\mathbf{x}^t, y^t)$ is also in A for all $t \in [0, 1]$. Thus,

$$f(\mathbf{x}^t) \geq y^t. \tag{P.4}$$

Now $y^t \equiv ty^1 + (1-t)y^2$, so we can substitute for y^i from (P.3) and write

$$y^t = tf(\mathbf{x}^1) + (1-t)f(\mathbf{x}^2). \tag{P.5}$$

Combining (P.4) and (P.5), we have $f(\mathbf{x}^t) \geq tf(\mathbf{x}^1) + (1-t)f(\mathbf{x}^2)$ $\forall\, t \in [0, 1]$, so f is a concave function.

Because we have established the assertions in both directions ($\Rightarrow$ and $\Leftarrow$), the proof is complete. ∎

We now have two equivalent ways of thinking about concave functions: one in terms of the value the function takes at convex combinations of any two points, and one in terms of the 'shape' of the set inscribed by the graph of the function. Either specification completely defines a concave function.

According to the definition of concave functions, Fig. A1.29 is concave. Nothing in the definition, or in Theorem A1.13, prohibits *linear segments* in the graph of the function. The set beneath is still convex. At x^t, the value of the function is exactly equal to the convex combination of $f(x^1)$ and $f(x^2)$, so the inequality $f(x^t) \geq tf(x^1) + (1-t)f(x^2)$ still holds there. Geometrically, the point $(x^t, f(x^t))$ simply lies *on*, rather than strictly *above*, the chord connecting x^1 and x^2 and that is quite all right.

It is sometimes convenient to exclude the possibility of linear segments in the graph of the function. *Strict concavity* rules out this kind of thing.

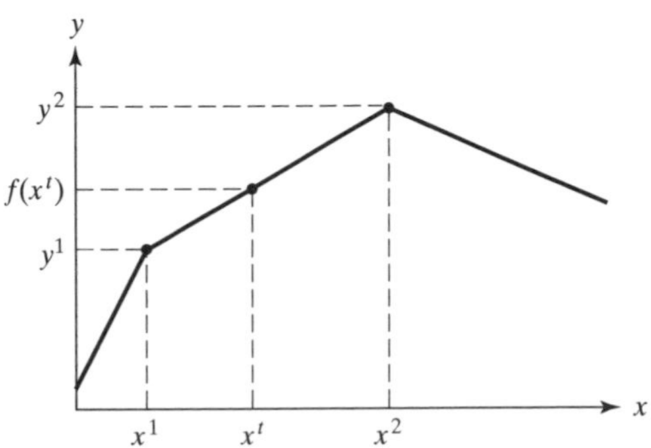

Figure A1.29. f is concave but not strictly concave.

DEFINITION A1.23 ***Strictly Concave Functions***

$f: D \to R$ is a strictly concave function iff, for all $\mathbf{x}^1 \neq \mathbf{x}^2$ in D,

$$f(\mathbf{x}^t) > tf(\mathbf{x}^1) + (1-t)f(\mathbf{x}^2) \text{ for all } t \in (0, 1).$$

Notice very carefully the small but important differences in the definitions of concave and strictly concave functions. First, strict concavity requires $f(\mathbf{x}^t)$ to be *strictly* greater than the convex combination of $f(\mathbf{x}^1)$ and $f(\mathbf{x}^2)$, rather than greater than or equal to it, as required for concave functions. Next, the strict inequality must hold for all t in the *open* interval $(0, 1)$, rather than the closed interval $[0, 1]$ as before. This makes perfect sense because if t were either zero or one, the convex combination $\mathbf{x}^t$ would coincide with either $\mathbf{x}^2$ or $\mathbf{x}^1$, and the strict inequality in the definition could not hold.

Geometrically, these modifications simply require the graph of the function to lie *strictly above* the chord connecting any two points on the graph, except at each of the two points themselves. This serves to rule out flat portions on the graph of the function.

A1.4.3 QUASICONCAVE FUNCTIONS

Concavity, whether strict or not, is a relatively strong restriction to place on a function. Often, one of the objectives in theoretical work is to identify and impose only the weakest possible restrictions needed to guarantee the result sought. *Quasiconcavity* is a related but weaker property that is often all that is required to get us where we want to go.

DEFINITION A1.24 ***Quasiconcave Functions***[7]

$f: D \to R$ is quasiconcave iff, for all $\mathbf{x}^1$ and $\mathbf{x}^2$ in D,

$$f(\mathbf{x}^t) \geq \min[f(\mathbf{x}^1), f(\mathbf{x}^2)] \text{ for all } t \in [0, 1].$$

Admittedly, this definition seems rather awkward at first. It says, if we take any two points in the domain and form any convex combination of them, the value of the function must be no lower than the lowest value it takes at the two points. Another way of describing quasiconcave functions is in terms of their level sets.

Suppose we have $y = f(x_1, x_2)$ and pick any two points $\mathbf{x}^1$ and $\mathbf{x}^2$ in its domain. Each of these gives rise to some value of the function and so each lies on some level set in the plane of its domain. When we form any convex combination of the two points, we get a point $\mathbf{x}^t$ somewhere on the chord connecting $\mathbf{x}^1$ and $\mathbf{x}^2$. The function has some value at the point $\mathbf{x}^t$, too, so $\mathbf{x}^t$ lies on some level set as well. Now consider the functions whose level sets are depicted in Fig. A1.30. In each instance, we will assume that $f(\mathbf{x}^1) \geq f(\mathbf{x}^2)$.

---

[7]The operator $\min[a, b]$ simply means 'the smaller of a and b'. If $a > b$, then $\min[a, b] = b$. If $a = b$, then $\min[a, b]$ equals a and b.

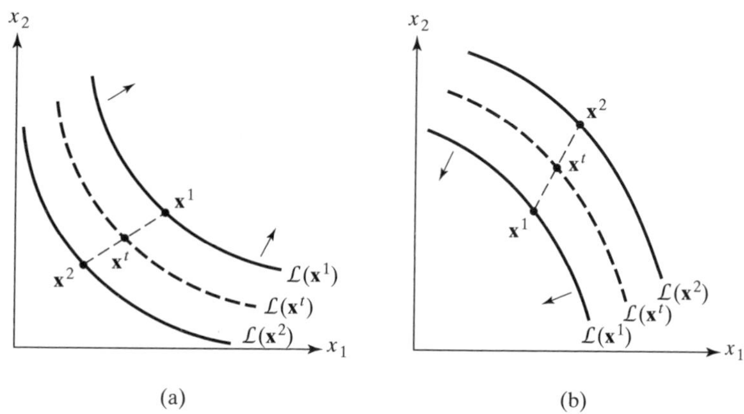

Figure A1. 30. Level sets for quasiconcave functions. (a) The function is quasiconcave and increasing. (b) The function is quasiconcave and decreasing.

When $f(\mathbf{x})$ is an increasing function, it will be quasiconcave whenever the level set relative to any convex combination of two points, $\mathcal{L}(\mathbf{x}^t)$, is always *on or above* the lowest of the level sets $\mathcal{L}(\mathbf{x}^1)$ and $\mathcal{L}(\mathbf{x}^2)$. This case is illustrated in Fig. A1.30(a). When $f(\mathbf{x})$ is a decreasing function, it will be quasiconcave whenever the level set relative to any convex combination of two points is always *on or below* the highest of the two level sets. This case is illustrated in Fig. A1.30(b).

The level sets in Fig. A1.30 were drawn nicely curved for a good reason. Besides requiring the relative positioning of level sets already noted, quasiconcavity requires very regular behaviour in its superior sets. As you may have guessed, these must be convex.

THEOREM A1.14 ***Quasiconcavity and the Superior Sets***

$f: D \to \mathbb{R}$ is a quasiconcave function iff $S(y)$ is a convex set for all $y \in \mathbb{R}$.

Proof: *Sufficiency*: First, we want to show that if f is quasiconcave, then $S(y)$ is a convex set for all $y \in \mathbb{R}$. To begin, let y be any point in $\mathbb{R}$, and let $S(y)$ be the superior set relative to y. Let $\mathbf{x}^1$ and $\mathbf{x}^2$ be any two points in $S(y)$. (If $S(y)$ is empty, our job is immediately done because the empty set is convex.) We need to show that if f is quasiconcave, all points of the form $\mathbf{x}^t \equiv t\mathbf{x}^1 + (1-t)\mathbf{x}^2$, $t \in [0, 1]$, are also in $S(y)$.

Because $\mathbf{x}^1 \in S(y)$ and $\mathbf{x}^2 \in S(y)$, the definition of the superior set tells us that $\mathbf{x}^1$ and $\mathbf{x}^2$ are both in D and satisfy

$$f(\mathbf{x}^1) \geq y \quad \text{and} \quad f(\mathbf{x}^2) \geq y. \tag{P.1}$$

Now consider any $\mathbf{x}^t$. We know $\mathbf{x}^t \in D$ because we are assuming D is a convex set. If f is quasiconcave, then

$$f(\mathbf{x}^t) \geq \min[f(\mathbf{x}^1), f(\mathbf{x}^2)] \geq y. \tag{P.2}$$

The first inequality is the definition of quasiconcavity, and the second follows from (P.1). But if $\mathbf{x}^t \in D$ and $f(\mathbf{x}^t) \geq y$, then $\mathbf{x}^t$ satisfies the requirements for inclusion in $S(y)$, so $S(y)$ must be a convex set. This completes the proof of sufficiency.

Necessity: Here we have to show that if $S(y)$ is a convex set for all $y \in \mathbb{R}$, then $f(\mathbf{x})$ is a quasiconcave function. To do that, let $\mathbf{x}^1$ and $\mathbf{x}^2$ be any two points in D. Without loss of generality, assume we have labelled things so that

$$f(\mathbf{x}^1) \geq f(\mathbf{x}^2). \tag{P.3}$$

By assumption, $S(y)$ is a convex set for any $y \in \mathbb{R}$, so clearly $S(f(\mathbf{x}^2))$ must be convex, too. Obviously, $\mathbf{x}^2 \in S(f(\mathbf{x}^2))$ and, by (P.3), $\mathbf{x}^1 \in S(f(\mathbf{x}^2))$. Then for any convex combination of $\mathbf{x}^1$ and $\mathbf{x}^2$ we must also have $\mathbf{x}^t \in S(f(\mathbf{x}^2))$. From the definition of $S(f(\mathbf{x}^2))$, this implies $f(\mathbf{x}^t) \geq f(\mathbf{x}^2)$. But in view of (P.3), this tells us

$$f(\mathbf{x}^t) \geq \min[f(\mathbf{x}^1), f(\mathbf{x}^2)],$$

so $f(\mathbf{x})$ is quasiconcave and the proof is complete. ∎

This theorem establishes an *equivalence* between quasiconcave functions and convex superior sets. To assume that a function is quasiconcave is therefore exactly the same as assuming that the superior sets are convex, and vice versa. Notice, however, that nothing we have said so far rules out the possibility of having 'linear segments' appear, this time in the level sets. Both the definition of quasiconcavity and Theorem A1.14 are consistent with the possibility depicted in Fig. A1.31. There, $\mathbf{x}^1$ and $\mathbf{x}^2$ lie on a flat portion of the same level set. The chord connecting them *coincides* with the linear segment in the level set, so that all convex combinations will also lie on the linear segment. Here, $f(\mathbf{x}^1) = f(\mathbf{x}^2) = f(\mathbf{x}^t)$, so the inequality $f(\mathbf{x}^t) \geq \min[f(\mathbf{x}^1), f(\mathbf{x}^2)]$ holds, but with equality. Naturally enough, this kind of thing is ruled out under *strict* quasiconcavity.

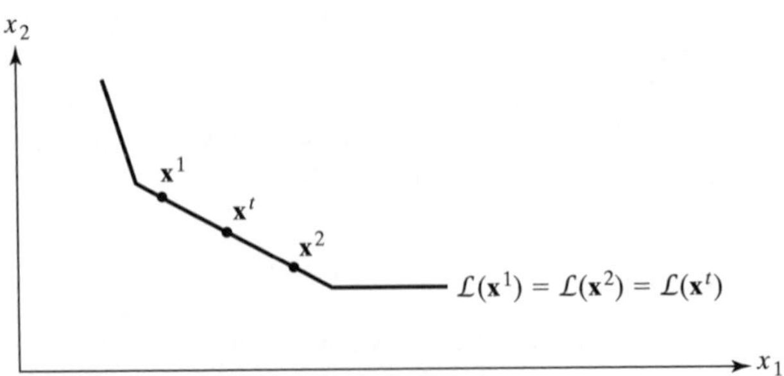

Figure A1.31. Quasiconcavity and linear segments in the level sets.

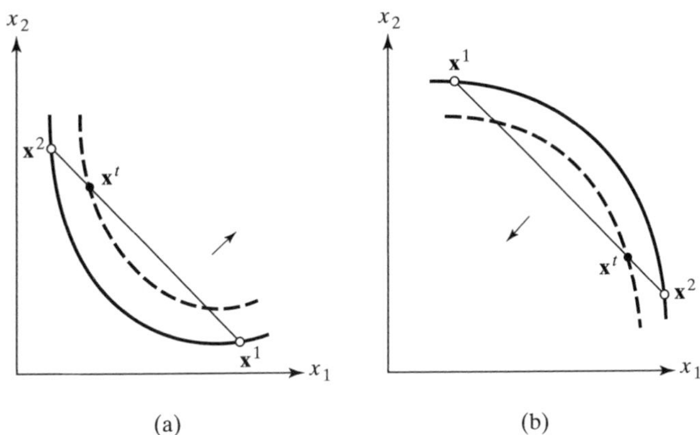

Figure A1.32. The function in (a) is strictly quasiconcave and increasing. The one in (b) is strictly quasiconcave and decreasing.

DEFINITION A1.25 *Strictly Quasiconcave Functions*

A function $f: D \to R$ is strictly quasiconcave iff, for all $\mathbf{x}^1 \neq \mathbf{x}^2$ in D, $f(\mathbf{x}^t) > \min[f(\mathbf{x}^1), f(\mathbf{x}^2)]$ for all $t \in (0, 1)$.

Once again, we require that t be in the open interval and that the inequality be strict. Constraining t to the open interval again prevents the definition from becoming vacuous. By requiring the strict inequality, we forbid the convex combination of two points in the same level set from also lying in that level set, as occurs in Fig. A1.31. Instead, such convex combinations must lie in *strictly* higher level sets, as occurs in Fig. A1.32. Thus, strictly quasiconcave functions must have superior sets with no flat segments in the boundary.

We began discussing quasiconcave functions by remarking that quasiconcavity is a *weaker* restriction than concavity. One might reason therefore that if a function is concave, it will satisfy all the properties of a quasiconcave function. This is indeed the case, and we conclude the discussion of quasiconcavity by stating this formally and giving a proof. (Note, however, that the converse is not true. A quasiconcave function *need not* be concave.)

THEOREM A1.15 *Concavity Implies Quasiconcavity*

A concave function is always quasiconcave. A strictly concave function is always strictly quasiconcave.

Proof: The theorem asserts that if f is (strictly) concave, then f is also (strictly) quasiconcave. We will give a constructive proof of the concave case, leaving the other as an exercise.

Assume that $f: D \to \mathbb{R}$ is concave. Take any $\mathbf{x}^1$ and $\mathbf{x}^2$ in D and assume, without loss of generality, that

$$f(\mathbf{x}^1) \geq f(\mathbf{x}^2). \tag{P.1}$$

From the definition of concavity, for $\mathbf{x}^t \equiv t\mathbf{x}^1 + (1-t)\mathbf{x}^2$, we must have

$$f(\mathbf{x}^t) \geq tf(\mathbf{x}^1) + (1-t)f(\mathbf{x}^2) \quad \text{for all } t \in [0, 1]. \tag{P.2}$$

Factor out $t \geq 0$ on the right-hand side, rearrange, and express (P.2) equivalently as

$$f(\mathbf{x}^t) \geq f(\mathbf{x}^2) + t\big(f(\mathbf{x}^1) - f(\mathbf{x}^2)\big) \quad \text{for all } t \in [0, 1]. \tag{P.3}$$

Now consider the product term on the right-hand side of (P.3). We know that $t \geq 0$ and, by (P.1), that $f(\mathbf{x}^1) - f(\mathbf{x}^2) \geq 0$, so the whole last term is non-negative and may be strictly positive. In either case, the whole right-hand side, together, must be greater than or equal to $f(\mathbf{x}^2)$. At the same time, we know from (P.1) that $f(\mathbf{x}^2) = \min[f(\mathbf{x}^1), f(\mathbf{x}^2)]$. Therefore, (P.1) and (P.3), together, tell us that

$$f(\mathbf{x}^t) \geq \min[f(\mathbf{x}^1), f(\mathbf{x}^2)] \quad \text{for all } t \in [0, 1],$$

so f satisfies the definition of a quasiconcave function. ∎

A1.4.4 CONVEX AND QUASICONVEX FUNCTIONS

The last type of real-valued functions we will consider are *convex* and *quasiconvex* functions. Although some confusion is possible because of the terminology, it is important to distinguish between the term 'convexity' as we have employed it in relation to a set and the same term as we now apply it in discussing a function. Basically, convexity of a function is just the 'flip side' of concavity of a function. Because we have treated concavity at some length, and because most important notions are mirror images of ones we have already encountered, this section can be briefer than the last. We begin with some definitions.

DEFINITION A1.26 ***Convex and Strictly Convex Functions***

1. *$f: D \to R$ is a convex function iff, for all $\mathbf{x}^1$, $\mathbf{x}^2$ in D,*

$$f(\mathbf{x}^t) \leq tf(\mathbf{x}^1) + (1-t)f(\mathbf{x}^2) \textit{ for all } t \in [0, 1].$$

2. *$f: D \to R$ is a strictly convex function iff, for all $\mathbf{x}^1 \neq \mathbf{x}^2$ in D,*

$$f(\mathbf{x}^t) < tf(\mathbf{x}^1) + (1-t)f(\mathbf{x}^2) \textit{ for all } t \in (0, 1).$$

Consider $f: D \to R$, where $D \subset \mathbb{R}$. The definition of a convex function requires that the value of the function evaluated at the convex combination of any two points be *no greater than* the value obtained when we form the corresponding convex combination of the values $f(x^1)$ and $f(x^2)$. Geometrically, this will be so only if the point $(x^t, tf(x^1) + (1-t)f(x^2))$ on the chord connecting $(x^1, f(x^1))$ and $(x^2, f(x^2))$ is *no lower* than the point

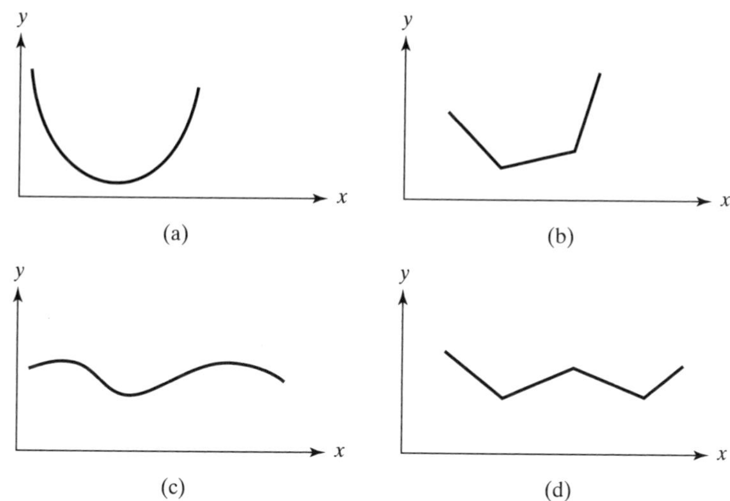

Figure A1.33. (a and b) Convex functions. (c and d) Non-convex. (a) Strictly convex.

$(x^t, f(x^t))$. Some examples of convex and non-convex functions are given in Fig. A1.33. As the examples show, a convex function may have 'linear segments' in its graph. As before, *strict* convexity is needed to rule out such things.

Concave and convex functions are very closely related – indeed, we said before that the one was the 'flip side' of the other. More precisely, there is an *equivalence* between concavity of a function and convexity of the *negative* of that function.

THEOREM A1.16 ***Concave and Convex Functions***

$f(\mathbf{x})$ is a (strictly) concave function if and only if $-f(\mathbf{x})$ is a (strictly) convex function.

Proof: The proof just requires manipulating the definitions. We will show sufficiency and leave necessity to the reader.

If $f(\mathbf{x})$ is concave, then $f(\mathbf{x}^t) \geq tf(\mathbf{x}^1) + (1-t)f(\mathbf{x}^2)$ for all $\mathbf{x}^1$ and $\mathbf{x}^2$ in D, and $t \in [0, 1]$. Multiply by -1 and get $-f(\mathbf{x}^t) \leq t(-f(\mathbf{x}^1)) + (1-t)(-f(\mathbf{x}^2))$, so $-f(\mathbf{x})$ is convex. ∎

Whereas concavity required points below the graph to form a convex set, convexity requires the set of points *on* and *above* the graph of the function to be a convex set.

THEOREM A1.17 ***Points On and Above the Graph of a Convex Function Form a Convex Set***

Let $A^* \equiv \{(\mathbf{x}, y) \mid \mathbf{x} \in D, f(\mathbf{x}) \leq y\}$ be the set of points 'on and above' the graph of $f : D \to R$, where $D \subset \mathbb{R}^n$ is a convex set and $R \subset \mathbb{R}$. Then

$$f \text{ is a convex function} \iff A^* \text{ is a convex set.}$$

Proof: By Theorem A1.16, $f(\mathbf{x})$ is convex iff $-f(\mathbf{x})$ is concave, and by Theorem A1.13, the latter holds iff the set

$$A \equiv \{(\mathbf{x}, y) \mid \mathbf{x} \in D, -f(\mathbf{x}) \geq y\}$$

is a convex set. Note that because y may be a positive or negative real number, we may rewrite the set A as

$$\begin{aligned} A &\equiv \{(\mathbf{x}, -y) \mid \mathbf{x} \in D, -f(\mathbf{x}) \geq -y\}, \\ &\equiv \{(\mathbf{x}, -y) \mid \mathbf{x} \in D, f(\mathbf{x}) \leq y\}. \end{aligned}$$

Hence, we have shown that $f(\mathbf{x})$ is convex iff the set $A \equiv \{(\mathbf{x}, -y) \mid \mathbf{x} \in D, f(\mathbf{x}) \leq y\}$ is convex.

Finally, note that A is convex iff A^* is convex because $(\mathbf{x}, y) \in A^*$ iff $(\mathbf{x}, -y) \in A$. We conclude that $f(\mathbf{x})$ is a convex function iff A^* is a convex set. ∎

A function may also be *quasiconvex*. As the name suggests, quasiconvexity is a weaker requirement than convexity. The definitions that follow are familiar in form, but pay close attention to the details.

DEFINITION A1.27 ***Quasiconvex and Strictly Quasiconvex Functions***[8]

1. *A function* $f: D \to R$ *is quasiconvex iff, for all* $\mathbf{x}^1, \mathbf{x}^2$ *in D,*

$$f(\mathbf{x}^t) \leq \max[f(\mathbf{x}^1), f(\mathbf{x}^2)] \qquad \forall\, t \in [0, 1].$$

2. *A function* $f: D \to R$ *is strictly quasiconvex iff, for all* $\mathbf{x}^1 \neq \mathbf{x}^2$ *in D,*

$$f(\mathbf{x}^t) < \max[f(\mathbf{x}^1), f(\mathbf{x}^2)] \qquad \forall\, t \in (0, 1).$$

Here again, these may seem rather awkward. Fortunately, we again know something about the level and other related sets for quasiconvex functions. The results are essentially the opposite of those obtained before. For a quasiconvex function, it is the *inferior sets* that are convex sets. If the quasiconvex function is *increasing*, this will be the set of points *below* the level set. If it is *decreasing*, this will be the set of points *above* the level set. These are illustrated in Fig. A1.34 and detailed in what follows. We leave the proof of the following theorem as an exercise.

THEOREM A1.18 ***Quasiconvexity and the Inferior Sets***

$f: D \to R$ is a quasiconvex function iff $I(y)$ is a convex set for all $y \in \mathbb{R}$.

[8]The operator $\max[a, b]$ means 'the larger of a and b'. If $a > b$, then $\max[a, b] = a$. If $a = b$, then $\max[a, b]$ equals a and b.

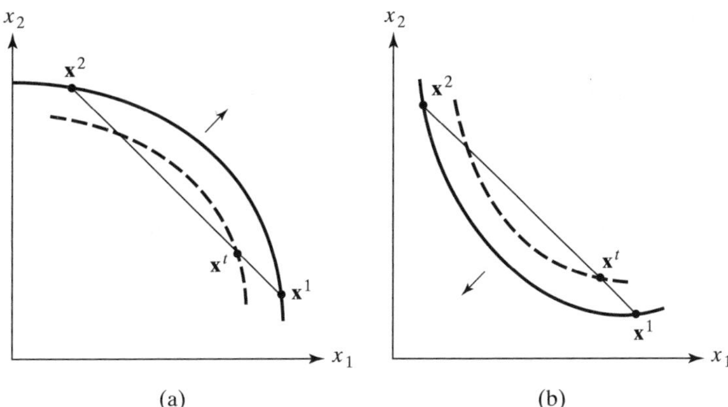

Figure A1.34. Quasiconvex functions have convex inferior sets. Strictly quasiconvex functions have no linear segments in their level sets. (a) Strictly quasiconvex and increasing. (b) Strictly quasiconvex and decreasing.

f is concave	$\Longleftrightarrow$ the set of points *beneath* the graph is convex
f is convex	$\Longleftrightarrow$ the set of points *above* the graph is convex
f quasiconcave	$\Longleftrightarrow$ superior sets are convex sets
f quasiconvex	$\Longleftrightarrow$ inferior sets are convex sets
f concave	$\Rightarrow$ f quasiconcave
f convex	$\Rightarrow$ f quasiconvex
f (strictly) concave	$\Longleftrightarrow$ $-f$ (strictly) convex
f (strictly) quasiconcave	$\Longleftrightarrow$ $-f$ (strictly) quasiconvex

Figure A1.35. Summary.

As we have seen, there is an *equivalence* between concavity of a function and convexity of the *negative* of that function. There is a similar equivalence relating quasiconcave and quasiconvex functions.

THEOREM A1.19 ***Quasiconcave and Quasiconvex Functions***

$f(\mathbf{x})$ is a (strictly) quasiconcave function if and only if $-f(\mathbf{x})$ is a (strictly) quasiconvex function.

Proof: Again, we will just show sufficiency. If $f(\mathbf{x})$ is quasiconcave, then $f(\mathbf{x}^t) \geq \min[f(\mathbf{x}^1), f(\mathbf{x}^2)]$. Multiply by -1 and get

$$-f(\mathbf{x}^t) \leq -\min[f(\mathbf{x}^1), f(\mathbf{x}^2)] = \max[-f(\mathbf{x}^1), -f(\mathbf{x}^2)],$$

so $-f(\mathbf{x})$ is quasiconvex. Necessity is just as easy. ∎

Finally, several of the important relationships between various real-valued functions we have studied are summarised in Fig. A1.35.

A1.5 EXERCISES

A1.1 The set operations of union and intersection obey the *commutative law* and the *distributive law*. The commutative law for unions states that $S \cup T = T \cup S$, and for intersections that $S \cap T = T \cap S$. The distributive law for intersections says that for three sets R, S, and T, $R \cap (S \cap T) = (R \cap S) \cap T$, and for unions that $R \cup (S \cup T) = (R \cup S) \cup T$. Verify these laws using diagrams similar to those in Fig. A1.1.

A1.2 The following are intuitively 'obvious'. Give a proof for each one.

(a) $S \subset (S \cup T)$.

(b) $T \subset (S \cup T)$.

(c) $(S \cap T) \subset S$.

(d) $(S \cap T) \subset T$.

A1.3 **De Morgan's laws** tell us that

$$(S \cap T)^c = S^c \cup T^c$$
$$(S \cup T)^c = S^c \cap T^c.$$

Prove De Morgan's laws.

A1.4 Extend De Morgan's laws to the case of an arbitrary number of sets. Prove that for any index set I,

$$\left(\bigcap_{i \in I} S_i\right)^c = \bigcup_{i \in I} S_i^c$$
$$\left(\bigcup_{i \in I} S_i\right)^c = \bigcap_{i \in I} S_i^c.$$

A1.5 Let A and B be convex sets. Show by counterexample that $A \cup B$ need not be a convex set.

A1.6 Extend Theorem A1.1 to the case of an arbitrary number of convex sets.

A1.7 Graph each of the following sets. If the set is convex, give a proof. If it is not convex, give a counterexample.

(a) $\{(x, y) \mid y = e^x\}$.

(b) $\{(x, y) \mid y \geq e^x\}$.

(c) $\{(x, y) \mid y \geq 2x - x^2; \quad x > 0, \ y > 0\}$.

(d) $\{(x, y) \mid xy \geq 1; \quad x > 0, \ y > 0\}$.

(e) $\{(x, y) \mid y \leq \ln(x)\}$.

A1.8 Let S be the set of all people on earth. Let the relation $\mathcal{R}$ be defined by the statement 'loves'. Is $\mathcal{R}$ complete? Transitive?

A1.9 Let A and B be two sets in domain D, and suppose that $B \subset A$. Prove that $f(B) \subset f(A)$ for any mapping $f \colon D \to R$.

A1.10 Let A and B be two sets in range R, and suppose that $B \subset A$. Prove that $f^{-1}(B) \subset f^{-1}(A)$ for any mapping $f: D \to R$.

A1.11 Consider the function $f(x) = x^2$. Describe the image set and determine whether the function is one-to-one and whether it is onto if

(a) $D = \mathbb{R}, \quad R = \mathbb{R}$.

(b) $D = \mathbb{R}, \quad R = \mathbb{R}_+$.

(c) $D = \mathbb{R}_+, \quad R = \mathbb{R}$.

(d) $D = \mathbb{R}_+, \quad R = \mathbb{R}_+$.

A1.12 Does an inverse function exist for the function depicted in Fig. A1.8(a)? How about Fig. A1.8(b)? Why or why not?

A1.13 Let $f: D \to R$ be any mapping and let B be any set in the range R. Prove that $f^{-1}(B^c) = (f^{-1}(B))^c$.

A1.14 For any mapping $f: D \to R$ and any two sets A and B in the range of f, show that

$$f^{-1}(A \cup B) = f^{-1}(A) \cup f^{-1}(B)$$
$$f^{-1}(A \cap B) = f^{-1}(A) \cap f^{-1}(B).$$

A1.15 Let $\{A_i\}_{i \in I} \subset R$ be any (finite or infinite) collection of sets in the range of f. Extend your proof in the preceding exercise to show that

$$f^{-1}\left(\bigcup_{i \in I} A_i\right) = \bigcup_{i \in I} f^{-1}(A_i)$$
$$f^{-1}\left(\bigcap_{i \in I} A_i\right) = \bigcap_{i \in I} f^{-1}(A_i)$$

A1.16 Let S and T be convex sets. Prove that each of the following is also a convex set:

(a) $-S \equiv \{\mathbf{x} \mid \mathbf{x} = -\mathbf{s}, \quad \mathbf{s} \in S\}$.

(b) $S - T \equiv \{\mathbf{x} \mid \mathbf{x} = \mathbf{s} - \mathbf{t}, \quad \mathbf{s} \in S,\ \mathbf{t} \in T\}$.

A1.17 Let $A_i \subset \mathbb{R}^m$ be a convex set for $i = 1, \ldots, n$. Prove that each of the following is a convex set.

(a) $\cap_{i=1}^n A_i$.

(b) $\times_{i=1}^n A_i$ (the Cartesian product).

(c) $\sum_{i=1}^n A_i \equiv \{\sum_{i=1}^n a_i \mid a_i \in A_i,\ i = 1, \ldots, n\}$ (the sum of sets).

(d) $\sum_{i=1}^n \alpha^i A^i \equiv \{\sum_{i=1}^n \alpha^i a_i \mid \alpha^i \in \mathbb{R},\ a_i \in A_i\}$ (the linear combination of sets).

A1.18 Let $f^i(\mathbf{x}) = \mathbf{a}^i \cdot \mathbf{x} + b^i$ for $\mathbf{a}^i \in \mathbb{R}^n$, $b^i \in \mathbb{R}$, and consider the inequalities, $f^i(\mathbf{x}) \geq 0$ for $i = 1, \ldots, n$. Let $\Omega = \{\mathbf{x} \mid f^i(\mathbf{x}) \geq 0,\ i = 1, \ldots, n\}$ be the set of solutions to these n linear inequalities. Show that Ω is a convex set.

A1.19 We sometimes write $\| \mathbf{x} \| \equiv \| \mathbf{x} - \mathbf{0} \|$ to denote the distance from the origin in $\mathbb{R}^n$ to the point $\mathbf{x}$. Consider any vector $t\mathbf{x}$, where $t \geq 0$ is a non-negative scalar. Prove that $\|t\mathbf{x}\| = t \| \mathbf{x} \|$.

A1.20 Consider any open interval (a, b). Show that

$$(a, b) = B_\varepsilon\left(\frac{a+b}{2}\right),$$

where $\varepsilon = (b-a)/2$.

A1.21 Prove part 4 in Theorem A1.2. Is the intersection of *infinitely* many open sets also an open set?

A1.22 Consider any two points $\mathbf{x}^1$ and $\mathbf{x}^2$ in $\mathbb{R}^n$. Let $B_\varepsilon(\mathbf{x}^1)$ be any open ball centred at $\mathbf{x}^1$.

(a) Let $Z \equiv \{\mathbf{z} \mid \mathbf{z} = t\mathbf{x}^1 + (1-t)\mathbf{x}^2, t \in [0, 1]\}$ be the set of all convex combinations of $\mathbf{x}^1$ and $\mathbf{x}^2$. Prove that $B_\varepsilon(\mathbf{x}^1) \cap Z \neq \emptyset$.

(b) Let $Z^* \equiv \{\mathbf{z} \mid \mathbf{z} = t\mathbf{x}^1 + (1-t)\mathbf{x}^2, t \in (0, 1)\}$ be the subset of Z that excludes $\mathbf{x}^1$ and $\mathbf{x}^2$. Prove that $B_\varepsilon(\mathbf{x}^1) \cap Z^* \neq \emptyset$.

A1.23 Prove part 4 in Theorem A1.4.

A1.24 Consider intervals in $\mathbb{R}$ of the form $[a, +\infty)$ and $(-\infty, b]$. Prove that they are both closed sets. Is the same true for intervals of the form $[a, c)$ and $(-c, b]$ for c finite?

A1.25 Let $S \subset \mathbb{R}$ be a set consisting of a single point, $S = \{s\}$. Prove that S is a closed, convex set.

A1.26 Let $(a, b) \subset \mathbb{R}$ be any open interval. Prove that its complement, $(a, b)^c = (-\infty, a] \cup [b, +\infty)$. Conclude that the complement of every open interval is the union of two closed sets.

A1.27 Any closed set of real numbers possesses a rather special property: it can be viewed as a (possibly infinite) intersection of unions of simple closed intervals. Specifically, for any closed set $S \subset \mathbb{R}$,

$$S = \bigcap_{i \in I}((-\infty, a_i] \cup [b_i, +\infty))$$

for some real numbers $a_i < b_i$ and some index set I. Give a proof of this claim.

A1.28 Let D be a subset of $\mathbb{R}^n$. Prove the analogues of Theorems A1.2 and A1.4 for open and closed sets in D. For example, the analogue of part 3 of Theorem A1.2 would read, 'The union of open sets in D is an open set in D'. Similarly for the others.

A1.29 Complete the following.

(a) Show that $[0, 1)$ is open in $\mathbb{R}_+$ but not in $\mathbb{R}$.

(b) Part (a) shows that open sets in $\mathbb{R}_+$ are not necessarily open in $\mathbb{R}$. Show, however, that closed sets in $\mathbb{R}_+$ are closed in $\mathbb{R}$.

(c) More generally, show that if D is a subset of $\mathbb{R}^n$ and D is open (closed) in $\mathbb{R}^n$, then $S \subset D$ is open (closed) in D if and only if it is open (closed) in $\mathbb{R}^n$.

A1.30 Prove that if b is the *l.u.b.* of $S \subset \mathbb{R}$ and S is an open set, then $b \notin S$. Prove that if b is the *l.u.b.* of $S \subset \mathbb{R}$ and S is closed, then $b \in S$.

A1.31 Let $\alpha_1 > 0$, $\alpha_2 > 0$, and $\beta > 0$ all be real numbers. Consider the subset of points in $\mathbb{R}^2$ given by $\Omega \equiv \{\mathbf{x} \in \mathbb{R}^2_+ \mid \alpha_1 x_1 + \alpha_2 x_2 \leq \beta\}$. Prove that Ω is a convex set. Sketch Ω in the plane. If $x_1 = 0$, what is the largest value that x_2 can take? If $x_2 = 0$, what is the largest value x_1 can take? Mark these points on your sketch. (Look familiar?) Prove that Ω is bounded.

A1.32 The set $S^{n-1} \equiv \{\mathbf{x} \mid \sum_{i=1}^{n} x_i = 1, x_i \geq 0, i = 1, \ldots, n\}$ is called the $(n-1)$-dimensional **unit simplex**.

(a) Sketch this set for $n = 2$.

(b) Prove that S^{n-1} is a convex set.

(c) Prove that S^{n-1} is a compact set.

A1.33 Prove the analogue of Theorem A1.6 for closed sets. That is, show that the following statements are equivalent:

(i) $f: D \to \mathbb{R}^n$ is continuous.

(ii) For every closed ball B in $\mathbb{R}^n$, the inverse image of B under f is closed in D.

(iii) For every closed subset S of $\mathbb{R}^n$, the inverse image of S under f is closed in D.

A1.34 Prove that $f: D \to \mathbb{R}^n$ is continuous if and only if $f^{-1}(T)$ is compact in the domain $D \subset \mathbb{R}^m$ for every compact set T in the range $\mathbb{R}^n$.

A1.35 To help convince yourself that the conditions of Theorem A1.10 are sufficient, but not necessary, illustrate a simple case like those in Fig. A1.18 where f is real-valued and continuous, $S \subset D$ is *not* compact, yet a minimum and a maximum over S both exist. Illustrate a case where neither is S compact, nor is f continuous, yet both a maximum and a minimum of f over S exist.

A1.36 Every **hyperplane** divides $\mathbb{R}^n$ into two 'half spaces': the set of points 'on and above' the hyperplane, $H^+ = \{\mathbf{x} \mid \mathbf{a} \cdot \mathbf{x} \geq \alpha\}$, and the set of points 'on and below' the hyperplane, $H^- = \{\mathbf{x} \mid \mathbf{a} \cdot \mathbf{x} \leq \alpha\}$. Prove that each of these two half spaces is a closed, convex set.

A1.37 Convince yourself that the conditions of Brouwer's theorem are sufficient, but not necessary, for the existence of a fixed point by illustrating the following situations:

(a) S is compact, S is convex, f is *not* continuous, and a fixed point of f exists.

(b) S is compact, S is *not* convex, f is continuous, and a fixed point of f exists.

(c) S is *not* compact, S is convex, f is continuous, and a fixed point of f exists.

(d) S is *not* compact, S is *not* convex, f is *not* continuous, and a fixed point of f exists.

A1.38 Let $f(x) = x^2$ and suppose that $S = (0, 1)$. Show that f has no fixed point even though it is a continuous mapping from S to S. Does this contradict Brouwer's theorem? Why or why not?

A1.39 Use Brouwer's theorem to show that the equation $\cos(x) - x - 1/2 = 0$ has a solution in the interval $0 \leq x \leq \pi/4$.

A1.40 Sketch a few level sets for the following functions:

(a) $y = x_1 x_2$.

(b) $y = x_1 + x_2$.

(c) $y = \min[x_1, x_2]$.

A1.41 Prove Theorem A1.12. Remember for parts 3 and 6 through 8 to prove that $A \subset B$ *and* $B \subset A$.

A1.42 Let $D = [-2, 2]$ and $f: D \to R$ be $y = 4 - x^2$. Carefully sketch this function. Using the definition of a concave function, prove that f is concave. Demonstrate that the set A is a convex set.

A1.43 Complete the proof of Theorem A1.15.

A1.44 Prove Theorem A1.18.

A1.45 Complete the proofs of Theorems A1.16 and A1.19.

A1.46 Consider any linear function $f(\mathbf{x}) = \mathbf{a} \cdot \mathbf{x} + b$ for $\mathbf{a} \in \mathbb{R}^n$ and $b \in \mathbb{R}$.

(a) Show that every linear function is both concave and convex, though neither strictly concave nor strictly convex.

(b) Show that every linear function is both quasiconcave and quasiconvex and, for $n > 1$, neither strictly so.

A1.47 Let $f(\mathbf{x})$ be a concave (convex) real-valued function. Let $g(t)$ be an increasing concave (convex) function of a single variable. Show that the composite function, $h(\mathbf{x}) = g(f(\mathbf{x}))$ is a concave (convex) function.

A1.48 Let $f(x_1, x_2) = -(x_1 - 5)^2 - (x_2 - 5)^2$. Prove that f is quasiconcave.

A1.49 Answer each of the following questions 'yes' or 'no', and justify your answer.

(a) Suppose $f(x)$ is an increasing function of one variable. Is $f(x)$ quasiconcave?

(b) Suppose $f(x)$ is a decreasing function of one variable. Is $f(x)$ quasiconcave?

(c) Suppose $f(x)$ is a function of one variable and there is a real number b such that $f(x)$ is decreasing on the interval $(-\infty, b]$ and increasing on $[b, +\infty)$. Is $f(x)$ quasiconcave?

(d) Suppose $f(x)$ is a function of one variable and there is a real number b such that $f(x)$ is increasing on the interval $(-\infty, b]$ and decreasing on $[b, +\infty)$. Is $f(x)$ quasiconcave?

(e) You should now be able to come up with a characterisation of quasiconcave functions of one variable involving the words 'increasing' and 'decreasing'.

CHAPTER A2

CALCULUS AND OPTIMISATION

A2.1 CALCULUS

A2.1.1 FUNCTIONS OF A SINGLE VARIABLE

Roughly speaking, a function $y = f(x)$ is **differentiable** if it is both continuous and 'smooth', with no breaks or kinks. The function in Fig. A2.1(b) is everywhere differentiable, whereas the one in Fig. A2.1(a) is not differentiable at x^0. Differentiability is thus a more stringent requirement than continuity. It is also a requirement we often impose because it allows us to use familiar tools from calculus.

The concept of the **derivative**, $f'(x)$, is no doubt familiar to you. The derivative is a function, too, giving, at each value of x, the slope or instantaneous rate of change in $f(x)$. We therefore sometimes write

$$\frac{dy}{dx} = f'(x), \tag{A2.1}$$

to indicate that $f'(x)$ gives us the (instantaneous) amount, dy, by which y changes per unit change, dx, in x. If the (first) derivative is a differentiable function, we can take its derivative, too, getting the second derivative of the original function

$$\frac{d^2y}{dx^2} = f'(x). \tag{A2.2}$$

If a function possesses continuous derivatives $f', f', \ldots, f^n$, it is called n-times continuously differentiable, or a C^n function. Some of the rules of differentiation are given in Fig. A2.2 for review.

Just as the derivative, $f'(x)$, gives the (instantaneous) rate of change of $f(x)$ per unit change in x, the second derivative, $f'(x)$, gives the rate of change of $f'(x)$ per unit change in x. That is, $f'(x)$ gives the rate at which the *slope* of f is changing. Consequently, the second derivative is related to the curvature of the function f.

For example, Fig. A2.3 depicts a concave function. The fact that it is 'curved downward' is captured by the fact that the slope of the function *decreases* as x increases, i.e., by

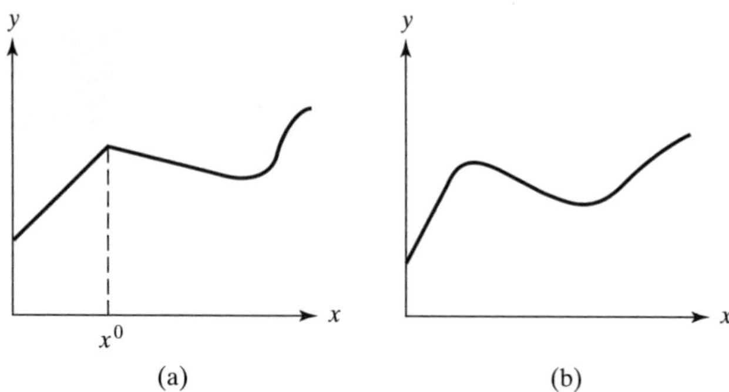

Figure A2.1. (a) Non-differentiable and (b) differentiable functions of a single variable.

For Constants, α : $\frac{d}{dx}(\alpha)=0.$

For Sums: $\frac{d}{dx}[f(x) \pm g(x)]=f'(x) \pm g'(x).$

Power Rule: $\frac{d}{dx}(\alpha x^n)=n\alpha x^{n-1}.$

Product Rule: $\frac{d}{dx}[f(x)g(x)]=f(x)g'(x)+f'(x)g(x).$

Quotient Rule: $\frac{d}{dx}\left[\frac{f(x)}{g(x)}\right]=\frac{g(x)f'(x)-f(x)g'(x)}{[g(x)]^2}.$

Chain Rule: $\frac{d}{dx}[f(g(x))]=f'(g(x))g'(x).$

Figure A2.2. Rules of differentiation.

the fact that its second derivative is non-positive. (Note that $f'(x^0)$, the slope of the line l_0, is greater than $f'(x^1)$, the slope of the line l_1.)

From Fig. A2.3, it appears that a function is concave precisely when its second derivative is always non-positive. In a moment, we shall state a theorem to this effect. Draw a few concave functions to convince yourself of this.

But something else is also apparent from Fig. A2.3. Note that both tangent lines, l_0 and l_1, lie entirely *above* (sometimes only weakly above) the function f. Let us focus on line l_0. This is a straight line with slope $f'(x^0)$ that goes through the point $(x^0, f(x^0))$. Consequently, the equation describing this straight line is

$$l_0(x) = f'(x^0)(x - x^0) + f(x^0).$$

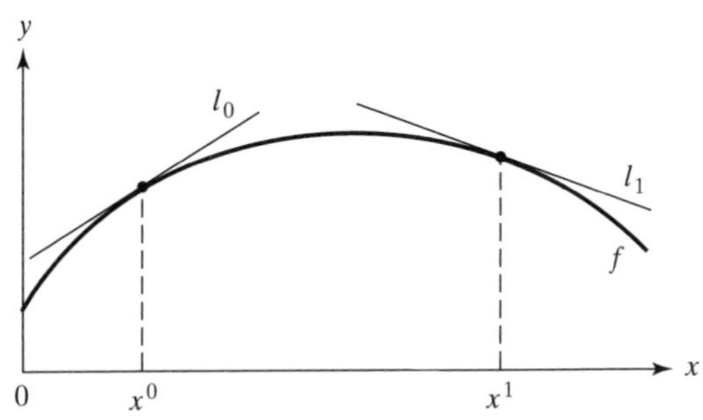

Figure A2.3. Curvature and the second derivative.

Now, saying that the line l_0 lies above f is just saying that $l_0(x) \geq f(x)$ for all x. But this then says that

$$f(x) \leq f(x^0) + f'(x^0)(x - x^0)$$

for all x. Thus, this inequality seems to follow from the concavity of f.

Theorem A2.1, which we state without proof, puts together the preceding observations to characterise concave functions of a single variable in two ways: one in terms of the function's second derivative, and the other in terms of its first derivative and the tangent lines it generates.

THEOREM A2.1 ***Concavity and First and Second Derivatives***

Let D be a non-degenerate interval of real numbers on the interior of which f is twice continuously differentiable. The following statements 1 to 3 are equivalent:

1. *f is concave.*
2. *$f''(x) \leq 0 \quad \forall$ non-endpoints $x \in D$.*
3. *For all $x^0 \in D: f(x) \leq f(x^0) + f'(x^0)(x - x^0) \quad \forall x \in D$.*

Moreover,

4. *If $f''(x) < 0 \quad \forall$ non-endpoints $x \in D$, then f is strictly concave.*

Because a function is convex if its negative is concave, Theorem A2.1 also gives a characterisation of convex functions. Simply replace the word 'concave' with 'convex', and reverse the sense of all the inequalities. One might think that the converse of statement 4 is true, i.e., that if f is strictly concave, then its second derivative must be strictly negative everywhere. You are asked in Exercise A2.20 to show that this is not the case.

A2.1.2 FUNCTIONS OF SEVERAL VARIABLES

We will usually be concerned with real-valued functions of several variables, and the ideas just discussed can be easily generalised.

In the single-variable case, it is easy to think of *the* derivative of the function giving us *the* slope or rate of change in y as x changes. There, the value of y, so any changes or increments in y, depends only on the value of the single variable x. However, with real-valued functions of n variables, y depends on the value of *all* n of the variables $x_1, \ldots, x_n$. It is therefore harder to think of *the* slope or *the* rate of change in y in the singular. It is quite natural, though, to think of *the slope as* x_1 *changes* and *the slope as* x_2 *changes*, and so on, for all n of the variables on which y depends. Rather than having a single slope, a function of n variables can be thought to have n *partial slopes*, each giving only the rate at which y would change if one x_i, alone, were to change. Each of these partial slopes is called a partial derivative. Formally, each partial derivative is defined just like an ordinary derivative, as the limiting value taken by the ratio of the increment in the value of the function from a change in one of its variables to the change in that variable itself.

DEFINITION A2.1 ***Partial Derivatives***

Let D be a subset of $\mathbb{R}^n$ *and suppose* $f\colon D \to \mathbb{R}$. *If* $\mathbf{x}$ *is an interior point of D, then the partial derivative of f with respect to* x_i *at* $\mathbf{x}$ *is defined as,*

$$\frac{\partial f(x)}{\partial x_i} \equiv \lim_{h\to 0} \frac{f(x_1, \ldots, x_i + h, \ldots, x_n) - f(x_1, \ldots, x_i, \ldots, x_n)}{h}.$$

Various other notations are sometimes used to denote partial derivatives. Among the most common are $\partial y/\partial x_i$ *or just* $f_i(\mathbf{x})$.

Notice some important things about partial derivatives. First, as remarked, there are n of them, one for each variable x_i. Second, like the derivative in the single-variable case, each partial derivative is itself a function. In particular, *each partial derivative is a function that depends on the value taken by every variable*, $x_1, \ldots, x_n$. Finally, notice that the partial derivative is defined at every point in the domain to measure how the value of the function changes as *one* x_i changes, leaving the values of the other $(n-1)$ variables *unchanged*. Thus, to calculate the partial derivative with respect to, say, x_i, one simply takes the ordinary derivative with respect to x_i, treating all other variables $x_j, j \neq i$, as constants. Consider the following example of a function of two variables.

EXAMPLE A2.1 Let $f(x_1, x_2) = x_1^2 + 3x_1x_2 - x_2^2$. This is a function of two variables, so there will be two partial derivatives. We obtain the partial with respect to x_1 by differentiating with respect to x_1, treating every appearance of x_2 as if it were some constant. Doing that, we obtain

$$\frac{\partial f(x_1, x_2)}{\partial x_1} = 2x_1 + 3x_2.$$

In the second term of the original function, we treated both multiplicative terms 3 and x_2 as constants. In the third term of the function, x_1 does not appear at all, so the entire term is treated as a constant. Because the derivative of a constant is zero, it contributes zero to the expression for the partial with respect to x_1.

Applying the same principles, we differentiate the original function with respect to x_2, this time treating all occurrences of x_1 as though they were constants. The partial with respect to x_2 is therefore

$$\frac{\partial f(x_1, x_2)}{\partial x_2} = 3x_1 - 2x_2.$$

Notice that *each* partial derivative in this example is a function of *both* x_1 and x_2. The value taken by each partial, therefore, will be different at different values of x_1 and x_2. At the point (1, 2), their values would be $f_1(1, 2) = 8$ and $f_2(1, 2) = -1$. At the point (2, 1), their respective values would be $f_1(2, 1) = 7$ and $f_2(2, 1) = 4$. □

It is easy to see that each partial derivative tells us whether the function is rising or falling as we change one variable alone, holding all others constant. But this is just like telling us how the value of the function changes as we move in the direction of one of the n unit vectors. It is sometimes useful to know whether the value of the function is rising or falling as we move in other directions away from a particular point in the domain.

So fix a point $\mathbf{x} = (x_1, \ldots, x_n)$ in the domain of f, and suppose we wish to know how the value of f changes from $f(\mathbf{x})$ as we move away from $\mathbf{x}$ in the direction $\mathbf{z} = (z_1, \ldots, z_n)$. The function

$$g(t) = f(\mathbf{x} + t\mathbf{z}),$$

defined for $t \in \mathbb{R}$, will help us in this regard. Note that $g(t)$ takes on the value $f(\mathbf{x})$ when $t = 0$, and as t increases from zero, $\mathbf{x} + t\mathbf{z}$ moves in the direction $\mathbf{z}$. Consequently, if $g(t)$ increases as t moves from being zero to being positive, then we know that f increases as we move from $\mathbf{x}$ in the direction $\mathbf{z}$. Thus, we are interested in whether $g'(0)$ is positive, negative, or zero.

We now give a heuristic description of how to calculate $g'(0)$. First, note that by definition, $g'(0)$ is just the rate at which f changes per unit change in t. Now, the ith coordinate in the domain of f increases at the rate z_i per unit change in t. Moreover, the rate at which f changes per unit change in the ith coordinate in the domain is just $f_i(\mathbf{x})$, the ith partial derivative of f at $\mathbf{x}$. Consequently, the rate at which f changes per unit change in t due to the change in the ith coordinate is $f_i(\mathbf{x})z_i$. The total rate of change of f is then just the sum of all of the changes induced by each of the n coordinates. That is,

$$g'(0) = \sum_{i=1}^{n} f_i(\mathbf{x})z_i.$$

The term on the right-hand side is known as the **directional derivative** of f at $\mathbf{x}$ in the direction $\mathbf{z}$.[1] This can be written more compactly using vector notation.

[1] Strictly speaking, for this calculation to be correct, f must be continuously differentiable.

Before doing so, a word on some vector-related conventions. All vectors should be assumed to be *column* vectors unless explicitly stated otherwise. In the text, we write $\mathbf{x} = (x_1, \ldots, x_n)$ even though $\mathbf{x}$ may be a column vector. This saves us from the inconvenient and constant use of the transpose notation such as $\mathbf{x} = (x_1, \ldots, x_n)^T$.

With this convention in mind, assemble all preceding n partial derivatives into a *row* vector $\nabla f(\mathbf{x}) \equiv (f_1(\mathbf{x}), \ldots, f_n(\mathbf{x}))$. The row vector $\nabla f(\mathbf{x})$ is called the **gradient** of f at $\mathbf{x}$. The directional derivative of f at $\mathbf{x}$ in the direction $\mathbf{z}$ then can be written as follows.

$$g'(0) = \nabla f(\mathbf{x})\mathbf{z}. \tag{A2.3}$$

Note that the partial derivative of f with respect to x_i is then just the directional derivative of f in the direction $(0, \ldots, 0, 1, 0, \ldots, 0)$, where the 1 appears in the ith position. Thus, all partial derivatives are just special kinds of directional derivatives. On the other hand, (A2.3) tells us that the rate at which f changes in any direction is determined by the vector of partial derivatives, i.e., the gradient of f. Thus, it is helpful to think of the gradient, ∇f, as being analogous to *the* derivative of a function of one variable. As before, the gradient is itself a function, because it maps every $\mathbf{x}$ in the domain into a vector of n 'partial slopes'. Also, as before, we can take the derivative of *these* derivatives and get something very much like the second derivative.

Let us consider one of the function's partial derivatives, for instance, the partial with respect to x_1. We note first that

$$\frac{\partial f(x_1, \ldots, x_n)}{\partial x_1}$$

is a function of n variables itself. Changes in any of the x_i could in principle affect its value. Thus, $f_1(\mathbf{x})$ itself has n partial derivatives.

There is no particular difficulty in calculating the n partial derivatives of the (first-order) partial $f_1(\mathbf{x})$. Each is calculated with respect to its given variable by simply treating all other variables as though they were constants, and applying the familiar rules of single-variable differentiation. The resulting derivative (itself also a function of n variables) is called a **second-order partial derivative**. When $f_1(\mathbf{x})$ is differentiated with respect to x_i, the result is the second-order partial of f with respect to x_1 and x_i, denoted

$$\frac{\partial}{\partial x_i}\left(\frac{\partial f(\mathbf{x})}{\partial x_1}\right), \qquad \text{or} \qquad \frac{\partial^2 f(\mathbf{x})}{\partial x_i \partial x_1}, \qquad \text{or} \quad f_{1i}(\mathbf{x}).$$

Because there are n of these partials of the partial with respect to x_1, one with respect to each of the x_i, $i = 1, \ldots, n$, they, too, can be arranged into a gradient vector. This time, though, the vector will be the gradient of the partial with respect to x_1, $f_1(\mathbf{x})$. We can write this gradient vector as

$$\nabla f_1(\mathbf{x}) = \left(\frac{\partial^2 f(\mathbf{x})}{\partial x_1 \partial x_1}, \ldots, \frac{\partial^2 f(\mathbf{x})}{\partial x_n \partial x_1}\right) \equiv (f_{11}(\mathbf{x}), \ldots, f_{1n}(\mathbf{x})).$$

Now, there are n first-order partial derivatives in our original gradient vector, $\nabla f(\mathbf{x})$. We can repeat the process we just completed for f_1 and get a total of n gradients, $\nabla f_i(\mathbf{x}), i = 1, \ldots, n$. In essence, when we do this, we are taking the 'gradient of the gradient' of the original function f, simply keeping in mind that each partial in the gradient n-vector itself has n partials. If we arrange all the $\nabla f_i(\mathbf{x})$ – each a vector of *second-order* partials – into a matrix by stacking one on top of the other, we get

$$\mathbf{H}(\mathbf{x}) = \begin{pmatrix} f_{11}(\mathbf{x}) & f_{12}(\mathbf{x}) & \ldots & f_{1n}(\mathbf{x}) \\ f_{21}(\mathbf{x}) & f_{22}(\mathbf{x}) & \ldots & f_{2n}(\mathbf{x}) \\ \vdots & \vdots & \ddots & \vdots \\ f_{n1}(\mathbf{x}) & f_{n2}(\mathbf{x}) & \ldots & f_{nn}(\mathbf{x}) \end{pmatrix}.$$

Notice that $\mathbf{H}(\mathbf{x})$ contains all possible second-order partial derivatives of the original function. $\mathbf{H}(\mathbf{x})$ is called the **Hessian matrix** of the function $f(\mathbf{x})$. Now recall the analogy between the gradient and the first derivative. Remembering that the Hessian was obtained by taking the gradient of the gradient, we can think of $\mathbf{H}(\mathbf{x})$ as analogous to the *second* derivative of a function of a single variable.

There is an important theorem on second-order partial derivatives to which we will have occasion to refer. It says that the order in which the partial derivatives are differentiated makes no difference. The theorem is offered here without proof.

THEOREM A2.2 ***Young's Theorem***

For any twice continuously differentiable function $f(\mathbf{x})$,

$$\frac{\partial^2 f(\mathbf{x})}{\partial x_i \partial x_j} = \frac{\partial^2 f(\mathbf{x})}{\partial x_j \partial x_i} \quad \forall\, i \text{ and } j.$$

While we will not prove Young's theorem, it is easily illustrated by considering an example.

EXAMPLE A2.2 Consider the function $f(x_1, x_2) = x_1 x_2^2 + x_1 x_2$. Its two first-order partials are

$$\frac{\partial f}{\partial x_1} \equiv f_1(\mathbf{x}) = x_2^2 + x_2 \quad \text{and} \quad \frac{\partial f}{\partial x_2} \equiv f_2(\mathbf{x}) = 2x_1 x_2 + x_1.$$

If we differentiate f_1 with respect to x_2, we get

$$\frac{\partial^2 f}{\partial x_2 \partial x_1} \equiv f_{12}(\mathbf{x}) = 2x_2 + 1.$$

Differentiating f_2 with respect to x_1, we get

$$\frac{\partial^2 f}{\partial x_1 \partial x_2} \equiv f_{21}(\mathbf{x}) = 2x_2 + 1.$$

Clearly, $f_{12} = f_{21}$ for any $\mathbf{x}$, just as Young's theorem promised. □

Like the second derivative, the Hessian is also a function. It maps each $\mathbf{x}$ in the domain into $n \times n = n^2$ second-order partial derivatives, and the values taken by each of these elements in the matrix $\mathbf{H}(\mathbf{x})$ will generally be different at each $\mathbf{x}$. Young's theorem tells us that the Hessian will be *symmetric*. One might well expect that, in analogy to the single-variable case, the matrix of second-order partials of f ought to provide information about its curvature. This is indeed correct, as we now explore.

In the single-variable case, Theorem A2.1 established that the curvature of a concave function was expressed by its second derivative as well as the relation of the function to its tangent lines. The same conclusions also hold in the multivariate case. A simple way to see this is first to understand the following result.

THEOREM A2.3 ***Single-Variable and Multivariable Concavity***

Let f be a real-valued function defined on the convex subset D of $\mathbb{R}^n$. Then f is (strictly) concave if and only if for every $\mathbf{x} \in D$ and every non-zero $\mathbf{z} \in \mathbb{R}^n$, the function $g(t) = f(\mathbf{x} + t\mathbf{z})$ is (strictly) concave on $\{t \in \mathbb{R} \mid \mathbf{x} + t\mathbf{z} \in D\}$.

Proof: We prove one direction for the concave case only, leaving the rest for you in Exercise A2.21. Suppose then that f is a concave function. Let $\mathbf{x} \in D$ and $\mathbf{z} \in \mathbb{R}^n$. We must show that $g(t) = f(\mathbf{x} + t\mathbf{z})$ is concave on $C = \{t \in \mathbb{R} \mid \mathbf{x} + t\mathbf{z} \in D\}$.

So, choose $t_0, t_1 \in C$, and $\alpha \in [0, 1]$. We must show that

$$g(\alpha t_0 + (1-\alpha)t_1) \geq \alpha g(t_0) + (1-\alpha)g(t_1). \tag{P.1}$$

First, note that C is a convex set, so that $\alpha t_0 + (1-\alpha)t_1 \in C$ and g is therefore defined there. To establish the desired inequality, we merely apply the definition of g. Indeed,

$$\begin{aligned} g(\alpha t_0 + (1-\alpha)t_1) &= f(\mathbf{x} + (\alpha t_0 + (1-\alpha)t_1)\mathbf{z}) \\ &= f(\alpha(\mathbf{x} + t_0\mathbf{z}) + (1-\alpha)(\mathbf{x} + t_1\mathbf{z})) \\ &\geq \alpha f(\mathbf{x} + t_0\mathbf{z}) + (1-\alpha)f(\mathbf{x} + t_1\mathbf{z}) \\ &= \alpha g(t_0) + (1-\alpha)g(t_1), \end{aligned}$$

where the inequality follows from the concavity of f. (Note that because $t_i \in C$, $\mathbf{x} + t_i\mathbf{z} \in D$ for $i = 1, 2$.) ∎

Theorem A2.3 says, in effect, that to check that a multivariate function is concave, it is enough to check, for each point $\mathbf{x}$ in the domain, and each direction $\mathbf{z}$, that the function of a *single* variable defined by the values taken on by f on the line through $\mathbf{x}$ in the direction $\mathbf{z}$ is concave. Because Theorem A2.1 characterises concave functions of a single variable, we can then put Theorems A2.1 and A2.3 together to characterise concave functions of many variables.

Before putting the two theorems together, it will be convenient to introduce some terminology from matrix algebra. An $n \times n$ matrix is called **negative semidefinite** if for all vectors $\mathbf{z} \in \mathbb{R}^n$,

$$\mathbf{z}^T A\mathbf{z} \leq 0.$$

If the inequality is strict for all non-zero $\mathbf{z}$, then A is called **negative definite**.[2] The matrix A is called **positive semidefinite** (respectively, **positive definite**) if $-A$ is negative semidefinite (negative definite). Think of negative semidefiniteness as the generalisation to matrices of the notion of non-positive numbers. Indeed, note that a 1×1 matrix (i.e., a number) is negative semidefinite if and only if its single entry is non-positive.

With this in mind, the analogue of a non-positive second derivative of a function of one variable would be a *negative semidefinite* matrix of second-order partial derivatives (i.e., the Hessian matrix) of a function of many variables. We can now put together Theorems A2.1 and A2.3 to confirm this.

THEOREM A2.4 ***Slope, Curvature, and Concavity in Many Variables***

Let D be a convex subset of $\mathbb{R}^n$ with a non-empty interior on which f is twice continuously differentiable. The following statements 1 to 3 are equivalent:

1. *f is concave.*
2. *$\mathbf{H}(\mathbf{x})$ is negative semidefinite for all $\mathbf{x}$ in the interior of D.*
3. *For all $\mathbf{x}^0 \in D : f(\mathbf{x}) \leq f(\mathbf{x}^0) + \nabla f(\mathbf{x}^0)(\mathbf{x} - \mathbf{x}^0) \qquad \forall\, \mathbf{x} \in D$.*

Moreover,

4. *If $\mathbf{H}(\mathbf{x})$ is negative definite for all $\mathbf{x}$ in D, then f is strictly concave.*

Proof: Because f is twice continuously differentiable, it is enough to establish the theorem on the interior of D. Continuity will then take care of the boundary points. So, fix $\mathbf{x} \in intD$ and $\mathbf{z} \in \mathbb{R}^n$. Let $C = \{t \in \mathbb{R} \mid \mathbf{x} + t\mathbf{z} \in D\}$, and let $g(t) = f(\mathbf{x} + t\mathbf{z})$ for all $t \in C$. Note that g inherits twice continuous differentiability from f.

Now, suppose that 1 holds so that f is concave. Then by Theorem A2.3, g is concave on C. Note that because $\mathbf{x}$ is in the interior of D, C is a non-degenerate interval, so that by Theorem A2.1

$$g''(t) \leq 0 \qquad \forall\, t \in C, \tag{P.1}$$

$$g(t) \leq g(t_0) + g'(t_0)(t - t_0) \qquad \forall\, t, t_0 \in C. \tag{P.2}$$

[2] If a_{ij} denotes the element in the ith row and jth column of A, then $\mathbf{z}^T A\mathbf{z} = \sum_{i=1}^n \sum_{j=1}^n z_j a_{ij} z_i$.

To make use of these results, we will have to calculate the first and second derivatives of g in terms of f.

Now, $g'(t)$ is simply the directional derivative of f at the point $\mathbf{x} + t\mathbf{z}$ in the direction $\mathbf{z}$. Consequently,

$$g'(t) = \nabla f(\mathbf{x} + t\mathbf{z})\mathbf{z}. \tag{P.3}$$

To calculate $g''(t)$, it is simplest to first write $g'(t)$ as

$$g'(t) = \sum_{i=1}^{n} f_i(\mathbf{x} + t\mathbf{z})z_i,$$

and then to differentiate the sum term by term. Now the derivative of $f_i(\mathbf{x} + t\mathbf{z})$ with respect to t is just the directional derivative of f_i at $\mathbf{x} + t\mathbf{z}$ in the direction $\mathbf{z}$, which can be written as

$$\sum_{j=1}^{n} f_{ij}(\mathbf{x} + t\mathbf{z})z_j.$$

Multiplying each of these by z_i and summing over i yields

$$g''(t) = \sum_{i=1}^{n}\sum_{j=1}^{n} z_i f_{ij}(\mathbf{x} + t\mathbf{z})z_j,$$

which can be written as

$$g''(t) = \mathbf{z}^T\mathbf{H}(\mathbf{x} + t\mathbf{z})\mathbf{z}. \tag{P.4}$$

Now, note that $0 \in C$. Consequently, by (P.1), we must have $g''(0) \le 0$. By using (P.4), this means that

$$\mathbf{z}^T\mathbf{H}(\mathbf{x})\mathbf{z} \le 0.$$

But because $\mathbf{z}$ and $\mathbf{x}$ were arbitrary, this means that $\mathbf{H}(\mathbf{x})$ is negative semidefinite for all $\mathbf{x}$. Thus, we have shown that $1 \Longrightarrow 2$.

Note that this also proves statement 4, because if $\mathbf{H}(\mathbf{x})$ is negative definite for all $\mathbf{x}$, then regardless of the chosen $\mathbf{x}$ and $\mathbf{z}$, so long as $\mathbf{z}$ is non-zero, $g''(t) < 0$ for all t, so that by Theorem A2.3, f must be strictly concave.

To see that $1 \Longrightarrow 3$, we must use (P.2). Choose any $\mathbf{x}^0 \in D$ and let the previous $\mathbf{z}$ be given by $\mathbf{x}^0 - \mathbf{x}$. (Recall that $\mathbf{z} \in \mathbb{R}^n$ was arbitrary.) Then both $0, 1 \in C$. Consequently, (P.2) implies that

$$g(0) \le g(1) - g'(1).$$

But using (P.3) and the definition of g, this just says that

$$f(\mathbf{x}) \leq f(\mathbf{x}^0) + \nabla f(\mathbf{x}^0)(\mathbf{x} - \mathbf{x}^0).$$

Therefore, statement 3 holds because both $\mathbf{x}$ and $\mathbf{x}^0$ were arbitrary. Hence, $1 \Longrightarrow 3$. The proofs that $2 \Longrightarrow 1$ and $3 \Longrightarrow 1$ are similar, and we leave these as an exercise. ∎

According to the theorem, a function is concave iff its Hessian is negative semidefinite at all points in the domain. It is therefore convex iff its Hessian is positive semidefinite at all points in the domain. At the same time, we know that the function will be strictly concave (convex) when the Hessian is negative (positive) definite on the domain, though the converse of this is not true.

There are many tests one can perform directly on the matrix $\mathbf{H}(\mathbf{x})$ to determine the concavity, convexity, quasiconcavity, or quasiconvexity of the function. The rules and regulations in this area are notoriously complicated. Their greatest applicability arises in the context of optimisation problems, to be considered later. It therefore seems best to postpone the details of these tests until then.

One fairly intuitive relation between the concavity/convexity of a function and its second partial derivatives does seem worthy of note here. In the single-variable case, a necessary and sufficient condition for a function to be concave (convex) is that its second derivative not be rising (falling). In the multivariable case, we can note a *necessary*, but not a sufficient, condition for concavity or convexity in terms of the signs of all 'own' second partial derivatives. The proof is left as an exercise.

THEOREM A2.5 ***Concavity, Convexity, and Second-Order Own Partial Derivatives***

Let $f: D \to R$ be a twice differentiable function.

1. *If f is concave, then $f_{ii}(\mathbf{x}) \leq 0$ for all $\mathbf{x}$ in the interior of D, $i = 1, \ldots, n$.*
2. *If f is convex, then $f_{ii}(\mathbf{x}) \geq 0$ for all $\mathbf{x}$ in the interior of D, $i = 1, \ldots, n$.*

A2.1.3 HOMOGENEOUS FUNCTIONS

Homogeneous real-valued functions arise quite often in microeconomic applications. In this section, we briefly consider functions of this type and use our calculus tools to establish some of their important properties.

DEFINITION A2.2 ***Homogeneous Functions***

A real-valued function $f(\mathbf{x})$ is called homogeneous of degree k if

$$f(t\mathbf{x}) \equiv t^k f(\mathbf{x}) \qquad \textit{for all } t > 0.$$

Two special cases are worthy of note: $f(\mathbf{x})$ is homogeneous of degree 1, or linear homogeneous, if $f(t\mathbf{x}) \equiv tf(\mathbf{x})$ for all $t > 0$; it is homogeneous of degree zero if $f(t\mathbf{x}) \equiv f(\mathbf{x})$ for all $t > 0$.

Homogeneous functions display very regular behaviour as *all* variables are increased simultaneously and *in the same proportion*. When a function is homogeneous of degree 1, for example, doubling or tripling all variables doubles or triples the value of the function. When homogeneous of degree zero, equiproportionate changes in all variables leave the value of the function unchanged.

EXAMPLE A2.3 The function

$$f(x_1, x_2) \equiv Ax_1^{\alpha}x_2^{\beta}, \qquad A > 0, \alpha > 0, \beta > 0,$$

is known as the **Cobb-Douglas** function. We can check whether this function is homogeneous by multiplying all variables by the same factor t and seeing what we get. We find that

$$\begin{aligned} f(tx_1, tx_2) \equiv A(tx_1)^{\alpha}(tx_2)^{\beta} &\equiv t^{\alpha}t^{\beta}Ax_1^{\alpha}x_2^{\beta} \\ &= t^{\alpha+\beta}f(x_1, x_2). \end{aligned}$$

According to the definition, the Cobb-Douglas function is homogeneous of degree $\alpha + \beta$. If the coefficients are chosen so that $\alpha + \beta = 1$, it is linear homogeneous. □

The partial derivatives of homogeneous functions are also homogeneous. The following theorem makes this clear.

THEOREM A2.6 ***Partial Derivatives of Homogeneous Functions***

If $f(\mathbf{x})$ is homogeneous of degree k its partial derivatives are homogeneous of degree $k - 1$.

Proof: Assume $f(\mathbf{x})$ is homogeneous of degree k. Then

$$f(t\mathbf{x}) \equiv t^k f(\mathbf{x}) \qquad \forall\, t > 0. \tag{P.1}$$

Differentiate the left-hand side with respect to x_i to get

$$\begin{aligned} \frac{\partial}{\partial x_i}(f(t\mathbf{x})) &= \frac{\partial f(t\mathbf{x})}{\partial x_i}\frac{\partial tx_i}{\partial x_i} \\ &= \frac{\partial f(t\mathbf{x})}{\partial x_i}t. \end{aligned} \tag{P.2}$$

Differentiate the right-hand side with respect to x_i to get

$$\frac{\partial}{\partial x_i}\left(t^k f(\mathbf{x})\right) = t^k \frac{\partial f(\mathbf{x})}{\partial x_i}. \tag{P.3}$$

Because (P.1) is an identity, (P.2) must equal (P.3), so

$$\frac{\partial f(t\mathbf{x})}{\partial x_i} t = t^k \frac{\partial f(\mathbf{x})}{\partial x_i}.$$

Dividing both sides by t gives

$$\frac{\partial f(t\mathbf{x})}{\partial x_i} = t^{k-1} \frac{\partial f(\mathbf{x})}{\partial x_i},$$

for $i = 1, \ldots, n$, and $t > 0$, as we sought to show. ∎

One frequent application arises in the case of functions that are homogeneous of degree 1. If $f(\mathbf{x})$ is homogeneous of degree 1, the theorem tells us its partial derivatives will satisfy

$$\frac{\partial f(t\mathbf{x})}{\partial x_i} = \frac{\partial f(\mathbf{x})}{\partial x_i} \qquad \forall\, t > 0.$$

This says that increasing (or decreasing) all variables in the same proportion leaves all n partial derivatives unchanged. Let us verify this for the Cobb-Douglas form.

EXAMPLE A2.4 Let $f(x_1, x_2) \equiv A x_1^{\alpha} x_2^{\beta}$, and suppose $\alpha + \beta = 1$ so that it is linear homogeneous. The partial with respect to x_1 is

$$\frac{\partial f(x_1, x_2)}{\partial x_1} = \alpha A x_1^{\alpha-1} x_2^{\beta}.$$

Multiply *both* x_1 and x_2 by the factor t, and evaluate the partial at (tx_1, tx_2). We obtain

$$\begin{aligned}\frac{\partial f(tx_1, tx_2)}{\partial x_1} &= \alpha A (tx_1)^{\alpha-1}(tx_2)^{\beta}\\ &= t^{\alpha+\beta-1}\alpha A x_1^{\alpha-1} x_2^{\beta}\\ &= \frac{\partial f(x_1, x_2)}{\partial x_1},\end{aligned}$$

as required, because $\alpha + \beta = 1$ and $t^{\alpha+\beta-1} = t^0 = 1$. □

Finally, **Euler's theorem** – sometimes called the **adding-up theorem** – gives us an interesting way to completely characterise homogeneous functions. It says a function is homogeneous if and only if it can always be written in terms of its own partial derivatives and the degree of homogeneity.

THEOREM A2.7 ***Euler's Theorem***

$f(\mathbf{x})$ is homogeneous of degree k if and only if

$$kf(\mathbf{x}) = \sum_{i=1}^{n} \frac{\partial f(\mathbf{x})}{\partial x_i} x_i \qquad \textit{for all } \mathbf{x}.$$

Proof: It will be useful to define the function of t,

$$g(t) \equiv f(t\mathbf{x}), \tag{P.1}$$

and to note some of its properties. Specifically, for fixed $\mathbf{x}$, differentiate with respect to t and obtain[3]

$$g'(t) = \sum_{i=1}^{n} \frac{\partial f(t\mathbf{x})}{\partial x_i} x_i, \tag{P.2}$$

which, at $t = 1$, gives

$$g'(1) = \sum_{i=1}^{n} \frac{\partial f(\mathbf{x})}{\partial x_i} x_i. \tag{P.3}$$

Now to prove necessity, suppose $f(\mathbf{x})$ is homogeneous of degree k, so that $f(t\mathbf{x}) = t^k f(\mathbf{x})$ for all $t > 0$ and any $\mathbf{x}$. From (P.1), we then have $g(t) = t^k f(\mathbf{x})$. Differentiating gives $g'(t) = kt^{k-1} f(\mathbf{x})$ and, evaluating at $t = 1$, we get $g'(1) = kf(\mathbf{x})$. Therefore, by using (P.3),

$$kf(\mathbf{x}) = \sum_{i=1}^{n} \frac{\partial f(\mathbf{x})}{\partial x_i} x_i, \tag{P.4}$$

which proves necessity.

[3]In case this is not crystal clear, remember that because $g(t) \equiv f(tx_1, \ldots, tx_n)$, t multiplies all n variables, so its effect enters separately through *each* of them. To get the derivative of $g(\cdot)$ with respect to t, we therefore have to *sum* the separate effects a change in t will have on $f(\cdot)$ through all those separate avenues. Moreover, in computing each of them, we have to remember to apply the *chain rule*. Thus $g'(t) = \sum_{i=1}^{n} \frac{\partial f(tx_1, \ldots, tx_n)}{\partial x_i} \frac{\partial (tx_i)}{\partial t}$.

But $\partial(tx_i)/\partial t = x_i$, so (P.2) results.

To prove sufficiency, suppose (P.4) holds. Evaluate at $t\mathbf{x}$ to get

$$kf(t\mathbf{x}) = \sum_{i=1}^{n} \frac{\partial f(t\mathbf{x})}{\partial x_i} t x_i. \tag{P.5}$$

Multiply both sides of (P.2) by t, compare to (P.5), and find that $tg'(t) = kf(t\mathbf{x})$. Substitute from (P.1) to get

$$tg'(t) = kg(t). \tag{P.6}$$

Now consider the function $t^{-k}g(t)$. If we differentiate this with respect to t, we obtain $d/dt\,[t^{-k}g(t)] = t^{-k-1}[tg'(t) - kg(t)]$. In view of (P.6), this derivative must be zero, so we conclude that $t^{-k}g(t) = c$ for some constant c. Rearrange and write this as $g(t) = t^k c$. To find c, evaluate at $t = 1$ and note $g(1) = c$. Then use definition (P.1) to obtain $c = f(\mathbf{x})$. Now we know that $g(t) = t^k f(\mathbf{x})$. Substituting from (P.1) once more, we conclude that

$$f(t\mathbf{x}) = t^k f(\mathbf{x})$$

for any $\mathbf{x}$, so the proof is complete. ∎

Once again we should note the implications for linear homogeneous functions. For $k = 1$, Euler's theorem tells us we can write $f(\mathbf{x})$ in terms of its partial derivatives as follows:

$$f(\mathbf{x}) = \sum_{i=1}^{n} \frac{\partial f(\mathbf{x})}{\partial x_i} x_i.$$

Let us verify this for the Cobb-Douglas form.

EXAMPLE A2.5 Let $f(x_1, x_2) = Ax_1^{\alpha}x_2^{\beta}$ and again suppose $\alpha + \beta = 1$. The partial derivatives are

$$\frac{\partial f(x_1, x_2)}{\partial x_1} = \alpha A x_1^{\alpha-1} x_2^{\beta}$$
$$\frac{\partial f(x_1, x_2)}{\partial x_2} = \beta A x_1^{\alpha} x_2^{\beta-1}.$$

Multiply the first by x_1, the second by x_2, add, and use the fact that $\alpha + \beta = 1$ to get

$$\begin{aligned}\frac{\partial f(x_1, x_2)}{\partial x_1} x_1 + \frac{\partial f(x_1, x_2)}{\partial x_2} x_2 &= \alpha A x_1^{\alpha-1} x_2^{\beta} x_1 + \beta A x_1^{\alpha} x_2^{\beta-1} x_2 \\ &= (\alpha + \beta) A x_1^{\alpha} x_2^{\beta} \\ &= f(x_1, x_2),\end{aligned}$$

just as we were promised by Euler's theorem. □

A2.2 OPTIMISATION

This section is devoted to the calculus approach to optimisation problems, the most common form of problem in microeconomic theory. After a very brief review of familiar results from single-variable calculus, we will see how they can be extended to the multivariable context. We then examine techniques to help solve optimisation problems involving constraints of the various kinds regularly encountered in theoretical economics. While we will not dwell here long enough to gain a highly sophisticated command of all the mathematical fine points in this area, we will strive for something deeper than a mere cookbook understanding of the techniques involved. Our goal will be to build from a good understanding of the single-variable case to a strong intuitive grasp of the principles at work in some very sophisticated and powerful methods, and to get some practice in their application. We begin with a review of familiar ground.

Consider the function of a single variable, $y = f(x)$, and assume it is differentiable. When we say the function achieves a **local maximum** at x^*, we mean that $f(x^*) \geq f(x)$ for all x in some neighbourhood of x^*. When we say the function achieves a **global maximum** at x^*, we mean that $f(x^*) \geq f(x)$ for all x in the domain of the function. The function achieves a *unique* local maximum at x^* if $f(x^*) > f(x)$ for all $x \neq x^*$ in some neighbourhood of x^*. It achieves a *unique* global maximum when $f(x^*) > f(x)$ for all $x \neq x^*$ in the domain. Similarly, the function achieves a **local minimum** (unique local minimum) at $\tilde{x}$ whenever $f(\tilde{x}) \leq f(x)$ $(f(\tilde{x}) < f(x))$ for all $x \neq \tilde{x}$ in some neighbourhood of $\tilde{x}$, and achieves a **global minimum** (unique global minimum) at $\tilde{x}$ whenever $f(\tilde{x}) \leq f(x)$ $(f(\tilde{x}) < f(x))$ for all $x \neq \tilde{x}$ in the domain.

Various types of optima are illustrated in Fig. A2.4. The function achieves local maxima at x^1, x^3, and x^5; a global maximum is achieved at x^3. The global maximum at x^3, however, is not unique. The local maxima at x^1 and x^3 are called **interior maxima**, because x^1 and x^3 are in the interior of the domain D, not at its 'edges'. Maxima such as the one achieved at x^5 are called **boundary maxima**. Likewise, at x^0, x^2, and x^4, there are local minima; at x^4, a global minimum. Those at x^2 and x^4 are interior minima, and that at x^0 is a boundary minimum.

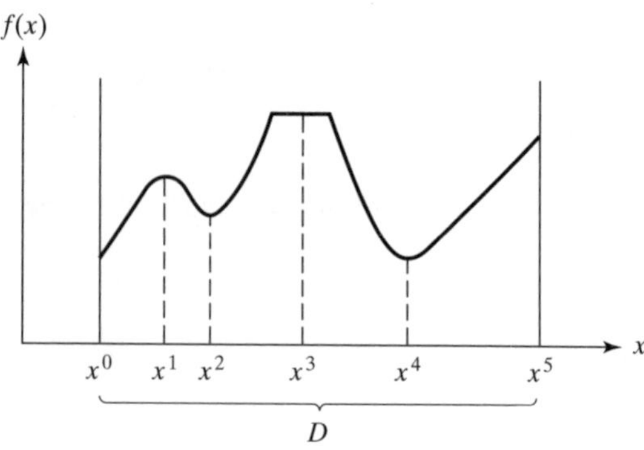

Figure A2.4. Local and global optima.

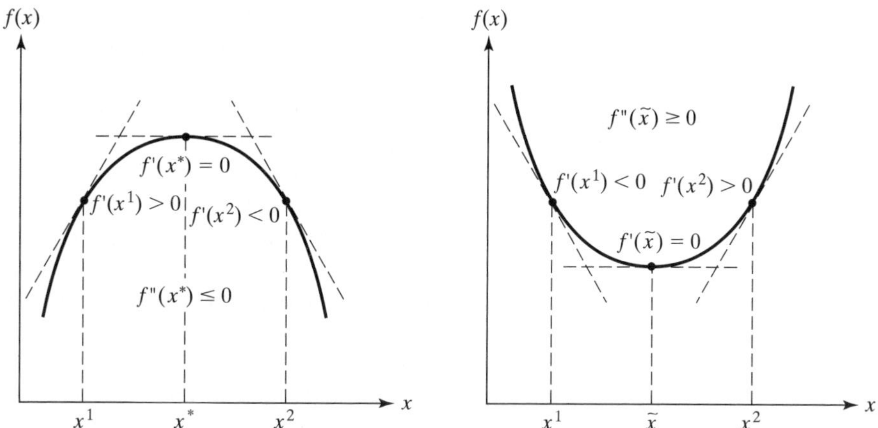

Figure A2.5. (a) $f'(x^*) = 0$ and $f'(x)$ is decreasing where $f(x)$ achieves a maximum. (b) $f'(\tilde{x}) = 0$ and $f'(x)$ is increasing where $f(x)$ achieves a minimum.

You are familiar with the calculus approach to problems of maximising or minimising functions of a single variable. In your calculus courses, you were probably introduced to the logic of 'first- and second-derivative tests', then given practice finding the optima of many different functions. The emphasis tended to be on applying these tests and learning how to calculate a function's optima. In theoretical economics, however, we seldom actually need to calculate optima. Instead, we usually just want to *characterise* them – to spell out the conditions that we know must hold at the optimum, and then work with those conditions, rather than with specific numbers.

For completeness, we recall the familiar **first-order necessary conditions (FONC)** and **second-order necessary conditions (SONC)** characterising optima of an arbitrary twice continuously differentiable function of one variable. The geometrical content of this theorem is contained in Fig. A2.5.

THEOREM A2.8 ***Necessary Conditions for Local Interior Optima in the Single-Variable Case***

Let $f(x)$ be a twice continuously differentiable function of one variable. Then $f(x)$ reaches a local interior

$$\begin{aligned} &1. \quad \textit{maximum at } x^* &&\Rightarrow f'(x^*) = 0 \quad (\textit{FONC}),\\ & &&\Rightarrow f''(x^*) \leq 0 \quad (\textit{SONC}).\\ &2. \quad \textit{minimum at } \tilde{x} &&\Rightarrow f'(\tilde{x}) = 0 \quad (\textit{FONC}),\\ & &&\Rightarrow f''(\tilde{x}) \geq 0 \quad (\textit{SONC}). \end{aligned}$$

A2.2.1 REAL-VALUED FUNCTIONS OF SEVERAL VARIABLES

Much of the intuition and familiar terminology carries over to real-valued functions of many variables. Suppose that $D \subset \mathbb{R}^n$, and let $f\colon D \to R$ be a twice continuously differentiable real-valued function of n variables. The function achieves a local maximum at $\mathbf{x}^*$ if no small movement away from $\mathbf{x}^*$ in any direction causes the value of the function to increase. In $\mathbb{R}^n$, some ε-ball centred at $\mathbf{x}^*$, $B_\varepsilon(\mathbf{x}^*)$, contains all the points as close to $\mathbf{x}^*$ as we choose to make them. Thus, a function achieves a local maximum at $\mathbf{x}^*$ whenever there exists some $\varepsilon > 0$ such that $f(\mathbf{x}^*) \geq f(\mathbf{x})$ for all $\mathbf{x} \in B_\varepsilon(\mathbf{x}^*)$. There is a *global* maximum at $\mathbf{x}^*$ if $f(\mathbf{x}^*) \geq f(\mathbf{x})$ for all $\mathbf{x}$ in the domain. The maximum is a unique local (global) maximum if there exists some $\varepsilon > 0$ such that $f(\mathbf{x}^*) > f(\mathbf{x}) \forall \mathbf{x} \in B_\varepsilon(\mathbf{x}^*)$ $(\forall\ \mathbf{x} \in D)$, $\mathbf{x} \neq \mathbf{x}^*$. Similarly, a local (global) minimum is achieved at $\tilde{\mathbf{x}}$ iff $f(\tilde{\mathbf{x}}) \leq f(\mathbf{x})$ $\forall \mathbf{x} \in B_\varepsilon(\tilde{\mathbf{x}})$ $(\forall\ \mathbf{x} \in D)$, $\mathbf{x} \neq \tilde{\mathbf{x}}$. These are unique if the inequalities hold strictly.

We would like to now generalise the first- and second-order necessary conditions for maxima and minima of functions of one variable to those of many variables. We have already seen how one can make good use of the function $g(t) = f(\mathbf{x} + t\mathbf{z})$ for various vectors $\mathbf{x}$ and $\mathbf{z}$ to reduce a question about functions of many variables to one about functions of just a single variable. The same technique will be used here.

The key is to note that if the function f of many variables is, say, maximised at $\mathbf{x}^*$, then for any vector $\mathbf{z}$, the function of a single variable, $g(t) = f(\mathbf{x}^* + t\mathbf{z})$, will be maximised at $t = 0$. Thus, we can apply the first- and second-order necessary conditions for functions of a single variable to g at the point $t = 0$. This will then lead to conditions on the gradient and Hessian of the function f at the point $\mathbf{x}^*$.

As one might expect, the analogy to the derivative being zero at an optimum for functions of one variable will be that the gradient vector must be zero at an optimum of a function of many variables. This is quite intuitive, for it simply says that if, say f is maximised at $\mathbf{x}^*$, then it had better not be possible to increase the value of f by increasing or decreasing any *one* of the x_i's while leaving all others fixed.

Thus, the single first-order equation $f'(\mathbf{x}^*) = 0$ characterising optima for functions of one variable generalises to the first-order *system of n simultaneous equations*, $\nabla f(\mathbf{x}^*) = \mathbf{0}$ characterising the optima of functions of n variables. This gives us our first-order necessary condition for any interior optima of real-valued functions.

THEOREM A2.9 ***First-Order Necessary Condition for Local Interior Optima of Real-Valued Functions***

If the differentiable function $f(\mathbf{x})$ reaches a local interior maximum or minimum at $\mathbf{x}^*$, then $\mathbf{x}^*$ solves the system of simultaneous equations,

$$\begin{aligned}
\frac{\partial f(\mathbf{x}^*)}{\partial x_1} &= 0\\
\frac{\partial f(\mathbf{x}^*)}{\partial x_2} &= 0\\
&\vdots\\
\frac{\partial f(\mathbf{x}^*)}{\partial x_n} &= 0.
\end{aligned}$$

Proof: We suppose that $f(\mathbf{x})$ reaches a local interior extremum at $\mathbf{x}^*$ and seek to show that $\nabla f(\mathbf{x}^*) = \mathbf{0}$. The proof we give is not the simplest, but it will be useful when we consider the second-order conditions. To begin, choose any vector $\mathbf{z} \in \mathbb{R}^n$. Then, for any scalar t, construct the familiar function of a single variable,

$$g(t) = f(\mathbf{x}^* + t\mathbf{z}). \tag{P.1}$$

Carefully recall a few things about g. First, for $t \neq 0$, $\mathbf{x}^* + t\mathbf{z}$ is just some vector different from $\mathbf{x}^*$, so $g(t)$ coincides with some value of f. For $t = 0$, $\mathbf{x}^* + t\mathbf{z}$ is the same as $\mathbf{x}^*$, so $g(0)$ coincides with the value of f at $\mathbf{x}^*$. Because $g(t)$ coincides with some value of f for every t, and with $f(\mathbf{x}^*)$ for $t = 0$, $g(t)$ must reach a local extremum at $t = 0$ because we have assumed that f reaches an extremum at $\mathbf{x}^*$. From Theorem A2.8, we know that if $g(t)$ reaches a local extremum at $t = 0$, then $g'(0) = 0$. As we have done before, we can differentiate (P.1) using the chain rule to obtain

$$g'(t) = \sum_{i=1}^{n} \frac{\partial f(\mathbf{x}^* + t\mathbf{z})}{\partial x_i} z_i$$

for any t. If we evaluate this at $t = 0$ and apply the condition $g'(0) = 0$, the local extremum of g at zero implies that

$$\begin{aligned} g'(0) &= \sum_{i=1}^{n} \frac{\partial f(\mathbf{x}^*)}{\partial x_i} z_i \\ &= \nabla f(\mathbf{x}^*)\mathbf{z} \\ &= 0. \end{aligned}$$

Because this must hold for every vector $\mathbf{z}$ in $\mathbb{R}^n$ – in particular for each of the n unit vectors – this implies that each of f's partials must be zero, or that

$$\nabla f(\mathbf{x}^*) = \mathbf{0},$$

as we sought to show. ∎

EXAMPLE A2.6 Let $y = x_2 - 4x_1^2 + 3x_1x_2 - x_2^2$. To find a critical point of this function, take each of its partial derivatives:

$$\begin{aligned} \frac{\partial f(x_1, x_2)}{\partial x_1} &= -8x_1 + 3x_2, \\ \frac{\partial f(x_1, x_2)}{\partial x_2} &= 1 + 3x_1 - 2x_2. \end{aligned}$$

We will have a critical point at a vector (x_1^*, x_2^*) where *both* of these equal zero simultaneously. To find x_1^* and x_2^*, set each partial equal to zero:

$$\frac{\partial f(x_1^*, x_2^*)}{\partial x_1} = -8x_1^* + 3x_2^* = 0$$
$$\frac{\partial f(x_1^*, x_2^*)}{\partial x_2} = 1 + 3x_1^* - 2x_2^* = 0, \tag{E.1}$$

and solve this system for x_1^* and x_2^*.

There are many ways to do this. The 'crudest' is to solve one equation for x_1^*, substitute for x_1^* into the other equation, and solve the second equation for x_2^*. Once you have x_2^*, plug that back into the original equation and solve for x_1^*. Because the system is (conveniently) linear, though, we can get a bit fancier. First, rewrite (E.1) as

$$-8x_1^* + 3x_2^* = 0$$
$$3x_1^* - 2x_2^* = -1,$$

or, in matrix form, as

$$\underbrace{\begin{pmatrix} -8 & 3 \\ 3 & -2 \end{pmatrix}}_{\mathbf{A}} \begin{pmatrix} x_1 \\ x_2 \end{pmatrix} = \begin{pmatrix} 0 \\ -1 \end{pmatrix}. \tag{E.2}$$

If we invert $\mathbf{A}$, we get

$$\mathbf{A}^{-1} = \frac{1}{|\mathbf{A}|} \begin{pmatrix} -2 & -3 \\ -3 & -8 \end{pmatrix} = \begin{pmatrix} \frac{-2}{7} & \frac{-3}{7} \\ \frac{-3}{7} & \frac{-8}{7} \end{pmatrix}$$

because the determinant $|\mathbf{A}| = 16 - 9 = 7$. If we premultiply both sides of (E.2) by $\mathbf{A}^{-1}$ and rearrange a bit, we obtain

$$\begin{pmatrix} x_1^* \\ x_2^* \end{pmatrix} = \begin{pmatrix} \frac{-2}{7} & \frac{-3}{7} \\ \frac{-3}{7} & \frac{-8}{7} \end{pmatrix} \begin{pmatrix} 0 \\ -1 \end{pmatrix} = \begin{pmatrix} \frac{3}{7} \\ \frac{8}{7} \end{pmatrix}.$$

Thus, the function reaches a critical point at $x_1^* = 3/7$ and $x_2^* = 8/7$. We do not yet know whether we have found a maximum or a minimum, though. For that we have to look at the second-order conditions. □

A2.2.2 SECOND-ORDER CONDITIONS

Intuitively, the second-order conditions in the multivariable case are the same as in the single-variable case. Once we have found a point where $\nabla f(\mathbf{x}) = \mathbf{0}$, we know we have a *maximum* if the function is 'locally concave' there, and we know we have a *minimum* if the function is 'locally convex'. Theorem A2.4 pointed out that curvature depends on the definiteness property of the Hessian of f. Intuitively, it appears that the function will be locally concave around $\mathbf{x}$ if $\mathbf{H}(\mathbf{x})$ is negative semidefinite, and will be locally convex if it is positive semidefinite. Intuition thus suggests the following *second-order necessary condition* for local interior optima.

THEOREM A2.10 ***Second-Order Necessary Condition for Local Interior Optima of Real-Valued Functions***

Let $f(\mathbf{x})$ be twice continuously differentiable.

1. *If $f(\mathbf{x})$ reaches a local interior maximum at $\mathbf{x}^*$, then $\mathbf{H}(\mathbf{x}^*)$ is negative semidefinite.*
2. *If $f(\mathbf{x})$ reaches a local interior minimum at $\tilde{\mathbf{x}}$, then $\mathbf{H}(\tilde{\mathbf{x}})$ is positive semidefinite.*

Proof: We can build directly from the proof of Theorem A2.9. Recall that we defined the function

$$g(t) = f(\mathbf{x} + t\mathbf{z})$$

for $\mathbf{z} \in \mathbb{R}^n$, and $\mathbf{x}$ a critical point of f. We observed that if f reaches a critical point at $\mathbf{x}$, then g reaches a critical point at $t = 0$. We further observed that, for any t,

$$g'(t) = \sum_{i=1}^{n} \frac{\partial f(\mathbf{x} + t\mathbf{z})}{\partial x_i} z_i.$$

Differentiating once again with respect to t, and again using the chain rule, we obtain the second derivative,

$$g''(t) = \sum_{j=1}^{n} \sum_{i=1}^{n} \frac{\partial^2 f(\mathbf{x} + t\mathbf{z})}{\partial x_i \partial x_j} z_i z_j. \tag{P.1}$$

Now, suppose that f is maximised at $\mathbf{x} = \mathbf{x}^*$. Again, by Theorem A2.8, it must be that $g''(0) \leq 0$. Evaluating (P.1) at $\mathbf{x}^*$ and $t = 0$, this says that

$$g''(0) = \sum_{j=1}^{n} \sum_{i=1}^{n} \frac{\partial^2 f(\mathbf{x}^*)}{\partial x_i \partial x_j} z_i z_j \leq 0,$$

or that $\mathbf{z}^T \mathbf{H}(\mathbf{x})\mathbf{z} \leq 0$. Because $\mathbf{z}$ was arbitrary, this means that $\mathbf{H}(\mathbf{x}^*)$ is negative semidefinite. Similarly, if f is minimised at $\mathbf{x} = \tilde{\mathbf{x}}$, then $g''(0) \geq 0$, so that $\mathbf{H}(\tilde{\mathbf{x}})$ is positive semidefinite, completing the proof. ∎

Theorems A2.9 and A2.10 are important and useful. We can use them to characterise an (interior) optimum whenever we know, or assume, one exists. Both are *necessary* conditions, allowing us to make statements like, '*If* $\mathbf{x}^*$ maximises $f(\mathbf{x})$, *then* $f_i(\mathbf{x}^*) = 0$, $i = 1, \ldots, n$, and $\mathbf{H}(\mathbf{x}^*)$ is negative semidefinite'. These conditions can help in locating potential maxima (or minima) of specific functions, but to verify that they actually maximise (or minimise) the function, we need *sufficient conditions*.

Sufficient conditions allow us to make statements like, '*If* such and such obtains at $\mathbf{x}$, *then* $\mathbf{x}$ optimises the function'. With conditions like this, we could solve for $\mathbf{x}$ and know that the function is optimised there. Sufficient conditions for optima can be derived, but as one would suspect, they are more stringent than necessary conditions. Simply stated, sufficient conditions for interior optima are as follows: (1) If $f_i(\mathbf{x}^*) = 0$ for $i = 1, \ldots, n$ and $\mathbf{H}(\mathbf{x}^*)$ is negative definite at $\mathbf{x}^*$, then $f(\mathbf{x})$ reaches a local maximum at $\mathbf{x}^*$; (2) if $f_i(\tilde{\mathbf{x}}) = 0$ for $i = 1, \ldots, n$, and $\mathbf{H}(\tilde{\mathbf{x}})$ is positive definite at $\tilde{\mathbf{x}}$, then $f(\mathbf{x})$ reaches a local minimum at $\tilde{\mathbf{x}}$. The sufficient conditions require the point in question to be a critical point, and require the curvature conditions to hold in their *strict* forms. (This serves to rule out the possibility of mistaking an inflection point for an optimum.) For example, when $\mathbf{H}(\mathbf{x}^*)$ is negative definite, the function will be strictly concave in some ball around $\mathbf{x}^*$.

Locating a critical point is easy. We simply set all first-order partial derivatives equal to zero and solve the system of n equations. Determining whether the Hessian is negative or positive definite there will generally be less easy.

Various tests for determining the definiteness property of the Hessian key on the sign pattern displayed by the determinants of certain submatrices formed from it at the point (or region) in question. These determinants are called the **principal minors** of the Hessian. By the first through nth principal minors of $\mathbf{H}(\mathbf{x})$ at the point $\mathbf{x}$, we mean the determinants

$$D_1(\mathbf{x}) \equiv |f_{11}| = f_{11}$$

$$D_2(\mathbf{x}) \equiv \begin{vmatrix} f_{11} & f_{12} \\ f_{21} & f_{22} \end{vmatrix}$$

$$\vdots$$

$$D_i(\mathbf{x}) \equiv \begin{vmatrix} f_{11} & \ldots & f_{1i} \\ \vdots & \ddots & \vdots \\ f_{i1} & \ldots & f_{ii} \end{vmatrix}$$

$$\vdots$$

$$D_n(\mathbf{x}) \equiv \begin{vmatrix} f_{11} & \ldots & f_{1n} \\ \vdots & \ddots & \vdots \\ f_{n1} & \ldots & f_{nn} \end{vmatrix},$$

where it is understood that f_{ij} is evaluated at $\mathbf{x}$. Each is the determinant of a matrix resulting when the last $(n - i)$ rows and columns of the Hessian $\mathbf{H}(\mathbf{x})$ are deleted, for $i = 1, \ldots, n$.

They are called the *principal* minors because they are obtained from submatrices formed as we move down the *principal diagonal* of the Hessian.

The following theorem gives requirements on its principal minors sufficient to ensure definiteness of the Hessian.

THEOREM A2.11 ***Sufficient Conditions for Negative and Positive Definiteness of the Hessian***

Let $f(\mathbf{x})$ be twice continuously differentiable, and let $D_i(\mathbf{x})$ be the ith-order principal minor of the Hessian matrix $\mathbf{H}(\mathbf{x})$.

1. *If $(-1)^i D_i(\mathbf{x}) > 0,\ i = 1, \ldots, n$, then $\mathbf{H}(\mathbf{x})$ is negative definite.*
2. *If $D_i(\mathbf{x}) > 0,\ i = 1, \ldots, n$, then $\mathbf{H}(\mathbf{x})$ is positive definite.*

If condition 1 holds for all $\mathbf{x}$ in the domain, then f is strictly concave. If condition 2 holds for all $\mathbf{x}$ in the domain, then f is strictly convex.

In particular, this theorem says that the function will be strictly concave if *the principal minors of the Hessian matrix always alternate in sign, beginning with negative*. It will be strictly convex if *the principal minors of the Hessian are all positive*.

Proof: A completely general proof would invoke part 4 of Theorem A2.4 and then reduce the problem to one of establishing that if the principal minors of a matrix alternate in sign, then the corresponding quadratic form is negative definite, and that if the principal minors are all positive, then the corresponding quadratic form is positive definite. This, in turn, is a well-known result in linear algebra. The interested reader may consult any standard text on this point. For example, see Hohn (1973). Here, we will give a simple proof for the case of *two* variables.

Suppose that $y = f(x_1, x_2)$ is twice continuously differentiable. The first and second principal minors of its Hessian are

$$D_1(\mathbf{x}) \equiv |f_{11}| = f_{11}$$
$$D_2(\mathbf{x}) \equiv \begin{vmatrix} f_{11} & f_{12} \\ f_{21} & f_{22} \end{vmatrix} = f_{11}f_{22} - (f_{12})^2, \tag{P.1}$$

where we have used the fact that $f_{12} = f_{21}$. For $\mathbf{z} = (z_1, z_2) \neq (0, 0)$, $\mathbf{z}^T\mathbf{H}(\mathbf{x})\mathbf{z}$ can be written

$$\mathbf{z}^T\mathbf{H}(\mathbf{x})\mathbf{z} = \sum_{j=1}^{2}\sum_{i=1}^{2} f_{ij}z_iz_j = f_{11}(z_1)^2 + 2f_{12}z_1z_2 + f_{22}(z_2)^2. \tag{P.2}$$

If we can show that $\mathbf{z}^T\mathbf{H}(\mathbf{x})\mathbf{z} < 0$ whenever those principal minors in (P.1) alternate in sign, beginning with negative, and that $\mathbf{z}^T\mathbf{H}(\mathbf{x})\mathbf{z} > 0$ whenever they are all positive, the theorem will be 'proved'.

Because (z_1, z_2) is not the zero vector, at least one of z_1, z_2 is non-zero. Suppose $z_2 \neq 0$. Note that we can add and subtract the same thing from the right-hand side of (P. 2) without changing anything. Adding and subtracting the quantity $(f_{12})^2(z_2)^2/f_{11}$, we get

$$\mathbf{z}^T\mathbf{H}(\mathbf{x})\mathbf{z} = f_{11}(z_1)^2 + 2f_{12}z_1z_2 + \frac{(f_{12})^2(z_2)^2}{f_{11}} + f_{22}(z_2)^2 - \frac{(f_{12})^2(z_2)^2}{f_{11}}.$$

Factoring out f_{11} from the first few terms and $(z_2)^2$ from the last two, we get

$$\mathbf{z}^T\mathbf{H}(\mathbf{x})\mathbf{z} = f_{11}\left((z_1)^2 + 2\frac{f_{12}}{f_{11}}z_1z_2 + \left(\frac{f_{12}}{f_{11}}\right)^2(z_2)^2\right) + \left(f_{22} - \frac{(f_{12})^2}{f_{11}}\right)(z_2)^2.$$

Recognising the first term as a square and putting the second term over a common denominator, we can write

$$\mathbf{z}^T\mathbf{H}(\mathbf{x})\mathbf{z} = f_{11}\left(z_1 + \frac{f_{12}}{f_{11}}z_2\right)^2 + \left(\frac{f_{11}f_{22} - (f_{12})^2}{f_{11}}\right)(z_2)^2. \tag{P.3}$$

Suppose that the principal minors in (P.1) alternate in sign, beginning negative. Then the first product in (P.3) is non-positive and the last is strictly negative because $z_2 \neq 0$ and because the numerator and denominator in the expression it multiplies have opposite signs by assumption. Consequently, $\mathbf{z}^T\mathbf{H}(\mathbf{x})\mathbf{z} < 0$. Similarly, if the principal minors in (P.1) are both positive, then both terms in (P.3) are non-negative and one is positive, so that $\mathbf{z}^T\mathbf{H}(\mathbf{x})\mathbf{z} > 0$. ∎

We are now prepared to state first- and second-order sufficient conditions for local interior optima. These conditions follow directly from what has already been established, so they need no further justification. We simply pull the threads together and write the conditions compactly to facilitate future reference.

THEOREM A2.12 ***Sufficient Conditions for Local Interior Optima of Real-Valued Functions***

Let $f(\mathbf{x})$ be twice continuously differentiable.

1. *If $f_i(\mathbf{x}^*) = 0$ and $(-1)^i D_i(\mathbf{x}^*) > 0$, $i = 1, \ldots, n$, then $f(\mathbf{x})$ reaches a local maximum at $\mathbf{x}^*$.*
2. *If $f_i(\tilde{\mathbf{x}}) = 0$ and $D_i(\tilde{\mathbf{x}}) > 0$, $i = 1, \ldots, n$, then $f(\mathbf{x})$ reaches a local minimum at $\tilde{\mathbf{x}}$.*

EXAMPLE A2.7 Let us check whether the critical point we found in the last example was a maximum or a minimum. We had

$$f(x_1, x_2) = x_2 - 4x_1^2 + 3x_1x_2 - x_2^2,$$

and found that

$$\frac{\partial f}{\partial x_1} = -8x_1 + 3x_2 \qquad \text{and} \qquad \frac{\partial f}{\partial x_2} = 1 + 3x_1 - 2x_2.$$

We compute the second-order partials,

$$\frac{\partial^2 f}{\partial x_1^2} = -8$$
$$\frac{\partial^2 f}{\partial x_1 \partial x_2} = 3$$
$$\frac{\partial^2 f}{\partial x_2 \partial x_1} = 3$$
$$\frac{\partial^2 f}{\partial x_2^2} = -2$$

and form the Hessian

$$\mathbf{H}(\mathbf{x}) = \begin{pmatrix} -8 & 3 \\ 3 & -2 \end{pmatrix}.$$

Before, we found a critical point at $\mathbf{x}^* = (3/7, 8/7)$. Checking the principal minors, we find that

$$D_1(\mathbf{x}) = |-8| = -8 < 0$$
$$D_2(\mathbf{x}) = \begin{vmatrix} -8 & 3 \\ 3 & -2 \end{vmatrix} = 16 - 9 = 7 > 0.$$

Because these alternate in sign, beginning with negative, Theorem A2.12 tells us that $\mathbf{x}^* = (3/7, 8/7)$ is a local maximum. □

You may have noticed in this example that the Hessian matrix was completely independent of $\mathbf{x}$. We would therefore obtain the same alternating sign pattern on the principal minors regardless of where we evaluated them. In Theorem A2.11, we observed that this is sufficient to ensure that the function involved is strictly concave. Now try to imagine the graph of some such strictly concave function in three dimensions. If it has any hills at all, it would seem that it can have only *one* and this must have a single highest point.

Indeed, from Fig. A2.5, it is intuitively clear that any local maximum (minimum) of a concave (convex) function must also be a global maximum (minimum). That intuition extends to the multivariable case as well. In multivariable (unconstrained) optimisation problems, local and global optima *coincide* when the function is either concave or convex. As usual, we treat only the case of concave functions.

THEOREM A2.13 ***(Unconstrained) Local–Global Theorem***

Let f be a twice continuously differentiable real-valued concave function on D. The following statements are equivalent, where $\mathbf{x}^*$ is an interior point of D:

1. $\nabla f(\mathbf{x}^*) = \mathbf{0}$.
2. *f achieves a local maximum at* $\mathbf{x}^*$.
3. *f achieves a global maximum at* $\mathbf{x}^*$.

Proof: Clearly, $3 \Longrightarrow 2$, and by Theorem A2.9, $2 \Longrightarrow 1$. Hence, it remains only to show that $1 \Longrightarrow 3$.

So, suppose that

$$\nabla f(\mathbf{x}^*) = \mathbf{0}.$$

Because f is concave, Theorem A2.4 implies that for all $\mathbf{x}$ in the domain,

$$f(\mathbf{x}) \le f(\mathbf{x}^*) + \nabla f(\mathbf{x}^*)(\mathbf{x} - \mathbf{x}^*).$$

But together, these two relations imply that for all $\mathbf{x}$,

$$f(\mathbf{x}) \le f(\mathbf{x}^*),$$

Therefore, f reaches a global maximum at $\mathbf{x}^*$. ∎

Theorem A2.13 says that under convexity or concavity, any local optimum is a global optimum. Notice, however, that it is still possible that the lowest (highest) value is reached at more than one point in the domain. If we want the highest or lowest value of the function to be achieved at a *unique* point, we have to impose *strict concavity* or *strict convexity*.

THEOREM A2.14 ***Strict Concavity/Convexity and the Uniqueness of Global Optima***

1. *If* $\mathbf{x}^*$ *maximises the strictly concave function f, then* $\mathbf{x}^*$ *is the unique global maximiser, i.e.,* $f(\mathbf{x}^*) > f(\mathbf{x})\ \forall\, \mathbf{x} \in D,\ \mathbf{x} \neq \mathbf{x}^*$.
2. *If* $\tilde{\mathbf{x}}$ *minimises the strictly convex function f, then* $\tilde{\mathbf{x}}$ *is the unique global minimiser, i.e.,* $f(\tilde{\mathbf{x}}) < f(\mathbf{x})\ \forall\, \mathbf{x} \in D,\ \mathbf{x} \neq \mathbf{x}^*$.

Proof: Again, we will prove the theorem for strictly concave functions. We again suppose the contrary and derive a contradiction.

If $\mathbf{x}^*$ is a global maximiser of f but $\mathbf{x}^*$ is not unique, then there exists some other point $\mathbf{x}' \neq \mathbf{x}^*$ such that $f(\mathbf{x}') = f(\mathbf{x}^*)$. If we let $\mathbf{x}^t = t\mathbf{x}' + (1 - t)\mathbf{x}^*$, then strict concavity requires that

$$f(\mathbf{x}^t) > tf(\mathbf{x}') + (1 - t)f(\mathbf{x}^*) \qquad \text{for all } t \in (0, 1).$$

Because $f(\mathbf{x}') = f(\mathbf{x}^*)$, this requires that

$$f(\mathbf{x}^t) > tf(\mathbf{x}') + (1 - t)f(\mathbf{x}'),$$

or, simply,

$$f(\mathbf{x}^t) > f(\mathbf{x}').$$

This, however, contradicts the assumption that $\mathbf{x}'$ is a global maximiser of f. Thus, any global maximiser of a strictly concave function must be unique. ∎

THEOREM A2.15 ***Sufficient Condition for Unique Global Optima***

Let $f(\mathbf{x})$ be twice continuously differentiable on the interior of its domain, D, and suppose that $\mathbf{x}^*$ and $\tilde{\mathbf{x}}$ are interior points of D.

1. *If $f(\mathbf{x})$ is strictly concave and $f_i(\mathbf{x}^*) = 0$, $i = 1, \ldots, n$, then $\mathbf{x}^*$ is the unique global maximiser of $f(\mathbf{x})$.*
2. *If $f(\mathbf{x})$ is strictly convex and $f_i(\tilde{\mathbf{x}}) = 0$, $i = 1, \ldots, n$, then $\tilde{\mathbf{x}}$ is the unique global minimiser of $f(\mathbf{x})$.*

Proof: This theorem has tremendous intuitive appeal. As usual, we only treat strictly concave functions, leaving strictly convex functions for you.

If f is strictly concave, then by Theorem A2.13, because $\nabla f(\mathbf{x}^*) = \mathbf{0}$, f achieves a global maximum at $\mathbf{x}^*$. Theorem A2.14 then implies that $\mathbf{x}^*$ is the unique global maximiser. ∎

A2.3 CONSTRAINED OPTIMISATION

Before, we were simply trying to characterise points where a function reached a local optimum when we were free to choose the variables $\mathbf{x}$ in any way we liked. In economics, we do not usually have that luxury. Scarcity is a pervasive fact of economic life – one could even *define* economics as the study of behaviour in the face of scarcity. Scarcity is most commonly expressed as *constraints* on permissible values of economic variables. Agents are then represented as seeking to do the best they can (in whatever sense is pertinent to the question at hand) within the constraints they face. This is the type of problem we will regularly encounter. We need to modify our techniques of optimisation and the terms that characterise the optima in such cases, accordingly. There are three basic types of constraints we will encounter. They are *equality* constraints, *non-negativity* constraints, and, more generally, any form of *inequality* constraint. We will derive methods for solving problems that involve each of them in turn. We will confine discussion to problems of maximisation, simply noting the modifications (if any) for minimisation problems.

A2.3.1 EQUALITY CONSTRAINTS

Consider choosing x_1 and x_2 to maximise $f(x_1, x_2)$, when x_1 and x_2 must satisfy some particular relation to each other that we write in implicit form as $g(x_1, x_2) = 0$. Formally, we write this problem as follows:

$$\max_{x_1,x_2} f(x_1, x_2) \quad \text{subject to} \quad g(x_1, x_2) = 0. \tag{A2.4}$$

Here, $f(x_1, x_2)$ is called the **objective function**, or **maximand**. The x_1 and x_2 are called **choice variables** and are usually written beneath the operator 'max' to remind us that it is values of x_1 and x_2 we seek. The function $g(x_1, x_2)$ is called the **constraint** and it jointly specifies those values of the choice variables that we are allowed to consider as *feasible* or permissible in solving the problem. The set of all x_1 and x_2 that satisfy the constraint are sometimes called the **constraint set** or the **feasible set**.

One way to solve this problem is by substitution. If the constraint function allows us to solve for one of the x_i in terms of the other, we can reduce the constrained problem in two variables to one without constraints, and with one less variable. For example, suppose that $g(x_1, x_2) = 0$ can be written to isolate x_2 on one side as

$$x_2 = \tilde{g}(x_1). \tag{A2.5}$$

We can substitute this directly into the objective function and it will guarantee that x_2 bears the required relation to x_1. This way, the two-variable constrained maximisation problem can be rephrased as the single-variable problem with no constraints:

$$\max_{x_1} f(x_1, \tilde{g}(x_1)). \tag{A2.6}$$

Now we just maximise this by our usual methods. The usual first-order conditions require that we set the *total* derivative, df/dx_1, equal to zero and solve for the optimal x_1^*. In doing that here, we have to keep in mind that x_1 now influences f in two ways: 'directly' through its 'own' position within f, and 'indirectly' through the original position of x_2. Thus, when we differentiate (A2.6), we must remember that f has two partial derivatives, and we must remember to use the *chain rule*. Keeping this in mind, we want x_1^*, where

$$\frac{\partial f(x_1^*, \tilde{g}(x_1^*))}{\partial x_1} + \underbrace{\frac{\partial f(x_1^*, \tilde{g}(x_1^*))}{\partial x_2} \frac{d\tilde{g}(x_1^*)}{dx_1}}_{\text{chain rule}} = 0.$$

When we have found x_1^*, we plug it back into the constraint (A2.5) and find $x_2^* = \tilde{g}(x_1^*)$. The pair (x_1^*, x_2^*) then solves the constrained problem, provided the appropriate second-order condition is also fulfilled.

Unfortunately, it is easy to imagine cases where the constraint relation is complicated and where it is not so easy to solve for one variable in terms of the other. What is more, many interesting problems involve more than two choice variables and more than one constraint. The substitution method is not well suited to these more complicated problems. In some cases, substitution would be unnecessarily burdensome. In others, it would simply be impossible. Fortunately, there is a better way – one capable of handling a much broader class of problems.

A2.3.2 LAGRANGE'S METHOD

Lagrange's method is a powerful way to solve constrained optimisation problems. In this section, we concentrate on learning the method itself and will only argue its plausibility in the relatively simple case of problems such as (A2.4). Once the principles are grasped, extending them to the more general case should seem straightforward.

Lagrange's method springs from a simple question: how can we use what we already know about optimising functions of several variables when constraints are not involved to help us solve problems when they *are* involved? We know that solving a problem that does not involve constraints is an easy matter. We simply find the first-order partial derivatives, set them equal to zero, and solve the system of equations. Lagrange's insight was to see that there always exists some *unconstrained* problem we can solve with our usual methods that gives us as a byproduct the solution we seek to the constrained optimisation problem.

To see this, let us reconsider our original problem:

$$\max_{x_1,x_2} f(x_1, x_2) \qquad \text{subject to} \qquad g(x_1, x_2) = 0.$$

Suppose we multiply the constraint equation by a new variable, call it λ (lambda), which we simply pull out of the air because it will prove useful. If we subtract this product from the objective function, we will have constructed a *new* function, called the Lagrangian function, or **Lagrangian** for short, and denoted by a script $\mathcal{L}(\cdot)$. This new function has *three* variables instead of two: namely, x_1, x_2, and λ:

$$\mathcal{L}(x_1, x_2, \lambda) \equiv f(x_1, x_2) - \lambda g(x_1, x_2).$$

Now, how would we determine the critical points of $\mathcal{L}(\cdot)$ if it were an ordinary (unconstrained) function of three variables? We would take all three of its partial derivatives and set them equal to zero. Doing this gives

$$\frac{\partial \mathcal{L}}{\partial x_1} = \frac{\partial f(x_1^*, x_2^*)}{\partial x_1} - \lambda^* \frac{\partial g(x_1^*, x_2^*)}{\partial x_1} = 0 \tag{A2.7}$$

$$\frac{\partial \mathcal{L}}{\partial x_2} = \frac{\partial f(x_1^*, x_2^*)}{\partial x_2} - \lambda^* \frac{\partial g(x_1^*, x_2^*)}{\partial x_2} = 0 \tag{A2.8}$$

$$\frac{\partial \mathcal{L}}{\partial \lambda} = g(x_1^*, x_2^*) = 0. \tag{A2.9}$$

These are three equations in the three unknowns, x_1, x_2, and λ. Lagrange's method asserts that if we can find values x_1^*, x_2^*, and λ^* that solve these three equations simultaneously, then we will have a critical point of $f(x_1, x_2)$ along the constraint $g(x_1, x_2) = 0$.

Suppose we can find x_1^*, x_2^*, and λ^* that solve (A2.7) through (A2.9). Notice something very important. Because they solve (A2.9), x_1^* and x_2^* must satisfy the constraint $g(x_1^*, x_2^*) = 0$. Showing that they *also* make $f(x_1, x_2)$ as large (or small) as possible subject to that constraint is a little harder, but it can be done.

Consider our contrived function $\mathcal{L}(\cdot)$ and take its total differential, remembering that λ is a full-fledged variable of the function:

$$d\mathcal{L} = \frac{\partial \mathcal{L}}{\partial x_1}dx_1 + \frac{\partial \mathcal{L}}{\partial x_2}dx_2 - \frac{\partial \mathcal{L}}{\partial \lambda}d\lambda.$$

By assumption, x_1^*, x_2^*, and λ^* satisfy the first-order conditions (A2.7) through (A2.9) for an optimum of $\mathcal{L}$, so $d\mathcal{L}$ evaluated there must equal zero. Substituting from those first-order conditions, we have

$$\begin{aligned} d\mathcal{L} = {} & \frac{\partial f(x_1^*, x_2^*)}{\partial x_1}dx_1 + \frac{\partial f(x_1^*, x_2^*)}{\partial x_2}dx_2 - g(x_1^*, x_2^*)d\lambda \\ & -\lambda^*\left[\frac{\partial g(x_1^*, x_2^*)}{\partial x_1}dx_1 + \frac{\partial g(x_1^*, x_2^*)}{\partial x_2}dx_2\right] = 0 \end{aligned} \tag{A2.10}$$

for all dx_1, dx_2, and $d\lambda$. To convince you that the solutions to the first-order conditions for an optimum of Lagrange's function *also* optimise the objective function $f(x_1, x_2)$ subject to the constraint $g(x_1, x_2)$, we have to show that at $(x_1^*, x_2^*, \lambda^*)$, the total differential of the objective function f is *also* equal to zero – at least for all *permissible* dx_1 and dx_2 that satisfy the constraint equation g. In essence, we want to show that $d\mathcal{L} = 0$ for *all* dx_1, dx_2, and $d\lambda$ implies that $df = 0$ for the *permissible* dx_1 and dx_2.

One thing we can do immediately to simplify things is to notice again that (A2.9) tells us the constraint is satisfied at x_1^* and x_2^*, so $g(x_1^*, x_2^*) = 0$. This means that the third term in (A2.10) is zero and our problem can be reduced to showing that

$$d\mathcal{L} = \frac{\partial f(x_1^*, x_2^*)}{\partial x_1}dx_1 + \frac{\partial f(x_1^*, x_2^*)}{\partial x_2}dx_2 - \lambda^*\left[\frac{\partial g(x_1^*, x_2^*)}{\partial x_1}dx_1 + \frac{\partial g(x_1^*, x_2^*)}{\partial x_2}dx_2\right] = 0 \tag{A2.11}$$

for all dx_i implies that $df = 0$ for those dx_i that satisfy the constraint g.

Next, we have to figure out what those permissible values of dx_1 and dx_2 are. Look again at the constraint equation. Clearly, if $g(x_1, x_2)$ must *always* equal zero, then after x_1 and x_2 change, it must again be equal to zero. Stated differently, permissible changes in x_1 and x_2 are those that lead to *no change* in the value of the constraint function $g(x_1, x_2)$. Let dx_1 and dx_2 stand for those 'permissible changes' in x_1 and x_2 from their values x_1^* and x_2^*, respectively. To say that there is no change in the value of g is to say that its total differential dg must equal zero. With this in mind, we can identify those changes dx_1 and dx_2 that make $dg = 0$ by totally differentiating the constraint equation and setting it equal to zero. Doing that, we find that the implicit relation,

$$dg = \frac{\partial g(x_1^*, x_2^*)}{\partial x_1} dx_1 + \frac{\partial g(x_1^*, x_2^*)}{\partial x_2} dx_2 = 0, \tag{A2.12}$$

must hold between permissible changes dx_1 and dx_2 from x_1^* and x_2^*, respectively,

Putting (A2.11) and (A2.12) together gives us the result. If we are only considering changes in the variables that satisfy (A2.12), then the third term in (A2.11) must be zero. Therefore, at (x_1^*, x_2^*), (A2.11) reduces to

$$d\mathcal{L} = \frac{\partial f(x_1^*, x_2^*)}{\partial x_1} dx_1 + \frac{\partial f(x_1^*, x_2^*)}{\partial x_2} dx_2 = 0$$

for all dx_1 and dx_2 satisfying the constraint. But this is precisely what we want. It says that the solutions $(x_1^*, x_2^*, \lambda^*)$ to the first-order conditions for an *unconstrained* optimum of Lagrange's function guarantee that the value of the objective function f cannot be increased or decreased for small changes in x_1^* and x_2^* that satisfy the constraint. Therefore, we must be at a maximum or a minimum of the objective function along the constraint.

To recapitulate, we have shown that if $(x_1^*, x_2^*, \lambda^*)$ solves $d\mathcal{L}(x_1^*, x_2^*, \lambda^*) = 0$ for all $(dx_1, dx_2, d\lambda)$, then $df(x_1^*, x_2^*) = 0$ for all dx_1 and dx_2 that satisfy the constraint. In words, (x_1^*, x_2^*) is a critical point of f *given* that the variables must satisfy the constraint and that any movement away from (x_1^*, x_2^*) must be a movement along the constraint. The first-order conditions (A2.7) through (A2.9) thus characterise the critical points of the objective function along the constraint. Whether those critical points are constrained maxima or minima cannot be determined from the first-order conditions alone. To distinguish between the two requires that we know the 'curvature' of the objective and constraint relations at the critical point in question. We will examine these issues later.

EXAMPLE A2.8 Let us consider a problem of the sort we have been discussing and apply Lagrange's method to solve it. Suppose our problem is to

$$\max_{x_1, x_2} -ax_1^2 - bx_2^2 \qquad \text{subject to} \qquad x_1 + x_2 - 1 = 0, \tag{E.1}$$

where $a > 0$ and $b > 0$.

First, form the Lagrangian,

$$\mathcal{L}(x_1, x_2, \lambda) \equiv -ax_1^2 - bx_2^2 - \lambda(x_1 + x_2 - 1).$$

Then set all of its first-order partials equal to zero:

$$\frac{\partial \mathcal{L}}{\partial x_1} = -2ax_1 - \lambda = 0 \tag{E.2}$$

$$\frac{\partial \mathcal{L}}{\partial x_2} = -2bx_2 - \lambda = 0 \tag{E.3}$$

$$\frac{\partial \mathcal{L}}{\partial \lambda} = x_1 + x_2 - 1 = 0. \tag{E.4}$$

To solve for x_1, x_2, and λ, notice that (E.2) and (E.3) imply

$$2ax_1 = 2bx_2,$$

or

$$x_1 = \frac{b}{a}x_2. \tag{E.5}$$

By substituting from (E.5) into (E.4),

$$x_2 + \frac{b}{a}x_2 = 1,$$

or

$$x_2 = \frac{a}{a+b}. \tag{E.6}$$

To find x_1, substitute from (E.6) into (E.5) and obtain

$$x_1 = \frac{b}{a+b}. \tag{E.7}$$

To find λ, we can substitute from (E.6) or (E.7) into (E.3) or (E.2), respectively. Either way, we get

$$-2b\left(\frac{a}{a+b}\right) - \lambda = 0,$$

or

$$\lambda = \frac{-2ab}{a+b}. \tag{E.8}$$

The solutions to (E.2) through (E.5) are therefore the three values

$$x_1 = \frac{b}{a+b}, \qquad x_2 = \frac{a}{a+b}, \qquad \lambda = \frac{-2ab}{a+b}. \tag{E.9}$$

Only x_1 and x_2 in (E.9) are candidate solutions to the problem (E.1). The additional bit of information we have acquired – the value of the Lagrangian multiplier there – is only 'incidental'. We may obtain the value the objective function achieves along the constraint by substituting the values for x_1 and x_2 into the objective function in (E.1):

$$y^* = -a\left(\frac{b}{a+b}\right)^2 - b\left(\frac{a}{a+b}\right)^2 = \frac{-(ab^2 + ba^2)}{(a+b)^2}. \tag{E.10}$$

Remember, from the first-order conditions alone, we are unable to tell whether this is a maximum or a minimum value of the objective function subject to the constraint. □

The Lagrangian method is quite capable of addressing a much broader class of problems than we have yet considered. Lagrange's method 'works' for functions with any number of variables, and in problems with any number of constraints, as long as the number of constraints is less than the number of variables being chosen.

Suppose we have a function of n variables and we face m constraints, where $m < n$. Our problem is

$$\max_{x_1,\ldots,x_n} f(x_1,\ldots,x_n) \quad \text{subject to} \quad \begin{aligned} g^1(x_1,\ldots,x_n) &= 0 \\ g^2(x_1,\ldots,x_n) &= 0 \\ &\vdots \\ g^m(x_1,\ldots,x_n) &= 0. \end{aligned} \tag{A2.13}$$

To solve this, form the Lagrangian by multiplying *each* constraint equation g^j by a *different* Lagrangian multiplier λ_j and subtracting them *all* from the objective function f. For $\mathbf{x} = (x_1,\ldots,x_n)$ and $\boldsymbol{\lambda} = (\lambda_1,\ldots,\lambda_m)$, we obtain the function of $n+m$ variables

$$\mathcal{L}(\mathbf{x}, \boldsymbol{\lambda}) = f(\mathbf{x}) - \sum_{j=1}^{m} \lambda_j g^j(\mathbf{x}). \tag{A2.14}$$

The first-order conditions again require that *all* partial derivatives of $\mathcal{L}$ be equal to zero at the optimum. Because $\mathcal{L}$ has $n+m$ variables, there will be a system of $n+m$ equations determining the $n+m$ variables $\mathbf{x}^*$ and $\boldsymbol{\lambda}^*$:

$$\begin{aligned} \frac{\partial \mathcal{L}}{\partial x_i} &= \frac{\partial f(\mathbf{x}^*)}{\partial x_i} - \sum_{j=1}^{m} \lambda_j^* \frac{\partial g^j(\mathbf{x}^*)}{\partial x_i} = 0 \qquad i = 1,\ldots,n \\ \frac{\partial \mathcal{L}}{\partial \lambda_j} &= g^j(\mathbf{x}^*) = 0 \qquad j = 1,\ldots,m. \end{aligned} \tag{A2.15}$$

In principle, these can be solved for the $n+m$ values, $\mathbf{x}^*$ and $\boldsymbol{\lambda}^*$. All solution vectors $\mathbf{x}^*$ will then be candidates for the solution to the constrained optimisation problem in (A2.13).

Lagrange's method is very clever and very useful. In effect, it offers us an algorithm for identifying the constrained optima in a wide class of practical problems. Yet the somewhat casual exposition given here presupposes a great deal. There is first the question of whether solutions to the constrained optimisation problems (A2.4) or (A2.13) even exist. In many of cases, there will at least be an easy answer to this question. If the objective function is real-valued and continuous (which it must be to be differentiable), and if the constraint set defined by the constraint equations is compact, we are assured by the Weierstrass theorem (Theorem A1.10) that optima of the objective function over the constraint set do exist.

Once this question is answered, however, there remains a more subtle question so far left open in our discussion of Lagrange's method. How, for instance, do we know that the Lagrangian multipliers we just 'picked out of thin air' even exist? More precisely, how do we know that there exists $\boldsymbol{\lambda}^*$ such that the critical points of $\mathcal{L}(\cdot, \boldsymbol{\lambda}^*)$ coincide with the constrained optima of f over the constraint set? Surely, there must be some conditions that have to be satisfied for this to be so.

In fact, there are some conditions of this sort, and they have primarily to do with requirements on the constraint set. In the simple two-variable, one-constraint problem, these conditions boil down to the requirement that at least one of the partial derivatives of the constraint equation be strictly non-zero. The plausibility of this restriction will become clearer when we examine the geometry of this simple problem in the next section. In the general case, this expands to the requirement that the gradient vectors of the m constraint equations, $\nabla g^j, j = 1, \ldots, m$, be *linearly independent*.

For the sake of completeness and to facilitate reference – if not for the sake of enlightenment – we will state Lagrange's theorem, which addresses these issues. The proof requires more advanced methods than we have attempted here, and so will be omitted. The interested reader can find it in any good text on multivariable calculus.

THEOREM A2.16 ***Lagrange's Theorem***

Let $f(\mathbf{x})$ and $g^j(\mathbf{x}), j = 1, \ldots, m$, be continuously differentiable real-valued functions over some domain $D \subset \mathbb{R}^n$. Let $\mathbf{x}^*$ be an interior point of D and suppose that $\mathbf{x}^*$ is an optimum (maximum or minimum) of f subject to the constraints, $g^j(\mathbf{x}^*) = 0$, $j = 1, \ldots, m$. If the gradient vectors $\nabla g^j(\mathbf{x}^*), j = 1, \ldots, m$, are linearly independent, then there exist m unique numbers $\lambda_j^*, j = 1, \ldots, m$, such that

$$\frac{\partial \mathcal{L}(\mathbf{x}^*, \boldsymbol{\lambda}^*)}{\partial x_i} = \frac{\partial f(\mathbf{x}^*)}{\partial x_i} - \sum_{j=1}^{m} \lambda_j^* \frac{\partial g^j(\mathbf{x}^*)}{\partial x_i} = 0 \qquad i = 1, \ldots, n.$$

A2.3.3 GEOMETRIC INTERPRETATION

The conditions characterising the Lagrangian solution to constrained optimisation problems have a geometrical interpretation that should be familiar from your intermediate economics courses. It is worth taking some time to learn to interpret these things with familiar graphical tools.[4]

[4]For more geometric intuition, see Fig. A2.12 and the discussion leading to it.

We again consider problem (A2.4). We can represent the objective function geometrically by its level sets, $L(y^0) \equiv \{(x_1, x_2) | f(x_1, x_2) = y^0\}$ for some y^0 in the range. (Keep in mind that there is one of these for every value y that the function can take.) By definition, all points in the set must satisfy the equation

$$f(x_1, x_2) = y^0.$$

If we change x_1 and x_2, and are to remain on that level set, dx_1 and dx_2 must be such as to leave the value of f unchanged at y^0. They must therefore satisfy

$$\frac{\partial f(x_1, x_2)}{\partial x_1} dx_1 + \frac{\partial f(x_1, x_2)}{\partial x_2} dx_2 = 0, \tag{A2.16}$$

which is obtained by totally differentiating each side of the equation for the level set and remembering that the total differential of the constant y^0 is equal to zero. This must hold *at any point along any level set of the function*.

We can derive an expression for the *slope* of any one of these level curves at some arbitrary point. In the (x_1, x_2) plane, the slope of any level curve will be 'rise' (dx_2) over 'run' (dx_1) for dx_2 and dx_1 satisfying (A2.16). By solving (A2.16) for dx_2/dx_1, the slope of the level set through (x_1, x_2) will be

$$\left.\frac{dx_2}{dx_1}\right|_{\text{along } L(y^0)} = (-1)\frac{f_1(x_1, x_2)}{f_2(x_1, x_2)}. \tag{A2.17}$$

The notation $|_{\text{along...}}$ is used to remind you of the very particular *sort* of changes dx_1 and dx_2 we are considering. Thus, as depicted in Fig. A2.6, the slope of the level set through any point (x_1, x_2) is given by the (negative) ratio of first-order partial derivatives of f at (x_1, x_2).

By the same token, suppose that the constraint g looks like Fig. A2.7 when plotted in the same plane. We can think of the constraint function, too, as a kind of level set. It is

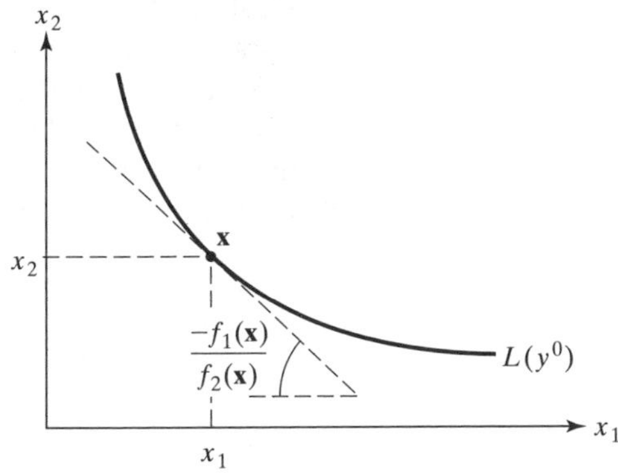

Figure A2.6. The slope of a level set.

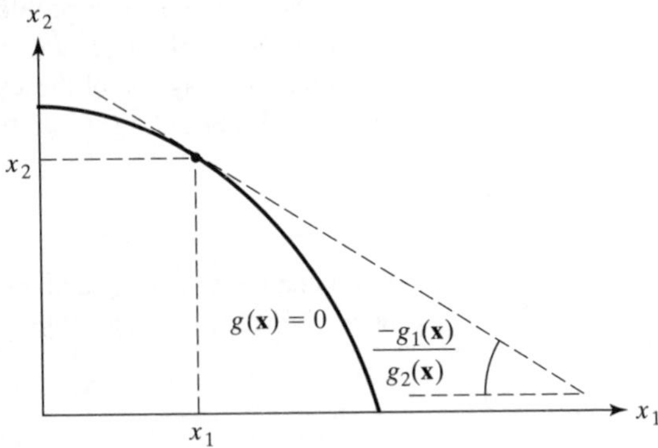

Figure A2.7. The slope of a constraint.

the set of all (x_1, x_2) such that

$$g(x_1, x_2) = 0.$$

Just as before, we can derive the *slope* of this constraint set at any point along it by totally differentiating both sides of this equation, remembering that the differential of (the constant) zero is zero. For any (x_1, x_2) satisfying the constraint, the relation

$$\frac{\partial g(x_1, x_2)}{\partial x_1} dx_1 + \frac{\partial g(x_1, x_2)}{\partial x_2} dx_2 = 0$$

must therefore hold for changes dx_1 and dx_2 along the constraint. By rearranging terms again, the slope of the constraint at the point (x_1, x_2) will be

$$\left.\frac{dx_2}{dx_1}\right|_{\text{along } g(\cdot)=0} = (-1)\frac{g_1(x_1, x_2)}{g_2(x_1, x_2)}. \tag{A2.18}$$

Now let us recall our problem (A2.4) and look at the first-order conditions for a critical point of the Lagrangian function given in (A2.7) through (A2.9). According to Lagrange's method, these conditions determine the solution values to our problem, (x_1^*, x_2^*), plus an 'incidental' Lagrangian multiplier, λ^*. Because we seek the solution values of the choice variables alone, and have no direct interest in the value of the Lagrangian multiplier, we can rewrite (A2.7) through (A2.9) to eliminate λ^* and get an expression for x_1^* and x_2^* alone. Simple rearrangement of (A2.7) through (A2.9) gives

$$\begin{aligned} \frac{\partial f(x_1^*, x_2^*)}{\partial x_1} &= \lambda^* \frac{\partial g(x_1^*, x_2^*)}{\partial x_1} \\ \frac{\partial f(x_1^*, x_2^*)}{\partial x_2} &= \lambda^* \frac{\partial g(x_1^*, x_2^*)}{\partial x_2} \\ g(x_1^*, x_2^*) &= 0. \end{aligned}$$

For the sake of this discussion, suppose $\lambda^* \neq 0$. Dividing the first of the equations by the second eliminates the variable λ^* altogether and leaves us with just two conditions to determine the two variables x_1^* and x_2^*:

$$\frac{f_1(x_1^*, x_2^*)}{f_2(x_1^*, x_2^*)} = \frac{g_1(x_1^*, x_2^*)}{g_2(x_1^*, x_2^*)} \tag{A2.19}$$

$$g(x_1^*, x_2^*) = 0. \tag{A2.20}$$

What do these two conditions say? Look again at (A2.17) and (A2.18) and consider the first condition (A2.19). The left-hand side of (A2.19) is -1 times the slope of the level set for the objective function through the point (x_1^*, x_2^*). The right-hand side is -1 times the slope of the level set for the constraint function. The condition says that the solution values of x_1 and x_2 will be at a point where the slope of the level set for the objective function and the slope of the level set for the constraint are equal. That is not all, though. The second condition (A2.20) tells us we must also be *on* the level set of the constraint equation. A point that is *on* the constraint and where the slope of the level set of the objective function and the slope of the constraint are *equal* is, by definition, a point of *tangency* between the constraint and the level set.

The situation for a maximum of the objective function subject to the constraint is depicted in Fig. A2.8(a). Clearly, the highest value of f along the constraint is the one achieved at the point of tangency picked out by (A2.19) and (A2.20) and hence, by the first-order conditions for the unconstrained optimum of the Lagrangian (A2.7) through (A2.9). The same principles apply in the case of minimisation problems, as depicted in Fig. A2.8(b).

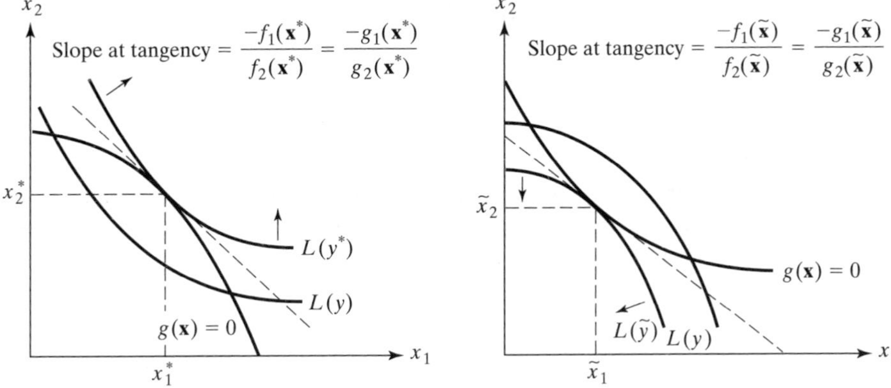

Figure A2.8. The first-order conditions for a solution to Lagrange's problem identify a point of tangency between a level set of the objective function and the constraint.

A2.3.4 SECOND-ORDER CONDITIONS

Second-order conditions for Lagrangian problems are very much in the same spirit as first-order conditions. Initially, one is tempted to reason as follows: if $(\mathbf{x}^*, \boldsymbol{\lambda}^*)$ satisfies the second-order conditions for a maximum of the unconstrained function $\mathcal{L}$, then we know we have a local maximum of f subject to the constraints. This is in fact a correct conjecture, but it turns out to be a much more stringent requirement than we really need in order to know that we have located a constrained optimum. In effect, we can reduce the 'dimensionality' of the curvature requirements by exploiting the interdependence between the $\mathbf{x}$'s imposed on the problem by the constraint relations. To know that we have a maximum, all we really need is that the second differential of the objective function at the point that solves the first-order conditions is decreasing *along the constraint.*

With two variables and one constraint, the conditions for this can be easily derived by exploiting the interdependence between x_1 and x_2 arising from the constraint. Suppose we arbitrarily view x_1 as free to take any value and think of $x_2(x_1)$ as the required value of x_2 imposed by the constraint. We then can think of the constraint as the identity

$$g(x_1, x_2(x_1)) \equiv 0.$$

Here, we view the constraint equation as defining x_2 as an implicit function of x_1. Differentiating with respect to x_1 and solving for dx_2/dx_1, we get the familiar relation

$$\frac{dx_2}{dx_1} = \frac{-g_1}{g_2} \tag{A2.21}$$

for the slope of the constraint relation in the (x_1, x_2) plane. Letting $y = f(x_1, x_2(x_1))$ be the value of the objective function subject to the constraint, we get y as a function of the single variable x_1. Differentiating with respect to x_1, we get $dy/dx_1 = f_1 + f_2(dx_2/dx_1)$. Substituting from (A2.21) gives

$$\frac{dy}{dx_1} = f_1 - f_2\frac{g_1}{g_2}. \tag{A2.22}$$

Differentiating again, remembering always that x_2 is a function of x_1, and that the f_i and g_i all depend on x_1 both directly and through its influence on x_2, we obtain the second derivative,

$$\begin{aligned}\frac{d^2y}{dx_1^2} &= f_{11} + f_{12}\frac{dx_2}{dx_1} - \left[f_{21} + f_{22}\frac{dx_2}{dx_1}\right]\frac{g_1}{g_2} \\ &\quad - f_2\left\{\frac{g_2[g_{11} + g_{12}(dx_2/dx_1)] - g_1[g_{21} + g_{22}(dx_2/dx_1)]}{g_2^2}\right\}.\end{aligned} \tag{A2.23}$$

Second-order necessary conditions for a maximum in one variable require that this second derivative be less than or equal to zero at the point where the first-order conditions are satisfied. Sufficient conditions require that the inequalities hold strictly at that point. The first-order conditions (A2.7) through (A2.9) require that $f_1 = \lambda g_1$ and $f_2 = \lambda g_2$. Young's theorem tells us that $f_{12} = f_{21}$ and $g_{12} = g_{21}$. Substituting from these, from (A2.21), and using some algebra, we can re-express (A2.23) as

$$\frac{d^2y}{dx_1^2} = \frac{1}{(g_2)^2}\left[(f_{11} - \lambda g_{11})(g_2)^2 - 2(f_{12} - \lambda g_{12})g_1g_2 + (f_{22} - \lambda g_{22})(g_1)^2\right]. \quad \text{(A2.24)}$$

Now look carefully at the terms involving λ inside the brackets. Recall that when we formed the first-order conditions (A2.7) through (A2.9), we found that the first-order partials of the Lagrangian function with respect to the x_i were

$$\mathcal{L}_i = f_i - \lambda g_i.$$

The second-order partials of $\mathcal{L}$ would then be

$$\begin{aligned} \mathcal{L}_{11} &= f_{11} - \lambda g_{11} \\ \mathcal{L}_{12} &= f_{12} - \lambda g_{12} \\ \mathcal{L}_{22} &= f_{22} - \lambda g_{22}. \end{aligned} \quad \text{(A2.25)}$$

It is clear that the terms involving λ inside the brackets are just the second-order partials of the Lagrangian with respect to the x_i. The entire bracketed term now can be seen to involve these second-order partials *plus* the first-order partials of the constraint. To the trained eye, the quadratic expression in the bracketed term can be recognised as the determinant of a symmetric matrix. Suppose we form the symmetric matrix

$$\bar{\mathbf{H}} \equiv \begin{pmatrix} 0 & g_1 & g_2 \\ g_1 & \mathcal{L}_{11} & \mathcal{L}_{12} \\ g_2 & \mathcal{L}_{21} & \mathcal{L}_{22} \end{pmatrix}.$$

This matrix is called the **bordered Hessian** of the Lagrangian function, because it involves the second-order partials of $\mathcal{L}$ *bordered* by the first-order partials of the constraint equation and a zero. If we take its determinant (e.g., by expanding along the last column), we see that

$$\bar{\mathbf{D}} \equiv \begin{vmatrix} 0 & g_1 & g_2 \\ g_1 & \mathcal{L}_{11} & \mathcal{L}_{12} \\ g_2 & \mathcal{L}_{21} & \mathcal{L}_{22} \end{vmatrix} = -[\mathcal{L}_{11}(g_2)^2 - 2\mathcal{L}_{12}g_1g_2 + \mathcal{L}_{22}(g_1)^2]. \quad \text{(A2.26)}$$

By combining (A2.24), (A2.25), and (A2.26), the second derivative of the objective function subject to the constraint can be written in terms of the determinant of the bordered

Hessian of the Lagrangian function as

$$\frac{d^2y}{dx_1^2} = \frac{(-1)}{(g_2)^2}\bar{D}. \tag{A2.27}$$

Thus, the curvature of the objective function along the constraint, indicated by the sign of the second derivative d^2y/dx_1^2, can be inferred directly from the sign of the determinant of the bordered Hessian of the Lagrangian function (assuming that $g_2 \neq 0$). Care is in order because the sign of the one will always be *opposite* the sign of the other, because the determinant in (A2.27) is multiplied by -1. We are now in a position to state a *sufficient* condition for the two-variable, one-constraint problem.

THEOREM A2.17 ***A Sufficient Condition for a Local Optimum in the Two-Variable, One-Constraint Optimisation Problem***

If $(x_1^*, x_2^*, \lambda^*)$ solves the first-order conditions (A2.7) through (A2.9), and if $\bar{D} > 0$ (< 0) in (A2.26) when evaluated at $(x_1^*, x_2^*, \lambda^*)$, then (x_1^*, x_2^*) is a local maximum (minimum) of $f(x_1, x_2)$ subject to the constraint $g(x_1, x_2) = 0$.

EXAMPLE A2.9 Let us consider whether the critical point we obtained in Example A2.8 is a minimum or a maximum. Referring back, it is easy to see that $\mathcal{L}_{11} = -2a$, $\mathcal{L}_{12} = 0$, $\mathcal{L}_{21} = 0$, and $\mathcal{L}_{22} = -2b$. From the constraint equation, $g_1 = 1$ and $g_2 = 1$. Constructing the bordered Hessian, its determinant will be

$$\bar{D} = \begin{vmatrix} -2a & 0 & 1 \\ 0 & -2b & 1 \\ 1 & 1 & 0 \end{vmatrix} = 2(a+b) > 0. \tag{A2.28}$$

Because here, $\bar{D} > 0$ for *all* values of x_1, x_2, and λ, it must be so at the solution (E.9) to the first-order conditions in Example A2.8. The value of the objective function in (E.10) must therefore be a *maximum* subject to the constraint. □

With n variables and $m < n$ constraints, the second-order sufficient conditions again tell us we will have a maximum (minimum) if the second differential of the objective function is less than zero (greater than zero) at the point where the first-order conditions are satisfied. The sign of the second differential can once more be reduced to knowing the definiteness of the bordered Hessian of the Lagrangian. In the multivariable, multiconstraint case, the bordered Hessian is again formed by bordering the matrix of second-order partials of $\mathcal{L}$ by all the first-order partials of the constraints and enough zeros to form a symmetric matrix. The test for definiteness then involves checking the sign pattern on the appropriate principal minors of this (monstrous-looking) bordered matrix:

$$\bar{\mathbf{H}} = \begin{pmatrix} 0 & \dots & 0 & g_1^1 & \dots & g_n^1 \\ \vdots & \ddots & \vdots & \vdots & \ddots & \vdots \\ 0 & \dots & 0 & g_1^m & \dots & g_n^m \\ g_1^1 & \dots & g_1^m & \mathcal{L}_{11} & \dots & \mathcal{L}_{1n} \\ \vdots & \ddots & \vdots & \vdots & \ddots & \vdots \\ g_n^1 & \dots & g_n^m & \mathcal{L}_{n1} & \dots & \mathcal{L}_{nn} \end{pmatrix}.$$

Its principal minors are the determinants of submatrices obtained by moving down the principal diagonal. The $n - m$ principal minors of interest here are those *beginning with the* $(2m + 1)$*-st and ending with the* $(n + m)$*-th, i.e., the determinant of* $\bar{\mathbf{H}}$. That is, the principal minors

$$\bar{\mathbf{D}}_k = \begin{vmatrix} 0 & \dots & 0 & g_1^1 & \dots & g_k^1 \\ \vdots & \ddots & \vdots & \vdots & \ddots & \vdots \\ 0 & \dots & 0 & g_1^m & \dots & g_k^m \\ g_1^1 & \dots & g_1^m & \mathcal{L}_{11} & \dots & \mathcal{L}_{1k} \\ \vdots & \ddots & \vdots & \vdots & \ddots & \vdots \\ g_k^1 & \dots & g_k^m & \mathcal{L}_{k1} & \dots & \mathcal{L}_{kk} \end{vmatrix}, \qquad k = m + 1, \dots, n. \qquad \text{(A2.29)}$$

We can summarise the sufficient conditions for optima in the general case with the following theorem.

THEOREM A2.18 *Sufficient Conditions for Local Optima with Equality Constraints*

Let the objective function be $f(\mathbf{x})$ *and the* $m < n$ *constraints be* $g^j(\mathbf{x}) = 0, j = 1, \dots, m$*. Let the Lagrangian be given by (A2.14). Let* $(\mathbf{x}^*, \boldsymbol{\lambda}^*)$ *solve the first-order conditions in (A2.15). Then*

1. $\mathbf{x}^*$ *is a local maximum of* $f(\mathbf{x})$ *subject to the constraints if the* $n - m$ *principal minors in (A2.29) alternate in sign beginning with positive* $\bar{D}_{m+1} > 0$, $\bar{D}_{m+2} < 0, \dots,$ *when evaluated at* $(\mathbf{x}^*, \boldsymbol{\lambda}^*)$.
2. $\mathbf{x}^*$ *is a local minimum* $f(\mathbf{x})$ *subject to the constraint if the* $n - m$ *principal minors in (A2.29) are all negative* $\bar{D}_{m+1} < 0$, $\bar{D}_{m+2} < 0, \dots,$ *when evaluated at* $(\mathbf{x}^*, \boldsymbol{\lambda}^*)$.

A2.3.5 INEQUALITY CONSTRAINTS

In many economic applications we are faced with maximising or minimising something subject to constraints that involve *inequalities*, instead of – or in addition to – simple equalities. For instance, a commonsense restriction in most problems is to require that the economic variables be available only in *non-negative* amounts. The Lagrangian analysis must be modified to accommodate problems involving this and more complicated kinds of inequality restrictions on the choice variables.

To help provide intuition for more complicated problems later, we begin with the simplest possible problem: maximising a function of one variable subject to a non-negativity constraint on the choice variable. Formally, we can write this problem as

$$\max_x f(x) \quad \text{subject to} \quad x \geq 0. \tag{A2.30}$$

As before, we are interested in deriving conditions to characterise the solution x^*. If we consider the problem carefully, keeping in mind that the *relevant region* for solutions is the non-negative real line, it seems that any one of three things can happen. These three possibilities are depicted in Fig. A2.9.

Let us consider each of these separately and try to characterise the solution in each case. In case 1, the (global) maximum is at x^1. But $x^1 < 0$ is not feasible because it violates the non-negativity constraint. Clearly, the maximum of f subject to $x \geq 0$ is achieved on the boundary of the feasible set at $x^* = 0$. Here, we say that the constraint is *binding*. At x^*, *two* things are true: x^* is equal to zero and the slope of f is negative. Thus, the two conditions, $x^* = 0$ and $f'(x^*) < 0$, characterise the solution in case 1. In case 2, the global maximum is achievable but only barely so. The function is maximised right at the point $x^* = 0$ on the boundary of the feasible set. The constraint on x is binding again, but it does not really matter. Again, *two* conditions characterise the solution in this case: $x^* = 0$ and $f'(x^*) = 0$. Case 3 alone corresponds to the kind we have encountered before. There, the maximum occurs at $x^* > 0$ inside the feasible set. The constraint is not binding, and we say that the problem admits of an *interior* solution because the solution is strictly inside

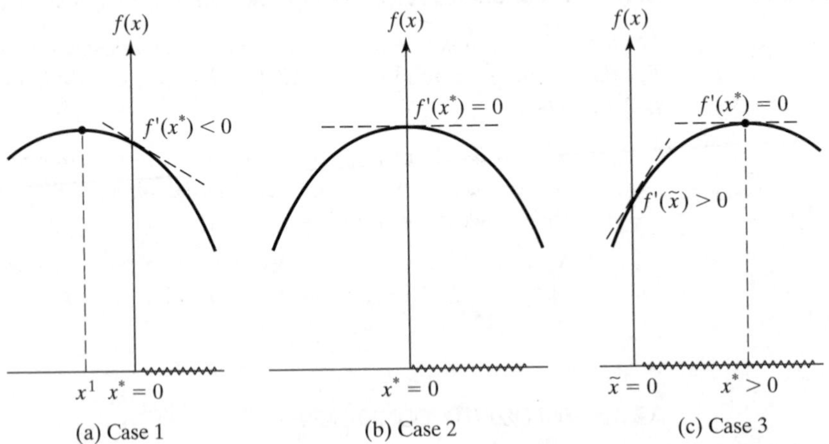

Figure A2.9. Three possibilities for maximisation with non-negativity constraints: (a) case 1, constraint is binding; (b) case 2, constraint is binding but irrelevant; and (c) case 3, constraint is not binding.

the feasible region. Once more, *two* things characterise the solution in case 3: $x^* > 0$ and $f'(x^*) = 0$.

At this point, the question arises: is there a convenient set of conditions that we can use to summarise all three possibilities? Again, the three possibilities are

$$\begin{array}{llll} \text{Case 1.} & x^* = 0 & \text{and} & f'(x^*) < 0 \\ \text{Case 2.} & x^* = 0 & \text{and} & f'(x^*) = 0 \\ \text{Case 3.} & x^* > 0 & \text{and} & f'(x^*) = 0. \end{array}$$

Is there something common to all three? Look carefully. In each case, multiply the two conditions together and notice that the product will always be zero! Thus, in all three cases, $x^*[f'(x^*)] = 0$.

This alone, however, is not quite enough. Look again at case 3. Clearly, $\tilde{x} = 0$ does *not* give a maximum of the function in the feasible region. There, $f'(\tilde{x}) > 0$, so as we increase x away from the boundary and into the feasible region, the value of the function will increase. Nonetheless, the product $\tilde{x}[f'(\tilde{x})] = 0$ even though $\tilde{x}$ is a minimum, not a maximum, subject to $x \geq 0$. We can rule out this unwanted possibility by simply requiring the function to be non-increasing as we increase x.

All together, we have identified *three* conditions that characterise the solution to the simple maximisation problem with non-negativity constraints. If x^* solves (A2.30), then all three of the following must hold:

$$\begin{array}{ll} \text{Condition 1.} & f'(x^*) \leq 0 \\ \text{Condition 2.} & x^*[f'(x^*)] = 0 \\ \text{Condition 3.} & x^* \geq 0. \end{array} \tag{A2.31}$$

Notice that these three conditions, together, rule out the 'minimum' problem just described. At $\tilde{x} = 0$, even though $\tilde{x}f'(x) = 0$, condition 1 is violated because $f'(\tilde{x}) > 0$.

EXAMPLE A2.10 Consider the problem

$$\max_x \; 6 - x^2 - 4x \qquad \text{subject to} \qquad x \geq 0.$$

Differentiating, we get $f'(x) = -2x - 4$. From (A2.31), x^* must satisfy

$$\begin{array}{lr} 1. & -2x^* - 4 \leq 0 \\ 2. & x^*[-2x^* - 4] = 0 \\ 3. & x^* \geq 0. \end{array}$$

Trying to solve conditions like these can sometimes get messy. A rule of thumb that usually works is to focus on the product term (2). Solve that first, then make sure the other conditions are satisfied. There, we can multiply through by -1, factor out a 2, and get

$$2x^*[x^* + 2] = 0.$$

The only values that satisfy this are $x = 0$ and $x = -2$. However, condition 3 rules out $x = -2$, leaving only $x = 0$ as a candidate. Making sure this satisfies condition 1 as well, we get $0 - 4 = -4 \leq 0$, so the solution must be $x^* = 0$. □

The conditions for a *minimum* of $f(x)$ subject to $x \geq 0$ can also be easily derived. The reasoning is just as before, except that this time the troublesome case arises if the function is *decreasing* at the boundary of the feasible set. We rule this out by requiring the derivative to be *non-negative* at the point in question. If x^* solves the minimisation problem with non-negativity constraints, then

$$\begin{aligned} &\text{Condition 1.} \quad f'(x^*) \geq 0 \\ &\text{Condition 2.} \quad x^*[f'(x^*)] = 0 \\ &\text{Condition 3.} \quad x^* \geq 0. \end{aligned} \tag{A2.32}$$

In quite sensible ways, (A2.31) and (A2.32) generalise to the case of optimising real-valued functions of any number of variables subject to non-negativity constraints on all of them. In the multivariable case, the three conditions must hold for each variable separately, with the function's partial derivatives being substituted for the single derivative. The following theorem is straightforward and its proof is left as an exercise.

THEOREM A2.19 ***Necessary Conditions for Optima of Real-Valued Functions Subject to Non-Negativity Constraints***

Let $f(\mathbf{x})$ be continuously differentiable.

1. *If $\mathbf{x}^*$ maximises $f(\mathbf{x})$ subject to $\mathbf{x} \geq \mathbf{0}$, then $\mathbf{x}^*$ satisfies*

$$\begin{aligned} &(i) && \frac{\partial f(\mathbf{x}^*)}{\partial x_i} \leq 0, && i = 1, \ldots, n \\ &(ii) && x_i^*\left[\frac{\partial f(\mathbf{x}^*)}{\partial x_i}\right] = 0, && i = 1, \ldots, n \\ &(iii) && x_i^* \geq 0, && i = 1, \ldots, n. \end{aligned}$$

2. *If* $\mathbf{x}^*$ *minimises* $f(\mathbf{x})$ *subject to* $\mathbf{x} \geq \mathbf{0}$*, then* $\mathbf{x}^*$ *satisfies*

$$\text{(i)} \quad \frac{\partial f(\mathbf{x}^*)}{\partial x_i} \geq 0, \qquad i = 1, \ldots, n$$

$$\text{(ii)} \quad x_i^*\left[\frac{\partial f(\mathbf{x}^*)}{\partial x_i}\right] = 0, \qquad i = 1, \ldots, n$$

$$\text{(iii)} \quad x_i^* \geq 0, \qquad i = 1, \ldots, n.$$

A2.3.6 KUHN-TUCKER CONDITIONS

Let us now consider optimisation subject to general inequality constraints. For example, consider the problem,

$$\max_{(x_1,x_2)\in\mathbb{R}^2} f(x_1, x_2) \text{ s.t. } g^1(x_1, x_2) \leq 0 \text{ and } g^2(x_1, x_2) \leq 0. \tag{A2.33}$$

Such a problem is commonly called a **non-linear programming** problem. In linear programming problems, a linear function is optimised subject to linear inequality constraints. In (A2.33), there are no such limitations on the form of the objective function and constraint relations, so you can see that linear programming problems are a special case of non-linear ones. The methods devised to handle the general non-linear programming problem owe much to the early study of the linear case.

Let us try to derive necessary first-order conditions for (x_1^*, x_2^*) to be a solution to (A2.33). For specificity, we shall assume that f, g^1 and g^2 are strictly increasing in each coordinate x_1 and x_2. Because this example involves only two variables, we can sketch the constraint sets in the plane. The shaded region of Fig. A2.10 is the set of points satisfying the two constraints. Because f is increasing, its level sets increase in value as we move outward from the origin. Fig. A2.11 depicts a situation in which f is maximised at the point $\mathbf{x}^* = (x_1^*, x_2^*)$ where the two constraints are both binding and equal to zero.

Note that at $\mathbf{x}^*$ the level set of f is not tangent to either of the lines on which the constraints are satisfied with equality. What can we say in general about the slope of the level set of f at $\mathbf{x}^*$? First, it must be weakly steeper than the slope of the level set of g^1 at $\mathbf{x}^*$. Otherwise, there would be feasible points to the north-west of $\mathbf{x}^*$ that achieve a higher value of f. (Make sure you see this before moving on!) Similarly, at $\mathbf{x}^*$ the slope of the level set of f must be weakly flatter than the slope of the level set of g^2. Since the slopes at $\mathbf{x}^*$ of the level sets of f, g^1 and g^2 are, respectively,

$$-\frac{\partial f(\mathbf{x}^*)/\partial x_1}{\partial f(\mathbf{x}^*)/\partial x_2}, \quad -\frac{\partial g^1(\mathbf{x}^*)/\partial x_1}{\partial g^1(\mathbf{x}^*)/\partial x_2}, \text{ and } -\frac{\partial g^2(\mathbf{x}^*)/\partial x_1}{\partial g^2(\mathbf{x}^*)/\partial x_2},$$

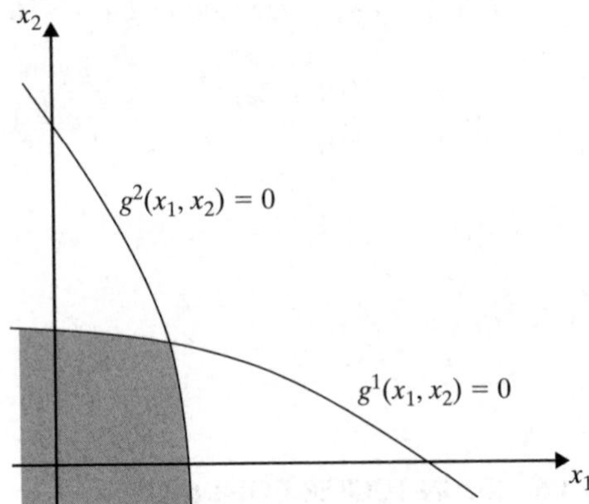

Figure A2.10. The feasible set.

we have just argued that,

$$-\frac{\partial g^1(\mathbf{x}^*)/\partial x_1}{\partial g^1(\mathbf{x}^*)/\partial x_2} \le -\frac{\partial f(\mathbf{x}^*)/\partial x_1}{\partial f(\mathbf{x}^*)/\partial x_2} \le -\frac{\partial g^2(\mathbf{x}^*)/\partial x_1}{\partial g^2(\mathbf{x}^*)/\partial x_2},$$

which, after multiplying by -1 and taking reciprocals, can be equivalently written as,

$$\frac{\partial g^1(\mathbf{x}^*)/\partial x_2}{\partial g^1(\mathbf{x}^*)/\partial x_1} \le \frac{\partial f(\mathbf{x}^*)/\partial x_2}{\partial f(\mathbf{x}^*)/\partial x_1} \le \frac{\partial g^2(\mathbf{x}^*)/\partial x_2}{\partial g^2(\mathbf{x}^*)/\partial x_1}. \tag{A2.34}$$

Let us now recall a bit of geometry with vectors. A vector (z_1, z_2), being the line segment from the origin to the point (z_1, z_2), has slope z_2/z_1. Thus, the first term in (A2.34) is the slope of the vector $\nabla g^1(\mathbf{x}^*) = (\partial g^1(\mathbf{x}^*)/\partial x_1, \partial g^1(\mathbf{x}^*)/\partial x_2)$ which is the gradient of g^1 at $\mathbf{x}^*$, the second term is the slope of the gradient vector $\nabla f(\mathbf{x}^*) = (\partial f(\mathbf{x}^*)/\partial x_1, \partial f(\mathbf{x}^*)/\partial x_2)$, and the third term is the slope of the gradient vector $\nabla g^2(\mathbf{x}^*) = (\partial g^2(\mathbf{x}^*)/\partial x_1, \partial g^2(\mathbf{x}^*)/\partial x_2)$.

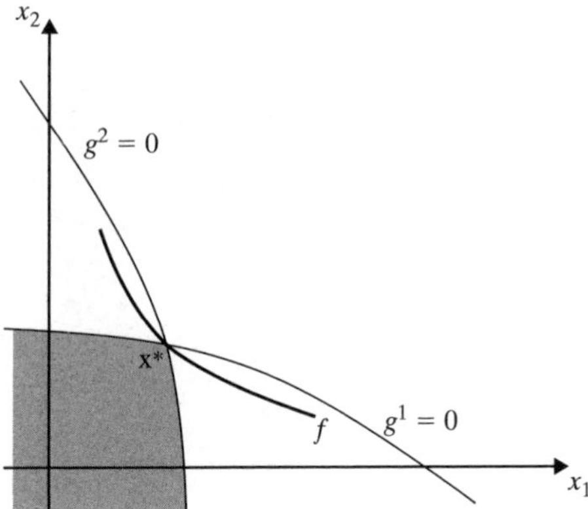

Figure A2.11. An optimal solution.

Consequently, (A2.34) tells us that the slope of the gradient vector $\nabla f(\mathbf{x}^*)$ lies between the slopes of the gradient vectors $\nabla g^1(\mathbf{x}^*)$ and $\nabla g^2(\mathbf{x}^*)$. Because a gradient vector is perpendicular to its level set,[5] the situation is therefore as shown in Fig. A2.12, where we have drawn each gradient vector as if $\mathbf{x}^*$ is the origin.

The north-east shaded cone in Fig. A2.12 is the set of all vectors (once again, think of $\mathbf{x}^*$ as the origin) that can be written as a non-negative linear combination of $\nabla g^1(\mathbf{x}^*)$ and $\nabla g^2(\mathbf{x}^*)$. Evidently, $\nabla f(\mathbf{x}^*)$ lies in this set and so we may conclude that if $\mathbf{x}^*$ solves (A2.33), there exist real numbers λ_1^*, λ_2^* such that,

$$\frac{\partial f(\mathbf{x}^*)}{\partial x_i} - \sum_{j=1}^{2} \lambda_j^* \frac{\partial g^j(\mathbf{x}^*)}{\partial x_i} = 0, \text{ for } i = 1, 2.$$

$$\lambda_1^* \geq 0, \lambda_2^* \geq 0,$$

and of course, in our example, the constraints are satisfied with equality, i.e.,

$$g^1(\mathbf{x}^*) = 0 \text{ and } g^2(\mathbf{x}^*) = 0.$$

[5]We have just shown that the slope of the gradient vectors are the negative reciprocals of the slopes of their level sets. Hence, they are perpendicular to their level sets.

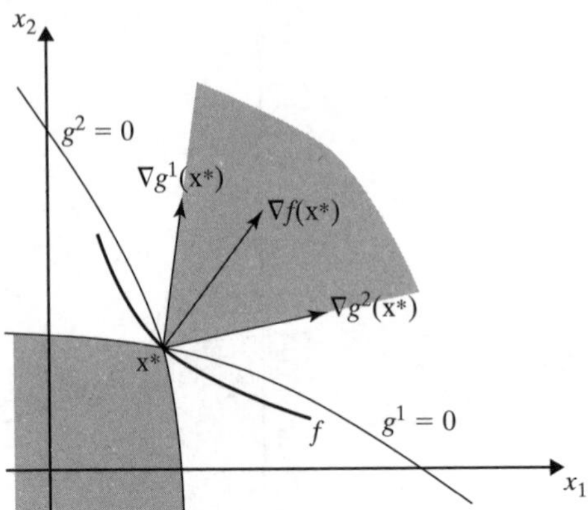

Figure A2.12. The gradient vectors.

In general, not all constraints need be satisfied with equality at the optimal solution. The Kuhn-Tucker theorem below provides necessary conditions of the sort we have just derived, while also handling situations in which some constraints are not binding at the optimum. The theorem shows that, at the optimum, the gradient of f can be expressed as a non-negative linear combination of the gradients of the g^j associated with binding constraints j. We state the theorem for maximisation problems only because any minimisation problem can be solved by maximising the negative of the objective function subject to the same constraints.

THEOREM A2.20 ***(Kuhn-Tucker) Necessary Conditions for Maxima of Real-Valued Functions Subject to Inequality Constraints***

Let $f(\mathbf{x})$ and $g^j(\mathbf{x})$, $j = 1, \ldots, m$ be continuous real-valued functions defined over some domain $D \in \mathbb{R}^n$. Let $\mathbf{x}^*$ be an interior point of D and suppose that $\mathbf{x}^*$ maximises $f(\mathbf{x})$ on D subject to the constraints $g^j(\mathbf{x}) \leq 0, j = 1, \ldots, m$, and that f and each g^j are continuously differentiable on an open set containing $\mathbf{x}^*$. If the gradient vectors $\nabla g^j(\mathbf{x}^*)$ associated with constraints j that bind at $\mathbf{x}^*$ are linearly independent, then there is a unique vector

$\lambda^* \in \mathbb{R}^n$, such that $(\mathbf{x}^*, \lambda^*)$ satisfies the Kuhn-Tucker conditions:

$$\frac{\partial \mathcal{L}(\mathbf{x}^*, \lambda^*)}{\partial x_i} = \frac{\partial f(\mathbf{x}^*)}{\partial x_i} - \sum_{j=1}^{m} \lambda_j^* \frac{\partial g^j(\mathbf{x}^*)}{\partial x_i} = 0, \quad i = 1, \ldots, n$$

$$\lambda_j^* \geq 0, \quad g^j(\mathbf{x}^*) \leq 0, \quad \lambda_j^* g^j(\mathbf{x}^*) = 0, \quad j = 1, \ldots, m.$$

Proof: Without loss, suppose that the first $K \geq 0$ constraints are binding and the remainder are not binding. Define $\lambda_j^* = 0$ for $j = K+1, \ldots, m$. Hence, regardless of the values of $\lambda_1^*, \ldots, \lambda_K^*$, it will be the case that $\lambda_j^* g^j(\mathbf{x}^*) = 0, j = 1, \ldots, m$. Define $B = \{\mathbf{b} \in \mathbb{R}^n \mid \mathbf{b} = \sum_{j=1}^{K} \lambda_j \nabla g^j(\mathbf{x}^*)$, for some $\lambda_1 \geq 0, \ldots, \lambda_K \geq 0\}$, and note that B is convex. It can also be shown that B is closed. See Exercise A2.29.

If $\nabla f(\mathbf{x}^*) \in B$, then $\nabla f(\mathbf{x}^*) - \sum_{j=1}^{K} \lambda_j^* \nabla g^j(\mathbf{x}^*) = 0$ for some $\lambda_1^* \geq 0, \ldots, \lambda_K^* \geq 0$. Moreover, such λ_i^* are unique since if also $\nabla f(\mathbf{x}^*) - \sum_{j=1}^{K} \hat{\lambda}_j \nabla g^j(\mathbf{x}^*) = 0$, then subtracting the two equalities gives $\sum_{j=1}^{K} (\lambda_j^* - \hat{\lambda}_j) \nabla g^j(\mathbf{x}^*) = 0$. The linear independence of $\nabla g^1(\mathbf{x}^*), \ldots, \nabla g^K(\mathbf{x}^*)$ implies $\lambda_j^* = \hat{\lambda}_j$ for $j = 1, \ldots, K$. Therefore, it suffices to show that $\nabla f(\mathbf{x}^*)$ is contained in B.

Let $\mathbf{a}^* = \nabla f(\mathbf{x}^*)$. Suppose, by way of contradiction, that $\mathbf{a}^* \notin B$. Then the two closed convex sets $A = \{\mathbf{a}^*\}$ and B are disjoint. By Theorem A2.24, there exists $\mathbf{p} \in \mathbb{R}^n$ such that,

$$\mathbf{p} \cdot \mathbf{a}^* > \mathbf{p} \cdot \mathbf{b} \tag{P.1}$$

for every $\mathbf{b} \in B$. In particular, $\mathbf{p} \cdot \mathbf{a}^* > \mathbf{0}$ because $\mathbf{0} \in B$. Also, $\mathbf{p} \cdot \nabla g^j(\mathbf{x}^*) \leq \mathbf{0}$ for every $j = 1, 2, \ldots, K$, since if this fails for some such j, (P.1) would be violated by setting $\mathbf{b} = \lambda \nabla g^j(\mathbf{x}^*)$ for $\lambda > 0$ large enough. Thus, we have

$$\nabla f(\mathbf{x}^*) \cdot \mathbf{p} > \mathbf{0} \quad \text{and} \quad \nabla g^j(\mathbf{x}^*) \cdot \mathbf{p} \leq \mathbf{0}, \quad \text{for } j = 1, \ldots, K. \tag{P.2}$$

Because $\nabla g^1(\mathbf{x}^*), \ldots, \nabla g^K(\mathbf{x}^*)$ are linearly independent vectors in $\mathbb{R}^n$, the $K \times n$ matrix G whose jth row is $\nabla g^j(\mathbf{x}^*)$ has range equal to all of $\mathbb{R}^K$.[6] In particular, if $\mathbf{w} \in \mathbb{R}^K$ is the column vector $(-1, -1, \ldots, -1)$, there exists $\mathbf{z} \in \mathbb{R}^n$ such that $G\mathbf{z} = \mathbf{w}$. So, in particular,

$$\nabla g^j(\mathbf{x}^*) \cdot \mathbf{z} < 0 \text{ for every } j = 1, \ldots, K. \tag{P.3}$$

[6]This is a basic fact from linear algebra. However, it can be proven quite directly using Theorem A2.24, a proof you might wish to try.

By (P.2), we may choose $\delta > 0$ small enough so that

$$\nabla f(\mathbf{x}^*) \cdot (\mathbf{p} + \delta \mathbf{z}) > \mathbf{0}. \tag{P.4}$$

Because $\mathbf{x}^*$ is in the interior of D, $f(\mathbf{x}^* + \varepsilon(\mathbf{p} + \delta\mathbf{z}))$ is well-defined as a function of ε so long as $|\varepsilon|$ is small enough. Moreover, all of the non-binding constraints $j = K + 1, \ldots, m$ are satisfied for $\varepsilon > 0$ small enough by continuity, and all of the binding constraints $j = 1, \ldots, K$ are satisfied for $\varepsilon > 0$ small enough because for each such j, (P.2) and (P.3) imply,

$$\frac{dg^j(\mathbf{x}^* + \varepsilon(\mathbf{p} + \delta\mathbf{z}))}{d\varepsilon} = \nabla g^j(\mathbf{x}^*) \cdot (\mathbf{p} + \delta\mathbf{z}) < 0.$$

Consequently, for $\varepsilon > 0$ small enough, $\mathbf{x}^* + \varepsilon(\mathbf{p} + \delta\mathbf{z})$ is feasible and must therefore yield a value of f that is no greater than the maximum value $f(\mathbf{x}^*)$. We must therefore have,

$$\left.\frac{df(\mathbf{x}^* + \varepsilon(\mathbf{p} + \delta\mathbf{z}))}{d\varepsilon}\right|_{\varepsilon = 0} \leq 0.$$

But according to (P.4),

$$\left.\frac{df(\mathbf{x}^* + \varepsilon(\mathbf{p} + \delta\mathbf{z}))}{d\varepsilon}\right|_{\varepsilon = 0} = \nabla f(\mathbf{x}^*) \cdot (\mathbf{p} + \delta\mathbf{z}) > 0,$$

which is the desired contradiction. ∎

The Kuhn-Tucker conditions of Theorem A2.20 are only necessary first-order conditions for local optima. Sufficient conditions are available when the objective function is concave or quasiconcave. The interested reader can consult Luenberger (1973) or Arrow and Enthoven (1961) on this point. For our purposes, the necessary conditions of Theorem A2.20 are enough.

The Kuhn-Tucker theorem is often written with the additional non-negativity constraints,

$$x_1 \geq 0, \ldots, x_n \geq 0,$$

given explicitly. Theorem A2.20 still applies to such a situation since each non-negativity constraint can be written as a constraint function g^j. Indeed, if the above non-negativity constraints are the only constraints, then Theorem A2.20 reduces to theorem A2.19. See Exercise A2.30.

The conclusion that $\lambda_j^* g^j(\mathbf{x}^*) = 0$ for $j = 1, \ldots, m$ is called **complementary slackness.** It says that if a constraint is slack its associated Lagrange multiplier must be zero, while if a Lagrange multiplier is positive its associated constraint must be binding. As you will be asked to show in exercise A2.33, the Lagrange multiplier λ_j^* can be interpreted as the marginal increase in the objective function when the jth constraint is relaxed.

The linear independence condition in Theorem A2.20 is one among a variety of possible **constraint qualifications**. To see that some such qualification is needed, consider the problem of maximising, $f(x) = x$ subject to $g(x) = x^3 \leq 0$, where $D = (-\infty, \infty)$. In this case, $x^* = 0$, $\nabla g(x^*) = 0$ and $\nabla f(x^*) = 1$. Hence, the conclusion of Theorem A2.20 fails. This does not contradict the theorem of course, because the singleton set of gradients $\{\nabla g(x^*)\}$ corresponding to the single binding constraint is not linearly independent. Thus, one cannot simply remove the constraint qualification. Exercise A2.31 provides several constraint qualifications, each of which can replace the linear independence condition given in Theorem A2.20 without changing the conclusion of the theorem except insofar as the uniqueness of the Lagrange multipliers is concerned.

A2.4 OPTIMALITY THEOREMS

Consider the maximisation problem,

$$\max_{\mathbf{x}\in\mathbb{R}^n} f(\mathbf{x}, \mathbf{a}) \quad \text{s.t.} \quad g^j(\mathbf{x}, \mathbf{a}) \leq 0, \quad j = 1, \ldots, m, \tag{A2.35}$$

where $\mathbf{x}$ is a vector of choice variables, and $\mathbf{a} = (a_1, \ldots, a_l)$ is a vector of parameters that may enter the objective function, the constraints, or both.

We maintain the following assumptions and notation throughout this section. The set of parameters is a subset A of $\mathbb{R}^l$ and each $g^j\colon \mathbb{R}^n \times A \to \mathbb{R}$. Let S be the set of $(\mathbf{x}, \mathbf{a}) \in \mathbb{R}^n \times A$ that satisfy all of the constraints, i.e., such that $g^j(\mathbf{x}, \mathbf{a}) \leq 0$, $j = 1, \ldots, m$. For every $\mathbf{a} \in A$ we assume there is at least one $\mathbf{x} \in \mathbb{R}^n$ such that $g^j(\mathbf{x}, \mathbf{a}) \leq 0$, $j = 1, \ldots, m$. The objective function f is defined on a subset D of $\mathbb{R}^n \times A$ containing S, i.e., $f\colon D \to \mathbb{R}$.

Suppose for a moment that for each $\mathbf{a} \in A$ there is at least one solution, $\mathbf{x}(\mathbf{a})$, to (A2.35). Then, for that vector of parameters, $\mathbf{a}$, the maximised value of the objective function is $f(\mathbf{x}(\mathbf{a}), \mathbf{a})$. This defines a new function, $V(\mathbf{a})$, called the *value function.* Formally,

$$V(\mathbf{a}) = \max_{\mathbf{x}\in\mathbb{R}^n} f(\mathbf{x}, \mathbf{a}) \quad \text{s.t.} \quad g^j(\mathbf{x}, \mathbf{a}) \leq 0, \quad j = 1, \ldots, m,$$

whenever the maximum exists. The maximum value of an objective function, f, subject to a single (binding) constraint, g, is illustrated in Fig. A2.13.

Clearly, the solutions to (A2.35) will depend in some way on the vector of parameters, $\mathbf{a} \in A$. Do the solutions vary continuously with $\mathbf{a}$? Does the maximised value $V(\mathbf{a})$ vary continuously with $\mathbf{a} \in A$. We will provide answers to both of these questions.

To ensure continuity of the value function or of the solution in the vector of parameters $\mathbf{a}$, we not only need to ensure that the objective function f is continuous, we need also to ensure that small changes in $\mathbf{a}$ have only a small effect on the set of feasible values of $\mathbf{x}$. There are essentially two ways this can fail. The set of feasible values of $\mathbf{x}$ might

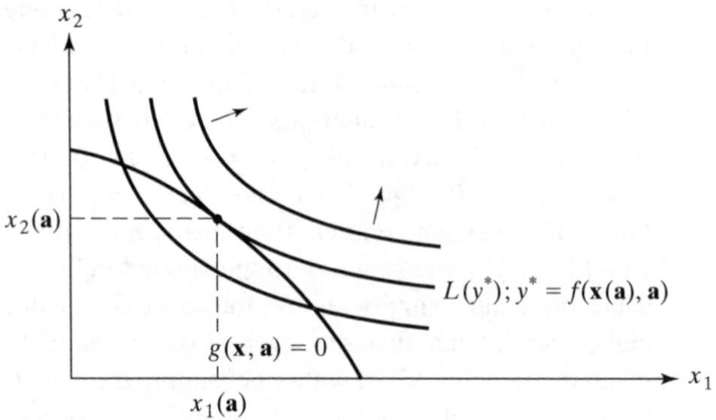

Figure A2.13. The maximum value of $f(\mathbf{x}, \mathbf{a})$, subject to the (binding) constraint $g(\mathbf{x}, \mathbf{a}) = 0$.

dramatically shrink or expand. Continuity of the g^j functions ensures that dramatic expansions cannot occur when $\mathbf{a}$ changes only slightly. To ensure that dramatic shrinkages do not occur requires an additional condition. Both conditions are contained in the following definition.

DEFINITION A2.3 ***Constraint-Continuity***

Say that constraint-continuity is satisfied if each $g^j: \mathbb{R}^n \times A \to \mathbb{R}$ is continuous, and for every $(\mathbf{x}^0, \mathbf{a}^0) \in \mathbb{R}^n \times A$ satisfying the m constraints, $g^1(\mathbf{x}, \mathbf{a}) \leq 0, \ldots, g^m(\mathbf{x}, \mathbf{a}) \leq 0$, and for every sequence $\mathbf{a}^k$ in A converging to $\mathbf{a}^0$, there is a sequence $\mathbf{x}^k$ in $\mathbb{R}^n$ converging to $\mathbf{x}^0$ such that $(\mathbf{x}^k, \mathbf{a}^k)$ satisfies the constraints for every k.[7]

THEOREM A2.21 ***The Theorem of the Maximum***

Suppose that S is compact, that $f: D \to \mathbb{R}$ is continuous, and that constraint-continuity is satisfied. Then,

(i) A solution to (A2.35) exists for every $\mathbf{a} \in A$, and therefore the value function $V(\mathbf{a})$ is defined on all of A.

(ii) The value function, $V: A \to \mathbb{R}$, is continuous.

(iii) Suppose that $(\mathbf{x}^k, \mathbf{a}^k)$ is a sequence in $\mathbb{R}^n \times A$ converging to $(\mathbf{x}^*, \mathbf{a}^*) \in \mathbb{R}^n \times A$. If for every k, $\mathbf{x}^k$ is a solution to (A2.35) when $\mathbf{a} = \mathbf{a}^k$, then $\mathbf{x}^*$ is a solution to (A2.35) when $\mathbf{a} = \mathbf{a}^*$.

(iv) If for every $\mathbf{a} \in A$ the solution to (A2.35) is unique and given by the function $\mathbf{x}(\mathbf{a})$, then $\mathbf{x}: A \to \mathbb{R}^n$ is continuous.

---

[7]This definition is equivalent to notions of upper and lower semicontinuity in the theory of correspondences.

Proof: Part (i) follows immediately from Theorem A1.10 because the compactness of S and the continuity of each g^j implies that for every $\mathbf{a} \in A$ the set of $\mathbf{x} \in \mathbb{R}^n$ satisfying the m constraints $g^1(\mathbf{x}, \mathbf{a}) \leq 0, \ldots, g^m(\mathbf{x}, \mathbf{a}) \leq 0$ is compact and because we have assumed throughout that it is non-empty.

Let us prove part (iii) next. Suppose, by way of contradiction, that (iii) fails. Then $\mathbf{x}^*$ is not a solution to (A2.35) when $\mathbf{a} = \mathbf{a}^*$. This means that there is some $\hat{\mathbf{x}} \in \mathbb{R}^n$ such that $(\hat{\mathbf{x}}, \mathbf{a}^*) \in S$ and $f(\hat{\mathbf{x}}, \mathbf{a}^*) > f(\mathbf{x}^*, \mathbf{a}^*)$. Because $\mathbf{a}^k$ converges to $\mathbf{a}^*$, constraint-continuity applied to $(\hat{\mathbf{x}}, \mathbf{a}^*)$ implies there is a sequence $\hat{\mathbf{x}}^k$ in $\mathbb{R}^n$ converging to $\hat{\mathbf{x}}$ such that $(\hat{\mathbf{x}}^k, \mathbf{a}^k)$ satisfies the constraints for every k. The continuity of f implies that (see Theorem A1.9) $f(\hat{\mathbf{x}}^k, \mathbf{a}^k)$ converges to $f(\hat{\mathbf{x}}, \mathbf{a}^*)$ and that $f(\mathbf{x}^k, \mathbf{a}^k)$ converges to $f(\mathbf{x}^*, \mathbf{a}^*)$. Consequently, because $f(\hat{\mathbf{x}}, \mathbf{a}^*) > f(\mathbf{x}^*, \mathbf{a}^*)$ we have,

$$f(\hat{\mathbf{x}}^k, \mathbf{a}^k) > f(\mathbf{x}^k, \mathbf{a}^k), \quad \text{for all } k \text{ large enough.}$$

But this contradicts the fact that $\mathbf{x}^k$ solves (A2.35) when $\mathbf{a} = \mathbf{a}^k$, and completes the proof of part (iii).

To prove part (ii), suppose that $\{\mathbf{a}^k\}_{k \in I}$ is a sequence in A converging to $\mathbf{a}^* \in A$. By Theorem A1.9 it suffices to show that $V(\mathbf{a}^k)$ converges to $V(\mathbf{a}^*)$. Suppose by way of contradiction, that $V(\mathbf{a}^k)$ does not converge to $V(\mathbf{a}^*)$. Then for some $\varepsilon > 0$, there is an infinite subset I' of I such that for every $k \in I'$, $V(\mathbf{a}^k)$ fails to be within ε of $V(\mathbf{a}^*)$. By definition of the value function, for each $k \in I'$ there is a solution $\mathbf{x}^k$ of (A2.35) when $\mathbf{a} = \mathbf{a}^k$ such that $V(\mathbf{a}^k) = f(\mathbf{x}^k, \mathbf{a}^k)$. Because each $(\mathbf{x}^k, \mathbf{a}^k)$ is in the compact set S, Theorem A1.8 implies that the sequence $\{(\mathbf{x}^k, \mathbf{a}^k)\}_{k \in I'}$ has a convergent subsequence, $\{(\mathbf{x}^k, \mathbf{a}^k)\}_{k \in I''}$, converging to, say $(\hat{\mathbf{x}}, \hat{\mathbf{a}})$, where I'' is an infinite subset of I'. Because $\{\mathbf{a}^k\}_{k \in I}$ converges to $\mathbf{a}^*$, the subsequence $\{\mathbf{a}^k\}_{k \in I''}$ also converges to $\mathbf{a}^*$. Consequently, $\{V(\mathbf{a}^k) = f(\mathbf{x}^k, \mathbf{a}^k)\}_{k \in I''}$ converges to $f(\hat{\mathbf{x}}, \mathbf{a}^*)$ by the continuity of f. But because for $k \in I''$ each $\mathbf{x}^k$ solves (A2.35) when $\mathbf{a} = \mathbf{a}^k$, part (iii) implies that $\hat{\mathbf{x}}$ solves (A2.35) when $\mathbf{a} = \mathbf{a}^*$. Hence, $V(\mathbf{a}^*) = f(\hat{\mathbf{x}}, \mathbf{a}^*)$, from which we conclude that $\{V(\mathbf{a}^k)\}_{k \in I''}$ converges to $V(\mathbf{a}^*)$. But this contradicts the fact that $V(\mathbf{a}^k)$ fails to be within $\varepsilon > 0$ of $V(\mathbf{a}^*)$ for every $k \in I' \supseteq I''$.

To prove part (iv), suppose that $\{\mathbf{a}^k\}_{k \in I}$ is a sequence in A converging to $\mathbf{a}^* \in A$. By Theorem A1.9 it suffices to show that $\mathbf{x}(\mathbf{a}^k)$ converges to $\mathbf{x}(\mathbf{a}^*)$. Suppose by way of contradiction, that $\mathbf{x}(\mathbf{a}^k)$ does not converge to $\mathbf{x}(\mathbf{a}^*)$. Then for some $\varepsilon > 0$, there is an infinite subset I' of I such that for every $k \in I'$, $\mathbf{x}(\mathbf{a}^k)$ fails to be within ε of $\mathbf{x}(\mathbf{a}^*)$. Defining $\mathbf{x}^k = \mathbf{x}(\mathbf{a}^k)$ for every k, the proof now proceeds as in the proof of part (ii) and is left as an exercise. ∎

If the solution to (A2.35) is always unique and the objective function, constraint, and solutions are differentiable in the parameter, $\mathbf{a}$, there is a very powerful theorem that can be used to analyse the behaviour of the value function $V(\mathbf{a})$ as the vector of parameters, $\mathbf{a}$, changes. This is known as the **Envelope theorem**. To keep the notation simple, we will prove the theorem when there is just a single constraint, i.e., when $m = 1$. You are invited to generalise the result to the case of many constraints in the exercises.

THEOREM A2.22 ***The Envelope Theorem***

Consider the problem (A2.35) when there is just one constraint and suppose the objective function, f, and the constraint function, g, are continuously differentiable in $(\mathbf{x}, \mathbf{a})$ on an open subset $W \times U$ of $\mathbb{R}^n \times A$. For each $\mathbf{a} \in U$, suppose that $\mathbf{x}(\mathbf{a}) \in W$ uniquely solves (A2.35), is continuously differentiable in $\mathbf{a}$ on U, and that the constraint $g(\mathbf{x}(\mathbf{a}), \mathbf{a}) \leq 0$ is binding for every $\mathbf{a} \in U$. Let $\mathcal{L}(\mathbf{x}, \mathbf{a}, \lambda)$ be the problem's associated Lagrangian function and let $(\mathbf{x}(\mathbf{a}), \lambda(\mathbf{a}))$ solve the Kuhn-Tucker conditions in Theorem A2.20. Finally, let $V(\mathbf{a})$ be the problem's associated value function. Then, the Envelope theorem states that for every $\mathbf{a} \in U$,

$$\frac{\partial V(\mathbf{a})}{\partial a_j} = \left.\frac{\partial \mathcal{L}}{\partial a_j}\right|_{\mathbf{x}(\mathbf{a}),\lambda(\mathbf{a})} \qquad j = 1, \ldots, m.$$

where the right-hand side denotes the partial derivative of the Lagrangian function with respect to the parameter a_j evaluated at the point $(\mathbf{x}(\mathbf{a}), \lambda(\mathbf{a}))$.

The theorem says that the *total* effect on the optimised value of the objective function when a parameter changes (and so, presumably, the whole problem must be reoptimised) can be deduced simply by taking the partial of the problem's Lagrangian with respect to the parameter and then evaluating that derivative at the solution to the original problem's first-order Kuhn-Tucker conditions. Although we have confined ourselves in the statement of the theorem to the case of a single constraint, the theorem applies regardless of the number of constraints, with the usual proviso that there be fewer constraints than choice variables. Because of the importance of this theorem, and because it is not so obviously true, we will work through a rather extended proof of the version given here.

Proof: First, form the Lagrangian for the maximisation problem:

$$\mathcal{L} \equiv f(\mathbf{x}, \mathbf{a}) - \lambda[g(\mathbf{x}, \mathbf{a})].$$

By hypothesis, $\mathbf{x}(\mathbf{a})$ and $\lambda(\mathbf{a})$ satisfy the first-order Kuhn-Tucker conditions given in Theorem A2.20. Therefore for every $\mathbf{a} \in U$, and because the constraint is binding, we have,

$$\begin{aligned} \frac{\partial f(\mathbf{x}(\mathbf{a}), \mathbf{a})}{\partial x_i} - \lambda(\mathbf{a})\frac{\partial g(\mathbf{x}(\mathbf{a}), \mathbf{a})}{\partial x_i} &= 0, \qquad i = 1, \ldots, n \\ g(\mathbf{x}(\mathbf{a}), \mathbf{a}) &= 0. \end{aligned} \tag{P.1}$$

The partial derivative of $\mathcal{L}$ with respect to the parameter a_j would be

$$\frac{\partial \mathcal{L}}{\partial a_j} = \frac{\partial f(\mathbf{x}, \mathbf{a})}{a_j} - \lambda\frac{\partial g(\mathbf{x}, \mathbf{a})}{\partial a_j}.$$

If we evaluate this derivative at the point $(\mathbf{x}(\mathbf{a}), \lambda(\mathbf{a}))$, we obtain

$$\left.\frac{\partial \mathcal{L}}{\partial a_j}\right|_{\mathbf{x}(\mathbf{a}),\lambda(\mathbf{a})} = \frac{\partial f(\mathbf{x}(\mathbf{a}), \mathbf{a})}{\partial a_j} - \lambda(\mathbf{a})\frac{\partial g(\mathbf{x}(\mathbf{a}), \mathbf{a})}{\partial a_j}. \tag{P.2}$$

If we can show that the partial derivative of the maximum-value function with respect to a_j is equal to the right-hand side of (P.2), we will have proved the theorem.

We begin by directly differentiating $V(\mathbf{a})$ with respect to a_j. Because a_j affects f directly and indirectly through its influence on *each* variable $x_i(\mathbf{a})$, we will have to remember to use the chain rule. We get

$$\frac{\partial V(\mathbf{a})}{\partial a_j} = \underbrace{\sum_{i=1}^{n}\left[\frac{\partial f(\mathbf{x}(\mathbf{a}), \mathbf{a})}{\partial x_i}\right]\frac{\partial x_i(\mathbf{a})}{\partial a_j}}_{\text{chain rule}} + \frac{\partial f(\mathbf{x}(\mathbf{a}), \mathbf{a})}{\partial a_j}.$$

Now, go back to the first-order conditions (P.1). Rearranging the first one gives

$$\frac{\partial f(\mathbf{x}(\mathbf{a}), \mathbf{a})}{\partial x_i} \equiv \lambda(\mathbf{a})\frac{\partial g(\mathbf{x}(\mathbf{a}), \mathbf{a})}{\partial x_i}, \qquad i = 1, \ldots, n.$$

Substituting into the bracketed term of the summation, we can rewrite the partial derivative of $V(\mathbf{a})$ as

$$\frac{\partial V(\mathbf{a})}{\partial a_j} = \lambda(\mathbf{a})\sum_{i=1}^{n}\left[\frac{\partial g(\mathbf{x}(\mathbf{a}), \mathbf{a})}{\partial x_i}\frac{\partial x_i(\mathbf{a})}{\partial a_j}\right] + \frac{\partial f(\mathbf{x}(\mathbf{a}), \mathbf{a})}{\partial a_j}. \tag{P.3}$$

The final 'trick' is to go back again to the first-order conditions (P.1) and look at the *second* identity in the system. Because $g(\mathbf{x}(\mathbf{a}), \mathbf{a}) \equiv 0$, we can differentiate both sides of this identity with respect to a_j and they must be equal. Because the derivative of the constant zero is zero, we obtain

$$\underbrace{\sum_{i=1}^{n}\left[\frac{\partial g(\mathbf{x}(\mathbf{a}), \mathbf{a})}{\partial x_i}\frac{\partial x_i(\mathbf{a})}{\partial a_j}\right]}_{\text{chain rule again}} + \frac{\partial g(\mathbf{x}(\mathbf{a}), \mathbf{a})}{\partial a_j} \equiv 0.$$

Rearranging yields

$$\frac{\partial g(\mathbf{x}(\mathbf{a}), \mathbf{a})}{\partial a_j} \equiv -\sum_{i=1}^{n}\left[\frac{\partial g(\mathbf{x}(\mathbf{a}), \mathbf{a})}{\partial x_i}\right]\frac{\partial x_i(\mathbf{a})}{\partial a_j}.$$

Moving the minus sign into the brackets, we can substitute the left-hand side of this identity for the entire summation term in (P.3) to get

$$\frac{\partial V(\mathbf{a})}{\partial a_j} = -\lambda(\mathbf{a})\frac{\partial g(\mathbf{x}(\mathbf{a}), \mathbf{a})}{\partial a_j} + \frac{\partial f(\mathbf{x}(\mathbf{a}), \mathbf{a})}{\partial a_j}. \tag{P.4}$$

The right-hand side of (P.4) is the same as the right-hand side of (P.2). Thus,

$$\frac{\partial V(\mathbf{a})}{\partial a_j} = \left.\frac{\partial \mathcal{L}}{\partial a_j}\right|_{\mathbf{x}(\mathbf{a}),\lambda(\mathbf{a})}$$

as we wanted to show. ∎

EXAMPLE A2.11 Let us see if we can verify the Envelope theorem. Suppose we have $f(x_1, x_2) \equiv x_1x_2$ and a simple constraint $g(x_1, x_2) \equiv 2x_1 + 4x_2 - a$. We are given the problem

$$\max_{x_1,x_2} x_1x_2 \quad \text{s.t.} \quad 2x_1 + 4x_2 - a = 0,$$

and would like to know how the maximum value of the objective function varies with the (single, scalar) parameter a. We will do this two ways: first, we will derive the function $V(a)$ explicitly and differentiate it to get our answer. Then we will use the Envelope theorem to see if we get the same thing.

To form $V(a)$, we must first solve for the optimal values of the choice variables in terms of the parameter. We would then substitute these into the objective function as in (A2.36) to get an expression for $V(a)$. Notice that this problem differs slightly from the one in (A2.35) because we do not require non-negativity on the choice variables. Thus, we can dispense with the Kuhn-Tucker conditions and just use the simple Lagrangian method. Forming the Lagrangian, we get

$$\mathcal{L} = x_1x_2 - \lambda[2x_1 + 4x_2 - a],$$

with first-order conditions:

$$\begin{aligned} \mathcal{L}_1 &= x_2 - 2\lambda = 0 \\ \mathcal{L}_2 &= x_1 - 4\lambda = 0 \\ \mathcal{L}_\lambda &= a - 2x_1 - 4x_2 = 0. \end{aligned} \tag{E.1}$$

These can be solved to find $x_1(a) = a/4$, $x_2(a) = a/8$, and $\lambda(a) = a/16$. We form the maximum-value function by substituting the solutions for x_1 and x_2 into the objective function. Thus,

$$V(a) = x_1(a)x_2(a) = \left(\frac{a}{4}\right)\left(\frac{a}{8}\right) = \frac{a^2}{32}.$$

Differentiating $V(a)$ with respect to a will tell us how the maximised value of the objective function varies with a. Doing that we get

$$\frac{dV(a)}{da} = \frac{a}{16}.$$

Now let us verify this using the Envelope theorem. The theorem tells us that to see how the maximised value of the function varies with a parameter, simply differentiate the Lagrangian for the maximisation problem with respect to the parameter and evaluate that derivative at the solution to the first-order conditions (E.1). Applying the theorem, we first obtain

$$\frac{dV(a)}{da} = \frac{\partial \mathcal{L}}{\partial a} = \lambda.$$

We then evaluate this at the solution to (E.1), where $\lambda(a) = a/16$. This gives us

$$\frac{dV(a)}{da} = \lambda(a) = \frac{a}{16},$$

which checks.

Besides verifying that the Envelope theorem 'works', this example has also given us some insight into what interpretation we can give to those 'incidental' variables, the Lagrangian multipliers. This is pursued further in the exercises. □

Although we have confined attention here to maximisation problems and their associated value functions, it should be clear that we could also construct value functions for *minimisation* problems analogously, and that the Envelope theorem would apply for them as well.

A2.5 SEPARATION THEOREMS

We end this mathematical appendix with a look at what are called 'separation' theorems. The idea is geometrically simple enough. Fig. A2.14 shows two disjoint convex sets, A and B, in $\mathbb{R}^2$. It is obvious that we can draw a line between them. Such a line is said to 'separate' the two sets. If we think of the line as being described by the equation,

$$p_1x_1 + p_2x_2 = I,$$

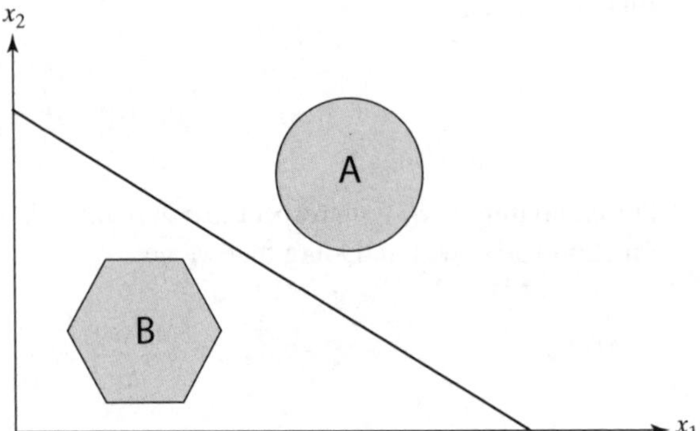

Figure A2.14. Separating convex sets.

where p_1, p_2, and I are positive constants, then every point $(a_1, a_2) \in A$ is such that

$$p_1a_1 + p_2a_2 > I,$$

and every point $(b_1, b_2) \in B$ is such that

$$p_1b_1 + p_2b_2 < I.$$

Consequently, if $\mathbf{p} = (p_1, p_2)$, then we see that the geometric notion of separation is expressed analytically as,

$$\mathbf{p} \cdot \mathbf{a} > \mathbf{p} \cdot \mathbf{b}, \text{ for every } \mathbf{a} \in A \text{ and every } \mathbf{b} \in B.$$

Imagine now two disjoint convex sets in $\mathbb{R}^3$, say a sphere and a box with the sphere entirely outside the box. Again, it is obvious that we can separate the two sets, this time with a plane, and an identical analytic expression, but now with all vectors in $\mathbb{R}^3$, describes the situation.

The separation theorems below generalise this to any number of dimensions. We will provide two theorems. The second theorem strictly generalises the first and allows the sets A and B to be, for example, open and 'tangent' to one another.

THEOREM A2.23 ***A First Separation Theorem***

Suppose that C is a closed and convex subset of $\mathbb{R}^n$ that does not contain the origin, $\mathbf{0}$. Then, there exists a vector $\mathbf{p} \in \mathbb{R}^n$ of length one and $\alpha > 0$ such that,

$$\mathbf{p} \cdot \mathbf{c} \geq \alpha, \textit{ for every } \mathbf{c} \in C.$$

Proof: If C is empty there is nothing to prove, so suppose that C is non-empty. Consider the minimisation problem,

$$\min_{\mathbf{c}\in C} \|\mathbf{c}\| . \tag{P.1}$$

If the closed set C were bounded, it would be compact. Then, because $\|\mathbf{c}\|$ is a continuous real-valued function of $\mathbf{c}$, we could apply Theorem A1.10 and conclude that a solution to (P.1) exists. But C need not be bounded. However, choose any $\mathbf{c}^0 \in C$, and consider the problem,

$$\min_{\mathbf{c}\in C'} \|\mathbf{c}\| , \tag{P.2}$$

where $C' = \{\mathbf{c} \in C : \|\mathbf{c}\| \leq \|\mathbf{c}^0\|\}$. Because C' is closed and bounded, (P.2) has a solution $\hat{\mathbf{c}}$, say. But $\hat{\mathbf{c}}$ is then also a solution to (P.1) because otherwise some $\mathbf{c}' \in C$ satisfies $\|\mathbf{c}'\| < \|\hat{\mathbf{c}}\| \leq \|\mathbf{c}^0\|$, contradicting that $\hat{\mathbf{c}}$ solves (P.2).

Because $\hat{\mathbf{c}}$ solves (P.1) and because C is convex, we have that for every $\mathbf{c} \in C$,

$$\|\alpha\mathbf{c} + (1-\alpha)\hat{\mathbf{c}}\|^2 = \alpha^2\mathbf{c}\cdot\mathbf{c} + 2\alpha(1-\alpha)\hat{\mathbf{c}}\cdot\mathbf{c} + (1-\alpha)^2\hat{\mathbf{c}}\cdot\hat{\mathbf{c}}$$

is minimised in $\alpha \in [0, 1]$ at $\alpha = 0$. Hence, by Theorem A2.19, this quadratic function of α, being differentiable, has a non-negative derivative with respect to α when evaluated at $\alpha = 0$. That is, for every $\mathbf{c} \in C$,

$$2\alpha\mathbf{c}\cdot\mathbf{c} + 2(1-2\alpha)\hat{\mathbf{c}}\cdot\mathbf{c} - 2(1-\alpha)\hat{\mathbf{c}}\cdot\hat{\mathbf{c}} \geq 0, \text{ when } \alpha = 0.$$

This says that for every $\mathbf{c} \in C$,

$$2\hat{\mathbf{c}}\cdot\mathbf{c} - 2\hat{\mathbf{c}}\cdot\hat{\mathbf{c}} \geq 0,$$

or equivalently that for every $\mathbf{c} \in C$,

$$\hat{\mathbf{c}}\cdot\mathbf{c} \geq \hat{\mathbf{c}}\cdot\hat{\mathbf{c}} = \|\hat{\mathbf{c}}\|^2 .$$

Because $\hat{\mathbf{c}} \in C$ and $\mathbf{0} \notin C$ imply that $\hat{\mathbf{c}} \neq \mathbf{0}$, we may conclude that,

$$\hat{\mathbf{c}}\cdot\mathbf{c} \geq \|\hat{\mathbf{c}}\|^2 > 0, \text{ for every } \mathbf{c} \in C.$$

Hence, setting $\mathbf{p} = \hat{\mathbf{c}}/\|\hat{\mathbf{c}}\|$ and $\alpha = \|\hat{\mathbf{c}}\| > 0$, we have

$$\mathbf{p}\cdot\mathbf{c} \geq \alpha, \text{ for every } \mathbf{c} \in C,$$

as desired. ∎

THEOREM A2.24 ***A Second Separation Theorem***

Suppose that A and B are disjoint convex subsets of $\mathbb{R}^n$*. Then, there exists a vector* $\mathbf{p} \in \mathbb{R}^n$ *of length one such that,*

$$\mathbf{p} \cdot \mathbf{a} \geq \mathbf{p} \cdot \mathbf{b}, \quad \textit{for every } \mathbf{a} \in A \textit{ and every } \mathbf{b} \in B.$$

If, in addition, the sets A and B are closed and at least one is bounded, $\mathbf{p} \in \mathbb{R}^n$ *can be chosen so that for some* $\alpha > 0$*,*

$$\mathbf{p} \cdot (\mathbf{a} - \mathbf{b}) \geq \alpha, \quad \textit{for every } \mathbf{a} \in A \textit{ and every } \mathbf{b} \in B.$$

Proof: Let us begin with the second part of the theorem, where it is assumed in addition that both A and B are closed and one is bounded. Define C to be the set difference $A - B$ consisting of all points of the form $\mathbf{a} - \mathbf{b}$ where $\mathbf{a} \in A$ and $\mathbf{b} \in B$. It is not difficult to argue that C is convex (try it!). With a little more effort it can also be shown that C is closed (see Exercise A2.37). Moreover, because A and B are disjoint, C does not contain the origin, $\mathbf{0}$. Hence, we may apply Theorem A2.23 and conclude that there is a vector $\mathbf{p} \in \mathbb{R}^n$ of length one and $\alpha > 0$ such that $\mathbf{p} \cdot \mathbf{c} \geq \alpha$ for every $\mathbf{c} \in C$. But, by the definition of C, this means that,

$$\mathbf{p} \cdot (\mathbf{a} - \mathbf{b}) \geq \alpha, \quad \text{for every } \mathbf{a} \in A \text{ and every } \mathbf{b} \in B,$$

as desired.

Let us turn now to the first part of the theorem, where neither A nor B need be closed or bounded. Once again letting $C = A - B$, it is still the case that $\mathbf{0} \notin C$ and C is convex, but C need no longer be closed. Thus, we cannot appeal directly to Theorem A2.23. Instead, let $\bar{C}$ be the set of all limits of convergent sequences of points in C. The set $\bar{C}$ is closed and convex (convince yourself!). Moreover, $\bar{C}$ contains C because every point $\mathbf{c}$ in C is the limit of the constant sequence $\mathbf{c}, \mathbf{c}, \ldots$. If $\mathbf{0} \notin \bar{C}$, then we may apply Theorem A2.23 exactly as when C is closed, and we are done. So, suppose that $\mathbf{0} \in \bar{C}$. By Exercise A2.38, it suffices to show that $\mathbf{0}$ is a member of $\partial\bar{C}$, the boundary of $\bar{C}$, because then there is a vector $\mathbf{p} \in \mathbb{R}^n$ of length one such that $\mathbf{p} \cdot \mathbf{c} \geq 0$ for every $\mathbf{c} \in C$ and the desired conclusion follows from the definition of C. Hence, it remains only to show that $\mathbf{0} \in \partial\bar{C}$.

Suppose, by way of contradiction, that $\mathbf{0} \in \bar{C}$ but that $\mathbf{0} \notin \partial\bar{C}$. Consequently, by the definition of the boundary of $\bar{C}$, $\mathbf{0} \in \bar{C}$ is not the limit of any sequence of points outside of $\bar{C}$. Therefore, there exists $\varepsilon > 0$ such that $B_\varepsilon(\mathbf{0})$, the ε-ball with centre $\mathbf{0}$, is contained in $\bar{C}$. (Think about why this must be so.) Let $\mathbf{e}_i$ denote the ith unit vector in $\mathbb{R}^n$ and let $\mathbf{1}$ be the n-vector of 1's. Choose $\delta > 0$ small enough so that $\delta\mathbf{e}_i$ and $-\delta\mathbf{1}$ are in $B_\varepsilon(\mathbf{0}) \subset \bar{C}$ for every $i = 1, \ldots, n$. By the definition of $\bar{C}$, for each $i = 0, 1, \ldots, n$, there is a sequence, $\{\mathbf{c}_i^k\}_{k=1}^\infty$, of points in C such that

$$\mathbf{c}_0^k \to -\delta\mathbf{1} \text{ and } \mathbf{c}_i^k \to \delta\mathbf{e}_i \text{ for } i = 1, \ldots, n. \tag{P.1}$$

For each k, let C^k be the set of all convex combinations of $\mathbf{c}_0^k, \mathbf{c}_1^k, \ldots, \mathbf{c}_n^k$. That is, $C^k = \{\mathbf{c} \in \mathbb{R}^n \mid \mathbf{c} = \sum_{i=0}^n \lambda_i \mathbf{c}_i^k$ for some non-negative $\lambda_0, \lambda_1 \ldots, \lambda_n$ summing to one$\}$. The set C^k is closed and convex (check this!). Moreover, C^k is contained in C because every point in C^k is a convex combination of points in the convex set C. Consequently, $\mathbf{0} \notin C^k$. We may therefore appeal to Theorem A2.23 to conclude that there is a vector $\mathbf{p}^k \in \mathbb{R}^n$ of length one such that $\mathbf{p}^k \cdot \mathbf{c} \geq 0$ for every $\mathbf{c} \in C^k$. In particular, for every $k = 1, 2, \ldots,$

$$\mathbf{p}^k \cdot \mathbf{c}_i^k \geq 0 \text{ for } i = 0, 1, \ldots, n. \tag{P.2}$$

Because the sequence $\{\mathbf{p}^k\}$ is bounded, Theorem A1.8 implies that it has a convergent subsequence, $\{\mathbf{p}^k\}_{k \in K}$, where K is an infinite subset of the the indices $1, 2, \ldots$. Let $\hat{\mathbf{p}}$ be the limit of this subsequence and note that $\|\hat{\mathbf{p}}\| = 1$ being the limit of vectors whose length is one. Taking the limit in (P.2) as $k \in K$ tends to infinity and using (P.1) gives,

$$\hat{\mathbf{p}} \cdot (-\delta \mathbf{1}) \geq 0 \text{ and } \hat{\mathbf{p}} \cdot (\delta \mathbf{e}_i) \geq 0 \text{ for } i = 1, \ldots, n. \tag{P.3}$$

The last n inequalities in (P.3) imply that $\hat{p}_i \geq 0$ for $i = 1, \ldots, n$. Together with the first inequality in (P.3), this implies that $\hat{\mathbf{p}} = \mathbf{0}$, contradicting the fact that $\hat{\mathbf{p}}$ has length one and completing the proof. ∎

The two separation theorems presented here are sufficient for most purposes. One might wonder about other such theorems. For example, can a point on the boundary of a convex set be separated from the set? Exercise A2.39 explores this question.

A2.6 EXERCISES

A2.1 Differentiate the following functions. State whether the function is increasing, decreasing, or constant at the point $x = 2$. Classify each as locally concave, convex, or linear at the point $x = 2$.

(a) $11x^3 - 6x + 8$.

(b) $(3x^2 - x)(6x + 1)$.

(c) $x^2 - (1/x^3)$.

(d) $(x^2 + 2x)^3$.

(e) $[3x/(x^3 + 1)]^2$.

(f) $[(1/x^2 + 2) - (1/x - 2)]^4$.

(g) $\int_x^1 e^{t^2}\, dt$.

A2.2 Find all first-order partial derivatives.

(a) $f(x_1, x_2) = 2x_1 - x_1^2 - x_2^2$.

(b) $f(x_1, x_2) = x_1^2 + 2x_2^2 - 4x_2$.

(c) $f(x_1, x_2) = x_1^3 - x_2^2 - 2x_2$.

(d) $f(x_1, x_2) = 4x_1 + 2x_2 - x_1^2 + x_1x_2 - x_2^2$.

(e) $f(x_1, x_2) = x_1^3 - 6x_1x_2 + x_2^3$.

(f) $f(x_1, x_2) = 3x_1^2 - x_1x_2 + x_2$.

(g) $g(x_1, x_2, x_3) = \ln(x_1^2 - x_2x_3 - x_3^2)$.

A2.3 Let $g(x_a, x_b) = f(x_a + x_b, x_a - x_b)$, where f is a differentiable function of two variables, say, $f = f(x_u, x_v)$. Show that

$$\frac{\partial g}{\partial x_a}\frac{\partial g}{\partial x_b} = \left(\frac{\partial f}{\partial x_u}\right)^2 - \left(\frac{\partial f}{\partial x_v}\right)^2.$$

A2.4 Show that $y = x_1^2x_2 + x_2^2x_3 + x_3^2x_1$ satisfies the equation

$$\frac{\partial y}{\partial x_1} + \frac{\partial y}{\partial x_2} + \frac{\partial y}{\partial x_3} = (x_1 + x_2 + x_3)^2.$$

A2.5 Find the Hessian matrix and construct the quadratic form, $\mathbf{z}^T\mathbf{H}(\mathbf{x})\mathbf{z}$, when

(a) $y = 2x_1 - x_1^2 - x_2^2$.

(b) $y = x_1^2 + 2x_2^2 - 4x_2$.

(c) $y = x_1^3 - x_2^2 + 2x_2$.

(d) $y = 4x_1 + 2x_2 - x_1^2 + x_1x_2 - x_2^2$.

(e) $y = x_1^3 - 6x_1x_2 + x_2^3$.

A2.6 Prove that the second-order own partial derivatives of a convex function must always be non-negative.

A2.7 Complete Example A2.4 for the partial with respect to x_2.

A2.8 Suppose $f(x_1, x_2) = \sqrt{x_1^2 + x_2^2}$.

(a) Show that $f(x_1, x_2)$ is homogeneous of degree 1.

(b) According to Euler's theorem, we should have $f(x_1, x_2) = (\partial f/\partial x_1)x_1 + (\partial f/\partial x_2)x_2$. Verify this.

A2.9 Suppose $f(x_1, x_2) = (x_1x_2)^2$ and $g(x_1, x_2) = (x_1^2x_2)^3$.

(a) $f(x_1, x_2)$ is homogeneous. What is its degree?

(b) $g(x_1, x_2)$ is homogeneous. What is its degree?

(c) $h(x_1, x_2) = f(x_1, x_2)g(x_1, x_2)$ is homogeneous. What is its degree?

(d) $k(x_1, x_2) = g(f(x_1, x_2), f(x_1, x_2))$ is homogeneous. What is its degree?

(e) Prove that whenever $f(x_1, x_2)$ is homogeneous of degree m and $g(x_1, x_2)$ is homogeneous of degree n, then $k(x_1, x_2) = g(f(x_1, x_2), f(x_1, x_2))$ is homogeneous of degree mn.

A2.10 A real-valued function h on $D \subset \mathbb{R}^n$ is called **homothetic** if it can be written in the form $g(f(\mathbf{x}))$, where $g\colon \mathbb{R} \to \mathbb{R}$ is strictly increasing and $f\colon D \to \mathbb{R}$ is homogeneous of degree 1. Show that if the differentiable function $h: D \to \mathbb{R}$ is homothetic, then for every $\mathbf{x} \in D$, and every i and j,

$$\frac{\partial h(t\mathbf{x})/\partial x_i}{\partial h(t\mathbf{x})/\partial x_j}$$

is constant in $t > 0$. What does this say about the level sets of the function h?

A2.11 Let $F(z)$ be an increasing function of the single variable z. Form the composite function, $F(f(\mathbf{x}))$. Show that $\mathbf{x}^*$ is a local maximum (minimum) of $f(\mathbf{x})$ if and only if $\mathbf{x}^*$ is a local maximum (minimum) of $F(f(\mathbf{x}))$.

A2.12 Suppose that $f(\mathbf{x})$ is a concave function and M is the set of all points in $\mathbb{R}^n$ that give global maxima of f. Prove that M is a convex set.

A2.13 Let $f(\mathbf{x})$ be a convex function. Prove that $f(\mathbf{x})$ reaches a local minimum at $\tilde{\mathbf{x}}$ if and only if $f(\mathbf{x})$ reaches a global minimum at $\tilde{\mathbf{x}}$.

A2.14 Prove that if $f(\mathbf{x})$ is strictly convex, and if $\tilde{\mathbf{x}}$ is a global minimiser of $f(\mathbf{x})$, then $\tilde{\mathbf{x}}$ is the unique global minimiser of $f(\mathbf{x})$.

A2.15 Check the calculations in Example A2.6 by using the substitution method to solve the system of first-order partials. Then evaluate the function at $x_1^* = 3/7$ and $x_2^* = 8/7$ and find y^*. Verify what we found in Example A2.7 by evaluating the function at *any other* point and comparing to y^*.

A2.16 Find the critical points when

(a) $f(x_1, x_2) = 2x_1 - x_1^2 - x_2^2$.

(b) $f(x_1, x_2) = x_1^2 + 2x_2^2 - 4x_2$.

(c) $f(x_1, x_2) = x_1^3 - x_2^2 + 2x_2$.

(d) $f(x_1, x_2) = 4x_1 + 2x_2 - x_1^2 + x_1x_2 - x_2^2$.

(e) $f(x_1, x_2) = x_1^3 - 6x_1x_2 + x_2^3$.

A2.17 Prove Theorem A2.15 for the case of strictly convex functions.

A2.18 Let $f(\mathbf{x})$ be a real-valued function defined on $\mathbb{R}^n_+$, and consider the matrix

$$\mathbf{H}^* \equiv \begin{pmatrix} 0 & f_1 & \cdots & f_n \\ f_1 & f_{11} & \cdots & f_{1n} \\ \vdots & \vdots & \ddots & \vdots \\ f_n & f_{n1} & \cdots & f_{nn} \end{pmatrix}.$$

This is a different sort of *bordered Hessian* than we considered in the text. Here, the matrix of second-order partials is bordered by the first-order partials and a zero to complete the square matrix. The principal minors of this matrix are the determinants

$$D_2 = \begin{vmatrix} 0 & f_1 \\ f_1 & f_{11} \end{vmatrix}, \quad D_3 = \begin{vmatrix} 0 & f_1 & f_2 \\ f_1 & f_{11} & f_{12} \\ f_2 & f_{21} & f_{22} \end{vmatrix}, \quad \ldots \quad D_n = |\mathbf{H}^*|.$$

Arrow and Enthoven (1961) use the sign pattern of these principal minors to establish the following useful results:

(i) If $f(\mathbf{x})$ is *quasiconcave*, these principal minors alternate in sign as follows: $D_2 \leq 0, D_3 \geq 0, \ldots$.

(ii) If for all $\mathbf{x} \geq \mathbf{0}$, these principal minors (which depend on $\mathbf{x}$) alternate in sign beginning with *strictly* negative: $D_2 < 0$, $D_3 > 0, \ldots$, then $f(\mathbf{x})$ is quasiconcave on the non-negative orthant. Further, it can be shown that if, for all $\mathbf{x} \gg \mathbf{0}$, we have this same alternating sign pattern on those principal minors, then $f(\mathbf{x})$ is *strictly* quasiconcave on the (strictly) positive orthant.

(a) The function $f(x_1, x_2) = x_1x_2 + x_1$ is quasiconcave on $\mathbb{R}^2_+$. Verify that its principal minors alternate in sign as in (ii).

(b) Let $f(x_1, x_2) = a\ln(x_1 + x_2) + b$, where $a > 0$. Is this function strictly quasiconcave for $\mathbf{x} \gg \mathbf{0}$? Is it quasiconcave? How about for $\mathbf{x} \geq \mathbf{0}$, but not equal to zero? Justify.

A2.19 Let $f(x_1, x_2) = (x_1x_2)^2$. Is $f(\mathbf{x})$ concave on $\mathbb{R}^2_+$? Is it quasiconcave on $\mathbb{R}^2_+$?

A2.20 Show that the converse of statement 4 of Theorems A2.1 and A2.4 are not true, by showing that $f(x) = -x^4$ is strictly concave on $\mathbb{R}$, but its second derivative is not everywhere strictly positive.

A2.21 Complete the proof of Theorem A2.3.

A2.22 Complete the proof of Theorem A2.4.

A2.23 Use part 2 of Theorem A2.4 to prove Theorem A2.5. In particular, consider the product $\mathbf{z}^T\mathbf{H}(\mathbf{x})\mathbf{z}$ when $\mathbf{z}$ is one of the n unit vectors in $\mathbb{R}^n$.

A2.24 Find the local extreme values and classify the stationary points as maxima, minima, or neither.

(a) $f(x_1, x_2) = 2x_1 - x_1^2 - x_2^2$.

(b) $f(x_1, x_2) = x_1^2 + 2x_2^2 - 4x_2$.

(c) $f(x_1, x_2) = x_1^3 - x_2^2 + 2x_2$.

(d) $f(x_1, x_2) = 4x_1 + 2x_2 - x_1^2 + x_1x_2 - x_2^2$.

(e) $f(x_1, x_2) = x_1^3 - 6x_1x_2 + x_2^3$.

A2.25 Solve the following problems. State the optimised value of the function at the solution.

(a) $\min_{x_1,x_2} x_1^2 + x_2^2$ s.t. $x_1x_2 = 1$.

(b) $\min_{x_1,x_2} x_1x_2$ s.t. $x_1^2 + x_2^2 = 1$.

(c) $\max_{x_1,x_2} x_1x_2^2$ s.t. $x_1^2/a^2 + x_2^2/b^2 = 1$.

(d) $\max_{x_1,x_2} x_1 + x_2$ s.t. $x_1^4 + x_2^4 = 1$.

(e) $\max_{x_1,x_2,x_3} x_1x_2^2x_3^3$ s.t. $x_1 + x_2 + x_3 = 1$.

A2.26 Graph $f(x) = 6 - x^2 - 4x$. Find the point where the function achieves its *unconstrained* (global) maximum and calculate the value of the function at that point. Compare this to the value it achieves when maximised subject to the non-negativity constraint $x \geq 0$.

A2.27 In minimising $f(x)$, subject to $x \geq 0$, there are thee possible cases that could arise. The constraint could be *binding, binding but irrelevant,* or *not binding*. Construct three graphs like those in Fig. A2.9 to illustrate these three cases. Convince yourself that the three conditions in (A2.32) account for all three cases. Construct a fourth case showing the 'troublesome' case alluded to in the text and explain why it would be ruled out by the conditions in (A2.32).

A2.28 State the Kuhn-Tucker theorem for the following minimisation problem

$$\min_{x_1,x_2} f(x_1,x_2) \quad \text{s.t.} \quad g(x_1,x_2) \leq 0 \quad \text{and} \quad x_1 \geq 0,\ x_2 \geq 0.$$

A2.29 In the proof of Theorem A2.20 we used the fact that the set of non-negative linear combinations of finitely many vectors in $\mathbb{R}^n$ is a closed set. This exercise will guide you towards a proof of this. Let $\mathbf{a}^1, \ldots, \mathbf{a}^N$ be vectors in $\mathbb{R}^n$ and let $B = \{\mathbf{b} \in \mathbb{R}^n \mid \mathbf{b} = \sum_{i=1}^N \lambda_i \mathbf{a}^i$, for some $\lambda_1 \geq 0, \ldots, \lambda_N \geq 0\}$. Suppose that $\mathbf{b}^1, \mathbf{b}^2, \ldots$ is a sequence of points in B converging to $\mathbf{b}^*$. We wish to show that $\mathbf{b}^*$ is in B.

(a) Argue that any $\mathbf{b}$ in B can always be written as a *minimal* non-negative linear combination of the $\mathbf{a}^i$, where minimal means that the number of $\mathbf{a}^i$'s given positive weight by the λ_i's cannot be reduced.

(b) Prove that if $\mathbf{b}^k = \sum_{i=1}^N \lambda_i^k \mathbf{a}^i$ for each $k = 1, 2, \ldots,$ and for each i the non-negative sequence $\{\lambda_i^k\}_{k=1}^\infty$ is bounded, then $\mathbf{b}^*$ is in B.

(c) Suppose that $\mathbf{b}^k = \sum_{i=1}^N \lambda_i^k \mathbf{a}^i$ for each $k = 1, 2, \ldots,$ and that for some i the non-negative sequence $\{\lambda_i^k\}_{k=1}^\infty$ is unbounded.

(i) Divide $\mathbf{b}^k$ by the sum $\lambda_1^k + \ldots + \lambda_N^k$ and conclude that $\sum_{i=1}^N \beta_i^* \mathbf{a}^i = \mathbf{0}$, the zero vector, for some non-negative $\beta_1^*, \ldots, \beta_N^*$ summing to one.

(ii) Argue that there exists $\beta_{i'}^* > 0$ and k such that,

$$\frac{\lambda_j^k}{\beta_j^*} \geq \frac{\lambda_{i'}^k}{\beta_{i'}^*} > 0, \text{ for all } j \text{ such that } \beta_j^* > 0.$$

(iii) Conclude from (i) and (ii) that for the i' and k identified there

$$\mathbf{b}^k = \sum_{i=1}^N \lambda_i^k \mathbf{a}^i = \sum_{j \neq i'} (\lambda_j^k - \beta_j^* \frac{\lambda_{i'}^k}{\beta_{i'}^*}) \mathbf{a}^j,$$

so that $\sum_{i=1}^N \lambda_i^k \mathbf{a}^i$ does not express $\mathbf{b}^k$ as a minimal non-negative linear combination of the $\mathbf{a}^i$.

(d) Conclude from (a)–(c) that because each term in the sequence $\mathbf{b}^1, \mathbf{b}^2, \ldots$ can be written as a minimal non-negative linear combination of the $\mathbf{a}^i$, the sequences of weights in those linear combinations must be bounded and therefore that $\mathbf{b}^*$ is in B as desired.

A2.30 Show that Theorem A2.20 reduces to Theorem A2.19 when the only constraints are $x_1 \geq 0, \ldots, x_n \geq 0$.

A2.31 Let $f(\mathbf{x})$ and $g^j(\mathbf{x})$, $j = 1, \ldots, m$, be real-valued functions over some domain $D \in \mathbb{R}^n$. Let $\mathbf{x}^*$ be an interior point of D and suppose that $\mathbf{x}^*$ maximises $f(\mathbf{x})$ on D subject to the constraints, $g^j(\mathbf{x}) \leq 0$ $j = 1, \ldots, m$. Assume that at the optimum, $\mathbf{x}^*$, f and each g^j are continuously differentiable and constraints $j = 1, \ldots, K$ are binding and constraints $j = K + 1, \ldots, m$ are not binding. Call constraint j linear if $g^j(\mathbf{x}) = a_j + \mathbf{b}^j \cdot \mathbf{x}$, some $a_j \in \mathbb{R}$ and $\mathbf{b}^j \in \mathbb{R}^n$. Otherwise, constraint j is non-linear. Consider the following collection of **constraint qualification** conditions.

(i) $\nabla g^1(\mathbf{x}^*), \ldots, \nabla g^K(\mathbf{x}^*)$ are linearly independent.

(ii) No convex combination of $\nabla g^1(\mathbf{x}^*), \ldots, \nabla g^K(\mathbf{x}^*)$ is the zero vector.

(iii) There exists $\mathbf{z} \in \mathbb{R}^n$ such that $\nabla g^j(\mathbf{x}^*) \cdot \mathbf{z} < 0$ for every $j = 1, \ldots, K$

(iv) There exists $\mathbf{z} \in \mathbb{R}^n$ such that $\nabla g^j(\mathbf{x}^*) \cdot \mathbf{z} \leq 0$ for every $j = 1, \ldots, K$ with the inequality strict for non-linear constraints.

(v) For every $\mathbf{p} \in \mathbb{R}^n$ such that $\nabla g^1(\mathbf{x}^*) \cdot \mathbf{p} \leq \mathbf{0}, \ldots, \nabla g^K(\mathbf{x}^*) \cdot \mathbf{p} \leq 0$ and for every $\delta > 0$, there exists $\varepsilon > 0$ and a continuously differentiable function $h\colon (-\varepsilon, \varepsilon) \to \mathbb{R}^n$ such that $h(0) = \mathbf{x}^*$, $\nabla h(0)$ is within δ of $\mathbf{p}$, and $g^j(h(s)) \leq 0$ for every $s \in (-\varepsilon, \varepsilon)$ and every $j = 1, \ldots, K$.

(a) Show that (i)⇒(ii)⇒(iii)⇒(iv)⇒(v).

(b) Show that (iv) is always satisfied if all the constraints are linear. Conclude, by (a), that (iv) and (v) are always satisfied if all the constraints are linear.

(c) Using the proof of Theorem A2.20 as a guide, prove that if (v) holds, there exist Lagrange multipliers, $\lambda_1^*, \ldots, \lambda_K^*$, all non-negative, such that,

$$\nabla f(\mathbf{x}^*) - \sum_{j=1}^{K} \lambda_j^* \nabla g^j(\mathbf{x}^*) = 0.$$

You need not prove that the λ_j^* are unique. Note that, by (a), you will then have proved that such λ_j^* exist when any one of the constraint qualification conditions (i)–(v) holds. (Of course, Theorem A2.20 covers the case when (i) holds, and in that particular case the λ_j^* are unique.) You will therefore have generalised Theorem A2.20.

A2.32 Arrow and Enthoven (1961) consider the *quasiconcave programming problem*

$$\max_{\mathbf{x}} f(\mathbf{x}) \quad \text{s.t.} \quad g(\mathbf{x}) \leq 0 \quad \text{and} \quad \mathbf{x} \geq \mathbf{0},$$

where $f(\mathbf{x})$ is quasiconcave, and $g(\mathbf{x})$ is quasiconvex.

(a) Show that if $\mathbf{x}^*$ is a local maximum, it is also a global maximum.

(b) Show that if $f(\mathbf{x})$ is strictly quasiconcave, then the global maximum is unique.

A2.33 Consider a maximisation problem where the objective function is $f(x_1, \ldots, x_n)$ and there are m constraints of the form $g^j(x_1, \ldots, x_n) - a_j = 0, j = 1, \ldots, m$. Here, none of the a_j enter the objective function and each enters just one constraint. In problems like this, a_j is called the **constraint constant** for the jth constraint. Under the assumptions of the envelope theorem, show that we can interpret the Lagrangian multiplier associated with each constraint as the effect on the maximised value of the objective function of a change in the relevant constraint constant. Repeat the exercise with m inequality constraints $g^j(x_1, \ldots, x_n) \leq a_j$ and show again that the Lagrange multiplier on the jth constraint is the derivative of the value function with respect to a_j. Thus, we may interpret the jth Lagrange multiplier as the marginal value of relaxing the jth constraint.

A2.34 Consider the non-linear programming problem

$$\max_{x_1,x_2} f(x_1, x_2) \quad \text{s.t.} \quad g(x_1, x_2) - a \leq 0.$$

It is obvious that increasing a cannot reduce the maximised value of f because the feasible set increases. Prove this another way by appealing to the envelope and Kuhn-Tucker theorems. (This second proof is of course not as good as the first, both because it is not as simple and because it requires additional assumptions.)

A2.35 Complete the proof of Theorem A2.21.

A2.36 Generalise the Envelope theorem to the case of many constraints. Assume that, locally (i.e., for all $\mathbf{a} \in U$), some constraints are always binding and the remainder are always non-binding.

A2.37 Suppose that A and B are closed subsets of $\mathbb{R}^n$ and that A is bounded.

(a) Prove that $A - B$ is closed.

(b) Let A be the subset of $\mathbb{R}^2$ weakly below the horizontal axis, and let B be the subset of $\mathbb{R}^2$ weakly above the hyperbola in the positive orthant defined by $y = 1/x$. Show that A and B are closed, but that $A - B$ is not.

A2.38 Suppose that A is a closed convex subset of $\mathbb{R}^n$ and that $\mathbf{a}^*$ is an element of the boundary of A.

(a) Use the definition of the boundary of a set to show that there is a sequence of points $\mathbf{a}^1, \mathbf{a}^2, \ldots$ not contained in A and converging to $\mathbf{a}^*$.

(b) For each k, use Theorem A2.23 to establish the existence of a vector $\mathbf{p}^k$ of length one satisfying,

$$\mathbf{p}^k \cdot \mathbf{a} \geq \mathbf{p}^k \cdot \mathbf{a}^k \text{ for every } \mathbf{a} \in A.$$

(c) By considering a convergent subsequence of $\{\mathbf{p}^k\}_{k=1}^{\infty}$, conclude that there is a vector $\hat{\mathbf{p}} \in \mathbb{R}^n$ of length one such that,

$$\hat{\mathbf{p}} \cdot \mathbf{a} \geq \hat{\mathbf{p}} \cdot \mathbf{a}^* \text{ for every } \mathbf{a} \in A.$$

A2.39 Repeat Exercise A2.38 without assuming that A is closed. In part (b) use Theorem A2.24 rather than Theorem A2.23.

List of Theorems

Chapter 1

Chapter 2

CHAPTER 3

CHAPTER 4

CHAPTER 5

CHAPTER 6

CHAPTER 7

CHAPTER 8

CHAPTER 9

MATHEMATICAL APPENDIX

CHAPTER A1

CHAPTER A2

List of Definitions

Chapter 1

Chapter 2

Chapter 3

CHAPTER 4

CHAPTER 5

CHAPTER 6

CHAPTER 7

CHAPTER 8

CHAPTER 9

MATHEMATICAL APPENDIX

CHAPTER A1

CHAPTER A2

Hints and Answers

Chapter 1

1.2 Use the definitions.

1.4 To get you started, take the indifference relation. Consider any three points $\mathbf{x}^i \in X$, $i = 1, 2, 3$, where $\mathbf{x}^1 \sim \mathbf{x}^2$ and $\mathbf{x}^2 \sim \mathbf{x}^3$. We want to show that $\mathbf{x}^1 \sim \mathbf{x}^2$ and $\mathbf{x}^2 \sim \mathbf{x}^3 \Rightarrow \mathbf{x}^1 \sim \mathbf{x}^3$. By definition of $\sim$, $\mathbf{x}^1 \sim \mathbf{x}^2 \Rightarrow \mathbf{x}^1 \succsim \mathbf{x}^2$ and $\mathbf{x}^2 \succsim \mathbf{x}^1$. Similarly, $\mathbf{x}^2 \sim \mathbf{x}^3 \Rightarrow \mathbf{x}^2 \succsim \mathbf{x}^3$ and $\mathbf{x}^3 \succsim \mathbf{x}^2$. By transitivity of $\succsim$, $\mathbf{x}^1 \succsim \mathbf{x}^2$ and $\mathbf{x}^2 \succsim \mathbf{x}^3 \Rightarrow \mathbf{x}^1 \succsim \mathbf{x}^3$. Keep going.

1.16 For (a), suppose there is some other feasible bundle $\mathbf{x}'$, where $\mathbf{x}' \sim \mathbf{x}^*$. Use the fact that B is convex, together with strict convexity of preferences, to derive a contradiction. For (b), suppose not. Use strict monotonicity to derive a contradiction.

1.22 Use a method similar to that employed in (1.11) to eliminate the Lagrangian multiplier and reduce $(n + 1)$ conditions to only n conditions.

1.23 For part (2), see Axiom 5′: Note that the sets $\succsim(\mathbf{x})$ are precisely the superior sets for the function $u(\mathbf{x})$. Recall Theorem A1.14.

1.27 Sketch out the indifference map.

1.28 For part (a), suppose by way of contradiction that the derivative is negative.

1.29 Set down all first-order conditions. Look at the one for choice of x_0^*. Use the constraint, and find a geometric series. Does it converge?

1.32 Feel free to assume that any necessary derivatives exist.

1.33 Roy's identity.

1.41 Theorem A2.6.

1.46 Euler's theorem and any demand function, $x_i(\mathbf{p}, y)$.

1.47 For part (a), start with the definition of $e(\mathbf{p}, 1)$. Multiply the constraint by u and invoke homogeneity. Let $\mathbf{z} \equiv u\mathbf{x}$ and rewrite the objective function as a choice over $\mathbf{z}$.

1.52 Take each inequality separately. Write the one as

$$\frac{\partial x_i(\mathbf{p}_i, y)/\partial y}{x_i(\mathbf{p}, y)} \leq \frac{\bar{\eta}}{y}.$$

Integrate both sides of the inequality from $\bar{y}$ to y and look for logs. Take it from there.

1.54 For part (b),

$$v(\mathbf{p}, y) = A^* y \prod_{i=1}^{n} p_i^{-\alpha_i},$$

where $A^* = A \prod_{i=1}^{n} \alpha_i^{\alpha_i}$.

1.60 Use Slutsky.

1.63 No hints on this.

1.66 For (b), u^0 must be $v(\mathbf{p}^0, y^0)$, right? Rewrite the denominator.

1.67 For (a), you need the expenditure function and you need to figure out u^0. For (b), $I = (u^0 - 1/8)/(2u^0 - 1)$. For (c), if you could show that the expenditure function must be multiplicatively separable in prices and utility, the rest would be easy.

CHAPTER 2

2.3 It should be a Cobb-Douglas form.

2.9 Use a diagram.

2.10 To get you started, $\mathbf{x}^2$ is revealed preferred to $\mathbf{x}^1$.

2.12 For (a), use GARP to show that, unless $\phi(\mathbf{x}^j)$ is zero, there is a minimising sequence of distinct numbers $k_1, ..., k_m$ defining $\phi(\mathbf{x}^j)$ such that no $k_1, ..., k_m$ is equal to j. Hence, $k_1, ..., k_m, j$ is a feasible sequence for the minimisation problem defining $\phi(\mathbf{x}^k)$. For (b), use (a). For (c), recall that each $\mathbf{p}^k \in \mathbb{R}^n_{++}$. For (e), the minimum of quasiconcave functions is quasiconcave.

2.13 Let $\mathbf{x}^0 = \mathbf{x}(\mathbf{p}^0, 1)$, $\mathbf{x}^1 = \mathbf{x}(\mathbf{p}^1, 1)$, and consider $f(t) \equiv (\mathbf{p}^0 - \mathbf{p}^1) \cdot \mathbf{x}(\mathbf{p}^1 + t(\mathbf{p}^0 - \mathbf{p}^1), (\mathbf{p}^1 + t(\mathbf{p}^0 - \mathbf{p}^1)) \cdot \mathbf{x}^0)$ for $t \in [0, 1]$. Show that if $\mathbf{x}^0$ is revealed preferred to $\mathbf{x}^1$ at $(\mathbf{p}^0, 1)$, then f attains a maximum uniquely at 0 on [0, 1].

2.14 In each of the two gambles, some of the outcomes in A will have zero probability.

2.16 Remember that each outcome in A is also a gamble in $\mathcal{G}$, offering that outcome with probability 1.

2.17 Axiom G4.

2.19 Which of the other axioms would be violated by the existence of two unequal indifference probabilities for the same gamble?

2.28 Risk averse.

2.32 Rearrange the definition and see a differential equation. Solve it for $u(w)$.

2.33 If you index his utility function by his initial wealth, then given two distinct wealth levels, how must the two utility functions be related to one another?

2.34 $u(w) = w^{\alpha+1}/(\alpha + 1)$.

2.38 For (a), $x_0 = x_1 = 1$. For (b), the agent faces *two* constraints, and $x_0 = 1, x_1^H = 3/2$ and $x_1^L = 1/2$. For (c), note that future income in the certainty case is equal to the expected value of income in the uncertain case.

CHAPTER 3

3.16 First find $MRTS_{ij}$ and write it as a function of $r = x_j/x_i$. Take logs and it should be clear.

3.17 For (a), first take logs to get

$$\ln(y) = \frac{1}{\rho} \ln\left(\sum_{i=1}^{n} \alpha_1 x_i^{\rho}\right).$$

Note that $\lim_{\rho\to 0} \ln(y) = 0/0$, so L'Hôpital's rule applies. Apply that rule to find $\lim_{\rho\to 0} \ln(y)$, then convert to an expression for $\lim_{\rho\to 0} y$. Part (b) is tough. If you become exasperated, try consulting Hardy, Littlewood, and Pólya (1934), Theorem 4.

3.20 Just work with the definitions and the properties of the production function.

3.23 For the second part, let $\mathbf{z}^2 = \Delta\mathbf{z}^1 \geq \mathbf{0}$.

3.32 $c(y) \equiv atc(y)y$.

3.43 Equations (3.3) and (3.4).

3.45 Work from the first-order conditions.

3.50 Define

$$\pi_v(p, \mathbf{w}, \bar{\mathbf{x}}) \equiv \max_{y,\mathbf{x}} py - \mathbf{w} \cdot \mathbf{x} \qquad \text{s.t.} \qquad f(\mathbf{x}, \bar{\mathbf{x}}) \geq y,$$

sometimes called the **variable profit function**, and note that $\pi_v(p, \mathbf{w}, \bar{\mathbf{x}}) = \pi(p, \mathbf{w}, \bar{\mathbf{w}}, \bar{\mathbf{x}}) + \bar{\mathbf{w}} \cdot \bar{\mathbf{x}}$. Note that π_v possesses *every* property listed in Theorem 3.7, and that the partial derivatives of π_v and $\pi(p, \mathbf{w}, \bar{\mathbf{w}}, \bar{\mathbf{x}})$ with respect to p and $\mathbf{w}$ are equal to each other.

3.55 $K^* = 5\sqrt{w_f/w_k}$.

CHAPTER 4

4.1 Exercise 1.65.

4.2 Try to construct a counterexample.

4.9 In part (b), $q^1 = 215/6$, $q^2 = 110/6$, and $p = 275/6$.

4.13 $p^{1*} = p^{2*} = 80/3$.

4.14 Exploit the symmetry here.

4.15 For (c), J^* is the largest integer less than or equal to $1 + 1\sqrt{2k}$.

4.18 For (a), just let $\eta(y) = \eta$, a constant, where $\eta \neq 1$. For (b), let $\eta = 0$. For (c), start over from the beginning and let $\eta(y) = 1$. For (d), according to Taylor's theorem, $f(t) \approx f(t_0) + f'(t_0)(t - t_0) + (1/2)f''(t_0)(t - t_0)^2$ for arbitrary t_0. Rearrange and view the expression for $CV + y^0$ as the function $y^0[t + 1]^{1/(1-\eta)}$. Apply Taylor's theorem and evaluate at $t_0 = 0$.

4.19 In (b), $v(p, y) = \ln(1/p) + y - 1$. For (d), will anything from Exercise 4.18 help?

4.20 Exercise 4.18.

4.25 For (a), $p^1 = p^2 = 4$. For (b), look at the tail.

4.26 Sketch it out carefully on a set of diagrams like Fig. 4.2. For (d), does it really make any difference to *consumers*? For (e), go ahead and assume that everyone is identical. Still, you will have to think about a lot of things.

CHAPTER 5

5.2 Differentiate the indirect utility function with respect to the price that rises and use Roy's identity.

5.10 Don't use fancy maths. Just think clearly about what it means to be Pareto efficient and what it means to solve the given set of problems.

5.12 Use x_2 as numéraire. For (b), remember that neither consumption nor prices can be negative.

5.15 Derive the consumers' demand functions.

5.16 The function $u^2(\mathbf{x})$ is a Leontief form.

5.17 The relative price of x_1 will have to be $\alpha/(1 - \alpha)$.

5.18 For (a), $\mathbf{x}^1 = (10/3, 40/3)$.

5.19 Calculate $\mathbf{z}(\mathbf{p})$ and convince yourself if $\mathbf{p}^*$ is a Walrasian equilibrium, then $\mathbf{p}^* \gg \mathbf{0}$. Solve the system of excess demand functions.

5.20 For (b), remember that total consumption of each good must equal the total endowment. Suppose that $\bar{p}$ is a market-clearing relative price of good x_1, but that $\bar{p} \neq p^*$. Derive a contradiction.

5.21 Consider the excess demand for good 2 when the price of good one is positive, and consider the excess demand for good one when the price of good one is zero.

5.22 For part (a), show first that if $u(\cdot)$ is strictly increasing and quasiconcave, then for $\alpha > 0$, $v(\mathbf{x}) = u\left(x_1 + \alpha \sum_{i=1}^n x_i, \ldots, x_n + \alpha \sum_{i=1}^n x_i\right)$ is strongly increasing and quasiconcave. Show next that if $u(\cdot)$ is strongly increasing and quasiconcave, then for $\varepsilon \in (0, 1)$, $v(\mathbf{x}) = u(x_1^\varepsilon, \ldots, x_n^\varepsilon)$ is strongly increasing and strictly quasiconcave. Now put the two together. For part (c), equilibrium prices can always be chosen to be non-negative and sum to one and hence contained in a compact set. Hence, any such sequence has a convergent subsequence.

5.23 See Assumption 5.2 for a definition of strong convexity.

5.26 $(p_y/p_h)^* = 4\sqrt{2}$ and he works an 8-hour day.

5.27 To show proportionality of the gradients, suppose they are not. Let $\mathbf{z} = (\nabla u^i(\bar{\mathbf{x}}^i)/\|\nabla u^i(\bar{\mathbf{x}}^i)\|) - (\nabla u^j(\bar{\mathbf{x}}^j)/\|\nabla u^j(\bar{\mathbf{x}}^j)\|)$, and show that $u^i(\bar{\mathbf{x}}^i + t\mathbf{z})$ and $u^j(\bar{\mathbf{x}}^j - t\mathbf{z})$ are both strictly increasing in t at $t = 0$. You may use the Cauchy-Schwartz inequality here, which says that for any two vectors, $\mathbf{v}$ and $\mathbf{w}$, $\mathbf{v} \cdot \mathbf{w} \leq \|\mathbf{v}\|\|\mathbf{w}\|$, with equality if and only if the two vectors are proportional.

5.38 Look carefully at the proof in the text. Construct the coalition of worst off members of *every* type. Give each coalition member the 'average' allocation for his type.

5.39 For (b), translate into terms of these utility functions and these endowments what it means to be (1) 'in the box', (2) 'inside the lens', and (3) 'on the contract curve'. For (d), consider the coalition $S = \{11, 12, 21\}$ and find a feasible assignment of goods to consumers that the consumers in S prefer.

5.40 Redistribute endowments equally. This will be envy-free. Invoke Theorem 5.5 and consider the resulting WEA, $\mathbf{x}^*$. Invoke Theorem 5.7. Now prove that $\mathbf{x}^*$ is also envy-free.

5.41 For (b), see the preceding exercise.

5.42 Fair allocations are defined in Exercise 5.40.

5.43 For (a), indifference curves must be tangent and all goods allocated. For (b), not in general.

5.46 Exercises 1.65 and 4.1 [Actually, this problem only tells you half the story. It follows from *Antonelli's theorem* that $\mathbf{z}(\mathbf{p})$ is both independent of the distribution of endowments *and* behaves like a single consumer's excess demand system if and only if preferences are identical and homothetic. See Shafer and Sonnenschein (1982) for a proof.]

CHAPTER 6

6.2 Show that *VWP* and *IIA* together imply *WP*.

6.4 Here is the proof mentioned in the stem of the question: Suppose we want $u(x^k) = a_k$ for $k = 1, 2, \ldots, m$, where the x^k are distinct members of X. Let $2\varepsilon > 0$ be the minimum Euclidean distance between any distinct pair of the x^k. Letting $\|\cdot\|$ denote Euclidean distance, define $u(x) = 0$ if for every k we have $\|x - x^k\| \geq \varepsilon$, and define $u(x) = \left(1 - \frac{\|x-x^k\|}{\varepsilon}\right) a_k$ if $\|x - x^k\| < \varepsilon$ for some k (by the triangle inequality there can be at most one such k). Prove that $u(\cdot)$ is continuous and that $u(x^k) = a_k$ for every k.

6.5 For part (b), what assumptions did we make about X? What additional assumptions did we make about social preferences? Do our additional assumptions about individual preferences play a role?

6.8 In part (b), notice that for $\varepsilon > 0$ small enough, $u^j - \varepsilon < u^j < \alpha + \varepsilon < u^i$. Now apply *HE*.

6.9 For part (e), consider changing individual 2's profile in (a) so that it becomes identical to 3's profile. What happens to the social preference between x and z?

6.11 For (a), if $\mathbf{x}^* \gg \mathbf{0}$ is a WEA, there must exist n prices $(p_i^*, \ldots, p_n^*)$ such that every $(\mathbf{x}^i)^*$ maximises agent i's utility over their budget set. Look at these first-order conditions and remember that the Lagrangian multiplier for agent i will be equal to the marginal utility of income for agent i at the WEA, $\partial v^i(\mathbf{p}^*, \mathbf{p}^* \cdot \mathbf{e}^i)/\partial y$. Next, note that W must be strictly concave. Thus, if we have some set of weights α^i for $i \in \mathcal{I}$ and an n-vector of numbers $\theta = (\theta_1, \ldots, \theta_n)$ such that $\alpha^i \nabla u^i((\mathbf{x}^i)^*) = \theta$ and $\mathbf{x}^*$ satisfies the constraints, then $\mathbf{x}^*$ maximises W subject to the constraints. What if we choose the α^i to be equal to the reciprocal of the marginal utility of income for agent i at the WEA? What could we use for the vector θ? Pull the pieces together.

6.12 For (b), consider this three-person, three-alternative case due to Sen (1970a). First, let xP^1yP^1z, zP^2xP^2y, and zP^3xP^3y. Determine the ranking of x versus z under the Borda rule. Next, let the preferences of 2 and 3 remain unchanged, but suppose those of 1 become $x\bar{P}^1z\bar{P}^1y$. Now consider the same comparison between x and z and make your argument.

6.13 Why can't (x, y) and (z, w) be the same pair? If $x = z$, invoke U and suppose that xP^ky, wP^jx, and yP^iw for all i. Use L^* and WP to show that transitivity is violated. If x, y, z, and w are all distinct, let xP^ky, zP^jw, and suppose that wP^ix and yP^iz for all i. Take it from here.

6.15 For (b) and (c), see Exercise A2.10 for the necessary definition. For (e),

$$E(w, \mathbf{y}) = \left(\sum_{i=1}^{N} \frac{1}{N}\left(\frac{y^i}{\mu}\right)^{\rho}\right)^{1/\rho}.$$

6.16 No, no, no, yes.

6.17 For parts (a) and (b), no, yes.

6.19 Argue by contradiction and change preferences monotonically so that all preferences are strict and x is at the top of n's ranking.

CHAPTER 7

7.3 For part (b), show first that if a strategy is strictly dominated in some round, then it remains strictly dominated by some remaining strategy in every subsequent round.

7.5 For (c), when is 99 a best response? To find W_i^1, follow these steps. Step 1: Show that if 14 results in a tie, then 15, 16, ..., 100 either lose or tie. Step 2: Show that 14 wins if all other players choose a number strictly above 14. Step 3: Show that 14 loses only if one-third the average of the numbers is strictly less than 14. Conclude from steps 2 and 3 that if 14 loses, so do 15, 16, ..., 100.

7.7 For (a), use the Nash equilibrium existence theorem.

7.8 Employ a fixed-point function similar to the one used to prove the existence of a Nash equilibrium to prove the existence of a strategy $m^* \in M_1$ for player 1, which maximises $u_1(m, m^*, \ldots, m^*)$ over $m \in M_1$. Then invoke symmetry.

7.9 See Exercise 7.7, part (c), for the definition of a game's value. See Exercise 7.8 for the definition of a symmetric game.

7.21 Would a player ever choose a strictly dominated strategy?

7.22 Do not rule out weakly dominated strategies. Are all of these equilibria in pure strategies? Verify that the high-cost type of a firm 2 earns zero profits in every Bayesian-Nash equilibrium.

7.32 Allow information sets to 'cross' one another.

7.42 Can 3's beliefs about 2 be affected by 1's choice?

CHAPTER 8

8.1 Recall that wealth in one state is a different commodity from wealth in another state and that the state in which consumer i alone has an accident is different than that in which only consumer $j \neq i$ does. Verify the hypotheses of the First Welfare Theorem and conclude that the competitive outcome of Section 8.1 is efficient in the sense described there.

8.5 For part (c), suppose there are at least three fixed points. Let x^* be a fixed point between two others and think about what would be implied if $f'(x^*) \geq 1$ and what would be implied if $f'(x^*) \leq 1$.

8.7 For (a), suppose not. Could demand for used cars equal supply?

8.12 For part (c), it is not a pooling contract.

8.13 First show that $\sum_{l=k}^{L}(\pi_l(0) - \pi_l(1)) > 0$ for all $k > 0$ by writing the sum instead as $\sum_{l=k}^{L}\left(\frac{\pi_l(0)}{\pi_l(1)} - 1\right)\pi_l(1)$ and arguing by contradiction. Finally, apply the following identity: $\sum_{l=0}^{L} a_l b_l \equiv \sum_{k=0}^{L}\left(\sum_{l=k}^{L} a_l\right)(b_k - b_{k-1})$ for every pair of real sequences $\{a_l\}_{l=0}^{L}$, $\{b_l\}_{l=0}^{L}$, and where $b_{-1} \equiv 0$.

8.16 For part (a), use the fact that the owner is risk neutral and the worker is risk-averse.

8.17 (a) Because the manager observes only output and not effort, the wage can depend only on output. Let $w(y)$ denote the worker's wage when output is y. The manager's problem is therefore as follows:

$$\max_{e, w(y_1), \ldots, w(y_m)} \sum_{i=1}^{m} p(y_i|e)(y_i - w(y_i)),$$

where $e \in \{e_1, \ldots, e_n\}$ and each $w(y_i) \in \mathbb{R}$, subject to

$$\sum_{i=1}^{m} p(y_i|e)u(w(y_i), e) \geq \sum_{i=1}^{m} p(y_i|e_j)u(w(y_i), e_j), \text{ for all } j = 1, \ldots, n$$

and

$$\sum_{i=1}^{m} p(y_i|e)u(w(y_i), e) \geq u(0, e_1).$$

(b) Let $e^* > e_1$ denote the effort level chosen by the worker in the optimal solution. Suppose, by way of contradiction, that the wage contract is non-increasing, i.e., that $w(y_i) \geq w(y_{i+1})$ for all i. Then, by the monotone likelihood ratio property, and Exercise 8.13,

$$\sum_{i=1}^{m} p(y_i|e^*)u(w(y_i), e^*) \leq \sum_{i=1}^{m} p(y_i|e_1)u(w(y_i), e^*),$$

because the function $u(w(y), e^*)$ is non-increasing in y. However, because $u(w, e)$ is strictly decreasing in e, we have

$$\sum_{i=1}^{m} p(y_i|e_1)u(w(y_i), e^*) < \sum_{i=1}^{m} p(y_i|e_1)u(w(y_i), e_1).$$

Putting the two inequalities together yields,

$$\sum_{i=1}^{m} p(y_i|e^*)u(w(y_i), e^*) < \sum_{i=1}^{m} p(y_i|e_1)u(w(y_i), e_1),$$

in violation of the incentive compatibility constraint. This contradiction proves the result.

CHAPTER 9

9.3 Note that (9.3) holds for all v, including $v = r$.

9.7 What are the first- and second-order conditions for bidder i implied by incentive compatibility? Because the first-order condition must hold for all v_i, it may be differentiated. Use the derivative to substitute into the second-order condition.

9.13 Did any of our results depend on the values being in [0, 1]?

9.15 (b) What is the induced direct selling mechanism?

9.17 (b) Use Theorem 9.5, and don't forget about individual rationality.

9.19 You will need to use our assumption that each $v_i - (1 - F_i(v_i))/f_i(v_i)$ is strictly increasing.

MATHEMATICAL APPENDIX

CHAPTER A1

A1.2 Just use the definitions of subsets, unions, and intersections.

A1.3 To get you started, consider the first one. Pick any $x \in (S \cap T)^c$. If $x \in (S \cap T)^c$, then $x \notin S \cap T$. If $x \notin S \cap T$, then $x \notin S$ or $x \notin T$. (Remember, this is the inclusive 'or'.) If $x \notin S$, then $x \in S^c$. If $x \notin T$, then $x \in T^c$. Because $x \in S^c$ or $x \in T^c$, $x \in S^c \cup T^c$. Because x was chosen arbitrarily, what we have established holds for all $x \in (S \cap T)^c$. Thus, $x \in (S \cap T)^c \Rightarrow x \in S^c \cup T^c$, and we have shown that $(S \cap T)^c \subset S^c \cup T^c$. To complete the proof of the first law, you must now show that $S^c \cup T^c \subset (S \cap T)^c$.

A1.13 To get you started, let $x \in f^{-1}(B^c)$. By definition of the inverse image, $x \in D$ and $f(x) \in B^c$. By definition of the complement of B in R, $x \in D$ and $f(x) \notin B$. Again, by the definition of the inverse image, $x \in D$ and $x \notin f^{-1}(B)$. By the definition of the complement of $f^{-1}(B)$ in D, $x \in D$ and $x \in (f^{-1}(B))^c$, so $f^{-1}(B^c) \subset (f^{-1}(B))^c$. Complete the proof.

A1.18 Let $\Omega^i = \{\mathbf{x} \mid \mathbf{a}^i \cdot \mathbf{x} + b^i \geq 0\}$. Use part (b) of Exercise A1.17.

A1.21 First, model your proof after the one for part 3. Then consider $\cap_{i=1}^{\infty} A_i$, where $A_i = (-1/i, 1/i)$.

A1.22 Draw a picture first.

A1.24 Look at the complement of each set.

A1.25 Use Theorem A1.2 to characterise the complement of S in $\mathbb{R}$.

A1.26 For the first part, sketch something similar to Fig. A1.12 and use what you learned in Exercise A1.24. The second part is easy.

A1.27 To get you started, note that the complement of S is open, then apply Theorem A1.3. Open balls in $\mathbb{R}$ are open intervals. Use what you learned in Exercise A1.26.

A1.31 Centre a ball at the origin.

A1.32 For part (c), you must show it is bounded *and* closed. For the former, centre a ball at the origin. For the latter, define the sets $F_0 \equiv \{\mathbf{x} \in \mathbb{R}^n | \sum_{i=1}^n x_i = 1\}$, $F_i \equiv \{\mathbf{x} \in \mathbb{R}^n | x_i \geq 0\}$, for $i = 1, \cdots, n$. Convince yourself that the complement of each set is open. Note that $S^{n-1} = \cap_{i=0}^n F_i$. Put it together.

A1.38 Look closely at S.

A1.39 Check the image of $f(x) = \cos(x) - 1/2$.

A1.40 Choose a value for y, some values for x_1, and solve for the values of x_2. Plot x_1 and x_2.

A1.46 In (b), it may help to remember that $\mathbf{x}^1$ and $\mathbf{x}^2$ can be labelled so that $f(\mathbf{x}^1) \geq f(\mathbf{x}^2)$, and that $tf(\mathbf{x}^1) + (1-t)f(\mathbf{x}^2) = f(\mathbf{x}^2) + t(f(\mathbf{x}^1) - f(\mathbf{x}^2))$.

A1.49 Yes, yes, no, yes. Look for convex sets. For (e), things will be a bit different if you assume $f(x)$ is continuous and if you do not.

CHAPTER A2

A2.1 For (g), $f'(x) = -\exp(x^2) < 0$.

A2.2 For (a), $f_1 = 2 - 2x_1$ and $f_2 = -2x_2$. For (e), $f_1 = 3x_1^2 - 6x_2$ and $f_2 = -6x_1 + 3x_2^2$.

A2.3 Chain rule.

A2.5 For (a),

$$\mathbf{H}(\mathbf{x}) = \begin{pmatrix} -2 & 0 \\ 0 & -2 \end{pmatrix}.$$

A2.11 Use the definition of an increasing function and the definitions of local optima.

A2.19 Strict quasiconcavity implies quasiconcavity.

A2.24 For (a), $\mathbf{x}^* = (1, 0)$ is a maximum. For (b), $\mathbf{x}^* = (0, 1)$ is a minimum.

A2.25 (a) $(1, 1)$ and $(-1, -1)$; $f(1, 1) = f(-1, -1) = 2$; (b) $(-\sqrt{1/2}, \sqrt{1/2})$ and $(\sqrt{1/2}, -\sqrt{1/2})$; (c) $(\sqrt{a^2/3}, \sqrt{2b^2/3})$ and $(\sqrt{a^2/3}, -\sqrt{2b^2/3})$; (d) $((1/2)^{1/4}, (1/2)^{1/4})$; (e) $(1/6, 2/6, 3/6)$.

A2.37 Use the fact that sequences in A are bounded and therefore have convergent subsequences.

References

Afriat, S. (1967). 'The Construction of a Utility Function from Expenditure Data', *International Economic Review*, 8: 67–77.

Akerlof, G. (1970). 'The Market for Lemons: Quality Uncertainty and the Market Mechanism', *Quarterly Journal of Economics*, 89: 488–500.

Antonelli, G. (1886). 'Sulla Teoria Matematica della Economia Politica': Pisa. Translated as 'On the Mathematical Theory of Political Economy', in J. L. Chipman et al. (eds.), *Preferences Utility and Demand: A Minnesota Symposium*. New York: Harcourt Brace Jovanovich, 333–364.

Arrow, K. (1951). *Social Choice and Individual Values*. New York: John Wiley.

——— (1970). 'The Theory of Risk Aversion', in K. Arrow (ed.), *Essays in the Theory of Risk Bearing*. Chicago: Markham, 90–109.

——— (1973). 'Some Ordinalist Utilitarian Notes on Rawls' Theory of Justice', *Journal of Philosophy*, 70: 245–263.

——— (1979). 'The Property Rights Doctrine and Demand Revelation under Incomplete Information', in M. Boskin (ed.), *Economics and Human Welfare*, New York: Academic Press, 23–39.

Arrow, K., and G. Debreu (1954). 'Existence of Equilibrium for a Competitive Economy', *Econometrica*, 22: 265–290.

Arrow, K., and A. Enthoven (1961). 'Quasi-Concave Programming', *Econometrica*, 29: 779–800.

Atkinson A. (1970). 'On the Measurement of Inequality', *Journal of Economic Theory*, 2: 244–263.

Aumann, R. J. (1964). 'Markets with a Continuum of Traders', *Econometrica*, 32: 39–50.

Barten A., and V. Böhm (1982). 'Consumer Theory', in K. Arrow and M. Intrilligator (eds.), *Handbook of Mathematical Economics*. Amsterdam: North Holland, 2: 382–429.

Bertrand, J. (1883). 'Review of Théorie Mathématique de la Richesse Sociale and Recherches sur les Principes Mathématiques de la Théorie des Richesses', *Journal des Savants*, 499–508.

Black, D. (1948). 'On the Rationale of Group Decision-Making', *Journal of Political Economy*, 56: 23–34.

Blackorby, C., and D. Donaldson (1978). 'Measures of Relative Equality and Their Meaning in Terms of Social Welfare', *Journal of Economic Theory* 18: 59–80.

Blackorby, C., D. Donaldson, and J. Weymark (1984). 'Social Choice with Interpersonal Utility Comparisons: A Diagrammatic Introduction', *International Economic Review*, 25: 327–356.

Cho, I. K., and D. M. Kreps (1987). 'Signaling Games and Stable Equilibria', *Quarterly Journal of Economics*, 102: 179–221.

Clarke, E. (1971). 'Multipart Pricing of Public Goods', *Public Choice*, 2: 19–33.

Cornwall, R. (1984). *Introduction to the Use of General Equilibrium Analysis*. Amsterdam: North Holland.

Cournot, A. (1838). *Recherches sur les principes mathématiques de la théorie des richesses*. Paris, Hachette. English trans. N. Bacon (1960). *Researches into the Mathematical Principles of the Theory of Wealth*. New York: Kelley.

Cramton, P., R. Gibbons, and P. Klemperer (1987). 'Dissolving a Partnership Efficiently', *Econometrica,* 55: 615–632.

d'Aspremont, C., and L. Gevers (1977). 'Equity and the Informational Basis of Collective Choice', *Review of Economic Studies*, 44: 199–209.

d'Aspremont, C. and L. A. Gérard-Varet (1979). 'Incentives and Incomplete Information', *Journal of Public Economics,* 11: 25–45.

Debreu, G. (1954). 'Representation of a Preference Ordering by a Numerical Function', in R. M. Thrall et al. (eds.), *Decision Processes*. New York: John Wiley, 159–165.

——— (1959). *Theory of Value*. New York: John Wiley.

——— (1972). 'Smooth Preferences', *Econometrica*, 40: 603–615.

Debreu, G., and H. Scarf (1963). 'A Limit Theorem on the Core of an Economy', *International Economic Review*, 4: 235–246.

Diewert, W. E. (1974). 'Applications of Duality Theory', in M. D. Intrilligator and D. A. Kendrick (eds.), *Frontiers of Quantitative Economics*. Amsterdam: North Holland, 2: 106–199.

Edgeworth, F. Y. (1881). *Mathematical Psychics*. London: Paul Kegan.

Eisenberg, B. (1961). 'Aggregation of Utility Functions', *Management Science*, 7: 337–350.

Geanakoplos, J. (1996). 'Three Brief Proofs of Arrow's Impossibility Theorem', mimeo, Cowles Foundation, Yale University.

Gibbard, A. (1973). 'Manipulation of Voting Schemes: A General result', *Econometrica*, 41, 587–601.

Goldman, S. M., and H. Uzawa (1964). 'A Note on Separability in Demand Analysis', *Econometrica*, 32: 387–398.

Green, J., and J-J. Laffont (1977). 'Characterization of Satisfactory Mechanisms for the Revelation of Preferences for Public Goods', *Econometrica*, 45: 727–738.

Grossman, S. J., and O. D. Hart (1983). 'An Analysis of the Principal-Agent Problem', *Econometrica*, 51: 7–45.

Groves, T. (1973). 'Incentives in Teams', *Econometrica*, 41: 617–631.

Hammond, P. J. (1976). 'Equity, Arrow's Conditions, and Rawls' Difference Principle', *Econometrica*, 44: 793–804.

Hardy, G., J. Littlewood, and G. Pólya (1934). *Inequalities*. Cambridge: Oxford University Press.

Harsanyi, J. (1953). 'Cardinal Utility in Welfare Economics and in the Theory of Risk-Taking', *Journal of Political Economy*, 61: 434–435.

——— (1955). 'Cardinal Welfare, Individualistic Ethics, and Interpersonal Comparisons of Utility', *Journal of Political Economy*, 63: 309–321.

——— (1967–1968). 'Games with Incomplete Information Played by "Bayesian" Players, Parts I, II, and III', *Management Science*, 14: 159–182, 320–334, and 486–502.

——— (1975). 'Can the Maximin Principle Serve as a Basis for Morality? A Critique of John Rawls's Theory', *American Political Science Review*, 69: 594–606.

Hicks, J. (1939). *Value and Capital*. Oxford: Clarendon Press.

——— (1956). *A Revision of Demand Theory*. Oxford: Clarendon Press.

Hildenbrand, W. (1974). *Core and Equilibria of a Large Economy*. Princeton: Princeton University Press.

Hohn, F. (1973). *Elementary Matrix Algebra*, 3rd ed. New York: Macmillan.

Holmstrom, B. (1979a). 'Moral Hazard and Observability', *Bell Journal of Economics*, 10: 74–91.

——— (1979b). 'Groves' Scheme on Restricted Domains', *Econometrica,* 47: 1137–1144.

——— (1982). 'Moral Hazard in Teams', *Bell Journal of Economics*, 13: 324–340.

Houthakker, H. (1950). 'Revealed Preference and the Utility Function', *Economica*, 17(66): 159–174.

Hurwicz, L., and H. Uzawa (1971). 'On the Integrability of Demand Functions', in J. S. Chipman et al. (eds.), *Utility Preferences and Demand; A Minnesota Symposium*. New York: Harcourt Brace Jovanovich, pp. 114–148.

Kakutani, S. (1941). 'A Generalization of Brouwer's Fixed-Point Theorem', *Duke Mathematical Journal*, 8: 451–459.

Knoblauch, V. (1992). 'A Tight Upper Bound on the Money Metric Utility Function', *American Economic Review*, 82(3): 660–663.

Kohlberg, E., and P. J. Reny (1997). 'Independence on Relative Probability Spaces and Consistent Assessments in Game Trees', *Journal of Economic Theory*, 75: 280–313.

Kreps, D. M., and B. D. Wilson (1982). 'Sequential Equilibria', *Econometrica*, 50: 863–894.

Krishna, V. and M. Perry (1998). 'Efficient Mechanism Design', mimeo, http://economics.huji.ac.il/facultye/perry/cv.html.

Kuhn, H. (1953). 'Extensive Games and the Problem of Information', in H. W. Kuhn and A. W. Tucker (eds.), *Contributions to the Theory of Games*, Volume II (Annals of Mathematics Studies 28). Princeton: Princeton University Press, 2: 193–216.

Kuhn, H., and A. W. Tucker (1951). 'Nonlinear Programming', in J. Neyman (ed.), *Proceedings of the Second Berkeley Symposium on Mathematical Statistics and Probability*. Berkeley: University of California Press, 481–492.

Luenberger, D. G. (1973). *Introduction to Linear and Nonlinear Programming*. New York: John Wiley.

McKenzie, L. (1954). 'On Equilibrium in Graham's Model of World Trade and Other Competitive Systems', *Econometrica* 22: 147–161.

Muller, E. and M. A. Satterthwaite (1977). 'The Equivalence of Strong Positive Association and Strategy-Proofness', *Journal of Economic Theory*, 14, 412–418.

Murata, Y. (1977). *Mathematics for Stability and Optimization of Economic Systems*. New York: Academic Press.

Myerson, R. (1981). 'Optimal Auction Design', *Mathematics of Operations Research*, 6: 58–73.

Myerson, R. and M. A. Satterthwaite (1983). 'Efficient Mechanisms for Bilateral Trading', *Journal of Economic Theory,* 29: 265–281.

Nash, J. (1951). 'Non-cooperative Games', *Annals of Mathematics*, 54: 286–295.

Nikaido, H. (1968). *Convex Structures and Economic Theory*. New York: Academic Press.

Osborne, M. J., and A. Rubinstein (1994). *A Course in Game Theory*. Cambridge, MA: The MIT Press.

Pareto, V. (1896). *Cours d'économie politique*. Lausanne: Rouge.

Pratt, J. (1964). 'Risk Aversion in the Small and in the Large', *Econometrica*, 32: 122–136.

Rawls, J. (1971). *A Theory of Justice*. Cambridge, MA: Harvard University Press.

Reny, P. J. (1992). 'Rationality In Extensive Form Games', *Journal of Economic Perspectives*, 6: 103–118.

—— (2001). 'Arrow's Theorem and the Gibbard-Satterthwaite Theorem: A Unified Approach', *Economics Letters*, 70: 99–105.

Richter, M. (1966). 'Revealed Preference Theory', *Econometrica*, 34(3): 635–645.

Roberts, K. W. S. (1980). 'Possibility Theorems with Interpersonally Comparable Welfare Levels', *Review of Economic Studies*, 47: 409–420.

Rothschild, M., and J. E. Stiglitz (1976). 'Equilibrium in Competitive Insurance Markets: An Essay in the Economics of Imperfect Information', *Quarterly Journal of Economics*, 80: 629–649.

Roy, R. (1942). *De l'utilité: contribution à la théorie des choix.* Paris: Hermann.

Royden, H. (1963). *Real Analysis*. New York: Macmillan.

Samuelson, P. A. (1947). *Foundations of Economic Analysis*. Cambridge, MA, Harvard University Press.

Satterthwaite, M. A. (1975). 'Strategy-Proofness and Arrow's Conditions: Existence and Correspondence Theorems for Voting Procedures and Social Welfare Functions', *Journal of Economic Theory*, 10: 187–217.

Selten, R. (1965). 'Spieltheoretische Behandlung eines Oligopolmodells mit Nachfrageträgheit', *Zeitschrift für die gesamte Staatswissenschaft*, 121: 301–324.

——— (1975). 'Reexamination of the Perfectness Concept for Equilibrium Points in Extensive Games', *International Journal of Game Theory*, 4: 25–55.

Sen, A. (1970a). *Collective Choice and Social Welfare*. Amsterdam: North Holland.

——— (1970b). 'The Impossibility of a Paretian Liberal', *Journal of Political Economy*, 78: 152–157.

——— (1984). 'Social Choice Theory', in K. Arrow and M. Intrilligator (eds.), *Handbook of Mathematical Economics.* Amsterdam: North Holland, 3, 1073–1181.

Shafer, W., and H. Sonnenschein (1982). 'Market Demand and Excess Demand Functions', in K. Arrow and M. Intrilligator (eds.), *Handbook of Mathematical Economics*. Amsterdam: North Holland, 2, 671–693.

Shephard, R. W. (1970). *Theory of Cost and Production Functions*. Princeton: Princeton University Press.

Slutsky, E. (1915). 'Sulla Teoria del Bilancio del Consumatore', *Giornale degli Economisti*, 51, 1, 26, English translation 'On the Theory of the Budget of the Consumer', in G. J. Stigler and K. E. Boulding (eds.), (1953) *Readings in Price Theory*. London: Allen and Unwin, 27–56.

Smith, A. (1776). *The Wealth of Nations*, Cannan Ed. (1976) Chicago: University of Chicago Press.

Spence, A. M. (1973). 'Job Market Signaling', *Quarterly Journal of Economics*, 87: 355–374.

Tarski, A. (1955). 'A Lattice-Theoretical Fixpoint Theorem and its Applications', *Pacific Journal of Mathematics*, 5: 285–309.

Varian, H. (1982). 'The Nonparametric Approach to Demand Analysis', *Econometrica*, 50(4): 945–973.

Vickrey, W. (1961). 'Counterspeculation, Auctions and Competitive Sealed Tenders', *Journal of Finance*, 16: 8-37.

Von Neumann, J., and O. Morgenstern (1944). *Theory of Games and Economic Behavior*. Princeton: Princeton University Press.

Wald, A. (1936). 'Uber einige Gleiehungssysteme der mathematischen Okonomie', *Zeitschrift für Nationalökonomic*, 7: 637–670. English translation 'Some Systems of Equations of Mathematical Economics', *Econometrica*, 19: 368–403.

Walras, L. (1874). *Eléments d'économie politique pure*. Lausanne: L. Corbaz. English trans. William Jaffé (1954) *Elements of Pure Economics*. London: Allen and Unwin.

Williams, S. (1999). 'A Characterization of Efficient Bayesian Incentive Compatible Mechanisms', *Economic Theory,* 14: 155–180.

Willig, R. D. (1976). 'Consumer's Surplus without Apology', *American Economic Review*, 66: 589–597.

Wilson, C. (1977). 'A Model of Insurance Markets with Incomplete Information', *Journal of Economic Theory*, 16: 167–207.

Index

Note: Figures are indicated by *italic page numbers* in the index, footnotes by suffix 'n'